R. Gupta's®

POPULAR MASTER GUIDE

CTET/STETs

Central Teacher Eligibility Test/State Teacher Eligibility Tests

PAPER-II

Mathematics & Science Teachers

(For Class VI to VIII)

Key Features

- Specialised Study Material Prepared by Experts
- Solved Multiple Choice Questions (MCQs)
- Solved Previous Years' Papers

2027 EDITION

RAMESH PUBLISHING HOUSE, NEW DELHI

Published by
O.P. Gupta *for* Ramesh Publishing House

Admin. Office
12-H, New Daryaganj Road, Opp. Officers' Mess,
New Delhi-110002 ✆ 23275224, 23245124

E-mail: info@rameshpublishinghouse.com
For Online Shopping: www.rameshpublishinghouse.com

Showroom
- Balaji Market, Nai Sarak, Delhi-110006 ✆ 23282525 📱 9354373464
- 4457, Nai Sarak, Delhi-110006

Book Code: R-1457

ISBN: 978-93-5012-166-5

Price: ₹ 610

Printed at: Deepak Offset, Delhi

Contents

❐❐❐

Scheme of Exam

PAPER II (FOR MATHEMATICS AND SCIENCE TEACHER)

PAPER-II will be for a person who intends to be a Teacher for Classes VI to VIII, for Mathematics and Science Subjects.

Duration of Examination —2½ hours

S.No.	Subjects	No. of Questions	Marks
1.	Child Development & Pedagogy (Compulsory)	30	30
2.	Language I (Compulsory)	30	30
3.	Language II (Compulsory)	30	30
4.	Mathematics and Science (For Mathematics and Science Teacher)	60	60
	Total	**150**	**150**

Nature and Standard of Questions:

- The test items on Child Development and Pedagogy will focus on educational psychology of teaching and learning, relevant to the age group of 11-14 years. They will focus on understanding the characteristics, needs and psychology of diverse learners, interaction with learners and the attributes and qualities of a good facilitator of learning.
- The Test items in Language I will focus on the proficiencies related to the medium of instruction.
- The Test items in Language II will focus on the elements of language, communication and comprehension abilities.
- Language II will be a language other than Language I. A candidate may choose any one language as Language I and other as Language II from the available language options and will be required to specify the same in the Confirmation Page.
- Opt two languages in which you wish to appear for CTET : List of languages and code are as follows:

Language	Code No.	Language	Code No.	Language	Code No.	Language	Code No.
English	01	Gujarati	06	Marathi	11	Sanskrit	16
Hindi	02	Kannada	07	Mizo	12	Tamil	17
Assamese	03	Khasi	08	Nepali	13	Telugu	18
Bengali	04	Malayalam	09	Oriya	14	Tibetan	19
Garo	05	Manipuri	10	Punjabi	15	Urdu	20

- The Test items in Mathematics and Science will focus on the concepts, problem solving abilities and pedagogical understanding and applications of the subjects. The test items of Mathematics and Science will be of 30 marks each. The test items will be evenly distributed over different divisions of the syllabus of that subject as prescribed for classes VI-VIII by the NCERT.
- The questions in the test for Paper II will be based on the topics prescribed in syllabus of the NCERT for classes VI - VIII but their difficulty standard as well as linkages, could be up to the Senior Secondary stage.
- Question paper shall be Bilingual (Hindi/English).

Previous Years' Paper

CTET—Paper-II, February-2026

For Mathematics and Science Teachers

(Exam held on 07-02-2026)

CHILD DEVELOPMENT AND PEDAGOGY

1. Read the following statements:

Assertion (A): The purpose of administering intelligence tests and extended observation should be to compare children in specific domains and abilities.

Reason (R): Intelligence is an innate ability and cannot be nurtured.

Choose the ***correct*** option.

1. Both (A) and (R) are true, but (R) is not the correct explanation of (A).
2. (A) is true, but (R) is false.
3. Both (A) and (R) are false.
4. Both (A) and (R) are true and (R) is the correct explanation of (A).

2. A teacher who consciously takes examples of scientists of all genders in her middle school classroom is trying to:

1. reinforce gender discrimination.
2. enable gender identity.
3. construct gender constancy.
4. break gender stereotypes.

3. Read the following statements:

Assertion (A): All girls are hardworking and sincere while boys are intelligent and dominating.

Reason (R): Two distinctive biological brains produce all differences in physical and cognitive skills as well as personalities and temperament in girls and boys.

Choose the ***correct*** option.

1. Both (A) and (R) are true, but (R) is not the correct explanation of (A).
2. (A) is true, but (R) is false.
3. Both (A) and (R) are false.
4. Both (A) and (R) are true and (R) is the correct explanation of (A).

4. Individual differences in learning preference of students should be seen as:

1. cognitive abnormality among some children.
2. developmental deficits among some children.
3. normal depiction of diversity.
4. abnormal parameter of their differing IQ levels.

5. The kind of assessment in which a student's scores are compared with the average performance of other students is called:

1. format-referenced
2. norm-referenced
3. self-referenced
4. criteria-referenced

6. Which of the following statements about classroom assessment are correct?

(*i*) Assessments should influence the students' cognitive processes while they study.

(*ii*) Assessments should serve as learning experiences in themselves.

(*iii*) Assessments should create fear and stress among students to get them to learn.

(*iv*) Assessments should be standardized and norm-referenced.

Choose the ***correct*** option.

1. (*i*), (*ii*)
2. (*ii*), (*iii*), (*iv*)
3. (*i*), (*ii*), (*iii*), (*iv*)
4. (*i*), (*iii*)

7. Which of the following questions would promote higher-order critical and analytical thinking skills among the students?

1. Identify the nouns mentioned in a specific newspaper article.
2. Read the newspaper articles and make a list of new words.
3. Read the newspaper article and think of a suitable title.
4. Identify the assumptions underlying two news-paper articles depicting the same event.

1. 3	**2.** 4	**3.** 3	**4.** 3	**5.** 2	**6.** 1	**7.** 4

8. Read the following statements:

Assertion (A): Students with poor writing abilities are often stereotyped by their teachers as 'intellectually disabled'.

Reason (R): Teachers tend to have implicit bias and hold assumptions about students' learning behaviours that can affect students' growth.

Choose the ***correct*** option.

1. Both (A) and (R) are true, but (R) is not the correct explanation of (A).
2. (A) is true, but (R) is false.
3. Both (A) and (R) are false.
4. Both (A) and (R) are true and (R) is the correct explanation of (A).

9. Which of the following is ***not*** a way to promote diversity in the classroom?

1. Encouraging students to express their unique identities and cultures
2. Adapting behaviour based on stereotyping students according to their backgrounds and cultures
3. Providing opportunities for students to interact with individuals from different backgrounds and cultures
4. Incorporating a variety of perspectives and experiences in the curriculum

10. Which of the following is the ***correct*** match of learning disability and challenge caused by it?

1. Dysgraphia—Impacts fine motor skills and spelling
2. Dyslexia—Impacts ability to learn numbers and arithmetic operations
3. Dyspraxia—Impacts ability to see, hear and talk properly
4. Dyscalculia—Impacts ability to read and language processing skills

11. Students struggling with 'autism' show ease at:

1. eye contact during conversation.
2. familiar and predictable routines.
3. rapid transitions between activities.
4. communication with strangers.

12. Which of the following statements is ***not*** correct about gifted children?

1. Children can be gifted in more than one kind of intelligence.
2. Gifted children are born with extraordinary abilities and potential that need to be nurtured.
3. Gifted children have lower sense of curiosity and poor imagination skills.
4. Children can be gifted at different levels and some can have some kind of disability also.

13. Error analysis by students

1. hinders metacognitive skills of students.
2. is a futile activity in process of learning.
3. supports students in retaining their learning.
4. creates further gaps in students' understanding.

14. Which of the following statements is ***correct*** regarding declarative knowledge and procedural knowledge?

1. Declarative knowledge is also known as analytical knowledge.
2. Procedural knowledge is generally process-oriented in nature.
3. Procedural knowledge tells the factual knowledge about something.
4. Declarative knowledge emphasizes how to do something.

15. Contents which require an extension or modification of existing cognitive structures take _____ time for learning and are retained for _____ duration.

1. long, short
2. short, short
3. short, long
4. long, long

16. Read the following statements:

Assertion (A): Teachers should encourage children to focus on questions such as "what is my learning goal and what do I need to do to get there".

Reason (R): When students understand how to self-assess their work performance, they can use this understanding to help themselves learn and progress.

Choose the ***correct*** option.

1. Both (A) and (R) are true, but (R) is not the correct explanation of (A).
2. (A) is true, but (R) is false.
3. Both (A) and (R) are false.
4. Both (A) and (R) are true and (R) is the correct explanation of (A).

17. In guided discovery approach of learning:

1. no prior planning or previous knowledge is required.
2. opportunities are provided to learners to construct knowledge for themselves.
3. teacher acts as a dictator and learners act as listeners.
4. learners are left on their own without any kind of intervention by teacher.

8. 4	**9.** 2	**10.** 1	**11.** 2	**12.** 3	**13.** 3	**14.** 2	**15.** 4	**16.** 4	**17.** 2

18. Which of the following strategies is ***not*** effective while developing conceptual understanding in children?

1. Presenting non-examples to show what the concept is not
2. Asking students to generate their own examples
3. Asking students to memorize the definition as it is
4. Presenting a wide range of examples in diverse contexts

19. An active middle school classroom should be founded on the theoretical principles of:

1. psychodynamism
2. social constructivism
3. psychoanalysis
4. behaviourism

20. Read the following statements:

Assertion (A): Empathy depends on the ability to understands that others have feelings and to gauge their feelings.

Reason (R): Emotions and cognition are not related to each other.

Choose the ***correct*** option.

1. Both (A) and (R) are true, but (R) is not the correct explanation of (A).
2. (A) is true, but (R) is false.
3. Both (A) and (R) are false.
4. Both (A) and (R) are true and (R) is the correct explanation of (A).

21. A middle school teacher can enable students become strategic self-motivated learners by—

1. providing varied forms of reinforcement for every task completed.
2. dictating well-prepared answers to questions in the textbook.
3. stressing upon objective-type testing at the end of the term.
4. encouraging students to develop their metacognitive knowledge and skills.

22. Which of the following exemplifies intrinsic motivation?

1. Motivation driven by personal interest or enjoyment of the task
2. Motivation driven by competition with others
3. Motivation driven by gaining the appreciation of others
4. Motivation driven by external rewards

23. Which debate is highlighted in the following question?
"Does an individual's biologically determined sex bring with it all the characteristics that define one's socially constructed gender?"

1. Continuous-Discontinuous view of development
2. Stable-Unstable view of development
3. Entity-Incremental view of ability
4. Nature-Nurture influences on development

24. A major developmental task during _____ is the search for identity–personal, sexual and occupational.

1. early childhood
2. adolescence
3. middle adulthood
4. middle childhood

25. Read the following statements:

Assertion (A): Children learn values and norms of the society in overt as well as covert ways.

Reason (R): Socialization is the simple process of passing on customs and rituals of the society.

Choose the ***correct*** option.

1. Both (A) and (R) are true, but (R) is not the correct explanation of (A).
2. (A) is true, but (R) is false.
3. Both (A) and (R) are false.
4. Both (A) and (R) are true and (R) is the correct explanation of (A).

26. As per Jean Piaget's theory of cognitive development, which of the following abilities distinguishes formal operational thinking from concrete operational thinking?

1. Conservation
2. Object permanence
3. Symbolic play
4. Abstract logic

27. A significant critique of Jean Piaget is that he failed to adequately consider the influence of _____ on development.

1. culture
2. experience
3. activity
4. maturation

28. Which of the following is a correctly matched pair?

1. Good boy-Good girl orientation–Greatest good for greater numbers
2. Law and Order orientation–Upholding principles of social justice for humanity
3. Social Contract orientation–Consideration of perception of others
4. Punishment and Obedience orientation–Avoidance of bad consequences

18. 3	**19.** 2	**20.** 2	**21.** 4	**22.** 1	**23.** 4
24. 2	**25.** 2	**26.** 4	**27.** 1	**28.** 4	

29. Jean Piaget and Lev Vygotsky are similar in their belief that:

1. language influences and determines thought.
2. culture has a profound effect on the learning.
3. development of children takes place in stage-like progression.
4. children are involved in the process of meaning making.

30. Lev Vygotsky proposed that:

1. children's thinking is 'quantitatively' different from adults.
2. children's thinking is 'qualitatively' different from adults.
3. children have a lot of potential which includes tasks they can do with the others' support.
4. children are born 'unruly' and society needs to teach them social behaviours.

MATHEMATICS AND SCIENCE

31. If

$$\begin{array}{r} 2\ A \\ \times\ A \\ \hline B\ 2\ A \\ \hline \end{array}$$

where A and B are digits, then

1. A = 1, B = 6 2. A = 1, B = 5
3. A = 5, B = 1 4. A = 6, B = 1

32. If $a - b = \frac{11}{5}$ and $ab = \frac{3}{4}$, then one of the values of $(a + b)$ is:

1. $2\frac{4}{5}$ 2. $3\frac{1}{5}$
3. $3\frac{2}{5}$ 4. $2\frac{3}{5}$

33. If $\frac{7x-1}{4} - \frac{1}{3}\left(2x - \frac{1-x}{2}\right) = \frac{10}{3}$, then what is the value of $\frac{11x+21}{2}$?

1. 29 2. 31
3. 32 4. 27

34. One of the factors of $5(2x - 4y) + 6(4x^2 + 16y^2 - 16xy) - 6$ is:

1. $4x - 8y + 3$ 2. $3x - 6y + 1$
3. $3x - 6y - 1$ 4. $2x - 4y - 3$

35. A shopkeeper buys a fan for ₹ 1,500 and marks it for ₹ 2,500. He sells it after giving a discount of 20% on its marked price and an additional discount of ₹ 250 on cash payment. If a customer buys it on cash payment, then what is the profit (in ₹) earned by the shopkeeper?

1. 225 2. 250
3. 300 4. 200

36. When x is added to each of the numbers 4, 10, 12 and 24, then the numbers so obtained in this order are in proportion. What is the value of $(3x + 1)$?

1. 13 2. 16
3. 19 4. 10

37. If $(3x - 30°)$ and $(2x + 20°)$ are two supplementary angles, then the value of $(2x - 4°)$ is:

1. 76° 2. 80°
3. 84° 4. 72°

38. Angles P and Q of a triangle PQR are respectively 30° and 50°. If the bisectors of angles P and Q meet at a point O, then the value of $(2\angle POQ - 10°)$ is:

1. 190° 2. 270°
3. 250° 4. 150°

39. Which of the following measurement (in cm) ***cannot*** form the sides of a right triangle?

1. 12, 16, 20 2. 4.5, 6, 7.5
3. 8, 16, 12 4. 2.5, 6.5, 6

40. Which of the following letters does ***not*** have rotational symmetry?

1. O 2. E
3. N 4. H

41. Diagonals PR and QS of a parallelogram PQRS intersect at point O. If OP = $(x + y)$ cm, OQ = 20 cm, OR = 16 cm and OS = $(y + 7)$ cm, then the value of $(7x - y)$ (in cm) is:

1. 8 2. 9
3. 13 4. 6

42. The perimeter and area of a trapezium are respectively 52 cm and 128 cm^2. If the sum of its non-parallel sides is 20 cm, then the distance between its parallel sides is:

1. 8 cm 2. 10 cm
3. 12 cm 4. 6 cm

29. 4	**30.** 3	**31.** 3	**32.** 1	**33.** 2	**34.** 1, 3	**35.** 2
36. 1	**37.** 4	**38.** 2	**39.** 3	**40.** 2	**41.** 1	**42.** 1

43. The area of a rectangular field is 48 m^2 and one of its sides is 6 m. How long will a person take to cross this field diagonally at a speed of 20 m per minutes?

1. 20 seconds
2. 30 seconds
3. 40 seconds
4. 15 seconds

44. Three metallic solid cubes of sides 8 cm, 6 cm and 10 cm are melted to form a single solid cube. The side of the new cube so formed is:

1. 20 cm
2. 18 cm
3. 12 cm
4. 24 cm

45. The mean of the median and mode of the observations 30, 61, 55, 56, 60, 20, 26, 45, 28 and 56 is:

1. 53
2. 55
3. 56
4. 52

46. A card is drawn from a well-shuffled deck of playing cards. What is the probability that the card drawn is a 10 a red king?

1. $\frac{1}{13}$
2. $\frac{3}{26}$
3. $\frac{2}{13}$
4. $\frac{1}{26}$

47. The greatest number that divides 87 and 123 leaving respectively 7 and 3 as remainders is:

1. 36
2. 40
3. 80
4. 20

48. The value of $0.\overline{4} + 0.\overline{6}$ is:

1. $1\frac{1}{9}$
2. $1\frac{2}{9}$
3. $1\frac{1}{10}$
4. 1

49. The difference between the largest and smallest fractions among $\frac{4}{7}, \frac{9}{16}, 1\frac{2}{7}$ and $\frac{3}{5}$ is:

1. $\frac{81}{112}$
2. $\frac{25}{28}$
3. $\frac{31}{56}$
4. $\frac{2}{7}$

50. The digit at units place of the square of a number is 2 more than the digit at units place of that number. Which of the following ***cannot*** be the digit at units place of the square of that number?

1. 5
2. 6
3. 9
4. 4

51. Which of the following should ***not*** be a part of assessment of students in mathematics?

1. Reason out mathematical facts
2. Recalling the definitions of mathematical terms
3. Use abstractions to perceive mathematical relationships
4. Apply mathematical concepts learnt to solve problems related to daily life situations

52. ______ was the first Indian mathematician who explained that the square root of negative number does not exist.

1. Baudhayana
2. Aryabhatta
3. Ramanujan
4. Mahavira

53. When asked to arrange the decimal numbers 1.5, 0.23, 1.6, 0.034, 1.13 in ascending order, one of the students arranged them as 0.23, 0.034, 1.5, 1.6, 1.13. Which among the following is ***most appropriate*** for the response of the student?

1. The student has made a careless mistake by arranging the decimal numbers in descending order
2. Teacher should ask the student to recall the rules of ordering decimal numbers and then arrange them
3. The student has developed a misconception of considering that decimal number as bigger number which has more digits in decimal part
4. The student has arranged the decimal numbers in the correct order

54. A teacher asked the children to cut out six squares of 'one' unit each and then asked, "How many different shapes can you make using these squares? Which shape formed would have the maximum perimeter?" The least appropriate objective of this activity is:

1. to provide opportunities for developing creativity and analytical skills
2. to assess children's learning about area and perimeter
3. to apply the formulae learnt in a new context
4. to engage children in group work

43. 2	**44.** 3	**45.** 1	**46.** 2	**47.** 2	**48.** 1
49. 1	**50.** 1	**51.** 2	**52.** 4	**53.** 3	**54.** 4

55. A child solved an equation $x + 7 = 15$ as

$$x + 7 - 7 = 15$$
$$x = 15$$

The best remedial strategy for this child is:

1. explain problems in simple language to the child
2. explain the concept of equality using alternate methods
3. ask the child to solve the same equation on the blackboard
4. give a lot of problems on solving equations to the child

56. According to the National Curriculum Framework, 2005, what are the important skills to be developed among learners while teaching arithmetic and algebra?

A. Looking for patterns in the relationships
B. Memorizing algebraic identities
C. Seeing relationship between numbers
D. Rigorous practice of writing algebraic notation

Choose the ***correct*** option.

1. A and C 2. B and C
3. B and D 4. A, B and D

57. After teaching 'shapes' in Class VIII, a teacher planned a trip to historical places. Which of the following is the ***most appropriate*** reason for this?

1. Teacher has completed most of the syllabus, so she planned the field trip just to have fun
2. Shapes are an integral part of any architecture and such trips encourage connection across the disciplines
3. It would be a break from the routine teaching of mathematics class and an opportunity to improve students' communication skill
4. Field trips are the recommendations of CBSE

58. Uma, a mathematics teacher, asked a student, "How many edges are there in a cylinder?" The student answered. "Two". Uma should

1. praise the student for correct answer
2. draw picture of the cylinder on the blackboard and show the edges
3. give cylinder in the hands of that students and ask the question again
4. give punishment to the student for wrong answer

59. A teacher gives an image drawn on a square grid to children and asks them to draw its enlarged and reduced size images. Which of the following would ***not*** be an objective of doing this exercise in a mathematics classroom?

1. To provide practice for application of fractions
2. To provide scope for integrating arithmetic and geometry
3. To introduce the concept of congruency and similarity
4. To apply the concept of ratio and proportion in different situations

60. Closed-ended questions in mathematics do ***not*** promote:

A. Divergent thinking
B. Convergent thinking
C. Creativity
D. Higher-order thinking skills

Choose the ***correct*** option.

1. A, B and C 2. B, C and D
3. A, C and D 4. A and B

61. You are provided with China rose indicator.
In the first test tube, you add two drops of solution A and observe no change in colour of the solution.
In the second test tube, you add two drops of solution B and get green colour.
In the third test tube, you add two drops of solution C and get magenta (dark pink) colour.
Identify the nature of solutions A, B and C.

1. A-Acidic; B-Basic; C-Neutral
2. A-Neutral; B-Basic; C-Acidic
3. A-Neutral; B-Acidic; C-Basic
4. A-Basic; B-Neutral; C-Acidic

62. Read the following statements:
Statement 1: An object can have non-zero mechanical energy but zero momentum.
Statement 2: An object can do zero work even if the force acting on the object is non-zero.
Choose the ***correct*** option.

1. Statement 1 is false, but Statement 2 is true.
2. Both Statement 1 and 2 are true.
3. Both Statement 1 and 2 are false.
4. Statement 1 is true, but Statement 2 is false.

63. Two identical metal containers are taken. Container A is painted black and the container B is painted white on the outside surface.
Step 1: Both the containers are kept in direct sunlight.
Step 2: After few hours, both the containers are kept in a shady area.
Which of the following will be observed?

1. Container B will gain heat faster than container A whereas container A will lose heat faster than container B.
2. Container A will gain as well as lose heat faster than container B.
3. Container B will gain as well as lose heat faster than container A.
4. Container A will gain heat faster than container B whereas container B will lose heat faster than container A.

55. 2	**56.** 1	**57.** 2	**58.** 3	**59.** 3	**60.** 3	**61.** 2	**62.** 2	**63.** 2

64. Why is it difficult to cut with a blunt knife as compared to a sharp one?

1. Force decreases
2. Area of contact increases
3. Area of contact decreases
4. Pressure increases

65. Which of the following can be used to increase the strength of an electromagnet?

1. Decreasing the number of turns of coil
2. Using a plastic core
3. Using at aluminium core
4. Increasing the flow of current

66. Which of the following is a set of organs that do ***not*** contribute to the digestive process?

1. Oesophagus, large intestine, rectum
2. Small intestine, large intestine, rectum
3. Large intestine, small intestine, oesophagus
4. Buccal cavity, oesophagus, rectum

67. Read the following statements:

A : Earthworm breathes through its skin and does not have lungs.

B : Tadpole breathes through gills and does not have lungs.

C : Snake breathes through its skin and does not have lungs.

Choose the ***correct*** option.

1. B and C are true
2. A and C are true
3. Only A is true
4. A and B are true

68. Read the following, and identify X, Y, Z and W respectively:

X : The part which produces pollen grains

Y : The part where the female gamete is formed

Z : The female reproductive part where pollen grains germinate

W: The part of the flower which attracts insects

Choose the ***correct*** option.

1. Anther, pistil, ovary, sepal
2. Anther, ovary, stigma, petals
3. Stamen, ovary, ovule, petals
4. Pistil, stigma, ovary, sepal

69. Read the following statements:

Assertion (A): Sewage treatment is essential to prevent diseases and deaths.

Reason (R): Sewage is a solid waste which causes water pollution and soil pollution.

Choose the ***correct*** option.

1. Both (A) and (R) are true, but (R) is not the correct reason for (A).
2. (A) is true, but (R) is false.
3. (A) is false, but (R) is true.
4. Both (A) and (R) are true and (R) is the correct reason for (A).

70. Read the following statements:

A : Spiracles and stomata are pores through which insects and leaves exchange gases respectively.

B : Spiracles in an insect are more in number as compared to stomata in a leaf.

C : Both stomata and spiracles are present on the lower surface of leaves and insect's body respectively.

Choose the ***correct*** option.

1. B and C are true
2. A and C are true
3. Only A is true
4. A and B are true

71. Fill in the blanks with the correct answer:

__A__ pushes the blood into pulmonary artery. __B__ take deoxygenated blood from the heart to the lungs. __C__ return oxygenated blood from the lungs to the heart. From the left atrium, blood flows to the __D__. __E__ receives blood from different parts of the body.

1. A-Left ventricle; B-Pulmonary arteries; C-Pulmonary veins; D-Right auricle; E-Right ventricle
2. A-Right ventricle; B-Pulmonary arteries; C-Pulmonary veins; D-Left ventricle; E-Right auricle
3. A-Right ventricle; B-Pulmonary veins; C-Pulmonary arteries; D-Left ventricle; E-Right auricle
4. A-Left ventricle; B-Pulmonary veins; C-Pulmonary arteries; D-Right auricle; E-Right ventricle

72. Read the following statements:

Assertion (A): Hypotheses become theories which in turn become laws.

Reason (R): Scientific laws such as law of gravitation are absolute.

Choose the ***correct*** option.

1. Both (A) and (R) are true, but (R) is not the correct reason for (A).
2. (A) is true, but (R) is false.
3. Both (A) and (R) are false.
4. Both (A) and (R) are true and (R) is the correct reason for (A).

64. 2	**65.** 4	**66.** 1	**67.** 4	**68.** 2	**69.** 2	**70.** 3	**71.** 2	**72.** 3

73. Sheena writes the following statements in her notebook:

A_1: Cactus is a desert plant.

A_2: A desert plant has very small-sized leaves.

A_3: Small-sized leaves help in reducing loss of water.

Which of the following is true about A_1, A_2 and A_3 respectively?

1. Inference, Inference, Inference
2. Observation, Hypothesis, Inference
3. Observation, Observation, Inference
4. Inference, Observation, Hypothesis

74. Which of the following ***cannot*** be regarded as a 'testable question'?

1. How does flu effect human immune system?
2. When will fossil fuels run out?
3. What does a earthworm eat?
4. What is the effect of cigarette smoke on lungs?

75. Read the excerpt given below:

A teacher arranged a fun trip to Qutub Minar for her learners. The learners saw the iron pillar in the Qutub complex. The teacher asked the learners to note down the details displayed about the pillar that is 1600 years old and rust-resistant. She also asked them to write those iron items in their house, which are being used regularly and are rusted and think of causes of rusting and ways to prevent rusting.

Which of the following process skills are being developed through the above mentioned activity?

1. Classification, observation, measurement
2. Inference, classification, observation
3. Classification, observation, hypothesis
4. Measurement, classification, inference

76. Which of the following does ***not*** satisfy 'process validity' of science curriculum as recommended by the National Curriculum Framework, 2005?

1. Students discussing the possible outcomes of connecting a piece of rubber, hairpin and lead to two open ends of an electric circuit
2. Students involved in developing hypothesis for germination of seeds kept in a dry cotton cloth and moist cotton
3. Students involved in making a list of elements given in the periodic table
4. Students investigating the acidity and basicity of different household items

77. The science textbooks often include interesting anecdotes from the past. One such story is that of accidental discovery of silk in China and the role of travellers and traders in introducing silk to the rest of the world through the 'Silk Route'.

What objectives of science teaching-learning are being fulfilled by including the above in the textbook?

A. To develop an understanding of nature of science
B. To develop a historical perspective
C. To develop an appreciation of how science is socially and culturally embedded
D. To reduce the burden of science content by including fun stories

Choose the ***correct*** option:

1. B, C and D 2. A, B and C
3. A, B and D 4. A, C and D

78. Which of the following tasks would ***not*** contribute to developing scientific temper among students?

1. Emphasizing the historical aspects of the development of scientific concepts
2. Reading out the tenets of nature of science
3. Encouraging the students to ask questions
4. Providing hands-on experiences to students

79. Which of the following is the most appropriate strategy to introduce physical properties of metals and non-metals to Grade VII learners as per the inquiry-based approach?

1. Initiate a discussion on students' everyday experiences of using metallic and non-metallic substances
2. Define the terms 'sonorous', 'boiling point' and 'melting point'
3. Give a set of materials to students and ask them to deduce the properties of metals and non-metals
4. List the differences between the physical properties of metals and non-metals on the blackboard

80. Read the following statements:

S_1 : Systematic experimentation needs to be introduced in upper primary stage to verify theoretical principles.

S_2 : Activities and experimental evidence play and important role in understanding nature of science.

S_3 : Most concepts should be arrived at by an inductive approach at upper primary level.

Choose the ***correct*** option.

1. Both S_1 and S_3 are true and S_3 is the correct reason for S_1
2. Both S_2 and S_3 are true, but S_1 is false
3. Both S_1 and S_3 are true, but S_2 is false
4. Both S_1 and S_2 are true and S_2 is the correct reason for S_1

73. 3	**74.** 2	**75.** 3	**76.** 3	**77.** 2	**78.** 2	**79.** 3	**80.** 2

81. Before beginning to formally teach a chapter of 'force' in Class VI, a teacher holds a discussion in which she asks children to imagine what would they do if they wish to keep a ball rolling on the ground for very long distance. How can she most suitably use the children's responses?

A. To evaluate students
B. To assess student's preconceptions
C. To determine the pedagogical strategy to be adopted to teach the concept
D. To equable students to define force

Choose the ***correct*** option.

1. B and C
2. C and D
3. A and C
4. A and B

82. Fill in the blanks with the ***correct*** answer:

At the onset of puberty, the size of ovaries in females __A__ and produce __B__. In males __C__ is produced by testes. The production of these hormones is controlled by __D__.

1. A–enlarges; B–thyroxine; C–testosterone; D-thyroid gland
2. A–reduces; B–estrogen; C–testosterone; D–pituitary gland
3. A–enlarges; B–estrogen; C–testosterone; D–pituitary gland
4. A–reduces; B–estrogen; C–sex hormone; D-adrenal gland

83. A circuit comprising three identical bulbs and a switch is connected in different arrangements as given below. In which arrangement will the bulbs glow the brightest?

1. Arrangement B–All bulbs in parallel
2. Arrangement C–Two bulbs in parallel connected in series with the third bulb
3. Arrangement D–Two bulbs in series connected in parallel with the third bulb
4. Arrangement A–All bulbs in series.

84. Read the following statements:

Assertion (A): Anodizing is a method of prevent metal from corrosion.

Reason (R): Anodizing is a process of coating iron with a layer of zinc.

Choose the ***correct*** option.

1. Both (A) and (R) are true, but (R) is not the correct reason for (A).
2. (A) is true, but (R) is false.
3. Both (A) and (R) are false.
4. Both (A) and (R) are true and (R) is the correct reason for (A).

85. Why do silver articles turn black when kept in the open for a few days?

1. Due to reaction with hydrogen sulphide present in air
2. Due to reaction with nitrogen oxides present in air
3. Due to reaction with carbon monoxide present in air
4. Due to reaction with oxygen in air

86. Identify A, B, C and D in the following table:

Name of the salt	Salt obtained from	
	Acid	Base
Ammonium chloride	HCl	A
Sodium nitrate	HNO_3	B
Sodium chloride	C	D

Choose the ***correct*** option.

1. A-NH_4; B-NaOH; C-HCl; D-NaOH
2. A-NH_3; B-NaOH; C-HCl; D-NaOH
3. A-NH_4OH; B-NaO; C-HCl; D-$NaHCO_3$
4. A-NH_4OH; B-$Na(OH_2)$; C-$HClO_2$; D-NaH

87. Read the following statements:

Step 1: A few spoons of sugar are dissolved in water to prepare a concentrated sugar syrup.

Step 2: The sugar syrup is heated on low flame till it caramelizes.

Choose the ***correct*** option.

1. Step 1 is a chemical change and Step 2 is a physical change
2. Both Step 1 and Step 2 are physical changes
3. Both Step 1 and Step 2 are chemical changes
4. Step 1 is a physical change and Step 2 is a chemical change

88. The ion of an element has two positive charges. The mass number of the atom is 27 and the number of neutrons is 14. What is the number of electrons in the ion?

1. 10
2. 11
3. 15
4. 13

81. 1	**82.** 3	**83.** 1	**84.** 2	**85.** 1	**86.** 2	**87.** 4	**88.** 2

89. A ray of light travels from air into three media A, B and C with different optical densities. Refer to the table given below and identify X, Y, Z and W.

	Change in speed of light	*Change in frequency of light*	*Change in wavelength of light*
Air to medium A	X	Y	Decreases
Air to medium B	Increases	No change	Z
Air to medium C	Remains same	W	No change

Choose the ***correct*** option.

1. X-Increases; Y-Increases; Z-Increases; W-Increases
2. X-Decreases; Y-Remains unchanged; Z-Increases; W-Remains unchanged
3. X-Decreases; Y-Decreases; Z-Increases; W-Remains unchanged
4. X-Increases; Y-Decreases; Z-Decreases; W-Increases

90. Read the following statements:

Situation A: Growth and branching of roots in the A-horizon and B-horizon is advantageous for absorption of water and minerals.

Situation B: C-horizon is rich in humus which makes soil soft and porous.

Choose the ***correct*** option.

1. Only Situation B is true
2. Both Situations A and B are true
3. Both Situations A and B are false
4. Only Situation A is true

LANGUAGE-I — ENGLISH

91. Read the following statements:

Assertion (A): Delaying the learning of languages in the early years makes it more difficult for children to acquire new languages.

Reason (R): Early years of the child are sensitive period for language acquisition.

Choose the ***correct*** option.

1. Both (A) and (R) are true, but (R) is not a correct explanation of (A).
2. (A) is not true, but (R) is false.
3. (A) is true, but (R) is not true.
4. Both (A) and (R) are true and (R) is a correct explanation of (A).

92. One of the key principles of National Curriculum Framework for Foundational Stage (2022) with respect to multilingualism is:

1. children are not able to pick up multiple oral languages in the early years
2. multilingualism has both cognitive and societal/ cultural benefits
3. children must be helped to unlearn their home language and focus of the school must shift on learning the language of the school
4. multilingual nature of a classroom acts as a barrier in effective curriculum transaction

93. In some of the speech communities, two different varieties of language coexist, each with a distinct range of social function. This situation is described as:

1. register
2. diglossia
3. dialect
4. code mixing

94. Children work in pairs. A text is divided in half. One child reads their text for the partner which the other child writes. Two of them work out the whole text. The activity is called:

1. word web
2. partial dictation
3. storytelling
4. running dictation

95. Which of the following statements is ***not*** true of study about the literary texts in language classroom?

1. Literary texts are cultural inputs for language learning.
2. Literary texts develop critical thinking and reflection.
3. Literary texts are for appreciation and enjoyment.
4. Literary texts should be used to teach grammar.

96. Naveen of Class VI struggles with reading the text. The teacher gives him simpler text to read. She conducts shared reading sessions for him. The support provided by the teacher is called:

1. scaffolding
2. brainstorming
3. ice breaking
4. reading readiness

97. Which approach in language teaching-learning believes 'language is a habit'?

1. Communicative language teaching
2. Natural approach
3. Cooperative language learning
4. Audiolingualism

89. 2	**90.** 4	**91.** 4	**92.** 2	**93.** 2	**94.** 2	**95.** 4	**96.** 1	**97.** 4

98. A child reads an unseen passage for which he is expected to answer the questions that following. This type of reading is referred to as:

1. exclusive reading
2. skimming
3. extensive reading
4. scanning

99. Teacher shows five pictures to the students and asks them to write story based on these pictures.

This is an example of:

1. jigsaw dictation
2. shared reading
3. creative writing
4. show and tell

100. Which of the following is the characteristic of performance-based assessment in language?

1. Non-interactive performance
2. Decontextualized test items
3. Contextualized communicative tasks
4. Multiple-choice questions

101. Read the following statements:

A : Reading is just to understand letter-sound relationships and pronounce the word correctly.

B : Reading is decoding symbols to arrive at meaning.

Choose the ***correct*** option;

1. A is true, but B is false
2. B is true, but A is false
3. Both A and B are false
4. Both A and B are true

102. A teacher has to assess listening skill of her students. Which of the following activities can she select as a listening assessment?

1. Teacher tells a story and after that asks comprehension-based questions
2. Teacher asks the children to read a story and after that asks comprehension-based questions
3. Teacher gives vocabulary-based tasks
4. Rating the children on their oral presentation

103. _____ is concerned with the aspects of meaning in language.

1. Semantics
2. Syntax
3. Morphology
4. Phonetics

104. Which of the following is ***not*** the principle of language learning?

1. Learners may vary in their preferred approaches to learning
2. Language is a tool for communication
3. Language is learnt through memorization of structures/rules of grammar
4. Learning a language involves mastery of both skills and knowledge

105. A teacher of Grade 6 writes a word in the centre of the blackboard and asks the learners brainstorm all the words they can think of which are connected to the central word. The major objective of this activity is:

1. improving vocabulary of learners
2. understanding grammar
3. enhancing reading skills
4. enhancing writing skills

Directions (Qs. No. 106-111): *Read the extract given below and answer the questions that follow:*

Your pretty bird in a gilded cage
Flutters its sorrowful wings
But there's never a cage-bird yet could sing
As my bird sings.

He's little and brown and wild and shy,
But free to build and thrive,
Your poor bit thing behind its bars
Is only half alive!

My bird sings out with a true wood-note,
Your pipes of sorrowful things,
And never, now, may he learn the song
That my bird sings.
Never, now, may he wheel and soar
With the sunshine on his wings,
O, a bird in a cage is a crippled thing
But my bird sings!

106. The speaker's bird can do a number of things. It is because:

1. the bird is caged
2. the bird is free
3. the bird is sorrowful
4. the bird is talented

107. The caged bird is described as 'a crippled thing' because:

1. it is not free to fly and soar
2. it is poor
3. it is wild
4. its one leg is broken

108. Which poetic device is used in the expression 'sorrowful wings'?

1. Simile
2. Transferred epithet
3. Personification
4. Metaphor

98. 4	**99.** 3	**100.** 3	**101.** 2	**102.** 1	**103.** 1
104. 3	**105.** 1	**106.** 2	**107.** 1	**108.** 2	

109. What is the theme of the poem?

1. The birds should be kept in a cage
2. The birds should be given good food
3. Birds living in the open enjoy their lives
4. The caged bird lives a fruitful life

110. "But my bird sings!" denotes that:

1. my bird is free
2. my bird doesn't feel free
3. my bird has regained her voice
4. my bird sings sweetly

111. The speaker says that the cage-bird flutters its sorrowful wings. The wings are being described as 'sorrowful' because:

1. the bird is sad as it is caged
2. the bird can't sing
3. the bird is hungry
4. the wings are broken

Directions (Qs. No. 112-120): *Read the passage given below and answer the questions that follow:*

1. Physical health affects the mind and vice versa. Which of the two is the more important is like asking the age-old question : what comes first, the chicken or the egg. For our present subject, let us be clear that a sound mind in a sound-body is prerequisite for high efficiency and good quality work in the office, factory or field, which leads to a sense of achievement and fulfilment.
2. Our health is, of course, important not only to us, but also to our families and even to our employers. No wonder then that companies everywhere have a stake in the health and fitness of their employee and are willing to spend considerable money towards this purpose. Japanese companies particularly excel in this and the more successful among them start off the day with a body-bending and stretching session and even singing the company song designed to promote loyalty and motivation among the workforce. This is considered an important factor contributing to high productivity and quality. Here is a lesson which has been emulated elsewhere in the world and could work wonders in India. It is estimated that some 20,000 American firms have established in-house health clubs. Typical of these is the soft drink manufacturer Pepsi Cola which has spent about $2 million in setting up a health club at its head office in New York State. Such expenditure has proved to be a wise investment in achieving better efficiency and higher productivity. It has, indirectly, also helped reduce the premium on the health insurance of its staff. This business has grown so large that hundreds of consultancies have sprung up for the management of health clubs and fitness centres. In some cases, there is a nominal contribution by the employees on the premise that this way they will value and use the facilities all the more. Some insurance companies have teamed up with employers in such ventures as better health contributes to a longer life and hence more premium! Though many firms in India have generous medical schemes, the movement towards health clubs and the like is yet to gain momentum.

112. 'The movement towards health clubs is yet to gain momentum in India' signifies that:

1. insurance companies are getting good premium due to health clubs
2. health clubs in Indian companies have not yet become popular
3. due to health clubs, many consultancies have opened up
4. health clubs are getting popular in Indian companies

113. What is directly affected by physical health?

1. Business 2. Efficiency
3. Insurance premium 4. Mind

114. Which one of the following words is opposite in meaning to the word 'nominal'?

1. Cursory 2. Simple
3. Substantial 4. Above-mentioned

115. Which one of the following words is nearest in meaning to the word 'prerequisite'?

1. Required 2. Optional
3. Secondary 4. Unnecessary

116. Which Part of Speech is the underlined word?

Japanese companies <u>particularly</u> excel in this.

1. Adverb 2. Noun
3. Conjunction 4. Adjective

117. Identify the clause in the underlined part of the sentence:

<u>It is estimated</u> that some 20,000 American firms have established in-house health clubs.

1. Adjective clause 2. Noun clause
3. Principal clause 4. Adverb clause

109. 3	**110.** 1	**111.** 1	**112.** 2	**113.** 4	**114.** 3	**115.** 1	**116.** 1	**117.** 3

118. What is the prerequisite for high effect and good quality work?

1. Health club
2. Exercising and stretching
3. Sound mind in a sound body
4. Good quality office

119. Japanese companies ensure loyalty and motivation by making their workers:

1. drink healthy drinks
2. sing the company's song
3. join health clubs
4. start off the day with exercising

120. Why do companies have health clubs?

1. They attract profit to the company
2. They help in better efficiency and high productivity of the workers
3. Health insurance companies can tie up with these health clubs
4. They attract more workforce

LANGUAGE-II — हिन्दी

121. 12-18 माह की आयु के बच्चे पहचाने जाने योग्य एक इकाईवाली ध्वनियाँ निकालना शुरू कर देते हैं, यह अवधि जिसके अंतर्गत प्रतिदिन की वस्तुओं के लिए एक ही पदावली बोली जाती है, क्या कहलाती है?

1. संक्षिप्त वाक् (टेलिग्राफिक)
2. एक-शब्दीय वाक्य अवस्था
3. बबलाना
4. कूजन (कूईंग)

122. पठन और लेखन कौशलों पर नीचे दिए गए कथनों पर विचार कीजिए:

A : पठन की समझ और योग्यता लेखन की योग्यता को प्रभावित करती है।

B : पठन और लेखन दोनों पृथक् प्रक्रियाएँ हैं और एक-दूसरे से स्वतंत्र होकर विकसित होती हैं।

सही विकल्प चुनिए।

1. A सही है, लेकिन B गलत है
2. A और B दोनों गलत हैं
3. A गलत है, लेकिन B सही है
4. A और B दोनों सही हैं

123. सभी भाषाओं में कुछ सर्वसामान्य गुणधर्म होते हैं, इन्हें क्या कहा जाता है?

1. भाषा सार्वभौमिक
2. प्रयुक्ति
3. बोलियाँ
4. द्विभाषारूपिता (डिग्लोसिया)

124. किसी भी कक्षा में भाषिक विविधता की स्वीकार्यता:

1. बच्चों के आत्मविश्वास को क्षति पहुँचाएगी जिससे कल्पनाशीलता और रचनात्मकता में क्षति आएगी
2. भाषा अधिगम में किसी प्रकार का प्रभाव नहीं पड़ेगा
3. बच्चों के आत्मविश्वास में वृद्धि होगी परिणामस्वरूप उनकी कल्पनाशीलता और रचनात्मकता में वृद्धि होगी
4. भाषा प्रवाह को प्राप्त करने में अवरोध पैदा करेगी

125. उद्‌गामी साक्षरता के संदर्भ में मुद्रित सामग्री के प्रति जागरूकता की कौन-सी विशेषता **नहीं** है?

1. अक्षरों और शब्दों के मध्य अंतर की पहचान कर पाना
2. बाएँ से दाएँ और ऊपर से नीचे की ओर पढ़ पाना
3. पूरे-पूरे वाक्य पढ़ना आरंभ करना
4. पुस्तक पकड़ना

126. नीचे बुनियादी चरण के संदर्भ में पठन कौशल के अधिगम प्रतिफल दिए गए हैं, उन्हें अनुक्रम में व्यवस्थित करें।

A. संक्षिप्त खंड उपयुक्त तान-अनुतान, विराम, ध्वनि में उतार-चढ़ाव के साथ सटीकता और प्रवाह के साथ पढ़ते हैं।

B. परिचित शब्दों के कुछ वाक्यों को सटीकता के साथ पढ़ते हैं।

C. संक्षिप्त खंड उपयुक्त तान-अनुतान और विराम के साथ सटीकता से पढ़ते हैं।

सही विकल्प चुनिए।

1. B, C, A
2. A, C, B
3. C, A, B
4. A, B, C

127. निम्नलिखित में से कौन-सा विस्तृत (एक्स्टेन्सिव) श्रवण का भाग **नहीं** है?

1. मुख्य विचार बिन्दु के लिए श्रवण
2. निष्कर्ष निकालना
3. कुछ तथ्यों व सूचनाओं के लिए श्रवण
4. सारांश के लिए श्रवण

128. निम्नलिखित में से कौन-सा कार्य पठन कौशल के आकलन हेतु प्रयोग में **नहीं** लाया जा सकता?

1. पढ़ी गई पाठ्य सामग्री के आधार पर बहुविकल्पीय प्रश्न
2. चित्र के माध्यम से संकेत आधारित शब्द सूचना
3. अध्यापक द्वारा कथा वाचन
4. सस्वर पठन

118. 3	**119.** 2	**120.** 2	**121.** 2	**122.** 1	**123.** 1
124. 3	**125.** 3	**126.** 1	**127.** 3	**128.** 3	

129. निम्नलिखित में से कौन-सा कथन जारी रहने वाले श्रुतलेख (रनिंग डिक्टेशन) को सही रूप से परिभाषित करता है?

1. बच्चे दो-दो के समूह में कार्य करते हैं। पाठ्य सामग्री को दो अंशों में विभाजित किया जाता है। एक बालक अपने जोड़ीदार के लिए अपना अंश पढ़ता है, दूसरा बालक उसे लिखता है। समूची पाठ्य सामग्री के लिए दोनों मिलकर कार्य करते हैं।
2. बच्चे दो-दो के जोड़ों में कार्य करते हैं। एक बालक दौड़कर पाठ्य सामग्री देखता है और अपने जोड़ीदार को श्रुतलेख बोलता है, जोड़ीदार उस सामग्री को लिखता है।
3. अध्यापक समूची कक्षा को शब्दों/पाठ्यसामग्री का श्रुतलेख बोलता है, विद्यार्थी उसे नोट करते हैं।
4. विद्यार्थी पाठ्य सामग्री के विभिन्न अंशों को पढ़ते हैं, तत्पश्चात् कार्य को पूरा करने के लिए एक-दूसरे के साथ सूचनाओं का आदान-प्रदान करते हैं।

130. ''बालक भाषा अर्जन की सहजात क्षमता के साथ जन्म लेते हैं'' भाषा अर्जन के इस विचार बिन्दु को किसके द्वारा समर्थन दिया गया है?

1. संज्ञानात्मक वादी
2. सामाजिक अन्तःक्रियावादी
3. व्यवहारवादी
4. प्राकृतवादी (नेटीविस्ट)

131. प्रक्रिया लेखन उपागम में लेखन प्रक्रिया का वह तत्व क्या कहलाएगा जिसके अंतर्गत लेखक औपचारिक रूप से अपने कार्य को बृहत्तर स्तर पर पाठकों के साथ साझा करते हैं?

1. प्रकाशन
2. संपादन
3. पुनरावृत्ति
4. प्रारूप तैयार करना

132. किसी पाठ्य सामग्री में आए कठिन शब्दों के संदर्भ में एक अध्यापक उस शब्द को मातृभाषा में बताता है और फिर विद्यार्थियों को याद करने के लिए कहता है। अध्यापक किस विधि का प्रयोग कर रहा है?

1. प्रत्यक्ष विधि (डायरेक्ट)
2. संरचनात्मक उपागम
3. सम्प्रेषणात्मक उपागम
4. व्याकरण अनुवाद विधि

133. एक शिक्षार्थी बिना मदद के क्या कर सकता है और किसी वयस्क या अधिक समर्थ सहपाठी के सहयोग से क्या कर सकती है, इन दोनों के बीच की स्थिति को क्या कहेंगे?

1. निकटस्थ विकास का क्षेत्र
2. उपलब्धि का क्षेत्र
3. दूरस्थ अधिगम
4. परिपक्वता का स्तर

134. प्रमस्तिष्क में क्षति के कारण भाषा के कार्य में विकार जिससे भाषिक स्वरूपों व नियमों को समझने और उत्पन्न करने में कठिनाई हो, उसे क्या कहेंगे?

1. पठन वैकल्य (डिस्लेक्सिया)
2. गणन वैकल्य (डिस्कैलकुलिया)
3. उच्चारण वैकल्य (डिसरथिया)
4. वाचाघात (अफेजिया)

135. उस प्रक्रिया का नाम बताइए जिसके द्वारा भाषा एक पीढ़ी से दूसरी पीढ़ी को स्थानांतरित होती हैं।

1. उत्पादकता
2. यादृच्छिकता
3. विस्थापन
4. सांस्कृतिक प्रसारण

निर्देशः (प्र. सं. 136 से 142 तक): *नीचे दिए गए गद्यांश को पढ़कर पूछे गए प्रश्नों के सबसे उपयुक्त उत्तर वाले विकल्प को चुनिए:*

समाज में पड़ते ही मनुष्य देखने लगता है कि उसकी स्थिति दोहरी हो गई है। वह देखता है कि मैं यह हूँ, और मैं बड़ा समझा जाता हूँ। इस निश्चय के साथ एक यह निश्चय और जुड़ जाने से कि मैं बड़ा समझा जाता हूँ मनुष्य के आनंद या सुख के अनुभव में वृद्धि होती है। इसी प्रकार मैं क्षुद्र हूँ इस धारणा के साथ मैं क्षुद्र समझा जाता हूँ इस धारणा के योग से दुःख के अनुभव की वृद्धि होती है। इस प्रकार स्थिति के एकांत और सामाजिक दो विभाग हो जाने से कोई तो दोनों विभागों पर दृष्टि रख सकते हैं और कोई एक ही पर। शक्तिशाली और प्रतिभा सम्पन्न मनुष्य पहले यह प्रयत्न करते हैं कि 'हम ऐसे हों'। फिर वैसे हो जाने पर यदि आवश्यक हुआ तो वह वे यह प्रयत्न भी करते हैं कि 'हम ऐसे समझे जाएँ'। इन दोनों के प्रयत्न जुदा-जुदा हैं। संसार में शक्ति सम्पन्न सब नहीं होते, इससे बहुत से लोग स्थिति के पहले विभाग के लिए जिन प्रयत्नों की आवश्यकता है उनमें अपने को असमर्थ देख दूसरे ही विभाग से किसी प्रकार अपना संतोष करना चाहते हैं और उसी पर दृष्टि रखकर प्रयत्न करते हैं। ईर्ष्या ऐसे लोगों के हृदय में बहुत जगह पाती है और उनके प्रयत्नों में सहायक भी होती है। भाव प्रवर्तन आदि के बल से जिस समुदाय के प्राणी परस्पर ऐसे बन गए हैं कि अपने इंद्रियानुभव और भावनाओं तक को जवाब देकर दूसरों के इंद्रियानुभव और भावनाओं द्वारा निर्वाह कर सकते हैं, उसी से ईर्ष्या का विकास हो सकता है। अतः ईर्ष्या का अनन्य अधिकार मनुष्य जाति ही पर है। एक कुत्ता किसी दूसरे कुत्तों को कुछ खाते देख उसे आप खाने की इच्छा कर सकता है, पर वह यह नहीं चाह सकता कि चाहे हम खाएँ या न खाएँ वह दूसरा कुत्ता न खाने पाए। दूसरे कुत्तों की दृष्टि में हमारी स्थिति कैसी है, इसकी चिंता उस कुत्ते को न होगी। अपने विषय में दूसरों के चित्त में अच्छी धारणा उत्पन्न करने का प्रयत्न अच्छी बात है। इस प्रयत्न को जो बुरा रूप प्राप्त होता है वह असत्य के समावेश के

129. 2	**130.** 4	**131.** 1	**132.** 4	**133.** 1	**134.** 4	**135.** 4

कारण, दूसरों की धारणा की अवास्तविकता और अपनी स्थिति की सापेक्षता के कारण, जब हम अपने विषय में दूसरों की झूठी धारणा और अपनी स्थिति के सापेक्ष रूप मात्र से संतोष करना चाहते हैं तभी बुराइयों के लिए जगह होती है और ईर्ष्या की राह खुलती है।

136. ईर्ष्या पर _____ का एकाधिकार है।

1. जानवरों
2. मानव जाति
3. न प्राणी जगत् का न मानव जगत् का
4. प्राणी जगत्

137. 'मानव की स्थिति दोहरी हो गई है' का आशय है:

1. जैसा हूँ वैसा ही समझा जाता हूँ
2. न समझता हूँ, न समझना चाहता हूँ
3. कोई कुछ भी समझे मुझे फर्क नहीं पड़ता
4. जैसा हूँ वैसा नहीं समझा जाता

138. 'ईर्ष्या ऐसे लोगों के हृदय में जगह पाती है', का आशय है:

1. ऐसे लोगों के हृदय में ईर्ष्या छिपी रहती है
2. ऐसे लोगों का हृदय ईर्ष्या से भर जाता है
3. ऐसे लोगों के हृदय में ईर्ष्या का घर होता है
4. ऐसे लोग ही ईर्ष्या करते हैं

139. सही कथन चुनिए:

1. ईर्ष्या का बहुवचन रूप है इर्ष्याएँ।
2. ईर्ष्या का बहुवचन रूप से ईर्ष्यायों।
3. ईर्ष्या का बहुवचन रूप नहीं होता।
4. ईर्ष्या का बहुवचन रूप है ईर्ष्ये।

140. "दृष्टि रखकर प्रयत्न करते है" में 'रखकर' _____ है।

1. वर्तमानकालिक कृदंत 2. भूतकालिक कृदंत
3. संयोजक 4. क्रिया

141. मनुष्य का दुःख बढ़ने का कारण है:

1. मैं जैसा हूँ उससे कम समझा जाता हूँ
2. मैं जैसा हूँ वैसा ही समझा जाता हूँ
3. मैं समझा ही नहीं जाता हूँ
4. लोग मुझे कुछ नहीं समझते

142. मनुष्य के लिए आनंददायक है:

1. मैं जैसा हूँ उससे निम्न समझा जाता हूँ
2. मैं जैसा हूँ वैसा ही जाना जाता हूँ
3. मैं जैसा हूँ उससे बड़ा समझा जाता हूँ
4. मैं जैसा हूँ उससे बहुत अधिक बड़ा समझा जाता हूँ

निर्देशः (प्र. सं. 143 से 150 तक): *नीचे दिए गए गद्यांश को पढ़कर पूछे गए प्रश्नों के सबसे उपयुक्त उत्तर वाले विकल्प को चुनिए:*

यह बात ध्यान देने की है कि ईर्ष्या व्यक्ति-विशेष से होती है। यह नहीं होता कि जिस किसी को ऐश्वर्य, गुण या मन से सम्पन्न देखा उसी से ईर्ष्या हो गई। ईर्ष्या उन्हीं से होती है जिनके विषय में यह धारणा होती है कि लोगों की दृष्टि हमारे साथ-साथ उन पर भी अवश्य पड़ती होगी। अपने से दूरस्थ होने के कारण अपने साथ-साथ जिन पर लोगों का ध्यान जाने का निश्चय नहीं होता उनके प्रति ईर्ष्या नहीं उत्पन्न होती। काशी में रहने वाली किसी धानी को अमेरिका के किसी धानी की बात सुनकर ईर्ष्या नहीं होगी। हिन्दी के किसी कवि को इटली के किसी कवि का महत्त्व सुनकर ईर्ष्या नहीं होगी। संबंधियों, बालसखाओं, सहपाठियों और पड़ोसियों के बीच ईर्ष्या का विकास अधिक देखा जाता है। लड़कपन से जो आदमी एक साथ उठते-बैठते देखे गए हैं उन्हीं में से कोई एक-दूसरे की बढ़ती से जलता हुआ भी पाया गया है। यदि दो साथियों में से कोई किसी अच्छे पद पर पहुँच गया तो वह इस उद्योग में देखा जाता है कि दूसरा किसी अच्छे पद पर न पहुँचने पाए। प्रायः अपनी उन्नति के गुप्त बाधकों का पता लगाते-लगाते लोग अपने किसी बड़े पुराने मित्र तक पहुँच जाते हैं। जिस समय संसर्ग सूत्र में बाँधकर हम औरों को अपने साथ एक पंक्ति में खड़ा करते हैं उस समय सहानुभूति, सहायता आदि की संभावना प्रतिष्ठित होने के साथ ही साथ ईर्ष्या और द्वेष की संभावना की नींव भी पड़ जाती है। अपने किसी विधान से हम भलाई ही भलाई की संभावना का सूत्रपात करें और इस प्रकार भविष्य के अनिश्चय में बाधा डालें, यह कभी हो ही नहीं सकता। भविष्य की अनिश्चयात्मकता अटल और अजेय है। अपनी लाख विद्या-बुद्धि से भी हम उसे बिल्कुल हटा नहीं सकते। अब ध्यान देने की बात यह निकली कि ईर्ष्या के संचार के लिए ईर्ष्या करने वाले और ईर्ष्या के पात्र के अतिरिक्त स्थिति पर ध्यान देने वाले समाज की भी आवश्यकता है। इसी समाज की धारणा पर प्रभाव डालने के लिए ही ईर्ष्या की जाती है; ऐश्वर्य, गुण या मन का गुप्त रूप से बिना किसी समुदाय को विदित कराए, सुख या संतोष भोगने के लिए नहीं।

143. किसी परिचित के प्रतिष्ठित हो जाने से:

1. हमें कोई फर्क नहीं पड़ता है
2. हम उसे पहले से अधिक इज्जत देते हैं
3. ईर्ष्या और द्वेष की नींव पड़ती है
4. उसके विकास को रोकने का मन करता है

144. ईर्ष्या पैदा करने के लिए आवश्यक नहीं है:

1. किसी का ऐश्वर्य
2. ईर्ष्या का पात्र
3. स्थिति पर ध्यान देने वाला समाज
4. ईर्ष्या करने वाला

136. 2 **137.** 4 **138.** 2 **139.** 3 **140.** 2 **141.** 1 **142.** 3 **143.** 3 **144.** 1

145. 'सूत्रपात करना' का आशय है:
1. कुछ न करना
2. प्रारम्भ करना
3. समाप्त करना
4. बहुत प्रयत्न करना

146. लड़कपन के साथी की बढ़ती से कोई:
1. खुश होता है
2. द्वेष करता है
3. सुखी होता है
4. जलता है

147. 'पड़ोसियों' पड़ोसी संज्ञा का _____ रूप है।
1. सामान्य बहुवचन
2. तिर्यक बहुवचन
3. तिर्यक एकवचन
4. सामान्य एकवचन

148. उन्नति के गुप्त बाधक को खोजने पर हमें क्या पता चलता है?
1. वह बालसखा था
2. वह पड़ोसी था
3. वह पुराना मित्र था
4. वह सहपाठी था

149. हम ईर्ष्या किससे करते हैं?
1. जिन्हें लोग हमारे साथ पढ़ता देखते हैं
2. जिन पर लोगों की हमारे साथ दृष्टि पड़ती है
3. जिन्हे लोग हमारे साथ नौकरी करते देखते है
4. जिन्हें लोग हमारे साथ खेलता देखते हैं

150. _____ के बीच ईर्ष्या नहीं फूलती-फूलती।
1. पड़ोसियों
2. दूर रहने वालों
3. रिश्तेदारों
4. सहपाठियों

EXPLANATORY ANSWERS

1. The assertion is incorrect because the main purpose of intelligence tests and extended observation is not to compare children with each other, but to understand each child's individual abilities, strengths, and areas requiring support. Modern educational psychology emphasizes individualized assessment rather than comparative ranking. The reason is also incorrect because intelligence is not purely innate or fixed; it is influenced by environmental factors such as education, experience, and socio-cultural context. Hence, both the assertion and the reason are false.

2. When a teacher deliberately includes examples of scientists of all genders, she is challenging the traditional belief that science is mainly a male field. This helps students see that ability, talent, and achievement are not limited by gender. Such classroom practice promotes equality, inclusion, and broader aspirations among children. Therefore, the purpose is to break gender stereotypes.

3. The assertion is false because statements like "all girls are hardworking and sincere" and "boys are intelligent and dominating" are generalized stereotypes, not valid educational truths. Children cannot be classified in such fixed ways on the basis of gender. The reason is also false because differences in behaviour, interests, personality, and achievement do not arise only from two biologically distinct brains. Socialization, environment, culture, opportunity, expectations, and upbringing also play a major role. Hence both the assertion and the reason are false.

4. Students differ in the ways they learn, respond, remember, express, and engage with knowledge. These differences are a natural part of human diversity and should be respected in the classroom. They should not be viewed as abnormalities, deficits, or proof of lower or higher intelligence. Good teaching accepts these variations and adapts methods accordingly. Therefore, individual differences in learning preference are a normal depiction of diversity.

5. In norm-referenced assessment, a student's performance is judged in relation to the performance of other students, usually a group average or standard norm group. The purpose is comparison and ranking rather than checking whether a fixed learning objective has been achieved. Since the question clearly says that the student's scores are compared with the average performance of other students, the assessment is norm-referenced.

6. Effective classroom assessment is meant to support learning rather than create pressure. Statement (*i*) is correct because good assessments guide students' thinking processes and help them reflect on how they learn. Statement (*ii*) is also correct as assessment itself can become a learning activity through feedback and reflection. Statement (*iii*) is incorrect since fear and stress hinder meaningful learning. Statement (*iv*) is also incorrect because classroom assessment need not always be standardized or norm-referenced; it should often be flexible and formative.

7. This question requires students to compare perspectives, analyze hidden meanings, and evaluate bias, which are key aspects of higher-order thinking. The other options mainly involve recall or simple comprehension, while this option demands critical analysis and deeper reasoning.

8. The assertion is true because students who struggle with writing are sometimes wrongly labeled due to superficial judgment. The reason is also true as teachers may hold implicit biases or assumptions that influence their perceptions. These biases directly lead to stereotyping, so the reason correctly explains the assertion.

9. Promoting diversity requires inclusion, respect, and equal opportunity. Stereotyping students leads to discrimination and limits their growth, which goes against the idea of diversity. The other options encourage inclusivity and cultural understanding.

145. 2	**146.** 4	**147.** 2	**148.** 3	**149.** 2	**150.** 2

10. Dysgraphia affects writing abilities, including handwriting, spelling, and fine motor coordination. Dyslexia is related to reading difficulties, dyscalculia to numerical understanding, and dyspraxia to motor coordination, so only the first match is correct.

11. Students with autism spectrum conditions typically prefer structure, repetition, and predictability. They often feel comfortable when activities follow a fixed routine because it reduces uncertainty and anxiety. Eye contact, sudden changes, and interacting with unfamiliar people can be challenging, so predictable routines provide a sense of stability and ease.

12. This statement is incorrect because gifted children generally show high curiosity, strong imagination, and creativity. They often explore ideas deeply and ask many questions. The other statements are valid as giftedness can be multi-dimensional, may coexist with disabilities, and requires nurturing.

13. Error analysis helps learners identify their mistakes, understand misconceptions, and correct them. This reflective process strengthens memory and conceptual clarity, thereby improving retention. It also promotes self-regulation and deeper understanding of the subject matter.

14. Procedural knowledge refers to knowing how to perform tasks or processes, such as solving a problem or carrying out an activity. It involves steps, methods, and sequences. Declarative knowledge, in contrast, refers to factual information or "knowing what."

15. When new learning requires modification or extension of existing cognitive structures, deeper processing is involved. This takes more time because learners must reorganize prior knowledge. However, such meaningful learning leads to stronger retention, so it is remembered for a longer duration.

16. The assertion is correct because encouraging students to think about their learning goals and the steps needed promotes self-regulated learning. The reason is also correct as self-assessment helps learners monitor their progress and improve performance. This ability directly explains why focusing on such reflective questions is important, as it strengthens independent learning and growth.

17. Guided discovery emphasizes active participation where learners explore, investigate, and build their own understanding with teacher support. It is neither completely unstructured nor teacher-dominated; instead, the teacher facilitates learning by providing direction and guidance.

18. Memorization alone does not promote conceptual understanding because it focuses on rote learning rather than meaning. Effective strategies include using examples, non-examples, and encouraging students to generate ideas, which deepen understanding and application of concepts.

19. An active classroom is based on interaction, collaboration, and knowledge construction through social processes. Social constructivism emphasizes learning through discussion, shared experiences, and active engagement, making it the most suitable theoretical base.

20. The assertion is correct because empathy involves recognizing and understanding others' emotions. The reason is false since emotions and cognition are closely connected; understanding others' feelings requires cognitive processing. Therefore, the assertion is true but the reason is false.

21. Strategic self-motivated learners are those who can plan, monitor, and evaluate their own learning. Metacognitive skills help students understand how they learn, set goals, and regulate their efforts. This internal control promotes independence and sustained motivation, unlike external reinforcement or rote methods.

22. Intrinsic motivation arises from within the individual, where the activity itself is satisfying and engaging. It does not depend on rewards, competition, or external approval, but on curiosity, interest, and enjoyment of learning.

23. The question directly explores whether biological factors (nature) determine gender characteristics or whether social and environmental influences (nurture) shape them. This reflects the classic debate about the relative role of heredity and environment in development.

24. Adolescence is the stage where individuals actively explore and form their identity in areas such as personal beliefs, career choices, and sexual identity. This phase is marked by self-reflection and questioning, making identity formation a key developmental task.

25. The assertion is correct because children acquire societal values both explicitly (through teaching) and implicitly (through observation and experience). The reason is incorrect as socialization is a complex, continuous process involving interaction, learning, and adaptation, not merely the simple transmission of customs and rituals.

26. In Jean Piaget's theory, formal operational thinking (around 11+ years) is marked by the ability to think abstractly, hypothetically, and logically beyond concrete situations. Concrete operational thinking is limited to tangible objects and real situations. Abilities like conservation and object permanence belong to earlier stages, so abstract logic is the key distinguishing feature.

27. A major criticism of Piaget's theory is that it underestimates the role of cultural and social influences in cognitive development. Later theorists, especially Lev Vygotsky, emphasized that learning is deeply shaped by cultural tools, language, and social interaction, which Piaget did not sufficiently highlight.

28. In Kohlberg's moral development theory, the punishment and obedience stage focuses on avoiding punishment and negative consequences. The other options are mismatched because they incorrectly link stages with unrelated moral principles.

29. Both Piaget and Vygotsky believed that children are active learners who construct their own understanding. While they differed in emphasis on social factors, both agreed that children are not passive recipients but actively engage in making sense of the world.

30. Vygotsky introduced the concept of the Zone of Proximal Development (ZPD), which highlights that children can perform certain tasks with guidance or collaboration that they cannot do alone. This emphasizes the importance of social interaction and support in learning.

31. Given number is 2A, so its value = 20 + A.
Multiplying by A:

$$(20 + A) \times A = 20A + A^2$$

This equals the number B2A = 100B + 20 + A.

So, $A^2 + 20A = 100B + 20 + A$

$$A^2 + 19A - 20 = 100B$$

Now checking digit values of A:
For A = 5:

$$5^2 + 19 \times 5 - 20 = 25 + 95 - 20 = 100 = 100 \times 1$$

So, B = 1.
Verification:

$$25 \times 5 = 125$$

Matches B2A = 125.

32. Given, $a - b = \frac{11}{5}, ab = \frac{3}{4}$

Use identity:

$$(a + b)^2 = (a - b)^2 + 4ab$$

$$(a + b)^2 = \left(\frac{11}{5}\right)^2 + 4\left(\frac{3}{4}\right)$$

$$= \frac{121}{25} + 3 = \frac{121}{25} + \frac{75}{25} = \frac{196}{25}$$

$$a + b = \sqrt{\frac{196}{25}} = \frac{14}{5} = 2\frac{4}{5}.$$

33. Given, $\frac{7x-1}{4} - \frac{1}{3}\left(2x - \frac{1-x}{2}\right) = \frac{10}{3}$

First simplify the bracket:

$$2x - \frac{1-x}{2} = \frac{4x-(1-x)}{2} = \frac{4x-1+x}{2} = \frac{5x-1}{2}$$

Now substitute:

$$\frac{7x-1}{4} - \frac{1}{3} \cdot \frac{5x-1}{2} = \frac{10}{3}$$

$$\frac{7x-1}{4} - \frac{5x-1}{6} = \frac{10}{3}$$

LCM = 12:

$$\frac{3(7x-1)-2(5x-1)}{12} = \frac{10}{3}$$

$$\frac{21x-3-10x+2}{12} = \frac{10}{3}$$

$$\frac{11x-1}{12} = \frac{10}{3}$$

$$11x - 1 = 40$$

$$11x = 41 \Rightarrow x = \frac{41}{11}$$

Now,

$$\frac{11x+21}{2} = \frac{41+21}{2} = \frac{62}{2} = 31.$$

34. $5(2x - 4y) + 6(4x^2 + 16y^2 - 16xy) - 6$

Since

$$4x^2 + 16y^2 - 16xy = (2x - 4y)^2$$

let, $t = 2x - 4y$

Then the expression becomes: $5t + 6t^2 - 6$

$$= 6t^2 + 5t - 6$$
$$= 6t^2 + 9t - 4t - 6$$
$$= 3t(2t + 3) - 2(2t+3)$$
$$= (3t - 2)(2t + 3)$$

Putting $t = 2x - 4y$,

$$= (3(2x - 4y) - 2)(2(2x - 4y) + 3)$$
$$= (6x - 12y - 2)(4x - 8y + 3)$$

Also, $6x - 12y - 2 = 2(3x - 6y - 1)$

So, $(6x - 12y - 2)(4x - 8y + 3)$

$$= 2(3x - 6y - 1)(4x - 8y + 3)$$

Hence $4x - 8y + 3$ is a factor, and $3x - 6y - 1$ is also a factor.

35.

Cost price = 1500
Marked price = 2500
First discount = 20% of 2500:

$$\frac{20}{100} \times 2500 = 500$$

Price after first discount:

$$2500 - 500 = 2000$$

Additional cash discount:

$$2000 - 250 = 1750$$

Selling price = 1750
Profit = 1750 − 1500 = 250.

36. In proportion means

$$\frac{4+x}{10+x} = \frac{12+x}{24+x}$$

Cross-multiplying:

$$(4 + x)(24 + x) = (10 + x)(12 + x)$$
$$96 + 28x + x^2 = 120 + 22x + x^2$$
$$28x - 22x = 120 - 96$$
$$6x = 24$$
$$x = 4$$

Now,

$$3x + 1 = 3(4) + 1$$
$$= 12 + 1 = 13.$$

37. Since the two angles are supplementary,

$$(3x - 30°) + (2x + 20°) = 180°$$
$$5x - 10° = 180°$$
$$5x = 190°$$
$$x = 38°$$

Now, $2x - 4° = 2(38°) - 4°$

$$= 76° - 4° = 72°.$$

38. In triangle PQR,

$$\angle P = 30°,\ \angle Q = 50°$$

So,

$$\angle R = 180° - (30° + 50°) = 100°$$

The bisectors of angles P and Q meet at the incenter O.

For the incenter,

$$\angle POQ = 90° + \frac{\angle R}{2}$$

$$\angle POQ = 90° + \frac{100°}{2}$$

$$= 90° + 50° = 140°$$

Now, $2\angle POQ - 10° = 2(140°) - 10°$

$$= 280° - 10° = 270°.$$

39. For a right triangle, the Pythagoras condition must be satisfied:

$(\text{largest side})^2 = (\text{other side})^2 + (\text{other side})^2$

Check each option:

For 12, 16, 20:

$12^2 + 16^2 = 144 + 256 = 400 = 20^2 \Rightarrow$ Right triangle

For 4.5, 6, 7.5:

$4.5^2 + 6^2 = 20.25 + 36 = 56.25 = 7.5^2 \Rightarrow$ Right triangle

For 8, 12, 16:

$8^2 + 12^2 = 64 + 144 = 208,\ 16^2 = 256$

$208 \neq 256 \Rightarrow$ Not a right triangle

For 2.5, 6, 6.5:

$2.5^2 + 6^2 = 6.25 + 36 = 42.25 = 6.5^2 \Rightarrow$ Right triangle

Hence, 8,16,12 cannot form a right triangle.

40. A figure has rotational symmetry if it looks the same after rotation by some angle less than 360°. Letter O has rotational symmetry, N has rotational symmetry of 180°, and H also has rotational symmetry of 180°. But capital E does not match itself on such rotation. Hence, E does not have rotational symmetry.

41. In a parallelogram, diagonals bisect each other ⇒

$$OP = OR,\ OQ = OS$$

$$x + y = 16 \quad \ldots(1)$$

$$y + 7 = 20 \Rightarrow y = 13$$

Substitute in (1):

$$x + 13 = 16 \Rightarrow x = 3$$

$$7x - y = 7(3) - 13 = 21 - 13 = 8.$$

42. Perimeter = 52, sum of non-parallel sides = 20

$$a + b = 52 - 20 = 32$$

$$\text{Area} = \frac{1}{2}(a+b)h$$

$$128 = \frac{1}{2}(32)h = 16h$$

$$h = 8 \text{ cm}.$$

43. Area = 48, one side = 6

$$\text{Other side} = \frac{48}{6} = 8$$

$$\text{Diagonal} = \sqrt{6^2+8^2} = \sqrt{36+64} = 10$$

$$\text{Time} = \frac{10}{20} = \frac{1}{2}\text{min} = 30\,\text{sec}.$$

44. $8^3 = 512, 6^3 = 216, 10^3 = 1000$

$$\text{Total volume} = 512 + 216 + 1000 = 1728$$

$$a^3 = 1728 \Rightarrow a = 12.$$

45. Arranged data: 20, 26, 28, 30, 45, 55, 56, 56, 60, 61

$$\text{Median} = \frac{45+55}{2} = 50$$

$$\text{Mode} = 56$$

$$\text{Mean} = \frac{50+56}{2} = 53.$$

46. The intended meaning of the question is "a 10 or a red king", because only then the options become meaningful.

Total number of cards in a standard deck: 52

Number of 10s: 4

Number of red kings: 2

A 10 and a king cannot be the same card, so there is no overlap.

Total favourable cards:

$$4 + 2 = 6$$

Therefore,

$$P = \frac{6}{52} = \frac{3}{26}$$

So the required probability is $\frac{3}{26}$.

47. Given remainders,

$$87 - 7 = 80,\ 123 - 3 = 120$$

Required number must exactly divide both 80 and 120.

HCF of 80 and 120

$$80 = 2^4 \times 5,\ 120 = 2^3 \times 3 \times 5$$

Common factors:

$$2^3 \times 5 = 8 \times 5 = 40$$

Hence, the greatest required number is 40.

48. $0.\bar{4} = \frac{4}{9},\ 0.\bar{6} = \frac{6}{9}$

$$0.\bar{4} + 0.\bar{6} = \frac{4}{9} + \frac{6}{9} = \frac{10}{9}$$

$$\frac{10}{9} = 1 + \frac{1}{9} = 1\frac{1}{9}.$$

49. Given fractions: $\frac{4}{7}, \frac{9}{16}, 1\frac{2}{7}, \frac{3}{5}$

$$1\frac{2}{7} = \frac{9}{7}$$

Compare:

$$\frac{9}{7} > \frac{3}{5} > \frac{4}{7} > \frac{9}{16}$$

$$\text{Largest} = \frac{9}{7}, \text{ smallest} = \frac{9}{16}$$

$$\frac{9}{7} - \frac{9}{16}$$

$$= \frac{144}{112} - \frac{63}{112} = \frac{81}{112}.$$

50. Let the unit digit of the number be d. Then unit digit of its square is d^2.

Given, $d^2 = d + 2$ (units place)

Check digits 0 to 9:

$0^2 = 0 \neq 2$, $1^2 = 1 \neq 3$

$2^2 = 4 \Rightarrow 4 = 2 + 2$ (valid)

$3^2 = 9 \neq 5$, $4^2 = 6 \Rightarrow 6 = 4 + 2$ (valid)

$5^2 = 5 \neq 7$, $6^2 = 6 \neq 8$

$7^2 = 9 = 7 + 2$ (valid)

Possible square digits: 4, 6, 9.

Hence, 5 cannot be the unit digit of the square.

51. Assessment in mathematics should focus on understanding, reasoning, application, and problem-solving. Simply recalling definitions promotes rote learning and does not reflect conceptual understanding. Therefore, it should not be the primary focus of assessment.

52. Mahavira, a 9th-century Indian mathematician, clearly stated that square roots of negative numbers do not exist in real numbers. This was an important early recognition in Indian mathematics regarding limitations of real number operations.

53. The student placed 0.23 before 0.034, showing misunderstanding. They likely assumed that more digits after the decimal indicate a larger number. Correct comparison requires place value understanding, not number of digits.

54. The activity primarily focuses on constructing different shapes using unit squares and analyzing their perimeters. Its core objectives include creativity, spatial reasoning, and understanding of area–perimeter relationships. While group work can be incorporated, it is not inherently required by the task itself. The activity can be effectively performed individually as well. Therefore, engaging children in group work is not a direct or essential objective of this activity, making it the least appropriate choice.

55. The child has not understood that whatever is done to one side of an equation must also be done to the other side. In the given work, 7 was subtracted only on the left side, which breaks the equality. So the real difficulty is conceptual, not linguistic or procedural speed. The best remedy is to rebuild the meaning of equality through balance models, concrete examples, or alternate methods so that the child understands why both sides must remain equal.

56. According to the spirit of NCF 2005, arithmetic and algebra teaching should help learners look for patterns and understand relationships between numbers instead of depending mainly on rote procedures. Skill development in mathematics should promote reasoning, structure, and meaning-making. Memorizing algebraic identities and repeated writing of notation may have some place, but they are not the central skills emphasized here. Hence A and C are the correct choices.

57. This is the most appropriate reason because historical buildings provide real-life examples of geometrical forms, symmetry, patterns, and spatial design. Such a trip helps students connect mathematics with architecture, art, and history. It makes learning meaningful by showing that shapes are not just textbook ideas but visible in the surrounding world. Therefore, the field trip supports interdisciplinary understanding in the best way.

58. In mathematics teaching, when a child gives an answer about a three-dimensional object, the best response is to provide a concrete experience. A cylinder can confuse children because its surfaces and curved boundaries are not understood clearly from words alone. By placing the cylinder in the student's hand and asking again, the teacher encourages observation, touch, and self-correction. This develops conceptual understanding better than mere praise, punishment, or only drawing a figure on the board.

59. Enlarging and reducing figures on a square grid mainly helps children understand scaling, ratio, proportion, and the connection between arithmetic and geometry. It may also involve fractional thinking when sizes are changed by a factor. However, such an activity is aimed at similarity, not congruency, because enlarged or reduced figures do not remain equal in size. Therefore, this combined objective is the least appropriate one.

60. Closed-ended questions usually lead students toward one fixed answer. Because of this, they mainly support convergent thinking, where the learner moves toward a single correct response. They do not usually encourage divergent thinking, creativity, or higher-order thinking skills such as open exploration, multiple strategies, and original reasoning. Hence A, C, and D are the correct set.

61. China rose indicator shows different colours with different kinds of solutions. If there is no change in colour, the solution is neutral. A green colour indicates a basic solution. A magenta or dark pink colour indicates an acidic solution. Therefore, solution A is neutral, solution B is basic, and solution C is acidic.

62. Statement 1 is true because an object may be at rest and still possess mechanical energy. For example, a body placed at a height has gravitational potential energy, so its mechanical energy is non-zero, but since it is at rest, its momentum is zero. Statement 2 is also true because work done is

$$W = Fs \cos \theta$$

If displacement is zero, or if force acts perpendicular to displacement, then work done becomes zero even though force is non-zero. Hence both statements are true.

63. Black surfaces are better absorbers and also better radiators of heat than white surfaces. Therefore, in sunlight, the black-painted container A will absorb heat faster than the white-painted container B. Later, when both are kept in shade, container A will also radiate and lose heat faster. Hence container A gains as well as loses heat faster than container B.

64. Pressure is given by

$$P = \frac{F}{A}$$

A blunt knife has a larger area of contact at its edge. For the same force, larger area produces less pressure, so cutting becomes difficult. Therefore, the correct reason is that the area of contact increases.

65. The strength of an electromagnet depends mainly on the amount of current, the number of turns in the coil, and the nature of the core. If current is increased, the magnetic field becomes stronger. Decreasing turns weakens it, and plastic or aluminium are not suitable ferromagnetic cores like soft iron. Hence increasing the flow of current increases the strength.

66. Digestion means breakdown of food into simpler substances. The oesophagus mainly transports food, the large intestine mainly absorbs water and salts, and the rectum stores faeces before egestion. These organs do not carry out digestion itself. Therefore, this set does not contribute to the digestive process.

67. Earthworms respire through their moist skin and do not have lungs, so statement A is correct. Tadpoles, being aquatic larval forms of frogs, respire through gills and not lungs, so statement B is also correct. Snakes, however, respire through lungs and not through skin, so statement C is false.

68. The anther produces pollen grains (male gametes). The ovary contains ovules where female gametes are formed. The stigma is the part where pollen grains land and germinate. Petals are brightly coloured and help in attracting insects for pollination.

69. Sewage treatment is essential because untreated sewage contains harmful microorganisms and pollutants that can spread diseases and contaminate water. However, the reason is incorrect because sewage is mainly liquid waste, not solid waste, though it may contain some solid impurities. Hence A is true but R is false.

70. Spiracles are openings on the body of insects for gas exchange, while stomata are pores on leaves for exchange of gases. Statement B is incorrect because stomata are far more numerous than spiracles. Statement C is incorrect because stomata are mainly on the lower surface of leaves, but spiracles are distributed along the sides of the insect's body, not specifically on the lower surface.

71. The right ventricle pumps deoxygenated blood into the pulmonary artery. Pulmonary arteries carry deoxygenated blood from the heart to the lungs. Pulmonary veins bring oxygenated blood back from the lungs to the heart. From the left atrium, blood flows into the left ventricle. The right auricle receives deoxygenated blood returning from different parts of the body. Therefore, the complete sequence matches option 2.

72. The assertion is false because in science, hypotheses do not automatically become theories and theories do not become laws. A hypothesis, theory, and law are different kinds of scientific knowledge, each serving a different purpose. A theory explains phenomena, while a law describes a consistent pattern or relationship. The reason is also false because scientific laws are not treated as absolute in the sense of being beyond revision; scientific knowledge remains open to refinement with new evidence. Hence both statements are false.

73. "Cactus is a desert plant" is a factual statement that can be directly known and recorded, so it is taken as an observation in this context. "A desert plant has very small-sized leaves" is also based on visible features and is therefore an observation. "Small-sized leaves help in reducing loss of water" goes beyond direct seeing and explains the functional reason, so it is an inference. Thus the correct order is Observation, Observation, Inference.

74. A testable question is one that can be investigated through observation, experiment, or available measurable evidence in a clear scientific way. The exact time when fossil fuels will run out cannot be tested directly in a classroom or standard scientific investigation because it depends on many changing factors such as consumption, discovery, technology, and policy. The other questions can be explored scientifically through evidence and study. Hence this is not a testable question.

75. In this activity, learners first observe the iron pillar and the details written about it. Then they identify and group iron objects at home, which involves classification. When they think about causes of rusting and ways to prevent it, they are forming possible explanations and predictions, which is hypothesis building. Therefore, the process skills developed here are classification, observation, and hypothesis.

76. Process validity emphasizes learning science through inquiry, exploration, hypothesis, and experimentation. Simply making a list of elements is a rote activity and does not involve scientific processes like observation, investigation, or reasoning. Hence it does not satisfy process validity.

77. Including such historical anecdotes helps students understand how scientific knowledge develops (nature of science), gives a historical perspective, and shows how science is influenced by social and cultural contexts. It is not primarily meant to reduce content burden, but to enrich understanding. Hence A, B, and C are correct.

78. Scientific temper develops through active engagement, questioning, experimentation, and understanding processes. Simply reading out principles does not ensure internalization or critical thinking. The other options promote inquiry and understanding, so this one does not contribute effectively.

79. Inquiry-based learning focuses on students discovering concepts through hands-on activities and reasoning. By experimenting with materials, students observe properties themselves and construct understanding, which is the most appropriate approach.

80. At the upper primary stage, science learning is centered around exploration, observation, and simple activities rather than formal, systematic experimentation aimed at verifying already established theories. Therefore, S1 is incorrect. S2 is correct because activities and experimental evidence help learners understand how scientific knowledge is built through observation and evidence. S3 is also correct as learners at this stage benefit from an inductive approach, where they move from specific examples and experiences to general principles. Hence, only S2 and S3 are true.

81. Before formally teaching the concept of force, such a discussion helps the teacher know what children already think about why a ball keeps rolling or stops. So it is useful for assessing students' preconceptions. It also helps the teacher decide the most suitable pedagogical strategy, because teaching should begin from learners' existing ideas and then gradually refine them. It is not mainly for evaluation in the formal sense, and it is not directly meant to make students define force at that stage.

82. At puberty, the ovaries in females increase in size and begin producing estrogen. In males, the testes produce testosterone. The secretion of these sex hormones is regulated by hormones released from the pituitary gland, which acts as an important control center for endocrine functions during adolescence. Therefore, the complete correct sequence is enlarges, estrogen, testosterone, and pituitary gland.

83. In a parallel circuit, each bulb is connected directly across the source and receives the full voltage. Since brightness depends on power ($P = V^2/R$), each bulb glows with maximum brightness. In contrast, in series circuits, the voltage is divided among bulbs, reducing brightness. Mixed arrangements give uneven brightness. Therefore, the arrangement where all bulbs are in parallel produces the brightest glow for each bulb.

84. Anodizing is indeed a method used to protect certain metals, especially aluminium, from corrosion by forming a thicker protective oxide layer on the surface. However, coating iron with zinc is not anodizing; that process is called galvanization. So the assertion is true, but the reason is false.

85. Silver articles turn black because silver reacts slowly with hydrogen sulphide present in air to form silver sulphide, which is black in colour. This black coating is called tarnish. It is not mainly due to oxygen, carbon monoxide, or nitrogen oxides. Hence the correct cause is reaction with hydrogen sulphide.

86. Salts are formed by neutralization of acids with bases.
Ammonium chloride is formed by:

$$NH_3 + HCl \rightarrow NH_4Cl$$

So, A = NH_3
Sodium nitrate is formed by:

$$HNO_3 + NaOH \rightarrow NaNO_3 + H_2O$$

So, B = NaOH
Sodium chloride is formed by:

$$HCl + NaOH \rightarrow NaCl + H_2O$$

So, C = HCl, D = NaOH.

87. Dissolving sugar in water does not change the chemical composition of sugar; it only forms a solution, so it is a physical change. Heating sugar syrup leads to caramelization, where sugar undergoes chemical reactions forming new substances with different colour and taste. Hence Step 1 is physical and Step 2 is chemical.

88. Mass number = 27, neutrons = 14
Number of protons = 27 - 14 = 13
For a neutral atom, electrons = 13
Given ion has +2 charge, so it has lost 2 electrons:

$$\text{Electrons} = 13 - 2 = 11.$$

89. When light passes from one medium to another:
Speed and wavelength may change depending on optical density.
Frequency always remains unchanged.
Air $\rightarrow$ Medium A:
Given wavelength decreases $\Rightarrow$ speed must decrease.
So, X = Decreases and Y = Remains unchanged.
Air $\rightarrow$ Medium B:
Given speed increases $\Rightarrow$ wavelength also increases.
So, Z = Increases.
Air $\rightarrow$ Medium C:
Given speed remains same $\Rightarrow$ wavelength remains same $\Rightarrow$ frequency also remains unchanged.
So, W= Remains unchanged.

90. In soil profile, A-horizon and B-horizon support root growth and branching, which helps plants absorb water and minerals effectively. So Situation A is correct. Situation B is incorrect because humus is mainly abundant in the topsoil, that is the A-horizon, not in the C-horizon. The C-horizon mainly contains partially weathered parent material and much less organic matter.

91. Early childhood is a highly sensitive period for language acquisition. During this stage, children acquire languages more naturally and with greater ease through exposure and interaction. If language learning is delayed, the process often becomes less effortless and more difficult later. Therefore, both the assertion and the reason are true, and the reason correctly explains the assertion.

92. The National Curriculum Framework for Foundational Stage recognizes multilingualism as a strength, not a problem. Young children can learn and use more than one language, and this supports thinking, communication, identity, and cultural connection. It also helps build inclusion and respect for diverse backgrounds. Hence this principle is the correct one.

93. Diglossia refers to a situation where two varieties of the same language, or two closely related varieties, coexist in a speech community with different social functions. Usually one variety is used in formal settings and the other in everyday conversation. Therefore, the correct term for this situation is diglossia.

94. In this activity, the text is divided into two parts, and each child has only one part. One reads while the other writes, and together they reconstruct the complete text.

This matches partial dictation. It is not running dictation, because that usually involves moving back and forth to read a displayed text and then dictating it to a partner.

95. Literary texts are primarily meant for appreciation, enjoyment, cultural exposure, and development of critical thinking. Using them mainly for teaching grammar reduces their aesthetic and interpretative value. Hence this statement is not true.

96. The teacher provides support by simplifying the text and engaging in shared reading. This temporary support helps the learner perform beyond current ability and gradually become independent. This guided assistance is known as scaffolding.

97. The audiolingual method is based on behaviourist theory, which views language learning as habit formation through repetition, drilling, and reinforcement. Hence it strongly believes that language is a habit.

98. In this situation, the child reads an unseen passage with the specific purpose of answering given questions. This requires locating particular information, keywords, or details from the text rather than reading for general understanding. Such goal-directed reading for specific answers is known as scanning, not extensive reading or skimming.

99. Students are asked to create a story using given pictures, which involves imagination, sequencing, and expression. This clearly reflects creative writing.

100. Performance-based assessment focuses on real-life use of language in meaningful contexts. It includes tasks like speaking, writing, or interacting in situations rather than answering objective questions. Hence contextualized communicative tasks are its key feature.

101. Statement A is incorrect because reading is not limited to letter-sound relationships and correct pronunciation; that is only decoding at a basic level. Reading is a meaning-making process. Statement B is correct as reading involves decoding written symbols to understand meaning. Hence B is true and A is false.

102. Listening skill is assessed when students listen to spoken input and respond to it. In this case, students listen to a story and then answer questions, which directly evaluates their listening comprehension. The other options involve reading, vocabulary, or speaking skills.

103. Semantics deals with meaning in language, including meanings of words, phrases, and sentences. Syntax deals with sentence structure, morphology with word formation, and phonetics with sounds.

104. Modern language learning emphasizes communication, interaction, and meaningful use rather than rote memorization of grammar rules. Therefore, this statement is not a principle of language learning, while the others reflect accepted principles.

105. Brainstorming words related to a central word helps students recall, connect, and expand their word knowledge. This directly enhances vocabulary development, which is the main objective of such an activity.

106. The speaker contrasts a free bird with a caged bird. The free bird can sing, fly, build, and thrive because it is not restricted. Its abilities come from its freedom, not from talent alone.

107. The caged bird is called a "crippled thing" because it cannot perform natural activities like flying freely or soaring in the sky. Its movement and life are restricted, which weakens its natural existence.

108. In "sorrowful wings," the wings themselves are not sorrowful; the sadness actually belongs to the bird. The quality of sorrow is transferred from the bird to its wings, which makes it a transferred epithet.

109. The poem highlights the contrast between freedom and captivity. It emphasizes that birds living freely in nature are happy and fulfilled, while caged birds suffer and are deprived of their natural life.

110. The repeated line "But my bird sings!" shows pride and happiness that the speaker's bird is free. Its ability to sing naturally symbolizes its freedom and joyful existence.

111. The wings are described as sorrowful because the bird is unhappy in captivity. Its inability to fly freely causes sadness, which is reflected in the description of its wings.

112. The passage clearly states that although such practices are common elsewhere, in India the movement has "yet to gain momentum," meaning it is still not widespread or popular.

113. The passage begins by stating that physical health affects the mind and vice versa. Hence, the mind is directly affected by physical health.

114. The word "nominal" means very small or minimal. Its opposite is "substantial," which means large or significant.

115. "Prerequisite" means something that is necessary or required beforehand. Hence, "required" is the closest in meaning.

116. The word "particularly" modifies the verb "excel," describing how Japanese companies excel. Therefore, it functions as an adverb.

117. A Principal Clause is a complete sentence that makes sense on its own. In this sentence, "It is estimated" is the Principal Clause. An Adjective Clause modifies a noun or pronoun and begins with words like "who", "which", or "that'. However, the underlined part does not function as an adjective clause. An Adverb Clause modifies verbs, adjectives, or other adverbs and answers questions like "how", "when", "where" or "why". The underlined part is not an adverb clause. A Noun Clause functions as a noun in the sentence and can act as a subject, object or complement. In the sentence, "that some 20,000 American firms have established in-house health clubs" is functioning as Noun Clause because it acts as the object of the verb "is estimated".

118. The passage explicitly states that a sound mind in a sound body is a prerequisite for high efficiency and good quality work.

119. The passage mentions that Japanese companies include singing the company song to promote loyalty and motivation among workers.

120. The passage emphasizes that investment in health clubs leads to improved efficiency, productivity, and overall performance of employees.

121. 12-18 माह की आयु में बच्चे एक-एक शब्द का प्रयोग करके पूरे वाक्य का अर्थ व्यक्त करते हैं, जैसे "मम्मी", "पानी" आदि। इस अवस्था में एक ही शब्द कई अर्थों को व्यक्त करता है, इसलिए इसे एक-शब्दीय वाक्य अवस्था कहा जाता है।

122. पठन और लेखन परस्पर संबंधित कौशल हैं। अच्छी पठन क्षमता से शब्दावली, संरचना और विचारों की समझ बढ़ती है, जो लेखन को बेहतर बनाती है। इसलिए A सही है। B गलत है क्योंकि दोनों प्रक्रियाएँ एक-दूसरे से स्वतंत्र नहीं हैं।

123. सभी भाषाओं में कुछ सामान्य विशेषताएँ होती हैं जैसे ध्वनि, व्याकरण, अर्थ आदि। इन सामान्य गुणों को भाषा सार्वभौमिक कहा जाता है।

124. भाषिक विविधता को स्वीकार करने से बच्चे अपनी भाषा में अभिव्यक्ति करने में सहज महसूस करते हैं। इससे उनका आत्मविश्वास बढ़ता है और वे अधिक रचनात्मक एवं कल्पनाशील बनते हैं।

125. उद्गामी साक्षरता में बच्चे प्रारंभिक स्तर पर अक्षरों, शब्दों और पुस्तक की दिशा (बाएँ से दाएँ) को पहचानते हैं। पूरे वाक्य पढ़ना एक उन्नत कौशल है, जो बाद के चरण में विकसित होता है, इसलिए यह इस संदर्भ में सही नहीं है।

126. पठन कौशल का विकास सरल से जटिल की ओर होता है। पहले बच्चे परिचित शब्दों के छोटे वाक्य सटीकता से पढ़ते हैं (B)। इसके बाद वे छोटे खंडों को तान-अनुतान और विराम के साथ पढ़ते हैं (C)। अंत में वे प्रवाह, सटीकता और ध्वनि के उतार-चढ़ाव के साथ पढ़ने लगते हैं (A)।

127. विस्तृत (extensive) श्रवण का उद्देश्य सामान्य अर्थ, मुख्य विचार, निष्कर्ष या सार समझना होता है। विशेष तथ्यों के लिए श्रवण 'intensive listening' का भाग है, इसलिए यह विस्तृत श्रवण का भाग नहीं है।

128. पठन कौशल के आकलन में छात्र द्वारा पढ़ना और समझना शामिल होता है। यदि शिक्षक कथा पढ़ता है, तो वह श्रवण कौशल का आकलन करता है, न कि पठन कौशल का।

129. यही 'running dictation' है, जिसमें एक विद्यार्थी पाठ को देखकर वापस आकर अपने साथी को बोलता है और दूसरा लिखता है। इसमें गति, स्मरण और सहयोग शामिल होते हैं।

130. यह विचार कि बच्चे भाषा अर्जन की जन्मजात क्षमता के साथ पैदा होते हैं, नोम चॉम्स्की के नेटीविस्ट सिद्धांत से संबंधित है, जो भाषा को मानव मस्तिष्क की अंतर्निहित क्षमता मानता है।

131. प्रक्रिया लेखन उपागम में अंतिम चरण वह होता है जब लेखक अपने लिखित कार्य को पाठकों के साथ साझा करता है। इसे प्रकाशन कहा जाता है, जहाँ लेखन को प्रस्तुत किया जाता है और उसका सामाजिक उद्देश्य पूरा होता है।

132. जब शिक्षक कठिन शब्द का अर्थ मातृभाषा में बताता है और विद्यार्थियों से उसे याद करने को कहता है, तो यह अनुवाद आधारित और रटने पर आधारित पद्धति होती है। यह व्याकरण अनुवाद विधि की विशेषता है।

133. यह अवधारणा लेव वाइगोत्स्की द्वारा दी गई है, जिसमें बताया गया है कि बच्चा अकेले क्या कर सकता है और सहायता से क्या कर सकता है, इनके बीच का अंतर ही निकटस्थ विकास का क्षेत्र होता है।

134. मस्तिष्क में क्षति के कारण भाषा को समझने और बोलने की क्षमता में जो विकार आता है, उसे अफेजिया कहते हैं। इसमें व्यक्ति को भाषिक नियमों और अभिव्यक्ति में कठिनाई होती है।

135. भाषा पीढ़ी दर पीढ़ी सीखी और सिखाई जाती है। यह जैविक रूप से नहीं, बल्कि सामाजिक और सांस्कृतिक प्रक्रिया के माध्यम से आगे बढ़ती है, जिसे सांस्कृतिक प्रसारण कहा जाता है।

136. गद्यांश में स्पष्ट कहा गया है कि "ईर्ष्या का अनन्य अधिकार मनुष्य जाति ही पर है", इसलिए ईर्ष्या केवल मनुष्यों में पाई जाती है।

137. 'स्थिति दोहरी' होने का अर्थ है कि व्यक्ति एक तो वास्तव में जैसा है और दूसरा समाज उसे जैसा समझता है। ये दोनों हमेशा समान नहीं होते, इसलिए सही अर्थ यही है।

138. 'जगह पाती है' का अर्थ है कि ईर्ष्या केवल थोड़ी नहीं, बल्कि उनके मन में प्रमुख रूप से स्थान बना लेती है और उनका हृदय ईर्ष्या से भर जाता है।

139. 'ईर्ष्या' एक भाववाचक संज्ञा है, जिसका सामान्यतः बहुवचन रूप नहीं होता।

140. 'रखकर' यहाँ क्रिया 'रख' में 'कर' प्रत्यय जुड़कर बना कृदंत रूप है, जो पहले घटित क्रिया को दर्शाता है और मुख्य क्रिया 'प्रयत्न करते हैं' से जुड़ता है। इसलिए यह भूतकालिक कृदंत है।

141. गद्यांश के अनुसार जब व्यक्ति स्वयं को छोटा समझे जाने की धारणा से जुड़ता है, तब दुःख बढ़ता है। इसलिए कम समझा जाना दुःख का कारण है।

142. गद्यांश में बताया गया है कि जब व्यक्ति को अपने से बड़ा समझा जाता है, तो उसके आनंद या सुख में वृद्धि होती है।

143. गद्यांश में स्पष्ट कहा गया है कि जब हम दूसरों को अपने साथ एक पंक्ति में रखते हैं, तो सहानुभूति के साथ-साथ ईर्ष्या और द्वेष की संभावना भी उत्पन्न होती है।

144. गद्यांश में कहा गया है कि ईर्ष्या केवल ऐश्वर्य, गुण या सम्पन्नता देखकर नहीं होती। इसके लिए ईर्ष्या करने वाला, ईर्ष्या का पात्र और समाज की उपस्थिति आवश्यक है। इसलिए ऐश्वर्य आवश्यक नहीं है।

145. 'सूत्रपात करना' का अर्थ है किसी कार्य या प्रक्रिया का आरम्भ करना।

146. गद्यांश में बताया गया है कि बचपन के साथी की उन्नति देखकर व्यक्ति जलता हुआ भी पाया जाता है, अर्थात उसमें ईर्ष्या होती है।

147. 'पड़ोसियों' में 'यों' प्रत्यय लगा है, जो तिर्यक बहुवचन रूप को दर्शाता है।

148. गद्यांश में कहा गया है कि उन्नति के गुप्त बाधकों को खोजते-खोजते लोग अपने किसी पुराने मित्र तक पहुँच जाते हैं।

149. ईर्ष्या उन्हीं लोगों से होती है जिनके बारे में हमें लगता है कि लोग उन्हें और हमें साथ-साथ देख रहे हैं।

150. गद्यांश में स्पष्ट कहा गया है कि जो लोग हमसे दूर होते हैं, उनसे ईर्ष्या नहीं होती, क्योंकि उनके साथ हमारी तुलना नहीं होती।

Previous Years' Paper

CTET—Paper-II, December-2024

For Mathematics and Science Teachers

(Exam held on 14-12-2024)

CHILD DEVELOPMENT AND PEDAGOGY

1. In an inclusive classroom the teacher:

A. Segregates children based on differing academic capabilities.

B. Modifies the curriculum and pedagogical strategies to suit varied needs of children.

C. Tries to encourage children to do better by promoting competitive spirit.

D. Identifies 'deficits' in children and correctly labels them.

2. Universal design for learning does NOT involve:

A. Providing all learners alternatives for demonstrating what the learners know.

B. Tapping into all learners' interests and offering challenges accordingly.

C. Practicing forms of labelling and categorization of learners.

D. Giving all learners various ways of acquiring information and knowledge.

3. Which of the following are effective strategies to teach new concepts?

(*i*) Presenting examples

(*ii*) Presenting non-examples

(*iii*) Promoting thinking about relationships amongst concepts.

(*iv*) Giving a definition and encouraging students to rote memorize it.

A. (*i*), (*iii*) B. (*i*), (*ii*), (*iii*)

C. (*iii*), (*iv*), (*i*) D. (*i*), (*ii*)

4. While proposing the relationship between language and thinking process, Lev Vygotsky conceptualized language as a/an:

A. form of egocentric speech used to only fulfill basic needs.

B. hinderance to the development of cognitive abilities.

C. Independent domain which is not related to cognition.

D. cultural tool which facilitates cognition in multiple ways.

5. While there exists a possibility of intra-group individual differences, yet most students with Autism:

A. demonstrate advanced communication skills.

B. express strict adherence to routine or steps.

C. perform superior skills of imaginative play.

D. acquire advanced socio-emotional reciprocity.

6. As per Jean Piaget's theory of Cognitive Development:

A. Learning experiences depend on children's current level of cognitive functioning.

B. Memorization should be prioritized over learning through experience.

C. Previous knowledge doesn't play any role in the process of learning.

D. Biological factors such as maturation don't play any role in cognitive development.

7. While engaging students who are visually challenged, teachers should use .... which ....

A. Braille, is an auditory system.

B. Frequency modulated transmission devices; are a tactile system.

C. Frequency modulated transmission devices; are an auditory system.

D. Braille, is a tactile system.

8. Fiza analyzes that she has more problems in learning topic X than in learning topic Z because she is interested in topic Z and is paying focused attention to it. Which of the following construct describes Fiza's abilities to analyze her thinking?

A. Memory B. Cognition

C. Cognitive conflict D. Metacognition

1. B	**2.** C	**3.** B	**4.** D	**5.** B	**6.** A	**7.** D	**8.** D

9. Howard Gardner's theory of multiple intelligence proposes that:

A. Intelligence is primarily inherited.
B. Intelligence can be measured accurately and predicated precisely.
C. Intelligence can successfully predict academic success.
D. Intelligences change over time.

10. Which of these statements would advocates of progressive education agree with?

A. Children are naturally 'uncivilized' and socialization is necessary to make them moral human beings.
B. Children are born in a social, cultural, economic context and this background influences their development.
C. Children are a distinct life-stage that hold importance because of 'what they would become as adults' rather than 'what they are as children'.
D. Children are naturally 'good' and society corrupts them.

11. **Assertion (A):** Creating an environment of fear and stress keeps students 'on their' toes and facilitates meaningful learning.

Reason (R): Learning is governed only by extrinsic factors.

Choose the **correct** option.

A. Both (A) and (R) are true but (R) is not the correct explanation of (A).
B. (A) is true but (R) is false.
C. Both (A) and (R) are false.
D. Both (A) and (R) are true and (R) is the correct explanation of (A).

12. Which of the following is an example of a performance goal orientation?

A. A student studies hard to get a good grade and be better than others.
B. A student studies hard to learn as much as possible from the teacher.
C. A student studies hard to further her own growth.
D. A student studies hard to achieve a deep understanding of a topic.

13. Which of the following is an example of assessment for student's learning?

A. A quiz and brainstorming at the beginning of class to check for prior knowledge.
B. A standardized test used to compare students across the country.
C. A rubric given to students at the beginning of a project, outlining what they need to do to achieve a certain grade.
D. A final exam that covers all the material learned throughout the term.

14. Which of the following statement aptly describes the purpose of a diagnostic assessment?

A. To identify the attitude patterns of students and design a career guidance programme as per their needs.
B. To provide feedback to the teacher about their teaching methods.
C. To identify the areas where students may need additional support or instruction.
D. To give students the opportunity to critically assess the work of their peers.

15. Lev Vygotsky views cognitive development as:

A. an individual activity
B. a unified process
C. effective adoption to the environment process
D. a collaborative process

16. Following Lev Vygotsky's ideas, a teacher should:

A. disseminate the knowledge to be memorized by the students.
B. encourage students to compete with each other.
C. practice reciprocal teaching with her students.
D. discourage the use of cultural tools by students.

17. Which of the following is an example of a question that promotes analytical thinking?

A. Which countries were directly involved in the World War II?
B. Which factors contributed to the outbreak of World War II?
C. Who was the leader of Germany during World War II?
D. In which year did World War II end?

18. **Assertion (A):** 12-year Amana gets scared every time the teacher asks her to answer or solve the maths problem on the blackboard because she fears that the teacher will scold her and she would be embarrassed.

Reason (R): When students feel unsafe and anxious their learning is adversely affected.

Choose the **correct** option.

A. Both (A) and (R) are true, but (R) is not the correct explanation of (A).
B. (A) is true, but (R) is false.
C. Both (A) and (R) are false.
D. Both (A) and (R) are true and (R) is the correct explanation of (A).

9. D **10.** B **11.** C **12.** A **13.** C **14.** C **15.** D **16.** C **17.** B **18.** D

19. Jean Piaget perceives .... to be .... Lev Vygotsky believes............ to be ....

A. Egocentric speech, effective in self-regulation; private speech, a sign of cognitive immaturity
B. Private speech, a sign of cognitive immaturity; egocentric speech, effective in self-regulation
C. Private speech, effective in self-regulation; egocentric speech, a sign of cognitive immaturity
D. Egocentric speech, a sign of cognitive immaturity; private speech, effective in self-regulation

20. Assertion (A): As compared to boys, girls have an innate tendency to be affected more by social and cultural factors.

Reason (R): Girls are genetically more sensitive and emotionally weaker than boys, making it more likely for them to conform to societal expectations.

Choose the **correct** option.

A. Both (A) and (R) are true, but (R) is not the correct explanation of (A).
B. (A) is true, but (R) is false.
C. Both (A) and (R) are false.
D. Both (A) and (R) are true and (R) is the correct explanation of (A).

21. Ten year old Kakuli is struggling with a difficult math problem. What can her teacher do to enhance her problem-solving skills?

A. Tell her to skip the problem and move on to the next one
B. Encourage her to keep trying and offer scaffolding when needed
C. Give severe punishment so that it is not repeated in future
D. Give her the solution to the problem

22. An example of 'class inclusion':

Assertion (A): Lokesh has trouble with classifying one concept (Delhi) as a subset of another (India).

Reason (R): Understanding how emotions affect memory and learning can lead to self-regulated learning.

Choose the **correct** option.

A. Both (A) and (R) are true, but (R) is not the correct explanation of (A).
B. (A) is true, but (R) is false.
C. Both (A) and (R) are false.
D. Both (A) and (R) are true and (R) is the correct explanation of (A).

23. In which of the following method teacher and student interchange their roles?

A. Receptive learning B. Expository teaching
C. Reciprocal teaching D. Conditioned learning

24. The behaviours, interests, attitudes, skills and personality traits that a culture considers appropriate for specific gender are referred to as .... and are ....

A. Gender roles; genetically determined
B. Gender identity; culturally defined
C. Gender identity; genetically determined
D. Gender roles; culturally defined

25. Assertion (A): Each child finds opportunities to play, experiment and discover their world.

Reason (R): Childhood is a universal construct.

Choose the **correct** option.

A. Both (A) and (R) are true, but (R) is not the correct explanation of (A).
B. (A) is true, but (R) is false.
C. Both (A) and (R) are false.
D. Both (A) and (R) are true and (R) is the correct explanation of (A).

26. You are a teacher who wants to encourage your students to think critically and creatively. Which of the following strategies is most likely to foster this type of thinking?

A. Providing students with open-ended questions to come up with their own solutions.
B. Giving students multiple-choice tests to assess their knowledge.
C. Lecturing on the topic and providing students with detailed notes.
D. Assigning a project in which students must memorize and present information on a topic.

27. Assertion (A): In an inclusive classroom, all curriculum adaptations should be directed to lower the educational standards for 'Special children'.

Reason (R): 'Special children' do not have any potential for learning in mainstream classroom.

Choose the **correct** option.

A. Both (A) and (R) are true, but (R) is not the correct explanation of (A).
B. (A) is true, but (R) is false.
C. Both (A) and (R) are false.
D. Both (A) and (R) are true and (R) is the correct explanation of (A).

19. D	**20.** C	**21.** B	**22.** A	**23.** C	**24.** D	**25.** C	**26.** A	**27.** C

28. Which of the following statements about Lawrence Kohlberg's theory is correct?

A. It is based on the study done through experimental methods.
B. It presents conflicting situations to children.
C. It takes into account effects of culture and gender on moral reasoning.
D. It does not specify exact stages for progression of moral development in children.

29. A teacher wants to enable meaningful and analytical learning in her class by providing opportunities for students to connect their prior knowledge to new concepts. Which of the following teaching strategies would be most effective?

A. Assign students to read the textbook chapter and answer questions at the end.
B. Ask students to share their own experiences related to the new material and then connect them to the topic.
C. Providing students with a step-by-step guide on how to complete a task related to the new material.
D. Lecturing on new material and providing students with a list of key terms to memorize.

30. Changes in emotion, self-perception and interpersonal relationships with families, peers and friends are studied under .... domain of development.

A. Cognitive B. Linguistic
C. Psycho-social D. Physical

MATHEMATICS AND SCIENCE

31. The value of 31096 ÷ (2704 ÷ 2) + 0.6738 + 0.63 + 0.059 − 0.79 is equal to:

A. 23.5728 B. 24.6728
C. 24.5728 D. 23.6728

32. Following data shows the number of wickets taken by a player in last 11 matches played by him/her:

1, 0, 2, 4, 0, 3, 1, 1, 2, 4, 1

What is the difference between the mean and mode of the above data?

A. $\frac{8}{11}$ B. $\frac{10}{9}$
C. $\frac{8}{9}$ D. $\frac{7}{11}$

33. The distance covered (in metres) by a wheel of radius 25 cm in 350 rounds is (use $\pi = 22/7$):

A. 550 B. 825
C. 1100 D. 275

34. The two corresponding angles formed by the intersection of two parallel lines by a transversal are $(3x - 20°)$ and $(5x - 60°)$. Then, the value of $(4x + 30°)$ is:

A. 110° B. 130°
C. 150° D. 90°

35. For teaching addition of integers at the upper primary stage which of the following is least useful:

A. use of lift
B. use of number line
C. use of chart paper
D. use of stairs

36. O is a point on line AB. Rays OC and OD are drawn on the same side of AB such that OC ⊥ OD. $\angle AOC = x$ and $\angle BOD = 3x$. Then, $\angle BOD$ is equal to:

A. 45° B. 60°
C. $67\frac{1}{2}°$ D. $22\frac{1}{2}°$

37. Which of the following statement is **correct** about assessment?

A. Summative Assessment helps to know to what extent the instructional objectives have been achieved while teaching a concept.
B. 'Assessment for learning' is a process with no scope of giving feedback.
C. Formative Assessment is used after the course completion to assign the grades.
D. Assessment as learning generates opportunities for self-assessment and peer assessment.

38. A sum of ₹ 8000 becomes ₹ 9500 at 7.5% p.a. in x years at simple interest. What will be the amount of the sum in same time at 20% p.a, if interest is compounded yearly?

A. ₹ 12144
B. ₹ 12672
C. ₹ 13824
D. ₹ 11616

28. B **29.** B **30.** C **31.** A **32.** A **33.** A **34.** A **35.** C **36.** C **37.** D **38.** B

39. Meenu wrote some numbers on the blackboard and arranged them in ascending order as $2 < 7 < 9 < 12$.

She then multiplied each number by $\left(-\frac{1}{2}\right)$.

Identify the **correct** statement regarding the above situation.

A. Mean of the numbers will remain the same.
B. Ascending order will now be changed to descending order.
C. Number of terms in the ascending order will change.
D. Ascending order of numbers will still remain the same.

40. Which one of the following is the most appropriate feature of mathematics textbooks at elementary level?

A. Books must contain a lot of similar questions to practice
B. Concepts should be presented from complex to simple
C. Concepts should be presented from concrete to abstract
D. The language of the book must be highly precise and technical

41. One of the factors of $20pq^2 + 4pq + 45pr^2 - 60pqr - 6rp$ is:

A. $2q - 3r$ B. $10p - 15r + 2$
C. $15p - 10r + 2$ D. $2r - 3q$

42. Which one of the following is a teacher-centred method of teaching mathematics?

A. Lecture Method
B. Heuristic Method
C. Group Discussion Method
D. Problem solving Method

43. The cost price of an article is ₹ 750. It is sold for ₹ 608 by giving 24% discount on its marked price. Had it been sold on its marked price, then what would have been the profit per cent?

A. 6% B. $5\frac{1}{3}\%$
C. $6\frac{2}{3}\%$ D. 5%

44. Cards bearing numbers 12, 13, 14, ..., 70, 71 (one number on one card) are kept in a box and then a card is drawn from the box without looking into it. What is the probability that the card drawn has the number which is **not** a prime?

A. $\frac{15}{59}$ B. $\frac{3}{4}$
C. $\frac{45}{59}$ D. $\frac{1}{4}$

45. Which of the following rational numbers lie between $\frac{-7}{10}$ and $\frac{-1}{4}$?

A. $\frac{-2}{3}, \frac{-3}{5}, \frac{-3}{4}$ B. $\frac{5}{-8}, \frac{2}{3}, \frac{-3}{5}$
C. $\frac{5}{-8}, \frac{-2}{3}, \frac{-3}{5}$ D. $\frac{-3}{5}, 0, \frac{-1}{5}$

46. Which of the following numbers is written in the standard form?

A. 8.5×10^{-12} B. 0.6×10^{15}
C. 83.7×10^{-9} D. 45×10^{3}

47. A nine-digit number $565x9274y$ is divisible by number 88. Then, the value of $(2x + 3y)$ is:

A. 25 B. 24
C. 22 D. 26

48. Which of the following represents the most important capabilities of learners to be assessed in mathematics?

(*a*) Ability to use abstractions to perceive relationships
(*b*) Ability to memorize all the formulae given in textbook
(*c*) Ability to apply mathematical concepts to solve problems related to daily life situations
(*d*) Ability to score full marks in mathematics

Choose the **correct** option.

A. (*a*) and (*d*) B. (*b*), (*c*) and (*d*)
C. (*b*) and (*d*) D. (*a*) and (*c*)

49. In a pentagon ABCDE, $\angle A = (2x + 9°)$, $\angle B = (2x + 1°)$, $\angle C = (2x - 1°)$, $\angle D = (2x + 5°)$ and $\angle E = (2x - 4°)$. Then, value of $(2x + 10°)$ is:

A. 116° B. 118°
C. 124° D. 114°

50. Many occupations such as accountancy, banking, shop-keeping, tailoring etc. requires mathematics directly or indirectly. This is an explanation of .... value of Mathematics.

A. Cultural B. Utilitarian
C. Professional D. Disciplinary

39. B	**40.** C	**41.** A	**42.** A	**43.** C	**44.** B	**45.** C	**46.** A	**47.** D	**48.** D
49. A	**50.** B								

51. Let A = $3x^2 - 8x + 11$, B = $-2x^2 + 12x$, C = $-4x^2 + 7$ and D = $x^2 - x - 11$.

If (A + B + C) – D = $px^2 + qx + r$, then the value of $(p + q + r)$ is:

A. 28 B. 30
C. 31 D. 27

52. For which of the following measurements, the construction of triangle ABC can be done?

A. AB = 8 cm, BC = 4 cm, ∠BCA = 90°, ∠ABC =60°
B. ∠ACB = 120°, ∠ABC = 25°, AC = BC = 4 cm
C. AB = 5 cm, BC = 6 cm, ∠ABC = 130°, ∠BAC = 25°
D. AB = 3 cm, BC = 4 cm, AC = 7 cm

53. Which of the following is used to record students' problem solving ability, measurement ability and experimentation ability?

A. Report Card B. Anecdotal Record
C. Teacher Diary D. Cumulative Record

54. PQRS is a parallelogram in which PQ = $(4x + 1)$ cm, QR = 26 cm, RS = 25 cm and PS = $(3y - 1)$ cm. Then, the value of $(3x + 2y)$ (in cm) is:

A. 36 B. 38
C. 39 D. 35

55. The distance between the parallel sides AB and CD of a trapezium ABCD is 12 cm. If AB < CD, CD = 24 cm and AD = BC =13 cm, then area of the trapezium (in cm^2) is:

A. 114 B. 247
C. 228 D. 123.5

56. If x is the smallest number which is to be subtracted from 2605 to make it a perfect square, then the value of $(4x + 7)$ is:

A. 23 B. 27
C. 31 D. 11

57. Nitu is always confused in identifying the transformations. Her mathematics teacher helped her by giving one simple word for each transformation namely: Reflection, Rotation, Translation and Enlargement.

Which of the following represents the **correct** sequence of meaning of each transformation as given above?

A. Flip, Turn, Slide and Bigger Figure
B. Slide, Flip, Turn and Bigger Figure
C. Flip, Slide, Turn and Bigger Figure
D. Turn, Slide, Flip and Bigger Figure

58. A solid cube of side 12 cm is cut into small solid cubes of side 4 cm each. What will be the relation between the total surface area of the original cube and the new total surface area of the small cubes so formed?

A. New total surface area will be twice the original total surface area.
B. New total surface area will be $\frac{1}{3}$ of the original total surface area.
C. New total surface area will be thrice the original total surface area.
D. New total surface area will be $\frac{1}{2}$ of the original total surface area.

59. On the basis of the information given in the statement, which of the suggested course of action logically follows?

Statement: Anamika does conceptual error while solving problems on mensuration.

Course of Action:

I. Teacher gives a lot of hands-on and visual practice to Anamika.
II. Teacher provides the scope of discussion while giving open-ended questions.

Choose the **correct** option.

A. Only course of action (II)
B. Neither course of action (I) nor course of action (II)
C. Both course of action (I) and (II)
D. Only course of action (I)

60. If $x = k$, is the solution of the equation:

$\frac{x-4}{7} - 1 = \frac{5-x}{3} + x$, then what is the value of $\frac{11k+18}{11k-12}$?

A. $\frac{3}{4}$ B. $\frac{5}{8}$
C. $\frac{4}{9}$ D. $\frac{1}{2}$

51. B	52. A	53. B	54. A	55. C	56. A	57. A	58. C	59. C	60. B

61. Which of the following statements is/are true regarding the function of bile juice in human digestive system?

(*a*) It makes the partly digested food coming from stomach alkaline.

(*b*) It helps in digestion of fats.

A. (*a*) is false and (*b*) is true
B. Both (*a*) and (*b*) are true
C. Both (*a*) and (*b*) are false
D. (*a*) is true and (*b*) is false

62. Which of the following represents correct matching set in the context of aquatic plants?

Adaptation	**Purpose**
(*a*) Large circular leaves	(*i*) helpful in protecting against decay
(*b*) Waxy coating	(*ii*) helpful in offering resistance to water currents
(*c*) Stems have large tunnels and holes	(*iii*) helpful in providing buoyancy
(*d*) Ribbon like leaves	(*iv*) helpful in staying afloat

	(*a*)	(*b*)	(*c*)	(*d*)
A.	(*ii*)	(*iii*)	(*i*)	(*iv*)
B.	(*ii*)	(*iv*)	(*iii*)	(*i*)
C.	(*iii*)	(*i*)	(*iv*)	(*ii*)
D.	(*iii*)	(*iv*)	(*ii*)	(*i*)

63. Assertion (A): Nichrome is used as a heating element in devices like electric toaster and electric geyser.

Reason (R): Nichrome has high melting point and low resistivity.

A. Both (A) and (R) are true, but (R) is not correct explanation for (A)
B. (A) is true and (R) is false
C. Both (A) and (R) are false
D. Both (A) and (R) are true and (R) is correct explanation for (A)

64. On the basis of the following information identify the substances which give flame on burning:

Substance	State	Vapourises on burning
A	Solid	No
B	Liquid	Yes
C	Solid	Yes
D	Liquid	No

A. A and B
B. B and C
C. C and D
D. A and D

65. ___(A)___ hormone regulates carbohydrate, protein and fat metabolism in our body. It is secreted by ___(B)___ gland and ___(C)___ in our diet impacts the functioning of this gland. (A), (B), (C) respectively are:

A. Adrenaline, Adrenal, Salts
B. Thyroxine, Thyroid, Iodine
C. Growth hormone, Pitutary, Proteins
D. Insulin, Pancreas, Sugar

66. The following activity is done in the class VII:

Students are given four iron bars out of which two are bar magnets. They are asked to identify the bar magnets. Which of the following process skills can be promoted through this activity?

A. Observation, Classification, Inferring
B. Observation, Classification, Communication, Measurement
C. Observation, Estimation, Experimentation, Controlling variables
D. Observation, Formulating hypothesis, Measuring

67. Which of the following have the most scope for promoting Art integrated learning in Science?

A. Projects, Portfolios
B. Anecdotal records, Journal writing
C. Journal writing, Field trips
D. Portfolios, Anecdotal records

68. Which of the following should not be the purpose of open book assessment in Science?

A. To gauge conceptual understanding of learners
B. To score more marks in tests
C. To give opportunity to explore the book
D. To reduce the fear of assessment in learners

69. Which of the following statements are true?

(*a*) Crystallisation is a chemical change.

(*b*) Photosynthesis is a chemical change.

(*c*) Ripening of fruit is a physical change.

(*d*) Formation of curd from milk is a chemical change.

A. (*b*) and (*d*)
B. (*b*) and (*c*)
C. (*c*) and (*d*)
D. (*a*) and (*b*)

70. Children of all age groups have various ideas which may be different from science concepts. Which of the following statements are true regarding these ideas?

(*a*) These ideas are usually stable.

(*b*) They are formed due to observable phenomenon.

(*c*) They tend to follow similar developmental pattern.

(*d*) They are easy to modify.

(*e*) They are often domain specific.

A. (*b*), (*c*), (*d*)
B. (*a*), (*b*), (*c*), (*d*)
C. (*a*), (*b*), (*c*), (*e*)
D. (*a*), (*b*), (*c*)

61. B **62.** C **63.** B **64.** B **65.** B **66.** A **67.** A **68.** B **69.** A **70.** C

71. Assertion (A): Arteries have thick and elastic walls as compared to veins.

Reason (R): The pressure of blood flow in arteries is low as compared to veins.

A. Both (A) and (R) are true but (R) is not correct explanation for (A).
B. (A) is true and (R) is false.
C. Both (A) and (R) are false.
D. Both (A) and (R) are true and (R) is correct explanation for (A).

72. S1. Self pollination can take place only in bisexual flowers.

S2. Cross pollination can take place only in Unisexual flowers.

A. Both S1 and S2 are false
B. S1 is true and S2 is false
C. S1 is false and S2 is true
D. Both S1 and S2 are true

73. Which of the following statements is correct?

S1. The normal temperature of the human body is 37°C.

S2. Heat flows from a body at a higher temperature to a body at lower temperature.

A. Both S1 and S2 are inferences
B. S1 is observation and S2 is inference
C. S1 is inference and S2 is observation
D. Both S1 and S2 are observation

74. The density of medium A is more than medium B but less than medium C. In which medium does the sound travels fastest?

A. B
B. C
C. Can't be inferred from this information
D. A

75. While ice melts at 0°C, its temperature:

A. decreases
B. remains same
C. first decreases and then remains same
D. increases

76. Which of the following strategies would support inquiry oriented science teaching?

A. Demonstrating the loss in weight of an object when immersed in water
B. Engaging students in floating and sinking activities
C. Explaining the difference between real and apparent weight
D. Define and explain Archimede's principle

77. Read the following statements in the context of Laws and theories in Science:

S1. Laws are generalisation statement whereas theories are explanations.

S2. Laws are very old and theories are contemporary.

S3. Laws can't be changed whereas theories are subject to change.

A. S1 and S2 are true whereas S3 is false
B. S1 and S3 are true whereas S2 is false
C. S3 is true whereas S1 and S2 are false
D. S1 is true; S2 and S3 are false

78. When a ray of light enters from medium A to medium B, its speed decreases and on further entering into medium C, its speed increases.

Which of the following conclusions can be drawn from this?

A. Refractive index of A is less than B but equal to C
B. Refractive index of A and C are less than B
C. Refractive index of A, B, C cannot be compared from above information
D. Refractive index of A is more than B and C

79. ___(A)___ is a technique of vegetative propagation in which a part of the stem or a young branch of a plant is pulled and buried in moist soil, such that the branch is still attached to the Parent Plant. After some time, roots develop in the buried part and it grows into a new plant. ___(B)___ is an example of plant usually grown through this technique.

(A) and (B) respectively are:

A. Grafting, Rose B. Budding, Hydra
C. Layering, Jasmine D. Cutting, Potato

80. The buoyant force on an object immersed in liquid acts in:

A. Downward direction
B. All direction
C. Parallel to liquid surface
D. Upward direction

81. Assertion (A): Achievement in STEM related courses is influenced by gender.

Reason (R): Problem solving strategies used by boys and girls are different.

A. Both (A) and (R) are true but (R) is not correct explanation of (A).
B. (A) is true and (R) is false.
C. Both (A) and (R) are false.
D. Both (A) and (R) are true and (R) is correct explanation of (A).

71. B	72. B	73. A	74. B	75. B	76. B	77. D	78. B	79. C	80. D	81. C

82. Which of the following statements is/are true regarding nature of science?

(*a*) Scientific ideas are not affected by cultural context.

(*b*) There is no single scientific method.

A. (*a*) is true and (*b*) is false
B. (*a*) is false and (*b*) is true
C. Both (*a*) and (*b*) are false
D. Both (*a*) and (*b*) are true

83. Which of the following statements are true in the context of respiration in whales and dolphins?

(*a*) They cannot use dissolved Oxygen.
(*b*) They have gills.
(*c*) They have large nostrils.
(*d*) They often come up to the water surface to breathe.

A. (*a*), (*c*), (*d*) B. (*b*), (*c*), (*d*)
C. (*a*), (*b*), (*d*) D. (*a*), (*b*), (*c*)

84. (*a*) Sunita takes 0.5 g of Sodium Carbonate in a test-tube and adds 5 ml of Dilute Hydrochloric acid.

(*b*) She passes the gas produced in the above reaction through Lime water.

Which of the following represents the chemical reactions taking place in (A) and (B)?

A. (*a*) – $Na_2CO_3 + 2HCl \rightarrow 2NaCl + H_2O + CO_2$
(*b*) – $Ca(OH)_2 + CO_2 \rightarrow CaCO_3 + H_2O$

B. (*a*) – $NaHCO_3 + HCl \rightarrow NaCl + H_2O + CO_2$
(*b*) – $Ca(OH)_2 + CO_2 \rightarrow CaCO_3 + H_2O$

C. (*a*) – $NaHCO_3 + HCl \rightarrow NaCl + H_2O + CO_2$
(*b*) – $CaCO_3 + H_2O + CO_2 \rightarrow Ca(HCO_3)_2$

D. (*a*) – $Na_2CO_3 + 2HCl \rightarrow 2NaCl + H_2O + CO_2$
(*b*) – $CaCO_3 + H_2O + CO_2 \rightarrow Ca(HCO_3)_2$

85. Which of the following statements are not true regarding compounds?

(*a*) Compounds show the properties of constituent substances.
(*b*) Only elements can react to form compounds.
(*c*) The composition of each compound is always fixed.
(*d*) Compounds can be separated by physical and chemical methods.

A. (*b*), (*c*), (*d*) B. (*a*), (*b*), (*d*)
C. (*a*), (*c*), (*d*) D. (*a*), (*b*), (*c*)

86. Which of the following statements is true?

A. Soil with low water holding capacity has good aeration and low percolation rate.
B. Soil with low water holding capacity has poor aeration and low percolation rate.
C. Soil with low water holding capacity has good aeration and high percolation rate.
D. Soil with low water holding capacity has poor aeration and high percolation rate.

87. Which of the following questions is a divergent question?

A. What if there was no gravity on the earth?
B. How does gravity vary with the altitude?
C. What would happen to gravity if the size of earth is reduced to half?
D. Why does a ball thrown up comes down?

88. Complete the following table:

Atomic number	Mass number	Number of electrons	Number of protons	Number of neutrons
9	A	B	C	10
D	24	E	12	F

A, B, C, D, E, F respectively are:

A. 19, 9, 9, 12, 12, 12
B. 9, 10, 9, 24, 12, 12
C. 9, 9, 10, 24, 12, 12
D. 19, 10, 9, 12, 12, 12

89. Assertion (A): Convex mirrors are used as rearview-mirrors in vehicles.

Reason (R1): They form erect and enlarged image.

Reason (R2): They have wider field of view.

A. (A) is true and only (R1) is correct explanation for (A).
B. (A) is true and only (R2) is correct explanation for (A).
C. (A) is true but neither (R1) nor (R2) are correct explanation for (A).
D. (A) is true and both (R1) and (R2) are correct explanations for (A).

90. Which of the following statements is/are true regarding relative reactivity of metals?

(*a*) Zinc is more reactive than Iron but less reactive than Aluminium.
(*b*) Sodium is more reactive than Potassium and Calcium.
(*c*) Aluminium is more reactive than Magnesium.

A. Only (*a*) B. (*b*) and (*c*)
C. Only (*c*) D. (*a*) and (*b*)

82. B **83.** A **84.** A **85.** B **86.** C **87.** A **88.** A **89.** B **90.** A

LANGUAGE-I : ENGLISH

Directions (Qs. No. 91-99): *Read the passage given below and answer the questions that follow:*

1. Colours have a deeper significance for a home than one can imagine. For if used right, they can give a perfect look. In today's time, when there is an abundance of everything but space, colour plays an important role in creating the right ambience and perhaps the space that you crave for. Besides having a tremendous potential to create mood through sheer appeal to the senses, right use of colours actually helps you create the spacious feeling.

2. For instance, instead of using a plain monotonous colour on all four walls, if you get a little imaginative, perhaps a little bold, you can create a sense of space within those four walls. One of the ways would be to blend light and dark colours. Or to paint two opposite sides in a lighter shade than the other two. Colour can add height to your room too. For instance, if the room is painted white and the upholstery of your furniture is in deep blue tone, the false ceilings could be painted in a light blue shade. Think out of the box to give even more interesting effects to your room.

3. Whatever your choice is, there are options in the market to help you realise your needs. These days you get special patterned stencils to decorate walls with interesting patterns like flowers, leaves, birds etc. Some people draw an entire scenery on one side of the wall to give the feeling of bringing the outdoors inside. The choices are many, so are the creative ways. Just let your imagination flow. Every room reflects the personality of the occupant, hence it is important to pay attention to every detail. Your walls are your canvases, freshly painted and all bare. Go ahead, splash colours and watch the effect unfold.

91. The word opposite in meaning to the underlined word in the given sentence is:

'Right use of colours actually helps you create the <u>spacious</u> feeling'.

A. airy
B. fresh
C. special
D. cramped

92. Read the following statements:

(*a*) Colours if used creatively can give the perfect look to a room.
(*b*) Space is abundant nowadays.
(*c*) The right colour-combination on walls and the roof creates a spacious feeling.

A. (*b*) and (*c*) are correct, (*a*) is incorrect
B. (*a*), (*b*) and (*c*) are all correct
C. (*a*) and (*c*) are incorrect, (*b*) is correct
D. (*a*) and (*c*) are correct, (*b*) is incorrect

93. As mentioned by the writer in para1, In today's times, what is a modern day home owner longing for?

A. Space B. Sheer appeal
C. Imagination D. Colours

94. Identify the parts of speech of the underlined words in the sentence given below:

'Right use of colours <u>actually</u> helps you create the spacious <u>feeling</u>'.

A. verb, adverb B. preposition, verb
C. conjunction, verb D. adverb, noun

95. According to the writer, it is important to pay attention to the colour scheme of your home because:

A. it reflects the personality of the owner
B. the walls reveal the secrets of your life
C. the monotonous shades add life to the rooms
D. the ambience created makes it look boring

96. As mentioned by the writer in para 2, some ways by which you can break the monotony of the room is:

A. by blending light and dark shades
B. painting all the 4 walls in plain colours
C. both (A) and (B)
D. (A) is correct, but not (B)

97. Complete the given word analogy:

monotonous : dull :: ambience : ?

A. temperature B. aura
C. weather D. room

98. 'To think out of the box' does not mean to think:

A. about novel ideas
B. in unusual ways
C. traditionally
D. creatively and imaginatively

91. D	**92.** D	**93.** A	**94.** D	**95.** A	**96.** D	**97.** B	**98.** C

99. Some people draw colourful sceneries on their home walls to:

A. bring nature into their homes
B. create a sense of space
C. blend dark and light colours
D. give a deeper significance to their home

Directions (Qs. No. 100-105): *Read the poem given below and answer the questions that follow:*

Between my finger and my thumb
The squat pen rests: snug as a gun.
Under my window, a clean rasping sound
When the spade sings into gravelly ground.
My father, digging, I look down
Till his straining rump among the flowerbeds
Bends low, comes up twenty years away
Stooping in rhythm through potato drills,
Where he was digging
The coarse boot nestled on the lug, the shaft
Against the inside knee was levered firmly.
He rooted out tall tops, buried the bright edge deep.
To scatter new potatoes that we picked,
Loving their cool hardness in our hands.

100. The poetic devices in line 2 and line 4 are:

A. hyperbole and metaphor
B. simile and alliteration
C. metaphor and simile
D. metaphor and personification

101. What is the overall tone of the poem?

A. pitiful and sympathetic
B. disgust and animosity
C. nostalgic and admiration
D. annoyance and anger

102. Complete the word analogy:

coarse : rough :: snug : ?

A. perfect B. lethal
C. comfortable D. lazy

103. '.......... loving their cool hardness in our hands'. What is the speaker referring to the given line?

A. the handles of the spade
B. the potatoes
C. the potato drills
D. the gun

104. In the second stanza, the poet is observing:

A. his father digging potatoes
B. farmers in the fields
C. potato growers in the countryside
D. a gardener tending flower beds

105. How does the speaker's father feel about his son's choice of career?

A. He wishes, his son choose a more practical path.
B. He is glad his son is not a farmer.
C. He is ambivalent towards the choice.
D. The poem doesn't make it clear.

106. 'Authenticity of materials' refers to:

A. materials written or developed by people in authority.
B. materials written or developed in real life content.
C. materials which children bring from home.
D. materials written by the teacher for her class.

107. Which of the following are known as receptive skills?

A. Reading and speaking
B. Speaking and writing
C. Listening and reading
D. Listening and writing

108. Aparna, a learner of class V understands that listening involves listening to each sound, words, then sentences to get the meaning of the speech or an audio. Which approach/strategy she believes in for learning to listen?

A. Bottom-up approach
B. Both top-down and bottom-up approach
C. It is neither top-down nor bottom-up approach
D. Top-down approach

109. Which of the following is NOT true of the National Education Policy (NEP) 2020 on the study of foreign languages?

A. Study of foreign languages included as one of the languages under the three language formula.
B. Foreign language does not include in the three languages studied under three language formula.
C. French is one of the language recommended to be studied as an additional option.
D. Study of foreign languages as an additional option during the secondary stage.

99. A **100.** B **101.** C **102.** C **103.** B **104.** A **105.** D **106.** B **107.** C **108.** A **109.** A

110. Many Indians who go abroad for jobs learn the language of the place. What is this motivation known as?

A. Integrative motivation
B. Instrumental motivation
C. It is neither instrumental nor integrative motivation
D. Both integrative and instrumental motivation

111. Here is text or some statements. Find out which language register does this text represent?

The Indian Constitution recognises every person as equal. This means that every individual in the country, including male and female, person from all castes, religions, tribes, educational and economic background are recognised as equal. This is not to say that inequity ceases to exist. It doesn't. But at least, in democratic India, the principle of the equality of all persons is recognised.

A. Social Science register
B. Legal register
C. Scientific register
D. Politic register

112. Which of the following statements is true of a dialect of a language?

A. Speakers of different dialects of one language can understand the other dialect speaker.
B. A dialect is a bigger category and language is a smaller category.
C. Sometime different social group may speak different dialects of the same language.
D. Dialects of language vary from region to region.

113. Which of the following tasks promotes integrated learning skills?

A. Assignment B. Project work
C. Writing an article D. Role play

114. Which of the following refers to 'Knowing about language'?

A Procedural knowledge
B. Grammatical knowledge
C. Strategic competence
D. Declarative knowledge

115. A teacher of class VI does a warm up activity to connect their previous knowledge and experience with the text they would read. She asks her learners to look at the illustrations of the reading text (the story) before she begin to teach the text. What does she want her learners to do?

A. Appreciate the illustrations.
B. Make prediction about the reading text.
C. Make them understand the illustrations.
D. Visualize the story through the illustrations.

116. Which of the following language is NOT a classical language?

A. Sanskrit B. Telugu
C. Hindi D. Tamil

117. A continuous record of instances of learning by the learners is known as:

A. Continuous Comprehensive Assessment
B. Proficiency assessment
C. Diagnostic test
D. Portfolio

118. What is the following strategy in the context grammar teaching known as?

Introducing language item in contexts, making learners notice the language items, enabling them to use in real life contexts and drawing the attention of learner to the form by discovering it.

A. Deductive method
B. Discovery methods
C. Consciousness Raising
D. Creating a Schema

119. What is 'systemic competence' in language learning?

A. Understanding and applying that languages have a grammatical system.
B. Understanding that all languages have a common structural system.
C. Understanding that all human have a systems of many languages.
D. Understanding and applying that language works as a system.

120. A teacher of class VI develops the following task for a speaking activity.

Speak five sentences about desert and its climatic conditions.

Is it a good task or not a good task? Select from option your response and reason for the same.

A. It is a good task because it makes the learner to talk about something i.e the desert.
B. It is not a good task because some of the learners may not know about desert.
C. It is not a good task because it lacks context as there is no input for speaking about desert and its conditions.
D. It is a good task because the learners may have studied about desert in their geography class and will have inputs to speak.

110. B	111. A	112. *	113. B	114. D	115. B	116. C	117. D	118. C	119. D	120. C

LANGUAGE-II : हिन्दी

निर्देश (प्र.सं. 121 से 128 तक): *निम्नलिखित गद्यांश को पढ़कर पूछे गए प्रश्नों के उत्तर के लिए सबसे उपयुक्त विकल्प का चयन कीजिए।*

एक स्वतंत्र और जनतांत्रिक समाज के लिए सामान्य संस्कृति को पोषित करने वाली उच्चस्तरीय शिक्षा बहुत आवश्यक है। यह तभी संभव है जब शिक्षा बहुत से कार्यकलापों का आयोजन करे। यह सब 'विद्यालय' जैसी संस्था में संभव हो सकता है। विद्यालय शिक्षा से जुड़ी नीतियों को कार्यान्वित करते हैं। जीवन की गुणवत्ता के संदर्भ में शिक्षा का एक विशिष्ट स्थान है। यह मानव जीवन के विभिन्न पक्षों पर बहुआयामी प्रभाव डालती है। शिक्षा का कार्य शिक्षार्थी को भय से मुक्ति दिलाना है। विद्यालय यह काम कर सकता है। विद्यालय में शिक्षा का वातावरण बच्चों को जानकारी देने, लिखना-पढ़ना सिखाने तक सीमित रखने के बजाय उन्हें स्वतः सीखने के लिए बढ़ावा देने वाला हो जिससे उनमें विभिन्न संस्कृतियों की समझ पैदा होगी।

121. 'जनतांत्रिक' में कौन-सा प्रत्यय है?

A. इत B. इक
C. त D. क

122. विद्यालय का परिवेश कैसा होना चाहिए?

A. पढ़ना सिखाने वाला।
B. स्वतः अधिगम को बढ़ावा देने वाला।
C. लिखना सिखाने वाला
D. जानकारी देने वाला

123. कौन-सा शब्द भिन्न है?

A. संस्कृति B. समाज
C. स्वतंत्र D. शिक्षा

124. गद्यांश के अनुसार शिक्षार्थी को भय से मुक्ति दिलाने का कार्य किसका है?

A. संस्कृति B. शिक्षा
C. नीति D. समाज

125. जनतांत्रिक समाज के लिए किस तरह की शिक्षा की आवश्यकता है?

A. वर्ग भेद पैदा करने वाली।
B. आजीविका के अवसर देने वाली।
C. जानकारी देने वाली।
D. संस्कृति का संवर्द्धन करने वाली।

126. शिक्षा किस प्रकार से संस्कृति को पोषित करने वाली बन सकती है?

A. बच्चों में पठन-लेखन का कौशल विकसित करके
B. बच्चों को विद्यालय में नामांकित करके
C. बच्चों के लिए बहुत-से कार्यकलापों का आयोजन करके
D. बच्चों को तरह-तरह की सूचनाएँ देकर

127. 'विद्यालय' का संधि विच्छेद होगा :

A. विद्या + अलय B. विद्य + आलय
C. विद्य + अलय D. विद्या + आलय

128. 'विद्यालय' के संदर्भ में कौन-सी बात सही है?

A. विद्यालय धर्म से जुड़ी नीतियों को कार्यान्वित नहीं करते हैं।
B. विद्यालय बच्चों पर बहुआयामी प्रभाव नहीं डालते हैं।
C. विद्यालय स्व-अधिगम को प्रेरित नहीं करते हैं।
D. विद्यालय में शिक्षा जैसा कार्य संभव नहीं है।

निर्देश (प्र.सं. 129 से 135 तक): *निम्नलिखित गद्यांश को पढ़कर पूछे गए प्रश्नों के उत्तर के लिए सबसे उपयुक्त विकल्प का चयन कीजिए।*

विभिन्न भाषाओं में साहित्य की विशिष्ट विधा के रूप में संस्मरण का महत्वपूर्ण स्थान है। हिन्दी में भी संस्मरण लिखने की एक सुदीर्घ परंपरा है। जनमन की जीवन-यात्रा की अंतरंग छवियों को संस्मरण कह सकते हैं। संस्मरणों में, जीवन में आने वाले व्यक्तियों, पात्रों, स्थानों और घटनाओं की अंतरंग छवियाँ प्रस्तुत की जाती हैं। इसीलिए इसमें साधारण से साधारण और महत्वपूर्ण से महत्वपूर्ण पात्र और प्रसंग शामिल होते हैं। कई बार साहित्यकार अपने संस्मरण को एक व्यापक यथार्थ से ही जोड़कर रखते हैं तो कई बार उसमें अपनी कल्पना का भी पुट भर देते हैं। कुछ साहित्यकार अपने संस्मरण के माध्यम से मानवीय सरोकारों को भी अभिव्यक्त करते हैं।

129. संस्मरण में साधारण से लेकर महत्वपूर्ण पात्र और प्रसंग शामिल होते हैं, क्योंकि :

A. यह विशिष्ट साहित्यकार द्वारा लिखे जाते हैं।
B. इसमें विशिष्ट घटनाओं व पात्रों का ही चित्रण किया जाता है।
C. इसमें जीवन में आने वाले किसी भी पात्र, प्रसंग, घटना का चित्रण होता है।
D. यह साधारण साहित्यकार द्वारा लिखे जाते हैं।

130. गद्यांश के अनुसार संस्मरण क्या है?

A. जीवन यात्रा की अंतरंग छवियाँ
B. शब्दों का सरस प्रयोग
C. विशिष्ट विचार दर्शन
D. स्मृतियों का संकलन

121. B	122. B	123. C	124. B	125. D	126. C	127. D	128. A	129. C	130. A

131. प्रस्तुत गद्यांश साहित्य की किस विधा के बारे में है?

A. कहानी
B. संस्मरण
C. निबंध
D. जीवनी

132. 'सुदीर्घ' का अर्थ है :

A. अति निपुण
B. अति सुंदर
C. बहुत लंबा
D. अति उत्तम

133. भिन्न शब्द समूह की पहचान करें :

A. सुदीर्घ परंपरा
B. अंतरंग छवि
C. व्यापक यथार्थ
D. जीवन यात्रा

134. कुछ साहित्यकार संस्मरण के माध्यम से क्या अभिव्यक्त करते हैं?

A. समाजवादी दृष्टिकोण
B. वैज्ञानिक चेतना
C. संघर्षशीलता
D. मानवीय सरोकार

135. गद्यांश के संदर्भ में कौन-सा वाक्य सही **नहीं** है?

A. संस्मरण का विशिष्ट विधा के रूप में महत्वपूर्ण स्थान है।
B. संस्मरण केवल हिंदी साहित्य की ही विधा है।
C. संस्मरण में साधारण व विशिष्ट हर तरह के प्रसंग शामिल होते हैं।
D. साहित्यकार संस्मरण में अपनी कल्पना का भी पुट भर देते हैं।

136. कृपा और कर्ण जुड़वाँ हैं और मणिपुरी की विशेष बोली बोलते हैं। हालाँकि उनके बोलने में विभिन्नता है। बोली बोलने के उनके व्यक्तिगत विशेष तरीके को किस रूप में जाना जाएगा?

A. बोली
B. वाक् क्रिया
C. मणिपुरी
D. व्यक्ति भाषा (आइडियोलैक्ट)

137. अदिति भूतकाल के नियम जानती है। परन्तु संदर्भ के अनुसार उनका प्रयोग नहीं कर पाती है। उसके पास किस प्रकार का ज्ञान है?

A. प्रक्रियात्मक ज्ञान
B. घोषणात्मक ज्ञान
C. ज्ञान का अनुप्रयोग
D. भाषा अर्जन उपकरण

138. शिक्षार्थी उस भाषा को समझते और व्यवहार में लाते हैं जो एक व्यवस्था की तरह कार्य करती है :

A. सर्वांगी (सिस्टमिक) दक्षता
B. सामाजिक भाषिक दक्षता
C. युक्तिपरक दक्षता
D. सम्प्रेषणात्मक दक्षता

139. कक्षा सात की एक अध्यापक अपने शिक्षार्थियों को एक लघु पठन सामग्री पढ़ने के लिए देती है, जिसके माध्यम से वे पाठ्य सामग्री में प्रस्तुत लोग और समुदाय की सत्ता व पहचान के बारे में समझ बना सके। अध्यापक शिक्षार्थियों में किस बात को समुन्नत करना चाहती है?

A. समालोचनात्मक साक्षरता
B. विश्लेषणात्मक पठन
C. साहित्यिक कौशल
D. भाषा साक्षरता

140. अश्विन जन्म से ही उड़िया भाषा जानता है। उसने अंग्रेजी और हिंदी भी पढ़ी है। इस कथन के आधार पर पता लगाइए कि कौन-सा कथन सही **नहीं** है?

A. उसका हिंदी अधिगम भाषा अधिगम है।
B. उसका अंग्रेजी अधिगम भाषा अधिगम है।
C. उसका अंग्रेजी अधिगम भाषा अर्जन है।
D. उसका उड़िया अधिगम भाषा अर्जन है।

141. यांत्रिक (इंस्ट्रूमेंटल) प्रेरणा कब होती है?

A. जब कोई व्यक्ति किसी भाषा को इसलिए सीखता है, जिससे कि वह उस भाषा के सहजात वक्ता के नजदीक आ सके।
B. जब कोई व्यक्ति अपने समुदाय के धार्मिक और सामाजिक उत्सवों (कार्यो) के लिए भाषा सीखता है।
C. एक व्यक्ति पुस्तक लिखने के लिए भाषा सीखता है।
D. जब कोई व्यक्ति उपयोगिता के कारण से भाषा सीखता है, जैसे कि रोजगार के लिए।

142. यहाँ एक पाठ्य सामग्री दी गई है। पता लगाइए कि यह पाठ्य सामग्री भाषा की किस प्रयुक्ति (रजिस्टर) से संबंधित है?

"अचानक, क्रान्ति के बाद, ऐसा संभव लगने लगा कि बदलाव आएगा। विश्व के कई भागों में यहाँ तक कि यूरोप और एशिया में भी व्यक्ति के अधिकारों के बारे में नए-नए विचार सामने आने लगे और जिनके नियंत्रण में सामाजिक सत्ता थी, उनकी भी चर्चा होने लगी। भारत में राजा राम मोहन राय और दिरोजियो ने फ्रेंच क्रान्ति के महत्व के बारे में बात की। सामाजिक परिवर्तन के इन विचारों को एक नया स्वरूप दिया गया।"

A. राजनीतिक प्रयुक्ति
B. सामाजिक विज्ञान प्रयुक्ति
C. क्रान्ति प्रयुक्ति
D. विज्ञान प्रयुक्ति

143. कक्षा आठ के अध्यापक सुभाष को कई बार दुख होता है कि भाषा आकलन ग्राह्यशील (रिसेप्टिव) कौशलों को महत्व नहीं देता है। ग्राह्यशील कौशलों से उनका क्या तात्पर्य है?

A. बोलना और पठन
B. श्रवण और पठन
C. बोलना और लेखन
D. श्रवण और लेखन

131. B	**132.** C	**133.** D	**134.** D	**135.** B	**136.** D	**137.** B	**138.** A	**139.** A	**140.** C
141. D	**142.** B	**143.** B							

144. श्रवण के शीर्ष अधोमुखी उपागम (टॉप डाउन) में क्या शामिल है?

A. वाक्, सामग्री या ऑडियो के सारांश (जिस्ट) को सुनना

B. सामग्री, वाक् या ऑडियो के समग्र संदेश को सुनना

C. प्रत्येक ध्वनि, शब्द, वाक्यांश, उपवाक्य और वाक्यों को सुनना

D. विशिष्ट वर्णनों की ओर ध्यान देना

145. निम्नलिखित में से कौन-सा कथन राष्ट्रीय शिक्षा नीति 2020 के द्वारा शास्त्रीय भाषाओं के अध्ययन के बारे में सही है?

A. त्रिभाषा सूत्र के अन्तर्गत एक विकल्प के रूप में शास्त्रीय भाषा का अध्ययन

B. प्रिप्रेटरी चरण के दौरान शास्त्रीय भाषा का अध्ययन

C. माध्यमिक चरण में एक केन्द्रक (कोर) भाषा के रूप में शास्त्रीय भाषा का अध्ययन

D. माध्यमिक चरण के दौरान एक अतिरिक्त विकल्प के रूप में शास्त्रीय भाषा का अध्ययन

146. भाषा की कक्षा में परियोजना कार्य की अभिकल्पना करने और उसे क्रियान्वित करने में क्या-क्या चरण संलग्न हैं?

A. समूह बनाना, टॉपिक की पहचान, योजना बनाना, आँकड़ों का संग्रहीकरण, आँकड़ों की व्याख्या, प्रारूप लेखन और रिपोर्ट फाइनल करना।

B. समूह बनाना, टॉपिक की पहचान, योजना बनाना, आँकड़ों का संग्रहीकरण, प्रारूप लेखन, आँकड़ों की व्याख्या और रिपोर्ट फाइनल करना।

C. अध्यापक और शिक्षार्थी मिलकर अपनी इच्छानुसार अपने तरीके से परियोजना कार्य की अभिकल्पना और क्रियान्वयन कर सकते हैं।

D. समूह बनाना, योजना बनाना, आँकड़ों का संग्रहीकरण, आँकड़ों की व्याख्या, प्रारूप लेखन, टॉपिक की पहचान और रिपोर्ट लेखन।

147. भाषा के बारे में कौन-सा सही **नहीं** है?

A. भाषा इतिहास का खजाना है।

B. भाषा मानव ज्ञान के कुल योग में योगदान देती है।

C. कुछ भाषाएँ केवल विज्ञान और अभियांत्रिकी को ही बेहतर रूप से सम्प्रेषित कर सकती है।

D. भाषा पहचान अभिव्यक्त करती है।

148. एक ऐसा परीक्षण जिसका उद्देश्य विद्यार्थी विशेष के कमजोर और प्रबल पक्ष के विशिष्ट क्षेत्रों की पहचान करना है, क्या कहलाता है?

A. वैधता परीक्षण B. निदानात्मक परीक्षण

C. रचनात्मक परीक्षण D. वस्तुनिष्ठ परीक्षण

149. भारत के संविधान में अंग्रेजी भाषा की क्या स्थिति है?

A. सह राजकीय भाषा

B. विदेशी भाषा

C. वैधानिक निकायों की भाषा

D. राजकीय (ऑफिशियल) भाषा

150. कक्षा सात की अध्यापिका किसी एक व्यक्ति के वर्णन से संबंधित लेखन कार्य देना चाहती है। वह कक्षा से बाहर गई और अपनी कक्षा में एक फेरी वाले को उसके सामान सहित लेकर आई। उसने उस फेरी वाले से कहा कि वह कक्षा में कोई सातेक मिनट के लिए रुके फिर शिक्षार्थियों को दो-दो के जोड़ों में उस व्यक्ति का वर्णन लिखने के लिए कहा। वह फेरी वाला इस गतिविधि में किस रूप में जाना जाएगा?

A. फेरी वाला B. गतिविधि का एक प्रतिभागी

C. सामग्री D. शिक्षण सहायक

EXPLANATORY ANSWERS

1. (B): An inclusive classroom is one where students with diverse abilities and needs learn together. To accommodate all learners, the teacher must adapt teaching methods and materials to cater to individual learning styles. This approach ensures that students with different academic capabilities, including those with disabilities or learning difficulties, receive the support they need to succeed in the classroom. Modifying curriculum and teaching strategies promotes equity and fosters a supportive learning environment where all students can thrive.

2. (C): Universal Design for Learning (UDL) is an educational framework that emphasizes flexible teaching methods to accommodate diverse learners. It ensures that students have multiple means of engagement, representation, and expression. However, labeling and categorization contradict the principles of UDL, as they can lead to stereotyping and lower expectations for students based on perceived deficiencies rather than fostering their unique strengths. UDL encourages personalized learning approaches that recognize diversity without rigid classifications.

3. (B): Effective teaching of new concepts involves helping students build meaningful connections. Presenting examples helps illustrate the concept, while non-examples clarify boundaries by showing what does not fit the concept. Encouraging students

144. B	**145.** D	**146.** A	**147.** C	**148.** B	**149.** A	**150.** C

to analyze relationships among concepts fosters deeper understanding. Unlike rote memorization, which focuses on recall without comprehension, these methods promote critical thinking and conceptual clarity, enabling students to apply their knowledge effectively in different contexts.

4. **(D):** Lev Vygotsky emphasized the role of language as a fundamental cultural tool that supports cognitive development. He argued that language enables higher-order thinking by allowing individuals to structure, organize, and reflect on their thoughts. Through social interactions, children internalize language, which helps them develop reasoning skills and problem-solving abilities. Language not only facilitates communication but also plays a crucial role in shaping cognitive functions such as planning, memory, and abstract thinking.

5. **(B):** Autism Spectrum Disorder (ASD) is characterized by a range of behavioural traits, including a strong preference for routines and structured patterns. Many individuals with autism exhibit resistance to change and may become distressed when their routines are disrupted. This adherence to routine provides a sense of predictability and control, helping them navigate daily life. While there are individual differences, a preference for structured environments and repetitive behaviours is a common characteristic of autism.

6. **(A):** Jean Piaget's theory of cognitive development suggests that children progress through stages of intellectual growth, each characterized by distinct ways of thinking and reasoning. Learning experiences must align with a child's current cognitive stage to be effective.

   Piaget emphasized the role of active exploration and interaction with the environment in cognitive development, highlighting that learning is most meaningful when it builds upon what a child can already understand rather than relying solely on memorization or passive reception of information.

7. **(D):** Braille is a system of raised dots used by individuals with visual impairments to read and write. It is a tactile system that allows users to recognize letters, words, and symbols through touch. Unlike auditory systems, which rely on sound, Braille provides an alternative way for visually challenged individuals to access information independently. Teachers should use Braille as an essential tool for literacy development among visually impaired students, ensuring they have equal opportunities for education and communication.

8. **(D):** Metacognition refers to an individual's ability to reflect on, regulate, and analyze their own thinking processes. Fiza's awareness of her difficulty in learning a specific topic due to differences in interest and attention demonstrates metacognitive awareness. This ability allows learners to assess their strengths and weaknesses, adjust their study strategies, and enhance their learning efficiency. Metacognition plays a crucial role in self-regulated learning, as it helps students make conscious decisions about how to approach different learning tasks.

9. **(D):** Howard Gardner's theory of multiple intelligences suggests that intelligence is not a fixed, singular entity but consists of various independent intelligences, such as linguistic, logical-mathematical, spatial, musical, and interpersonal intelligences. These intelligences are dynamic and can develop over time based on experiences, education, and environmental influences. Unlike traditional views that see intelligence as static and measurable through IQ tests, Gardner's theory emphasizes the adaptability and evolving nature of human intelligence.

10. **(B):** Advocates of progressive education recognize that children's development is deeply influenced by their social, cultural, and economic backgrounds. Education should be designed to accommodate these influences, ensuring that learning experiences are meaningful and relevant to students' lived realities. Progressive education focuses on experiential learning, active participation, and critical thinking, emphasizing that education should not be isolated from the societal and cultural contexts in which children grow.

11. **(C):** Fear and stress do not facilitate meaningful learning; instead, they can hinder cognitive engagement, creativity, and retention. A positive and supportive environment enhances learning by encouraging students to take risks and actively participate. Learning is influenced by both intrinsic and extrinsic factors, including motivation, prior knowledge, and social interactions, rather than being governed solely by extrinsic rewards or pressures.

12. **(A):** Performance goal orientation focuses on demonstrating ability, gaining recognition, and outperforming peers rather than mastering a subject. Students with a performance goal mindset are primarily driven by external validation, such as grades or teacher approval, rather than intrinsic motivation to learn. This type of orientation can sometimes lead to anxiety and a fear of failure, reducing deep learning and problem-solving skills.

13. (C): Assessment for learning provides students with ongoing feedback to help them understand their progress and improve their learning. A rubric serves this purpose by clarifying expectations, guiding students in self-monitoring their work, and allowing for adjustments before final evaluation. Unlike summative assessments, which judge final performance, assessments for learning support continuous improvement.

14. (C): Diagnostic assessments help teachers identify students' strengths, weaknesses, and learning gaps before instruction begins. This allows for targeted interventions and personalized support. Unlike summative assessments, which measure learning outcomes after instruction, diagnostic assessments provide crucial information to modify teaching strategies and ensure that all students receive the help they need.

15. (D): Vygotsky emphasized that cognitive development occurs through social interactions and cultural experiences. He proposed that learning is facilitated by collaboration with peers and more knowledgeable individuals, such as teachers or parents. Through guided participation and scaffolding, students gradually develop higher cognitive abilities, making learning a collective and interactive process rather than an isolated one.

16. (C): Reciprocal teaching is an instructional strategy based on Vygotsky's theories, where students engage in dialogue with the teacher and peers to develop comprehension skills. This technique involves summarizing, questioning, clarifying, and predicting, allowing students to take an active role in their learning. Unlike rote memorization, reciprocal teaching fosters critical thinking and enhances students' ability to process and retain information.

17. (B): Analytical thinking requires students to examine relationships, causes, and underlying principles rather than merely recalling facts. This question promotes deeper understanding by encouraging students to evaluate historical events, analyze multiple causes, and consider different perspectives. Unlike factual recall questions, analytical questions help students develop reasoning and problem-solving skills.

18. (D): Anxiety and fear negatively impact a student's ability to learn and perform. When students feel threatened or embarrassed, their cognitive abilities are compromised, leading to avoidance behaviours and reduced participation. A supportive and safe learning environment is essential for fostering confidence and academic success, making emotional well-being a key factor in effective learning.

19. (D): Piaget viewed egocentric speech as a stage children outgrow as they develop social awareness. In contrast, Vygotsky saw private speech as a crucial tool for self-regulation and problem-solving. Private speech helps children guide their actions and internalize thinking processes, playing a vital role in cognitive development and independent learning.

20. (C): Social and cultural factors influence all individuals, regardless of gender. Research does not support the claim that girls are genetically more sensitive or emotionally weaker than boys. Instead, societal expectations and stereotypes shape behaviours and opportunities. Both boys and girls are affected by cultural norms, and their development is influenced by a complex interplay of biological, social, and environmental factors.

21. (B): Scaffolding is a teaching approach in which a teacher provides temporary support to help a student reach a higher level of understanding and problem-solving ability. Encouraging persistence helps students develop resilience, while guided assistance ensures they acquire the necessary skills to solve problems independently. This approach aligns with Vygotsky's Zone of Proximal Development, which emphasizes learning through gradual assistance.

22. (A): Class inclusion is a cognitive ability that allows children to understand hierarchical relationships between categories, such as recognizing that Delhi is a part of India. Lokesh's difficulty with this concept is a typical characteristic of Piaget's preoperational or early concrete operational stage. However, reasoning about emotions and memory pertains to metacognition, which is unrelated to class inclusion.

23. (C): In reciprocal teaching, students and teachers take turns leading discussions, summarizing, questioning, clarifying, and predicting content. This method fosters interactive learning and helps students develop comprehension skills through active engagement. Unlike traditional teacher-led methods, reciprocal teaching encourages students to become independent learners by assuming instructional roles themselves.

24. (D): Gender roles refer to behaviours, interests, and expectations that a society considers appropriate for men and women. These roles are shaped by cultural norms rather than being biologically determined. Societal influences such as media, education, and family upbringing play a crucial role in defining and reinforcing gender roles.

25. (C): Not all children have equal opportunities to play, experiment, and discover due to socio-economic, cultural, and environmental differences. Additionally, childhood is not a universal construct but is shaped by cultural and historical contexts. Different societies define childhood in various ways, affecting children's experiences and access to education and play.

26. (A): Open-ended questions promote critical and creative thinking by allowing students to explore multiple perspectives, analyze information, and develop original ideas. Unlike rote memorization or multiple-choice tests, open-ended tasks encourage deeper cognitive engagement and problem-solving skills.

27. (C): Inclusive education does not mean lowering educational standards for children with special needs. Instead, it focuses on modifying teaching strategies and providing necessary accommodations to help all students learn effectively. Special children have learning potential and can benefit from mainstream classrooms when given appropriate support, making Reason (R) incorrect.

28. (B): Kohlberg's theory of moral development is based on presenting moral dilemmas to children and analyzing their reasoning. This approach helps determine how individuals progress through different stages of moral understanding. Kohlberg's model emphasizes justice and ethical decision-making rather than cultural or gender influences.

29. (B): Meaningful learning occurs when new information is linked to prior knowledge. Encouraging students to relate concepts to their personal experiences fosters deeper understanding and retention. This approach aligns with constructivist theories, which emphasize active engagement in learning rather than passive memorization.

30. (C): The psycho-social domain of development includes emotional growth, self-perception, and interpersonal relationships with family, peers, and friends. Changes in these areas influence personality development, identity formation, and social skills, making them crucial aspects of human development. This domain is distinct from cognitive, linguistic, and physical development.

31. (A): $31096 \div (2704 \div 2) + 0.6738 + 0.63 + 0.059 - 0.79$

$= 31096 \div 1352 + 0.6738 + 0.63 + 0.059 - 0.79$

$= 23 + 0.6738 + 0.63 + 0.059 - 0.79$

$= 23 + 1.3628 - 0.79$

$= 24.3628 - 0.79 = 23.5728.$

32. (A): Arranging the given data in ascending order: 0, 0, 1, 1, 1, 1, 2, 2, 3, 4, 4

$$\text{Mean} = \frac{0+0+1+1+1+1+2+2+3+4+4}{11}$$

$$= \frac{19}{11}$$

and mode = 1 (maximum 4 times)

$\therefore$ The difference between the mean and mode

$$= \frac{19}{11} - 1 = \frac{8}{11}.$$

33. (A): Here, radius of wheel = 25 cm

circumference of wheel $= 2\pi r$

$= 2\pi \times 25 = 50\pi$ cm

$\therefore$ The distance covered by a wheel in 350 rounds

$= 350 \times 50\pi$ cm

$= 350 \times 50 \times \frac{22}{7}$

$= 50 \times 50 \times 22$

$= 55000$ cm

$= \frac{55000}{100}$ m $= 550$ m.

34. (A): The two corresponding angles formed by the intersection of two parallel lines by a transversal are $(3x - 20°)$ and $(5x - 60°)$

$\because$ The two corresponding angles are equal

$\therefore \quad (3x - 20°) = (5x - 60°)$

$\Rightarrow \quad 5x - 3x = -20 + 60$

$\Rightarrow \quad 2x = 40° \Rightarrow x = 20°$

$\therefore \quad 4x + 30° = 4 \times 20° + 30°$

$= 80° + 30° = 110°.$

35. (C): Teaching addition of integers requires interactive and visual methods that help students grasp the concept effectively. Tools such as a number line, stairs, and lift provide hands-on experiences that facilitate understanding of positive and negative numbers. In contrast, using chart paper is less effective because it is a static representation and does not actively engage students in the process of visualizing integer operations.

36. (C):

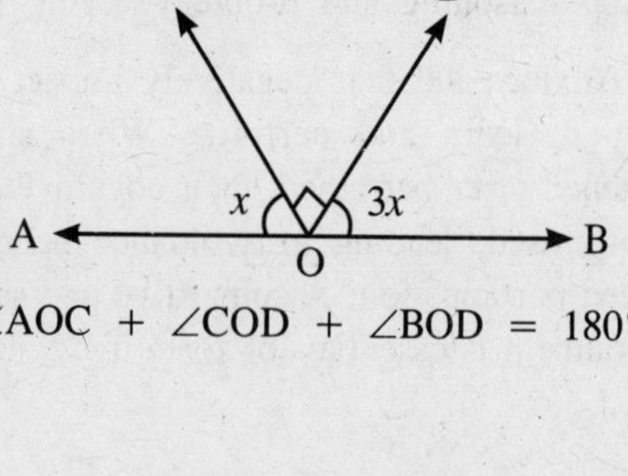

$\because \angle AOC + \angle COD + \angle BOD = 180°$

$\therefore \quad x + 90° + 3x = 180°$

$\Rightarrow \quad 4x = 180° - 90°$

$\Rightarrow \quad 4x = 90°$

$\Rightarrow \quad x = \frac{45°}{2}$

$\therefore \quad \angle BOD = 3x$

$= 3 \times \frac{45°}{2} = \frac{135°}{2} = 67\frac{1}{2}°.$

37. (D): Assessment as learning emphasizes the active involvement of students in monitoring their progress through self-reflection and peer feedback. This method encourages learners to develop critical thinking and metacognitive skills, allowing them to understand their strengths and areas for improvement. Unlike summative assessments, which evaluate final outcomes, assessment as learning fosters continuous growth and deeper engagement in the learning process.

38. (B): $\text{Time} = \frac{\text{Simple Interest} \times 100}{\text{P} \times r}$

$= \frac{(₹\ 9500 - ₹\ 8000) \times 100}{₹\ 8000 \times 7.5}$

$= \frac{1500 \times 100}{8000 \times \frac{15}{2}} = \frac{150 \times 2}{8 \times 15} = \frac{20}{8}$

$= \frac{5}{2} = 2\frac{1}{2}$

$\Rightarrow \quad t = 2\frac{1}{2}$ years

Now, Amount = ?, in same time at 20% p.a. interest is compounded yearly.

$\therefore \quad A = P\left(1 + \frac{r}{100}\right)^2 \left(1 + \frac{r \times \frac{1}{2}}{100}\right)$

$= 8000\left(1 + \frac{20}{100}\right)^2 \left(1 + \frac{20 \times \frac{1}{2}}{100}\right)$

$= 8000\left(1 + \frac{1}{5}\right)^2 \left(1 + \frac{1}{10}\right)$

$= 8000\left(\frac{36}{25}\right)\left(\frac{11}{10}\right)$

$= 32 \times 36 \times 11$

$= ₹\ 12672.$

39. (B): When each number is multiplied by (-1/2), all values become negative, and their relative order is reversed. The original sequence ($2 < 7 < 9 < 12$) transforms into ($-1 > -3.5 > -4.5 > -6$), which follows a descending order. This transformation occurs because multiplying by a negative fraction maintains the inverse relationship between numbers.

40. (C): At the elementary level, students understand mathematical ideas better when they are introduced through concrete experiences before progressing to abstract concepts. Using real-life objects and visual models helps build foundational understanding before moving to symbolic representations and abstract reasoning, making learning more effective and meaningful.

41. (A): To determine a factor of the given polynomial, factorizing common terms and identifying binomial expressions is essential. By factoring, one of the possible binomial factors is found to be $2q - 3r$, which satisfies the polynomial factorization rules. This method helps in simplifying algebraic expressions and solving polynomial equations effectively.

42. (A): The lecture method is a traditional, teacher-centered approach where the teacher delivers content while students passively receive information. Unlike heuristic or problem-solving methods, which encourage student engagement and exploration, the lecture method prioritizes direct instruction and transmission of knowledge without much student interaction.

43. (C): Let marked price of an article be ₹ x

Then, $\quad \text{S.P.} = x \times \frac{100 - 24}{100}$

$\Rightarrow \quad 608 = x \times \frac{76}{100}$

$\Rightarrow \quad x = \frac{608 \times 100}{76} = 800$

$\Rightarrow \quad x = ₹\ 800$

$\therefore \quad$ Marked price = ₹ 800

Now, $\quad$ Selling price = Marked price = ₹ 800

Given, $\quad$ Cost price = ₹ 750

$\because \quad$ Profit = S.P. − C.P.

$= 800 - 750 = 50$

$\therefore \quad \text{Profit per cent} = \frac{\text{Profit} \times 100}{\text{C.P.}}$

$= \frac{50 \times 100}{750} = \frac{100}{15} = \frac{20}{3}$

$= 6\frac{2}{3}\%.$

44. (B): Given, numbers 12, 13, 14, ..., 70, 71

$\therefore$ Total numbers = 60

Here, Prime numbers: 13, 17, 19, 23, 29, 31, 37, 41, 43, 47, 53, 59, 61, 67, 71

Total number of prime numbers = 15

$\therefore$ Probability (the card drawn has the numbers which is not a prime)

$$= \frac{60-15}{60} = \frac{45}{60} = \frac{3}{4}.$$

45. (C): Rational numbers lie between $\frac{-7}{10}$ and $\frac{-1}{4}$

$\Rightarrow$ between -0.70 and -0.25

(A) $\frac{-2}{3}, \frac{-3}{5}, \frac{-3}{4}$

$\Rightarrow -0.66, -0.60, -0.075$

(B) $\frac{-5}{8}, \frac{2}{3}, \frac{-3}{5}$

$\Rightarrow -0.62, 0.66, -0.60$

(C) $\frac{-5}{8}, \frac{-2}{3}, \frac{-3}{5}$

$\Rightarrow -0.62, -0.66, -0.60$

(D) $\frac{-3}{5}, 0, \frac{-1}{5}$

$\Rightarrow -0.60, 0, -0.20$

Here, Option (C) lies between -0.70 and -0.25.

46. (A): A number is written in standard form when it is expressed as $a \times 10^n$, where $1 \leq a < 10$ and n is an integer. In option (A), 8.5 falls within the required range, and the exponent -12 follows the proper scientific notation format. The other options either do not satisfy this condition or are not written in the correct standard form.

47. (D): $\because$ $565x9274y$ is divisible by number 88

$\Rightarrow$ $565x9274y$ is divisible by 8 and 11

$\therefore$ $74y$ is divisible by 8

$\Rightarrow \quad \frac{74y}{8} = 93$, when $y = 4$

and $565x9274y$ is divisible by 11

$\Rightarrow (y + 7 + 9 + 5 + 5) - (4 + 2 + x + 6)$
$= 0$ or divisible by 11

$\Rightarrow (y + 26) - (x + 12) = 0$

$\Rightarrow \quad y - x + 14 = 0$

$\Rightarrow \quad 4 - x + 14 = 0$ (putting $y = 4$)

$\therefore \quad 18 - x = 0$ or divisible by 11

when $x = 7$ then $18 - x = 11$

Hence, $x = 7$ and $y = 4$

Hence, $2x + 3y = 2 \times 7 + 3 \times 4$
$= 14 + 12 = 26$

$\Rightarrow \quad 2x + 3y = 26.$

48. (D): The ability to use abstractions to perceive relationships and apply mathematical concepts to real-life situations are crucial indicators of mathematical understanding. Mathematics is not about memorizing formulas but about reasoning, problem-solving, and making connections. The ability to transfer mathematical knowledge to practical contexts demonstrates true mathematical competency.

49. (A): In a pentagon, ABCDE

The sum of all angles = 540°

$\therefore \angle A + \angle B + \angle C + \angle D + \angle E = 540°$

$\Rightarrow 2x + 9° + 2x + 1° + 2x - 1° + 2x + 5° + 2x - 4° = 540°$

$\Rightarrow \quad 10x + 10° = 540°$

$\Rightarrow \quad 10x = 540° - 10°$

$\Rightarrow \quad 10x = 530°$

$\Rightarrow \quad x = 53°$

Hence, $(2x + 10°) = 2 \times 53° + 10°$
$= 106° + 10° = 116°$

$\Rightarrow \quad 2x + 10° = 116°.$

50. (B): The utilitarian value of mathematics refers to its practical applications in daily life and various professions. Fields such as accountancy, banking, and tailoring rely on mathematical calculations and problem-solving skills. Mathematics is essential for managing finances, measurements, and logical decision-making, making it a fundamental tool in multiple occupations.

51. (B): Given, $A = 3x^2 - 8x + 11$

$B = -2x^2 + 12x$

$C = -4x^2 + 7$ and

$D = x^2 - x - 11$

$(A + B + C) - D = px^2 - qx + r$

$\Rightarrow (3x^2 - 8x + 11 - 2x^2 + 12x - 4x^2 + 7)$
$- (x^2 - x - 11) = px^2 + qx + r$

$\Rightarrow -4x^2 + 5x + 29 = px^2 + qx + r$

Comparing both sides by co-efficient of x^2, x and constant

$\therefore \quad p = -4, q = 5$

and $\quad r = 29$

Hence, $p + q + r = -4 + 5 + 29$

$\Rightarrow \quad p + q + r = 30.$

52. (A): AB = 8 cm, BC = 4 cm,

$\angle BCA = 90°$

$\angle ABC = 60°$

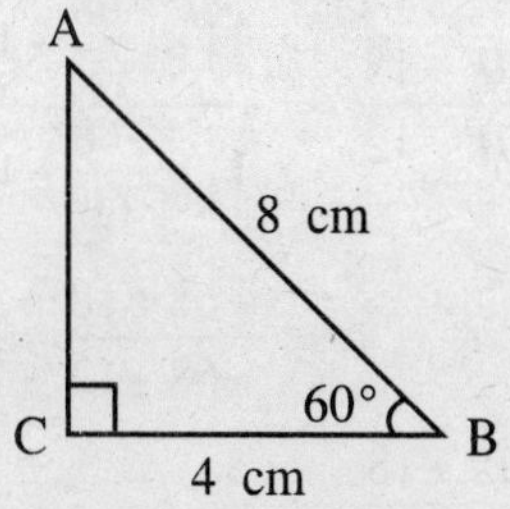

$\because \quad \cos 60° = \frac{1}{2}$

$\Rightarrow \quad \cos 60° = \frac{BC}{AB} = \frac{4}{8} = \frac{1}{2}$

$\Rightarrow \quad \cos 60° = \frac{1}{2}$

$\therefore$ Option (A), the construction of triangle ABC can be done.

53. (B): Anecdotal records are brief written observations documenting significant incidents of a student's performance or behaviour. They capture qualitative details about how students approach and solve problems, measure quantities, or conduct experiments. This makes them useful for tracking skills like problem-solving, measurement, and experimentation in a descriptive, context-specific manner.

54. (A): Given, In parallelogram PQRS,

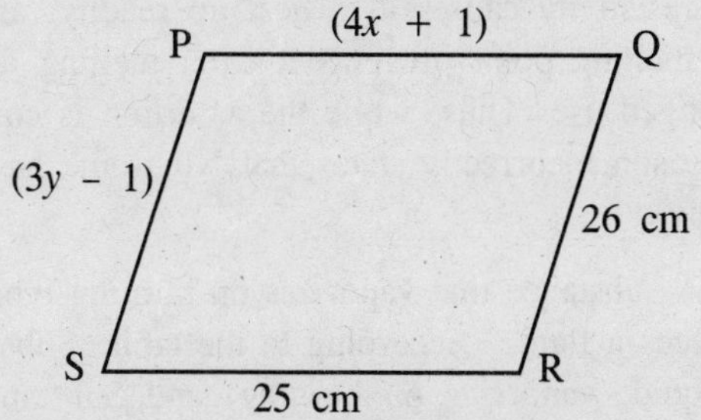

$PQ = (4x + 1)$ cm

$QR = 26$ cm

$RS = 25$ cm,

$PS = (3y - 1)$ cm

$\because \quad PQ = RS$

$\therefore \quad 4x + 1 = 25$

$\Rightarrow \quad 4x = 24 \Rightarrow x = 6$

and $\quad PS = QR$

$\therefore \quad 3y - 1 = 26$

$\Rightarrow \quad 3y = 27 \Rightarrow y = 9$

Hence, $\quad (3x + 2y) = 3 \times 6 + 2 \times 9$

$= 18 + 18 = 36$ cm

$\Rightarrow \quad (3x + 2y) = 36$ cm.

55. (C): Given, ABCD is a trapezium,

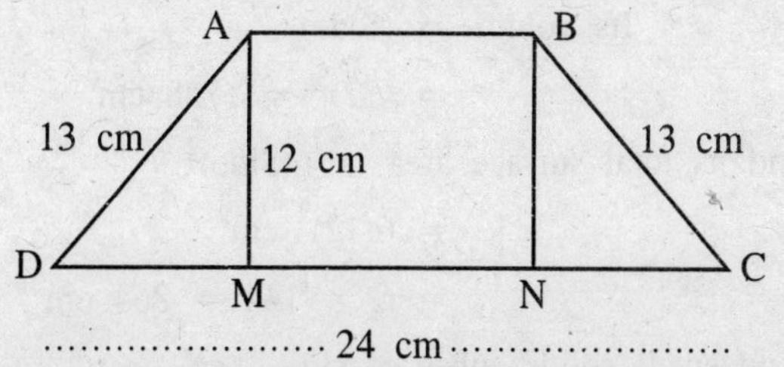

$AB < CD, \quad CD = 24$ cm

and $\quad AD = BC = 13$ cm

Let $AM \perp CD$ and $BN \perp CD$

$\therefore \quad AM = 12$ cm,

$BN = 12$ cm

In ΔAMD,

$AM^2 + DM^2 = AD^2$

$\Rightarrow \quad 12^2 + DM^2 = 13^2$

$\Rightarrow \quad DM^2 = 169 - 144 = 25 = (5)^2$

$\Rightarrow \quad DM = 5$ cm

$\therefore \quad CN = 5$ cm

$[\because AM = BN \text{ and } AD = BC]$

$\therefore \quad MN = 24 - (5 + 5) = 14$ cm

$\Rightarrow \quad AB = MN = 14$ cm

$\therefore$ Area of the trapezium,

$= \frac{1}{2}$ (Sum of parallel sides) $\times$ height

$= \frac{1}{2}(AB + CD) \times AM$

$= \frac{1}{2}(14 + 24) \times 12$

$= \frac{1}{2} \times 38 \times 12$

$= 19 \times 12 = 228 \text{ cm}^2$.

56. (A): $\quad 2605 - x = (51)^2$

$\Rightarrow \quad 2605 - x = 2601$

$\Rightarrow \quad x = 2605 - 2601$

$\Rightarrow \quad x = 4$

$\therefore \quad (4x + 7) = 4 \times 4 + 7$

$= 16 + 7$

$\Rightarrow \quad (4x + 7) = 23$ cm.

57. (A): Reflection is often described as a "flip" across a line, Rotation as a "turn" around a point, Translation as a "slide" along a particular direction, and Enlargement as creating a "bigger figure." Associating each transformation with these simple terms helps students differentiate them clearly and avoid confusion.

58. (C): Given, A solid cube of side 12 cm

$$\text{Its volume} = (\text{Side})^3 = (12)^3 = 1728 \text{ cm}^3$$

and its total surface area $= 6(\text{Side})^2$

$$= 6(12)^2 \text{ cm}^2 = 6 \times 144 = 864 \text{ cm}^2$$

And small solids cubes of side 4 cm each

$$\text{Its volume} = (\text{Side})^3 = (4)^3 = 64 \text{ cm}^3$$

and its total surface area $= 6(\text{Side})^2$

$$= 6(4)^2 = 96 \text{ cm}^2$$

and total number of small cubes

$$= \frac{1728}{64} = 27$$

$\therefore$ The new total surface area of the small cubes

$$= 27 \times 96 \text{ cm}^2 = 2592 \text{ cm}^2$$

Hence, new total surface area/the original total surface area

$$= \frac{2592}{864} = 3$$

Hence, new total surface area will be thrice the original total surfae area.

59. (C): Hands-on and visual practice (I) helps solidify understanding in mensuration by letting students see and manipulate shapes and measurements concretely. Open-ended questions with discussion (II) allow students to articulate their thinking, address misconceptions, and learn from peers. Combined, these methods effectively target and correct conceptual errors.

60. (B): Given, $x = k$ is the solution of the equation,

$$\frac{x-4}{7} - 1 = \frac{5-x}{3} + x$$

$$\Rightarrow \quad \frac{x-4}{7} - \frac{5-x}{3} = 1 + x$$

$$\Rightarrow \quad \frac{3(x-4) - 7(5-x)}{21} = (1 + x)$$

$$\Rightarrow \quad 3x - 12 - 35 + 7x = 21(1 + x)$$

$$\Rightarrow \quad 10x - 47 = 21 + 21x$$

$$\Rightarrow \quad 10x - 21x = 47 + 21$$

$$\Rightarrow \quad -11x = 68$$

$$\Rightarrow \quad x = \frac{-68}{11}$$

$$\Rightarrow \quad k = \frac{-68}{11}$$

Hence,
$$\frac{11k+18}{11k-12} = \frac{11 \times \frac{-68}{11} + 18}{11 \times \frac{-68}{11} - 12} = \frac{-68+18}{-68-12} = \frac{-50}{-80} = \frac{5}{8}$$

$$\Rightarrow \quad \frac{11k+18}{11k-12} = \frac{5}{8}.$$

61. (B): Bile juice neutralizes the acidic chyme coming from the stomach (making it alkaline) and assists in the digestion of fats by emulsifying them into smaller droplets. Both functions are essential steps in the overall digestive process, ensuring that nutrients are properly broken down and absorbed.

62. (C): Large circular leaves help provide buoyancy (*iii*). A waxy coating on leaves and stems helps protect against decay (*i*). Stems with tunnels and holes assist in staying afloat (*iv*). Ribbon-like leaves can endure water currents, effectively offering resistance or reducing damage (*ii*). Each adaptation aligns with the specific needs of aquatic plants.

63. (B): Nichrome is indeed used as a heating element in devices like toasters and geysers because it has a high melting point and high resistivity, not low. Its high resistivity causes it to heat up readily, and its high melting point prevents it from melting during prolonged use. Thus, while the assertion is correct, the reason incorrectly states that Nichrome has low resistivity.

64. (B): A substance that vaporizes on burning typically produces a flame. According to the table, Substance B (liquid, vaporizes on burning) and Substance C (solid, vaporizes on burning) both give a flame. Substances A and D do not vaporize on burning and therefore do not produce a flame.

65. (B): Thyroxine regulates the body's metabolism of carbohydrates, proteins, and fats. It is secreted by the thyroid gland, whose proper functioning depends on adequate iodine intake. A deficiency of iodine in the diet can lead to thyroid-related problems, underscoring the critical link between thyroxine production and iodine.

66. (A): Students closely watch the bars' behaviour (observation) when they test for magnetism, categorize which bars show magnetic properties (classification), and draw conclusions on which ones are magnets (inferring). Measurement or more advanced processes are not strictly necessary for identifying the bar magnets, making observation, classification, and inferring the most relevant skills.

67. (A): Art integrated learning in Science is effectively fostered through projects that allow students to create models, drawings, or multimedia artifacts, and through portfolios where they can compile diverse creative works. These approaches promote reflective thinking and deeper engagement, blending artistic expression with scientific understanding.

68. (B): The true purposes of open book assessment include assessing conceptual understanding, providing opportunities for exploration, and reducing anxiety. Merely aiming for higher marks undermines the spirit of open book assessments, which is to encourage deeper learning rather than rote memorization.

69. (A): Photosynthesis and the formation of curd both involve chemical changes, as new substances are formed and the original composition is altered. Crystallization is typically a physical change (not chemical), and the ripening of fruit involves biochemical processes, making it a chemical change rather than a physical one.

70. (C): Children's ideas are often stable, formed from observable experiences, follow similar developmental patterns, and are domain-specific. They are not easy to modify, as they can persist unless carefully addressed through targeted instruction and experiences that challenge misconceptions.

71. (B): Arteries do have thick, elastic walls due to the high pressure of blood flow. However, the reason is incorrect because it states that arteries have lower pressure than veins, which is not true. Instead, arteries carry blood at a higher pressure as blood is pumped directly from the heart.

72. (B): Self-pollination does require bisexual (hermaphroditic) flowers that have both stamens and pistils within the same flower. Cross pollination is not limited to unisexual flowers; it can happen between two bisexual flowers or a unisexual flower and a different flower with complementary reproductive parts.

74. (B): In standard elementary science contexts, it is typically taught that denser media (especially solids) allow sound to travel faster due to closer particle arrangement, assuming the same general conditions. Since C is denser than A (and A is denser than B), medium C is presented as having the fastest speed of sound among the three.

75. (B): While ice melts at 0°C, the temperature stays constant. The latent heat of fusion absorbed by the ice is used to change its state from solid to liquid, not to raise its temperature. Consequently, the melting ice-water mixture remains at 0°C until the entire solid has melted.

76. (B): This strategy aligns with inquiry-based learning by allowing learners to make predictions, explore objects in water, and observe real outcomes. Such hands-on exploration fosters curiosity and helps students generate questions, collect data, and draw conclusions. It moves beyond passive listening to active discovery, deepening conceptual understanding of buoyancy.

77. (D): Laws are indeed generalized statements describing patterns in nature, and theories offer explanations of these patterns. Laws can also be revised if new evidence emerges, and some theories have existed for many years, so S2 and S3 are not universally valid. Hence, only S1 holds true while S2 and S3 stand incorrect.

78. (B): When light travels from medium A to medium B and slows down, it indicates B has a higher refractive index than A. When it then enters medium C and speeds up again, B must also have a higher refractive index than C. Hence, for both transitions (A to B, and B to C), B is the densest optical medium among the three. Therefore, A < B and C < B in terms of refractive index.

79. (C): Layering involves bending a stem or branch downward into moist soil while it remains attached to the parent plant. After developing roots, this buried section can grow into a new plant when severed. Jasmine is commonly propagated using this method, which ensures high success rates by maintaining a live connection until rooting.

80. (D): Buoyant force always acts opposite to the direction of gravity, pushing upwards on the immersed object. This upward push results from the fluid's pressure, which increases with depth, thereby creating a net upward thrust. It is what makes objects seem lighter or able to float in a liquid.

81. (C): Assertion (A) suggests that gender influences achievement in STEM courses. While there are studies and discussions on gender disparities in STEM, attributing achievement solely to gender is an oversimplification and not universally accurate.

Reason (R) suggests that the problem-solving strategies used by boys and girls are different. While there may be individual differences in problem-solving strategies, generalizing this difference to all boys and girls is not supported by conclusive evidence.

Therefore, both the assertion and the reason can be considered inaccurate or false in this context. The correct answer remains: C. Both (A) and (R) are false.

82. (B): Scientific ideas are shaped by historical, cultural, and social contexts, so they are not entirely isolated from culture. There is also no single rigid "scientific method," since researchers employ diverse procedures, problem-solving tactics, and investigative strategies in advancing science.

83. (A): Whales and dolphins cannot directly use dissolved oxygen; they breathe atmospheric air through nostrils (blowholes), which are relatively large. They regularly surface for fresh air, an adaptation necessary because they lack gills. This combination explains their need to breathe at the water's surface rather than extracting oxygen from the water.

84. (A): Sodium carbonate reacts with dilute hydrochloric acid, releasing carbon dioxide. Passing the carbon dioxide through lime water forms a milky precipitate of calcium carbonate.

These balanced reactions confirm the products formed at each step of the process.

(*a*) $Na_2CO_3 + 2HCl \rightarrow 2NaCl + H_2O + CO_2$

(*b*) $Ca(OH)_2 + CO_2 \rightarrow CaCO_3 + H_2O$.

85. (B): Compounds do not retain the properties of their constituent elements, so (*a*) is not true. They can form from reactions between not only elements but also other compounds, making (*b*) incorrect. Physical and Chemical methods generally cannot separate compounds, so (*d*) is also not true. The composition of a compound is always fixed, which means (*c*) remains valid.

86. (C): When pores in soil are large and loosely packed, water drains quickly, leading to low water retention. The same porous structure allows adequate air circulation, resulting in good aeration. A higher rate of water movement through the soil indicates faster percolation, which is typically linked to lower water holding capacity.

87. (A): 19, 9, 9, 12, 12, 12. This question allows for multiple ideas and perspectives with no single definitive answer. It encourages creative thinking about how daily life, the environment, and physical laws would change. Such open-ended exploration characterizes a divergent question, promoting imaginative and critical thinking rather than a factual response.

88. (A): Atomic number = number of protons = number of electrons for a neutral atom.

For the first row, atomic number 9 gives 9 protons and 9 electrons.

With 10 neutrons, the mass number is 19 (9 + 10). In the second row, having 12 protons and a mass number of 24 implies 12 electrons and 12 neutrons (24 – 12).

89. (B): Convex mirrors are used as rearview mirrors in vehicles because they always form an erect, though diminished, image and also provide a wider field of view. The larger viewing area is the main reason they are preferred over flat or concave mirrors, making (R2) the correct explanation rather than (R1), which incorrectly mentions an enlarged image.

90. (A): Zinc is more reactive than iron but less reactive than aluminum in the typical metal reactivity series. Sodium is not more reactive than potassium, and aluminum does not exceed magnesium in reactivity. Since (a) is the only accurate statement concerning relative metal reactivities, it stands correct on its own.

91. (D): The word "spacious" refers to something that has ample space or feels open. The opposite of spacious is "cramped," which means confined or lacking space. In the context of the passage, the correct antonym is "cramped," as it describes a space that feels restricted and small.

92. (D): The passage states that the right use of colours can create a spacious feeling, supporting (*c*). It also mentions that creatively using colours can enhance a room's look, making (*a*) correct. However, it clearly states that space is limited in modern times, which makes (*b*) incorrect.

93. (A): The passage highlights that modern homeowners long for more space, given the abundance of everything except space. The focus is on how colour schemes can create an illusion of spaciousness in homes with limited physical space.

94. (D): In the sentence, "actually" modifies the verb "helps" and describes the manner in which something occurs, making it an adverb. "Feeling" is used as a noun in this context, referring to an experience or perception.

95. (A): The passage states that a room's colours and design reflect the personality of its occupant. This suggests that the colour scheme of a home is an expression of individuality, making it an important aspect of home décor.

96. (D): The passage suggests that blending light and dark shades can break monotony and create a more dynamic room design. However, painting all four walls in a plain colour does not contribute to this effect, making (B) incorrect.

97. (B): "Ambience" refers to the atmosphere or mood of a place, much like "aura" refers to the distinct character or atmosphere surrounding something. The analogy follows the pattern of a synonym relationship.

98. (C): "Thinking out of the box" means approaching a problem or idea in a novel and unconventional manner. The opposite of this is thinking traditionally, which follows conventional methods rather than exploring new or creative approaches.

99. (A): The passage mentions that some people draw scenery on their walls to create the effect of bringing the outdoors inside. This artistic approach enhances the sense of space and connects the indoor environment with elements of nature.

100. (B): In line 2, "snug as a gun" is a simile because it directly compares the pen to a gun using "as." In line 4, "spade sings" is an example of alliteration, as the repetition of the 's' sound creates a rhythmic effect that enhances the imagery of the digging process.

101. (C): The poet recalls memories of his father's labour in the fields with a sense of nostalgia. He admires the dedication and rhythm of his father's work, recognizing the strength and tradition associated with it. The poem reflects deep respect for the hard work of past generations while the speaker acknowledges his own different path.

102. (C): The word "snug" means fitting closely and securely in a comfortable manner. In the analogy, "coarse" corresponds to "rough," so "snug" logically matches "comfortable" as both describe a sense of physical ease and fit.

103. (B): The phrase "cool hardness in our hands" refers to freshly dug potatoes. The poet describes the sensory experience of handling them, emphasizing their firmness and temperature, which contrasts with the effort involved in digging them from the soil.

104. (A): In the second stanza, the poet observes his father engaged in the act of digging potatoes. He describes the physical effort, posture, and movement of his father as he works, highlighting the routine and rhythm of his labour.

105. (D): The poem focuses on the poet's admiration for his father's work and his recognition of his own different career path. However, it does not explicitly state how the father feels about his son's choice, leaving it open to interpretation.

106. (B): Authentic materials refer to resources created for real-world purposes rather than educational exercises. These materials include newspapers, advertisements, and real-life conversations, helping learners engage with language as it is naturally used.

107. (C): Receptive skills involve understanding and processing information rather than producing it. Listening and reading require learners to receive and interpret meaning from spoken or written language, whereas speaking and writing are productive skills that involve creating language output.

108. (A): In the bottom-up approach, listening comprehension starts with recognizing individual sounds and words, then constructing meaning from them. Aparna's method of listening by processing sounds first and then understanding full sentences aligns with this approach.

109. (A): The National Education Policy (NEP) 2020 does not include foreign languages in the three-language formula. Instead, foreign languages like French and German are recommended as additional subjects at the secondary level, separate from the three-language requirement.

110. (B): Instrumental motivation refers to learning a language for practical purposes, such as employment, travel, or academic requirements.

In this case, Indians who go abroad learn the language to secure jobs and communicate effectively in their workplace, making their motivation instrumental rather than integrative, which is more related to cultural assimilation.

111. (A): The text discusses the principles of equality and democracy as recognized in the Indian Constitution. This type of language and content is commonly found in Social Science discourse, which deals with political, social, and legal concepts. It does not specifically follow the structure of a legal or scientific register, making "Social Science register" the most appropriate choice.

113. (B): Project work integrates multiple language skills, including reading, writing, speaking, and listening. It requires students to research, analyze, collaborate, and present their findings, making it an effective approach for promoting integrated learning. Unlike isolated assignments or role play, project work engages students in a comprehensive learning process.

114. (D): Declarative knowledge refers to knowing facts, rules, and information about a language, such as grammar rules and vocabulary meanings. It contrasts with procedural knowledge, which involves the ability to use language in communication. Knowing about the language's structure and components is part of declarative knowledge.

115. (B): By examining illustrations before reading, learners activate prior knowledge and anticipate what the text may be about. This pre-reading strategy helps students engage with the material, make connections, and develop better comprehension as they read.

116. (C): A classical language is one with a long history of literary tradition and significant ancient texts. Sanskrit, Telugu, and Tamil have been recognized as classical languages in India, while Hindi, despite its wide usage, does not meet the criteria of antiquity and literary depth in the same way, making it not a classical language.

117. (D): A portfolio is a continuous record of a student's learning progress over time. It includes various types of work such as essays, assignments, projects, and reflections, helping both teachers and students assess development in multiple skill areas. Unlike assessments that provide a one-time evaluation, portfolios offer an ongoing record of growth.

118. (C): Consciousness-raising in grammar teaching involves drawing learners' attention to language structures by providing contextual examples, encouraging them to notice patterns, and helping them discover grammatical rules on their own. This strategy enhances language awareness and facilitates deeper understanding rather than simply memorizing rules.

119. (D): Systemic competence in language learning refers to the awareness that language follows a structured system, including grammar, syntax, and phonetics. This competence enables learners to recognize patterns, form coherent expressions, and apply rules appropriately in communication.

120. (C): A good speaking task should provide learners with sufficient input or background knowledge to structure their responses. Simply asking students to talk about a topic without prior input or context may lead to difficulty in generating ideas, making it an ineffective activity for developing speaking skills.

121. (B): 'जनतांत्रिक' शब्द में 'इक' प्रत्यय जुड़ा हुआ है। यह प्रत्यय संज्ञा या विशेषण बनाने में सहायक होता है, जो किसी विशेष विचारधारा या शासन प्रणाली का संकेत देता है। इस शब्द में 'जनतंत्र' से 'इक' प्रत्यय जोड़ने पर 'जनतांत्रिक' बना, जिसका अर्थ है लोकतांत्रिक प्रणाली से संबंधित।

122. (B): गद्यांश के अनुसार विद्यालय का वातावरण ऐसा होना चाहिए जो बच्चों को केवल पढ़ने-लिखने तक सीमित न रखे, बल्कि उन्हें स्व-अधिगम की प्रेरणा दे। जब बच्चे स्वयं सीखने की प्रवृत्ति विकसित करेंगे, तो वे विभिन्न संस्कृतियों की समझ भी विकसित कर सकेंगे।

123. (C): दिए गए विकल्पों में 'संस्कृति', 'समाज' और 'शिक्षा' परस्पर संबंधित शब्द हैं क्योंकि ये सामाजिक और सांस्कृतिक विकास से जुड़े हैं। जबकि 'स्वतंत्र' का अर्थ स्वतंत्रता या मुक्ति से है, जो अन्य शब्दों से अलग संदर्भ को दर्शाता है।

124. (B): गद्यांश के अनुसार शिक्षा का कार्य शिक्षार्थी को भय से मुक्त करना है। शिक्षा केवल जानकारी देने तक सीमित नहीं होती, बल्कि यह व्यक्ति के मानसिक, सामाजिक और सांस्कृतिक विकास में सहायक होती है। विद्यालय का उत्तरदायित्व है कि वह भयमुक्त वातावरण प्रदान कर बच्चों को आत्मनिर्भर और आत्मविश्वासी बनाए।

125. (D): गद्यांश में स्पष्ट रूप से कहा गया है कि जनतांत्रिक समाज के लिए आवश्यक है कि शिक्षा संस्कृति का संवर्द्धन करे। केवल जानकारी देना या वर्ग भेद बढ़ाना शिक्षा का उद्देश्य नहीं होना चाहिए, बल्कि यह समाज में समानता और जागरूकता को बढ़ावा देने वाली होनी चाहिए।

126. (C): गद्यांश के अनुसार शिक्षा केवल लिखना-पढ़ना सिखाने तक सीमित नहीं होनी चाहिए, बल्कि उसमें विभिन्न गतिविधियों का समावेश होना चाहिए। इन गतिविधियों के माध्यम से बच्चों में रचनात्मकता और सांस्कृतिक समझ विकसित की जा सकती है, जिससे शिक्षा संस्कृति को पोषित करने वाली बन सकती है।

127. (D): 'विद्यालय' शब्द का संधि विच्छेद 'विद्या + आलय' होता है। 'विद्या' का अर्थ ज्ञान या शिक्षा से है और 'आलय' का अर्थ स्थान से है। अतः विद्यालय का शाब्दिक अर्थ हुआ–विद्या प्राप्त करने का स्थान।

128. (A): गद्यांश में स्पष्ट किया गया है कि विद्यालय शिक्षा से जुड़ी नीतियों को कार्यान्वित करते हैं, न कि धर्म से जुड़ी नीतियों को। विद्यालय का मुख्य उद्देश्य बच्चों को ज्ञान, आत्मनिर्भरता,

और सांस्कृतिक समझ प्रदान करना होता है, जिससे वे समाज में सकारात्मक भूमिका निभा सकें।

129. (C): संस्मरण का उद्देश्य लेखक के जीवन से जुड़े छोटे-बड़े अनुभवों, घटनाओं और व्यक्तियों का चित्रण करना होता है। इसमें साधारण और विशिष्ट दोनों तरह के पात्र और प्रसंग शामिल किए जाते हैं, जिससे पाठकों को वास्तविक जीवन का अनुभव प्राप्त हो सके।

130. (A): गद्यांश के अनुसार, संस्मरण को 'जनमन की जीवन-यात्रा की अंतरंग छवियाँ' कहा गया है। यह लेखक के जीवन में घटित घटनाओं, अनुभवों और पात्रों का वर्णन करता है, जो पाठकों को लेखक की भावनाओं और विचारों से जोड़ता है।

131. (B): गद्यांश में साहित्य की एक विशेष विधा 'संस्मरण' की चर्चा की गई है। इसमें लेखक अपने व्यक्तिगत अनुभवों, जीवन की घटनाओं और समाज से जुड़े प्रसंगों को अभिव्यक्त करता है, जिससे पाठक वास्तविकता और मानवीय सरोकारों से परिचित होते हैं।

132. (C): 'सुदीर्घ' का अर्थ होता है अत्यधिक लंबा या विस्तृत। गद्यांश में इसे हिन्दी में संस्मरण लिखने की लंबी परंपरा के संदर्भ में प्रयोग किया गया है, जो इस विधा के ऐतिहासिक महत्व को दर्शाता है।

133. (D): दिए गए विकल्पों में 'सुदीर्घ परंपरा', 'अंतरंग छवि' और 'व्यापक यथार्थ' साहित्यिक और वर्णनात्मक शब्द-समूह हैं, जबकि 'जीवन यात्रा' एक भिन्न समूह है, क्योंकि यह व्यक्तिगत जीवन की प्रक्रिया को दर्शाता है, जो एक विशेष दिशा में आगे बढ़ती है।

134. (D): गद्यांश में उल्लेख किया गया है कि कुछ साहित्यकार अपने संस्मरणों के माध्यम से मानवीय सरोकारों को अभिव्यक्त करते हैं। इसका अर्थ यह है कि वे सामाजिक, सांस्कृतिक और मानवीय मूल्यों को अपने लेखन के केंद्र में रखते हैं और उनके माध्यम से समाज को जागरूक करने का कार्य करते हैं।

135. (B): गद्यांश में कहा गया है कि संस्मरण विभिन्न भाषाओं में साहित्य की एक विशिष्ट विधा के रूप में महत्वपूर्ण स्थान रखता है। यह कथन स्पष्ट करता है कि संस्मरण केवल हिंदी साहित्य तक सीमित नहीं है, बल्कि अन्य भाषाओं में भी इसकी समृद्ध परंपरा है।

136. (D): व्यक्ति भाषा (आइडियोलैक्ट) किसी व्यक्ति द्वारा बोली जाने वाली विशिष्ट भाषा शैली को संदर्भित करता है। कृपा और कर्ण एक ही भाषा की विशेष बोली बोलते हैं, फिर भी उनके बोलने के तरीके अलग-अलग हैं। यह अंतर उनकी व्यक्तिगत भाषा शैली को दर्शाता है, जिसे 'आइडियोलैक्ट' कहा जाता है।

137. (B): घोषणात्मक ज्ञान (Declarative Knowledge) में व्यक्ति को किसी विषय या नियमों की जानकारी होती है, लेकिन वह उन्हें संदर्भानुसार सही तरीके से लागू नहीं कर पाता। अदिति को भूतकाल के नियमों की जानकारी है, परंतु वह उनका सही उपयोग नहीं कर पाती, इसलिए उसके पास घोषणात्मक ज्ञान है।

138. (A): सर्वांगी (Systemic) दक्षता का अर्थ भाषा को एक व्यवस्थित संरचना के रूप में समझना और उसका प्रयोग करना है। शिक्षार्थी भाषा की इस संरचनात्मक प्रणाली को समझकर और लागू करके भाषा का सही उपयोग करते हैं, जिससे वे प्रभावी संप्रेषण करने में सक्षम होते हैं।

139. (A): शिक्षिका द्वारा दी गई पठन सामग्री का उद्देश्य यह सुनिश्चित करना है कि शिक्षार्थी समाज में विभिन्न समुदायों और उनकी पहचान के बारे में गहराई से सोच सकें। समालोचनात्मक साक्षरता (Critical Literacy) शिक्षार्थियों को सामाजिक सत्ता, पहचान और असमानताओं को पहचानने और उनका विश्लेषण करने में सक्षम बनाती है।

140. (C): भाषा अर्जन (Language Acquisition) जन्मजात प्रक्रिया होती है, जिसमें बच्चा बिना औपचारिक शिक्षा के भाषा सीखता है। अश्विन जन्म से उड़िया जानता है, इसलिए यह उसका अर्जित ज्ञान है। हिंदी और अंग्रेजी उसने औपचारिक रूप से पढ़ी है, अतः वे अधिगम की श्रेणी में आती हैं। लेकिन दिए गए विकल्पों में 'अंग्रेजी अधिगम भाषा अर्जन है' गलत कथन है, क्योंकि अंग्रेजी उसने पढ़कर सीखी है, न कि स्वाभाविक रूप से अर्जित की है।

141. (D): यांत्रिक (Instrumental) प्रेरणा तब होती है जब कोई व्यक्ति भाषा को किसी विशेष उद्देश्य, जैसे कि रोजगार, यात्रा, या व्यापार के लिए सीखता है। यह भाषा अधिगम की व्यावहारिक प्रेरणा होती है, न कि सामाजिक या सांस्कृतिक जुड़ाव से प्रेरित।

142. (B): गद्यांश में सामाजिक परिवर्तन, क्रांति और सामाजिक सत्ता जैसे विषयों की चर्चा की गई है। यह सामाजिक विज्ञान की भाषा प्रयुक्ति से संबंधित है, क्योंकि इसमें इतिहास, समाजशास्त्र और राजनीतिक सिद्धांतों के संदर्भ दिए गए हैं।

143. (B): ग्राह्यशील (Receptive) कौशल वे होते हैं जिनमें शिक्षार्थी जानकारी प्राप्त करते हैं, जैसे श्रवण (Listening) और पठन (Reading)। इसके विपरीत, बोलना और लेखन उत्पादक (Productive) कौशल माने जाते हैं, क्योंकि इनमें भाषा का सृजन किया जाता है।

144. (B): शीर्ष अधोमुखी (Top-down) श्रवण प्रक्रिया में शिक्षार्थी पहले संपूर्ण संदेश को समझने का प्रयास करते हैं और फिर आवश्यकतानुसार विवरणों पर ध्यान देते हैं। वे पहले वाक्य या प्रसंग की मुख्य अवधारणा को समझते हैं, फिर विशिष्ट विवरणों पर ध्यान केंद्रित करते हैं।

145. (D): राष्ट्रीय शिक्षा नीति 2020 के अनुसार, माध्यमिक स्तर पर शास्त्रीय भाषाओं को एक अतिरिक्त भाषा विकल्प के रूप में पढ़ने की अनुमति दी गई है। यह अनिवार्य नहीं है, लेकिन इच्छुक विद्यार्थी इसे अपनी रुचि के अनुसार चुन सकते हैं।

146. (A): भाषा की कक्षा में परियोजना कार्य की अभिकल्पना और क्रियान्वयन के लिए एक चरणबद्ध प्रक्रिया का पालन किया जाता है। सबसे पहले, शिक्षार्थियों को समूहों में विभाजित किया जाता है, फिर टॉपिक की पहचान की जाती है। इसके बाद योजना बनाई जाती है, आँकड़ों का संग्रह और उनकी व्याख्या की जाती है। अंतिम चरण में प्रारूप लेखन और रिपोर्ट को अंतिम रूप दिया जाता है ताकि परियोजना का निष्कर्ष प्रस्तुत किया जा सके।

147. (C): भाषा का उद्देश्य केवल विज्ञान और अभियांत्रिकी तक सीमित नहीं होता। सभी भाषाएँ मानव ज्ञान, विचारों और संस्कृति को संप्रेषित करने में सक्षम होती हैं। विज्ञान और अभियांत्रिकी जैसे विशिष्ट क्षेत्रों के लिए कुछ भाषाओं में अधिक तकनीकी शब्दावली हो सकती है, लेकिन इसका अर्थ यह नहीं कि अन्य भाषाएँ इन विषयों को व्यक्त नहीं कर सकतीं।

148. (B): निदानात्मक परीक्षण (Diagnostic Test) का उद्देश्य विद्यार्थियों की कमजोरी और ताकत के विशिष्ट क्षेत्रों की पहचान करना होता है। यह परीक्षण यह जानने में मदद करता है कि किसी विद्यार्थी को किन विषयों या अवधारणाओं पर अधिक ध्यान देने की आवश्यकता है, जिससे उनकी सीखने की प्रक्रिया को बेहतर बनाया जा सके।

149. (A): भारत के संविधान में अंग्रेजी को हिंदी के साथ एक सह-राजकीय (संवैधानिक) भाषा के रूप में मान्यता दी गई है। संविधान के अनुच्छेद 343 के अनुसार, हिंदी भारत की आधिकारिक भाषा है, लेकिन प्रशासनिक कार्यों और विधायी उद्देश्यों के लिए अंग्रेजी का उपयोग भी किया जाता है।

150. (C): फेरी वाला इस गतिविधि में शिक्षण सामग्री के रूप में कार्य कर रहा है, क्योंकि उसका उपयोग विद्यार्थियों के लिए वर्णनात्मक लेखन गतिविधि को अधिक प्रभावी बनाने के लिए किया गया है। वह स्वयं शिक्षण प्रक्रिया में सक्रिय भूमिका नहीं निभा रहा, बल्कि एक दृश्य सामग्री के रूप में प्रस्तुत किया गया है, जिससे विद्यार्थी उसका अवलोकन कर सकें और उसका वर्णन लिखने का अभ्यास कर सकें।

Previous Years' Paper

CTET—Paper-II, July-2024

For Mathematics and Science Teachers

(Exam held on 07-07-2024)

CHILD DEVELOPMENT AND PEDAGOGY

1. In progressive education children are perceived as:

A. Innocent and dependent

B. Compliant and capable of only consuming knowledge

C. Knowledgeable and meaning-makers

D. Vulnerable and in need of protection

2. Feedback to the students in a classroom is most effective when:

A. It assigns comparative ranks to the students.

B. It occurs during as well as after the learning activity.

C. It focuses on what the child cannot do rather than what they can do.

D. It centres around tests and exams at the end of the year.

3. **Assertion (A):** During adolescence the pressures to conform to gender expectations and follow conventions of feminity or masculinity increases.

Reason (R): Gender and gender roles are determined biologically.

Choose the **correct** option.

A. Both (A) and (R) are true and (R) is the correct explanation of (A).

B. Both (A) and (R) are true but (R) is not the correct explanation of (A).

C. (A) is true but (R) is false.

D. Both (A) and (R) are false.

4. Sunita, a 12 year old girl, shows exceptional musical ability. Both her parents are accomplished singers, and they send her for classes for voice training after school. Her capabilities are most likely to be the result of an interaction between:

A. growth and maturation

B. nutrition and discipline

C. heredity and environment

D. gender identity and genetic make-up

5. Sensitive periods are those time periods during which certain __________ are especially important for course of 'normal' development.

A. genetic predispositions

B. ethnic factors

C. environmental factors

D. hereditary factors

6. In order to develop critical thinking among students a teacher should:

A. ask only those questions which carry single answers.

B. discourage the students from asking doubts and questions.

C. give questions that involve inferences and explanations.

D. avoid questions which need inference and analysis.

7. A teacher asks herself—"How can I provide experiences that require students to classify different types of objects in the environment and analyse their classification schemes?" Which intelligence is she trying to promote in students?

A. Linguistic Intelligence

B. Inter-personal Intelligence

C. Naturalistic Intelligence

D. Bodily-Kinesthetics Intelligence

8. How does setting mastery goals impact a student's motivation and views of ability?

A. It often implies enhanced intrinsic motivation and belief in the entity view of ability.

B. It often implies enhanced intrinsic motivation and belief in the incremental view of ability.

C. It often implies enhanced extrinsic motivation and belief in the entity view of ability.

D. It often implies enhanced extrinsic motivation and belief in the incremental view of ability.

1. C	2. B	3. C	4. C	5. C	6. C	7. C	8. B

9. Rama is a teacher who is implementing Vygotsky's theory in her classroom and she assigns her students to work in groups to complete a challenging task. During the task, one student struggles to understand a key concept. What would be the most effective way for Rama to help this student?

A. Provide the student with the answer to the problem so the group can move on.
B. Encourage the student to try to solve the problem on her own.
C. Assign a different task to the student that is better suited to her abilities.
D. Work through the problem with the student and providing guidance and feedback as needed while involving other group members.

10. **Assertion (A):** Teachers should encourage debates, discussions and collaborations among students.

Reason (R): Knowledge production is an inactive process and engagement in group activities hinders meaningful learning.

Choose the **correct** option.

A. Both (A) and (R) are true and (R) is the correct explanation of (A).
B. Both (A) and (R) are true but (R) is not the correct explanation of (A).
C. (A) is true but (R) is false.
D. Both (A) and (R) are false.

11. Change and stability in emotions, personality and social relationships together constitute:

A. Personality development
B. Emotional development
C. Psychosocial development
D. Cognitive development

12. Which of the following correctly describes 'culturally responsive teaching' to cater to diverse groups of students?

(*i*) Intentional (*ii*) Adaptive
(*iii*) Differentiated (*iv*) Standardized

A. (*i*), (*iv*) B. (*ii*), (*iii*)
C. (*i*), (*ii*), (*iii*) D. (*i*), (*ii*), (*iii*), (*iv*)

13. **Assertion (A):** Schools should function within frameworks which assess the finished product and learning outcomes.

Reason (R): Learning is tightly sequential and hierarchical.

Choose the **correct** option.

A. Both (A) and (R) are true and (R) is the correct explanation of (A).
B. Both (A) and (R) are true but (R) is not the correct explanation of (A).
C. (A) is true but (R) is false.
D. Both (A) and (R) are false.

14. According to Lev Vygotsky what is the relationship between language and thought?

A. Language does not shape thought
B. Thought shapes language
C. Language and thought are independent of each other
D. Language and thought are complex interrelated processes of development

15. Which of the following is a correctly matched pair?

A. Criterion - referenced assessment: includes mastery of specific topics
B. Norm - references assessment: compares performance to that of peers
C. Formative assessment: determining what the students can do before and after the class
D. Summative assessment: involves paper - pencil tests as well as detailed accounts of non-written behaviours

16. Which of the following hinders the participation of students with visual impairment in classroom?

A. electronically formatted lecture transcriptions
B. printed textbooks and notes
C. raised-line drawings and maps
D. tactile models of graphic materials

17. Which method did Lawrence Kohlberg used to study moral development of children?

A. Quantitative research approach
B. Posing moral dilemmas to children and analyzing responses
C. Conducting observations of children during play
D. Experimental method

18. Constructivist teaching leads to __________ learning by students.

A. discovery B. meaningless
C. rote D. receptive

19. Students struggling with dyslexia can be taught to read:

A. Through systematic phonological training.
B. By providing higher grade level reading texts.
C. By giving long and complex passages.
D. Through association method of conditioning.

20. Jean Piaget's theory of cognitive development implicates that:

A. Behaviour should be conditioned using rewards and punishments.
B. Concepts should be taught in a sequence of complex to simple.
C. Curriculum should be designed keeping children's age-group and stage in mind.
D. Focus of teaching should be the outcome of the activity instead of the process of thinking.

9. D **10.** C **11.** C **12.** C **13.** D **14.** D **15.** B **16.** B **17.** B **18.** A **19.** A **20.** C

21. You are a teacher who wants to help your students develop metacognitive skills. Which of the following strategies is most likely to foster this type of thinking?

A. Giving students marks instead of qualitative feedback on their performance.
B. Encouraging students to reflect on their own learning and thinking processes.
C. Providing students with summarised notes for assignments.
D. Assigning homework that requires memorization and recall.

22. Which of the following statement is correct about 'Autism'?

A. All autistic people have at least one exceptional skill.
B. Autism is a neuro-developmental disorder.
C. Autism is caused solely by environmental factors.
D. Autism can be cured and improves with age.

23. A key commonality in Piaget and Vygotsky's theories is:

A. Their views of relationship between language and thought.
B. Focus on stage-like progression in children's development.
C. Involvement and engagement of children in their own learning.
D. The role of culture in the cognitive processes.

24. Assertion (A): Teachers should respect the individual differences among learners and adapt their teaching to cater to needs of all students.

Reason (R): Collaborations, group works and interactions among students should be avoided while teaching a class of diverse learners.

Choose the **correct** option.

A. Both (A) and (R) are true and (R) is the correct explanation of (A).
B. Both (A) and (R) are true but (R) is not the correct explanation of (A).
C. (A) is true but (R) is false.
D. Both (A) and (R) are false.

25. Which learning strategy involves children teaching others what they have learned?

A. Conditioned learning
B. Rote learning
C. Expository teaching
D. Reciprocal teaching

26. Assertion (A): In Asian cultures which stress social harmony, expressions of 'anger' are 'discouraged' and 'shame' is encouraged.

Reason (R): Emotions are subjective and do not play any role in learning.

Choose the **correct** option.

A. Both (A) and (R) are true and (R) is the correct explanation of (A).
B. Both (A) and (R) are true but (R) is not the correct explanation of (A).
C. (A) is true but (R) is false.
D. Both (A) and (R) are false.

27. According to Jean Piaget how are children different from adults?

A. Children are dependent on adults while adults are independent.
B. Adults are much more knowledgeable than children.
C. Children's thinking is qualitatively different from that of adults.
D. Children's thinking is quantitatively different from that of adults.

28. Which of the following question promotes analytical thinking?

A. The capital city of India is __________.
B. How many States are there in India?
C. What is the total population of India?
D. What are the various causes of increase of population in India?

29. Inclusive classrooms:

A. Recognize that every child will learn at the same rate and at the same time.
B. Is an educational program offered to cater to the needs of 'special children'.
C. Are meant to offer differentiated instructions as per individual differences.
D. Aim to remove all kinds of differences among the children.

30. Assertion (A): Teachers should give lot of opportunities to children for experimentation and discuss examples and non-examples.

Reason (R): A constructive way of dealing with misconceptions in children is to provide counter examples.

Choose the **correct** option.

A. Both (A) and (R) are true and (R) is the correct explanation of (A).
B. Both (A) and (R) are true but (R) is not the correct explanation of (A).
C. (A) is true but (R) is false.
D. Both (A) and (R) are false.

21. B	22. B	23. C	24. C	25. D	26. C	27. C	28. D	29. C	30. A

MATHEMATICS AND SCIENCE

31. Perimeter of a quadrilateral ABCD is 120 cm. If BC = 48 cm, CD = 17 cm, AD = 40 cm and $\angle A = \angle B = 90°$, then area of quadrilateral ABCD (in cm^2) is:

A. 660 B. 690
C. 720 D. 750

32. Which of the following statement is least appropriate regarding the proofs in mathematics?

A. It explains why a particular mathematical result must be true.
B. It helps to reveal the connections and provide insights into the underlying structure of mathematics.
C. It can help the students to validate their own reasoning.
D. Proofs are built on intuitive knowledge and not reasoning.

33. PQRS is a parallelogram whose diagonals PR and QS intersect at a point O such that OP = $(x + 7)$ cm, OQ = $(x + y)$ cm, OR = 20 cm and OS = 16 cm. Then, value of $(7y + 5)$ (in cm) is:

A. 21 B. 23
C. 26 D. 28

34. The value of $52 \times 3 \div 4 + \sqrt{441} \div 7 \times 3 + 5 - 32 \div 8 \times 12$ is:

A. 0 B. 5
C. 15 D. 21

35. Arun is three years older than Varun. Eight years ago, $\frac{5}{6}$th of Arun's age exceeded $\frac{3}{5}$th of Varun's age by 6 years. If the present age of Varun is x years, then the value of x can be determined by solving the equation:

A. $\frac{5}{6}(x-5) - \frac{3}{5}(x-8) = 6$

B. $\frac{5}{6}(x-8) - \frac{3}{5}(x-5) = 6$

C. $\frac{3}{5}(x+5) - \frac{5}{6}(x-6) = 6$

D. $\frac{3}{5}(x+3) - \frac{5}{6}(x-8) = 6$

36. The domain of learning that deals with attitudes and values is known as:

A. Knowledge domain B. Cognitive domain
C. Affective domain D. Psychomotor domain

37. The height and base radius of a right circular cylinder are 9 cm and 6 cm respectively. If the base radius becomes half and height increases by 3 cm, then which of the following describes the new volume of the cylinder?

A. The new volume will be twice the original volume.
B. The new volume will be half the original volume.
C. The new volume will be thrice the original volume.
D. The new volume will be one-third the original volume.

38. Arrange the following statements according to ascending levels of geometrical thinking as per Van-Hiele's theory of geometrical learning.

(*a*) Identification of properties of geometrical shapes
(*b*) Classification of different shapes
(*c*) Finding relationship between the properties of geometrical shapes
(*d*) Identification of geometrical shapes as they are

Choose the **correct** option:

A. (*a*), (*b*), (*c*), (*d*) B. (*d*), (*b*), (*a*), (*c*)
C. (*d*), (*c*), (*b*), (*a*) D. (*a*), (*c*), (*b*), (*d*)

39. In a pie chart, the marks obtained by a student in Mathematics, Science, Social Science, Hindi and English are respectively represented by sectors of central angles 90°, 80°, 65°, 75° and 50°. If the total marks obtained by the students were 540, then what is the difference of the marks obtained by him/her in Mathematics and English?

A. 60 B. 50
C. 40 D. 30

40. At upper primary stage, as per NCERT, which of the following topics have NOT been included under number system?

A. Complex Numbers
B. Fractions
C. Exponents and Powers
D. Square roots and cube roots

31. A **32.** D **33.** C **34.** B **35.** A **36.** C **37.** D **38.** B **39.** A **40.** A

41. Which of the following statement is NOT correct with respect to Rubrics as a tool of assessment?

A. Rubrics has a fixed scale.
B. Rubrics has a list of characteristics describing performance for each point on the scale.
C. Rubrics consist of a clear performance target for students.
D. Rubrics make evaluation more subjective.

42. The number of faces (F), edges (E) and vertices (V) of a polyhedron are 7, 15 and x, respectively. Then, the value of $(2F + 3E - 4x)$ is:

A. 20 B. 19
C. 18 D. 17

43. If $(2x + 5y)^2 - 5(2x + 5y) - 14 = (2x + 5y + p)(2x + 5y + q)$, then the value of $(p + q)$ is:

A. 7 B. −14
C. 9 D. −5

44. Two parallel lines are intersected by a transversal and the two interior angles so formed on the same side of the transversal are $(2x + 15°)$ and $(3x - 20°)$. Then, the value of $(4x + 6°)$ is:

A. 154° B. 150°
C. 148° D. 146°

45. The sum of the largest and smallest fractions among $\frac{6}{7}$, $2\frac{3}{5}$, $\frac{3}{8}$ and $2\frac{8}{15}$ is:

A. $2\frac{9}{35}$ B. $2\frac{37}{40}$
C. $2\frac{7}{35}$ D. $2\frac{39}{40}$

46. Which of the following does **not** imply the meaning of assessment?

A. It is evaluation.
B. It helps to label the students.
C. It helps to diagnose individual differences.
D. It is a procedure to gather information of student's performance.

47. Which of the following is NOT an indicator of creativity in Mathematics?

A. Students use convergent thinking in different contexts.
B. Students are able to think flexibly.
C. Students use multiple and alternate problem solving strategies.
D. Students can pose questions.

48. If x is the least number which must be added to 955 to make it a perfect square, then value of $3x + 2$ is equal to:

A. 20 B. 14
C. 11 D. 5

49. How many natural numbers between 1 and 500 are divisible by each of the numbers 3, 5 and 7?

A. 3 B. 4
C. 5 D. 6

50. According to National Curriculum Framework 2005 which of the following process is least important in mathematics?

A. Solving day to day problems.
B. Understanding when and how a mathematical technique is to be used.
C. Finding short-cuts in mathematics.
D. Generalizing a mathematical formula.

51. M is a point on side AB of a triangle ABC such that AM = BM = CM. If angles A and B are respectively x and 70°, then the value of $(3x + 25°)$ is equal to:

A. 70° B. 85°
C. 100° D. 115°

52. A sum invested at 10% p.a. for 2 years becomes ₹ 3,267, when the interest is compounded annually. What will be the simple interest on the same sum at the same rate in $2\frac{1}{2}$ years?

A. ₹ 625 B. ₹ 650
C. ₹ 675 D. ₹ 700

53. D is a point on side AB of a ΔABC such that CD is the bisector of $\angle ACB$. If $\angle A = 50°$ and $\angle B = 70°$, then $\angle ADC$ is equal to:

A. 30° B. 50°
C. 70° D. 100°

54. Marks obtained by some students of a class are 36, 37, 31, 42, 23, 38, 17, 18, 35, 25, 29 and 35. The difference of the mean and the range of the data is:

A. 4.5 B. 5.0
C. 5.5 D. 6.0

55. A trader buys 12 fans for ₹ 24,000. He marks each fan at 25% above the cost price. If he sells all fans by giving 10% discount on the marked price, then his overall profit (in ₹) is:

A. 2700 B. 3000
C. 3200 D. 3500

41. D	**42.** B	**43.** D	**44.** A	**45.** D	**46.** B	**47.** A	**48.** A	**49.** B	**50.** C
51. B	**52.** C	**53.** D	**54.** C	**55.** B					

56. $\dfrac{(a-b+c)^2-(a-b-c)^2}{b-a}$ is equal to:

A. $b - c$ B. $c - a$
C. $-4c$ D. $2c$

57. Area of a right triangle is 240 cm^2. If its one side other than the hypotenuse is 30 cm, then perimeter (in cm) of the triangle is:

A. 80 B. 84
C. 92 D. 100

58. A teacher distributes different types of triangle shaped paper cuttings to the learners and tells them to measure and tabulate the angles in order to find the sum of angles. He tells them to note the result in each case.

This method of teaching is an example of:

A. Discovery method
B. Teacher centered approach
C. Deductive method
D. Analytical approach

59. Which of the following is NOT true?

A. 3 + 4 × 5 is not a mathematical expression.
B. Operations of multiplication can be done on mathematical expressions.
C. The expression (x^2 + 10x + 25) cannot be simplified further.
D. The value of the variable in an equation which satisfy the equation is called a solution of the equation.

60. The ratio of two numbers is 3 : 7 and their LCM is 630. Then, sum of the LCM and HCF of these numbers is:

A. 30 B. 300
C. 600 D. 660

61. (A) Metal oxides are basic in nature.
(B) Air expands on heating.
(C) Lime water turns milky on passing carbon dioxide.
(D) Sodium hydroxide and hydrochloric acid neutralize each other.

If observation is represented by O and inference by I, which of the following statements is correct?

A. O - C, D; I - A, B
B. O - B, C; I - A, D
C. O - C; I - A, B, D
D. O - A, B; I - B, C

62. Which of the following is not a feature of alternate conceptions in science?

A. Ideas are stable.
B. Ideas are resistant to change.
C. Ideas are developed from observable features.
D. Ideas do not demonstrate cause and effect reasoning.

63. Read the statements given below and choose the **correct** option:

Assertion (A): It is recommended that acid should be added to water for diluting the acid and not vice-versa.

Reason (R): Dilution of acid is a highly exothermic reaction.

A. Both (A) and (R) are true and (R) is correct explanation of (A).
B. Both (A) and (R) are true but (R) is not correct explanation of (A).
C. (A) is true but (R) is false.
D. Both (A) and (R) are false.

64. Read the statements given below and choose the **correct** option:

Assertion (A): The rate of breathing in aquatic animals is slower than land animals.

Reason (R): Presence of large amounts of dissolved oxygen affects rate of breathing of aquatic animals.

A. Both (A) and (R) are true and (R) is correct explanation of (A).
B. Both (A) and (R) are true but (R) is not correct explanation of (A).
C. (A) is true but (R) is false.
D. Both (A) and (R) are false.

65. **Assertion (A):** The ceilings of cinema halls and concert halls are generally curved.

Reason (R): Sound waves after striking a curved surface get reflected in all directions.

A. Both (A) and (R) are true and (R) is correct explanation for (A).
B. Both (A) and (R) are true but (R) is not correct explanation for (A).
C. (A) is true but (R) is false.
D. Both (A) and (R) are false.

66. Which of the following is/are **true** regarding scientific investigations?

(*a*) Results are not influenced by procedure.
(*b*) Social context may influence conclusions in any investigation.
(*c*) Data and evidence are same.
(*d*) There is no universal scientific method.

A. (*a*) and (*b*) B. (*b*) and (*d*)
C. (*a*) and (*c*) D. (*c*) and (*d*)

56. C	57. A	58. A	59. C	60. D	61. C	62. D	63. A	64. D	65. A	66. B

67. Read the statements given below and choose the **correct** options:

Assertion (A): The filament of an incandescent bulb is made up of tungsten.

Reason (R): Tungsten has low resistance and high melting point.

A. Both (A) and (R) are true and (R) is correct explanation of (A).
B. Both (A) and (R) are true but (R) is not correct explanation of (A).
C. (A) is true and (R) is false.
D. Both (A) and (R) are false.

68. Three identical holes are punched at different levels (heights) in a plastic bottle. The bottle is filled with water. Which of the following statements is true regarding the flow of water from the holes?

(*a*) Water from lowest hole comes out with greatest force
(*b*) Water from highest hole comes out with greatest force
(*c*) Water from all holes comes out with equal force
(*d*) Water from lowest hole falls at maximum distance
(*e*) Water from highest hole falls at maximum distance
(*f*) Water from all holes falls at same distance

A. (*c*) and (*f*) B. (*a*) and (*e*)
C. (*b*) and (*e*) D. (*a*) and (*d*)

69. Which of the following characterizes human circulatory system?

A. open, single circulation
B. open, double circulation
C. closed, single circulation
D. closed, double circulation

70. A class VII teacher plans to identify alternate conceptions of students in the topic 'Adaptations in plants and animals'. Which of the following sets of strategies is best suited for this purpose?

A. Drawings, checklist, interview
B. Portfolio, group discussion, diagnostic questionnaire
C. Diagnostic questionnaire, interview, drawings
D. Project, checklist, drawings

71. Which of the following is **not** caused due to excessive use of fertilizer and pesticides?

A. Soil erosion
B. Nitrification
C. Eutrophication
D. Bio-magnification

72. An odometer in a car measures:

A. distance travelled by the car
B. instantaneous speed of the car
C. average speed of the car
D. acceleration of the car

73. Which of the following is **true** regarding scientific laws?

A. They describe relationships between observable phenomena.
B. They are formed from scientific theories.
C. They can't be challenged.
D. They provide reasoning for physical phenomena.

74. Which of the following statements is/are **true**?

(*a*) Self pollination takes place only in bisexual flowers.
(*b*) Bisexual flowers can pollinate both by self and cross pollination.

A. (*a*) is true and (*b*) is false.
B. (*a*) is false and (*b*) is true.
C. Both (*a*) and (*b*) are false.
D. Both (*a*) and (*b*) are true.

75. Which of the following activities is best suited to develop inductive reasoning?

A. asking students to state laws of reflection
B. asking students to measure angle of reflection for various cases of angle of incidence in a plane mirror
C. verify laws of reflection experimentally
D. solve numerical problems based on law of reflection

76. Two sperms of a man fuse with two eggs of a woman. The twins formed are:

A. identical
B. fraternal
C. may be identical or fraternal
D. always conjoint

77. Which of the following statements is/are **true** regarding Rainwater harvesting?

(*a*) It conserves ground water.
(*b*) It reduces local flooding.
(*c*) It creates drainage problems.
(*d*) It can be used for irrigation of crops.

A. (*a*), (*b*), (*c*) B. (*a*), (*c*), (*d*)
C. (*a*), (*b*), (*d*) D. (*b*), (*c*), (*d*)

67. C **68.** D **69.** D **70.** B, C **71.** A **72.** A **73.** A **74.** B **75.** B **76.** B **77.** C

78. Discussion on socio-scientific issues in class helps in:

(*a*) developing argumentative skills in learners
(*b*) developing multiple perspectives on an issue
(*c*) encouraging citizen science activities
(*d*) appreciating the role of society in development of science

A. (*b*) and (*c*) B. (*a*), (*b*) and (*c*)
C. (*c*) and (*d*) D. (*b*), (*c*) and (*d*)

79. Which of the following illustrates 'science as inquiry'?

A. Classify the given plants into herbs, shrubs and trees
B. Explore factors which affect the rate of germination in gram seeds
C. List five uses of coconut tree
D. Observe the types of venation in various leaves

80. A gender responsive pedagogy in science entails.

(*a*) Use of gender sensitive language
(*b*) Engaging students in examining stereotypes
(*c*) Making gender based groups
(*d*) Using differentiated instruction and assessment

A. (*a*), (*b*) and (*c*)
B. (*a*), (*c*) and (*d*)
C. (*a*) and (*b*)
D. (*c*) and (*d*)

81. Read the following statements and choose the **correct** option:

S1 - Photosynthesis is endothermic reaction.
S2 - Respiration is exothermic reaction.

A. Both S1 and S2 are true.
B. Both S1 and S2 are false.
C. S1 is true and S2 is false.
D. S1 is false and S2 is true.

82. Following table depicts colour changes in acids and bases when various indicators are added:

Indicator	Colour change in acids	Colour change in bases
Turmeric	No change	A
China rose	Dark Pink	B
Phenolphthalein	C	Pink
Methyl orange	D	Pink

A, B, C, D respectively are:

A. reddish brown, green, colourless, orange
B. yellow, green, orange, colourless
C. reddish brown, pink, orange, colourless
D. yellow, orange, pink, colourless

83. The colour of flame depends on:

(*a*) Nature of combustible substance
(*b*) Oxygen supply
(*c*) Temperature of the surroundings

A. (*a*) only B. (*b*) only
C. (*a*) and (*b*) D. (*a*) and (*c*)

84. Which of the following factors are responsible for generation and flow of winds on the earth?

(*a*) Uneven heating of the earth
(*b*) Uneven heating of the oceans
(*c*) Distance between earth and sun
(*d*) Gravitational force on the earth

A. only (*a*) B. (*a*) and (*c*)
C. (*a*) and (*b*) D. (*a*) and (*d*)

85. The atomic number of A is 13 and the atomic number of B is 17. The chemical formula of the compound formed from A and B could be:

A. A_3B B. AB_3
C. AB_2 D. AB

86. Which of the following statement is **not** true regarding conduction of heat?

A. Conduction is faster in solids than liquids.
B. Two objects should be in contact with each other for heat flow.
C. Conduction does not take place in gases.
D. All materials do not allow heat to flow through them in same way.

87. An object floats with $\frac{1}{4}$ th part of its volume outside the liquid when put in liquid A and $\frac{3}{4}$ th part of its volume outside the liquid when put in liquid B. Which of the following statements is **true**?

A. Density of liquid A is greater than density of liquid B.
B. Both liquids have same density.
C. Density of liquid B is greater than density of liquid A.
D. The densities of liquid cannot be compared on the basis of above information.

88. Sunita drops a piece of potassium metal in a beaker of cold water and notes down the observations. Which of the following observation is **not** correct?

A. Potassium reacts violently with water.
B. It is endothermic reaction.
C. Hydrogen gas is evolved.
D. Pop sound is heard.

78. B **79.** B **80.** C **81.** A **82.** A **83.** C **84.** C **85.** B **86.** C **87.** C **88.** B

89. The purpose of divergent questions in science classroom can be:

(*a*) to promote critical thinking

(*b*) to discern between students

(*c*) to develop communication

(*d*) to identify gifted students

(*e*) to identify alternate conceptions

(*f*) to appreciate subjectivity in science

A. (*a*), (*b*), (*d*) and (*e*)
B. (*a*), (*b*), (*c*) and (*f*)
C. (*a*), (*c*), (*e*) and (*f*)
D. (*b*), (*d*), (*e*) and (*f*)

90. Identify the mirrors on the basis of information given in the following table:

Mirror	Nature of image	Size of image
A	virtual and erect	same as object
B	real and inverted	same as object
C	real and inverted	enlarged
D	virtual and erect	diminished

A. A - Plane, B - Convex, C - Concave, D - Convex
B. A - Convex, B - Concave, C - Convex, D - Concave
C. A - Plane mirror, B - Concave, C - Concave, D - Convex
D. A - Concave, B - Plane, C - Convex, D - Concave

LANGUAGE-I—ENGLISH

Directions (Qs.No. 91-99): *Read the passage given below and answer the questions that follow:*

1. On 15 January 2009, several interesting things happened. A plane crash landed into the Hudson River, right in the middle of New York City. The pilot, crew and 155 passengers escaped safely. But then, something else happened... Jim was nearby and watched the event happen. He immediately tweeted that he had just seen a plane crash in the Hudson. From there the news spread quickly. People contacted him immediately and asked him what was happening, and other people on the street took photos and videos with their phones and posted them online. Ordinary people suddenly became journalists. It was 15 minutes before the news broke on official news channels.

2. Photos, videos and tweets from ordinary people at the scene of dramatic events now provide the words and images that describe events in the news. When a meteor exploded over a Russian city in 2013, millions of people around the world watched videos and photos of the event on Facebook and YouTube. Social media can also save lives. In January 2010, an earthquake hit the Caribbean island of Haiti. The government said that there had been an earthquake, but they didn't give many details at first. Meanwhile, people living in the disaster area were posting photos and eye witness accounts on Twitter and Facebook and telling the world that it was an emergency and houses were collapsing. A local radio presenter used this information to help people find family members, and people even phoned his program to ask if their relatives were safe.

3. News travels fast on social media, but false stories spread just as quickly as the truth. Some of these "facts" are erroneous, others are deliberate hoaxes. Hoaxes remind us that not everything people post and publish is reliable. But social media can change our lives for the better.

91. The meteor explosion in 2013 in Russia was watched by people on:

A. Twitter
B. YouTube
C. All social media handles
D. Facebook and YouTube

92. 'Some of these facts are erroneous'. The antonym for the underlined word in the given sentence is:

A. faultless
B. inaccurate
C. invalid
D. surprising

93. Why should we not take news on social media lightly?

A. The facts are erroneous.
B. Strangers can call you to seek information.
C. They can change our lives for the better.
D. News posted are hoax and confusing.

94. Arrange the following events as mentioned in para 1 in the correct sequential order.

(*a*) Jim watched the crash and tweeted.

(*b*) People started contacting Jim for updated news.

(*c*) A plane crashed into the Hudson River.

(*d*) The news of the crash was broadcast 15 minutes later.

A. (*c*) → (*b*) → (*d*) → (*a*)
B. (*b*) → (*c*) → (*a*) → (*d*)
C. (*d*) → (*c*) → (*a*) → (*b*)
D. (*c*) → (*a*) → (*b*) → (*d*)

89. A **90.** C **91.** D **92.** A **93.** C **94.** D

95. Read the following statements:

(*a*) A plane crashed on 15 January, 2009

(*b*) 155 passengers escaped, but the pilot lost his life.

(*c*) Jim, an onlooker, posted pictures on Facebook

A. (*a*) and (*b*) are correct, but (*c*) is incorrect
B. (*c*) is correct, but (*a*) and (*b*) are incorrect
C. (*a*) is correct, but (*b*) and (*c*) are incorrect
D. (*a*), (*b*) and (*c*) are all incorrect

96. Complete the given word analogy:

dramatic : exciting :: hoax : ___?___ .

A. media posts B. deception
C. example D. excuse

97. News on social media:

A. are reliable B. travel fast
C. are deliberate hoaxes D. are insignificant

98. Identify Parts of Speech of the underlined words in the sentence given below:

'But social media can change our lives for the better.'

A. noun, adverb B. verb, adjective
C. verb, adverb D. noun, adjective

99. Ordinary people suddenly became journalists means:

A. they started posting news-bits pictures and videos on social media
B. they headed towards media houses to seek employment
C. they started contacting Jim to know the details
D. they left the jobs where they were employed

Directions (Qs. No. 100-105): *Read the poem given below and answer the questions that follow:*

Great, wide, beautiful, wonderful world,
With the wonderful water round you curled.
And the wonderful grass upon your breast
World, you are beautifully drest.
The wonderful air is over me,
And the wonderful wind is shaking the tree,
It walks on the water, and whirls the mills,
And talks to itself on the tops of the hills.
You friendly Earth! How far do you go,
With the wheat-fields that nod and the rivers that flow.
With cities and gardens, and cliffs, and isles,
And people upon you for thousands of miles?
Ah, you are so great, and I am so small,
I tremble to think of you, World, at all;
And yet, when I said my prayers today,
A whisper inside me seemed to say,
'You are more than the Earth, though you are such a dot,
You can love and think, and the Earth cannot!'

100. What does the underlined word refer to?

'It walks on the water, ...'

A. river B. grass
C. wind D. Earth

101. In the line, 'with the wonderful water round you curled', the word 'curled' means:

A. arched B. surrounded
C. mounted D. turbulent

102. In this poem, the poet describes the:

A. the Earth, its present and past
B. the plants that grow on the Earth
C. beauty and vastness of Earth
D. life in the cities

103. The wind in the poem talks to:

A. itself B. trees
C. clouds D. hills

104. Identify the figures of speech in line 1 and line 4.

A. anaphora, personification
B. alliteration, metaphor
C. alliteration, personification
D. simile, alliteration

105. List the 3 different things (in stanza 3) found on Earth that make it great.

A. rivers, gardens, cliffs
B. isles, oceans, people
C. wheatfields, trees, whisper
D. cities, grass, mills

106. The impact of tests and assessments on teachers, learners, and materials is called ________.

A. Corpus effect B. Washback effect
C. Classroom effect D. Reinforcement

107. Schools should follow additive bilingualism because it:

A. values the culture and language of the child
B. gives importance to teaching English as a second language
C. promotes the child's language but not the culture
D. hinders the development of the first language

95. C **96.** B **97.** B **98.** D **99.** A **100.** C **101.** B **102.** C **103.** A **104.** C
105. A **106.** B **107.** A

108. Linguistic function such as intonation, tone, stress, and rhythm are known as:

A. Poetry B. Prosody
C. Phonetics D. Pragmatics

109. Which of the following statements is NOT true about languages in India?

A. According to the Indian Constitution, English is an Associate Official Language.
B. According to the list of Eighth schedule of the Constitution of India, there are 22 languages.
C. Sanskrit is a Modern Indian Language.
D. Hindi is the lingua franca of the Indian sub-continent.

110. In a language class, students form groups under the guidance of a teacher and present an advertisement on a given topic. Learning a language in this way is called ________.

A. Collaborative learning
B. Competition and rivalry
C. Language games
D. Guidance and counseling

111. A teacher gives a task to familiarise the learners with the vocabulary used in restaurants. What among the following should be objective of the lesson?

A. To acquaint the learner with the lexical items
B. To familiarise with the grammatical items
C. To introduce the text about a holiday destination
D. To develop critical thinking

112. Which school of learning believed that language, whether verbal or non-verbal, takes place through the process of habit formation?

A. Functionalist B. Behaviourist
C. Cognitivist D. Interactionalist

113. The time and place of the story are called the ____.

A. Theme B. Setting
C. Plot D. Climax

114. In a language class, a teacher asks a group of students to act as purchasers, property sellers, landlords and tenants while other students are asked to watch them and enjoy their conversation. This activity is called ________.

A. Roleplay B. Drama
C. Acting class D. Guidance

115. A language teacher brings everyday objects such as newspapers, menu cards and train tickets to teach the students of class V. What is she doing to make learning happen?

A. She is using authentic materials to make her teaching more realistic and useful.
B. She is trying to help her students to learn multiple languages.
C. She wants her students to learn English through real life like situations.
D. She is creating awareness in the students.

116. Which of the following is NOT an important factor in planning a listening lesson?

A. Pausing the recording B. Speed of delivery
C. Gender of speakers D. Number of speakers

117. Multilingualism in India intends teachers to understand:

A. communication happens, and social cohesion is maintained
B. minority languages should be clubbed with dominant languages
C. 'a language' policy should be framed in a diverse society
D. language, identity and culture are separate entities

118. Which skill of language is known as receptive skills?

A. Listening and Speaking
B. Speaking and Writing
C. Reading and Writing
D. Listening and Reading

119. Listening involves:

A. hearing the sound, decoding the sounds as they are
B. guessing the content
C. using prior knowledge of the subject
D. recognising sounds and deducing the meaning from it

120. Match the language teaching methods in Column-A with their understanding or related activities in Column-B:

Column-A	Column-B
(*a*) Communicative Language Teaching	(*i*) Socially acceptable and contextually appropriate language
(*b*) Direct method	(*ii*) Silent reading
(*c*) Grammar Translation	(*iii*) Written literary texts
(*d*) West's New Method	(*iv*) Grammar is taught inductively

	(*a*)	(*b*)	(*c*)	(*d*)
A.	(*i*)	(*iv*)	(*iii*)	(*ii*)
B.	(*iv*)	(*ii*)	(*iii*)	(*i*)
C.	(*iii*)	(*i*)	(*ii*)	(*iv*)
D.	(*ii*)	(*i*)	(*iv*)	(*iii*)

108. B **109.** C **110.** A **111.** A **112.** B **113.** B **114.** A **115.** A **116.** C **117.** A
118. D **119.** D **120.** A

LANGUAGE-II—हिन्दी

निर्देश (प्र. सं. 121 से 128 तक) : *निम्नलिखित गद्यांश को पढ़कर पूछे गए प्रश्नों के सही/सर्वाधिक उपयुक्त विकल्प का चयन कीजिए।*

जिंदगी की सबसे बड़ी सिफत हिम्मत है। व्यक्ति के और सारे गुण उसके हिम्मती होने से ही पैदा होते हैं। कुछ लोग ऐसी गोधूलि में बसते हैं जहाँ न तो जीत हँसती है और न कभी हार के रोने की आवाज सुनाई पड़ती है। साहस की जिंदगी सबसे बड़ी जिंदगी होती है। ऐसी जिंदगी की पहचान यह है कि वह बिल्कुल निडर, बिल्कुल बेखौफ होती है। साहसी मनुष्य की पहली पहचान यह है कि वह इस बात की चिंता नहीं करता कि तमाशा देखने वाले लोग उसके बारे में क्या सोच रहे हैं। अड़ोस-पड़ोस को देखकर चलना, यह साधारण जीव का काम है। जिंदगी के उस पन्ने को उलटकर पढ़ना चाहिए जिसके सभी अक्षर फूलों से नहीं, कुछ अंगारों से भी लिखे गए हों।

121. 'निडर' में प्रयुक्त उपसर्ग 'नि' की अर्थगत विशेषता है :

A. अधिकता B. अभाव
C. रहित D. सहित

122. 'गोधूलि' से तात्पर्य है :

A. रात्रि वेला B. प्रभात वेला
C. मध्य रात्रि D. संध्या वेला

123. 'सिफत' का अर्थ है :

A. उद्देश्य B. स्वीकृति
C. विशेषता D. अनुभव

124. 'अड़ोस-पड़ोस को देखकर चलना' से क्या अभिप्राय है?

A. अपने दाएँ-बाएँ देखकर चलना।
B. अपने पड़ोसियों का ध्यान रखना।
C. दूसरों के अनुसार जिंदगी जीना।
D. सबका हित देखना।

125. किस गुण के होने से व्यक्ति के और बाकी गुण स्वतः पैदा होते हैं?

A. नेतृत्व B. साहस
C. संतोष D. निष्कपट

126. जिंदगी के किस तरह के पन्ने को पढ़ने की बात कही गई है?

A. जिसमें चुनौतियाँ हों।
B. जिसमें सुख ही सुख हों।
C. जिसमें असफलताएँ हों।
D. जिसमें फूलों की सुगंध हो।

127. साहसी मनुष्य की सबसे पहली पहचान क्या है?

A. वह सदा आगे बढ़ता जाता है।
B. बहुत निडर होता है।
C. बाधाओं से नहीं घबराता है।
D. लोगों के सोच की परवाह नहीं करता है।

128. गोधूलि में बसने वाले लोगों से अभिप्राय है :

A. विवशता और अभाव में जीने वाले लोग।
B. जय-पराजय के अनुभव से परे लोग।
C. फल की कामना न करने वाले लोग।
D. जीवन में परिश्रम करने वाले लोग।

निर्देश (प्र. सं. 129 से 135 तक) : *निम्नलिखित गद्यांश को पढ़कर पूछे गए प्रश्नों के सही/सर्वाधिक उपयुक्त विकल्प का चयन कीजिए।*

मनुष्य के आनंद की सहज अभिव्यक्ति है संगीत। संगीत जीवन की अनमोल धरोहर है। संगीत प्रकृति प्रदत्त कला है। ललित कलाओं में संगीतकला को सर्वोच्च स्थान प्राप्त है। संगीत वह ललित कला है जिसमें हम अपने मन की भावनाओं को स्वर और लय के माध्यम से प्रकट करते हैं। प्रत्येक कला भावनाओं को व्यक्त करने का माध्यम है। संगीत एक सार्वभौमिक कला है। संगीत का जन्म आनंद से होता है और हमारे लिए आनंद का सृजन भी संगीत करता है। संगीत के आनंद को पाने के लिए सुनने की कला विकसित करनी पड़ती है। संगीत केवल हमारा मनोरंजन ही नहीं करता अपितु हमें संस्कारित भी करता है। संगीत हमारे भीतर की अच्छाई को उद्वेलित करता है।

129. संगीत द्वारा भावनाओं को प्रकट करने का प्रमुख माध्यम क्या हैं?

A. रंग, आकृति B. स्वर, लय
C. छंद, अलंकार D. मुद्रा, भाव

130. 'सर्वोच्च' का संधि विच्छेद है :

A. सर्व + उच्च
B. स + र्वोच्च
C. सर्वो + उच्च
D. सर्व + ऊच्च

131. संगीत के आनंद की प्राप्ति के लिए क्या आवश्यक है?

A. सुरीला कंठ होना चाहिए।
B. सुनने की कला विकसित करनी चाहिए।
C. संगीत का ज्ञान होना चाहिए।
D. संगीतज्ञ से पहचान करनी चाहिए।

121. C **122.** D **123.** C **124.** C **125.** B **126.** A **127.** D **128.** B **129.** B **130.** A **131.** B

132. संगीत हमें किस प्रकार से संस्कारित करता है?
A. हमारा मनोरंजन करके।
B. अभिव्यक्ति का माध्यम बनके।
C. हमें आनंदित करके।
D. हमारे मन की अच्छाई को सामने लाकर के।

133. प्रस्तुत गद्यांश में किस कला की बात की गई है?
A. नृत्य B. स्थापत्य
C. संगीत D. नाटक

134. संगीत को जीवन की अनमोल धरोहर कहा गया है, क्योंकि :
A. यह आनन्द का सृजन करता है।
B. यह प्रकृति प्रदत्त है।
C. यह ख्याति प्रदान करता है।
D. यह सर्वसुलभ है।

135. 'सार्वभौमिक' का अर्थ है :
A. सभी धर्मों में व्याप्त।
B. समान भाव से व्याप्त।
C. स्वदेश में व्याप्त।
D. संपूर्ण जगत में व्याप्त।

136. कौन-सा उपकरण समक्रमिक और अतुल्यकालिक ऑनलाइन शिक्षण अवसरों की उपलब्धता देता है?
A. पाठ्य-पुस्तकें B. रेलयात्रा टिकट
C. टेलीविजन D. पैडलेट

137. रचनात्मक आकलन के लिए कौन-सा उपकरण उपयुक्त **नहीं** है?
A. प्रदत्त कार्य B. लिखित परीक्षा
C. परियोजना D. कक्षा प्रस्तुतीकरण

138. भाषा शिक्षण के लिए प्रतिदिन काम में आने वाली सामग्री का प्रयोग करना क्या कहलाता है?
A. वास्तविक वस्तुएँ (रीयलिया)
B. भाषा खेल
C. शिक्षण सामग्री
D. पाठ्य सामग्री

139. भारत की 'शिक्षा नीति में भाषा' (त्रिभाषा सूत्र) किसे समुन्नत करने के लिए कहती है?
A. बहुभाषा शिक्षा
B. एक भाषिक शिक्षा
C. हिन्दी पर मुख्य बल देते हुए द्विभाषिक शिक्षा
D. मातृभाषा आधारित बहुभाषावाद

140. शीर्ष अधोमुखी प्रक्रिया (टॉप डाउन) के बारे में क्या सही **नहीं** है?
A. सुनने वाले अपने पूर्व ज्ञान पर निर्भर होते हैं
B. सुनने वाले जो सुनना चाहते हैं उसके बारे में अनुमान लगाते हैं
C. सुनने वाले संसार के बारे में प्राप्त ज्ञान का प्रयोग करते हैं
D. सुनने वाले को प्रत्येक शब्द का अर्थ सुनने की आवश्यकता है

141. अन्तर्राष्ट्रीय मातृभाषा दिवस कब मनाया जाता है?
A. पहली जनवरी B. चौदह फरवरी
C. इक्कीस फरवरी D. तेरह अप्रैल

142. ई-मेल के उस प्रकार की पहचान करिए जो आप अपने उस सहयोगी को लिखना चाहेंगे जो आपका मित्र भी है?
A. अनौपचारिक
B. औपचारिक
C. व्यापार संबंधी
D. लिखा-पढ़ी (कॉरिसपॉन्डेंस) पत्र व्यवहार

143. विद्यार्थियों के अधिगम और समझ में स्पष्टता लाने के लिए समूची शिक्षण अधिगम प्रक्रिया के दौरान किया जाने वाला आकलन क्या है?
A. अधिगम के लिए आकलन
B. अधिगम का आकलन
C. अधिगम में आकलन
D. अधिगम के रूप में आकलन

144. द्वितीय भाषा की कक्षा में एक अध्यापक ने 'स्वास्थ्य ही धन है' पर ऑडियो रिकॉर्डिंग सुनायी। उसके बाद उसने कार्यपत्रक (वर्कशीट) बाँटी और कहा कि दिए गए विकल्पों में से सही उत्तर पर निशान लगाएँ।

इस पाठ का उद्देश्य विद्यार्थियों को इस योग्य बनाना है कि :
A. स्वास्थ्य पर पाठ का श्रवण करें।
B. विद्यार्थियों को कार्य में संलग्न किया जाए।
C. विचार बिन्दुओं को सुनकर विश्लेषण किया जाए।
D. स्वास्थ्य और धन पर पाठ को कंठस्थ किया जाए।

145. भाषा अधिगम में गलतियों के बारे में क्या **सही** नहीं है?
A. गलतियाँ भाषा अधिगम प्रक्रिया में अवरोध पैदा करती है
B. गलतियाँ हमेशा बुरी नहीं होती हैं और अधिगम में मदद करती हैं
C. गलतियाँ भाषा अधिगम प्रक्रिया का महत्वपूर्ण पहलू हैं
D. गलतियाँ द्वितीय भाषा अर्जन की प्रक्रिया को समझने में मदद करती हैं

132. D **133.** C **134.** A **135.** D **136.** D **137.** B **138.** A, C **139.** D **140.** D **141.** C
142. A **143.** A **144.** B, C **145.** A

146. भाषा शिक्षा में रचनात्मकता क्या है?

A. खुले अन्त वाले कक्षायी प्रदत्त कार्य जिनकी भिन्न-भिन्न व्याख्याएँ हो सकती हैं और भिन्न-भिन्न उत्तर निकल सकते हैं

B. किसी अवधारणा के प्रति समझ बनाने के लिए विभिन्न विषयों से प्राप्त तत्वों को मिलाना

C. शिक्षण की नवीन विधियों का प्रयोग करते हुए कक्षायी गतिविधि

D. सम्प्रेषणात्मक भाषा शिक्षण का प्रयोग करते हुए कक्षा सामग्री

147. "शिक्षार्थियों को समृद्ध भाषायी परिवेश मिलना चाहिए और गलतियाँ इस बात का साक्ष्य हैं कि अधिगम हो रहा है।" यह किसके द्वारा अनुशंसित है?

A. व्यवहारवादी B. संज्ञानात्मकवादी

C. मानवतावादी D. मनोविश्लेषणवादी

148. निम्नलिखित में से कौन-से कथन **सही** हैं?

(*a*) पठन वैकल्य (डिस्लैक्सिया) पठन विकार है।

(*b*) लेखन वैकल्य (डिस्ग्रैफिया) लेखन विकार है।

(*c*) लेखन वैकल्य (डिस्ग्रैफिया) पठन विकार है।

(*d*) पठन वैकल्य (डिस्लैक्सिया) लेखन विकार है।

A. केवल (*a*) सही है

B. केवल (*b*) और (*d*) सही हैं

C. (*a*) और (*b*) दोनों सही हैं

D. (*c*) और (*d*) दोनों सही हैं

149. सरकारी विद्यालय की अध्यापिका रीता सातवीं कक्षा के विद्यार्थियों को अंग्रेजी पढ़ाने के लिए दृश्य उपकरण और भाषा खेल खिलाती है। रीता शिक्षण के किस सिद्धान्त का अनुपालन कर रही है?

A. स्वाभाविक प्रक्रिया का सिद्धान्त

B. अभ्यास और आदत निर्माण का सिद्धान्त

C. अभिप्रेरणा और रुचि का सिद्धान्त

D. जीवन से सम्बद्धता का सिद्धान्त

150. उस लघु कथा को क्या कहेंगे जिसमें मुख्य पात्र पशु हैं और नैतिक मूल्यों को उभारते हैं?

A. फंतासी B. जंतुकथा (फेबल)

C. विज्ञान फिक्शन D. यात्रा वृत्तान्त

EXPLANATORY ANSWERS

1. (C): Progressive education views children as active participants in their own learning process, emphasizing their ability to construct knowledge and meaning from their experiences. This approach encourages exploration, inquiry, and critical thinking, positioning children not just as passive recipients of information but as active agents who interact with and shape their understanding of the world.

Progressive education can be traced back to the works of John Locke and Jean-Jacques Rousseau, both of whom are known as forerunners of ideas that would be developed by theorists such as John Dewey. Considered one of the first of the British empiricists, Locke believed that "truth and knowledge... arise out of observation and experience rather than manipulation of accepted or given ideas". He further discussed the need for children to have concrete experiences in order to learn. Rousseau deepened this line of thinking in Emile, or On Education, where he argued that subordination of students to teachers and memorization of facts would not lead to an education.

2. (B): Effective feedback is immediate and ongoing, which helps students reflect on their learning process continuously rather than just at the end. This approach allows students to make adjustments in real-time, enhancing learning outcomes by providing them with the opportunity to understand and correct their mistakes as they occur.

Effective feedback in the classroom is essential for student learning. It helps students to understand their strengths and weaknesses, to identify areas where they need to improve and to set goals for themselves. Feedback can also help students to develop a growth mindset and to believe in their ability to learn and grow. When giving feedback, it is important to keep the following in mind:

- **Be specific and constructive:** Instead of saying "good job" or "nice work," try to be more specific about what the student did well. For example, you could say "I liked the way you explained the steps to solving the problem" or "I noticed that you used evidence from the text to support your claims."

146. A	**147.** B	**148.** C	**149.** C	**150.** B

- **Focus on the process, not the product:** Instead of praising the student's grade or test score, praise their effort and their willingness to learn. For example, you could say "I'm proud of the way you worked hard on this project" or "I appreciate the way you asked questions to clarify your understanding."
- **Make it timely:** Feedback is most effective when it is given as soon as possible after the student has completed their work. This allows them to reflect on the feedback and to apply it to their future work.
- **Provide opportunities for students to respond to feedback:** Students should have a chance to ask questions about the feedback and to explain how they plan to improve. This helps to ensure that they understand the feedback and that they are committed to improving.

3. **(C): Assertion (A):** During adolescence, the pressures to conform to gender expectations and follow conventions of femininity or masculinity increase. It is true. Adolescence is a key developmental stage where individuals begin to form a stronger sense of identity, including gender identity. This is a period of self-discovery, but it's also a time when external influences become particularly powerful. During adolescence, societal norms and cultural expectations around gender roles often become more pronounced. These norms dictate what is considered appropriate behaviour, appearance, and interests for males and females. For example, boys might be encouraged to exhibit traits like assertiveness and strength, while girls might be expected to be nurturing and empathetic. Adolescents are highly influenced by their peers. The desire to fit in and be accepted can lead to increased pressure to conform to traditional gender roles. Peer groups often reinforce gender norms, making it difficult for adolescents to deviate from expected behaviours without facing social consequences like teasing or exclusion.

   Reason (R): Gender and gender roles are determined biologically. It is false. Gender roles are not biologically determined; they are socially and culturally constructed. Different societies have different expectations for how individuals of different genders should behave, dress, and interact. These roles and expectations can change over time and can vary greatly between cultures.

4. **(C):** Her genetic background from her parents, both accomplished singers, likely predisposes her to musical talent (heredity). However, her environment, including the specialized voice training and the support from her parents, also plays a critical role in nurturing and developing this talent. This illustrates the concept of gene-environment interaction, where both genetic predispositions and environmental factors contribute significantly to the development of specific skills.

5. **(C):** Sensitive periods refer to specific times in an individual's development when the influence of environmental factors is particularly profound. It is the period for the child to develop particular capabilities. It is the time when the brain of a child is most receptive to a certain type of stimuli. A sensitive period is one when the child is maturational ready to acquire a skill. During this period the child must have favourable experiences which will help her to acquire the skill. If the favourable experiences come after the sensitive period is over, the child finds it difficult to learn. During this period, specific experiences affect the development of the child more than they do at other times. Such periods are sensitive for development because during these periods the child is ready to learn a particular skill. For example, a child begins to speak only when she is able to control the movements of the tongue, lips and vocal cords and the brain has developed further. That is, the child must be biologically ready to speak.

6. **(C):** Encouraging critical thinking requires tasks that challenge students to go beyond mere recall of facts. Questions that demand analysis, inference, and synthesis promote deeper understanding and engagement with the material, helping students develop the ability to think independently and apply knowledge in varied contexts.

7. **(C):** This form of intelligence involves understanding and organizing the natural environment, which aligns with activities like classifying natural objects. Such tasks leverage students' capacity to discern patterns, categorize items based on their characteristics, and engage with the physical world in a meaningful way.

   Linguistic Intelligence is an understanding of the rules, rhythm, meaning, and function of languages. A person with this type of intelligence can easily explain words or phrases to others, learn different languages, and excel at using language.

   Inter-personal intelligence is, the ability to understand and interact effectively with others. It involves effective verbal and non-verbal communication, the ability to note distinctions among others, sensitivity to the moods and temperaments of others, and the ability to entertain multiple perspectives.

Bodily-kinesthetics intelligence is the capacity to manipulate objects and use a variety of physical skills. This intelligence also involves a sense of timing and the perfection of skills through mind–body union. Athletes, dancers, surgeons, and crafts people exhibit well-developed bodily-kinesthetics intelligence.

8. (B): Mastery goals focus on developing competence and learning new skills rather than competing with others. This orientation fosters intrinsic motivation, as students are driven by personal growth and understanding. It also aligns with the incremental theory of intelligence, which posits that abilities can be developed through effort and perseverance.

Mastery orientation is described as a focus on learning and improvement. Mastery orientation focuses on learning, not grades; improvement, not appearances; competency, not competition. This person wants to understand and grow, not just prove how smart he or she is. Students who are more mastery motivated see learning as incremental. They believe abilities can be improved with practice and that they have control over their learning, these students exhibit academic behaviours that positively impact their learning successes. These behaviours include persevering through difficult tasks and using feedback to improve their performance.

9. (D): Implementing Vygotsky's theory, this approach utilizes the zone of proximal development (ZPD), where learners achieve more with skilled guidance than they could independently. By scaffolding the learning process and facilitating peer interaction, Rama can help the student build understanding through collaborative learning, enhancing cognitive development effectively.

10. (C): Assertion (A) is true as active engagement in debates and collaborative learning fosters critical thinking and knowledge construction. However, Reason (R) is false because knowledge production is inherently active, and group activities are valuable for deepening understanding and promoting interactive learning environments.

11. (C): This term encapsulates the developmental changes in emotions, personality traits, and social relationships. It emphasizes the combined influence of psychological factors and the social environment in shaping an individual's development throughout life.

Personality development refers to the process by which the organized thought and behaviour patterns that make up a person's unique personality emerge over time. Many factors influence personality, including genetics and environment, how we were parented, and societal variables.

Emotional development involves learning what feelings and emotions are, understanding how and why they occur, recognising your own feelings and those of others, and developing effective ways for managing those feelings.

Cognitive development is a field of study in neuroscience and psychology focusing on a child's development in terms of information processing, conceptual resources, perceptual skill, language learning, and other aspects of the developed adult brain and cognitive psychology.

12. (C): Culturally responsive teaching acknowledges and utilizes the cultural backgrounds of students as assets in the learning process. It involves intentional planning and adaptive strategies to meet the diverse learning needs of students, employing differentiated methods to ensure all students are engaged and supported in their learning environment.

13. (D): Schools should not solely focus on assessing the finished product and learning outcomes as this can neglect the importance of the learning process itself, which is not always tightly sequential and hierarchical. Learning is often a dynamic and recursive process where students may need to revisit concepts multiple times in different contexts to build understanding.

Hence, both the Assertion and Reason are false.

14. (D): Vygotsky posited that language and thought develop together and influence each other throughout a child's development. He believed that thought is internalized language and that language is a tool that significantly shapes cognitive processes.

Vygotsky was a Russian psychologist who believed that social interactions play a key role in development. According to Lev Vygotsky, language development changes the nature of human thought. According to him, learning occurs when children interact with people and the environment. His greatest contribution was the emphasis on the role of socio-cultural influences in our development. He asserted that the cognitive development of children is enhanced through social interaction with other people, particularly those who are more skilled. He explains this with the concept of the Zone of Proximal Development (ZPD), which refers to a range of tasks that a child can achieve only with assistance from a more skilled adult or peer called the More Knowledgeable Other (MKO). Adult assistance is provided wherever necessary which is called scaffolding.

15. (B): Norm-referenced assessments are designed to evaluate and rank students in relation to one another, typically to establish a distribution of achievement where individuals are compared against a norm group, usually represented by their peers.

Criterion-referenced assessment is related to the performance of the students in a well defined learning task. It has nothing to do with the norms or relative rank or position of students in any well defined group. A criterion-referenced test is used to ascertain a status with respect to the individual's status with respect to a defined achievement domain.

Formative assessment is a type of assessment that is used to monitor student progress and provide feedback during the teaching and learning process. It is typically used to identify students who need additional support and to adjust the curriculum as needed.

Summative Assessment commonly known as "Assessment of learning" refers to measure, classify, certify and report the level of student learning by assessing them at the end of the term. It is conducted at the end of a teaching-learning process to grade or rank the learners. Summative assessment is useful for awarding grades to students and promotion to the next grades.

16. (B): Traditional printed materials are not accessible to students with visual impairments, who require alternative formats like braille, audio books, or digital texts that can be used with screen reading software to fully participate and access information in the classroom.

17. (B): Kohlberg's approach involved presenting children with hypothetical moral dilemmas and discussing their reasoning behind their decisions. This method helped to explore how moral reasoning changes with age and cognitive development.

Kohlberg's theory is broken down into three primary levels. At each level of moral development, there are two stages:

Level 1. Pre-conventional Morality (4 to 10 years): Pre-conventional morality is the earliest period of moral development. At this age, children's decisions are primarily shaped by the expectations of adults and the consequences for breaking the rules. There are two stages within this level:

- Stage 1 (Obedience and Punishment)
- Stage 2 (Instrumental purpose orientation)

Level 2. Conventional Morality (10 to 13 years): The next period of moral development is marked by the acceptance of social rules regarding what is good and moral. During this time, adolescents and adults internalize the moral standards they have learned from their role models and from society:

- Stage 3 (Good-Boy Good-girl orientation)
- Stage 4 (Maintaining Social Order)

Level 3. Post-conventional Morality (13 to 16 years): At this level of moral development, people develop an understanding of abstract principles of morality. The two stages at this level are:

- Stage 5 (Social Contract and Individual Rights)
- Stage 6 (Universal Principles).

18. (A): Constructivist approaches to teaching focus on students actively constructing their own understanding and knowledge of the world, through experiencing things and reflecting on those experiences. This philosophy supports the idea that learners construct new ideas or concepts based upon their current/past knowledge and by discovery through hands-on, experiential learning activities.

19. (A): Phonological training involves teaching the awareness of phonemes, or the sounds that make up words, which is critical for reading. Systematic phonological training helps dyslexic students decode text by understanding and manipulating sounds, which significantly aids their reading development.

20. (C): Piaget's theory is based on the concept that cognitive development occurs in stages, and each stage represents a new way of thinking and understanding the world. This implies that educational content and approaches should be tailored to match the developmental stage of the child to maximize understanding and learning effectiveness.

Piaget's theory of cognitive development, or his genetic epistemology, is a comprehensive theory about the nature and development of human intelligence. It was originated by the Swiss developmental psychologist Jean Piaget (1896–1980). The theory deals with the nature of knowledge itself and how humans gradually come to acquire, construct, and use it. Piaget's theory is mainly known as a developmental stage theory.

Piaget's four stages of intellectual (or cognitive) development are:

- Sensory-motor stage (0 to 2 years)
- Pre-operational stage (2 to 6 years)
- Concrete operational stage (6 to 11 years)
- Formal Operational stage (11+ years to adolescence).

21. (B): Metacognitive skills involve understanding and managing one's own learning processes. By encouraging students to reflect on how they learn, what strategies they use, and how they can improve their thinking processes, teachers foster deeper metacognitive awareness, leading to better self-regulation and more effective learning strategies.

22. (B): Autism Spectrum Disorder (ASD) is characterized by challenges with social skills, repetitive behaviours, speech, and non-verbal communication. It is a complex developmental condition involving persistent challenges in social interaction, speech, and non-verbal communication, often accompanied by restricted/repetitive behaviours. The exact cause of autism is unknown, but it is understood to involve a combination of genetic and environmental factors, not solely environmental influences as some might suggest.

23. (C): Both Jean Piaget and Lev Vygotsky emphasized the active role children play in their cognitive development. Piaget saw children as little scientists who learn through active experimentation and problem-solving, while Vygotsky emphasized the social context of learning, where children learn through interactions with more knowledgeable others, highlighting the engagement and active participation in their learning processes.

24. (C): While it is essential for teachers to respect and adapt to individual differences among learners, it is false that collaborations and group works should be avoided in a diverse class. Collaborative learning can be very effective in leveraging diverse perspectives and strengths, thereby enriching the learning experience for all students.

25. (D): Reciprocal learning strategy involves students teaching each other what they have learned, which helps deepen understanding through explanation and discussion. It typically involves students working in pairs or small groups to teach one another and ask questions, enhancing comprehension and retention.

26. (C): In many Asian cultures, societal norms do discourage the expression of anger and encourage the management of shame to maintain social harmony. However, the reason provided is incorrect as emotions play a significant role in learning by influencing engagement, attention, and memory processes. Emotional experiences can deeply impact cognitive functions and learning outcomes.

27. (C): Jean Piaget emphasized that children think differently from adults. He proposed that cognitive development proceeds through a series of stages, each characterized by unique ways of thinking and understanding the world. Children do not just know less; their cognitive processes function differently.

28. (D): This question promotes analytical thinking by requiring students to consider multiple factors and their interrelations rather than merely recalling facts. Analytical questions encourage evaluation, synthesis, and critical thinking, as students must analyze various components and their impacts on population growth.

29. (C): Inclusive education involves tailoring teaching environments and practices to accommodate the diverse learning needs of all students. This ensures that every student, regardless of their abilities or disabilities, receives appropriate educational opportunities and supports tailored to their individual needs.

30. (A): Providing students with opportunities for experimentation allows them to explore and test their understandings, which is essential for conceptual learning. Discussing examples and non-examples helps address misconceptions by clarifying what a concept is and is not, effectively utilizing counterexamples to challenge and refine students' understanding, aligning with constructive educational practices.

31. (A):

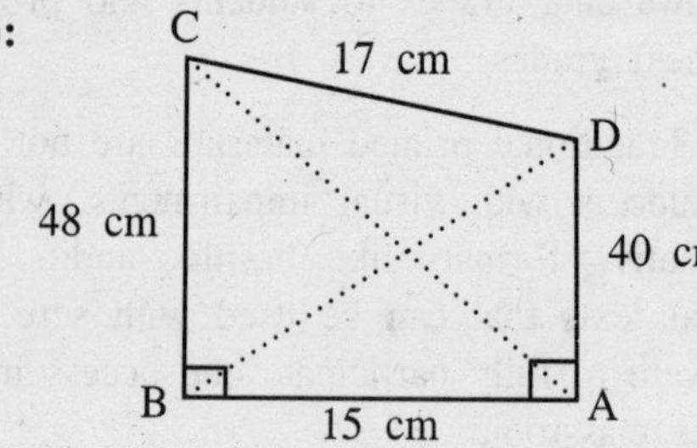

$\because$ Perimeter of quadrilateral ABCD = 120 cm

$\therefore$ AB = 120 − (40 + 17 + 48)

= 120 − 105 = 15 cm

Area of ABCD = ar ΔABC + ar ΔBAD

$$= \frac{1}{2} \times 15 \times 48 + \frac{1}{2} \times 15 \times 40$$

$$= 360 + 300 = 660 \text{ cm}^2.$$

32. (D): This statement is least appropriate regarding the proofs in mathematics. Mathematical proofs are fundamentally based on logical reasoning and the application of defined rules and principles, rather than on intuition alone. They involve a systematic process of deriving conclusions from axioms, definitions, and previously established theorems, ensuring that the result must necessarily follow from the premises. The core of mathematical proof lies in its rigor and the objective verification of claims through logical deduction, not merely intuitive understanding.

33. (C):

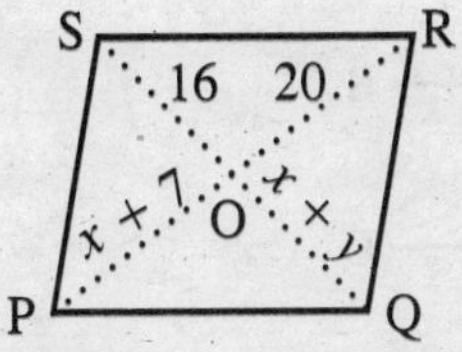

$\because$ PQRS is a parallelogram

$$x + y = 16$$

and $x + 7 = 20$

$\Rightarrow \quad x = 13$

$\Rightarrow \quad 13 + y = 16$

$\Rightarrow \quad y = 3$

$\therefore$ Value of $7y + 5 = 7 \times 3 + 5$

$= 21 + 5$

$= 26$ cm.

34. (B): The value of

$52 \times 3 \div 4 + \sqrt{441} \div 7 \times 3 + 5 - 32 \div 8 \times 12$

$= 39 + 21 \div 7 \times 3 + 5 - 4 \times 12$

$= 39 + 3 \times 3 + 5 - 48$

$= 39 + 14 - 48$

$= 53 - 48 = 5.$

35. (A): $\because$ Present age of Varun $= x$ years

$\therefore$ Present age of Arun $= (x + 3)$ years

According to the question,

8 years ago, Varun's age $= x - 8$

Arun's age $= (x - 5)$ years

$\therefore \quad \frac{5}{6}(x-5) - \frac{3}{5}(x-8) = 6$

$\Rightarrow \quad \frac{5x-25}{6} - \frac{3x+24}{5} = 6$

$\Rightarrow \quad \frac{25x-125-18x+144}{30} = 6$

$\Rightarrow \quad 7x + 19 = 180$

$\Rightarrow \quad 7x = 161$

$\Rightarrow \quad x = \frac{161}{7} = 23$

Hence, the present age of Varun = 23 years.

36. (C): The domain of learning that deals with attitudes and values is known as the affective domain. This domain encompasses the manner in which people deal with things emotionally, such as feelings, values, appreciation, enthusiasms, motivations, and attitudes. It is distinct from the cognitive domain, which covers knowledge and intellectual skills, and the psychomotor domain, which relates to physical or manual skills. The affective domain is crucial for understanding how individuals are likely to react emotionally to different learning experiences and environments.

37. (D):

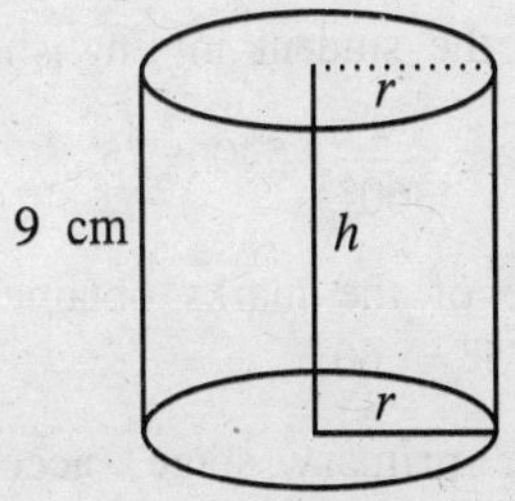

$r = 6$ cm

$h = 9$ cm

Original volume of cylinder $= \pi \times 6 \times 6 \times 9$

$= 324\ \pi$ cm^3

Now, $\quad r = \frac{6}{2} = 3$ cm

and $h = 9 + 3 = 12$ cm

New volume of cylinder $= \pi \times 3 \times 3 \times 12$

$= 108\ \pi$ cm^3

$\therefore \quad \frac{\text{New Volume}}{\text{Original Volume}} = \frac{108}{324} = \frac{6}{18} = \frac{1}{3}$

Clearly, the new volume will be one-third the original volume.

38. (B): According to Van Hiele's theory of geometrical learning, there are levels that describe how students understand geometry. Starting from the lowest level:

(*d*) **Identification of geometrical shapes as they are:** This is the first level, where students are able to recognize and name geometric shapes based on their appearance, without understanding their properties.

(*b*) **Classification of different shapes:** At the second level, students can group shapes into categories based on their properties such as having parallel sides or equal angles.

(*a*) **Identification of properties of geometrical shapes:** In the third level, students focus on identifying and understanding the specific properties of shapes, such as the attributes that define squares versus rectangles.

(*c*) **Finding relationship between the properties of geometrical shapes:** The fourth level involves understanding the relationships between different properties of shapes, such as how the properties of parallelism, angle measures, and side lengths interrelate in polygons.

This ascending order of levels reflects a progression from recognizing and naming shapes to deeper understanding of their characteristics and the relationships between those characteristics.

39. (A): Marks obtained by the student in Maths

$$= \frac{90°}{360°} \times 540 = 135$$

Marks obtained by the student in English

$$= \frac{50°}{360°} \times 540 = 75$$

Required difference of the marks obtained by the student = 135 – 75 = 60.

40. (A): At the upper primary stage, according to NCERT, the curriculum does not include complex numbers as part of the number system topic. The number system typically covered at this level includes concepts like fractions, decimals, exponents and powers, and square and cube roots. Complex numbers, which involve the use of the imaginary unit 'i', are typically introduced at higher educational levels due to their abstract and advanced mathematical nature.

41. (D): This statement is not correct with respect to rubrics as a tool of assessment. Rubrics are designed to make evaluation more objective and consistent by providing a detailed set of criteria and a fixed scale that describes the expected performance at each level. Each criterion within a rubric is clearly defined, helping assessors evaluate work consistently across different students and different assessors. The primary goal of a rubric is to clarify expectations for students and provide a transparent method for scoring or grading, thus reducing subjectivity in assessment.

42. (B): In polyhedron, we have,

$$V - E + F = 2$$

$$\Rightarrow \quad x - 15 + 7 = 2$$

$$\Rightarrow \quad x - 8 = 2 \Rightarrow x = 10$$

The Value of $2F + 3E - 4x$

$$= 2 \times 7 + 3 \times 15 - 4x$$

$$= 14 + 45 - 40$$

$$= 59 - 40 = 19.$$

43. (D): Let, $2x + 5y = a$

$$a^2 - 5a - 14 = (a + p)(a + q)$$

$$\Rightarrow \quad a^2 - 7a + 2a - 14 = (a + p)(a + q)$$

$$\Rightarrow \quad a(a - 7) + 2(a - 7) = (a + p)(a + q)$$

$$\Rightarrow \quad (a + 2)(a - 7) = (a + p)(a + q)$$

$$\Rightarrow \quad a + 2 = a + p$$

or $\quad a - 7 = a + q$

$$\Rightarrow \quad p = 2,\ q = -7$$

$$\therefore \quad p + q = 2 - 7 = -5.$$

44. (A):

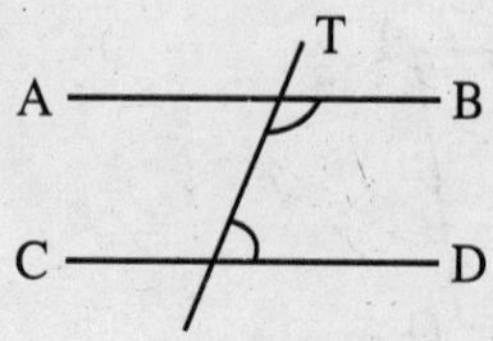

$\because$ Sum of two interior angles = 180°

$$2x + 15° + 3x - 20° = 180°$$

$$\Rightarrow \quad 5x - 5° = 180°$$

$$\Rightarrow \quad 5x = 180° + 5° = 185°$$

$$\Rightarrow \quad x = \frac{185}{5} = 37°$$

Value of $4x + 6° = 4 \times 37° + 6°$

$$= 148° + 6° = 154°.$$

45. (D):

$$\frac{6}{7} = 0.85$$

$$2\frac{3}{5} = 2.6$$

$$\frac{3}{8} = 0.37$$

$$2\frac{8}{15} = 2.5$$

Clearly, $2\frac{3}{5}$ is the largest and $\frac{3}{8}$ is the smallest

$\therefore$ Sum of largest and smallest fraction

$$= 2\frac{3}{5} + \frac{3}{8}$$

$$= \frac{13}{5} + \frac{3}{8} = \frac{104 + 15}{40} = \frac{119}{40} = 2\frac{39}{40}.$$

46. (B): Assessment in education does not imply labeling students. Instead, its primary purpose is to evaluate, inform, and enhance teaching and learning processes. Effective assessment is used to diagnose individual differences, guide instructional decisions, and provide feedback to improve student performance and understanding. Labeling students based on assessments can lead to negative educational outcomes by creating fixed mindsets about abilities and potential.

47. (A): Convergent thinking, which involves focusing on a single, correct solution to a problem, is not an indicator of creativity in mathematics. Creativity in mathematics is typically indicated by the ability to think flexibly, use multiple and alternative problem-solving strategies, and pose new questions. These characteristics allow students to explore different ways of understanding and solving problems, which is crucial for creative mathematical thinking.

48. (A): 955 is lying between $(30)^2$ and $(31)^2$

$$(30)^2 = 900$$
$$(31)^2 = 961$$
$$\therefore \quad 961 - 955 = 6$$

Hence, $955 + 6 = 961$

when, we add 6 in 955 then it becomes a perfect square, Hence, $x = 6$

Value of $3x + 2 = 3 \times 6 + 2 = 20$.

49. (B): LCM of 3, 5 and 7 = 105

Natural numbers between 1 to 500 are divisible by 3, 5 and 7 are,

$$105 \times 1 = 105$$
$$105 \times 2 = 210$$
$$105 \times 3 = 315$$
$$105 \times 4 = 420$$

Hence, required number = 4.

50. (C): According to the National Curriculum Framework 2005, the emphasis in mathematics education should be on understanding concepts, solving real-world problems, applying mathematical techniques appropriately, and generalizing mathematical formulas to new situations. Finding short-cuts, while sometimes useful in specific contexts, is considered least important compared to these other objectives. The framework prioritizes deep understanding and the ability to think critically and creatively about mathematical problems over merely finding quicker ways to solve them. This approach is aimed at developing a robust mathematical foundation rather than just focusing on speed and efficiency.

51. (B):

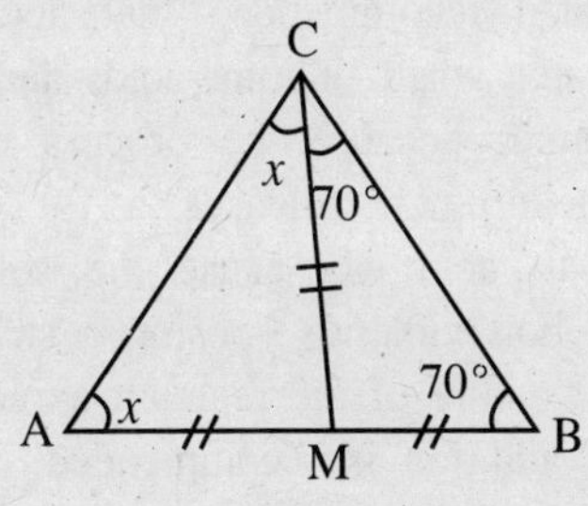

$\because \quad AM = MB = CM$

$\Rightarrow \quad AM = CM = \angle A = \angle C$

$\therefore \quad CM = MB \Rightarrow \angle C = \angle B$

$\Rightarrow \quad \angle C = 70°$

[Given, $\angle B = 70°$, $\angle A = x°$]

In ΔABC,

$\angle A + \angle B + \angle C = 180°$

$\Rightarrow x + 70° + x + 70° = 180°$

$\Rightarrow \quad 2x + 140° = 180°$

$\Rightarrow \quad 2x = 40° \Rightarrow x = 20$

Value of $3x + 25° = 3 \times 20 + 25 = 85°$.

52. (C): $A = P\left(1 + \frac{r}{100}\right)^t$

$$\frac{3267}{P} = \left(1 + \frac{10}{100}\right)^2 = \left(\frac{11}{10}\right)^2 = \frac{121}{100}$$

$$\Rightarrow \quad P = \frac{3267 \times 100}{121} = ₹\ 2700$$

$$S.I. = \frac{P \times r \times t}{100} = \frac{2700 \times 10 \times 5}{100 \times 2}$$

$$= 27 \times 25 = ₹\ 675.$$

53. (D):

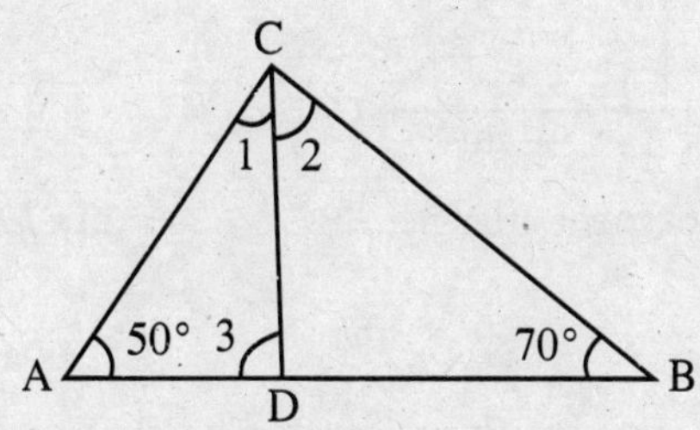

In ΔABC,

$\angle A + \angle B + \angle C = 180°$

$\Rightarrow \quad 50° + 70° + \angle C = 180°$

$\Rightarrow \quad \angle C = 180° - 120° = 60°$

$\because$ CD is the bisector of $\angle C$

$\therefore \quad \angle 1 = \angle 2 = 30°$

In ΔACD,

$\angle 1 + \angle 50° + \angle 3 = 180°$

$\Rightarrow \quad 30° + 50° + \angle 3 = 180°$

$\Rightarrow \quad \angle 3 = 180° - 80° = 100°$

Hence, $\angle ADC = 100°$.

54. (C): Mean

$$= \frac{36 + 37 + 31 + 42 + 23 + 38 + 17 + 18 + 35 + 25 + 29 + 35}{12}$$

$$= \frac{366}{12} = 30.5$$

Range $= 42 - 17 = 25$

Required difference $= 30.5 - 25 = 5.5$.

55. (B): Cost of 12 fans = ₹ 24000

Cost of 1 fan = ₹ 2000

Marked price of each fan $= 2000 + \frac{25}{100} \times 2000$

$= ₹\ 2500$

Discount $= \frac{10}{100} \times 2500 = ₹\ 250$

S.P. of each fan $= 2500 - 250 = ₹\ 2250$

Profit on each fan $= 2250 - 2000 = ₹\ 250$

Hence, overall profit $= 12 \times 250 = ₹\ 3000$.

56. (C): $\dfrac{(a-b+c)^2-(a-b-c)^2}{b-a}$

$= \dfrac{(a-b+c+a-b-c)(a-b+c-a+b+c)}{b-a}$

$= \dfrac{(2a-2b)(2c)}{b-a} = \dfrac{-2(b-a)(2c)}{(b-a)} = -4c.$

57. (A):

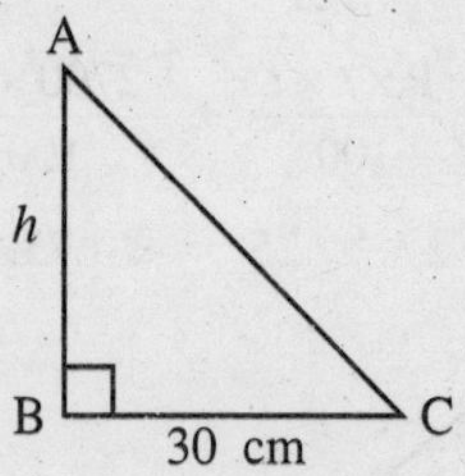

Area of right triangle ABC $= \dfrac{1}{2}\times 30\times h$

$\Rightarrow \quad 240 = 15h$

$\Rightarrow \quad h = \dfrac{240}{15} = 16$

$\Rightarrow \quad AB = 16$ cm

We have, $(AC)^2 = (AB)^2 + (BC)^2$

$= (16)^2 + (30)^2$

$= 256 + 900 = 1156$

$\Rightarrow \quad AC = \sqrt{1156} = 34$ cm

Perimeter of $\Delta ABC = AB + BC + AC$

$= 16 + 30 + 34 = 80$ cm.

58. (A): This teaching method Discovery method of learning involves students actively engaging in exploring and investigating the properties of triangles through hands-on activities. By measuring and tabulating the angles of different triangle shapes themselves, students are likely to discover the fundamental principle that the sum of the angles in a triangle is always 180 degrees. This approach is characteristic of the discovery method, where students learn by direct interaction with materials and concepts, leading to the formation of their own conclusions, rather than being directly told by the teacher. This fosters deeper understanding and retention of the concept as students see firsthand how it manifests in various examples they work with themselves.

59. (C): The expression $(x^2 + 10x + 25)$

$= (x^2 + 5x + 5x + 25)$

$= x(x + 5) + 5(x + 5)$

$= (x + 5)(x + 5) = (x + 5)^2$

Hence, the expression $(x^2 + 10x + 25)$ can not be simplified further is not true.

60. (D): Let two numbers are $3x$ and $7x$

LCM = 630 (given)

LCM of two numbers are $21x$

$21x = 630$

$\Rightarrow \quad x = \dfrac{630}{21} = 30$

Numbers are $3 \times 30 = 90$ and $7 \times 30 = 210$

HCF $= x = 30$

Hence, Sum of LCM and HCF

$= 630 + 30 = 660.$

61. (C): The statement (C) "Lime water turns milky on passing carbon dioxide" is an observation because it describes a direct observable event. Statements (A) "Metal oxides are basic in nature," (B) "Air expands on heating," and (D) "Sodium hydroxide and hydrochloric acid neutralize each other" are inferences, as they involve conclusions or generalizations based on experimental data or chemical properties, not just straightforward observations.

62. (D): Alternate conceptions in science are often stable, resistant to change, and developed from observable features. However, the idea that alternate conceptions do not demonstrate cause and effect reasoning is incorrect. In fact, many alternate conceptions arise precisely because individuals attempt to construct cause and effect explanations based on their observations and prior knowledge, albeit sometimes inaccurately.

63. (A): It is indeed recommended that acid should be added to water when diluting acid, and not the other way around, because the process is highly exothermic—meaning it releases a lot of heat. Adding water to acid can cause the solution to splash or even boil violently, posing a safety risk. The exothermic nature of the reaction explains why this method of addition is recommended.

64. (D): The assertion that the rate of breathing in aquatic animals is slower than in land animals is generally false, as aquatic animals often have adaptations that allow them to maximize oxygen extraction from water, which contains less dissolved oxygen than air. The reason provided—that the presence of large amounts of dissolved oxygen affects the rate of breathing—is also incorrect, as dissolved oxygen levels in water are typically lower compared to the oxygen concentration in air, and this scarcity usually necessitates more efficient or faster breathing in aquatic animals, not slower.

65. (A): The assertion that ceilings of cinema halls and concert halls are generally curved is true, as this architectural design helps in the distribution of sound waves evenly throughout the hall. The reason given—that sound waves after striking a curved surface get reflected in all directions—is accurate and is indeed the correct explanation for why such a design is effective. The curvature helps to scatter sound waves uniformly, avoiding sound focusing and ensuring that sound quality is maintained throughout the space.

66. (B): In scientific investigations, (*b*) social context may influence conclusions because cultural, economic, and political contexts can shape what questions are asked and how information is interpreted. (*d*) There is no universal scientific method acknowledges that the process of scientific inquiry can vary greatly depending on the discipline, the nature of the inquiry, and the specific methods required for each research question, rather than following a single, rigid procedure.

67. (C): The filament of an incandescent bulb is indeed made of tungsten because it has a very high melting point, which allows it to glow white-hot without melting. However, the reason provided in (R) is incorrect; tungsten is actually chosen for its high resistance, not low resistance, which allows it to heat up to high temperatures necessary for light emission.

68. (D): Water from the lowest hole comes out with the greatest force due to the higher water pressure at deeper levels in the bottle. This greater force also causes the water from the lowest hole to fall at maximum distance from the bottle, as the initial velocity is higher, overcoming air resistance more effectively and traveling further before hitting the ground. So, There are two statements (*a*) and (*d*) is true regarding the flow of water from the holes.

69. (D): The human circulatory system is characterized by being closed, meaning that the blood is contained within the vessels, and double circulation, which involves two distinct circuits: the pulmonary circuit (between the heart and lungs) and the systemic circuit (between the heart and other organs). This system efficiently delivers oxygen and nutrients to body tissues and removes carbon dioxide and other wastes.

70. (B & C): Both sets of strategies are well-suited for identifying alternate conceptions about adaptations in plants and animals. Portfolios, group discussions, and diagnostic questionnaires collectively provide a robust framework for assessing understanding over time, fostering peer interaction, and pinpointing specific misconceptions. Similarly, diagnostic questionnaires, interviews, and drawings offer a comprehensive approach, combining structured assessment, in-depth personal exploration, and visual expression, which together enhance the detection and understanding of student misconceptions.

71. (A): Soil erosion primarily results from physical factors like water runoff and wind, which remove topsoil. While the misuse of fertilizers and pesticides can lead to soil degradation and loss of soil structure, which may indirectly influence erosion, they are more directly linked to problems like eutrophication, nitrification, and biomagnification due to nutrient runoff and chemical accumulation in ecosystems.

72. (A): An odometer is a device specifically designed to track the total distance a vehicle has traveled over its operational lifetime. It does not measure speed, acceleration, or any other variable but strictly the cumulative distance covered, making it a crucial tool for maintenance schedules, resale value assessments, and legal documentation of vehicle use.

73. (A): Scientific laws are statements based on repeated experiments or observations that describe some aspect of the world under specific conditions. They are empirical, concise, and universally applicable, often expressed in mathematical form. Laws do not explain why the phenomena occur but rather how they occur, and they are not derived from theories but can inform them.

74. (B): Self-pollination can occur in both bisexual and unisexual flowers if they possess mechanisms to facilitate it, not exclusively in bisexual flowers. Bisexual flowers, which contain both male and female reproductive structures, indeed have the capability to undergo both self-pollination and cross-pollination, depending on the presence of vectors and the flower's compatibility and design.

75. (B): This activity involves observing specific instances and deriving a general rule, which is the essence of inductive reasoning. By measuring angles of reflection and incidence in multiple instances, students can observe the consistent patterns that emerge, thereby forming a basis for understanding and articulating the law of reflection through their empirical observations, enhancing their inductive reasoning skills.

76. (B): When two sperms fuse with two separate eggs, the twins formed are fraternal, or dizygotic. This occurs when two different eggs are fertilized by two different sperms, each developing into a separate embryo with its own genetic material. Fraternal twins are genetically similar to regular siblings and not genetically identical.

77. (C): Rainwater harvesting helps in conserving groundwater by capturing rainwater and allowing it to seep into the ground, enhancing water table levels. It also reduces local flooding by minimizing the volume of runoff water during heavy rains. Additionally, harvested rainwater can be used for irrigation, providing a sustainable water source for agricultural purposes. It does not inherently create drainage problems but instead often alleviates such issues by reducing surface runoff.

78. (B): Discussion of socio-scientific issues in the classroom helps in developing argumentative skills as students learn to articulate their positions and defend them with evidence. It also fosters the development of multiple perspectives, as students are exposed to and must consider different viewpoints on an issue. Furthermore, such discussions can encourage citizen science activities by engaging students with real-world problems and science that affects societal outcomes.

79. (B): This activity illustrates 'science as inquiry' as it involves actively questioning and investigating to discover how different variables influence a biological process, namely the germination of seeds. Students set up experiments, manipulate variables, and observe outcomes, embodying the inquiry-based approach which is fundamental to scientific learning and understanding.

80. (C): A gender-responsive pedagogy in science includes the use of gender-sensitive language, which avoids reinforcing stereotypes and promotes inclusion. It also involves engaging students in examining and challenging stereotypical notions about gender roles in science, thereby fostering a more inclusive and reflective learning environment. Making gender-based groups and using differentiated instruction are strategies that can be part of an inclusive pedagogy but are not specifically required for a gender-responsive approach.

81. (A): Photosynthesis is an endothermic reaction because it absorbs energy, specifically light energy from the sun, to convert carbon dioxide and water into glucose and oxygen. Respiration is an exothermic reaction because it releases energy by breaking down glucose in the presence of oxygen to produce carbon dioxide, water, and energy in the form of ATP.

82. (A): Turmeric changes to reddish brown in bases, indicating its base-sensitive color change. China rose changes to green in bases, reflecting its unique pH indicator properties. Phenolphthalein changes from colourless in acidic conditions to pink in basic conditions. Methyl orange changes from orange in acidic conditions to pink in basic conditions.

83. (C): The color of a flame depends on the nature of the combustible substance, which influences the flame's color by the specific elements being burned (e.g., sodium producing a yellow flame, copper producing a green flame). Additionally, the oxygen supply affects the flame color, as variations in oxygen levels can alter the combustion process and thereby the flame's appearance and color.

84. (C): The generation and flow of winds on Earth are primarily influenced by uneven heating of the earth and oceans. This differential heating creates areas of high and low pressure, causing air to move from high-pressure zones to low-pressure zones, generating winds. The uneven heating results from variations in solar radiation absorbed at different locations due to Earth's curvature and the varied absorption capacities of land and water.

85. (B): Given the atomic numbers, element A is Aluminum (Al) with 13 electrons, typically forming a +3 ion (Al^{3+}), and element B is Chlorine (Cl) with 17 electrons, typically forming a -1 ion (Cl^-). The formula of the compound formed would be AB_3, where one Al^{3+} ion combines with three Cl ions to form Aluminum Chloride ($AlCl_3$), ensuring electrical neutrality.

86. (C): This statement is not true regarding conduction of heat. Conduction can occur in gases, though it is much less effective compared to solids due to the larger distances between molecules in gases, which makes the transfer of kinetic energy between molecules less efficient. However, heat conduction still occurs to some degree.

87. (C): When an object floats in a liquid, the proportion of the object's volume that remains outside the liquid is inversely proportional to the density of the liquid. The fact that a larger fraction (3/4) of the object's volume is outside liquid B compared to liquid A (1/4) implies that liquid B has a higher density than liquid A. This is because a denser liquid displaces more weight per unit volume, allowing a greater proportion of the object to float above the liquid's surface.

88. (B): This statement is not correct. The reaction of potassium with water is highly exothermic, not endothermic. When potassium reacts with water, it does so violently, generating heat and causing the hydrogen gas that is evolved to ignite, often heard as a pop sound. The reaction releases a significant amount of energy, hence it is exothermic.

89. (A): Divergent questions in a science classroom serve multiple purposes. They promote critical thinking by encouraging students to think in various directions and consider multiple outcomes or solutions. They can also help discern between students by identifying different levels of understanding or thought processes. Identifying gifted students and alternative conceptions are further benefits, as these questions allow teachers to see which students can think beyond standard responses and who might hold misunderstandings that need addressing.

90. (C): The nature and size of the images produced by mirrors align with the properties of specific types of mirrors. A plane mirror creates virtual and erect images that are the same size as the object. A concave mirror can produce real and inverted images; when the object is outside the focal point, the image can be the same size or enlarged, depending on the object's distance from the mirror. A convex mirror always creates virtual and erect images that are diminished, regardless of the object's distance from the mirror.

91. (D): The passage specifically mentions that millions of people around the world watched videos and photos of the meteor explosion over a Russian city on Facebook and YouTube. These platforms are highlighted as primary sources for viewing the event, indicating their significant role in disseminating visual content quickly to a global audience.

92. (A): The antonym for "erroneous," which means incorrect or wrong, is "faultless," implying something that is free from error or defects. The other options, such as "inaccurate" and "invalid," are actually synonyms of "erroneous," while "surprising" does not relate directly to the concept of correctness or accuracy.

93. (C): While the passage mentions that false stories and hoaxes can spread on social media, it also points out that social media can change our lives for the better, emphasizing the positive impact and potential of social media platforms to disseminate useful information and aid in situations like disasters.

94. (D): The correct sequence of events as mentioned in paragraph 1 starts with the plane crashing into the Hudson River. Then, Jim, who watched the crash, tweeted about the event. Following his tweet, people began contacting Jim for updates. Finally, it was noted that the news of the crash was broadcast on official news channels 15 minutes later.

95. (C): Statement (*a*) is accurate as the passage confirms that a plane crashed on 15 January, 2009. However, statement (*b*) is incorrect because the passage specifies that the pilot, crew, and all 155 passengers escaped safely, implying no loss of life. Statement (*c*) is incorrect as there is no mention of Jim posting pictures on Facebook; it only states that he tweeted about the event.

96. (B): In the analogy "dramatic : exciting," the relationship is that of a characteristic or description, where dramatic events are often exciting. Similarly, "hoax : deception" fits because a hoax is inherently a form of deception, misleading people intentionally.

97. (B): The passage highlights that news travels fast on social media, underscoring the rapid dissemination of information through platforms like Twitter and Facebook, regardless of the accuracy of the content.

98. (D): In the sentence "But social media can change our lives for the better," "lives" functions as a noun as it is the object being affected by the potential change, and "better" serves as an adjective describing in what way the lives can be changed, implying an improvement.

99. (A): The phrase "Ordinary people suddenly became journalists" means that regular individuals took on the role of reporting news by using social media to share pictures, videos, and updates about events, effectively performing journalistic functions without formal employment by media outlets.

100. (C): In the context of the poem, the line "It walks on the water, and whirls the mills" describes actions that are characteristics of the wind. The wind is personified as moving across the water's surface and causing the mills to turn, emphasizing its dynamic and pervasive influence in the natural world.

101. (B): The poet uses "curled" to describe the water enveloping the Earth, creating a vivid image of the water as a continuous, embracing presence around the globe. This description conveys the interconnectedness and comprehensive embrace of the oceans and waters.

102. (C): The entire poem is a celebration of the Earth's grandeur and splendor, highlighting the awe-inspiring aspects of the natural world, from the grass and waters to the air and winds, and the expansive reach of the Earth's landscapes and human inhabitations.

103. (A): As mentioned in the poem, "And talks to itself on the tops of the hills," the wind is personified as engaging in a monologue, adding a layer of mystery and animation to the natural element, suggesting its capacity for movement and sound generation.

104. (C): The first line "Great, wide, beautiful, wonderful world," uses alliteration with the repetition of the initial 'w' sound, enhancing the lyrical quality of the line. The fourth line, "World, you are beautifully drest," personifies the Earth, attributing it with the characteristic of being adorned as if it were a person.

105. (A): The stanza lists "wheat-fields that nod and the rivers that flow, with cities and gardens, and cliffs, and isles, and people upon you for thousands of miles," highlighting the diverse and abundant elements that contribute to the Earth's grandeur. Specifically, the elements that capture the essence of the Earth's greatness in this stanza are rivers, gardens, and cliffs, showcasing the natural beauty and varied landscapes of the planet.

106. (B): The impact of tests and assessments on teachers, learners, and materials is known as the washback effect. This term is used to describe how the nature and use of assessment influence instruction and learning in the classroom, often shaping what is taught and how teaching is conducted based on what will be tested.

107. (A): Schools should follow additive bilingualism because it values both the child's native culture and language by adding a second language without diminishing the first. This approach supports maintaining and developing the first language while learning a second, enhancing cognitive and cultural benefits.

108. (B): Linguistic functions such as intonation, tone, stress, and rhythm are collectively known as prosody. These elements of speech contribute to the patterns of rhythm and sound used in oral language, playing a critical role in communication by affecting meaning, emotion, and emphasis.

109. (C): This statement is NOT true about languages in India. Sanskrit is considered a classical language of India, not a modern language. It has a foundational status in the cultural history of India but is not classified under the category of Modern Indian Languages, which typically refers to languages currently in widespread use.

110. (A): In a language class, when students form groups under the guidance of a teacher to present an advertisement on a given topic, this method is known as collaborative learning. This approach involves students working together to solve problems, complete tasks, or create products, promoting engagement and interaction, which are beneficial for language acquisition.

111. (A): The objective of a lesson that familiarizes learners with vocabulary used in restaurants is to acquaint them with specific lexical items related to that context. This includes terms and phrases commonly used in restaurant settings, which aids in practical language usage for dining out scenarios.

112. (B): The school of learning that believed language acquisition, whether verbal or non-verbal, occurs through the process of habit formation is the Behaviourist school. This theory emphasizes that learning takes place through repetition and reinforcement, with language skills being developed as learners respond to stimuli and form associations.

113. (B): The time and place of a story are collectively known as the setting. This element of a narrative provides the background against which the story's events unfold, contributing to the mood, atmosphere, and context that influence characters and plot developments.

114. (A): In a language class, when students act out specific roles such as purchasers, property sellers, landlords, and tenants, while others observe, this activity is termed roleplay. It involves participants adopting and acting out characters in predefined scenarios to practice and enhance their language skills in a simulated environment, which is particularly effective in language teaching for developing conversational skills and applying vocabulary in context.

115. (A): By incorporating everyday objects such as newspapers, menu cards, and train tickets in her language teaching, the teacher is utilizing authentic materials. These real-world items provide students with practical, contextual experiences that help bridge the gap between classroom learning and the outside world, enhancing the relevance and application of the language skills being taught.

116. (C): The gender of speakers is not typically an important factor in planning a listening lesson. Key considerations in a listening lesson include the speed of delivery, the clarity of the recording, the accent of the speakers, the complexity of the content, and the number of speakers as these elements directly affect the ability of students to understand and interpret the spoken language.

117. (A): Multilingualism in India requires teachers to understand that communication across multiple languages facilitates social cohesion and integration within diverse communities. Teachers need to recognize the role of language in social interactions and community belonging, rather than merely focusing on linguistic skills.

118. (D): Listening and reading are known as receptive skills in language learning. These skills involve receiving and processing information, as opposed to productive skills like speaking and writing, which involve producing language. Receptive skills are fundamental in language acquisition, as they form the basis for language understanding and interpretation.

119. (D): Listening involves more than just hearing sounds; it includes the ability to recognize those sounds and deduce their meaning within a linguistic and situational context. Effective listening requires integrating known language structures with contextual clues to understand spoken communication fully.

120. (A):

- Communicative Language Teaching (CLT) focuses on enabling learners to communicate effectively and appropriately in social situations. Hence, it aligns with socially acceptable and contextually appropriate language use.
- The Direct method emphasizes teaching grammar inductively, where learners are exposed to the language and deduce the rules through its use.
- Grammar Translation often involves the use of written literary texts as a central component, focusing on translating texts from one language to another.
- West's New Method includes activities like silent reading, aiming to improve language comprehension and fluency through intensive reading exercises.

121. (C): 'निडर' शब्द में प्रयुक्त 'नि' उपसर्ग का अर्थ होता है 'बिना' या 'रहित', जो अभाव को दर्शाता है। इसलिए, 'निडर' का अर्थ होता है 'डर रहित' या 'बिना डर के', जो व्यक्ति की डर के प्रति अनुपस्थिति को दर्शाता है।

122. (D): 'गोधूलि' शब्द का अर्थ है–संध्या का समय, जब सूरज ढलने वाला होता है और आसमान में धूलि की एक परत-सी बन जाती है। इस समय को विशेष रूप से 'गोधूलि' कहा जाता है।

123. (C): 'सिफत' शब्द का अर्थ होता है–किसी चीज या व्यक्ति की विशेषता या गुण। इसका उपयोग उन खासियतों को बताने के लिए होता है जो किसी व्यक्ति या वस्तु में पाई जाती हैं।

124. (C): 'अड़ोस-पड़ोस को देखकर चलना' से अभिप्राय है कि व्यक्ति अपनी जिंदगी दूसरों के हिसाब से जीता है, यानी समाज के अनुसार अपना निर्णय लेता है और दूसरों की राय को महत्व देता है।

125. (B): गद्यांश के अनुसार, साहस ही वह मुख्य गुण है जिसके होने से व्यक्ति के अन्य गुण स्वतः पैदा होते हैं। साहस व्यक्ति को चुनौतियों का सामना करने और जीवन में आगे बढ़ने की प्रेरणा देता है।

126. (A): गद्यांश में जिंदगी के उन पन्नों को पढ़ने की बात कही गई है जो केवल सुखमय न होकर कुछ कठिनाइयों और चुनौतियों से भी भरे हों, जैसे कि अंगारों से लिखे हुए।

127. (D): साहसी व्यक्ति की पहचान यह है कि वह दूसरों के विचारों की परवाह किए बगैर अपना निर्णय लेता है और अपने मार्ग पर आगे बढ़ता है।

128. (B): 'गोधूलि में बसने वाले लोग' से अभिप्राय उन लोगों से है जो जीत और हार के द्वंद्व से परे हैं, जो न तो जीत की खुशी मनाते हैं और न ही हार के गम में डूबते हैं।

129. (B): संगीत में भावनाओं को प्रकट करने का प्रमुख माध्यम 'स्वर और लय' होते हैं। इसमें स्वर से तात्पर्य संगीत की ध्वनि से है और लय से तात्पर्य संगीत में नियमितता और गति से है। ये दोनों ही तत्व संगीत में भावनाओं को व्यक्त करने के लिए अत्यंत महत्वपूर्ण हैं।

130. (A): 'सर्वोच्च' शब्द का संधि विच्छेद 'सर्व' और 'उच्च' में होता है। यहाँ 'सर्व' का अर्थ होता है 'सभी' और 'उच्च' का अर्थ होता है 'उच्चतम'।

131. (B): संगीत के आनंद की प्राप्ति के लिए 'सुनने की कला' का विकसित होना आवश्यक है। इससे संगीत के हर स्वर और लय की बारीकियों को समझने में मदद मिलती है, जिससे संगीत का सही आनंद उठाया जा सकता है।

132. (D): संगीत हमें इस प्रकार से संस्कारित करता है कि जिससे हमारे मन की अच्छाई उद्वेलित हो। संगीत सुनने से हमारे भीतर के सकारात्मक भावों को बल मिलता है, जो हमें बेहतर इंसान बनाने में मदद करता है।

133. (C): प्रस्तुत गद्यांश में संगीत कला की बात की गई है, जिसमें इसे जीवन की अनमोल धरोहर और सार्वभौमिक कला के रूप में वर्णित किया गया है।

134. (A): संगीत को जीवन की अनमोल धरोहर इसलिए कहा गया है क्योंकि यह आनंद का सृजन करता है। संगीत सुनने से मनुष्य को गहरा सुकून और आनंद प्राप्त होता है, जो जीवन की गुणवत्ता को बढ़ाता है।

135. (D): 'सार्वभौमिक' का अर्थ है—कुछ ऐसा जो संपूर्ण जगत में व्याप्त हो। इस संदर्भ में, संगीत को सार्वभौमिक कला कहा गया है क्योंकि यह सभी संस्कृतियों और समाजों में पाई जाती है और सभी मानव समुदायों द्वारा इसका आनंद लिया जाता है।

136. (D): 'पैडलेट' एक डिजिटल टूल है जो शिंक्षकों और छात्रों को समक्रमिक (सिंक्रोनस) और अतुल्यकालिक (असिंक्रोनस) ऑनलाइन शिक्षण अवसर प्रदान करता है। इसके माध्यम से छात्र विभिन्न समयों पर कार्य कर सकते हैं और उनका जवाब दे सकते हैं, जो शिक्षण को अधिक लचीला और पहुंच योग्य बनाता है।

137. (B): रचनात्मक आकलन के लिए लिखित परीक्षा उपयुक्त नहीं है क्योंकि यह आमतौर पर छात्रों की रचनात्मकता और अभिनव सोच को प्रकट करने में सीमित होती है। रचनात्मक आकलन में प्रोजेक्ट्स, क्लास प्रेजेंटेशन्स और अन्य प्रयोगात्मक तरीके अधिक प्रभावी होते हैं।

138. (A & C): भाषा शिक्षण में प्रतिदिन काम में आने वाली सामग्री का प्रयोग करना 'रीयलिया' के रूप में जाना जाता है, जो वास्तविक वस्तुएं जैसे मेनू कार्ड्स, टिकट्स आदि का उपयोग करता है। इसके साथ ही, यह शिक्षण सामग्री के रूप में भी वर्गीकृत हो सकता है क्योंकि यह शिक्षण-अधिगम प्रक्रिया को सहायता प्रदान करता है।

139. (D): भारत की 'शिक्षा नीति में भाषा' (त्रिभाषा सूत्र) मातृभाषा आधारित बहुभाषावाद को समुन्नत करने के लिए कहती है, जिसमें छात्रों को उनकी मातृभाषा के साथ-साथ अन्य भारतीय भाषाओं और अंतर्राष्ट्रीय भाषाओं की शिक्षा दी जाती है।

140. (D): यह टॉप-डाउन प्रक्रिया के बारे में सही नहीं है क्योंकि इस प्रक्रिया में सुनने वाले अपने पूर्व ज्ञान का प्रयोग करते हुए अनुमान लगाते हैं और संदर्भ से सार्थकता निर्मित करते हैं, प्रत्येक शब्द का विश्लेषण नहीं करते।

141. (C): अंतर्राष्ट्रीय मातृभाषा दिवस हर वर्ष 21 फरवरी को मनाया जाता है। यह दिवस मातृभाषा के महत्व और विविध भाषाओं के संरक्षण के लिए समर्पित है।

142. (A): अगर आप अपने एक सहयोगी को ई-मेल लिख रहे हैं जो आपका मित्र भी है, तो ई-मेल का स्वर अनौपचारिक होना चाहिए। इससे संवाद में एक सहजता और मैत्रीपूर्ण भाव आता है, जो दोस्ताना संबंधों में सामान्य होता है।

143. (A): विद्यार्थियों के अधिगम और समझ में स्पष्टता लाने के लिए समूची शिक्षण अधिगम प्रक्रिया के दौरान किया जाने वाला आकलन 'अधिगम के लिए आकलन' है। इस प्रकार का आकलन शिक्षण प्रक्रिया के साथ-साथ निरंतर चलता है और अधिगम प्रक्रिया को गहराई से समझने में सहायक होता है।

144. (B & C): द्वितीय भाषा की कक्षा में ऑडियो रिकॉर्डिंग सुनाने और उसके बाद वर्कशीट बाँटने का उद्देश्य यह है कि विद्यार्थियों को कक्षा की गतिविधियों में सक्रिय रूप से भाग लेने के लिए प्रेरित किया जाए और उन्हें सुनी गई सामग्री से विचार बिन्दुओं को समझने और उनका विश्लेषण करने का अवसर प्रदान किया जाए।

145. (A): गलतियाँ भाषा अधिगम प्रक्रिया में अवरोध पैदा करती हैं। यह कथन सही नहीं है क्योंकि गलतियाँ वास्तव में भाषा अधिगम की प्रक्रिया में सहायक होती हैं। गलतियाँ करने से विद्यार्थी अपनी त्रुटियों को समझते हैं और सीखने में सुधार करते हैं।

146. (A): भाषा शिक्षा में रचनात्मकता उन गतिविधियों और कार्यों को कहते हैं जो छात्रों को विभिन्न तरीकों से सोचने और उत्तर देने की स्वतंत्रता देते हैं। जिसमें खुले अन्त वाले कक्षायी प्रदत्त कार्य जिनकी भिन्न-भिन्न व्याख्याएँ हो सकती हैं और भिन्न-भिन्न उत्तर निकल सकते हैं।

147. (B): यह विचार कि गलतियाँ भाषा अधिगम के दौरान होती हैं और यह दर्शाती हैं कि अधिगम हो रहा है, संज्ञानात्मक दृष्टिकोण से अनुशंसित है। इस दृष्टिकोण में गलतियों को एक अनुकूलनीय और संवर्धनात्मक भाग के रूप में देखा जाता है, जो भाषा अधिगम प्रक्रिया में छात्रों की सक्रिय भागीदारी और स्व-संशोधन के माध्यम से अधिक समझ और क्षमता को विकसित करता है।

148. (C): पठन वैकल्य (डिस्लैक्सिया) पठन विकार है और लेखन वैकल्य (डिस्ग्रैफिया) लेखन विकार है। ये दोनों शिक्षण और अधिगम में विशेष चुनौतियाँ प्रस्तुत करते हैं।

149. (C): रीता द्वारा दृश्य उपकरण और भाषा खेलों का उपयोग छात्रों की रुचि और अभिप्रेरणा बढ़ाने के लिए किया जा रहा है, जो उन्हें अंग्रेजी सीखाने में सहायक होता है और उन्हें शिक्षण प्रक्रिया में सक्रिय रूप से भाग लेने के लिए प्रेरित करता है।

150. (B): एक लघु कथा जिसमें मुख्य पात्र पशु होते हैं और जो नैतिक मूल्यों को उभारते हैं, उसे 'जंतुकथा' या 'फेबल' कहा जाता है। इस प्रकार की कथाएं सामान्यतः नैतिक सबक देने के उद्देश्य से लिखी जाती हैं।

Previous Paper (Solved)

CTET—Paper-II, January 2024

For Mathematics and Science Teachers

(Exam Held on 21-01-2024)

Child Development and Pedagogy

1. According to Vygotsky, what is the role of the teacher in facilitating cognitive development ?

A. To provide information and knowledge to the student.

B. To guide and support the student's learning through scaffolding.

C. To allow the student to learn completely independently.

D. To give only those tasks that the student can currently do independently.

2. Which of the following statements about adolescence is not correct?

A. Adolescence is a social construction.

B. Adolescence is generally considered to begin with puberty - the process that leads to sexual maturity and the ability to reproduce.

C. Adolescence is developmental transition between childhood and adulthood entailing physical, cognitive and psychosocial changes.

D. Children across different cultures usher in and experience adolescence in a similar manner.

3. Sujata participates eagerly in the dance competition only because she is interested in winning the first prize of cash. Sujata is:

A. Intrinsically motivated

B. Extrinsically motivated

C. Mastery-Oriented learner

D. Failure-avoiding learner

4. In order to address the individual differences among learners, a teacher should:

A. acknowledge differences as abnormal and kind of deficit

B. be indifferent towards individual differences

C. consider differences as obvious feature of human diversity

D. implement a rigid and uniform curriculum for all learners

5. Jean Piaget believed that knowledge is :

A. constructed by the child rather than being passed passively from the environment.

B. innate and given rather than acquired through interactions.

C. co-constructed in interactions with more knowledgeable others.

D. a visible behavioural change that can be measured with reliability.

6. In a progressive classroom assessment is :

A. Dynamic B. Objective

C. Summative D. Normative

7. Which of the following process is essential in meaning-making of the information received from environment and store it further in memory?

A. Attention

B. Decay

C. Forgetting

D. Retrieval

8. Which of the following is an example of a question that requires students to analyze information?

A. What is the plot of the novel "To Kill a Mockingbird"?

B. What is the theme of the novel "To Kill a Mockingbird"?

C. How does the author use symbolism in "To Kill a Mockingbird"?

D. Who is the protagonist of "To Kill a Mockingbird"?

1. B	**2.** D	**3.** B	**4.** C	**5.** A	**6.** A	**7.** A	**8.** C

9. Assertion (A): Teachers should constantly reflect on their own stereotypes and bias.

Reason (R): Culturally responsive teaching means that teachers are reflective.

Choose the correct option:

A. Both (A) and (R) are true and (R) is the correct explanation of (A).
B. Both (A) and (R) are true, but (R) is not the correct explanation of (A).
C. (A) is true, but (R) is false.
D. Both (A) and (R) are false.

10. The central argument of Carol Gilligan's critique of Kohlberg's theory of moral development is around:

A. Ethics of care and the feminist perspective.
B. Overestimation of children's moral abilities.
C. Use of experimental design in studying children.
D. Educational implications of the study for school going children.

11. Assertion (A): Learning from real-life problems and concrete experiences gives the children multiple pathways for learning and retrieving information.

Reason (R): Development is relatively orderly and sequential.

Choose the correct option:

A. Both (A) and (R) are true and (R) is the correct explanation of (A).
B. Both (A) and (R) are true, but (R) is not the correct explanation of (A).
C. (A) is true, but (R) is false.
D. Both (A) and (R) are false.

12. Dyslexia is a ________ condition which impacts learner's ability to ________.

A. emotional, draw pictures
B. neurological, link sounds with symbols
C. physiological, socialize with peers
D. sensory, coordinate body movements

13. A middle school teacher wants to enable meaningful learning by helping students make connections between concepts and real-world applications. Which of the following activities would be an appropriate pedagogical strategy?

A. Let the students memorize terms and definitions.
B. Let the students complete worksheets with multiple choice questions.
C. Let the students learn by the method of stimulus-response conditioning.
D. Let the students research on a current issue in small groups and present their findings to the class.

14. In which stage of Kohlberg's moral development do children's reasoning revolve around ethics of law?

A. Pre-conventional morality
B. Conventional morality
C. Heteronomous morality
D. Autonomous morality

15. Which of the following does not exemplify an inclusive classroom?

A. Incorporation of diverse perspectives
B. Following reasonable accommodation
C. Offering differentiated instruction
D. Encouraging competitive ethos

16. Work in progress Portfolios are an effective tool for formative assessment because :

(*a*) They involve students in the process of assessment.
(*b*) They offer insights about the progress of individual students.
(*c*) They focus mainly in the presentation of the final product.
(*d*) They offer tangible evidence of student learning.

A. (*b*), (*c*) B. (*a*), (*d*)
C. (*a*), (*b*), (*c*) D. (*a*), (*b*), (*d*)

17. Which of the following describes a mastery goal orientation?

A. focus on achieving a certain level of performance for competing with others.
B. focus on improving ones' skills and understanding of a task.
C. focus on achieving a high grade for receiving external rewards.
D. focus on avoiding failure or punishment for fear of humiliation.

18. Which of the following best describes the role of the teacher in progressive education?

A. The teacher is the primary source of knowledge and authority in the classroom.
B. The teacher provides diverse materials for children to experiment and provides scaffolding as and when required.
C. The teacher is responsible for ensuring strict adherence to curriculum standards.
D. The teacher lets the children learn independently and does not interfere in their learning.

9. A	**10.** A	**11.** B	**12.** B	**13.** D	**14.** B	**15.** D	**16.** D	**17.** B	**18.** B

19. Asking Critical questions such as "how much and in what ways are various gender represented in textbooks and media" would encourage:
A. Questioning gender stereotypes
B. Strengthening gender constancy
C. Reinforcing gender identity
D. Discouraging gender role flexibility

20. According to Jean Piaget the ability to use symbols for symbols such as letting the letter X stand for an unknown numeral develops during ________ and enables the children to learn ________.
A. concrete operational stage; algebra and calculus
B. concrete operational stage; conservation and seriation
C. formal operational stage; algebra and calculus
D. formal operational stage; conservation and seriation

21. Alok shows the following behaviours : Holds head in an awkward position when reading; squinting and rubbing the eye frequently; redness/swelling of eyes; confusing letters. These can be symptoms of potential:
A. Visual problems
B. Language comprehension problems
C. Autistic spectrum disorder
D. Communication disorder

22. **Assertion (A):** In an inclusive classroom, adaptations should be made in learning goals, pedagogical strategies as well as assessment.

Reason (R): The philosophy of inclusion advocates elimination of all individual differences through pedagogical approaches and assessment.

Choose the correct option:
A. Both (A) and (R) are true and (R) is the correct explanation of (A).
B. Both (A) and (R) are true, but (R) is not the correct explanation of (A).
C. (A) is true, but (R) is false.
D. Both (A) and (R) are false.

23. According to Lev-Vygotsky children benefit from the experience of interacting with ________ while working ______ their zone of proximal development.
A. more knowledgeable others; within
B. more knowledgeable others; just outside
C. the physical environment; within
D. the physical environment; just outside

24. A teacher notices that one of her students is highly distractible and has trouble paying attention during class. Which of the following strategies would is an effective strategy in helping the student stay focused?
A. Giving the student repeated tasks to do during class.
B. Strictly telling the student to increase their attention span.
C. Giving a timer to student for self-regulation and time-management.
D. Calling the parents and taking strict disciplinary action against the student.

25. **Assertion (A):** Students are more likely to do well and stay in school if they have emotional attachment to their school and believe that they matter.

Reason (R): Emotions play a significant role in learning.

Choose the correct option:
A. Both (A) and (R) are true and (R) is the correct explanation of (A)
B. Both (A) and (R) are true, but (R) is not the correct explanation of (A)
C. (A) is true, but (R) is false
D. Both (A) and (R) are false

26. Which of the following is a core principle of constructivist learning theory?
A. Teachers should provide direct instruction and explicit guidance to students.
B. Learning occurs when students receive correct answers and feedback from teachers.
C. Students construct their own knowledge through active engagement with their environment.
D. Learning is primarily a passive process that involves receiving and memorizing information.

27. **Assertion (A):** The less able a child is to do a task the more directions the teachers should give and as the child can do more and more the teacher should help less and less.

Reason (R): Intelligence cannot be accurately measured by calculating IQ.

Choose the correct option:
A. Both (A) and (R) are true and (R) is the correct explanation of (A).
B. Both (A) and (R) are true, but (R) is not the correct explanation of (A).
C. (A) is true, but (R) is false.
D. Both (A) and (R) are false.

19. A	20. C	21. A	22. C	23. A	24. C	25. A	26. C	27. B

28. Which of the following characterise the process of socialization?
(*a*) It is a linear process.
(*b*) It is a complex process.
(*c*) It is a multidimensional process.
(*d*) It takes place uniquely in different cultures.
A. (*a*), (*b*)
B. (*b*), (*c*)
C. (*b*), (*c*), (*d*)
D. (*a*), (*b*), (*c*), (*d*)

29. **Assertion (A):** There is no objectively definable moment when a child enters middle childhood or adolescence.

Reason (R): Development is continuous in nature.

Choose the correct option:
A. Both (A) and (R) are true and (R) is the correct explanation of (A).
B. Both (A) and (R) are true, but (R) is not the correct explanation of (A).
C. (A) is true, but (R) is false.
D. Both (A) and (R) are false.

30. An elementary school teacher can strongly influence students' development of academic self-concept by:
A. Keeping very low expectations from all students
B. Punishing autonomy and initiative in students
C. Rewarding autonomy and initiative in students
D. Keeping very low expectations from special students

Mathematics and Science

31. BD is the diagonal of parallelogram ABCD such that $\angle CBD = 12x$, $\angle ABD = 7y$, $\angle ADB = 60°$ and $\angle CDB = 28°$. Then, the value of $2x + 3y$ is:
A. 20° B. 21°
C. 22° D. 23°

32. A student listed the following properties of Rational Numbers. Which one/ones is/are correct?
(*a*) A rational number includes integers.
(*b*) 0 (zero) is not a rational number.
(*c*) All fractions are rational numbers.

Choose the correct options:
A. (*a*) and (*c*) B. Only (*b*)
C. Only (*c*) D. (*a*) and (*b*)

33. One of the factors of $p^3x + p^2(x - y) - p(y + z) - z$ is :
A. $p^2x - py + z$
B. $p^2x + py + z$
C. $p^2x - py - z$
D. $p^2x + py - z$

34. If the median of the data 30, 8, 7, 3, 17, 15, 21, 24, 29, 23 is x and the median of the data obtained by replacing 3 by 33 and 8 by 18 in the above data is y, then what is the difference between y and x?
A. 1 B. 2
C. 3 D. 4

35. Three numbers are in the ratio 2 : 3 : 4 and the sum of their cubes is 33957. What is the sum of the three numbers?
A. 54 B. 63
C. 72 D. 81

36. The number of vertices (V), edges (E) and faces (F) of a polyhedron are respectively 10, 15 and x. Then, the value of $(3x - 12)$ is:
A. 7 B. 9
C. 14 D. 18

37. If $\frac{x}{y} = \left(\frac{-1}{3}\right)^{-3} \div \left(\frac{2}{3}\right)^{-4}$, then what is the value of $\left(\frac{x}{y} + \frac{y}{x}\right)^{-1}$?
A. $-\frac{3}{16}$ B. $\frac{19}{48}$
C. $\frac{38}{73}$ D. $-\frac{48}{265}$

38. Concept was labelled as 'Schema' by:
A. Vygotsky B. Piaget
C. Bruner D. Van Hieles

39. If $x = 1.011 + 10.11 - 12.101 + 0\ 1011$, then what should be added to x to get the sum as 1.1?
A. 1.9789 B. 0.3111
C. 0.2211 D. 1.1311

28. C	29. A	30. C	31. C	32. A	33. C
34. C	35. B	36. B	37. D	38. B	39. A

40. Teacher conducted an oral assessment in class and found that Ram can speak definition of all types of numbers - odd, even, prime and composite accurately, but not able to identify the numbers accurately when given a set of numbers.

Which of the following is most appropriate for the above situation?

A. Ram has good memory but lacks practice.
B. Ram has good memory but lacks concentration.
C. Ram has good memory but lacks conceptual understanding.
D. Ram has analytical ability.

41. A shopkeeper sells an article for ₹324 after giving a discount of 28% on its marked price. The cost price of the article is ₹300. If he sells the article by giving 18% discount on its same marked price, then what will be his profit percent?

A. 10% B. 19%
C. 23% D. 24%

42. The product of two rational numbers is $-\frac{40}{3}$. If one of the two numbers is $-\frac{5}{2}$, then the reciprocal of the other number lies between:

A. $\frac{3}{20}$ and $\frac{9}{50}$ B. $\frac{9}{50}$ and $\frac{1}{5}$

C. $\frac{1}{5}$ and $\frac{1}{4}$ D. $\frac{1}{4}$ and $\frac{1}{3}$

43. A class VI mathematics teacher posed the following problem to her students :

"In a morning walk, three persons started together. Their steps measure 70 cm, 85 cm and 95 cm respectively. What is the minimum distance each should walk so that all can cover the same distance in complete steps?"

Which of the following concepts would be required to solve the given problem?

A. Concept of HCF
B. Concept of LCM
C. Concept of division
D. Concept of proportion

44. A student was given the following problem on percentage to solve, "Find the percentage of decrease if the population of a city decreased from 28,000 to 26,500." She wrote the following solution,

Original population = 28,000;

New population = 26,500

$$\% \text{ decrease} = \frac{26500}{28000} \times 100\% = 94.6\%$$

Which of the following is most appropriate with respect to the response of the student?

A. Student is able to understand the concept of percentage but is not able to understand percentage of which quantity is to be found.
B. Student has solved the question correctly but has used wrong symbols in solution.
C. Student does not know the concept of percentage.
D. Student has made a careless mistake.

45. The difference between two supplementary angles is 20°. If the smaller of these angles is p, then the value of $3p - 50°$ is:

A. 310° B. 270°
C. 250° D. 190°

46. x varies inversely as y. When $x = 3.5$, then $y = 2.4$. What is the value of y when $x = 5.6$?

A. 1.4 B. 1.5
C. 2.1 D. 2.8

47. Which among the following Learning-Teaching Resources (LTRs) are most appropriate for visually challenged students in mathematics classroom?

(*a*) Geogebra
(*b*) Taylor's abacus
(*c*) Computer
(*d*) Spreadsheet

Choose the correct options:

A. (*a*) and (*b*) B. (*c*) and (*d*)
C. (*b*) and (*c*) D. (*b*), (*c*) and (*d*)

48. National Education Policy (NEP) 2020 recommends that Sports Integrated Pedagogy needs to be used in classroom teaching. Which among the following are correct in the context of using sports integrated pedagogy in mathematics classroom?

(*a*) Teaching-learning process shall become joyful.
(*b*) It is not possible to use sports for teaching mathematics.
(*c*) It will be time consuming and hence needs to be avoided.
(*d*) Apart from popular sports, there are many indigenous sports which can be used in teaching mathematics.

Choose the correct options:

A. (*a*) and (*c*) B. (*b*) and (*c*)
C. (*a*) and (*d*) D. (*b*), (*c*) and (*d*)

40. C	**41.** C	**42.** B	**43.** B	**44.** A	**45.** D	**46.** B	**47.** C	**48.** C

49. The area of the curved surface of a right circular cylinder is 4400 cm^2 and the circumference of its base is 110 cm. Its volume (in m^3) is:

$\left(\text{Use } \pi = \frac{22}{7}\right)$

A. 0.0284 B. 0.0385
C. 0.0285 D. 0.0382

50. A box opened at the top is made of wood of thickness 3 cm. Its external length, breadth and height are respectively 1.48 m, 1.16 m and 83 cm (base = length × breadth). What will be the cost of painting its inner surface at ₹150 per m^2?

A. ₹838.20 B. ₹839.10
C. ₹841.40 D. ₹842.50

51. In triangles ABC and DEF; ∠B = 90°, BC = 8 cm, ∠A = 40°, DE = 8 cm, ∠F = 40° and ∠E = 90°. Then, which of the following statements is true?

A. ΔABC ≅ ΔDEF, by RHS
B. ΔABC ≅ ΔFED, by RHS
C. ΔABC ≅ ΔDFE, by AAS
D. ΔABC ≅ ΔFED, by AAS

52. Three consecutive integers are such that when they are taken in increasing order and multiplied by 3, 5 and 2, respectively, they add up to 99. What is the sum of the original first and third integers?

A. 16 B. 18
C. 20 D. 24

53. A middle school mathematics teacher poses the following question to her class.

"Which type of graph would you use to show the following data?
(*a*) The heights of participants in an athletics meet
(*b*) The number of passengers boarding trains from 9:00 am to 9:00 pm at a station."

The intention of the teacher is to:

A. Help learners understand the difference between bar graph and line graph.
B. Introduce the concept of pie charts.
C. Teach line graph through contextual situations.
D. Teach the use of histograms for data representation.

54. If a 8-digit number 9 4 7 1 x 9 y 2 is divisible by 72, then which of the following statements is not true?

A. x = 8 and y = 5 B. x = 4 and y = 9
C. x = 9 and y = 5 D. x = 3 and y = 1

55. Mathematics is a way of thinking since:

(*a*) It provides an opportunity for students to engage in proofs and examining patterns.
(*b*) Students reproduce formulae and symbols during problem solving.
(*c*) Students use appropriate strategies for solving various new problems.

Choose the correct option:

A. (*a*) and (*b*) B. (*b*) and (*c*)
C. (*a*) and (*c*) D. Only (*b*)

56. The following table shows the number of different fruits kept in a carton :

Type of fruits	Mangoes	Apples	Oranges	Guavas	Pomegranates
Number	44	56	42	30	38

If a pie chart is constructed for the above data, what will be the angle of the sector representing apples?

A. 79.2° B. 72°
C. 96° D. 100.8°

57. The lengths of the parallel sides of a trapezium are 11 cm and 25 cm and the distance between them is 12 cm. Its area is equal to the area of a rectangle whose sides are in the ratio 3 : 2. What is the perimeter (in cm) of the rectangle?

A. 40 B. 50
C. 60 D. 70

58. If A = $-2x^2 + 12x$, B = $11 - 8x + 3x^2$, C = $17 - 4x^2$ and D = $x^2 - x - 3$, then what is the sum of the co-efficients of x^2 and x in (A + B + C − D)?

A. 0 B. −1
C. 1 D. 3

59. Which of the following is not a dimension of assessment of mathematics learning?

A. Communication
B. Patterns and procedures
C. Disposition towards mathematics
D. Mathematical reasoning

60. In triangle PQR, ∠P = 55° and QR = 18 cm. In which of the following cases, ΔPQR can be an obtuse scalene triangle?

A. ∠R = 25° and PQ = 18 cm
B. ∠R = 15° and PR > 18 cm
C. ∠R = 65° and PQ > 18 cm
D. ∠R = 35° and PR = 18 cm

49. B	**50.** B	**51.** D	**52.** C	**53.** D	**54.** C
55. C	**56.** C	**57.** C	**58.** C	**59.** C	**60.** B

61. Read the following paragraph carefully and select the option which would correctly fill the blanks in the given order.

Sound is produced by vibration and different musical instruments have specific vibrating parts. In a __X__ the sound is produced by stretched strings, in a __Y__ it is the stretched membrane that vibrates and in a __Z__ the vibrating part that produces sound is the air column.

X, Y and Z can respectively be:

A. sitar, harmonium, dholak
B. dholak, ektara, mouth organ
C. guitar, tabla, shehnai
D. ektara, violin, piano

62. Identify the set of micronutrients (nutrients required by plants in small quantities):

A. Potassium, Magnesium, Copper
B. Copper, Phosphorous, Calcium
C. Sulphur, Aluminium, Chlorine
D. Zinc, Iron, Manganese

63. Read the following statements carefully and select the correct option.

Assertion (A) : The stars in the night sky appear to move from east to west.

Reason (R) : The earth rotates from west to east.

A. (A) and (R) are both correct and (R) is the correct explanation for (A)
B. (A) and (R) are both correct but (R) is not the correct explanation for (A)
C. (A) is correct but (R) is incorrect
D. (A) and (R) are both incorrect

64. Which of the following statements regarding rusting of iron are true?

(*a*) It involves a chemical reaction between iron and oxygen.
(*b*) It is an exothermic reaction.
(*c*) It can take place at room temperature.
(*d*) It is reversible reaction.

A. (*a*), (*b*), (*d*) B. (*b*) and (*c*)
C. (*a*) and (*d*) D. (*a*), (*b*) and (*c*)

65. Match the substances in column A with their chemical names in column B.

(A)	(B)
(*a*) Slaked lime	(*i*) Calcium oxide
(*b*) Table salt	(*ii*) Sodium bicarbonate
(*c*) Limestone	(*iii*) Calcium carbonate
(*d*) Caustic soda	(*iv*) Calcium hydroxide
(*e*) Quick lime	(*v*) Sodium hydroxide
(*f*) Baking soda	(*vi*) Sodium chloride

	(*a*)	(*b*)	(*c*)	(*d*)	(*e*)	(*f*)
A.	(*iv*)	(*vi*)	(*iii*)	(*v*)	(*i*)	(*ii*)
B.	(*vi*)	(*ii*)	(*v*)	(*i*)	(*iii*)	(*iv*)
C.	(*i*)	(*vi*)	(*iii*)	(*v*)	(*ii*)	(*iv*)
D.	(*iv*)	(*v*)	(*iii*)	(*ii*)	(*i*)	(*iv*)

66. Identify the correct statement(s) :

(*a*) : A fact is an observation that has repeatedly been found to be true over the time.
(*b*) : A law is a theory that has repeatedly been found to be true over the time.

A. Only (*a*) B. (*a*) and (*b*)
C. Only (*b*) D. Neither (*a*) nor (*b*)

67. Read the following text :

When a negatively charged rod is brought near an uncharged electroscope,

(*a*) the electroscope leaves move further apart
(*b*) both the electroscope leaves acquire similar charge
(*c*) the negative charges pass on to the electroscope causing its leaves to move further apart

Of the above three statements:

A. (*a*) is an observation while (*b*) and (*c*) are inferences
B. (*a*) and (*b*) are observations and (*c*) is an inference
C. (*a*), (*b*) and (*c*) are observations
D. (*a*), (*b*) and (*c*) are inferences

68. Which of the following gases are responsible for acid rain?

(*a*) Nitrogen (*b*) Oxygen
(*c*) Ozone (*d*) Sulphur dioxide
(*e*) Nitric oxide

A. (*a*) and (*b*) B. (*b*) and (*c*)
C. (*c*) and (*d*) D. (*d*) and (*e*)

69. Which of the following is NOT indicative of the hypothesising skill?

A. Formulating questions which lead to inquiry
B. Attempting to explain observations or relationships in terms of some principle
C. Using the senses to gather information
D. Identifying variables for an experiment

70. Identify the correct statements from the following:

(*a*) Generally non-metals do not react with water.
(*b*) Generally non-metals do not react with acids.

Choose the correct option:

A. Only (*a*) B. Only (*b*)
C. Both (*a*) and (*b*) D. Neither (*a*) nor (*b*)

61. C **62.** D **63.** A **64.** D **65.** A **66.** A **67.** A **68.** D **69.** C **70.** C

71. A ball is thrown up in the air. It reaches a maximum height and then returns to the thrower.

Which of the following quantities have the same values during the upward and downward motion of the ball?

A. Acceleration B. Force of gravity
C. Displacement D. Work done by gravity

72. A body has a linear momentum of p and a mass of m. The kinetic energy of the body is :

A. p^2m B. $2p^2m$
C. $\frac{p^2}{2m}$ D. pm

73. Which of the following is the most suitable strategy for introducing the students to the concept of 'chemical reactions' at upper primary level?

A. Explain the concept of valence electrons and electronic configuration
B. Write the chemical equations in symbolic form and ask students to observe
C. Define a chemical reaction and give examples
D. Hold a discussion on chemical reactions which students are likely to have observed in their lives

74. Which of the following is a set of animals in which all show external fertilization?

A. Hens, lizards, butterflies
B. Lizards, butterflies, frogs
C. Butterflies, frogs, fish
D. Frogs, fish, starfish

75. Consider the test item given below and match the following:

Column-A	**Column-B**
Unit of force	Joule
Symbol of iron	HCl
Formula of hydrochloric acid	Ag
Unit of work	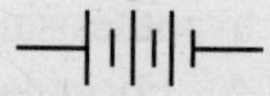
Symbol of silver	Calorie
Symbol of battery	Fe
	Newton

Which of the following is not a reason that can be given to justify that the item is poorly constructed?

A. For an entry in column A there are at the most two plausible entries in column B
B. There are unequal entries in column A and B
C. The matching pairs can be easily guessed
D. There is inconsistency among entries

76. Read the following statements and select the correct option.

Assertion (A): Dried raisins when left in plain water for some time swell due to osmosis.

Reason (R): Plant cells have a selectively permeable cell membrane.

A. (A) and (R) are both correct and (R) is the correct explanation for (A)
B. (A) and (R) are both correct but (R) is not the correct explanation for (A)
C. (A) is correct but (R) is incorrect
D. (A) is incorrect but (R) is correct

77. Which of the following would be a most suitable strategy to introduce the topic 'deficiency diseases' at upper primary level?

A. Provide a definition of balanced diet and introduce the concept of deficiency
B. Arrange for a doctor's prescription pertaining to a deficiency disease and hold a discussion around it
C. List the various nutrients and the functions they perform in human body
D. Hold a discussion on common human diseases

78. Which of the following best explains the statement 'science promotes scepticism'?

A. Scientists judge the validity of a claim based on objective empirical evidence
B. Science is purely inductive in nature
C. Scientists do not trust the findings of other scientists
D. Scientists are open-minded and willing to modify their ideas

79. A box of mass 500 gm is lying on a horizontal table. Which of the following statements is true regarding the force(s) acting on it? [g = 10 m/s^2]

A. No force acts on it
B. An unbalanced force of 5 N acts on it in downward direction
C. A pair of balanced forces acts on it
D. An unbalanced force of 5 N acts on it in the upward direction

80. __X__ is a device which is used to see around corners and is based on the principle of __Y__. X and Y respectively are:

A. Telescope, reflection
B. Kaleidoscope, refraction
C. Periscope, reflection
D. Periscope, dispersion

71. A,B	**72.** C	**73.** D	**74.** D	**75.** B	**76.** A	**77.** B	**78.** A	**79.** C	**80.** C

81. X and Y are thick, black liquids which can be used for metalling the roads. X is derived from petroleum and Y is derived from coal. Which of the following can X and Y respectively be?

A. Bitumen, Coal Tar B. Coal Tar, Charcoal
C. Charcoal, Bitumen D. Coal Tar, Bitumen

82. Which of the following is not desirable with respect to carrying out of a classroom demonstration by a teacher?

A. Rehearse the demonstration before carrying it out in class
B. Emphasise beforehand the linkages that students are required to make
C. Supplement the demonstration with explanations
D. Follow up the demonstration with discussion

83. Which of the following statement(s) is correct?

A. Fertilisers are richer in specific nutrients as compared to manure
B. Fertilisers enhance the water holding capacity of the soil
C. Fertilisers provide a lot of humus to the soil
D. Fertilisers increase the number of friendly microbes in soil

84. Find the set that correctly matches the plants in column A with the mode of asexual reproduction which they exhibit:

Column-A	Column-B
(*a*) Rose	(*i*) Budding
(*b*) Yeast	(*ii*) Spore formation
(*c*) Ferns	(*iii*) Fragmentation
(*d*) Spirogyra	(*iv*) Pollination
	(*v*) Vegetative propagation

	(*a*)	(*b*)	(*c*)	(*d*)
A.	(*v*)	(*i*)	(*ii*)	(*iv*)
B.	(*iv*)	(*i*)	(*v*)	(*iii*)
C.	(*v*)	(*iii*)	(*ii*)	(*ii*)
D.	(*iv*)	(*iii*)	(*i*)	(*ii*)

85. Which of the following plant disease(s) are caused by bacteria?

(*a*) Rust of wheat
(*b*) Citrus tanker
(*c*) Yellow vein mosaic of bhindi

A. (*a*) and (*b*) B. Only (*b*)
C. (*b*) and (*c*) D. Only (*c*)

86. The difference between maximum and minimum resistance that can be obtained by connecting three resistances of $\frac{1}{3}\Omega$ each is:

A. $\frac{2}{3}\Omega$ B. $\frac{8}{9}\Omega$
C. $1\ \Omega$ D. $\frac{1}{9}\Omega$

87. A teacher, while teaching the chapter 'Body Movements' to class VI students shows the following images to her students :

A sailing boat, swimming fish and a flying aeroplane. She then asks the students to reflect on the shape of the images and the manner of movement. Which of the following are likely to be employed by students in answering?

(*a*) Classifying
(*b*) Observing
(*c*) Inductive reasoning
(*d*) Measuring

A. (*a*) and (*b*)
B. (*b*) and (*c*)
C. (*c*) and (*d*)
D. (*a*) and (*d*)

88. Seed dispersal may be said to help the plants in all of the following except :

A. over crowding
B. avoid competition for sunlight, water and minerals
C. invade new habitats
D. produce new varieties

89. Which of the following is the most suitable reason behind Newtons theory of gravitation being regarded as an excellent theory?

A. It explains larger number of observations by making fewer assumptions
B. It has been arrived at after thorough experimentation
C. It has been formulated using the precise language of mathematics
D. It has been developed over a long period of time

90. Read the following statements carefully and select the correct option.

S1 : Rayon is a synthetic fibre.
S2 : Rayon is made without using any natural raw material.

A. Both S1 and S2 are true
B. S1 is true and S2 is false
C. S1 is false and S2 is true
D. Both S1 and S2 are false

81. A	82. B	83. A	84. A	85. B	86. B	87. B	88. A	89. A	90. B

Language-I—English

Directions (Q.No. 91-99): *Read the given passage and answer the questions that follow.*

1. We were walking across the garden when my daughter spotted a cluster of familiar red flowers. She pulled me to one side and then, looking excitedly at me as though she had a secret to share, she pulled me down to her height and whispered in my ears. I shot up straight almost as soon as she had finished her sentence. With my mouth ajar, I was about to tell her that it was probably not a good idea to do so when I was transported to the time when I was around her age.

2. It had been a rather long day from school and I was dead tired. I was walking along the pathway that was lined with many ixora plants when my friend grabbed me by the arm. Before I could do anything, he gleefully plucked a single flower from the cluster and showed it to me. Unimpressed, I was not about to be swayed by a puny flower and was about to admonish him when he turned the flower upside down to show me a tiny almost invisible thread-like thing that protruded out from its stalk.

3. He pulled the faint yellowish thread and right at the end of it, a tiny drop of nectar appeared. At least, that was what I think it was, as it was really quite sweet. That day we raided the ixora plants. We really had a lot of fun. I could still taste the sweetness till today. My daughter's urgent tug brought me back to reality. I turned to my daughter and decided that she too needed to know the joy of tasting sweet nectar from beautiful blooms.

91. Identify the parts of speech of the underlined words.

I was transported to the <u>time</u> when I was <u>around</u> her age.

A. noun, verb B. adjective, preposition
C. noun, preposition D. noun, adverb

92. From the given anecdote, one can assume that the 2 characters shared the relationship of:

A. best friends
B. mother and daughter
C. school-mates
D. grandmother and grand-child

93. 'to be transported in time' means ________.

A. travel backwards
B. to indulge in time travel
C. recollect memories of the past
D. to take future decisions

94. 'I was about to <u>admonish</u> him ....'.

The underlined word can be replaced by the word:

A. appreciate B. reprimand
C. refuse D. cajole

95. Complete the word analogy :

cluster : bunch :: puny : ?

A. delicate B. colourful
C. prickly D. long-stalked

96. In para 1, according to the mother it was not a good idea to:

A. taste sweet nectar from flowers
B. raid the ixora plants
C. walk in the garden the whole day long
D. walk along the pathway alone

97. 'To be dead tired' does not mean:

A. to feel too tired to walk
B. to be exhausted
C. to be completely exhausted
D. to feel refreshed

98. Read the following sentences:

Assertion (A): The child was excited to share a secret with her mother.

Reason (R): The mother was in disbelief and went down memory lane.

A. (A) is correct, but (R) is incorrect
B. Both (A) and (R) are correct
C. Both (A) and (R) are true, but (R) is not the correct explanation of (A)
D. Both (A) and (R) are true and (R) is the correct explanation of (A)

99. Read the following sentences:

(*a*) The writer is traumatised by the memories of her childhood.
(*b*) The daughter's secret brings back nostalgic memories of the school days.
(*c*) The writer wants her child to be connected to the sweet pleasures of nature.

A. (*a*) and (*c*) are correct, (*b*) is incorrect
B. (*b*) and (*c*) are incorrect, (*a*) is correct
C. (*a*) and (*b*) are correct, (*c*) is incorrect
D. (*b*) and (*c*) are correct, (*a*) is incorrect

91. C	**92.** B	**93.** C	**94.** B	**95.** A	**96.** A	**97.** D	**98.** D	**99.** D

Directions (Q.No. 100-105): *Read the given extract and answer the questions that follow.*

My tea is nearly ready and the sun has left the sky;
Its time to take the window to see Leerie going by;
For every night at tea time and before you take your seat,
With lantern and with ladder he comes posting up the street.

Now Tom would be a driver and Maria may go to the sea;
And my papa's a banker and as rich as he can be;
But I, when I'm stronger and choose what I'm to do,
O Leerie, I'll go around at night and light the lamps
with you

For we are very lucky, with a lamp before the door;
And Leerie stops to light it as he lights so many more;
And O ! Before you hurry by with ladder and with light,
O Leerie, see a little child and nod to him tonight!

100. Why does the poet consider himself to be fortunate?
A. He has a rich banker father.
B. He doesn't have to light other peoples' doors.
C. He has light at night by his door.
D. He is strong and doesn't have to make a choice in life.

101. The phrase, 'the sun has left the sky' indicates that:
A. it is morning B. it is forenoon
C. it is afternoon D. it is evening time

102. Read the following sentences:
(*a*) The poet occasionally has a light outside his door.
(*b*) The poet wants to be a banker like his father when he grows up.
(*c*) The poet is fascinated by the lamp lighter's profession.
A. (*a*) and (*c*) are correct, (*b*) is incorrect
B. (*b*) and (*c*) are correct, (*a*) is incorrect
C. (*a*) and (*b*) are incorrect, (*c*) is correct
D. (*a*) and (*b*) are correct, (*c*) is incorrect

103. With reference to the poem, complete the word analogy :

Leerie : lamplighter :: father : ?
A. rich businessman B. driver
C. sailor D. banker

104. Identify the rhyme scheme in lines 5 - 8.
A. abba B. aabb
C. abab D. aaba

105. The poet looks at the lamp-lighter's profession with:
A. wonder B. jealousy
C. curiosity D. confusion

106. Malayalam spoken by a particular community in Kozhikodi is slightly different from the Malayalam spoken by others in the same place. What is the Malayalam spoken by the particular community known as?
A. Two varieties of Malayalam
B. Regional dialect of Malayalam
C. Social dialect of Malayalam
D. They are two different languages

107. Following learning task was given to learners in different groups. Find out what is this vocabulary learning activity known as.

Find words and phrases which relate to the following words.

(Family) (Relationship) (Feeling)

A. Thematic Vocabulary
B. Word clusters
C. Cluster Vocabulary
D. Word Web

108. The language we use for day-to-day, face-to-face interaction is known as:
A. Cognitive Academic Language Proficiency (CALP)
B. Basic Interpersonal Communication Skills (BICS)
C. Communicative language skills
D. Interpersonal language proficiency

109. A teacher at the secondary stage gives a text/short story and asks them to read and discuss the meaning and ideas of the text from the point of view of power and justice. What does the teacher attempt to develop in the learners?
A. Critical literacy skills
B. Critical pedagogy
C. Critical language development
D. Higher order language skills

110. Procedural knowledge in the teaching-learning grammar is _________.
A. knowing how to do the grammatical item.
B. knowledge about the grammatical item.
C. knowing the rules of the grammatical item.
D. knowing the language and its culture.

100. C	101. D	102. C	103. D	104. B	105. A	106. C	107. A	108. B	109. A	110. A

111. A teacher of Class VII conducts a pair work activity in which the pairs are given a story of ten sentences. One in the pair reads out the first sentences and the other in the pair writes that sentence. Then other in the pair read out second sentence and the first in the pair writes the second sentence. Likewise the pairs complete the whole story. Later they compare their writing with the original text given to them. What is this activity known as?

A. Mutual Writing B. Mutual Listening
C. Sentence Dictation D. Mutual Dictation

112. Which of the following is NOT true of Sign Language?

A. Sign language has many varieties.
B. Sign language is a natural language.
C. Sign language does not have a grammar.
D. Sign language has a grammar.

113. Which one of the following is true of the three language formula?

A. Mother tongue/home language/regional language as the first language.
B. English/Hindi/home language/local language as the first language.
C. Mother tongue/home language/Hindi as the first language.
D. Mother tongue/home language/English as the first language.

114. Remedial teaching is for:

A. learners who need attention on certain aspects of language learning.
B. teachers who need to modify their teaching for certain student to learn the language.
C. learners and teachers to understand and modify/improve their teaching/learning strategies.
D. learners and teachers to enhance the scores in the examination in language paper

115. A method of teaching in which a teacher and four students form a collaborative learning group with different roles. Dialogues occur on the content of the text passage, which creates a zone of proximal development in which reading comprehension improves. This method is referred to as :

A. Grammar Translation Method
B. Reciprocal Teaching
C. Structural Approach
D. Model Reading

116. A language teacher tells a story in English and asks learners to work in group to tell the story in the languages known to them and then in the common language of the classroom. What is this pedagogical strategy known as?

A. Translanguaging
B. Multilingual policy
C. Multilanguage teaching
D. Language acquisition

117. A learner reads through the news item in the newspaper to know specific information. This reading is known as __________.

A. Critical reading B. Skimming
C. Scanning D. Study skill

118. What is 'interlingual identification'?

A. Learner's judgment that something in the native language and something in the target language are similar.
B. Learner's judgment that something in the native language and something in the target language are dissimilar.
C. Learner's judgment that the knowledge of the native language interferes in the learning of second language.
D. Learner's understanding that learning of different languages warrants different abilities.

119. Shreya is a Class VI learner who moves from the Jalander in Punjab to Madurai in Tamil Nadu as her father has been transferred. She knows Punjabi as her mother tongue and English language she studies as her second language in school. She is able to speak and read Tamil learning from her neighbourhood. Which one of the following statements is true based on the languages she now knows?

A. Her Punjabi and Tamil come under language acquisition and English comes under language learning.
B. Her Tamil comes under language acquisition and English and Punjabi come under language learning.
C. All the three languages, Punjabi, Tamil and English under language learning.
D. Her English comes under language acquisition and Punjabi and Tamil come under language learning.

120. Which of the following is NOT the purpose of extensive reading?

A. Reading for appreciation
B. Reading for extrapolation
C. Reading for learning grammar
D. Reading for pleasure

111. D	112. C	113. A	114. C	115. B	116. A	117. C	118. A	119. A	120. C

Language-II—हिन्दी

निर्देश (प्र.सं. 121 से 128): *निम्नलिखित गद्यांश को पढ़कर पूछे गए प्रश्नों के सही/सर्वाधिक उपयुक्त विकल्प का चयन कीजिए।*

हाल ही में मेडिकल इंडस्ट्री के एक जानकार दावा कर रहे थे कि भविष्य में डॉक्टरों, सर्जनों की जरूरत भी कम होने वाली है। एआई के जरिए लक्षणों को समझा जाएगा। आपकी केस हिस्ट्री एआई को पता होगी। ताजा हालत पूछ ली जाएगी और प्रिस्क्रिप्शन आपके हाथ में होगा। शारीरिक श्रम से जुड़े कामों पर शायद सबसे कम असर पड़ने वाला है। यह समझने का वक्त है कि एआई से फायदे होंगे या नुकसान। अभी तो इस नकली बुद्धिमत्ता को इंसान ने ही जन्म दिया है। उसका नियंत्रण है, लेकिन एआई वरदान ही रहे और भस्मासुर न बने, उसके लिए यह सोचने की जरूरत भी है कि मानवीय बुद्धिमत्ता के स्तर को इतना ऊँचा कैसे उठाया जाए कि एआई उस पर हावी न हो सके। अब अगर चैट जीपीटी बनाया है तो फिर पढ़ाई-लिखाई और इम्तहानों का वह तरीका कौन-सा हो, जो बिना एआई के युवाओं और बच्चों के बौद्धिक स्तर को परख सके।

यह सवाल ऐसे हैं जिनके जवाब दे पाना मुश्किल है, पर नजर जरूर रखनी चाहिए। वैज्ञानिकों को भी तय करना चाहिए कि एआई ऐसी हो जो इंसानियत फैलाने में मददगार हो।

121. गद्यांश के आधार पर कहा जा सकता है कि एआई ऐसी होनी चाहिए जो :
A. मानवीय क्षमताओं को कम करे
B. मानवीय गुणों का संस्कार दे
C. कम समय में अधिक कार्य करे
D. बिना बुद्धि के सारे जवाब दे दे

122. समूह से भिन्न शब्द है :
A. पढ़ाई-लिखाई B. रात-दिन
C. कंकड़-पत्थर D. चाय-वाय

123. 'मानवीय' शब्द में प्रत्यय है :
A. वीय B. य
C. ईय D. इय

124. एआई शारीरिक श्रम से जुड़े कार्यों पर संभवतः सबसे कम प्रभाव डाले। इससे कौन-सा कार्य प्रभावित नहीं होगा?
A. चिकित्सा B. शिक्षण
C. खेती-बाड़ी D. आविष्कार

125. एआई को जन्म देने वाला कारक है :
A. आवश्यकता B. तकनीक
C. सभ्यता D. मानव

126. 'एआई' का अर्थ है :
A. एपल इंटेलिजेंस
B. आर्टिफिशियल इंटेलीजेंस
C. आर्टिफिशियल इंस्टीट्यूट
D. एपल इंस्टीट्यूशन

127. एआई से शिक्षा जगत भी प्रभावित होगा। यह प्रभाव :
A. नकारात्मक होगा B. शून्य होगा
C. सकारात्मक होगा D. अधिक होगा

128. चिकित्सा से जुड़े कार्य करने में एआई भविष्य में क्या सहयोग करेगा?
A. डॉक्टरों को जॉब देगा
B. केस हिस्ट्री बना देगा
C. अस्पतालों की संख्या कम कर देगा
D. अस्पतालों की संख्या बहुत बढ़ा देगा

निर्देश (प्र.सं. 129 से 135): *निम्नलिखित गद्यांश को पढ़कर पूछे गए प्रश्नों के सही/सर्वाधिक उपयुक्त विकल्प का चयन कीजिए।*

प्रश्न उठता है कि प्राण का शरीर के साथ बेहतर तालमेल कैसे बैठाकर रखा जाए। ऐसा क्या करें कि प्राण शरीर के हर अंग की तरफ संतुलित और व्यवस्थित होकर बहे। देखा जाए तो बीमारी और कुछ भी नहीं, बल्कि प्राण का उस अंग विशेष में असंतुलित हो जाना ही है। स्वास्थ्य का अर्थ ही होता है–प्राण का समुचित तरीके से समस्त अंगों की तरफ बहना। योग में इस प्राण को बल देने के लिए अनेक अभ्यास हैं। इनके जरिए हम अपने प्राण को रोज बल दे सकते हैं और शरीर में होने वाली बीमारियों की रोकथाम कर सकते हैं। यह प्राण केवल हमारे शरीर की ही संभाल नहीं करता, यह मन, बुद्धि आदि प्रत्येक आयाम को जीवन देता रहता है।

129. जीवन के लिए सर्वाधिक महत्वपूर्ण है :
A. योग के माध्यम से प्राणायाम करना
B. प्राण के माध्यम से योग करना
C. प्राण और शरीर का दीर्घायु होना
D. प्राण और शरीर का सामंजस्य

121. B **122.** D **123.** C **124.** C **125.** D **126.** B **127.** A **128.** B **129.** D

130. विशेषण शब्द का उदाहरण नहीं है :

A. संतुलित B. स्वस्थ

C. स्वास्थ्य D. व्यवस्थित

131. प्राण वायु को सशक्त बनाने के अभ्यास .... में है।

A. शिक्षा B. योग

C. चिकित्सक D. शिक्षक

132. प्राण वायु शरीर के हर अंग में संतुलित और .... होकर बहती है।

A. व्यवस्थित B. अव्यवस्थित

C. उत्तेजित D. मंद-मंद

133. रोग का कारण है :

A. प्राण वायु का बहुत अधिक बढ़ जाना

B. प्राण वायु का अंग विशेष में असंतुलन

C. योग के माध्यम से शारीरिक शक्ति घटाना

D. अपने शरीर की उचित देखभाल न करना

134. अच्छे स्वास्थ्य का संबंध .... से है।

A. अच्छे शरीर

B. प्राण वायु

C. योगाभ्यास

D. बीमारियों के अभाव

135. 'बुद्धि' में 'इक' प्रत्यय लगने पर शब्द बनेगा :

A. बुद्धिक B. बौद्धिक

C. बोद्धिक D. बौद्धीक

136. निम्नलिखित में से कौन-सी विधि भाषा अधिगम के लिए ड्रिल और 'भाषा के औपचारिक गुणधर्म में निपुणता' को आवश्यक रूप की तरह अनुशंसा करती है?

A. श्रव्य भाषावाद

B. सम्प्रेषणात्मक भाषा शिक्षण

C. व्याकरण अनुवाद विधि

D. कुल भौतिक प्रतिक्रिया

137. कक्षा सात का विद्यार्थी ऐलम कन्नड़, मराठी, हिंदी और अंग्रेजी चार भाषाएँ जानता है। घर में जब वह अपने माता-पिता के साथ बात करता है तो प्रवाह के साथ चारों भाषाएँ बोलता है और विद्यालय में वह हिंदी, कन्नड़ तथा अंग्रेजी बोलता है क्योंकि उसके मित्र व अध्यापकों को यही भाषाएँ आती हैं। इस स्थिति को किस रूप में जाना जाएगा?

A. परभाषिक (ट्रांसलिंग्युल) योग्यता

B. कोड जाल (कोड मैशिंग)

C. कोड से आगे जाना (कोड मूविंग)

D. अन्तरभाषा (इंटरलैंग्युएज)

138. भाषा अधिगम के बारे में कौन-सा कथन सही है?

A. सहजात/प्रथम भाषा का ज्ञान द्वितीय भाषा के अधिगम में अवरोध डालता है।

B. सहजात/प्रथम भाषा के ज्ञान का द्वितीय भाषा अधिगम से कोई लेना-देना नहीं है।

C. सहजात/प्रथम भाषा का ज्ञान द्वितीय भाषा के अधिगम को समर्थित करता है।

D. प्रथम भाषा अधिगम और द्वितीय भाषा दोनों पूरी तरह से अलग-अलग हैं।

139. कक्षा छह की अध्यापिका शब्दावली समृद्ध करने के लिए चम्मच, प्लेट, डिब्बे, परात कक्षा में लेकर आती है। इन्हें दिखाकर वह रसोई में इस्तेमाल होने वाली वस्तुओं का विवरण लिखना चाहती है। भाषा शिक्षण के संदर्भ में इन वस्तुओं को क्या कहेंगे?

A. शिक्षण सामग्री

B. वास्तविक वस्तुएँ (रीयलिया)

C. खाना पकाने के बर्तन

D. वास्तविक जीवन के कार्य

140. घोषणात्मक ज्ञान क्या है?

A. किसी भाषा के शब्द का उच्चारण करना जानना।

B. व्याकरणिक तत्वों के बारे में ज्ञान।

C. व्याकरणिक तत्वों में त्रुटि की पहचान करना सीखना।

D. किसी व्याकरणिक तत्व पर कैसे कार्य किया जाए, यह जानना।

141. यहाँ एक ऐसी स्थिति दी जा रही है जहाँ विद्यार्थियों को विषय के प्रति समझ बनाने के लिए विषय के विपरीत वाले दृष्टिकोण से परिचित करवाया जाता है। इस प्रक्रिया द्वारा विद्यार्थियों में किसके विकास का प्रयास किया जा रहा है?

A. समालोचनात्मक विश्लेषण

B. प्रक्रिया आधारित शिक्षणशास्त्र

C. समालोचनात्मक साक्षरता

D. साक्षरता विकास

130. C	**131.** B	**132.** A	**133.** B	**134.** B	**135.** B
136. A	**137.** A	**138.** C	**139.** B	**140.** B	**141.** C

142. 'परभाषा व्यवहार' (ट्रान्सलैंग्युजिंग) क्या है?

A. भाषाओं के शिक्षण अधिगम के दौरान एक भाषा से दूसरी भाषा में व्यवहार करने से संबंधित है।

B. भाषाएँ किस तरह से एक समय अवधि के दौरान अपना रूप बदलती हैं।

C. एक कक्षा में एक से अधिक भाषाओं को संसाधन के रूप में इस्तेमाल करने की शिक्षण शास्त्रीय प्रक्रिया है।

D. विद्यालय में कितनी भाषाएँ पढ़ानी चाहिए इस मुद्दे पर 'शिक्षा नीति में भाषा' है।

143. निम्नलिखित में से कौन-सी प्रक्रियाएँ भाषा को अच्छी तरह से लिखना सीखने में शामिल है?

A. मानस मंथन - रूपरेखा तैयार करना - प्रारूपण - मुख्य बिन्दु नोट करना - संपादन - अन्तिम स्वरूप देना

B. मानस मंथन - मुख्य बिन्दु नोट करना - प्रारूप लिखना - रूपरेखा तैयार करना - संपादन - अन्तिम स्वरूप देना

C. मानस मंथन - मुख्य बिन्दु नोट करना - प्रारूप लिखना - संपादन - रूपरेखा तैयार करना - अन्तिम स्वरूप देना

D. मानस मंथन - मुख्य बिन्दु नोट करना - रूपरेखा तैयार करना - प्रारूप लिखना - संपादन - अन्तिम स्वरूप देना

144. सामाजिक विज्ञान की कक्षा में शिक्षार्थी कक्षा में दिए जा रहे वक्तव्य से मुख्य बिन्दु समझने की कोशिश कर रहे हैं और मुख्य बिन्दु लिख रहे हैं। इस कौशल को क्या कहेंगे?

A. अध्ययन कौशल   B. श्रवण कौशल

C. लेखन कौशल   D. संज्ञानात्मक कौशल

145. नीचे दिए गए प्रश्न को पढ़ें। पता करें कि यह प्रश्न किस प्रारूप (टाइपोलोजी) का है?

''छोटी बालिका की कहानी पढ़ने के बाद, आपने उसके दुखों और कठिनाइयों का सामना करने वाले साहस को महसूस किया। आप उस लड़की को उसकी प्रशंसा के लिए पत्र लिखना चाहेंगे। लगभग 120 शब्दों में पत्र लिखिए।''

A. अभिव्यक्तिपरक प्रश्न

B. दीर्घ उत्तरीय प्रश्न

C. पाठ का विस्तार करने वाला प्रश्न (एक्स्ट्रापोलेटिव)

D. विमर्श संबंधी प्रश्न

146. कक्षा आठ की अध्यापिका एक पाठ्य सामग्री के पाँच वाक्यों को दो बार अंग्रेजी में पढ़ती है और शिक्षार्थियों को ध्यानपूर्वक सुनने के लिए कहती है। इसके बाद वह शिक्षार्थियों को चार-चार के समूह में काम करने के लिए कहती है कि वे पढ़ी गई पाठ्य सामग्री का पुनर्लेखन करें जो एकदम मूल जैसा ना हो। इस गतिविधि को क्या कहेंगे?

A. लेखन कार्य   B. अनुच्छेद श्रुतलेख

C. सामूहिक श्रुतलेख   D. श्रवण कार्य

147. यह अकादमिक भाषा या विभिन्न प्रकार के विषयों के लिए आवश्यक भाषा में निपुणता से संबंधित है :

A. अंतरभाषा निपुणता

B. बुनियादी अंतरवैयक्तिक सम्प्रेषण कौशल (BICS)

C. सम्प्रेषणात्मक भाषा निपुणता

D. संज्ञानात्मक अकादमिक भाषा निपुणता (CALP)

148. भाषा शिक्षा पर राष्ट्रीय शिक्षा नीति 2020 के संदर्भ में कौन-सा कथन सही नहीं है?

A. त्रिभाषा सूत्र के अन्तर्गत शास्त्रीय भाषा का अध्ययन।

B. त्रिभाषा सूत्र के अन्तर्गत मातृभाषा/घर की भाषा का अध्ययन।

C. त्रिभाषा सूत्र के अन्तर्गत भारतीय भाषाओं का अध्ययन।

D. त्रिभाषा सूत्र के अन्तर्गत भाषा के रूप में अंग्रेजी भाषा का अध्ययन।

149. निम्नलिखित में से त्रिभाषा सूत्र के संबंध में कौन-सा कथन सही है?

A. सभी बच्चे अपनी विद्यालयी शिक्षा अंग्रेजी माध्यम/घर की भाषा में शुरू करते हैं और दसवीं पूरी करने तक कम से कम दो और भाषाएँ सीखते हैं।

B. सभी बच्चे अपनी विद्यालयी शिक्षा अपने राज्य की भाषा में शुरू करते हैं और दसवीं पूरी करने तक कम से कम दो और भाषाएँ सीखते हैं।

C. सभी बच्चे अपनी विद्यालयी शिक्षा राज्य भाषा हिंदी में शुरू करते हैं और दसवीं पूरी करने तक कम से कम दो और भाषाएँ सीखते हैं।

D. सभी बच्चे अपनी विद्यालयी शिक्षा मातृभाषा/घर की भाषा में शुरू करते हैं और दसवीं पूरी करने तक कम से कम दो और भाषाएँ सीखते हैं।

150. अधिगम प्रतिफल शिक्षार्थियों को समर्थ बनाते हैं :

A. व्याकरणिक ज्ञान को मापन के संदर्भ में प्राप्त करना

B. दक्षताओं को मापन के संदर्भ में प्राप्त करना

C. सभी कौशलों के अधिगम के न्यूनतम स्तरों को प्राप्त करना

D. भाषागत तथ्यों को मापन के संदर्भ में प्राप्त करना

142. C   **143.** D   **144.** A   **145.** C   **146.** B,C   **147.** D   **148.** A   **149.** D   **150.** B

EXPLANATORY ANSWERS

1. **(B):** Vygotsky's theory of cognitive development emphasizes the crucial role of social interaction in learning and development. He introduced the concept of the Zone of Proximal Development (ZPD), which is the difference between what a learner can do without help and what they can achieve with guidance and encouragement from a skilled partner. According to Vygotsky, the teacher's role is to scaffold learning within the ZPD, providing support structures to help the student progress. The teacher guides the learning process, offering assistance with tasks that are just beyond the student's current capabilities, thereby facilitating cognitive development. This approach contrasts with the idea of simply delivering information or allowing students to learn entirely on their own.

2. **(D):** The statement that "Children across different cultures usher in and experience adolescence in a similar manner" is not correct. Adolescence is significantly influenced by cultural, social, and environmental factors, leading to considerable variability in how it is experienced across different societies. While biological aspects of adolescence, such as puberty, are universal, the social constructions and expectations associated with adolescence vary widely. Different cultures have unique rites of passage, norms, and definitions of what constitutes adulthood, indicating that the transition from childhood to adulthood is not uniform but deeply embedded in cultural contexts.

3. **(B):** Sujata is extrinsically motivated because her primary drive to participate in the dance competition is the external reward of winning the first prize of cash, rather than the joy of dancing or personal satisfaction. Extrinsic motivation refers to behavior that is driven by external rewards such as money, fame, grades, and praise. This type of motivation contrasts with intrinsic motivation, where actions are driven by internal rewards, such as personal satisfaction or the joy of doing something.

4. **(C):** Acknowledging individual differences as an obvious feature of human diversity is essential for effective teaching. Teachers should recognize and value the unique backgrounds, abilities, interests, and learning styles of their students. This understanding enables the adaptation of teaching strategies to meet the diverse needs of learners. By considering differences as a natural and valuable aspect of human diversity, teachers can create inclusive learning environments that support and engage all students, fostering a sense of belonging and respect for diversity within the classroom.

5. **(A):** Jean Piaget believed that children actively construct knowledge through their interactions with the environment. According to Piaget, learning is a process of adaptation where children use assimilation and accommodation to incorporate new information into their existing cognitive structures. Knowledge construction is an active process where learners build their understanding through experiences, exploration, and problem-solving. Piaget's theory emphasizes the role of the learner in seeking knowledge and understanding, rather than passively receiving information from the external world. This view highlights the importance of providing opportunities for hands-on learning and discovery, allowing children to explore and understand the world around them through their actions and reflections.

6. **(A):** In a progressive classroom, assessment is dynamic. This approach to assessment is ongoing and evolves with the learning process, focusing on the continuous observation of students' progress over time. Dynamic assessment is formative in nature, aimed at understanding and improving learning in real-time rather than measuring learning at a fixed point. It involves interactive and adaptive methods to gauge students' abilities, learning needs, and progress, allowing for immediate feedback and adjustments to teaching strategies. This contrasts with traditional objective, summative, or normative assessments, which are more static and measure learning outcomes against a fixed standard or benchmark.

7. **(A):** Attention is essential in the meaning-making of the information received from the environment and its further storage in memory. It is the process of selectively concentrating on one aspect of the environment while ignoring other things. Attention is critical because it determines which information gets processed further. Without adequate attention, information may not be effectively encoded into memory, making it difficult for further storage and retrieval. This focus allows individuals to filter out irrelevant or less important information and concentrate on what is critical for learning or task completion.

8. (C): Asking students how the author uses symbolism in "To Kill a Mockingbird" is an example of a question that requires them to analyze information. Analysis involves breaking down information into its component parts to understand its structure and meaning. This type of question encourages students to think critically about the text, examining how specific elements like symbolism contribute to the overall message, themes, or characters' development. It goes beyond simple recall or description (found in options A and D) and requires a deeper understanding and interpretation of the text, distinguishing it from questions about plot or character identification.

9. (A): Both Assertion (A) and Reason (R) are true, and (R) is the correct explanation of (A). Teachers' reflection on their own stereotypes and biases is crucial for culturally responsive teaching. This process involves recognizing and understanding one's own cultural lens and biases that might influence interactions with students and pedagogical choices. Culturally responsive teaching is grounded in teachers being reflective about their practices and assumptions. By examining their biases, teachers can better support all students' cultural backgrounds and learning needs, making (R) a valid explanation for (A).

10. (A): The central argument of Carol Gilligan's critique of Kohlberg's theory of moral development centers around ethics of care and the feminist perspective. Gilligan argued that Kohlberg's model was based on a male-centric view of morality that emphasized justice and rights. She proposed that this perspective overlooked the moral reasoning based on relationships, care, and responsibility, which she found to be more prevalent in females. Gilligan's critique introduced a significant dimension to moral development theories, emphasizing that moral reasoning is not solely based on justice but also on caring and relational aspects, underscoring the importance of diversity in understanding moral development.

11. (B): Both Assertion (A) and Reason (R) are true, but (R) is not the correct explanation of (A). Learning from real-life problems and concrete experiences indeed provides children with multiple pathways for learning and retrieving information, as it engages them in context-rich activities that enhance understanding and memory recall. This approach aligns with experiential learning theories, which suggest that learning is more effective when it is active and situated in meaningful contexts. However, while development being relatively orderly and sequential is a true statement in the context of psychological development theories, it does not directly explain why learning from real-life problems and experiences offers multiple pathways for learning. The orderly and sequential nature of development refers to the progression through developmental stages, not necessarily to the mechanisms of learning and information retrieval in experiential contexts.

12. (B): Dyslexia is a neurological condition that impacts a learner's ability to link sounds with symbols. It primarily affects reading and related language-based processing skills. Dyslexia is characterized by difficulties with accurate and/or fluent word recognition and by poor spelling and decoding abilities. These challenges stem from a deficit in the phonological component of language that is unrelated to intelligence. Dyslexia is not related to emotional issues, physiological conditions affecting social interactions, or sensory problems affecting body movements but is a specific learning disability in reading.

13. (D): Letting the students research on a current issue in small groups and present their findings to the class is an appropriate pedagogical strategy for enabling meaningful learning by helping students make connections between concepts and real-world applications. This approach engages students actively in the learning process, encourages collaboration, and fosters critical thinking and communication skills. It contrasts with more passive or rote learning strategies, such as memorizing terms or completing worksheets, and is more aligned with constructivist principles that advocate for learning through discovery and application in real-world contexts.

14. (B): In Kohlberg's theory of moral development, children's reasoning that revolves around the ethics of law is most characteristic of the Conventional morality stage. This stage typically emerges in adolescence and is marked by an individual's adherence to rules and conventions of society. Individuals in this stage view morality based on societal rules and laws, which they believe maintain social order and ensure the welfare of the group. It is differentiated from the Pre-conventional morality stage, where moral reasoning is based on personal consequences, and the Post-conventional (or Autonomous morality) stage, where individuals base their moral decisions on abstract principles and values that may transcend societal rules.

15. (D): Encouraging a competitive ethos does not exemplify an inclusive classroom. Inclusive education focuses on accommodating diverse learning needs, ensuring accessibility, and promoting a supportive and cooperative learning environment. It emphasizes the importance of incorporating diverse perspectives, providing reasonable accommodations for students with disabilities, and offering differentiated instruction to meet the varied learning styles and abilities of all students. A competitive ethos, by contrast, may create a learning environment that prioritizes winning and comparison over collaboration, potentially marginalizing or excluding students who may not perform well in competitive settings.

16. (D): Work in progress portfolios are an effective tool for formative assessment because they involve students in the process of assessment (*a*), offer insights about the progress of individual students (*b*), and offer tangible evidence of student learning (*d*). These portfolios allow students and teachers to see the development of skills and knowledge over time, facilitating personalized feedback and adjustments in learning strategies. The focus is not primarily on the presentation of the final product (*c*), but on the learning process, reflection, and growth over time. This approach emphasizes student involvement and provides a comprehensive view of student progress and achievements.

17. (B): A mastery goal orientation focuses on improving one's skills and understanding of a task. Individuals with a mastery orientation are motivated by the desire to learn, understand, and develop their competencies. They view challenges as opportunities to expand their abilities and are less concerned with comparing their performance to that of others. This contrasts with a performance orientation, where the focus is on achieving a certain level of performance relative to others or avoiding failure.

18. (B): In progressive education, the role of the teacher includes providing diverse materials for children to experiment with and offering scaffolding as and when required. Progressive education emphasizes active learning, critical thinking, and the development of problem-solving skills. Teachers in this approach act more as guides or facilitators of learning rather than traditional authoritative sources of knowledge. They create learning environments that encourage exploration and inquiry, supporting students' learning processes through scaffolding rather than dictating or controlling the learning experience.

19. (A): Asking critical questions such as "how much and in what ways are various genders represented in textbooks and media" would encourage questioning gender stereotypes. This approach promotes critical thinking about societal norms and representations of gender, encouraging students to recognize and challenge stereotypes and biases. By examining the content and portrayal of different genders in educational and media resources, students can become more aware of how gender stereotypes are perpetuated and consider the implications for gender equality and representation.

20. (C): According to Jean Piaget, the ability to use symbols for symbols, such as letting the letter X stand for an unknown numeral, develops during the formal operational stage and enables the children to learn algebra and calculus. The formal operational stage, which typically begins around age 12, is characterized by the development of abstract thinking and the ability to use hypothetical-deductive reasoning. During this stage, children and adolescents become capable of thinking about abstract concepts, including mathematical symbols and complex problem-solving, which are essential for understanding and learning algebra and calculus. This contrasts with the concrete operational stage, where children develop logical thinking about concrete events but still struggle with abstract concepts.

21. (A): Alok's behaviors, including holding his head in an awkward position when reading, squinting and rubbing his eyes frequently, redness or swelling of the eyes, and confusing letters, are indicative of potential visual problems. These symptoms suggest that he may be experiencing difficulties with vision, which could include issues like refractive errors (e.g., myopia, hyperopia, astigmatism), eye strain, or other visual impairments that affect his ability to read comfortably and accurately. It is important for children showing such signs to be evaluated by a vision care specialist to determine the underlying cause and to receive appropriate treatment or accommodations.

22. (C): Assertion (A) is true: In an inclusive classroom, adaptations should indeed be made in learning goals, pedagogical strategies, and assessment to accommodate the diverse needs of all students, ensuring that each student has access to the curriculum and can participate fully in the learning process. However, Reason (R) is false: The philosophy of inclusion does not advocate for the elimination of all individual differences through pedagogical approaches and assessment. Instead, it emphasizes valuing and embracing individual differences and providing the necessary supports and accommodations to enable all students to succeed. Inclusion is about adapting the educational environment to the students rather than expecting the students to fit into a one-size-fits-all model.

23. **(A):** According to Lev Vygotsky, children benefit from the experience of interacting with more knowledgeable others while working within their zone of proximal development (ZPD). The ZPD is the difference between what a learner can do without help and what he or she can achieve with guidance and encouragement from a skilled partner. Vygotsky's theory emphasizes the importance of social interaction in cognitive development, suggesting that learning occurs most effectively when children are supported by others who are more skilled, enabling them to progress beyond their current level of independent capability.

24. **(C):** Giving a timer to the student for self-regulation and time-management is an effective strategy in helping the student stay focused. This approach encourages the student to become more aware of how they use their time and to develop skills in managing their attention and efforts during class. Timers can be used to break down tasks into manageable intervals, helping students to maintain focus for shorter periods and gradually increasing their attention span over time. This strategy supports the development of executive function skills, including planning, time management, and self-regulation, which are crucial for academic success.

25. **(A):** Both Assertion (A) and Reason (R) are true, and (R) is the correct explanation of (A). Students are indeed more likely to do well and stay in school if they feel an emotional attachment to their school and believe that they matter. This sense of belonging and significance can motivate students to engage more deeply with their learning and to persist through challenges. Reason (R) supports this by highlighting the significant role of emotions in learning. Emotions affect motivation, engagement, and the overall learning experience, influencing students' connections to their educational environment and their belief in their own value within that context. Emotional factors are critical in shaping students' attitudes towards school and their academic outcomes.

26. **(C):** Students construct their own knowledge through active engagement with their environment. This is a core principle of constructivist learning theory, which posits that learning is an active, constructive process. Learners are not passive recipients of information; instead, they actively construct their own understanding and knowledge of the world, through experiencing things and reflecting on those experiences. Constructivism emphasizes the importance of learners being engaged in meaningful tasks, problem-solving, and critical thinking, and it suggests that teachers should facilitate rather than direct learning, providing environments where students can explore and build their understanding.

27. **(B):** Assertion (A) is true: The teaching strategy where the teacher provides more direction when a child is less able to do a task and gradually reduces support as the child becomes more capable reflects the educational principle of scaffolding, which is part of Vygotsky's theory of the Zone of Proximal Development. This approach helps to optimize learning and supports the child's development. However, Reason (R) is also true but it is not the correct explanation of (A). The statement about intelligence not being accurately measured solely by calculating IQ addresses the complexities and limitations of intelligence testing but does not directly relate to the principles of scaffolding and instructional support based on a child's capability.

28. **(C):** Socialization is characterized as being a complex, multidimensional process that takes place uniquely in different cultures. Socialization is not linear; it involves various agents (such as family, schools, peers, and media) and dimensions (including values, norms, behaviors, and social skills), and it is influenced by cultural contexts. This process is essential for individuals to learn and internalize the norms, values, and behaviors that are necessary for functioning effectively in their society. The uniqueness of socialization in different cultures highlights the diverse ways in which societies impart and individuals acquire social norms and practices.

29. **(A):** Both Assertion (A) and Reason (R) are true, and (R) is the correct explanation of (A). There is no objectively definable moment when a child enters middle childhood or adolescence because development is a continuous process. Developmental stages transition smoothly from one to the next without distinct boundaries, and the timing of these transitions can vary widely among individuals, influenced by biological, environmental, and cultural factors. The continuous nature of development means that changes are gradual and cumulative, making it difficult to pinpoint a specific moment when a child moves from one developmental stage to another.

30. (C): Rewarding autonomy and initiative in students can strongly influence the development of academic self-concept. When teachers support and reward students' autonomy and initiative, they help foster a sense of competence, independence, and a positive self-concept. Encouraging students to take initiative in their learning and recognizing their efforts and achievements contributes to their belief in their own abilities, which is crucial for their academic motivation and success. This approach contrasts with keeping low expectations or punishing autonomy, which can undermine students' confidence and motivation.

31. (C): Given, BD is the diagonal of parallelogram ABCD.

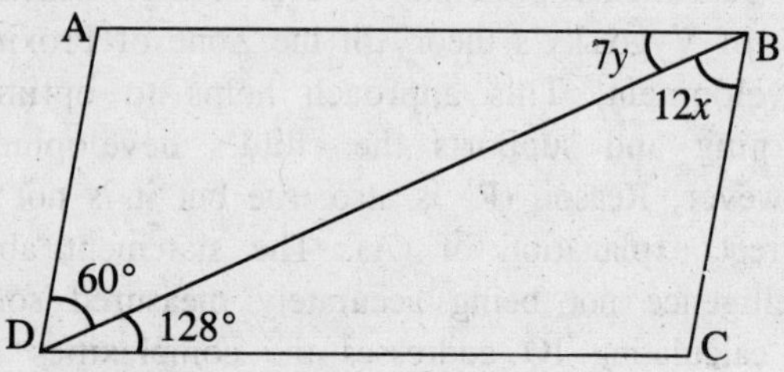

Such that,

$\angle CBD = 12x$, $\angle ABD = 7y$, $\angle ADB = 60°$ and $\angle CDB = 28°$

$\because$ AB || DC and AD || BC

$\therefore \angle ABD = \angle BDC$

$\Rightarrow \quad 7y = 28°$

$y = 4°$

and $\angle ADB = \angle CBD$

$\Rightarrow \quad 60° = 12x$

$x = 5°$

Hence, $2x + 3y = 2 \times 5 + 3 \times 4 = 22°$.

32. (A): (*a*) **A rational number includes integers:** A rational number is any number that can be expressed as a fraction where both the numerator and the denominator are integers, and the denominator is not zero. Integers are whole numbers, including positive, negative, and zero. Integers can be represented as rational numbers by expressing them as a fraction with a denominator of 1. For example, 5 can be represented as 5/1, –3 can be represented as –3/1, and 0 can be represented as 0/1. Therefore, integers are indeed included in the set of rational numbers.

(*c*) **All fractions are rational numbers:** A fraction is a representation of a part of a whole, expressed as one integer divided by another. For example, 3/4, -2/5, and 7/2 are all fractions. By definition, rational numbers are numbers that can be expressed as fractions where both the numerator and denominator are integers. Since fractions meet this criteria—they consist of integers in the numerator and denominator—they are all rational numbers.

33. (C): $p^3x + p^2(x - y) - p(y + z) - z$

$= p^3x + p^2x - p^2y - py - pz - z$

$= (p^3 + p^2)x - (p^2 + p)y - (p + 1)z$

$= p^2(p + 1)x - p(p + 1)y - (p + 1)z$

$= (p^2 x - py - z)(p + 1)$

Hence, one of the factors is $(p^2x - py - z)$.

34. (C): Arranging the given data in ascending order

3, 7, 8, 15, 17, 21, 23, 24, 29, 30

Here, $n = 10$ (even no.)

$\therefore x = \text{Median} = \frac{1}{2}\left[\frac{n}{2}\text{th term} + \left(\frac{n}{2}+1\right)\text{th term}\right]$

$\Rightarrow \quad x = \frac{1}{2}[17+21]$

$= \frac{1}{2}[38]$

$= 19$

Again, replacing 3 by 33 and 8 by 18

$\therefore$ New Data: 33, 7, 18, 15, 17, 21, 23, 24, 29, 30

In ascending order:

7, 15, 17, 18, 21, 23, 24, 29, 30, 33

$\therefore y = \text{Median} = \frac{1}{2}[\text{5th term} + \text{6th term}]$

$\Rightarrow \quad y = \frac{1}{2}[21 + 23]$

$= \frac{1}{2}[44]$

$= 22$

Hence, $(y - x) = 22 - 19 = 3$

Hence, the difference between y and x is 3.

35. (B): Let the three numbers are $2x$, $3x$ and $4x$

Then, $(2x)^3 + (3x)^3 + (4x)^3 = 33957$

$\Rightarrow 8x^3 + 27x^3 + 64x^3 = 33957$

$\Rightarrow 99x^3 = 33957$

$\Rightarrow x^3 = 343$

$\Rightarrow x^3 = (7)^3$

$\Rightarrow x = 7$

Hence, the sum of the three numbers

$= 2x + 3x + 4x$

$= 9x$

$= 9 \times 7$

$= 63.$

36. (B): Given, V = 10, E = 15 and F = x of a polyhedron

$\because F + V - E = 2$

$\therefore x + 10 - 15 = 2$

$\Rightarrow x - 5 = 2$

$\Rightarrow x = 7$

Hence, $(3x - 12) = 3 \times 7 - 12 = 21 - 12 = 9$

Hence, $(3x - 12) = 9$

37. (D): Given $\frac{x}{y} = \left(\frac{-1}{3}\right)^{-3} \div \left(\frac{2}{3}\right)^{-4}$

$$= \left(\frac{3}{-1}\right)^{3} \div \left(\frac{3}{2}\right)^{4}$$

$$= (-3)^3 \times \left(\frac{2}{3}\right)^{4}$$

$$= (-1)(3)^3 \times \frac{(2)^4}{(3)^4}$$

$$\Rightarrow \frac{x}{y} = (-1)\frac{(2)^4}{3} = \frac{-16}{3}$$

$$\therefore \left(\frac{x}{y} + \frac{y}{x}\right)^{-1} = \left(\frac{-16}{3} + \frac{3}{-16}\right)^{-1}$$

$$= -\left(\frac{16}{3} + \frac{3}{16}\right)^{-1}$$

$$= -\left(\frac{256 + 9}{48}\right)^{-1}$$

$$= -\left(\frac{265}{48}\right)^{-1}$$

$$= -\frac{48}{265}$$

38. (B): Jean Piaget, a renowned developmental psychologist, introduced the concept of "Schema" as a fundamental cognitive structure in his theory of cognitive development. A schema can be defined as a mental framework or organized pattern of thought that individuals use to understand and interpret the world around them. These mental structures evolve and adapt over time through processes such as assimilation and accommodation, enabling individuals to make sense of new information and experiences. Piaget proposed that schemas serve as the building blocks of cognitive development, shaping how individuals perceive, think, and interact with their environment as they progress through different stages of development.

39. (A): Given,

$x = 1.011 + 10.11 - 12.101 + 0.1011$

$\Rightarrow x = -0.8789$

Let y should be added to x to get sum as 1.1

$\therefore x + y = 1.1$

$\Rightarrow -0.8789 + y = 1.1$

$\Rightarrow y = 1.1 + 0.8789$

$\Rightarrow y = 1.9789.$

40. (C): This option suggests that although Ram can recall and repeat definitions accurately, he struggles with applying conceptual understanding when identifying numbers within a set. Ram's ability to accurately recite the definitions of various types of numbers, such as odd, even, prime, and composite, suggests that he has a good memory for information. However, his difficulty in identifying numbers accurately within a given set indicates a lack of conceptual understanding rather than issues related to memory, concentration, or analytical ability. This suggests that while he can memorize and repeat information, he may struggle to apply that knowledge in real-world contexts or to understand the underlying principles behind the definitions.

41. (C): Here SP of an article = ₹324

CP of an article = ₹300

Discount = 28%

Let Marked price of an article = ₹(300 + x)

Then, SP = $(300 + x) \times \frac{100 - 28}{100}$

$\Rightarrow 324 = (300 + x) \times \frac{72}{100}$

$\Rightarrow (300 + x) = 324 \times \frac{100}{72} = 450$

$\Rightarrow (300 + x) =$ ₹450

Again, discount = 18%

$\therefore$ SP $= 450\times\frac{100-18}{100}$

$= \frac{9}{2}\times 82$

$= 9 \times 41$

$= 369$

Now, profit = SP – CP

$= 369 - 300$

$= 69$

Hence, profit percent $= \frac{\text{Profit}\times 100}{\text{CP}}$

$= \frac{69\times 100}{300}$

$= 23\%$.

42. (B): Given, the product of two rational numbers $= \frac{-40}{3}$

$\Rightarrow pq = \frac{-40}{3}$

$\Rightarrow p\times\frac{-5}{2} = \frac{-40}{3}$

$\Rightarrow p = \frac{-40}{3}\times\frac{-2}{5} = \frac{16}{3}$

The reciprocal $= \frac{1}{p} = \frac{3}{16} = 0.1875$

Here, $\frac{1}{p}$ lies between $\frac{9}{50} = 0.18$ and $\frac{1}{5} = 0.2$

43. (B): To solve this problem, we need the concept of the Least Common Multiple (LCM). The LCM of the step lengths (70 cm, 85 cm, and 95 cm) will give us the minimum distance each person should walk so that they can cover the same distance in complete steps. The LCM represents the smallest distance that is divisible by all three step lengths without any remainder, ensuring that each person can complete an equal number of steps.

44. (A): Student is able to understand the concept of percentage but is not able to understand percentage of which quantity is to be found. The student correctly calculated the percentage decrease, but it seems that they misunderstood what the percentage represents. The percentage decrease should be calculated with respect to the original population, not the new population. Therefore, while the student understands the concept of percentage, they are not clear about which quantity the percentage decrease should be calculated relative to.

45. (D): Let $p < q$

Then, $q - p = 20°$ ...(*i*)

and $q + p = 180°$ ...(*ii*)

Adding (*i*) and (*ii*),

$2q = 200°$

$\Rightarrow q = 100°$

Putting $q = 100$ in (*i*), we get

$p = 80°$

Hence, $3p - 50° = 3 \times 80° - 50°$

$= 240° - 50°$

$= 190°$

46. (B): Given, $x \propto \frac{1}{y} \Rightarrow x = \frac{k}{y}$, when $x = 3.5$

then, $y = 2.4$

$\Rightarrow 3.5 = \frac{k}{2.4}$

$\Rightarrow k = 3.5 \times 2.4$

$\Rightarrow k = 8.4$

Now, when, $x = 5.6$

then, $x = \frac{k}{y}$

$\Rightarrow 5.6 = \frac{8.4}{y}$

$\Rightarrow y = \frac{8.4}{5.6}$

$\Rightarrow y = \frac{6}{4} = \frac{3}{2}$

$\Rightarrow y = 1.5$

47. (C): The following Learning-Teaching Resources (LTRs) are most appropriate for visually challenged students in mathematis classroom:

- **Taylor's abacus:** An abacus is a physical tool that consists of beads or counters on rods or wires. Visually challenged students can use their sense of touch to manipulate the beads, helping them perform various mathematical operations such as addition, subtraction, multiplication, and division.

The tactile feedback provided by the abacus allows visually challenged students to develop a concrete understanding of mathematical concepts and enhances their spatial reasoning skills.

- **Computer:** Computers equipped with accessibility features such as screen readers and Braille displays can provide visually challenged students with access to a wide range of mathematical software and online resources. Screen readers convert on-screen text into synthesized speech or refreshable Braille displays, allowing visually challenged students to navigate mathematical content, input mathematical expressions, and receive feedback audibly or through Braille output. Additionally, specialized software applications designed for visually challenged students can provide interactive tutorials, exercises, and simulations to facilitate learning and reinforce mathematical concepts.

Hence, options (*b*) and (*c*) are correct.

48. (C): Sports integrated pedagogy in mathematics classroom:

- **Teaching-learning process shall become joyful:** Integrating sports into the mathematics classroom can make the teaching-learning process more enjoyable and engaging for students. By incorporating physical activities and games related to mathematics concepts, students can experience hands-on learning and have fun while learning mathematical concepts.
- **Apart from popular sports, there are many indigenous sports which can be used in teaching mathematics:** Sports integrated pedagogy encourages the exploration and utilization of various sports, including indigenous sports, as tools for teaching mathematics. These sports can provide unique contexts and scenarios for students to apply mathematical concepts, fostering creativity, cultural appreciation, and a deeper understanding of mathematics.

Hence, options (*a*) and (*d*) are correct.

49. (B): Given, the area of the curved surface of a right-circular cylinder = 4400 cm²

$$\Rightarrow \quad 2\pi rh = 4400 \quad \ldots(i)$$

and the circumference of its base = 110 cm

$$\Rightarrow \quad 2\pi r = 110 \quad \ldots(ii)$$

$$\therefore \quad r = \frac{110}{2\pi} = \frac{55}{\frac{22}{7}}$$

$$= \frac{55}{22}\times 7$$

$$= \frac{5}{2}\times 7$$

$$= \frac{35}{2} \text{ cm}$$

$$\Rightarrow \quad r = \frac{35}{2} \text{ cm}$$

From (*i*) and (*ii*)

$$110h = 4400 \Rightarrow h = 40 \text{ cm}$$

$$\therefore \text{ Volume of cylinder } = \pi r^2 h$$

$$= \frac{22}{7}\times\left(\frac{35}{2}\right)^2\times 40$$

$$= \frac{22}{7}\times\frac{35}{2}\times\frac{35}{2}\times 40$$

$$= 22 \times 5 \times 35 \times 10$$

$$= 1100 \times 35$$

$$= 38500 \text{ cm}^3$$

$$= \frac{38500}{100\times100\times100} \text{ m}^3$$

$$= 0.0385 \text{ m}^3$$

50. (B): Here, A box opened of the top

$$\therefore \text{ Internal length } = 1.48 \times 100 - 6 = 142 \text{ cm}$$

$$\text{Breadth } = 1.16 \times 100 - 6 = 110 \text{ cm}$$

$$\text{and height } = 83 - 3 = 80 \text{ cm}$$

$$\therefore \text{ Inner surface area of a box } = lb + 2(bh + lh)$$

$$= 142 \times 110 + 2(110 \times 80 + 142 \times 80) \text{ cm}^2$$

$$= 15620 + 2[80(110 + 142)] \text{ cm}^2$$

$$= 15620 + 160\ (252) \text{ cm}^2$$

$$= 15620 + 40320 \text{ cm}^2$$

$$= 55940 \text{ cm}^2$$

$$= \frac{55940}{100\times100} \text{ m}^2$$

$$= 5.594 \text{ m}^2$$

Hence, the cost of painting its inner surface area

$$= ₹150 \times 5.594$$

$$= ₹839.10.$$

51. (D): Given, in ΔABC and ΔDEF

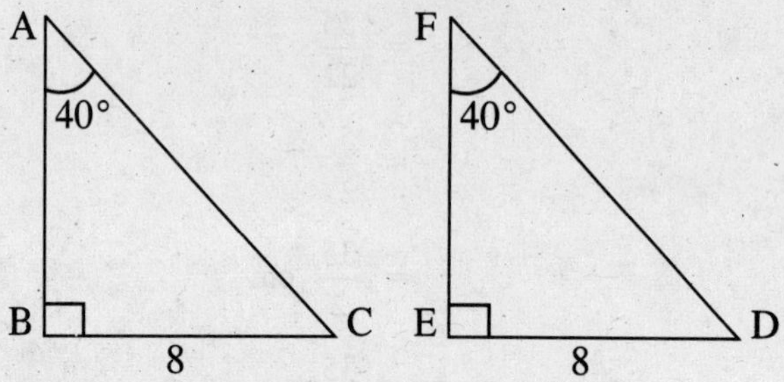

Given, $\angle A = \angle F = 40°$

$\angle B = \angle E = 90°$

$BC = DE = 8$ cm

$\therefore AB = FE$

By AAS-congruence criteria

$\Delta ABC \cong \Delta FED$.

52. (C): Let three consecutive integers are x, $x + 1$ and $x + 2$

Then, $3(x) + 5(x + 1) + 2(x + 2) = 99$

$\Rightarrow 3x + 5x + 5 + 2x + 4 = 99$

$\Rightarrow 10x + 9 = 99$

$\Rightarrow 10x = 90$

$\Rightarrow x = 9$

$\therefore$ The sum of the original first and third integers

$= x + x + 2$

$= 2x + 2$

$= 2 \times 9 + 2$

$= 18 + 2$

$= 20$

53. (D): Teaching the use of histograms for data representation aligns with the scenarios provided in the question. Histograms are used to represent the frequency distribution of continuous data by grouping it into intervals or bins. Let's examine the scenarios:

(*a*) The heights of participants in an athletics meet: Although heights could be considered continuous data, they could also be grouped into intervals or ranges (e.g., 150-160 cm, 160-170 cm, etc.). In this case, a histogram could effectively display the frequency distribution of participant heights within each interval, providing insights into the distribution of heights among the participants.

(*b*) The number of passengers boarding trains from 9:00 am to 9:00 pm at a station: In the scenario of the number of passengers boarding trains from 9:00 am to 9:00 pm at a station, a histogram could indeed be used if the time intervals were converted into continuous time periods. The histogram would then display the frequency distribution of passenger boarding's across these continuous time intervals, providing a visual representation of passenger flow throughout the day. This approach allows for a more nuanced understanding of passenger boarding patterns over time, which can be valuable for analyzing and managing train station operations effectively.

54. (C): Given, 9 4 7 1 x 9 y 2 is divisible by 72 $(72 = 8 \times 9)$

$\Rightarrow$ 9 4 7 1 x 9 y 2 is divisible by 8 and 9

$\therefore \quad \frac{9y2}{8} = 119$ when $y = 5$

$= 124$ when $y = 9$

$= 114$ when $y = 1$

and 9 4 7 1 x 9 y 2 is divisible by 9

$\therefore \quad \frac{9+4+7+1+x+9+y+2}{9} = \frac{32+5+x}{9}$

$= \frac{37+x}{9} = 5$

when $x = 8$

and $\frac{32+x+9}{9} = 5$, when $x = 4$

and $\frac{32+x+1}{9} = 4$, when $x = 3$

Hence, option (C) $x = 9$ and $y = 5$ is not true.

55. (C): Mathematical thinking is a way of thinking to involves mathematics to solve real-world problems. Thinking, reasoning, and working mathematically involve students in identifying and posing problems, and selecting and applying appropriate strategies to find solutions.

Mathematics is a way of thinking since:

- It doesn't involve rote memorization, nothing can be blindly memorized in mathematics, and even the formulas can be proved.
- It provides an opportunity for the students to engage in proofs and examining patterns as mathematics involves a lot of proofs to be learned to deal with the problems.
- It enhances the mental state of the child as he/she tries to explore, understand and apply the concept.
- Make students use appropriate strategies for solving new and different problems in their way even if it is beyond the textbook.

Hence, (*a*) and (*c*) are correct.

56. (C): From given table

Total number of fruits

$= 44 + 56 + 42 + 30 + 38$

$= 210$

$\because$ pie-chart is constructed

$\therefore 360° = 210$

$\Rightarrow 1 \text{ fruit} = \frac{360°}{210} = \frac{12°}{7}$

$\therefore 56 \text{ fruits} = \frac{12°}{7} \times 56 = 96°$

Hence, the angle of the sector representing Apples = 96°.

57. (C): Let the sides of rectangle are $3x$ and $2x$

Then, area of rectangle $= 3x \times 2x = 6x^2$

and area of trapezium

$= \frac{1}{2}$ (sum of parallel sides) $\times$ height

$= \frac{1}{2}(11+25)\times 12$

$= 6(36)$

$= 216 \text{ cm}^2$

According to question,

$6x^2 = 216$

$\Rightarrow x^2 = 36$

$\Rightarrow x = 6$

Hence, the perimeter of the rectangle $= 2(l + b)$

$= 2(3x + 2x) = 10x$

$= 10 \times 6 = 60$ cm.

58. (C): $(A + B + C - D)$

$= -2x^2 + 12x + 11 - 8x + 3x^2 + 17 - 4x^2 - (x^2 - x - 3)$

$\Rightarrow (A + B + C - D) = -4x^2 + 5x + 31$

$\therefore$ The sum of the co-efficients of x^2 and x in $(A + B + C - D) = -4 + 5 = 1$.

59. (C): Disposition towards mathematics refers to students' attitudes, beliefs, and feelings towards mathematics. While disposition towards mathematics is an essential aspect of mathematics education and can influence students' motivation and engagement with the subject, it is not typically considered a dimension of assessment of mathematics learning. Assessment of mathematics learning usually focuses on dimensions such as mathematical knowledge and skills, problem-solving abilities, mathematical reasoning, and communication of mathematical ideas.

60. (B): Given, in ΔPQR, $\angle P = 55°$ and $QR = 18$ cm

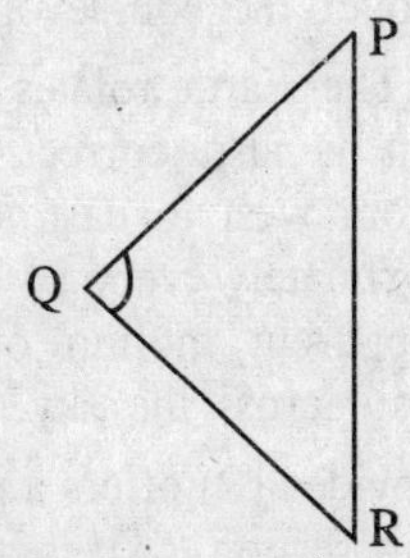

$\therefore \angle R = 15°$ and $PR > 18$ cm

$\therefore \angle Q > 90°$

Hence, ΔPQR can be an obtuse scalene triangle.

61. (C): guitar, tabla, shehnai

- In a guitar, the sound is produced by stretched strings.
- In a tabla, it is the stretched membrane that vibrates.
- In a shehnai, the vibrating part that produces sound is the air column.

62. (D): Set of micronutrients (nutrients required by plants in small quantities):

- **Zinc (Zn):** Zinc is essential for several enzymatic reactions within plants, including the synthesis of certain proteins and the regulation of growth hormones. It is involved in processes such as photosynthesis, seed germination, and root development. Zinc deficiency can lead to stunted growth, reduced yield, and abnormal leaf development in plants.
- **Iron (Fe):** Iron is a crucial component of chlorophyll, the pigment responsible for photosynthesis. It plays a vital role in electron transport chains, enzyme activation, and nitrogen fixation. Iron deficiency can result in chlorosis (yellowing of leaves) due to decreased chlorophyll production, ultimately impairing the plant's ability to produce energy through photosynthesis.
- **Manganese (Mn):** Manganese functions as a cofactor for several enzymes involved in photosynthesis, respiration, and nitrogen metabolism. It plays a role in antioxidant defense mechanisms and helps plants cope with environmental stresses. Manganese deficiency can lead to interveinal chlorosis, reduced growth, and poor reproductive development in plants.

63. (A): Assertion (A): The stars in the night sky appear to move from east to west. This statement is correct. When we observe the night sky, we notice that the stars appear to move across the sky from east to west over the course of the night.

Reason (R): The Earth rotates from west to east. This statement is also correct. The Earth rotates on its axis from west to east, completing one full rotation approximately every 24 hours. This rotation causes the apparent motion of celestial objects, including stars, across the sky.

The reason provided (R) offers a plausible explanation for why the assertion (A) is true. As the Earth rotates from west to east, an observer on the Earth's surface will perceive celestial objects, such as stars, to move in the opposite direction, from east to west. This apparent motion is an effect of the Earth's rotation and is consistent with the observed movement of stars in the night sky.

64. (D): Rusting of iron:

- **It involves a chemical reaction between iron and oxygen:** Rusting of iron is a chemical process that occurs when iron reacts with oxygen in the presence of water. The presence of water, particularly moisture from the atmosphere or water vapor, is crucial for the rusting process to occur. The chemical reaction between iron, oxygen, and water results in the formation of iron oxide, commonly known as rust. The reaction can be represented by the equation:

$$34\ Fe + 3\ O_2 + 6H_2O \rightarrow 4\ Fe(OH)_3$$

- **It is an exothermic reaction:** The rusting of iron is indeed an exothermic process. An exothermic reaction is one that releases energy in the form of heat to its surroundings. When iron undergoes rusting, energy is released in the form of heat, contributing to the warming of the surroundings. This energy release is a characteristic feature of exothermic reactions.
- **It can take place at room temperature:** Rusting of iron can occur at room temperature, although the rate of rusting may vary depending on environmental conditions such as humidity and the presence of salts or acids. Water vapor in the atmosphere or moisture on the surface of the iron provides the necessary moisture for the rusting process. Oxygen from the air reacts with the iron in the presence of this moisture to initiate the rusting process. While higher temperatures can accelerate the rusting process, rusting can still occur at room temperature given sufficient moisture and oxygen.

Hence, (*a*), (*b*) and (*c*) are correct.

65. (A): Substances and their chemical names are:

- Slaked lime is also known as calcium hydroxide, which is represented chemically as $Ca(OH)_2$. It is produced by adding water to quicklime (calcium oxide), resulting in a chemical reaction that produces calcium hydroxide.
- Table salt is the common name for sodium chloride, which is represented chemically as NaCl. Sodium chloride is a compound composed of sodium ions (Na^+) and chloride ions (Cl^-).
- Limestone is primarily composed of calcium carbonate ($CaCO_3$). It is a sedimentary rock formed from the accumulation of calcium carbonate deposits over time.
- Caustic soda is the common name for sodium hydroxide, which is represented chemically as NaOH. Sodium hydroxide is a strong base and is commonly used in various industrial processes, including the manufacture of soap and paper.
- Quicklime is also known as calcium oxide, which is represented chemically as CaO. It is produced by heating limestone (calcium carbonate) in a kiln, resulting in the decomposition of calcium carbonate to calcium oxide and carbon dioxide.
- Baking soda is the common name for sodium bicarbonate, which is represented chemically as $NaHCO_3$. Sodium bicarbonate is commonly used as a leavening agent in baking and as an antacid to relieve heartburn.

66. (A): A fact is an observation that has repeatedly been found to be true over time: This statement is true. In science, a fact is an empirical observation that is objectively verifiable and has been confirmed through repeated experimentation and observation. Facts are considered to be true based on evidence and are not dependent on interpretation or opinion. For example, the fact that water freezes at 0 degrees Celsius at standard atmospheric pressure is based on repeated observations and experiments.

67. (A): When a negatively charged rod is brought near an uncharged electroscope:

(*a*) **The electroscope leaves move further apart:** This statement describes a direct and measurable change in the position of the electroscope leaves when a negatively charged rod is brought near it. Therefore, it is indeed an observation.

(*b*) **Both the electroscope leaves acquire similar charge:** This statement proposes a conclusion based on the observation described in statement (a). It infers that the electroscope leaves acquire similar charges due to the influence of the negatively charged rod. Therefore, it is an inference.

(*c*) The negative charges pass on to the electroscope causing its leaves to move further apart: Similar to statement (*b*), this statement also proposes a mechanism or explanation for the observation described in statement (*a*). It infers that the negative charges from the rod cause the electroscope leaves to move further apart. Therefore, it is also an inference.

68 (D): Gases responsible for acid rain:

- **Sulphur dioxide (SO_2):** Sulphur dioxide is primarily produced by the combustion of fossil fuels, such as coal and oil, in industrial processes and power plants. When sulphur dioxide is released into the atmosphere, it can react with oxygen and water vapor to form sulphuric acid (H_2SO_4). This reaction occurs in the presence of sunlight and atmospheric moisture. The sulphuric acid formed from the reaction with sulphur dioxide contributes to the acidity of rainwater, resulting in acid rain.
- **Nitric oxide:** Nitric oxides are produced by the combustion of fossil fuels in vehicles, industrial processes, and power plants, as well as by natural processes such as lightning and wildfires. In the atmosphere, nitrogen oxides can react with oxygen and water vapor to form nitric acid (HNO_3) and other nitrogen-containing acids, such as nitrous acid (HNO_2). These acids contribute to the acidity of rainwater, further contributing to the phenomenon of acid rain.

69. (C): Using the senses to gather information: This option refers to the process of gathering information through sensory perception, such as seeing, hearing, touching, etc. While this is an important aspect of the scientific process, it is not directly related to hypothesizing, which focuses more on proposing explanations or hypotheses based on existing knowledge or observations. Hypothesizing involves formulating educated guesses or proposed explanations for observed phenomena based on existing knowledge or observations, rather than simply collecting sensory data. However, sensory information serves as the foundation upon which hypotheses and explanations are developed, as it provides the empirical basis for scientific inquiry and investigation.

70. (C): Correct statements are:

(*a*) Generally non-metals do not react with water: This statement is generally true. Most non-metals do not react with water, especially at room temperature and under normal conditions. However, some non-metals, such as sulphur and phosphorus, can react with water under specific conditions to form acidic or basic solutions.

(*b*) Generally non-metals do not react with acids: This statement is also generally true. Non-metals typically do not react with acids under normal conditions. While some non-metals, such as hydrogen and carbon, can react with certain acids under specific conditions, the general trend is that non-metals do not readily react with acids.

72. (C): Kinetic energy, K.E. $= \frac{1}{2}mv^2$ ...(*i*)

Let the speed of the body be v.

Momentum, p = mv

$$v = \frac{p}{m} \quad ...(ii)$$

Substituting the value of v from eqn. (*ii*) in eqn. (*i*), we get:

$$\text{K.E.} = \frac{1}{2}m\left(\frac{p}{m}\right)^2 = \frac{p^2}{2m}$$

Hence, the kinetic energy of the body is $\frac{p^2}{2m}$.

73. (D): Introducing students to the concept of chemical reactions through a discussion on observable phenomena in their daily lives is effective because it makes the topic more relatable and engaging. Students are likely to have encountered various chemical reactions in their surroundings, such as rusting of iron, burning of wood, baking of bread, or formation of bubbles when baking soda reacts with vinegar. By discussing these familiar examples, students can begin to understand the concept of chemical reactions in a practical context. It also provides an opportunity for students to share their observations and experiences, fostering active participation and inquiry-based learning. This approach sets a foundation for further exploration and understanding of chemical reactions in subsequent lessons.

74. (D): The set of animals which show external fertilization include:

- **Frogs:** Frogs lay their eggs in water, such as ponds or streams. During mating, the male frog releases sperm, which fertilizes the eggs externally as they are laid by the female. This process allows for the sperm to swim to the eggs and fertilize them in the water.

- **Fish:** Most fish species reproduce through external fertilization. Female fish release eggs into the water, and male fish release sperm to fertilize the eggs externally. This process often occurs in large groups during spawning events, where both eggs and sperm are released into the water simultaneously.
- **Starfish:** Starfish, or sea stars, are marine invertebrates that also exhibit external fertilization. During spawning, male and female starfish release their gametes into the water. Fertilization occurs externally as the sperm swim to the eggs, resulting in the development of larvae that eventually settle and grow into new starfish.

75. (B): This option highlights the issue of unequal entries in column A and column B of the test item. In a well-constructed matching test item, each entry in column A should have a corresponding and unique match in column B, and vice versa. However, in this particular item, there are six entries in column A but seven entries in column B. This discrepancy creates confusion and inconsistency for the test-taker because they may not know which entry in column B corresponds to which entry in column A. As a result, the unequal entries make it challenging to accurately match the items and undermine the reliability of the assessment. Therefore, option B correctly identifies this flaw in the construction of the test item.

76. (A): Assertion (A) states that dried raisins swell when left in plain water for some time due to osmosis. This is correct because osmosis is the movement of water molecules across a selectively permeable membrane from an area of lower solute concentration to an area of higher solute concentration, resulting in the swelling of the raisins.

Reason (R) states that plant cells have a selectively permeable cell membrane. This is also correct because plant cells, like all cells, have a cell membrane that regulates the movement of substances in and out of the cell. The cell membrane in plant cells is selectively permeable, allowing certain molecules to pass through while blocking others.

The reason (R) provides a correct explanation for assertion (A) because it links the process of osmosis occurring in dried raisins to the presence of a selectively permeable membrane, which is characteristic of plant cells.

77. (B): Arranging for a doctor's prescription related to a deficiency disease and holding a discussion around it is a suitable strategy to introduce the topic of deficiency diseases at the upper primary level. This approach provides a real-life context for understanding deficiency diseases, making the topic more tangible and relevant for students. By examining the prescription, students engage in active learning as they analyze its contents, discuss the diagnosis and treatment of deficiency diseases, and ask questions about the condition mentioned. The doctor's prescription serves as a visual aid that supports students' comprehension of how deficiency diseases are diagnosed and treated in medical practice, while also promoting critical thinking and interdisciplinary learning across science, mathematics, and language arts domains. Overall, this strategy fosters deeper understanding and interest in deficiency diseases among students, paving the way for further exploration and learning in the topic area.

78. (A): Science encourages skepticism by emphasizing the importance of critically evaluating claims and hypotheses through rigorous empirical investigation. Scientists approach new ideas with skepticism, questioning their validity and seeking evidence to support or refute them. In the scientific method, hypotheses are tested through observation and experimentation, and conclusions are drawn based on objective evidence rather than preconceived notions or beliefs. This commitment to evidence-based reasoning promotes skepticism as scientists continuously evaluate and scrutinize claims in pursuit of truth and knowledge. Options B, C, and D do not directly address the fundamental role of empirical evidence in promoting skepticism within the scientific process.

79. (C): A pair of balanced forces acts on the box. This means that the box experiences two forces that are equal in magnitude but opposite in direction. Firstly, the weight of the box acts downward due to gravity, which is calculated to be 5 N given the mass of the box and the acceleration due to gravity. Secondly, the table exerts a normal force on the box in the upward direction, also with a magnitude of 5 N. According to Newton's third law of motion, these two forces form a pair of action-reaction forces, ensuring that the box remains at rest on the horizontal table. This balanced force situation implies that the net force acting on the box in the vertical direction is zero, leading to the conclusion that a pair of balanced forces acts on it.

80. (C): A periscope is a device used to see around corners, typically in submarines or military tanks. It works based on the principle of reflection. A periscope consists of a system of mirrors or prisms that reflect light, allowing the viewer to observe objects or scenes that are not directly in their line of sight. When light enters the periscope, it undergoes multiple reflections inside the device before reaching the observer's eye, enabling them to see around obstacles or corners. Therefore, this option accurately pairs the device (X) and the principle (Y) as periscope and reflection, respectively.

81. (A): Bitumen and coal tar are thick, black liquids derived from petroleum and coal, respectively, and are commonly used for metalling roads. Bitumen, derived from petroleum, is a common binder used in road construction for its adhesive properties and ability to bind aggregates together. Coal tar, derived from coal, is another type of black, viscous liquid used for road surfacing and roofing materials. Therefore, this option correctly identifies X and Y as bitumen and coal tar, respectively, making it the correct choice.

82. (B): A good demonstration should allow students to discover the connections and takeaways on their own. Pre-emphasizing the linkages takes away the element of discovery and can stifle critical thinking and engagement. The goal is for students to understand the concepts demonstrated, not simply memorize specific connections. Providing the linkages beforehand can lead to rote memorization rather than deep understanding. Demonstrations are most effective when they spark curiosity and encourage students to explore the concepts further. Telling them exactly what they need to learn beforehand can hinder their natural curiosity and exploration process.

83. (A): Fertilisers are synthetic substances or chemical compounds containing specific nutrients such as nitrogen, phosphorus, and potassium in concentrated forms. They are manufactured to provide plants with essential nutrients necessary for their growth and development. In contrast, manure is organic matter derived from decomposed animal or plant materials. While manure also contains nutrients, it tends to be less concentrated and may not provide nutrients in the specific ratios required by plants. Therefore, fertilisers are indeed richer in specific nutrients compared to manure.

84. (A): The correct match is:

- Rose exhibits vegetative propagation, a form of asexual reproduction where new plants grow from specialized structures such as runners, rhizomes, bulbs, or tubers.
- Yeast reproduces asexually mainly through budding, where a small bud forms on the parent cell and eventually detaches to become a new individual.
- Ferns reproduce asexually through spore formation. Spores are single-celled reproductive structures produced by ferns and released into the environment to germinate and develop into new individuals.
- Spirogyra reproduces asexually through fragmentation, where the filament breaks into fragments, and each fragment grows into a new individual.

85. (B): Citrus canker: Citrus canker is a bacterial disease caused by the bacterium *Xanthomonas citri*. It affects citrus plants, including oranges, lemons, and grapefruits, causing characteristic lesions or cankers on leaves, stems, and fruits. These cankers are raised, corky lesions that may ooze bacterial exudates. Citrus canker can lead to defoliation, premature fruit drop, and reduced fruit quality, impacting citrus production.

87. (B): (*b*) **Observing:** When presented with images of a sailing boat, swimming fish, and flying airplane, students are likely to carefully observe the characteristics of each image. They may pay attention to details such as the shapes of the objects and the way they are depicted in motion. By observing these details, students can gather information that will help them analyze and respond to the teacher's question effectively.

(*c*) **Inductive Reasoning:** Inductive reasoning involves drawing general conclusions based on specific observations. After observing the shapes and movements of the images, students may use inductive reasoning to generalize principles about the relationship between an object's shape and its mode of movement. For instance, they might infer that streamlined shapes are suitable for movement through water or air, while more solid and stable shapes are suited for movement on land. By applying inductive reasoning, students can make logical connections between the observed characteristics of the images and broader principles of motion and design.

88. (A): Seed dispersal mechanisms, such as wind, water, animals, or self-dispersal strategies, help plants spread their seeds away from the parent plant. By dispersing seeds, plants reduce the likelihood of overcrowding in their immediate vicinity. Overcrowding can lead to competition among plants for essential resources such as sunlight, water, and nutrients, which can hinder the growth and development of individual plants. Therefore, seed dispersal plays a crucial role in maintaining plant populations by preventing overcrowding and promoting the successful establishment of offspring in diverse environments. Therefore, this option is the correct answer as it does not align with the benefits of seed dispersal.

89. (A): Newton's theory of gravitation is considered excellent because it successfully explains a wide range of observations related to the motion of celestial bodies, such as the orbits of planets, the motion of moons, and the tides, among others. Despite its simplicity, the theory accounts for complex phenomena in the universe by relying on fundamental principles of mass, distance, and gravitational attraction. Additionally, Newton's theory is elegant in its simplicity, as it requires fewer assumptions to explain diverse observations compared to alternative theories. This parsimony in assumptions enhances the theory's explanatory power and contributes to its status as a cornerstone of modern physics.

90. (B): Statement 1 (S1): "Rayon is a synthetic fiber." This statement is true. Rayon is classified as a semi-synthetic fiber, as it is derived from natural cellulose sources such as wood pulp, bamboo, or cotton, but undergoes extensive chemical processing to convert these materials into fiber form. While it is not purely synthetic, it is often categorized as a synthetic fiber due to its manufacturing process.

Statement 2 (S2): "Rayon is made without using any natural raw material." This statement is false. Rayon is indeed made using natural raw materials, primarily cellulose from wood pulp, bamboo, or cotton. Although the manufacturing process involves significant chemical processing, the raw material used in rayon production originates from natural sources. Therefore, S2 is false.

91. (C): "time" is a noun referring to a specific period, while "when" is a preposition that introduces a dependent clause, indicating a specific point in time.

92. (B): The characters share a mother and daughter relationship, as indicated by the narrative's context and the use of "my daughter" by the narrator.

93. (C): "To be transported in time" means to recollect memories of the past, as the phrase suggests a mental return to a previous moment or experience.

94. (B): "Admonish" means to reprimand or scold someone, suggesting a context of intended correction or warning.

95. (A): In this analogy, "cluster" relates to "bunch" as a group of things; similarly, "puny" relates to "delicate" in describing something small or weak.

96. (A): The mother initially thought it was not a good idea to taste sweet nectar from flowers, reflecting a moment of hesitation before recalling her own childhood joy.

97. (D): "To be dead tired" means to be extremely exhausted. It does not mean "to feel refreshed," which is the opposite of being tired.

98. (D): Assertion (A) states that the child is excited to share a secret with her mother, indicating a positive emotional response from the child. Reason (R) provides an explanation for this excitement by suggesting that the mother's reaction, characterized by disbelief and reminiscing about past memories, contributes to the child's excitement. Essentially, the child's anticipation of the mother's reaction, along with the emotional connection between them, influences the child's excitement. Therefore, Reason (R) is a plausible explanation for Assertion (A)

99. (D): The daughter's secret revives nostalgic memories of the mother's school days (*b*), and the narrative focuses on connecting the child to the simple pleasures of nature (*c*). The writer is not traumatised by her childhood memories, making (*a*) incorrect.

100. (C): The poet considers himself fortunate because he has a lamp lit by Leerie outside his door every night, providing light and safety.

101. (D): "The sun has left the sky" indicates it is evening time, as it describes the transition period after sunset.

102. (C): The poet is clearly fascinated by the lamp lighter's profession, as evidenced by his expressed desire to accompany Leerie and light the lamps. There's no indication he wants to follow in his father's footsteps as a banker, making (*b*) incorrect, and the light is regularly outside his door, not occasionally, making (*a*) incorrect.

103. (D): Leerie's profession is a lamplighter, and the father's profession is explicitly mentioned as a banker, making the correct analogy "father : banker".

104. (B): The rhyme scheme in lines 5 - 8 is "aabb," as "sea" rhymes with "be" and "do" rhymes with "you".

105. (A): The poet looks at the lamp-lighter's profession with wonder, admiring the role and expressing a wish to join Leerie in his nightly duties.

106. (C): The Malayalam spoken by a particular community in Kozhikode that is slightly different from the Malayalam spoken by others in the same place is known as a social dialect of Malayalam. Social dialects vary based on social groups rather than geographical differences.

107. (A): Thematic vocabulary activities, as demonstrated in this learning task, involve learners identifying and exploring words and phrases that are thematically related to a specific topic or theme. In this case, the theme revolves around concepts like "Family", "Relationship", and "Work". Students are tasked with finding words and phrases that are associated with these themes, thereby expanding their vocabulary within the context of these topics. This activity encourages learners to make connections between words and concepts, thereby deepening their understanding and retention of vocabulary in a meaningful and contextualized manner.

108. (B): The language used for day-to-day, face-to-face interaction is known as Basic Interpersonal Communication Skills (BICS). This term refers to the conversational language skills necessary for social interactions.

109. (A): By giving a text/short story and asking learners to discuss its meaning and ideas from the perspective of power and justice, the teacher attempts to develop critical literacy skills in the learners. This approach encourages students to analyze and critique the text for underlying messages about societal structures.

110. (A): Procedural knowledge in the teaching-learning of grammar is knowing how to do the grammatical item. It involves the practical use of grammar in constructing sentences, as opposed to merely knowing about its rules.

111. (D): The described activity is known as Mutual Dictation. It involves partners alternating between reading and writing sentences from a text, engaging both listening and writing skills, and then checking their work against the original text.

112. (C): It is not true that Sign Language does not have a grammar. Sign languages, like spoken languages, have their own complex grammars. This includes rules for sentence structure, tense, and other linguistic elements.

113. (A): The three-language formula typically involves the mother tongue/home language/regional language as the first language, ensuring the learner's cultural and linguistic roots are emphasized in their education.

114. (C): Remedial teaching serves as a targeted intervention for both learners and teachers to identify and address specific areas of difficulty in language learning. It provides learners who struggle with certain aspects of language acquisition with personalized attention and support to overcome their challenges. Additionally, it enables teachers to adapt their teaching methods and approaches to better meet the needs of individual students, ultimately enhancing the effectiveness of language instruction. By fostering a deeper understanding of learning strengths and weaknesses, remedial teaching facilitates the development and refinement of strategies for both learners and teachers, leading to improved language learning outcomes.

115. (B): This teaching method is referred to as Reciprocal Teaching. It is a collaborative learning activity where the teacher and students take turns leading a dialogue on the text's content, enhancing reading comprehension within a supportive group structure.

116. (A): This pedagogical strategy is known as Translanguaging. It involves using multiple languages in the teaching and learning process, allowing students to switch between languages to enhance understanding and expression.

117. (C): Reading through a news item to locate specific information is known as Scanning. It is a reading technique used to find particular facts or figures, focusing on key details rather than understanding the text's overall meaning.

118. (A): Interlingual identification refers to a learner's judgment that something in the native language and something in the target language are similar. This can sometimes lead to correct understanding but also to errors if the assumed similarities do not actually exist.

119. (A): Shreya's Punjabi and Tamil would be considered as acquired languages because she learned them in natural, immersive environments (Punjabi at home and Tamil in her neighborhood). English, studied formally in school as a second language, comes under language learning, involving more explicit instruction and study.

120. (C): The purpose of extensive reading is not primarily focused on learning grammar. Extensive reading is aimed at reading for pleasure, appreciation, and extrapolation, encouraging a broader and more engaged interaction with texts beyond the specifics of grammar.

121. (B): गद्यांश के आधार पर यह कहा जा सकता है कि एआई ऐसी होनी चाहिए जो मानवीय गुणों का संस्कार दे। इससे इंसानियत फैलाने में मदद मिलेगी।

122. (D): शब्द समूह में 'चाय-वाय' भिन्न है क्योंकि यह विशेष तरीके से अभिव्यक्ति के लिए प्रयोग होता है, जबकि अन्य विकल्प सामान्य शब्द जोड़े हैं।

123. (C): 'मानवीय' शब्द में 'ईय' प्रत्यय है, जो मानव से बना है और 'मानव से संबंधित' का भाव देता है।

124. (C): एआई शारीरिक श्रम से जुड़े कार्यों पर सबसे कम प्रभाव डालेगा, इसलिए खेती-बाड़ी प्रभावित नहीं होगी क्योंकि यह शारीरिक श्रम पर निर्भर करता है।

125. (D): एआई को जन्म देने वाला कारक मानव है, क्योंकि मानव ने ही इस तकनीक का विकास किया है।

126. (B): 'एआई' का अर्थ है आर्टिफिशियल इंटेलीजेंस, जो मशीनों द्वारा बुद्धिमत्ता के प्रदर्शन को संदर्भित करता है।

127. (A): एआई से शिक्षा जगत पर प्रभाव नकारात्मक भी हो सकता है अगर इसे सही दिशा में नहीं ले जाया जाए, क्योंकि इससे शिक्षा के पारंपरिक तरीके बदल सकते हैं।

128. (B): एआई भविष्य में चिकित्सा से जुड़े कार्य करने में मदद करेगा, जैसे कि केस हिस्ट्री बनाने में, लक्षणों की पहचान में, और सही उपचार प्रदान करने में।

129. (D): जीवन के लिए सर्वाधिक महत्वपूर्ण प्राण और शरीर का सामंजस्य है, क्योंकि गद्यांश में यही बात बार-बार उल्लेखित है कि प्राण शरीर के हर अंग में संतुलित और व्यवस्थित होने से ही स्वास्थ्य बना रहता है।

130. (C): 'स्वास्थ्य' विशेषण शब्द का उदाहरण नहीं है, बल्कि यह एक संज्ञा है। शेष विकल्प विशेषण हैं जो गुणवाचक शब्द होते हैं।

131. (B): प्राण वायु को सशक्त बनाने के अभ्यास योग में है। गद्यांश के अनुसार योग में प्राण को बल देने के लिए अनेक अभ्यास हैं।

132. (A): प्राण वायु शरीर के हर अंग में संतुलित और व्यवस्थित होकर बहती है। यह स्वास्थ्य और बीमारी के संदर्भ में बताया गया है।

133. (B): रोग का कारण प्राण वायु का अंग विशेष में असंतुलन होता है। गद्यांश के अनुसार, बीमारी प्राण का उस अंग विशेष में असंतुलित हो जाना ही है।

134. (B): अच्छे स्वास्थ्य का संबंध प्राण वायु से है। गद्यांश में स्वास्थ्य को प्राण का समुचित तरीके से समस्त अंगों की तरफ बहने के रूप में परिभाषित किया गया है।

135. (B): 'बुद्धि' में 'इक' प्रत्यय लगने पर शब्द 'बौद्धिक' बनेगा। यह शब्द 'बुद्धि से संबंधित' अर्थ देने के लिए प्रयोग किया जाता है।

137. (A): इस स्थिति को परभाषिक (ट्रांसलिंग्युल) योग्यता के रूप में जाना जाएगा, जहाँ एक व्यक्ति विभिन्न सामाजिक और पारिवारिक परिस्थितियों में बहुभाषिकता का प्रदर्शन करता है।

138. (C): सहजात/प्रथम भाषा का ज्ञान द्वितीय भाषा के अधिगम को समर्थित करता है। यह ज्ञान नई भाषा सीखने की प्रक्रिया में एक सकारात्मक आधार के रूप में कार्य करता है और अधिगम को आसान बनाता है।

139. (B): चम्मच, प्लेट, डिब्बे, परात जैसी वस्तुएँ भाषा शिक्षण में वास्तविक वस्तुएँ (रीयलिया) के रूप में जानी जाती हैं। इन्हें विद्यार्थियों को शब्दावली सिखाने और उन्हें वास्तविक दुनिया से जोड़ने के लिए इस्तेमाल किया जाता है।

140. (B): घोषणात्मक ज्ञान का अर्थ है व्याकरणिक तत्वों के बारे में ज्ञान। यह भाषा सीखने की प्रक्रिया में उस ज्ञान को संदर्भित करता है जो व्यक्ति को भाषा के नियमों, वाक्य रचना और व्याकरणिक संरचनाओं की समझ होती है।

141. (C): यहाँ विषय के विपरीत वाले दृष्टिकोण से परिचित करवाकर विद्यार्थियों में समालोचनात्मक साक्षरता के विकास का प्रयास किया जा रहा है। इससे विद्यार्थियों को विषय की गहराई से समझ बनाने और विभिन्न दृष्टिकोणों की पहचान करने में मदद मिलती है।

142. (C): 'परभाषा व्यवहार' (ट्रान्सलैंग्युजिंग) एक ऐसी शिक्षण शास्त्रीय प्रक्रिया है जिसमें एक कक्षा में एक से अधिक भाषाओं को संसाधन के रूप में इस्तेमाल किया जाता है। यह विद्यार्थियों को अपनी भाषाई संपदा का उपयोग करने के लिए प्रोत्साहित करता है।

143. (D): भाषा को अच्छी तरह से लिखना सीखने में शामिल प्रक्रियाएँ हैं : मानस मंथन - मुख्य बिन्दु नोट करना - रूपरेखा तैयार करना - प्रारूप लिखना - संपादन - अन्तिम स्वरूप देना। यह प्रक्रिया विचारों की सृजनात्मकता, संरचना, और अंतिम लेखन को संशोधित करने और परिमार्जित करने के चरणों को दर्शाती है।

144. (A): सामाजिक विज्ञान की कक्षा में वक्तव्य से मुख्य बिन्दु समझने और लिखने की कोशिश एक अध्ययन कौशल है। इस कौशल में सुनकर मुख्य बिन्दुओं को पहचानना और उन्हें लिखना शामिल है, जो सूचना को प्रभावी ढंग से संसाधित करने और समझने में मदद करता है।

147. (D): अकादमिक भाषा या विभिन्न प्रकार के विषयों के लिए आवश्यक भाषा में निपुणता 'संज्ञानात्मक अकादमिक भाषा निपुणता' (CALP) से संबंधित है। यह शैक्षणिक संदर्भों में भाषा के जटिल उपयोग की क्षमता को दर्शाता है।

149. (D): त्रिभाषा सूत्र के संबंध में सही कथन यह है कि सभी बच्चे अपनी विद्यालयी शिक्षा मातृभाषा/घर की भाषा में शुरू करते हैं और दसवीं पूरी करने तक कम से कम दो और भाषाएँ सीखते हैं। इससे भाषाई विविधता और बहुभाषिकता को बढ़ावा मिलता है।

150. (B): अधिगम प्रतिफल शिक्षार्थियों को विभिन्न दक्षताओं को मापन के संदर्भ में प्राप्त करने में समर्थ बनाते हैं। यह उन्हें भाषा अधिगम, संचार कौशल, और विभिन्न विषयों में ज्ञान को समझने और लागू करने में सक्षम बनाता है।

Child Development & Pedagogy

SECTION a

CHILD DEVELOPMENT

CONCEPT OF DEVELOPMENT

Development refers to interaction of a person with his environmental surroundings whose after product is to increase:

- The strength
- The degree of differentiation
- The organization of personality

Development refers to those effects upon the person's cognitive and emotional systems which strengthen one or more abilities of the person in the desired manner. Thus, development is the qualitative changes in the organism. Environment has very important role to play in the process of development.

Three Concepts of Development

1. *Development is maturation :* According to **Arnold Gessell**, the role of physical changes is very important in development. The development from infancy to adolescence is governed by physical changes. When physical growth of the particular stage gets matured only then development in that stage is possible. For example, a growing nervous system changes systematically and automatically and this results in predictable changes in bones and muscles. Thus major changes in the organism are based on maturation.

   According to Gessell, there is internal programming toward physical and cognitive growth and each year is characterized by certain behavioural changes. Development is always guided and controlled by these changes.

2. *Development is learning :* According to **Baer**, "development is the behavioural changes which require programming and programming requires time but not enough of it to call it age."

   Programming here means the sequence of learning which may happen naturally or it may be arranged in the life of an individual with the help of the environment. Thus, according to this definition, development is genetic and environmental both. Whatever we learn in the process of our life is related to development of us.

3. *Development is the synthesis of abilities :* According to **Jean Piaget**, there are four basic elements that take part in the process of development and development is the result of synthesis of all these elements. They are given below:

I. Maturation	An automatic and innate process
II. Social transmission	Learning through language, schooling or training given by parents
III. Experiences	Obtained from the outer environment informally
IV. Equilibration	Whatever is learnt or gained internally or externally is equilibrated here.

STAGES OF DEVELOPMENT

From infancy to adulthood human being undergoes the following stages of development.

1	Infancy	-	0-2 years
2	Early childhood	-	3-6 years
3	Later childhood	-	7-12 years
4	Adolescence	-	13-17 years
5	Adulthood	-	18-25 years

At each stage of human development, certain physical, intellectual, language, emotional and social changes occur which may be similar or entirely different from the preceding age. We will describe all these stages one by one.

Dimensions (Areas) of Development

Before coming to the stages of development it is better to know what the physical, intellectual, emotional and social development are:

1. **Physical development :** Important characteristics of physical growth and development are given below:
   - Physical growth is curvilinear not steady or regular. Rapid growth is followed by slow growth and then again rapid growth may be there.
   - Different parts (organs) of the body have its own unique way of development. Whatever changes we see in hands and legs cannot be seen in heart or lung.
   - Physical growth and development is affected by climatic conditions. For example, cold countries have more favourable conditions of growth and development than hot or humid countries.
   - Heredity fixes a limit of physical growth and development. The descendents of five feeted man is not supposed to have a height of more than 6 feet or 5½ feet.
   - Physical growth is very rapid in the infancy and in the later childhood. It is again fast in the start of adolescence.

Dimensions of Physical Growth : Important dimensions of physical growth and development are as follows:

(i) *Height :* A new born baby is 19-20 inches in length at the time of birth. As soon as the baby grows, his height also increases.

(ii) *Weight :* Human baby has a weight of 2.5 kg. –3.5 kg. at the time of birth. Girl babies are generally lighter than male babies here. When a baby becomes an adult he acquires a weight of 55 kg. at the height 5.5 feet. The weight of boys are generally higher than girls due to increased height. If height is more, weight will also be high.

(iii) *Body proportion :* Some organs of the body are more developed at the time of birth than others. But as soon as the baby grows and reaches to the period of adulthood, proportionate change and growth are seen. For example, head is already somewhat developed at the time of birth but it grows less proportionately than other parts of body.

(iv) *Internal organs :* Internal organs of the body also develop with age. As the child grows, the heart beat which is 100-120 per minute in infancy, becomes regular and normal, *i.e.*, 72 times per minute. Respiration also becomes slower, deeper and regular, food takes longer time to pass the digestive tract, the body temperature becomes stable and so on and all this happens due to growth and development of the internal organs of the body. This increase in efficiency enables the older children and adults to adapt to the environmental changes.

It is pitutory gland which is responsible for growth in the early years of life. Sex gland is also activated under the influence of this gland, and influence the pitutory gland as well. If sex hormones did not restrain the function of pitutory gland the human being would become a giant.

2. **Motor development :** Motor development includes movement of hands, lags, mouth and other related muscles of the body. Important features of motor development are as follows:
   - Motor development occurs in those structures which lie nearest to the main axis especially near the vaist, thighs, legs etc. The child learns to control the muscles of his arms earlier than those of fingers.
   - Bilateral to unilateral trend in the coordination and control of muscles is seen. The child first uses both of his hands then he gradually learns to use only one hand in specialized manner.
   - From general to specific trend in motor development is seen.
   - An orderly sequence of motor development is also seen. **Hurlock** found that motor development in the head region takes place first, followed by the motor development of arms, hands, legs, etc. This trend is not reversed any how.
   - If motor development of the child is delayed by any reason, his emotional and social development will also be delayed or disturbed.

3. **Intellectual development :** Intellectual development includes attending, perceiving, observing, thinking, recalling, analyzing, evaluating, problem solving and the development of language and concepts. These aspects of mind grow and change with age. Generally these activities of mind are inter related. Important features of intellectual development are as follows:

- Mental development is a continuous but steady process and all activities of mind are inter-related also.
- As long as the experiences of the child increase, his mental horizon expands. He learns not only to differentiate but to integrate different elements of the physical as well as meta-physical world.
- Factors affecting mental development are maturation and learning.
- Mental activities are guided and controlled by nervous system. Brain which is an important part of nervous system plays the key role in the mental development of the child.
- Sensation and perception are the primary aspects of mental activities. In fact, mental activities start from these two aspects. Sensation is the first step to knowledge which is accompanied by perception.
- Perceptual experience leads to concept formation. Concept formation takes place on the basis of general and common qualities of an object, e.g., concept of "book" is developed after seeing so many things like books and then we say that books are for reading. Thus, concept is developed on the basis of common qualities of an object. It involves discrimination and generalization both.
- Concept of an object or idea changes with the change in experiences for example, cold season of December may have different meaning for the people of Kolkata and Srinagar due to difference of experiences.
- Child's concepts change with the increase in his age. For example, a small child may develop a unique concept of ghost. But when he becomes an adult, his concept of ghost changes.

4. **Language development :** Language development is actually the verbalization of concepts which is learnt by imitation (hearing). If child is deaf, his language development will be zero. Important features of language development are given below.
   - Language is a tool to be used for all types of communication. Without proper language development, no communication from one person to the other is possible.
   - Language is used as a tool in acquiring knowledge. When knowledge increases, vocabulary also increases.
   - Language development starts with mere names of objects or events and when it reaches at its peak it develops ideas into universal concepts.
   - Growth and maturity of speech is an important aspect of language development. Four needs of the child motivates him to learn speech.

Desire to secure information more and more (Interrogative sentences).

(a) Desire to give commands or to do requests (Imperative sentences).

(b) Desire to come into social relationship with others.

(c) Desire to express feelings and thoughts (Exclamatory and Assertive sentences)

- There are spurts or rest in the speech development. It is not constant throughout life. Sometimes it is very rapid and sometimes very slow.
- The development of thinking moves from simple to complex and from the concrete to the abstract.
- An individual stops growing intellectually upto the age of 20 years in general.

5. **Emotional development :** Emotion is a strong feeling that is so strong that it can be observed overtly. There are **four qualities of emotional experiences:**
   - Every emotional experience involves feeling
   - Every emotional experience is accompanied by marked physiological changes
   - An emotional experience includes an impulse towards some kind of action, ie, overt response is seen
   - Emotion involves awareness or perception of what it is or what it might be that causes these impulses and feelings

Important features of emotional development are as follows :

(a) Emotions start immediately after birth. For example, an infant shows fear, anger, love etc, though his emotions are not clear at this age, according to Sherman.

(b) Children's emotions are very intense as compared to adults. As they grow they begin to exercise restraint over their emotions. They learn to modify and hide their emotions also.

(c) Child's emotions last only for a few minutes and then it ends all of a sudden. The transitory nature of the child's emotions lies in a rapid shift from one emotion to another. When he shows anger, he at the next moment smiles.

(d) In the beginning, the emotional expression is diffused and generalized. It becomes stable, differentiated, selective, moderate and graded as the child grows older.

(e) Emotional development is also determined by the socio-economic background of the child. If a child belongs to a cultured family, he will show more emotional maturity.

(f) Emotional development is affected by the physical development of the child also. For example, if a child is physically weak due to malnutrition or diseases, his emotions will be less stable and less subtle.

6. **Social development :** Human baby is the only organism in the world that takes maximum and longer time to be socially and economically self dependent. He needs help from others more than any other creature. This dependence of the child on others helps him to learn how to interact with others in diverse situations. The more a person is healthy in his social interactions, the more he is said to be socially developed. Important features of social development are as follows:

- Social development starts with the process of socialization, a process which enables a child to acquire his social status according to his age. It is the process of socialization that helps the child to learn social traditions, customs and culture.
- The child increases his social circles gradually. These circles increase further when the child grows with age. It makes very difficult for the child to adjust with different types of people in the society. Thus, social development is actually an adjustment training.
- Social development means to share joy and sorrows with others, to work as a member of a group, to cooperate with others and to develop social perception for the purpose of developing belongingness with the rest of the society.
- The end points of social development is social maturity, ie, to adapt successfully to the social environment without frustration. A socially matured person is one who is fair in his dealing, courteous in his behaviour and honest in his character. His sense of responsibility, his self confidence, and his leadership quality make him distinct from others. He confirms what is acceptable to others and denies what is antagonistic to him.

Lifespan and Development

(A) Infancy and development : Various dimensions of development during the period of infancy are given below.

1. **Physical development :** This period is marked by following characteristics of physical development.

(i) Physical development is very rapid during this period. For example size increases ten inches upto second year. Weight also becomes almost double at the age 4½ months, i.e., from 3 kg at birth to almost 6 kg. At the age of 4½ month.

(ii) Though sex organs are totally undeveloped and inactive during this period, yet a tendency to sexual development is seen in the second year of life. Child actually passes through three stages of sexual development. First stage, the stage of self love belongs to infancy. Here the child derives pleasure from his body, by sucking his thumbs of hand or legs or by touching his sex organs. The other two stages- homosexual or hetero sexual belong to early childhood.

(iii) At the time of birth, boys are heavier than girls. 7% weight loss is seen in the first seven days then the baby start to gain weight.

(iv) Study shows that boys are on the average heavier than girls at all age levels except from 11-14 years of age in which girls are found heavier than boys.

(v) Head is more developed than other parts of the body at birth. It grows proportionately at lesser speed than other parts of the body. At 6 years, the child gains 90% of the adult size of head.

(vi) Facial skeleton is found larger in proportion to cranium from birth to seven years of age.

(vii) Nose is proportionately small and flat on the face in the first four years. It gains full size at the age of 13 or 14.

(viii) Trunk is found heavy during the period of infancy. It along with legs lengthens gradually.

(ix) At birth, the weight of the brain is one fourth of an adult brain. It is one half by the age of 9 months and three fourth by the age of two years.

(x) In the first year of the baby the heart beat is very irregular and its speed is very high. As the child grows, the heart beat becomes regular and slower. Other physical changes are given below.

- Food takes longer time to pass through the digestive tract and to reach the intestines.
- Urine bladder can retain urine for a longer period of time.
- Body temperature becomes more stable.
- Composition of blood does not change.

(xi) The weight becomes almost three times the birth weight at the end of first year. By the age of 2, it becomes 3½ times the birth weight.

2. Nervous system :

(i) Nerve cells attain maturity during this period

(ii) Brain also grows rapidly and its size and weight increases

(iii) Improvement in the functioning and structure of sensory organs is seen. Thus, by the end of this period the child is able to perform all the functions of seeing, hearing, smelling, tasting and touching properly.

3. Motor development :

(i) Co-ordination and control of bodily movements are seen.

(ii) The child starts grasping objects in the fourth month of his life.

(iii) He sits in the sixth month. He crawls in the seventh or eighth month. He stands with the help of support in the ninth month and in the 12th month he begins to walk slowly without support.

(iv) Running begins in the second year of his life

(v) Greater muscular involvement is seen during infancy

4. Language development :

(i) It starts with vocalization in the form of cries or explosive sounds. This vocalization may be described as pre speech form.

(ii) The child only cries at the time of birth to express his emotions or desires. This crying is used even in the second year of life to express desires and needs.

(iii) He begins to utter few words by the end of the first year like mama, dada etc. Some unintelligible words spoken by the child may be seen in the seventh or eighth month.

(iv) Language development properly begins in the beginning of the second year. The rate of language development becomes rapid at the age of 1.5 years and the child crames any new learnt word just in order to retain it in his mind.

(v) By the end of two years he begins to speak proper but short sentences, though grammatical mistakes may be there.

5. Intellectual development :

(i) No clear cut sign of intellectual development is seen during infancy. His capacity to grasp new words is totally based on rote memory, though his cramming is without reason or intellect.

(ii) He lacks abstract understanding. His understanding is exclusively restricted to concrete materials but he thinks that heavier is one which is bigger in size. Thus, a plastic ball of bigger size is heavier than a metal ball of smaller size for the child.

(iii) Sign of creativity is seen at the end of the 2nd year. The infant often engages himself in collecting many articles.

(iv) This is a period of make belief. When he attains the age of 2, he believes in what he is told by his elders.

(v) A baby perceives an unfamiliar object as a form or as a figure. He has an innate tendency to organize his sense field and to perceive the object as a whole but this perception lacks definiteness.

6. Social development :

(i) He learns social skills in the company of his mother and fathers. When he is responded by them he learns how to respond to others. Thus, he learns all his social experiences from his family members in the first year but in the second year his horizon expands to his neighbourhood.

(ii) By the end of two years he begins to take the notice of other infants and plays with them.

(iii) He totally depends upon his family members for the fulfillment of his social, psychological and physical needs.

(iv) He expects that every body around him should love him and care him. When this expectation is not fulfilled he becomes irritated and cries.

(v) The baby becomes aware of other persons around him at the age of one month. In the second month, he smiles in response to the attentions of adults and he is able to distinguish his mother and other women. In the third month he waves his hands and legs when he is talked to. In the fourth month, he makes anticipatory adjustment to being lifted by someone. In the fifth month, he attends to the human face and looks in the direction of the person who leaves him. He smiles in response to the person who speaks and plays with him. In the sixth month, he reacts differently to smiling and scolding and shows negative responses to strangers. In the ninth month, he tries to imitate the speech of others. He copies simple acts and gestures of others after observation in the tenth month. In the 12th month, he can refrain from doing things when he is forbidden to do so.

In the second year of life he exhibits fear and dislike for strangers by crying or withdrawing. When the baby attains the age of 18 months, he shows negativism in the form of stubborn resistance to the demands of adults.

(vi) In the first two years, the child's play is self centred. He does not like to be interfered by other children or adults. He plays in his own way. He is generally non-cooperative and has to be handled with patience and tacts. In short, the baby is socially underdeveloped.

(vii) Hurlock has presented the social development taking place during first two years of infancy as under :

1. First month	Understand human and other voices
2. Second month	Recognizes human voices and greets with smile
3. Third month	Recognizes mother and distresses on her being away
4. Fourth month	Recognizes human faces
5. Fifth month	Understands the tone of voices i.e. love and hate
6. Sixth or Seventh month	Welcomes the known with smile
7. 8th or 9th month	Plays with his own shadow
8. 24th month	Participates in elder's work

7. Emotional development:

(i) He is completely egocentric and selfish. When he reaches the age of 2, he even does not want to share his toys.

(ii) He is irritated and cries when he is chided by his family members.

(iii) His emotions are intense, frequent and totally unstable though emotional reactions become distinct in the beginning of the second year. These emotions are spontaneous and he can not control them.

(iv) He cannot hide his feelings thus, his entire emotions are in the overt form.

(v) Emotions of anger, fear, disgust, elation, love and affections are seen. For example, when he is loved by his mother, he shows his affection by his activities. Similarly, when he is not attended by his family members, he feels disgusted. He also feels pleasure in the company of his mother or his father.

(vi) A number of psychologists are of the view that infants are able to undergo emotional experiences. Emotions of fear, anger, joy, hate etc. are seen in them even in the first year.

(vii) During the period of infancy only those conditions arouse emotional responses which affect the child's immediate needs and well being, but when the child grows, his spectrum increases and he becomes responsive to a number of stimuli.

(viii) It has been noticed that babies and children show their pronounced emotional disturbance just before eating, sleeping, or waking up. For example, when a baby wakes up after sleep, he cries whether he is hungry or not.

(ix) Intellectually dull children are less emotionally disturbed than the normal children.

(x) Infants show smiling response to any human face whether familiar or stranger between eight and twenty weeks of age. Negative responses to strangers starts after 20 weeks of age and continues upto 40 weeks.

(B) Early childhood and development : Various dimensions of development during the period of early childhood (3-6 years) are as follows:

1. Physical and motor development :

(i) He acquires many motor skills like catching, throwing, running, jumping, climbing, using simple tools, riding a tricycle etc.

(ii) Growth in outer parts of the body especially height, weight, formation of muscles etc. is not as fast as it was during infancy. The child, however begins to assume the body proportion of an adult.

(iii) The growth of legs is rapid and it acquires about half of an adult size. The growth of head is, however, very slow and that of trunk is medium.

(iv) The height of a three years old child is 38 inches on an average though Indian children may be slightly lower than this size. Similarly, the weight should also be 33 pounds at the age of three. By the age of five years, the average weight of children is 43 pounds and average height for boys is 43 inches.

Motor	2 years	3 years	4 and 5 years
Development	Walks without help, jumps, runs	Skips, hops	Free and active movement responds to music
Fine motor coordination	Copying	Can match shapes, sees similarities and differences	Can name colours
Perceptual	Identifies self, matches colours	Can fit nuts, boxes	Matches shapes and colours, distinguishes names
Vocalization	200 words, uses few words	900 words, follows commands	Can repeat 4 digits-2000 to 3000 words, can define familiar words
Adaptive behaviour	Bowel control	Builds blocks, can draw a man	4 digits, draws body with details

(v) Muscles develop at a very rapid speed due to excess involvement of the child in motor activities.

(vi) The rate of heart beat and pulse slow down and blood pressure goes up steadily.

(vii) By the age of 5-6 the child acquires 90% of the adult weight of brain. Nerve fibres in the brain areas also come to almost maturity by the end of the period of early childhood. It should be noted that the growth of brain and nerve fibres is very rapid from birth to four years.

(viii) Self feeding, self dressing, self bathing, combing the hair, brushing the teeth, playing with toys, using pencils for writing or sketching etc are also seen during this period.

2. Intellectual development :

(i) Perceptual development begins from mass movement to differentiation. Norms for perceptual development is given in the callout table.

(ii) The child perceives those things quickly and clearly which are concerned with his mental set and interest.

(iii) The child begins to explore his social environment and acquire new experiences at the age of three.

(iv) By the age of six, the child develops clear perception of size, shape, colour, time and distance. He does not consider all bigger objects as heavier too.

(v) The child begins to form concepts of physical and social reality. For example, he does not do any thing against the wishes of his family members. If he does so, he hides the same.

(vi) The child starts learning many materials by rote memorization. His capacity to retain learnt material increases.

(vii) Imagination begins to grow and creativity is seen. He manipulates or breaks his toys to understand its mechanism. But his thinking process is restricted to concrete objects only.

(viii) Span of attention increases from 7 minutes to 20 minutes.

(ix) His curiosity forces him to explore the environment. He asks so many questions from his elders for this purpose.

(x) The child is now able to use symbols in language and mathematics.

(xi) The child develops a lot of concepts during this period but many of his concepts cannot be verbalized by him due to limited vocabulary.

(xii) During this period, children's concepts of spatial relations, distance and depth are vague. This makes the children awkward in their behaviour. For example they calculate height and distance wrongly.

(xiii) By the age of five, they are able to distinguish between past, present and future, ie, between yesterday, tomorrow and day after tomorrow etc.

(xiv) The concepts of number and quantity also become clear to them. According to Piaget, children acquire concept of number even before they are able to count.

(xv) Children's social concepts are influenced by the nature of inter-personal relationship.

(xvi) This stage is also called the stage of fantasy. The child takes shelter into his imaginary world in order to escape the harsh realities of his world at home and neighbourhood. If he is given more chance to interact with people, his social concepts will be rich.

3. Language development

(i) The child has to master four major tasks in the process of learning to speak properly.

- Comprehension of the speech of others
- Building a vocabulary
- Using and combining words into sentences
- Pronouncing the words correctly

By the end of the period of early childhood, the child is able to master all these four tasks.

(ii) Language development of a child actually begins from birth cry. When he is responded by his mother after crying, he comes to understand the meaning and importance of crying.

(iii) A ten month old child is able to use one or two words only but by the end of the first year his vocabulary increases to four, as **Smith** has observed. By the end of 2nd year, he can use 272 words. In the third year, his vocabulary increase to 896. when he attains the age of four, he can use 1560 words and at the age of 6 he can use 2562 words as Smith has observed.

(iv) Language development of children is not uniform. It depends upon better socio-economic environment at home, better schooling and independent living of the child.

4. Social development:

(i) Feeling of autonomy develops in children. They try to explore and manipulate their environment independently.

(ii) The child learns how to behave, talk and interact with the family members and neighbourhood.

(iii) The child may be frustrated if social atmosphere of the neighbourhood is not similar to that of the atmosphere at home.

(iv) The child's play no longer remains a solitary play after the age of three. The child selects his playmates and develops casual friendship with them. He learns cooperation, competition, sympathy, jealousy, teasing, bullying, quarrelling, etc. in the company of his playmates.

(v) Imitation, timidity, shyness, desire for possession etc. are other forms of social behaviour that develop during this period.

(vi) The child who is resistive upto the age of three years becomes cooperative and friendly and seeks approval of adults upto the age of four years. That is why he does not object to exchange his toys with his best friends.

(vii) At the age of 5-6 he begins to pride about his parents and boast about other members of his family after six.

(viii) Most of the children want to dominate in their respective groups at the age of six. Thus group leader changes every time in the group. In this way, the child learns how to adjust in the society in varied situations.

(ix) Children of both sexes play together without any discrimination.

(x) They also take part in those games which involve physical energy and motor activity like hide and seek.

(xi) They take interest in fairy tales and animal stories in which they want that someone should win in the fighting. They are very much interested to know which animal is stronger and strongest out of so many at the age of 4-5.

(xii) Negativism increases during this period. It is believed that the more a child is frustrated by the interference of adults, the more negativistic his behaviour will be.

(xiii) Girls have been found more dominating than boys in social and group situations.

5. Emotional development : Contributions of emotions are very much recognized in the personal and social adjustment of the individuals. Important features of emotional development during this period are given below.

(i) Emotions of the child are exhibited only for a very short period. It means that child shifts from one emotion to another very rapidly. For example, if a three or four years old child who is weeping loudly is given a toffee, he will become pleased at once.

(ii) Emotions of children are intense irrespective of the intensity of the stimulus. A very simple stimulus can create a very intense emotional experience.

(iii) Children are helpless to hide their emotions and they express them by different activities like crying, throwing objects, nail biting, bullying, thumb sucking and speech difficulties. Emotions of hope, disappointment, fear, anxiety, shame, jealousy, hatred etc. are expressed during this period in different ways.

(iv) He is still guided by his innate tendencies and instincts.

(v) His moral behaviour is also guided by his emotions-pleasure and pain.

(vi) Emotions of submission and elation are alternately seen in the child.

(vii) At the age of five his emotions begin to organize into sentiment. The most primitive sentiment is his love for his own self and his love for his toys. Due to this reason, this stage is also called "Narcissism autoerotism" or self love. This word **narcissism** has been derived from Greek language which means falling in love with one self.

(viii) The child also develops a deep sentiment of affection for his parents. At the age of 6-7 it is very painful for the child to see his/her father or mother ailing. Here Freud is of the opinion that girl is very much attached to her father and boy feels more attachment to his mother. Former is called Elektra complex and later is called Oedipus complex.

(ix) The child begins to show "moodiness" expressed in sulking and bad emotions at the age of four. This emotion reaches to its peak during the period of adolescence.

(x) Most of the emotional responses are learned by children by imitating parents and other family members. Thus, emotions are innate but emotional responses are innate and learnt both.

Educational Implications of the Period of Early Childhood

Early childhood is basically a pre-school period. The formal education of the child begins when he attains the age of five so, sixth year of life of the child is very important from point of view of educating the child. Since success of education of this period will depend on the pre-school education, so, the whole period from 3-6 becomes very important. Following strategies must be adopted by the school to develop the child educationally.

(i) The teacher in the school should first see whether the child has proper physical and motor development. Regular medical and health check up programme should be organized in the school for this purpose.

(ii) Parents should also be consulted if teacher finds some problem in the physical or motor development of the child.

(iii) It is the teacher who will first notice the physical or motor problems of the child. Hence, he should know the norms of physical and social development of children. On the basis of his very report, the child will be sent to the doctor for further diagnosis and investigation.

(iv) Various types of games and play activities should be organized in the school according to the age of children and they should be motivated to participate in those activities.

(v) The child is very active physically during this period. He mostly takes part in those activities, which involve muscular movement. Seeing this, he should be given rich diet to eat. If child is not getting proper nutrition, he will not gain height or weight properly.

(vi) This is a period of taking shift from dependence to self help, so child should be given more and more freedom to do in whatever manner he likes and to manipulate his environment in his own way.

(vii) This is a period of rapid intellectual growth. Hence, he should be sent to pre-primary school for learning through plays.

(viii) He should also be taught religious and moral principles so that he may become an acceptable member of the society.

(ix) He should be given freedom to manipulate objects so that he may develop his creative potentials.

(x) The teacher should narrate the stories of animals before such children. It will develop their vocabulary and imaginative power.

(xi) The child can concentrate for a longer period. Hence, the teacher can teach him any thing systematically. Even mathematics can be taught to him because he can understand symbols.

(xii) Efforts should be made to increase the vocabulary of the child as much as possible so that he can verbalize all the concepts that he knows.

(xiii) In order to save the child from frustration, he should not be interfered by the adults or parents.

(xiv) The child can increase his vocabulary mostly by hearing, so, he should be talked more and more. Better environment created at home means better language development.

(xv) Group activities are most suitable for such children. They should be given chance to get involve in such activities. Through these activities they would learn competition, cooperation, sympathy and the like feeling.

(xvi) The child seeks approval of adults. Adults should not be miserly in giving such approvals. They should rather love him.

(xvii) Girls and boys can be educated in a co-setting. This arrangement will create no administrative problem.

(xviii) If the child disobeys the parents they should not mind it. It is a natural phenomenon and will come down in the later childhood.

(xix) Girls should be preferred to be given the role of group leaders.

(xx) A teacher can control intense emotions of the child by his loving behaviour.

(xxi) Since children of this age can not hide their emotions, it is very easier for the teacher to deal these children effectively.

(xxii) Early childhood is a period in which the child can be emotionally attached to any body who loves him. The emotional attachment with parents may be generalized and extended to teachers in the school. A teacher can exploit this tendency and get the students involved in so many types of tasks.

(C) Later childhood and development : This is the period between the age of 6-12 years. At the end of this period, puberty symptoms begin to grow and the period of adolescence starts. This period is marked by **pseudo maturity** and excellence in different fields. As far as sexual maturity is concerned, it remains completely dormant during this period, but this sex emerges with a great force at the end of this period. Because of the dormant nature of sex, this stage is also called **latency period**. Various dimensions of development during this period are given below.

1. Physical development :

(i) Steady and slow but uniform growth in the external as well as internal organs are seen.

(ii) Milk teeth are replaced by permanent set.

(iii) Auscification of bones takes place due to increase in height and weight.

(iv) Refinement in motor skills are seen.

(v) The child is physically restless during this period. He finds himself engaged in one activity or the other.

(vi) The brain acquires the size of an adult.

(vii) It is the period of best health of the individual during his whole life. During this period children never get tired. They burn their calories in physical activities and eat to the maximum level possible.

(viii) Girls are ahead of boys by two years in height and weight physiologically. Girls at the age of 11 are ahead of boys by at least one year.

(ix) Shedding of milk teeth and growth of permanent teeth change the shape of mouth, like flattening of forehead, sharpening nose and broadening of the chest.

(x) Important physical characteristics of this period are increased manual dexterity, high muscular strength, increased resistance to fatigue, increased endurance for play activities and so on.

2. Intellectual development :

(i) The child develops the powers of observation, reasoning and abstract thinking.

(ii) He can accumulate huge amount of knowledge in his mind. He can derive information and pleasure from books.

(iii) His perceptual ability, memory, and application of mental powers become keener.

(iv) The IQ of the child becomes stable and determines his IQ level in future. In short, it is a period of intellectual maturity.

(v) Boys love adventure and fairy tales and girls love mild form of romance and biographies.

(vi) The child begins to admire things and people around him and he begins to imitate the behaviour of those people who he likes.

(vii) The child begins to make clear distinction between himself and the outer world. He starts working on reality principles according to Freud.

(viii) The concept of natural laws becomes fully developed at the end of this period.

(ix) Capacity of logical thinking and power of reasoning increases.

(x) Interest in science fictions and stories reaches at its peak by the end of later childhood.

(xi) Courage and loyalty both increase simultaneously.

(xii) The child starts day dreaming and he defeats his rivals in his imaginative plays.

(xiii) The early imaginary fears are disappeared by the end of 12 years.

(xiv) When a child attains the age of ten, he shows high ability of generalization.

(xv) Children of this age are concerned with immediate cause and effect relationship and current happening. They live in the realm of present and don't care for future.

(xvi) The child begins to understand conceptual problem very well. He can analyse it and can give suggestions for its solutions.

(xvii) The physical growth is slow and steady during this period but intellectual growth and the functioning of mind are very rapid during this period.

(xviii) The child develops clear concepts of length, breath, time and distance.

3. Sexual development :

(i) From this angle this stage of the child is called latency period. Generally sexual energy at this age remains dormant but it becomes very active immediately after the age of 12 years.

(ii) Indifferent and antagonistic attitude towards the opposite sex are seen by the age of 10-11. As a result of this attitude, boys do not like to mix up with girls and girls are antagonistic to mix up with boys. Due to this reason upper primary education (from VIth –VIIIth) in co educational setting is not suited in school.

4. Emotional development :

(i) Rapid shift from one type of emotion to another is not seen and the child learns how to control his emotions in a variety of social situations. For example, he avoids weeping in the company of his friends.

(ii) Emotional responses of the child become less diffused and undifferentiated, ie, intensity of emotions is reduced.

(iii) Emotions are expressed even in the absence of concrete materials.

(iv) Fear of animals, ghosts, loneliness and high place that was found in the early childhood, no longer persists in the later childhood.

(v) Certain new fear appear during this stage like fear of failing in the attempt such as games examinations, etc, fear of supernatural objects, such as heaven or hell etc and fear of being ridiculed etc.

(vi) The child gets angry if he is thwarted, teased or prejudiced. If he is compared with other children wrongly, he is interfered in his activities or he is ridiculed by elders, all these things will make the child angry.

(vii) If child thinks that some other children are being favoured by elders, he again gets angry. He becomes jealous of those children who are favoured. Emotion of jealousy is found in girls more than in boys.

(viii) All emotions like joy, love, curiosity, grief and affection appear during this stage in a stable manner. The child can hide his emotions. He expresses only those emotions which are approved socially.

(ix) Emotions are structured into sentiments. Various types of sentiments like religious, moral, patriotic and aesthetic sentiments develop during this period.

(x) Complex of superiority develops during this period. Boys consider themselves superior to girls.

5. Social development :

(i) He loves to play in groups and shares his toys with other children. Team spirit and group loyalties are commonly seen in such children in a more matured form.

(ii) Social horizon of the child increases to neighbourhood and school and he looses the shackles of his family ties. He becomes independent of his parents and does many things against their wishes.

(iii) He wants to become hero or leader in the group in the same way as we see in the period of early childrenhood.

(iv) He cares himself more than others. His self centred behaviour sometimes gives rise to rivalries and aggression.

(v) He accepts social norms. He feels pride to be ruled by public opinions. He is so much attached with his group that he can defy even the orders of his parents if they do not match with the norms of the group to which the child belongs. This tendency in children continues upto the age of 17-18.

(vi) Social development of the child mostly takes place in the play ground. The child mostly takes interest in those games which require stiff competition like football, hockey, kabaddi and kho kho.

(vii) Girls mostly prefer indoor games but if they are exposed to outdoor games they enjoy more than boys. Badminton, tennis and skipping are their favorite games.

(viii) When something wrong happens, boys indulge into physical combat and girls into verbal fights or pulling each others hairs. The behaviour of the child is largely influenced by the group to which child belongs.

(ix) The age from 10-12 is referred to gang age when children take much interest in gang activities and adhere to gang loyalties. That is why we see that every child in the age group of 10-12 necessarily joins a group and follows its rules and regulations strictly.

(x) Sex differentiation becomes sharp,i.e., girls play with girls only. The child does not like to play with girls during this period.

He accepts only those girls in his group which are very energetic and courageous.

(xi) It is the period of peak unruliness in schools and homes especially when child is thwarted by his peers and relatives. Here, the child rejects many of the standards set by the adults or his family members and tries to live an independent life in his own circle.

(xii) Some delinquent acts like bullying, stealing, gang activities etc begin at the end of this period.

(xiii) Boys are more rebellion than girls and their groups or gangs are more organized than girls.

(xiv) Because of the excess involvement of boys and girls in their respective groups, this period is particularly known as gang age period.

6. Moral development:

(i) When the child attains the age of six, his capacity to understand relationship increases. He accepts lawful and unlawful social matters, though his concept of right and wrong may be different from his peers.

(ii) At the age of 8 he moves from specific response to generalized response and thus his concepts become more generalized. For example, he comes to realize that stealing of any thing is bad whether it be the matter of money or books.

(iii) During the period of later childhood morality is defined as performing good acts and maintaining the conventional social order. Children of this age are not deficient of this respect in any way.

(iv) At the age of 11-12, moral behaviour is oriented towards authority and maintaining the status quo which is considered to be a primary value. When the child changes his group loyalties, moral values may also change. It is because their conduct is mostly governed by the mores of his group.

(v) The development of right and wrong concepts begins at home in the period of early childhood. but it actually matures in the group. That is why we see that the child may float the authority of his parents but he may not go against the wishes of his gang. Such moral behaviour is dangerous only when the group is not following social and moral norms properly.

Educational Implications of the Period of Later Childhood

(i) Suitable freedom should be given to children to develop physically, emotionally and intellectually.

(ii) These children like games, sports and group activities very much. School should organize such activities and should make them an indispensable part of the curriculum.

(iii) A teacher should not try to compare boys with girls. It is because girls feel themselves superior to boys and vice versa. If a teacher does not follow this maxim, it will create hatred for girls in the minds of boys.

(iv) Most of the lessons should be taught to children of this age through group activities.

(v) A teacher must be democratic in dealing such children. If anything is imposed on them irrationally, they will not follow it.

(vi) It is also necessary for the teacher to express faith in such children. He should not suspect the integrity and honesty of these children without reason.

(vii) Many desirable behaviours come to light during this period. Such behaviours should be reinforced regularly.

(viii) Children should be allowed to go to neighbourhood to learn community experiences. Remember that only school experiences are not enough.

(ix) The parents should not take the gang activities of their sons and daughters with anger. The only thing that is needed is that the gang should be good in behaviour.

(x) Certain hobbies are developed during this period. They should be encouraged by teachers and parents.

(xi) Interest and liking of boys and girls differ. Hence, they should be assigned different types of works according to their liking.

(xii) Children should be motivated to take rich diet in order to develop their muscles and bones.

(xiii) Child is never at rest during this period. So, a teacher should always get them involve in certain activities—physical or mental. If child is free, he may be destructive and problematic for the family.

(xiv) If a teacher knows the norm of physical growth of these boys and girls, he can guide them accordingly in the class. If the child is not growing on a satisfactory line, the

teacher can report to the parents of the child.

(xv) If a teacher is successful in developing reading habits as a part of their routine activity in students, they can accumulate huge amount of information and knowledge.

(xvi) The teacher should take the child to the laboratory for observation and experimentation. Lab work must start at the age of 12.

(xvii) Children of this age should be taught stories full of adventure and romance.

(xviii) The tendency of hero worshiping in such children should be exploited by the teacher.

(xix) Power of reasoning of the child should be utilized in understanding religion and mythology.

(xx) Parents should not forbid the child from doing a particular thing in a straight forward manner. They should give reason to the child why it should not be done.

(xxi) The child should be given chance to generalize laws and principles as mush as possible.

(xxii) Children of this age do not care much for their tomorrow. Hence, whatever good is done by them should be reinforced immediately.

(xxiii) At the age of ten, girls do not like to mix up with boys and vice versa. So, a teacher should guide them separately and co-education at the junior level is not recommended at all.

(xxiv) Children can hide any of their emotions at this age. So, a teacher should not study them in hurry and draw conclusion about the child.

(xxv) The behaviour of the teacher should be completely unbiased. He should not discriminate any child on any ground. Biased attitude and discrimination make the child angry.

(xxvi) The child should be given opportunity to lead at least one group in any curricular or co-curricular activities.

(xxvii) Religious and moral educations should properly begin at this stage.

(xxviii) Gang activities of children should not be discouraged by the teacher. Such activities are essential for self expression and exposure.

THEORIES OF CHILD DEVELOPMENT

Theories of child development can be classified into three broad categories. The first is psycho analytic theory propounded by Sigmund Freud and his associates. This theory gives much importance to unconscious motivation developed especially in the early period's of life and it determines the personality of the individual in the later parts of life also. The second is behaviouristic theory of child development which lays stress on the connection between stimulus and response. The major advantage of this category of theories is that it can be experimented and verified in clinical setting and thus these theories are more scientific in nature. The last category is cognitive theory of child development. It is a molar approach of explanation of human development and it takes the total situation facing the mind into account. It lays stress on perception and its organization responsible for learning and development.

Some of these theories are being described below:

1. Psychoanalytic Theory (Freud) : According to this theory, every child passes through five stages of psycho-sexual development. These stages are given below.

(a) Oral stage: At this stage focus of pleasure is mouth. When child sucks milk from the breast of her mother, he not only quenches his hunger but also gets pleasure by the excitement of mouth.

(b) Anal stage : When child attains the age of two the focus of pleasure shifts from mouth to anus. The child obtains pleasure from the activities related to anus during this period. That is why defecating is enjoying for the child.

(c) Phallic stage : This period starts at the age of three and lasts at the age of six. Here the focus of pleasure shifts from anus to sexual organs like pennis or vagina. That is why habit of masturbation is common in children. Two special complexes also develop during this period (1) Oedipus complex-here the male child wants his mother more but finds his father as a powerful rival. He wants to destroy this rival but he is unable to do so. (2) Elektra complex-Here female child comes closer to her father and hates her mother.

(d) Latency stage : During this period all earlier forms of sexual activities are stopped. The child takes interest in learning skills and in the development of social and religious values. This stage helps the child to develop his super ego on the basis of his ego.

(e) Genital stage : The focus of pleasure shifts to the member of the opposite sex by using genital organs here. This stage starts after 13 years.

2. Ericksons' Theory of Psychosocial Stages : Erickson has proposed another theory of stages of child development. He divides stages of development into eight phases marked by specific developmental characteristics. The stages are as follows :

S.No.	STAGE	PSYCHOSOCIAL CRISES
1	Birth to first year	Trust Vs mistrust
2	1 to 2 years	Autonomy Vs shame, doubt
3	3 to 5 years	Initiative Vs Guilt
4	6 to 12 years	Industry Vs inferiority
5	Adolescence	Identity Vs identity diffusion
6	Early adult period	Intimacy Vs Isolation
7	Young and middle adult	Generativity Vs self-absorption
8	Later adult period	Integrity Vs despair

A brief explanation of these stages are given below:

(i) The infant develops a sense of trust in himself as well as in the environment. This trust is developed when he finds others at the beck and call of his physiological needs. Contrary to this, if his needs are not fulfilled by the people around him, he aches and cries. As a result, he loses his faith in the people around him.

(ii) When the child attains the age of 1.5 years, he develops the sense of autonomy in him. He does not want help from others. If parents give them reasonable freedom, it will develop confidence in them. Children who are not given such freedom to explore the environment, develop suspicion and doubt about their abilities. When they perform a task they become shy and hesitant. They are afraid of their mistakes which can bring about shame for them.

(iii) At the age of three, rapid growth of children in all dimensions is seen. At this age, the child starts to take initiatives on various tasks. The social horizon of the child begins to spread from home to neighbourhood and then to school. At this age, children also begin to develop the sense of right or wrong. Feeling of guilt is developed when they do not follow moral principles and codes given by their parents and teachers.

(iv) Fourth stage of development in the life of a child starts at age of six and comes to an end just before adolescence. During this period child utilizes his energies for self improvement and for the conquest of the outer world. He shows his industry and hard labour in all directions with special emphasis to motor field. The child wants to understand different mechanisms of the world through his toys and other usable articles. If the above opportunities are not given to him and the child is still treated as a child of low mind, it develops inferiority complex in him.

(v) When the child attains the age of thirteen he begins to fight for his identity in his group. He wants to become a leader in various activities and through this he wants to gain popularity among girls. Contrary to this if he is completely disregarded in the group to which he belongs, his identity is diffused.

(vi) Adulthood period starts at the age of 17. In the early years of adulthood, the individual wants to increase his social circle as large as possible. If he is amiable by nature, he is liked by others and if he is selfish, self centred or intolerant or he is hated by others especially by the girls, he starts to live in isolation. Many tragic songs and dramas are written during this period.

(vii) In the middle years of adulthood, generativity is seen. The individual exposes himself through any outstanding efforts in any field. He wants to live for others. That is why he is very much interested to see a better and disciplined world around him. The condition of self absorption is seen when an individual does not receive any encouragement for his tasks from anywhere.

(viii) Last stage is known for the integrity of the person to his profession, group, organization and institution to which he belongs. When justice is not maintained or an individual is not paid and recognized according to his efforts, his integrity is turned into despair.

3. Robert Sears' Development Theory: This theory represents the behavioural approach to the study of child development. According to Robert Sears learning experiences of the child are the result of stimulus-response associations that may result either classical or operant conditioning procedures . Thus according to this theory, development is a process of observable social interaction. The more there is social interaction, the more there is learning which is enhanced by reinforcement also.

There are three broad phases of human development according to this theory which are given below-

(a) *Phase (I) Rudimentary behaviour :* Initial behavioural training starts during this period. The period of this stage is birth to sixteen months of age. During this period the infant is activated by his innate needs of hunger, thirst, motor movement, defecation etc. These needs create tension in him and in order to reduce this tension, the infant is motivated for action. When action of the infant is reinforced by positive response, his needs are satisfied. The infant is very much selfish in his behaviour in the beginning and does not care for any social world. But when social world (parents and relatives) fulfills his needs and infant is reinforced for his action of say crying learning takes place which makes the learner more learned and goal directed.

Since, the infant here depends on someone else for the gratification of needs, the development becomes a process of social interaction. It is a type of operant behaviour here. The social environment in which the child is born greatly influences the development of the child. If child is not reinforced by anybody, *i.e*, his needs are not fulfilled, no development will be there. Socio-economic condition of the family, birth order of the child, his sex, the education or profession of his parents etc., affect the development of the child.

In other words, we can say that the first phase of the child's development interlinks the biological endowments (innate abilities) of the child with his social environment. The more the social environment is conducive to the fulfillment of biological needs of the child, the more learning and development will be there.

(b) *Phase II (Secondary behaviour) :* When child is reinforced by his parents and other members of the family, and the child's biological needs are gratified, he comes to develop secondary behaviour system, *i.e.*, he has to respond to others. If his response is fine he will be motivated. If response of the child is not upto the mark, it will be corrected by others and thus the process of development of correct secondary behaviour goes on.

The secondary behaviour of children starts by imitation. If model to be imitated is good, behaviour of the child will also be fine. The secondary behaviour of children should also be reinforced by parents and others and use of punishment as a technique should be avoided as much as possible because it can create behaviour problems in the child.

During this phase when the child begins to fulfil his needs himself by learning some new behaviour, his dependency on others decreases with age till the child is grown up fully and becomes an independent member of the society.

(c) *Phase III (Behaviour motivated) :* After the age of 11-12 the social boundary of the child expands a lot. The child comes in contact with other parents and their sons and with many people in his school and thus his process of socialization is accelerated. His dependency on others is reduced further but some new dependency in the school increases also. If child is given approval by his parents and other persons of the society that his behaviour is fine, he motivated to repeat that behaviour again and thus the process of development expands.

As the number of environmental **reinforcers** increases, the child comes to identify those persons well who satisfy his needs and he accepts those people as his model.

4. **Bandura's Theory of Development :** He gives equal importance to reward and punishment in the development of behaviour. Thus Bandura is mainly concerned with the social development of the individual. He believed that responses which are reinforced are more likely to recur than those responses of children which are not reinforced. Behaviour is learned either through conditioning or observational learning. In early childhood many behaviours of children are not approved by parents. Children are rather punished for the execution of such behaviour. Due to this fear, children are conditioned not to repeat that behaviour even in the later periods of life. Thus reward and punishment both are necessary for the moral and social development of the child.

   Observation (imitation) is the second mechanism responsible for learning (or acquisition of behaviour. The child creates some models in his mind or he is impressed by the behaviour of some people and accepts them as his model. These models are imitated by the child. Imitation follows certain principles such as competency, social status, power and similarity of the model with the imitator.

5. **Jean Piaget's Theory of Development :** He has explained his theory in the context of cognitive (mental) development of the child. Before coming to various stages of

development according to this theory it is better to know various related concepts to understand the theory in detail. These concept are given below:

1. **The schema :** The concept of schema is applied to the sensory motor behaviour of the infant. The infant does various activities such as sucking milk from the mother's breast, looking at the objects of the environment and pointing at it and in the process he tries to comprehend and conceptualize the objects, animals or space. This process of conceptualization depends on the sequence of behaviour employed by the infant to adapt to his environment. This is called schema which is not the same in all the individuals. Basic structure, is however the same. Although a particular scheme derives its name from the sequence of behaviour which the schema denotes yet some internal organizational disposition is there to enable the sequence to adapt itself to a number of conditions. As the development of the individual takes place, each schema is enlarged, modified and co-ordinated with other schemas. In this way, more complex schemas are formed.

   The sensory motor scheme develops out of reflex behaviour of the infant. When this behaviour is repeated by the infant many times and is responded by others, it is internalized and is gradually converted into cognitive schema. For example, in northern India when a child says mum and is given water by the parents the child conceptualizes mum as water. Many such defects are corrected in the later stage of life.

   Piaget believes that schemed a (cognitive structure) exists in primitive form even at conception and develops progressively with age.

2. **Assimilation and accommodation :** The schemas which are acquired in infancy period are practiced and modified in the later stages of life. This process of practice and change is called assimilation and accommodation by the cognitive field theorists. These assimilation and accumulation processes go hand in hand. For example, during infancy when infant acquires grasping schema he pick up objects and grasps them. This grasping of objects is called assimilation. But if that particular object is too big or too small to grasp it., the child changes his schema in order to manage the new situation. It is called accommodation.

   The cognitive structure (schema) changes from one stage to another by the process of equilibration. Through this process the child tries to adapt to his changing environment every time to maintain equilibrium between him and the environment.

PRINCIPLES OF DEVELOPMENT

1. *Development is a product of interaction :* Development is a process which is the result of constant interchange of energy within the organism and his environment. Thus hereditary forces interact with environmental forces and the process of development goes further. These two forces are so closely interacted that it is very difficult to isolate the contribution of either of them. The contribution of gene may be 10% as compared to 90% contribution of environment in the process of development.

2. *Development follows an orderly sequence :* The rate of growth and development is different in different individuals depending upon a number of factors but it does follow an orderly sequence in all the individuals. The psychologists have reported three important directional trends in the process of development:

   (a) *Cephaulo caudal :* Development starts from head and proceed toward heel. We see that development of head of a child is well advanced as compared to other parts of the body.

   (b) *Proximodigital :* Development starts from the central part of the body. Then it spread to other outer or more distant parts of the body. We see that an infant uses his shoulders and elbows first to reach an object and then he uses his fingers and wrists.

   (c) *Locomotion :* Locomotion develops in a sequence in all the individuals belonging to different cultures of the world. The rate of development for different infants may be different but every infant wili have to pass through these stages at all cost. For example, an infant first learns to crawl, then to sit, then to stand and finally to walk. No infant can walk directly in the first stage.

3. *Development is a continuous process :* Development is a continuous process which begins from the time of conception in the womb of the mother and continues till death. But this process is not always smooth or gradual. Ups and downs are most of the time seen in every stage of development. There are spurts in physical growth and psychological functioning. Sharp growth rate is seen at the time of spurts. For example, a sharp increase in height and weight in the early adolescent period, a fast rise in vocabulary during pre-school period, sudden improvement in problem solving abilities during adolescence and so on.
4. *Development goes from bilateral to unilateral trend :* Infants up to the age of 2.5 years use both of their hands with equal ease. Then they learn to use any of their hands preferably. Similarly, in the beginning of cycle learning we use both the hands to control it but when we become fully experts in cycle learning we can control the cycle single handedly. Thus, development is a process of specialization also.
5. *Inter-relationship of different aspects of development:* Different aspects of development are interdependent and inter related. For example child's social behaviour is interrelated with his physical development. If child is physically handicapped, his emotional development may also be slow with aggressive development in some emotions. Similarly, if social development of an individual is poor, his mental or physical development will also be slow.
6. *Development is individualized process :* All individuals develop in their own way depending on their genetic characteristics and the training received from the environment. Thus, each child has his own rate of physical, social, mental or emotional development. If we observe ten years old children in a society, we find that there are great differences in their height, weight, sociability, emotional expressions and learning readiness. Similarly, the rate of growth is very high during infancy or pre-adolescent period as compared to other periods of life. Thus, rate of growth also changes with the change in stages of life.
7. *Development is positive and negative both :* Up to a certain period of human's life all the faculties of the individual develop but after that retardation starts specially after the age of 70. Physical and emotional retardations are seen during this age with zero social development. Mental development still continues but it too ultimately starts diminishing with the increase in age. Death is nothing but the collapse of all these processes of development.
8. *Development is cumulative :* Development is a cumulative process. Certain changes impress the observer and it looks as these changes are sudden but actually they are not sudden. They are the cumulative effect of all the changes in the individual. The child climbs the steps of the development one by one and then he reaches the zenith. The child first of all learns the words, then he learns the phrases, then sentences and finally he comes to know how the stories or essays are written. Thus, each change in the child is the culmination of his prior growth and experiences.
9. *Development proceed from general to specific:* In all types of development we find the principle of mass differentiation and integration. At the time of birth, the world is like big blooming confusion for the child. Then by and by his behaviours are refined and become goal directed responses.
10. *Rate of development differs with sex :* There is slight difference in the process of development between boys and girls. Girls mature earlier than boys at least emotionally. Girls are taller and heavier than boys in pre adolescence period but by the end of this period boys surpass them.

Dimensions of Growth and Development

1. *Physical growth and development :* It refers to strengthening of body and muscles with better proficiency and coordination of motor organs, if a person is able to do heavy work with ease, if he is able to do the task in lesser time, if he is able to do the task with accuracy and if he is able to do the task with neatness and beauty, then it is said that physical growth and development of the person is satisfactory.
2. *Social growth and development :* It refers to improvement and refinement of behaviour of an individual in social situations. If a person is stable in his behaviour even in adverse situations, if the behaviour of the person is fully acceptable to the society and if he is able to influence the society by his behaviour, then it is said that the social growth and development of the person is satisfactory.

3. *Emotional growth and development :* It refers to the accuracy of responses that an individual will exhibit under the influence of his emotions. These exhibited responses will be real as well. For example, if anger is not exhibited at the abuse given by any other person, it means that emotional growth and development is not satisfactory. Expressing sorrow at losses but not so much sorrow as it is beyond control is emotional maturity. If a person gets angry at his insults but he fully controls his anger according to the situation, then it is said that his emotional growth and development is satisfactory. Same is the case with other emotions also.
4. *Intellectual growth and development :* It refers to the ability to draw out conclusion from jumbled informations and to apply the inferences to real life situations in order to make the life happy and meaningful. If a person normally does what he is expected to do, if he is able to mould the situation in his own favour, if he is able to manipulate the situation against the other and if he is not backward in any way in mental operations, then it is said that his mental growth and development is satisfactory.
5. *Language growth and development :* Language is means of expressing, thinking and action. Had we not been given this power, we would not have been able to interact with others and our social existence was not possible. Language may be verbal and non verbal both. Human being uses both types of languages at a time to inform others about his thinking and behaviour and to be informed about their thinking and behaviour. Thus, language development refers to the ability of a person to convince the people what he thinks right.

Factors Affecting Growth and Development

Many factors affect to these dimensions of growth and development. Some of them affect mental or social growth and development and some factors affect all of them. Important such factors are given below:

1. *Proper Diet :* There is direct relationship between nutrition and physical growth. If diet is not taken according to the physical activities, physical growth will be retarded which will in turn affect the social, mental and emotional growth and development also.
2. *Exercise :* Physical exercise on regular basis will also improve physical growth and development. If a person is slow in his physical activities, his health might be worsened. The more an organ of the body is used, the more it will become strong.
3. *Sanitation and hygiene :* A disease free body is likely to grow more freely. This is possible only when the person is following the norms of hygiene and live in a good sanitary condition. It will save the person from communicable diseases.
4. *Genetic factors :* Genes play very important role in the process of growth and development. Nobody can surpass his genetic characteristics. If a person belongs to a race which is genetically short in height he can not increase his height by taking nutritious food and doing exercises.
5. *Recognition in the society :* If the individuality of a person is recognized in the society and he is given full freedom to grow his potentialities, his physical as well as social growth and development will be maximum. Unnecessary restrictions imposed on a person hampers the process of growth and development.
6. *Sociability :* Social relations also affect growth and development of a person. If a person is discarded by the society and people are biased against him, he will get less chance of socialization. As a result, his social horizon will be limited which will reduce his social learning. This will deteriorate the social growth and development. In that case the person will get less chance of exposure in the society. It will reduce his physical development also. As far as language development is concerned, sociability is a must.
7. *Training :* Growth and development is science in itself. If proper training on scientific lines is given to the individual, he is likely to grow and develop by leaps and bounds. Physical and health education serves this purpose.
8. *Games and sports :* Games and sports are necessary for all types of growth and development. They release pent up feeling of the person on one hand and give more chance of physical activities on the other. They are an important source of recreation as well. All these things are very conducive to physical, social and emotional growth and development.
9. *Protection :* A person must feel secure in the society only then his growth and development will be natural and spontaneous. If an

individual is living in a surcharged atmosphere and his life and property is always in danger, he will develop negative thinking. Negative attitude towards life and society is an enemy of growth and development in general.

10. *Manipulation of the environment :* If a person is given full enhance to manipulate the environment, his thinking will expand. It will have a positive bearing on his mental and emotional development.
11. *Free exchange of ideas :* Language development takes place only when a person is exposed in the society. In such an environment free exchange of ideas takes place. It increase word power of a person.
12. *Self contentment :* Human desires have no ends. If first desire of the wants is satisfied, another desire replaces the first, thus man always becomes slave of desires. It creates a tension in the mind of man. On the other, if a man is fully contended with what he has, he becomes tension free. It can improve his process of growth and development to a great extent.

HEREDITY AND ITS INFLUENCE

All that which we inherit from our parents, grandparents, great grandparents and so on as a free gift is called heredity. It is of two types: (i) Biological heredity and (ii) *Social heredity*

Biological heredity is that which a person inherits from his forefathers in the forms of chromosomes and genes.

Social heredity means all that one generation receives from the preceding generation in the form of social traditions customs and skills.

Person belonging to Rajput race is generally found muscular with strong and wide bones. It is an example of biological heredity. And the son of a carpenter is also likely to be an expert carpenter. It is an example of social heredity.

We will talk in this part only about biological heredity which is determined by genes. These genes are located in chromosomes. A person inherits chromosomes from his forefathers. With the transfer of these chromosomes genes are also transferred which are actually the carrier of heredity. Sex of an individual is also determined by genes. In order to know how traits are fixed by genes, we must first of all know the principles of heredity.

Principles of Heredity

There are two principles in this regard :

(a) *Principle of resemblance* : This principle states that like begets like. A cat can only give birth to a kitten, a human can only give birth to a baby and so on. According to this principle children generally resemble their parents or relatives.

(b) *Principle of Variability* : Many children do not resemble their parents. There are many instances where intelligent parents have dull children or ugly parents have beautiful children. This variation is universal in nature. That is why we see every individual unique in certain respect. This is called principle of variability of inheritance.

Mechanism of Heredity

When human sperm and egg unite, they are fertilized into zygote. Each zygote has 23 pairs of chromosomes. Every egg in the body contains the same number of chromosomes. The number of chromosomes in a given species are same but different species have different number of chromosomes.

For example, all humans contain 46 chromosomes. Half of them come from mother and half of them come from father. Within the chromosomes there are thousands of minute particles called genes. They are actually the carriers of hereditary traits from one generation to another.

Chromosomes are made up of long organic molecules whose main substance is deoxyribo nucleic acid (DNA). It is found in the chromosomes as two long strands periodically connected by chemical bonds.

Our heredity information is not found in the two long strands of DNA but in their order of appearance between the two strands of DNA. One pair of chromosomes is related to sex (gender) also. Females have two x chromosomes and males have an x and a y chromosome. If sperm of x chromosomes unite with the egg of y chromosomes, then the child will be a girl. If on the other hand, the sperm of y unite with the egg of x chromosomes, then the offspring will be a male child.

The story of hereditary influence will not be complete without knowing the influence of genes on our traits. It is because traits are determined exclusively by genes.

Genes are of two types **(i) dominant and (ii) recessive**. We inherit the same qualities of our parents because of dominant genes. If same characteristics are not inherited it means that recessive gene is active there. If marriages between blood relations take place, the recessive genes are developed which can cause many deformities in the body, i.e., offspring may become physically or mentally handicapped.

Law of Inheritance

Gregor Mendel (1866) discovered the law of inheritance in hybrid peas growing in the garden of an Austrain monastery. His law was found applicable to animals also. His law can be summarized as under.

"If a man who is homozygous for blue eyes marries a woman who is homozygous for brown eyes, the children of the couple will have brown eyes only" (Homozygous condition is that condition in which information concerning a given characteristic differ in the paired gene position)

If a homozygous man marries to a heterozygous woman the distribution of children from the couple will be such that one fourth of them will be homozygous for brown eyes, one half of them, will he heterozygous and one fourth of them will be homozygous for blue eyes.

By this law, Mendel concluded that all genetic informations come to the individual in units rather than in graduated series. In other words, we receive from our ancestors genes controlling the development of specific unitary characteristics not a composite of traits called tendencies.

The second conclusion that can be drawn from this law is that characteristics of men do not remain constant. They tend to vary continuously along a dimension of genes.

Some Studies on Influence of Heredity

How great the role of inheritance is in shaping the personality of an individual by the process of growth and development can be understood by the following studies:

1. **Galton :** He was the first psychologist who conducted studies on the nature and extent of genetic influences in man. He studied 997 eminent British people and found that there were 322 people out of 997 who were also distinguished. He also studied 997 average people and found that only one of them was eminent. He thus concluded that eminent men were found in families which have already one eminent member at least. He also found that decreased instances of imminence were seen when eminent people decreased their relationship with eminent persons. Thus, according to him eminence is inherited from generation to generation.

   He also studied some people of U.S.A. who were given better educational facilities and compared them with the eminent people of U.K. who were given average educational facilities. He found that people of USA were not better performed than that of UK.

2. **Goddard (1914) :** He studied a Kalikak family of USA. Martia Kalikak who was a soldier in the American revolution, developed illegal sexual relation with a feeble-minded lady and an illegitimate child was born. 480 descendents were traced from the family tree of this illegitimate boy. Out of them 143 were feeble-minded, 291 were borderline normal and only 46 were found normal in intelligence.

   After the revolution when Mr. Kalikak married a normal lady a legitimate child was born. 496 descendents were traced from the family tree of this boy. All of them except two were found normal or above normal in intelligence and they became teachers, lawyers, businessmen etc. This study proves that intelligence is inherited from one generation to the next.

   These two studies show that heredity plays an important role in determining the traits. But the conclusions derived from these two studies can not be fully relied upon because of the following reasons.

   (i) They do not distinguish between biological and social inheritance. Their studies combine these two factors. So, it is very difficult to isolate the contribution of gene in shaping the personality.

   (ii) Testing material used in these studies was not perfect and the survey is also unsystematic and unreliable.

   (iii) The researchers were already biased in favour of hereditary factors. So, their conclusions can not be relied upon.

3. **Kellogg and Kellogg :** In order to study the relative influence of heredity and environment they conducted a systematic research by taking their own son and a chimpanzee. Their respective ages were 10 months and 7.5 months. Both of them were brought up in the same environment with similar type of facilities given to them. Their behaviours were systematically studied at regular intervals. It was found that in the beginning the chimpanzee surpassed the son in motor skills of jumping, running, climbing, etc. Chimpanzee also learned some social skills such as eating with spoon and drinking from a glass, but he could learn 93 words only. But later on, the son caught him up in all areas of development except physical strength.

   This study shows that heredity sets a limit for maximum development which can not be improved even by providing the best environment.

ENVIRONMENT AND ITS INFLUENCE

Environment here means social and cultural environment especially. Physical environment also becomes the part of social environment when it is used in the learning process. When an individual lives in a society, in a family, he learns many things from the social and cultural environment. These learnings bring about certain changes in his behaviour. Some of these changes may be of permanent nature. These permanent changes become the part and parcel of his habits. When these habits are converted into values after maturity, they become the representative traits of the individual. Individual is now recognized with these traits.

Influence of Environment in Shaping the Personality

The role or contribution of environment is no less than that of the heredity. In fact human being is a by product of heredity and environment both. The importance of environment in the process of growth and development can be understood by the following example.

A missionary in (Midnapur) Bihar found two children who were taken by wolves in early children hood. These children were reared in the company of wolves in beast environment. They learned to walk on four feet, ate raw flesh and verbalized like wolves. These children were brought back from the forest and kept in a hospital. One of them died next day and the other could hardly learn elementary things. This study shows that if suitable environment is not provided to a person, his genetic qualities will not flourish at all.

On the basis of studies on heredity and environment with regard to growth and development following conclusions can be drawn:

1. Heredity and environment both play combined role in the development of personality of an individual.
2. Heredity does not determine any trait of the personality in isolation. It only provides a base and then environment develops the trait.
3. Subjective traits of the individual like physique, colour of skin, resistance level of the body etc are determined by the hereditary factors. Certain diseases are also inherited because of low resistability of the body of the individual.
4. Bad environment can surpass good inheritance but good environment is not a substitute for poor heredity. It means heredity sets a limit for the maximum development. Even good training and experiences will not enable the person to cross this limit. On the other hand, even good man by genes can be made corrupt in a bad environment.
5. Training and experiences can improve the traits of an individual to a great extent. Even intelligence level can be improved to some extent.

Environmental Factors Affecting Growth and Development

Environmental influences begin since the time of conception of the child into the womb of his mother. Mental, physical and emotional conditions of mother, also influence the development of foetus in the womb. When child opens his eyes in the physical world, he immediately comes in contact with the environment. Since he takes birth in a society, he is also influenced by a number of social and cultural factors. The impact of some of these factors on his growth and development is given below:

1. **Physical factors of the environment :** Physical and geographical conditions of the environment play an important role in shaping the personality of an individual. People living in deserts, hilly areas and plains have great difference in their body strength, height, structure, mode of living, habits etc. Climate of the region also affects the behaviour, body built and resistance to fight the environmental forces. For example, people living in Siberian region can tolerate lower degree of temperature than those who live in Indian sub continent. Personality traits are also determined by these environmental factors, for example, people living in African continent are more aggressive and get easily annoyed than those living in North America.
2. **Family of the individual :** Personality of an individual develops fully only when interaction between biological inheritance and environmental forces take place. Home is the first place of these interactions. Whatever early changes take place in the nature and pattern of personality formation in the initial life of an individual at home, they are generally upheld in the whole life. In the family, child comes in contact with his parents, grandparents, uncles, aunties and cousins. These people give full recognition to the child. They also respond him keeping his likes and dislikes. Several empirical evidences support that childhood experiences are decisive determinants of his personality in later life. For example, if a child is deprived of family love and other facilities, he may grow into

either an aggressive or totally submissive person in future. Margarets Ribble in 1944 started a series of investigations on the effects of some psychological deprivations in infancy. She studied 600 children in this regard and concluded that lack of adequate cuddling and other close physical contact with some friendly adults can impose serious handicaps on the growing infants.

Each and every characteristic of the family affects the personality of the child in future. We are taking here one more example of morale of the family. A low morale home does not present a good model before the child for imitation. Stort in 1939 on the basis of a questionnaire administered on 1800 adolescents concluded three things given below-

- Children coming from homes where good morale pattern dominated were better adjusted, more independent in thinking and action and more satisfactorily related to their parents than those who were average in this dimension.
- Adolescents who came from discarded and nagging families were poorly adjusted in the society.
- Economic factors also influence the development of personality. Poverty of parents and lack of money even to fulfil legitimate needs of their children led to certain kinds of frustrations in adolescents.

3. **School :** School is a miniature society in itself. Here individual stays for almost six hours daily in the early quarter period of his life. His personality is shaped by the school in the following ways.
   - School poses new problems before the child to be acquired and new models for imitation.
   - School provides new knowledge and expands the horizon of the child. These behavioural changes determine the pattern and direction of growth and development.
   - Social interaction with teachers, classmates and peers is possible in schools. These interaction also shape the personality of the individual.
4. **Teacher :** Teacher can play a very crucial role in shaping the personality of the individual. The way the teacher behaves and handles his students and the personality traits exhibited by him have an important effect on the future personality of students. He influences a child in the following ways.
   - The way the teacher carries out his role in the class will affect the emotional climate of the classroom. An authoritarian teacher will establish an autocratic climate and a democratic teacher will create a permissive climate in the classroom. Autocratic climate will tend to create aggression and bostility among students. If climate is democratic, it will develop constructive, thoughtful and cooperative behaviour among students. All good personality traits can be developed by democratic climate in the class. Because of this reason democratic dealing is preferred to autocratic dealing. The more a teacher is democratic in his attitude and behaviour, the more his students will be accommodative to others.
   - Studies have shown that children who repeatedly fail in the class are likely to be cruel, selfish, unfriendly, unhappy, impolite, boastful and quarrelsome. Thus, teacher tries to reduce the occurrence of failures in the class by his dedicated efforts.
   - Whatever model of character is presented by the teacher in the class, it is immediately copied down by the students. If teacher has ideal traits in him, students, are also likely to be idealistic.
5. **Language :** Language is the medium by which the society is structured and experiences of the race are transmitted from generation to generation. The child learns the languages of the society. He learns many experiences and knowledge by these languages. He also communicates the other members of the society by these languages. Thus, by these processes he becomes an integral part of the social environment.
6. **Social roles :** The word role has been derived from the theatre world. In theatres the actors play the role of different characters as the situation demands. Worlds is also a stage and human beings are just actors who play their respective roles. Man is a social animal. He comes in contact with different people in the society. As a result he has to play the role of a father, son, brother, friend, student etc. throughout his life at various stages of his development. Social roles are the process by which an individual interacts with other members of the society. Thus, social roles are the collection of behaviour and relevant attitudes towards others. These roles are learned by individuals through observation and imitation.

7. **Self concept :** Self concepts are the means by which we create our unique image and identity in the society. Self concept in the child is initiated by physical awareness. The other means of developing self concept are how we maintain our social status, how we dress ourselves and how we speak and respond to others. Self concept influences our personality development in two ways. The first is that if people hold us in high esteem, we feel exalted. And the second is that if others hold negative attitude towards us, it creates the feeling of worthlessness and it may lead to self defence or withdrawl from the social situation. If self concept is fully developed in an individual his rate of growth and development will be high.
8. **Identification :** Identification is the process by which we imitate the physical, social or mental characteristics of our model. When a boy identifies himself with his father by coping father's behaviour it means that he wants to be like him. If identifying models are solid physically, mentally or socially, the identification process will also be solid and healthy.
9. **Living standard :** Physical and mental health of a person is directly related to his living standard. If he is getting nutritious food and sufficient amount of time for sports and exercise, his rate of development will be high. People of developed countries are found very advanced because of this reason.
10. **Cultural heritage :** Every society is identified by its cultural heritage which is transmitted from one generation to the next. The transmission of cultural heritage may also be termed as social heredity. The personality of an individual is gradually shaped by the culture he is born in.

E.R. Tyler defined culture in the following words.

"It is that complex whole which includes knowledge, beliefs, morals law, customs and many other capabilities (skills) and habits acquired by man as a member of society."

Thus, culture refers to total life activities of a society. Whatever a person learns from the society by the process of interaction is called culture. In other words, what the people think, feel and do constitute the culture of a society. Biological inheritance is more or less the same all over the world but whatever differences are seen in the process of growth and development of personality among individuals it is because of the differences of social inheritance (culture). We can easily identify people reared in different cultures by the personality patterns they possess. English, Africans, Arabs and Indians can be identified by their cultural background more than by their biological heredity.

No single culture dominates in big countries. Sub cultures within the culture is also seen which brings about social conflicts. This conflict distorts the personality of individuals as well. Culture or sub cultures are silent educators and they mould the personality of individuals very silently.

The influence of cultural forces is so powerful that if three identical twins of a Hindu family are reared in three different cultures such as houses of Muslims, Christians and jews, the impact of their respective cultures will produce three distinct type of personality. These twins will not have any thing of their original Hindu culture.

The influence of culture can also be understood by the following words:

"Culture regulates our lives at every turn. From the moment we are born until we die, whether we are conscious of it or not, constant pressure on us forces us to follow certain types of behaviour that other men have created for us".

Culture influences the personality development of an individual in the following ways:

- Ideas, values, beliefs, customs and traditions are internationalized through the process of learning. A child who takes birth in a particular culture is reared in that very culture. He learns ideas, beliefs, values, customs etc. of his society and thus he acquires distinctive personality characteristics in the process.
- Various cultures are propagated by various institutions. When individual takes part in these activities actively or in a passive manner, he gets attached to these cultural institutions. Thus, his culture is institutionalized. This is the **second stage of culture formation**. When culture of a region reaches this stage it becomes very difficult to wipe it out by other cultures.

PIAGET'S STAGES OF COGNITIVE DEVELOPMENT

According to him, there is an orderly sequence of stages in cognitive development. Thus progression from one stage to another is always fixed. The child can not adopt the strategies of a later stage at an early stage of development. It is because he must have to acquire and exercise the strategies and schemas of earlier stages. For example, in order to understand words, the child must know letters first or we can not teach Electronic Physics to a child of primary class.

Ausbel commenting upon the development stages of Piaget writes "Piaget's stages are identifiable, sequential phases in an orderly progression of development that are qualitatively discriminable from adjacent phases and generally characteristic of most members of a broadly defined age range".

The stages of cognitive development are related in the sense that they represent forms of adaptation, but these forms are qualitatively different, that is the adaptive functions are transformed as the child moves from one stage to the next. This theory of development is quite different from the theory of associationists who emphasize the gradual accumulation of responses.

Important stages of Piaget's theory of mental development are given below.

I. Period of sensorimotor adaptation (from 0-2 years): The infant starts this stage by his reflex activities and then he reaches to the stage of sensorimotor schemes by practice and accommodation. The intellectual development at this stage is marked by the following characteristics.

(a) *Object concept formation :* Objects exist in the mind of an adult whether they are present before the person or not. But in the psychological world of a child, only those objects exist which have a psychological presence for the child, ie, he can look and touch it. As soon as they are removed from the eyes of the child, they cease to exist for the child. When the child experiences the same object repeatedly, he develops the concept of permanence of objects. This concept is developed in the first year of life. When this type of structure is formed in the mind, practice of concepts is started by the child.

(b) *Coordinated space :* Spatial world at first is totally uncoordinated for the child. Each sensory modality has its own space. By the end of two years, the child develops the concepts which are marked by the coordination among different objects and between objects and body of the child

(c) *Objectified causalty :* The concept of cause and effect relationship is established when action of the child brings about an effect. Then this effect is taken as the cause of that event.

(d) *Objectification of time :* By the end of two years the child is also able to objectify time.

II. Period of symbolic and preconceptual thought (2-4 years): Ideas begin to develop in the mind of the child at the third year. By imitation and observation, he demonstrates that he is capable of extending his physical world to metaphysics. He begins to use symbols in the 4th year. Now he can represent the environment in the absence of perceptual cues only on the basis of ideas.

III. Period of intuitive thought (4-8 years): At this stage the child can use various concepts in different situations, *i.e.*, he is able to generalize his past and present experiences. His thoughts are not based on logical reasoning. It is rather governed by intution. The child can talk about this and that momentary static condition in a separate manner but he can not properly integrate various sets of conditions into an integrated whole due to lack of logical weakness, *i.e.*, logical coherence is not found here. For example, a child can write fine sentences representing various topics but he can not write a compact essay.

IV. The period of concrete operation (8-12 years): Here the child is able to direct his attention away from the static condition, ie, he can accommodate with all the successive changes taking place in the system. It means that he can reorganize his future on the basis of his past experience as well as trends at present. Reasoning power of the child is well developed during this period. Some examples of what a child can do are handling and manipulating the numbers in various ways by various operations, arrangement of objects and materials into various groups and sub groups, ordering of objects according to one or more attributes and so on. Piaget has described a term "grouping" for this stage of cognitive development.

This period also shows some logical inconsistency in the thinking of the child. Piaget has coined a term "syncretism" for this defect. Despite this, beginning of abstract operation is seen during this stage.

V. Period of formal (abstract) operation (12-18 years): During this period, the thought process of the child becomes systematic, consistent and reasonably well integrated. Reality guides the contemplation process of the child. The formal operation of thinking starts with the formulation of hypothesis, (deductive reasoning) and reaches at its peak when hypothesis is tested by experiments, ie, inductive reasoning. At this stage, the boy can manipulate any abstract idea in his own way and form new idea entirely different from the old one. His wisdom lies in the expertise administration of the unforeseen. Whenever an adolescent faces any problem with the help of formal operation of thought he identifies various relevant variables which may be helpful in the solution of that problem and then all these variables are manipulated by him.

Thus, development of formal operation capacity enables the adolescent to transfer understanding from one situation to another and to evaluate the results on the basis of its pros and cons. Physical (concrete) objects are never required for thinking (operation) during this period. The thought process is completely abstract here.

KOHLBERG'S THEORY OF DEVELOPMENT

According to him moral development of the child proceeds in sequential but distinctive stages. These stages are given below:

(a) **Stage-I :** In the early years of a child's life (from zero-four years) the physical consequences of an action determines its goodness or badness. If fire burns the child, he does not touch it. The child is ego-centric and standards of morality are external here.

(b) **Stage-II :** The child gives importance to his own point of view, (his self) and is able to take account of other's roles insofar as he can use them in his own way. This is a period of make belief. Right action is what which satisfies the needs of the child. The role of others is also important in the sense that a child does only what can bring approval of others. Thus, only that behaviour is moral which can satisfy not only self needs of the child but it must please others also.

(c) **Stage-III :** At this stage the child adopts the view pints of others on the basis of their consequences. He does not question the views of others. The child considers only that thing as right which are considered as right by others. Thus, the child is totally conformist to the standard of the society.

(d) **Stage-IV:** At this stage, the child is able to make any moral decision on his own without caring for the thinking of others. Though he considers laws and regulations set by the society as the essence of morality, yet he develops his own principles of morality on various occasions. Thus, he is a non-conformist to the norms of the society to a great extent.

(e) **Stage-V :** Standards and norms are more internalized here. The adolescents examine various view points prepared by different societies and recognize them. They think that the laws prepared by their own society are correct. Other societies may have good moral principles that must be adopted after careful appraisal.

(f) **Stage-VI :** This is the last stage of moral development according to Kohlberg. Here the universality of the view points of the individual is seen. He formulates his own universal moral principles which he thinks that all societies should adhere to it. True understanding of right and wrong is developed at this stage.

HAVIGHURST'S THEORY OF DEVELOPMENT

According to him at each stage of development, there are certain tasks, skills and understanding that must be completed before a person can proceed to a higher level of development.

Havighurst Says –

"At or about a certain period in the life of the individual, successful achievement leads to his happiness and to success with later tasks, while failure leads to unhappiness in the individual, disapproval by society and difficulty with later tasks".

LIST OF DEVELOPMENT TASKS GIVEN BY HAVIGHURST

S.No.	Birth to 6 years	6 to 12 years
1	Learning to walk	Learning physical skills, ordinary games.
2	Learning to take solid food	Building wholesome attitudes towards oneself as a growing organism
3	Learning to talk	Learning to get along with age mates
4	Learning to control the elimination of body wastes.	Learning an appropriate masculine or feminine role.
5	Learning sex differences	Developing fundamental skills in reading, writing and calculating.

6	Achieving physiological stability	Developing concepts necessary for everyday living
7	Forming simple concepts of social and physical reality	Developing the ability of manipulating the ideas and concepts.
8	Learning to relate oneself emotionally to parents, siblings and other people	Achieving personal independence
9	Learning to distinguish right and wrong and developing a conscience	Developing attitudes towards social groups and institutions

COMPARISON OF THREE CATEGORIES OF THEORIES

S. No.	Psycho analytic	Behaviouristic	Cognitive
1	Feeling is important here	Stimulus and behaviour of others are important here	Thinking is all responsible for development
2	In order to acquire moral principles, parental values are internalized	Moral values are adopted from either models or they are acquired by conditioning	Moral principles are acquired automatically with age, ie, mental development
3	Super ego, a moral conduct is formed at the age of five	Learning of morality is a life long process	Super ego is formed during the period of adolescence
4	Moral values are not free from culture	Same	Moral values are universal
5	Parents and relatives are agents of socialization	Adults and peers who give reinforcement are the main agents of socialization	People of the matured age are the agents of socialization

VYGOTSKY'S SOCIOCULTURAL THEORY

Both Jean Piaget and Lev Vygotsky believed that children build knowledge through experiences. Piaget believed this happened through exploration with hands-on activities. Vygotsky, on the other hand, believed that children learn through social and cultural experiences. Interactions with peers and adults help children in this process. While interacting with others, children learn the customs, values, beliefs, and language of their culture. For this reason, families and teachers should provide plently of social interaction for young children.

Vygotsky believed language is an important tool for thought and plays a key role in cognitive development. He introduced the term ***private speech***, or self-talk. This refers to when children ''think out loud''. After learning language, children engage in this self-talk to help guide their activity and develop their thinking. Generally, self-talk continues until children reach school age.

One of Vygotsky's most important contributions was the *zone of* ***proximal development*** (ZPD). This concept presents learning as a scale. One end of the scale or ''zone'' includes the tasks that are within the child's current development level. The other end of the scale includes tasks too difficult for children to accomplish, even with help. In the middle are the tasks children cannot accomplish alone. These are achieved with help from another knowledgeable peer or adult. The term used for this assistance is ***scaffolding***. Just as a painter needs a structure on which to stand and point a building, scaffolding provides the structure for learning to occur. For example, a teacher could scaffold a child's learning while constructing a puzzle. The teacher might demonstrate how a piece fits or provide clues regarding colour, shape or size. The ''zone'' is constantly changing. In contrast to Piaget, Vygotsky believed that learning was not limited by stage or maturation. Children move forward in their cognitive development with the right social interaction and guided learning.

CONCEPTS OF CHILD-CENTERED AND PROGRESSIVE EDUCATION

Child-Centered Education

Child-centered education is the idea that the needs and desires of the child should take precedence in structuring the learning day. The whole idea is that learning should be fun and engaging for the child, and is most likely to be that way if the child is incharge of the learning experience, rather than the adult parent or teacher.

Child-centered education is most characterised by learning 'centers' in a classroom that promote hands-on, active participation by the child. There may be magnifying glasses and bug slides in the science center, books and puppets that could be used to re-tell the stories in the language arts center, and wood blocks and shapes in the math center. The children are free to manipulate the objects in these centers. It is the process, the activity, the experience, that is valuable, not the facts, ideas, concepts or skills.

It is a relatively new approach to education. For centuries past, adults defined what education should be and children were the ones who did the adjusting. Education was considered work, not play.

Then came the softening influences of child psychologist Jean-Jacques Rousseau, as well as Dr. Marria Montessori, John Dewey, Jean Piaget and Lev Vygotsky, who all contended that a child's self-esteem and self-concept should be built up in order to create a better learner. Soon, the colleges of education were promoting child-centered education instead of instructionally centered education.

Role of Learner in Child-Centered Education

Learners are active as opposed to passive recipients of knowledge. Learners may assume a decision-making role in the classroom. Learners often decide what is to be learned, through which activities and at what pace. Learners can also produce materials and provide activities for the classroom.

Role of Teacher in Child-Centered Education

To put this approach into practice, teachers need to help students set achievable goals; they encourage students to assess themselves and their peers; help them to work co-operatively in groups and ensure that they know how to make use of all the available resources for learning.

Progressive Education

During most of the twentieth century, the term 'progressive education' has been used to describe ideas and practices that aim to make schools more effective agencies of a democratic society. Although there are numerous differences of style and emphasis among progressive educators, they share the conviction that democracy means active participation by all citizens in social, political and economic decisions that will affect their lives. The education of engaged citizens, according to this perspective, involves two essential elements: (1) respect for diversity, meaning that each individual should be recognised for his or her own abilities, interests, ideas, needs, and cultural identity, and (2) the development of critical, socially engaged intelligence, which enables individuals to understand and participate effectively in the affairs of their community in a collaborative effort to achieve a common good. These elements of progressive education have been termed 'child-centered' and 'social reconstruction' approaches, and while in extreme forms they have sometimes been separated, in the thought of John Dewey and other major theorists they are seen as being necessarily related to each other.

The term 'progressive' arose from a period (roughly 1890–1920) during which many Americans took a more careful look at the political and social effects of vast concentrations of corporate power and private wealth. Dewey, in particular, saw that with the decline of local community life and small scale enterprise, young people were losing valuable opportunities to learn the arts of democratic participation, and he concluded that education would need to make up for this loss. In his Laboratory School at the University of Chicago, where he worked between 1896 and 1904, Dewey tested ideas he shared with leading school reformers such as Francis W. Parker and Ella Flagg Young. Between 1899 and 1916 he circulated his ideas in works such as The School and Society, The Child and the Curriculum, Schools of Tomorrow, and Democracy and Education, and through numerous lectures and articles. During these years other experimental schools were established around the country, and in 1919 the Progressive Education Association was founded, aiming at "reforming the entire school system of America".

Therefore, progressive education is a reaction against the traditional style of teaching which teaches facts largely at the expense of understanding what is being taught. According to **John French,** "The progressive school teaches the child to think for himself instead of passively accepting stereotyped ideas. It keeps always in mind that each child is different from every other, and that what makes an educated person useful in his particular walk of life, what makes him interesting, what makes him an individual, is not his resemblance to other people, but his differences".

Philosophies and Practices of Progressive Education

1. Curriculum is strongly influenced by what the children are interested in, and is child-centered rather than adult driven.
2. Learning is 'hands-on', experiential and the emphasis is on process rather than product children are 'learning to learn'.
3. Children learn through integrated, theme-based units or inquiry projects and the 'theme' often emerges from the children.
4. Assessment is authentic and holistic. Children are well known by their teachers and peers. There are no tests or letter grades. Instead, narrative reports are written about children

that cover all aspects of their development: social, emotional, personal, physical and intellectual level.

5. Classes are usually of mixed ages and no ability grouping is used. Children are able to work at their own pace and cross-age friendships are encouraged.
6. Progressive education practices a developmental approach which holds that each child is a unique being unfolding and developing at their own pace according to a specific pattern. At each stage of development there are things that can be learned and things that should not be learned. Respecting a child's development is central to progressive education.

Types of Progressive Education

1. **Humanistic :** The humanistic form of progressive education focuses on the humanities, arts and social sciences. Its emphasis is on the individual child and not the curriculum. This type of progressivism aims to build a well-rounded individual with highly developed critical thinking and reasoning skills. The children learn think for themselves instead of accepting everything teachers tell them. Social development and interaction among the students are seen as valuable learning techniques.
2. **Constructivism :** Constructivism is a type of child-centered progressivism. It focuses on the child's creativity and learning abilities. Teachers should build the curriculum around the requirements and interests of the child. It maintains that education should consider children's developmental stages. Swiss psychologist **Jean Piaget** influenced the theories of constructivist education. Experiential learning, or learning by doing, allows students to construct their own knowledge.
3. **Montessori :** Italian doctor Marria Montessori started the Montessori progressive educational system. She developed her teaching theories by clinical observation and analysis of how children learn. Her method of education focused on how children naturally learn, all by themselves, without the help of adults. Maria Montessori concluded that children teach themselves, and it's the job of teachers to facilitate this process, not dominate it. Montessori teachers provide a sensory-rich environment and hands-on activities.

CRITICAL PERSPECTIVE OF THE CONSTRUCT OF INTELLIGENCE

Introduction

The most important variable that affects schooling or performance on a job is intelligence. Psychologists have interpreted the term intelligence in different ways and there is no consensus among them on the term even so far. In psychology this term is treated as a construct whose structure is different in different individuals.

The vagueness of the term arises due to the fact that intelligence is not a concrete material. It is rather abstraction from the behaviour of the individual which is indirectly inferred and elaborated as an adjective.

The dictionary meaning of term "intelligence" is the capacity to acquire and apply knowledge. **Boring** defines intelligence as intelligence is what an intelligence test measures.

Definitions of Intelligence

Several psychologists have classified and defined intelligence in several ways. Some of them are given below:

1. Vernon's Classification of Intelligence

(a) *Biological Approach:* Man is an organism among millions living on earth. Environment works as a foe for him. Intelligence is the capacity to adapt to the environment or new situations of life at every moment.

This definition of intelligence can be criticized on the ground that there have been many intelligent and renowned persons who were ill adapted to their social and physical environment. Besides, if we want to study individual differences in a society, this definition serves no practical purpose.

(b) *Psychological Approach :* According to psychologists intelligence is the relative effects of heredity and environment both. An English psychologist, **C. Burt** defined intelligence as the innate general cognitive ability.

In support of psychological definitions of intelligence **Hebb** and **R.B. Catell** distinguished two kinds of intelligence. The first is intelligence "A" which is Fluid intelligence and which is related to genetic potentialities or innate qualities of the individual's nervous system. Second is intelligence "B" which is crystalised "intelligence" and which is related to experiences, learning and environmental factors. These two types of intelligence in normal circumstances so much overlap on each other that they are practically indistinguishable.

(c) *Operational Approach :* These definitions help us to understand the concept of intelligence in clear and definite terms. In this approach scientific terms are first of all defined operationally and then observations are conducted with reference to these terms. For example, in order to determine a child's IQ, we first administer a test of a specific kind. Then we observe his performance on the test and finally draw certain conclusions in the context of the pre-determined objectives.

2. Freeman's Classification

(a) *Ability of adjustment :* An individual is intelligent to the extent to which he is able to adjust to new situations and problems of life. The more a person is intelligent, the more he is able to adapt to his environment in antagonistic conditions. The person who is low in intelligence has less capacity to adjust to the new situations of life.

(b) *Ability of learning :* Learning ability is also an index of intelligence. The more a person is intelligent, the more he will be able to learn new things.

(c) *Ability to carry on abstract thinking :* This category of definitions of intelligence is related to the effective use of concepts and symbols in dealing with situations and solving the problems through the use of verbal and numerical symbols. According to **Terman**, an individual is intelligent to the extent he is able to carry on abstract thinking.

3. E.L. Thorndike's Classification

(a) *Concrete intelligence :* The intellectual ability in relation to concrete materials is called concrete intelligence. It is the ability of a person to comprehend the actual situations and react to them adequately. This kind of intelligence is measured by using performance tests or picture tests in which the subject manipulates the concrete materials.

(b) *Abstract intelligence :* It is the ability to respond to words, letters, numbers or symbols. This type of intelligence is required in all academic activities in schools or outside the schools. The highest level of abstract intelligence is manifested in the thoughts of philosophers or in the inventions of scientists and mathematicians.

(c) *Social intelligence :* It is the ability of an individual to react to social situations of life. It is the ability to understand others and to react to them in such a manner that they may not feel unjust attitude regarding them.

4. Intelligence as a Global Capacity

A comprehensive definitions of intelligence : **Stoddard** (1943) and **Wechsler** (1944) have defined intelligence in the following words :

"Intelligence is the aggregate or the global capacity of the individual to act purposefully, to think rationally and to deal with the environment effectively".

Stoddard further elaborated that intelligence is the capacity of a person to undertake such activities which are: (*i*) difficult (*ii*) complex (*iii*) abstract (*iv*) economical (*v*) goal directed (*vi*) valuable from social view points (*vii*) original. These activities demand concentration of energy and a resistance to emotional forces.

Characteristics of Intelligence

From the above definitions of intelligence, we can draw the following characteristics of intelligence:

(*i*) Intelligence is the composite of several intellectual skills, such as thinking, doing, reasoning, dealing, learning etc.

(*ii*) Intelligence is displayed by the behaviour of the individual as a whole and intelligent behaviour is always goal directed.

(*iii*) Intelligence is the ability to adjust to abnormal and challenging situations of life.

(*iv*) Intelligence is not related to ordinary tasks of life. It is always related to extra ordinary manipulation.

(*v*) Wechsler has included the concepts of drive and incentive which are implied in his statement. "To act purposefully" and "to deal effectively". But many psychologists are of the view that drive and incentive are non-intellectual traits of personality and if they are included in a test of mental ability, more confusions will be created thereof.

(*vi*) There are seven fundamental elements of intelligence according to **Stoddard.** Intelligent person can undertake difficult and abstract tasks with ease. He can manipulate and deal the abstract ideas and concepts efficiently. Similarly, economy refers to the rate at which a mental task is done or a problem is solved. If "A" solves a problem sooner than 'B' then 'A' will be considered more intelligent than 'B'. The term social value indicates whether a mental task performed by a person is in accordance with the socially desirable and acceptable norms or not. The last term original refers to a person's, ability to discover something new and different, *i.e.*, this term is directly related to creative potential of a person. Discovery of some new facts and principles and inventions of new concrete materials by the scientists are few examples of originality.

Stoddard's definition of intelligence has been criticized on two grounds :

(a) It includes social values in intelligence, *i.e.*, intelligent task must be socially desirable. Psychologists criticize this point by saying that social value is a subjective phenomenon, *i.e.*, what is desirable for me, may not be necessarily desirable for others. So, there is no scope of subjectivity in an objective intelligence test.

(b) He has included two conditions of intelligent behaviour in his definition. First is concentration of energy and second is resistance to emotional forces. Psychologists say that these elements are non-intellectual traits and hence they should not be included in mental abilities at any cost.

Theories of Intelligence

1. Faculty theory of intelligence:

This is the oldest theory of intelligence given during the period of pre-experimental psychology. According to this theory mind is made up of different faculties like reasoning, logic, memory, imagination and discrimination. These faculties are independent of each other and can be developed by rigorous mental exercises of the difficult subject-matter.

This theory does not take the hereditary factors of intelligence into account and thus this theory was discarded by the later psychologists who believed that we can never improve the intellectual capacity of a person if he is mentally slow by birth.

2. Unifactor theory:

According to Alfred Binet (1916) intelligence is a general intellectual ability which is made up of several discrete abilities. These abilities include

(i) to reason well with abstract material

(ii) to comprehend well

(iii) to have a clear direction of thoughts

(iv) to relate thinking with the attainment of a desirable end and

(v) to be self-critical.

All these abilities combined together is called general mental ability. Thus, intelligence is a single but complex mental process which can be measured by different kinds of materials designed for the purpose.

3. Two factors theory:

This theory was developed by an English psychologist, **Charles Spearman** in 1904. According to him, intellectual abilities consist of two factors, general ability known as 'G' factors and specific abilities known as 'S' factors.

Characteristics of G factors

(i) It is universal inborn ability.

(ii) It is general mental energy.

(iii) It is constant, *i.e.*, it remains the same in all the individuals and does not change with time.

(iv) The amount of G differs from person to person depending on his genes.

(v) It is used in every life activity.

(vi) Greater the amount of G in an individual, larger is the chance of his success in life.

Characteristics of 'S' factors

(i) It is learnt and hence acquired in the environment.

(ii) It varies from activity to activity in the same individual.

(iii) The amount of S also differs from person to person due to his accessibility to learning situations.

(iv) 'S' factors are related to the specific activity. A low correlation between two or more functions or activities indicates the presence of 'S' factor involved in the activity. A person can be expert only in one or few activities because of the specific factors involved in the activity.

According to Spearman, out of these two factors 'G' factor is more important and thus it is an important measure of intelligence. So, any intelligence test should measure only 'G' factor because it provides most important basis of predicting a person's behaviour in different situations. Raven's Progressive Matrices and Catell's Culture Fair Test both measure 'G' factor.

Spearman has explained his theory with the help of a tetrad equation which is given below :

$$rap \times rbq - raq \times rbp = 0$$

Here,

a = opposites
b = discrimination
p = completion
q = cancellation

Thus, rap means correlation between opposites and completions, rbq means correlation between cancellation and discrimination, raq means correlation between opposite and cancellation and rbp means correlation between discrimination and completion. This theory can also be explained with the help of a diagram given below :

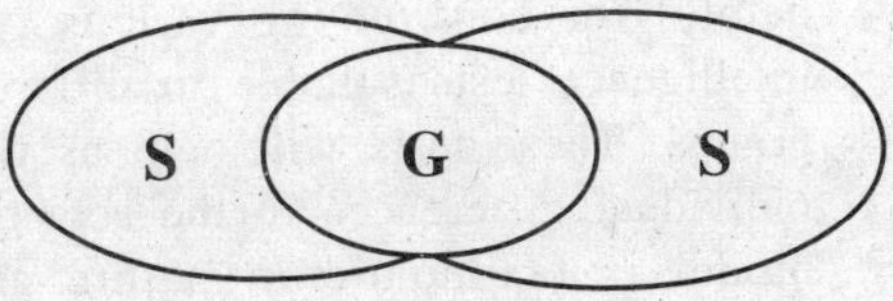

4. Multi-factors theory :

This theory was developed by an American psychologist, **E.L. Thorndike.** He opposed the theory of general intelligence by saying that there are specific stimuli and specific mental responses. Intelligence is nothing more than a potential specific connections between these stimuli and responses. Differences of intelligence among people are due to the different number of such connections in the neurological system. This theory is also called **atomistic theory** of intelligence. There are **four attributes of intelligence** according to him:

(a) *Level :* It refers to the difficulty of a task that can be removed by using intelligence. If different tasks are arranged in increasing difficulty order, then the height that a person can attain determines his level of intelligence. It is a kind of power test.

(b) *Range :* It refers to the number of tasks of the same difficulty value that a person can do in a certain period of time. Theoretically, an individual possessing a certain level of intelligence should be able to solve the whole range of tasks at a given level. It is a kind of speed test.

Range and level can not be completely isolated from each other. We can not measure range without altitude (level) and vice versa.

(c) *Area :* It refers to the total numbers of situations at each level to which the individual is able to respond. Area is the summation of all ranges at each level of intelligence. Area = Level × Range.

(d) *Speed :* It refers to the rapidity with which an individual can respond to a test items. Speed and level are positively correlated. It is different from range in the sense that no specific time is given here to complete a task.

Every intelligence test should consist of these four attributes.

5. Group factor structure of intelligence (PMA Test) :

This theory was developed by **L.L. Thurstone.** According to him, intelligence is not an expression of general factor but a combination of group of traits. They are intermediate factors, *i.e.*, they are not so universal as 'G' factor and they are not so specific as 'S' factor. This primary group of factors give the common mental abilities, a functional cohesiveness and then constitute a group. Another group of common mental abilities is said to have another primary factor and so on. In this way, there are a number of groups of mental abilities each of which has its own primary factors. On the basis of factor analysis of these groups, Thurstone identified the following seven group factors which are termed as primary mental abilities (PMA).

1. Number factor (N) : It is the ability to do numerical calculations rapidly and accurately.
2. Verbal factor (V) : They are related to the operations involving verbal comprehension.
3. Space factor (S) : It is related to the tasks in which subject manipulates an object imaginary in space.
4. Word fluency factor (W) : It is involved to the situation when the subject is asked to think of isolated words at a fast rate.
5. Reasoning factors (R) : It is used in those tasks that require the subject to discover a rule or principles involved in series or groups of letters.
6. Rote memory (M) : It is the ability to memorize a fact quickly.
7. Perceptual speed (P) : It is the ability to note perceptual (visual) details rapidly.

The point to be noted here is that these seven abilities are significantly correlated with each other.

6. Structure of intelligence (SI) model :

This model was given by **J.P. Guilford** in 1966 in the University of California on the basis of factor analysis of many tests. According to him human mind is composed of at least three dimensions—operations, contents and products, and each dimension of intellect is sufficiently distinct which can be detected by factor analysis. These three dimensions of mind are given below:

(A) **Operations :** Operations can be divided into five major groups of intellectual abilities.

- **Cognition :** It includes discovery, recognition of informations and new understanding of the facts.
- **Memory :** It is the ability to recognize or recall previously learnt material.
- **Divergent thinking :** This operation is closely associated with creative potential. It refers to the ability to search out and think in a novel out of track way.
- **Convergent thinking :** It refers to the generation of information from given information and drawing conclusion from the given facts.

- **Evaluation :** It is the ability to make judgement on the basis of merits and demerits of a phenomenon. Here, value judgement on knowledge and thoughts is placed after critically examining them.

(B) Contents : Five kinds of contents are involved here. Operations are performed on these contents.

- **Figural content :** It is the concrete material perceived through the senses. Visual materials have three properties, size, form and colour.
- **Auditory content :** It includes nature and characteristics of sound perceived.
- **Symbolic content :** It includes letters, digits and other conventional signs usually organised in general pattern.
- **Semantic content :** It refers to those verbal meanings, ideas and concepts for which no examples are necessary.
- **Behavioural content :** It includes knowledge regarding other persons.

(C) Products : When five operations are applied to five types of contents, six kinds of products are made.

- **Units :** It refers to the production of a single word, definition or isolated bits of informations.
- **Classes :** It refers to the production of a concept.
- **Relations :** It refers to the production of any form of relationship, such as, analogy, opposite or similar ones.
- **System :** It refers to the production of internally consistent set of classification of various forms.
- **Transformation :** It refers to the production of changes in meaning, organisation or some other arrangement.
- **Implication :** It refers to the production of such information which is beyond the data given.

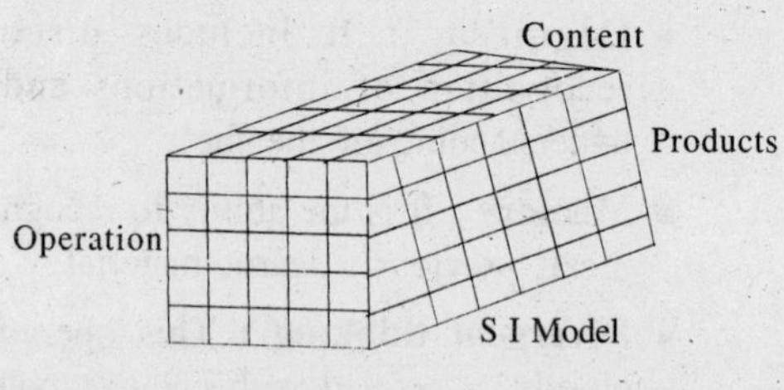

S I Model

On the basis of the model given above it can be stated that there are $5 \times 5 \times 6 = 150$ factors involved in intelligent acts.

Educational Implication of the Model

(a) In psychology : This model is very much helpful for constructing various types of intelligence tests suitable to different age groups. These tests will help us to study individual differences in the society. This model is taxonomic in nature and has discovered many abilities which were not known before. If test maker has included items representing contents and operations, he can see whether products are same or different. Conversely, if products are shown by the subject through the test, the test maker can find out the content and operation and match them with the items given in the test.

(b) In vocational testing : This model shows that there are 150 intellectual abilities. This model predicts five kinds of mental abilities classified as content. This means that different kinds of test items are needed in vocational testing. Six types of products are also tested on the basis of items representing the products. For example, if a person is able to deal with items of figural contents, he can deal with machines, operators, engineers etc. and any or all of the six types of products can be made by him, such as, he can define a machine or any operator. He can give clear concept about how a machine is operated and so on.

(c) In the field of education : Conventionally, learner was considered to be a kind of stimulus response device. Once the stimulus is given to him, he will respond but the new conception of the learner in the light of SI model is that of electronic computer which not only stores information but uses that information to generate new information either by divergent or convergent thinking.

Thus, this model gives the idea that learning is not merely the association of informations but it is the discovery of information as well. Model suggests that in order to understand human learning and higher mental processes of thinking, some drastic modifications are to be made in our theory of curriculum construction and pedagogy of instruction. Similarly, education is no longer considered to be the training of mind. Now, main emphasis on education is given to the learning of specific skills and modification of behaviour and all these materials are not taught merely for the purpose of training the mind of humans.

7. Two Level Process Theory of Intelligence :

This theory was developed by **Jensen** in 1968. According to him intelligence is a combination of two levels of processes. One is associative intelligence and the other is abstract intelligence. Associative intelligence includes those kinds of tests that depend upon memory and simple verbal association. Abstract intelligence includes those factors as concept learning, thinking, problem solving skills, multiple discrimination, principle learning etc.

8. Burt and Vernon's Hierarchy Theory :

Burt (1940) separated four factors of intelligence by using statistical techniques :

- General factors (common to all traits)
- Group factors (common to some of the traits)
- Specific factors (limited to few traits)
- Error factors (limited to a particular trait when it is measured)

When human mind is put at the top, there will be 5 level hierarchical model of intelligence where general factors will come next to intelligence and error factors will come in the last.

Vernon, on the other hand, suggested that intelligence tests measure an overall factor G as well as two other mental abilities. First are related to verbal, numerical and educational. Second are related to practical, mechanical, spatial and physical. These two major factors can be divided into minor group factors. These minor factors can further be divided into various specific factors and so on.

MEASUREMENT OF INTELLIGENCE

Historical development of mental testing can be divided into three periods for the purpose of convenience.

(A) Pre-Binet Period :

In the 19th century, there was a good deal of interest in the field of psychophysics in which attempts were made to develop general rule of sensory judgement. The functioning of sensory reactions of the typical individuals is actually studied in psycho-physics. Method of limits procedure was used here to measure the extent to which people were able to differentiate between stimuli. But the limitation of these experiments was that accurate generalization of the result was not possible.

Francis Galton was the first psychologist who took interest in studying whether individual characteristics are acquired or inherited. For this purpose, he studied the lives of prominent English men and in his book "Hereditary Genius" he demonstrated that personal characteristics, (mental and physical) of men are inherited. He developed a series of tests to measure these characteristics. It was the starting point of mental measurement.

The first laboratory of experimental psychology was established by **Wundt** in 1879 in Leiping. He employed two methods to test vision, hearing, reaction time and psychosomatic problems—*(i)* psycho-physical method *(ii)* Introspection method. He also developed mental tests which could measure the keenness of vision and hearing, muscular strength, reaction time and other sensory motor functions of body.

Many of **Galton's** ideas were brought to USA by an American psychologist **J.M. Catell.** Like **Galton** he also believed that intellectual functions can best be measured by the reaction time and sensory discrimination tests.

In the last quarter of the 19th century, many psychological laboratories came into existence and studies of individual differences in mental abilities started.

The word "**Mental Test**" was first used by Catell in 1890 but his tests were actually tests of sensory discrimination, speed of motor responses and the like.

Thus, upto this period mental ability was identified as sensory acuity of an individual. The correlation between mental abilities and academic achievements was not known at the time.

Drawbacks of this period:

- Psychologists were unable to identify and define the nature of intelligence. Keenness of sensory motor reactions were related to intelligence.
- They were unable to measure the complex functions of the body.
- Intelligence tests developed during this period were measuring other than intelligence.

(B) Binet Period :

An important incident led the people to think about mental measurement during this period. In the beginning of the 20th century in France, a large number of students failed in the examination. For this teachers and students blamed each other. Seeing this, superintendent of public instruction appointed a committee to device some techniques to screen out slow learners in the schools. Binet and Simon were among members of the committee. They developed a variety of paper pencil tests in their psychological laboratory established in 1889, to administer them on children of different ages. Through these tests Binet tried to measure more complex mental functions such as power of judgement and reasoning, memory, arithmetic ability, etc.

An important contribution of Binet and Simon is that they categorised their tests in terms of age levels by administering their test items to children of different ages. In this way, an age scale of intelligence was also developed. For example, if an item was correctly answered by majority of seven years old children but only few six years old children could respond it correctly, then this item was reserved for seven years old children. In this way, Binet and Simon developed separate tests for different ages.

Similarly, if an item suited to eight years old child was correctly answered by a child of 6 years and if the same trend was shown by the six years old child in most of the cases of a test, then the mental age of the child was considered to be eight years not six years, though his chronological age is six years only. Thus, the concept of mental age was also introduced by Binet and Simon for the first time in the history of mental testing and with the help of this concept we could assess the intellectual ability of a person. Some of the tests developed during this period are given below:

Binet-Simon Scale

The first scale of Binet-Simon was published in 1905. This scale consisted of 30 items arranged in increasing order of difficulty. This scale was a crude measure of intelligence of school going children.

In order to remove some of its defects they revised their scale in 1908. It was the first age based scale and it created a lot of interest among the psychologists across the world. The items in the tests were grouped according to the appropriate age levels from 3 to 13 years.

Some items for three years age

- Point to your nose, eyes and mouth.
- Repeat two digits 3, 5.
- Repeat sentences of six syllables.
- Enumerate objects in a picture.
- Give family names.

Some items of eight years age

- Read a passage and remember two lines.
- Add up the value of five coins.
- Name four colours.
- Count reverse from 20 to zero.
- Give differences between two objects.

1908 revision of Binet-Simon Scale was adopted by many psychologists of America, Switzerland and Germany and many suggestions were given by them for the improvement of the scale. Binet-Simon accepted their suggestions and revised their scale again in 1911.

Some sample items of 1911 scale are given below:

(A) Age = 8 years

- Gives difference between two objects.
- Counts reverse from 20 to zero.
- Points out omissions from unfinished pictures.
- Tells the dates correctly.
- Repeats the digits.

(B) Age = 10 years

- Arranges five blocks in order of increasing weights.
- Reproduces two geometric designs by using memory.
- Criticizes absurd statements.
- Comprehends and answers difficult questions.
- Uses three given words in two sentences.

Main Features of Binet-Simon Scale

(i) They are really scales, *i.e.*, items of the tests are arranged in the increasing difficulty order. Easiest items are put in the beginning and the most difficult item is put in the last. Thus, these scales measure the level or aptitude of an examinee and not their speed.

(ii) These tests measure the general abilities of intelligence instead of specific abilities.

(iii) They can also measure the mental growth of the subject because they are arranged according to different ages from 3 to 14 years.

(iv) They are administered on subjects individually.

(v) Their system of scoring is tied to age norms. A child's performance on the scale will be compared to that of children of his own age.

L.M. Terman's revision of Binet–Simon Scale: L.M. Terman of **Stanford** University revised this scale in 1916 to adapt to American situations. He introduced one new concept which was intelligence Quotient (IQ) in his revision. His scale consisted of 90 items ranging from 3 to 14 years of age. Some items of this scale are given below:

Age = 7 years

- Knows number of fingers on both hands.
- Describes pictures.
- Repeats five digits.
- Gives differences between paired objects.
- Ties a bowknot.

1937 Revision of Binet-Simon Scale : Terman along with his associate Merill revised 1916 scale again in 1937. This revision had two equivalent forms L and M. The number of items in the test was raised to 129 in each L M. forms. A new change was also introduced in the test which was the calculation of chronological age. Upto 13 years CA was taken to be as original but after 13 years CA was computed in the following manner.

At 14 years = 13 yrs+2/3 of 14th year = 13 2/3 years.

At 15 years = 13+2/3 of 2 years = 14 1/3 years.

At 16 years = 13+2/3 of 3 years = 15 years.

Besides, 16 years was taken to be the last age for calculation of IQ. After that, CA was taken to be constant.

LM form revision of 1960 : Binet-Simon scale was last revised in 1960 in which items of both L and M forms were included in the scale. This revision has a range of 2 years of mental age scores to 22 years and 11 months of mental age score. This form of the test measures abilities from 7 categories namely, language, memory, reasoning, social intelligence, conceptual phenomenon, numerical, reasoning and visual motor. Test items are in the form of words, objects and pictures and the responses given by the examinees are in the form of drawing, calculating, writing and speaking. Administration of the test requires one full hour. In this revision intelligence is expressed in terms of standard scores of the deviation IQ.

Wechsler Scale : This scale may be considered an improvement over Binet-Simon scale as it can measure the intelligence of adults very effectively. David Wechsler developed this scale in 1939. This scale was developed in two equivalent forms, each form consisted of ten subtests of which five tests were verbal and five were non-verbal or performance type. This scale was revised in 1955 and was renamed as Wechsler Adult Intelligence Scale (WAIS). It comprised of 11 sub tests of which six were verbal and five were non-verbal. This scale is used on persons above 16 years of age upto 64 and administration time of the scale is one hour. The detail of these 11 subtests are given below:

(a) Verbal subtests :

1. *Information* : 29 questions are given here to test the recall of knowledge concerning wide varieties of information.
2. *Comprehension* : 14 questions are given here to test understanding of knowledge concerning a particular subject or event.
3. *Arithmetic* : 14 questions are given here to test numerical ability. These questions are solved orally without using paper and pencil at all.
4. *Similarity* : 13 questions are given here to measure abstract verbal reasoning. Examinees are required here to compare two objects and find out the relationship between them.
5. *Digit span* : Memory for digits are measured here. In the first half, the examinee is asked to repeat in the same order, three to nine digits presented in the forward directions and in the second half, the digits are repeated in a backward direction.
6. *Vocabulary* : 40 words of increasing difficulty value are presented before the examinees here and they are asked to tell the meaning of these words.

(b) Non-verbal or performance subtests:

1. *Digit symbol* : Nine digits each with different digit symbols are given to the examinees here and they are asked to give the right code for each digits or symbols.
2. *Picture completion* : This subtest measures the ability of the examinees to analyse the parts from the whole. Examinees are given 21 cards containing incomplete pictures and they are asked to fill the missing part of each picture.
3. *Block design* : Its purpose is to measure the ability to analyse the complex whole. There are only 7 designs in these blocks which have red, white and red-white sides. Examinees are asked to produce a given design with the help of these blocks.
4. *Picture arrangement* : Its purpose is to measure the ability to identify the whole from the parts. Here six set of pictures are given to the examinees and they are asked to arrange them in an order which tells a meaningful story.
5. *Object assembly* : Its purpose is to measure the ability to synthesise the whole with the help of parts. Here examinees are given some puzzle pictures each representing some parts of the human body and they are asked to assemble them in the form of a complete man.

Speed and accuracy factors are also scored in Arithmetic, digit symbol, block design, picture arrangement and object assembly. Raw scores of each subject are converted into normalized standard scores with a mean of 10 and SD of 3. This makes the scores of each sub tests comparable. Separate IQ for verbal and non-verbal subtest forms is calculated by adding up the respective subtests of the two forms and if we add up scores on all the 11 subtests, we obtain total scale score. These standard scores are expressed in the form of deviation IQ with a mean of 100 and SD of 15.

Wechsler developed another scale known as Wechsler intelligence Scale for Children in 1949 to test the intelligence of children from 5 to 15 years of age. It also takes one hour to administer, though there are 12 subtests in this scale. Maze test is the only test which is extra in WISC. Maze subtest has eight mazes to be traced by the examinee with a pencil. These mazes are given in increasing order of difficulty.

The scoring system of both the tests WAIS and WISC are the same. Here also the total scores are converted into deviation IQ with a mean of 100 and SD of 15.

Advantages of Wechsler Scales

(i) Though Binet's scale and Wechsler's scale both are individual scales, yet the later can be

administered on small groups of children and adults.

(ii) Wechsler's scale is easier to administer than Binet's Scale and its scoring is also less complex than the former.

(iii) Wechsler has prepared separate scales for children and adults Binet's scale does not possess this advantage.

Other differences of Wechsler Scales and Stanford Binet Scale

(i) In Wechsler scale, items are not grouped in terms of mental age as is the case of Stanford-Binet scale. Points are given here for all correct responses. Thus, WAIS or WISC is a point scale.

(ii) In Stanford-Binet scale items are interpreted in terms of different age levels of the examinees but in WAIS or WISC similar types of items are grouped together to form subtests.

(iii) WAIS has separate age norms for adults but in SB Scale all the individuals above 18 are treated in a similar manner as far as computation of IQ is concerned. Thus, people of all age levels are treated as 18 years of age after 18.

(iv) In SB tests items are varied, unrelated and upgraded but in WAIS and WISC tests, items are graded according to various range of ages.

(v) SB scale is internally standardized and rigid but WAIS is externally standardized and flexible.

(vi) SB scale refers to qualitative evaluation while WAIS refers to quantitative evaluation.

(vii) Slight chance of statistical treatment is possible in SB scale but WAIS is fully subject to all statistical analysis.

(c) Post Binet period :

This period is particularly known for testing intelligence in groups and thus group test of intelligence became popular during this periods.

A group test is one that can be given to a number of subjects at a time by a single examiner. This type of test came into being during first World War for the purpose of classifying soldiers for various jobs in accordance with their mental abilities. Army Alpha and Army Beta, two tests were developed during this period. Army Alpha is a verbal group test of intelligence meant for literate people. Army beta is a non-verbal group test of intelligence meant for illiterate persons.

We will discuss here some more group test of intelligence :

1. **Catell's Culture Fair Test :** This test was developed by RB Catell and was published by IPAT (Institute for Personality and Ability Testing) in 1961. The test has three scales and can be administered on children and adults both.

   Scale I meant for 4-8 years

   Scale II meant for 8-15 years

   Scale III meant for 15 years and above

   This test measures the general intelligence factor and takes 30-60 minutes to administer. The test has been prepared in such a manner that previously learnt skill or knowledge does not help the examinee to score more on this test. That is why, it is said to be independent of school achievement, social advantages and environmental influences.

2. **Large Thorndike's Intelligence Test :** This test is meant for primary and secondary school children graded into five different levels. The purpose of the test is to measure verbal comprehension, numerical skill and reasoning abilities. Test has verbal as well as non-verbal items. Only non-verbals items are, however, included at the lower levels. The administration of the test takes 30 minutes in all.

3. **Raven Progressive Matrices Test :** This test was developed in England. It consists of geometric figures and designs. The subjects find out the relationship between figures and select appropriate parts for completion of each pattern of relations.

Classification of Intelligence Test

(A) Classification from the point of view of administration

1. **Individual intelligence test :** An individual intelligence test is one which is administered to only one person at a time. Binet-Simon is an example.

2. **Group intelligence test :** A group intelligence test is one which can be administered to more than one persons at a time. Army Alpha and Army Beta are two examples of such tests.

Some general characteristics of group intelligence tests are as follows :

(i) They have been developed on the assumption that intelligence is a general capacity and can be measured by sampling a variety of mental activities.

(ii) In group tests the similar types of items are pooled together in different subtests.

(iii) Every group test is standardized for a special range of ages or school grades.

(iv) Construction of individual test is also very difficult and costly as compared to group tests.

Their scoring and standardization is also time consuming process.

(v) It is very difficult to establish rapport between the examiner and the examinees and hence examinees can not be motivated properly in group tests of intelligence. These two limitations are not seen in individual tests.

(vi) Group tests are superior to individual tests in the sense that norms established here are more dependable than that of individual tests. It is because these norms are calculated on the basis of a very large sample.

(vii) Individual test provides qualitative performance of the individual while group tests are mostly point scale and express the performance in quantities.

(B) Classification from the point of view of nature of items of the test

1. **Verbal test :** Verbal test of intelligence is one in which instructions and items are produced before the examinees through the written language. So, examinees must be literate to take these tests. Mohsin's General intelligence Test, Joshi's General Mental Ability test and Jalota's Group General Mental Ability Test are some examples of verbal tests of intelligence of Indian origin.

2. **Non-verbal test :** A non-verbal test is one which requires the use of language only to impart instructions. The examinees are asked to manipulate the test materials in their own way. Since language is not needed to respond to items here, it can be administered to illiterate persons as well. They are also culturally free and hence they can be applied to any situation representing any culture. Test items are usually of figured relation type. Army Beta is a good example of non-language test.

3. **Performance test :** A performance test is one in which a subject has to perform some thing or to manipulate some concrete materials without much use of the language ability. Non-verbal and performance tests are useful for the following groups of people:

   (a) *Deaf and Dumb :* Those children who cannot hear or speak can be tested with the help of performance test.

   (b) *Illiterates :* Verbal test of intelligence is useless for those who cannot read or write. Performance test is useful for them.

   (c) *Shy children :* Many withdrawn children are hesitant to express before others. Performance and non-verbal test of intelligence will suit them very much.

   (d) *Educationally deficient children :* Verbal test of intelligence generally measure learning along with intelligence. If children are educationally poor, they will perform poorly on intelligence test too and thus they will be wrongly declared as children of below average intelligence. Such a problem can be overcome by using performance test or non-verbal intelligence test.

   (e) *Useful for children of other culture :* A particular culture dominates in every verbal intelligence test and thus the test can not be adopted by other cultures. Due to free from culture, performance test is suitable for these foreign students.

Some performance tests of intelligence are given below :

(a) **Pintner Paterson Scale :** This is the first systematic performance test. This scale was standardized in 1917. It consists of 15 subtests.

(b) **Goodenough Drawing Test :** This scale was developed by Florence Goodenough in 1926. Here child is asked to draw the picture of a man as best as possible without any time limit. This is especially useful for those children who are suspected to be mentally retarted.

Weaknesses of performance test :

- Here the subject can score high due to practice effect and chance success is more frequent than verbal tests. Because of this reason, reliability coefficient is very low.
- They fail to distinguish between gifted and average children due to limited scope of these tests.
- These scales fail to test fine mental abilities such as, ability to make abstraction or concept formation or evaluation abilities of mind.

Interpretation of Intelligence Test Scores : Intelligence test scores can be interpreted in the following three ways:

1. **Mental age :** This concept was first introduced by **Afred Binet** of France in 1908. It refers to a score that is determined by comparing a child's score with the scores obtained by younger or older children in the norming group. Here a child's score is compared with the average score of his own age. For example, if a 9-year-old child scores 60 on an intelligence test and suppose mental age norms for that scale are as follows:

   Mental age of 8 years = 60
   Mental age of 9 years = 70
   Mental age of 10 years = 80

Then, in that case, mental age of the child will be considered as 8 years instead of 9 though his chronological age is 9 years.

Similarly, if another child of 8 years obtains a score of 80, then his mental age will be 10 years, though his chronological age is 8 years only.

Thus, we can say that the mean performance of each age level becomes the mental age for that age level.

2. **Intelligent Quotient (IQ) :** IQ is also based on the concept of mental age. It is the ratio of mental age to the chronological age multiplied by 100.

$$IQ = \frac{MA}{CA} \times 100.$$

Suppose, the mental age of a 10-year-old child is 12 years on the basis of his scores on an intelligence test, his IQ will be

$$\frac{12}{10} \times 100 = 120.$$

Similarly, if mental age of a person is nine years two months and his age is 12 years 6 months, then his IQ will be

$$\frac{110}{150} \times 100 = 73.3.$$

General classification of persons in terms of IQ

IQ	Classification
140 and above	Genius
130-140	Very superior
120-130	Superior
110-120	Bright
90-110	Average
80-90	Dull
70-80	Borderline
Below 70	Mentally retarded.

Shortcomings of IQ: Some of the main short comings of IQ are as follows:

(i) It is a well-known fact that after 18 years, the mental age of a person tends to stabilize. Thus, if IQ is calculated after this age, the result will be misleading, *i.e.*, a person will be less intelligent if he grows in age.

(ii) Variability of IQ scores from one test to another is not the same. As a result IQ scores for different tests would not be directly comparable.

(iii) It has also been found that variability in IQ scores for the different age levels on the same test is not the same. In that case IQ scores would be a misleading index because it would indicate that a person's IQ may increase or decrease as he grows in age. An example will illustrate this point.

Age	IQ	SD
9 years old child	120	12
7 years old child	120	9

Here IQ of 120 of both the children is not the same due to difference in SD.

3. **Deviation IQ :** Now-a-days IQ ratio is converted into a normalized standard score with a fixed mean of 100 and SD of 15. This is known as DIQ. This fixed mean and SD remain constant through all the age levels. It means that if a child's score is 1 SD above the mean his DIQ will be 100 + 15 = 115. Similarly, if his score is 1 SD below the mean his DIQ will be 100 – 15 = 85 and so on. Thus, with the help of these **DIQ** scores inter age comparison is also possible.

Uses of Intelligence Test

Intelligence tests can be applied in the following situations.

1. **Measurement of general learning abilities:** Intelligence and achievement in schools are highly correlated. If a person is high on an intelligence test, he is expected to score high on school achievements also. Conversely if a person scores high on an intelligence test and still his school achievement is very poor, we can find out other reasons for his educational backwardness.
2. **Assessment of individual differences and categorization :** With the help of intelligence tests we can categories a particular class into several convenient groups and plan our instructional strategies accordingly. Thus, intelligence testing is very useful for educational guidance.
3. **Exact definition of mental retardation is possible :** It is said that those who are below 70 in IQ are retarded but to what extent they are mentally retarded can further be studied with the help of higher screening. We may define the three groups of mentally retarted in the following ways.

Category	IQ level
Morons	45-69
Imbeciles	25-45
Idiots	Below 25

4. **Identification of gifted children :** Gifted children are the treasure of the society. They must be identified in the earlier stages of their

lives so that they can be fully guided and helped for their better advancement which is directly related to the advancement of the society as well. Intelligence testing will help the concerned organisations to chalk out plans in the desired manner.

5. **Vocational guidance :** Some children are very forward in verbal abilities and some are superior in non-verbal abilities. This identification is possible only with the help of intelligence tests. Since academic subjects need verbal intelligence and technical subjects need non-verbal or performing abilities, hence children may be guided accordingly.
6. **Screening :** In today's age of competition and rush, screening has become a necessity. Every school has limited seats of admission and it has to select only those students who can raise the academic level of the school high and get name for it. Same is the case with appointments in jobs. For all these purposes, intelligence testing is a must.
7. **Study of mental growth :** Mental abilities develop in a sequential order onward. We can use intelligence tests for studying the trends of mental development of individuals. Intelligence tests have made it clear that mental development of children is a steady consistent process from year-to-year till the age of 25. Intelligence tests show that mind does not develop rapidly in the period of adolescence like the physical and emotional development, but in childhood, it develops rapidly.

Limitations of Intelligence Tests

1. Generally intelligence test shows what a person can do at a certain point of time. These abilities are tested on the basis of certain items included in the test. In order to make the results dependable, a proper size of the sample must be selected for standardization of the test.
2. Some people may be fatigued earlier than others when take a test. This extent of fatigue may reduce their scores and hence intelligence testing will not be accurate. So scores should be taken with caution.
3. No intelligence test is fully free from cultural influences. So, home or school background may affect the intelligence test scores of subjects.
4. Administration of the test also affects the scores of subjects. If proper rapport is there between the examiner and the examinee. IQ scores may be high. On the other hand, if children are frightened with the testing situation as is case of slow learners they will perform poorly on the test.
5. Taking intelligence scores in absolute form is misleading. Intelligence tests do not reveal all the mental abilities in most of the cases. So, intelligence test must be supplemented with clinical setting and case history method to collect detailed information about a subject as is done in clinics by physician who does not entirely believe in physical investigations. He rather takes the help of clinical diagnosis before giving remedial treatment to the patients.

THOUGHT AND LANGUAGE

In this section we examines the relationship between language and thought: that language determines thought, that thought determines language, and that thought and language have different origins. Let us examine these three viewpoints in some detail.

Language as Determinant of Thought

In Hindi and other Indian languages we use a number of different words for various kinship relationships. We have different terms for mother's brother, father's elder brother, father's younger brother, mother's sister's husband, father's sister's husband and so on. An English person uses just one word *uncle* to describe all these kinship relationships. In the English language there are dozens of words for colours whereas some tribal languages have only two to four colour terms. Do such differences matter for how we think? Does an Indian child find it easier to think about and differentiate between various kinship relationships compared to her English-speaking counterpart? Does our thinking process depend on how we describe it in our language?

Benjamin Lee Whorf was of the view that language determines the contents of thought. This view is known as **linguistic relativity hypothesis**. In its strong version, this hypothesis holds what and how individuals can possibly think is determined by the language and linguistic categories they use **(linguistic determinism).** Experimental evidence, however, maintains that it is possible to have the same level or quality of thoughts in all languages depending upon the availability of linguistic categories and structures. Some thoughts may be easier in one language compared to another.

Thought as Determinant of Language

The noted Swiss psychologist, Jean Piaget believed that thought not only determines language, but also precedes it. Piaget argued that children form an internal representation of the world through thinking. For example, when children see something and later copy it (a process called imitation), thinking does take place, which does not involve language. A child's observation of other's behaviour and imitation of the same behaviour, no doubt involves thinking but not language. Language is just one of the vehicles of thinking. As actions become internalised, language may affect children's range of symbolic thinking but is not necessary for the origins of thought. Piaget believed that though language can be taught to children, understanding of the words require knowledge of the underlying concepts (*i.e.* thinking). Thus, thought is basic, and necessary if language is to be understood.

Different Origins of Language and Thought

The Russian psychologist, Lev Vyogotsky, argued that thoughts and language develop in a child separately until about two years of age, when they merge. Before two years thought is preverbal and is experienced more in action (Piaget's sensory motor stage). The child's utterances are more automotic reflexes—crying when uncomfortable—than thought-based. Around two years of age, the child expresses thought verbally and her/his speech reflects rationality. Now children are able to manipulate thoughts using soundless speech. He believed that during this period the development of language and thinking become interdependent; the development of conceptual thinking depends upon the quality of inner speech and vice versa. Thought is used without language when the vehicle of thinking is non-verbal such as visual or movement-related. Language is used without thought when expressing feelings or exchanging pleasantries, for example "Good morning! How are you?" "Very well, I am fine". When the two functions overlap, they can be used together to produce verbal thought and rational speech.

Development of Language

Language is a complex system and unique to human beings. Psychologists have tried to teach sign language, use of symbols to chimpanzees, dolphins, parrots, etc. But it is observed that, human language is more complex, creative, and spontaneous than the system of communication other animals can learn. There is also a great deal of **regularity** with which children all over the world seem to be learning the language or languages to which they are exposed. When we compare individual children, we find that they differ a great deal in the rate of their language development as well as in how they go about it. But when we take a general view of children's acquisition of language all over the world we find some *predictable pattern* in which children proceed from almost no use of language to the point of becoming competent language users. Language develops through some of the stages discussed below.

Newborn babies and young infants make a variety of sounds, which gradually get modified to resemble words. The first sound produced by babies is crying. Initial crying is undifferentiated and similar across various situations. Gradually, the pattern of crying varies in its pitch and intensity to signify different states such as hunger, pain, and sleepiness, etc. These differentiated crying sounds gradually become more meaningful *cooing sounds* (like 'aaa', 'uuu', etc). usually to express happiness.

At around six months of age children enter the *babbling* stage. Babbling involves prolonged repetition of a variety of consonants and vowel sounds (for example, da—, aa—, ba—). By about nine months of age these sounds get elaborated to strings of some sound combinations, such as 'dadadadadada' into repetitive patterns called *echolalia.* While the early babblings are random or accidental in nature, the later babblings seem to be imitative of adult voices. Children show some understanding of a few words by the time they are six months old. Around the first birthday (the exact age varies from child-to-child) most children enter the *one-word-stage.* Their first word usually contains one syllable—*ma or da*, for instance. Gradually they move to one or more words which are combined to form whole sentences or phrases. So they are called *holophrases*. When they are 18 to 20 months of age, children enter a *two-word stage* and begin to use two words together. The two-word stage exemplifies *telegraphic speech.* Like telegrams (got admission, send money) it contains mostly nouns and verbs. Close to their third birthday, *i.e.* beyond two-and-a-half years, children's language development gets focused on rules of the language they hear.

How is language acquired? You must be wondering: "How do we learn to speak?" As with many other topics in psychology, the questions of whether a behaviour develops as a result of inherited characteristics (nature) or from the effects of learning (nurture) has been raised with regard to language. Most psychologists accept that both nature and nurture are important in language acquisition.

Behaviourist B.F. Skinner believed we learn language the same way as animals learn to pick keys or press bars. Language development, for the behaviourists follow the learning principles, such as association (the sight of bottle with the word 'bottle'), imitation (adults use of word "bottle"), and reinforcement (smiles and hugs when the child says something right). There is also evidence that children produce sounds that are appropriate to a language of the parent or care-giver and are reinforced for having done so. The principle of shaping leads to successive approximation of the desired responses so that the child eventually speaks as well as the adult. Regional differences in pronunciation and phrasing illustrate how different patterns are reinforced in different areas.

Linguist Noam Chomsky put forth the innate proposition of development of language. For him the *rate at which children acquire words and grammar* without being taught can not be explained only by learning principles. Children also *create all sorts of sentences* they have never heard and, therefore, could not be imitating. Children throughout the world seem to have a *critical period*—a period when learning must occur if it is to occur successfully—for learning language. Children across the world also go through the same stages of language development. Chomsky believes language development is just like physical maturation given adequate care, it "just happens to the child". Children are born with "universal grammar". They readily learn the grammar of whatever language they hear.

Skinner's emphasis on learning explains why infants acquire the language they hear and how they add new words to their vocabularies. Chomsky's emphasis on our built-in readiness to learn grammar helps explain why children acquire language so readily without direct teaching.

GENDER AS A SOCIAL CONSTRUCT; GENDER ROLES, GENDER-BIAS AND EDUCATIONAL PRACTICE

Gender refers to the social distinctions between boys and girls and men and women that are socially constructed rather than biologically determined. These distinctions are reflected in the roles that boys and girls play in society and the status that they occupy within it. Gender roles tend to be dynamic. They vary from one culture and time period to another and are characterized by unequal power relationships.

Ending gender bias and discrimination is crucial to the empowerment of women and girls and to the achievement of gender equality in education. Applying a gender perspective helps to make differences in power relations visible. It also helps us to see more clearly the needs and rights of girls and boys in particular geographical, cultural and economic contexts.

The ultimate goal is to eliminate gender biases and discriminatory practices and policies, both overt and covert. This is at the heart of gender analysis. Gender analysis should therefore be a prerequisite for identifying and understanding problems as they relate to education, and especially to the continued exclusion of girls from quality schooling. Gender analysis guides the process of finding viable and sustainable solutions to the problems of access, quality and learning achievement.

Gender analysis of what learners bring to education (including early childhood socialization, feeding and health access, cultural heritage and language), the content of education, teaching and learning processes, learning environments and learning outcomes help to highlight bad (and good) educational practices and policies. This analysis, in turn, should form the basis for educational interventions that are sensitive to both gender and human rights.

Gender Bias in Teaching

A common response from teachers when asked about gender inequity in classrooms is that they treat all their students the same. There are two problems with this statement. First, students are diverse and have different learning issues, thus treating all students in the same way means that some students will have a better learning experience than their peers. Second, teachers may be ignoring their unconscious gender biases towards their students, their schools and themselves. If ignored, these gender biases, which may have developed from cultural norms, may lead to bias in the classroom.

Gender bias occurs when people make assumptions regarding behaviours, abilities or preferences of others based upon their gender. Because there are strong gender role stereotypes for masculinity and femininity, students who do not match them can encounter problems with teachers and with their peers. For example, the expectation is that boys naturally exhibit boisterous, unruly behaviour, are academically able, rational, and socially uncommunicative, whereas girls are quiet, polite, and studious. Girls are also expected to possess better social skills than boys and to excel at reading and the language arts. So girls who present discipline problems for teachers, or quiet, studious boys, may encounter a lack of understanding from peers and teachers. Within the classroom, these biases unfold in students' practices and teachers' acceptance of certain behaviours from one student or another based upon the students' gender. Also, bias due to a person's gender is not mutually exclusive of other social categories such as race, ethnicity, class, religion, and language. For example, some teachers may perceive African American or other Black girls as loud and uncontrollable because the girls do not exhibit the feminine behaviours associated with White women, such as quiet, self-effacing and malleable.

Gender bias can occur within subject areas and school activities. For example, in subjects such as mathematics and the sciences, there are different participation patterns for girls and boys. Gender bias promulgates a myth that boys are naturally better at mathematics and science than girls. The implications are that if girls succeed in these subjects it is due to their hard work, not their intelligence, whereas boys' success is credited to their natural talent. There are some signs that gender bias in schools may be decreasing in some areas. The percentage of girls participating in science has increased and achieved parity with boys in biology, chemistry and algebra. However, subjects that are prerequisites for college majors such as engineering or physics remain dominated by men. Only 25% of high school students enrolled in physics are female. Moreover, there has been little increase in the percentage of women in engineering programs.

Males are also more likely than females to be in remedial programs and students' race also impacts these patterns. For example, African American males are more likely than White or female peers to enroll in remedial reading and mathematics courses. And non-White students have a higher representation in vocational and noncollege preparatory courses than their White peers. Teachers are critical components in challenging gender bias in schooling, but they also can be major contributors to it as well, through their pedagogical practices, curriculum choices, and assessment strategies.

Gender Bias in Teachers

Teachers' unconscious gender biases can produce stereo-typic expectations for students' success and participation in the classroom. Teachers view male students' domination of the classroom and their time as typical masculine behaviour. However, these biases have consequences for the students and the classroom climate. More than two decades ago, researchers identified and named groups of students who dominated the teacher's time and the classroom resources as ''target students'' (Tobin & Gallagher, 1987). Target students were typically white and male. They answered most of the teacher's questions and also asked most of the questions. This behaviour pattern was particularly insidious in mathematics and science classrooms because teachers did not expect girls to have competent knowledge in these subject areas. Classroom observations documented that target students typically called out answers to the teacher's questions, thus denying other students the opportunity to engage in dialogue with the teacher or get to grips with the subject matter. Furthermore, because boys are perceived as having natural talent in science, teachers asked boys harder and more complicated questions than girls. If girls attempted to answer more difficult questions than boys and faltered, teachers often repeated the question and asked that another student. typically a boy, provide the answer. However, if a boy failed to answer correctly, teachers reframed the question or broke it into a series of simpler questions that could help the student find the answer. Teachers' unconscious stereotyped gender bias that boys are smarter than girls, especially in mathematics and the sciences, meant they were willing to work with boys to reach the answer because they perceived boys were capable of achieving that goal but girls were not. Conversely, teachers of subjects perceived as feminine will spend more time engaged with girls.

Teachers' gendered perceptions of students' ability is also reflected in the type of praise and expectations they have of their students. Teachers often give girls less meaningful and less critical praise than boys. Boys' work is described as unique or brilliant, while girls' work is often undervalued, critically ignored and praised for its appearance. This aspect of teachers' behaviour is particularly detrimental to girls because it means they do not receive feedback on their work that could help them develop deeper understandings of concepts (Liu, 2006).

Teachers also use target students to maintain the tempo and pace of classroom instruction. For example, in a lecture or whole class discussion when a teacher is posing questions to the class, he or she may encourage target students to call out answers in order to keep the lesson moving, rather than wait for the other students to process the question and provide an answer. This short ''wait time'' may be detrimental to learning. More than three decades ago, researchers found that if teachers waited three to five seconds before accepting a student's answer, more students became engaged in the classroom and also improved their understanding of the content. Moreover, the longer wait time meant that teachers began to ask more cognitively challenging questions. However, the existence of target students in classes who often call out answers without direction from teachers meant that fewer students, especially girls, engaged in the lessons. In the absence of proactive teacher intervention, these patterns in which males dominate classroom interactions also occur in mixed-gender, small groups.

Target students dominate classroom interactions and exchanges at all education levels. In the early 2000s, researchers identified these same patterns of engagement in a professional development program for science teachers. When alerted to the invasive behaviours of the male teachers in the cohort, faculty began using overt breaching strategies to stop the target students calling out answers, dominating the human and materials resources of the classroom, and showing disrespect to their peers (Martin Milne & Scantlebury, 2006).

Teachers' gender bias towards students can also extend to their response to students who challenge their authority. Such risk-taking behaviour in boys is expected and at times praised, but assertiveness in girls is viewed negatively and labelled unfeminine. Similarly, boys who do not exhibit stereotypic masculine behaviours may be ridiculed (Renold, 2006).

Teachers use gender expectations as a means of maintaining classroom control. For example, teachers will seat undisciplined boys next to girls as a classroom management strategy. Further, teachers use the gendered expectation that girls' nurturing characteristics will lead them to place others' needs before their own. In other words, teachers often ask girls to assume mothering roles towards students who have fallen behind with learning because of inattentiveness, absenteeism through truancy, or in-school disciplinary procedures, and often those students are male.

Effects of Gender Bias

Gender bias can impact students' attitudes towards learning and their engagement with the subject. If affected by gender bias, girls will tend to believe that any success they have is due to hard work rather than any innate talent or intelligence. Boys may be encouraged to believe that success in science and mathematics should come easily to them because of their gender. Some males report dropping out of college science and mathematics programs because they no longer perceive these subjects as easy. Overall, teachers have lower expectations for girls' academic success compared to boys, and their attitudes are shown through the type and quality of the student-teacher interaction. The type and quality of critique teachers give their students can also have an impact. Teachers' comments on girls' work focuses on its appearance but with boys' work teachers focus on the content. Girls often do not receive substantive comments or criticism from teachers from which they could improve their ability to learn. During the many hours spent in classrooms, girls receive less time and attention from teachers than their male peers. Teachers usually ask girls easier questions than they ask boys. Typically, girls receive fewer opportunities to engage in classroom discourse, use equipment and assert their knowledge in classrooms.

Reducing Gender Bias

Gender bias in education is a series of microinequities whose impact is cumulative and often ignored. Girls are rewarded and praised for compliant behaviour. Teachers do not challenge girls with questions and rarely offer criticisms of their works. Teachers can reduce and challenge gender bias through an examination of their pedagogical practices and by posing simple questions about their practices. For example, which students do they frequently interact with? Are target students evident in their classroom? If so, how does the teacher deal with those students? What questioning techniques does the teacher use to engage students? Does the teacher ask complicated questions to girls as well as boys? Does the teacher use a variety of pedagogical and assessment practices? Which students are engaged with the curriculum?

Another way of reducing gender bias would be for teachers to videotape their classes and review their interactions with the students. Or they could invite a colleague to watch their teaching and record which students are being asked questions and what type of questions. However, teachers must also prepare for the consequences of changing their practices. Girls are conditioned to receiving less of the teacher's attention, and they do not usually cause discipline problems if they are not receiving their fair share, but boys can react negatively to losing the teacher's attention, causing disruption to lessons and becoming discipline problems. Moreover, research has also shown that boys avoid written work and often have poor communication skills when asked to work in singlesex groups.

However, the gains in reducing gender bias in education may disappear with the requirements of high-stakes testing required by No Child Left Behind (NCLB). NCLB requires that states report academic achievement data in most social categories, except gender (Kahle, 2004). This may result in less attention being placed on gender bias and less data that might reveal it. Continued monitoring of gender bias is necessary to minimize its impact on students' opportunities for learning and achievement.

INDIVIDUAL DIFFERENCES AMONG LEARNERS

It is not unusual to find a wide range of differences among students in a class or a group. These differences are invariably identified in terms of student's characteristics such as physical (appearance, height, size, sex, colour, etc.), demographic (age, caste, socio-economic status, etc.) and cognitive behaviour (thinking, remembering, problem solving, creating idea, etc.). The differences that exist among students due to physical, demographic, affective behaviour and cognitive behaviour characteristics are referred to as individual differences.

Differences due to physical and demographic characteristics are conspicuous and easy to identify. However, the differences that exist in the way they solve problem in Mathematics or in their ability to interpret and explain ideas are not easily visible but are identified through their performance. Let us examine, for instance, the answers given by Bitto and

Neha, two students of the same class to the following proverb.

Interpret the saying, "Pen is mighter than the sword".

Bitto's Interpretation

It means that writing had always been able to influence mankind more than any amount of sheer physical strength; writing undoubtedly makes a more lasting impact in the minds of the people than any form of physical demonstration. In the case of the latter the impact might be forceful though less lasting. Great thinkers, writers and philosophers have from time immemovial been able to hold sway over the minds of the people by means of their profound knowledge through their writings. For example, Socrates won the wrath of a powerful state, because of his great ability to hold spellbound the young through his discourses. Similarly, the writing of Voltaire and Rousseau inspired the French to rise up in revolt.

Neha's Interpretation

It is a common proverb which simply means that through writing it is possible to win more victories than by using physical force and weapons. When any good book is read it is possible to retain in our memory the message it contains. On the other hand, success achieved through physical might is not for mankind.

The above illustration reflects the differences between Bitto and Neha in their interpretation of the proverb. While Bitto delves deep in her interpretation, Neha states only the meaning.

According to Skinner, individual differences in learner behaviours are the result of the organism's genetic endowment and reinforcement. Thus, Skinner believed that defective genetic endowment and/or defective reinforcement contingencies in an individual's experience result in a failure to acquire a variety of learned behaviours.

The process of an individual's mental activities such as remembering, analysing, interpreting, reasoning, problem solving and thinking are cognitive domain behaviours and are essential for learning and achievement. How we think, what and how we remember, how we solve problem and how we create ideas are cognitive domain behaviours and individuals differ by these behaviours. Such differences are often identified by psychologists in terms of intelligence, aptitude, creating and academic achievement.

Individual differences are crucial for teachers who are responsible for guiding all forms of learning. In fact, many educators would suggest that the primary role of teachers is to provide education to meet the individual differences and to develop student cognitive process.

Do Individuals Differ in Intelligence?

Well, they do differ. But how? Differences are due to the differences in the level of general intellectual ability and the underlying cognitive process among individuals.

How do we identify differences in intelligence?

Using suitable intelligence tests we can measure and identify the difference. An intelligence test may contain sub-tests (sub-sections) and each sub-test represents a different set of ability. The scores obtained in all sub-tests are added up to obtain a single score to represent the general ability of the student. Thus, the single score obtained for each individual in a test is expressed in terms of **intelligence quotient** (IQ). IQ is a measure of intelligence and is defined as the ratio of mental age (average age of children who give correct responses/ answers in an intelligence test) to the chronological age (actual age) multiplied by 100 (to avoid fraction). Thus mental age is:

$$IQ = \frac{\text{Mental age}}{\text{Chronological age}} \times 100$$

IQ scores help us estimate individual differences by categorising individuals on the basis of their IQs. These differences have important consequences for learning and performance. Let us examine the different categories of students based on their intelligence level.

Gifted : Those students who possess IQs of 130 or above are called gifted students. They are superior in intelligence and have high ability to reason. As compared to other children, they can perform academic activities grasping concepts, memorising, perceiving, seeing relationships, generalising, dealing with abstract ideas, critical thinking and solving problems more effectively and quickly. They have a broad attention span that permits concentration and the ability for a high level of academic performance. They take initiative in intellectual work and follow complex directions. Such individuals are small in number as compared to normal or average children. Normal groups have those children whose IQs range from 90 to 110 and they are able to profit from regular school programmes with varying degrees of effort.

Disabled : There are children with **disability** due to low level to intellectual functioning or specific learning deficits. Children with low level or below-average intellectual functioning are called mentally retarded. The children with inadequate level of intelligence are impaired in their ability to learn and to adapt to the demands of society. Mentally retarded children are of different categories. They can be:

- **Border line** (IQ ranges 90-70) and **educable mentally retarded** (IQ ranges 70-50) children can perform academic activities but are slow in their learning. Special instructional strategies can help them to profit from learning activities. They can take care of themselves and live independently as adults.
- **Trainable mentally retarded** (IQ ranges 50-35) are capable of learning only certain rudimentary literacy materials and simple occupational skills. They possess some ability to take care of their personal needs and can be trained in daily living skills. Such children require special classes or schools to study in.
- **Severely retarded** (IQ below 35) have quite limited adaptive behaviour and are never found in school. They are dependent on their families for their personal needs.

Children with specific learning defects are called learning disabled group. They are normal to above-average on intelligence but have difficulties in one or more psychological processes involved in understanding or in using language or numbers (written or spoken). The difficulties manifest in their ability to listen, think, speak, read, write, spell or do mathematical calculations. These difficulties are identified as **aphasia** (difficulty in grasping spoken language), **dylesia** (difficulty in reading), **hyperlexia** (little or no comprehension), **dyscalculia** (difficulty in doing arithmetic) and **dysgraphia** (difficulty in writing). Some are hyperactive in the sense that they are excessively active inattentive and behave impulsively. They follow instructions poorly and do not often complete the assigned tasks.

Instructional Strategies for Handling Individual Differences

- Organise instruction for the development of cognitive process.
- Use existing cognitive level as base.
- Strengthen memory.
- Formulate level specific instructional strategy.
- Use individual meeting.
- Provide instructions to overcome learning disability.

Do Individuals Differ in Aptitude?

Yes, they do differ. An individual may have a mechanical aptitude, another may have an aptitude for mathematics or yet another may have an aptitude for language, music or athletics. Such differences are due to the differences in the combination of abilities related to the cognitive processes, and the sensory and psychomotor components. For instance, when we talk of mechanical aptitude, we may deal with ability for spatial relations, ability to acquire information on mechanical matters and ability to comprehend mechanical relations, besides sensory and psychomotor abilities. Similarly, when we discuss aptitude in music, we may identify ability for musical memory, pitch discrimination, loudness discrimination, time discrimination and judgement of rhythm. Likewise, abilities required for science or mathematics are different and each requires a separate set of abilities.

The differences in aptitude can be identified using aptitude tests. Aptitude tests for areas such as mechanical skills, mathematics, science, language, music and graphic art can be used to identify the aptitude of students in each area of performance. You might have heard of the use of aptitude tests in medicine, engineering, business management, law or teacher training for selection of students for studies in the respective fields. The aptitude test, in fact, provides a measure of the candidates promise or teachability in a field of study, say, medicine. In other words, the test would tell whether the candidate possesses the required aptitude or readiness to profit from studies in the concerned field of study.

Instructional Strategy for Handling Individual Differences

The suggested approach for handling individual differences is **adaptive instructional system**. In this approach at least two alternative instructional treatments are needed to ensure academic success. Which is the most appropriate instructional treatment for the student depends upon his or her existing level of aptitude (learning readiness). Students with high aptitude may choose unstructured instructional strategy. With minimum guidance from teacher, they may be encouraged to learn through the discovery oriented approach. You may use the inductive process but instructional treatment is essentially learner-centered.

In contrast, highly structured instructional treatment for low aptitude learners is designed in small units through sequential steps and feedback. Frequent summary and review with simplified illustration, analogy and precise explanation of concepts and principles to be learned will facilitate progressive learning. Periodic achievement and aptitude assessments and comparison of these scores with the aptitude scores obtained at the start of instruction would tell the degree to which each learner in the specific treatment group has achieved.

However, for those who are unable to profit from either of the alternative treatments presented above, **compensatory aptitude training** is suggested. This consists of directed reading skill, study habits, self-learning skills, note taking and related activities. The main aim of compensatory aptitude training is to develop readiness for entry into structured treatment. Periodic monitoring should be formulated to identify the students who reach the required level for entry into alternative treatment.

Do Learners Differ in their Academic Achievements?

They do differ, but how? We have seen that those who possess appropriate pre-requisite knowledge learn more effectively than those who lack such knowledge. Differences in pre-requisite knowledge possessed by students create differences in the attainment of knowledge. Further, knowledge is attained progressively. Progressive differences in knowledge attainment leads to cumulative differences in knowledge attainment and this form of differences is often called **Mathew Effect.** It means that academically rich get richer and those who are poor continue to be poor. Thus, differences in pre-requisites and cumulative knowledge lead to differences in the knowledge possessed by the students likewise, they also differ in their capabilities to manipulate the knowledge in a given situation and the differences are identified in terms of the abilities to apply, analyse, synthesise and evaluate knowledge. In fact, ability is an essential condition for learning and the abilities related to intelligence, aptitude and creativity are important for academic achievement. We have seen the instructional strategies for meeting the differences in intelligence, aptitude and creativity through classroom situations. It means that differences in intelligence, aptitude and creativity do create differences in academic achievement.

The differences in academic achievement can be identified using an achievement test in the concerned subject. However, if the achievement test contains only knowledge level items (questions), it tells only knowledge level differences. On the other hand, if it contains items (questions) on knowledge and capabilities—comprehension, application, analysis, synthesis and evaluation—the various levels of differences can be identified. Besides, the total marks, each level-wise total is needed to identify the strengths and weaknesses of every student as well as the differences among students. As a teacher, if you know the strengths and weaknesses of your students in a subject, you may be able to adopt appropriate instructional strategies to suit their strenghts and weaknesses in that subject.

Apart from these achievement differences are quite often identified in terms of categories of achievers by classifying students as high, average and low achievers. Though there is no strict cut-off points, these categories can be created using marks. High achievers are those who possess higher level of knowledge and capabilities (say, with marks 66% and above) than the rest and those who possess average level of knowledge and capabilities (say. with marks 36% to 65%) are called average achievers. On the other extreme, you may find learners with low level knowledge and capabilities (with 35% and below marks). They are called low achievers. If you are interested in identifying the high, average and low achievers in a subject, say Science or language, the categories are created using the marks obtained in the concerned subject. However, categories can also be created based on the overall achievement in a class.

As a teacher, you may be curious to know the strategies for meeting the achievement differences in your classroom or the challenges posed by the strengths and weaknesses of the students in teaching-learning situations. Let us discuss important instructional strategies.

What are Instructional Strategies?

Let us discuss the major strategies to cope up with the differences in academic achievement.

- Provide appropriate pre-requisites to organise and learn new information.
- Use visual aids.
- Use analogy, example and illustration.
- Ensure learner's active involvement in learning.
- Periodic assessment.

EVALUATION AND ASSESSMENT

Evaluation

Evaluation, particularly educational evaluation is a series of activities designed to measure the effectiveness of the teaching-learning systems as a whole. According to Mary Thorpe (1980), "Evaluation is the collection, analysis and interpretation of information about any aspect of a programme of education." Teaching-learning process is a continuous activity. It needs to be evaluated from beginning to end. Evaluation during the learning process (continuous assessment), often termed as "formative evaluation", is important for learners and teachers alike.

The bases of evaluation are learning objectives, performance standards and achievement tests on the one hand, and learners' and experts' opinions on the other. Evaluation helps to build an educational programme, assess its achievement and improve upon its effectiveness. It also provides valuable feedback on the design, development and implementation of the programme. It is, of course, an important component of the teaching-learning process. It helps in making the value judgement, determining educational status, or measuring achievement of learners.

The scope of evaluation in schools extents to almost all the areas of learner's personality development. It includes both scholastic and non-scholastic areas. It reveals the strengths and weaknesses of the learners, so that the learners have better opportunity to understand and improve themselves.

Evaluation is helpful to teachers also. It provides feedback to them to reshape their teaching strategies according to the needs of the learners. Evaluation in education in general and in distance education in particular becomes imperative to know as to what extent the goals of education have been achieved.

Thus, evaluation is not merely assigning grades to learners. It is a continuous process of acquiring and processing information in order to improve one's learning and to assess decisions made in designing an instructional system. If we analyse the above statement we easily notice that it has three important implications for the entire teaching-learning system. They are as follows:

1. Evaluation is a continuous process and not a one time performance measurement, effected at the end of a course/programme. It starts at the stage of curriculum development and continues until the instruction ends.
2. Evaluation process is goal-directed. It is aimed at finding ways and means to improve learning and thereby to achieve learning objectives more effectively and more efficiently.
3. Evaluation requires the use of accurate and appropriate measuring instructions to collect information for taking decisions about the quality and operation of education.

It is clear that in designing an effective learning system, one of the earliest steps we need to take is to prepare a comprehensive evaluation plan, which should be developed soon after the learning objectives have been formulated. This practice will help us to:

- determine whether the objectives are attainable or need revisions before we start designing the instructional system;
- collect data/information in a form that suits our purposes adequately and at a time when it is available, otherwise the opportunity to collect specific information may be lost; and
- have sufficient time to test the effectiveness of a design.

Continuous and Comprehensive Evaluation (CCE)

Continuous and Comprehensive Evaluation (CCE) refers to a system of school based evaluation of a student that covers all aspects of a student development. It is a developmental process of student which emphasizes on two fold objectives. These objectives are continuity in evaluation and assessment of broad based learning and behaviourial outcomes on the other.

The term **'continuous'** is meant to emphasise that evaluation of identified aspects of students **'growth and development'** is a continuous process rather than an event, built into the total teaching-learning process and spread over the entire span of academic session. It means regularity of assessment, frequency of unit testing, diagnosis of learning gaps, use of corrective measures, retesting and feedback of evidence to teachers and students for their self evaluation.

The second term **'comprehensive'** means that the scheme attempts to cover both the scholastic and the co-scholastic aspects of the students' growth and development. Since abilities, attitudes and aptitudes can manifest themselves in forms other than the written word, the term refers to application of variety of tools and techniques (both testing and non-testing) and aims at assessing a learner's development in areas of learning, like:

- Knowledge
- Understanding
- Applying
- Analyzing
- Evaluating
- Creating

Objectives of CCE

- To help develop cognitive, psychomotor and affective skills.
- To lay emphasis on thought process and de-emphasise memorization.
- To make evaluation an integral part of teaching-learning process.
- To use evaluation for improvement of students achievement and teaching-learning strategies on the basis of regular diagnosis followed by remedial instructions.
- To use evaluation as a quality control device to maintain desired standard of performance.
- To determine social utility, desirability or effectiveness of a programme and take appropriate decisions about the learner, the process of learning and the learning environment.
- To make the process of teaching and learning a learner-centered activity:

Features of CCE

- The **'continuous'** aspect of CCE takes care of **'continual'** and **'periodicity'** aspect of evaluation.

- Continual means assessment of students in the beginning of instructions (placement evaluation) and assessment during the instructional process (**formative evaluation**) done informally using multiple techniques of evaluation.
- Periodicity means assessment of performance done frequently at the end of unit/term (**summative evaluation**).
- The **'comprehensive'** component of CCE takes care of assessment of all round development of the child's personality. It includes assessment in **Scholastic as well as Co-Scholastic** aspects of the pupil's growth.
- Scholastic aspects include curricular areas or subject specific areas, whereas Co-Scholastic aspects include Life Skills, Co-Curricular Activities, Attitudes and Values.
- Assessment in Scholastic areas is done informally and formally using multiple techniques of evaluation continually and periodically. The diagnostic evaluation takes place at the end of unit/term test. The causes of poor performance in some units are diagnosed using diagnostic tests. These are followed with appropriate interventions followed by retesting.
- Assessment in Co-Scholastic areas is done using multiple techniques on the basis of identified criteria, while assessment in Life Skills is done on the basis of Indicators of Assessment and Checklists.

Functions of CCE

- It helps the teacher to organize effective teaching strategies.
- Continuous evaluation helps in regular assessment to the extent and degree of Learner's progress (ability and achievement with reference to specific Scholastic and Co-Scholastic areas).
- Continuous evaluation serves to diagnose weaknesses and permits the teacher to ascertain an individual learner's strengths and weaknesses and her needs. It provides immediate feedback to the teacher, who can then decide whether a particular unit or concept needs a discussion again in the whole class or whether a few individuals are in need of remedial instruction.
- By continuous evaluation, children can know their strengths and weaknesses. It provides the child a realistic self assessment of how he/she studies. It can motivate children to develop good study habits, to correct errors, and to direct their activities towards the achievement of desired goals. It helps a learner to determine the areas of instruction in where more emphasis is required.
- Continuous and comprehensive evaluation identifies areas of aptitude and interest. It helps in identifying changes in attitudes and value systems.
- It helps in making decisions for the future, regarding choice of subjects, courses and careers.
- It provides information/reports on the progress of students in Scholastic and Co-Scholastic areas and thus helps in predicting the future success of the learner.

Continuous evaluation helps in bringing awareness of the achievement to the child, teachers and parents from time-to-time. They can look into the probable cause of the fall in performance if any, and may take remedial measures of instruction in which more emphasis is required. Many times, because of some personal reasons, family problems or adjustment problems, the children start neglecting their studies, resulting in sudden drop in their performance. If the teacher, child and parents do not notice the sudden drop in the performance of the child in academics, it could result in a permanent deficiency in the childs' learning.

The major emphasis of CCE is on the continuous growth of students ensuring their intellectual, emotional, physical, cultural and social development and therefore, it will not be merely limited to assessment of learner's scholastic attainments. CCE uses assessment as a means of motivating learners to provide feedback and follow up work to improve upon the learning in the classroom and to present a comprehensive picture of a learner's profile. It is this that has led to the emergence of the concept of **School Based Continuous and Comprehensive Evaluation.**

Scholastic and Co-Scholastic Assessment

In order to have Continuous and Comprehensive Evaluation, both Scholastic and Co-Scholastic aspects need to be given due recognition. Such a holistic assessment requires maintaining an ongoing and comprehensive profile for each learner that is honest, encouraging and discreet. While teachers frequently reflect, plan and implement remedial strategies, the child's ability to retain and articulate what has been learned over a period of time also requires periodic assessment. These assessments can take many forms but all of them should be as comprehensive and discreet as possible. **Weekly**, **fortnightly**, or **quarterly** reviews (depending on the learning area), that do not openly compare one learner with another are generally recommended. The objective is to promote and enhance not just learning and retention among children, but their soft skills as well.

Scholastic Assessment

The objectives of the Scholastic domain are:-

- Desirable behaviour related to the learner's knowledge, understanding, application, evaluation, analysis and the ability to apply it in an unfamiliar situation.
- To improve the teaching learning process.
- Assessment should be both **Formative** and **Summative**.

Summative and Formative Assessment

Assessment is often divided into formative and summative categories for the purpose of considering different objectives for assessment practices.

Summative Assessment

Summative assessment is intended to measure learning outcomes and report those outcomes to students, parents and administrators. In an educational setting, it generally occurs at the conclusion of a class, course, semester or academic year. In the context of a course summative assessments are typically used to assign students a course grade. It is also referred to in a learning context as **"assessment of learning". Performance-based assessment** is similar to summative assessment, as it focuses on achievement. A well-defined task is identified and students are asked to create, produce, or do something, often in settings that involve real-world application of knowledge and skills. Proficiency is demonstrated by providing an extended response. Performance formats are further differentiated into products and performances. The performance may result in a product, such as a painting, portfolio, paper, or exhibition, or it may consist of a performance, such as a speech, athletic skill, musical recital, or reading.

Definitions of Summative Assessment

- "Good summative assessments—tests and other graded evaluations—must be demonstrably reliable, valid, and free of bias" (Angelo and Cross, 1993).
- '...assessment (that) has increasingly been used to sum up learning' (Black and William, 1999).
- '...looks at past achievements ... adds procedures or tests to existing work ... involves only marking and feedback grades to student ... is separated from teaching ... is carried out at intervals when achievement has to be summarized and reported.' (Harlen, 1998).

Features of Summative Assessment

- Assessment of learning.
- Generally taken by students at the end of a unit or semester to demonstrate the **"sum"** of what they have or have not learned.
- Summative assessment methods are the most traditional way of evaluating student work.

Formative Assessment

Formative assessment is generally carried out throughout a course or project. In an educational setting, formative assessment is used by teachers to consider approaches to teaching and next steps for individual learners and the class, and would not necessarily be used for grading purposes. Formative assessment, also referred to as **"educative assessment"** or **"assessment for learning"**, is used to aid learning. Assessment for learning is defined as "all those activities undertaken by teachers and/or students, which provide information to be used as feedback to modify the teaching and learning activities in which they are engaged" (Black and William 2004).

Definitions of Formative Assessment

- '... often means no more than that the assessment is carried out frequently and is planned at the same time as teaching'. (Black and William, 1999)
- '... provides feedback which leads to students recognizing the (learning) gap and closing it ... it is forward looking ...' (Harlen, 1998).
- '... includes both feedback and self-monitoring'. (Sadler, 1989)
- '... is used essentially to get a feedback into the teaching and learning process.' (Tunstall and Gipps, 1996)

Features of Formative Assessment

- Is diagnostic and remedial.
- Makes provision for effective feedback.
- Provides a platform for the active involvement of students in their own learning.
- Enables teachers to adjust teaching to take account of the results of assessment.
- Recognizes the profound influence assessment has on the motivation and self-esteem of students, both of which are crucial influences on learning.
- Recognizes the need for students to be able to assess themselves and understand how to improve.
- Builds on students' prior knowledge and experience in designing what is taught.
- Incorporates varied learning styles to decide how and what to teach.
- Encourages students to understand the criteria that will be used to judge their work.

- Offers an opportunity to students to improve their work after they get the feedback.
- Helps student to support their peer group and vice-versa.

A common form of formative assessment is **"diagnostic assessment"**. Diagnostic assessment measures a student's current knowledge and skills for the purpose of identifying a suitable program of learning. **"Self-assessment"** is a form of diagnostic assessment which involves students assessing themselves. **"Forward-looking assessment"** asks those being assessed to consider themselves in hypothetical future situations.

Co-Scholastic Assessment

The desirable behaviour related to learner's life skills, attitudes, interests, values, co-curricular activities and physical health are described as skills to be acquired in co-scholastic domain.

The process of assessing the students' progress in achieving objectives related to scholastic and co-scholastic domain is called comprehensive evaluation. It has been observed that usually under the scholastic domain such as knowledge and understanding of the facts, concepts, principles etc. of a subject are assessed. The Co-Scholastic elements are either altogether excluded from the evaluation process or they are not given adequate attention. For making the evaluation comprehensive, both Scholastic and Co-Scholastic aspects should be given importance. Simple and manageable means of assessment of Co-Scholastic aspects of growth must be included in the comprehensive evaluation scheme.

Comprehensive evaluation would necessitate the use of a variety of tools and techniques. This will be so because both different and specific areas of learner's growth can be evaluated through certain special techniques.

School Based CCE

School based Evaluation is held at school level unlike external examination conducted by the Boards of School Education. This is done by the teachers according to the schedule developed by the school and guidelines given by the Board. Though this evaluation has been done at school level all along, certain shortcomings have crept into this system. These shortcomings can be attributed to various factors. The basic factor is the misconception of teachers regarding the place of evaluation and its importance in the educational process. The other factor has been the imitation of the practice of external examination which is generally held at the end of the session.

In the School Based System of evaluation, the focus on the purpose of assessment has changed. Now, it includes readiness testing, screening of development, evaluation of performance in cognitive, affective and psychomotor domains more frequently, systematically and effectively.

In other words, School Based Evaluation is child-centred, school-centred and multidimensional evaluation. Hence, in its true spirit, it triggers an all round development of the learner. It encourages all kinds of learning in life both inside the school as well as outside it. It is child-centered as it attempts to consider the learner as a unique entity for its individual pattern of development. It builds on individual child's abilities, progress and development in achieving already set goals and objectives of education as an individual and not just his/her position in relation to other learners.

Further, this evaluation helps a learner to use his/her potential in a better manner and also provides insight to the teachers to discover the methods which may be helpful to the individual learner in resolving his/her problems and difficulties.

Besides being ***child-centred,*** this evaluation is ***school-centred*** as well. It means that no outside agency interferes in this evaluation process. It is entirely school based and done by the teacher. The teacher is trusted and given full responsibility of evaluating students with the brief that the teacher knows best about his/her students.

School Based Evaluation is ***multidimensional.*** Its multidimensional nature is reflected in recognizing and taking care of learners' social, emotional, physical, intellectual and other areas of development which are interrelated and cannot be considered in isolation. It also calls for the use of multiple techniques and tools of evaluation.

Aim of School Based CCE

- Elimination of chance element and subjectivity (as far as possible), de-emphasis on memorization, encouraging comprehensive evaluation incorporating both Scholastic and Co-Scholastic aspects of learners development.
- Continuous evaluation spread over the total span of the instructional time as an integral built-in aspect of the total teaching-learning process.
- Functional and meaningful declaration of results for effective use by teachers, students, parents and the society.
- Wider uses of test results for purposes not merely of the assessment of levels of pupils' achievements and proficiencies, but mainly for their improvement, thorough diagnosis and remedial/enrichment programmes.

- Improvement in the mechanics of conducting examinations for realizing a number of other allied purposes.
- Introduction of concomitant changes in instructional materials and methodology.
- Introduction of the semester system.
- The use of grades in place of marks in determining and declaring the level of pupil performance and proficiency.

Its Characteristics

School Based Evaluation has the following characteristics:

- Is broader, more comprehensive and continuous than traditional system.
- Aims primarily to help learners for systematic learning and development.
- Takes care of the needs of the learner as responsible citizens of the future.
- Is more transparent, futuristic and provides more scope for association among learners, teachers and parents.

School based evaluation provides opportunities to teachers to **know the following about their learners:**

- What they learn?
- How they learn?
- What type of difficulties/limitations they face in working in tandem?
- What do the children think?
- What do the children feel?
- What are their interests and dispositions?

The focus has shifted to developing a deep learning environment. There is a paradigm shift in the pedagogy and competencies from 'controlling' to 'enriching' to 'empowering' schools.

Traditional Schooling	Enriching Schooling	Empowering Schooling
• Teacher centred • Subjects and classes-teacher directed • Sorting and ranking individuals **Competency:** • Memory • Competitive	• Student centred • Self directed • Continuous assessment **Competency:** • Critical thinking • Collaborative • Creative	• Experience centred • Virtual authenticity • Multi literacies **Competency:** • Risk taking • Ethical • Interactive

Implementing School Based Assessment would mean:

- Elimination of chance element and subjectivity (as far as possible), de-emphasis of memorization, encouraging Comprehensive evaluation incorporating both scholastic and co-scholastic aspects of learners development.
- Continuous evaluation spread over the total span of the instructional time as an integral built-in aspect of the total teaching-learning process.
- Functional and meaningful declaration of results for effective use by teachers, students, parents and the society.
- Wider uses of test results for purposes not merely of the assessment of levels of pupils' achievements and proficiencies, but mainly for its improvement, through diagnosis and remedial/enrichment programmes.
- Improvements in the mechanics of conducting examinations for realizing a number of other allied purposes.
- Introduction of concomitant changes in instructional materials and methodology.
- Introduction of the semester system from the secondary stage onwards.
- The use of grades in place of marks in determining and declaring the level of pupil performance and proficiency.

The above goals are relevant for both external examination and evaluation in schools.

Shortcoming of Traditional External Examination

- It is a one shot examination at the end of a year at the terminal stage of schooling.
- It mainly evaluates only the scholastic aspects of learning of the students.
- It does not evaluate all the abilities of the children. On the basis of marks obtained in written examination the students are declared pass or fail and further classified into predetermined divisions.

- Pass and fail system causes frustration and is inhumane because the failed candidates come to feel that they are good for nothing.
- Co-scholastic areas are almost totally ignored and have no place in the currently prevalent scheme of education and evaluation.
- The practice of testing of untaught content also reflects poor learning achievement.
- Only limited techniques of evaluation without potential for judging a student are being used.
- The aim of evaluation is to improve learner's quality which is not served by external examination.
- The current practice of awarding marks suffers from many discrepancies due to variety of errors.
- The varied ranges of obtained scores of students in different subjects create the problem in declaring reliable results.
- Analysis and interpretation of test results is not done in a scientific way.

School Based Continuous and Comprehensive Evaluation System should be Established to:

- reduce stress on children.
- make evaluation comprehensive and regular.
- provide space for the teacher for creative teaching.
- provide a tool of diagnosis and remediation.
- produce learners with greater skills.

Four Assessment Paradigms

Assessment *of* Learning

The 'assessment **of** learning' is defined as a process whereby someone attempts to describe and quantify the knowledge, attitudes or skills possessed by another. Teacher direction is paramount and the student has little involvement in the design or implementation of the assessment process in these circumstances.

- Teacher designs learning
- Teacher collects evidence
- Teacher judges what has been learnt (and what has not been learnt)

Assessment *for* Learning

The 'assessment **for** learning' involves increased level of student autonomy, but not without teacher guidance and collaboration. The assessment **for** learning is sometimes seen as being akin to 'formative assessment'. There is more emphasis towards giving useful advice to the student and less emphasis on the giving of marks and the grading function.

- Teacher designs learning
- Teacher designs assessment with feedback to student
- Teacher judges what has been learnt (student develops insight into what has not)

Assessment *as* Learning

The 'assessment **as** learning' is perhaps more connected with diagnostic assessment and can be constructed with more of an emphasis on peer learning. Assessment **as** learning generates opportunities for self assessment and peer assessment. Students take on increased responsibility to generate quality information about their learning and that of others.

- Teacher and student co-construct learning
- Teacher and student co-construct assessment
- Teacher and student co-construct learning progress map

Assessment **for** learning and assessment **as** learning activities should be deeply embedded in teaching and learning and be the source of interactive feedback, allowing students to adjust, re-think and re-learn.

Assessment *in* Learning

The 'assessment **in** learning' places the question at the centre of teaching and learning. It deflects the teaching from its focus on a 'correct answer' to a focus on 'a fertile question'. Through enquiry students engage in processes that generates feedback about their learning, which come from multiple sources and activities. It contributes to the construction of other learning activities, line of enquiry and the generation of other questions.

- Student as the centre of learning
- Student monitors, assesses and reflects on learning
- Student initiates demonstration of learning (to self and others)
- Teacher as coach and mentor.

Teachers and students need to understand the purpose of each assessment strategy. The overall assessment 'package' being used by learners and teachers should accurately capture, generate and use meaningful learning information to generate deep learning and understanding.

ASSESSING LEARNERS

Any meaningful report on the quality and extent of a child's learning needs to be comprehensive. We need a curriculum whose creativity, innovativeness, and development of the whole being, the hallmark of a good education makes uniform tests that assess memorised facts and textbook-based learning obsolete. We need to redefine and seek new parameters for and ways of evaluation and feedback. In addition to the learner's achievements in specific subject areas that lend themselves to testing easily, assessment would need to encompass attitudes to learning, interest, and the ability to learn independently.

ASSESSMENT IN THE COURSE OF TEACHING

Preparing report cards is a way for the teacher to think about each individual child and review what she/he has learnt during the term, and what she/he needs to work on and improve. To be able to write such report cards, teachers would need to think about each individual child, and hence pay attention to them during their everyday teaching and interaction. One does not need special tests for this; learning activities themselves provide the basis for such ongoing observational and qualitative assessments of children. Maintaining a daily diary based on observation helps in continuous and comprehensive evaluation. An extract from the diary of a teacher for a week notes the following: "Kiran enjoyed his work. He took an instant liking to the books that were informative and brief. He says that he likes simple and clear language. In noting down facts, he goes for short answers. He says that it helps him understand things easily. He favours a practical approach." Similarly, keeping samples and notes of the child's work at different stages provides both the teacher and the learner herself or himself with a systematic record of his/her learning progress.

The belief that assessment must lead to finding learning difficulties to then be remediated is often very impractical and not founded on a sound understanding of pedagogic practice. Problems regarding conceptual development cannot and do not wait for formal tests in order to be detected. A teacher can, in the course of teaching itself, come to know of such problems by asking questions that make children think or by giving them small assignments. She can then attend to them in the process of teaching—by ensuring that her planning is flexible and responsive to the learners and their learning.

CURRICULAR AREAS THAT CANNOT BE 'TESTED FOR MARKS'

Each area of the curriculum may not lend itself to being 'tested'; it may even be antithetical to the nature of learning in the curricular area. This includes areas such as work, health, yoga, physical education, music and art. While the skill-based component of physical education and yoga could be tested, the health aspect needs continuous and qualitative assessments. Currently, this has the effect of making these subjects and activities 'less important' in the curriculum; these areas are inadequately provided for in terms of material resources and curricular planning, and marked by a lack of seriousness. Further, the time allocated for them is also frequently sacrificed to accommodate special classes. This is a serious compromise with parts of the curriculum that have deep educational significance and potential.

Even if 'marks' cannot be given, children can be assessed for their development in these areas. Participation, interest, and level of involvement, and the extent to which abilities and skills have been honed, are some markers that can help teachers to gauge the benefits of what children learn and gain through such activities. Asking children to self-report on their learning can also provide teachers with insight into children's educational progress and give them feedback on improving curriculum or pedagogy.

DESIGN AND CONDUCT OF ASSESSMENT

Assessments and examinations must be credible, and based on valid ways of gauging learning.

As long as examinations and tests assess children's ability to remember and recall textbook knowledge, all attempts to redirect the curriculum towards learning will be thwarted. First, tests in knowledge-based subject areas must be able to gauge what children have learnt, and their ability to use this knowledge for problem solving and application in the real world. In addition, they must also be able to test the processes of thinking to gauge if the learner has also learnt where to find information, how to use new information, and to analyse and evaluate the same.

The types of questions that are set for assessment need to go beyond what is given in the book. Often children's learning is restricted as teachers do not accept their answers if they are different from what is presented in the guidebooks.

Questions that are open-ended and challenging could also be used. Designing good test items and questions is an art, and teachers should spend time thinking about and devising such questions. The interest and ability of teachers to design good questions can be promoted through district—or state-level competitions. All question papers must be designed graded for difficulty in order to permit all children to experience a level of success, and to gain confidence in their ability to answer and solve problems.

Trying to devise a good and effective open-book examination can be a challenge that we must try to take up in our curricular efforts at all levels of school. This would require teachers and examination setters to emphasise the interpretation and application of learning over the arguments and facts that can be located in the book. There have been successful demonstrations that such examinations can be carried out on a large scale, and that teachers can themselves be trusted with moderating the results of such examinations. In this way, the assessment of projects and lab work can also be made credible and sound.

It is important that after receiving their corrected papers, children rewrite the answers and that these are again reviewed by teachers to ensure that children have learnt and gained something out of the ordeal.

Competition is motivating, but it is an extrinsic rather than intrinsic form of motivation. It is, of course, much easier to establish and to manipulate, and therefore frequently resorted to by teachers and school systems as a way creating and nurturing the drive for excellence. Schools begin 'ranking' children as early as their pre-primary years as a way of inculcating in them a competitive spirit. Such a competitive drive has several negative side effects on learning, often superficial learning is sufficient to create and maintain impressions, and over time students lose their ability to take initiative or do things for the fulfilment of one's own interest; hence, areas that cannot be 'marked' are neglected. This has unhealthy consequences for classroom culture, making children individualistic and unsuited to team work. There is an absurd and unnecessary importance given to term examinations, often accompanied by extreme arrangements of invigilation and secrecy. While the physical and psychological effects of this may not be readily visible until middle school, they frequently lead to high levels of stress in children, and cause early burnout. Schools and teachers need to ask themselves whether there is really much to be gained out of such practices and to what extent learning requires such systems of marking and ranking.

SELF-ASSESSMENT AND FEEDBACK

The role of assessment is to gauge the progress that both learner and teacher have made towards achieving the aims that have been set and appraising how this could be done better. Opportunity for feedback, leading to revision and improvement of performance, should constantly be available, without exams and evaluations being used as a threat to study.

Grading and correction carried out in the presence of students and providing feedback on the answers they get right and wrong, and why. Asking children about why they answered what they did assists teachers in going beyond the written answer to engage with children's thinking. Such processes also take away the frightening judgemental quality of marks obtained in a test, and enable children to understand and focus on their mistakes and learn through these mistakes. Sometimes head teachers object, claiming that correction in the presence of the child reduces 'objectivity'. This is a misplaced concern for 'objectivity', stemming from a competitive system that believes in judging children. Such a concern for 'objectivity' is misplaced in evaluation, which is consistent with educational goals.

Not only learning outcomes but also learning experiences themselves must be evaluated. Learners happily comment on the totality of their experience. Exercises, both individual and collective, can be designed to enable them to reflect on and assess their learning experiences. Such experiences also provide them with self-regulatory capabilities essential for 'learning to learn'. Such information is also valuable feedback to the teacher, and can be used to modify the learning system as a whole.

Every classroom interaction with children requires their evaluation of their own work, and a discussion with them about what should be tested and the ways of finding out whether the competencies are being developed or not. Even very young children are able to give correct assessments of what they can or cannot do well. The role of teaching is to provide an opportunity to each child to learn to the best of his or her ability and provide learning experiences that develop cognitive qualities, physical well-being and athletic qualities, as also affective and aesthetic qualities.

Report cards need to present to children and parents a comprehensive and holistic view of the child's development in many fields. Teachers must be able to say things about each child/student, that conveys to them a sense of individualised attention, reaffirms a positive self-image, and communicates personal goals for them to work towards. Whether it is marks or grades that are reported, a qualitative statement by the teacher is necessary to support the assessment. Only through such a relationship with each child can any teacher succeed in influencing him/her, and contributing to his/her learning. Along with the teacher assessing each child, each student could also assess himself or herself and include this self-assessment in the report card.

Currently, many report cards carry information on subject areas and have nothing to say about other aspects of the child's development, including health, physical fitness and abilities in games, social skills, and abilities in art and craft. Qualitative statements about these aspects of children's education and development would provide a more holistic assessment of educational concerns.

AREAS THAT REQUIRE FRESH THINKING

There are many areas of the curriculum that can be assessed but for which we still do not have reliable and efficient instruments. This includes assessing learning that is carried out in groups, and learning in areas such as theatre, work and craft where skills and competencies develop over longer time scales and require careful observation.

Continuous and comprehensive evaluation has frequently been cited as the only meaningful kind of evaluation. This also requires much more careful thinking through about when it is to be employed in a system effectively. Such evaluation places a lot of demand on teachers' time and ability to maintain meticulous records if it is to be meaningfully executed and if it is to have any reliability as an assessment. If this simply increases stress on children by reducing all their activities into items for assessment, or making them experience the teacher's 'power', then it defeats the purpose of education. Unless a system is adequately geared for such assessment, it is better for teachers to engage in more limited forms of evaluation, but incorporating into them more features that will make the assessment a meaningful record of learning.

Finally, there is a need to evolve and maintain credibility in assessment so that they perform their function of providing feedback in a meaningful way.

ASSESSMENT AT DIFFERENT STAGES

ECCE and Classes I and II of the Elementary Stage: At this stage, assessment must be purely qualitative judgements of children's activities in various domains and an assessment of the status of their health and physical development, based on observations through everyday interactions. On no account should they be made to take any form of test, oral or written.

Class III to Class VIII of the Elementary Stage: A variety of methods may be used, including oral and written tests and observations. Children should be aware that they are being assessed, but this must be seen by them as a part of the teaching process and not as a fearful constant threat. Grades or marks along with qualitative judgements of achievement and areas requiring attention are essential at this stage. Children's own self-evaluation can also be a part of the report card from Class V onwards. Rather than examinations, there could be short tests from time-to-time, which are criterion based. Term-wise examinations could be commenced from Class VII onwards when children are more psychologically ready to study large chunks of material and, to spend a few hours in an examination room, working at answering questions. Again, the progress card must indicate general observations on health and nutrition, specific observations on the overall progress of the learner, and information and advice for the parents.

Class IX to Class XII of the Secondary and Higher Secondary Stages: Assessment may be based more on tests, examinations and project reports for the knowledge-based areas of the curriculum, along with self-assessment. Other areas would be assessed through observation and also through self-evaluation.

Reports could include much more analysis about the students, various skill/knowledge areas and percentiles, etc. This would assist them by pointing out the areas of study that they need to focus on, and also help them by providing a basis for further choices that they make regarding what to study thereafter.

SECTION b

CONCEPT OF INCLUSIVE EDUCATION & UNDERSTANDING CHILDREN WITH SPECIAL NEEDS

CONCEPT OF INCLUSIVE EDUCATION

Every child is special for his/her parent and, every child has a special need for love, acceptance and a feeling of belongingness. Here, we call **children with special needs** to those who are "different" from their cohorts. They are born equal with some limitations and with the help of inclusion be able to actively participate as equal citizens in all aspects of society and community life. Thus, children with special needs refer to "all those children who require adaptations to the normal process of education due to problems of vision, hearing, movement, learning and intellect." In other words, these children have some kind of **disability**.

Inclusive Education denotes that all children irrespective of their strengths and weaknesses will be part of the mainstream education. Thus, inclusive education means, "the act of ensuring that all children despite their differences, receive the opportunity of being part of the same classroom as other children of their age, and in the process get the opportunity to being exposed to the curriculum to their optimal potential."

EDUCATIONAL PROVISIONS FOR CHILDREN WITH SPECIAL NEEDS

The last two decades of the 19th century has witnessed the knowledge and processes of educating the disabled children through Christian Missionaries. The first school for the deaf was established in Mumbai in 1883 and the first school for the blind in Amritsar in 1887. At that time, it was believed that children with disabilities could not be educated alongwith normal children. Therefore, education to disabled children was offered through special school. This trend continued early sixties of the last century with the help of some international agencies who developed programme of integrated education. Here, children disabilities were placed in regular school so that they could study alongwith their non-disabled 'peers". The integrated education adopts various models for service deliver. Presently the emphasis is on the need to provide education for all in appropriate environment with inclusive philosophy through inclusive education.

INTEGRATED EDUCATION FOR THE DISABLED CHILDREN (IEDC)

With the development of science and technology and improvement in Medical Services and Aggressive neo-natal intervention has ensured that a large number of babies who would earlier have not survived but often with different abilities. The number of differently abled children is on the increasing trend but it is not possible to create the required number of special schools throughout the country to meet this challenge due to the high cost and also due to the fact that the population is so scattered. The best alternative under these situations is to make use of the infrastructural facilities already present in terms of regular schools and integrate children into the mainstream of education.

Consequent on the success of international institutions in introducing differently abled children in regular schools, the planning commission, Govt. of India, in 1971 includes in its plan a programme for integrated education. In 1974, the Union Government introduced a scheme called "Integrated Schools" to do just this. This scheme was later revised and a plan of action formulated. The important aims of IEDC includes:

- Provide educational opportunity to differently abled children in regular schools.
- Facilitate retention of differently abled in the school system.

- Integrate children from special school to common schools.

The scope of the scheme of IEDC includes pre-school training, counselling for the parents, and special training in skills for all kinds of differently abled children. It provides facilities in the form of books, stationary, uniforms and allowances for transport, reader and escort etc.

Project Integrated Education for the Disabled (PIED)

This scheme was launched by MHRD Govt. of India in collaboration with UNICEF in 1987 to strengthen the integration of differently abled into regular schools. Under this scheme, a cluster instead of individual school is given importance. This scheme is an improvement over the special schools in one or many ways and provides a way towards universalisation of elementary education and Education for All including for differently abled children.

Assumption About Integrated Education

Integrated education assumes a process of bringing disabled children into mainstream schools, where the system remains the same. As per the system, the child is the problem. So, it is essential to change the child where the resources are focused on the individual child. The failure is due to the child's problem; he is not able, not ready, not good enough to cope up with the system.

In integrated education; it is the children with disabilities who are seen as the problem, who must be "fixed", "changed" & "adapted" to suit the existing regular, mainstream school. It is the disabled child who is seen as a square peg in a round table. The system remains the same. The onus for successful integration therefore, is on the disabled child.

Assumption About Inclusive Education

Assumptions of inclusive education is opposite to integrated education. Inclusive education assumes that changes the system to fit the child. It is essential to addresses all types of individual needs, not just disability. Teachers and schools are held responsible for children's learning. It focuses on flexibility of curriculum, teacher training and change in environmental. Failure is the problem with the system not with the child. It is quite essential to assumes that all children can learn and that all children need their learning to be supported in diverse ways.

In this model of inclusive education, it is not the child, but the education system, which is seen as a problem. Therefore, it is the system (with all its components) with should be changed, modified & made flexible enough to accommodate the diverse needs of all learners, including children with disabilities. The onus for success is therefore on the flexibility of the system. It focuses on the environment, as the "disabling" cause because it fails to provide appropriate access to equal opportunities for all persons to participate fully in social life.

Though integrated education of differently abled children has gained momentum all over the country since 1974, there are some other possibilities too for these children to get education. For example, the NIOS (National Institute of Open Schooling) offers education which have the advantage of being specially adopted to the needs of every child as well as aimed at giving the child every opportunity to progress at his/her pace. Another example is alternative schooling and community-based rehabilitation programmes.

EDUCATION FOR A COHESIVE SOCIETY

Despite more than half a century of independence, India is struggling for freedom from various kinds of biases and imbalances such as rural/urban, rich/poor, and differences on the basis of caste, religion, ideology, gender etc. Education can play a very significant role in minimising and finally eliminating these differences by providing equality of access to quality education and opportunity.

Equality of opportunity means ensuring that every individual receives suitable education at a pace and through methods suited to his/her being. Children of the disadvantaged, and socially discriminated groups and also those suffering from specific challenges must be paid special attention.

Provision for equal opportunity to all not only in access, but also in the conditions for success is a precondition for the promotion of equality. The curriculum must create an awareness of the inherent equality of all with a view to removing prejudices and complexes transmitted through the social environment and the factor of birth.

EDUCATION OF GIRLS

Equality among sexes is a fundamental right under the constitution of India. The state, however, also has the right to exercise positive protective discrimination in favour of the disadvantaged population groups including women. Emphasis in education has moved from 'Equality of Educational Opportunity' (NPE, 1968) to 'Education for Women's Equality and Empowerment' (1986). As a result, the curricular and training strategies for the education of girls now demand more attention. Besides, making education accessible to more and more girls, especially rural girls, removing all gender discrimination and gender bias in school curriculum, textbooks and the process of transaction is absolutely necessary. There is a need to develop and implement gender inclusive and gender sensitive curricular strategies to nurture a generation of girls and boys who are equally competent and are sensitive to one another, and grow up in a caring and sharing mode as equals, and not as adversaries.

EDUCATION OF LEARNERS FROM DISADVANTAGED GROUPS

For achieving a cohesive society it would be essential to respond to specific educational needs of learners from different sections of the society with special emphasis on the Scheduled Castes, the Scheduled Tribes and the other socially and economically disadvantaged groups. In order to do so, there is a need for integrating the socio-cultural perspectives partly by showing concern for their linguistic specificities and pedagogic requirements. Implications of the multilingual and multicultural environment shall have to be taken care of through specifically devised methodology. Contextualisation of curriculum shall have to be effected through curricular materials. The fundamental rights of the disadvantaged groups have to be consciously in-corporated in the curriculum. Even the problem of educating the migrating population shall have to be handled through specific condensed educational programmes based on the main ingredients of the national curriculum.

EDUCATION OF THE GIFTED AND TALENTED

An educational system has the dual role of promoting equality as well as excellence. Education is increasingly called upon to liberate all the creative potentialities of human consciousness. Man essentially fulfils himself in and through creation. It is in the context of this, that education of gifted and talented children assumes great importance. A curricular programme while on the one hand should identify such children, on the other it should also nurture their diverse creative abilities by paying them special attention. It is also important that the identification and nurturance begins right from the earliest stage of education. Moreover, the task of identifying the gifted and talented must be accomplished on the basis of a broad conceptualisation of the process from multiple perspectives rather than as a search for a unitary human attribute. Not only their IQ (Intelligence Quotient) but also their EQ (Emotional Quotient) and SQ (Spiritual Quotient) ought to be assessed.

NATIONAL LEVEL POLICY AND LEGISLATION

Kothari Commission (1964-66)

The Kothari Commission first suggested that the education of handicapped children has to be organised not merely on humanitarian grounds, but also an aspects of utility. The commission emphasised that the education of children with disability should be "an inseparable part of the general education system. The commission also specifically emphasised that the education of children with disability should be "an inseparable part of the general education system. The commission also specifically emphasised. the importance of integrated education in meeting this target as it is cost effective and useful in developing mutual understanding between children with and without disabilities.

National Policy on Education (1986)

The National Policy on Education was adopted by Indian Parliament in 1986. The policy emphasized the removal of disparities, and ensuring equalisation of educational opportunity under its para education of the disabled.

National Policies for Persons with Disabilities (2006)

This recognises that persons with disabilities are valuable human resources for the country and seek to create an environment that provides them equal opportunities, protection of their rights and full participation in society.

Persons with Disabilities (Equal Opportunities, Protection of Rights & Full Participation) Act, 1995

Landmark legislation in the history of special education in India is the persons with Disabilities Act, 1995. This comprehensive Act covers seven disabilities, namely blindness, low vision, hearing impaired, loco-motor impaired, mental retardation, leprosy cured and mental illness.

The Rehabilitation Council of India (RCI) Act, 1992

This Act was passed in 1992 for the purpose of constituting the Rehabilitation Professionals and for maintenance of a Central Rehabilitation Register. It was amended by Rehabilitation Council of India (Amendment) Act, 2000 to provide for monitoring the training of rehabilitation professionals and personal, promoting research in rehabilitation and special education as additional objectives of the council.

SECTION C

LEARNING AND PEDAGOGY

LEARNING

A considerable change in the behaviour of the organism is called learning. When organism comes in contact with his environment certain necessary adjustment in the behaviour is needed. This adjustment in behaviour is the result of acquision of various habits, skills, attitudes and knowledge which is actually learning in simple term

Thus, learning means change in response or behaviour (modification, elimination or acquisition of responses involving some degree of performance) caused partly or wholly by conscious or unconscious experiences. This learning does not include physiological changes such as fatigue, temporary sensory resistance or non functioning even after continued stimulation.

Definition of Learning

It is very difficult to give a universally acceptable definition of learning because psychologists have defined the concept from different angles on the basis of their experiments. The common feature among these definitions is that learning in psychology has the status of a construct which means an idea or image that can not be directly observed like electrons or genes but they are inferred from the behaviour of the organism.

Melvin H Marx has defined learning in the following words;

"Learning is a relatively enduring change in behaviour which is a function of prior behaviour (usually called practice)

Explanation : According to the definition given above learning has three attributes:

1. Learning is a some what permanent change in behaviour. Changes occurred due to illness, fatigue, maturation or the consumption of intoxicants is not learning.
2. Learning is not directly observable. It is inferred from the behaviour of the organism in the form of construct.
3. Learning is a function of practice and experience. Experiences adds learning and practice gives it an enduring nature.

Some other **definitions** of learning are given below;

"Learning is modification of behaviour through experiences." — **Gates**

"Learning involves the acquisition of habit knowledge and attitudes". —**Crow and Crow**

"Learning is any change in behaviour resulting from behaviour." —**Guilford**

"Learning includes both acquisition and retention." —**Skinner**

"Any activity can be called learning so far as it develops the individual (in any respect good or bad) and makes him after behaviour and experiences different from what that would otherwise have been."

—**Woodworth**

"The term learning covers every modification in behaviour to meet environmental requirement".

—**Gardner Murply**

"Learning is the process by which behaviour (in the broader sense) is originated or changed through practice or training." —**Kingsley and Garry**

"Learning is the acquisition of new behaviour or the strengthening or weakening of old behaviour as a result of experience." —**Henry P. Smith**

"Learning is an episode in which a motivated individual attempts to adapt his behaviour so as to succeed in a situation which he perceives as requiring action to attain a goal."

— Presey, Robinson & Horrocks

"Learning is the process by which an activity originates or is changed through reacting to an encountered situation, provided that the characteristics of the changes in activity can not be explained on the basis of native response tendencies maturation or temporary state of the organism (e.g. fatigue or drugs etc.)

—Milgard

Characteristics of Learning

On the basis of the meaning and definitions given above following characteristics of learning can be derived:

1. **Learning is a relatively permanent change in behaviour :** Temporary changes in behaviour brought about due to some accidents or consuming any drugs is not learning at all. Learning is a relatively permanent change in behaviour. It is in this context we can say that reading some selected material to pass an examination is not learning. It is because learnt material is forgotten immediately after the exam.
2. **Learning is a progress or growth of the organism :** Learning is a fundamental need of life. Without it, no progress or growth is possible. This process of growth is unending also. One achievement of the organism motivates him to go for further achievement and thus excellence in many cases is achieved.
3. **Learning is a life long process :** An organism needs learning (behavioural change) at every moment of life to adjust to new situations at every moment. He can not sit idle at any time. Situations all the time force him for the acquisition of new learning.
4. **Learning is not directly observable :** How much learning has taken place in an organism can not be directly observed. It is inferred from his behaviour which is manifested by some activities, mental or physical.
5. **Learning is the result of experiences :** Experiences are gained at every moment of life. Learning is the other name of these experiences.
6. **Learning is a goal directed process :** Learning is a purposeful activity. It is a goal directed process. Learning which is the result of unconscious efforts of the individual is not learning in actual sense.
7. **Learning is retained through practice :** Practice or exercise is a must to retain learning. If practice is not made, learning will be forgotten and the nature of learning will no longer remain permanent. Thus, learning is acquisition and retention both.
8. **Learning reinforces further learning :** Learning definitely gives satisfaction to the individual which further motivates him for higher level of learning. Similarly, learning which is accompanied by reinforcement is more likely to become permanent and motivating for further learning.
9. **Learning is motivated by adjustment :** Man has to adjust himself according to the new environment. In this way learning is an adjustment.
10. **Learning is aroused by individual and social needs :** Learning depends upon our social needs, problems, desires, and ideals. There are certain persons who learn very fast whereas others are slow in learning. It should be noticed that social environment affects learning. It is impossible to learn in the absence of environment.
11. **Learning is transferable :** It means that learning may change place but the quantum of change in the place may be different. Change in the place is caused by techniques, ideals and the process. Change of place takes place from one field of education to the other field and from one class to other class.
12. **Learning is a process not a product :** Learning is a product for public at large but a psychologist considers it a process which has got the following four shapes-Need, Goal, adjustment and change.
13. **Improvement in the behaviour through learning :** When man reacts to the environment there is progressive modification of behaviour through learning. That is why, learning is known as improvement.
14. **Learning is active and creative :** Learning is active and creative i.e. learning depends upon the active involvement of the learner. It is said that if the learner is not self active, he cannot learn.

    It is, therefore, said that learning is the result of active involvement and experience from the sender and the receiver both.
15. **Learning is universal :** Humans are not the only organism that learn ie, react to the environment for adjustment. Animals also go through the process of learning though their speed of learning may be slower than humans.

Learning differentiated from Some Concepts

1. **Learning and instinct :** Some behaviour of every organism is reflexive or inborn, eg, breathing, breast feeding etc. All such activities take place without the process of learning. As we move to lower animals reflexes or instincts are seen more and more in their behaviour. The least example of instincts are found in humans. These instincts are not the result of any learning or experiences. They are relatively invariant in form and are reliably elicited or released by a particular and usually very simple stimulus (R Habber 1966) Thus learning is not needed for instincts or reflexive behaviour.

2. **Learning and maturation :** Maturation means physiological development of the individual according to the norms of a particular age. Learning and maturation are very closely related in the sense that for a successful learning, a definite level of maturation is a must. Thus learning is induced by maturation. For example, we can not teach quantum mechanics to a six year old child due to lack of maturation.

   Maturation on the other hand, is qualitative changes in the organism which are not induced by learning. Maturation is an increase in competency and adaptability according to Baldwin.

   Thus, we see that maturation is purely an internal process in the organism and learning is an external process more than an internal change in the behaviour of the organism. Learning and training should start only when a child must have reached an appropriate level of maturation. Maturation is actually the readiness for an activity due to physiological preparation.

3. **Leaning and cramming :** Cramming does not bring about any change in the behaviour of a student. So, cramming can never be called as learning. Despite this fact, in order to make a durable or permanent change in the behaviour of an organism, cramming will be very much helpful.

4. **Learning and acquisition of knowledge :** Acquisition of knowledge and skills is generally termed as learning but if that change of behaviour in the organism is not applied in any situation in any manner, mere accumulation of facts and information is not learning in real sense.

5. **Learning and education :** As the meaning of education suggested by the Good's dictionary of education, education is the aggregate of all the processes, by means of which a persons develops his abilities, attitudes and other forms of behaviour of positive value in the society in which the organism lives. Learning is also a process of change in the behaviour of the organism but this change may be of positive and negative value both.

Mental Process Involved in Learning

Learning may be the result of conditioning of behaviour but following mental processes are also involved in learning:

1. **Direction :** The person must be directed to the process of learning. It means that he must be full attentive to the process. He must have a clear cut goal for learning and he must take full interest to achieve that goal.
2. **Interpretation :** Learning needs perception, reaction to the stimuli and then concepts formation. The organism must realize all these relations in his mind.
3. **Selection :** So many stimuli or experiences may be there before the organism at the time of learning. He selects and recalls only those stimuli and experiences which are relevant to the situation.
4. **Insight :** When organism comes across a number of stimuli and experiences, he tries to find out various types of relationship among them. An insight helps him to reach the correct relationship.
5. **Creation :** When learning takes place, certain new mental pattern is formed which forces the organism to think and act in a new way.
6. **Criticism :** When an organism learns something (his behaviour is changed) he does not accept it so easily. he evaluates all workable solutions in his mind before putting it into application or practice.

TYPES OF LEARNING

Different criteria of classification of learning are given below:

(A) Learning according to the development of body organs

Such type of learning can broadly be classified into two categories:

1. **Motor learning :** It involves motor and muscular parts of the body. Motor learning is

also of two types sensory motor and perceptual motor. Sensory motor learning is related to the acquisition of simple habits through sense organs. Learning of skills in nursery school play ground is a good example of sensory motor learning.

Perceptual motor learning is related to the acquisition of social habits and complex motor skills. Dancing, cycling, handwriting, typing, swimming, driving, playing a musical instrument, etc, are some examples of perceptual motor learning. It is very much objective in nature.

2. **Ideational learning :** In this type of learning, muscular or motor activity is not needed. It is related to the acquisition of concepts, ideas and mental associations. This type of learning is mostly subjective in nature.

Ideational learning can also be classified into the following categories.

(i) Perceptual learning which mostly comes through senses (direct experiences with the objects). Learning through concrete materials, learning through written or spoken symbols,, drawing a picture, nature study and sight seeing are some examples of perceptual learning

(ii) Conceptual learning is the other name of abstract learning. It is related to the acquisition of concepts and abstract ideas.

(iii) Associative learning is learned incidentally or by connecting two different types of learning. Prescribed sequence is followed while linking one information with the other.

(iv) Imaginative learning is the process by which things of the past, present and future are given a definite form. It involves the acquisition of images and understanding of things beyond the normal range of sensory experiences.

(B) Learning according to the domains of behaviour involved

Domains of human behaviour are three, cognitive, affective, and psychomotor so, learning can also be classified into these three categories.

1. **Cognitive learning :** It is related to the acquisition of knowledge, understanding of concepts, inter-relationship of various concepts and ideas etc. This type of learning is 90% emphasized in the classroom. Here only mind is brought into action. When this type of learning is well developed, a learner is able to generalize and evaluate concepts as well as personal experiences.

2. **Attitudinal learning :** Attitudes, values and social systems are also learnt by the individual. This type of learning begins with the feeling of belongingness of a person to his group. How a person should react to others in various types of emotional situations is the result of this type of learning.

3. **Skill learning and habit formation :** Motor behaviour of the individual along with feeling is involved here. Practice is an important aspect of this type of learning. Reading, writing, playing a certain game or doing some physical job with perfection is the result of this type of learning.

(C) Gagne's classification of learning

Gagne has classified learning into eight categories in a hierarchical order as given below.

1. **Signal learning :** This is called classical conditioning learning developed by Russian psychologist Pavlov. In this learning unconditioning stimulus (food) and conditioned stimulus, (sound of the bell are paired together and presented to a dog a number of times. Due to this paring sound of the bell (conditioned) stimulus also forces the dog to elicit the response (to salivate) This secretion of saliva by the sound of the bell is called conditioning. Sound of the bell works as signal here.

2. **Stimulus-response learning (operant conditioning) :** This study of operant conditioning started with the work of E.L. Thorndike He placed a hungry cat in a box and dish of food was kept outside. When cat manipulated the lever of the box correctly, it opened and cat could get food. Here manipulation of lever as a response is instrumental in producing the reward (food) here hence, this learning is also called instrumental conditioning. Instrumental conditioning is more flexible than classical one in the sense that responses are conditioned here to a variety of efforts. Such experiments were conducted and improved further by Skinner to explain operant nature of behaviour in a set form with the help of reinforcement.

3. **Chain learning :** Chaining means connection between S-R is formed in sequence Chaining is of two types, motor and verbal. Using remote controller to switch on or off a T V is an example of motor sequence and greeting a guest at home is an example of verbal sequence.

In verbal chaining, two or more previously learned verbal sequences in stimulus response form are chained. If first member or the second member word of the sequence comes, the other member will automatically come, such as mummy daddy, chhola bhatora, old, young etc. Opposite words are also used in the sequence to form a chain.

In motor chaining, a number of related activities are tied in such a sequence that one activity will necessarily be followed by the other. Driving a car or weaving cloth on a handloom are best examples of motor chain. The driver of a car comes to the next activity taking the gear into neutral position immediately after applying the brakes. This second activity is chained in a sequence.

It must be noted here that a chain can not be established unless the organism is capable of linking various acts in a sequence.

4. **Verbal associate learning :** In this type of learning verbal language is also used along with showing an object, ie, seeing is associated with a word. For example, we show an object to a child and say that it is monkey. Next time when the child will see an object exactly or almost similar to the object previously seen by him, he will name it as monkey.

Two types of chaining are involved here:

(i) Observing S-R connection that connects the appearance of the object and distinguishes it from other objects, i.e., the child distinguishes the object before him from the other objects not similar to it.

(ii) When object is clearly distinguished from the other objects it becomes next stimulus for the child and when the child say it is monkey, it is the second response. Thus, a connection between S-R is formed

In order to make this type of learning a success, the following points must be kept in mind:

(i) Verbal units must be presented in a proper sequence, *i.e.*, one chain must come after the other and the whole chain at a time.

(ii) Learner must be active enough to make responses required by every chain.

(iii) Cues may be used to facilitate verbal association.

(iv) Span of retention power of the individual determines the length of the chain. There is however, a limit of these verbal chains. Unlimited number of chains can not be retained at all.

(v) There must be provision for the confirmation of correct responses in the learning situation.

5. **Learning by discrimination :** When specific behaviour is shown to only one given stimulus and other stimuli are totally excluded it is called discrimination. This type of learning is seen from the beginning of life of the organism. An infant does not consider all women having breast or feeding him by their breast as mothers. Only one out of so many is her mother and that is well discriminated. The child discriminates a feeding bottle and other bottles, the child of the home and the child outside the home etc. thus, a relatively higher mental operation is involved in discrimination.

The concept opposite to discrimination is generalization. When after conditioning to a particular stimulus, other similar stimuli also cause to elicit same response, the process is called stimulus generalization. The point to be noted here is that without perfection in stimulus generalization, nobody will be able to learn by discrimination.

Fine discrimination takes place only out of the process of stimulus generalization. Initially the infant accepts every woman as mummy but when he does not get required response from every one, he narrows down the spirit of generalization and recognizes his real mummy on the basis of her responses.

Discrimination is also not similar to the word of differentiation. In discrimination, emphasis is placed on stimulus side, but in differentiation, emphasis is placed on the response side. In discrimination, we eliminate the unwanted responses to the other stimuli through selective reinforcement but in differenciation, we develop a very specific type of response on the basis of the stimuli presented through selective reinforcement after examining a number of related responses too.

6. **Concept learning :** Concept is developed on the basis of common characteristics of an object. When we identify an object or an idea on the basis of its common properties, which a class of objects share in common not specific to other objects or ideas, it is called concept learning. The properties of shape, size, colour, form, nature etc are used to discriminate an object from other objects of the same class. For example, trees are many but the concept of a mango tree is applied to a tree which has some very specific property.

Concept learning is the pre-requisite for learning a law or principle. Learning of abstract concept is more difficult than concrete concepts ;because discrimination is done here on the basis of ideation only.

7. **Learning of principles :** Learning of principles or laws takes place only after concept learning. It is because regular and constant relationship between two or more concepts is established in a principle. Knowledge of so many principles and laws are necessary to function properly in the environment and to save our time in repeated experimentations. Most of the learning obtained in schools is concentrated to laws, principles, systems etc.

8. **Problem solving :** It is the highest stage of learning in the hierarchy. When an individual has learned all laws and principles, he evaluates them from the point of view of utility or facticity. This evaluation helps him to solve various problems of life.

IMPORTANCE OF LEANING FOR TEACHERS

Learning is important for a teacher in the following ways:

1. A teacher can adopt learning centred approach of teaching such as, activity programme, project method, problem solving method etc., and avoid teaching centred approach. Former is autonomous process and later is a burden on students.
2. A teacher can use the whole and part learning methods alternately to benefit the poor and talented students equally in the class.
3. Verbalization on the part of the teacher along with other motor activity can explain and clarify the concepts and remove the difficulties of students. Cue is also used by the teacher in the class.
4. A teacher will not bank upon memorization from the very beginning of teaching. Desired change of behaviour is not related to memorization,
5. A teacher can keep the maturity level and inborn capacity of students in mind for effective learning.
6. A teacher can provide varied experiences to students in such a way that they can identify similarities and differences in objects, situations and concepts. This approach of learning will facilitate learning in the class.
7. The primary objective of schooling is to bring about desirable changes in the behaviour of learners through the process of learning. A teacher must know all these approaches and operations of learning and their relative significance. A teacher can adopt a better teaching strategy in the class only after knowing different approaches and operations of teaching.
8. A teacher can accommodate his teaching according to the individual differences of students only after knowing the process and theories of learning.
9. An important contribution of leaning psychology is that it has propounded and popularized the concept of motivation and its uses on scientific lines. We are now in a better position to use different techniques to motivate the students for verbal, mental or motor activity. The teacher can motivate the students in the class according to their age levels.
10. A teacher can know various procedures of remembering and forgetting and he can utilize various techniques of learning to minimize the share of forgetting in the class. He can help the students to transfer skills and informations acquired in the classroom to daily life situations outside the school and vice versa.
11. Modern psychology of learning lays much stree on social psychology of leaning and group dynamics. A teacher can improve social learning environment of the class by putting various theories and procedures of learning into practice.

THEORIES OF LEARNING

We may categories all these theories of learning into two groups.

1. Laboratory psychologists' theories of association or connection (S-R theories)
2. Cognitive field theories or gestalt psychology of learning. S-R theories of learning can further be classified into two categories as under

(A) S-R theories without Reinforcement	(B) S-R theories with reinforcement
1. Pavlov's conditioning theory	Thorndike's theory
2. Watson's learning theory	Hull's theory
3. Guthrie's learning theory	Skinner's theory

As far as field theories are concerned there are three important theories which are given below:

1. Gestalt theory of learning
2. Lewin's theory of leaning
3. Tolman's sign gestalt theory of learning

HOW CHILDREN THINK AND LEARN

Children learn from anything and everything they see and act upon. They have learnt a lot before they join school, and they continue to learn outside the school hours. If we believe that children learn only in school, it is because of what we wrongly regard as learning. When a child spends hours on trying to solve a Jigsaw puzzle (say), he/she is often reprimanded by adults for wasting study time. Little do the grown-ups realise that it is through such interesting games that this child may be increasing his/her understanding of shapes and size. And, this learning is taking place outside the school hours, without formal instruction. A curriculum built upon assumptions about children's learning, that ignore this aspect, is also responsible for children losing interest in mathematics or in any formal learning.

From the time a child is born, his/her interaction with the world around his/her starts. He/she perceives things around his/her, and gradually makes sense of them. He/she slowly begins to recognise people and objects, relate more and more to the environment, and observe things through the senses of touch, sight, taste, smell and sound. There are **four different stages** of learning or development that each child goes through.

Sensorimotor

This is from the ages of birth to about two years old. During this time the child's primary mode of learning occurs through the five senses. He/she learns to experience environment. The child touches things, holds, looks, listens, tastes, feels, bangs, and shakes everything in sight. When the child adds motor skills such as creeping, crawling and walking, his/her environment expands by leaps and bounds. The child is now exploring their environment with both senses and the ability to get around.

Preoperational

This is the stages between ages two and seven. During this stage the child is busy gathering information or learning, and then trying to figure out ways that they can used what they have learned to begin solving problems.

During this stage of his/her life child will be thinking in specifics and will find it very difficult to get generalise anything. This is the time when a child learns by asking questions. The child generally will not want a real answer to his question at this point. When he asks why do we have grass .... He simply wants to know that it is for him to play in. No technical answers for know. The child in this age group judges everything on the 'me' basis—How does it affect me? Do I like it?

Concrete Operations Period

This is the period of time when child is between the ages of seven to ten. This is a wonderful age as this is when children begin to manipulate data mentally. They take the information at hand and begin to define, compare and contrast it. They, however, still think concretely.

The concrete operational child is capable of logical thought. This child still learns through their senses, but no longer relies on only them to teach him. He now thinks as well. A good teacher for this age group would start each lesson at a concrete level and then more toward a generalised level. The child, during this period, is very literal in their thinking.

Formal Operations Period

The period begins at about age eleven. At this time the child will break through the barrier of literalism and more on to thinking in more abstract terms. He no longer restricts thinking to time and space. This child now starts to reflect, hypothesize and theorize. In the formal operation period, children need to develop cognitive abilities. The following is a list of six simple categories of cognitive abilities. The following is a list of six simple categories of cognitive abilities:

1. **Knowledge of facts and principals:** This is the direct recall of facts and principals. **Examples:** memorisation of dates, name, definition, vocabulary words.
2. **Comprehension:** Understanding of facts and ideas.
3. **Application:** Needs to know, rules, principles, and procedures and how to use them.
4. **Analysis:** Breaking down concepts into parts.
5. **Synthesis:** Putting together information or ideas.
6. **Evaluation:** Judging the value of information.

BASIC PROCESSES OF TEACHING AND LEARNING

Teaching-learning process is the heart of education. On it depends the fulfilment of the aims & objectives of education. It is the most powerful instrument of education to bring about desired changes in the students. Teaching learning are related terms. In teaching-learning process, the teacher, the learner, the curriculum & other variables are organised in a systematic way to attain some pre-determined goal.

Essential Aspects of the Teaching-learning Process

According to Diana Laurillard, there are four aspects of the teaching-learning process:

1. **Discussion**—between the teacher and learner.
2. **Interaction**—between the learner and some aspect of the world defined by the teacher.
3. **Adaptation**—of the world by the teacher and action by the learner.
4. **Reflection**—on the learner's performance by both teacher and learner.

According to **Burton** in the figure above

1. Teaching can become effective only by relating it to process of learning.
2. Teaching objective cannot be realised without being related to learning situation.
3. We may create and use teaching aids to create some appropriate learning situation.
4. The strategies and devices of teaching may be selected in such a manner that the optimal objectives of learning area achieved.
5. To understand principles, goals, objectives of education in right perspective.
6. Appropriate learning situation condition may be created for congenial and effective teaching.

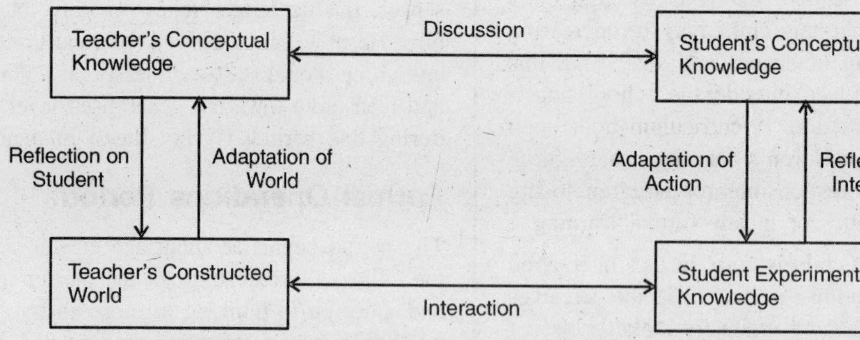

Fig. 1: *Essential aspects of the ideal teaching-learning process*

Approaches to Learning Theories

Aspect	Behaviourist	Cognitivist	Humanist
Learning theorists	Thorndike, Pavlov, Watson, Guthrie, Hull, Tolman, Skinner	Koffka, Kohler, Lewin, Piaget, Ausubel, Bruner, Gagne	Maslow, Rogers
View of the learning process	Change in behaviour	Internal mental process (including insight, information processing, memory, perception)	A personal act to fulfil potential
Locus of learning	Stimuli in external environment	Internal cognitive structuring	Affective and cognitive needs
Purpose in education	Produce behavioural change in desired direction	Develop capacity and skills to learn better	Become self-actualized autonomous
Educator's role	Arranges environment to elicit desired response	Structures content of learning activity	Facilitates development of the whole person
Manifestations in adult learning	Behavioural objectives	Cognitive development	Andragogy
	Competency-based education	Intelligence, learning and memory as function of age	Self-directed learning
	Skill development and training	Learning how to learn	

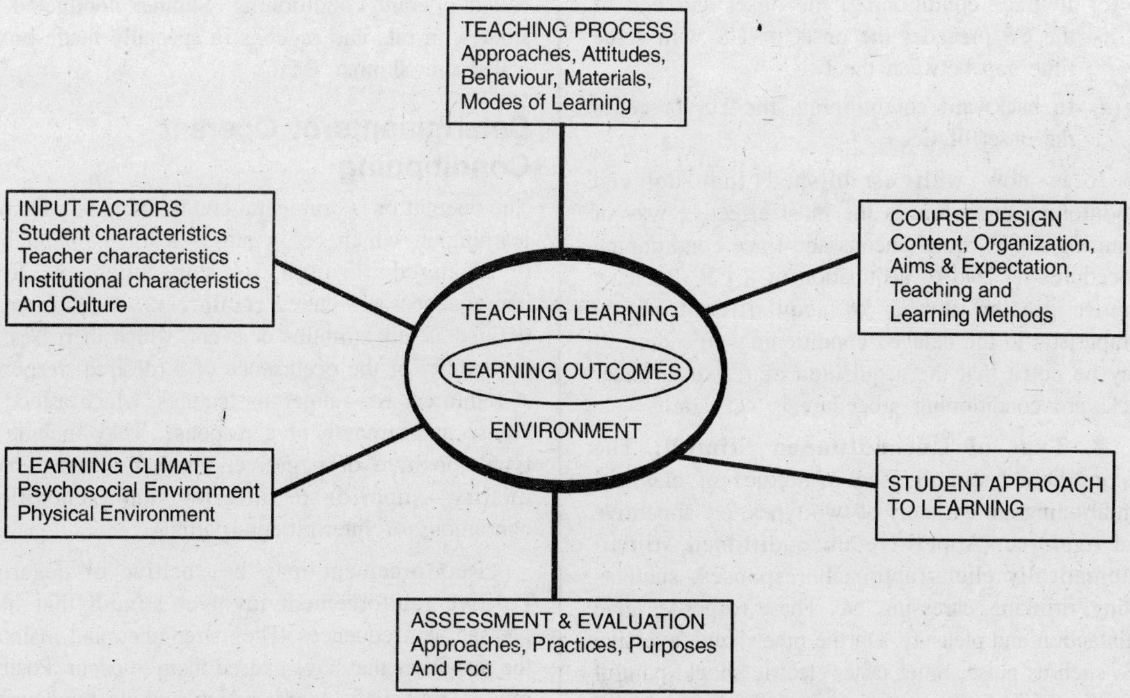

Fig. 2: *Teaching-Learning Environment*

PARADIGMS OF LEARNING

Learning takes place in many ways. There are some methods that are used in acquisition of simple responses while other methods are used in the acquisition of complex responses. The simplest kind of learning is called conditioning. Two types of conditioning have been identified. The first one is called classical conditioning and the second instrumental/operant conditioning. In addition, we have observational learning, cognitive learning, verbal learning, concept learning and skill learning.

Classical Conditioning

This type of learning was first investigated by Ivan P. Pavlov. Like many great scientific advances, classical conditioning was discovered accidentally. The nineteenth-century Russian physiologist Ivan Pavlov was looking at salivation in dogs in response to being fed, when he noticed that his dogs would begin to salivate whenever he entered the room, even when he was not bringing them food. However, when Pavlov discovered that any object or event which the dogs learnt to associate with food (such as the food bowl) would trigger the same response, he realised that he had made an important scientific discovery, and he devoted the rest of his career to studying this type of learning.

Classical conditioning is 'classical' in that it is the first systematic study of basic laws of learning. Classical conditioning involves learning to associate an unconditioned stimulus that already brings about a particular response (*i.e.* a reflex) with a new (conditioned) stimulus, so that the new stimulus brings about the same response. The unconditioned stimulus (or UCS) is the object or event that originally produces the reflexive/natural response.

Once the neutral stimulus has become associated with the unconditioned stimulus, it becomes a conditioned stimulus (CS). The conditioned response (CR) is the response to the conditioned stimulus. Thus, learning situation in classical conditioning is one of S-S learning in which one stimulus becomes a signal of another stimulus.

Determinants of Classical Conditioning

How quickly and strongly acquisition of a response occurs in classical conditioning depends on several factors. Some of the major factors influencing learning a CR are described below:

1. Time Relations between Stimuli: The classical conditioning procedures, discussed below, are basically of four types based on the time relations between the onset of conditioned stimulus (CS) and unconditioned stimulus (US). The first three are called forward conditioning procedures, and the fourth one is called backward conditioning procedure. The basic experimental arrangements of these procedures are as follows:

(*a*) When the CS and US are presented together, it is called simultaneous conditioning.

(*b*) In delayed conditioning, the onset of CS precedes the onset of US. The CS ends before the end of the US.

(*c*) In trace conditioning, the onset and end of the CS precedes the onset of US with some time gap between the two.

(*d*) In backward conditioning, the US precedes the onset of CS.

It is now well established that delayed conditioning procedure is the most effective way of acquiring a CR. Simultaneous and trace conditioning procedures do lead to acquisition of a CR, but they require greater number of acquisition trials in comparison to the delayed conditioning procedure. It may be noted that the acquisition of response under backward conditioning procedure is very rare.

2. Type of Unconditioned Stimuli: The unconditioned stimuli used in studies of classical conditioning are basically of two types, *i.e.* appetitive and aversive. Appetitive unconditioned stimuli automatically elicits approach responses, such as eating, drinking, caressing, etc. These responses give satisfaction and pleasure. On the other hand, aversive US, such as noise, bitter taste, electric shock, painful injections, etc. are painful, harmful, and elicit avoidance and escape responses. It has been found that appetitive classical conditioning is slower and requires greater number of acquisition trials, but aversive classical conditioning is established in one, two or three trials depending on the intensity of the aversive US.

3. Intensity of Conditioned Stimuli: This influences the course of both appetitive and aversive classical conditioning. More intense conditioned stimuli are more effective in accelerating the acquisition of conditioned responses. It means that the more intense the conditioned stimulus, the fewer are the number of acquisition trials needed for conditioning.

Operant/Instrumental Conditioning

B.F. Skinner is regarded as the father of operant conditioning, but his work was based on **Thorndike's law of effect.** In the late nineteenth century, psychologist Edward Thorndike proposed the law of effect. The law of effect states that any behaviour that has good consequences will tend to be repeated, and any behaviour that has bad consequences will tend to be avoided. In the 1930s, B.F. Skinner, extended this idea and began to study operant conditioning. Operant conditioning is a type of learning in which responses come to be controlled by their consequences.

Operants are those behaviours or responses, which are emitted by animals and human beings voluntarily and are under their control. The term operant is used because the organism operates on the environment. Conditioning of operant behaviour is called operant conditioning. Skinner conducted his studies on rats and pigeons in specially made boxes, called the Skinner Box.

Determinants of Operant Conditioning

The operant or instrumental conditioning is a form of learning in which behaviour is learned, maintained or changed through its consequences. Such consequences are called **reinforcers**. A reinforcer is defined as any stimulus or event, which increases the probability of the occurrence of a (desired) response. A reinforcer has numerous features, which affect the course and strength of a response. They include its type—positive or negative, number or frequency, quality—superior or inferior, and schedule—continuous or intermittent (partial).

Reinforcement may be positive or negative. Positive reinforcement involves stimuli that have pleasant consequences. They strengthen and maintain the responses that have caused them to occur. Positive reinforcers satisfy needs, which include food, water, medals, praise, money, status, information, etc. Negative reinforcers involve unpleasant and painful stimuli. Responses that lead organisms to get rid of painful stimuli or avoid and escape from them provide negative reinforcement. Thus, negative reinforcement leads to learning of avoidance and escape responses. For instance, one learns to put on woollen clothes, burn firewood or use electric heaters to avoid the unpleasant cold weather. One learns to move away from dangerous stimuli because they provide negative reinforcement. It may be noted that negative reinforcement is not punishment. Use of punishment reduces or suppresses the response while a negative reinforcer increases the probability of avoidance or escape response. For instance, drivers and co-drivers wear their seat belts to avoid getting injured in case of an accident or to avoid being fined by the traffic police.

Classical and Operant Conditioning : Differences

1. In classical conditioning, the responses are under the control of some stimulus because they are reflexes, automatically elicited by the appropriate stimuli. Such stimuli are selected as US and responses elicited by them as UR. Thus Pavlovian conditioning, in which US elicits responses, is often called respondent conditioning.

   In instrumental conditioning, responses are under the control of the organism and are voluntary responses or 'operants'. Thus, in the two forms of conditioning different types of responses are conditioned.

2. In classical conditioning, the CS and US are well-defined, but in operant conditioning CS is not defined. It can be inferred but is not directly known.
3. In classical conditioning, the experimenter controls the occurrence of US, while in operant conditioning the occurrence of the reinforcer is under the control of the organism that is learning. Thus, for US in classical conditioning the organism remains passive, while in operant conditioning the subject has to be active in order to be reinforced.
4. In the two forms of conditioning, the technical terms used to characterise the experimental proceedings are different. Moreover what is called reinforcer in operant conditioning is called US in classical conditioning. An US has two functions. In the beginning, it elicits the response and also reinforces the response to be associated and elicited later on by the CS.

OBSERVATIONAL LEARNING

The other form of learning takes place by observing others. Earlier this form of learning was called **imitation**. Bandura and his colleagues in a series of experimental studies investigated observational learning in detail. In this kind of learning, human beings learn social behaviours, therefore, it is sometimes called **social learning**. In many situations individuals do not know how to behave. They observe others and emulate their behaviour. This form of learning is called **modelling**.

Examples of observational learning abound in our social life. Fashion designers employ tall, pretty, and gracious young girls and tall, smart, and well-built young boys for popularising clothes of different designs and fabrics. People observe them on televised fashion shows and advertisements in magazines and newspapers. They imitate these models. Observing superiors and likeable persons and then emulating their behaviour in a novel social situation is a common experience.

The children observe adults' behaviours, at home and during social ceremonies and functions. They enact adults in their plays and games. For instance, young children play games of marriage ceremonies, birthday parties, thief and policeman, house keeping, etc. Actually they enact in their games what they observe in society, on television, and read in books.

Children learn most of the social behaviours by observing and emulating adults. The way to put on clothes, dress one's hair, and conduct oneself in society are learned through observing others. It has also been shown that children learn and develop various personality characteristics through observational learning. Aggressiveness, prosocial behaviour, courtesy, politeness, diligence, and indolence are acquired by this method of learning.

COGNITIVE LEARNING

Some psychologists view learning in terms of cognitive processes that underlie it. They have developed approaches that focus on such processes that occur during learning rather than concentrating solely on S-R and S-S connections. Thus, in cognitive learning, there is a change in what the learner knows rather than what he/she does. This form of learning shows up in insight learning and latent learning.

Insight Learning

Kohler demonstrated a model of learning which could not be readily explained by conditioning. He performed a series of experiments with chimpanzees that involved solving complex problems. Kohler placed chimpanzees in an enclosed play area where food was kept out of their reach. Tools such as poles and boxes were placed in the enclosure. The chimpanzees rapidly learned how to use a box to stand on or a pole to move the food in their direction. In this experiment, learning did not occur as a result of trial and error and reinforcement, but came about in sudden flashes of insight. The chimpanzees would roam about the enclosure for some time and then suddenly would stand on a box, grab a pole and strike a banana, which was out of normal reach above the enclosure. The chimpanzee exhibited what Kohler called insight learning—the process by which the solution to a problem suddenly becomes clear.

In a normal experiment on insight learning, a problem is presented, followed by a period of time when no apparent progress is made and finally a solution suddenly emerges. In insight learning, sudden solution is the rule. Once the solution has appeared, it can be repeated immediately the next time the problem is confronted. Thus, it is clear that what is learned is not a specific set of conditioned associations between stimuli and responses but a cognitive relationship between a means and an end. As a result, insight learning can be generalised to other similar problem situations.

Latent Learning

Another type of cognitive learning is known as latent learning. In latent learning, a new behaviour is learned but not demonstrated until reinforcement is provided for displaying it. Tolman made an early contribution to the concept of latent learning. To have an idea of latent learning, we may briefly understand his experiment. Tolman put two groups of rats in a maze and gave them an opportunity to explore. In one group, rats found food at the end of the maze and soon learned to make their way rapidly through the maze. On the other hand, rats in the second group were not rewarded and showed no apparent signs of learning. But later, when these rats were reinforced, they ran through the maze as efficiently as the rewarded group.

Tolman contended that the unrewarded rats had learned the layout of the maze early in their explorations. They just never displayed their latent learning until the reinforcement was provided. Instead, the rats developed a cognitive map of the maze, *i.e.* a mental representation of the spatial locations and directions, which they needed to reach their goal.

LEARNING AS A SOCIAL ACTIVITY

Learning is a social activity. Our learning is intimately associated with our connection with other human beings, our teachers, our peers, our family as well as casual acquaintances, including the people before us or next to us. We are more likely to be successful in our efforts to educate, if we recognise this principle rather than try to avoid it. Much of traditional education, as Dewey pointed out, is directed towards isolating the learner from all social interaction, and towards seeing education as a one-on-one relationship between the learner and the objective material to be learned. In contrast, progressive education (to continue to use Dewey's formulation) recognizes the social aspect of learning and uses conversations interaction with others, and the application of knowledge as an integral aspect of learning.

SOCIAL CONTEXT OF LEARNING

Social Learning theory

Social learning theory focuses on the learning that occurs within a social context. It considers that people learn from one another, including such concepts as observational learning, imitation, and modelling. Among others **Albert Bandura** is considered the leading proponent of this theory.

General Principles of Social Learning Theory Follows:

1. People can learn by observing the behaviour is of others and the outcomes of those behaviours.
2. Learning can occur without a change in behaviour. Behaviourists say that learning has to be represented by a permanent change in behaviour, in contrast social learning theorists say that because people can learn through observation alone, their learning may not necessarily be shown in their performance. Learning may or may not result in a behaviour change.
3. Cognition plays a role in learning. Over the last 40 years social learning theory has become increasingly cognitive in its interpretation of human learning. Awareness and expectations of future reinforcements or punishments can have a major effect on the behaviours that people exhibit.
4. Social learning theory can be considered a bridge or a transition between behaviourist learning theories and cognitive learning theories.

How the Environment Reinforces and Punishes Modelling:

People are often reinforced for modelling the behaviour of others. Bandura suggested that the environment also reinforces modelling. This is in several possible ways:

1. The observer is reinforced by the model. For example, a student who changes dress to fit in with a certain group of students has a strong likelihood of being accepted and thus reinforced by that group.
2. The observer is reinforced by a third person. The observer might be modelling the actions of someone else, for example, an outstanding class leader or student. The teacher notices this and compliments and praises the observer for modelling such behaviour thus reinforcing that behaviour.
3. The imitated behaviour itself leads to reinforcing consequences. Many behaviours that we learn from others produce satisfying or reinforcing results. For example, a student in my multimedia class could observe how the extra work a classmate does is fun. This student in turn would do the same extra work and also receive enjoyment.
4. Consequences of the model's behaviour affect the observers behaviour vicariously. This is known as vicarious reinforcement. This is where in the model is reinforced for a response and then the observer shows an increase in that same response. Bandura illustrated this by having students watch a film of a model hitting a inflated clown doll. One group of children saw the model being praised for such action. Without being reinforced, the group of children began to also hit the doll.

Contemporary Social Learning Perspective of Reinforcement and Punishment

1. Contemporary theory proposes that both reinforcement and punishment have indirect effects on learning. They are not the sole or main cause.
2. Reinforcement and punishment influence the extent to which an individual exhibits a behaviour that has been learned.
3. The expectation of reinforcement influences cognitive processes that promote learning. Therefore, attention pays a critical role in learning. And attention is influenced by the expectation of reinforcement. An example would be, where the teacher tells a group of students that what they will study next is not on the test. Students will not pay attention, because they do not expect to know the information for a test.

Cognitive Factors in Social Learning

Social learning theory has cognitive factors as well as behaviourist factors (actually operant factors).

1. **Learning without performance:** Bandura makes a distinction between learning through observation and the actual imitation of what has been learned.
2. **Cognitive processing during learning:** Social learning theorists contend that attention is a critical factor in learning.
3. **Expectations:** As a result of being reinforced, people form expectations about the consequences that future behaviours are likely to bring. They expect certain behaviours to bring reinforcements and others to bring punishment. The learner needs to be aware however, of the response reinforcements and response punishment. Reinforcement increases a response only when the learner is aware of that connection.
4. **Reciprocal causation:** Bandura proposed that behaviour can influence both the environment and the person. In fact each of these three variables, the person, the behaviour, and the environment can have an influence on each other.
5. **Modelling:** There are different types of models. There is the live model, and actual person demonstrating the behaviour. There can also be a symbolic model, which can be a person or action portrayed in some other medium, such as television, videotape, computer programs.

Behaviours that can be learned through modelling:

Many behaviours can be learned, at least partly, through modelling. Examples that can be cited are, students can watch parents read, students can watch the demonstrations of mathematics problems, or seen someone acting bravely and a fearful situation. Aggression can be learned through models. Much research indicate that children become more aggressive when they observed aggressive or violent models. Moral thinking and moral behaviour are influenced by observation and modelling. This includes moral judgments regarding right and wrong which can in part, develop through modelling.

Conditions Necessary for Effective Modelling to Occur:

Bandura mentions four conditions that are necessary before an individual can successfully model the behaviour of someone else:

1. **Attention:** the person must first pay attention to the model.
2. **Retention:** the observer must be able to remember the behaviour that has been observed. One way of increasing this is using the technique of rehearsal.
3. **Motor reproduction:** the third condition is the ability to replicate the behaviour that the model has just demonstrated. This means that the observer has to be able to replicate the action, which could be a problem with a learner who is not ready developmentally to replicate the action. For example, little children have difficulty doing complex physical motion.
4. **Motivation:** the final necessary ingredient for modelling to occur is motivation, learners must want to demonstrate what they have learned. Remember that since these four conditions vary among individuals, different people will reproduce the same behaviour differently.

Effects of Modelling on Behaviour:

Modelling teaches new behaviours.

Modelling influences the frequency of previously learned behaviours.

Modelling may encourage previously forbidden behaviours.

Modelling increases the frequency of similar behaviours. For example, a student might see a friend excel in basketball and he tries to excel in football because he is not tall enough for basketball.

Educational implications of social learning theory:

Social learning theory has numerous implications for classroom use.

1. Students often learn a great deal simply by observing other people.
2. Describing the consequences of behaviour is can effectively increase the appropriate behaviours and decrease inappropriate ones. This can involve discussing with learners about the rewards and consequences of various behaviours.
3. Modelling provides an alternative to shaping for teaching new behaviours. Instead of using shaping, which is operant conditioning, modelling can provide a faster, more efficient means for teaching new behaviour. To promote effective modelling a teacher must make sure that the four essential conditions exist; attention, retention, motor reproduction, and motivation.
4. Teachers and parents must model appropriate behaviours and take care that they do not model inappropriate behaviours.
5. Teachers should expose students to a variety of other models. This technique is especially important to break down traditional stereotypes.
6. Students must believe that they are capable of accomplishing school tasks. Thus, it is very important to develop a sense of self-efficacy for students. Teachers can promote such self-efficacy by having students receive confidence-building messages, watch others be successful, and experience success on their own.
7. Teachers should help students set realistic expectations for their academic accomplishments. In general in my class that means making sure that expectations are not set too low. I want to realistically challenge my students. However, sometimes the task is beyond a student's ability, example would be the cancer group.
8. Self-regulation techniques provide an effective method for improving student behaviour.

PLANNING FOR PROBLEM SOLVING

A curriculum that accommodates a variety of developmental levels as well as individual differences in young children sets the stage for problem solving. Choices, decision-making, and a curriculum framework that integrates learning, such as Katz and Chard's project method, are especially appropriate for young learners. The project approach facilitates cooperative learning and promotes diverse ideas. Donna Ogle's K-W-L (what you KNOW, what you WANT to know, and what you have LEARNED) is another method of organizing work that promotes problem solving. Themes, units, webbing, and the KWL method are all ways of organizing curriculum that can support problem solving. Beginning with the needs and interests of the children, problem solving develops from meaningful experiences important to the children. The teacher-designed curriculum provides the classroom basis for these experiences.

For example, a second grade investigation of waste materials from a classroom led one group of young children to explore the topic in an integrated way. Reading, writing, counting, measuring, interviews of community people, and science experiments were planned, initiated and reported. Solutions to many problems posed during the investigation were tried out and some were found to be successful. Through group work, individuals were able to participate and communicate as cognitive and social needs were met. Each child, at individual levels and in individual ways, was successful within the group experience. Problem solving empowers children.

Providing for Problem Solving

Problem solving is a skill that can be learned and must be practiced. It is facilitated by a classroom schedule that provides for integrated learning in large blocks of time, space for ongoing group projects, and many open-ended materials. The teacher provides the time, space, and materials necessary for in-depth learning.

1. Time: Teachers can provide for problem solving by enlarging blocks of learning time during the school day. Because making choices, discussing decisions, and evaluating mistakes takes time, large time blocks best suit the problem-solving process. It is important that children know they have time to identify and solve problems.

2. Space: Projects and group meetings may require an assessment of classroom space. Moving desks and tables together facilitates communication and cooperation in the classroom. Once the teacher has observed the patterns of traffic in the classroom, equipment can be moved or eliminated to promote problem solving.

3. Materials: The open-ended materials that are needed for the construction and concrete solving of problems should be safe, durable, and varied. Well-marked storage units should be easily accessible to children, and materials should be available for ongoing exploration and manipulation. Access to a variety of materials encourages children to use materials in new and diverse ways. This freedom promotes problem solving.

The Problem-Solving Model

Individuals or groups can solve problems. Group problem solving is important to young children because many diverse ideas are generated. Both individual and group processes should be included in the early childhood classroom. Becoming skillful at problem solving is based on the understanding and use of sequenced steps. These steps are:

1. Identifying the problem,
2. Brainstorming a variety of solutions,
3. Choosing one solution and trying it out, and
4. Evaluating what has happened.

Choosing Good Problems

Goffin provides teachers with guiding questions that will help them identify appropriate problems for young children. Some of these are:

1. Is the problem meaningful and interesting?
2. Can the problem be solved at a variety of levels?
3. Must a new decision be made?
4. Can the actions be evaluated?

Problem solving is a way to make sense of the environment and, in fact, control it. The process allows children in an increasingly diverse world to be active participants and to implement changes. By including problem solving in the early childhood classroom, we equip children with a life-long skill that is useful in all areas of learning.

Obstacles to Solving Problems

Two major obstacles to solving a problem are mental set and lack of motivation.

Mental Set

Mental set is a tendency of a person to solve problems by following already tried mental operations or steps. Prior success with a particular strategy would sometimes help in solving a new problem. However, this tendency also creates a mental rigidity that obstructs the problem solver to think of any new rules or strategies. Thus, while in some situations mental set can enhance the quality and speed of problem solving, in other situations it hinders problem solving. You might have experienced this while solving mathematical problems. After completing a couple of questions, you form an idea of the steps that are required to solve these questions and subsequently you go on following the same steps, until a point where you fail. At this point you may experience difficulty in avoiding the already used steps. Those steps would interfere in your thought for new strategies. However, in day-to-day activities we often rely on past experiences with similar or related problems.

Like mental set, **functional fixedness** in problem solving occurs when people fail to solve a problem because they are fixed on a thing's usual function. If you have ever used a hardbound book to hammer a nail, then you have overcome functional fixedness.

Lack of Motivation

People might be great at solving problems, but all their skills and talents are of no use if they are not motivated. Sometimes people give up easily when they encounter a problem or failure in implementing the first step. Therefore, there is a need to persist in their effort to find a solution.

ALTERNATIVE CONCEPTIONS OF LEARNING

When teachers provide instruction on concepts in various subjects, they are teaching students who already have some pre-instructional knowledge about the topic. Student knowledge, however, can be erroneous, illogical or misinformed. These erroneous understandings are termed alternative conceptions or misconceptions (or intuitive theories). Alternative conceptions (misconceptions) are not unusual. In fact, they are a normal part of the learning process. We quite naturally form ideas from our everyday experience, but obviously not all the ideas we develop are correct with respect to the most current evidence and scholarship in a given discipline. Moreover, some concepts in different content areas are simply very difficult to grasp. They may be very abstract, counterintuitive or quite complex. Hence, our understanding of them is flawed. In addition, things we have already learned are sometimes unhelpful in learning new concepts/theories. This occurs when the new concept or theory is inconsistent with previously learned material. Accordingly, as noted, it is very typical for students (and adults) to have misconceptions in different domains (content knowledge areas). Indeed, researchers have found that there is a common set of alternative conceptions (misconceptions) that most students typically exhibit. There is one class of alternative theories (or misconceptions) that is very deeply entrenched. These are "ontological misconceptions," which relate to ontological beliefs (*i.e.*, beliefs about the fundamental categories and properties of the world).

Alternative conceptions (misconceptions) can impede learning for several reasons. First, students generally are unaware that the knowledge they have is wrong. Moreover, misconceptions can be very entrenched in student thinking. In addition, new experiences are interpreted through these erroneous understandings, thereby interfering with being able to correctly grasp new information. Also, alternative conceptions (misconceptions) tend to be very resistant to instruction because learning entails replacing or radically reorganizing student knowledge. Hence, conceptual change has to occur for learning to happen. This puts teachers in the very challenging position of needing to bring about significant conceptual change in student knowledge. Generally, ordinary forms of instruction, such as lectures, labs, discovery learning, or simply reading texts, are not very successful at overcoming student misconceptions. For all these reasons, misconceptions can be hard nuts for teachers to crack. However, several instructional strategies have been found to be effective in achieving conceptual change and helping students leave their alternative conceptions behind and learn correct concepts or theories.

Instructional strategies that can lead to change in students' alternative conceptions (misconceptions) and to learning of new concepts and theories

1. Present new concepts or theories that you are teaching in such a way that students see as plausible, high-quality, intelligible and generative.
2. Use students' correct conceptions and build on those by creating a bridge of examples to the new concept or theory that students are having trouble learning due to misconceptions they hold.
3. Use model-ased reasoning, which helps students construct new representations that vary from their intuitive theories.
4. Use diverse instruction, wherein you present a few examples that challenge multiple assumptions, rather than a larger number of examples that challenge just one assumption.
5. Help students become aware of (raise student metacognition about) their own alternative conceptions (misconceptions).
6. Present students with experiences that cause cognitive conflict in students' minds. Experiences (as in strategy 3 above) that can cause cognitive conflict are ones that get students to consider their erroneous (misconception) knowledge side-by-side with, or at the same time as, the correct concept or theory.
7. Engage in Interactive Conceptual Instruction (ICI).
8. Develop students' epistemological thinking, which incorporates beliefs and theories about the nature of knowledge and the nature of learning, in ways that will facilitate conceptual change. The more naive students' beliefs are about knowledge and learning, the less likely they are to revise their misconceptions.
9. Help students "self-repair" their misconceptions.
10. Once students have overcome their alternative conceptions (misconceptions).

Presenting new concepts or theories

In presenting new concepts or theories, teachers should be sure to show these theories or concepts as:

1. Plausible: The new information should be shown to be consistent with other knowledge and able to explain the available data. Learners must see how the new conception (theory) is consistent with other knowledge and a good explanation of the data.

2. High quality: Of course, the theory/concept to be taught is of high quality from a scientific point of view, since it is a correct theory. However, the presented theory should take a better account of the data than what students currently have available to them. For example, the instructor should deal with the problem from the perspective of the students (*e.g.*, students for whom a "flat earth" theory provides a better account of the data available than does a "spherical earth" theory). Hence, the quality of the new theory must be considered along with the kind of data that students know about.

3. Intelligible: Teachers should do what they can to increase the intelligibility of the new theory. Learners must be able to grasp how the new conception works. To increase intelligibility, teachers can use methods such as use of:

(*a*) analogies,

(*b*) models, and

(*c*) direct exposition.

4. Generative/fruitful: Teachers should show that the new concept/theory can be extended to open up new areas of inquiry. Learners must be able to extend the new conception to new areas of inquiry. Teachers might accomplish this by illustrating the application of the new concept/theory to a range of problems. These problems can include familiar ones and new ones.

UNDERSTANDING CHILDREN'S 'ERRORS' AS SIGNIFICANT STEPS IN THE LEARNING PROCESS

The legacy of Jean Piaget to the world of early childhood education is that he fundamentally altered the view of how a child learns. And a teacher, he believed, was more than a transmitter of knowledge she was also an essential observer and guide to helping children build their own knowledge.

As a university graduate, Swiss-born Piaget got a routine job in Paris standardizing Binet-Simon IQ tests, where the emphasis was on children getting the right answers. Piaget observed that many children of the same ages gave the same kinds of incorrect answers. What could be learned from this?

Piaget interviewed many hundreds of children and concluded that children who are allowed to make mistakes often go on to discover their errors and correct them, or find new solutions. In this process, children build their own way of learning. From children's errors, teachers can obtain insights into the child's view of the world and can tell where guidance is needed. They can provide appropriate materials, ask encouraging questions, and allow the child to construct his own knowledge.

Piaget's continued interactions with young children became part of his life-long research. After reading about a child who thought that the sun and moon followed him wherever he went, Piaget wanted to find out if all young children had a similar belief. He found that many did indeed believe this. Piaget went on to explore children's countless "why" questions, such as, "Why is the sun round?" or "Why is grass green?" He concluded that children do not think like adults. Their thought processes have their own distinct order and special logic. Children are not "empty vessels to be filled with knowledge" (as traditional pedagogical theory had it). They are "active builders of knowledge-little scientists who construct their own theories of the world."

COGNITION & EMOTIONS

What is Cognition?

Cognition is the ability to preceive, memorise, reason and understand. These abilities change with age. As the child grows, her thinking becomes more mature and efficient. Therefore, cognition can simply be defined as the process of acquiring, processing, organising and using knowledge. The development of cognition means development of all these abilities. A child's thinking changes as result of both age (maturation) and increased experiences.

Major Cognitive Characteristics of Children

Infancy

It is interesting to see the number of changes that take place in the first two years. Children at this stage are very active learners. Even when it seems the child is only lying and looking at nothing (e.g. 2 month old) she is actually looking at and trying to understand the things around her.

The first two years children begin by exploring their own bodies and move to the outside objects. Children at 2/3 months discover their thumb or hand or occasionally their own foot. These fascinate them they try to play with them. For a two month old a toy is not as satisfying as her/his own thumb in her/his mouth. Gradually, by about six months, children begin to play with objects outside the body. This could be the toy, the sheet, the bottle, etc. Later, by two years they can even indulge in pretend play [example doctor-doctor, house-house, etc.].

What children also achieve by two years is the understanding of object permanance. **Object permanance is the understanding that things exist even if you can not see them.** Let us take an example. If you show a five month old a toy she gets excited. If you hide the toy the child soon forgets that any toy even existed. This is because she thinks out of sight is out of mind. Do the same thing with a 1½ year old and you will find the child is either looking for it or asks you to find it. This is because she knows the toy exists even if she can not see it. This understanding, that things exist even if you can not see them, is called object permanance.

The other major development that happens by two years is that children begin to learn the symbols. What are symbols? A two year old can convey her thoughts and desires through language. All these are essential processes of cognition.

Early Childhood

This is a period when the childs mastery in use of symbols increases. We can observe this in the everyday behaviour and activities of the child, *i.e.* in what she plays, her language etc. Gradually her representations of objects become more flexible and less self centred. A one year old while playing does not need a toy phone to pretend speaking on the phone. She can use any object. This is indicative of flexibility in thinking. Gradually, children also start directing play between dolls, *e.g.,* one doll is the mother and the other doll the child. This is indicative of the child moving away from self to becoming less self centred.

Children at this stage also believe that all objects have feelings like human beings. That is why you will often see the child feeding her teddy bear.

Children at this stage can also focus on only one aspect of a situation and can not go back. Let us now take an example. You offer cola to a 4 yr old in a tall glass. You then change your mind and pour the coke from the tall glass to a short glass and give it to the child. You will find the child will say I want the big glass. This is because she can only focus on one aspect (height) at a time. Also, she is not able to go back mentally and realise that in the process of pouring from big to small glass, no cola was taken away.

Similarly, take two plates and put in one 6 pieces of chocolate spreadout and in the other make a tower of 6 pieces of chocolate. You will find the child thinking the spread out chocolate is more. This is because the child can only focus on one aspect at a time. This limitation seriously restricts the problem solving and logical thinking abilities of the child.

It also indicates the child's inability to understand that another point of view different from her own can exist, *e.g.,* you often find children responding to your question by nodding their heads, even if they are not in the same room as you. This is because they do not see another's point of view.

Middle Childhood

During this period, children begin to understand that another view point can exist. They are also able to focus on more than one aspect of a situation and go back and forth on their thinking. This makes their thinking more logical and efficient. However, children are only comfortable with concrete ideas/objects. It means, something that is real for them, *i.e.,* either something they have seen, *e.g.,* a house or something is in front of them, a plant or something linked to what they know, *e.g.,* blue like the sky. They are not able to think about abstract ideas, *e.g.,* what would happen if everyone could fly?

Emotion

Emotions, put simply, are feelings. In infants we can see these very clearly in the form of joy, anger and fear. These are similar to the emotions that adults have.

1. **The variety of emotions increases with age:** The basic emotions of joy, fear, anger are visible in infants. Gradually, as a sense of self develops; children begin to relate with people around them and value their opinions. Then we can see the emotion like pride, shame, sympathy, guilt also developing in them.
2. **The expression of emotion also changes with age:** Emotions are both innate and learnt. The instinctive response to a stimulus is innate but how to express that feeling is learnt, *e.g.* taking away of a toy makes the child angry (innate) but instead crying she is encouraged to ask for it back (learnt). Frustration tolerance increases with age. As children grow older, their responses change in both as well as instinctive method of expression, *e.g.,* when 2 year old falls downs she cries loudly and later forgets quickly. A 6 year old on the other hand, may not cry but forgets far less easily.
3. **The triggers or cause of emotions change with age:** The stimuli that elicit emotion also change with age, *e.g.,* an infant may cry on hearing the loud explosion of a cracker but a middle childhood child may laugh. Sucking a thumb may give great joy to an infant but provides no pleasure to a child is middle childhood.
4. **The coping techniques change with age:** Methods of coping with frustration and stress change with age. While a younger child may cry, or cling to the adult, an older child is likely to suppress the emotion.

Factors Affecting Emotional Development

If we look round in our environment, we will find that people differ in the emotions they experience and express. Some are happy, some are angry, some moody, some helpful. What then affects our emotional development?

1. **Parenting style:** Democratic parenting where induction is used as a method of disciplining allows for more mature emotional development and also for development of personal behaviour.
2. **Role model:** There are two factors which influence what a child ultimately learns:
   (i) How adults and others in the child's environment handle their emotions.
   (ii) How successful is the emotional expression in achieving their needs.
3. **Violence in the child's environment:** The kind of behaviour the child see in the community (*e.g.* during riots) or on TV will affect her expressions of emotions.
4. **Cultural norms:** Emotional expressions are learnt from the environment. It is the environment that tells us how to react in a situation (*e.g.* some people feel the emotion of fear when a black cat crosses their path). It is also the environment that tells us the acceptable way of expressing ones emotions (*e.g.* in many families it is unacceptable for boys to express their distress by crying). Therefore, our cultural beliefs and values also influence our emotional development.

MOTIVATION AND LEARNING

Definition of Motivation

1. **J.P. Guilford :** Motivation is any internal factor or conditions that needs to initiate or sustain an activity.
2. **B.F. Skinner :** Motivation in school learning involves arousing, persisting, sustaining and directing desirable behaviour .

3. **Lowell :** Motivation is psycho-physiological and internal process initiated by some needs which led to activity and which will satisfy those needs.
4. **Thompson :** Motivation is the act of stimulating interest in the pupils (individuals) where there is no such interest.
5. **Woodworth :** Motivation is the state of the individual which disposes him of certain behaviour for seeking goals.

Nature and Characteristics of Motivation

On the basis of above definitions following nature and characteristics of motivation are established:

1. Motivation is such a psychological factor which is controlled by physical conditions. This is an internal process. When this process becomes active in the body of an organism, he starts activity. This very process furthers the activity and directs the activity as well. As soon as the process stops activity also stops immediately.
2. In school environment motivation arouses the behaviour of pupils, directs it and helps the pupils to persist on it. A teacher can make any thing do by the students in the class by it.
3. A person is motivated to do an activity only when he is driven by any internal need for that job. When study becomes the need of the pupil, he is motivated to study. If this need is not there in him, it is created by the teacher from outside. This need gets satisfied at the fulfillment of the activity. The same job is performed by all sports and games coach in fields and playgrounds.
4. Need of life depends upon the objectives of life. If the student has fixed the objective of scoring 80% marks in the examination, this objective works as a need for him. Thus, teacher, by making the aimless students sensitive to objectives of life, motivates them to do better and better.
5. Motivation is an art of increasing the interest of students. Students can not be motivated to teaching learning process just by arousing their interest without creating the needs.

In conclusion we can say that need is the main factor behind motivation. Other factors are interest, objectives of life, curiosity, intelligence etc.

Needs : The feeling of want of something is called need. Condition of restlessness continues until the need is fulfilled. Man manifests any specific type of behaviour because of this very tension.

Maslow's Hierarchy of Human Needs

Abraham Maslow explained the theories of motivation in 1954 in the perspective of needs. He classified human needs in five levels in a continuum of pyramid. He termed the physiological, safety and belongingness needs as lower level needs and esteem and self-actualization needs as higher level needs.

1. **Physiological needs:** These primary needs are created in an individual by nature. Needs of air, water, food, defecation etc. are such needs. Unless these needs of the individual are satisfied, he can not even think of higher level needs. Meaning thereby, we can not motivate a hungry or thirsty pupil for learning in the class. If a child does not have even resources to fulfil these needs, he can defer these needs by his will power but only for a short duration, but ultimately these needs will have any how to be fulfilled.
2. **Safety needs:** After fulfilling the physiological needs an organism wants to be protected in the environment from his enemies whether they are his fellow being or the fury of the environment in the form of heat, cold, rain etc. In the school situation a child wants that he should not be teased by any body. If the school is unable to protect the child, the child can never be motivated for learning.
3. **Needs of belongingness:** Having the above two needs been fulfilled an individual wants to be associated with others. He wants love, affection and friendship from his fellow beings. In order to satisfy these very needs child participates in different types of programmes in the school. In order to draw the attention and love of his teachers, he fulfills the home works given to him. Those teachers who fail to satisfy these needs of their pupils, they cannot motivate them for learning as well.
4. **Esteem needs :** After the lower level of needs being fulfilled, an organism wants respects and recognition in the society. For this purpose he exhibits some extra ordinary performance on certain affairs. The organism wants some powers in his hand to use it in the society. For example, he wants to become monitor of the class or captain of football or cricket team. In order to motivate such students for learning, it is necessary that such needs of these students must be fulfilled to the maximum level possible.
5. **Needs of self actualization :** An individual comes to recognise his strengths and weakness fully before coming to this last level of needs.

On the basis of potentialities he wants to do such an extra-ordinary work so that he may acquire the top place in the eyes of the people. For example, talented students after a period of time come to know that they can top the class. In order to achieve this target they try their best. If a teacher fails to recognise the abilities of these students and does not respond properly at their achievement, these students lag behind their actual level of performance.

It is clear from the above classification that there are five groups of people found in every society. The first group gets satisfied only at the fulfillment of its first level needs and does not care for the next. Second group can be satisfied only at fulfilling the two levels of needs. The next two groups are smaller than these. They can be motivated only when their higher levels of needs are fulfilled. The last group is actually never contended. It always tries its best to excel more and more.

Types of Motivation

1. **Extrinsic Motivation :** In such type of motivation efforts are made to create such environment from outside that individual starts taking interest in the task. For example, if a student does not take interest in teaching learning process because of his hunger, thirst or lack of safety, first of all, these needs of the students are satisfied. Important other extrinsic motivations are reward and punishment, praise and blame, success and failure, competition and cooperation, and so on.
2. **Intrinsic Motivation :** These motivations are related to subject matter or activities of the students. This motivation stresses to fulfil the higher level of needs such as esteem or self actualization needs. Such type of individuals can hardly be motivated by extrinsic motivation. Here efforts are made to create such an environment from within the individual that higher performance becomes his needs and objective of life. Unless and until these needs are fulfilled, he never sits idle. Knowledge of progress, novelty in the procedure, and higher aspiration level, goals, etc, are important intrinsic motivating factors.
3. **External Internal Motivation :** This is the joint technique of motivation and is applied simultaneously on the individual.

Techniques of Motivation

Important extrinsic and intrinsic techniques of motivation are as follows:

1. Reward and Punishment

Student endeavours to do the best in order to get reward. He becomes pleased when he is given reward and greater enthusiasm on the part of the student is shown. Following things must be kept in mind while giving reward to an individual.

(*a*) The nature or amount of reward should be according to the level of performance. Additional reward is always fatal for the future progress of an individual.

(*b*) Individual must know the importance of reward. If reward is given to so many individuals at a time, the reward loses its validity.

(*c*) Reward should not be traditional or a routine activity. Different types of rewards should be given at different occasions.

(*d*) Reward should have some monetary or social value.

As far as punishment is concerned its fear leads an individual not to do unwanted jobs. The child comes to the class with full preparation in order to avoid punishment. Following things must be kept in mind before assigning any punishment:

(*a*) Punishment should not be regular. Such punishment can make the children habitual to punishment.

(*b*) Punishment should not be so severe. Such punishment can create hatred in the minds of children towards the whole system.

(*c*) Punishment should be given keeping in view the mental and physical resistance of children.

(*d*) Punishment should be judiciously distributed to all guilty persons.

Researches have made it clear that reward is better technique of motivation than punishment. Punishment is fatal to the psychological development of the organism also. So, punishment should be avoided as much as possible.

2. Praise and Blame

When a child is praised at his successes, he is overjoyed. As a result he works better than before. Following points must be kept in view while using praise as a technique of motivation:

(*a*) If an organism is praised at every big or small successes randomly, he will be addicted to listening the words of praise.

As a result no new behaviour is created due to praise.

(b) Weaker children should be praised even at their small bits of successes while talented children should be praised only when they have really done something very unique.

(c) Praise technique should be applied according to changing ratio schedule, i.e., sometimes, it should be used and sometimes not and the subject must not know at what time this is to be given.

As far as blame is concerned, students are directly blamed for their failures and they are made ashamed. But excess use of blame as a technique of motivation may frustrate the child. Following points must be kept in mind before blaming the students on their failures:

(a) Positive efforts of a child must be praised first before blaming him on his failure.

(b) Students should not be solely made responsible for their failure. Other related factors and conditions must also be included in the list of factors causing failures in life.

(c) The language of the blame should not be insulting for students. The self respect of every individual must be recognised.

3. Success and Failure

Success creates self confidence among individuals and possibility of more successes increases. Teacher creates such an environment in the class in which all the barriers in the way of success are removed.

Failure can also work as a source of motivation. Especially the talented students accepts the failure as a challenge for them. In order to use this technique in the classroom situation, the teacher presents such problems in the class which students are unable to solve. The bright students accept this challenge for future and thus they are motivated for work.

4. Competition and Cooperation

The feeling of competition is universal in humans. In the classroom situations weak students compare themselves with their own group and bright students compare their achievements with that of bright group of students. In this way the whole class is motivated. In games and sports too, competitions works as the best motivator. Every sports person does harder and harder efforts to raise his performance level. Such type of competition is called individual competition. Team competition also works as a good motivating force. These two types of competitive feelings are aroused by the teacher in the class in order to motivate the pupils.

The utility of cooperation as a technique of motivation is very limited. Here. Students are asked to work with mutual cooperation so that every one in the group may get opportunity to develop. Project method of teaching is a good example of this technique.

5. Knowledge of Progress

It is a traditional method of motivating the students that they are regularly told about their progress on the basis of formative evaluations. When they come to know about their achievements, they work harder to raise this level due to the feedback obtained from the knowledge of their progress. Teacher and sports teacher should regularly evaluate the achievement of students and students should be informed immediately about this. If any delay is made in evaluation or its reporting, the teachers will not be able to give any feedback to his students. For this purpose, regular tests should be conducted in the class and they should be evaluated with no delay. If evaluation and its reporting takes much time, students forget their mistakes or actual activities and, as a result, they do not get any feedback from these.

6. Novelty

Researches have proved that monotony makes a man bored. In order to motivate such persons in their task novelty and change in the approach is essential. In the class room situation a teacher brings about novelty in his method of teaching at regular intervals. This makes the students come across to new experiences at every movement. Level of students must be kept in view while introducing novelty in the situation so that this novelty may not work as a bouncer.

7. Aspiration Level

Level of aspiration has a direct relationship with the objectives of life. An individual can achieve the objectives of his life when his aspiration level is high. A teacher tries to raise this level as much high as possible but it is always matched with the mental or physical potentialities of the pupils. If this level of aspiration is higher than physical or mental level, student will get frustrated at their successive failures. Contrary to this if this level is lower than the physical or mental level, it will reduce the activities of students and they will develop inferiority complex.

THEORIES OF MOTIVATION

1. Instinct Theory

This theory of motivation was propounded by an English psychologist **Mc Dougall**. He pleaded that every human being has some innate powers or instincts. These instincts work as motives also and influence our behaviour. Under the influence of these instincts relationship between the object and the individual is established. Sentiments are aroused as a result of this. These sentiments organise an individual's emotional life and bring about stability in his behaviour. Thus, sentiments are an important factor behind the force of motivation. He explained the importance of self respect regarding sentiments. An individual's character is evaluated in terms of the stability of his self respect. If organisation of moral sentiments is more stable than the sentiments regarding the self respect, the character of the person will be strong.

2. Psychoanalytic Theory : (By Freud, Young and Adler)

According to them conscious plays main role in controlling an individuals' behaviour. As against unconscious mind there is the role of repression. Repression is the elimination of painful and unhealthy experiences from the conscious mind. Thus, repression is a defense mechanism with the help of which an individual tries to adjust partially. This repression is necessary because as child grows, many of his needs and feelings are disliked by the people which were earlier liked. When these needs are eliminated from the conscious mind, they are collected into unconscious mind and affect human behaviour indirectly. Sometimes these repressed needs come to the conscious level also when they receive any stimulus from outside. Thus, according to these psychologists, human behaviour is influenced by such motives also about which he is totally unaware.

3. Maslow's Need Theory

This theory has already been explained under the head of Maslow's Hierarchy of needs.

4. Social Theory

This theory is of two type :

(a) **Cultural Pattern Theory** (by **Mead & Benedict**) **:** According to this theory, behaviour of a person is influenced by the respective culture in which he lives. For example, individuals of those castes which have strict controlling system on their members become foolish, dry and short tempered when they grow. On the contrary, the castes in which children are behaved affectionately, they manifest considerate behaviour when they grow. Thus, behaviour is very much influenced by the pattern of rearing of a person. In the classroom situation, a teacher can motivate his students by his own behaviour.

(b) **Field Theory** (by **Kurt Levin**) **:** According to this theory, the behaviour of an individual is not determined by his qualities or personality traits but all those forces which act between an individual and his environment. Thus, there is a close relationship between an individual and his environment. In the class room situation a child can be motivated by creating an environment suitable to the child.

5. Drive Theory

This theory is somewhat similar to need theory of Maslow. According to this theory an individual is driven to act when certain biological needs create some inner tension which is called drive. Thus drive is the primary cause of motivation.

The drawback of this theory is that it is helpless to explain why an individual, in the absence of inner drive behaves in a particular situation due to the effect of his environment as is explained by the social theory of motivation.

6. Incentive Theory

According to this theory, external incentives such as rewards, monetary benefits, promotion in the social status etc. can also motivate an individual to act in a certain direction.

7. Expectancy Theory

According to this theory an individual is not actually getting any reward or monetary benefits but the expectation of getting such a reward or benefits can motivate him to do the job in the best manner possible. In the field of games, a sportsman can be motivated to perform his best by giving him some incentive not at present but in the future.

8. Learning of behaviour Theory (Clark Hall)

According to this theory an individual's behaviour depends on the satisfaction or dissatisfaction of his needs. When his needs are satisfied, his psychological tensions are reduced and he retains the reaction of his learnt behaviour. When his organic needs are satisfied, he learns to link the social conditions with his primary needs and retains that particular behaviour.

9. Motivation Hygiene Theory (Fredrick Herzberg)

This theory was indoctrinated in the field of industry and commerce first. Herzberg interviewed farmers, account officers, nurses and house wives in Pistbarg University in 1966 and propounded this theory.

According to this theory motives enhance the efficiency by providing comforts and satisfactions to the pupils. Motives keep them delighted by increasing their achievement on one hand and pupils get satisfied by their motives on the other. This in turn enriches learning. Since the effect of motives are positive and persists for a longer period of time, as a result motives develop the following feelings in the pupils:

(*a*) Achievement
(*b*) Recognition
(*c*) Responsibility
(*d*) Advancement
(*e*) Personal growth

The above feeling are directly affected by hygiene factors. They are given below :

(*a*) Methods of supervision
(*b*) Condition of work
(*c*) Inter-personal relations
(*d*) Social policy and administration
(*e*) Status
(*f*) Security

If level of these factors is low, the individual becomes unhappy, and as a result, learning outcome will fall. It can also develop negative attitude among the learner. The learner can be motivated by raising the level of these six hygiene factors.

This theory has direct application in the field of education and sports along with other field of life. Performance of students of government schools is low only because of low level of some of hygiene factors. If organizational climate of the school is made good, it will automatically increase the achievement of pupils.

10. Operant Conditioning Model of Motivation

This model was presented by Skinner. It suggests that behaviour would change by the consequence of that very behaviour. If the result of a particular behaviour is satisfactory, it will be automatically reinforced and repeated in future. Reinforcement is given from outside also for the recurrence of desired behaviour.

Thus, this model does not give importance to the inner motivation of the individual. It ignores drives and needs of learners as well. Level of aspiration is also ignored by this model. This model is rather based on the observable and measurable overt behavioural responses which are modified slowly by giving proper reinforcement.

According to this model the desirable behaviours are first identified. Then conditions are created for the occurrence of these behaviours. And finally, once they occur, reinforcement is given for the recurrence of these behaviours.

Techniques of motivation and students' needs, teaching objectives and learning structures

Need (lower needs)	Teaching structure	Teaching objectives	Techniques of motivation (Extrinsic)
1. Physiological	1. Signal learning	1. Knowledge	1. Reward
2. Safety	2. Chain learning	2. Comprehension or understanding	2. Praise and reward
3. Belongingness (higher needs)	3. Multiple discrimination learning	3.Above + Analysis	3. Success and failure (extrinsic and intrinsic)
4. Esteem	4. Cocept learning	4.Application	4. Competition and cooperation
5. Self actualization	5. Principle learning	5.Creativity	5. Knowledge of result 6. Novelty 7. Level of aspiration 8. Self-motivation

Techniques of motivation and students' needs : The teacher should first of all find out the needs of his student's *i.e.*, at what level of needs the students are. Only then the teacher can give intrinsic or extrinsic motivation to his students. It is also likely that students do not have the capacity to think beyond the third level of Maslow's needs. In that case the teacher should create the other two needs in his students by telling the students about the goals of life and its related difficulties.

These very needs will motivate the students for effort and desired behaviour will be seen in future.

Motivation techniques and learning objectives

While selecting suitable techniques of motivation the teacher keeps this fact into account what learning objectives he had formulated in the beginning. Thus, a teacher takes 6 × 3 = 18 objectives into account while selecting motivation techniques. We will discuss these three domains of objectives in relation to motivation techniques below :

(a) *Cognitive Domain Objectives :* If teacher has restricted his objectives to the level of application only, then for realising these three levels of objectives, a composite techniques of motivation may be proved to be successful. But if the objectives are extended to analysis, synthesis or evaluation, motivation techniques will not work much. The teacher will rather have to take the help of teaching strategies and tactics such as self study, problem solving group discussion, symposium and seminars etc.

(b) *Affective objectives :* Lower level of affective objectives like receiving, responding and valuing etc, can be achieved by using techniques of motivation. But techniques of motivation are not very much helpful for achieving higher level of objectives and in that case, the teacher should use strategies of teaching like self study, brain storming , CAI etc. more than motivation techniques.

(c) *Psychomotor objectives :* Techniques of motivation are most helpful for realising objectives of psychomotor domain and extrinsic techniques are more powerful than intrinsic techniques here.

Motivation and Learning Structure

Various techniques of motivation should also he selected according to different structures of learning. These five structures are given here:

(a) **Signal learning** : Stimulus and responses are directly connected here. Extrinsic techniques of motivation are most suitable here.

(b) **Chain learning** : Chain is formed between stimuli and responses here. Environment is especially significant here so, extrinsic techniques are most suitable in chain learning.

(c) **Multiple discrimination learning** : So many stimuli are presented before the students simultaneously here and they respond to these stimuli on the basis of similarities and differences. Environment and content both are important here. In this type of learning structure, both types of motivation techniques are useful.

(d) **Concept learning** : In such type of learning content and its presentation are given preference here. Therefore, only intrinsic techniques of motivation are useful here.

(e) **Principle learning** : In this structure, various concepts are presented in the form of chain here. When this is done, they take the form of laws or principles. It means that only content is important here. So, only intrinsic techniques of motivation is useful here.

FACTORS CONTRIBUTING TO LEARNING

Introduction

Learning, can be considered as the process by which skills, attitudes, knowledge and concepts are acquired, understood, applied and extended. All human beings, whether grown ups or children engage in the process of learning, either consciously, sub-consciously or subliminally. It is through learning that their competence and ability to function in their environment get enhanced. It is important to understand that while we learn some ideas and concepts through instruction or teaching, we also learn through our feelings and experiences. Feelings and experiences are a tangible part of our lives and these greatly influence what we learn, how we learn and why we learn.

Learning has been considered partly a cognitive process and partly a social and affective one. It qualifies as a cognitive process because it involves the functions of attention, perception, reasoning, analysis, drawing of conclusions, making interpretations and giving meaning to the observed phenomena. All of these are mental processes which relate to the intellectual functions of the individual. Learning is a social and affective process, as the societal and cultural context in which we function and the feelings and experiences which we have, greatly influence our ideas, concepts, images and understanding of the world. These constitute inner subjective interpretations and represent our own unique, personalized constructions of the specific universe of functioning. Our knowledge, ideas, concepts, attitudes, beliefs and the skills which we acquire are a consequence of these combined processes.

CLASSIFICATION OF FACTORS: PERSONAL & ENVIRONMENT

To understand how we categorise the factors affecting learning, let us begin by considering the following examples:

- Ravi is sixteen year old and wants to please his mother by getting good results in his board examinations. He is so eager to please her, that he spends long hours of concentrated time and energy on his studies. He consciously tries to control other sources of distraction in his life and reduces the time spent on watching television, playing games and chatting with his friends.

- Rita Williams wants to be a famous tennis player. To achieve her goal, she practices tennis whenever she can, even though she gets no encouragement from her family. She makes it a point to watch tennis matches and maintain a good rapport with her sports teacher.
- Yuvraj is a good student, but lately he has been scoring very low marks at school. He is not able to concentrate or pay attention and his class work and home assignments reflect a very poor quality. Sources revealed that his parents fight a lot with each other and are about to get divorced.
- Arti and Kavita are two sisters. Arti is very good at art and craft and can sketch just about anything she sees. Kavita has a ear for music. She knows most songs and can sing them even if she has heard them only once. Both of them spend hours together pursuing their respective interest areas.
- Sayeeda is tall, attractive and has a very good figure. She wants to be a model or an air-hostess and nurtures this secretly as her dream. She is too scared to share her wishes with her family, since she belongs to an orthodox family, where girls at best can pursue teaching as a career. When she tries telling her mother what she wants, she is firmly told that she can only do her B.Ed and can go to the coaching classes for these.

The above cited examples illustrate that learning is a universal phenomenon mediated by a number of factors, both personal and environmental in nature. The dictum "everybody learns" is as true as its corollary, *i.e.*, everybody learns in accordance with his/her unique, individualized blend of personal and environmental factors. For example, in case of Ravi, the desire to please his mother, striving to do well in his board exams and managing his life situations appropriately constitute the key factors which influence him. For Rita Williams, it is her intrinsic desire to be a good tennis player which is paramount. She is not deterred by the lack of family support and continues to make efforts to promote her love for tennis on her own and fulfil her desire to be successful.

In case of Yuvraj, in spite of his innate capacity to study and perform well, his lack of achievement can be attributed to the emotional insecurity stemming from his parents' divorce. As far as Arti and Kavita are concerned, their special interests and talent in art and music respectively, seem to guide their activities.

For Sayeeda, the home environment and family culture and values determine her professional choice. Her own inner interests, desires and wishes are not to be taken into cognizance.

In all the examples cited, we can find evidence of both personal and environmental factors influencing the process of learning. Learning can thus be defined as a function of the interaction of personal and environmental factors.

$$L = f\,(EF \times PF)$$

L = learning; f = function; EF = environmental factors; PF = personal factors.

Personal factors are the intra individual factors like motivation, interests, abilities etc which predispose an individual towards learning as in the case of Rita Williams, Arti and Kavita. Environmental factors on the other hand, are those contextual factors which highlight the role of the environment in learning, such as the socio-emotional, societal and cultural factors as seen in the case of Yuvraj and Sayeeda. Although the two factors represent different categories, they operate in a common system. The environmental factors provide the context within which the personal factors, operate. The learner and the learning process can only be completely understood with reference to the interaction of both environmental and personal factors. This may be diagrammatically represented as follows:

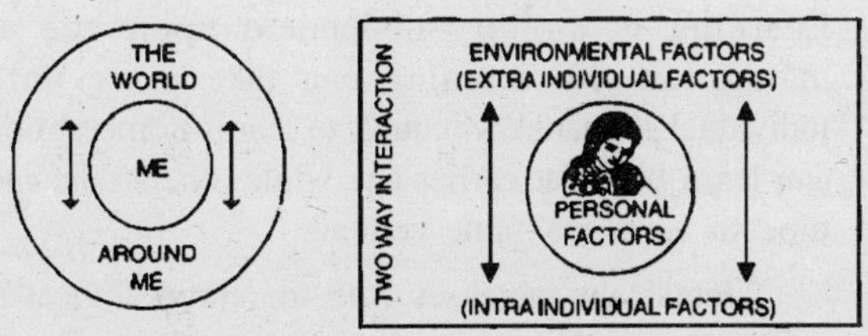

Fig: *Factors affecting learning*

Personal Factors Influencing Learning

The process of learning is influenced by a variety of personal factors. A thorough knowledge of these factors will prove very helpful for teachers and parents in understanding and guiding their children's learning. Some of the personal factors that influence the learning process may be classified as under : sensation and perception, fatigue and boredom, maturation, emotional condition, needs, interests, motivation, attention, intelligence, aptitude, attitude, etc. Let us discuss the important personal factors in the following sub-sections.

Sensation and Perception

Apart from the general health of the students, sensation and perception are the psychological factors which help in learning. Sensation is at the core of perception. There are five sense organs *i.e.*, skin, ears, tongue, eyes and nose. These sense organs are the gateways of knowledge and help in perception of various stimuli in the environment. Any defect in any of the sense organs will affect learning and hence acquisition of knowledge. For example, defects of vision such as myopia, hypermetropia, astigmatism, etc., cause headaches, nausia and general disinclination to study. A blind person depends upon the sense of touch or skin for learning and thus acquires knowledge and skills, as he can not visualise the objects. The stimuli are preceived and assimilated, and hence learnt through various sense organs. In this way we can say that sensation and perception is the bases of knowledge and learning.

Fatigue and Boredom

It is virtually boredom or lassitude rather than fatigue which bothers the students. The difference between the two is that fatigue is mental or physical tiredness which decreases in efficiency and competency to work. Boredom, on the other hand, is a lack of desire on an aversion to work. Such an aversion makes one feel fatigued without being actually fatigued. Studying seldom causes fatigue. It is mainly boredom which, besides causing the impression of fatigue, decreases student efficiency in learning.

Age and Maturation

Learning is directly dependent upon age and maturation. No learning can take place unless individual is matured enough to learn. Some children can learn better at earlier age while others take more time to learn the same content.

Mental age increases with the chronological age and ceases at about the age of sixteen years. Increase in age means intellectual maturation which helps in solving difficult problems. The principle of maturation warns us against enforcing learning on a child when he is not mature enough to learn the specific skills. Teachers should explain this principle to parents who are over ambitious or over enthusiastic in sending their children to school at the very early age.

Emotional Conditions

Desirable emotional conditions enhance the quality and speed of learning. Happiness, joy and satisfaction are always favourable for any type of learning. Adverse emotional conditons, on the other hand, hinder learning. Many studies have established the fact that emotional strain, stress, tensions, disturbances, etc., are extremely inimical to scholastic pursuits.

Needs

A need is the lack of something which, if provided, would facilitate child's usual behaviour. The lack of something is experienced by the child. The child then tries to perform that activity which culminates in the satisfaction of the need. Thus, the needs are associated with goals. Among human beings, the needs are realtively permanent tendencies which seek satisfaction in achieving certain specific goals. When these goals are achieved, the particular need is satisfied or met for the time being, but it recurs sooner or later and energises further activity. The needs in human beings can be physiological such as need for oxygen, food, water, etc. They may be social such as the need for affection, recognition, self-regard, etc. Social needs are however, quite different from physiological needs. Social needs might originate after physiological needs are satisfied. These needs have a complex structure and dominate the individual's behaviour.

There is not equal urgency in the satisfaction of all needs. Some have to be satisfied before others can manifest themselves.

In schools, children are not expected to do any intellectual thinking unless their physiological needs are satisfied. Poor, starved children may concentrate less on attainment of knowledge than on food. Similarly, very cold or hot classrooms or over-crowded seats will not be conducive to good learning. Likewise the need for safety, love and esteem, all act as powerful motives in the learning situations. If the child is afraid of the teacher or feels unsafe while in the school on account of too much beating or some other form of punishment, no learning can take place. Similarly, his needs for warmth and affection are very stimulating and hence results in effective learning.

Interests

Various types of interests of the students can be exploited to facilitate their learning. The interests during early infancy are mostly limited and short lived. As the child grows older his interests diversify and stabilize. You, a school teacher, should have thorough knowledge of children's interests. You can eliminate much drudgery, monotony and boredom from the school work if you make your instruction lively and stimulating and arouse student interest in it.

Once the students' interest is aroused in an activity you should expend more effort on it. No learning can be achieved without proper expenditure of effort on it. Students can even overcome distraction, fatigue and boredom if they feel interested in your instruction and class activities. It has often been found that, in most cases, fatigue in reality is loss of interest in the learning activity. Interest, should be exploited to yield results of greater quantity and quality learning in school.

Life is so exciting that many interesting things and activities often clamor to attract our attention.

Children frequently face the dilemma of mutually conflicting interests. Immediate interests often seem to be clashing with the remoter ones. A student might be in a quandary at least for the time being when his interest in sports impels him towards the play-field and his interest in studies force him to concentrate on books.

In such cases of conflicting interests a lot of hesitancy, wastage, frustration and unhappiness is bound to follow. What is needed is education at home and school which helps/trains children to achieve a healthy balance in their interests. They should be trained to budget their time in such a manner as to pay a reasonable attention to various interests, scholastic, athletic, social etc., within the time at their disposal.

Motivation

Motivation is the heart of the learning process. It generates the will in an individual to do something. Adequate motivation not only engages the student in an activity which results in learning, but also sustains and directs learning. Two types of motivation are commonly recognised. These are: intrinsic and extrinsic motivation.

Intelligence

Intelligence as expressed by an I.Q. score on an intelligence test is positively related to learning. Generally, students with higher I.Q. learn rapidly. However, higher I.Q. in itself is no guarantee for rapid learning, since other factors such as needs, interest, motivation, etc., of the students and the methods used for learning are also important.

Aptitude

A student who possesses appropriate aptitude for a particular subject of study or skill, will learn better and retain it for a longer time. On the other hand, he will require relatively longer time to study a subject for which he lacks natural aptitude. He is liable to forget it soon besides feeling bored and unhappy all the time while learning it. Hence, it is extremely desirable to analyse the aptitude of students before prescribing courses of study for them.

Attitude

The learning process is also influenced considerably by the attitude of the student. If he is alert, attentive and interested in the material to be learnt, he is bound to have a favourable attitude towards it. Such an attitude will enable him to tackle the learning situation economically, pleasantly and effectively. Conversely, if he is inattentive and is uninterested in the material his attitude is bound to be unfavourable. This will hinder the smooth learning of the material in hand besides involving undue strain and tension in the learner.

Environmental Factors

Environmental influences begin since the time of the conception of the child in the womb of the mother. Mother's mental, physical and emotional conditions influence the development of foetus in the womb. The external environment starts from the time of birth of the child. It (external environment) refers to the surroundings which prevail in home, school and locality. At these places, the child interacts with members of the family, teachers, classmates or peers and neighbours and establishes relationship with them. The relationship with the members of the society, and the surroundings may affect the development of the child and also the way he learns. Some of the environmental factors are discussed as follows:

Surrounding : Natural, Social and Cultural

As the title of the sub-section indicates, we shall discuss here natural, social and cultural environment the child interacts with and get influenced.

Natural surrounding covers the climatic and atmospheric condition. These conditions affect learning directly. It has been found that high temperature and humidity reduces mental efficiency. For a limited time, humidity and high temperature can be tolerated but prolonged humidity and high temperature become unbearable and decrease mental efficiency. The intellectual productivity and creativeness of people living in hot regions are much low. Likewise, the morning time is always better for mastering difficult tasks. Mental efficiency decreases due to increased humidity and temperature. Studies on the academic progress of evening school students shows losses of efficiency varying from one to six per cent.

Social surrounding includes especially the environment of home, school and locality. Physical conditions at home such as large family, small family, (specific place of the study), insufficient ventilation, improper lighting, uncomfortable temperature, noisy home environment due to use of radio, TV, etc., noisy neighbourhood, constant visits by friends or relatives, etc., influence the intellectual learning of the student. The socio-emotional factors such as child rearing practices, reward and punishment, scope for freedom and independence in activities and decision making, play and study facilities, ambitions and aspirations of the parents, disorganisation and discord among birth positions such as eldest, youngest or single child have their definite influence on learning. For example, a student who comes from a very poor family and never had any intellectual stimulation at home remains dull and unresponsive in the class. In some societies there is a strong sex bias. Girls are directly or indirectly told that education is not meant for them. In the middle class families, on the other hand, parents are rather over-ambitious. They wish their children to make quick academic progress, grow-up and find a respectable vocation preferably a white collar job. Such children, therefore get sufficient incentive from their families. This, of course, is most favourable to scholastic learning, although an overdose of family emphasis on acquiring academic excellence might affect the child's mental and physical health adversely. Similarly, school activities, study facilities and teaching methods and behaviour of teachers, principals and non-teaching staff have an impact upon learning. If the school atmosphere is unconducive, it adversely affects the learning process. Locality also has an influence on a child. If the locality is bad, the learning will be ineffective to some extent.

Cultural demands and social expectations also influence learning. The spirit of culture is reflected in its social and educational institutions. Children's learning, therefore, is greatly determined by the demands and expectations of their culture. Thus, for instance, in an industrialized culture the emphasis mostly centres mechanical sciences and preparing children for highly mechanised vocations. In an agriculture based community, on the other hand, the educational process focusses on preparing its members for those skills which are suited to the needs of an agrarian community.

The philosophical elements of culture also influence the spirit of children's learning. Children in a democratic culture tend to acquire democrative and values and attitudes. A feudal, aristocratic or dictatorial culture, on the other hand, promotes autocratic modes of thought and behaviour.

Relationship with Teacher, Parents and Peers

The teacher is an important constituent in the instructional process. She/he plays an important role in shaping the behaviour of students. The way he teaches and manages the students has an affect on their learning. An authoritarian teacher will create an aggression and hostility among students while a democratic teacher will create a participatory climate for learning. The democratic environment leads students to constructive, thoughtful and cooperative behaviour. Generally, students learn better in a democratic set up because they like democratic procedures. The teacher is no more an instructor or the director of learning in a democratic set up. She/he helps his/her students in their learning. The teachers no more dominate the scene, they can get better results by decentralizing authority, increasing independence of students. They can attend to the comments and questions of the students. They can encourage students to participate in learning activities in and outside the class. There should be more emphasis on activity-centred classroom where student's active participation in the teaching-learning process is encouraged and the teacher acts as a guide to promote learning.

Relationship with parents plays a vital role in the learning process of the student. If the child-parents relationship is based on mutual respect and faith, it can provide the child a congenial atmosphere which in turn can facilitate his/her learning. A distorted and unhealthy environment, on the other hand, adversely affects the learning of the student. The upward mobility brings resistance on the part of the student to learn. Students in such families find themselves unable to cope up. A subtle but powerful influence on the growing child arises from his/her position among the children in the family. The parents of the first born expect the child to act like miniature adults and hence the first-born are found to encounter a variety of expectations and stresses. Whereas parents tend to be more relaxed in their do's and dont's with the last-born. Factors like traumatic events at home, separation or death can also precipitate learning problems in the normal child.

A healthy peer group relationship also plays an important role in learning. Student-student relationship in the classroom, school, society, etc., create a particular type of emotional climate. The climate solely depends upon their relationships. A sound relationships provides a tension free environment to the student to learn more and to compete in the class. If the relationship among peers is not good, it adversely affects their learning. Therefore, to improve the classroom learning climate, free discussion should be there. You should help your students understand each other in formal or informal meetings. They should be encouraged to meet each other and their teachers freely. If any mis-understanding is created or developed, it should be immediately clarified so as to maintain the healthy climate and cordial relationship among peers.

Mass Media Influence on Learning

Today, mass media is all pervaive and omnipresent. Our day-to-day life is inundated with the presence of mass media. We can access mass media through television, radio and print. If, some years ago, radio and print were the main tools of mass communication, television seems to have taken over the place now.

Mass media is informative and influence the thinking of people. It creates a learning environment. Mass media is not controlled by a single agency and what it represents is neither organized learning (as in schools) nor the immediate reality surrounding you (as in home and community). Mass media offers a wide range of information and reality far removed from immediate reality. The informal learning environment created by mass media is intense and far reaching in impact than any other informal learning environment.

Learning through print medium presupposes the ability to read alike. Hence, its reach as an informal learning agency is limited. Radio is more effective than print as the listener requires only comprehension skill. The advent of twenty four hours television channels have redefined the role of mass media as an agency of informal learning. Television is more powerful and effective than radio and print as it exercises greater influence on the viewers through visual images.

Both radio and television appeal to literates and illiterates alike. The mass media-is not an agency of organized learning. However, the mass media is sometimes used by state agencies to effect purposeful and specific learning at a mass level. For example, the family planning, pulse polio, and HIV/AIDS programmes on mass media sponsored by the state are intended to bring about behaviour modification among the masses.

For children who have access to the mass media, especially the television, it becomes an additional and supportive source of learning in the context of organized learning. Children who are exposed to the mass media are well informsd and that often facilitate their reddiness for new learning in the organized learning context. However, learning through the mass media, especially the television is not always positive or constnictive learning. Through television viewing, children often pick up values that are not in conformity with the values of the family, school, or community. Thus, television or any other mass media teaches academic and cognitive skills and social behaviours but it can have both positive and negative influences on children.

These days television and radio are used as supportive agencies in imparting organized learning. For example, the Indira Gandhl National Open University utilizes the electronic media (television and radio) for teaching-learning purposes. We can say that the electronic media is used for creating a virtual learning environment. Through interactive radio counselling students sitting across the country are able to tune in to listen to their teachers and interact with them. Teleconferencing creates interactive virtual classroom. The virtual learning environment created on television or computer is found effective due to the presence of visual images and the use of multimedia. Then, there are noninteractive virtual learning environments, like the telecast of UGC's country-wideclassrooms. Decades ago when television was a rarity, the government of India used All India Radio to educate the Indian fanners about the technological advances in farming to bring in India's Green Revolution. Thus, mass media can play a significant role in formal and non-formal learning.

MULTIPLE CHOICE QUESTIONS

1. According to Piaget, during the first stage of development (birth to about 2 years age), a child learns best
   (*a*) by thinking in an abstract fashion
   (*b*) by applying newly acquired knowledge of language
   (*c*) by using the senses
   (*d*) by comprehending neutral words
2. The most intense and crucial socialization takes place
   (*a*) during early childhood
   (*b*) during adulthood
   (*c*) throughout the life of a person
   (*d*) during adolescence
3. Heredity is considered as a .... social structure.
   (*a*) dynamic (*b*) static
   (*c*) primary (*d*) secondary
4. Theory of learning which totally and only depends on '*observable behaviour*' is associated with .... theory of learning.
   (*a*) Behaviourist (*b*) Constructivist
   (*c*) Cognitivist (*d*) Developmental
5. Which of the following does ***not*** reflect 'teaching for understanding'?
   (*a*) Help students see similarities and differences and generate analogies
   (*b*) Enable students to memorize isolated facts and procedures
   (*c*) Ask students to explain a phenomenon or a concept in their own words
   (*d*) Teach students to provide examples to illustrate how a law works
6. Which of the following is ***not*** a characteristic feature of intrinsically motivated children?
   (*a*) They display a high level of energy while working
   (*b*) They like challenging tasks
   (*c*) They always succeed
   (*d*) They enjoy doing their work
7. A teacher wants the gifted children of her class to achieve their potential. Which of the following should she ***not*** do to achieve her objective?
   (*a*) Segregate them from their peers for special attention
   (*b*) Challenge them to enhance their creativity
   (*c*) Teach them to enjoy non-academic activities
   (*d*) Teach them to manage stress
8. Which of the following is ***not*** a sign of reading difficulty among young learners? Difficulty in
   (*a*) understanding words and ideas
   (*b*) spelling consistency
   (*c*) letter and word recognition
   (*d*) reading speed and fluency
9. 'Self-regulation' of learners refers to
   (*a*) rules and regulations made by the student body
   (*b*) self-discipline and control
   (*c*) their ability to monitor their own learning
   (*d*) creating regulations for student behaviour
10. Which of the following statements ***cannot*** be considered as a feature of 'learning'?
    (*a*) Study of behaviour is learning
    (*b*) Unlearning is also a part of learning
    (*c*) Learning is a process that mediates behaviour
    (*d*) Learning is something that occurs as a result of certain experiences
11. Constructivism as a theory
    (*a*) emphasises on memorising information and testing through recall
    (*b*) emphasises on the dominant role of the teacher
    (*c*) focuses on the role of imitation
    (*d*) emphasises the role of the learner in constructing his own view of the world
12. A creative learner refers to one who is
    (*a*) capable of scoring consistently good marks in tests
    (*b*) good at lateral thinking and problem solving
    (*c*) very talented in drawing and painting
    (*d*) highly intelligent
13. Development of concepts is primarily a part of
    (*a*) physical development
    (*b*) social development
    (*c*) emotional development
    (*d*) intellectual development

14. Individual learners differ from each other in
(*a*) sequence of development
(*b*) general capacity for development
(*c*) principles of growth and development
(*d*) rate of development

15. The statement : 'An important precondition for the proper development of a child is ensuring her/his healthy physical development'
(*a*) is true because physical development occupies the topmost place in the sequence of development
(*b*) is true because physical development is interrelated with other domains of development
(*c*) is untrue as physical development does not affect other domains of development in any way
(*d*) may be incorrect as development varies from individual to individual

16. Irfan breaks toys and dismantles them to explore their components. What would you do?
(*a*) Encourage his inquisitive nature and channelise his energy
(*b*) Make him understand that toys should not be broken
(*c*) Never let Irfan play with toys
(*d*) Always keep a close watch

17. Understanding the principles of development of a child helps a teacher in
(*a*) rationalizing why the learner ought to be taught
(*b*) effectively catering to the different learning styles of learners
(*c*) identifying the social status of the learner
(*d*) identifying the economic background of the learner

18. Every learner is unique means that
(*a*) A common curriculum for all learners is not possible
(*b*) It is impossible to develop the potential of learners in a heterogeneous class
(*c*) No two learners are alike in their abilities, interests and talents
(*d*) Learners do not have any common qualities, nor do they share common goals

19. The statement 'Men are generally more intelligent than women'
(*a*) shows gender bias
(*b*) is true for different domains of intelligence
(*c*) is ture
(*d*) may be true

20. Christina took her class for a field trip and after coming back, she discussed the trip with her students. It may be connotated as
(*a*) Learning for Assessment
(*b*) Learning of Assessment
(*c*) Assessment of Learning
(*d*) Assessment for Learning

21. Human development is based on certain principles. Which of the following is ***not*** a principle of human development?
(*a*) General to Specific
(*b*) Reversible
(*c*) Continuity
(*d*) Sequentiality

22. Centrally sponsored scheme of Integrated Education for disabled children aims at providing educational opportunities to children with disabilities in
(*a*) Open schools
(*b*) Blind Relief Association schools
(*c*) Regular schools
(*d*) Special schools

23. Which of the following statements is true about 'learning'?
(*a*) Learning is not affected by emotional factors at any stage of learning.
(*b*) Learning is fundamentally a mental activity.
(*c*) Errors made by children indicate that no learning has taken place.
(*d*) Learning is effective in an environment that is emotionally positive and satisfying for the learners.

24. The main purpose of assessment should be
(*a*) to decide if a student should be promoted to the next class
(*b*) to diagnose and remedy gaps in learning
(*c*) to point out the errors of the learners
(*d*) to measure the achievement of learners

25. Helping learners recapitulate or recall what they have already learnt is important because
(*a*) it is an effective way of revising old lessons
(*b*) it enhances the memory of learners thereby strengthening learning
(*c*) it is a convenient beginning for any classroom instruction
(*d*) relating new information to prior knowledge enhances learning

26. Creative answers require
(*a*) open-ended questions
(*b*) a highly disciplined classroom
(*c*) direct teaching and direct questions
(*d*) content-based questions

27. Learners should ***not*** be encouraged to
(*a*) participate in as many co-curricular activities as possible
(*b*) memorize all the answers to questions which the teacher may ask
(*c*) ask as many questions as possible both inside and outside the class

(*d*) actively interact with other learners in group work

28. Which of the following is ***not*** an appropriate tool for Formative Assessment?
(*a*) Term test (*b*) Quiz and games
(*c*) Assignment (*d*) Oral questions

29. Diagnosis of the gaps in the learning of students should be followed by
(*a*) systematic revision of all lessons
(*b*) reporting the findings to learners and parents
(*c*) appropriate remedial measures
(*d*) intensive drill and practice

30. Multilingual character of Indian society should be seen as
(*a*) a challenge to teacher's capacity to motivate students to learn
(*b*) a factor that makes school life a complex experience for the learners
(*c*) a hindrance in teaching-learning process
(*d*) a resource for enrichment of school life

31. Which of the following statements regarding personality traits is correct?
(*a*) Traits of personality can not be developed in isolation without taking the help of environment
(*b*) Subjective traits of the individual are determined by genetic factors
(*c*) Bad environment can surpass good inheritance but good environment is not a substitute for poor heredity
(*d*) All of these

32. Which of the following characteristics denote infancy period?
(*a*) Physical growth is curvilinear
(*b*) Physical growth is rapid
(*c*) Head grows at relatively slower rate as compared to other parts of the body
(*d*) All of these

33. Which of the following is not the characteristic of infancy period?
(*a*) From bilateral to unilateral trend in motor organs
(*b*) From general to specific trend in motor organs
(*c*) Emotional/social development is not associated with motor development
(*d*) Steady mental development

34. Which of the following illustrates conceptual development?
(*a*) Perception is the beginning of concept formation
(*b*) Concept changes with changes in experiences
(*c*) Concept changes with age
(*d*) All of these

35. There is one thing common in language and physical development what is that?
(*a*) Spurts of development at different ages
(*b*) Dependence on experience
(*c*) Dependence on training
(*d*) None of these

36. Which of the following characteristics is not associated with emotional development?
(*a*) Emotion is accompanied by physiological changes
(*b*) Emotions start immediately after birth
(*c*) Intense form of emotions are seen during early childhood period
(*d*) Emotions are unrelated to physical development

37. The child acquires about three fourth of the brain weight by the age of
(*a*) 2½ years (*b*) 2 years
(*c*) 6 years (*d*) 8 years

38. Social development of an infant depends on
(*a*) his chance of interaction with others
(*b*) love and affection shown to the child
(*c*) the extent to which he is able to attract the attention of others
(*d*) all of the above

39. In which of the following stages the child looks self centred?
(*a*) Infancy (*b*) Early childhood
(*c*) Adolescence (*d*) Adulthood

40. In the period of infancy, emotions are
(*a*) intense, frequent and unstable
(*b*) like an open book(overt)
(*c*) need based
(*d*) all of these

41. Which of the following organs of the body shows rapid growth in infancy?
(*a*) growth of hands (*b*) growth of head
(*c*) growth of legs (*d*) growth of fingers

42. In normal learning environment, forgetting is caused
(*a*) due to back of practice for a long time
(*b*) due to the interference of other learnt material
(*c*) due to lack of consolidation of memory traces
(*d*) all of these

43. Clear conception of size, weight, colour, time etc., is seen at the age of
(*a*) six (*b*) four
(*c*) four and half (*d*) five

44. Which of the following is not the characteristics of intellectual development of early childhood?
(*a*) increased span of attention
(*b*) exploration of the environment
(*c*) ability to verbalize all known concepts
(*d*) ability to distinguish past, present and future

45. Social development by the end of early childhood is marked by
(a) the feeling of autonomy
(b) the end of solitary plays
(c) the temperament of co-operation and friendliness
(d) all of these

46. Fictional world of the child starts at the age of
(a) 5-6 (b) 6-8
(c) 3-4 (d) 4-5

47. Girls are more dominating than boys in social situations in which of the following periods?
(a) pre-adolescent period
(b) early childhood period
(c) both of these
(d) none of these

48. In the period of early childhood, child is
(a) helpless to hide his emotions
(b) seen shifting his emotions very rapidly and frequently
(c) guided by his innate tendencies and instincts
(d) all of these

49. A nursery teacher should organize
(a) group games in the school
(b) those games which involve motor organs of the body
(c) those games which help the child to manipulate the environment
(d) all of these

50. Later childhood is called latency period because
(a) creative potentials are dormant
(b) sex remains dormant
(c) it is a period of inactivity
(d) all of these

51. Physical development of later childhood is marked by
(a) Auscification of bones
(b) Permanent teeth
(c) Excessive motor activity
(d) All of these

52. Girls surpass boys physically in
(a) infancy
(b) later childhood
(c) early childhood
(d) adolescence

53. The period of later childhood is marked by
(a) intellectual maturity
(b) high muscular energy
(c) hero worship
(d) all of these

54. Which of the following is not the characteristics of intellectual development of later childhood?
(a) High interest in science fiction
(b) Increased logical power
(c) Careful for future
(d) End of imaginary fears

55. Children are very much hateful or indifferent to opposite sex at the age of
(a) 11-12 (b) 13-14
(c) 10-11 (d) 15-16

56. Period of later childhood is marked by
(a) slow and steady physical growth
(b) stability in emotions
(c) anger against injustice
(d) all of these

57. At the end of later childhood period, the child
(a) feels himself superior to girls
(b) becomes independent of his family
(c) wants to become hero
(d) all of these

58. The best place of social development for a 12 years old child is
(a) neighbourhood
(b) family
(c) playground
(d) school

59. Group activities and group loyalties are at its peak at the age of
(a) 10-12 (b) 13-15
(c) 8-10 (d) 18-20

60. A teacher should not let a 12 years old child any time free because
(a) child is always interested to get involve in physical or mental activities
(b) spurts of creativity are seen at this age
(c) child is frustrated
(d) all of these

61. Elektra complex refers to
(a) daughter comes closer to the father
(b) son comes closer to the mother
(c) inferiority complex in the presence of girls
(d) none of these

62. According to Freud, super-ego is properly developed during
(a) latency period (b) anal period
(c) phallic period (d) none of these

63. Development is a process of observable social interaction. This is the opinion of
(a) Erikson (b) Skinner
(c) Robert Sears (d) None of these

64. The secondary behaviour of the child according to Robert Sears starts with
(a) reinforcement (b) imitation
(c) modelling (d) none of these

65. The period of sensory motor adoptation of Piaget is
(a) 0-2 years (b) 1-3 years
(c) 3-5 years (d) 4-6 years

66. The child adopts the view points of others on the basis of consequences of these views in the
(*a*) third stage of Kohlberg's theory
(*b*) second stage of Kohlberg's theory
(*c*) fourth stage of Kohlberg's theory
(*d*) fifth stage of Kohlberg's theory

67. Which of the following is not the view point of cognitive theories of development?
(*a*) moral principles are acquired automatically with age
(*b*) super ego is formed during the period of adolescence
(*c*) Moral values are determined by culture
(*d*) Mural principles are universal

68. Organization of sensory experiences about a particular object is called
(*a*) percepts (*b*) reasoning
(*c*) concept (*d*) none of these

69. The concept building in a person depends on
(*a*) the age and maturity of the person
(*b*) past experiences of the learner
(*c*) intelligence of the learner
(*d*) all of these

70. Agreement on a concept is possible because
(*a*) concepts are subjective
(*b*) concepts are objective
(*c*) concepts are hierarchical
(*d*) b and c both

71. Which of the following statements about concepts is correct?
(*a*) Some concepts are more powerful than others
(*b*) All concepts are universal
(*c*) Concepts are differentiated on the basis of their attributes
(*d*) None of these

72. Which is the highest level of concept formation?
(*a*) formal level (*b*) sensory level
(*c*) concrete level (*d*) none of these

73. How many steps of problem solving has been given by Gates?
(*a*) Six (*b*) Seven
(*c*) Five (*d*) Ten

74. Freeman considers intelligence as an ability
(*a*) to adjust in an adverse situation
(*b*) to learn better and faster
(*c*) to manipulate abstract materials
(*d*) all of these

75. Single factor theory of intelligence was given by
(*a*) Alfred Binet (*b*) Thorndike
(*c*) Freeman (*d*) None of them

76. Which of the following is not the characteristics of 'S' factor according to Spearman ?
(*a*) It is the acquired capacity of the individual
(*b*) Specialization in only one trade is possible
(*c*) It varies from activity to activity in the same individual
(*d*) Individuals differ only in 'S' factor of intelligence

77. In multifactor theory, range is related to
(*a*) Number of tasks that a person can do in a limited period of time
(*b*) Difficulty level of items
(*c*) General intelligence of learners
(*d*) None of these

78. SI model of intelligence was given by I P Guilford in
(*a*) 1911 (*b*) 1904
(*c*) 1966 (*d*) 1975

79. Hierarchy theory of intelligence was given by
(*a*) Jenson
(*b*) Thorndike
(*c*) Burt and Vernon
(*d*) None of them

80. In the pre-Binet period, intelligence was considered as
(*a*) Sensory acuity of the individual
(*b*) Verbal ability of the individual
(*c*) Associative ability of the individual
(*d*) All of these

81. An age scale of intelligence was first developed by
(*a*) Spearman (*b*) Terman
(*c*) Binet-Simon (*d*) None of them

82. Binet-Simon scale of intelligence measures
(*a*) General mental abilities not specific ones.
(*b*) Mental growth of the individual over a period of time
(*c*) The aptitude or level of an examinee not their speed
(*d*) All of these

83. WAIS came into being in
(*a*) 1939 (*b*) 1955
(*c*) 1960 (*d*) 1964

84. Wechsler developed an intelligence test for children in
(*a*) 1939 (*b*) 1949
(*c*) 1955 (*d*) 1956

85. Catell's culture fair test of intelligence was developed in
(*a*) 1960 (*b*) 1961
(*c*) 1965 (*d*) 1955

86. Non-verbal test of intelligence is suitable for
(*a*) deaf and dumb
(*b*) illiterates
(*c*) backward children
(*d*) all of these

87. Intelligence testing is useful for knowing
(*a*) individual difference
(*b*) mental retardation

(*c*) educational backwardness
(*d*) all of these

88. Scores on intelligence tests can not be fully relied on because
(*a*) fatigue level can influence the performance
(*b*) cultural factors can influence the score
(*c*) they generally do not reveal all the mental abilities of a person
(*d*) all of these

89. Who among the following psychologists is of the view that a learner can be motivated by satisfying his needs?
(*a*) Henry Murray (*b*) Abraham Maslow
(*c*) Both of these (*d*) None of these

90. Permanent change in behaviour brought about by experience or training is called.
(*a*) Learning (*b*) Motivation
(*c*) Assimilation (*d*) None of these

91. The book "**Theory of Motivation**" has been written by
(*a*) K B Madson (*b*) Maslow
(*c*) Murray (*d*) None of them

92. Motivated behaviour of a person is
(*a*) Well directed and well guided towards the goal
(*b*) Agitated until the goal is achieved
(*c*) Both of these
(*d*) None of these

93. Factors affecting motivations are
(*a*) Physiological factors only
(*b*) Psychological factors only
(*c*) Psycho-social factors
(*d*) All of these

94. Process of motivation is affected by all except
(*a*) Habits
(*b*) Mental sets and values
(*c*) Physical factors
(*d*) None of these

95. Which of the following does not come under the category of social motives?
(*a*) Prestige and Status
(*b*) Social approval
(*c*) Personal goal
(*d*) Money hoarding

96. Our action and behaviour is motivated by the desire for getting pleasure and avoiding pain. This is the opinion of
(*a*) Thomas Hobbes (*b*) Descartes
(*c*) Kant (*d*) John Locke

97. Fundamental instincts of humans are inherited rather than acquired. These instincts are the spring of human behaviour. The above opinion was held by
(*a*) Charles Darwin (*b*) Mc Dougall
(*c*) Both of these (*d*) None of these

98. Instinct theory of behaviour was rejected by psychologists on which of the following grounds?
(*a*) Adult behaviour is guided by experience and learning also. It is not always guided by instinct
(*b*) Human behaviour is affected by the cultural factors also
(*c*) Human being is a rational animal. He is not supposed to be directed by instincts only
(*d*) All of these

99. Central motive state was explained by
(*a*) Morgan
(*b*) Mc Dougall
(*c*) Murray
(*d*) None of them

100. Abraham Maslow was basically a
(*a*) Pragmatist (*b*) Humanist
(*c*) Realist (*d*) All of them

101. A self actualized person is one who
(*a*) Does not accept restrictions imposed by the society
(*b*) Always seeks perfection
(*c*) Is very good in inter personal relationship with others
(*d*) All of these

102. The theory of achievement motivation was developed by Mc Clelland of Harward University in
(*a*) 1949 (*b*) 1951
(*c*) 1965 (*d*) 1944

103. Achievement motive in a child can be developed by
(*a*) Proper guidance and high expectation from the child
(*b*) Telling the stories of great men to the child
(*c*) Setting a realistic goal for the child
(*d*) All of these

104. Which of the following is not a characteristic of learning?
(*a*) Learning is a relatively permanent change in behaviour
(*b*) Learning is a growth of the organism
(*c*) Learning is directly observed
(*d*) Learning is a goal directed process

105. In the beginning of life, the baby is guided by
(*a*) maturation
(*b*) instincts
(*c*) learning
(*d*) none of these

106. Accumulation of knowledge or facts becomes learning when
(*a*) It is applied in real life situation
(*b*) It is done by the learner himself
(*c*) It is provided by the teacher
(*d*) None of these

107. Dancing, driving, writing etc are the examples of
(*a*) Mechanical learning
(*b*) Perceptual motor learning
(*c*) Psychomotor learning
(*d*) both (*b*) and (*c*)

108. In Gagne's hierarchy, learning has been divided into
(*a*) eight parts (*b*) nine parts
(*c*) seven parts (*d*) none of the above

109. Match the following:

	(A)	(B)
(*i*)	Classical conditioning	1. Kohler
(*ii*)	Drive reduction	2. Hull
(*iii*)	Sign gestalt	3. Pavlov
(*iv*)	Learning by insight	4. Tolman

	(*i*)	(*ii*)	(*iii*)	(*iv*)
(*a*)	1	2	3	4
(*b*)	3	2	4	1
(*c*)	2	1	3	4
(*d*)	4	3	2	1

110. Reflexes are of two types according to Pavlov. They are physiological and
(*a*) Psychic (*b*) Neural
(*c*) Mental (*d*) None of these

111. In classical conditioning, extinction will take place when
(*a*) Organism is poor in generalization
(*b*) CS is given without UCS for a long time
(*c*) CS > UCS
(*d*) None of these

112. Backward conditioning will take place when
(*a*) UCS is presented prior to CS
(*b*) CS is presented prior to UCS
(*c*) Reward is not given to the organism
(*d*) None of these

113. When connection is not established between a CS and CR, due to any factor, that is called
(*a*) Spontaneous recovery
(*b*) Extinction
(*c*) Inhibition
(*d*) None of these

114. When a child responds to all women who wear black suit because of the black suit of her mother, it is the example of
(*a*) internal inhibition
(*b*) generalization
(*c*) assimilation
(*d*) all of these

115. Which of the following is not a behaviourist?
(*a*) Watson
(*b*) Skinner
(*c*) Pavlov
(*d*) Lewin

116. Learning according to Watson is
(*a*) the shifting of old responses to the new stimuli
(*b*) the result of connection between S-R formed in the brain
(*c*) both of these
(*d*) none of these

117. Which of the following points differentiates the theories of Watson and Guthrie?
(*a*) law of contiguity
(*b*) law of recency
(*c*) generalization
(*d*) law of frequency

118. In operant conditioning reward works as motives but in Guthrie's theory motives are
(*a*) Stimuli given to the learner
(*b*) Actions done by the learner
(*c*) Both of these
(*d*) None of these

119. We forget something not by disuse but by other learning. This is the theory of
(*a*) contiguity
(*b*) trial and error
(*c*) learning by insight
(*d*) perception

120. Which of the following is not an essential requirement for trial and error learning?
(*a*) Drive
(*b*) Barrier
(*c*) Chance success
(*d*) Selective movement of the organism

121. According to the law of trial and error, learning occurs when
(*a*) it is satisfying for the learner
(*b*) bond between S-R is strengthened by the repeated use
(*c*) drive is there in the learner to act
(*d*) all of these

122. Which of the following facilitates learning according to Thorndike?
(*a*) Transfer of training
(*b*) Mental set of the learner
(*c*) Law of contiguity
(*d*) All of these

123. In Hull's theory, for learning to occur, the S-R connection must be associated with the
(*a*) cognitive field of the learner
(*b*) diminution of the need
(*c*) both of these
(*d*) none of these

124. Reinforcement in Skinner's theory is similar to drive reduction in which theory
(*a*) Hull's theory
(*b*) Guthrie's theory
(*c*) Lewin's theory
(*d*) None of these

125. Which of the following theories is most quantitatively measurable?
(*a*) Pavlov's
(*b*) Skinner's
(*c*) Hull's
(*d*) None of these

126. In drive reduction theory, the effective stimulus in learning is the trace. It is formed
(*a*) in the brain
(*b*) by the bond of S-R
(*c*) in the nervous system
(*d*) none of these

127. In drive reduction theory, habit formation is a function of
(*a*) stimulus potential
(*b*) stimulus generalization
(*c*) reaction potential
(*d*) all of these

128. Hull may be considered superior to other S-R Theorists in the sense that he was able to measure
(*a*) latency of response
(*b*) reinforcement potential
(*c*) both of these
(*d*) none of these

129. Which of the following points differentiates Skinner from other S-R theorists?
(*a*) His operant conditioning (type R learning)
(*b*) His schedule of reinforcement
(*c*) His way of shaping behaviour
(*d*) All of these

130. Skinner's theory is more objective in nature than the others because
(*a*) operant behaviour is external
(*b*) reflexes never have zero strength
(*c*) reinforcement is followed by responses
(*d*) all of these

131. Aversive stimuli in operant conditioning means
(*a*) individual will not do a particular act because of fear of such stimuli
(*b*) individual will not do a particular act because of the disapproval from others
(*c*) both of these
(*d*) none of these

132. In Skinner's theory, reinforcement is given to the learner when
(*a*) his response is 100% correct
(*b*) his response is closer to the correct behaviour
(*c*) both of these
(*d*) none of these

133. Which of the following statements regarding S-R theories is not correct?
(*a*) Man behaves like a machine
(*b*) Behaviour is overt and can be objectively measured
(*c*) Learning proceeds from simple to complex
(*d*) Things are perceived in the context of figure ground *i.e.*, in relation to other things

134. Which of the following statements regarding field theories are correct?
(*a*) Learning is not additive
(*b*) Molar approach of behaviour is followed here
(*c*) Interaction between organism and the environment is essential for learning
(*d*) All of these

135. Operant conditioning is different from respondent conditioning in which of the following points
(*a*) In OC reinforcement is given after the response is made
(*b*) In operant conditioning, behaviour is controlled by central nervous system
(*c*) A chain of responses is needed for shaping the behaviour (learning)
(*d*) All of these

136. Thorndike and Skinner do not differ at all in
(*a*) the law of effect
(*b*) law of readiness
(*c*) law of contiguity
(*d*) all of these

137. According to gestalt psychologists, behaviour can not be quantified because
(*a*) it is always changeable
(*b*) it is governed by the configuration produced in the mind
(*c*) it is rarely overt
(*d*) all of these

138. Law of pragnanz is the other name of the law of
(*a*) continuity
(*b*) closure
(*c*) contiguity
(*d*) none of these

139. How does the law of similarity work according to field theorists?
(*a*) Similar ideas and experiences get associated to form a whole
(*b*) Similar objects or experiences are easily learnt
(*c*) Both of these
(*d*) None of these

140. Learning by insight looks similar to some extent to which of the following theories?
(*a*) Need reduction theory
(*b*) R type of learning
(*c*) Trial and error theory
(*d*) None of the above

141. The other name of conditioned reflexes is
(*a*) psychic reflexes
(*b*) motor reflexes

(*c*) physiological reflexes
(*d*) none of the above

142. According to Renzuli, a gifted child is one
(*a*) Who possesses above average ability in almost every field
(*b*) Who is committed to task and highly motivated
(*c*) Who is definitely creative
(*d*) All of these

143. Gifted and talented children must be identified as early as possible because
(*a*) If their potentials are not developed by proper guidance of the teacher, it is a loss of the society
(*b*) They are likely to create problems for others, if they are not given work according to their ability
(*c*) Ordinary level of curriculum will not suit to these children
(*d*) All of these

144. Achievement test can be a good indicator of intellectual power if
(*a*) It is conducted immediately after the teaching is over
(*b*) A student shows good performance consistently on different achievement test
(*c*) Both of these
(*d*) None of these

145. Which of the following skills does not require high intellectual ability?
(*a*) Technical skills
(*b*) Mechanical skills
(*c*) Teaching skills
(*d*) Management skills

146. Cognitive abilities related to giftedness are all except
(*a*) High comprehensive and analytical abilities
(*b*) High level of verbal intelligence
(*c*) High retention power
(*d*) None of these

147. A superior child is advanced to a normal child by at least
(*a*) 2½ years
(*b*) Four years
(*c*) 1 years
(*d*) 1½ years

148. A gifted child is
(*a*) realistic in his approach
(*b*) highly interested in solving social problems
(*c*) more frequently chosen by his age mates and peers
(*d*) all of these

149. Which of the following enrichment programmes is suitable for gifted children in the school?
(*a*) Mathematics or Science Olympiad
(*b*) Challenging home assignments
(*c*) Map work during studies
(*d*) All of these

150. Which of the following does not come under the category of acceleration for gifted children?
(*a*) Skipping of classes
(*b*) Early admission
(*c*) Extra laboratory work
(*d*) Organizing summer camps

151. Under achievers are those who
(*a*) Score low on intelligence tests
(*b*) Achieve low in the class consistently despite their superior intelligence
(*c*) Are unable to correspond their achievement to the level of their innate abilities
(*d*) Both (*b*) and (*c*)

152. Which of the following conditions must be satisfied in order to designate a person mentally retarded?
(*a*) Sub-normal intellectual functioning
(*b*) Very poor adaptive ability
(*c*) Dependability on others
(*d*) All of these

153. The best measure of identifying mildly mentally retarded is
(*a*) Administration of standardized intelligence test
(*b*) Administration of behaviour test
(*c*) Administration of adjustment test
(*d*) A combination of all

154. Physical trauma during pregnancy may cause
(*a*) Mental retardation
(*b*) Blindness
(*c*) Deafness
(*d*) All of these

155. All of the following may cause mental retardation except
(*a*) Blood incompatibility
(*b*) Action of toxic agent
(*c*) Radio-activity
(*d*) None of these

156. Which of the following is an important postnatal cause of mental retardation?
(*a*) Brain injury
(*b*) Infection
(*c*) Severe malnutrition
(*d*) All of these

157. Dullers do not differ from normal children in
(*a*) Physical characteristics
(*b*) Level of social expectancy
(*c*) Both of these
(*d*) None of these

158. Which of the following things is not required for educating mildly mentally retarded children?
(*a*) Regular counseling
(*b*) Remedial teaching

(c) Modification in the curriculum
(d) Regular evaluation

159. Teaching of which of the following skills is not suitable to borderline cases?
(a) Electric fitting
(b) Repairing of electric or electronic equipments
(c) Oratory skills
(d) Activity based skills

160. IQ range of morons are in the range of
(a) 60-90 (b) 50-75
(c) 60-80 (d) 30-50

161. Morons are slow in
(a) Physical growth
(b) Thinking and planning
(c) Taking initiative
(d) All of these

162. Unsatisfactory relation of a mentally retarded child with the environment is technically called
(a) Autism
(b) Maladjustment
(c) Pseudo-dullness
(d) None of these

163. All of the following are characteristics of morons except
(a) They are restricted to unskilled or semi skilled occupations
(b) They are likely to be delinquent more easily
(c) They have stronger sex drives than the normals
(d) They are educable upto normal level but at a slower rate

164. Which of the following modifications in the curriculum is needed for morons?
(a) Activity based curriculum
(b) Skill dominated curriculum
(c) Emphasis on social training
(d) All of these

165. Which of the following things can not be taught to Imbeciles?
(a) Self help skills
(b) Unskilled job to be performed under supervision
(c) Writing skills
(d) Social skills

166. In which of the following cases divergent thinking is required?
(a) Attempting a multiple choice items
(b) Writing an essay
(c) Doing a research activity
(d) Both (a) and (c)

167. Which of the following tests is similar to Guilford's test of cognitive abilities?
(a) Word association test
(b) Things test
(c) Hidden shapes test
(d) None of these

168. In Hidden shapes test of creativity, which of the following things is used?
(a) Pictures
(b) Words
(c) Things
(d) None of them

169. A creative child in the class can not be satisfied unless
(a) He is given freedom to manipulate ideas or things
(b) He is allowed to ask questions in his own way
(c) Both of these
(d) None of these

170. A creative child is one who
(a) Is ideationally productive and unconventional
(b) Does not stick to social and religious norms in a hard manner
(c) Is all the time restless to do something uncommon and unique
(d) All of these

171. For the development of creative potential of a child, the teacher should
(a) Allow him to be critical to ideas and people
(b) Give them chance of problem solving
(c) Both of these
(d) None of these

172. New ideas (Eureka) suddenly comes in the minds of the creative children in the stage of
(a) Preparation
(b) Illumination
(c) Revision
(d) Incubation

173. The technique to foster creativity in children is
(a) Brain storming
(b) Problem solving
(c) Both of these
(d) None of these

174. A teacher can foster creativity in children by
(a) Developing confidence in them
(b) Giving them opportunity to express
(c) Both of these
(d) None of these

175. Learning disabled children are
(a) Deficient in using potentials
(b) Low in intelligence
(c) Slow in activity
(d) None of these

176. Learning disabled children perform very poorly in
(a) academic areas
(b) technical areas

(c) both of these
(d) none of these

177. Problem of learning disability is more complex than that of other disabilities because
(a) Its causes can not be easily ascertained by applying usual tests
(b) It is associated to behaviour problems
(c) Both of these
(d) None of these

178. Educationally, learning disabled look similar to
(a) dullers
(b) backward children
(c) both of these
(d) none of these

179. In which of the following physical characteristics learning disabled children differ from the normal ones?
(a) They are all the time clumsy and awkward
(b) Poor coordination of motor abilities
(c) Height, weight and health
(d) All of these

180. Which of the following methods is most suitable for learning disabled children?
(a) Behaviour guidance method
(b) Remedial teaching
(c) Brain storming
(d) None of them

181. In order to improve work habits of learning disabled what should be done?
(a) Unattending behaviour should be penalized
(b) Close monitoring of the behaviour is needed
(c) Cues and prompt should be given
(d) All of these

182. Those who are normal in intelligence but slow in academic achievement due to psycho-social reasons are called
(a) Backward children
(b) Gifted under achievers
(c) Both of these
(d) None of these

183. Consistent low achievement leads to low intelligence because
(a) 50% intellectual ability is expressed in verbal form
(b) Learning develops thinking and reasoning power
(c) Both of these
(d) None of these

184. Which of the following situations may lead to educational backwardness?
(a) Sensory impairment
(b) Motor disability
(c) Long diseases and health problems.
(d) All of these

185. Emotional disturbances may lead to educational backwardness because
(a) Proper emotional development is necessary for social interactions
(b) Emotions will develop intellectual power, *i.e.*, emotional intelligence
(c) Both of these
(d) None of these

186. Which of the following factors will not lead to educational backwardness?
(a) Poor socio economic status of the family
(b) Poor educational environment of the school
(c) Occupation of the family
(d) Poor emotional climate of the family

187. Which of the following is an important cause of educational backwardness at primary level of education in India?
(a) Poor school organisation
(b) Lack of accountability
(c) Attitude of the masses towards education
(d) All of these

188. Which of the following measures should be adopted by the teacher to check educational backwardness?
(a) Continuous evaluation and regular feedback
(b) Remedial teaching
(c) Adjustment and behaviour training
(d) All of these

189. Teaching by small steps and frequent short assignment techniques are useful for
(a) Slow learners
(b) Learning disabled
(c) Educationally backward children
(d) Children of all types of disabilities

190. Special schools are required for backward children when
(a) Backwardness is due to any serious physical handicap
(b) The size of population of backward children in the society is very large as is the case of Gujarat where the achievement of students in mathematics is always seen very low
(c) Both of these
(d) None of these

191. Which of the following should be considered the most important quality of a teacher at primary level?
(a) Patience and perseverance
(b) Competence in methods of teaching and knowledge of subjects
(c) Competence to teach in highly standardised language
(d) Eagerness to teach

192. A teacher, because of his/her democratic nature, allows students to sit all over the class. Some sit together and discuss or do group reading. Some sit quietly and read themselves. A parent does not like it. Which of the following may be the best way to handle the situation?

(*a*) Parents should request the principal to change the section of their ward
(*b*) Parents should show trust in the teacher and discuss the problem with the teacher
(*c*) Parents should take away the child from that school
(*d*) Parents should complain against the teacher to the principal

193. The stage in which a child begins to think logically about objects and events is known as
(*a*) Formal operational stage
(*b*) Pre-operational stage
(*c*) Concrete operational stage
(*d*) Sensori-motor stage

194. 'Mind mapping' refers to
(*a*) a plan of action for an adventure
(*b*) drawing the picture of a mind
(*c*) researching the functioning of the mind
(*d*) a technique to enhance comprehension

195. The best way, specially at primary level, to address the learning difficulties of students is to use
(*a*) expensive and glossy support material
(*b*) easy and interesting textbooks
(*c*) story-telling method
(*d*) a variety of teaching methods suited to the disability

196. Which of the following will foster creativity among learners?
(*a*) Providing opportunities to question and to nurture the innate talents of every learner
(*b*) Emphasizing achievement goals from the beginning of school life
(*c*) Coaching students for good marks in examination
(*d*) Teaching the students the practical value of good education

197. According to Piaget, at which of the following stages does a child begin to think logically about abstract propositions?
(*a*) Formal operational stage (11 years and up)
(*b*) Sensori-motor stage (Birth–02 years)
(*c*) Pre-operational stage (02–07 years)
(*d*) Concrete operational stage (07–11 years)

198. Learning can be enriched if
(*a*) more and more teaching aids are used in the class
(*b*) teachers use different types of lectures and explanation
(*c*) due attention is paid to periodic tests in the class
(*d*) situations from the real world are brought into the class in which students interact with each other and the teahcer facilitates

199. Which of the following statements ***cannot*** be considered as a feature of the process of learning?
(*a*) Learning is a comprehensive process
(*b*) Learning is goal-oriented
(*c*) Unlearning is also a learning process
(*d*) Educational institutions are the only place where learning takes place

200. A student of V-grade with 'visual deficiency' should be
(*a*) helped with his/her routine-work by parents and friends
(*b*) treated normally in the classroom and provided support through Audio CDs
(*c*) given special treatment in the classroom
(*d*) excused to do a lower level of work

201. Which of the following is ***not*** related to the socio-psychological needs of the child?
(*a*) Need for emotional security
(*b*) Regular elimination of waste products from the body
(*c*) Need for company
(*d*) Need for appreciation or social approval

202. Which is the place where the child's 'cognitive' development is defined in the best way?
(*a*) School and classroom environment
(*b*) Auditorium
(*c*) Home
(*d*) Playground

203. .... is considered a sign of motivated teaching.
(*a*) Remedial work given by the teacher
(*b*) Questioning by students
(*c*) Pin drop silence in the class
(*d*) Maximum attendance in the class

204. Which of the following is ***not*** a sign of an intelligent young child?
(*a*) One who has the ability to communicate fluently and appropriately
(*b*) One who carries on thinking in an abstract manner
(*c*) One who can adjust oneself in a new environment
(*d*) One who has the ability to cram long essays very quickly

205. "Children actively construct their understanding of the world" is a statement attributed to
(*a*) Pavlov (*b*) Kohlberg
(*c*) Skinner (*d*) Piaget

206. Kritika who does ***not*** talk much at home, talks a lot at school. It shows that
(*a*) teachers demand that children should talk a lot at school
(*b*) she does not like her home at all
(*c*) her thoughts get acknowledged at school
(*d*) the school provides opportunities to children to talk a lot

207. A teacher should make an attempt to understand the potentialities of her/his students. Which of the following fields is related to this objective?
(*a*) Social Philosophy
(*b*) Media – Psychology
(*c*) Educational Psychology
(*d*) Educational Sociology

208. Motivation, in the process of learning,
(*a*) differentiates new learning from old learning
(*b*) makes learners think unidirectionally
(*c*) creates interest for learning among young learners
(*d*) sharpens the memory of learners

209. The term 'curriculum' in the field of education refers to
(*a*) overall programme of the school which students experience on a day-to-day basis
(*b*) evaluation process
(*c*) text-material to be used in the class
(*d*) methods of teaching and the content to be taught

210. At lower classes, play-way method of teaching is based on
(*a*) principles of methods of teaching
(*b*) psychological principles of development and growth
(*c*) sociological principles of teaching
(*d*) theory of physical education programmes

211. "A young child responds to a new situation on the basis of the response made by him/her in a similar situation as in the past." This is related to
(*a*) 'Law of Effect' of learning
(*b*) 'Law of Attitude' of learning process
(*c*) 'Law of Readiness' of learning
(*d*) 'Law of Analogy' of learning

212. .... is ***not*** considered a sign of 'being gifted'.
(*a*) Fighting with others
(*b*) Novelty in expression
(*c*) Curiosity
(*d*) Creative ideas

213. Education of children with special needs should be provided
(*a*) by methods developed for special children in special schools
(*b*) in special schools
(*c*) by special teachers in special schools
(*d*) along with other normal children

214. To make assessment a 'useful and interesting' process, one should be careful about
(*a*) labelling students as intelligent or average learners
(*b*) using a variety of ways to collect information about the student's learning across the scholastic and co-scholastic boundaries
(*c*) using technical language to give feedback
(*d*) making comparisons between different students

215. 'Dyslexia' is associated with
(*a*) Mathematical disorder
(*b*) Reading disorder
(*c*) Behavioural disorder
(*d*) Mental disorder

216. Parents should play a .... role in the learning process of young children.
(*a*) proactive
(*b*) sympathetic
(*c*) neutral
(*d*) negative

217. "Development is a never ending process." This idea is associated with
(*a*) Principle of continuity
(*b*) Principle of integration
(*c*) Principle of interaction
(*d*) Principle of interrelation

218. The 'insight theory of learning' is promoted by
(*a*) Pavlov
(*b*) Jean Piaget
(*c*) Vygotsky
(*d*) 'Gestalt' theorists

219. In which of the following stages do children become active members of their peer group?
(*a*) Adulthood
(*b*) Early childhood
(*c*) Childhood
(*d*) Adolescence

220. Four distinct stages of children's intellectual development are identified by
(*a*) Erikson (*b*) Skinner
(*c*) Piaget (*d*) Kohlberg

221. Mass media, cinema and library are passive agencies of education because
(*a*) learner can not react to the feedback system of these agencies directly
(*b*) they provide informal education
(*c*) they can not come closer to the educant
(*d*) all of these

222. Education of a child really begins
(*a*) Once he takes birth
(*b*) Once he attains the age of three
(*c*) Once he is admitted to post nursery schools
(*d*) Once he learns to speak

223. Family is the original social institution from which all other institutions emerged, who said this
(*a*) Brown (*b*) Ballard
(*c*) Machiver (*d*) None of them

224. Which of the following is not the primary function of schools
(*a*) reorganization and reconstruction of Human experiences

(b) all-round development of the child
(c) to make the children self reliant
(d) advancement of culture

225. In a democratic country, school should reflect
(a) National aspirations
(b) Community related local aspirations
(c) Both of these
(d) None of these

226. The best teacher in a village school is he who
(a) carries community experiences to the class room
(b) prepares instructional programmes in the interest of the community
(c) carries classroom experiences to the community
(d) all of these

227. Universalisation of education is the concept adopted by
(a) modern state (b) democratic state
(c) totalitarian state (d) religious state

228. Secular education in India means
(a) an education opposed to religion
(b) an education indifferent to religion
(c) an education emphasizing equality of religions
(d) none of these

229. School works as a social sub system for
(a) transmission of culture
(b) preservation of culture
(c) advancement of culture
(d) all of these

230. "Society is nothing but a process of interaction among people." Who said this?
(a) Lapier (b) Cuber
(c) Reuter (d) Payne

231. The best model of schooling is
(a) Close interaction between education of society
(b) Self reliant society by education
(c) Reflection of openness by schools
(d) All of these

232. Special provisions have been made for socially and educationally backward classes of the nation under article
(a) 29 (b) 31
(c) 15 (d) 19

233. Religious education is prohibited in government schools and colleges under Article
(a) 29 (b) 28 (1)
(c) 39 (2) (d) 15 (a)

234. Religious and linguistic minorities shall have the right to establish and administer their own educational institutions under Article
(a) 30(1) (b) 31(2)
(c) 40 (d) 41

235. Article 351 is about
(a) education of tribals
(b) promotion of Hindi
(c) promotion of secularism
(d) English as official language

236. Status of central university is given to any educational institution under union list of
(a) Entry 65 (b) Entry 63
(c) Entry 66 (d) None of these

237. Entry 25 of concurrent list states about
(a) vocational and technical training of labour
(b) the education of working class
(c) the education of disabled
(d) none of the above

238. Education in the mother tongue at primary stage to children belonging to linguistic minorities has been mentioned in Article
(a) 250 (b) 350
(c) 349 (d) 351

239. Educational and economic interests of SCs and STs have been safeguarded under Article
(a) 46 (b) 45(a)
(c) 351 (d) 52

240. Education of union territories is administered by the central government under Article
(a) 350 (b) 229
(c) 239 (d) 50

241. Education was transferred from state list of subjects to concurrent list in
(a) 1976 (b) 1972
(c) 1980 (d) 1950

242. Which of the following statements about growth and development is not correct?
(a) Growth generally refers to quantitative changes while development refers to qualitative changes
(b) Growth is a function of the environment
(c) Growth is not possible without development and vice versa
(d) Growth is determined by intrinsic and genetic factors of the organism

243. The limit of growth is fixed by
(a) internal factors of the organism
(b) nutrition and exercise
(c) both of these
(d) none of these

244. Development is
(a) Maturation
(b) Learning
(c) Synthesis of abilities
(d) All of these

245. Development takes place when
(a) environmental forces work on the organism
(b) environmental forces interact with the hereditary forces in an organism

(c) both of these
(d) none of these

246. Which of the following statements about development is correct?
(a) Process of development can be improved by exercise and nutrition
(b) Development may be positive and negative both
(c) Development proceeds from general to specific
(d) All of these

247. The son of a goldsmith becomes an expert goldsmith. It is an example of a
(a) biological heredity
(b) social heredity
(c) transfer of instinct
(d) none of these

248. All humans contain .... chromosomes.
(a) 26 (b) 36
(c) 46 (d) 42

249. DNA test helps us to know
(a) the genetic traits of a person
(b) nature of personality and its composition
(c) both of these
(d) none of these

250. The law of inheritance was discovered by Gregor Mendel in
(a) 1866 (b) 1911
(c) 1888 (d) 1920

251. Everything which influences child's development is categorised under the 'Environment' other than 'Heredity.' This statement is given by
(a) Boring (b) Woodworth
(c) Douglas (d) Holland

252. During infancy which of the following aspect of development is not completed?
(a) Moral Development
(b) Emotional Development
(c) Social Development
(d) Language Development

253. A teacher who has given the responsibility of 'Infant education,' he must pay attention on
(a) The education must be child-centred
(b) The education must be mother-centred
(c) The education must be sport-centred
(d) The education must be school-centred

254. Which one of the following stage of child's development is popularly nicknamed as Mysterious period of the life?
(a) Infancy (b) Childhood
(c) Adolescence (d) Adulthood

255. Which one of the following is the defect of language development in children?
(a) Stammering (b) Talktiveness
(c) Scribbled writing (d) Reserve nature

256. The major change occurs in adolescent period is
(a) In voice
(b) In Bodily shape and organs
(c) In gestures and manners
(d) In all the above

257. In adolescent girls the following abilities are much better in comparison than the adolescent boys
(a) Language Abilities
(b) Functional Abilities
(c) Thinking Abilities
(d) Scientific Abilities

258. The psychologist who has given much importance to individual difference in children is
(a) Galton (b) Young
(c) Freud (d) Robert

259. In which age-group a child can differentiate between the anger and affection?
(a) In infancy (b) In childhood
(c) In adolescence (d) In adulthood

260. The chief social behaviour of infancy is
(a) Birth of group-feelings
(b) Exchange of toys
(c) Imitation of approved nouns
(d) All the above

261. The nearest emotion of distress which is developed after three months of the age in children
(a) Anger (b) Hate
(c) Fear (d) All the above

262. The best controlling powers of emotionally are displayed by
(a) Gifted children
(b) Mentally retarded
(c) Physically powerful children
(d) The children having escaping tendencies from work

263. Which one of the following does not having maximum development during adolescent stage?
(a) Intellectual abilities
(b) Mental abilities
(c) Interest-related abilities
(d) All of the above

264. In order to develop group-feelings among children, the provision in education required as
(a) The co-operative games and sports in school
(b) The group activities like dance, music and drama
(c) The mass drills and physical exercises on the games field
(d) All the above

265. It is said that in childhood, the children should be exposed to adventurous stories of great historical journeys which may develop the quality of
(*a*) Elimination of fear syndrome
(*b*) Discipline and obedience
(*c*) Delightfulness
(*d*) Enthusiasm and motivation

266. In early childhood, the children should be given education through
(*a*) Toys and games (*b*) Paper-Pencil
(*c*) Models (*d*) Plants

267. Which one of the following is not associated with the social development in childhood?
(*a*) Gang formation
(*b*) Formation of sex-groups
(*c*) Desire for social acceptance in children
(*d*) Attraction towards girls in boys

268. According to Piagent, infants in the sensorimotor thought stage cannot
(*a*) use sensory (*b*) use motor actions
(*c*) form symbolic (*d*) display reflexes

269. According to Piaget, the imaginary audience and the personal fable are both parts of
(*a*) intuitive (*b*) object
(*c*) conservation (*d*) adolescent

270. What is the term that Erikson coined?
(*a*) Oedipus Complex
(*b*) Self-fulfilling Prophecy
(*c*) Identity Crisis
(*d*) Positive Reinforcement

271. The two main personality differences identified by Eysenck are
(*a*) extroversion/introversion and neuroticism/stability
(*b*) pessimism/optimism and sufficiency/insecurity
(*c*) extroversion/introversion and shrewdness/insecurity
(*d*) neuroticism/stability and optimism/pessimism

272. Erik Erikson's theory is a good example of the .... approach.
(*a*) proactive (*b*) idiographic
(*c*) nomothetic (*d*) psychoanalytic

273. Attitudes are .... throughout life and are embodied our socialization process.
(*a*) constant (*b*) seen
(*c*) rigid (*d*) learned

274. Who is called as father of Conditioning?
(*a*) Pavlov (*b*) Koffka
(*c*) Wertheimer (*d*) Skinner

275. Which of the following concept in the basic element of conditioned Response?
(*a*) Associative Reflex
(*b*) Association Response
(*c*) Stimulus effect
(*d*) Latercy Response

276. When a child is asked that chocolate is not given to you, if you are telling-a-lie. This conditioning is an example of
(*a*) Non-reinforced training
(*b*) Discriminatory punishment training
(*c*) Escape training
(*d*) Discriminatory training

277. The meaning of the word conditioning is
(*a*) Relationship between the stimuli
(*b*) Substitution of organism behaviour with another behaviour
(*c*) Accommodation with new stimuli
(*d*) Learning through exercise

278. Which one of the following is not associated with Classical conditioning?
(*a*) Contemporary conditioning
(*b*) Delayed conditioning
(*c*) Trace conditioning
(*d*) Non-reinforced conditioning

279. Instrumental conditioning is also called as
(*a*) S-type conditioning
(*b*) Q-type conditioning
(*c*) C-type conditioning
(*d*) R-type conditioning

280. In which type of conditioning the reward is depend on the response?
(*a*) Classical conditioning
(*b*) Instrumental conditioning
(*c*) Respondents behaviour
(*d*) Operant behaviour

281. The ability of the learner to utilize or apply the acquired knowledge or skills in school to solve problems in similar or related situations at some future date is known as
(*a*) Knowledge acquisition
(*b*) Reinforcement
(*c*) Motivation
(*d*) Transfer of learning

282. In the learning of sciences and math's, scientifically their is no difference in performance as a result of gender. Which of the following influence gender based performance?
(*a*) Culture (*b*) Attitude
(*c*) Stereotyping (*d*) Race

283. Learning is best defined as a process that involves:
(*a*) Two stimuli being paired that produce a conditioned response over time
(*b*) An organism interacting with its environment, becoming changed by

experience, and thereby modifying subsequent behaviours
(c) An organism interacting with its environment through autoshaping and conditioning
(d) An organism responding to its environment based on reinforcement or punishment for behaviours

284. The basic understanding of the relationship between unconditoned response (UR) and conditioned response (CR) included which of the following ideas?
(a) The UR and Cr are not always the same response
(b) Organisms come to generally behave toward conditioned stimulus as they do unconditioned stimulus
(c) Stimulus substitution
(d) The UR and Cr are always the same response

285. Which of the following is accurate in relation to the law of effect?
(a) The law of effect relates to Pavlov's proposal that reward will strengthen the connection between the response that proceeded it and any stimuli present when it is delivere(d)
(b) In modern terminology, Thorndike's 'satisfiers' and 'annoyers' are called enforcers and punishers
(c) In the law of effect, a stimulus-response (S-R) association is learne(d)
(d) It is generally thought that the likelihood of an animal responding in a particular way cannot be controlled by the consequence of that response.

286. Which of the following statements applies to instrumental learning?
(a) Instrumental learning is the process by which an animal learns about the relationship between its behaviour and the consequence of that behaviour.
(b) Instrumentally trained responses are not entirely elicited by identifiable stimuli.
(c) Instrumental learning allows the animal to control the occurrence of environmental events.
(d) All of the above

287. Generally the construct of Personality can be defined in terms of
(a) Biological Approaches
(b) Psycho-sexual Approaches
(c) Psycho-physical Approaches
(d) Bio-chemical Approaches

288. The consistent and distinct style of behavioural tendencies are called as
(a) Habit (b) Trait
(c) Learning (d) Instinct

289. The personal changes that occur among the students through socialization can be judged through
(a) Inter-personal relationship among the specialised groups of the students
(b) The activities of the student
(c) Collecting the information from the parents
(d) Asking to the students

290. Co-operation is the fundamental basis of inter-personal relations which means
(a) It is self-centred in the early development of the children
(b) It is society-centred which is expressed in interpersonal relationship
(c) It can be learned through imitation and suggestibility
(d) It is voluntary in nature and can not be imposed

291. Personality is the sum total of all reactions which a person exhibits
(a) In context of environment
(b) In context of a person
(c) In context of society
(d) In context of himself

292. According to Sri Aurobindo, the basic elements of personality can be sequentially arranged as under
(a) Physical-Emotional-Intellectual-Spiritual-Super Mental
(b) Physical-Intellectual-Super Mental
(c) Physical-Intelecutual-Spiritual
(d) Physical-Emotional-Spiritual

293. Which of the following statements is correct in relation to values?
(a) Value is the dimension of arriving at an aim
(b) Value is a process which activated by a stimulus
(c) Value is a feeling which form through acts
(d) All the above

294. The need of the development of interest is felt in children
(a) They are playful in nature which leads them towards the development of constructive tendencies
(b) The interests make children's feelings more mature
(c) The interests enrich children's instincts
(d) All the above

295. The propounder of the Single factor theory of intelligence was
(a) Alfred Binet (b) Charles Spearman
(c) Burt (d) Guilford

296. Which of intelligence is accepted (recognised) by Trorndike?
(a) Simple-factor theory

(b) Bi-factor theory
(c) Multi-factor theory
(d) Three-dimensional theory

297. The two-factor theory of intelligence has been put forth by
(a) Burt and Vernon (b) Terman
(c) Spearman (d) Skinner

298. The factor which is most important in influencing the intellectual development of the individual is
(a) Family environment
(b) School environment
(c) Neighbourhood
(d) Cultural environment

299. The most important school related factor influencing child's intelligence is
(a) Curriculum
(b) Discipline
(c) Curriculum Activities
(d) All the above

300. Verbal intelligence tests are the better option for
(a) Literate persons (b) Illiterate persons
(c) Small children (d) Special children

ANSWERS

1	2	3	4	5	6	7	8	9	10
(c)	(d)	(b)	(a)	(b)	(c)	(a)	(a)	(c)	(a)
11	12	13	14	15	16	17	18	19	20
(d)	(b)	(d)	(d)	(b)	(a)	(b)	(c)	(a)	(c)
21	22	23	24	25	26	27	28	29	30
(b)	(c)	(d)	(d)	(d)	(a)	(b)	(a)	(c)	(d)
31	32	33	34	35	36	37	38	39	40
(d)	(d)	(c)	(d)	(a)	(d)	(b)	(d)	(a)	(d)
41	42	43	44	45	46	47	48	49	50
(c)	(d)	(a)	(c)	(d)	(a)	(c)	(d)	(d)	(b)
51	52	53	54	55	56	57	58	59	60
(d)	(b)	(d)	(c)	(a)	(d)	(d)	(c)	(a)	(a)
61	62	63	64	65	66	67	68	69	70
(a)	(a)	(c)	(b)	(a)	(a)	(c)	(a)	(d)	(d)
71	72	73	74	75	76	77	78	79	80
(b)	(a)	(c)	(d)	(a)	(d)	(a)	(c)	(c)	(a)
81	82	83	84	85	86	87	88	89	90
(c)	(d)	(b)	(b)	(b)	(d)	(d)	(d)	(c)	(a)
91	92	93	94	95	96	97	98	99	100
(a)	(c)	(d)	(d)	(c)	(a)	(c)	(d)	(a)	(b)
101	102	103	104	105	106	107	108	109	110
(d)	(b)	(d)	(c)	(b)	(a)	(d)	(a)	(b)	(a)
111	112	113	114	115	116	117	118	119	120
(b)	(a)	(c)	(b)	(d)	(c)	(d)	(a)	(a)	(d)
121	122	123	124	125	126	127	128	129	130
(d)	(d)	(b)	(a)	(c)	(c)	(a)	(a)	(d)	(a)
131	132	133	134	135	136	137	138	139	140
(a)	(c)	(d)	(d)	(d)	(a)	(b)	(b)	(a)	(c)
141	142	143	144	145	146	147	148	149	150
(a)	(d)	(d)	(c)	(a)	(d)	(a)	(d)	(d)	(c)
151	152	153	154	155	156	157	158	159	160
(d)	(d)	(d)	(d)	(d)	(d)	(c)	(c)	(c)	(b)
161	162	163	164	165	166	167	168	169	170
(d)	(a)	(d)	(d)	(d)	(d)	(b)	(a)	(c)	(a)

171	172	173	174	175	176	177	178	179	180
(c)	(b)	(c)	(c)	(d)	(a)	(a)	(b)	(b)	(a)
181	**182**	**183**	**184**	**185**	**186**	**187**	**188**	**189**	**190**
(d)	(a)	(c)	(d)	(c)	(c)	(d)	(d)	(d)	(c)
191	**192**	**193**	**194**	**195**	**196**	**197**	**198**	**199**	**200**
(a)	(b)	(c)	(c)	(d)	(a)	(d)	(d)	(d)	(b)
201	**202**	**203**	**204**	**205**	**206**	**207**	**208**	**209**	**210**
(b)	(a)	(b)	(d)	(d)	(c)	(c)	(c)	(a)	(b)
211	**212**	**213**	**214**	**215**	**216**	**217**	**218**	**219**	**220**
(a)	(a)	(d)	(b)	(b)	(a)	(a)	(d)	(d)	(c)
221	**222**	**223**	**224**	**225**	**226**	**227**	**228**	**229**	**230**
(a)	(a)	(b)	(d)	(c)	(d)	(a)	(c)	(d)	(c)
231	**232**	**233**	**234**	**235**	**236**	**237**	**238**	**239**	**240**
(a)	(c)	(b)	(a)	(b)	(b)	(a)	(b)	(a)	(c)
241	**242**	**243**	**244**	**245**	**246**	**247**	**248**	**249**	**250**
(a)	(b)	(a)	(d)	(c)	(d)	(b)	(c)	(c)	(a)
251	**252**	**253**	**254**	**255**	**256**	**257**	**258**	**259**	**260**
(a)	(a)	(c)	(b)	(a)	(d)	(a)	(a)	(a)	(d)
261	**262**	**263**	**264**	**265**	**266**	**267**	**268**	**269**	**270**
(d)	(a)	(d)	(d)	(d)	(a)	(d)	(c)	(d)	(c)
271	**272**	**273**	**274**	**275**	**276**	**277**	**278**	**279**	**280**
(a)	(b)	(d)	(a)	(a)	(a)	(a)	(d)	(a)	(d)
281	**282**	**283**	**284**	**285**	**286**	**287**	**288**	**289**	**290**
(d)	(b)	(b)	(b)	(a)	(b)	(d)	(c)	(a)	(b)
291	**292**	**293**	**294**	**295**	**296**	**297**	**298**	**299**	**300**
(a)	(a)	(d)	(d)	(a)	(c)	(c)	(a)	(d)	(a)

Mathematics

SECTION a MATHEMATICS

NUMBER SYSTEM

KNOWING OUR NUMBERS

Counting thing is a common thing in our daily life and it is easy for us now. When we count things and give specific names or symbols for our countings, that is known as number.

We use numbers and know many things about them. Numbers help us count concrete objects. They help us to say which collection of objects is bigger and arrange them in order, *e.g.*, first, second, etc.

Numbers are used in many different contexts and in many ways.

In our System of numeration, numbers are written by using the symbols 0, 1, 2, 3, 4, 5, 6, 7, 8 and 9 with each symbol getting a value depending on the place it occupies. These symbols are called digits. A number related to the objects in a collection gives an idea of how many objects are there in the collection.

The number 789345126 can be represented as:

Ten crores	Crores	Ten Lacs (Millions)	Lacs	Ten Thousands	Thousands	Hundreds	Tens	Units
10^8	10^7	10^6	10^5	10^4	10^3	10^2	10^1	10^0
7	8	9	3	4	5	1	2	6

This number can be read and written in words as : "Seventy-eight crores, ninety-three lacs, forty-five thousands, one hundred twenty six". The above pattern is known as Indian/Hindu Arabic System.

Types of Numbers

1. **Natural Numbers or Positive Integers (N = 1, 2, 3, 4, 5, ...):** These are also called counting numbers. When two natural numbers are added or multiplied together, the result is always a natural number. Therefore, all positive integers, used for counting objects, are always **natural numbers** whereas zero together with negative integers and fractional numbers are not natural numbers.
2. **Whole Numbers (W = 0, 1, 2, 3, 4, 5, ...):** The number '0' together with the natural numbers gives us the numbers which are called **whole numbers,** *e.g.,* 0, 1, 2, 3, 4, ... etc. whereas –10, –15, –12 ..... or $\frac{1}{5}, \frac{2}{9}, \frac{4}{5}$..... etc. are not whole numbers.

7. **Even Numbers:** All those numbers which are exactly divisible by 2, are called 'even numbers', *e.g.,* 2, 8, 14, 28, 52 etc. are even numbers.
8. **Odd Numbers:** All those numbers which are not exactly divisible by 2, are called 'odd numbers', *e.g.,* 1, 3, 5, 7, 9, 19 etc. are odd numbers.
9. **Composite Numbers:** The numbers which are divisible not only by 1 or themselves, but by some other numbers also, are called the 'composite numbers'. In other words, the numbers which have more than two factors are called 'composite numbers.', *e.g.,* 4, 9, 15, 18, 27, ... etc. are composite numbers.
10. **Prime Numbers:** The numbers which have only two factors, 1 and the number itself are called 'prime numbers', *e.g.,* 2, 5, 11, 19, 23, 31, ... etc. are prime numbers.
11. **Co-primes:** Two numbers which have only 1 as the common factor are called 'co-primes'. 5 and 7 are co-primes. So are 15 and 16.
12. **Twin Primes:** Two prime numbers which differ by 2, are called 'twin primes', *e.g.,* 3, 5; 5, 7; 11, 13; 71, 73 are some pairs of twin primes.

13. **Consecutive Numbers:** The numbers which are following or coming after other numbers in regular order, are called consecutive numbers. 4, 6, 8, 10 are consecutive even numbers and 9, 11, 13, 15 are consecutive odd numbers. 3, 4, 5, 6, 7 ..... etc. are consecutive numbers in the natural order of the number series.

Comparing Numbers: By comparing the numbers we can find out that which is the greatest and which is the smallest number. Through this process we can arrange the numbers in ascending or descending order.

To compare the numbers at first we consider the number of digits. If a number has more digits obviously, it will be greater.

If the numbers of digit are same in two numbers then we compare the digits of left ends. The greater digit shows the greater number. Again if the digits of left ends of the given number are same then we compare rightward and so on, *e.g.*, in the given numbers 4752, 6838, 5927 and 4769 the greatest number is 6838 and the smallest number is 4752.

Ascending Order: If in a given number series, numbers are written in increasing order, then the number series is said to be written in ascending order. *e.g.*, 25, 30, 41, 50 or –10, –8, –6, –2 etc. are series in ascending order.

Descending Order: If in a given number series, numbers are written in decreasing order, then the number series is said to be written in descending order. *e.g.*, 50, 41, 30, 25, or –2, –6, –8, –10 etc. are series in descending order.

Formation of Number

Suppose, we have four digits 7, 0, 5, 9. Using these digits we have to make different 4 digit numbers such that no digits are repeated in a number. Hence, 7059 is allowed, but 7759 is not. Thus, we can make 18 numbers from the given digits. Since, 0759 is actually a three digit number. So, we can not start to make a number with zero.

Estimation

When a number is not written exactly. It is only a rough counting of a thing. Then it is called estimate and the process is called 'estimation'.

We use this process where exact counting is not possible or where the exact counting is not necessary. *e.g.*, the total number of stars in the sky, distance between the sun and the earth, quantity of water flowed through a river etc.

To estimate to the nearest tens by rounding off we observe that which is the nearest tens of the given number and the colser one is the approximate of the number. *e.g.*, if we have to round the number 273 to the nearest tens. Then we will have to observe that which tens is closer to 273, 270 or 280? Obviously, 270 is closer to 273. So it is rounded off as 270.

Same process is used to estimate to the nearest hundreds, thousand and so on.

There are no rigid rules when you want to estimate the outcomes of numbers. The procedure depends on the degree of accuracy required and how quickly the estimate is needed. The most important thing is, how sensible the guessed answer would be.

To estimate products we round off each factor to its greatest place, then multiply the rounded off factors. *e.g.* to estimate the product of 73 and 547, 73 is rounded off to 70 and 547 is rounded off to 500.

$\therefore$ Estimated product = 70 × 500 = 35,000.

Roman Numerals

We have been using the Hindu-Arabic numeral system so far. This is not the only system available. One of the early systems of writing numerals is the system of Roman numerals. This system is still used in many places.

The rules for the system are:

(*a*) If a symbol is repeated, its value is added as many times as it occurs: i.e. II is equal 2, XX is 20 and XXX is 30.

(*b*) A symbol is not repeated more than three times. But the symbols V, L and D are never repeated.

(*c*) If a symbol of smaller value is written to the right of a symbol of greater value, its value gets added to the value of greater symbol.
VI = 5 + 1 = 6, XII = 10 + 2 = 12
and LXV = 50 + 10 + 5 = 65

(*d*) If a symbol of smaller value is written to the left of a symbol of greater value, its value is subtracted from the value of the greater symbol.
IV = 5 – 1 = 4, IX = 10 – 1 = 9
XL = 50 – 10 = 40 XC = 100 – 10 = 90

(*e*) The symbols V, L and D are never written to the left of a symbol of greater value, i.e. V, L and D are never subtracted,
The symbol I can be subtracted from V and X only.
The symbol X can be subtracted from L, M and C only.

Following these rules we get,

1 = I	6 = VI
2 = II	7 = VII
3 = III	8 = VIII
4 = IV	9 = IX
5 = V	

10 = X	60 = LX
20 = XX	70 = LXX
30 = XXX	80 = LXXX
40 = XL	90 = XC
50 = L	100 = C

PLAYING WITH NUMBERS

Playing is the common nature of the children. They feel a great pleasure in game. If we use game in mathematics or mathematics in game then the student will get pleasure and also the knowledge of mathematics. For this purpose mathematics teachers should be attaintive and they should create the appropriate games to teach the different topics.

Factors and Multiples

A factor of number is an exact divisor of that number. *e.g.,* 1, 2, 3, 4, 6 and 12 are the exact divisor of 12. Hence, these are the factors of 12.

If 'm' is the number divided by 'n' then 'm' will be said the multiple of 'n'. *e.g.,* 3, 6, 9, 12, ... are divided by 3. Hence 3, 6, 9, 12 .... are the multiples of 3.

IMPORTANTS

- A number is a multiple of each of its factors.
- 1 is a factor of every number.
- Every number is a factor of itself.
- Every factor of a number is an exact divisor of that number.
- Every factor is less than or equal to the given number.
- Number of factors of a given number are finite.
- Every multiple of a number is greater than or equal to that number.
- The number of multiples of a given number is infinite.
- Every number is a multiple of itself.
- A number for which sum of all its factors is equal to twice the number is called a perfect number.
- 1 is neither a prime nor a composite number.
- 2 is the smallest prime number which is even.
- Every prime number except 2 is odd.

Prime Factorisation

When a number is expressed as a product of its factors we say that the number has been factorised and if only prime factors are used in this process when it is known as prime factorisation.

e.g., factorisation of 54 = $2 \times 3 \times 3 \times 3$

Since all the factors are prime number. Therefore it is the prime factorisation of 54. Prime factorisation is used to find LCM and HCF of numbers.

Highest Common Factor (HCF)

The Highest Common Factor (HCF) of two or more given numbers is the highest (or greatest) of their common factors. It is also known as Greatest Common Divisor (GCD).

e.g., the common factors of 20, 28 and 36 are 1, 2, and 4. Hence, 4 is the highest common factor of 20, 28 and 36.

Lowest Common Multiple (LCM)

The Lowest Common Multiple (LCM) of two or more given numbers is the lowest (or smallest or least) of their common multiples.

e.g., the common multiple of 4 and 9 are 36, 72, 108, 144, ... Hence, 36 is the lowest common multiple of 4 and 9.

Relationship Between Two Numbers and Their L.C.M. and H.C.F.

Product of the H.C.F. and the L.C.M. of two numbers is equal to the product of the given numbers.

i.e., 1st number × 2nd number = H.C.F. × L.C.M.

SOME FACTS AND FORMULAE

(i) The smallest natural number or positive integer is (+1).
(ii) The greatest negative integer is –1.
(iii) The number '0' is neither positive nor negative integer.
(iv) 1 is only such number which is neither a prime number nor a composite number.
(v) 2 is only such number which is an even number as well as a prime number.
(vi) 2 is the smallest prime number.
(vii) The number of prime numbers between 1 to 100 is 25.
(viii) A square number may have 0, 1, 4, 5, 6 or 9 in its unit's place.
(ix) A cubic number may have any digit from 0 to 9 in its unit's place.

Things to remember while solving problems on whole numbers

A. Sum of numbers from 1 to $n = \frac{n(n+1)}{2}$ (where n is the number of terms)

B. Number of odd numbers from 1 to $n = \left(\frac{\text{Last odd number} + 1}{2}\right)$

C. Sum of odd numbers from 1 to n = (Number of odd numbers)^2

D. Number of even numbers from 1 to $n = \left(\frac{\text{Last even number}}{2}\right)$

MATHEMATICS

E. Sum of even numbers from 1 to n = Number of even numbers × (Number of even numbers + 1)

Test for Divisibility of Numbers

1. **Divisibility by 2:** A number is divisible by 2, if its units digit is 0, 2, 4, 6 or 8. For example, each of the numbers 130, 244, 566, 278, ... etc. is divisible by 2.
2. **Divisibility by 3:** A number is divisible by 3, if the sum of its digits is a multiple of 3. For example, each of the numbers 312, 213, 456 is divisible by 3 since sum of digits in each of these numbers is (3 + 1 + 2 = 6), (2 + 1 + 3 = 6) and (4 + 5 + 6 = 15) respectively, each of which is a multiple of 3.
3. **Divisibility by 4:** A number is divisible by 4, if the number formed by its digits in ten's and unit's places is divisible by 4. For example, numbers formed by ten's and unit's digits of 1132, 1312, 1400 and 1348 are 32, 12, 00 and 48 respectively which are divisible by 4. Hence, these numbers also are divisible by 4.
4. **Divisibility by 5:** A number is divisible by 5, if its unit's digit is either 0 or 5. For example, each of the numbers 100, 205, 315, 435 is divisible by 5 since unit's digit in each of these numbers is either 0 or 5.
5. **Divisibility by 6:** A number is divisible by 6, if it is divisible by both 2 and 3.
6. **Divisiblity by 8:** A number is divisible by 8, if the number formed by its digits in hundred's, ten's and unit's places is divisible by 8. For example, numbers formed by hundred's, ten's and unit's digits of 1864, 1024, 2008 and 5000 are 864, 024, 008 and 000 respectively which are divisible by 8. Hence, these numbers also are divisible by 8.
7. **Divisibility by 9:** A number is divisible by 9, if the sum of its digits is a multiple of 9. For example, each of the numbers 23409, 454554, 66636 is divisible by 9 since sum of digits in each of these numbers is (2 + 3 + 4 + 0 + 9 = 18), (4 + 5 + 4 + 5 + 5 + 4 = 27) and (6 + 6 + 6 + 3 + 6 = 27) respectively, each of which is a multiple of 9.
8. **Divisibility by 10:** A number is divisible by 10, if its unit's digit is zero. For example, each of the numbers 50, 80, 1310, 1400 is divisible by 10 since unit's digit in each of these numbers is 0.
9. **Divisibility by 11:** A number is divisible by 11, if the difference of the sum of its digits in even places and the sum of its digits in odd places (starting from unit's place) is either 0 or a multiple of 11. For example, each of the numbers 909183, 540045 and 184712 is divisible by 11 since in each of the numbers difference of the sum of digits in even places and sum of the digits in odd places is [(9 + 9 + 8) – (0 + 1 + 3) = 22], [(5 + 0 + 4) – (4 + 0 + 5) = 0] and [(8 + 7 + 2) – (1 + 4 + 1) = 11] respectively, each of which is either '0' or a multiple of '11'.

Properties of Consecutive Numbers

(*a*) The product of two consecutive numbers is exactly divisible by 2.
e.g., 3 × 4 = 12 which is exactly divisible by 2.

(*b*) The product of three consecutive numbers is exactly divisible by 6.
e.g., 2 × 3 × 4 = 24, which is exactly divisible by 6.

(*c*) The product of four consecutive numbers is exactly divisible by 24.
e.g., 2 × 3 × 4 × 5 = 120, which is exactly divisible by 24.

(*d*) The product of five consecutive numbers is exactly divisible by 120.
e.g., 2 × 3 × 4 × 5 × 6 = 720, which is exactly divisible by 120.

(*e*) The difference between the squares of two consecutive odd numbers is always exactly divisible by 8.
e.g., $5^2 - 3^2 = 25 - 9 = 16$, which is exactly divisible by 8.

(*f*) If 1 is added to the product of either two odd consecutive numbers or two even consecutive numbers, the result obtained will be a perfect square number,
e.g., $5 \times 7 + 1 = 35 + 1 = 36 = 6^2$, which is a perfect square number.

(*g*) The sum of two consecutive numbers is equal to the difference between their squares.
e.g., $4 + 5 = 9 = 5^2 - 4^2 = 9$.

(*h*) The sum of the cubes of three consecutive numbers is exactly divisible by their own sum.
e.g., $4^3 + 5^3 + 6^3 = 64 + 125 + 216 = 405 = (4 + 5 + 6) \times 27$.

WHOLE NUMBERS

We know that the number 1 has no predecessor in natural number. If we add zero as the predecessor for 1 in the collection of natural numbers. The including collection will be the collection of whole numbers. In other words, the natural numbers along with zero form the collection of whole number.

Thus, the whole numbers are 0, 1, 2, 3, 4.....

Properties of Whole Numbers

- All natural numbers are whole numbers.
- All whole numbers are natural number except zero.
- Smallest whole number is zero.
- Greatest whole number can not be determined because adding 1 we can get the next whole number.
- The sum of whole numbers is always a whole number.
- Also the multiplication of whole numbers is always a whole number.
- The above two properties are known as the closer property of addition and multiplication respectively.
- Subtraction and division do not show the closer property. It means difference of two whole numbers as well as quotient of two whole numbers may or may not be a whole number.
- Division of zero by a whole number gives zero.
- Division of a whole number by zero is not defined.
- We can add two whole numbers in any order,

  e.g., $5 + 6 = 6 + 5$

  This is known as the commutative property of addition for whole numbers.
- We can multiply two whole numbers in any order, *e.g.,* $9 \times 4 = 4 \times 9$

  This is known as the commutative property of multiplication for whole numbers.
- We can group the whole numbers for convenience of adding,

  e.g., $(2 + 3) + 7 = 2 + (3 + 7)$

  This is known as the associative property of addition.
- We can group the whole number for convenience of multiplying, *e.g.,* $(7 \times 5) \times 4 = 7 \times (5 \times 4)$

  This is known as the associative property of multiplication.
- We can distribute the multiplicant for the convenience of multiplication,

  e.g., $138 \times 15 = (100 + 38) \times 15$

  $= 100 \times 15 + 38 \times 15 = 1500 + 570$

  $= 2070$

  This is known as the distributive property of multiplication over addition.

NEGATIVE NUMBERS AND INTEGERS

The numbers whose value is less than zero is called negative numbers. The minus mark (–) is used to represent the negative numbers. Negative number is the part of integers which is located in the left of zero on the number line.

Properties of Negative Numbers

- The product of two negative number is always positive, *e.g.,* $(-3) \times (-5) = 15$
- In an application of multiplication if the number of negative numbers are odd then the product is always negative. But if the number of negative numbers are even the product is always positive,

  e.g., $(-2) \times (-3) \times (-7) \times -(10) \times (-4) = -1680$

  and $(-3) \times (-4) \times (-10) \times (-6) = 720$
- The sum of two negative numbers is equal to the negative sum of the negative number,

  e.g., $(-5) + (-7) = -12$
- The difference of two same negative numbers is always zero, *e.g.,* $(-21) - (-21) = 0$
- The quotient of two negative numbers is always positive,

  e.g., $(-45) \div (-5) = 9$

Integers

The first numbers to be discovered were natural numbers, *i.e.,* 1, 2, 3, 4,... . If we include zero to the collection of natural numbers, we get a new collection of numbers known as whole numbers, *i.e.,* 0, 1, 2, 3, 4,... We have earlier found that there are negative numbers too. If we put the whole numbers and the negative numbers together, the new collection of numbers will look like 0, 1, 2, 3, 4, 5,...., –1, –2, –3, –4, –5, ... and this collection of numbers is known as Integers. In this collection, 1, 2, 3, ... are said to be positive integers and –1, –2, –3, ... are said to be negative integers.

Representation of Integers on a number line

We draw a line and mark some points at equal distance on it. Mark a point as zero on it. Points to the right of zero are positive integers and are marked 1, 2, 3 etc. Points to the left of zero are negative integers and are marked –1, –2, –3 etc.

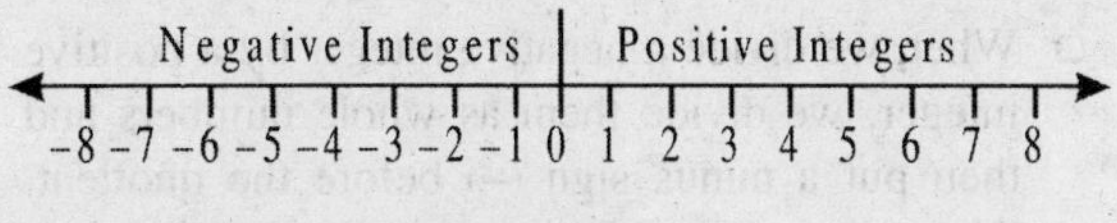

Properties of Integers

- For any two integers a and b, $a + b$ is an integer, *e.g.,* $(-5) + (-7) = -12$ or $(-5) + 7 = 2$

  This is called the closer property for addition of the integers.
- If a and b are two integers then $a - b$ is also an integer, *e.g.,* $(-8) - (-15) = 7$ and $7 - 11 = -4$

This is called the closer property for substraction of the integers.

- ❑ We can add two integers in any order.

  e.g.,, $(-5) + 6 = 6 + (-5)$

  This is known as the commutative property of addition for integers.
- ❑ Subtraction is not commutative for integers. It means if a and b are two integers then $a - b \neq b - a$.
- ❑ We can group the integers for convenience for adding. *e.g.,* $\{(-3) + (-5)\} + 6 = (-3) + \{(-5) + 6)\}$

  This is known as the associative property of addition.
- ❑ When we add zero to any integer we get the same integer. Thus, zero is an additive identity for integers.
- ❑ If a and b are two integers then $a \times b$ is also an integer.

  This is called the closer property for multiplication of the integers.
- ❑ We can multiply two integers in any order,

  e.g., $(-5) \times (-7) = (-7) \times (-5)$

  This is known as the commutative property of addition for integers.
- ❑ The product of three integers does not depend upon the grouping of integers and this is called the associative property for multiplication of integers,

  e.g., $(2 \times 3) \times (-4) = 2 \times \{3 \times (-4)\}$
- ❑ We can distribute the multiplicant for the convenience of multiplication,

  $$\begin{aligned} e.g.,\ (-127) \times (25) &= \{(-100) + (-27)\} \times 25 \\ &= (-100) \times 25 + (-27) \times 25 \\ &= (-2500) + (-675) \\ &= -3175. \end{aligned}$$

  This is known as the distributive property of multiplication over addition for integers.
- ❑ Any integer which is multiplied by zero gives zero, *e.g.,* $(-13) \times 0 = 0$.
- ❑ When we multiply by 1 to any integer we get the same integer. Thus, 1 is known as multiplicative identity for integers.
- ❑ When we divide a negative integer by a positive integer, we divide them as whole numbers and then put a minus sign (–) before the quotient. We, thus, get a negative integer.
- ❑ When we divide a positive integer by a negative integer, we first divide them as whole numbers and then put a minus sign (–) before the quotient. Thus we get a negative integer. In general, for any two positive integers a and b.

  $a \div (-b) = (-a) \div b$ where $b \neq 0$
- ❑ When we divide a negative integer by a negative integer, we first divide them as whole numbers and then put a positive sign (+). Thus we get a positive integer.

  In general, for any two positive integers a and b

  $(-a) \div (-b) = a \div b$ where $b \neq 0$
- ❑ Division is not communitative for integers like whole number,

  i.e., $a \div b \neq b \div a$.
- ❑ Like whole numbers, any integer divided by zero is meaningless and zero divided by an integer other than zero is equal to zero i.e., for any integer a, $a \div 0$ is not defined but $0 \div a = 0$ for $a \neq 0$.
- ❑ Negative integer divided by 1 gives the same negative integer. So, any integer divided by 1 gives the same integer. In general, for any integer a, $a \div 1 = a$.

FRACTIONS

A fraction is a number that represents a ratio or division of two whole numbers. It is represented as $\frac{p}{q}$ where, $q \neq 0$ and p and q are integers eg; $\frac{3}{4}, \frac{5}{8}, \frac{6}{10}$ etc. The number which is written above the line is known as numerator and another one which is written below the line is known as denominator. The denominator tells how many equal parts are there while the numerator tells how many of these equal parts are teken.

Fraction on the Number Line

We have already learnt to show whole numbers like 0, 1, 2, 3, 4, ... on the number line. Similarly, we can show the fraction also on the number line. Suppose we have to show $\frac{2}{3}$ on a number line. Then we will have to divide the length between 0 and 1 into 3 equal parts and show as follows

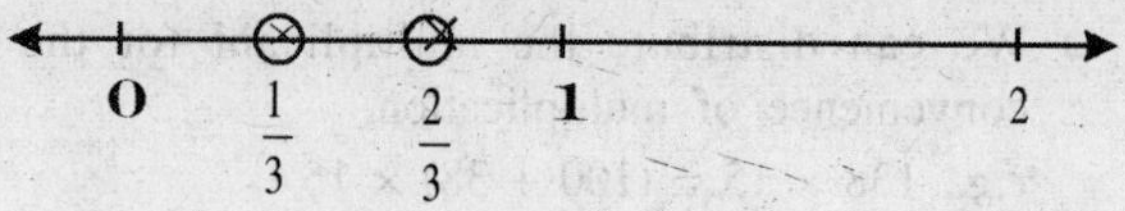

Kinds of Fractions

- ❑ **Like Fraction:** Those fractions whose denominators are same are known as like fractions,

  e.g., (*i*) $\frac{1}{3}, \frac{2}{3}, \frac{3}{3}$ (ii) $\frac{2}{7}, \frac{3}{7}, \frac{4}{7}$ etc.
- ❑ **Unlike Fractions:** Those fractions whose denominators are not same are known as unlike fractions,

  e.g., (*i*) $\frac{2}{3}, \frac{2}{5}, \frac{5}{7}$.

- **Proper Fractions:** Fractions in which numerator is smaller than denominator are known as proper fractions, e.g., (i) $\frac{1}{3}, \frac{2}{3}, \frac{4}{5}$.
- **Improper or Odd Fraction:** Fractions in which numerator is greater than or equal to denominator are known as improper fraction or odd fractions, *e.g.*, $\frac{7}{5}, \frac{5}{2}, \frac{17}{3}, \frac{11}{9}, \frac{7}{7}$
- **Unit Fraction:** Fraction whose numerator is 1, is known as unit fraction, *e.g.*, $\frac{1}{1}, \frac{1}{3}, \frac{1}{5}, \frac{1}{7}$.
- **Mixed Fraction:** Any improper fraction written by the combination of a whole number and a proper fraction, is known as a mixed fraction.

e.g., $3\frac{1}{4} = 3 + \frac{1}{4}$

$= \frac{3 \times 4}{4} + \frac{1}{4} = \frac{12+1}{4}$

$= \frac{13}{4}$ (Improper fraction)

- **Inverse Fraction:** In two fractions, when the numerator of one is the denominator of other and the denominator of one is the numerator of other fraction, they are called inverse fractions of each other. For example:

Inverse fraction of $\frac{2}{3}$ is $\frac{3}{2}$.

Equivalent Fraction

When numerator and denominator are multiplied or divided by the same number then the resultant fraction is known as equivalent fraction, *e.g.*, $\frac{4}{5} = \frac{4 \times 3}{5 \times 3} = \frac{12}{15}$

here $\frac{12}{15}$ is the equivalent fraction of $\frac{4}{5}$. Thus we can get many equivalent fractions of a particular fraction.

Simplest Form of a Fraction

A fraction is said to be in the simplest (or lowest) form if its numerator and denominator have no common factor except 1. The shortest way to find the equivalent fraction in the simplest form is to find the HCF of the numerator and denominator, and then divide both of them by the HCF,

e.g., $\frac{36}{24}$.

The HCF of 36 and 24 is 12.

Hence, $\frac{36}{24} = \frac{36 \div 12}{24 \div 12} = \frac{3}{2}$. Hence, the fraction $\frac{3}{2}$ is in the lowest form.

Comparing Fractions

If the numerator are same in the fractional number then that fractions whose denominator is smaller represent a bigger fraction, *e.g.*, in $\frac{5}{6}$ and $\frac{5}{7}$, bigger fraction is $\frac{5}{6}$.

If the denominator is same then that fraction whose numerator is greater reprsent a bigger fraction, *e.g.*, in $\frac{15}{17}$ and $\frac{13}{17}$ bigger fraction is $\frac{15}{17}$.

If the numerator and the denominator both are different (unlike fraction), we first get their equivalent fractions with the same denominator then compare the numerator of the corresponding fractions, *e.g.*, $\frac{5}{9}$ and $\frac{3}{5}$ the equivalent fraction of $\frac{5}{9}$ and $\frac{3}{5}$ with the same denominator is $\frac{5}{9} = \frac{5 \times 5}{9 \times 5} = \frac{25}{45}$ and $\frac{3}{5} = \frac{3 \times 9}{5 \times 9} = \frac{27}{45}$.

Obviously, $\frac{5}{9}$ is bigger fraction.

Addition of Fractions

If the fractions have same denominator, then the denominator is called a common denominator. In such cases, add the numerators and use this sum as the new numerator with the common denominator as the denominator of the sum.

For example:

$\frac{7}{17} + \frac{6}{17} = \frac{13}{17}$

If the fraction has different denominators:

For example:

$\frac{1}{3} + \frac{9}{4} + \frac{3}{5} = ?$

L.C.M. of 3, 4, 5 which is equal to 60:

$\frac{1}{3} = \frac{20}{60}, \frac{9}{4} = \frac{135}{60}, \frac{3}{5} = \frac{36}{60}$

$\frac{20}{60} + \frac{135}{60} + \frac{36}{60} = \frac{191}{60}$

Subtraction of fractions

When the fractions have the same denominator, subtract the numerator and place the result over the denominator. *For example:*

$\frac{7}{9} - \frac{5}{9} = \frac{7-5}{9} = \frac{2}{9}$

MATHEMATICS

When the fractions have different denominators,

$\frac{5}{8}-\frac{1}{5}=?$

Common denominator in this case is 40

$\frac{5}{8}=\frac{25}{40},\frac{1}{5}=\frac{8}{40}$

$\therefore \frac{25}{40}-\frac{8}{40}=\frac{25-8}{40}=\frac{17}{40}$

Multiplication of Fractions

While multiplying two fractions, multiply their numerators and divide this by the product of their denominators, *e.g.*, $\frac{3}{4}\times\frac{7}{12}=\frac{21}{48}=\frac{7}{16}$.

Division of Fractions

This can be done either by multiplying by the L.C.M. of the denominators of the fractions, or by multiplying by such a number which can make the denominator 1. It may be noted that one fraction is a reciprocal of another if their product is 1. So $\frac{1}{2}$ and 2 are reciprocals.

To find the reciprocal of a fraction, simply interchange the numerator and denominator. This is known as inverting fractions. To divide one fraction by another fraction, invert the divisor and multiply.

For example: $\frac{5}{8}\div\frac{1}{2}=\frac{5}{8}\times\frac{2}{1}=\frac{10}{8}=\frac{5}{4}$.

SOLVED QUESTIONS

Example 1 : What is the sum of first four prime numbers?

Solution: Sum of first four prime numbers = 2 + 3 + 5 + 7 = 17.

Example 2 : What is the number of prime factors of $(6)^{10}\times(7)^{17}\times(55)^{27}$?

Solution: $(6)^{10}\times(7)^{17}\times(55)^{27}=2^{10}\times3^{10}\times7^{17}\times5^{27}\times11^{27}$

$\therefore$ No. of prime factors = 10 + 10 + 17 + 27 + 27 = 91.

Example 3 : Prime factors of a number are 2, 2, 3, 7. Find the number.

Solution: The number is equal to the product of prime factors.

$\therefore$ 2 × 2 × 3 × 7 = 84 is the required number.

Example 4 : What is the sum of all primes between 70 and 100?

Solution: Prime numbers between 70 and 100 are 71, 73, 79, 83, 89 and 97.

$\therefore$ Sum of 71 + 73 + 79 + 83 + 89 + 97 = 492.

Example 5 : What will be the sum of odd numbers between 1 to 200?

Solution: Number of odd numbers between

$1 \text{ to } n=\left(\frac{\text{Last odd number}+1}{2}\right)$

$\therefore$ Number of odd numbers between 1 to 200 =

$\frac{199+1}{2}=100$

$\therefore$ Sum of odd numbers between 1 to 200 = (Number of odd numbers)^2 = $(100)^2$ = 10000.

Example 6 : If 30 *x* 0103 is divisible by 11, then, what is the value of *x*?

Solution: If a number is divisible by 11, the difference between the sum of the digits at the even places and sum of digits at odd places should be zero or a multiple of 11.

$\because$ The sum of the digits in the even places = 0 and the sum of the digits in the odd places = 3 + *x* + 1 + 3 = 7 + *x*

$\therefore$ (7 + *x*) − 0 = 11

x = 11 − 7 = 4.

Example 7 : If $\frac{72\times x}{27\times48}$ is a natural number then what will be the least value of *x*?

Solution: $\frac{72\times x}{27\times48}$ is a natural number or a positive integer.

$\because$ 1 is the smallest positive integer

$\therefore \frac{72\times x}{27\times48}=1\Rightarrow x=\frac{27\times48}{72}=18$

Hence, the least value of *x* will be 18.

Example 8 : What is additive inverse of $\frac{3}{7}$?

Solution: We know that if sum of two numbers is 0, then each of the numbers is additive inverse of the other.

Therefore, additive inverse of $\frac{3}{7}$ is $-\frac{3}{7}$, because $\frac{3}{7}-\frac{3}{7}=0$.

Example 9 : What will be the multiplicative inverse of $-\frac{7}{8}$?

Solution: Multiplicative inverse (reciprocal) of $-\frac{7}{8}$ is $-\frac{8}{7}$ because $\left(-\frac{7}{8}\right)\times\left(-\frac{8}{7}\right)=1$.

MULTIPLE CHOICE QUESTIONS

1. 2, 4, 6, 8, 10, ..., are:
A. prime numbers B. odd numbers
C. even numbers D. natural numbers

2. 2, 3, 5, 7, 11 and 13 are:
A. even numbers B. odd numbers
C. prime numbers D. natural numbers

3. The prime numbers between 1 to 100 are:
A. 20 B. 22
C. 25 D. 30

4. The only even prime number is:
A. 2 B. 67
C. 79 D. 98

5. Which of the following is not a prime number?
A. 79 B. 83
C. 87 D. 97

6. Which of the following is a prime number?
A. 117 B. 147
C. 149 D. 159

7. The smallest whole number which is divisible by 3 and also by the next two greater prime number is:
A. 15 B. 21
C. 60 D. 105

8. If '*a*' is an odd number, '*b*' is an even number and '*c*' is odd then, $a + b + c$ is:
A. odd number B. even number
C. prime number D. any number

9. The product of two prime numbers is a:
A. prime number B. even number
C. odd number D. composite number

10. Prime factors of a number are 2, 2, 3, 7. The number is:
A. 14 B. 41
C. 48 D. 84

11. The largest number which is a factor of 56 as well as 84 is:
A. 2 B. 7
C. 14 D. 28

12. L.C.M. of 6, 9, 12, 18 is:
A. 28 B. 36
C. 38 D. 42

13. $a + b + c + d$ is a positive number, a minimum of '*x*' of the number *a, b, c* and *d* must be positive, where '*x*' is equal to:
A. –1 B. 2
C. 3 D. 4

14. If the sum of two numbers '*x*' and '*y*' is equal to twice the first number, the second number '*y*' is:
A. $> x$ B. $< x$
C. $= x$ D. negative number

15. The difference between the squares of two consecutive numbers is 25. The numbers are:
A. 11, 12 B. 12, 13
C. 15, 14 D. 14, 13

16. The sum of two digits of a number is 15. If 9 is added to the number, the digits are reversed. The number is:
A. 78 B. 87
C. 69 D. 96

17. If the number $(10^n - 1)$ is divisible by 11, then n is:
A. odd number B. even number
C. any number D. multiple of 11

18. $\left(1-\frac{1}{3}\right)\left(1-\frac{1}{4}\right)\left(1-\frac{1}{5}\right)...\left(1-\frac{1}{n}\right) = ?$
A. $\frac{42}{29}$ B. $\frac{n-1}{n}$
C. $\frac{2}{n}$ D. 0

19. $\left(2-\frac{1}{3}\right)\left(2-\frac{3}{5}\right)\left(2-\frac{5}{7}\right)...\left(2-\frac{997}{999}\right) = ?$
A. $\frac{997}{999}$ B. ∞
C. $\frac{997}{3}$ D. $\frac{1001}{3}$

20. What should be added to the product of four consecutive odd numbers to make it a perfect square?
A. 13 B. 14
C. 15 D. 16

21. What is the value of $1+\cfrac{1}{1+\cfrac{1}{1+\cfrac{1}{3}}}$?
A. $1\frac{4}{7}$ B. $2\frac{4}{7}$
C. $3\frac{4}{7}$ D. $4\frac{4}{7}$

22. $\dfrac{\left(2\frac{2}{3}+3\frac{4}{7}\right)^2+\left(2\frac{2}{3}-3\frac{4}{7}\right)^2}{\left(\frac{8}{3}\right)^2+\left(\frac{25}{7}\right)^2} = ?$
A. 1 B. $\frac{1}{2}$
C. 2 D. 4

MATHEMATICS

23. $\dfrac{4\frac{1}{7}-2\frac{1}{4}}{3\frac{1}{2}+1\frac{1}{7}} \div \dfrac{1}{2+\dfrac{1}{2+\dfrac{1}{5-\frac{1}{5}}}} = ?$

A. 3 B. $\frac{1}{8}$
C. 8 D. 1

24. $\dfrac{180\times15-12\times20}{140\times8+2\times55} = ?$

A. 2 B. 4
C. $\frac{4}{5}$ D. 6

25. $\dfrac{(6+6+6+6)\div6}{4+4+4+4+4\div4} = ?$

A. $3\frac{6}{13}$ B. $\frac{4}{13}$
C. $\frac{3}{2}$ D. 1

26. $\dfrac{-\frac{1}{2}-\frac{2}{3}+\frac{4}{5}-\frac{1}{3}+\frac{1}{5}+\frac{3}{4}}{\frac{1}{2}+\frac{2}{3}-\frac{4}{3}+\frac{1}{3}-\frac{1}{5}-\frac{4}{5}} = ?$

A. 1 B. –2
C. $\frac{-10}{3}$ D. $-\frac{3}{10}$

27. If $\frac{1}{3}+\frac{1}{2}+\frac{1}{x}=4$, then find the value of x is:

A. $\frac{24}{11}$ B. $\frac{18}{5}$
C. $\frac{6}{19}$ D. $\frac{5}{18}$

28. $\dfrac{1}{\left(2\frac{1}{3}\right)}+\dfrac{1}{\left(1\frac{3}{4}\right)} = ?$

A. 1 B. 2
C. $\frac{1}{2}$ D. $4\frac{1}{12}$

29. Which of the following pairs of fractions adds up to a number greater than 5?

A. $\frac{13}{5}, \frac{11}{6}$ B. $\frac{11}{4}, \frac{8}{3}$
C. $\frac{7}{3}, \frac{11}{5}$ D. $\frac{5}{3}, \frac{3}{4}$

30. $1+\frac{1}{2}+\frac{1}{4}+\frac{1}{7}+\frac{1}{14}+\frac{1}{28}$ is equal to:

A. 2 B. 3
C. 2.5 D. 3.5

31. The difference of $1\frac{3}{16}$ and its reciprocal is equal to:

(A) $\frac{105}{304}$ B. $\frac{15}{34}$
C. $\frac{15}{16}$ D. $\frac{4}{3}$

32. Supply the two missing figures in order indicated by x and y in the given equation, the fraction being in their lowest terms:

$$5\frac{1}{x}\times y\frac{3}{4}=20$$

A. 5, 3 B. 4, 1
C. 3, 3 D. 3, 1

33. $5\frac{2}{3}\div ?\frac{5}{6}=2$

A. 5 B. 4
C. 3 D. 2

34. Find the value of ★ in the following:

$$1\frac{2}{3}\div\frac{2}{7}\times\frac{★}{7}=1\frac{1}{4}\times\frac{2}{3}\div\frac{1}{6}$$

A. 6 B. 0.6
C. $\frac{1}{6}$ D. 0.006

35. $6\frac{5}{6}\times5\frac{1}{3}+17\frac{2}{3}\times4\frac{1}{2}=?$

A. $112\frac{1}{3}$ B. $116\frac{17}{18}$
C. $115\frac{17}{18}$ D. $112\frac{17}{18}$

36. $4\frac{1}{2}\times4\frac{1}{3}-8\frac{1}{3}\div5\frac{2}{3}=?$

A. $18\frac{1}{34}$ B. $11\frac{33}{34}$
C. $\frac{7}{17}$ D. 8

37. $2\frac{3}{4}\div2\frac{2}{3}\div1\frac{1}{12}=?$

A. $\frac{169}{144}$ B. $\frac{99}{104}$
C. $1\frac{1}{4}$ D. $\frac{39}{48}$

38. If $\frac{4}{5}$ of an estate be worth Rs. 16,800, then the value of $\frac{3}{7}$ of the estate will be:

A. Rs. 90,000 B. Rs. 72,000
C. Rs. 21,000 D. Rs. 9,000

39. By how much does $\frac{6}{7/8}$ exceed $\frac{6/7}{8}$?

A. $7\frac{5}{6}$ B. $7\frac{3}{4}$

C. $6\frac{3}{4}$ D. $6\frac{1}{8}$

40. The H.C.F. of 72 and 18 is:

A. 9 B. 72

C. 18 D. 36

41. The L.C.M. of 6, 8, 10 and 12 is:

A. 120 B. 60

C. 240 D. 130

42. The H.C.F. of $\frac{5}{6}, \frac{6}{7}, \frac{7}{8}, \frac{8}{9}$ and $\frac{9}{10}$ is:

A. $\frac{1}{2420}$ B. $\frac{1}{2520}$

C. $\frac{1}{2660}$ D. $\frac{1}{2540}$

43. The L.C.M. of two numbers is 85 and their product is 1020. Their H.C.F. will be:

A. 16 B. 27

C. 12 D. 22

44. The L.C.M. and H.C.F. of two numbers are 4284 and 32 respectively. If one of the numbers is 204, the other is:

A. 672 B. 576

C. 676 D. 572

45. L.C.M. of 24, 28, 36 and 44 is a multiple of 24 and which of the following numbers?

A. 441 B. 231

C. 337 D. 197

46. H.C.F. of 420, 315 and 462 is:

A. 24 B. 28

C. 27 D. 21

47. The smallest number exactly divisible by 3, 4, 6 and 8 is:

A. 26 B. 24

C. 25 D. 28

48. Which of the following is the greatest common divisor of 1170 and 102?

A. 8 B. 4

C. 6 D. 3

49. A number, when 3 is added to it, becomes divisible by 36, 45 and 50. The smallest such number is:

A. 987 B. 798

C. 986 D. 897

50. The least perfect square number which is completely divisible by 10, 20, 30 and 40 is:

A. 4800 B. 3600

C. 4400 D. 2500

51. The sum of two numbers is 216 and their H.C.F. is 27. These numbers are:

A. 60 and 90 B. 81 and 135

C. 64 and 128 D. 30 and 84

52. The L.C.M. of two numbers is 45 times their H.C.F. If the sum of the L.C.M. and the H.C.F. of these two numbers is 1150 and one of the numbers is 125, then the other number is:

A. 256 B. 225

C. 250 D. 255

53. The H.C.F. and the L.C.M. of two numbers are 50 and 250 respectively. On dividing one of these numbers by 2, 50 is obtained as quotient. The numbers are:

A. 100, 125 B. 80, 100

C. 125, 100 D. 200, 250

54. The H.C.F. of three numbers is 12. If the three numbers are in the ratio of 1 : 2 : 3, then the numbers are:

A. 14, 28, 42 B. 12, 24, 36

C. 15, 30, 45 D. 24, 48, 72

55. The greatest four-digit number completely divisible by 2, 3, 4 and 5 is:

A. 9960 B. 9690

C. 8990 D. 9980

56. Which of the following has most numbers of divisors?

A. 182 B. 176

C. 101 D. 99

57. Expressed in simplest form : $\frac{1095}{1168}$

A. $\frac{25}{26}$ B. $\frac{17}{26}$

C. $\frac{15}{16}$ D. $\frac{13}{16}$

58. Expressed in lowest terms : $\frac{128352}{238368}$

A. $\frac{9}{13}$ B. $\frac{7}{13}$

C. $\frac{5}{13}$ D. $\frac{3}{4}$

59. HCF of $4 \times 27 \times 3125$, $8 \times 9 \times 25 \times 7$ and $16 \times 81 \times 5 \times 11 \times 49$ is:

A. 1260 B. 540

C. 360 D. 180

60. The ratio of two numbers is 3 : 4 and their H.C.F. is 4. Find their L.C.M.

A. 48 B. 24

C. 16 D. 12

61. Three numbers are in the ratio 1 : 2 : 3 and their HCF is 12. Find the numbers.

A. 12, 24, 36 B. 10, 20, 30
C. 5, 10, 15 D. 4, 8, 12

62. If the sum of two numbers is 55 and the H.C.F. and L.C.M. of these numbers are 5 and 120 respectively. Find the sum of their reciprccals.
A. $\frac{120}{11}$ B. $\frac{11}{120}$
C. $\frac{601}{55}$ D. $\frac{55}{601}$

63. The L.C.M. of two numbers is 495 and their H.C.F. is 5. If the sum of the numbers is 100, then find their difference.
A. 90 B. 70
C. 46 D. 10

64. The LCM and HCF of two numbers are 84 and 21 respectively. If the ratio of the two numbers is 1 : 4. Find the larger of two numbers.
A. 108 B. 84
C. 48 D. 12

65. The HCF of two numbers is 11 and their LCM is 7700. If one of the number is 275, then find the second number.
A. 318 B. 308
C. 283 D. 279

66. Three numbers are in the ratio of 3 : 4 : 5 and their LCM is 2400. Find their HCF.
A. 200 B. 120
C. 80 D. 40

67. The LCM of two numbers is 48. The numbers are in the ratio of 2 : 3. The sum of the numbers is:
A. 64 B. 40
C. 32 D. 28

68. The product of two numbers is 2028 and their HCF is 13. The number of such pair is
A. 4 B. 3
C. 2 D. 1

69. Find the greatest number that will divide 43, 91 and 183 so as to leave the same remainder in each case.
A. 13 B. 9
C. 7 D. 4

70. What is the difference between the real value and place value of 7 in the number 87569 is:
A. 6000 B. 6939
C. 6993 D. 9693

71. In the given fractions $\frac{7}{12}, \frac{11}{16}, \frac{13}{18}$ and $\frac{12}{17}$ the greatest is:
A. $\frac{7}{12}$ B. $\frac{11}{16}$
C. $\frac{13}{18}$ D. $\frac{12}{17}$

72. In the given fractions $\frac{7}{12}, \frac{17}{22}, \frac{15}{16}$ and $\frac{5}{6}$ the smallest is:
A. $\frac{5}{6}$ B. $\frac{15}{16}$
C. $\frac{11}{12}$ D. $\frac{17}{22}$

73. The simplest form of $\frac{4550}{7735}$ is:
A. $\frac{17}{10}$ B. $\frac{91}{65}$
C. $\frac{35}{17}$ D. $\frac{10}{17}$

74. Product of three consecutive numbers is exactly divided by:
A. 4 B. 6
C. 8 D. None of these

75. If a and b are two rational numbers such that $a \times b = 1$, then each is called:
A. Multiplicative Inverse
B. Additive Inverse
C. Multiplicative Identity
D. None of there

76. Zero is a:
A. Positive integer
B. Negative integer
C. Neither positive nor negative integers
D. None of these

77. The estimated product of 376 and 57 is:
A. 15000 B. 21432
C. 24000 D. None of these

78. HCF of 38, 72 and 46 is:
A. 2 B. 4
C. 6 D. 8

79. The smallest negative integer is:
A. Can not be determined
B. −1
C. 0
D. None of these

80. If a prime number is divided by zero then the quotient is:
A. 0
B. 1
C. The prime number itself
D. Not defined

81. If Zero is divided by an integer then the quotient is:
A. 0
B. 1
C. The integer itself
D. Not defined

82. The closer property for whole number is not shown by:
A. Subtraction B. Division
C. Both A and B D. Addition

83. If *a*, *b* and *c* are integers then which one of the following is incorrect.
A. $a \times b = b \times A$
B. $A - B \neq B - A$
C. $A \div B = B \div A$
D. $(A + B) + C = A + (B + C)$

84. Which of the following represents the correct form of associative property of multiplication for whole numbers?
A. $(a + b) + c = a + (b + c)$
B. $(a \times b) \times c = a \times (b \times c)$
C. $(a + b) \times c = a + c \times b + c$
D. $(a + b) \times c = a \times c + b \times c$

85. When we divide a negative integer by a negative integer, then we get:
A. Negative integer B. Zero
C. 1 D. Positive integer

86. Integer is the collection of:
A. Even and Odd numbers
B. Positive and negative numbers
C. Prime and composite numbers
D. None of these

ANSWERS

1	2	3	4	5	6	7	8	9	10
C	C	C	A	C	C	D	B	D	D
11	**12**	**13**	**14**	**15**	**16**	**17**	**18**	**19**	**20**
D	B	A	C	B	A	B	C	D	D
21	**22**	**23**	**24**	**25**	**26**	**27**	**28**	**29**	**30**
A	C	D	A	B	D	C	A	B	A
31	**32**	**33**	**34**	**35**	**36**	**37**	**38**	**39**	**40**
A	C	D	A	C	A	B	D	C	C
41	**42**	**43**	**44**	**45**	**46**	**47**	**48**	**49**	**50**
A	B	C	A	B	D	B	C	D	B
51	**52**	**53**	**54**	**55**	**56**	**57**	**58**	**59**	**60**
B	B	A	B	A	B	C	B	D	A
61	**62**	**63**	**64**	**65**	**66**	**67**	**68**	**69**	**70**
A	B	D	B	B	D	B	C	D	C
71	**72**	**73**	**74**	**75**	**76**	**77**	**78**	**79**	**80**
C	D	D	B	A	C	C	A	A	D
81	**82**	**83**	**84**	**85**	**86**				
A	C	C	B	D	B				

SOME SELECTED EXPLANATORY ANSWERS

1. The numbers divisible by 2 are called even numbers, since, 4, 6, 8, 10 are divisible by 2, hence these are even numbers.

2. 2, 3, 5, 7, 11 and 13 are prime numbers.

3. The prime numbers between 1 to 100 are : 2, 3, 5, 7, 11, 13, 17, 19, 23, 29, 31, 37, 41, 43, 47, 53, 59, 61, 67, 71, 73, 79, 83, 89 and 97 i.e., 25 numbers.

4. 2 is the only even prime number.

5. 87 is divisible by 3, therefore, it is not a prime number.

6. 149 is not divisible by any number, therefore, it is a prime number.

7. The number should be divisible by 3, 5 and 7. Thus L.C.M. of 3, 5, 7 is equal to 105 which is the required number.

8. Out of *a, b, c*; *a* is odd and *c* is odd while *b* is even. The sum of two odd numbers is even, *i.e.,* $a + c$ = even = d. Also, the sum of two even numbers is even, *i.e.,* $d + b$ = even.
$\therefore a + b + c$ = Even number.

9. Product of two prime numbers is never a prime number but it is either an odd number or an even number.

10. The number is equal to the product of prime factors.
$\therefore 2 \times 2 \times 3 \times 7 = 84$ is the required number.

11. Find H.C.F. of 56, 84 which is equal to 28.

12. L.C.M. of 6, 9, 12, 18, is 36.

13. If all numbers were not positive, then the sum could not be positive. If *a, b, c* were all – 1 and *d* were 5, then $a + b + c + d$ would be positive, so B., C., D. are incorrect.

14. $x + y = 2x$

$\therefore \quad y = 2x - x = x$

15. Let the numbers are x and $(x + 1)$

$\therefore \quad (x+1)^2 - x^2 = 25$

$\Rightarrow \quad x^2 + 1 + 2x - x^2 = 25$

$\Rightarrow \quad 2x + 1 = 25$

$\Rightarrow \quad 2x = 25 - 1 = 24$

$\therefore \quad x = \frac{24}{2} = 12$

$\therefore \quad x + 1 = 12 + 1 = 13$

Hence, the numbers are 12, 13.

16. Let x be the digit in units place. Digit in ten's place is then $15 - x$.

$\therefore$ The number $= 10\,(15 - x) + x$

The new number with reverse digits $= 10 \times x + (15 - x)$

$\therefore \quad 10(15 - x) + x + 9 = 10x + 15 - x$

$\Rightarrow \quad 150 - 10x + x + 9 = 9x + 15$

$\Rightarrow \quad 18x = 144 \quad x = \frac{144}{18} = 8$

The digit of ten's place $= 15 - 8 = 7$

$\therefore$ The required number = 78.

17. n is even number.

18. $\frac{2}{3}\times\frac{3}{4}\times\frac{4}{5}\times\ldots\times\frac{n-1}{n} = \frac{2}{n}$.

19. $\frac{5}{3}\times\frac{7}{5}\times\frac{9}{7}\times\ldots\times\frac{1001}{999} = \frac{1001}{3}$.

20. Let the four consecutive odd numbers be $(2x - 3)$, $(2x - 1)$, $(2x + 1)$ and $(2x + 3)$

$\therefore$ Their product $= (2x - 1)(2x + 1)(2x - 3)(2x + 3)$

$= (4x^2 - 1)(4x^2 - 9)$

$= 16x^4 - 40x^2 + 9$

$= (4x^2 - 5)^2 - 16$

Hence, on adding 16, the result will be a perfect square.

24. $\frac{180\times15-12\times20}{140\times8+2\times55} = \frac{2700-240}{1120+110} = \frac{2460}{1230} = 2$.

25. $\frac{(6+6+6+6)\div6}{4+4+4+4\div4} = \frac{24\times\frac{1}{6}}{4+4+4+1} = \frac{4}{13}$.

26. $\frac{-\frac{1}{2}-\frac{2}{3}+\frac{4}{5}-\frac{1}{3}+\frac{1}{5}+\frac{3}{4}}{\frac{1}{2}+\frac{2}{3}-\frac{4}{3}+\frac{1}{3}-\frac{1}{5}-\frac{4}{5}}$

$= \frac{\frac{3}{4}-\frac{1}{2}-\frac{2}{3}-\frac{1}{3}+\frac{4}{5}+\frac{1}{5}}{\frac{1}{2}-\frac{1}{3}-1} = \frac{\frac{1}{4}-1+1}{-5/6}$

$= \frac{1}{4}\times-\frac{6}{5} = -\frac{3}{10}$.

27. $\frac{1}{3}+\frac{1}{2}+\frac{1}{x} = 4 \quad \Rightarrow \frac{1}{x} = 4-\frac{5}{6} = \frac{19}{6}$

$\therefore x = \frac{6}{19}$.

28. $\frac{1}{\left(2\frac{1}{3}\right)}+\frac{1}{1\frac{3}{4}} = \frac{1}{7/3}+\frac{1}{7/4} = \frac{3}{7}+\frac{4}{7} = 1$.

29. $\frac{13}{5}+\frac{11}{6} = \frac{78+55}{30} = \frac{133}{30} = 4\frac{13}{30} < 5$

$\frac{11}{4}+\frac{8}{3} = \frac{33+32}{12} = \frac{65}{12} = 5\frac{5}{12} > 5$.

30. $1 + \frac{1}{2}+\frac{1}{4}+\frac{1}{7}+\frac{1}{14}+\frac{1}{28}$

$= \frac{28+14+7+4+2+1}{28} = \frac{56}{28} = 2$.

31. The required difference

$= \frac{19}{16}-\frac{16}{19} = \frac{361-256}{304} = \frac{105}{364}$

32. $5\frac{1}{x}\times y\frac{3}{4} = 20 \quad \Rightarrow \frac{5x+1}{x}\times\frac{4y+3}{4} = 20$

$\Rightarrow (5x + 1)(4y + 3) = 80x$

By putting $x = y = 3$, we get the required result.

Hence, $x = 3$, $y = 3$.

33. Let, $5\frac{2}{3}\div x\frac{5}{6} = 2$

$\Rightarrow \frac{17}{3}\div\frac{6x+5}{6} = 2$

$\Rightarrow \frac{6x+5}{6} = \frac{17}{6} \quad \Rightarrow 6x = 12. \quad \therefore x = 2$

34. Let, $\frac{5}{3}\div\frac{2}{7}\times\frac{x}{7} = \frac{5}{4}\times\frac{2}{3}\div\frac{1}{6}$

$\Rightarrow \frac{5}{3}\times\frac{7}{2}\times\frac{x}{7} = \frac{5}{4}\times\frac{2}{3}\times6$

$\Rightarrow \frac{5}{6}x = 5 \quad \therefore x = 6.$

35. $\frac{41}{6}\times\frac{16}{3}+\frac{53}{3}\times\frac{9}{2} = \frac{656}{18}+\frac{477}{6}$

$= \frac{656+1431}{18} = \frac{2087}{18} = 115\frac{17}{18}$.

36. $\frac{9}{2}\times\frac{13}{3}-\frac{25}{3}\div\frac{17}{3} = \frac{9}{2}\times\frac{13}{3}-\frac{25}{3}\times\frac{3}{17} = \frac{39}{2}-\frac{25}{17}$

$= \frac{613}{34} = 18\frac{1}{34}$

37. $\frac{11}{4} \div \frac{8}{3} \div \frac{13}{12} = \frac{11}{4} \times \frac{3}{8} \times \frac{12}{13} = \frac{99}{104}$.

38. Let, $\frac{4}{5} \times x = 16,800$

$\therefore \quad \frac{3}{7} \times x = 16800 \times \frac{5}{4} \times \frac{3}{7}$ = Rs. 9000.

39. $\frac{6}{7/8} - \frac{6/7}{8} = \frac{48}{7} - \frac{6}{56} = \frac{384-6}{56} = \frac{378}{56} = \frac{27}{4}$

$= 6\frac{3}{4}$.

40. $72 = 2 \times 2 \times 2 \times 3 \times 3$

$18 = 2 \times 3 \times 3$

$\therefore$ Common factors $= 2 \times 3 \times 3 = 18$

$\therefore$ H.C.F. $= 18$

41. $6 = 2 \times 3$; $8 = 2 \times 2 \times 2$

$10 = 2 \times 5$; $12 = 2 \times 2 \times 3$

It is clear that 2 occurs as prime factor maximum three times, 3 one time and 5 one time.

Hence, required L.C.M.

$= 2 \times 2 \times 2 \times 3 \times 5 = 120$.

42. H.C.F. of $\frac{5}{6}, \frac{6}{7}, \frac{7}{8}, \frac{8}{9}$

and $\frac{9}{10} = \frac{\text{H.C.F. of } 5, 6, 7, 8 \text{ and } 9}{\text{LCM of } 6, 7, 8, 9 \text{ and } 10}$

Now, H.C.F. of 5, 6, 7, 8 and 9 = 1

and L.C.M. of 6, 7, 8, 9 and 10 = 2520

$\therefore$ Required H.C.F. $= \frac{1}{2520}$.

43. L.C.M. of two numbers × H.C.F. of the numbers = Product of the numbers

$\therefore$ 85 × H.C.F. = 1020

$\therefore$ H.C.F. $= \frac{1020}{85} = 12$.

44. 1st number × 2nd number = LCM × HCF

$\therefore$ 204 × 2nd number = 4284 × 32

$\therefore$ 2nd number $= \frac{4284 \times 32}{204} = 672$

$\therefore$ 2nd number = 672

45. $24 = 2 \times 2 \times 2 \times 3$

$28 = 2 \times 2 \times 7$

$36 = 2 \times 2 \times 3 \times 3$

$44 = 2 \times 2 \times 11$

$\therefore$ Required LCM

$= 2 \times 2 \times 2 \times 3 \times 3 \times 7 \times 11 = 24 \times 231$

Therefore, it is obvious that LCM of the given number is a multiple of 24 and 231.

47. L.C.M. of 3, 4, 6 and 8

2	3,	4,	6,	8
2	3,	2,	3,	4
3	3,	1,	3,	2
	1,	1,	1,	2

$\therefore$ The required number = LCM of the given numbers $= 2 \times 2 \times 3 \times 2 = 24$.

48. $1170 = 2 \times 5 \times 3 \times 3 \times 13$

$102 = 2 \times 3 \times 17$

$\therefore$ Greatest common divisor $= 2 \times 3 = 6$.

51. Let the numbers be x and y.

$\therefore x + y = 216 = 27 \times 8$

Since HCF of these two numbers is 27, hence, common factor of these two numbers is 27. Therefore, these numbers will be of the form of 27 × 1, 27 × 2, 27 × 3, ... etc.

According to the condition of the problem, sum of these numbers is 216.

$\therefore$ The numbers will be 27 × 3 = 81

and 27 × 5 = 135.

53. According to the condition of the problem, 50 is obtained on dividing one of the numbers by 2

$\therefore$ One of the numbers = 50 × 2 = 100

Now, 1st number × 2nd number = LCM × HCF

$\therefore$ 100 × 2nd number = 250 × 50

$\therefore$ 2nd number $= \frac{250 \times 50}{100} = 125$

Hence, numbers are 100 and 125.

54. Let the numbers be x, $2x$ and $3x$ respectively. Here, HCF of the three numbers is 12, therefore 12 is the largest common factor of these three numbers. Thus, it is clear that $x = 12$

$\therefore$ These numbers are 12, 24 and 36 respectively.

55. LCM of 2, 3, 4 and 5 = 60

Largest 4-digit number = 9999

Now, 60) 9999 (166

60

399

360

× 399

360

39

$\therefore$ Largest 4-digit number completely divisible by 2, 3, 4 and 5

= 9999 – 39 = 9960

$\therefore$ Required number = 9960.

56.

Numbers	*Their divisors*
182	→ 1, 2, 7, 13, 14, 26, 91 and 182
176	→ 1, 2, 4, 8, 16, 22, 44, 88 and 176
101	→ 1 and 101
99	→ 1, 3, 9, 11, 33 and 99

Therefore, 176 has the most number of divisors.

57. 1095) 1168 (1
1095
73) 1095 (15
73
365
365
×

Hence, HCF of 1095 and 1168 is 73.

Then, $\frac{1095}{1168}=\frac{1095\div73}{1168\div73}=\frac{15}{16}$.

58. 128352) 238368 (1
128352
110016) 128352 (1
110016
18336) 110016 (6
110016
×

Hence, HCF of 128352 and 238368 is 18336.

Then, $\frac{128352\div18336}{238368\div18336}=\frac{7}{13}$.

59. $4 \times 27 \times 3125 = 2^2 \times 3^3 \times 5^5$
$8 \times 9 \times 25 \times 7 = 2^3 \times 3^2 \times 5^2 \times 7$
$16 \times 81 \times 5 \times 11 \times 49 = 2^4 \times 3^4 \times 5 \times 7^2 \times 11$
$\therefore$ HCF $= 2^2 \times 3^2 \times 5 = 4 \times 9 \times 5 = 180$.

60. Let the numbers be $3x$ and $4x$;
HCF = 4; Hence, $x = 4$
Then, numbers will be 12 and 16;
$\therefore$ Their LCM = 48.

61. Let the numbers are x, $2x$ and $3x$;
Their HCF = 12
Then, $x = 12$, so the numbers will be 12, 24, 36.

62. Let the number be x and y.
Then, $x + y = 55$; xy = HCF × LCM = 5 × 120
$\therefore$ Sum of their reciprocals

$$=\frac{1}{x}+\frac{1}{y}=\frac{x+y}{xy}=\frac{55}{5\times120}=\frac{11}{120}.$$

63. Let the number be x and $(100 - x)$
Now, $x(100 - x) = 5 \times 495$
$\Rightarrow x^2 - 100x + 2475 = 0$
$\Rightarrow x^2 - 55x - 45x + 2475 = 0$
$\Rightarrow x(x - 55) - 45(x - 55) = 0$
$\Rightarrow (x - 45)(x - 55) = 0$
Either, $x = 45$ or, $x = 55$
Hence, the numbers are 45 and 55
So, their difference = 55 – 45 = 10.

64. Let the two numbers be x and $4x$.
Then, $x \times 4x = 21 \times 84 \Rightarrow x^2 = 21 \times 21$
$\therefore x = 21$
Hence, larger of two numbers = $4x = 4 \times 21 = 84$

65. Second number $= \frac{11\times7700}{275} = 308$.

66. Let the numbers be $3x$, $4x$ and $5x$.
Then, L.C.M. = $60x$

Now, $60x = 2400 \quad \therefore x = \frac{2400}{60} = 40$

Since, the numbers are 3 × 40, 4 × 40, 5 × 40.
Hence, their HCF = 40.

67. Let the two numbers be $2x$ and $3x$;
their LCM = $6x$
Now, $6x = 48 \quad \therefore x = 8$
Hence, the numbers are 2 × 8, 3 × 8 = 16, 24
Their sum = 16 + 24 = 40.

68. Let the two numbers be $13x$ and $13y$
Now, $13x \times 13y = 2028$

$\therefore \quad xy=\frac{2028}{13\times13}=12$

Then, co-primes with product 12 are (1, 12) and (3, 4)
Hence, the requried numbers are (13 × 1, 13 × 12) and (13 × 3, 13 × 4).
So, there are two such pairs.

69. Greatest number = HCF of (91 – 43), (183 – 91) (183 – 43)

$$\left[\begin{array}{r}\because 48=2\times2\times2\times3\\ 92=2\times2\times23\\ 140=2\times2\times5\times7\end{array}\right]$$

= HCF of 48, 92, 140
= 4.

ALGEBRA

INTRODUCTION TO ALGEBRA

Algebra is a branch of mathematics in which we study about the calculation of letters or symbols. It follows the general principles and features of applications ie; Algebra generalises the mathematical concepts. We can represent the values, the sizes and the quantities through algebra in different situations. The variables represented by the letters do not have any definite numerical value rather these may have different values. It is also a science like arithmatic, but there is only one difference that it uses a new language and signs. Algebra is related with carefull evaluation and its study rather than source of specific problems.

Objectives of Algebra Teaching

(i) To develop the analytical ability.

(ii) To develop the skill of systematically generalisation of facts.

(*iii*) To develop the skill of using general formulae in special situation.

(*iv*) To establish carefully and increase the concepts of Arithmatic.

(*v*) To study minutely the mathematical relationship through the new terminology and signs.

Variables: A variable is a sign or a letter which does not have a fixed value, *e.g.,* The number 50 or any other number have their fixed value but $4p$ does not have the fixed value because the value of p may be 0, 1, 2, 3, ...

Clearly, variables can take different values; they have no fixed value. But they are numbers. That is why as in the case of numbers, operations of addition, subtraction, multiplication and division can be done on them.

Expressions: A group of signs that represent an idea or a quantity is called an expression, *e.g.,* $4x + 5$, $9x + y$, $3y^3 + z$ etc.

Terms: A sign or a group of signs that is added together to form an expression is called a term. *e.g.,* In expression $5x^2 - 6y$; $5x^2$ and $- 6y$ are terms.

Factors: The variables and constants of a term is called factors, *e.g.,* In $5xy$, the factors are 5, x and y.

Coefficient: The numerical factor of a term is called numerical coefficient or coefficient, *e.g.,* In $6yz$ the coefficient is 6.

Monomial: The algebraic expression which has only one term is called monomial, *e.g.,* $7xy$, $-3z$ etc.

Binomial: The algebraic expression which has two unlike terms is called binomial, *e.g.,* $x + 2y$, $2a + c$ etc.

Trinomial: The algebraic expression which has three unlike terms is called trinomial, *e.g.,* $a + b + c$, $3x + 2y + 4$ etc.

Polynomial: In the comprehensive form, the expression which has one or more than one terms is called polynomial.

Like and unlike terms: When two or more terms have similar algebraic factors then these are called like terms rather than two or more terms have different algebraic factors then these are unlike terms, *e.g.,* In $2ab - 3ac + 5ab - 4$, algebraic factors of $2ab$ and $5ab$ are same so, both are like terms. But $2ab$ and $- 3ac$ are unlike terms.

The sum of two or more like terms is a like term with a numerical coefficient equal to the sum of the numerical coefficient of all the like terms.

The difference between two like terms is a like term with a numerical coefficient equal to the difference between the numerical coefficients of the two like terms.

To Evaluate the Expression: The value of an expression depends upon the variables used to form the expression. To evaluate the expression we put the given value of variables and calculate them.

Addition and Subtraction of Algebraic Expressions: We write each expression to be added in a separate row. While doing so we write like terms one below the other and then add them, *e.g.,*

(*i*) $5xy + 7yz - 3xz$, $4yz + 10\,xz - 9y$, $- 6xz + 9x - 4xy$

Writing the three expressions in separate rows, with like terms one below the other,

$$\begin{array}{l} \quad 5xy + 7yz - 3xz \\ + \qquad\quad 4yz + 10xz - 9y \\ + \ -4xy \quad - 6xz + 9x \\ \hline \quad xy + 11yz + xz + 9x - 9y \end{array}$$

(*ii*) $9x^2 - 5xy + 6y - 5$ from
$11x^2 - 6xy + 8y^2 + 8x - 7y$

$$\begin{array}{r} 11x^2 - 6xy + 8y^2 + 8x - 7y \\ 9x^2 - 5xy \qquad + 6y - 5 \\ (-) \quad (+) \qquad\quad (-) \;\; (+) \\ \hline 2x^2 - xy + 8y^2 + 8x - 13y + 5 \end{array}$$

Multiplication of Algebraic Expression: By using the distributive law, we are able to carry out the multiplication term by term, *e.g.*,,

(*i*) $3a\ (6a^2 + 5b + 9)$
$= 3a + 6a^2 + 3a \times 5b + 3a \times 9)$
$= 18a^3 + 15ab + 27a$

(*ii*) $(4p + 5q) \times (7p - 4q)$
$= 4p\ (7p - 4q) + 5q\ (7p - 4q)$
$= 4p \times 7p - 4p \times 4q + 5q \times 7p - 5q \times 4q$
$= 28p^2 - 16pq + 35pq - 20q^2$
$= 28p^2 + 19pq - 20q^2$

Equation: An equation is a condition on a variable which is satisfied only for a definite value of the variable, *e.g.*, $5x + 9 = 24$ is an equation where $x = 3$ satisfies it.

The value of the variable in an equation which satisfies the equation is called a solution to the equation.

Identity: Such an equality, true for every value of the variable in it, is called an identity.

Thus, $(x + 1)\ (x + 2) = x^2 + 3a + 2$ is an identity.

An equation is true for only certain values of the variable in it. It is not true for all values of the variable. This is the difference between an equation and an identity.

Some standard identities

(*i*) $(a + b)^2 = a^2 + 2ab + b^2$
(*ii*) $(a - b)^2 = a^2 - 2ab + b^2$
(*iii*) $a^2 - b^2 = (a + b)\ (a - b)$
(*iv*) $(a + b)^2 + (a - b)^2 = 2(a^2 + b^2)$
(*v*) $(a + b)^2 - (a - b)^2 = 4ab$
(*vi*) $(a + b)^2 = (a - b)^2 + 4ab$
(*vii*) $(a - b)^2 = (a + b)^2 - 4ab$
(*viii*) $(a + b + c)^2 = a^2 + b^2 + c^2 + 2ab + 2bc + 2ca$
(*ix*) $(a + b)^3 = a^3 + b^3 + 3ab\ (a + b)$
(*x*) $(a - b)^3 = a^3 - b^3 - 3ab\ (a - b)$
(*xi*) $a^3 + b^3 = (a + b)\ (a^2 - ab + b^2) = (a + b)^3 - 3ab\ (a + b)$
(*xii*) $a^3 - b^3 = (a - b)\ (a^2 + ab + b^2) = (a - b)^3 + 3ab\ (a - b)$
(*xiii*) $a^3 + b^3 + c^3 - 3abc = (a + b + c)\ (a^2 + b^2 + c^2 - ab - bc - ca)$
(*xiv*) If, $a + b + c = 0$, then, $a^3 + b^3 + c^3 = 3abc$

Linear Equation in One Variable

An equation which is formed by an expression with only one variable and the highest power of the variable appearing in the expression is 1. Such type of equation is known as Linear Equation in One Variable, *e.g.*, $2x + 5 = 9$, $4p - 9 = 7$ etc.

(*a*) An algebraic equation is an equality involving variables. It has an equality sign. The expression on the left of the equality sign is the Left Hand Side (LHS). The expression on the right of the equality sign is the Right Hand Side (RHS).

(b) In an equation the values of the expressions on the LHS and RHS are equal. This happens to be true only for certain values of the variable. These values are the solutions of the equation.

(c) To find the solution of an equation. We assume that the two sides of the equation are balanced. We perform the same mathematical operations on both sides of the equation, so that the balance is not disturbed. As few such steps give to solution,

e.g., (*i*) $4x - 7 = 29$

Solution: Adding 7 to both sides,

$4x - 7 + 7 = 29 + 7$ or, $4x = 36$

Now dividing both sides by 4,

$$\frac{4x}{4} = \frac{36}{4} \quad \text{or, } x = 9$$

(*ii*) $5x - 13 = 3x - 9$

Solution: We have, $5x - 13 = 3x - 9$
or, $2x - 13 = -9$ (Subtracting $3x$ from both sides)
or, $2x = 4$ (Adding 13 is both sides)
or, $x = 2$ (Dividing both sides by 2)

Factorisation

When we factorise an algebraic expression, we write it as a product of factors. These factors may be numbers, algebraic variables or algebraic expression.

Expressions like $3xy$, $5x^2y$, $2x(y + 2)$, $5(y + 1)\ (x + 2)$ are already in factors form. Their factors can be just read off from them, as we already know.

On the other hand consider expressions like $2x + 4$, $3x + 3y$, $x^2 + 5x$, $x^2 + 5x + 6$. It is not obvious what their factors are, we need to develop systematic methods to factorise these expressions, *i.e.*, to find their factors.

Methods of common factors

To factorise $6x^2y + 9xy^2$

$$6x^2y = 2 \times \boxed{3} \times \boxed{x} \times x \times \boxed{y}$$
$$9xy^2 = 3 \times \boxed{3} \times \boxed{x} \times y \times \boxed{y}$$

Here common factors are 3, x and y

Hence, $6x^2y + 9xy^2 = 2 \times 3 \times x \times x \times y + 3 \times 3 \times x \times y \times y$
$= 3 \times x \times y\,[(2 \times x) + (3 \times y)]$
$= 3xy\,(2x + 3y)$

Factorisation by regrouping terms

To factorise $15xy - 6x + 5y - 2$

We have, $15xy - 6x + 5y - 2$
$= 15xy + 5y - 6x - 2$
$= 5y\,(3x + 1) - 2(3x + 1)$
$= (5x - 2)\,(3x + 1)$

Factorisation using identities

To factorise $49p^2 - 36$

These are two terms; both are squares and the second is negative, The expressions is of the form $(a^2 - b^2)$.

$49p^2 - 36 = (7p)^2 - (6)^2 = (7\,p - 6)\,(7p + 6)$

Factors of the form $(x + a)\,(x + b)$

To factorise $p^2 + 6p - 16$

We have, $p^2 + 6p - 16 = p^2 + 8p - 2p - 16$
$= p(p + 8) - 2\,(p + 8) = (p - 2)\,(p + 8)$

Division of Algebraic Expressions

(i) Polynomial by monomial

To divide $(3y^8 - 4y^6 + 5y^4)$ by y^4

We have $\dfrac{3y^8 - 4y^6 + 5y^4}{y^4} = \dfrac{y^4\left(3y^4 - 4y^2 + 5\right)}{y^4}$
$= 3y^4 - 4y^2 + 5$

(ii) Polynomial by polynomial

To divide $x(x + 1)\,(x+ 2)\,(x + 3)$ by $x(x + 1)$

We have, $\dfrac{x(x+1)(x+2)(x+3)}{x(x+1)} = (x+2)(x+3)$

RATIO AND PROPORTION

Ratio

In ratio we compare two quantities of the same kind and consider what multiple, part or parts one is of the other. In comparing 8 with 4, observe that it is 2 times 4. This comparison can be represented as $8 \div 4$ or $\dfrac{8}{4}$.

Hence, ratio is that relation between two numbers which is expressed by the fraction, the numerator is which is the measure of the first quantity and denominator is the measure of the second quantity.

If the terms of a ratio be multiplied or divided by the same quantity the value of the ratio remains unaltered.

Thus, 3 : 4 is the same as 9 : 12 and 9 : 12 is the same as 3 : 4.

Proportion

The equality of two ratios is called proportion.

Consider the two ratios:

Ist ratio	2nd ratio
5 : 15	7 : 21

Since, 5 is one-third of 15 and 7 is one-third of 21, the two ratios are equal. The equality of two ratios is called proportion and the numbers 5, 15 and 7, 21 are said to e in proportion.

The proportion may be written as 5 : 15 : : 7 : 21 (5 is to 15 as 7 is to 21)

$\Rightarrow$ 5 : 15 = 7 : 21

$\Rightarrow \dfrac{5}{15} = \dfrac{7}{21}$

The numbers 5, 15, 7 and 21 are called the terms. 5 is the first term, 15 the second, 7 the third, and 21 the fourth.

The first and fourth terms, *i.e.*, 5 and 21 are called extremes (end terms), and the second and the third terms, *i.e.*, 15 and 7 are called the means (middle terms), 21 is called the fourth proportional.

Some Important Facts

1. If a and b are two quantities, then
   (*a*) Duplicate ratio of $a : b = a^2 : b^2$
   (*b*) Sub-duplicate ratio of $a : b = \sqrt{a} : \sqrt{b}$
   (*c*) Triplicate ratio of $a : b = a^3 : b^3$
   (*d*) Sub-triplicate ratio $a : b = \sqrt[3]{a} : \sqrt[3]{b}$
   (*e*) Inverse or reciprocal ratio of $a : b = \dfrac{1}{a} : \dfrac{1}{b}$
   (*f*) Third proportional to 'a' and 'b' $= \dfrac{b^2}{a}$
2. If A : B = $x : y$ and B : C = $p : q$, then
   (*a*) $A : C = \dfrac{x \times p}{y \times q}$
   (*b*) A : B : C = $px : py : qy$
3. In what ratio the two kinds of tea must be mixed together one at Rs. x per kg and another at Rs. y per kg, so that the mixture may cost Rs. z per kg?
   $$\text{Ratio} = \frac{z - y}{x - z}$$
4. A grey hound persues a hare as takes J_1 leaps for every J_2 leaps of the hare. If K_1 leaps of the hound are equal to K_2 leaps of the hare, then the Ratio of speeds of the hound and hare is
   $$\frac{J_2 \times K_1}{J_1 \times K_2}$$

5. The incomes of two persons are in the ratio of $a : b$ and their expenditure are in the ratio of $x : y$. If the saving of each person is Rs. s, then income of each is Rs. $\frac{as(y-x)}{ay-bx}$ and Rs. $\frac{bs(y-x)}{ay-bx}$ respectively.
6. In a mixture of z litre, the ratio of milk and water is $x : y$. If another p litres of water is added to the mixture, the ratio of milk and water in the resulting mixture $= \frac{xz}{yz + p(x+y)}$
7. There are four members a, b, c and d, then formula for
   A. What should be added to each of these numbers so that the remaining numbers may be proportional $= \frac{ad - bc}{(b+c)-(a+d)}$
   B. What should be subtracted from each of these numbers so that the remaining numbers may be proportional $= \frac{ad - bc}{(a+d)-(b+c)}$
8. In a mixture the ratio of milk and water is $a : b$. If in this mixture another K litre of water is added, then the ratio of milk and water in the resulting mixture becomes $a : m$. Then the quantity of milk in the original mixture $= \frac{ak}{m-b}$ and quantity of water $= \frac{bk}{m-b}$

Unitary Method

The method in which first we find the value of one unit and then the value of required number of units is known as Unitary Method.

Equivalent Ratio: We compare the various ratios. To know that the given ratios are whether equivalent or not. To do this first we write the ratios in the form same denominator. Now we campare the fractions. If these are similar then we say that the ratios are equivalent,

e.g., Comparision of 5 : 6 and 20 : 24

$$\frac{5}{6} = \frac{5\times4}{6\times4} = \frac{20}{24} \text{ and } \frac{20}{24}$$

Obviously the given ratios are equivalent.

Percentage

The word 'per cent' or 'percentage' means 'for every one hundred'. In other words, it gives an indication of rate per hundred. It is denoted by the symbol %.

For example, 5% means 5 out of one hundred or $\frac{5}{100}$.

Remember :

(*i*) For converting a per cent into a fraction, divide it by 100.

(*ii*) For converting a fraction into a per cent, multiply it by 100.

(*iii*) For converting a per cent into a decimal, shift the decimal point two places to the left.

(*iv*) For converting one given quantity (x) as a percentage of another given quantity (y), find $\frac{x}{y}\times100$.

(*v*) There is no unit of percentage.

(*vi*) For converting a decimal into per cent first convert it into fraction then multiply it by 100.

(*vii*) To find the number by percentage convert the per cent into fraction and multiply with the number.

(viii) To find per cent by ratio, put the part of ratio as as numerator first which percent you have to find. Then put the sum of ratio as denominator and multiply by 100.

Important Facts

For quickly solving the problems related to percentage, remember following rules:

Rule 1:

A. Of the given two numbers if the first is x% more than the second, then the second will be $\left(\frac{100\times x}{100+x}\right)$% less than the first.

B. Of the given two numbers if the first is x% less than the second, then the second will be $\left(\frac{100\times x}{100-x}\right)$% more than the first.

C. If two numbers are respectively x% and y% more than a third number, then the first number will be $\left(\frac{100+x}{100+y}\times100\right)$% of the second.

D. If two numbers are respectively x% and y% less than a third number, then the first number will be $\left(\frac{100-x}{100-y}\times100\right)$% of the second.

Profit and Loss

A consumer who goes to the market and buys certain goods. The buyer is called a customer and the shopkeeper who sells the goods to him is called a retailer. The retailer purchases goods in turn in bulk from a wholesaler who keeps a large stock of good and in this case, the retailer becomes the customer.

1. Cost Price (C.P.) : Cost price is that price at which a particular article is bought. Profit and loss both are marked at cost price.

2. Selling Price (S.P.) : Selling price is that price at which a particular article is sold.

3. Overheads : The expenses incurred on transportation, maintenance, packaging, advertisements and the like are included as Overhead. These overheads and the profit when added to the cost price determine the selling price.

4. Profit or Gain : Whenever a person sells an article at price greater than the cost price he is said to have made a profit or gain.

Profit or Gain = S.P. – C.P.

5. Loss : If S.P. is less than the C.P. there is loss.

Loss = C.P – S.P.

Some Basic Formulae :

(i) Gain = S.P. – C.P.

(ii) Loss = C.P. – S.P.

(iii) $\text{Gain\%} = \dfrac{\text{Gain} \times 100}{\text{C.P.}}$

(iv) $\text{Loss\%} = \dfrac{\text{Loss} \times 100}{\text{C.P.}}$

From these we can write direct expressions for S.P. and C.P.

(v) $\text{S.P.} = \left(\dfrac{100 + \text{Gain\%}}{100}\right) \times \text{C.P.}$ in case of gain or profit

(vi) $\text{S.P.} = \left(\dfrac{100 - \text{Loss\%}}{100}\right) \times \text{C.P.}$ in case of loss

These can be rewritten as

$$\text{C.P.} = \frac{100}{100 + \text{Gain\%}} \times \text{S.P.}$$

in case of profit

$$\text{C.P.} = \frac{100}{100 - \text{Loss\%}} \times \text{S.P.}$$

in case of loss

(vii) If the C.P. of x goods = S.P. of y goods, then

A. $\text{Gain\%} = \dfrac{x - y}{y} \times 100$

[In case of $x > y$]

B. $\text{Loss\%} = \dfrac{y - x}{y} \times 100$

[In case of $y > x$]

(viii) When a man sells two things at the same price each and in this process his loss on first things is $x\%$ and gain on second things is $x\%$, then in such a type question, there is always a loss.

$$\text{Loss\%} = x\% \text{ of } x = \frac{x^2}{100} = \left(\frac{x}{10}\right)^2.$$

and $$\text{Loss} = \frac{2 \times \text{S.P.}}{\left(\frac{100}{x}\right)^2 - 1}$$

(ix) An article is sold at a profit of $x\%$. Had it been sold for Rs. a some more, $y\%$ would have gained. Then,

C.P. of an article

$$= \frac{\text{More gain} \times 100}{\text{Difference in percentage profit}}$$

(x) A dishonest shopkeeper prefers to sell goods at his cost price but uses a false weight of x grams for each kilogram. Then his gain per cent,

$$\text{gain\%} = \frac{\text{Error}}{\text{True value} - \text{Error}} \times 100$$

$$= \frac{1000 - x}{x} \times 100$$

$$\text{or, gain\%} = \frac{\text{True weight} - \text{False weight}}{\text{False weight}} \times 100.$$

Simple Interest

Interest is the money paid for the use of money borrowed, *i.e.*, extra money paid for using other's money is called interest.

The sum borrowed is called the principal. The sum of interest and principal is called the *Amount.*

If the interest on a certain sum borrowed for a certain period is reckoned uniformly, then it is called simple interest, denoted by S.I.

Thus, if A = Amount, P = Principal, I = Interest, T = Time (in year), R = Rate per cent per annum, then

A. $I = \dfrac{P \times R \times T}{100}$ B. $P = \dfrac{100 \times I}{R \times T}$

C. $T = \dfrac{100 \times I}{P \times R}$ D. $R = \dfrac{100 \times I}{P \times T}$

(e) $P = \dfrac{100A}{100 + RT}$ *(f)* A = P + I.

Compound Interest

In business transaction if interest as it becomes due is not paid to the lender but is added on to the principal, the money is said to be lent at compound interest and the total sum owed after a given time is called the amount at compound interest for that time.

After a certain period, the difference between the amount and the original principal is called the Compound Interest (C.I.).

Some Important Formulas :

Let, Principal = P

Time = n years

Rate = $r\%$ p.a.

then, the amount,

A. when interest is compounded annually:

then, $\text{Amount} = P\left(1+\frac{r}{100}\right)^n$

B. when interest is compounded half yearly:

then, $\text{Amount} = P\left(1+\frac{r/2}{100}\right)^{2n}$

C. when interest is compounded quarterly :

then, $\text{Amount} = P\left(1+\frac{r/4}{100}\right)^{4n}$

D. when time is fraction of a year, say $4\frac{1}{3}$ years,

then, $\text{Amount} = P\left(1+\frac{r}{100}\right)^4 \times \left(1+\frac{\frac{1}{3}r}{100}\right)$

E. when rates are $r_1\%$, $r_2\%$ and $r_3\%$ for Ist, IInd and IIIrd year respectively;
then,

$$\text{Amount} = P\left(1+\frac{r_1}{100}\right)\left(1+\frac{r_2}{100}\right)\left(1+\frac{r_3}{100}\right).$$

SOLVED QUESTIONS

Example 1: Choose the variables and write their numerical coefficient from the following expressions:

$6xy + 4$, $3 - y^2$, $12 - y$, $12 - y + 3y^2$, $4ab^2 - 3ab + 5$

Solution:

Expressions	Variables	Numerical Coefficient
$6xy+4$	$6xy$	6
$3-y^2$	$-y^2$	−1
$12-y+3y^2$	$-y, 3y^2$	−1, 3
$4ab^2-3ab+5$	$4ab^2, -3ab$	4, −3

Example 2: Simplify $12x^2 - 9x + 5x - 4x^2 - 7x + 10$

Solution: Rearranging the terms,

$12x^2 - 4x^2 + 5x - 9x - 7x + 10$

$= (12 - 4)x^2 + (5 - 9 - 7)x + 10$

$= 8x^2 + (-11)x + 10 = 8x^2 - 11x + 10$

Example 3: Evaluate the expression $5a^2 + 5a - 2$ if $a = -2$

Solution: Putting the value of a in the given expression $5a^2 + 5a - 2$

$= 5 \times (-2)^2 + 5 \times (-2) - 2$

$= 5 \times 4 + (-10) - 2 = 20 - 10 - 2 = 8$

Example 4: Simplify: $(a + b)(2a - 3b + c) - (2a - 3b)c$.

Solution: We have,

$(a + b)(2a - 3b + c)$

$= a(2a - 3b + c) + b(2a - 3b + c)$

$= 2a^2 - 3ab + ac + 2ab - 3b^2 + bc$

$= 2a^2 - ab - 3b^2 + bc + ac$

and $(2a - 3b)c = 2ac - 3bc$

Hence,

$(a + b)(2a - 3b + c) - (2a - 3b)c$

$= 2a^2 - ab - 3b^2 + bc + ac - (2ac - 3bc)$

$= 2a^2 - ab - 3b^2 + bc + ac - 2ac + 3bc$

$= 2a^2 - ab - 3b^2 + (bc + 3bc) + (ac - 2ac)$

$= 2a^2 - 3b^2 - ab + 4bc - ac$

Example 5: Solve $2y + \frac{5}{3} = \frac{26}{3} - y$

Solution: We have, $2y + \frac{5}{3} = \frac{26}{3} - y$

or, $2y + y = \frac{26}{3} - \frac{5}{3}$ or, $3Y = \frac{21}{3}$

or, $3y = 7$ $\therefore$ $y = \frac{7}{3}$

Example 6: The difference between two whole numbers is 66. The ratio of the two numbers is 2 : 5. What are the two numbers?

Solution: Since the ratio of the two numbers is 2 : 5, we may take one number to be $2x$ and the other to be $5x$. It is given that the difference is 66. Hence,

$5x - 2x = 66$

or $3x = 66$

or $x = 22$

Since the numbers are $2x$ and $5x$, they are $2 \times 22 = 44$ or $5 \times 22 = 110$, respectively.

Example 7: Length and breadth of a rectangular field are 50 m and 15 m respectively. Find the ratio of the length to the breadth of the field.

Solution: Length of the rectangular field = 50 m

Breadth of the rectangular field = 15 m

The ratio of the length to the breadth is 50 : 15

The ratio can be written as $\frac{50}{15} = \frac{50 \div 5}{15 \div 5} = \frac{10}{3}$

= 10 : 3

Thus, the required ratio is 10 : 3.

Example 8: Divide Rs. 60 in the ratio 1 : 2 between Anu and Madhu.

Solution: The two parts are 1 and 2.

Hence, sum of the parts = 1 + 2 = 3.

This means Anu gets 1 part and Madhu gets 2 parts out of every 3 parts.

Hence, Anu's share = $\frac{1}{3} \times 60 = \text{Rs. } 20$

And Madhu's share = $\frac{2}{3} \times 60 = \text{Rs. } 40$.

MULTIPLE CHOICE QUESTIONS

1. In algebra we study about the calculation of:
A. digits
B. numerals
C. letters and symbols
D. None of these

2. A letter or a sign which does not have a fixed value that is:
A. Algebra B. Variable
C. Term D. None of these

3. A group of signs that represent an idea or a quantity is:
A. a term B. a factor
C. an expression D. None of these

4. In $7xy^2$ the numerical coefficient is:
A. x B. y^2
C. 2 D. 7

5. The factors of the term $4x^2yz$ are:
A. 4, x^2, y and z
B. x, y and z
C. 4 and 2
D. Can not be determined

6. $5xy + 2z + 5$ is a:
A. Monomial B. Trinomial
C. Binomial D. None of these

7. $(3m^2 - 17m + 10) \div (3m - 2)$ equals to:
A. $5 - m$ B. $m + 5$
C. $m - 5$ D. $m + 4$

8. HCF of $(2x - 7)(3x + 4)$; $(2x - 7)^2(4x + 3)$ and $(2x - 7)^4(3x - 4)$ is:
A. $(2x - 7)(3x + 4)$ B. $(2x - 7)(3x - 4)$
C. $(3x + 4)$ D. $(2x - 7)$

9. LCM of $(m + 3)^2(m - 2)(m + 1)^2$; $(m + 1)^3(m + 3)(m + 4)$ is:
A. $(m + 3)^2(m + 1)^3$
B. $(m + 1)^2(m + 3)$
C. $(m + 3)^2(m + 1)^3(m - 2)(m + 4)$
D. None of these

10. Factors of $3x^2(y - z) + 9x(y - z)^2$ are:
A. $3x(y - z)$ B. $3x(y - z)[x + 3(y - z)]$
C. $3x^2(y - z)$ D. None of these

11. Factors of $x^2 - 6x + 8$ are:
A. $(x - 2)(x - 4)$ B. $(4x - x)(2 - x)$
C. $(4x + x)(2 + x)$ D. None of these

12. $(3m + n)^2$ is equal to:
A. $9m^2 + n^2 + 3n$ B. $9m^2 + n^2$
C. $9m^2 + n^2 + 6mn$ D. None of these

13. What will the value of y in equation $2x + 3y = 13$ if $x = 2$?
A. 4 B. 3
C. 2 D. None of these

14. If $x = -3$ and $y = 2$ the value of $4x - 3xy + 3y - 2x + y^2$ is:
A. 49 B. 94
C. 90 D. None of these

15. $9a^2c + 7b^2a$ is a:
A. Binomial B. Monomial
C. Trinomial D. None of these

16. Coefficient of $-3x^2y^2z^2$ is:
A. −2 B. 2
C. −3 D. 3

17. Like terms of $-5a^2bc$ is:
A. $5abc$ B. abc
C. a^2bc D. None of these

18. Sum of $9a - 2b + 5c$ and $-3a + 6b - 12c$ is:
A. $6a + 4b + 3c$ B. $6a - 4b + 3c$
C. $6a + 4b - 7c$ D. None of these

19. What should be added in $4x^4 - 2x^2y^2 + y^4$ to become $x^4 - y^4$?
A. $-3x^2 - 2y^2 + 2x^2y^2$
B. $-3x^4 - 2y^4 + 2x^2y^2$
C. $3x^4 + 2x^2y^2 - 2y^4$
D. $-3x^4 - 2y^4 + 2x^2y^2$

20. What is the difference between $4a + 2b - 8c$ and $-3a + 2b - 5c$?
A. $3a - c$ B. $a - 3c$
C. $7a - 3c$ D. None of these

21. Simplify $2a + [5b - \{9a - (10b + 4a)\}]$.
A. $3a - 15b$ B. $ab(5 - 3)$
C. $-3a + 15b$ D. None of these

22. $(4x + 5y)(3x - y)$ equals to:
A. $12x^2 + 11xy - 5y^2$
B. $12x^2 - 11xy + 5y^2$
C. $12x^2 - 11xy - 5y^2$
D. None of these

23. $(-14x^4y^3z) \div (-7x^2yz)$ equal to:
A. $2x^2y^2$ B. $-2x^2y^2$
C. $2x^2y^2z$ D. $3xyz$

24. $(p^2 - p + 2)(p^2 + p + 2)$ equals to:
A. $p^4 + 3p^2 - 4$ B. $p^4 - 3p^2 + 4$
C. $p^4 + 3p^2 + 4$ D. None of these

25. Factors of $a^3 - \frac{1}{a^3} - 36$ are:
A. $\left(a + \frac{1}{a} + 3\right)\left(a^2 + \frac{1}{a^2} + 10 - \frac{3}{a} + 3a\right)$
B. $\left(a + \frac{1}{a} - 3\right)\left(a + \frac{1}{a}\right)$
C. $\left(a + \frac{1}{a} + 3\right)\left(a - \frac{1}{a}\right)$
D. None of these

26. Correct value of $a^4 - 6b^2c + 3c^2 + 5ac$ if $a = 2$, $b = -2$ and $c = 3$
A. 0 B. -1
C. 2 D. 1

27. Sum of $5x + 3y - 2z$ and $-6x - 9z + 2y$ is:
A. $11x + 5y - 11z$ B. $-x + 5y - 11z$
C. $x - 5x + 11z$ D. None of these

28. Difference of $9x - 2y + 4z$ and $-x - 6y + 4z$ is:
A. $8x - 4y$ B. $10x + 4y$
C. $10x - 4y$ D. $8x + 4y$

29. If $x + 5$, $y = 3$ and $z = 2$ then correct value of $x^2 + y^2 + z^2 + 2xy + 2yz + 2zx$ is:
A. -25 B. 10
C. 0 D. 125

30. Correct factorisation of $\left(x^2 + x + \frac{1}{4}\right)$ is:
A. $\left(x + \frac{1}{2}\right)^2$ B. $\left(x + \frac{1}{2}\right)(x + 2)$
C. $\left(x - \frac{1}{2}\right)^2$ D. None of these

31. If sum of two numbers is 173 and difference between them is 73 then smaller one is:
A. 37 B. 123
C. 50 D. None of these

32. If sum of three consecutive numbers is 129 then the least number is:
A. 43 B. 41
C. 42 D. 44

33. What will the value of $x^4 + 2 + \frac{1}{x^4}$ if $x = \sqrt{3}$?
A. $11\frac{1}{9}$ B. 130
C. $44\frac{1}{2}$ D. 100

34. HCF of two algebraic expression is $(a + 1)$ and LCM is $(a^2 + 4a + 3)$ if one of them is $(a + 1)$ the another one is:
A. $a^2 + 4a$ B. $a^2 - 4a - 1$
C. $a^2 + 4a + 1$ D. $a^2 + 4a + 3$

35. If the price of seven books and four copies is Rs. 100 while the price of nine books and eight copies is Rs. 140. The price of 1 book and 1 copy is:
A. Rs. 12 and Rs. 8
B. Rs. 12 and Rs. 4
C. Can not be determined
D. None of these

36. The equivalent of ratio 6 : 4 is
A. 3 : 2 B. 9 : 6
C. Both A and B D. None of these

37. If the cost of 6 cans of juice is Rs 210 then what will be the cost of 4 cans of juice?
A. Rs 104 B. Rs 410
C. Rs 140 D. None of these

38. A car travels 90 km in $2\frac{1}{2}$ hours then how much distance will it travel in 4 hours:
A. 144 km B. 140 km
C. 114 km D. 142 km

39. Solution of $\frac{15}{4} - 7x = 9$ is
A. $\frac{3}{4}$ B. $-\frac{4}{3}$
C. $-\frac{3}{4}$ D. $\frac{4}{3}$

40. Alok is twice old as Ashok. Five year ago his age was three times of Ashok's age. Then his present age is:
A. 10 years B. 15 years
C. 20 years D. 25 years

41. If 10% of x is the same as 20% of y, then x : y is equal to :
A. 1 : 2 B. 2 : 1
C. 5 : 1 D. 10 : 1

42. The mean proportional between 0.32 and 0.02 is:
A. 0.34 B. 0.3
C. 0.16 D. 0.08

43. Rs. 425 is divided among 4 men, 5 women and 6 boys such that the share of a man, a woman and a boy may be in the ratio of 9 : 8 : 4. What is the share of a woman?
A. Rs. 34 B. Rs. 24
C. Rs. 44 D. None of these

44. The monthly salary of A, B, C is in the proportion of 2 : 3 : 5. If C's monthly salary is Rs. 1200 more than that of A, then B's annual salary is:

A. Rs. 14400 B. Rs. 24000
C. Rs. 1200 D. Rs. 2000

45. Rs. 1050 is divided among P, Q and R. The share of P is $\frac{2}{5}$ of the combined share of Q and R. Thus P gets:

A. Rs. 200 B. Rs. 300
C. Rs. 400 D. Rs. 420

46. The ratio between Sumit's and Prakash's age at present is 2 : 3. Sumit is 6 years younger than Prakash. The ratio of Sumit's age to Prakash's age after 6 years will be:

A. 1 : 2 B. 2 : 3
C. 3 : 4 D. 3 : 8

47. The areas of two spheres are in the ratio 1 : 4. the ratio of their volumes is:

A. 1 : 2 B. 1 : 4
C. 1 : 8 D. 1 : 6

48. A certain amount was divided between Kavita and Reena in the ratio 4 : 3. If Reena's share was Rs. 2400, the amount is:

A. Rs. 5600 B. Rs. 3200
C. Rs. 9600 D. None of these

49. The prices of scooter and television set are in the ratio 3 : 2. If a scooter costs Rs. 6000 more than the television set, the price of the television set is:

A. Rs. 6000 B. Rs. 10000
C. Rs. 12000 D. Rs. 18000

50. In a class, the number of boys is more than the number of girls by 12% of the total strength. The ratio of the boys to girls is:

A. 11 : 14 B. 14 : 11
C. 25 : 28 D. 28 : 25

51. A right circular cylinder and a right circular cone have the same radius and the same volume. The ratio of the height of the cylinder to that of the cone is:

A. 3 : 5 B. 2 : 5
C. 3 : 1 D. 1 : 3

52. A circle and a square have same area. Therefore, the ratio of the side of the square and the radius of the circle is :

A. $\sqrt{\pi}:1$ B. $1:\sqrt{\pi}$
C. $1 : \pi$ D. $\pi : 1$

53. If Rs. 782 be divided into three parts, proportional to $\frac{1}{2}:\frac{2}{3}:\frac{3}{4}$; then the first part is:

A. Rs. 204 B. Rs. 196
C. Rs. 190 D. Rs. 182

54. If 10% of x = 20% of y, then $x : y$ is equal to:

A. 10 : 1 B. 5 : 1
C. 2 : 1 D. 1 : 2

55. In a school ratio of boys to girls is 4 : 5. When 100 girls leave the school ratio becomes 6 : 7. How many boys are there in the school?

A. 1200 B. 1300
C. 1500 D. 1600

56. A sum of Rs. 1300 is divided among P, Q, R and S such that $\frac{\text{P's share}}{\text{Q's share}} = \frac{\text{Q's share}}{\text{R's share}} = \frac{\text{R's share}}{\text{S's share}} = \frac{2}{3}$. Then P's share is:

A. Rs. 320 B. Rs. 240
C. Rs. 160 D. Rs. 140

57. If A : B = 6 : 7 and B : C = 8 : 9, then A : B : C is:

A. 24 : 28 : 63 B. 48 : 28 : 63
C. 48 : 56 : 63 D. None of these

58. The sum of two numbers is 20 and their difference is $2\frac{1}{2}$. What is the ratio of the numbers?

A. 11 : 7 B. 9 : 11
C. 9 : 7 D. None of these

59. Two numbers are in the ratio 3 : 5. If each number is increased by 10, the ratio becomes 5 : 7. The numbers are:

A. 3, 5 B. 7, 9
C. 13, 22 D. 15, 25

60. One man adds 3 litres of water to 12 litres of milk and another 4 litres of water to 10 litres of milk. What is the ratio of the strengths of the milk in the two mixtures?

A. 15 : 25 B. 25 : 28
C. 28 : 25 D. None of these

61. Gold is 19 times as heavy as water and copper 9 times as heavy as water. The ratio in which these two metals be mixed so that the mixtures is 15 times as heavy as water is:

A. 1 : 2 B. 2 : 3
C. 3 : 2 D. 19 : 135

62. The ratio between the ages of Kamla and Savitri is 6 : 5 and the sum of their ages is 44 years. The ratio of their ages after 8 years will be:

A. 5 : 6 B. 7 : 8
C. 8 · 7 D. 14 : 13

63. Vinay got thrice as many marks in Maths as in English. The proportion of his marks in Maths and History is 4 : 3. If his total marks in Maths, English and History is 250 then, what is his marks in English?

A. 120 B. 90
C. 40 D. 80

64. 13 books cost Rs 273, then the cost of 2 books is equal to:
A. Rs 18 B. Rs 21
C. Rs 42 D. Rs 27

65. If 13 pens cost Rs 29.90, then what will be the cost of 1 pen?
A. Rs 2 B. Rs 2.30
C. Rs 2.40 D. Rs 2.50

66. 20 trucks can hold 150 metric tonnes, how much will 18 trucks hold?
A. 125 m tonnes B. 135 m tonnes
C. 145 m tonnes D. 147 m tonnes

67. 500 copies of a book cost Rs 3125, what will 100 copies cost?
A. Rs 525 B. Rs 575
C. Rs 625 D. Rs 635

68. A horse eats $27\frac{1}{2}$ kg of corn in 22 days. How much does he eat in 7 days?
A. $8\frac{3}{4}$ kg B. $9\frac{1}{4}$ kg
C. $9\frac{1}{2}$ kg D. $9\frac{3}{4}$ kg

69. A boy runs a km in 7 min 10 seconds. How long will he take to run 400 m?
A. 2 min B. 2 min 32 sec
C. 2 min 52 sec D. 1 min 58 sec

70. What will 12 dozens knives cost when 3 dozens cost Rs 37?
A. Rs 111 B. Rs 135
C. Rs 148 D. Rs 444

71. What is the cost of 205 sticks at Rs 24 per score?
A. Rs 205 B. Rs 240
C. Rs 246 D. Rs 248

72. What is the cost of 3 quintals 20 kg of coal if 3 quintals cost Rs 300?
A. Rs 302 B. Rs 320
C. Rs 640 D. Rs 600

73. 5 men can do a piece of work in 3 days, in how many days will 1 man do it?
A. $\frac{3}{5}$ B. $\frac{5}{3}$
C. 15 D. $\frac{1}{15}$

74. Simplest form of the ratio 25 to 275 is:
A. 1 : 5 B. 2 : 5
C. 1 : 11 D. 1 : 13

75. 2.25 : .75 is the same as:
A. 1 : 3 B. 2 : 4
C. 2 : 5 D. 7 : 5

76. Compound ratio of 2 : 3, 3 : 4, 4 : 5 is:
A. 3 : 5 B. 2 : 4
C. 2 : 5 D. 1 : 20

77. $\frac{2}{3}:\frac{7}{9}$ is the same as:
A. 3 : 2 B. 7 : 6
C. 2 : 3 D. 6 : 7

78. 12 seconds : 10 hours is:
A. 1 : 300 B. 300 : 1
C. 1 : 3000 D. 3000 : 1

79. A number exceeds 20% of itself by 40. The number is :
A. 50 B. 60
C. 80 D. 320

80. The price of an article is cut by 10%. To restore it to the former value, the new price must be increased by :
A. 10% B. $9\frac{1}{11}$%
C. $11\frac{1}{9}$% D. 11%

81. 5% income of A is equal to 15% income of B and 10% income of B is equal to 20% income of C. If income of C is Rs. 2000, then total income of A, B and C is :
A. Rs. 6000 B. Rs. 18000
C. Rs. 20000 D. Rs. 14000

82. A student who secures 20% marks in an examination fails by 30 marks. Another student who secures 32% gets 42 marks more than those required to pass. The percentage of marks required to pass is:
A. 20 B. 25
C. 28 D. 30

83. In a college election, a candidate secured 62% of the votes and is elected by a majority of 144 votes. The total number of votes polled is :
A. 600 B. 800
C. 925 D. 1200

84. What will be 80% of a number whose 200% is 90?
A. 144 B. 72
C. 36 D. None of these

85. The price of an article has been reduced by 25%. In order to restore the original price, the new price must be increased by :
A. $33\frac{1}{3}$% B. $11\frac{1}{9}$%
C. $9\frac{1}{11}$% D. $66\frac{2}{3}$%

86. In an organisation, 40% of the employees are matriculates, 50% of the remaining are graduates and the remaining 180 are postgraduates. How many employees are graduates?

A. 360 B. 240
C. 300 D. 180

87. The population of a town increases by 5% annually. If its population in 2008 was 138915, what it was in 2005?
A. 110000 B. 100000
C. 120000 D. 90000

88. The population of a village is 4500. $\frac{5}{9}$th of them are males and rest females. If 40% of the males are married, then the percentage of married female is :
A. 35 B. 40
C. 50 D. 60

89. A candidate needs 35% marks to pass. If he gets 96 marks and fails by 16 marks, then the maximum marks are :
A. 250 B. 320
C. 300 D. 425

90. In an election one of the two candidates gets 40% votes and loses by 100 votes. Total number of votes is :
A. 500 B. 400
C. 600 D. 1000

91. The gross income of a person is Rs. 20000. 10% of his income is exempted from income tax and his net income is Rs. 19100. The rate of income tax is :
A. 3% B. 2%
C. 4% D. 5%

92. One-eight of a number is 17.25. What will 73% of number be?
A. 82.66 B. 96.42
C. 100.75 D. 138.00

93. If 58% of 960 – x% of 635 = 277.4, find the value of x.
A. 24 B. 36
C. 44 D. 58

94. There are 1225 employees in an organisation, out of which 40% got transferred to different places. How many such employees got transferred?
A. 490 B. 540
C. 630 D. 710

95. 56% of a number is 1064. What is 38% of the number?
A. 666 B. 722
C. 856 D. 912

96. The owner of a cell phone shop charges his customer 32% more than the cost price. If a customer paid Rs. 6600 for the cell phone, then what was the cost price of the cell phone?
A. Rs. 5000 B. Rs. 5500
C. Rs. 5800 D. Rs. 6100

97. The difference between 89% of a number and 73% of the same number is 448. What is 49% of that number?
A. 1124 B. 1218
C. 1372 D. 1426

98. Nupur invests Rs. 89856, what is 26% of her annual income in mutual funds. What is her monthly income?
A. Rs. 23980.50 B. Rs. 28800
C. Rs. 28990 D. Rs. 33606.25

99. The difference between 70% and 55% of a number is 72. The number is:
A. 370 B. 460
C. 480 D. 520

100. 20% of a number is 10% of :
A. half the number
B. double the number
C. ten times the number
D. twenty times the number

101. 75% of what area is 15 sq. metres?
A. 10 sq. metres B. 15 sq. metres
C. 20 sq. metres D. 25 sq. metres

102. Profit after selling a commodity for Rs. 425 is same as loss after selling it for Rs. 355. The cost of the commodity is :
A. Rs. 285 B. Rs. 390
C. Rs. 295 D. Rs. 400

103. Bhajan Singh purchased 120 reams of paper at Rs. 80 per ream. He spent Rs. 280 on transportation, paid octroi at the rate of 40 paise per ream and paid Rs. 72 to the coolie. If he wants to have a gain of 8%, what must be the selling price per ream?
A. Rs. 86 B. Rs. 86.48
C. Rs. 79 D. Rs. 90

104. Subhash purchased a taperecorder at $\frac{9}{10}$ of its selling price and sold it at 8% more than its S.P. His gain is :
A. 8% B. 10%
C. 18% D. 20%

105. A dealer marks his goods 20% above cost price. He then allows some discount on it and makes a profit of 8%. The rate of discount is :
A. 12% B. 10%
C. 6% D. 4%

106. A trader lists his articles 20% above C,P. and allows a discount of 10% on cash payment. His gain per cent is :
A. 10% B. 8%
C. 6% D. 4%

107. Tarun bought a T.V. with 20% discount on the labelled price. Had he bought it with 25%

discount, he would have saved Rs. 500. At what price did he buy the T.V.?

A. Rs. 5000 B. Rs. 8000
C. Rs. 10000 D. Rs. 12000

108. While selling a watch, a shopkeeper gives a discount of 5%. If he gives a discount of 7%, he earns Rs. 15 less as profit. The marked price of the watch is :

A. Rs. 697.50 B. Rs. 712.50
C. Rs. 787.50 D. None of these

109. Kabir buys an article with 25% discount on its marked price. He makes a profit of 10% by selling it at Rs. 660. The marked price is :

A. Rs. 600 B. Rs. 700
C. Rs. 800 D. Rs. 885

110. A man bought a horse and cart. If he sold the horse at 10% loss and the cart at 20% gain he would not loss anything. If he sold the horse at 5% loss and the cart at 5% gain he would lose Rs. 10 in the bargain. What did he pay for each?

A. Rs. 400, Rs. 200 B. Rs. 300, Rs. 300
C. Rs. 250, Rs. 350 D. Rs. 350, Rs. 250

111. The marked price of a radio is 20% more than its cost price. If a discount of 10% is given on the marked price, the gain percentage is:

A. 8 B. 10
C. 12 D. 15

112. A fan is listed at Rs. 1400 and the discount offered is 10%. What additional discount must be given to bring the net selling price to Rs. 1200?

A. $4\frac{16}{21}\%$ B. 5%
C. 6% D. $16\frac{2}{3}\%$

113. Sanjay buys a field of agricultural land for Rs. 3,60,000. He sells one-third at a loss of 20% and two-fifth at a gain of 25%. At what price must he sell the remaining field so as to make an overall profit of 10%?

A. Rs. 1,00,000 B. Rs. 1,15,000
C. Rs. 1,20,000 D. Rs. 1,25,000

114. Saurabh bought a radio for Rs. 800 and spent Rs. 400 on it. He sold it for Rs. 1500. What is his gain per cent?

A. 25% B. 35%
C. 52% D. 55%

115. Samir purchased 150 quintals of wheat. One-fourth of the total quantity, he sold at a loss of 10%. At what gain per cent should he sell the remaining wheat to gain 10% on the whole transaction?

A. $14\frac{1}{2}\%$ B. $15\frac{2}{3}\%$
C. $16\frac{2}{3}\%$ D. $18\frac{2}{3}\%$

116. What sum of money will produce Rs 75 interest in 3 years at 5% simple interest?

A. Rs 750 B. Rs 600
C. Rs 500 D. Rs 112.5

117. At what rate per cent will a sum of money double itself in 20 years with simple interest?

A. 4% B. 5%
C. 10% D. 20%

118. At what rate per cent, the simple interest on a sum of money treble itself in 25 years?

A. 4% B. 6%
C. 8% D. 10%

119. A sum of money doubles itself in 16 years. In what time will it treble itself?

A. 24 years B. 32 years
C. 64 years D. 20 years

120. If the interest on money be 1 paisa per rupee per month, what is the rate per cent per annum?

A. 4% B. 100%
C. 10% D. 12%

121. What sum of money lent out at 5% per annum will give one rupee as interest per day? (1 year = 365 days).

A. Rs 7300 B. Rs 7200
C. Rs 7500 D. Rs 3650

122. Neeraj took a loan at 10% per annum simple interest. After 4 years he returned the principal along with the interest. If he returns in all Rs 3500, what is the principal amount?

A. Rs 2500 B. Rs 3250
C. Rs 3150 D. Rs 2100

123. In what time will the interest on a given sum at $4\frac{1}{2}\%$ amount to nine sixteenth of the sum?

A. 10 years B. 12 years
C. $12\frac{1}{2}$ years D. 25 years

124. If the simple interest on a sum of money is $\frac{1}{9}$ of the principal, and the number of years is equal to the rate%. The rate % is:

A. 9% B. $4\frac{1}{2}\%$
C. 3% D. $3\frac{1}{3}\%$

125. If Rs 1000 be placed at interest at 5% and the interest be added to the principal every 10 years, in how many years will it amount to Rs 2000?

A. 12 years B. 20 years

C. 16 years D. $16\frac{2}{3}$ years

126. If a, b, c are three sums of money such that b is the simple interest on a and c is the simple interest on b for the same rate and time, then the relation between three sums is:

A. $b^2 = ac$ B. $b = ac$

C. $b^2 = \sqrt{ac}$ D. $a = bc$

127. A house costs Rs 10000. Incidental expenses and taxes amount to Rs 360 a year. What rent per month must the owner receive to earn 6% on his investment?

A. Rs 85 B. Rs 80

C. Rs 70 D. Rs 60

128. A certain sum of money at simple interest amounts to Rs 896 in three years' and Rs 960 in five years. The sum is:

A. Rs 600 B. Rs 700

C. Rs 750 D. Rs 800

129. What sum of money lent out at 6% per annum simple interest amount to Rs 690 in 3 years?

A. Rs 550 B. Rs 500

C. Rs 600 D. Rs 684

130. The simple interest of Rs 200 for 4 years is Rs 60. What will be the interest of Rs 800 for 3 years at the same rate of interest?

A. Rs 90 B. Rs 60

C. Rs 180 D. Rs 120

131. The compound interest of Rs 3000 for 2 years at 5% is:

A. Rs 300 B. Rs 307

C. Rs 307.50 D. Rs 317.50

132. Find the amount of Rs 2400 after 3 years, when the interest is compounded annually at the rate of 20% per annum.

A. Rs 4000 B. Rs 4100

C. Rs 4147 D. Rs 4147.20

133. The interest on a certain deposit at 4.5% is Rs 202.5 in one year. How much the additional interest in one year be on the same deposit at 5% per annum?

A. Rs 225 B. Rs 20.25

C. Rs 22.50 D. Rs 202.50

134. The difference between compound interest and simple interest on a certain sum for 2 years at the rate of 5% per annum is Rs 1. What is the sum?

A. Rs 200 B. Rs 300

C. Rs 400 D. Rs 500

135. A sum becomes Rs 1352 in 2 years at 4% compound interest. The sum is:

A. Rs 1225 B. Rs 1245

C. Rs 1250 D. Rs 1270

ANSWERS

1	**2**	**3**	**4**	**5**	**6**	**7**	**8**	**9**	**10**
D	B	C	D	A	B	C	D	C	B
11	**12**	**13**	**14**	**15**	**16**	**17**	**18**	**19**	**20**
A	C	B	B	A	C	C	C	D	C
21	**22**	**23**	**24**	**25**	**26**	**27**	**28**	**29**	**30**
C	A	A	B	A	D	B	C	C	A
31	**32**	**33**	**34**	**35**	**36**	**37**	**38**	**39**	**40**
C	C	A	D	B	C	C	A	C	C
41	**42**	**43**	**44**	**45**	**46**	**47**	**48**	**49**	**50**
B	D	A	C	B	C	C	A	C	B
51	**52**	**53**	**54**	**55**	**56**	**57**	**58**	**59**	**60**
D	A	A	A	A	C	C	C	D	C
61	**62**	**63**	**64**	**65**	**66**	**67**	**68**	**69**	**70**
C	C	C	C	B	B	C	A	C	C
71	**72**	**73**	**74**	**75**	**76**	**77**	**78**	**79**	**80**
C	B	C	C	B	C	D	C	A	C
81	**82**	**83**	**84**	**85**	**86**	**87**	**88**	**89**	**90**
B	B	A	C	A	D	C	C	B	A
91	**92**	**93**	**94**	**95**	**96**	**97**	**98**	**99**	**100**
D	C	C	A	B	A	C	B	C	B
101	**102**	**103**	**104**	**105**	**106**	**107**	**108**	**109**	**110**
C	B	D	D	B	B	B	D	C	A
111	**112**	**113**	**14**	**115**	**116**	**117**	**118**	**119**	**120**
A	A	C	A	C	C	B	C	B	D

121	122	123	124	125	126	127	128	129	130
A	A	C	D	D	A	B	D	C	C
131	**132**	**133**	**134**	**135**					
C	D	C	C	C					

SOME SELECTED EXPLANATORY ANSWERS

8. Factors of $(2x - 7)(3x + 4) = (2x - 7), (3x + 4)$

$(2x - 7)^2 (4x + 3) = (2x - 7), (4x + 3)$

$(2x - 7)^4 (3x - 4) = (2x - 7), (3x - 4)$

Hence, HCF $= (2x - 7)$.

10. Since, $3x(y - z)$ is common in $3x^2(y - z) + 9x(y - z)$

Hence, $3x^2(y - x) + 9x(y - z)^2$

$= 3x(y - z)[x + 3(y - z)]$

11. $x^2 - 6x + 8 = x^2 - 4x - 2x + 8$

$= x(x - 4) - 2(x - 4)$

$= (x - 2)(x - 4)$.

12. $(3m + n)^2 = 9m^2 + n^2 + 6mn$

$(\because (a + b)^2 = a^2 + b^2 + 2ab)$.

13. Putting the value of x in equation.

$2 \times 2 + 3y = 13$

$\Rightarrow \quad 4 + 3y = 13 \Rightarrow 3y = 13 - 4 = 9$

$\therefore \quad y = \frac{9}{3} = 3$.

18.
$$\begin{array}{r} 9a - 2b + 5c \\ -3a + 6b - 12c \\ \hline 6a + 4b - 7c \\ \hline \end{array}$$

19.
$$\begin{array}{r} x^4 - y^4 \\ 4x^4 + y^4 - 2x^2y^2 \\ - \quad - \quad + \\ \hline -3x^4 - 2y^4 + 2x^2y^2 \\ \hline \end{array}$$

20.
$$\begin{array}{r} 4a + 2b - 8c \\ -3a + 2b - 5c \\ + \quad - \quad + \\ \hline 7a \qquad - 3c \\ \hline \end{array}$$

22.
$$\begin{array}{r} 4x + 5y \\ 3x - y \\ \hline 12x^2 + 15xy \\ -4xy - 5y^2 \\ \hline 12x^2 - 11xy - 5y^2 \\ \hline \end{array}$$

23. $(-14x^4y^3z) \div (-7x^2yz)$

$= \frac{-14}{-7} x^{4-2} y^{3-1} z^{1-1}$

$= 2x^2y^2$

26. Putting the value of a, b and c in the given expression,

$2^4 - 6 \times (-2)^2 \times 3 + 3 \times 3^2 + 5 \times 2 \times 3$

$= 16 - 72 + 27 + 30 = 73 - 72 = 1$.

27.
$$\begin{array}{r} 5x + 3y - 2z \\ -6x + 2y - 9z \\ \hline -x + 5y - 11z \end{array}$$

28.
$$\begin{array}{r} 9x - 2y + 4z \\ -x - 6y + 4z \\ + \quad + \quad - \\ \hline 10 + 4y \\ \hline \end{array}$$

29. $x^2 + y^2 + z^2 - 2xy + 2yz - 2xz$

$= (x - y - z)^2$

Now putting the value of x, y and z

$= (5 - 3 - 2)^2 = 0$.

30. $x^2 + x + \frac{1}{4} = x^2 + 2.\frac{1}{2}.x + \left(\frac{1}{2}\right)^2$

$= \left(x + \frac{1}{2}\right)^2$

$\left(\because a^2 + 2ab + b^2 = (a + b)^2\right)$.

31. Smaller number $= \frac{173 - 73}{2} = \frac{100}{2} = 50$.

32. Let the number are x, $x + 1$ and $x + 2$

From question, $x + x + 1 + x + 2 = 129$

or $\quad 3x + 3 = 129 \quad \therefore 3x = 129 - 3 = 126$

$\therefore \quad x = \frac{126}{3} = 42$.

Hence, least number = 42.

33. Putting the value of x in

$x^4 + 2 + \frac{1}{x^4} = \left(\sqrt{3}\right)^4 + 2 + \frac{1}{\left(\sqrt{3}\right)^4}$

$= 9 + 2 + \frac{1}{5} = 11\frac{1}{9}$

34. LCM × HCF = Fist number × Second number

$\therefore$ Second number $= \frac{(a+1)(a^2 + 4a + 3)}{(a+1)}$

$= a^2 + 4a + 3$.

37. Cost of 6 cans of juice = Rs 210

$\therefore$ Cost of 1 can of juice $= \frac{210}{6}$ = Rs 35

$\therefore$ Cost of 4 cans of juice $= 35 \times 4$ = Rs 140.

38. In $2\frac{1}{2}$ hours the car travels 90 km

$\therefore$ In 1 hour the car travels $\frac{90}{5} \times 2 = 36$ km

$\therefore$ In 4 hours the car travels $36 \times 4 = 144$ km.

39. $\frac{15}{4} - 7x = 9 \Rightarrow 7x = \frac{15}{4} - 9 = -\frac{21}{4}$

$\therefore \quad x = -\frac{21}{7 \times 4} = -\frac{3}{4}.$

42. Mean proportional $= \sqrt{0.32 \times 0.02}$

$= \sqrt{0.0064} = 0.08.$

44. Let the monthly salary of A, B, C be $2x$, $3x$ and $5x$

Then, $5x - 2x = 1200$

or, $3x = 1200 \quad \therefore x = 400$

B's monthly salary $= 3x = 3 \times 400 =$ Rs. 1200.

45. P : (Q + R) = 2 : 5

$\therefore$ P's share = Rs. $\left(1050 \times \frac{2}{7}\right)$ = Rs. 300.

46. Let their ages be $2x$ and $3x$ years.

$\Rightarrow \quad 3x - 2x = 6 \quad \Rightarrow x = 6$

Sumit's age = 12 years

Prakash's age= 18 years

After 6 years, Sumit's age = 18 years and Prakash's age = 24 years

$\therefore$ Ratio of their ages = 18 : 24 = 3 : 4.

48. Let their shares be Rs. $4x$ and Rs. $3x$

Then, $3x = 2400 \Rightarrow x =$ Rs. 800

$\therefore$ Total amount $= 7x = 7 \times 800 =$ Rs. 5600.

49. Let the price of a scooter be Rs. $3x$ and that of a television set be Rs. $2x$

Then, $3x - 2x = 600 \Rightarrow x = 6000$

$\therefore$ Cost of a television set $= 2x = 2 \times 6000$ = Rs. 12000.

51. Let the heights of the cylinder and cone be h and H respectively.

Then, $\pi r^2 h = \frac{1}{3}\pi r^2 H \Rightarrow \frac{h}{H} = \frac{1}{3}$

So, their heights in the ratio = 1 : 3.

52. Let the side of the square be x and the radius of the circle be y. Then,

$x^2 = \pi y^2$

$\Rightarrow \quad \frac{x^2}{y^2} = \pi \quad \Rightarrow \frac{x}{y} = \sqrt{\pi}$

$\therefore \quad x : y = \sqrt{\pi} : 1.$

53. Here ratio $= \frac{1}{2} : \frac{2}{3} : \frac{3}{4} = 6 : 8 : 9$

Hence, 1st part $= \frac{6}{6+8+9} \times$ Rs. 782

$= \frac{6}{23} \times$ Rs.782 = Rs. 204.

54. Here, $\frac{10}{100} \times x = \frac{20}{100} \times y \quad \Rightarrow \frac{x}{y} = \frac{2}{1}$

$\therefore \quad x : y = 2 : 1.$

55. Let initially number of boys and girls be $4x$ and $5x$.

Now, $\frac{4x}{5x - 100} = \frac{6}{7} \quad \Rightarrow 15x - 300 = 14x$

$\therefore \quad x = 300.$

57. A : B = 6 : 7

B : C = 8 : 9

$\therefore$ A : B : C = 6 × 8 : 7 × 8 : 7 × 9

= 48 : 56 : 63

58. Ratio $= \dfrac{20 + \frac{5}{2}}{20 - \frac{5}{2}} = \frac{22.5}{17.5} = \frac{225}{175} = \frac{9}{7} = 9 : 7$

59. Let the number be $3x$ and $5x$.

Then, $\frac{3x + 10}{5x + 10} = \frac{5}{7}$

$\Rightarrow \quad 7(3x + 10) = 5(5x + 10)$

$\Rightarrow \quad 21x + 70 = 25x + 50$

$\Rightarrow \quad 4x = 20 \Rightarrow x = 5$

So, the numbers are 15, 25.

60. Strength of milk in the first mixture

$= \frac{12}{12+3} = \frac{12}{15}$

Strength of milk in the second mixture =

$\frac{10}{10+4} = \frac{10}{14}$

$\therefore$ The ratio of their strengths $= \frac{12}{15} : \frac{10}{14} = 12 \times 14 : 15 \times 10 = 28 : 25.$

62. Let their ages be $6x$ and $5x$ years.

$\therefore 6x + 5x = 44 \quad \Rightarrow 11x = 44 \Rightarrow x = 4$

So, their present ages are 24 years and 20 years

$\therefore$ Ratio of their ages after 8 years = 32 : 28 = 8 : 7.

63. M = 3E and $\frac{M}{H} = \frac{4}{3}$

$\therefore H = \frac{3}{4}M = \frac{3}{4} \times 3E = \frac{9}{4}E$

Now, $M + E + H = 250 \Rightarrow 3E + E + \frac{9}{4}E = 250$

$\therefore$ 25E = 1000 or, E = 40.

64. $\because$ Cost of 13 books = Rs 273

$\therefore$ Cost of 1 book = Rs 273 ÷ 13 = Rs 21

$\therefore$ Cost of 2 books = Rs 21 × 2 = Rs 42.

73. 5 men can do a piece of work in 3 days

1 man can do a piece of work in 3 × 5 = 15 days.

76. Compound ratio of 2 : 3, 3 : 4, 4 : 5 is

$= \frac{2}{3} \times \frac{3}{4} \times \frac{4}{5} = \frac{2}{5}$

i.e. 2 : 5.

MATHEMATICS

78. 12 seconds : 10 hours

12 second : 16 × 3600 seconds

1 : 3000.

79. $x - 20\%$ of $x = 40 \Rightarrow x - \frac{x}{5} = 40$

$\Rightarrow \frac{4x}{5} = 40 \Rightarrow x = \frac{40 \times 5}{4} = 50.$

80. Required percentage $= \frac{10}{100-10} \times 100$

$= \frac{10}{90} \times 100 = 11\frac{1}{9}\%$.

81. 5% A = 15% B, and 10% B = 20% C

Then, A = 3B and B = 2C

$\therefore$ B = 2C = 2 × 2000 = Rs. 4000

And A = 3B = 3 × 4000 = Rs. 12000

$\therefore$ A + B + C = 12000 + 4000 + 2000

= Rs. 18000.

82. 20% of x + 30 = 32% of x – 42

$\Rightarrow$ 12% of x = 72

$\Rightarrow x = \frac{72 \times 100}{12} = 600$

Pass Mark = 20% of 600 + 30 = 150

Pass percentage $= \left(\frac{150}{600} \times 100\right)\% = 25\%$.

83. (62% of x – 38% of x) = 144 $\Rightarrow$ 24% of x = 144

$\Rightarrow x = \frac{144 \times 100}{24} = 600.$

84. 200% of x = 90

$\Rightarrow x = \frac{90 \times 100}{200} = 45$

$\therefore$ 80% of $x = \left(\frac{80}{100} \times 45\right) = 36.$

85. Required percentage

$= \frac{25}{100-25} \times 100 = \frac{25}{75} \times 100 = 33\frac{1}{3}\%$.

87. $x \times \left(1 + \frac{5}{100}\right)^3 = 138915$

$\Rightarrow x \times \frac{21}{20} \times \frac{21}{20} \times \frac{21}{20} = 138915$

$\Rightarrow x = \frac{138915 \times 20 \times 20 \times 20}{21 \times 21 \times 21}$

= 120000.

88. Males $= \left(\frac{5}{9} \times 4500\right) = 2500$

Females = 2000

$\therefore$ Married males $= \frac{40}{100} \times 2500 = 1000$

and married females = 1000

$\therefore$ Percentage of married females

$= \left(\frac{1000}{2000} \times 100\right)\% = 50\%.$

89. 35% of x = 96 + 16 = 112

$\Rightarrow \frac{35}{100} \times x = 112 \Rightarrow x = \frac{112 \times 100}{35} = 320.$

90. Out of 100, difference in votes = (60 – 40) = 20

20% of x = 100

$\therefore x = \frac{100 \times 100}{20} = 500$.

92. The number = 8 × 17.25 = 138.00

73% of the number $= \frac{73}{100} \times 138 = \frac{10074}{100}$

= 100.75.

93. 58% of 60 – x% of 635 = 277.4

$\Rightarrow \frac{58}{100} \times 960 - \frac{x}{100} \times 635 = 277.4$

$\Rightarrow \frac{127x}{20} = 556.8 - 277.4$

$\therefore x = \frac{20 \times 279.4}{127} = 44.$

94. The number of employess got transferred

$= \frac{40}{100} \times 1225 = 490.$

95. Let the number be x; then

$\frac{56}{100} \times x = 1064 \quad \therefore x = \frac{1064 \times 100}{56} = 1900$

Now, 38% of 1900 $= \frac{38}{100} \times 1900 = 722.$

96. Let cost price of the cell phone be Rs. x; then

$x + \frac{32}{100} \times x = 6600 \quad \Rightarrow \frac{132x}{100} = 6600$

$\therefore x = \frac{100 \times 6600}{132} =$ Rs. 5000.

97. Let the number be x; then

$(89 - 73) \times \frac{x}{100} = 448 \quad \therefore x = \frac{448 \times 100}{16} = 2800$

49% of 2800 $= \frac{49}{100} \times 2800 = 1372.$

98. Let the Nupur's monthly income = Rs. x, then

$\frac{26}{100} \times x = \frac{89856}{12}$

$\therefore x = \frac{7488 \times 100}{26} =$ Rs. 28800.

99. Let the number be x; then

$(70-55) \times \frac{1}{100} \times x = 72 \quad \therefore x = \frac{100 \times 72}{15} = 480.$

100. Let number be 100, then 20% and 10% of the number be 20 and 10 respectively.
Hence, 20% of a number is 10% of double the number.

101. Let required area be x sq. metre; then

$$\frac{75}{100} \times x = 15 \quad \therefore x = \frac{15 \times 100}{75} = 20 \text{ sq. metre.}$$

102. Let C.P. = Rs. x

Then, $425 - x = x - 355 \Rightarrow 2x = 780$

$\therefore$ x = Rs. 390.

103. C.P. of 1 ream $= 80 + \frac{280}{120} + \frac{72}{120} + 0.40$

$$= 80 + \frac{7}{3} + \frac{3}{5} + \frac{2}{5} = \text{Rs. } \frac{250}{3}$$

$$\therefore \text{S.P. of 1 ream} = \text{Rs.}\left(\frac{108}{100} \times \frac{250}{3}\right) = \text{Rs. } 90.$$

104. Let S.P. = Rs. 100; C.P. for Subhash $= \frac{9}{10} \times 100 =$ Rs. 90 and S.P. = Rs. 108
Hence, gain % for Subhash

$$= \frac{108 - 90}{90} \times 100 = 20\%.$$

105. Let C.P. be Rs. 100; then Marked price = Rs. 120 and S.P. = Rs. 108

$$\therefore \quad \text{Discount} = \left(\frac{12}{120} \times 100\right)\% = 10\%.$$

106. Let C.P. be Rs. 100
Then, marked price = Rs. 120

$$\text{S.P.} = \text{Rs.}\left(\frac{90}{100} \times 120\right) = \text{Rs. } 108$$

$$\therefore \text{Gain } \% = \left(\frac{8}{100} \times 100\right)\% = 8\%.$$

107. Here, 5% = 500 $\therefore$ 100% $= \frac{500}{5} \times 100$
= Rs. 10,000
Hence, labelled price = Rs. 10,000

$$\therefore \text{ S.P.} = \frac{80}{100} \times \text{Rs. } 10{,}000 = \text{Rs. } 8000.$$

108. Let the marked price = Rs. x

Then, $\frac{7x}{100} - \frac{5x}{100} = 15 \Rightarrow \frac{x}{50} = 15$

$\therefore$ x = Rs. 750.

109. C.P. $= \frac{100}{75} \times 660$ = Rs. 600

Hence, M.P. $= \frac{100}{75} \times 600$ = Rs. 800.

110. Here, 10% C.P. of horse = 20% C.P. of cart; Hence, C.P. of horse = 2 × C.P. of cart;
Let C.P. of cart and horse be Rs. x and Rs. $2x$ respectively; then,

$$\frac{5}{100} \times 2x - \frac{5}{100} \times x = 10 \Rightarrow \frac{1}{20}x = 10$$

$\therefore$ $x = 200$

Hence, C.P. of a cart = Rs. 200 and C.P. of a horse = 2 × 200 = Rs. 400.

111. Let C.P. be Rs. 100; then marked price = Rs. 120

Since, S.P. $= \frac{90}{100} \times 120$ = Rs. 108

$\therefore$ Profit = 108 – 100 = Rs. 8, Hence, gain = 8%.

112. Let second discount = x%; then

$$\frac{90}{100} \times \frac{(100 - x)}{100} \times 1400 = 1200 \quad \Rightarrow (100 - x)$$

$$= \frac{2000}{21} \quad \therefore x = 100 - \frac{2000}{21} = \frac{100}{21} = 4\frac{16}{21}\%.$$

114. Net C.P. = 800 + 400 = Rs. 1200
Gain = 1500 – 1200 = Rs. 300

$$\text{Hence, Gain\%} = \frac{300}{1200} \times 100 = 25\%.$$

116. S.I. = Rs 75, T = 3 years, R = 5%

$$\text{P} = \frac{100 \times \text{S.I.}}{\text{R} \times \text{T}} = \frac{100 \times 75}{3 \times 5} = \text{Rs } 500.$$

117. Rs 100 becomes Rs 200 in 20 years *i.e.* interest earned on Rs 100 is Rs 100 over a period of 20 years.

$$\therefore \text{Rate } \% = \frac{100}{20} = 5\%.$$

123. Let P = Re 1, then S.I. Rs. $\frac{9}{16}$, R $= \frac{9}{2}\%$

$$\therefore \text{T} = \frac{\frac{9}{16} \times 100}{\frac{9}{2} \times 1} = \frac{25}{2} = 12\frac{1}{2} \text{ years.}$$

125. Interest earned in 10 years on Rs 1000 at 5% per annum is Rs 500, so after 10 years, principal becomes Rs 1500.
Now Rs 1500 becomes Rs 2000 means that the interest on Rs 1500 should be Rs 500.

$$\therefore \text{T} = \frac{500 \times 100}{1500 \times 5} = 6\frac{2}{3} \text{ years}$$

Hence total time $= 16\frac{2}{3}$ years.

GEOMETRY

BASIC GEOMETRICAL IDEAS (2-D)

The term 'Geometry' is the English equivalent of the Greek word '*Geometron*'. '*Geo*' means Earth and 'metron' means Measurement. According to historians, the geometrical ideas shaped up in ancient times, probably due to the need in art, architecture and measurement. Even today geometrical ideas are reflected in all forms of art, measurements, architecture, engineering, cloth designing etc. We observe and use different objects like boxes, tables, books, the tiffin box we carry to your school for lunch, the ball with which we play and so on.

(*i*) **Point:** A minute geometrical figure that only determines a location is known as point. Point is a tiny dot which has no length or breadth.

Example: Tip of a compass, the pointed end of a needle etc.

(*ii*) **Line Segment:** A geometrical figure which has length but no breadth. It has two end points. Line segment is a part of line. It is the shortest route between two points. If a line segment has two end points X and Y then it is denoted as $\overline{XY}$ or $\overline{YX}$.

Example: An edge of box, An edge of book, pencil etc.

(*iii*) **Line:** If a line segment is extended endlessly in both directions is known as line. We can not draw a complete line and also can not determine its length because it has no end point in the both directions. So, we put arrow marks to indicate its endlessness.

e.g., 

We put minimum two points to determine the line and indicate the line as $\overleftrightarrow{AB}$ or $\overleftrightarrow{BA}$.

(*iv*) **Ray:** A ray is a portion of a line. It has only one end point. It start from a point and goes endlessly to the another direction. Length of ray is also can not be determined. Ray is drawn as 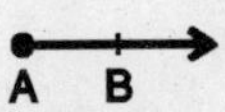

and indicated as $\overrightarrow{AB}$.

Example: Sun rays, Ray of light from a torch etc.

(*v*) **Parallel lines:** If two lines do not intersect up to thier endless points is called parallel lines. In other words, lines like these which do not meet to each-other are said to be parallel; these lines are called parallel lines.

Example: Railway tracks, opposite edges of scale, opposite edges of table etc.

(*vi*) **Curves:** The doodling line is called curve. If we draw some drawing without lifting the pencil from the paper and without using a rular, all are curves.

(*a*) **Simple curve:** If a curve does not cross itself. It is also known as open curve.

(*b*) **Closed curve:** If a curve crosses to each other and surround some space is called closed curve.

(*vii*) **Concurrent Lines:** The point where three or more lines intersect.

(*viii*) **Angle:** A geometrical figure which have two rays with single end point is called angle.

(*ix*) **Triangle:** A closed figure with three sides which has three angles and three vertices is called triangle.

(*x*) **Quadrilateral:** A figure which is made up of joining four non-collinear points called quadrilateral. Or, A figure which is made up of four sides, angles and four vertices is called quadrilateral. The sum of all angles of a quadrilateral is 360°.

(*x*) **Circle:** A circle is a set of points in a plane which are at a constant distance from a given fixed point.

UNDERSTANDING ELEMENTARY SHAPES (2-D AND 3-D)

All the shapes around us are formed by lines and curves. Edges, planes, corners, open curves and closed curves are commonly found in our surroundings. We organise the aforesaid components to form angles, triangles, polygons and circles. They may have different size and measures.

To measure a line segment: We can compare between two or more line segment through observation, with tracing paper, ruler and divider.

But ruler is a proper tool for the measurement of line segment.

We should aware of the error of measurement. It may occur due to thickness of ruler and wrong position of our eyes during the measurement.

KINDS OF ANGLES

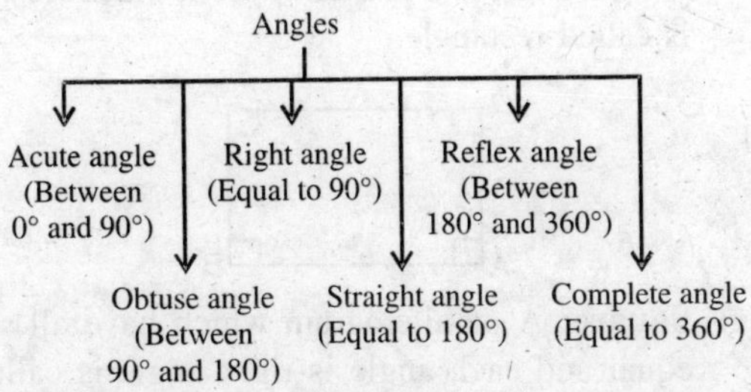

Complementary Angles: Two angles whose sum is 90º is said to be complementary to each other *i.e.*, complement of $\theta = (90^\circ - \theta^\circ)$.

Supplementary Angles: Two angles whose sum is 180º is said to be supplementary to each other. *i.e.*, supplementary of $\theta = (180^\circ - \theta^\circ)$.

Adjecent Angles: If two angles have a common vertex then they are said to be adjecent.

Linear pair: If the pair of adjacent angles are also the supplementary to each-other then it is said to be a linear pair.

Vertically opposite Angles: If two lines intersect at a point, the pair of alternative angles is called vertically opposite angles.

Vertically opposite angles are always equal.

Intersecting line: If two lines have a common point they are called intersecting lines.

Example: X (the letter of english alphabet; the sign of mathematical operation.)

Angles on Parallel Lines

Transversal: If a straight line crosses two or more than two parallel lines then it is called transversal.

When a transversal crosses a pair of parallel lines then it forms eight angles.

Corresponding Angles: Let AB and CD are two parallel lines and l is transversal, then, pair of corresponding angles are equal *i.e.*,

$\angle 1 = \angle 6 \quad \angle 3 = \angle 8$

$\angle 2 = \angle 5 \quad \angle 4 = \angle 7$

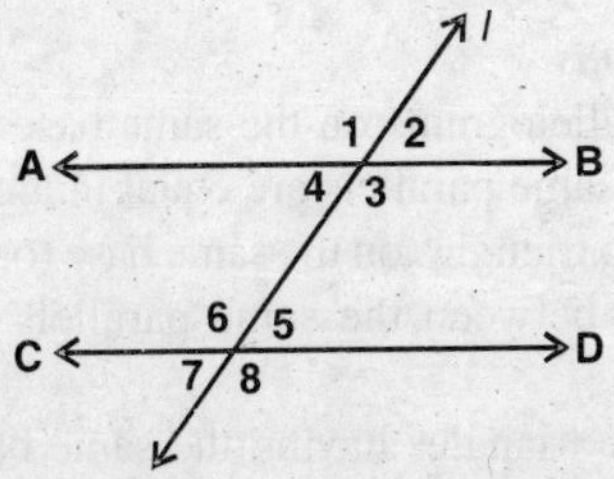

Alternate Interior Angles: In the above figure $\angle 4$ and $\angle 5$ also $\angle 3$ and $\angle 6$ are the pairs of alternate interior angles. The pair of alternate interior angles are equal.

Hence, $\angle 4 = \angle 5$ and $\angle 3 = \angle 6$.

The sum of interior angles on the same side of transversal is 180°.

i.e., $\angle 3 + \angle 5 = 180^\circ$ also $\angle 4 + \angle 6 = 180^\circ$.

Axioms and Theorems on Lines and Angles

Axioms:

1. If a ray stands on a line, then the sum of two adjacent angles so formed is 180º.
2. If the sum of two adjacent angles is 180º, then the non-common arms of the angles form a line.
3. If a transversal intersects two parallel lines, then each pair of corresponding angles is equal.
4. If a transversal intersects two lines such that a pair of corresponding angles is equal, then the two lines are parallel to each other.

Theorems

1. If two lines intersect each other, then the vertically opposite angles are equal.
2. If a transversal intersects two parallel lines, then each pair of alternate interior angles is equal.
3. If a transversal intersects two lines such that a pair of alternate interior angles is equal, then the two lines are parallel.
4. If a transversal intersects two lines, then each pair of interior angles on the same side of the transversal is supplementary.
5. If a transversal intersects two lines such that a pair of interior angles on the same side of the transversal is supplementary, then the two lines are parallel.
6. Lines which are parallel to the same line are parallel to each other.
7. The sum of the angles of a triangle is 180º.
8. If a side of a triangle is produced, then the exterior angle so formed is equal to the sum of the two interior opposite angles.

CLASSIFICATION OF TRIANGLES

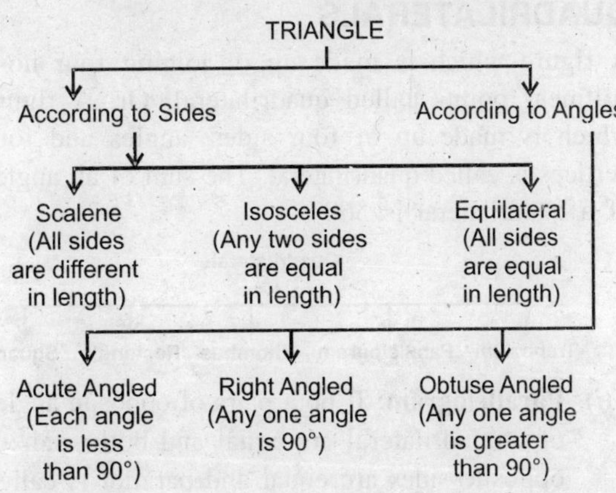

Pythagoras Theorem: In a right angled triangle the square of the hypotenuse equals the sum of the square of its sides.

i.e., $AC^2 = AB^2 + BC^2$

$\Rightarrow \quad b^2 = c^2 + a^2$

$= a^2 + c^2$

Median: A line segment joining the vertex of triangle and mid-point of its opposite side is called median.

Axiom and Theorems on Triangles

Axiom 1. (SAS congruence rule) : Two triangles are congruent if two sides and the included angle of one triangle are equal to the corresponding two sides and the included angle of the other triangle.

Theorems

1. **(ASA congruence rule):** Two triangles are congruent if two angles and the included side of one triangle are equal to two angles and the included side of other triangle.
2. Angle opposite to equal sides of an isosceles triangle are equal.
3. The sides opposite to equal angles of a triangle are equal.
4. **(SSS congruence rule):** If three sides of one triangle are equal to the three sides of another triangle, then the two triangles are congruent.
5. **(RHS congruence rule):** If in two right triangles the hypotenuse and one side of one triangle are equal to the hypotenuse and one side of the other triangle, then the two triangles are congruent.
6. If two sides of a triangle are unequal, the angle opposite to the longer side is larger (or greater).
7. In any triangle, the side opposite to the larger (greater) angle is longer.
8. The sum of any two side of a triangle is greater than the third side.

CLASSIFICATION OF QUADRILATERALS

A figure which is made up of joining four non-collinear points called quadrilateral. Or, A figure which is made up of four sides, angles and four vertices is called quadrilateral. The sum of all angles of a quadrilateral is 360°.

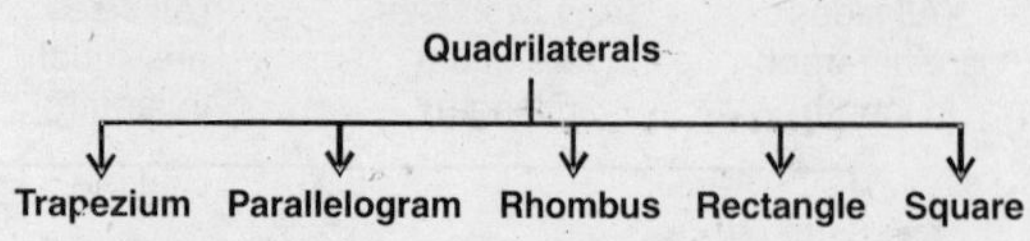

(*i*) **Parallelogram:** If both pairs of opposite angles of a quadrilateral are equal and both pair of opposite sides are equal and parallel is called parallelogram.

(*ii*) **Trapezium:** If one pair of opposite sides are parallel of a quadrilateral, then it is called a trapezium.

(*iii*) **Rhombus:** A parallelogram in which all the sides are equal is called a rhombus.

(*iv*) **Rectangle:** A parallelogram in which each angles is right angle and pair of opposite sides are equal is called rectangle.

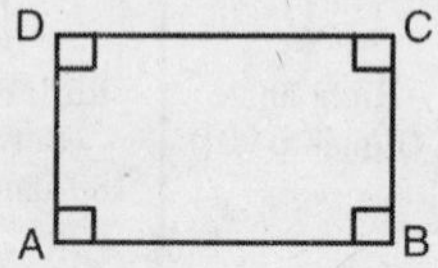

(*v*) **Square:** A parallelogram which have all sides equal and each angle is right angle is called a square.

(*vi*) **Kite:** A quadrilateral whose two pairs of adjacent sides and one pair of opposite angle are equal is called kite.

Theorems on Quadrilateral

Theorems

1. A diagonal of a parallelogram divides it into two congruent triangles.
2. In a parallelogram, opposite sides are equal.
3. If each pair of opposite sides of a quadrilateral is equal, then it is a parallelogram.
4. In a parallelogram, opposite angles are equal.
5. If in a quadrilateral, each pair of opposite angles is equal, then it is a parallelogram.
6. The diagonals of a parallelogram bisect each other.
7. If the diagonals of a quadrilateral bisect each other, then it is a parallelogram.
8. A quadrilateral is a parallelogram if a pair of opposite sides is equal and parallel.
9. The line segment joining the mid-points of two sides of a triangle is parallel to and half of the third side.
10. The line drawn through the mid-point of one side of a triangle, parallel to another side bisects the third side.

Theorems on Areas of Parallelograms and Triangles

Theorems

1. Parallelograms on the same base and between the same parallels are equal in area.
2. Two triangles on the same base (or equal bases) and between the same parallels are equal in area.
3. Two triangles having the same base (or equal bases) and equal areas lie between the same parallels.

COMPONENTS OF CIRCLE

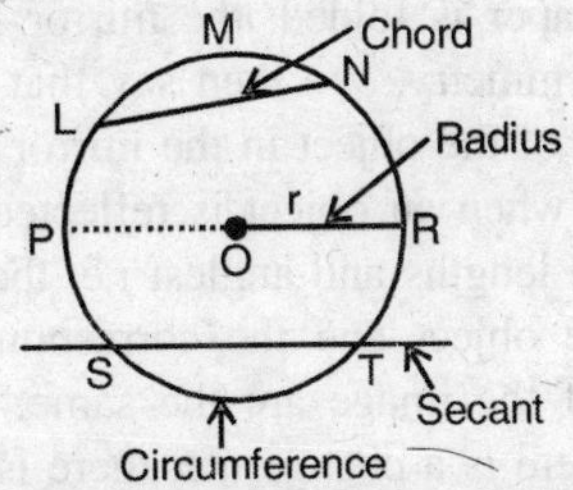

Here, the fixed point O is called the centre.

The constant distance is called radius. PR is the diameter of the circle.

Diameter is twice of radius.

Arch: A continuous part of a circle.

Secant: A line which intersect a circle in two distinct points.

Chord: A line segment joining any two points on the circle.

Segment: A chord divides the circle into two parts and each parts is called segment.

Semicircle: A diameter divides the circle into two equal parts and each part is called semicircle.

Central Angle: An angle whose vertex is centre of a circle is called central angle.

Sector: A region in the interior of a circle enclosed by an arc on one side and a pair of radii on the other two sides is called a sector.

Circumference: The distance around a circle is called circumference.

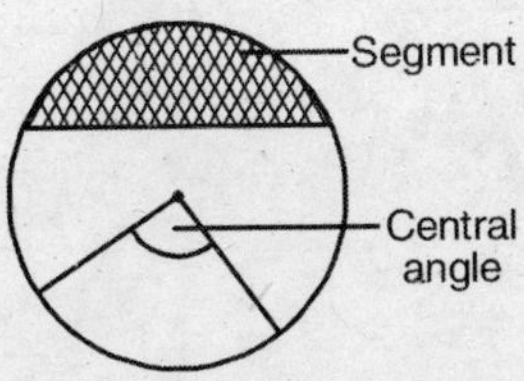

Cyclic Quadrilateral: If all four vertices of a quadrilateral lie on the circumference of a circle, then such a quadrilateral is called a cyclic quadrilateral.

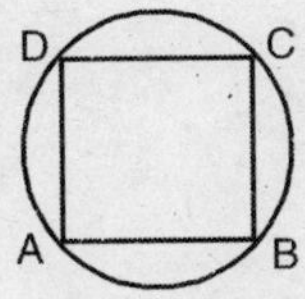

SOME IMPORTANT FACTS ON CIRCLE

- The perpendicular from the centre to any chord bisects the chord.
- The line joining the centre of the mid-point to any chord of a circle is perpendicular to the chord.
- Equal chords of congruent circles are equidistant from the corresponding centres.
- Chords of congruent circles which are equidistant from the corresponding centres, are equal.
- Equal chords of a circle are equidistant from the centre.
- Equal chords of a circle subtend equal angle at the centre.
- The angle subtended by an arc at the centre of a circle is double the angle subtended by it at any point on the remaining part of the circle.
- Angles in the same segment of a circle are equal.
- If the sum of any pair of opposite angles of a quadrilateral is 180°, then the quadrilateral is cyclic.
- The angle made in a semicircle is always a right angle.
- The arc of a circle subtending a right angle at any point of the circle in its alternate segment is a semicircle.

Theorems on Circles

1. Equal chords of a circle subtend equal angles at the centre.
2. If the angles subtended by the chords of a circle at the centre are equal, then the chords are equal.
3. The perpendicular from the centre of a circle to a chord bisects the chord.
4. The line drawn through the centre of a circle to bisect a chord is perpendicular to the chord.
5. There is one and only one circle passing through three given non-collinear points.
6. Equal chords of a circle (or of congruent circle) are equidistant from the centre (or centres).
7. Chords equidistant from the centre of a circle are equal in length.
8. The angle subtended by an arc at the centre is double the angle subtended by it at any point on the remaining part of the circle.
9. Angles in the same segment of a circle are equal.
10. If a line segment joining two points subtends equal angles at two other points lying on the same side of the line containing the line segment, the four points lie on a circle (*i.e.* they are concyclic).
11. The sum of either pair of opposite angles of a cyclic quadrilateral is 180°.
12. If the sum of a pair of opposite angles of a quadrilateral is 180°, the quadrilateral is cyclic.

THREE DIMENSIONAL SHAPES

Sphere: A solid that is completely round, with every point on its surface at an equal distance from the centre is called sphere eg. ball, marble, globe etc.

Cone: A solid sides or hollow object with a round flate base and sides that slope up to a point, is called cone. eg.– ice cream cone, traffic cone, top etc.

Cuboid: A solid object which has six rectangular sides at right angles to each other is called cuboid. *e.g.,* bricks, box, match-box, etc.

Cube: A solid or hollow figure with six equal square sides at right angles to each other is called cube, *e.g.,* dice, rubic-rostrum.

Cylinder: A solid or hollow figure with round ends and why straight sides is called cylinder, *e.g.,* glass, bottle, gas cylinder etc.

Pyramid: A solid shape with a square or triangular base and sloping side that meet in a point at the top is called pyramid. eg. Pyramid of Egypt etc.

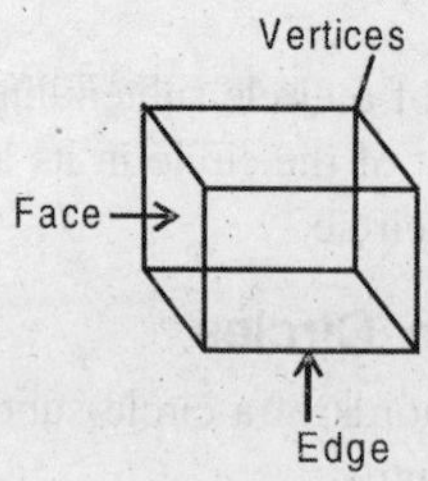

Faces: The polygonal regions of a solid surface called faces.

Edges: Where two faces meet that is called edge.

Vertices: Where two or more edges meet that point is called vertex.

SYMMETRY

Symmetry is very a common term used in our daily life. When we see certain figures with evenly balanced proportions, we say "The figures are symmetrical".

If we could fold a picture in half such that the left and right halves match exactly then the picture is said to have line symmetry. If a mirror is placed on the fold then the image of one side of the picture will fall exactly on the other side of the picture. When it happens, the fold, which is the mirror line, is a line of symmetry (or an axis of symmetry) for the picture.

When we fold the figure along the dotted line, one-half of the drawing would fit exactly over the other half. If show that the figure is symmetrical.

Figure with two lines of symmetry — Kite, rectangle, a cut out from double fold.

Figure with multiple (more than two) lines symmetry — Three lines of symmetry for an equilateral triangle, square, pentagon, hexagon.

Symmetry in daily life — road, signs, crabs, starfish, playing cards, scissors, Koch's snowfllke, swastik, flowers, butterfly, lock, etc.

Reflection and Symmetry

Line symmetry and mirror reflection are naturally related and linked to each other. The object and its image are symmetrical with reference to the mirror line. If the paper is folded, the mirror line becomes the line of symmetry. We then say that the image is the reflection of the object in the mirror line. We can also see that when an object is reflected, there is no change in the lengths and angles; i.e. the lengths and angles of the object and the corresponding lengths and angles of the image are the same. However, in one aspect there is a change, i.e. there is a difference between the object and the image.

English Alphabet and their symmetrical mirror image

Letter	Symmetrical Mirror Images
A	A
B	ꓭ
C	Ɔ
D	ᗡ
E	Ǝ
F	ꟻ
G	ꓨ
H	H
I	I
J	Ⴑ
K	ꓘ
L	
M	M
N	
O	O
P	ꟼ
Q	Ϙ
R	Я
S	
T	T
U	U
V	V
W	W
X	X
Y	Y
Z	Ƨ

Some Objects those show symmetry—Paper cutting to show decoration, Kaleidoscope, Album etc.

Rotational Symmetry

When an object rotates, its shapes and size do not change and this type of symmetry is called rotational symmetry, e.g., paper windmill, cross section of lemon, road sign, wheel etc. The rotation turns an object about a fixed point. This fixed point is the centre of rotation and the angle of turning during rotation is called the angle of rotation.

CONSTRUCTIONS

As it has earlier told that even today geometrical ideas are reflected in our forms of art, measurement, architecture, engineering, cloth designing and many other skills. We see a number of shpaes and these are very familier to us. We draw pictures which include different shapes and we know about some of these shapes. But only knowing about the shapes is not enough. We should learn how to make these shapes, which tools are used to make these shapes. What is the process and how can we use these shapes.

TOOLS AND THEIR USES

SN.	Name & Fig.	Description	Use
1.	The Ruler [or the straight edge]	A ruler ideally has no markings on it. However, the ruler in your instruments box is graduated into centimetres along one edge (and sometimes into inches along the other edge).	To draw line segments and to measure their lengths.
2.	The Compasses	A pair—a pointer on one end and a pencil on the other.	To mark off equal lengths but not to measure them. To draw arcs and circles.
3.	The Divider	A pair of pointers	To compare lengths.
4.	Set-Squares	Two triangular pieces—one of them has 45°, 45°, 90° angles at the vertices and the other has 30°, 60°, 90° angles at the vertices.	To draw perpendicular and parallel lines.
5.	The Protractor	A semi-circular device graduated into 180° parts. The measure starts from 0° on the right hand side and ends with 180° on the left hand side and vice-versa.	To draw and measure angles.

To draw a parallel line through the point which is not on the given line

Using ruler and compass

Step 1. A line l is drawn and a point P is taken not on the line l.

Step 2. A point Q is taken on line l and joined both the point P and Q.

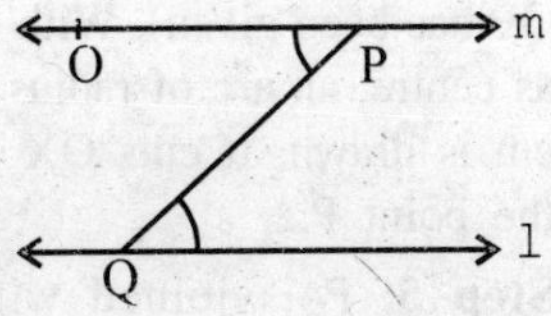

Step 3. An angle $\angle OPQ$ of the same measurement of $\angle Q$ is constructed.

Step 4. Now OP is extended in both direction and named as m.

Since, $\angle P = \angle Q$ (Alternate interior angle)

Hence, $l \parallel m$, and point P is located at m.

Construction of a triangle when the lengths of its three sides as given (SSS criterion)

To construct a trianlge ABC, given that AB = 7 cm, BC = 8 cm and AC = 9 cm.

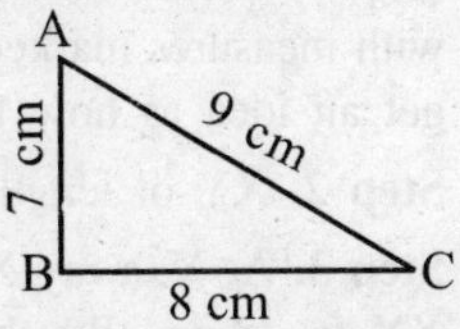

Step 1. First, a rough sketch with given measure is drawn, (This will help us in deciding how to proceed).

Step 2. A line segment BC of length 8 cm is drawn.

Step 3. From B, point A is at a distance of 7 cm. So, with B as centre, an arc of radius 7 cm is drawn. (Now A will be somewhere on this arc. Now we should find where exactly A is).

Step 4. From C, point A is at a distance of 9 cm. So, with C as centre, an arc of radius 9 cm is drawn. (A will be somewhere on this arc, we have to fix it).

Step 5. A has to be on both the arcs drawn. So, it is the point of intersection of arcs. The point of intersection of arcs as A is marked. AB and AC is joined. Thus ΔABC is constructed.

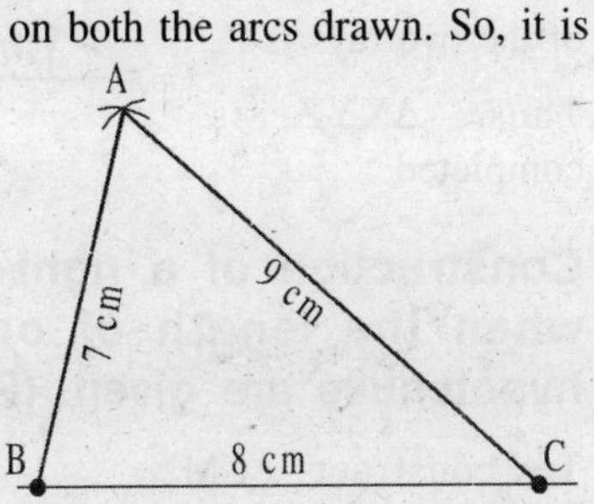

Construction of a triangle when the lengths of two sides and the measure of the angle between them are given. (SAS Criterion)

To construct a triangle PQR, given that PQ = 4 cm, QR = 7 cm and $\angle PQR = 60°$.

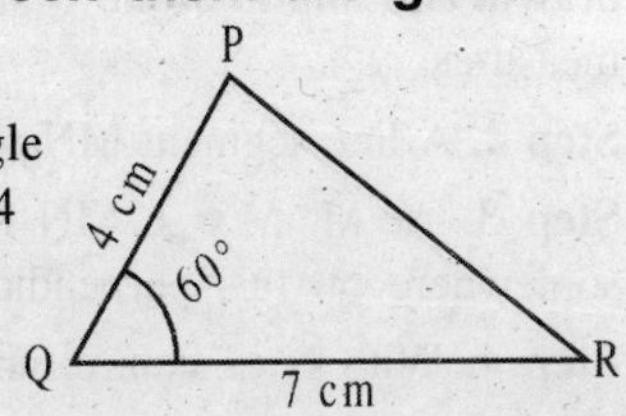

Step 1. First, a rough sketch with given measures. (This helps us to determine the procedure in construction) is drawn.

Step 2. A line segment QR of length 7 cm is drawn.

Step 3. At Q, QX making 60° with QR is drawn. (The point P must be somewhere on this ray of the angle).

Step 4. (To fix P, the distance QP has been given). With Q as centre, an arc of radius 4 cm is drawn. It cuts QX at the point P.

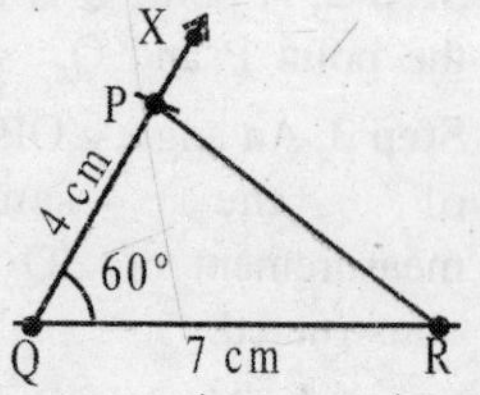

Step 5. P is joined with R. Now, ΔPQR is obtained.

Construction of a triangle when the measures of two of its angles and the length of the side included between them is given. (ASA Criterion)

To construct ΔXYZ if it is given that XY = 8 cm, $m\angle ZXY = 30°$ and $m\angle XYZ = 100°$.

Step 1. Before actual construction, a rough sketch with measures marked on it is drawn. (This is just to get an idea as how to proceed).

Step 2. XY of length 8 cm is drawn.

Step 3. At X, a ray XP making an angle of 30° with XY is drawn. By the given condition, Z must be somewhere on the XP.

Step 4. At Y, a ray YQ making an angle of 100° with YX is drawn. By the given condition, Z must be on the ray YQ also.

Step 5. Z has to lie on both the rays XP and YQ. So, the point of intersection of the two rays is Z.

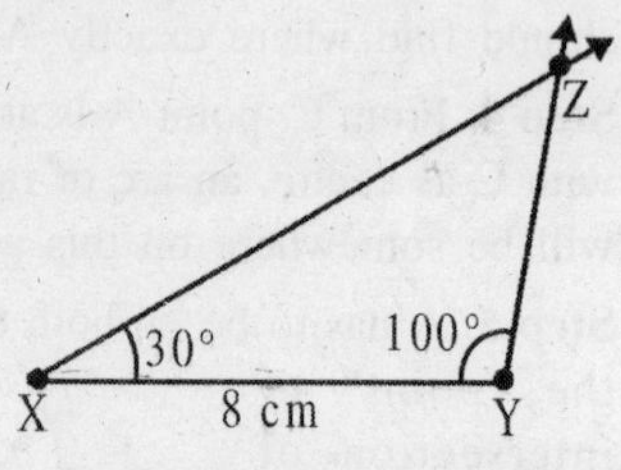

Thus, ΔXYZ is completed.

Construction of a right-angled triangle when the length of one leg and its hypotenuse are given. (RHS Criterion)

To construct ΔLMN, right-angled at M, given that LN = 8 cm and MN = 5 cm.

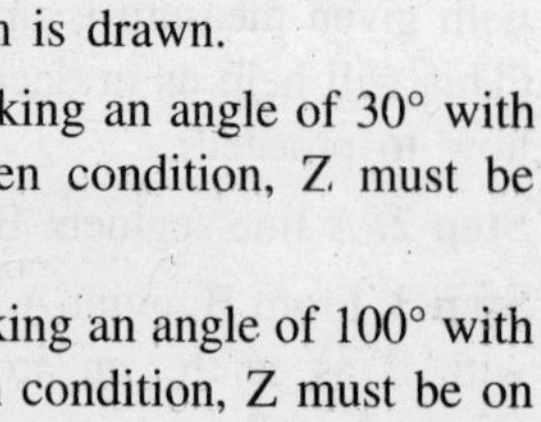

Step 1. A rough sketch is drawn and marked the measures.

Step 2. A line segment MN of length 5 cm is drawn.

Step 3. At M, MX ⊥ MN is drawn. (L should be somewhere on this perpendicular).

Step 4. With N as centre, an arc of radius 8 cm is drawn. (L must be on this arc, since it is at a distance of 8 cm from N).

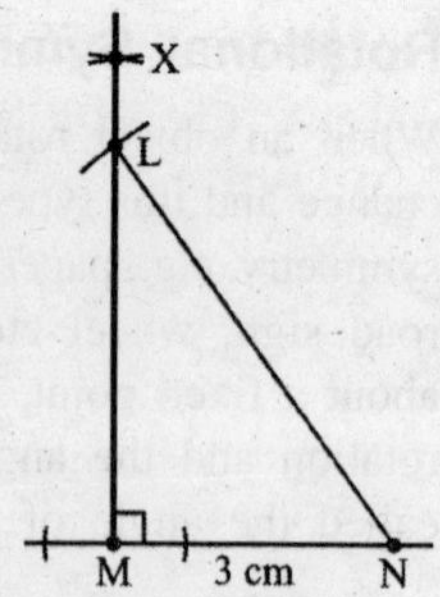

Step 5. L has to be on the perpendicular line MX as well as on the arc drawn with centre N. Therefore, L is the meeting point of these two.

Thus, ΔLMN is obtained.

Construction of a quadrilateral when the length of four sides and a diagonal are given

To construct a quadrilateral PQRS where PQ = 5 cm, QR = 8 cm, RS = 6 cm, PS = 7 cm and PR = 9 cm.

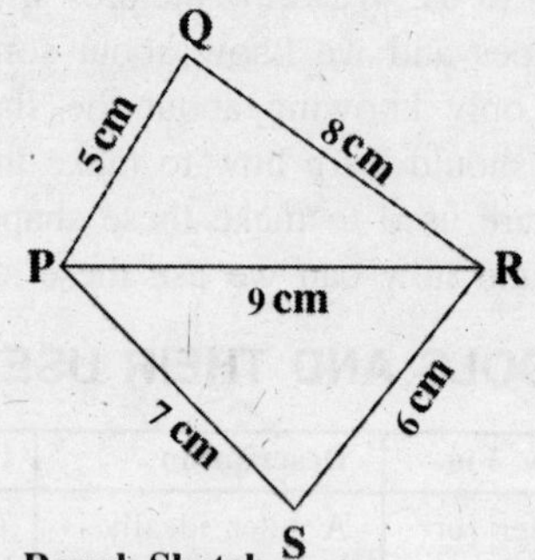

Rough Sketch

A rough sketch helps us in visualising the quadrilateral. So we should draw this first and mark the measurements.

Step 1. According to the rough sketch, DPQR is constructed using SSS construction condition.

Step 2. Now, we have to locate the fourth point S. It would be opposite to Q with reference to PR.

With P as centre, an arc of radius 7 cm is drawn. (The point S is somewhere on this arc).

Step 3. S is 6 cm away from R. So with R as centre, an arc of radius 6 cm is drawn. (The point S is somewhere on this arc also!).

Step 4. S should lie on both the arcs drawn. So it is the point of intersection of the two arcs. Point S is marked and quadrilateral PQRS is completed.

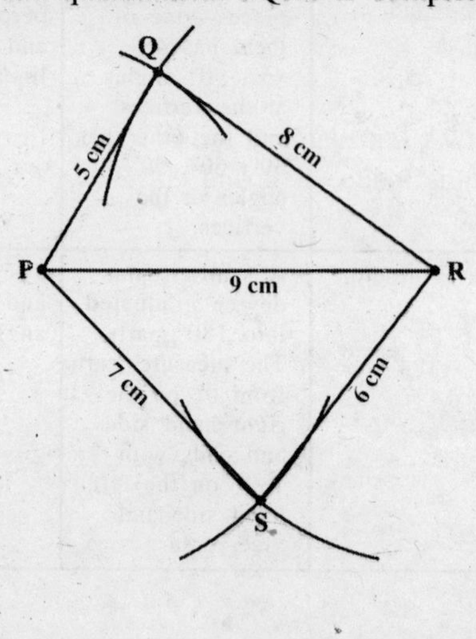

Construction of a quadrilateral when two diagonals and three sides are given

To construct a quadrilateral ABCD, given that BC = 4.5 cm, AD = 5.5 cm, CD = 5 cm the diagonal AC = 5.5 cm and diagonal BD = 7 cm.

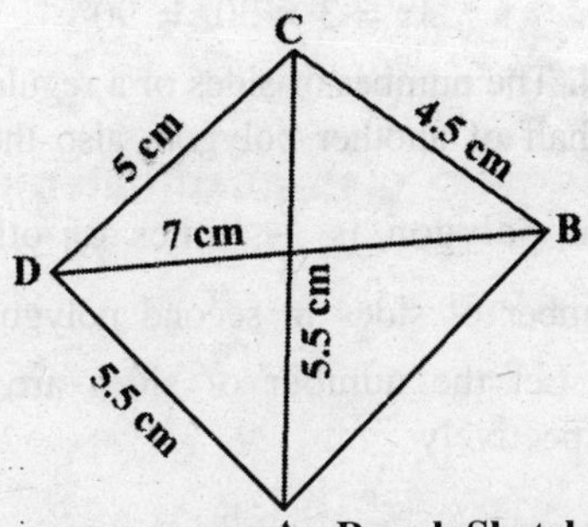

Rough Sketch

Through the rough sketch of the quadrilateral ABCD we can easily see that it is possible to draw Δ ACD first.

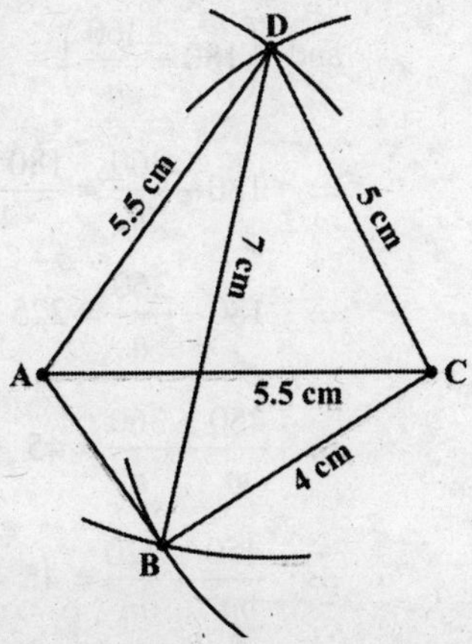

Step 1. ΔACD is drawn using SSS construction. (We now need to find B at a distance of 4.5 cm from C and 7 cm from D).

Step 2. With D as centre, an arc of radius 7 cm is drawn. (B is somewhere on this arc).

Step 3. With C as centre, an arc of radius 4.5 cm is drawn. (B is somewhere on this arc also).

Step 4. Since B lies on both the arcs, B is the point intersection of the two arcs. Point B is marked and quadrilateral ABCD completed.

Construction of a quadrilateral when two adjacent sides and three angles are given

To construct a quadrilateral ABCD where AB = 3.5 cm, BC = 6.5 cm, ∠A = 75°, ∠B = 105° and ∠C = 120°.

Step 1. A line segment AB = 3.5 cm drawn. ∠ABX = 105° is made on B and out BC = 6.5 cm.

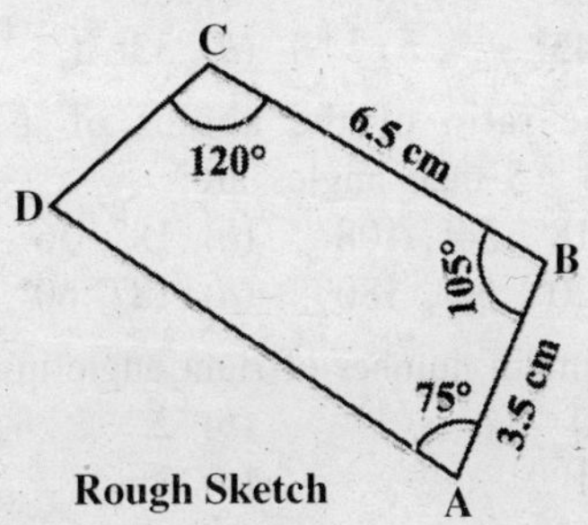

Rough Sketch

Step 2. ∠BCY = 120° is made at C.

Step 3. ∠BAZ = 75° at A is made. The point D is marked as interesecting point. Thus, quadrilateral ABCD is constructed.

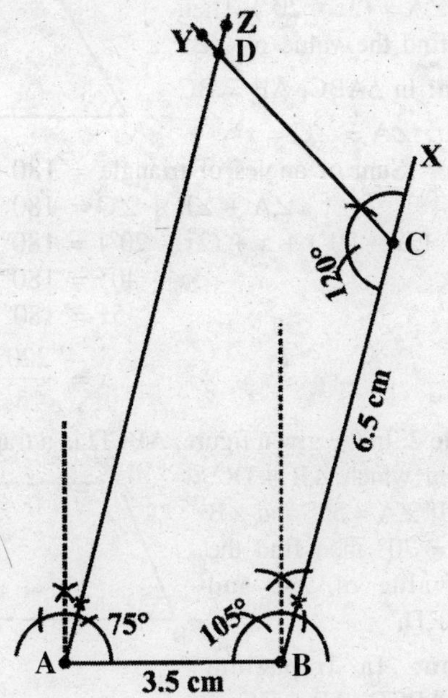

Construction of a quadrilateral when three sides and two included angles are given

To construct a quadrilateral ABCD, where AB = 4 cm, BC = 5 cm, CD = 6.5 cm and ∠B = 105° and ∠C = 80°.

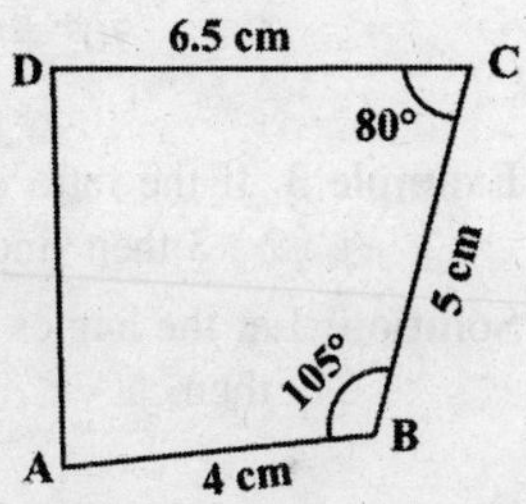

Step 1. Starting with taking BC = 5 cm on B. An angle of 105° along BX is drawn. A 4 cm away on this is marked.

Step 2. The fourth point D is on CY which is inclined at 80° to BC. So ∠BCY = 80° is made at C on BC.

Step 3. D is at a distance of 6.5 cm on CY. With C as centre, an arc of length 6.5 cm is drawn. It cuts CY at D.

Step 4. The quadrilateral ABCD is completed.

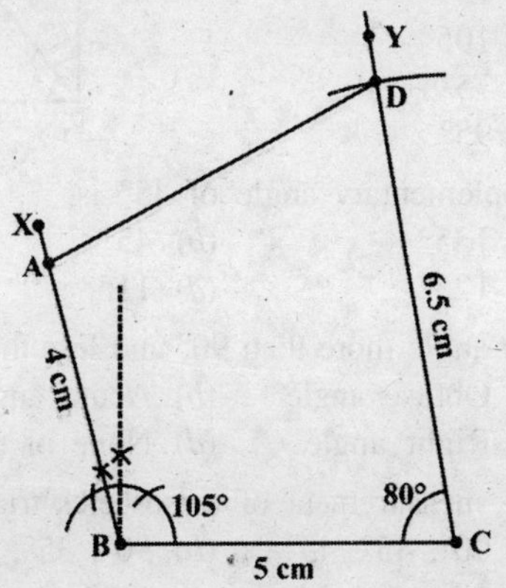

MATHEMATICS

SOLVED QUESTIONS

Example 1. In the given figure, AB = BC, ∠B = x and ∠A = (2x – 20°). Then find the value of ∠B.

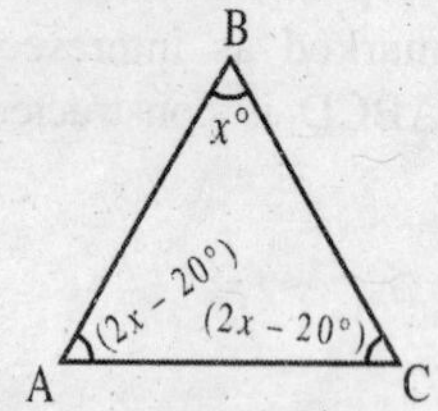

Solution: In ΔABC, AB = BC

$\therefore$ ∠A = ∠C = $x°$

$\because$ Sum of angles of triangle = 180°

$$\angle A + \angle B + \angle C = 180°$$
$$(2x - 20°) + x + (2x - 20°) = 180°$$
$$5x - 40° = 180°$$
$$5x = 180° + 40°$$
$$x = \frac{220°}{5} = 44°$$

Example 2. In the given figure, ABCD is a trapazium, in which AB ∥ DC. If ∠A = 55° and ∠B = 70° then find the value of ∠C and ∠D.

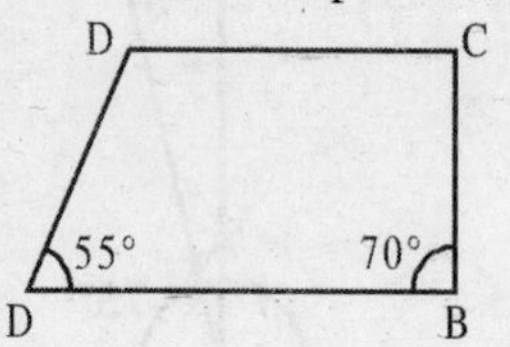

Solution: In trapazium ABCD, AB ∥ DC

$$\therefore \quad \angle A + \angle C = 180°$$
$$55° + \angle C = 180°$$
$$\therefore \quad \angle C = 180° - 55° = 125°$$
and
$$\angle B + \angle D = 180°$$
$$70° + \angle D = 180°$$
$$\angle D = 180° - 70° = 110°$$

Example 3. If the ratio of the angles of a triangle is 1 : 2 : 3 then find the value of greatest angle.

Solution: Let the angles of the triangle are x, 2x and 3x, then

From question,
$$1x + 2x + 3x = 180°$$
$$\Rightarrow \quad 6x = 180°$$
$$\therefore \quad x = \frac{180°}{6} = 30°$$
$$\therefore \quad 1x = 1 \times 30° = 30°$$
$$2x = 2 \times 30° = 60°$$
or
$$3x = 3 \times 30° = 90°$$

Example 4. The number of sides of a regular polygon is half of another polygon, also the angle of that polygon is $\frac{5}{4}$ times of other, than, number of sides in second polygon is?

Solution: Let the number of sides are n and m respectively

From question, $n = \frac{m}{2}$

and $\left(180 - \frac{360}{n}\right) = \frac{5}{4}\left(180 - \frac{360}{m}\right)$

$$\Rightarrow \quad 180 - \frac{360}{n} = \frac{180 \times 5}{4} - \frac{360 \times 5}{4 \times m}$$
$$\Rightarrow \quad 180 - \frac{360}{n} = 225 - \frac{450}{m}$$
$$\Rightarrow \quad \frac{450}{m} - \frac{360}{n} = 45$$
$$\Rightarrow \quad \frac{450}{m} - \frac{720}{m} = 45 \Rightarrow \frac{-270}{m} = 45$$

$\therefore$ m = –6 but negative value of m is not. Practical Hence, number of side = 6.

MULTIPLE CHOICE QUESTIONS

1. What is the total number of points in a line?
(*a*) 0 (*b*) 2
(*c*) Innumerable (*d*) None of these

2. What will be the value of x is the given figure?

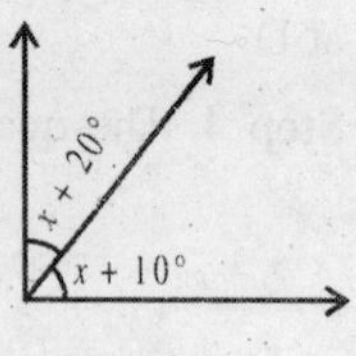

(*a*) 15°
(*b*) 105°
(*c*) 75°
(*d*) 95°

3. Supplementary angle of 45° is:
(*a*) 135° (*b*) 45°
(*c*) 125° (*d*) 115°

4. The angle more than 90° and less than 180° is:
(*a*) Obtuse angle (*b*) Acute angle
(*c*) Right angle (*d*) None of these

5. The measurement of a isosceles triangle is:
(*a*) 90°, 45°, 45° (*b*) 90°, 35°, 35°
(*c*) 90°, 45°, 30° (*d*) 90°, 60°, 60°

6. Value of x in the given figure is

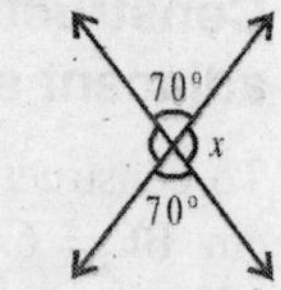

(*a*) 170°
(*b*) 120°
(*c*) 110°
(*d*) 70°

7. If the three angles of a triangle are $x°$, $(x + 30)°$ and $(x + 51)°$ then value of x is—
(*a*) 35° (*b*) 66°
(*c*) 45° (*d*) 33°

8. If the ratio of the angles of a triangle is 2 : 3 : 5 then angles are:
(*a*) 18°, 54°, 108° (*b*) 18°, 36°, 126°
(*c*) 20°, 60°, 180° (*d*) 18°, 60°, 102°

9. Maximum number of right angle in a triangle is
(*a*) 0 (*b*) 2
(*c*) 1 (*d*) 3

10. In the given figure, BC = 5 cm, AP = 6 cm. Then what is the value of AB?

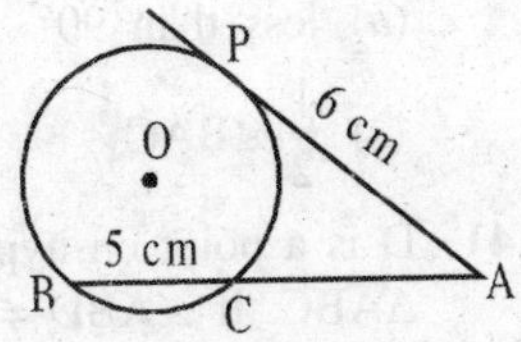

(a) 6 cm
(b) 9 cm
(c) 7 cm
(d) None of these

11. In the given figure, O is the centre of the circle and ∠ABC = 30° then value of ∠BAC is:

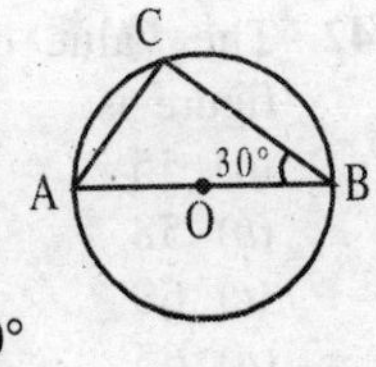

(a) 70° (b) 60°
(c) 80° (d) 50°

12. What will be the value of A in the given figure?

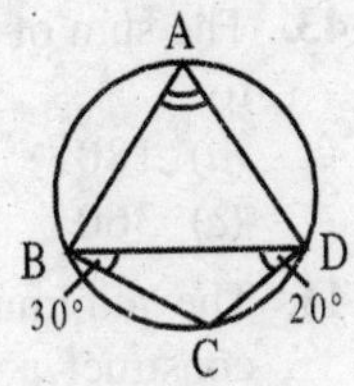

(a) 70°
(b) 40°
(c) 50°
(d) 100°

13. In the given figure, O is the centre of the circle. If ∠BOC = 100° then ∠BAC = ?

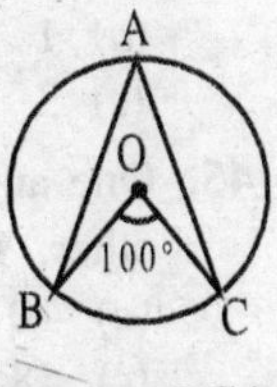

(a) 50° (b) 100°
(c) 40° (d) 70°

14. In the given figure, ∠BOA = 124° then ∠BCA equals to:

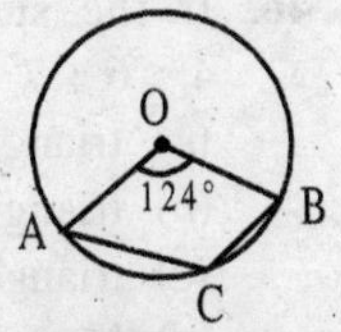

(a) 140°
(b) 100°
(c) 120°
(d) 118°

15. In the given figure, O is the centre of the circle, ABCD is a cyclic quadrilateral and ∠A = 105° then ∠DBC = ?

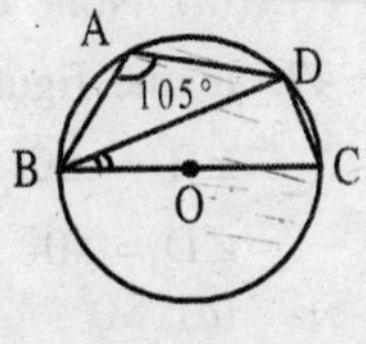

(a) 20° (b) 17°
(c) 25° (d) 15°

16. If the two sides of Δ are perpendicular to each other Δ each to each then which of the following is satisfied:
(a) RHS (b) ASA
(c) SSA (d) SSS

17. If angle between two straight lines is acute angle, then angle between their prependiculars will be:
(a) acute (b) obtuse
(c) right angle (d) cannot be determined

18. If a point inside a triangle is equidistant from the three side of the triangle, then the point is:
(a) Orthocentre (b) Incentre
(c) Centroid (d) Circum centre

19. Which of the following statement is correct?
(a) Tow triangles are always similar
(b) Two parallelograms are always similar
(c) Two rhombus are always similar
(d) Two squares are always similar

20. Two circles intersect each other at maximum:
(a) 2 points (b) 3 points
(c) 1 point (d) 0 point

21. If a straight line drawn from the vertex of a triangle parallel to the base of triangle bisect the exterior vertical angle, then the triangle is:
(a) equilateral (b) right angled
(c) obtuse angled (d) iscoceles

22. The locus of the centres of all circles of given radius, r, in the same plane, passing through a fixed point is:
(a) a point (b) a straight line
(c) a plane (d) a circle

23. A rectangle has ______ lines of symmetry.
(a) 1 (b) 2
(c) 3 (d) 4

24. Of all the triangles on the same base and between two parallel lines, the perimeter is least if the triangle is:
(a) iscoleces (b) right angled
(c) equilateral (d) obtuse angled

25. The sum of length of altitudes drawn from any point inside a triangle, whose all sides are equal, to all three sides is:
(a) equal to side of triangle
(b) 1/3 of side of triangle
(c) 1/2 of side of triangle
(d) equal to perimeter of triangle

26. If the mid points of base of a triangle is equidistant from the sides, then the triangle will be
(a) equilateral (b) iscoceles
(c) scalene (d) right angled

27. How many lines of symmetry are there in a square?
(a) 1 (b) 2
(c) 4 (d) 3

28. The line joining the middle points of non parallel sides of trapezium is:
(a) 1/4 of length of parallel sides
(b) 1/3 of length of parallel sides
(c) 1/2 of length of parallel sides
(d) 2/3 of length of parallel sides

29. In a square ABCD, the diagonal BD is produced to L, such that DL = CD, then
(a) $CL^2 = BL + BD$ (b) $CL^2 = BL \times BD$
(c) CL = BL – BD (d) None of these

30. In the sides of square ABCD, points X and Y are taken such that DY = DX, then:
(a) BX = BY (b) BX < BY
(c) BX > BY (d) None of the above

31. In the given figure, if ∠B = ∠ACB = 48° and ∠D = 37°, then the value of ∠CAD is:

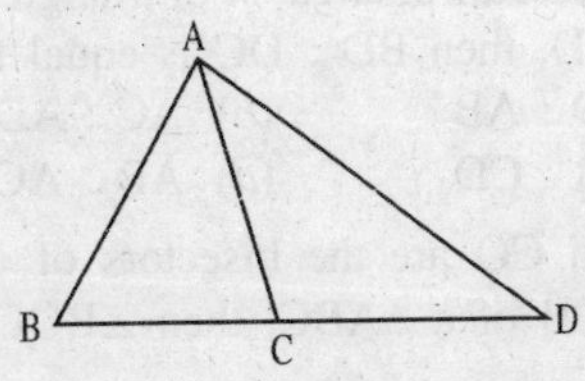

MATHEMATICS

(*a*) 11 (*b*) 10
(*c*) 12 (*d*) 13

32. ABC is a triangle; AD is $\perp$ to BC and AE, the bisector of angle A. The measure of $\angle$DAE is:
(*a*) $\frac{\angle B - \angle C}{3}$ (*b*) $\frac{1}{4}(\angle B + \angle C)$
(*c*) $\angle B - \angle C$ (*d*) $\frac{2}{5}(\angle B - \angle C)$

33. In the given figure the value of x is:

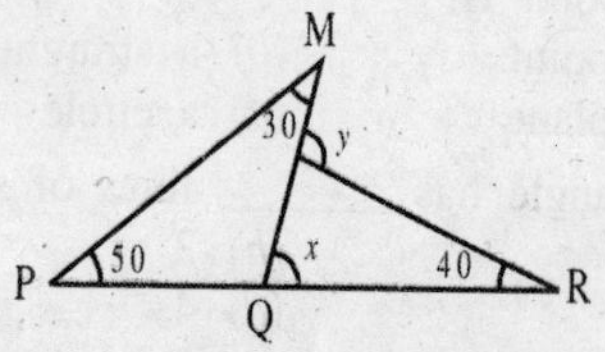

(*a*) 60 (*b*) 80
(*c*) 90 (*d*) 100

34. In a triangle ABC, AD the bisector of angle A is $\perp$ to CD such that AD meets BC at D, then
(*a*) AB = BC (*b*) AB = AC
(*c*) AC = BC (*d*) None of these

35. In a parallelogram shown below, X is mid point of AD and Y is mid point of BC, XY divides DB in the ratio.

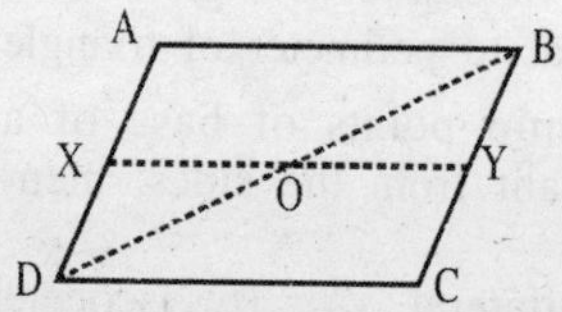

(*a*) 1 : 2 (*b*) 1 : 1
(*c*) 1 : 3 (*d*) 2 : 3

36. On the sides of a triangle PQR, equilateral triangles SQR, TRR and UPQ are drawn externally. If ratio of sides of triangle is 2 : 3 : 4, then ratio of PU : RT : QS is:
(*a*) 1 : 1 : 1 (*b*) 2 : 3 : 5
(*c*) 2 : 3 : 4 (*d*) Can't be determined

37. ABC is an equilateral triangle. If straight line $\perp$ to AB, BC, CA through the points B, C, A respectively form a ΔPQR. The ratio of ΔPQR and ΔABC is:
(*a*) 2 : 1 (*b*) 4 : 1
(*c*) 3 : 2 (*d*) 3 : 1

38. ABC is a right angled iscosceles triangle in which AB is hypotenuse, the bisector of $\angle$BAC is AD meeting BC in D, then
(*a*) AC + CD < AB (*b*) AC + CD > AB
(*c*) AC – CD = AB (*d*) AC + CD = AB

39. If the bisector of angle A of triangle ABC meets BC in D, then BD : DC is equal to:
(*a*) AD : AB (*b*) AC : AD
(*c*) AB : CD (*d*) AB : AC

40. BO and CO are the bisectors of angles ABC and ACB of a ΔABC, then $\angle$BOC is:
(*a*) less than 90° (*b*) greater than 90°
(*c*) $\frac{1}{2}\angle BAC$ (*d*) a right angle

41. D is a point on hypotenuse BC of right angled ΔABC. If $\angle$ABD = $\angle$BAD, then
(*a*) AD $\neq$ BD $\neq$ CD (*b*) AD $\neq$ BD = CD
(*c*) AD = CD = BD (*d*) AD = BD $\neq$ CD

42. The value of x in following figure is:

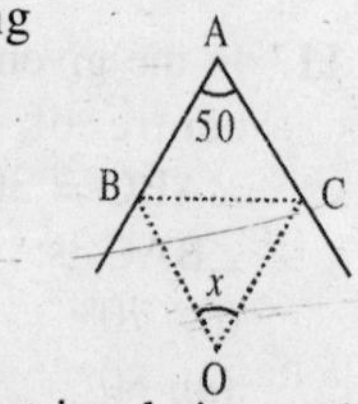

(*a*) 55
(*b*) 58
(*c*) 60
(*d*) 65

43. The sum of exterior angles of a triangle is equal to:
(*a*) 180 (*b*) 270
(*c*) 360 (*d*) 420

44. The minimum number of elements required to construct a square is:
(*a*) 1 (*b*) 2
(*c*) 3 (*d*) 4

45. One angle of a cyclic trapazium is 3 times the other. The measure of smaller angle is:
(*a*) 40 (*b*) 45
(*c*) 48 (*d*) 50

46. If the sides of a triangle are in the ratio 4 : 6 : 7 then the
(*a*) triangle is acute angled
(*b*) triangle is obtuse angled
(*c*) triangle is right angled
(*d*) None of these

47. In the figure the $\angle$BAD is equal to:
$\angle$B = $\angle$C = 60
$\angle$D = 40

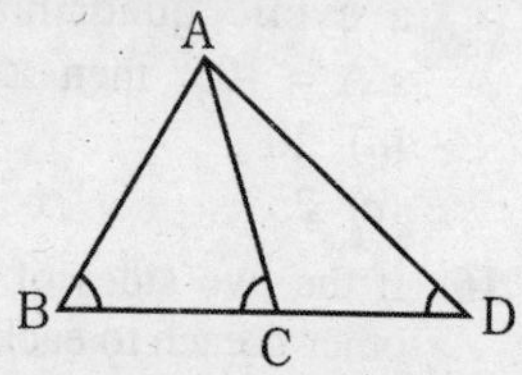

(*a*) 80
(*b*) 60
(*c*) 20
(*d*) 100

48. If all the sides of a parallelogram touch a circles, then parallelogram is a:
(*a*) Square (*b*) Rhombus
(*c*) Rectangle (*d*) None of these

49. Any cyclic parallelogram is:
(*a*) Rhombus (*b*) Square
(*c*) Rectangle (*d*) Trapezium

50. The value of $\angle$BAC in following figure is

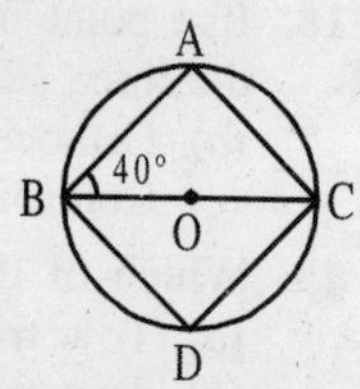

(*a*) 90
(*b*) 45
(*c*) 50
(*d*) 60

51. If the sides of a rhombus are 5 cm each and one of diagonal is 6 cm, the value of other diagonal is?

(a) 8 cm (b) 10 cm
(c) 4 cm (d) 5 cm

52. If each exterior angle of a regular polygon is 1/3 of interior angle then the number of sides is:
(a) 4 (b) 6
(c) 10 (d) 8

53. A quadrilateral can be drawn with:
(a) Four sides are given
(b) Four sides, one angle are given
(c) Three sides and diagonal is given
(d) None of these

54. The orthocentre of an obtuse angled triangle lies.............. the triangle.
(a) Outside
(b) Inside
(c) On smallest side of
(d) None of these

55. In a right angled ΔABC, AD is $\perp$ the hypotenuse BC then AD^2 is:
(a) AC × CD (b) AC × BA
(c) DC × BD (d) None of these

56. A circle is entirely in another circle, it is possible to draw
(a) One common tangent
(b) 2 common tangents
(c) Many tangents
(d) No common tangent

57. If ratio of base of two similar triangles is 2 : 5 then ratio of their area is:
(a) 2 : 25 (b) 4 : 5
(c) 4 : 25 (d) 4 : 9

58. ABCD is a rhombus. If $\angle ACB = 56°$, then $\angle ADB$ is
(a) 32 (b) 34
(c) 134 (d) 124

59. If G is the centroid of ΔABC and the median AD is 21 cm then value of DG is:
(a) 14 cm (b) 15 cm
(c) 18 cm (d) 7 cm

60. In ΔABC, AB = AC, then < BAC is:

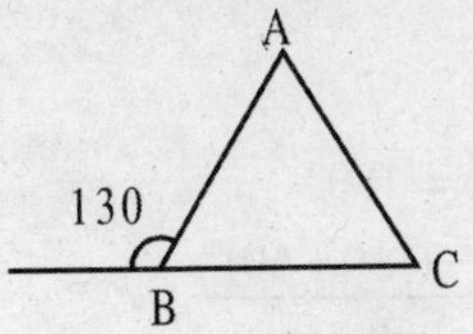

(a) 80° (b) 90°
(c) 100° (d) 130°

61. If AD and BE are medians of ΔABC and BE ‖ DF. Then

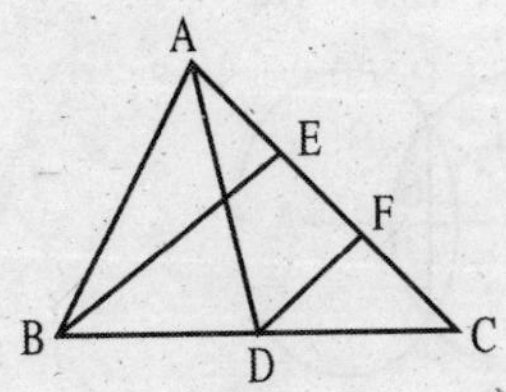

(a) $CF = \frac{1}{4}AC$ (b) $CF = \frac{1}{3}AC$
(c) $CF = \frac{1}{2}AC$ (d) $CF = \frac{2}{3}AC$

62. In the figure $\angle QPR$ is equal to:

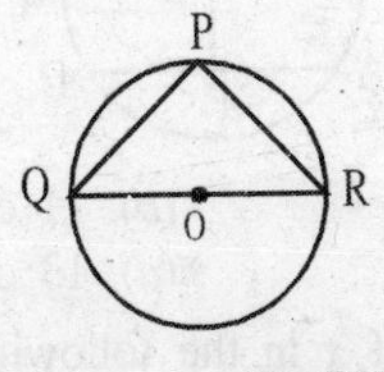

(a) 60° (b) 70°
(c) 90° (d) 80°

63. In the figure the value of x is:

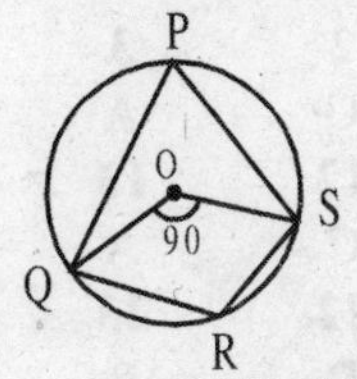

(a) 135° (b) 140°
(c) 145° (d) None of these

64. What will be the value of x in the figure?

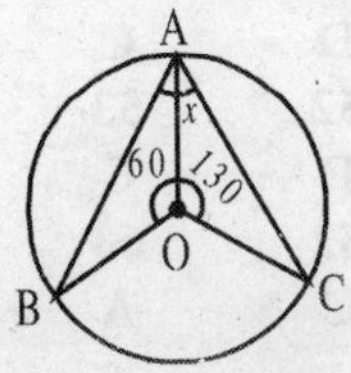

(a) 70° (b) 75°
(c) 80° (d) 90°

65. The perimeter of a triangle is P times the sum of its altitutdes, then value of P is:
(a) 0.5
(b) 0.8
(c) 1
(d) greater than 1

66. In given figure if EF ‖ AD and ED ‖ AC. If BF = 4 cm, FD = 6 cm and BE = 8 cm. Then BC is equal to:

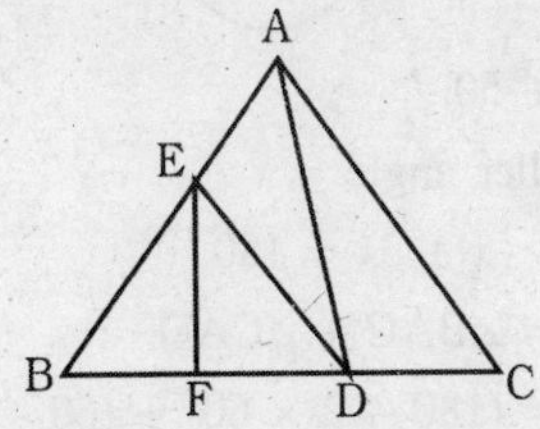

(a) 20 cm (b) 25 cm
(c) 30 cm (d) 35 cm

67. Two circles of radii 10 cm and 8 cm intersect and the length of the common chord is 12 cm. Distance between their centres is:
(a) 13 cm (b) 13.3 cm
(c) 13.8 cm (d) None of these

68. In the figure, if AB = 10 cm, CD = 24 cm and distance between AB and CD is 17 cm, then radius of circle is:

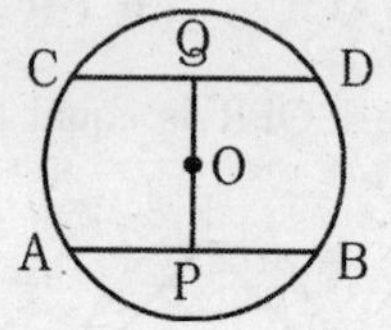

(*a*) 10 cm (*b*) 11 cm
(*c*) 12 cm (*d*) 13 cm

69. The value of x in the following figure is:

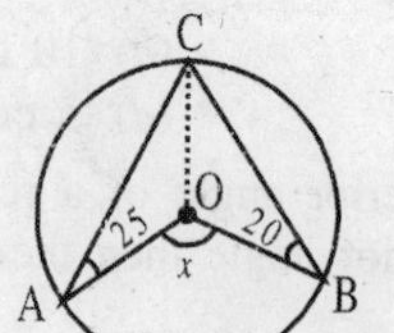

(*a*) 98° (*b*) 45°
(*c*) 90° (*d*) 48°

70. If the radius of a circle is 8 cm, then the side of regular hexagon inscribed in it is:
(*a*) 8 cm (*b*) 10 cm
(*c*) 12 cm (*d*) 16 cm

ANSWERS

1	2	3	4	5	6	7	8	9	10
C	C	A	A	A	D	D	A	C	B
11	**12**	**13**	**14**	**15**	**16**	**17**	**18**	**19**	**20**
B	C	A	D	D	A	B	B	D	A
21	**22**	**23**	**24**	**25**	**26**	**27**	**28**	**29**	**30**
D	D	B	A	A	B	C	C	B	A
31	**32**	**33**	**34**	**35**	**36**	**37**	**38**	**39**	**40**
A	C	B	B	B	C	D	D	D	B
41	**42**	**43**	**44**	**45**	**46**	**47**	**48**	**49**	**50**
C	D	C	B	B	A	A	B	C	A
51	**52**	**53**	**54**	**55**	**56**	**57**	**58**	**59**	**60**
A	D	C	A	C	D	D	B	D	A
61	**62**	**63**	**64**	**65**	**66**	**67**	**68**	**69**	**70**
A	C	A	B	D	B	B	D	C	A

SOME SELECTED EXPLANATORY ANSWERS

22. The locus of centres of all circles in same plane passing through a fixed plane is a circle.

33. $x = 30 + 50$.

45. Let smaller angle = x

$$x + 3x = 180.$$

47. $\angle BAD = \angle BAC + \angle CAD$

$$= (180 - 2 \times 60) + (60 - 40)$$

50. Angle in a semicircle is right angle.

56.

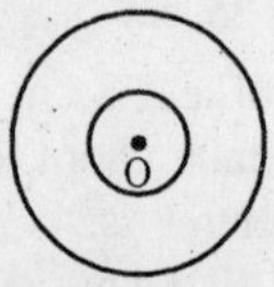

57. Ratio of area = (ratio of base)^2.

59. Distance from line = $\frac{1}{3}$ of median.

61. D is mid point of BC and DF ∥ BE
So in ΔBCE

$$CF = \frac{1}{2}CE = \frac{1}{2} \times \left(\frac{1}{2}AC\right).$$

62. $\angle QPR = 90°$ (angle in a semicircle)

63. $\angle P = \frac{90}{2}$

$\angle P + \angle R = 180°$

64. $x = \frac{360° - (130 + 60)°}{2}$

66. In Δ ABD, $\frac{BF}{FD} = \frac{BE}{EA}$

In Δ ABC, $\frac{BE}{EA} = \frac{BD}{BC}$

67.

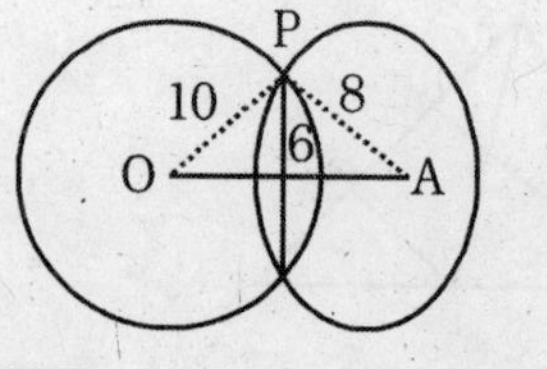

MENSURATION

Mensuration is a branch of mathematics in which we study about length of lines, area of planes and volume of solids. It is a base of architecture and engineering. More over it is useful in our daily life. Often we use mensuration to find the volume of tank, required number of bricks to build a house, area of fields etc. The main objectives of mensuration in mathematics teaching as follows:

(i) To apprise the students about the concept of length, perimeter, area and volume.

(ii) To develop the skill of transformation of various units.

(iii) To apprise the students to find area and volume of the geometrical figure with the formulae of mensuration.

(iv) To make capable students to recognise the similarity of some formulae.

Perimter: Perimeter is the distance covered along the boundary forming a closed figure when you go round the figure once.

Area: The amount of surface enclosed by a closed figure is called its area.

Volume: Amount of space occupied by a three dimensional object is called its volume.

AREA AND PERIMETER OF PLANES

Triangle

1. Perimeter = 3 × side (Equilateral triangle)
2. Area = $\frac{1}{2} \times \text{base} \times \text{height}$, or

Area = $\sqrt{s(s-a)(s-b)(s-c)}$

where *a*, *b*, *c*, are the lengths of the sides of triangle and $s = \frac{a+b+c}{2}$

Right Angled Triangle : It is one whose one of the angles is right angle, *i.e.*, 90°.

1. $(\text{Hypotenuse})^2 = (\text{Perpendicular})^2 + (\text{Base})^2$
2. Area = $\frac{1}{2} \times \text{Base} \times \text{Perpendicular}$

Equilateral Triangle : All three sides are equal in length and all three angles are equal to 60°.

1. Area = $\frac{\sqrt{3}}{4} \times (\text{Side})^2$
2. Area = $\frac{(\text{Height})^2}{\sqrt{3}}$
3. Height = $\frac{\sqrt{3}}{2} \times \text{side}$
4. Perimeter = 3 × side

Isosceles Triangle : Two sides are equal in lengths.

1. Area = $\frac{b}{4}\sqrt{4a^2 - b^2}$

where a = lengths of equal sides
b = length of unequal side

2. In an isosceles right triangle,

(a) Hypotenuse = $\sqrt{2} \times \text{congruent side (a)}$

(b) Area = $\frac{1}{2} \times a^2$

(c) Perimeter = $\sqrt{2} \times a(\sqrt{2}+1)$

Rectangle :

1. Area = length(l) × breadth(b)
2. Perimeter = $2(l + b)$
3. Diagonal = $\sqrt{l^2 + b^2}$

Square :

1. Area = $(\text{Side})^2$
2. Perimeter = 4 × side
3. Diagonal = $\text{side} \times \sqrt{2}$

Parallelogram: Area = Base × Height.

Trapezium : Area = $\frac{1}{2} \times \text{Height} \times$ (Sum of parallel sides). Here, height is the distance between the two parallel sides.

Rhombus :

1. Area = $\frac{1}{2} \times \text{Product of diagonals}$
2. Side = $\sqrt{\left(\frac{d_1}{2}\right)^2 + \left(\frac{d_2}{2}\right)^2}$, where d_1 and d_2 are diagonals
3. Perimeter = 4 × side

Quadrilateral : Area = $\frac{1}{2} \times \text{One diagonal} \times$ (Sum of perpendicular to it from the opposite vertices)

$= \frac{1}{2} \times d \times (a+b)$

Circle :

1. Diameter = 2 × Radius
2. Area = $\pi r^2 = \frac{\pi}{4}d^2$;

   where d = diameter = $\sqrt{\frac{4A}{\pi}}$
3. Circumference = $2\pi r = \pi d$
4. Radius = $\frac{\text{Circumference}}{2\pi} = \frac{\sqrt{\text{Area}}}{\pi}$
5. Length of an Arc = $\frac{\theta}{360°}\times 2\pi r$
6. Area of sector = $\frac{\theta}{360°}\times \pi r^2 = \frac{1}{2}\times \text{Arc}\times r$

Polygon :

1. Interior angle + Exterior angle = 180°
2. Each interior angle = $\left(\frac{2n-4}{n}\right)\times 90°$

   where n = number of sides
3. Sum of Exterior angles = 360°
4. Perimeter = Number of sides × Length of side.
5. For an equilateral triangle of side 'a'

   (a) radius of inscribed circle = $\frac{a}{2\sqrt{3}}$

   and side of the triangle = $2\sqrt{3}r$,

   (b) radius of circumcircle = $\frac{a}{\sqrt{3}}$
6. Area of regular polygon = $\frac{1}{2}$(No. of sides) (Radius of the inscribed circle)
7. Area of regular hexagon = $\frac{3\sqrt{3}}{2}(\text{side})^2$ = 2.598 $(\text{side})^2$
8. Area of a regular octagon = $2\left(\sqrt{2}+1\right)(\text{side})^2$ = 4.828 $(\text{side})^2$
9. Area of quadrilateral, A = $\sqrt{s(s-a)(s-b)(s-c)(s-d)}$

   where, $s = \frac{a+b+c+d}{2}$

VOLUME AND SURFACE AREA OF SOLIDS

Cuboid : A cuboid has six faces, each one a ractangle. It has 12 edges. For example, a rectangular brick.

Let Length = l, Breadth = b and Height = h, then,

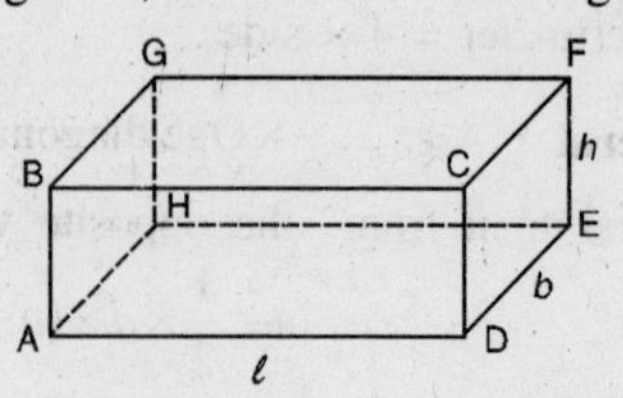

1. Volume = (Length × Breadth × Height)
2. Whole Surface Area = $2(lb + bh + lh)$
3. Diagonal = $\sqrt{l^2+b^2+h^2}$
4. Area of 4 walls of a room = $2 \times h\,(l + b)$

Cube : In a cube, Length = Breadth = Height

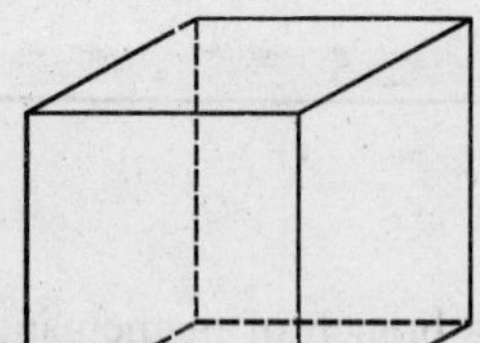

1. Volume = $(l)^3$
2. Length = $\sqrt[3]{\text{Volume}}$
3. Whole Surface Area = $6\,l^2$
4. Diagonal = $l\times\sqrt{3}$
5. Lateral Surface Area = $4\,l^2$

Cylinder :

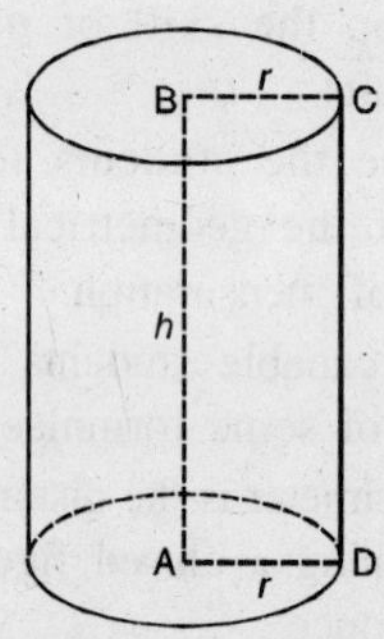

1. Volume = $\pi r^2 h$
2. Curved Surface Area = $2\pi rh$
3. Total Surface Area = $2\pi r(r + h)$

   where r = radius, h = height .

Spherical Cell :

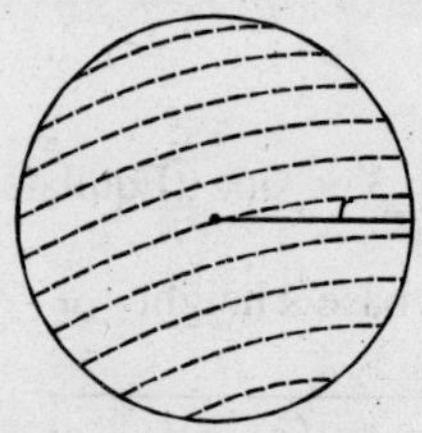

1. Volume = $\frac{4}{3}\pi\left(R^3 - r^3\right)$
2. Total Surface Area= $4\pi(R^2 - r^2)$

   where R = Outer radius

   r = Inner radius

Sphere :

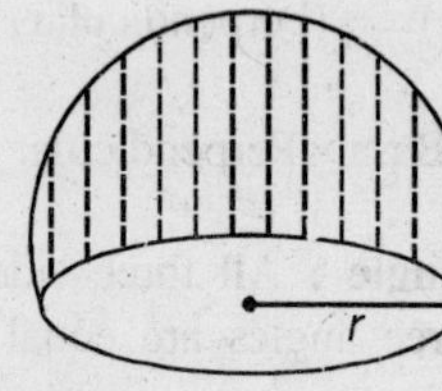

1. Volume = $\frac{4}{3}\pi r^3$

2. Surface Area = $4\pi r^2$

Semi-sphere :

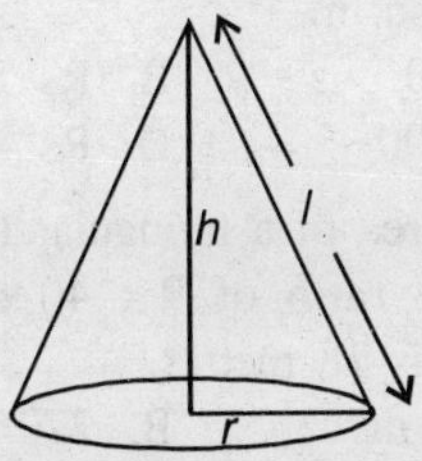

1. Volume = $\frac{2}{3}\pi r^3$
2. Curved surface area = $2\pi r^2$
3. Total surface area = $3\pi r^2$

Cone :

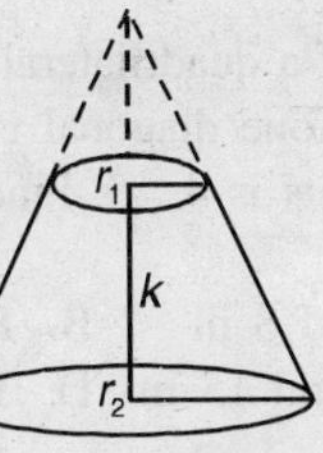

1. Slant height (l) = $\sqrt{r^2 + h^2}$
2. Volume = $\frac{1}{3}\pi r^2 h$
3. Curved surface area = πrl
4. Total surface area = $\pi r\,(l + r)$
5. If the depth of the frustum of a cone be k and the radii of its ends are r_1 and r_2, then
   (i) Slant height of the frustum of a cone
   $$= \sqrt{k^2 + (r_1 - r_2)^2}$$
   (ii) Curved surface of the frustum
   $$= \pi(r_1 + r_2)\, l.$$
   (iii) Volume = $\frac{\pi k}{3}\left(r_1^2 + r_1 r_2 + r_2^2\right)$

SOLVED QUESTIONS

Example 1: The length of a rectangular field is 20 m greater than its breadth. If the perimeter of field is 280 m, find the area of the field.

Solution: Let x and $x + 20$ be the breadth and length of the rectangle, so that

$2\,(x + 20 + x) = 280$

or $2x + 40 + 2x = 280$

or $4x = 240$

or $x = 60$ metres

and $x + 20 = 80$ metres

$\therefore$ Area = 80 × 60 = 4800 sq. metres.

Example 2: What will be the cost of surrounding with a fence a square field of 16 hectares at 20 paise per metre?

Solution: Area of square field = 16 hectares

= 160000 sq. m.

$\therefore$ Side of square field = $\sqrt{160000}$

= 400 m

Perimeter of the field = 4 × 400

= 1600 m

Cost of fencing = $1600 \times \frac{20}{100}$

= Rs 320.

Example 3 : The sides of a triangle are 5 cm, 5 cm and 6 cm respectively. Find its area?

Solution: $s = \frac{a+b+c}{2} = \frac{5+5+6}{2} = 8$ cms.

Now $\Delta = \sqrt{s(s-a)(s-b)(s-c)}$

$= \sqrt{8 \times 3 \times 3 \times 2}$

$= \sqrt{2 \times 2 \times 2 \times 3 \times 3 \times 2}$

$= \sqrt{2^2 \times 2^2 \times 3^2}$

= 12 sq. cm.

Example 4 : One of the diagonals of a quadrilateral is 120 metres and the perpendiculars upon it from the opposite corners are 15.4 m and 28.6 m. What will be the area of the quadrilateral?

Solution: Area of quadrilateral

$= \frac{1}{2} \times \text{Diagonal} \times \text{Sum of offsets}$

$= \frac{1}{2} \times 120 \times (15.4 + 28.6)$

$= \frac{1}{2} \times 120 \times 44$

= 2640 sq. m.

Example 5 : The circumference of a circle is 44 m, then find its area.

Solution: Circumference of a circle is $2\pi r$

$\therefore$ $2 \times \frac{22}{7} \times r = 44$

or $r = \frac{44 \times 7}{44} = 7$ m

Now area of circle = $\frac{22}{7} \times 7 \times 7$

= 154 sq. m.

MULTIPLE CHOICE QUESTIONS

1. The area of a ground is 12500 m^2. If its length is 125 m, then its perimeter is:
A. 1250 m^2 B. 450 m^2
C. 450 m D. 100 m

2. The length and breadth of a rectangle are 4 metres and 3 metres respectively. The length of the diagonal of a rectangle is:
A. 2 m B. 3 m
C. 4 m D. 5 m

3. The area of a square plot is 6050 sq. m. The length of its diagonal is:
A. 120 m B. 110 m
C. 100 m D. 90 m

4. The length and breadth of a garden are in the ratio of 2 : 1. If its perimeter is 60 m, then its length is:
A. 40 m B. 20 m
C. 30 m D. 25 m

5. Perimeters of two squares are 24 and 32 metres. Find the perimeter of the square which is equal to area of these two?
A. 30 m B. 40 m
C. 45 m D. 50 m

6. A map is drawn to scale of 120 cm to a kilometre. How many square cm on the map will represent a hectare of ground?
A. 144 sq. cm B. 1245 sq. cm
C. 204 sq. cm D. 144 sq. cm

7. A rectangular ground 12 metres long and 10 metres broad is surrounded by a road 2 metres wide. Find the area of the road
A. 108 sq. m. B. 102 sq. m.
C. 104 sq. m. D. 114 sq. cm

8. How long a man take to walk four times round the boundary of a square field containing 9 hectares as area at the rate of 6 km. per hour?
A. 12 minutes B. 24 minutes
C. 48 minutes D. 36 minutes

9. The length and breadth of a room are in the ratio 3 : 2. If its area is 216 sq. m., then its perimeter is:
A. 50 m B. 60 m
C. 72 m D. 76 m

10. Find the length of the diagonal of a square whose area is 24200 sq. m.
A. 200 m B. 120 m
C. 210 m D. 220 m

11. The length of a hall exceeds its breadth by 12 m. If the perimeter of the hall is 76 m, find the cost of carpeting it at 25 paise per sq. m.
A. Rs 80 B. Rs 81
C. Rs 81.25 D. Rs 81.75

12. The sides of a triangular field are 120 m, 160 m and 200 m. Find the cost of ploughing it at 25 paise per sq. m.
A. Rs 240 B. Rs 2400
C. Rs 2000 D. Rs 4200

13. Find the area of a traingular field whose sides are in the ratio of 9 : 40 : 41 and whose perimeter is 18 metres.
A. 72 sq. m B. 270 sq. m
C. 720 sq. m D. 7200 sq. m

14. Area of an isosceles triangle is 60 cm^2 and the length of its equal sides is 13 cm. Find the base of Δ.
A. 10 cm B. 12 cm
C. 15 cm D. 16 cm

15. The area of a quadrilateral piece of land is 486 sq. m. and one diagonal is 36 m and the ratio of the offsets is 4 : 5. Find the length of these offsets.
A. 6 m and 8 m B. 8 m and 10 m
C. 12 m and 15 m D. 16 m and 20 m

16. A hall whose length is 16 metres and breadth twice its height, takes 168 metres of paper 2 metres wide for its four walls. Find the area of the floor.
A. 196 sq. m B. 172 sq. m
C. 192 sq. m D. 152 sq. m

17. The diameter of a wheel is 1.26 m. How far will it travel in 500 revolutions?
A. 2000 m B. 1980 m
C. 1900 m D. 1860 m

18. A wire is in the form of a circle of radius 42 cm. It is bent into a square. The side of the square is:
A. 11 m B. 22 m
C. 44 m D. 66 m

19. If the radius of one circle is twelve times the radius of another. How many times does the greater contain the area of the smaller?
A. 12 times B. 144 times
C. 6 times D. 169 times

20. Find the radius of a circle whose area is equal to the sum of two circles whose radii are 5 metres and 12 metres.
A. 13 metres B. 12.5 metres
C. 14.5 metres D. $\sqrt{119}$ metres

21. The area of a sector is one-tenth that of the complete circle. Find the angle of sector.
A. 3° B. 13°
C. 30° D. 36°

22. Find the length of the longest rod that can be placed in a room 12 metres long, 9 metres broad and 8 metres high.
A. 1.7 m B. 17 m
C. 0.17 m D. 2.7 m

23. Find the edge of a cubical block whose volume is equal to that of a rectangular bar measuring 27 cm long, 16 cm wide and 4 cm thick.
A. 10 cm B. 10.5 cm
C. 11 cm D. 12 cm

24. The rectangular solid beam is 15 units long and 8 units thick. Find its breadth if its cost at the rate of Rs 30 per cubic unit is Rs 2700.
A. 75 units B. 7.5 units
C. .75 units D. .7 units

25. The area of 4 walls of a room is 660 square metres and the length is twice its breadth. If height of the room is 11 metres, then area of the ceiling is:
A. 50 sq. m B. 100 sq. m
C. 150 sq. m D. 200 sq. m

26. A circular lawn whose diameter is 100 metres is surrounded by a uniform road 5 metres wide. Area of the road is:
A. 1450 sq. m B. 1550 sq. m
C. 1650 sq. m D. 1750 sq. m

27. Circumference of a circle is 44 m. Its area is:
A. 142 sq. m B. 152 sq. m
C. 154 sq. m D. 158 sq. m

28. The perimeter of a circle is equal to that of a square. The areas are in the ratio of:
A. 11 : 11 B. 11 : 12
C. 13 : 11 D. 14 : 11

29. How many cubes of edge 4 cm can be cut from a cube of 12 cm edge.
A. 64 B. 27
C. 18 D. 9

30. The volume of a metallic cylindrical pipe is 748 cu. cm. Its length is 14 cm and its external radius is 9 cm. Find its thickness.
A. 10 cm B. 11 cm
C. 1.1 cm D. 1 cm

31. A cylindrical bucket 28 cm in diameter and 72 cm high is full of water. The water is emptied into a rectangular tank 66 cm long 28 cm wide. Find the height of water level in the tank.
A. 2.4 cm B. 24 cm
C. 12 cm D. 1.2 cm

32. The height of a right circular cylinder is 6 m. Three times the sum of the areas of its two circular faces is twice the area of its curved surface. Find the radius of the base.
A. 2 m B. 4 m
C. 6 m D. 8 m

33. Three cubes of metals whose edges are 3, 4 and 5 dm, respectively, are melted and formed into a single cube. If there be no waste in the process, find the edge of new cube.
A. 16 dm B. 60 dm
C. 6 m D. 6 dm

34. The radius of the base of a cone 6 cm high is 3.5 cm. Find the volume of cone.
A. 231 cu cm B. 77 cu cm
C. 232 cu cm D. 156 cu cm

35. The circumference of the base of a right circular cylinder is 88 cm. The height of the cylinder is 42 cm. Its volume is:
A. 22782 cu cm B. 23278 cu cm
C. 24872 cu cm D. 25872 cu cm

36. Volume of a cone is 616 cubic metres. If its perpendicular height is 27 metres, then find the radius of the base.
A. $5\frac{2}{3}$ m B. 4 m
C. $1\frac{2}{3}$ m D. $4\frac{2}{3}$ m

37. A hollow cylindrical tube open at both ends is made of iron 2 cm thick. If the external diameter be 50 cm and the length of the tube be 140 cm, find the number of cubic cm of iron in it.
A. 42240 cu cm B. 42440 cu cm
C. 4240 cu cm D. 40240 cu cm

38. The diameter of base of a right circular cone is 7 cm and slant height 10 cm. Find its area.
A. 11 cm^2 B. 100 cm^2
C. 110 cm^2 D. 154 cm^2

39. 11 cubic metres of steel is converted into bars of 10 cm diameter and 1.4 metre length. The number of bars formed is:
A. 10 B. 100
C. 1000 D. 10000

40. How many bullets can be made out of a cube of lead whose edge measures 22 cm, each bullet being 2 cm in diameter?
A. 2154 B. 2541
C. 2514 D. 1271

41. The length of a rectangle is increased by $\frac{1}{3}$ and width is decreased by $\frac{1}{3}$, the area of the rectangle is diminished by the fraction.
A. $\frac{2}{3}$ B. $\frac{1}{6}$
C. $\frac{1}{9}$ D. $\frac{1}{8}$

42. A room is 15 metres long and 12 metres wide. The area of its four walls is 270 sq. metres. Its height is:
A. 4 m B. 5 m
C. 6 m D. 8 m

43. The base of a right prism is a trapezium whose parallel sides are 40 cm and 20 cm while the perpendicular distance between them is 10 cm. If height of the prism is 10 cm, its volume is:
A. 3000 cu cm B. 4000 cu cm
C. 5000 cu cm D. 6000 cu cm

44. If the radius of a circle is increased by 100%, the area is increased by:
A. 400% B. 300%
C. 200% D. 100%

45. If the diameter of the wire is decreased by 5 per cent, by how much per cent will the length be increased if the volume remains the same?
A. $2\frac{1}{2}$% B. 5%
C. 10% D. 10.8%

46. Find the area of the quadrilateral piece of ground whose diagonals is 60 metres long and the perpendiculars from the opposite vertices are 48 and 22 metres respectively.
A. 1800 sq. m. B. 2100 sq. m.
C. 4200 sq. m. D. 4000 sq. m.

47. How many metres of wall paper 2 metres wide will be required for a room 8.3 metres long, 4.2 metres wide and 4 metres high?
A. 60 metres B. 50 metres
C. 100 metres D. 150 metres

48. The difference between the circumference and radius of a circle 74 metres. Find the diameter of the circle.
A. 37 m B. 28.5 m
C. 28 m D. 2.8 m

49. A circular road runs round a circular garden. If the difference between the circumferences of the outer circle and the inner circle is 44 metres, then the width of the road is:
A. 14 m B. 7 m
C. 21 m D. 2.1 m

50. A rectangle measures 50 cm × 25 cm. Its area is
A. 1150 sq. cm B. 1250 sq. cm
C. 1275 sq. cm D. 1280 sq. cm

51. A field is in the form of a square whose perimeter is 580 m. Area of this field is
A. 21025 sq. m B. 20225 sq. m
C. 30025 sq. m D. 19975 sq. m

52. Area of a circle is 154 sq. cm. Its circumference will be
A. 44 cm B. 48 cm
C. 54 cm D. 68 cm

53. The base and the height of a triangle is 8 cm and 10 cm respectively. Its area will be
A. 40 sq. cm B. 20 sq. cm
C. 49 sq. cm D. 64 sq. cm

54. If it is given that the parallel sides of a trapezium are 15 m and 25 m while the distance between them is 10 m. Its area will be:
A. 150 sq. m B. 225 sq. m.
C. 200 sq. m D. 270 sq. m.

55. Perimeter of a rectangular field is 760 m and its length and breadth are in the ratio 11 : 8. Area of this rectangular field is
A. 35200 sq. m B. 34700 sq. m
C. 35600 sq. m D. 45200 sq. m

56. The perimeter of a square is 24 m and that of another is 32 m. Find the perimeter of a third square, area of which is equal to sum of the areas of these two squares
A. 40 m B. 51 m
C. 37 m D. 42 m

57. If the perimeter of an equilateral triangle is 72 cm, its area will be
A. $144\sqrt{3}$ sq. cm B. $142\sqrt{3}$ sq. cm
C. $154\sqrt{2}$ sq. cm D. $144\sqrt{2}$ sq. cm

58. Find the perimeter of a rhombus whose diagonals measure 16 cm and 12 cm.
A. 38 cm B. 40 cm
C. 41 cm D. 46 cm

59. If area of a traingle whose base is 6 cm is equal to the area of a square of side 6 cm, find the height of this triangle.
A. 10 cm B. 22 cm
C. 12 cm D. 18 cm

60. A garden is 24 m long and 14 m wide. There is a path 1 m wide outside the garden along its sides. If the path is to be constructed with square marble tiles 20 cm × 20 cm, find the number of tiles required to cover the path.
A. 1800 B. 2200
C. 2000 D. 2150

61. Two adjacent sides of a parallelogram are 40 m and 30 m respectively. If one diagonal of the parallelogram measures 50 m, find its area.
A. 1100 sq. m B. 1200 sq. m
C. 1400 sq. m D. 1500 sq. m

62. Four sides of a trapezium are 50 cm, 17 cm, 25 cm and 12 cm respectively. If the first of the four sides is parallel to the third, find the area of this trapezium.
A. 280 sq. cm B. 810 sq. cm
C. 270 sq. cm D. 225 sq. cm

63. A solid in the form of a cuboid is 4 cm × 3 cm × 2 cm. Its volume will be

A. 20 cu cm B. 22 cu cm
C. 28 cu cm D. 24 cu cm

64. A reservoir is 3 m long, 2 m wide and 1 m deep. Its capacity in litres is
A. 8000 litres B. 10000 litres
C. 6500 litres D. 6000 litres

65. Surface area of a cube is 1014 sq. cm. Its volume will be
A. 2197 cu cm B. 2297 cu cm
C. 2179 cu cm D. 2117 cu cm

66. Circumference of the base of a cylinder is 88 cm and height of the cylinder is 42 cm. Its volume is
A. 25872 cu cm B. 28572 cu cm
C. 25870 cu cm D. 22584 cu cm

67. If two cubes each of 10 cm side are kept close to each other, then the cuboid so formed will have surface area equal to
A. 1200 sq. cm B. 5000 sq. cm
C. 1000 sq. cm D. 1250 sq. cm

68. A room is in the form of a cube of side 10 m. How many bales of cotton can be kept in it if each bale covers 5 cu m space?
A. 100 B. 175
C. 200 D. 225

69. The surface area of a cube is 600 sq. m. Its diagonal is
A. $10\sqrt{3}$ cm B. $5\sqrt{3}$ cm
C. $4\sqrt{2}$ cm D. $10\sqrt{2}$ cm

ANSWERS

1	**2**	**3**	**4**	**5**	**6**	**7**	**8**	**9**	**10**
C	D	B	B	B	A	C	C	B	D
11	**12**	**13**	**14**	**15**	**16**	**17**	**18**	**19**	**20**
C	B	C	A	C	C	B	D	B	A
21	**22**	**23**	**24**	**25**	**26**	**27**	**28**	**29**	**30**
D	B	D	C	D	C	C	D	B	D
31	**32**	**33**	**34**	**35**	**36**	**37**	**38**	**39**	**40**
B	B	D	B	D	D	A	C	C	B
41	**42**	**43**	**44**	**45**	**46**	**47**	**48**	**49**	**50**
C	B	A	B	D	B	B	C	B	B
51	**52**	**53**	**54**	**55**	**56**	**57**	**58**	**59**	**60**
A	A	A	C	A	A	A	B	C	C
61	**62**	**63**	**64**	**65**	**66**	**67**	**68**	**69**	
B	C	D	D	A	A	C	C	A	

SOME SELECTED EXPLANATORY ANSWERS

1. Area of rectangular ground = 12500 m^2
Length of rectangular ground = 125 m
∴ Breadth of rectangular ground

$$= \frac{12500}{125} = 100 \text{ m}$$

Perimeter = 2 (L + B) = 2 × (125 + 100)
= 2 × 225 = 450 m.

3. Diagonal of square plot

$$= \sqrt{2 \times \text{Area}}$$

$$= \sqrt{2 \times 6050}$$

$$= \sqrt{12100} = 110 \text{ m}.$$

6. 1 hectare = 10000 sq. m.

$$\therefore \text{No. of sq. cm of map} = \frac{120 \times 120 \times 10000}{1000 \times 1000}$$

= 144 sq. cm.

8. Area of field = 9 × 10000 = 90000 sq. m.

Side of field = $\sqrt{90000}$ = 300 m

Perimeter = 4 × 300 = 1200 sq. m.

4 times perimeter = 4 × 1200 = 4800 sq. m.

$$\text{Time taken} = \frac{60}{6000} \times 4800 = 48 \text{ minutes.}$$

15. Let offsets be $4x$ m and $5x$ m
∴ Area of quadrilateral

$$= \frac{1}{2} \times \text{diagonal} \times (\text{sum of the offsets})$$

$$486 = \frac{1}{2} \times 36(4x + 5x)$$

$$486 \times 2 = 36 \times 9x$$

or $x = \dfrac{4.86\times2}{36\times9} = 3$

$\therefore$ Offsets are 4×3 m, 5×3 m *i.e.* 12 m and 15 m.

26. Inner radius of circular lawn $r_1 = 50$ m

Outer radius of circular lawn $r_2 = 50 + 5 = 55$ m

$$\text{Area of road} = \pi\left(r_2^2 - r_1^2\right) = \frac{22}{7}(55^2 - 50^2) = \frac{22}{7}\times525 = 1650 \text{ sq. m.}$$

31. Let the height of water level in the tank = x m

$\therefore \pi r^2 h = l \times b \times x$

or $\dfrac{22}{7}\times14\times14\times72 = 66 \times 28 \times x$

or $x = \dfrac{\frac{22}{7}\times14\times14\times72}{66\times28} = 24$ cm.

38. Radius of base of cone 'r' $= \dfrac{7}{2}$ cm

Slant height of cone 'l' = 10 cm

$$\text{Area of cone} = \pi rl = \frac{22}{7}\times\frac{7}{2}\times10 = 110 \text{ sq. cm.}$$

46. Area of quadrilateral

$$= \frac{1}{2}\times \text{diagonal} \times \text{(Sum of the offsets)} = \frac{1}{2}\times60\times(48+22) = \frac{1}{2}\times60\times70 = 2100 \text{ sq. m.}$$

50. Area of the rectangle $= l \times b = 50 \times 25 = 1250$ sq. cm

51. Here, $4 \times \text{side} = 580$

$\Rightarrow$ side $= \dfrac{580}{4} = 145$ m

$\therefore$ Area = $(\text{side})^2$

$(145)^2 = 21025$ sq. m.

52. Area of the circle $= \pi r^2$

$\Rightarrow \pi r^2 = 154$

$\Rightarrow r^2 = \dfrac{154\times7}{22}$

$\Rightarrow r = 7$ cm

$\therefore$ Circumference of the circle $= 2\pi r$

$$= 2\times\frac{22}{7}\times7 = 44 \text{ cm.}$$

53. Area of the triangle $= \dfrac{1}{2}\times8\times10 = 40$ sq. cm.

54. Area of the trapezium $= \dfrac{1}{2}\times(15+25)\times10 = 200$ sq. m.

55. Suppose length and breadth of the rectangular field are $11x$ m and $8x$ m.

$\therefore$ Perimeter of the field $= 2(11x + 8x) = 2 \times 19x = 38x$ m.

Now, $38x = 760$

$\Rightarrow x = \dfrac{760}{38} = 20$

$\therefore$ Length of the field $= 11 \times 20 = 220$ m

Breadth of the field $= 8 \times 20 = 160$ m

$\therefore$ Area of the field $= 220 \times 160 = 35200$ sq. m.

56. Side of the 1st square $= \dfrac{24}{4} = 6$ m

And side of the 2nd square $= \dfrac{32}{4} = 8$ m

Now, area of the third square $= 6^2 + 8^2 = 36 + 64 = 100$ sq. m.

$\therefore$ Side of the third square $= \sqrt{100} = 10$ m

Hence, Perimeter of the third square $= 4 \times \text{side} = 4 \times 10 = 40$ m.

57. Here, $3x = 72$

$\Rightarrow x = \dfrac{72}{3} = 24$ cm.

$\therefore$ Area of the equilateral triangle

$$= \frac{\sqrt{3}}{4}\times x^2 = \frac{\sqrt{3}}{4}\times(24)^2 = 144\sqrt{3} \text{ sq. cm.}$$

58. Side of rhombus $= \sqrt{\left(\dfrac{16}{2}\right)^2 + \left(\dfrac{12}{2}\right)^2} = \sqrt{8^2 + 6^2} = \sqrt{100} = 10$ cm.

$\therefore$ Perimeter of the rhombus $= 4 \times \text{side} = 4 \times 10 = 40$ cm.

59. Area of the square = 36 sq. cm

Now, $\dfrac{1}{2}\times\text{base}\times\text{height} = 36$

$\Rightarrow \dfrac{1}{2}\times6\times\text{height} = 36$

$\therefore$ Height of the triangle $= \dfrac{36\times2}{6} = 12$ cm.

60. Area of the garden $= 24 \times 14 = 336$ sq. m

Area of the (garden + path) $= 26 \times 16 = 416$ sq. m

$\therefore$ Area of the path $= 416 - 336 = 80$ sq. m

Area of 1 tile $= 20 \times 20 = 400$ sq. cm $= .04$ sq. m

$\therefore$ Number of tiles required to cover the path

$$= \frac{80}{.04} = 2000.$$

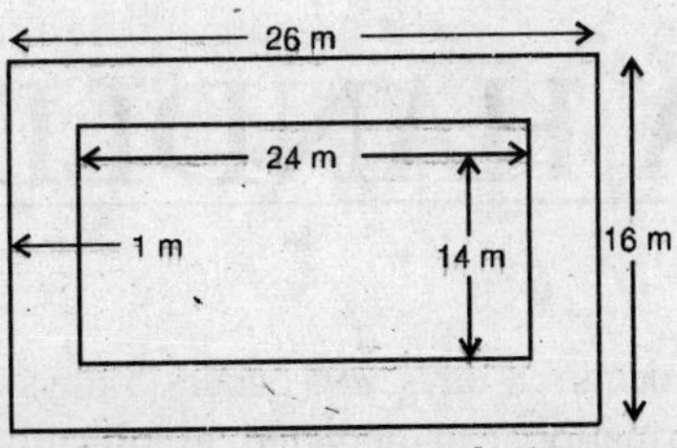

61. Here, $50^2 = 40^2 + 30^2$

$\therefore$ Two triangles, *i.e.*, ΔABC and ΔADC are right angled triangle.

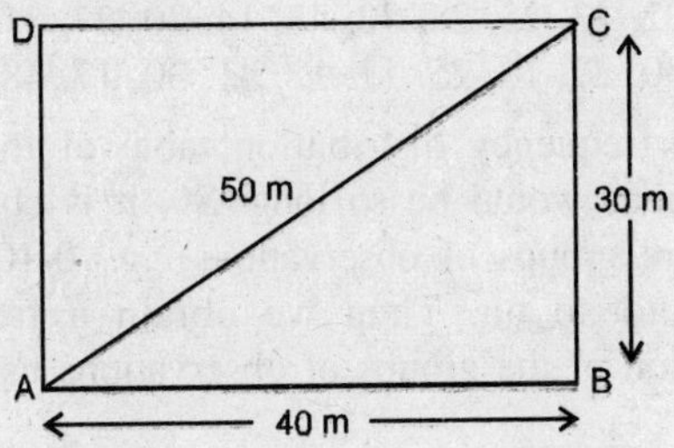

$\therefore$ Area of parallelogram ABCD = 2 × Area of

$\Delta ABC = 2 \times \frac{1}{2} \times 40 \times 30 = 1200$ sq.m.

63. Volume of the cuboid $= l \times b \times h$

$= 4 \times 3 \times 2 = 24$ cu. cm.

64. Volume of the reservoir $= l \times b \times h$

$= 3 \times 2 \times 1 = 6$ cu. m

($\because$ 1 cu m = 1000 litres)

$\therefore$ Capacity of the reservoir

$= 6 \times 1000 = 6000$ litres.

65. Here, $6 \times (\text{side})^2 = 1014$

$\Rightarrow$ $(\text{side})^2 = \frac{1014}{6} = 169$

$\therefore$ $\text{side} = \sqrt{169} = 13$ cm

Hence, Volume of the cube $= (\text{side})^3$

$= (13)^3 = 2197$ cu cm.

66. Here, $2\pi r = 88$

$\therefore$ $r = \frac{88}{2\pi} = \frac{88 \times 7}{2 \times 22} = 14$ cm

Since, volume of the cylinder $= \pi r^2 h$

$= \frac{22}{7} \times (14)^2 \times 42 = 22 \times 2 \times 14 \times 42$

$= 25872$ cu cm.

67. Here, length of the cuboid = Edge of the first cube + Edge of the second cube

$= 10 + 10 = 20$ cm

$\therefore$ Surface area of the cuboid

$= 2(20 \times 10 + 10 \times 10 + 10 \times 20)$

$= 2(200 + 100 + 200)$

$= 2 \times 500 = 1000$ sq. cm.

68. Volume of the cubical room $= (10)^3 = 1000$ cu m

Number of cotton bales which can be placed in the room

$$= \frac{\text{Volume of the room}}{\text{Volume of each cotton bale}} = \frac{1000}{5} = 200.$$

69. Here, $6 \times (\text{side})^2 = 600$

$\Rightarrow$ $\text{side}^2 = 100$

$\Rightarrow$ $\text{side} = \sqrt{100} = 10$ cm

$\therefore$ Diagonal of the cube $= \sqrt{3} \times \text{side}$ cm.

$= \sqrt{3} \times 10 = 10\sqrt{3}$ cm

DATA HANDLING

We are required to understand the trends important variations and typical results after manipulating the data, in whatever from it may be. Then, we will be required to either answer some questions or verify a few statements on the basis of the trends, variations and results.

Data handling is a tool to express or depict the given information using various types of symbols. In our day-to-day life we come across several kinds of information such as—

(*i*) Distance covered by a car in 10 hours.

(*ii*) Books sold by a shopkeeper in the last week.

(*iii*) Runs scored by Sachin in World Cup. etc.

The information collected in all such cases is called 'data'. In other words, "Data is a collection of numbers gathered to give some information." It is usually gathered in the context of a situation that we want to study. To give a clear idea of what it represents the data is represented in graphic form.

Organising Data

Generally data is given in unorganised or raw form. We organise it systematically to draw meaningful conclusions. *e.g.,* the temperature of 30 days of a city was given as : 30°, 25°, 29°, 28°, 25°, 30°, 30°, 26°, 29°, 28°, 30°, 30°, 28°, 26°, 30°, 28°, 22°, 29°, 28°, 30°, 26°, 28°, 30°, 27°, 30°, 25°, 28°, 29°, 30° and 29° then how many days the city faced the highest temperature?

It's not easy to answer the question looking at the given temperatures which are written haphazardly. So we arrange the data using tally marks. Thus we easily give the answer.

Temperatures	Tally marks	No. of Days
25°	|||	3
26°	|||	3
27°	|	1
28°	~~||||~~ |||	8
29°	~~||||~~	5
30°	~~||||~~ ~~||||~~	10
		N = 30

Thus, we can easily determine that the city faced the highest temperature 30° till 10 days.

Grouping Data

In the above example we have seen that same degree of temperatures occurs frequently *e.g.,* 30° occurs 10 days, 28° occurs 8 days, 29° occurs 5 days and so on. This information can depicted graphically.

In our daily life we often deal with different type of data. Some of them are small but some of them are large data. For example, following is the daily attendence of employees of an office in April. 14, 16, 46, 24, 22, 43, 25, 24, 32, 43, 14, 30, 27, 31, 32, 28, 18, 19, 30, 27, 16, 25, 11, 12, 31, 30, 17, 48, 19, 23.

The frequency distribution table of the above observations would be so long. So, it is convenient to prepare groups of observations *e.g.,* 0-10, 10-20, 20-30 and so on. Then we obtain a frequency distribution of the groups of observations using tally marks.

Groups	Tally Marks	Frequency
10-20	~~||||~~ ~~||||~~	10
20-30	~~||||~~ ||||	9
30-40	~~||||~~ ||	7
40-50	||||	4
		N = 30

Data arranged in this manner is known as the grouped and the distribution is called a grouped frequency distribution. Now we can derive many meaningful inferences like—

(*i*) Most of the days the attendences were poor.

(*ii*) Only four days the attendence were maximum and so on.

Variate: The quantity that we measure from observation to observation is called a variate.

Class Interval: Every data is generally divided into small group using some interval is said to be in class-interval, *e.g.,* 0-5, 5-10, 10-15, etc.

Class-size: The difference between the true upper limit and true lower limit of a class gives the size of the class-interval, *e.g.,* class-size of the class interval 0-5 is 5.

Mid-value: The variable value which is midway between the lower and upper limit of a class is called its mid-value, *e.g.,* mid-value of class interval 0-5 is $\frac{0+5}{2} = 2.5$.

Frequency: The number of observations corresponding to particular class is said to be the frequency of that class, *e.g.,* frequency of the interval

5-10 is 6. It means 6 persons have got 5 or more articles but less than 10.

Cumulative Frequency: The sum of the preceding frequencies is called cumulative frequency. Last frequency of cumulative frequency column is equal to the sum of the frequencies.

Class Limits: Every interval has two limits. Lower number of the interval is called lower limit while upper number of the interval is called upper limit, *e.g.*, in interval 0-5, 0 is the lower limit while upper number of the interval 5 is called upper limit.

Diagrammatic representation of data

(a) One-dimensional diagrams are (i) Bar diagram, (ii) Sub-divided bar diagram, (iii) Multiple bar diagram.

(b) Two-dimensional diagrams are (i) Squares, (ii) Circles, (iii) Pie-diagrams.

(c) Three-dimensional diagrams are (i) Cubes, (ii) Cylinders, (iii) Spheres.

(d) Pictograms.

(e) Cartograms.

Graphical representation of data

(a) Histogram

(b) Frequency polygon

(c) Frequency curve

(d) Cumulative frequency curve or ogive.

Histogram: A statistical graph that represents by the height of a rectangular column the number of times that each class of result occurs in a sample or experiment, *e.g.*, the following table presents the number of matured persons in the age group (15-50) in a city.

Age Group	No. of Persons	Age Group	No. of Persons
15-20	200	35-40	750
20-25	350	40-45	900
25-30	475	45-50	100
30-35	600		

Then the histogram of the data is given below:

HISTROGRAM

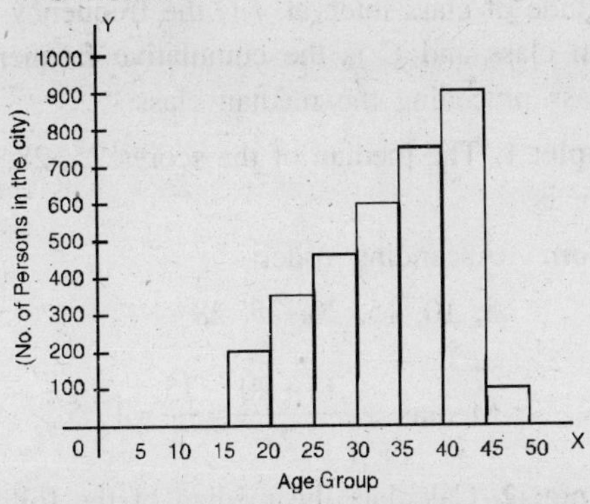

Frequency Polygon: The graph obtained when the mid-point of the tops of the rectangle in a histogram with equal class interval are joined by line segment. The area under the polygon is equal to the total area of the rectangle, *e.g.*, the frequency polygon of above given data is shown in figure.

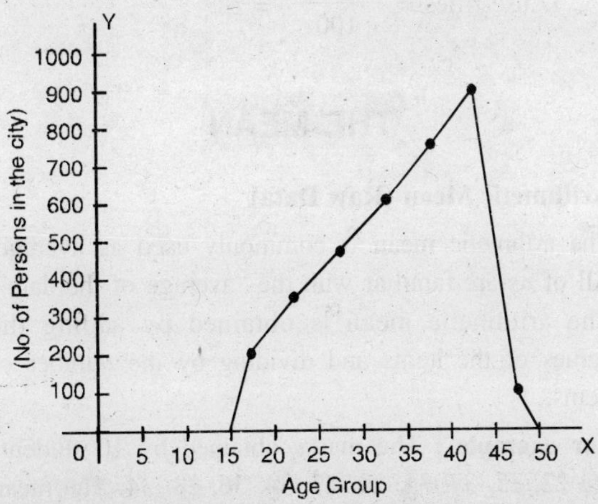

Bar Graph: A graph consisting of bars whose lengths are proportional to quantities in a set of data. It can be used when one axis cannot have a numerical scale, *e.g.*, to show how many different columns of flowers grow from a packet of mixed seeds given in figure.

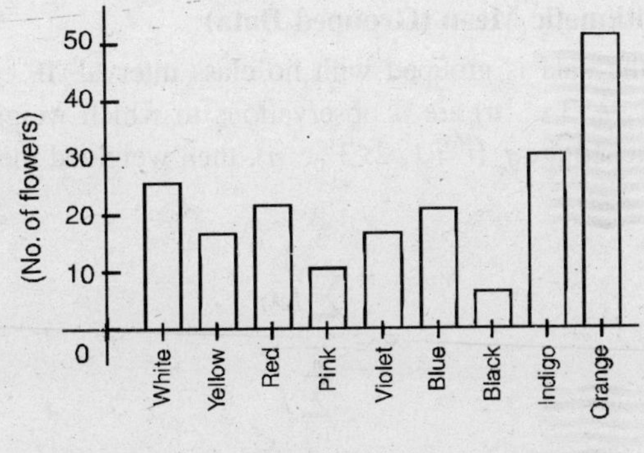

Pie-chart: A diagram in which proportions are illustrated as sectors of a circle. The relative area of the sectors representing the different proportions, *e.g.*, if out of 100 military personnels 25 personnels use tank, 30 personnels use warship, 40 personnels use aircraft and rest of them use rifles. Then pie-chart of the above data is

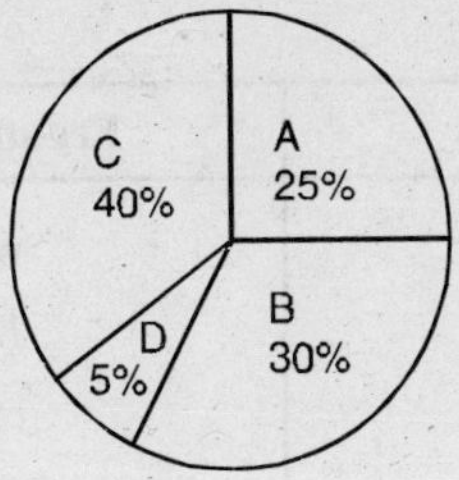

$$\text{A use tank} = \frac{25 \times 360}{100} = 90^\circ$$

$$\text{B use warship} = \frac{30 \times 360}{100} = 108^\circ$$

C use aircraft = $\frac{40 \times 360}{100}$ = 144°

D use rifles = $\frac{5 \times 360}{100}$ = 18°

THE MEAN

Arithmetic Mean (Raw Data)

The arthmetic mean is commonly used as average. All of us are familiar with the "average of the data". The arithmetic mean is obtained by adding the values of the items and dividing by the number of items.

For example : The marks obtained by 10 students are 22, 35, 37, 38, 29, 27, 34, 36, 28, 34. The mean of marks is:

Solution: No. of students = 10

$$\text{Mean } (\bar{x}) = \frac{22+35+37+38+29+27+34+36+28+34}{10}$$

$$= \frac{320}{10} = 32 \text{ marks.}$$

Arithmetic Mean (Grouped Data)

If the data is grouped with no class interval. If x_i (i = 1, 2, 3 .... n) are n observations to which weights attached are f_i (i = 1, 2, 3 .... n), then weighted mean is:

$$\bar{x} = \frac{\sum_{i=1}^{n} f_i x_i}{\sum_{i=1}^{n} f_i}$$

Again, if the data is grouped with class interval and frequencies are gien with these then,

mean $\bar{x} = \frac{\Sigma fx}{\Sigma f}$ where, f = frequency

x = mid-value

For example: Calculate the mean for the following distribution:

Marks	Frequency
10-20	6
20-30	8
30-40	15
40-50	7
50-60	3
60-70	0
70-80	1

Solution:

Marks	Mid-value (x)	Frequency (f)	$f \times x$
10-20	15	6	15 × 6 = 90
20-30	25	8	25 × 8 = 200
30-40	35	15	35 × 15= 525
40-50	45	7	45 × 7 = 315
50-60	55	3	55 × 3 = 165
60-70	65	0	65 × 0 = 0
70-80	75	1	75 × 1 = 75
		$\sum f = 40$	$\sum fx = 1370$

$$\text{Mean } \bar{x} = \frac{\sum fx}{\sum f} = \frac{1370}{40} = 34.25.$$

THE MEDIAN

It is defined as the value of that item of the arrayed series which divides the whole series into two equal parts. The middle item of the array is called the median. For example, in the 3, 5, 9, 13, 15, 21, 22, 25, 29, the median is 15. When the data is ungrouped and the number of items is odd, the median is $\left(\frac{n+1}{2}\right)$ th value. If n is even, there will be two central items, *i.e.,* $\left(\frac{n}{2}\right)$ th item and $\left(\frac{n}{2}+1\right)$ th item. The average value of these two items will be median in such case.

When the data is grouped,

$$\text{Median} = l + \frac{\frac{N}{2} - C}{f} \times i$$

Where l is the lower limit of the class in which median lies. N is the sum of frequencies, i is the magnitude of class interval, f is the frequency of the median class and C is the cumulative frequency of the class preceding the median class.

Example: 1. The median of the scores 25, 28, 20, 8, 10, 15, is:

Solution: Ascending order:

8, 10, 15, 20, 25, 28

$$\text{Median} = \frac{15+20}{2} = \frac{35}{2} = 17.5.$$

Example: 2. Calculate the median of the following:

Income in Rs :	20	21	22	23	24
No. of Persons :	2	4	4	3	6

Solution:

Income (x)	Frequency (f)	C. frequency (c)
20	2	2
21	4	6
22	4	10
23	3	13
24	6	19

Here N = 19, which is odd.

$\therefore$ Median = Income of $\left(\frac{n+1}{2}\right)$th term

= Income of $\left(\frac{19+1}{2}\right)$th term

= Income of 10th term = Rs 22.

THE MODE

Mode is defined as that item of the series which occurs most frequently. In a frequency distribution, mode is that variable which has the maximum frequency. When we say that average age of Indians is 60 years, it means that model age of the people in India is 60 years *i.e.* most of the people in India die after 60 years.

For example: Find the mode of given set of numbers: 2, 2, 3, 5, 4, 3, 2, 3, 3, 3, 5

Solution: Arranging the number with same value together, we get, 2, 2, 2, 3, 3, 3, 3, 4, 5, 5 mode of this data is 3 because it occurs more frequently then other observations.

In case of grouped data the formula to be used is $l+\frac{f-f_1}{2f-(f_1+f_2)}\times i$

Where l = lower limit of the model class

f = frequency of the model class

f_1 = frequency of the class preceding the model class

f_2 = frequency of the class succeeding of the model class

i = class interval

For example: Find the mode of the following frequency distribution.

Class interval	Frequency
24.5-29.5	1
29.5-34.5	1
34.5-39.5	3
39.5-44.5	4
44.5-49.5	7
49.5-54.5	9
54.5-59.5	3
59.5-64.5	8
64.5-69.5	4

Solution: Mode = $l+\frac{f-f_1}{2f-(f_1+f_2)}\times i$

$= 49.5+\frac{9-7}{2\times 9-7-3}\times 5$

= 49.5 + 1.2 = 50.7.

SOLVED QUESTIONS

Example 1 : The average of 6 numbers is 30. If the average of first 4 numbers is 25 and that of last 3 number is 35, then what is the fourth number?

Solution: Average of 6 numbers = 30

$\therefore$ Total of 6 numbers = 30 × 6 = 180

Again, average of first 4 numbers = 25

$\therefore$ Total of first 4 numbers = 25 × 4 = 100

Again, average of last 3 numbers = 35

$\therefore$ Total of last 3 numbers = 35 × 3 = 105

Hence, the fourth number

= 100 + 105 − 180 = 205 − 180 = 25.

Example 2 : If the average weight of a group of 20 boys was calculated to be 89.4 kg and it was later discovered that one weight was misread as 78 kg instead of the correct one of 87 kg. Then, what is the correct average weight?

Solution: Average weight of 20 boys = 89.4 kg.

$\therefore$Total weight of 20 boys = 89.4 × 20

= 1788 kg

Correct average weight = $\frac{1788-78+87}{20}$

$= \frac{1797}{20} = 89.85$ kg.

Example 3 : What is the average of $1^2, 2^2, 3^2, 4^2, 5^2, 6^2$, and 7^2?

Solution: Average of $1^2, 2^2, 3^2, 4^2, 5^2, 6^2, 7^2$ is

$$A = \frac{1^2+2^2+3^2+4^2+5^2+6^2+7^2}{7}$$

$$= \frac{1}{7}\cdot\frac{7(7+1)(2\times 7+1)}{6}$$

$$= \frac{1}{7}\cdot\frac{7\times 8\times 15}{6} = 20.$$

Example 4 : Find the median for the data : 35, 31, 12, 16, 29, 74, 45, 40, 49, 57, 62.

Solution: Arranging the given scores in the ascending order of magnitude, we have

12, 16, 29, 31, 35, 40, 45, 49, 57, 62, 74

Hence, n = 11 (an odd number)

Hence, median = $\left(\frac{11+1}{2}\right)$th score

$= \left(\frac{12}{2}\right)$th score = 6th score, which is 40.

Hence, median is 40.

Example 5 : Find the median for the data : 29, 34, 11, 17, 36, 21, 46, 23, 39, 41.

Solution: Arranging the given scores in the ascending order of magnitude, we have

11, 17, 21, 23, 29, 34, 36, 39, 41, 46

Here, n = 10 (an even number)

Hence, median = average of middle terms

= average of 5th and 6th terms

$$= \frac{29+34}{2} = \frac{63}{2} = 31.5$$

Hence, median is 31.5.

MULTIPLE CHOICE QUESTIONS

1. The median for the data 205, 170, 131, 174, 153, 142, 147, 157, 196, 148 is:

A. 155 B. 157
C. 170 D. 174

2. The median of the following data is 32.5.

Class Interval	Frequency
0–10	x
10–20	5
20–30	9
30–40	12
40–50	y
50–60	3
60–70	2
Total	**40**

The values of x and y are:

A. 6, 3 B. 3, 6
C. 4, 7 D. 7, 4

3. The mode of the data 12, 6, 7, 6, 9, 12, 6, 8, 6, 4 is:

A. 8 B. 7
C. 6 D. 4

4. The mode of the data 15, 8, 26, 25, 24, 15, 18, 20, 24, 15, 19, 15 is:

A. 15 B. 24
C. 25 D. 26

5. The shirt sizes worn by a group of 200 people, who bought the shirt from a store, are as follows:

Shirt size	37	38	39	40	41	42	43	44
No. of people buying it	15	25	39	41	36	17	15	12

The mode of shirt size worn by the group is:

A. 39 B. 40
C. 41 D. 42

6. A frequency table is a table which displays the manner in which frequencies are distributed over?

A. One class B. Ten classes
C. Several classes D. Class interval

7. The total of frequencies of a particular class and of all classes prior to the particular class is known as:

A. frequency B. cumulative frequency
C. distribution table D. None of the above

8. The sum of upper class limit and lower class limit divided by two is called:

A. Midway value B. True class limits
C. Frequency value D. Class size

9. Class size is the difference between the class marks of two:

A. classes B. alternate classes
C. adjacent classes D. first and last classes

10. If a score is repeated n times in a distribution, then n is called that score's:

A. variate B. frequency
C. variable D. mean

11. A tabular representation in which scores are classified is called:

A. a frequency distribution
B. a discrete series
C. a continuous series
D. a cumulative frequency distribution

12. Information collected by an individual or a group for some study is called:

A. statistics B. data
C. statistical data D. investigation

13. Data collected by an investigator for his personal study is called:

A. primary data B. secondary data
C. list value D. collection

14. Data collected by an investigator for someone else is called:

A. primary data
B. secondary data
C. frequency distribution
D. a continuous distribution

15. Which one of the following is the best job for an investigator?

A. Collection of data
B. Planning of the project
C. Classification of data
D. Tabulation of data

16. The gap between the highest and the lowest score is called:
A. class interval
B. data
C. range
D. length of the class interval

17. Which of the following is not true?
A. Statistics deals with quantitative facts
B. Statistics deals with the individuals
C. Statistics can be misused
D. Statistical results are true on an average

18. The mean of four numbers is 10. When the numbers 6 and 8 are added, the new mean is:
A. 24 B. 17
C. 9 D. 4

19. The arithmetic mean of 16 numbers is 18. One of the numbers namely, 33 is removed. The arithmetic mean of the remaining 15 numbers is:
A. 14 B. 15
C. 17 D. 18

20. The mean of a certain frequency distribution with sample size 20 is 7. If each item is increased by 1.5, the mean of the new distribution will be:
A. 21.5 B. 8.5
C. 5.5 D. 18.5

21. The arithmetic mean of 10 numbers is 20. The arithmetic mean of first 9 numbers is 21. The last number is:
A. 10 B. 11
C. 20 D. 21

22. The arithmetic mean of 20 numbers is 18. One number 60 is added. What is the arithmetic mean of 21 numbers?
A. 18 B. 19
C. 20 D. 21

23. The arithmetic mean of four observations is found to be 120. While calculating this, one observation whose value is 33 is taken as 13. The correct mean is:
A. 115 B. 125
C. 140 D. 153

24. A student was asked to find the arithmetic mean of the following 10 items 4, 15, 9, 7, 13, 18, 14, 12, 6 and x. He found the mean to be 10. He could not read clearly the value in place of x, the value of x he substituted is:
A. 2 B. 12
C. 3 D. 13

25. For the series 2, 5, 7, 8, 12, 14, 17 median is equal to:
A. 4 B. 8
C. 7 D. 5

26. The median of the following items 5, 17, 15, 16, 19, 27, 29 will be:
A. 27 B. 15
C. 19 D. 16

27. The weighted average of the score 35 and 55 is 40. The ratio of the weights attached to the scores is:
A. 3 : 1 B. 1 : 3
C. 7 : 11 D. 15 : 19

28. The mode of the data 25, 26, 27, 30, 25, 26, 25, 34 is:
A. 26 B. 30
C. 27 D. 25

29. The mode of the following data is 1, 5, 3, 4, 5, 3, 4, 3, 7, 1, 3, 4, 3, 8 is:
A. 4 B. 3
C. 5 D. 1

30. The median of ungrouped scores 31, 35, 27, 29, 32, 43, 37, 41, 34, 28, 36, 44, 45, 42, 30 is:
A. 32 B. 35
C. 34 D. 36

31. When the scores are distributed symmetrically around a central point, the best measure of central tendency is:
A. G.M. B. Median
C. Mode D. Mean

32. When the exact mid point of the distribution is wanted, the best measure of central tendency is:
A. G.M. B. Median
C. Mode D. Mean

33. When a quick and approximate measures of central tendency is all that is wanted, it is the:
A. G.M. B. Median
C. Mode D. Mean

34. If the median of a distribution is 23 and mean is 22.5, then the mode is:
A. 23 B. 22.5
C. 24 D. 23.5

35. Calculate the mode, for the following data:

Marks:	50	58	65	68	70	75	78	80
Frequency:	4	6	8	4	5	3	4	1

A. 60 B. 61
C. 63 D. 65

ANSWERS

1	2	3	4	5	6	7	8	9	10
A	B	C	A	B	C	B	A	C	B

11	12	13	14	15	16	17	18	19	20
A	C	A	B	B	C	B	C	C	B
21	**22**	**23**	**24**	**25**	**26**	**27**	**28**	**29**	**30**
B	C	B	A	B	D	A	D	B	B
31	**32**	**33**	**34**	**35**					
D	B	C	C	C					

SOME SELECTED EXPLANATORY ANSWERS

1. Here, $n = 10$

Arranging the given scores in the ascending order of magnitude, we have

131, 142, 147, 148, 153, 157, 170, 174, 196, 205

$$\text{Median} = \frac{\text{Fifth term + Sixth term}}{2}$$

$$= \frac{153+157}{2} = \frac{310}{2} = 155.$$

4. As 15 has been repeated maximum (= 4) number of times. Hence, the mode of the data is 15.

5. From the given table, it is clear that the size 40 has maximum frequency hence 40 is the mode.

MATHEMATICS

SECTION b **PEDAGOGICAL ISSUES**

NATURE OF MATHEMATICS

A systemic goal that needs to be underlined and internalised in the entire system is universal inclusion. This means acknowledging that forms of social discrimination work in the context of mathematics education as well and addressing means for redress. For instance gendered attitudes which consider mathematics to be unimportant for girls, have to be systematically challenged in school. In India, even caste based discrimination manifests in such terms, and the system cannot afford to treat such attitudes by default.

Inclusion is a fundamental principle. Children with special needs, especially children with physical and mental disabilities, have as much right as every other child to learn mathematics, and their needs (in terms of pedagogy, learning material etc) have to be addressed seriously. The conceptual world of mathematics can bring great joy to these children, and it is our responsibility not to deprive them of such education.

What is Mathematics?

Mathematics is the science of measurement and calculations. It is the science of logical reasoning. It is a systematically organised and exact branch of science.

A universal definition of mathematics can not be given due to its immensity (wide extent). Many mathematicians have defined the mathematics as a subject. But they could not even touched the every factors of mathematics.

e.g., ''Mathematics is the science of measurement, quantity and magnitude''.

—Oxford dictionary

''Mathematics may be defined as the subject in which we never know what we are talking about nor wheather what we are saying true.''

—Bertrand Russel

''Mathematics is the language in which God has written the universe.''

—Galeleo

''Mathematics is the study of abstract system built of abstract elements. These elements are not described in concrete fashion.''

—Marshal H. Stone

''Mathematics is a way to settle in mind of children a habit of reasoning.''

—Locke

''Mathematics is the science that draws necessary conclusions.''

—Benjamin Peirce

''As far as the laws of mathematics refer to reality they are not certain; and as far as they are certain, they do not refer to reality.''

—Albert Einstien

According to above definitions, we can conclude that

(*i*) Mathematics is the science that draws necessary conclusions.
(*ii*) It is a systematic, organised and exact branch of science.
(*iii*) It settles in the mind a habit of reasoning.
(*iv*) It is a science of logical reasoning.
(*v*) It is a science of number and calculation also.
(*vi*) Mathematics is the science of space, measurement, magnitude and quantity.
(*vii*) It deals with relationships and quantitative facts.
(*viii*) Mathematics is an abstract experimental and inductive science.

Importance of Mathematics

Mathematical thinking is a very significant factor in a modern society as a habit of mind for its usage at the workplace, business and finance; and for personal decision-making. Mathematics is essential for the prosperity of a nation in providing devices for comprehending science, engineering, technology and other related subjects. It is a very important tool in public decision-making and for involvement in the knowledge economy. Mathematics provides students with great and powerful ways to describe, analyse and transform the world. It has the power to create moments of pleasure and wonder for all students when they solve a problem for the very first time, discover a better solution, or observe hidden links. Pupils who are very good at mathematics and capable of intelligent thinking are able to think independently in applied and abstract ways, and can reason, solve problems and calculate risk. In fact education should always begin with mathematics because it creates well designed brains that are capable of reasoning right. It is even proved that those who have learned math from their childhood should be trusted, for they have procured solid foundation for arguing which becomes to them a kind of second nature.

Mathematics is not a mere subject that prepares students for higher academic attainment or job qualification in the future. It is not all about practicing calculations in algebra, statistics and algorithms that, after all, computers are capable of doing. It is more about how it compels the human brain to formulate problems, theories and methods of solutions. It prepares children to face a variety of simple to multifaceted challenges every human being encounters on a daily basis. Irrespective of your status in life and however basic your skills are, you apply mathematics. Daily activities including the mundane things you do memorizing phone numbers, buying groceries, cooking food, balancing a budget, paying bills, estimating gasoline consumption, measuring distance and managing your time. In the fields of business and economy, including the diverse industries existing around you, basic to complex math applications are crucial.

Anywhere in the world, mathematics is employed as a key instrument in a diversity of fields such as medicine, engineering, natural science, social science, physical science, tech science, business and commerce, etc. Application of mathematical knowledge in every field of study and industry produces new discoveries and advancement of new disciplines. All innovations introduced worldwide, every product of technology that man gets pleasure from is a by product of Science and Math. The ease and convenience people enjoy today from the discoveries of computers, automobiles, aircraft, household and personal gadgets would never have happened if it were not for this essential tool used in technology.

Every branch of Mathematics has distinct applications in different types of careers. The skills enhanced from practicing math such as analyzing patterns, logical thinking, problem solving and the ability to see relationships can help you prepare for your chosen career and enable you to compete for interesting and high-paying jobs against people around the globe. Even if you do not take up math-intensive courses, you have the edge to compete against other job applicants if you have a strong mathematical background, as industries are constantly evolving together with fast-paced technology.

Since mathematics encompasses all aspects of human life, it is unquestionably important in education to help students and all people from all walks of life perform daily tasks efficiently and become productive, well-informed, functional, independent individuals and members of a society where Math is a fundamental component.

NATURE OF MATHEMATICS

Students must understand aims and objectives of the subjects which are included in the curriculum. Because it decides the nature of the subject. Mathematics has an unbreakable and strong position as compared to other subjects. It is more stable and important also than the other subjects which is taught in school curriculum. These are the factors which decide the structure, truthfulness, prediction and reliability of the subject. The nature of mathematics is also determined on the basis of these factors like the other subjects.

Mathematics relies on both logic and creativity, and it is pursued both for a variety of practical purposes and for its intrinsic interest. For some people, and not only professional mathematicians, the essence of mathematics lies in its beauty and its intellectual challenge. For others, including many scientists and engineers, the chief value of mathematics is how it applies to their own work. Because mathematics plays such a central role in modern culture, some basic understanding of the nature of mathematics is requisite for scientific literacy. To achieve this, students need to perceive mathematics as part of the scientific endeavour, comprehend the nature of mathematical thinking, and become familiar with key mathematical ideas and skills.

Mathematics is the science of patterns and relationships. As a theoretical discipline, mathematics explores the possible relationships among abstractions without concern for whether those abstractions have counterparts in the real world. The abstractions can be anything from strings of numbers to geometric figures to sets of equations. In addressing, say, "Does the interval between prime numbers form a pattern?" as a theoretical questions, mathematicians are interested only in finding a pattern or providing that there is none, but not in what use such knowledge might have. In deriving, for instance, an expression for the change in the surface area of any regular solid as its volume approaches zero, mathematicians have no interest in any correspondence between geometric solids and physical objects in the real world.

A central line of investigation in theoretical mathematics is identifying in each field of study a small set of basic ideas and rules from which all other interesting ideas and rules in that field can be logically deduced. Mathematicians, like other scientists, are particularly pleased when previously unrelated parts of mathematics are found to be derivable from one another, or from some more general theory. Part of the sense of beauty that many people have perceived in mathematics lies not in finding the greatest elaborateness or complexity but on the contrary, in finding the greatest economy and simplicity of representation and proof. As mathematics has progressed, more and more relationships have been found between parts of it that have been developed separately—for example, between the symbolic representations of algebra and the spatial representations of geometry. These cross-connections enable insights to be developed into the various parts; together, they strengthen belief in the correctness and underlying unity of the whole structure.

Mathematics is also an applied science. Many mathematicians focus their attention on solving problems that originate in the world of experience. They too search for patterns and relationships, and in the process they use techniques that are similar to those used in doing purely theoretical mathematics. The difference is largely one of intent. In contrast to theoretical mathematicians, applied mathematicians, in the examples numerical information, rather than as an abstract problem. Or they might tackle the area/volume problem as a step in producing a model for the crystal behaviour.

The results of theoretical and applied mathematics often influence each other. The discoveries of theoretical mathematicians frequently turn out—sometimes decades later—to have unanticipated practical value. Studies on the mathematical properties of random events, for example, led to knowledge that later made it possible to improve the design of experiments in the social and natural sciences. Conversely, in trying to solve the problem of billing long-distance telephone users fairly, mathematicians made fundamental discoveries about the mathematics of complex networks. Theoretical mathematics, unlike the other sciences, is not constrained by the real world, but in the long run it contributes to a better understanding of that world.

Because of its abstractness, mathematics is universal in a sense that other fields of human thought are not. It finds useful applications in business, industry, music historical scholarship, politics, sports, medicine, agriculture, engineering, and the social and natural sciences. The relationship between mathematics and the other fields of basic and applied science is especially strong. This is so for several reasons, including the following:

- The alliance between science and mathematics has a long history, dating back many centuries. Science provides mathematics with interesting problems to investigate, and mathematics, provides science with powerful tools to use in analyzing data. Often, abstract patterns that have been studied for their own sake by mathematicians have turned out much later to be very useful in science. Science and mathematics are both trying to discover general patterns and relationships, and in this sense they are part of the same endeavor.
- Mathematics is the chief language of science. The symbolic language of mathematics has turned out to be extremely valuable for expressing scientific ideas unambiguously. The statement that $a = F/m$ is not simply a shorthand way of saying that the acceleration of an object depends on the force applied to it and its mass; rather, it is a precise statement of the quantitative relationship among those variables. More important, mathematics provides the grammar of science—the rules for analyzing scientific ideas and data rigorously.
- Mathematics and science have many features in common. These include a belief in understandable order; and interplay of imagination and rigorous logic; ideas of honesty and openness; the critical importance of peer criticism; the value placed on being the first to make a key discovery; being international in scope; and even, with the development of powerful electronic computers, being able to use technology to open up new fields of investigation.
- Mathematics and technology have also developed a fruitful relationship with each other. The mathematics of connections and logical chains, for example, has contributed greatly to the design of computer hardware and programming techniques. Mathematics also contributes more generally to engineering, as in describing complex systems whose behaviour can then be simulated by computer. In those simulations, design features and operating conditions can be varied as a means of finding optimum designs. For its part,

computer technology has opened up whole new areas in mathematics, even in the very nature of proof, and it also continues to help solve previously daunting problems.

It is not necessary that all subjects should be same nature. Comparatively mathematics has unique nature thus on the basis of which we generally compare it with other subjects. Of course, the basis of comparision of two or more subjects is their nature. Understanding the nature of mathematics may be easy on the basis of following features—

(*i*) Mathematics relies on logic and creativity.

(*ii*) It is pursued for a variety of practical purposes and for its intrinsic interest.

(*iii*) Mathematics plays a central role in modern culture.

(*iv*) It is the science of patterns and relationships.

(*v*) Mathematics explores the possible relationships among abstractions as a theoretical discipline.

(*vi*) It is an applied science.

(*vii*) The result of theoretical and applied mathematics influence each - other.

(*viii*) Mathematics is universal in a sense that other fields of human thought are not.

(*ix*) It finds useful applications in business, music industry, politics, sports, medicines, agriculture, engineering, historical scholarship, social and natural science and many other region of human life.

(*x*) The relationship between mathematics and the other fields of basic and applied science is especially strong.

(*xi*) Mathematics is the chief language of science.

(*xii*) Mathematics and science have many common features.

(*xiii*) It involves conversion of abstract concepts into concrete form.

(*xiv*) It draws numerical inferences on the basis of given information and data.

(*xv*) Mathematical rules, law and formulae are universal.

(*xvi*) It has its own language and the language is well defined useful and clear. The language consists mathematical terms, concepts, formulae, theories, principles and signs etc.

(*xvii*) It helps to develop the habit of self confidence and self reliance.

(*xviii*) It provides doubtless and errorless theories, principles, concepts etc.

(*xix*) It helps in the development of sense of appreciation and scientific attitude.

(*xx*) It provides the training of scietific method.

(*xxi*) It provides accurate and reliable knowledge based on sense-organs.

Now, we can understand the nature of mathematics and conclude that really the structure of mathematics is the basis of its nature. It is stronger than the other subjects. Roger Becon has also said that Mathematics is the gateway and key of all sciences.

LOGICAL THINKING

Logical thinking is the process in which one uses reasoning consistently to come to a conclusion. Problems or situations that involve logical thinking call for structure, for relationships between facts, and for chains of reasoning that make sense.

According to Dr. Karl Albrecht sequential thought is the basis of all logical thinking. The process involves taking the important ideas, facts, and conclusions involved in a problem and arranging them in a chain-like progresssion that takes on a meaning in and of itself. To think logically is to think in steps.

It has been proven that specific training in logical thinking processes can make people smarter. Logical thinking allows a child to reject quick answers, such as "I don't know," or "this is too difficult," by empowering them to delve deeper into their thinking processes and understand better the methods used to arrive at a solution and even the solution itself.

Logical thinking is also an important foundational skill of math. Learning mathematics is a highly sequential process. If you don't grasp a certain concept, fact, or procedure, you can never hope to grasp others that come later, which depend upon it. For example, to understand fractions you must first understand division. To understand simple equations in algebra requires that you understand fractions. Solving 'world problems' depends on knowing how to set up and manipulate equations, and so on.

Logical thinking is not a magical process or a matter of genetic endowment, but a learned mental process.

One of the aims of the mathematics is to teach a child to think logically. Logical thinking exercises are carefully graded. For example, in the first example of *Logical Thinking exercise* a child would be asked to arrange a sequence of coloured blocks in front of them, from left to right.

One would then ask the child : "If you had to add one more colour to the above sequence, which colour would you choose?" The answer, of course, is dark.

PLACE OF MATHEMATICS IN CURRICULUM

"Science and Mathematics should be taught on a compulsory basis to all pupils as a part of general education during first ten years of schooling.

—Kothari Commission (1964-66)

"The progress of Mathematics is linked to the prosperity of the state."

—Nepolean

"Mathematics is a queen of all sciences without any king."

—Unknown

Mathematics is most important subject in curriculum. Actually except our mother tongue there is no other subject which is such closely related to our daily life but mathematics. Now-a-days it has been given an important position in curriculum. Because it not only has the utility in daily life but also the social and cultural importance. It is helpful in the development of mental descipline. Mathematics has own desciplinary value and it does not need any special evaluation or testing to get a place in curriculum. When one sends his or her child to school he or she generally expects that the child will be able to cash the knowledge, skills, attitude and ideas. Parents expects that the child will earn intellectual habits and different powers *i.e.* discipline, value, morality etc. Of course matematics helps the child to achieve the aforesaid qualities. Moreover there are many advantage of giving due importance to mathematics and making it compulsory subject.

CURRICULUM EXPECTATIONS

The expectations identified for each course describe the knowledge and skills that students are expected to acquire, demonstrate, and apply in their class work, on tests, and in various other activities on which their achievement is assessed and evaluated. Two sets of expectations are listed for each strand, or broad curriculum area, of each course.

- The overall expectations describe in general terms the knowledge and skills that students are expected to demonstrate by the end of each course.
- The specific expectations describe the expected knowledge and skills in greater detail. The specific expectations are arranged under subheadings that reflect particular aspects of the required knowledge and skills and that may serve as a guide for teachers as they plan learning activities for their students. The organization of expectations in subgroupings is not meant to imply that the expectations in any subgroup are achieved independently of the expectations in the other subgroups. The subheadings are used merely to help teachers focus on particular aspects of knowledge and skills as they develop and present various lessons and learning activities for their students.

PLACE OF MATHEMATICS IN CURRICULUM

Everybody stands in need of some knowledge of mathematics. But in the case of an ordinary citizen, it is felt that the knowledge acquired during the primary and middle stage will suffice. Consequently there is some controversy over the place of mathematics in the school curriculum.

Some people are also of the view that mathematics is an exceptionally difficult subject, *i.e.,* its study demands special ability and intelligence. It is felt that everybody is not able enough to learn it successfully. Therefore, everybody should not be burdened with the study of this tough subject. References are also made to low pass percentage and heavy failures in this subjects in examinations. These poor results also support the view that mathematics should be made an optional subject.

There appears some justification for the view that mathematics should be made an optional subject at the high school stage. Since mathematics is primarily taught for its disciplinary value and mental discipline being a myth, no mathematics need be taught beyond the middle school stage.

It is also true that mathematics is indispensable in various sciences and professions. But everybody is not going to become an engineer or a statistician. Only those who have to go to such vocations may continue to study it. There is no need of burdening an average student with the study of this subjects, especially when an average citizen can lead to a successful life with the help of an elementary knowledge of mathematics and without any specialised or advanced knowledge in it.

If we take a broader view of the situation, we can infer that the belief of the critics is erroneous.

So far as the need of special ability in the learning of mathematics is concerned, it has been established with the help of experiments that in mathematics more of general intelligence (G) than specific ability (S) is needed.

Mathematics is a useful subject for most of the vocations and specialised courses. Although everybody studying in the school is not going to become an engineer or a scientist, but at a very early stage, it may not be possible to determine finally as to who is not going to join a profession like that. Therefore, the duty of the school is to give to the high school student a broad view of what he is capable of achieving in future. He should get a broader view of what he is capable of achieving in future. To deprive the student of the knowledge of this subject at the high school stage means narrowing the choice of semi-vocational courses, preparatory courses, vocational courses and vocations for him. Ignorance of mathematics will be a great handicap in the way of his future studies and occupations.

Educationists have begun to feel that education upto middle standard is not sufficient for the citizen of today. The period of compulsory education needs to be extended from the middle to the high school standard. After this extension of the period of compulsory education from eight to ten or eleven years, mathematics will have to be retained as a compulsory subject for as many number of years.

When foreigners talk of making this subject optional, they do so on a different fotting. Their pupils are two years older at the high school stage. In India, the pupils at high school stage are too young and immature to choose subjects and vocations for themselves. The parents being mostly illiterate are also not in a position to make any final choice at this stage regarding the future education and occupation.

While keeping it compulsory the interests of both types of students will have to be safeguarded. So the syllabus shall contain such subject matter as it useful for those who are going to discontinue their education after the high school stage and are entering into life. It shall also contain such knowledge as elucidates mathematical principles and processes so that the students who will later join a university course, shall not feel handicapped because of sudden rise in standard.

However, there cannot be any two opinions about the necessity of diversification and specialization in the final year of the higher secondary school stage. Here mathematics has to be treated as an optional or specialized subject like other subject of study.

The unprecedented changes that are taking place in today's world will profoundly affect the future of today's students. To meet the demands of the world in which they will live, students will need to adapt to changing conditions and to learn independently. They will require the ability to use technology effectively and the skills for processing large amounts of quantitative information. Today's mathematics curriculum must prepare students for their future roles in society. It must equip them with essential mathematical knowledge and skills; with skills of reasoning, problem solving, and communication; and, most importantly, with the ability and the incentive to continue learning on their own. This curriculum provides a framework for accomplishing these goals.

The choice of specific concepts and skills to be taught must take into consideration new applications and new ways of doing mathematics. The development of sophisticated yet easy-to-use calculators and computers is changing the role of procedure and technique in mathematics. Operations that were an essential part of a procedures-focused curriculum for decades can now be accomplished quickly and effectively using technology, so that students can now solve problems that were previously too time-consuming to attempt, and can focus on underlying concepts. "In an effective mathematics program, students learn in the presence of technology. Technology should influence the mathematics content taught and how it is taught. Powerful assistive and enabling computer and handheld technologies should be used seamlessly in teaching, learning, and assessment." This curriculum integrates appropriate technologies into the learning and doing of mathematics, while recognizing the continuing importance of students' mastering essential numeric and algebraic skills...

The development of mathematical knowledge is a gradual process. A coherent and continuous program is necessary to help students see the "big pictures", or underlying principles, of mathematics... These courses reflect the belief that students learn mathematics effectively when they are initially given opportunities to investigate ideas and concepts and are then guided carefully into an understanding of the abstract mathematics involved...

A balanced mathematics program at the secondary level includes the development of algebraic skills. This curriculum has been designed to equip students with the algebraic skills they need to understand other aspects of mathematics that they are learning, to solve meaningful problems, and to continue to meet with success as they study mathematics in the future. The algebraic skills required in each course have been carefully chosen to support the other topics included in the course. Calculators and other appropriate technology will be used when the primary purpose of a given activity is the development of concepts or the solving of problems, or when situations arise in which computation or symbolic manipulation is of secondary importance.

WHY MATHEMATICS IS KEPT IN CURRICULUM?

Before starting to teach a particular subject it is essential to know why we are goint to teach the subject. Aimlessness makes a work uninteresting and it is wastage of time, energy and other resourses. Hence we first determine aims and objectives of a work. Thus, teaching mathematics also has some aims and objectives. Because aimless teaching of mathematics may be uninteresting and it will be wastage of time, energy and other resourses for both the pupil and the teacher. Some aims of teaching mathematics are as follows—

(*i*) To develop their intellectual powers and disciplines.

(*ii*) To enable to make use of the learning in mathematics in their daily life.

(*iii*) To help the student in recieving social and moral virtues.

(*iv*) To help in the study of other subjects and future learning in mathematics.

(*v*) To give the insight to recognise relationships between different branches and topics of mathematics.

(*vi*) To meet this different interests, to develop their aesthetic abilities and to help them in their power of utilisation of their leisure time.

(*vii*) To help them in becoming self-dependent for mastering new topics and problems of mathematics.

(*viii*) To make them understand the contribution of mathematics in the development of culture and civilizaiton.

(*ix*) To prepare for the future vocation or occupation.

LANGUAGE OF MATHEMATICS

WHAT IS A LANGUAGE?

Here are some definitions of language:

1. A set (finite or infinite) of sentences, each finite in length and constructed out of a finite set of element —Noam Chomsky
2. The code we all use to express ourselves and communicate to others—Speech & Language Therapy Glossary of Terms
3. A systematic means of communicating by the use of sounds or conventional symbols —Word Net
4. A system of words used in a particular discipline —Word Net

These definitions describe language in terms of the following components:

- A vocabulary of symbols or words
- a grammar consisting or rules or how these symbols may be used
- A community of people who use and understand these symbols
- A range of meanings that can be communicated with these symbols

Each of these components also found in the language of mathematics.

The language of mathematics is the system used by mathematicians to communicate mathematical ideas among themselves. This language consists of a substrate of some natural language (for example English) using technical terms and grammatical conventions that are peculiar to mathematical discourse, supplemented by a highly specialized symbolic notation for mathematical formulas.

Like natural languages in general, discourse using the language of mathematics can employ a scala of registers. Research article in academic journals use a more formal tone than oral exchanges over a scribbled-upon napkin in the university cafeteria.

THE VOCABULARY OF MATHEMATICS

Mathematical notation has assimilated symbols from many different alphabets and typefaces. It also includes symbols that are specific to mathematics, such as $\forall\exists\nabla\wedge\infty$

Mathematical notation is central to the power of modern mathematics. Though the algebra of Al-Khwarizmi did not use such symbols, it solved equations using many more rules than are used today with symbolic notation, and had great difficulty working with multiple variables (which using symbolic notation can simply be called *x, y, z*, etc.). Sometimes formulas cannot be understood without a written or spoken explanation, but often they are sufficient by themselves, and sometimes they are difficult to read aloud or information is lost in the translation to words, as when several parenthetical factors are involved or when a complex structure like a matrix is manipulated.

Like any other profession, mathematics also has its own brand of technical terminology. In some cases, a word in general usage has a different and specific meaning within mathematics—example are group, ring, field, category, term, and factor etc.

In other cases, specialist terms have been created which do not exist outside of mathematics—examples are tensor, fractal, functor. Mathematical statements have their own moderately complex taxonomy, being divided into axioms, conjectures, theorems, lemmas and corollaries. And there are stock phrases in mathematics, used with specific meanings, such as "*if and only if*", "*necessary and sufficient*" and "*without loss of generality*". Such phrases are known as mathematical jargon.

When mathematicians communicate with each other informally, they use phrases that help to convey ideas. Examples of some of the more idiomatic phrases are "kill this term", "vanish this interval" and "grow this variable".

The vocabulary of mathematics also has visual elements. Diagrams are used informally on blackboards, as well as more formally in published work. When used appropriately, diagrams display schematic information more easily. Diagrams also help visually and aid intuitive calculations. Sometimes, as in a visual proof, a diagram even serves as complete justification for a proposition. A system of diagram conventions may evolve into a mathematical notation.

THE GRAMMAR OF MATHEMATICS

The grammar used for mathematical discourse is essentially the grammar of the natural language used as substrate, but with several mathematics-specific peculiarities.

Most notably, the mathematical notation used for formulas has its own grammar, not dependent on a specific natural language, but shared internationally by mathematicians regardless of their mother tongues. This includes the conventions that the formulas are written predominantly left to right, also when the writing system of the substrate language is right-to-left, and that the Latin alphabet is commonly used for simple variables and parameters. A formula such as

$\sin x + a \cos 2x \geq 0$ is understood by Chinese and Israeli mathematicians alike.

Such mathematical formulas can be a part of speech in a natural-language phrases, or even assume the role of a full-fledged sentence. For example, the formula above, an equation, can be considered a sentence or sentential phrase in which the greater than or equal to symbol has the role of a verb. In careful speech, this can be made clear by pronouncing "$\geq$" as "is greater than or equal to", but in an informal context mathematicians may shorten this to "greater or equal" and yet handle this grammatically like a verb.

Mathematical formulas can be vocalized (spoken aloud). The vocalization system for formulas has to be learned, and is dependent on the underlying natural language. For example, when using English, the expression "$f(x)$" is conventionally pronounced "eff of eks", where the insertion of the preposition "of" is not suggested by the notation per se. The expression "$\frac{dy}{dx}$" on the other hand, is vocalized like "dee-why-dee-eks", with complete omission of the fraction bar, in other contexts often pronounced "over".

Characteristic for mathematical discourse – both formal and informal – is the use of the inclusive first person plural "we" to mean: "the audience (or reader) together with the speaker (or author)".

THE LANGUAGE COMMUNITY OF MATHEMATICS

Mathematics is used by mathematicians, who form a global community composed of speakers of many languages. It is also used by students of mathematics. As mathematics is a part of primary education in almost all countries almost all educated people have some exposure to pure mathematics. It is interesting to note that there are very few cultural dependencies or barriers in modern mathematics. There are international mathematics competitions, such as the International Mathematical Olympiad, and international co-operation between professional mathematicians in commonplace.

MATHEMATICS IS A LANGUAGE

"My own attitude, which I share with many of my colleagues is simply that mathematics is a language. Like English, Latin or Chinese, these are certain concepts for which mathematics is particularly well suited, it would be as foolish to attempt to write a love poem the fundamental theorem of Algebra using the English language."

—RLE Schwarzenberger (2000)

Mathematics can communicate a range of meanings that is as wide as (althought different from) that of a natural language. Here are there broad categories:

- **Mathematics describes the real world:** Many areas of mathematics originated with attempts to describe and solve real world phenomena from measuring farms (geometry) to falling apples (calculus) to gambling (probability). Mathematics is widely used in modern physics and engineering, and has been hugely successful in helping us to understand more about the universe around us from its largest scales (physical cosmology) to its smallest (quantum mechanics). Indeed, the very success of mathematics in this respect has been a source of puzzlement for some philosophers.
- **Mathematics describes abstract structures:** On the other hand, there are areas of pure mathematics which deal with abstract structures, which have no known physical counterparts at all. However, it is difficult to give any categorical examples here, as even the most abstract structures can be co-opted as models in some branch of physics.
- **Mathematics describes mathematics:** Mathematics can be used reflexively to describe itself—this is an area of mathematics called metamathematics.

As a language mathematics has own symbols, word and rules of sentence. Which is based on a certian consistant set of assumptions and built up from there according to the rules of logic. Such logic is necessary for developing mathematical thought. It's understanding and applications depend upon the level of development of ordinary language. *e.g.,* ''Every rectangle is a parallelogram but every parallelogram is not a rectangle. Here, only after developing the use of conjuctions *i.e.* but, hence, so therefore, or and etc. the children become ready for or ordinary language are also used in mathematics. But these words have an exact mathematical meaning. For example — sum, difference, addition, power, multiplication, division, subtraction etc.

The Language of Mathematics

The Language of Mathematics was designed so we can write about:

1. Things like Numbers, Sets, Functions, etc.
2. What we do with those things (add, subtract, multiply, divide, join together, etc)

Symbols

Mathematics uses symbols instead of words:

- There are the 10 digits: 0, 1, 2,...9
- There are symbols for operations: $+ - \times /$
- And symbols that ''stand in'' for values x, y,...
- And many special symbols: $= < \leq$, ...

Letter Conventions

Often (but not always) letters have special uses:

	Examples	What they usually mean
Start of the alphabet:	a, b, c, ...	constants (fixed values)
From i to n:	i, j, k, ..., n	positive integers (for counting)
End of the alphabet:	...x, y, z	(variables unknowns)

Those are no rules, but they are often used that way.

Example:

$$y = ax + b$$

People would assume that a and b are fixed values.

And that x is the one that changes, which in turn makes y change.

Nouns, Verbs, Sentences

Even though we don's actually use the words ''noun'', ''verb'', or ''pronoun'' in Mathematics, it might help you understand Mathematics by thinking about its similarlies to English.

Nouns

Nouns could be fixed things, such as numbers, or expressions with numbers

15   2(3-1/2) 4^2

Verbs

And the verb could be the equals sign ''='', or may be an inequality like $<$ or $>$

Pronouns

In English pronouns are things that stand in for nouns (it, he, you, etc). In Mathematics they could be variables like x or y:

5x-7 xy^2 -3/x

Sentence

And they could be put together into a sentence like this:

$$3x + 7 = 22$$

(And we actually do use the word sentence in mathematics)

Alternative views

Some definitions of language, emphasize the spoken nature of language. Mathematics would not qualify as a language under these definitions, as it is primarily a written form of communication. However, these definitions would also disqualify sign languages, which are now recognized as languages in their own right, independent of spoken language.

Other linguists believe no valid comparison can be made between mathematics and language, because they are simply too different.

EVALUATION

Education is concerned with preparing citizens for a meaningful and productive life, and evaluation should be a way of providing credible feedback on the extent to which we have been successful in imparting such an education. Seen from this perspective, current process of evaluation, which measure and assess a very limited range of faculties, are highly inadequate and do no provide a complete picture of an individual's abilities or progress towards fulfilling the aims of education.

But even this limited purpose of evaluation, of providing feedback on scholastic and academic development, can be achieved only if the teacher is prepared even before the course of teaching begins, armed with not only the techniques of assessment but also the parameters for evaluation and the various tools that will be employed. In addition to judging the quality of the students' achievements, a teacher would also need to collect, analyse and interpret their performances on various measures of the assessment to come to an understanding of the extent and nature of the students' learning in different domains. The purpose of assessment is necessarily to improve the teaching-learning process and materials, and to be able to review the objectives that have been identified for different school stages by guaging the extent to which the capabilities of learners have been developed. Needless to say, this does not mean that tests and examinations will have to conducted frequently. On the contrary, routine activities and exercises can be employed effectively to assess learning.

WHAT IS EVALUATION?

"Evaluation is systematic, continuous process of determining the effectiveness of the learning experiences provided in the class room."

—NCERT

"Evaluation is a continuous process; it forms an integral part of the total system of education and is intimately related to educational objectives. It exercises a good influence on pupils study habits and the teacher's methods of instruction and thus helps not only to measure educational achievement but also to improve it. The techniques of evaluation are means of collecting evidences about the students' development in desirable directions."

—Kothari Commission

"Evaluation is relatively a new technical term, introduced to designate a more comprehensive concept of measurement that is implied in conventional test and examinations."

—The Encyclopaedia of Education Research

"Evaluation may be defined as a systematic process of determining the extent to which educational objectives are achieved by the pupils."

—Dandekar

"Evaluation is an inclusive concept which indicates all kinds of means to ascertain the quality, value and effectiveness of desired outcomes. It is a compound of objective evidence and objective observation. It is total and final estimate. It is a valuable, an indispensable guide to the modification of policies and to further action." —Wesley

Evaluation is consistently identified in the professional literature as both a critical component and a weak link in the delivery of professional development, but it must not be overlooked. Any effective evaluation should concern itself with changes that take place in instructional practices.

Both formal and informal methods of evaluation can be employed in determining the impact of the Workshop/Presentation on instructional behaviour. More formal methods use some type of instrument to assess changes in instructional behaviour, before and after the workshop. Practitioners can complete self-evaluations, or a peer or supervisor can complete an evaluation instrument after classroom observations. Analysis of the completed instruments enables practitioners and supervisors to identify areas of strength and weakness and to work on improving instruction. Other less formal or more qualitative approaches include maintaining records/journals of an instructor's own reflections of what occurs in the classroom, or conducting ethnographic studies that describe what happens in the classroom when new instructional strategies are implemented.

In the Indian education system, the term evaluation is associated with examination, stress and anxiety. All efforts at curriculum definition and renewal come to naught if they cannot engage with the bulwark of the evaluation and examination system embedded in schooling. We are concerned about the ill effects that examinations have on efforts to make learning and teaching meaningful and joyous for children. Currently, the board examinations negatively influence all testing and assessment through out the school years, beginning with pre-school.

At the same time, a good evaluation and examination system can become an integral part of the learning process and benefit both the learners themselves and the educational system by giving credible feedback. This section addresses evaluation and assessment as they are relevant to the normal course of teaching-learning in the school, as a part of the curriculum.

RELATIONSHIP BETWEEN OBJECTIVES, LEARNING EXPERIENCES AND EVALUATION

The objectives, learning experiences and evaluation are all interrelated to each other. Evaluation is based on objectives of teaching and learning experiences and also evaluates the objectives at the same time. Thus, in the classroom teaching the teacher organises suitable teaching- learning activities in order to promote desired expected changes in behaviour. It is much broader term than text or examination. It concerned not only with assessment of the students but also with the whole process of education. After

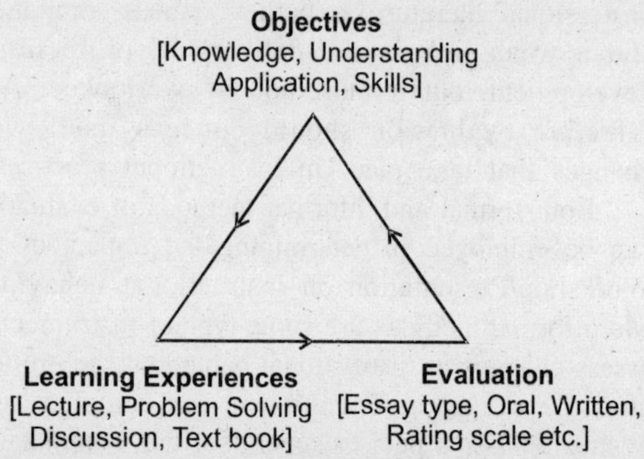

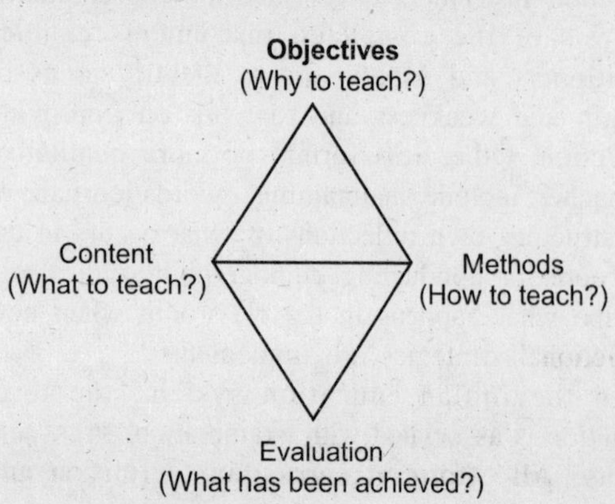

deciding what to teach? (content) and how to teach? (Methods). Why to teach? (object). The question arises what has been achieved? Thus evaluation helps to answer the question what has been achieved by the student? Thus evaluation is the process through which assessment, achievement and effectiveness of educational programme is determined.

PURPOSE & FUNCTION OF EVALUATION

1. **Motivation :** To motivate the children for better learning.
2. **Present Status of the Children :** Evaluation helps in determining the present status of the children in the teaching-learning process.
3. **Guidance and Counselling :** Evaluation provides basis for guidance and counselling to children, by recognising individual differences of children.
4. **To Diagnose the Problems :** Evaluating procedures help the teacher to know the shortcomings of his students, and to diagnose children's weaknesses and strength for further instructions.
5. **Measure Examination System :** Evaluation helps the teacher to measure examination system *i.e.* the topper in the class or failure in the class, etc.
6. **Rate of Progress in Children :** Evaluation helps to determine the rate of progress in children *i.e.* how much marks did Ritu achieved in her 1st term examination and final examinations etc.
7. **Classification of Students :** Evaluation helps in the classification of students into different categories *i.e.* gifted, backward or average students.
8. **Basis for Selection :** With the help of various aptitude and attitude test for selection in various course of study, placement etc. evaluation plays a vital role.
9. **Discover Innovative and Effective Teaching Methods :** Evaluation helps to discover innovative and effective teaching methods by diagnosing children's weakness and strengths.
10. **Improvement in Curriculum :** By evaluation the teacher collect evidences for improvement in curriculum.
11. **Success in Teaching :** Evaluation helps the teacher to assess the success in her teaching.
12. **Improvement in Teaching-learning Process :** Evaluation helps to know the teacher the weaknesses of the student and on those base she brings improvements in teaching-learning process.

13. **Grading the Students :** Evaluation helps in grading the students on the basis of their quarterly, half-yearly and annual examinations and thus knowing the rank of the students of a class.
14. To measure behavioural changes of the children *i.e.* their interest, physical, emotional, moral and social development, etc.
15. **Encourage Teachers for Action Research :** The teacher adopt new strategies for action research on the basis of evaluation.
16. **Feedback to Teacher & Students :** Evaluation helps to give reinforcement and feedback to both the teacher and pupils.
17. **For Remedial Work :** Evaluation helps the students to find out remedies for the problems, so that better results can be achieved.
18. **Clarification of Objectives of Education :** Evaluation is based on objectives. The teacher tries to understand the objectives of each topic in the light of their utility in education.
19. **Basis of Admission :** The students's progress is evaluated by various method *i.e.* tests, annual examination and on its basis the students is given admission in the next class.
20. **In Giving Scholarships :** Evaluation helps in judging the progress of the students and on the basis of this scholarships are provided to students with very high grade.

IMPORTANT FEATURES OF EVALUATION

1. It may be used to emprove curriculum, instructions, methods and examination etc.
2. It is diagnostic so that it may provide basis for remedial teaching.
3. It measures the direction and extent behavioural change.
4. Evaluation offers feedback to the entire educational system.
5. It is pupil oriented and activity based programme.
6. It is directly related with the teaching process.
7. It is continuous process.
8. It helps in determining the potentialities and interests of children.
9. It not only measures the educational achievement of the students but also helps in their progress.
10. There is a close relationship between instructional objectives, teaching process and evaluation.
11. It is helpful to a teacher in diagnosing children's difficulties.
12. It makes the reaching-learning process dynamic and innovative.
13. It is a wider concept than testing examination and measurement.
14. It becomes easy to know the present status of the children from their day-to-day record.
15. Evaluation is comprehensive (complete) as it includes everything that can be evaluated.
16. Evaluation is systematic and scientific.
17. Evaluation is both quantitative and qualitative aspects.
18. It is a judgment giving process.
19. Evaluation makes education purpose-centred.
20. Evaluation is concerned with growth and development of the student and not with the status in the group.

PROCESS OF EVALUATION

Evaluation process involves the following steps:

1. Selection and formulation of objectives.
2. Defining objectives in terms of behavioural changes.
3. Selection of tools and techniques of evaluation.
4. Interpretation and generalisation of results.
5. Feedback the results for improvement of teaching learning process.

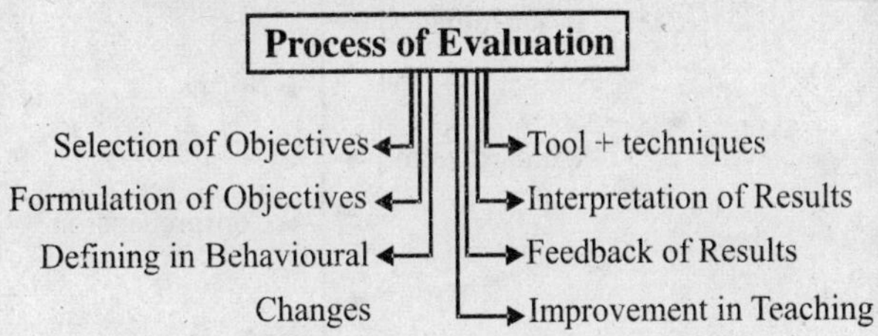

1. **Selection and Formulation of Objectives :** The objectives to be tested are selected in advance before conducting evaluation. The teacher must be very careful in the instructions. On the basis of instructions for objectives given the test items are constructed.
2. **Formulation of Objectives :** A teacher has to be very careful about the instructional objectives of various classes and on that basis of the objective specified various test items are formed for various classes, etc.
3. **Defining Objectives in Behavioural Terms :** After determining and formulation of objectives to be tested teacher should define the objectives clearly in terms of expected changes in pupils' behaviour *i.e.*

(a) Knowledge
(b) Understanding
(c) Application
(d) Skills

4. **Selection of Tools and Techniques of Evaluation :** Selection of suitable tools and techniques depends upon the types of evidence required. Tools and techniques must provide evidence to the teaching objectives to which they are concerned. They should also satisfy criteria of a good measuring rod or good evaluation.
5. **Use of Tools and Techniques and Making Results :** After selecting and developing the tools, teacher applies them in testing situations, she scores or other evidence regarding the behavioural changes are recorded. On the basis of recorded evidences and information conclusions are drawn.
6. **Interpretation and Generalisation of Results :** The evidence which we get through various tools and technique of evaluation are not meaningful to the learner, the teacher or the parents unless the scores are i terpreted properly. Then the results are analysed in terms of objective to rate the progress of an individuals's comparative performance in the class. This collected data helps to generalise the level of achievements required for each class or individual student etc.
7. **Feedback of the Results for Improvement of Teaching Learning Process :** On the basis of analysis of test results or evidences recorded, pupil's progress is made and shown to the parents. This is necessary for parents to know child's self-evaluation strengths and weakness of their ward for proper diagnosis.
8. **Improvements in Teaching-Learning Process:** On the basis of the feedback of the results, and after for diagnostic measures, re-teaching and remedial teaching is arranged and the teacher tries to adopt some new strategies in her teaching-learning process for better achievements in student's progress.

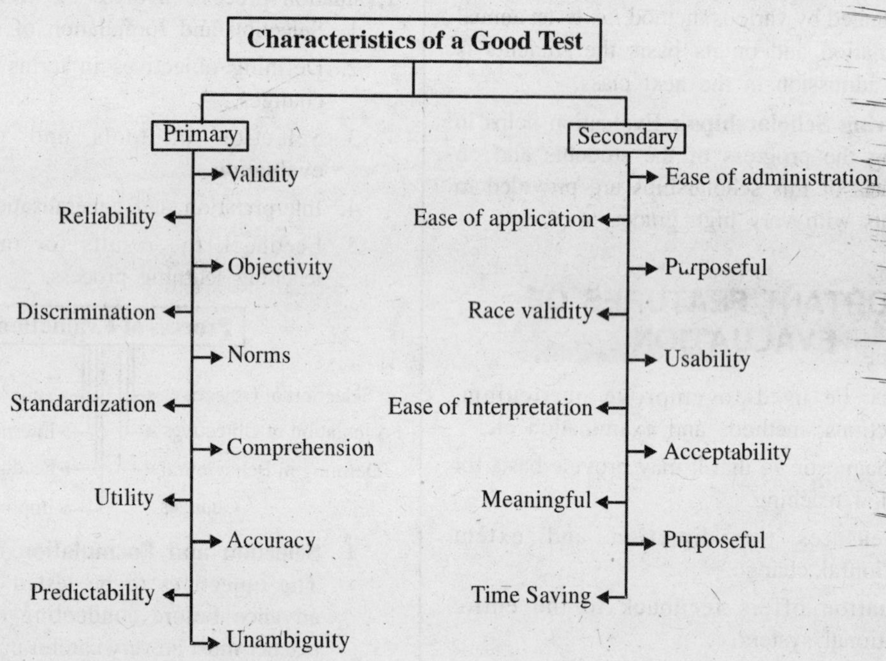

BASIC PRINCIPLES OF EVALUATION

The foundation or base of any building should be very strong, if the building is very beautiful but the foundation or base *i.e.* the pillars on which the building stands are weak, the building will collapse. Similarly, if evaluation is not based on certain basic principles, the evaluation system cannot said to be effective and teaching aims will not be achieved. Some of the basic principles of evaluation are:

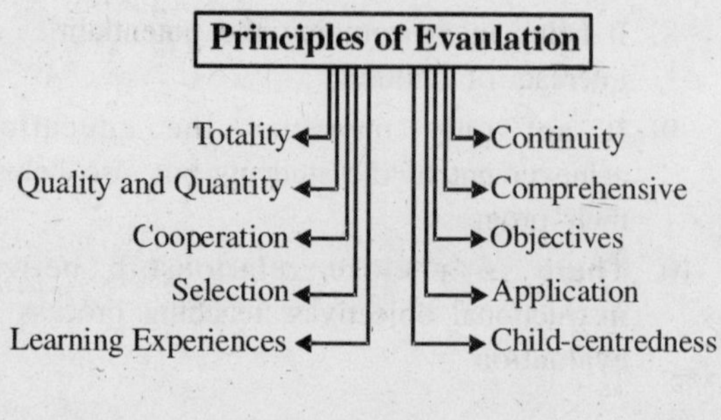

TYPES OF EVALUATION

1. Diagnostic Evaluation
2. Prognosis Evaluation
3. Formative Evaluation
4. Summative Evaluation
5. Comprehensive Evaluation
6. Continuous Evaluation

FORMATIVE EVALUATION

When a teacher has taught a part of unit or some topics or content or any learning concepts he or she wants to judge the outcome of the students. In the same manner the student also need to know their progress in the path of learning. The formative evaluation is a great help to the teacher as well as student as it provides the information to both about the strength and weakness of their teaching and learning.

The term formative means the ongoing or systematic assessment of student's achievement in the course of teaching programme. Formative evaluation occurs between the formative stage that it when the process of teaching and learning is going on and not after it is completed.

According to New Education Policy (1986)— Formative evaluation is an integral part of teaching-learning process. The formative evaluation also is helpful in the process of curriculum construction at the formative stage.

The formative evaluation is carried out both in formal [*i.e.*, question-answer, assignments, tests, quizzes, draft-work, concept maps, peer response, groups porfolio, reviews, conference etc) as well as informal (*e.g.*, listening students comments, conversations, observations etc.)

Features/Need/Importance of Formative Evaluation

1. **Minimum Level of Learning :** The formative evaluation can be used by the teachers to ensure that the minimum levels of learning are attained by all children in the classroom teaching.
2. **Monitor the Teaching Process :** The purpose of formative evaluation is to monitor the teaching process to know that learning process is taking place or not.
3. **Enhance Teaching Learning Process :** It is mainly meant to enhance the teaching-learning process and not designed to make final judgements.
4. **Pupils Weaknesses Diagnosed :** Pupils weaknesses are diagnosed throughout in the process of classroom teaching. Hence formative evaluation is a continuous feedback to both the teacher and the student determining the success and failure of learning.
5. **Feedback to Students and Teacher :** On one side formative evaluation provides feedback to the children and on the other hand it provides feedback to the teacher also and can modify her teaching process accordingly.
6. **Monitoring Pupil's Learning Process :** It is helpful in monitoring pupils learning progress.
7. **Helps to Increase Retention :** It makes easy for the students and helps to increase retention and transfer of learning of the unit or topic being taught.
8. **Self Evaluation :** Formative evaluation can also be used as a self-evaluation. Can also be used as a self-evaluation devices by the children.
9. **Correcting Learning Deficiencies :** It also helps the teacher for correcting her learning deficiencies and weaknesses.
10. **Keep Students Attentive :** Formative test also keep the students attentive.
11. **Immediate Decision Making :** Formative evaluation is most useful for the immediate decision making that students face.
12. **Variety of Techniques Used :** This is a continuous and integral part of teaching where one uses variety of techniques *i.e.* attitude, aptitude, inventories, rating scale, checklists, etc. and alert listeners, and students remain informative for the topic being taught.
13. **Assimilation of Various Concepts :** Formative evaluation determines how well the students are assimilating various concepts, skills and behavioural changes.
14. **Helps to Improve Instructional Behaviour :** Formative evaluation helps to improve the instructional behaviour in the development phase, rather than being in trouble over its failure after the programme is completed.
15. **No Reason for Failure :** When student is continuously evaluated and guided through formative evaluation, there is no reason for the failure in the final summative evaluation.

SUMMATIVE EVALUATION

When the students become fully familiar with the whole syllabus, summative evaluation is conducted. Thus summative evaluation occurs in the end of the academic year session to declare pass/fail of the student result and on that basis they are promoted to new classes.

The turm summative means to assigning a grade for students achievement at the end of a term of the teaching programme. Such type of evaluation is carried out at the end of a lesson or unit, and it represent a find test or measure of the students progress made by him as the result of his progress of teaching.

Thus where formative evaluation reaches its last stage. There is an urgent need of summative evaluation. It occurs at the end of a term or a sesson to measure the success of students and to know what has been achieved by him. For summative evaluation both types of techniques *i.e.*, formal and informal techniques may be used. The formal techniques includes—standardised as well as teacher made test, questionaire, interviews, rating scale, assignments etc. Internal techniques include—observations, discussions, comments and feedback given by the student etc.

Features/Need/Importance of Summative Evaluation

1. **Final Progress :** It tells about the final progress of the students as a result after the course of full units or topic.
2. **Feedback is Less :** Interaction of the teacher and pupil is very limited and the feedback is much less as compared to formative evaluation.
3. **End of the Academic Year :** It occurs at the end of the academic year of the session.
4. **Declared Pass or Fail :** The students are declared pass or fail on the basis of summative evaluation and on its basis they are promoted to new classes.
5. **Examination Conducted :** It is in the form of annual examination, terminal examination, external examination (board examination *i.e.* CBSE etc.).
6. **Promotion of Students :** Helps in the classification of grades and promotion of students.
7. **End of Course :** It is treated as an end of the course activity.
8. **Results Help to Choose Career :** The result of the students helps them to choose their careers, placements and are predictions for their future success.

On the basis of above description it is clear that formal and informal methods are techniques which are equally used in formative and summative evaluation. But objectives of the techniques are different in both the evaluations.

Why Evaluate?

Effective teachers use a variety of means, some formal and others informal, to determine how much and how well their students are learning. For example, to formally evaluate student learning, most teachers use quizzes, tests, examinations, term papers, lab reports, and homework.These formal evaluation techniques help the instructor to evaluate student achievement and assign grades.

To evaluate classroom learning informally, teachers also use a variety of techniques. For example, teachers pose questions, listen carefully to student questions and comments, and monitor body language and facial expressions. Informal, often implicit evaluations permit the teacher to make adjustments in their teaching: to slow down or review material in response to questions, confusion, and misunderstandings; or to move on when student performance exceeds expectations.

When teaching at a distance, educators must address a different teaching challenge than when teaching in a traditional classroom. For example, instructors no longer have:

- A traditional, familiar classroom.
- A relatively homogeneous group of students.
- Face-to-face feedback during class (*e.g.*, students' questions, comments, body language, and facial expressions).
- Total control over the distance delivery system.
- Covenient opportunities to talk to students individually.

For these reasons, distance educators may find it useful to not only formally evaluate students through testing and homework, but to use a more informal approach in collecting data determine.

DIAGNOSTIC TESTING & REMEDIAL TEACHING

Before understanding the meaning of diagnostic evaluation let us know what diagnostic means?

Just as a doctor diagnosis a patient to find out the nature, type and extent of his disease before prescribing medicine, a teacher applies diagnostic test to diagnose the particular strength and weakness of the students.

The main aim of diagnostics is to find out the specific weakness and general difficulties:

(a) Diagnosis of general difficulties

(b) Diagnosis of specific difficulties

Diagnosis not only helps in finding out the problems faced by the students but also helps in finding remedies for them. If a student is weak in solving problems then remedial teaching can be arranged for him. The main aims of diagnosis is to locate specific learning and instructional difficulties, and if possible to determine their cause. In educational psychology several tests and instruments are used for diagnostic purpose.

Our main role as a teacher is to promote quality learning among the students. This is possible only when we act as a guide and the students actively participate in the process of learning. During the teaching-learning process, we have to locate and identify the areas where the learner commits mistakes. It is the crucial stage of the teaching-learning process where we have to diagnose and prepare instructional material for Remedial Teaching to ensure the desired quality of learning.

At this stage the role of a teacher is just like a doctor's. The doctor takes all the steps necessary to diagnose the disease by performing different tests and then prescribes medicines for the particular disease.

In the case of education the process of diagnostic testing is the step and remedial teaching is the prescription. Hence diagnostic testing and remedial teaching are very essential for ensuring effective learning and in improving the quality of education.

Objectives of Diagnostic Testing

- To understand the meaning and importance of diagnostic testing;
- To understand the nature and purpose of diagnostic testing;
- To follow the steps and stages of diagnostic testing in the classroom teaching-learning process; and
- To conduct remedial teaching in mathematics in classroom situations

FUNCTIONS OF DIAGNOSTIC TEST

Classification	Assessment of Specific Abilities with Regard to	Remediation	Etology
(*i*) Aptitude/Musical level	(*i*) Level of Abnormality	(*i*) Special education for handicapped	(*i*) Study of diagnosis
(*ii*) Vocational level	(*ii*) Level of Adjustment	(*ii*) Counselling for mental Ailment	
(*iii*) Intellectual level	(*iii*) Level of Depression and Anxiety	(*iii*) Remedial teaching for learning weakness	
		(*iv*) Clinical treatment for Physical Ailment	

Features of Diagnostic Test

- It is an effective tool for teachers that helps in planning and organising remedial teaching.
- If finds out deficiency and weakness of student in learning of a contents.
- It is a base to form tutorial groups so as helps the poor students to develop their performance removing their differences.
- It is a qualitative test not a quantitative.
- In these tests no scores are made for correct answers only wrong responses are taken into view in the sequence of contents.

- It adopts objective type tests only.
- In needs an expert or specialist to identify the cause for wrong answers.
- It fully emphasises on all learning and teaching points.
- It arranges the items in hearing sequence so as to help transfer of learning position.

DIAGNOSTIC TESTING : MEANING AND IMPORTANCE

In general, after completing a particular unit/topic we conduct a test to assess the achievements of learners. After evaluation we draw some conclusions and we find that some of the students have fared very well and a particular group of students have achieved below your expectations. Now we will have to find out the causes for this low achievement or slow learning. There would be certain reasons for this low achievement. Now it is very essential to find out the particular area where the difficulty lies or the particular concept where the learner commits errors. To locate and identify the areas of learning difficulties leads to Diagnostic Testing.

After identifying the areas where the error lies, we have to find out the reasons due to which the particular child/group of students have not responded well. At this stage we have to play the role of a doctor. If a patient visits the doctor's clinic he suggests different tests relevant to the symptoms observed by him. After getting reports he is in a position to identify and diagnose the disease and then prescribe the medicine for it.

Likewise, as a teacher, we have to first identify and locate the area where the error lies. The process adopted for this purpose in educational situations is known as diagnostic testing. We may say that diagnostic testing implies a detailed study of learning difficulties.

In diagnostic testing the following points must be kept in mind:

(*i*) Who are the pupils who need help?

(*ii*) Where are the errors located ?

(*iii*) Why did the error occur ?

Suppose we have taught the simple method of subtraction of two-digit numbers without borrowing and then conducted a test which indicates the solutions as follows :

Student's name—Anshu.

98	77	85	81	97
– 62	– 52	– 35	– 40	– 67
36	25	55	41	37

After conducting test we are in a position to assess the whole group. This assessment is followed by an analysis *i.e.*, we have to find out about each individual the area of difficulty or the concept where the learner commits errors. For example, Student 'Anshu' has solved all the questions of subtraction of two-digit numbers without borrowing correctly except for the subtraction of one digit from another one-digit number. We find that her answers are $5 - 5 = 5$, $7 - 7 = 7$. We are in a position to diagnose the particular concept which Anshu could not understand. This is known as diagnostic testing.

While performing a diagnostic test you have the specific aim to analyse the exact nature of the progress made by the learner in a particular topic/unit and to know the particular area of weakness/error which requires a series of carefully graded tests. The main aim of diagnostic testing is to analyse not to assess. It will be more clear in the following example.

Student's name – Ashish

370	590	860	870
– 210	– 230	– 330	– 353
160	360	530	520

513	654	845
– 206	– 352	– 203
307	202	602

Careless slip

260	280	370
– 109	– 140	– 143
100	240	230

Skill analysis of subtraction performance

We have conducted a test in the classroom to assess subtraction skill. After this assessment we have to find out how many students have not acquired this skill and who they are. For that particular group we will have to prepare a list to find the concept which is not clear to the learner or the particular step where the learner makes mistakes. For instance, in Ashish's case we have found that he makes a mistake when the question involves subtraction of zero from a number or of a number from zero through borrowing from the next digit. Ashish knows how to subtract zero from zero. You can conclude from this analysis that Ashish's makes a mistake only when the concepts of zero and a number come together in subtraction. This is identification of the area of learning difficulties, and the process involved in identifying and testing the problem is called diagnostic testing.

Construction of Diagnostic Test

- Formulate the objectives or outline of contents.
- Analyise the contents into subtopics and its elements.
- Identify the difficulties in the orders of sub-topics.
- Analyse the items and modify them.
- Prepare the final draft of the test.
- Prepare manual of test.
- Remedial devices and measures.

NATURE AND PURPOSE OF DIAGNOSTIC TESTING

If we consider arithmetical attainments from both a qualitative and quantitative standpoints, we can distinguish four main points (*i*) accuracy, (*ii*) speed of writing, (*iii*) methods of work and (*iv*) extent of the arithmetic process mastered.

It is obvious that we will try to find the feedback through the medium of class work or through weekly or monthly tests which indicate pupils' ability in each of the four aforesaid directions. But it is not enough for teaching purposes particularly with those pupils/learners who are slow learners. With this group of learners we are required to have a more analytical estimate of their achievements. Let us take the following example :

After teaching basic operations (addition, subtraction, multiplication and division) to a group of students, we conduct a test of say 10 items and the results are summarized as below :

Items	Errors	Items	Errors
1	2	6	10
2	1	7	8
3	3	8	9
4	2	9	32
5	3	10	32

From the above data it is possible to analyse the test items. It is clear that items 9 and 10 have been missed by most of the students. At this stage we have to re-think to make some modifications in items 9 and 10. This is the stage where we have identified and located the problem and hence diagnosed the area of error committed by the learners. Similarly, for items 6, 7 and 8, we will re-think and evolve instructional material to improve the quality of learning.

The above example suggests that Diagnostic Testing is analytical in nature where the teacher has to look at the performance of pupils in order to examine why they have not learned or mastered the particular concept or competency. For each pupil individually one has to pinpoint the specific kind of mistake he makes. This analysis is based on the date of performance rather than the general opinion of the teacher. It may be interpreted in terms of each students, a group of students, each concept/competency and for each of the questions.

Why should the teacher undertake this kind of probe into the performance of pupils? The obvious response is that he/she wants to ensure the quality of learning (at the level of mastery) and is curious to know what specific action should be taken to obtain the desired results. Thus the main purpose of diagnostic testing is to spot the learning difficulties of pupils with a view to developing corrective measures, termed as remedial teaching.

STEPS AND STAGES IN DIAGNOSTIC TESTING

The essential steps in educational diagnosis are:

(*i*) Identifying the students who are having trouble or need help.

(*ii*) Locating the errors or learning difficulties.

(*iii*) Discovering the causal factors of slow learning.

(*i*) Identifying the students who are having trouble or need help

First, one must know the learners who require help. For this we can administer a general achievement test based on the topics already taught. After evaluation we will be in a position to make lists of students who are below average, average or above average. Next, one has to locate the area where the error occurs in order to have a deeper insight into the pupils' difficulties.

(*ii*) Locating the errors or learning difficulties

After identifying the students who need help and visualising the necessity of additional instructional material to improve the quality of learning, our main role is to find out the area where the learner commits mistakes or which is the area where learning difficulties lie. For example we examine the pupils' responses as follows:

(*i*) $\frac{3}{4}+\frac{5}{4}=\frac{8}{4}$ (*ii*) $\frac{7}{12}+\frac{4}{12}=\frac{11}{12}$

(*iii*) $1+\frac{3}{4}=\frac{④}{4}$ (*iv*) $5+\frac{1}{7}=\frac{⑦}{7}$

(*v*) $\frac{1}{2}+\frac{1}{3}=\frac{②}{⑤}$ (*vi*) $\frac{3}{7}+\frac{4}{5}=\frac{⑦}{⑫}$

From the above example we would realise that the learner has the knowledge of adding fractions having the same denominator but the concept of addition of fractions having different denominators is not clear to him even though it was taught in the

MATHEMATICS

classroom. Thus we have located the area where the learning difficulty lies.

***(iii)* Discovering the causal factors of slow learning**
In some cases of learning difficulties, the causal factors are relatively simple. A student may be inattentive during teaching-learning or may be committing errors due to insufficient practice or irregular attendance.

Sometimes the cause is ill-health or faulty work habits etc. It has also been observed sometimes that the basic cause of low achievement is a feeling of helplessness or the complexity of the subject-matter which perhaps is much above the level of their comprehension.

Sequential presentation in below shows how diagnosis leads to improved quality of learning.

Teaching-learning ⟶ Evaluation ⟶ Unsatisfactory performance of pupils
↓
A case for diagnosis ⟶ Administer a General Achievement Test or use the data of previous testing ⟶ Identify students who need help
↓
Locate the area of difficulty ⟶ Identify causal factors ⟶ Provide remedial measures ⟶ Improved quality of learning

REMEDIAL TEACHING

While diagnosis is the process of investigating the learners' difficulties and the reasons for this, its follow up leads to actions that may help children make up their deficiencies. This step is generally termed Remedial Teaching. So you have to be skilled in preparing or arranging for such materials which may be used to undertake corrective instruction and thus enhancing the quality of learning.

Selection of Materials

The following points should be kept in mind while selecting appropriate instructional material:

(*i*) The corrective material should be designed to correct the students' individual difficulties.

(*ii*) You have to analyse the work of slow learners by means of observation, interview and diagnostic testing. A careful consideration of the three may help decide what kind of corrective material is to be designed and whether material will be adequate to correct the specific difficulties of learners.

(*iii*) The corrective material should be graded, self-directive and should permit students to work independently. Written directions, which accompany the material, should be easily readable and comprehensible by the students.

(*iv*) The corrective material must permit individuals to progress according to their pace.

(*v*) The material should encourage systematic recording of evidence of pupils' progress.

The following examples will illustrate the points discussed above.

For preparing the material for remedial teaching, let us explain the example discussed above. (steps and stages in dignostic testing) In this we had diagnosed that the learners had not understood the concept of adding fractions of the following type:

$1+\frac{3}{4}, 2+\frac{5}{7}, 3+\frac{6}{7}$, etc.

On the other hand, they had attained mastery over adding fractions of the type

$\frac{1}{2}+\frac{3}{2}; \frac{3}{2}+\frac{5}{2}; \frac{3}{4}+\frac{5}{4}; \frac{4}{5}+\frac{7}{5}$; etc.

Accordingly, now, we will have to prepare material where the learner should have plenty of opportunity to exercise on equalization of denominators in the given fractions.

(*i*) $1+\frac{3}{4}=\frac{1}{1}+\frac{3}{4}=\frac{1\times4}{1\times4}+\frac{3}{4}=\frac{4}{4}+\frac{3}{4}=\frac{4+3}{4}=\frac{7}{4}$

(*ii*) $2+\frac{5}{7}=\frac{2}{1}+\frac{5}{7}=\frac{2\times7}{1\times7}+\frac{5}{7}=\frac{14}{7}+\frac{5}{7}=\frac{14+5}{7}=\frac{19}{7}$

Enough practice should be provided to pupils on similar questions until they attain mastery. While selecting and implementing the instructional material the most important thing is the individual need of the student in a particular area. We have to give differential treatment. Different methodologies have to be adopted for different kinds of students. Other modes of interaction such as learner-learner interaction and learner-material interaction may also be utilized, besides the traditional teacher-learner interaction, using appropriate instructional material.

We have learnt about diagnostic testing which is the most important part of the teaching-learning process. It implies a detailed study of learning difficulties. Its aim is to analyse, not to assess. The nature and purpose of diagnostic testing is to identify the areas of difficulties where the learner commits errors.

After locating the area where the difficulty lies, as a teacher we will devise some strategy to remove problems in learning and the causes due to which the learner has faced the difficulties. The strategy used by us to remove the weakness of the learner is known as remedial teaching. Diagnostic testing leads to remedial teaching in which we have to prepare instructional material for quality learning, adopting different methodologies as per needs of the individual or a particular group.

PROBLEMS OF TEACHING

Vision for School Mathematics

- Children learn to enjoy mathematics rather than fear it.
- Children learn important mathematics.
- Mathematics is more than formulas and mechanical procedures.
- Children see mathematics as something to talk about, to communicate through, to discuss among themselves, to work together on.
- Children pose and solve meaningful problems.
- Children use abstractions to preceive relationships, to see structures, to reason out things, to argue the truth or falsity of statements.
- Children understand the basic structure of Mathematics: Arithmetic, algebra, geometry and trigonometry, the basic content areas of school. Mathematics, all offer a methodology for abstraction, structuration and generalisation.
- Teachers engage every child in class with the conviction that everyone can learn mathematics.

PROBLEMS OF TEACHING

Any analysis of mathematics education in our schools will identify a range of issues as problematic. We structure our understanding of these issues around the following four problems which we deem to be the core areas of concern:

1. A sense of fear and failure regarding mathematics among a majority of children,
2. A curriculum that disappoints both a talented minority as well as the non-participating majority at the same time,
3. Crude methods of assessment that encourage perception of mathematics as mechanical computation, and
4. Lack of teacher preparation and support in the teaching of mathematics.

Each of these can and need to be expanded on, since they concern the curricular framework in essential ways.

Fear and Failure

If any subject area of study evokes wide emotional comment, it is mathematics. While no one educated in Tamil would profess (or at the least, not without a sense of shame) ignorance of any Tirukkural, it is quite the social norm for anyone to proudly declare that (s)he never could learn mathematics. While these may be adult attitudes, among children (who are compelled to pass mathematics examinations) there is often fear and anxiety. Mathematics anxiety and 'math phobia' are terms that are used in popular literature.

In the Indian context, there is a special dimension to such anxiety. With the universalisation of elementary education made a national priority, and elementary education a legal right, at this historic juncture, a serious attempt must be made to look into every aspect that alienates children in school and contributes towards their non-participation, eventually leading to their dropping out of the system. If any subject taught in school plays a significant role in alienating children and causing them to stop attending school, perhaps mathematics, which inspires so much dread, must take a big part of the blame.

Such fear is closely linked to a sense of failure. By Class III or IV, many children start seeing themselves as unable to cope with the demands made by mathematics. In high school, among children who fail only in one or two subjects in year-end examinations and hence are detained, the maximum numbers fail in mathematics. This statistic pursues us right through to Class X, which is when the Indian state issues a certificate of education to a student. The largest numbers of Board Exam failures also happen in mathematics.

There are many perceptive studies and analyses on what causes fear of mathematics in schools. Central among them is the cumulative nature of mathematics. If you struggle with decimals, then you will struggle with percentages; if you struggle with percentages, then you will struggle with algebra and other mathematics subjects as well. The other principal reason is said to be the predominance of symbolic language. When symbols are manipulated without understanding, after a point, boredom and bewilderment dominate for many children, and dissociation develops.

Failure in mathematics could be read through social indicators as well. Structural problems in Indian education, reflecting structures of social discrimination, by way of class, caste and gender, contribute further to failure (and perceived failure) in mathematics education as well. Prevalent social attitudes which see girls as incapable of mathematics, or which, for centuries, have associated formal computational abilities with the upper castes, deepen such failure by way of creating self-fulfilling expectations.

A special mention must be made of problems created by the language used in textbooks, especially at the elementary level. For a vast majority of Indian children, the language of mathematics learnt in school is far removed from their everyday speech, and especially forbidding. This becomes a major force of alienation in its own right.

Disappointing Curriculum

Any mathematics curriculum that emphasises procedure and knowledge of formulas over understanding is bound to enhance anxiety. The prevalent practice of school mathematics goes further a silent majority give up early on, remaining content to fail in mathematics, or at best, to see it through, maintaining a minimal level of achievement. For these children, what the curriculum offers is a store of mathematical facts, borrowed temporarily while preparing for tests.

On the other hand, it is widely acknowledged that more than in any other content discipline, mathematics is the subject that also sees great motivation and talent even at an early age in a small number of children. These are children who take to quantisation and algebra easily and carry on with great facility.

What the curriculum offers for such children is also intense disappointment. By not offering conceptual depth, by not challenging them, the curriculum settles for minimal use of their motivation. Learning procedures may be easy for them, but their understanding and capacity for reasoning remain underexercised.

Crude Assessment

We talked of fear and failure. While what happens in class may alienate, it never evokes panic, as does the examination. Most of the problems cited above relate to the tyranny of procedure and memorization of formulas in school mathematics, and the central reason for the ascendancy of procedure is the nature of assessment and evaluation. Tests are designed (only) for assessing a student's knowledge of procedure and memory of formulas and facts, and given the criticality of examination performance in school life, concept learning is replaced by procedural memory. Those children who cannot do such replacement successfully experience panic, and suffer failure.

While mathematics is the major ground for formal problem solving in school, it is also the only arena where children see little room for play in answering questions. Every question in mathematics is seen to have one unique answer, and either you know it or you don't. In Language, Social Studies, or even in Science, you may try and demonstrate partial knowledge, but (as the students see it), there is no scope for doing so in mathematics. Obviously, such a perception is easily coupled to anxiety.

Amazingly, while there has been a great deal of research in mathematics education and some of it has led to changes in pedagogy and curriculum, the area that has seen little change in our schools over a hundred years or more is evaluation procedures in mathematics. It is not accidental that even a quarterly examination in Class VII is not very different in style from a Board examination in Class X, and the same pattern dominates even the end-of chapter exercises given in textbooks. It is always application of some piece of information given in the text to solve a specific problem that tests use of formalism. Such antiquated and crude methods of assessment have to be thoroughly overhauled if any basic change is to be brought about.

Inadequate Teacher Preparation

More so than any other content discipline, mathematics education relies very heavily on the preparation that the teacher has, in her own understanding of mathematics, of the nature of mathematics, and in her bag of pedagogic techniques. Textbook-centred pedagogy dulls the teacher's own mathematics activity.

At two ends of the spectrum, mathematics teaching poses special problems. At the primary level, most teachers assume that they know all the mathematics needed, and in the absence of any specific pedagogic training, simply try and uncritically reproduce the techniques they experienced in their school days. Often this ends up perpetuating problems across time and space.

At the secondary and higher secondary level, some teachers face a different situation. The syllabi have considerably changed since their school days, and in the absence of systematic and continuing education programmes for teachers, their fundamentals in many concept areas are not strong. This encourages reliance on 'notes' available in the market, offering little breadth or depth for the students.

While inadequate teacher preparation and support acts negatively on all of school mathematics, at the primary stage, its main consequence is this: mathematics pedagogy rarely resonates with the findings of children's psychology. At the upper primary stage, when the language of abstractions is formalised in algebra, inadequate teacher preparation reflects as inability to link formal mathematics with experiential learning. Later on, it reflects as incapacity to offer connections within mathematics or across subject areas to applications in the sciences, thus depriving students of important motivation and appreciation.

Other Systematic Problems

We wish to briefly mention a few other systematic sources of problems as well. One major problem is that of compartmentalisation. There is very little systematic communication between primary school and high school teachers of mathematics, and none at all between high school and college teachers of mathematics. Most school teachers have never even seen, let alone interacted with or consulted, research mathematicians. Those involved in teacher education are again typically outside the realm of college or research mathematics.

Another important problem is that of curricular acceleration: a generation ago, calculus was first encountered by a student in college. Another generation earlier, analytical geometry was considered college mathematics. But these are all part of school curriculum now. Such acceleration has naturally meant pruning of some topics: there is far less solid geometry or spherical geometry now. One reason for the narrowing is that calculus and differential equations are critically important in undergraduate sciences, technology and engineering, and hence it is felt that early introduction of these topics helps students proceeding further on these lines. Whatever the logic, the shape of mathematics education has become taller and more spindly, rather than broad and rounded.

While we have mentioned gender as a systematic issue, it is worth understanding the problem in some detail. Mathematics tends to be regarded as a 'masculine domain'. This perception is aided by the complete lack of references in textbooks to women mathematicians, the absence of social concerns in the designing of curricula which would enable children questioning received gender ideologies and the absence of reference to women's lives in problems. A study of mathematics textbooks found that in the problem sums, not a single reference was made to women's clothing, although several problems referred to the buying of cloth, etc.

Classroom research also indicates a fairly systematic devaluation of girls as incapable of 'mastering' mathematics, even when they perform reasonably well at verbal as well as cognitive tasks in mathematics. It has been seen that teachers tend to address boys more than girls, which feeds into the construction of the normative mathematics learner as male. Also, when instructional decisions are in teachers' hands, their gendered constructions colour the mathematical learning strategies of girls and boys, with the latter using more invented strategies for problem-solving, which reflects greater conceptual understanding. Studies have shown that teachers tend to attribute boys' mathematical 'success' more to ability, and girls' success more to effort. Classroom discourses also give some indication of how the 'masculinising' of mathematics occurs, and the profound influence of gender ideologies in patterning notions of academic competence in school. With performance in mathematics signifying school 'success', girls are clearly at the losing end.

RECOMMENDATIONS

While the litany of problems and challenges magnifies the distance we need to travel to arrive at the vision articulated above, it also offers hope by way of pointing us where we need to go and what steps we may/must take.

We summarise what we believe to be the central directions for action towards our stated vision. We group them again into four central themes:

1. Shifting the focus of mathematics education from achieving 'narrow' goals to 'higher' goals,
2. Engaging every student with a sense of success, while at the same time offering conceptual challenges to the emerging mathematician,
3. Changing modes of assessment to examine students' mathematisation abilities rather than procedural knowledge,
4. Enriching teachers with a variety of mathematical resources.

MULTIPLE CHOICE QUESTIONS

1. "Mathematics is a way to settle in mind of children a habit of reasoning." This is the statement of:
   A. Locke B. Galeleo
   C. Bertrand Russel D. None of these
2. A major fault of laboratory method is:
   A. It does not emphasise students to prepare as a scientist.
   B. It imagines a studnent as a tiny scientist.
   C. It makes foolish of students.
   D. It exploits the students mentally.
3. Geometry is related with:
   A. Numbers
   B. Digits
   C. Signs
   D. Expansion and extension
4. Which of the following is included in audio materials:
   A. Television B. Gramophone
   C. Black-board D. Toys
5. The oldest branch of mathematics is:
   A. Geometry B. Algebra
   C. Arithmatic D. None of these
6. The teacher should ask the questions:
   A. Standing amidst the pupils
   B. Speaking loudly
   C. Following the principle of variety
   D. All of the above
7. Which one of the following is not a teaching technique?
   A. Seminar B. Symposium
   C. Film and Chart D. Interview
8. At Primary stage, which method for teaching of writing is useful?
   A. French method
   B. Kindergarten method
   C. Play way method
   D. All of the above
9. Which teaching technique is not suitable for primary stage?
   A. Symposium B. Explanation
   C. Drill D. Questioning
10. Mathematics provides training for:
    A. Teaching
    B. Scientific methods
    C. Solving problems
    D. None of these
11. Which material can you use for teaching reading at primary stage?
    A. Flannel Board B. Lecture by experts
    C. Flash cards D. All of these
12. Objective type questions have:
    A. reliability B. validity
    C. coverage D. All of these
13. Which is not related to affective domain?
    A. Knowledge B. Characterisation
    C. Valueing D. Receiving
14. Which one is the teaching technique?
    A. Interview B. Note making
    C. Review D. All of the above
15. The devices used to make teaching method more effective are known as:
    A. principle of teaching
    B. techniques of teaching
    C. methodology of teaching
    D. None of the above
16. We, as mathematics teacher, evaluate pupil performance for:
    A. upgrading the students
    B. motivating the students
    C. assessing teacher's performance
    D. All of the above
17. The introductory questions should:
    A. be based on previous knowledge of the students
    B. be easy and not difficult
    C. have linkage
    D. All of the above
18. Internal qualities of a good mathematics book are:
    A. good printing
    B. psychological presentation of the subject-matter
    C. suitable font type and size
    D. All of the above

19. Which one of the following is not the principle of teaching:
A. exposure B. gradation
C. review D. phonology

20. Logical thinking allows a child to:
A. reject quick answers
B. to give quick answers
C. give the best solution
D. None of these

21. Logical thinking is:
A. a common teaching process
B. a special teaching process
C. learned method process
D. None of these

22. Solving mistakes take place due to:
A. poor text books
B. lack of writing exercises
C. defective pronunciation
D. All of the above

23. Which is not a method of teaching mathematics?
A. Grammar B. Translation
C. Direct method D. Enquiry method

24. Giving assignment of the students is a:
A. Technique
B. A.V. Aids
C. Principle of teaching
D. Maxim of teaching

25. What are the points of informative and summative assessment?
A. Objectives
B. Tests
C. Level of Generalisation
D. All of the above

26. Understanding children's thinking helps the teachers to:
A. use their knowledge in instructional planning
B. predict about the mischief of students
C. know about the problem of students
D. None of these

27. Which of the following is false in the context of keeping mathematics in curriculum?
A. It enables to make use of learning in mathematics in their daily life.
B. It prepares students for the future vocation or occupation.
C. It developes intellectual powers and disiplines of the students.
D. None of these.

28. Main defects of essay type questions are that:
A. they evaluate theory aspect only
B. they are not so reliable
C. they are not so valid
D. All of the above

29. At primary level, we should use .... method for teaching reading.
A. Story method B. Sentence method
C. Phonic method D. All of these

30. For evaluation, teacher should use:
A. essay type questions
B. oral testing
C. objective type questions
D. All of the above

31. The administration of a teaching unit involves:
A. introduction B. presentation
C. evaluation D. All of these

32. An ideal lesson plan is:
A. Objective based
B. Based on Previous knowledge
C. Based on Teaching levels
D. All of the above

33. Characteristics of good questions are:
A. realisation of aims
B. thought provoking
C. brief and direct
D. All of the above

34. What is the basis of teaching method?
A. Objective B. Content
C. Both 'A' and 'B' D. None of these

35. The most effective teaching aid:
A. Non-projected B. Direct experience
C. Projected D. None of these

36. In the scope of educational diagnosis use is made of:
A. interview B. diagnostic test
C. observation D. All of these

37. The lesson plan helps in:
A. applying theoretical knowledge in class
B. giving practical shape to the concept of management of teaching-learning
C. Both 'A' and 'B'
D. None of the above

38. What are the tests of performance?
A. Essay type tests B. Objective tests
C. Test of skills D. None of these

39. Multiple choice tests require thinking the ..... alternative.
A. incorrect
B. correct
C. Both 'A' and 'B'
D. None of the above

40. "if and only if" is known as:
A. Mathematical term
B. Mathematical phrase
C. Mathematical concept
D. None of these

41. Mathematics is a language because:
A. it can communicate a range of meanings
B. it has own symbols, words and rules of sentence
C. it discribes the concepts of science
D. All of these

42. 'How to teach' is related with
A. Teaching method
B. Evaluation
C. Objectives
D. Contents

43. The curriculum means:
A. Courses of Study
B. Race Course
C. Syllabus
D. Educational Programme

44. Type of curriculum used in our education is:
A. Learner-centred
B. Teacher-centred
C. Objective-centred
D. Content-centred

45. The curriculum is developed in view of:
A. Educational objectives
B. Child development
C. National development
D. All of the above

46. Evaluation is a process of:
A. qualitative B. quantitative
C. Both 'A' and 'B' D. None of these

47. Mathematics is the sciences of:
A. space B. numbers
C. calculations D. All of these

48. Who said that, 'Mathematics is the science which draws necessary conclusions'?
A. Hogben B. Locke
C. Benjamin Peirce D. None of these

49. Evaluation helps to answer the question:
A. What should be taught?
B. How can be achieved?
C. What has been achieved?
D. None of these.

50. Knowledge, Understanding, Application and Skills are components of:
A. Evaluation B. Methods
C. Objectives D. Content

51. What is characteristic of essay type examination?
A. Validity B. Reliability
C. Objectivity D. Depends on memory

52. Which is the main remedial teaching strategy?
A. Tutorial
B. Supervised
C. Both 'A' and 'B'
D. None of these

53. The more comprehensive plan is:
A. Resource Plan B. Unit Plan
C. Lesson Plan D. All of these

54. A unit plan should:
A. be flexible
B. provide a variety
C. consists of familiar topics
D. All of the above

55. Purpose(s) of evaluation is/are:
A. Motivation
B. Selection
C. Remedial work
D. All of these

56. Evaluation gives the feedback to:
A. teachers
B. students
C. the entire educational system
D. None of these

57. Evaluation may be used to improve:
A. Examination
B. Curriculum
C. Teaching methods
D. All of these

58. Preparation of daily lesson planning includes:
A. determination of objectives
B. selection of content
C. determination of methods
D. All of the above

59. Achievement tests are:
A. teacher-made
B. standardised
C. Both 'A' and 'B'
D. None of these

60. Evaluation helps the teachers to:
A. diagnose students' difficulties
B. make the teaching-learning process dynamic and innovative
C. motivate the children for better learning
D. All of these

61. Which of the following is not the process of evaluation?
A. Interpretation and generalisation of results
B. Selection of tools and techniques
C. Understand the students thinking
D. Feedback the results for improvement of teaching-learning process

62. What is the basis of remedial teaching?
A. Diagnosis
B. Weakness of the students
C. Individual difference
D. All of the above

63. The function of measurement is:
A. prognosis B. diagnosis
C. research D. All of these

64. Which of the following is not the characteristics of good test?
A. Validity B. Discrimination
C. Confidence D. Utility

65. Formative evaluations occurs:
A. at the end of session
B. during the teaching-learning process
C. at the end of year
D. at home

66. The most useful teaching aid in mathematics is:
A. visual aid
B. audio aid
C. audio visual aid
D. None of these

67. The most use of teaching aids are in:
A. arithmetic B. algebra
C. science D. trigonometry

68. A good objective should be:
A. related to teacher
B. testable
C. small
D. attractive

69. Summative evaluation:
1. tells about the final progress of the student.
2. helps in the classification of grades and promotion of the students.
3. helps to choose career and placement to the students.
4. helps to monitor the teaching process.
5. give the feedback to students and teachers.
A. 2, 3 and 4 B. 3, 4 and 5
C. 1, 2 and 3 D. 1, 2 and 4

70. Which of the following is not the problem of teaching mathematics:
A. biasness of gender
B. compartmentalisation
C. lack of curiosity in students
D. crude assessment

71. What is characteristic of the unit approach of curriculum?
A. Child centred
B. Content centred
C. Objective centred
D. Teacher centred

72. The team teaching is a method of:
A. playing game
B. teaching
C. physical exercise
D. None of these

73. Students make errors in mathematics due to:
A. poor attention
B. carelessness
C. lack of knowledge
D. all of these

74. In team teaching, the participant teachers decide their:
A. objectives B. activities
C. ideas D. All of these

75. Error of evaluation is:
A. personal error B. constant error
C. variable error D. All of the above

76. Errors due to evaluators can be eredicated:
A. by construction of appropriate tools and methods
B. being objective during measurement and evaluation
C. by making the test objective
D. None of these

77. Which of the following point should not be kept in the mind during remedial teaching?
A. Who is going to help the students?
B. Where are the errors located?
C. Why did the error occur?
D. Who need help?

78. Which of the following is not the feature of diagnostic test?
A. It is a quantitative test
B. It adopts objective type test only
C. It is an effective tool for teachers that helps in planning and organising remedial teaching
D. None of these

79. The nature of mathematics is:
A. ornamental B. logical
C. difficult D. not for common

80. Which work is not related with a teacher?
A. Planning B. Teaching
C. Guidance D. Budgeting

81. Introductory questions are asked:
A. in the beginning of the lesson
B. in midway
C. at the end
D. at every stage

82. Memory questions are used to test:
A. previous knowledge of pupils
B. present knowledge of pupils
C. interest of the pupils
D. discipline

83. The aims of questioning are:
A. to motivate the pupils
B. to create interest and curiosity
C. to test the previous knowledge
D. All of the above

84. Achievement test for:
A. test of minimum performance
B. test of maximum performance
C. test of natural performance
D. test of performance

85. Micro-teaching helps in:
A. controlling indiscipline
B. encouraging indiscipline
C. Both 'A' and 'B'
D. None of the above

86. Which is the teacher-centred method?
A. Source method B. Lecture method
C. Project method D. Socialised Recitation

87. Which problem in classroom is due to curriculum?
A. Cleanliness B. Indiscipline
C. Teaching D. Discipline

88. Formal techniques of evaluation are:
1. teacher made test
2. questionaire
3. observations
4. intervews
5. comments

A. 1, 2 and 3 B. 1, 2 and 4
C. 1, 2 and 5 D. 1 and 2

89. Which of the following is not the type of evaluation?
A. Comprehensive evaluation
B. Prognosis evaluation
C. Spasmodic evaluation
D. Summative evaluation

90. In distance education the instructors don't have:
A. Opportecnity to talk to students
B. Face to face feed back during class
C. A triaditional of familiar classroom
D. All of these

ANSWERS

1	2	3	4	5	6	7	8	9	10
A	B	D	B	C	D	C	D	A	B
11	**12**	**13**	**14**	**15**	**16**	**17**	**18**	**19**	**20**
C	D	A	D	B	D	D	D	C	A
21	**22**	**23**	**24**	**25**	**26**	**27**	**28**	**29**	**30**
C	D	D	A	D	A	D	A	B	D
31	**32**	**33**	**34**	**35**	**36**	**37**	**38**	**39**	**40**
D	D	D	B	A	D	C	C	B	B
41	**42**	**43**	**44**	**45**	**46**	**47**	**48**	**49**	**50**
D	A	B	C	C	B	D	C	B	C
51	**52**	**53**	**54**	**55**	**56**	**57**	**58**	**59**	**60**
D	C	C	D	D	C	D	D	C	D
61	**62**	**63**	**64**	**65**	**66**	**67**	**68**	**69**	**70**
C	D	D	C		A	C	B	C	C
71	**72**	**73**	**74**	**75**	**76**	**77**	**78**	**79**	**80**
B	D	D	B	D	B	A	A	B	D
81	**82**	**83**	**84**	**85**	**86**	**87**	**88**	**89**	**90**
A	A	D	D	A	B	B	B	C	D

Science

SECTION a

SCIENCE

FOOD

It is a nutritive substance taken by an organism for growth, work, repair and maintaining life processes. It provides energy to do work and maintain body heat, provides materials for the growth of the body, makes necessary materials for reproduction and provides materials for the repair of damaged cells and tissues of our body. Food has many different components and each one is necessary for one or the other function. Major ones are — carbohydrates, fats, proteins, minerals, vitamins, water and roughage.

COMPONENTS OF FOOD

Carbohydrates

They are made up of three elements - carbon, hydrogen and oxygen, the proportion of hydrogen and oxygen being the same as in water. Glucose $C_6H_{12}O_6$ Sucrose, $C_{12}H_{22}O_{11}$ and Starch $(C_6H_{10}O_5)_n$ are examples of carbohydrates. They are the main source of energy in our body, with 1 gm of carbohydrates producing about 17 kilojoules of energy upon oxidation. For a normal person, 400 to 500 gms of carbohydrates are required daily but for sportspersons, growing children and nursing mothers, it is on higher side. Cellulose, which forms the cell walls of plants is also a carbohydrate but not a food for human because the enzyme capable of digesting cellulose is not produced in human beings. Cellulose, however, helps in maintaining a healthy digestive system. Sugar is a type of carbohydrate which is sweet in taste. Glucose, Fructose and Sucrose are examples of sugar. The carbohydrates in our food is obtained mainly from plant sources like wheat, rice, maize, potatoes, peas, beans and fruits. During respiration, oxidation of carbohydrates takes place. It is represented as

$$C_6H_{12}O_6 + 6O_2 \rightarrow 6CO_2 + 6H_2O + \text{Energy}$$

Fats

They are esters of long chain fatty acids and an alcohol called glycerol. Fats also contain atoms of carbon, hydrogen and oxygen. However, fats contain less proportion of oxygen as compared to carbohydrates. The main function of fats in the body is to provide a steady source of energy and for this purpose, they are deposited within the body. One gm of fat gives 37 kilojoules of energy which is more than double of that given by carbohydrates. Fats, the richest source of energy to our body, can be stored in the body for subsequent use. Fats, soluble in organic solvents and insoluble in water, also supply fat-soluble vitamins to our body. Fats, as such cannot be absorbed by our body due to insolubility in water and needs to be hydrolysed into simpler substances, soluble in water. A normal diet should contain about 75 gms of fat per day. Fats are supplied to our body by butter, ghee, cheese, milk, egg-yolk, meat, nuts, soyabean and cooking oils. Fats containing saturated fatty acids are solid at ordinary room temperature while those containing. unsaturated fatty acids are in the liquid form. Saturated fats are stable and hence get deposited in the body. Our body can convert carbohydrates into some fatty acids but a few others have to be taken with the food as they cannot be synthesised within the body. These fatty acids, which have to be supplied through the food, are called essential fatty acids. These are unsaturated in nature. Therefore, it is better to use unsaturated fats in our diet.

Energy Requirements: The energy requirement of a body varies according to age, sex, lifestyle, occupation, climate and special situations like pregnancy and lactation. Lesser intake of food gives insufficient energy and leads to sick-ness. Excess intake of food also creates problems. Following table gives average daily requirements of energy, with women generally needing less energy than men of the same age group.

Age	*Energy requirements*
5 years	6000 kJ per day
11 years	9000 kJ per day
18 years	11000 kJ per day
Adult (normal work)	9600 kJ per day
Adult (heavy work)	12000 kJ per day
Adult (very heavy work)	16000 kJ per day

Proteins

They are complex organic compounds made up of carbon, hydrogen, oxygen and nitrogen. The building blocks of Protein are Amino acids and there are large number of amino acids. Some proteins also contain sulphur and phosphorus. Proteins are essential for the growth of children and teenagers, and for maintenance and making good the wear and tear of the body tissues in adults. Proteins are made up of nitrogen containing compounds called amino acids. An adult needs about 1 gm of protein per kg of body weight. Proteins can be obtained from the plant as well as animal sources, with groundnuts, beans, whole cereals like wheat and maize and pulses belonging to the former category and fish, eggs, milk, cheese and lean meat belonging to the latter. Milk, meat and eggs contain all the amino acids required by our body.

Minerals

Our body also needs some inorganic substances like metals, non-metals and their salts, though in small amounts. These minerals are needed to build bones, teeth, formation of Red Blood Corpuscles, coagulation of blood, functioning of muscles, nerves and glands, etc. Some of the important minerals needed by our body are — iron, iodine, calcium, phosphorus, sodium, potassium, zinc, copper, magnesium, chloride, fluoride and sulphur. We get most of the minerals in combined form from plant sources. Deficiency of these minerals causes many diseases. The quantity of minerals required vary with about 30 milligram of iron requirement, 1 milligram of iodine requirement and 1 gm of calcium and phosphorus requirement daily for a normal person.

Vitamins

They are complex organic compounds which are necessary for normal growth, good health, good vision, proper digestion and healthy teeth, gums and bones. They act as catalysts in certain chemical reactions of metabolism in our body. They don't provide energy to our body nor form body tissues. Vitamins are needed in small quantities and their deficiency effects eyes, skin, bones, hair and general growth. More than 15 types of vitamins are known and only 2 vitamins — D and K can be formed in our body. Rest are either provided through our diet or taken separately in synthetic form. Vitamin B-complex and C are water soluble vitamins while vitamin A, D, E and K are oil soluble. Vitamin B-Complex is a mixture of 11 vitamins. Following table gives necessity and sources of vitamins.

Vitamin	*Necessity*	*Source*
Vitamin A	For maintaining healthy eyesight, normal skin and hair	Cod liver oil, fish, eggs, milk, carrot, leafy vegetables.
Vitamin B_1	For growth, carbohydrate metabolism, functioning of heart, nerves and muscles.	Milk, soya-food, meat, whole cereals, green vegetables.
Vitamin C	For keeping teeth, gums and joints healthy, for increasing resistance of body to infection	Citrus fruits, guava, tomatoes.
Vitamin D	For normal growth of bones and teeth	Milk, eggs, butter, cod liver oil, sun light.
Vitamin E	For normal reproduction, functioning of muscles and protection of liver	Green leafy vegetables, milk, butter, tomato.
Vitamin K	For normal clotting of blood and normal functioning of liver	Green leafy vegetables, soyabean, tomato.

Water

It is essential for our body because it helps in the assimilation of food. About two-thirds of a man's body is the water in his tissues. Water also helps in digestion, transport, excretion and regulating body temperatures. The survival time without water is very short. Amount of water needed depends on one's age, type of work and the climate. Dehydration is caused by excessive loss of water from the body.

Roughage

It is the fibrous material present in plants and their products. It mainly consists of the indigestible plant carbohydrates called cellulose. Though it does not provide any energy to the body, yet keeps the digestive system in order, by helping in retaining water in the body and preserving constitution. The main source of roughage are salads, cabbage, corn cob, porridge, vegetables and fruits with stems.

DISEASES

Communicable Diseases

They are the diseases which can be transmitted from reservoirs of infection or infected person to the healthy but susceptible persons. The disease causing agent or the pathogen can be transmitted directly or indirectly. Direct transmission occurs:

(i) By direct contact with an infected person, e.g., chickenpox, smallpox, measles, leprosy, ringworm, gonorrhea, syphilis etc.,

(ii) Through sneezing, coughing, talking with infected person or spitting, e.g., diphtheria, influenza, common cold, measles, tuberculosis, pneumonia, mumps, whopping cough.

(iii) Through contact of injuries with soil, e.g., tetanus.

(iv) Through animal bites, e.g., rabies.

(v) Through placenta from mother to the foetus, e.g., German measles.

Indirect transmission takes place through some intermediate agents:

(i) Through agency of some vectors, e.g., African sleeping sickness is spread by Tse Tse fly, Kala-azar by sand fly, malaria by female Anopheles, Yellow fever by Aedes mosquito, Filariasis by Culex mosquito, Bubonic plague by Rat flea and Typhoid, cholera, amoebic dysentery by housefly.

(ii) By agencies like blood, water, food, e.g., cholera, dysentery, typhoid, AIDS.

(iii) Through contaminated articles like towels, handkerchief, toys, soap, utensils, surgical instruments.

(iv) By wind currents, aerosol sprays and dust.

(v) Through unclean hands, e.g., Enterobiesis.

Deficiency Diseases

These occur due to deficiency of some nutrients in the diet or some hormone due to hypo activity or damage to endocrine glands.

Diet Deficiency	*Disease*	*Symptoms*
Protein	Kwashiorkor	Swelling of abdomen and feet; enlarged liver; skin becomes dark and scaly.
Protein-energy malnutrition	Marasmus	Rapid weight loss; body growth and brain weight lowered.
Vitamin A	Night-blindness, Xerophthalmia	Inability to see in dim light; defective teeth formation; dry skin; retarded growth.
Vitamin B_1	Beri-Beri	Swelling and Pain in legs, loss of appetite; weakness; palpitation; headache.
Vitamin B_2	Cheilosis	Cracking of skin; inflammation of mouth and tongue; retarded growth.
Vitamin B_5	Pellagra	Skin eczema; swelling of gums; mental disturbances; disturbance of digestive tract.
Vitamin C	Scurvy	Swelling and bleeding of gums; pain in the muscles and joints; General weakness and fatigue; decreased resistance to cold; long time for wound healing.
Vitamin D	Rickets (in children), (in adult) Osteomalacia	Twisting of bones; bending of bones.
Vitamin K	Hypothrombinemia	Reduced capacity of clotting.
Iron	Anaemia	Loss of appetite; loss of weight; body looks pale; early tiredness.
Iodine	Goitre	Retarded growth; mental disability; enlargement of thyroid gland.
Fluoride	Dental caries	Loosing of teeth; swelling and bleeding of gums.
Calcium and phosphorus	Affects formation of bones and teeth	Weakening of bones; loss of teeth enamel; pain in the bones
Insulin	Diabetes	Sugar level in blood increases; person be-comes more susceptible to infections.
Thyroxine	Cretinism (child), Goitre	Mental retardation; physical growth stunted; small skeleton.
STH	Dwarfism	Diminished growth of the bones; person becomes dwarf, caused by lower activity of pituitary gland.
	Gigantism	Hyperactivity of pituitary gland causes excessive growth of the bones; person becomes abnormally tall.

Allergic Disease

In these diseases, body becomes hypersensitive to some foreign agents, allergens, which cause inflammation when come in contact with the body or enter inside the body. Foreign agents can be dust, pollens, certain-foods, serum, certain drugs or fabrics. The unfavourable response of the body to allergens is called allergic reaction. Asthma and hay fever are allergic diseases.

Degenerative Diseases

These occur due to degenerative changes in some vital organs of the body. Deposition of calcium salts or cholesterol in the walls of the blood vessels, hypertension or high blood pressure, reduced blood supply to heart muscles, clot formation in the coronary artery and back flow of blood from the ventricles to auricles are degenerative diseases of heart and blood vessels of the body. Obstruction of blood circulation to brain and stroke, epilepsy and inflammation of joints (arthritis) also belong to this category of diseases.

Cancer: It is characterised by uncontrolled growth and division of certain body tissues, forming a tumour. The rate of cell division is much higher than that of normal cells. All tumours are not cancerous. These cells have less survival capability than the normal cells and due to less adhesiveness, generally wander through the tissues to cause cancerous growth in different parts of the body. Cancer is neither contagious nor hereditary disease. The agents inducing cancer growth fire called carcinogens. Cancer can be caused by radiations (X-rays, gamma rays and particulate radiations); physical irritants (certain foods causing continued abrasion of the linings of the intestinal tract), chemical agents (caffeine, polycyclic hydrocarbons, heavy metallic ions, hormones), biological agents (viruses). The body organs, affected by cancerous cells are breast, stomach, lung, skin, pancreas, bones, muscles, lymph nodes, urinary bladder, vagina, liver and blood. Blood cancer is called Leukaemia. It is characterised by increased WBC count of the blood. The malignant tumour that grow rapidly and damage the normal cells, needs to be removed immediately otherwise could cause death. Danger signs of cancer are: persisting tumour, any wound not healing, any wound with continuous bleeding, persistent indigestion, rapid change in appearance of warts, persistent changes in bowel movements, persistent hoarseness in voice or coughing or swallowing or unexpected loss of weight.

Congenital Diseases

These are inborn diseases which are present from the birth. These are inheritable and are generally caused by gene or chromosomal mutations. These are Albinism, Sickle cell anaemia, Thalassemia, Hemophilia, Wilson's diseases and Anophthalmia. Some genetic disorders are caused due to changes in chromosomes number in the offsprings e.g. Dow's syndrome (mongolism), Klinefelter's syndrome, Turner's syndrome or super males/females.

Bacterial Diseases

Bacteria are minute organisms which are known to cause a number of diseases:

Disease	*Incubation period*	*Spread through*	*Symptoms*
Tuberculosis	2-10 weeks	Air-borne, droplet infection	Fever, coughing, chest pain and bloody sputum. Any part of body can be effected but lung is most common.
Diptheria	2-6 days	Air-borne droplet infection	Inflammation of mucus membrane of nose, throat and tonsils. In severe cases respiratory tract is blocked. Generally affects children below the age of 5 years.
Cholera	6 hours to 2-3 days	Contaminated food and water. House flies are the vectors	Acute diarrhoea, muscular cramps, sunken eyes, low blood pressure, dehydration, loss of min-erals in urine.
Leprosy	Upto 5 years	Prolonged and intimate contact	Deformity of fingers and toes, formation ulcers, scaly and nodulated skins, infected skin becomes senseless.
Whopping cough	7-14 days	Droplet infection	Mild fever, severe coughing, vomiting, accumulation of muscles in respiratory track, interfering in respiration.
Tetanus	3-21 days	Entry of cysts through any wound made by sharp object, dog bite or fall on the road	Restlessness, pulling pain in the wound, convulsions, stiffness of neck, rigid jaw muscles, contraction of muscles and paralysis.
Typhoid	1-3 weeks	Directed and Contact	Headache, classic typhoid fever, haemorrhage and ulceration of intestines, lashes on chest and upper abdomen.
Plague	2-6 days	Rats and bedbugs transmit the germs	High fever, extreme weakness, enlargement of lymph nodes, haemorrhage of bronchi and lungs.
Pneumonia	1-3 days	Air-borne	Collection of lymph, mucus in the bronchioles and alveoli. Reduced respiratory efficiency.

Gonorrhoea, syphilis, diarrhoeal diseases, food poisoning and meningitis are also caused by bacterias.

Viral Diseases

Disease	*Incubation period*	*Spread through*	*Symptoms*
Chicken-pox	12-20 days	Direct contact with infected persons or infected objects	Fever, headache, loss of appetite followed by dark red coloured rashes on the whole body. After some days rashes dry forming crusts which finally fall and patient recovers. Children below age of 5 years are more likely to catch the virus.
Smallpox	12 days	Droplet infection	Sudden high fever, headache, painful whole body followed by rashes. Rashes change into postulates with fluid. Rashes dry up leaving permanent pockmarks.
Poliomyelitis	7-14 days	Direct and oral	Headache and fever followed by stiffness of neck and convulsions. Finally, legs become paralysed. If respiratory centres are damaged, breathing fails and causes death.
Measles	10 days	Droplet infection	Common cold, headache, fever followed by coughing, sneezing, skin eruptions, conjuctivitis.
Mumps	12-26 days	Droplet infection	Painful enlargement of salivary gland high fever, difficulty in the movement of jaws and opening of mouth.
Rabies	1-3 months	Bite of rabied animal like dogs, monkeys, cates	100% fatal disease, causes severe headache, high fever and painful contraction of muscles ofz throat and chest. Patient fears from water. So, the disease is also called hydrophobia.
Influenza	24-28 hours	Air-borne	Bronchitis, coughing, bronchopneumonia.

AIDS

Acquired Immuno Deficiency Syndrome (AIDS) is caused by a virus which weakens the human body's immunity or self defence mechanism. Since natural immunity of the body gets reduced, AIDS makes body prone to many other infections. The patient suffering from AIDS actually die from other infections or diseases. AIDS disease usually spreads through sexual contact, transfusion of infected blood, use of infected needles for injections or from infected mother to the foetus. No medicine or vaccine has been developed to cure AIDS. Precaution is recommended to avoid AIDS.

Diseases Caused by Protozoa

Amoebiasis (Amoebic dysentery), Malaria, Kala-azar, Trypanosomiasis and Giardiasis are main diseases caused by protozoans. Malaria is a parasitic infection. When mosquito bites man to suck blood, it introduces the saliva containing the malarial parasite into blood stream of the man.

MULTIPLE CHOICE QUESTIONS

1. Consumption of 'Khesari dal' with Arhar dal leads to which of the following disease:
(*a*) Lathyrism (*b*) Anaemia
(*c*) Dropsy (*d*) Kala-Azar

2. ORS, Which is used for the treatment of Diarrhea stands for:
(*a*) Oral Recharging Solution
(*b*) Oral Reducing Solution
(*c*) Oral Replenishing Solution
(*d*) Oral Rehydration Solution

3. Ragi is richest source of:
(*a*) Iron (*b*) Calcium
(*c*) Iodine (*d*) Vitamin B complex

4. Why does a piece of bread when chewed tastes sweet ?
(*a*) The sugar content of bread is drawn out
(*b*) The taste buds are stimulated by chewing
(*c*) Saliva's action converts starch into maltose
(*d*) It does not taste sweet; it is just an illusion

5. Cereals are mainly rich in :
(*a*) Glucose (*b*) Maltose
(*c*) Proteins (*d*) Starch

6. Pulses are a good source of :
(*a*) Carbohydrates (*b*) Fats
(*c*) Proteins (*d*) Vitamins

7. Which of the following statement is correct :
(*a*) Plants carry on photosynthesis all the time.
(*b*) Plants carry on photosynthesis during the night and respiration during the day.
(*c*) Plants carry on photosynthesis during the day and respiration all the time.
(*d*) Plants carry on respiration and photosynthesis alternately all the time.

8. Plants absorb most part of water needed by them through their :
(*a*) Embryonic zone (*b*) Growing point
(*c*) Root hairs (*d*) Zone of elongation

9. Which of the following is used by green plants for the manufacture of sugar ?
(*a*) Carbon dioxide (*b*) Sun light
(*c*) Water (*d*) All of the above

10. Roughage, a necessary constituent of diet, consists largely of indigestible :
(*a*) carbohydrates such as cellulose and lignin
(*b*) carbohydrates (cellulose and lignin) and unsaturated fatty acids
(*c*) carbohydrates (cellulose and lignin) and semi-cooked meat
(*d*) all of these

11. What should be given to an athlete for instant energy?
(*a*) carbohydrates (*b*) protein
(*c*) fat (*d*) vitamin

12. The largest part of most diet is made up of :
(*a*) nucleic acid (*b*) proteins
(*c*) carbohydrates (*d*) lipids

13. A vegetarian may get the required phosphorous for his body from :
(*a*) fish (*b*) milk
(*c*) rice (*d*) soyabean

14. In the human body, fats are stored in :
(*a*) epithelial cells (*b*) adipose tissues
(*c*) epidermis (*d*) liver

15. Match the following :

	List I		List II
A.	Beri-beri	1.	Vitamin A
B.	Night-blindness	2.	Vitamin E
C.	Scurvy	3.	Vitamin K
D.	Haemorrhage	4.	Vitamin C
		5.	Vitamin B

	A	B	C	D
(*a*)	4	3	5	2
(*b*)	3	4	5	2
(*c*)	4	1	5	3
(*d*)	5	1	4	3

16. Which of the following is the principal organ of digestion and absorption of food in our body ?
(*a*) Large intestine
(*b*) Liver
(*c*) Pancreas
(*d*) Small intestine

17. Workers in deep mines usually suffer from dehydration because :
(*a*) water is lost due to evaporation
(*b*) water is lost due to defecation
(*c*) water is lost in the form of urine
(*d*) water is lost along with salts in the form of sweat.

18. All of the following are constituents of chlorophyll molecules, except :
(*a*) calcium
(*b*) carbon
(*c*) hydrogen
(*d*) magnesium

19. Which of the following is rich in all the three foods—carbohydrates, proteins and fats ?
(*a*) Rice grains
(*b*) Soyabean seeds
(*c*) Mango fruit
(*d*) Cabbage leaves

20. Rheumatic heart patients are specially advised against taking—
(*a*) fats (*b*) salt
(*c*) carbohydrates (*d*) proteins

21. What converts glycogen to glucose?
(*a*) glucagon (*b*) insulin
(*c*) adrenalin (*d*) both (*a*) and (*b*)

22. What is the term used for the synthesis of glycogen from glucose?
(*a*) gluconeogenesis (*b*) glycolysis
(*c*) glycogenesis (*d*) glycogenolysis

23. Which is the first proteolytic enzyme to act on proteins?
(*a*) peptidase (*b*) trypsin
(*c*) erepsin (*d*) pepsin

24. The digestion of which of the following releases nitrogenous wastes into the body?
(*a*) carbohydrates (*b*) fats
(*c*) proteins (*d*) all the above

25. Where does the digestion of starch in mammals start?
(*a*) duodenum (*b*) oesophagus
(*c*) mouth (*d*) stomach

26. What is the bolus of food in acidic medium after digestion called?
(*a*) acidified bolus (*b*) bile bolus
(*c*) chime (*d*) chile

27. Which is the essential mineral for the synthesis of protein in the body?
(*a*) iron (*b*) sodium
(*c*) potassium (*d*) sulphur

28. Which respiratory disease is associated with excess of histamine?
(*a*) asthma (*b*) bronchitis
(*c*) emphysema (*d*) all

29. What is the disease that develops since birth called?
(*a*) communicable (*b*) acquired
(*c*) congenital (*d*) degenerative

30. Which of the following organ is primarily concerned with immunity?
(*a*) liver (*b*) kidney
(*c*) lymphatic tissue (*d*) thyroid

31. What is a cell coded protein found in response to infection with host animal virus called?

(a) antigen (b) antibody
(c) histamine (d) interferon

32. Which of the following causes AIDS?
(a) Rubella virus
(b) Varicella virus
(c) Corynebacterium diptheriae
(d) HIV

33. Which of the following causes the viral disease of chicken pox?
(a) Echo virus (b) Herpes roster
(c) Herpes simplex (d) Varicella

34. Entamoeba histolytica is a human parasite. Where is it usually found?
(a) mouth (b) liver
(c) intestine (d) blood

35. Which mosquito transmits malaria?
(a) male anopheles (b) female anopheles
(c) male culex (d) female culex

36. Which of the following marks the second line of defense?
(a) lever (b) blood
(c) antibodies (d) WBC

37. Which parasite causes sleeping sickness?
(a) Plasmodium (b) Entamoeba
(c) Trympanosoma (d) Gregarina

38. Which among the following is/are the element/s of carbohydrates?
(a) carbon (b) hydrogen
(c) oxygen (d) all of these

39. Which among the following is deposited in the body to provide a steady source of energy?
(a) Fats (b) Carbohydrates
(c) Proteins (d) Vitamins

40. Which vitamin/s is/are souluble in water?
(a) Vitamin B (b) Vitamin C
(c) Vitamin A (d) Vitamin B and C

ANSWERS

1	2	3	4	5	6	7	8	9	10
(a)	(d)	(b)	(c)	(d)	(c)	(c)	(c)	(d)	(a)
11	**12**	**13**	**14**	**15**	**16**	**17**	**18**	**19**	**20**
(a)	(c)	(b)	(b)	(d)	(d)	(d)	(a)	(b)	(b)
21	**22**	**23**	**24**	**25**	**26**	**27**	**28**	**29**	**30**
(a)	(c)	(d)	(c)	(c)	(c)	(d)	(a)	(c)	(c)
31	**32**	**33**	**34**	**35**	**36**	**37**	**38**	**39**	**40**
(d)	(d)	(d)	(c)	(b)	(d)	(c)	(d)	(a)	(d)

❑❑❑

MATERIALS

We need different types of materials to meet our daily needs. Some of them are obtained from nature while others are prepared by man. The materials that we get from nature are called natural materials. Wood, silk, cotton, leather, rubber, coal, etc. are natural materials. However, some materials that we use are man-made. Synthetic textiles like terylene and nylon, cement, glass, plastics, dyes, soap, detergents, fertilizers, insecticides and pesticides are some man-made materials which are commonly used.

CANDLES

Candles are used as emergency light source and for decorative and ceremonial purposes. Usually they are made from a mixture of paraffin wax or some other slow-burning substance like tallow (stearic acid). They are commonly made in cylindrical form but are also made in fanciful designs. They contain a wick at their centre. When lighted with a matchstick heat from its flame liquefies the wax of the candle. This liquefied wax rises up along the wick where it is converted into vapour form, which then catches fire.

INKS

Ink is used in various writing instruments like fountain pens, ball pens, gel pens, roller pens, soft tip pens, etc. Ink is a coloured fluid or a paste that is used for writing or printing. Earlier, black ink, also called India ink,was most widely used. It was made by mixing lamp black or carbon black in water or oil to which some gum was added which stabilized the mixture and also gave it better sticking property. This ink is used even these days but more commonly used inks are solutions of water or alcohol soluble dyes. Inks used in printing are similar in nature but are in the form of thick paste, which has a better sticking property.

SOAP AND DETERGENTS

Soap and detergents are used to wash our clothes. We wash our hands and take bath with soap. Soap and detergents help in removing dirt, oil and grease. Soap has been in use for at least last three thousand years. Soaps are sodium or potassium salts of long chain organic acids (called fatty acids) like stearic acid and palmitic acid. It is made by heating oil with sodium hydroxide. The oil and sodium hydroxide solution are fed into an enclosed reaction vessel under high pressure and heated at high temperature. At this temperature, the reaction is completed in a few minutes. The mixture of soap and glycerol is cooled and a concentrated solution of sodium chloride is added. Glycerol dissolves readily in salt solution but soap does not. So, solid soap separates out from the mixture. It is then removed by centrifugation. While still hot it is sprayed into a hot vacuum chamber to dry it. Perfume is added and the particles are compressed into soap cake.

Soaps and detergents form lather or foam with water. Lather removes grease and dirt particles from clothes. Water by itself cannot do it as it does not wet oily or greasy dirt. Addition of soap or detergents improves the wetting property of water and thus helps in removing oily or greasy dirt.

MATCHBOX

The head of matchstick consists of a mixture of potassium chlorate and antimony trisulphide bound together by glue. The striking surface on the matchbox is a mixture of red phosphorus and powdered glass held by glue. When a matchstick is struck against the coated surface of the matchbox, some heat is produced that makes the chemicals in the match head react. The heat of this reaction ignites the wood.

CEMENT

Cement is one of the most important building materials. It is employed in the construction of buildings, roads, bridges, dams, etc. For general uses like plastering or laying of bricks, this powder is mixed with sand and water and the resulting thick paste is used for construction purposes. As a result of chemical reactions between water and cement this mixture sets into a hard mass.

Concrete is a mixture of cement, sand, gravel or small pieces of stone and water. It sets to an extremely hard structure. It is used for making floors and roads. Concrete may be further strengthened by filling it around or over a network of steel rods and allowing it to set. It is known as reinforced concrete cement or R.C.C. Such structures are very strong and are used in construction of pillars, roofs of buildings, roads, bridges and dams.

Manufacture: Limestone and clay are mixed in definite proportion and ground to a fine powdery state. This dry powder is used as such or mixed with water to form a paste and heated in a rotary kiln (a type of furnace). It is slowly made to pass through the kiln wherein limestone and clay combine chemically and form a mixture of calcium silicate, $CaSiO_3$ and calcium aluminate, $CaAl_2O_3$. This mixture is in the form of small greenish black or grey-coloured.

GLASS

Glass is used for various purposes. You must have seen glasses fitted in windows and doors, looking mirrors, windscreens of vehicles, reading glasses, sunglasses, etc.

The basic raw materials needed for making glass are: Washing soda, Limestone and Sand.

The raw materials are mixed in a definite proportion. These are then ground and the mixture is heated in a furnace. Sometimes scrap glass is also mixed with other raw materials. By doing so glass can be recycled and it also helps in melting of the mixture. The fused mixture is then allowed to cool. The glass so produced is transparent, non-crystalline and brittle.

Types of glass and their uses: There are various types of glasses depending upon their composition and the purpose of their use.

Soda-lime glass: The glass produced as given above is called soda-lime glass or soft glass. It is used for manufacture of bottles ordinary crockery, ordinary laboratory glass apparatus like soda glass test tubes etc.

Hard glass: If instead of sodium carbonate, potassium carbonate is used for making glass another variety of glass known as hard glass is produced. It can withstand very high temperatures. It is used for making hard glass laboratory apparatus like hard glass test tubes, beakers, conical flasks etc.

Borosilicate glass: It is sodium aluminium borosilicate. It can withstand rapid heating and cooling without breaking. It is used for making kitchenware and laboratory apparatus. It is sold under the trade names Borosil and Pyrex.

Flint or optical glass: It is used for making lenses, prisms, spectacles, etc. because of its excellent optical properties. It is composed of alkalis, lead oxide and silica. It is also known as flint glass. A superior variety of optical glasses is made by adding cerium oxide. It cuts harmful ultra violet rays that are harmful to eyes. It is known as Crooke's glass.

Coloured glass: It is made by adding small quantities of oxides of different metals to basic ingredients. Blue glass contains traces of cobalt or copper oxide, green glass contains chromium ferrous oxide, red glass contains selenium oxide.

Fibre glass: It is produced by passing molten glass through rotating spinners when it gets converted into fine threads. It is used as an insulating material for heat, electricity and sound in different equipment like electric ovens, geysers, refrigerators, etc. It is also used for reinforcing plastics and rubber to make bodies of cars and scooters and safety helmets.

WASHING SODA

Washing soda is used for washing of clothes. It is because of this chemical used that the clothes washed by a washerman appear so white. Chemically, washing soda is sodium carbonate decahydrate ($Na_2CO_3.10H_2O$). It is an important chemical required as basic raw material in hundreds of industries.

Washing soda is manufactured by Solvay process. In this process, firstly, carbon dioxide is obtained by heating limestone strongly.

It is then passed through cold brine (a solution of concentrated NaCl in water), which has previously been saturated with ammonia.

Being sparingly soluble in water, crystallizes out. It is calcinated (heated strongly in a furnace) to get sodium carbonate.

Ammonia used in this process is regenerated by first converting the quicklime obtained earlier with water and then reacting it with ammonium chloride obtained from carbonating tower.

BAKING SODA

Baking soda is mainly used in the baking industry. When sodium hydrogen carbonate or its solution is heated, it gives off carbon dioxide. It is this carbon dioxide which raises the dough during baking. The sodium carbonate produced during the heating of sodium hydrogen carbonate gives bitter taste. Therefore, usually baking powder is used, which is a mixture of baking soda, $NaHCO_3$ and an acid like tartaric acid. The latter is added to neutralize the sodium carbonate formed in the reaction given above, to avoid its bitter taste. Cakes are made so soft and fluffy by using baking powder. Baking soda is also used in medicines to neutralize the excessive acidity in the stomach. Mixed with a solid acid such as citric or tartaric acid, it finds use in effervescent drinks used to cure indigestion. Another important use of baking soda is in certain types of fire extinguishers.

SCIENCE

BLEACHING POWDER

It is prepared in a vertical tower made of cast iron with inlets for chlorine and hot air near the base. The dry slaked lime, calcium hydroxide, is fed into the chlorinating tower from the top. It moves downward slowly and meets the upcoming current of chlorine. As a result of the reaction between them it is converted into bleaching powder which collects at the bottom.

It is used mainly for bleaching cotton, linen and wood pulp in textile and paper factories. Apart from this, it is used as a disinfectant and germicide for the sterilization of water, in rendering wool unshrinkable and for the manufacture of chloroform. It also finds use as an oxidizing agent in many chemical industries.

POLYMERS

Polymers are large molecules of relatively high molecular masses, They are obtained by joining

IMPORTANT POLYMERS

	NAME OF POLYMER	MONOMER	USES
1.	Polythene	Ethene	As insulator, anti-corrosive, packing material, household and laboratory wares.
2.	Polystyrene	Styrene	As insulator, wrapping material, manufacture of toys and household articles.
3.	Polyvinylchloride (PVC)	Vinyl Chloride	In manufacture of raincoats, hand bags, vinyl flooring and leather clothes.
4.	Polytetrafluoro ethylene (PTFE) or Teflon	Tetrafluoroethylene	As lubricant, insulator and making cooking wares.
5.	Polymethyl metha acrylate (PMMA) or Plexi glass	Methylmetha acrylate	As substitute of glass and making decorative materials.
6.	Polyacrylonitrile (Orlon)	Acrylonitrile	In making synthetic fibres and synthetic wool.
7.	Styrene butadiene rubber (SBR)	(a) Styrene (b) Butadiene	In making automobile tyres and footwear.
8.	Nitrile rubber (Buna-N)	(a) Acrylonitrile (b) Butadiene	In making oil seals, manufacture of hoses and tank linings.
9.	Neoprene	Chloroprene	As insulator, making conveyor belts and printing rollers.
10.	Poly ethyl acrylate	Ethylacrylate	In making films, hose pipes and finishing fabrics.
11.	Terylene (Dacron)	(a) Ethylene glycol (b) Tetraphthalic acid or methyl ester	For making fibres, safety belts, tyre cords, tents etc.
12.	Glyptal	(a) Ethylene glycol (b) Phthalic acid	As binding material in preparation of mixed plastics and paints.
13.	Nylon 6	Caprolactam	In making fibres, plastics, tyre cords and ropes.
14.	Nylon 66	(a) Hexamethylenediamine (b) Adipic acid	In making brushes, synthetic fibres, parachutes, ropes and carpets.
15.	Bakelite	(a) Formaldehyde (b) Phenol	For making gears, protective coatings and electrical fittings.
16.	Urea-formaldehyde resin	(a) Formaldehyde (b) Urea	For making unbreakable cups and laminated sheets.
17.	Melanine formaldehyde resin	(a) Melamine (b) Formaldehyde	In making plastic crockery, un-breakable cups and plates.
18.	Poly-β-hydroxy butyrate-co β hydroxy valerate(PHBV)	(a) Hydroxy butyric acid (b) Hydroxy propionic acid	As packaging, orthopaedic devices and in controlled drug release.

together a large number of small molecules (monomer). Structurally, they are characterised by many repeating molecular subunit, units which form linear chains or a cross-linked network.

The process of formation of polymers from their starting materials is called polymerization and the small molecules that combine with each other are termed as monomers. A polymer may be made by polymerization of one or more compounds.

Classification

(*i*) ***Naturally Occurring Polymers*** **:** These occur in plants and animals. For example, proteins, nucleic acids, cellulose and rubber.

(*ii*) ***Semi-Synthetic Polymers*** **:** These are mostly derived from naturally occurring polymers by chemical modifications. Cellulose on acetylation with acetic anhydride in presence of sulphuric acid forms cellulose diacetate rayon used in making threads and materials like films, glasses etc. Vulcanized rubber has much improved properties and is used in making tyres. Gun-cotton, is a cellulose nitrate, is used in making explosives.

(*iii*) ***Synthetic Polymers*** **:** A large number of man-made polymers are now available, which can be synthesized in laboratory. These include fibres, plastics and synthetic rubbers etc., and find diverse uses as in clothing, electric fittings, eye lenses, substitute for wood and metals.

Some Inorganic Polymers

Glass is made up of rings and chains of repeating silicate units. Glass fibres (fibreglass) are used in textiles and in many construction materials. Bricks, concrete and ceramics are three-dimensional polymers. Polyphosphazenes is formed from reacting NH_4Cl with PC_{15} at 250°C for several hours. Can be substituted to alter properties.

NATURAL RUBBER

It is a natural polymer and possesses remarkable elasticity. It undergoes long range reversible extension under relatively small applied force. This elasticity makes it valuable for a variety of uses. It is manufactured from rubber latex which is a colloidal suspension of rubber in water and is obtained by making incisions in the bark of rubber trees found in tropical and semi-tropical countries such as India (southern part), Indonesia, Malaysia, Sri Lanka, South America etc.

Vulcanization of Rubber

Rubber is used in the temperature range 283 to 335 K as it becomes soft at higher temperatures and brittle at lower temperatures. It has large water absorption capacity, is non-resistant to non-polar solvents and is attacked by oxidizing agents.

In 1893, Charles Goodyear discovered accidently that addition of sulphur to hot rubber causes changes that improve its physical properties in a spectacular manner. This process is called vulcanization. It was originally performed by heating a mixture of raw rubber and sulphur at 373 to 415 K. This process is slow and therefore zinc oxide is used to accelerate the rate of vulcanization. On vulcanization, sulphur establishes cross-links at these reactive sites. Thus, the rubber gets stiffened and intermolecular movement of rubber springs is prevented resulting in change of stiffness. The stiffness of vulcanized material depends upon the amount of sulphur added. About 5% sulphur is used for making tyre rubber and 30% of it for making battery case rubber.

Synthetic Rubbers

Synthetic rubber is the vulcanized rubber which has high elasticity. Most of the synthetic rubber is butadiene derivatives. Some of the important synthetic rubbers is given in the table here

SYNTHETIC RUBBERS	MONOMERS	USES
1. Neoprene (Polychloroprene)	Chloroprene	It is stable to aerial oxidation, and resistant to vegetable or mineral oils. It is used in hoses, gaskets shoe heels, stoppers, conveyor belt, printing rollers etc.
2. Buna-S	Styrene butadiene	Good electric insulator ; used for toys, combs, radio and television parts, etc.
3. Buna N	Butadiene and acrylnitrile	Resistant to action of petrol lubricant oils organic solvent ; used in making oil seals, hoses, tank lining etc.
4. Thiokol (Polysulphide rubber)	Dichloroethane sodium tetrasulphide	It has high tensile strength than natural rubber. It is resistant to the action of mineral oil oxygen, ozone etc.

RAYON, The First Synthetic Fibre

Rayon, Louis Marie Hilaire Bernigaut, Comte de Chardonnet worked on a process of producing threads of an artifical silk" made from collodion in 1884. Chardonnet's silk was finally marketed in 1891, but was short-lived after a young lady's ball gown went up in a puff of smoke after being touched by the lighted cigar of her escort. Charles F. Cross and Edward J. Bevan patened their formula for viscose, a cellulose polymer, in 1892 and were soon manufacturing items of their new Viscoid. The first viscose thread was made by Charles Topham Jr. and commericially produced in 1899. Rayon, made from regenerated cellulose in 1926, marketed by Du Pont, was finally used as a replacement for silk.

PLASTICS

Plastics are synthetic polymers which can be easily moulded or set into a desired shape. Plastics are polyamide, polyesters, polythene, bakelite, terylene etc.

A variety of plastics have been made by replacing one or more hydrogen atoms in ethene and polymerising the resulting monomer (basic unit).

Plastics are of two types : ***thermoplastic*** and ***thermosetting*** plastics. A plastic substance which can be melted repeatedly by heating and can be moulded again and again into different shapes is called **thermoplastic polymer** e.g. Polyvinyl chloride (PVC), Polythene, Nylon and Terylene. A plastic substance which does not soften much on heating and cannot be moulded a second time is called a thermosetting plastic. e.g. bakelite and melamine.

FERTILIZERS

A chemical fertilizer is a salt or some other chemical substance, containing the necessary plant nutrients. By repeated growing of crops, the agricultural land suffers loss of certain elements, largely nitrogen, phosphorus and potassium, which are known as primary nutrients. Other nitrient elements essential for plant growth but required in lesser amount are: calcium, magnesium and iron. Certain elements required in trace amount called *micro-nutrients, e.g.,* copper, manganese, cobalt, zinc and boron.

Fertilizers having only one primary nutrient (*i.e.,* N, P or K) are called **single fertilizers**. Examples are: ***(i) Nitrogenous fertilizers*** such as ammonium sulphate, ammonium nitrate, sodium nitrate, urea ; ***(ii) Phosphoric fertilizers*** such as superphosphate; and ***(iii) Potassium fertilizer*** such as potassium chloride.

Except urea NH_2CONH_2 (organic fertilizer), rest other fertilizers mentioned above are inorganic fertilizers.

Fertilizers having more than one primary nutrients are known are **mixed fertilizers.** Depending on the nature of nutrients, these may be classified as NK, NP, PK or NPK type. For example, potassium nitrate (KNO_3) is a mixed fertilizer of NK type; Ammonium hydrogen phosphate, $(NH_4)\ H_2PO_4$, also called ammophos is of the NP type. Fertilizers of NPK type are known as complete fertilizers because they supply all the essenital primary nutrients.

As compared to fertilizers, the manures are not very rich in the plant nutrients (*i.e.,* N,P,K,). But they do provide to the soil abundant organic matter such as humus. This helps to improve both the physical and chemical properties of the soil. The indiscriminate use of inorganic fertilizers leads to problem of soil pollution.

PESTICIDES

Pesticides for Control of Weeds and Pests

A weed is an unwanted plant that grows with a crop and consumes a lot of nutrients added to the soil for promotion of the growth of crops. The growth of weed reduces the crop yield, so it becomes necessary to control the growth of weed.

Pests are harmful to plants as well as to animals. Some pests are rats (a rodent), locusts (an insect) etc. which cause tremendous damage to crops. They are controlled by using chemicals, these chemicals which inhibit the action of plant and animal pests are known as **pesticide**. Pesticides include chemicals such as *insecticides, herbicides, rodenticides, miticides,* etc. Some common pesticides are : Dichloro-diphenyl-trichloroethane (DDT) and Benzene hexachloride (BHC) or gammexane, zinc phosphide, methyl-parathion. Except zinc phosphide (inorganic pesticide) rest other pesticides mentioned above are organic pesticides.

A good pesticide should be cheap, effective, easy to apply in solution, and biodegradable. It should not be harmful to man and animals.

MEDICINE

The treatment of diseases in Ayurvedic, Unani or the modern allopathic system, the chemical compounds are used in the forms of drugs. Some of these drugs are :

1. Analgesics

Analgesics are the drugs used for relieving pain. Aspirin, (2–acetoxybenzoic acid) a common analgesics with antipyretic properties. Some other analgesics like *naproxen, Ibuprofen* and *diclofenac sodium* or *potassium* find uses as alternatives to them. Certain narcotics (which induce sleep and unconsciousness) like morphine and its derivatives codeine and heroine are used in severe pain as analgesics.

2. Tranquillizers

Tranquillizers are used for the treatment of stress, and severe mental diseases. They form an important component of sleeping pills. They are also called psychotherapeutic drugs. Some of the famous drugs of this class are; derivatives of barbiturate acid such as *veonal, amytal, nembutal, luminal* and *seconal*, which are called barbiturates. These barbiturates are hypnotic *i.e.,* sleep producing agents. Some non-hypnotic tranquillizer are also known which are *chlordiazepoxide, Maprobamate*, etc. used in relieving tension equanil is used in controlling depresssion and hypertension.

3. Antiseptics

Antiseptics are either used to kill or prevent the growth of micro-organisms. Some antiseptic creams like forcing, soframycin, etc. are used.

4. Disinfectants

Disinfectants are also used to kill microorganisms but are not safe for living tissues. Disinfectants are applied for inanimate objects like floors, drainage systems, instruments, etc.

Chlorine is used as disinfectant for drinking water. *Sulphurdioxide* at lower concentrations are used for sterilizing and preservation of squashes. *Dettol,* the commonly used antiseptic is a mixture of chloroxylenol and terpeneol. In soap *Bithional* is added to eliminate undesirable odours resulting from bacterial decomposition of organic matter on the skin. *Iodine* is a powerful antiseptic, which is employed as tincture of iodine (an alcohol-water solution containing 2–3 per cent iodine). Iodoform has been used for antiseptic powder of wound. *Boric acid* is used as a weak antiseptic for eyes and baby talcum powders. *Hydrogen peroxide* is used as non-irritating strong antiseptics.

5. Antibiotics

Antibiotics are chemical substances which are produced by micro-organisms that inhibit the growth or even destroy micro-organisms. The first antibiotics, discovered by Alexander Flemming in 1929 from the mould was *Penicillium notatum.* The antibiotics can be either bactericidal or bacteriostatic.

The range of micro-organisms attacked by an antibiotic is called its spectrum, Chloramphenicol is a broad spectrum antibiotic which is rapidly absorbed in the gastro–intestinal tract and hence can be given orally in case of typhoid, dysentery, and acute fever, meningitis and pneumonia. Penicillin manufactured at Hindustan Antibiotics in Pimpri.

(a) ***Penicillin :*** There are at least six natural penicillins isolated so far. *Ampicillin and amoxicillin* are semi-synthetic modifications of *penicillin.* One of the biggest disadvantage with penicillin is that certain persons are sensitive to it. Therefore it has become absolutely essential to test the patients for sensitivity to penicillin before it is administered.

(b) ***Chloramphenicol :*** It is a broad-spectrum antibiotic, isolated in 1947. It is rapidly absorbed from the gastro-intestinal tract and hence can be given orally. It is very effective against, typhoid, dysentery, acute fever, certain form of urinary infections, meningitis and pneumonia.

(c) ***Streptomycin :*** It is highly effective against micro-organism that cause *tuberculosis.* Therefore, it is widely used for the treatment of tuberculosis.

DYES

Dyes *are the coloured substances used to impart permanent colour to the textiles, foodstuffs, silk, wool,* etc. All coloured substances, however, are not dyes. The requisites of a true dye are:

(i) It should be non-toxic.

(ii) It should be able to fix itself to the material.

(iii) When fixed it should not be fade by light and washing.

(vi) The dye should resist the action of water, acids and alkalies.

The colour of a particular dye is linked with the nature of wavelengths absorbed and released in the visible region of light (400–750 nm). For example, if a dye absorbs radiations corresponding to yellowish green colour, it will appear as violet which is a complementary colour of green. Dyes impart colours to a fabric by absorbing the complementary colours.

COSMETICS

Cosmetics became important in our life. Coal tar which at one time was dumped in pits because of its extremely unpleasant smell happens to be the major source of various cosmetics such as creams, perfumes, talcum powders, deodorants etc. A list of chemicals that constitute some of the cosmetics has been given in the table here :

CHEMICAL	COSMETICS
Acetone	Cologne, nail enamel remover
Benzaldehyde	Perfumes, cologne, hair spray, vaseline, shaving cream, shampoo, soaps
Benzyl acetate	Perfumes, detergent, soaps, after shave lotions, deodorants
Benzyl alcohol	Cologne, nail enamel remover, fabric softener
Camphor	Perfumes, shaving cream, Nail polish
Methylene chloride	Shampoo, cologne
Ethanol	Shampoo, hair spray, perfumes, Shaving creams.
Phthales	Hair sprays, skin moisturisers.
Toluene	Lacquers nail polishes
Benzoic acid	Cream and lotion
Cetyl alcohol	Moisturising cream, lotions
Hydroquinone	Moisturising cream
Linalool	Perfumes, bar soaps, hand lotions
Terpinene	Cologne, perfume, air freshner
Terpineol	Perfumes and colognes.

MULTIPLE CHOICE QUESTIONS

1. A drug that prevents infection and decay is called a/an:
(a) Antiseptic (b) Anti-malarial drug
(c) Germicide (d) Analgesic

2. The substance that is not polymeric in nature is:
(a) nylon (b) polyvinyl chloride
(c) starch (d) glucose

3. Match the following :

	List-I		List-II
A.	Freon	1.	Anti-Knocking agent
B.	Tetraethylo lead	2.	Refrigerant
C.	Banzene Hexachloride	3.	Fire extinguisher
D.	Carbon Tetrachloride	4.	Insecticide

Codes :

	A	B	C	D
(a)	2	1	4	3
(b)	4	2	1	3
(c)	3	4	2	1
(d)	2	4	3	1

4. The substance that is added to make natural rubber strong and more bouncy is:
(a) sulphuric acid (b) sponge
(c) sulphur (d) chlorine

5. The element not present in fertilizers is:
(a) nitrogen (b) hydrogen
(c) chlorine (d) phosphorous

6. Teflon is a:
(a) Insecticide (b) Drug
(c) Polymer (d) Dye

7. Which of the following is a natural polymer ?
(a) Cellulose (b) Plastic
(c) Rubber (d) Silk

8. The substance that is least prone to catch fire is:
(a) nylon (b) terrycot
(c) cotton (d) polyester

9. Which compound of mercury is used as an antiseptic?
(a) Mercuric oxide (b) Cinnabar
(c) Mercuric chloride (d) Mercuric sulphide

10. Match the following:

	List I	List II
I.	Natural rubber	(A) Buna-S
II.	Synthetic rubber	(B) Latex
III.	Natural fibre	(C) Wool
IV.	Synthetic fibre	(D) Nylon

	I	II	III	IV
(a)	B	A	C	D
(b)	A	B	C	D
(c)	B	C	A	D
(d)	C	D	A	B

11. Chemotherapy deals with:
(a) industrial engineering
(b) the use of chemicals in warfare
(c) use of chemicals for the cure of diseases
(d) none of these

12. The following is used as a moth-repellant and insecticide:
(a) Urea (b) Naphthalene
(c) Benzoic acid (d) Citric acid

13. Point out the wrong statement :
(a) Penicillin was discovered by Fleming
(b) Phenacetin is a very important antibiotic
(c) Chloroquine is an antimalarial drug
(d) Ether is an anaesthetic

14. 'Placedo' is often given to patients. It is :
(a) an anti-depressant
(b) a broad-spectrum antibiotic
(c) a sugar pill
(d) a tonic

15. Novalgin is a common :
(a) Analgesic (b) Antibiotic
(c) Antipyretic (d) both (a) and (c)

16. The antiseptic action of Dettol is due to:
(a) Chlorobenzol (b) Chloroxyphenol
(c) Chloroquine (d) Chloroamphenicol

17. The compound used as an antibiotic is :
(a) Ampicillin (b) Aspirin
(c) Sulphuryl (d) Chloroquine

18. A medicine which promotes secretion of urine is called :
(a) Uretic (b) Monouretic
(c) Diuretic (d) Triuretion

19. Which of the following is a general anaesthetic?
(a) Xylocaine
(b) Para-aminosalicyclic acid
(c) Nitrous oxide
(d) None of the above

20. Which of the following is used in lowering the blood pressure ?
(a) Resprine (b) Morphine
(c) Cocaine (d) Diethyl ether

21. Which one of the following is the common example of Fibres ?
(a) Bakelite (b) Buna-S rubber
(c) Nylon-66 (d) Nylon-6

22. The polymer used in the manufacture of electrical goods like switches, plugs, etc, is :
(a) chloroprene (b) bakelite
(c) teflon (d) none of these

23. Hydrazine is :
(a) Biliquid propellant
(b) Mono-liquid propellant

(c) Hybrid propellant
(d) None

24. Which of the following is a solid propellant :
(a) a mixture of paraffin and potassium nitrate
(b) ammonia
(c) hydrogen peroxide
(d) hydrazine

25. Which of the following is not an organic pesticide ?
(a) DDT (b) BHC
(c) Zinc Phosphide (d) Methyl parathian

26. Which of the following is organic fertilizer ?
(a) Potassium chloride
(b) Ammonium hydrogen phosphate
(c) Urea
(d) Super phosphate

27. Coloured glasses for goggles contain:
(a) ferrous oxide (b) lanthanide oxide
(c) nickel oxide (d) ferric oxide

28. Ordinary glass is a mixture of :
(a) sodium silicate (Na_2SiO_3), calcium silicate ($CaSiO_3$) and silica (SiO_2)
(b) sodium silicate and calcium silicate ($CaSiO_3$)
(c) only sodium silicate and silica
(d) none

29. Which chemical is used in the place of sodium carbonate to make the soft glass hard ?
(a) Calcium carbonate
(b) Sodium sulphate
(c) both (a) and (b)
(d) Potassium carbonate

30. Which Chemical is found is shampoo?
(a) Toluene (b) Ethanol
(c) Acetone (d) Terpineol

31. The striking surface of the matchbox contains—
(a) Phosphorus (b) Potassium
(c) Antimony (d) Clorine

32. Which of the followings is used as insulator?
(a) Polythene (b) Polystyrene
(c) Neoprene (d) All of these

33. Baking Soda is—
(a) $NaHCO_3$ (b) Na_2CO_3
(c) Na_22CO_3 (d) None of these

34. Which of the followings is the first synthetic fibre?
(a) Dycron (b) Teryline
(c) Rayon (d) None of these

35. Which chemical among the following is pesticide?
(a) insecticides (b) herbicides
(c) rodenticides (d) All of these

36. Analgesics are used
(a) for relieve pain
(b) for the treatment of stress
(c) to prevent the growth of micro-organism
(d) None of these

37. Which among the following is/are known as primary nutrients of soil?
(a) Nitrogen (b) Phosphorus
(c) Potassium (d) All of these

38. Ammonium sulphate is—
(a) Nitrogenous fertilizer
(b) Phosphoric fertilizer
(c) Potassium fertilizer
(d) All of these

39. The nail enamel remover contains—
(a) Benzyl acetate
(b) Acetone
(c) Methylene chloride
(d) Benzoic Acid

40. Streptomycin is—
(a) an Antibiotics (b) an Antiseptics
(c) an Analgesics (d) a Tranquillizers

ANSWERS

1	2	3	4	5	6	7	8	9	10
(a)	(d)	(a)	(c)	(c)	(c)	(a)	(c)	(c)	(a)
11	**12**	**13**	**14**	**15**	**16**	**17**	**18**	**19**	**20**
(c)	(b)	(b)	(c)	(d)	(b)	(a)	(c)	(c)	(a)
21	**22**	**23**	**24**	**25**	**26**	**27**	**28**	**29**	**30**
(c)	(b)	(b)	(a)	(c)	(c)	(a)	(a)	(d)	(b)
31	**32**	**33**	**34**	**35**	**36**	**37**	**38**	**39**	**40**
(a)	(d)	(a)	(c)	(d)	(a)	(d)	(a)	(b)	(a)

❑❑❑

THE WORLD OF LIVING

Biology is the study of living organisms, that is, all plant and animal life, including man, and even the microbes.

There are well-defined characteristics that differentiate the 'living' from the 'non-living'. Living organisms are characterised by the following features:

(i) **Organization :** Every organism has a definite biological organization. Every organism is composed of single cells. These single cells are organised to form multicellular organisation. which gives different size, shape and function to organisms.

(ii) **Metabolism :** The sum total of biochemical reactions involved in the release and utilization of energy within the organism is called *metabolism.* Metabolism consists of two broad patterns of chemical reactions that are inter-dependent and continuous. The *anabolism* consisting of chemical reactions that form complex substances from simpler substances resulting in the formation of more protoplasm and therefore growth; and the *catabolism* consisting of chemical reactions that break down complex substances resulting in the release of energy.

(iii) **Growth** : Growth is defined as an irreversible increase in weight, size or volume of an organism.

(iv) **Reproduction** : Organisms tend to perpetuate their kind through reproduction. The living organisms are multiplied to forrı new individuals by sexual or asexual means.

(v) **Responsiveness** : All living organisms respond to physical or chemical stimuli like, temperature, light, chemicals, touch, etc. Some plants such as *Mimosa* leaves are sensitive to touch.

(vi) **Adaptation :** All living organisms (Plants and Animals) have a capacity to adapt themselves to changing environmental conditions. Plants and animals are adapted by changing their structure, physiology or behaviour.

(vii) **Movement :** Living organisms have the capacity to move from one place to another.

(viii) **Respiration :** All living organism takes Oxygen and release CO_2. This process is called Respiration.

The earth shows a remarkable variety of living organisms. Some sort of classification is needed when dealing with such diversity if we are to understand living things. Aristotle and other ancient Greeks (4th and 3rd century B.C.), possibly made the earliest serious efforts to classify living things in the world they knew as plants and animals. They identified a few thousands types. ***Charaka*** (first century A.D.) the father of Ayurveda listed the names of over 200 kinds of animals and about 340 kinds of plants in his book 'Charaka Samhita".

In the modern classification system, each living thing belongs to a species, genus, family, order, class, phylum (or division, in plants), and kingdom. These groups are sometimes divided into subgroups.

The five kingdoms are *Monera, Protista, Fungi, Plantae* (plants) and *Animalia* (animals).

LIVING WORLD

Monera Protista Fungi Plantae Animalia

KINGDOM MONERA

Bacteria

Having appeared about 3,500 million years ago, bacteria are one of the oldest and smallest group of organisms with cellular length ranging from 0.1 to 10 μm and possessing an average diameter of about 1 μm. Found in soil, dust, water, air, in and on plants and animals, most bacteria are enclosed by a tough protective layer called *cell wall.* Some species are enclosed by a *capsule,* a slimy layer making the wall resistant to destructive chemicals. All bacteria have a cell membrane, an elastic bag -like structure just inside the cell wall. Small molecules of food enter the cell through pores in this membrane, but larger molecules cannot pass through.

Inside the membrane is *cytoplasm,* a jelly-like substance containing chemicals called *enzymes,* required for food breakdown and building cell parts. These cells also contain DNA, vital for growth, reproduction and other activities. It forms an area of the cytoplasm called *nuclear body.* Other parts of bacterias cell structure are *mesosomes*–unfoldings of cell surface membrane; *ribosomes* sites for protein synthesis *pilus* numerous fine protein rods concerned with attachment to specific cells or surfaces; *plasmids*-small, self-replicating circles of extra DNA, processing a few genes that give extra survival and *flagellum*-the tail-like structure enabling movement of bacteria cells.

Viruses

Viruses are the smallest living organisms, but without a cellular structure. They have a simple structure, consisting of a small piece of nucleic acid, either DNA or RNA, surrounded by a protein or lipoprotein coat. They can reproduce by invading living cells, therefore, are all parasitic. While outside a host cell they are inert, inside they enter a dynamic phase in which they replicate, pirating the host cell's enzymes, nucleic and amino acids and machinery to accomplish what they are not equipped to do alone. Viral replication is often carried out at the expense of the host. Diseases such as herpes, rabies, influenza, some cancers, poliomyelitis and yellow fever are of viral origin. Of the estimated 1,000-1,500 types of viruses, approximately 250 cause diseases to humans (over 100 of which cause the common cold) and 100 infect animals.

Discovery of Viruses

It was in 1898 that Beijerink, a Dutchman, for the first time described the infectious nature of certain plant fluids as 'virus'. Later, viruses were found to be the smallest living organisms, their size ranging from 20 to 300 nm, and about 50 times smaller than bacteria. They cannot be seen with a light microscope and pass through filters that retain bacteria.

KINGDOM PROTISTA

Algae

Believed to be the best photosynthetic eukaryotes, algae are found in water and form a group of protists that are of great biological importance to humans. Algae lack true stem, roots and leaves and, therefore, are given the special name *thallus.* Spread throughout intertidal zone, most algae have specialized adaptations for protection against drying when exposed during low tide. Some large algae, like kelps, are edible and considered staple food in some parts of the world. Extracts from kelp and other algae are used to produce products like ice cream and cosmetics.

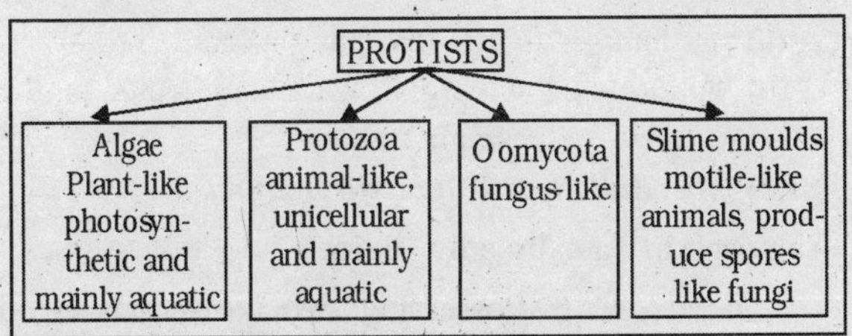

Classification of Protists Kingdom

Classification

Algae are differentiated according to the presence of photosynthesis pigments

(a) **Green algae:** Appearing as single-celled amorphous sheets or a collection of long filamentous strands, green algae belong to phylum *Chlorophyta* category. Most species are *found* in fresh water habitats even as they can survive in marine waters, damp soils, snow and ice.

(b) **Red algae:** Belong to phylum *Rhodophyta* group, red coralline algae can incorporate calcium carbonate into their cell walls, thereby, lending their body a rigid, segmented appearance and texture. Most of these species have the ability to carry out photosynthesis at much greater depths than other types.

(c) **Brown algae:** These are multicellular algae (such as kelps), which can have leaf-like blades and stems and grow in marine waters near the coast. And due to the presence ef pigment *fucoxanthin,* their texture is of brown or olive colour.

(d) **Diatoms:** Significant components of phytoplankton, diatoms are tiny, floating, photosynthetic organisms that form the base of aquatic food chains. They are single-celled algae with a cell wall made of silica or glass.

(e) **Golden brown or yellow brown algae:** Alike brown algae, this category too receives its characteristic colour from the carotenoid pigment *fucoxanthin.* Usually, they are unicellular and colonial and swim or float in lakes and oceans as phytoplankton.

(f) **Blue-green algae:** Probably the most ancient organisms on Earth, blue-green algae are also called as cyanobacteria. They are single-celled and connect in a filament form or are arranged in simple colonies.

KINGDOM FUNGI

Kingdom Fungi comprises of numerous moulds that grow on damp organic matter (such as bread, leather, decaying vegetation and dead fish) and unicellular yeasts that are abundant on sugary surfaces of the ripe fruits and many parasite plants. Though botanists classified fungi in the plant kingdom, biologists later considered it as a separate kingdom. Most fungi can be seen through naked eye and its study is called *mycology* (*'mykes'* mushrooms). They are sub-divided on the basis of mycelium morphology and mode, nutrition and reproduction.

SCIENCE

CHARACTERISTICS OF FUNGI

- The absence of chlorophyll makes fungi non-photosynthetic; therefore, they resort to heterotrophic nutrition.
- Can be mutualists, parasites or saprotrophs.
- Digestion takes place outside the body and nutrients are absorbed directly.
- Body is usually a *mycelium,* a network of five tubular filaments called *hyphae.* These may be septate (have cross-walls, like Penicillium) or *aseptate* (no cross-walls, e.g., Mucor).
- Rigid cell walls containing *chitin* as the fibrillar material. (Chitin is nitrogen-containing, polysac charide, very similar in structure to *cellulose* with high tensile strength). It, therefore, gives shape to the hyphae and prevents osmotic bursting of cells.
- If carbchydrate is stored, it is usually as glycogen and not starch. They reproduce by means of spores and are non-motile organisms.

KINGDOM PLANTAE (PLANT KINGDOM)

Bryophytes

Found mostly in moist places, bryophytes are simple, non-vascular small plants with thallus-like body, which remains attached to the soil by *rhizoids.* The mode of reproduction is mainly sexual and they lack roots, flowers and seeds. Bryophytes are embryo-bearing plants of three plant divisions: Bryophyta (mosses), Hepatophyta (liverwort) and Anthocerophyta (hornworts). In their level of organization, bryophytes lie between chlorophyta (from which they are likely to be evolved) and simpler, lower vascular plants like the Lycopododophyta.

Tracheophytes

Found only on land, tracheophyte are a collective term applied to vascular plants of a division or phyla. The nine divisions can be divided into two main groups: pteridophytes and spermatophytes.

A. Pteridophytes

Lycopododophyta

Multicellular, terrestrial plants with vascular tissues, lycopododophyta's body are differentiated into roots, stem and leaves. The spores are produced in the axils of fertile leaves, mostly aggregated into club-like terminal cones. Club mosses, spike mosses, quillworts are common examples.

Arthrophyta

Possessing upright stems that grow from underground branches, arthrophyta, too, are multicellular plants with vascular tissues. The plant body is divided into roots, stem and small whorled leaves. They are largely an extinct group, represented by a single living genus the *Equisetum* (the horsetails). Horsetails are conspicuously jointed rushes with spokes of short, pine-needle like leaves radiating from each joint. Found in wet, swampy soil, they occur in all land masses except Australia. The stem contains silica and is used for polishing wood.

Pterophyta

They contain spores for reproduction, which usually are produced on the lower surface ofleaves or on their margins. Pterophyta also are multicellular plants with vascular tissues, their body differentiated into roots, stem and leaves. Here, seeds are not produced.

B. Spermatophytes

These plants have seeds and are divided as (i) *Gymnosperm* (Latin *gymn* 'naked' and Greek *sperma* 'seed') and (ii) *Angiosperm* (Latin *angi* 'enclosed' and Greek *sperma* 'seed' meaning seed inside fruits).

Gymnosperm

These are further divided into

Cycadophyta: These are multicellular terrestrial plants with vascular tissues (without vessels). The plant body is divided into root, stem and leaves. The stem is large and woody, leaves are large and fern-like. Example: Cycas (sago palm), Zamia (sago tree).

Coniferophyta: Multicellular plants with well-developed tissues, the main plant body of *coniferophyta* is large and woody leaves are simple, smaller than cycodophyta and needle-like. Example: Cedrus (deodar) and Taxus (yew).

Angiosperms (or Anthrophyta)

This category includes more advanced flowering plants with well-developed vascular tissues and makes up for more than half of all known species of plantsabout 20,000. They are predominantly saprophytic, possess a well-differentiated body of roots, stem and leaves, and occur in almost all places. Angiosperms range vary in size from minute floating duckweeds to giant eucalyptus and silk-cotton trees, and include plants of great variety and form cacti, water lilies, sunflowers, orchids, pitcher plants, Indian pipe, etc. The reproductive organs of these plants are flowers and seeds are enclosed within an ovary, which develops into a fruit-wall. On the basis of age they are grouped as:

(a) *Perennials-living* for many years,
(b) *Annuals-producing* flowers and fruits in the course of a single season,
(c) *Biennials-living* for two seasons.

Angiosperms are broadly divided into two classes:

Dicotyledons: Possessing two cotyledons (seed leaves that usually do not become foliage leaves but serve to provide food for the new seedling) in their seeds, these plants may be annuals, biennials or perennials. Example: Gram.

Monocotyledons: Mostly annuals with a single cotyledon in their seeds, these plants do not have any secondary growth and their features include flower parts in threes: one cotyledon leaf venis (which are usually parallel) and vascular tissues (present in scattered bundles in the stem).

Other Classifications

(a) Terrestrial plants-grow on soil.

(b) Hydrophytes-grow in water.

(c) Epiphytes-perch on other plants, but do not take nourishment from them. They are not rooted in the soil but upon branches and stems of other plants. Example: *Urn.*

(d) Xerophytes-grow in dry habitats like deserts. Example: *Cacti.*

(e) Mesophytes-thrive under conditions intermediate between very wet and very dry. A great variety of crops like beans, tomatoes, peas, etc. belong to this category.

(f) Parasitic-lack chlorophyll and, therefore, cannot prepare their own food.

(g) Carnivorous-trap insects and other small creatures on their sticky leaves and digest them to obtain nitrogen and other material essential for their growth. Example: Insectivorous plants like pitcher plant and bladderwort.

KINGDOM ANIMALIA (ANIMAL KINGDOM)

Protozoa

Protozoa, the single-celled microscopic organisms, include flagellated Zoomastigina as its members, many of which live as parasites on plants and animals. All functions of protozoa are performed within the single cell itself. Examples: Amoeba, sarcodina. The protozoa, however, are placed in kingdom Protista with other single-celled organisms in many classifications. They can be classified as Sarcomastigophora (flagellates), Sarcodina (Sarcodines), Sporozoa (Spore-formers) and Ciliophora (Ciliates).

Metazoa

All animals, including humans, are placed under the metazoa sub-kingdom. They are multicellular organisms in which cells are grouped together to form tissues, organs and systems. Metazoas are divided into two main groups:

Invertebrates (Non-Chordata Phyla)

Commonly called sponges, non-chordates do not possess a vertebral column; they lack a backbone and up till now the most abundant species on Earth. Nearly 2 million such animals have been identified so far, constituting about 98 per cent of the total members identified in the entire animal kingdom.

Vertebrates (Phylum Chordata)

These are animals that possess a backbone or spinal column, made of interlocking units called vertebrate. Also called as phylum Chordata, vertebrates have a strong, but flexible, structure that supports the body and anchors the limbs. They also protect the nerves of the spinal cord. They include fish, amphibians and reptiles, as well as birds and mammals.

Amphibians

Amphibians are members of the class Amphibia, subphylum Vertebrata, phylum Chordata. The class Amphibia includes frogs, toads, salamanders, etc. Amphibians are characterized by a glandular skin without external scales, by gills during development (and in adulthood in some) and by eggs that may have jelly coats but develop without formation of extra-embryonic membranes such as the amnion. Most amphibians also have four limbs. Limbs and lungs are adaptations for life on land; .he limbs evolved from the ancestral fishes' lobed fins. The scales and amniote egg evolved by reptiles are further adaptations for life on land and distinguish reptiles from amphibians.

Reptiles

Reptiles are characterized *by* a combination of features, none of which alone could separate all reptiles from all other animals. Among these features are (i) cold-bloodedness; (ii) the presence of lungs; (iii) direct development without larval forms as in amphibians; (iv) a dry skin with scales but not feathers (a characteristic of birds) or hair (a characteristic of mammals); (v) an amniote egg; (vi) internal fertilization; (vii) a 3-4 chambered heart; (viii) two aortic arches (blood vessels) carrying blood from the heart to the body; mammals have only one aorta on the left; birds also have one but on the right; (ix) a metanephric kidney; (x) 12 pairs of head (cranial) nerves; amphibians have 10; and (xi) some special skeletal features.

Mammals

Mammals belong to subphylum Vertebrata. The mammals evolved from a lineage of reptiles about 225 million years ago. Presently, nearly 4,500 species of mammals are found on Earth. The order **Primates** contains our species, H. *sapiens.* Primates belong to class Mammalia and show all the features of mammals, including hair and milk glands for nursing the young. They are endothermic, have vertebrae and a skeleton and are segmented deuterostomes, with a coelom made from an outgrowth of the digestive tract. Primates are eutherians, that is, they have a placenta that provides an intimate mother-child relationship where the mother nurses the child.

Characteristics of Primates

Primates are characterized by certain uniting features, including limber shoulders and hip joints to allow a great range of movement, opposable thumbs and big toes to grab food or hang on to branches, presence of a clavicle (a nail on the first toe) and a large' brain. Besides, primates have highly sensitive hands, which lend them the sense of touch. Their eyes are set close together to enhance depth perception. Having evolved from an arboreal ancestor during the Mesozoic era, most primates still live on trees. The most advanced known primates are humans.

Family Hominidae

The family that humans belong to *Family Hominidae* also includes chimpanzees, gorillas and orangutans. There are only four generae and six species in this family, but it is a very diverse group. Male hominids are larger than females, and they have opposable thumbs and big toes, except for humans. Hominids, probably the most advanced family in the world, possess developed forearms with legs longer than the arms. They lack a tail and all the species in this family, other than humans, are good tree climbers. Hominids also have a unique structure of their teeth with canines that have not developed into tusks and broad incisors. Even chimpanzees can learn human sign language and show innovation when solving problems. Following species are included under the Family Hominidae.

Homo sapiens-Humans

Homo sapiens (our species) are the only living species in the *Homo* genus. The main characteristics here are bipedal posture, excellent eyesight and a large brain that allows problem-solving capabilities and innovative thinking. The head is larger than other primates because the skull requires room to enclose the large brain. Humans also have a highly developed nervous system and strong senses.

Alike other apes, humans too have opposable thumbs and nails on their fingers but lack tails. The upper legs have very strong muscles, thereby allowing them to stand upright. A curve in the spine near the lower back allows upright posture because the centre of gravity of a human is directly over the pelvis.

CELL : THE BASIC UNIT OF LIFE

All organisms are composed of cells. The cell is the structural basis of life. Organisms may be made up of one or more cells. If the organisms are made up of a single cell, they are called *unicellular organisms*, e.g. amoeba, chalamydomonas, bacteria, and many fungi; while the organisms made up of a few cells (e.g. some algae and fungi) to several million cells are called *multicellular organisms*.

Robert Hooke in 1665, was the first to identify cells. In the early 19th century, Matthias Schleiden, Theodor Schwan, and others recognized the universal occurence and importance of cells and formulated a comprehensive cell theory in 1838-39 which states that:

(i) The cell is the smallest unit of living matter capable of assimilation, respiration, growth and reproduction; and

(ii) The cell can live independently and reproduce its own kind (in other words, all cells come from pre-existing cells).

Max Schutze (1861) proposed that living matter of an organism is protoplasm and the cell is simply an accumulation of protoplasm limited by an outer membrane and containing a nucleus.

TYPES OF CELLS

The living organisms have two types of cells.

- **Prokaryotic Cells:** These are the cells without definite nucleus, i.e. nucleus is not bound by a nuclear membrane. It is called nucleoid *e.g.* bacteria, Blue-Green Algae. (Cyanobacteria) PPLO, etc.
- **Eukaryotic Cells :** These have a definitely organised nucleus with a definite nuclear membrane which surrounds the genetic material and it has membrane bound cell organelle such as mitochondria, lysosomes, chloroplasts etc., *e.g.* animal cells, plant cells, fungi, algae, etc.

STRUCTURE OF THE CELL

Plasma or Cell Membrane

It is the outer covering of each cell, which separates its contents from the surounding medium. It is a living, ultra thin, porous, semi-permeable membrane. It provides the mechanical support and external protection to the protoplasm. It acts as a efficient barrier to exterior environment and allows selective permeability to necessary materials to and from the cell.

Mitochondria

These are double membrane, rod-like or spherical, extremely small organelles. The outer membrane of a mitochondria is smooth whereas the inner membranes show many infoldings called cristae. Mitochondria are the sites of energy release (in the form of ATP) for all the cellular purposes and hence are also known as the 'power houses' of the cell.

Ribosomes

The ribosomes are granular masses which are either associated with the endoplasmic reticulum, or dispersed freely in the cytoplasm. They contain RNA and are the sites of protein synthesis in the cell.

Ribosomes are sub-microscopic, polypeptide manufacturings naked nucleoproteins. Robinson and Brown (1953) discovered ribosome in plant cells and Palade (1955) discovered it in animal cells.

Golgi Bodies

The Golgi apparatus consists of an irregular network or rod-like globular or granular bodies in animal cells. It is often concentrated around the nucleus and associated with endoplasmic reticulum. Large number of golgi bodies occurs in gland and nerve cells, but less number of golgi bodies occurs in muscle cells. For the given type of cell, golgi bodies are uniform in shape. The chief function of golgi bodies in gland cells is to collect protein secretions from the endoplasmic reticulum and pass them outside the cell. Golgi bodies add carbohydrates to these secretions to stiffen them into material called zymogen granules. The golgi apparatus in plants is known as ***dictysome***.

Golgi apparatus is present in all eukaryotic cells except RBC and sieve tube elements. It is also absent in prokaryotes and sperm cells of seedless embryophytes.

Centrosomes

The Centrosome, found in most of the animals cells is a rather dense area of protoplasm, lies close to the nucleus. The Centrosome containing two cylindrical structure are called centrioles. Each Centrioles is surrounded by pericentriolar material. They play an important part in cell division, species lacking them include amoebae, unicellular red algae, pines and the flowering plants.

Lysosomes

Lysosomes are vacuole-like bodies that secrete enzymes to digest food substances. Lysosomes are also involved in various other functions like, in defence against bacteria and viruses, in destroying old and worn out organelles and often resulting in the death of the cells. Because of this last role, they are referred to as *suicide bags* of the cells.

The Lysosomal membrane is impermeable to the digestive enzymes stored within it capable of withstanding their digestive action against macromolecules within the cells.

Nucleus

It is the central component of cell which control and regulate all activities of cell. There are generally one nucleus per cell, though some cells possess two or more nucleus. The nucleus is usually round and confining a watery fluid, the *nucleoplasm*, bounded by two porous membranes (nuclear membrane) that are often continuous with the endoplasmic reticulum. The nucleoplasm contains the substance called *chromatin*, which carries the genes, or determiners of heredity. Besides this, one or several spherical bodies called *nucleoli* are enmeshed in the chromatin network. The chromatid is composed of nucleoproteins - a combinations of proteins and nucleic acids - DNA (deoxyribonucleic acid) and RNA (ribonucleic acid). Thus, chromatin bears the genetic information units - the genes. The various cellular activities are controlled by the nucleus through its chromosomes.

Chromosomes

It is a rod-shaped structure visible under the light microscope during the cell division. Each chromosome is made up of chromatin material. Some portions of chromatin take a darker stain during interphase. This region is called **heterochromatin**.

Chromosomes are 0.5 to 30μm in length and 0.2 to 3μm in diameter. Major exceptions include several insects whose giant chromosomes may reach a length of nearly 300μm and a width of 10μm.

Cell Wall

The cell wall is the second layer of the cell envelope below the glycocalyx. This layer determines the shape of the cell and provides a kind of strong structural support to prevent the bacterium from bursting or collapsing in a hypotonic solution.

CELL DIVISION

To divide and duplicate is one of the fundamental properties of cells. In fact, the growth and development of all organisms are dependent upon the enlargement and division of their cells.

Plants and animals are usually composed of millions of cells when they are fully grown, yet they all begin life from only one cell: a fertilized egg cell or zygote. The zygote divides to produce 'daughter' cells which eventually become specialized into all the body tissues.

SCIENCE

There are two major types of cell division *mitosis* and *meiosis*. Each of these is divided into two events—nuclear division (Karyokinesis) which is followed by the division of the cytoplasm (Cytokinesis).

Mitosis

In cells with nuclei, an important step in cell division is the division of the nucleus. The nucleus (except in sex cell) divides by the process called mitosis. Mitosis occurs in four successive stages; prophase, metaphase, anaphase, and telophase. There are no sharp dividing lines separating the various stages, and the events of each stage vary somewhat in different organism. The four stages are preceded by a resting stage, called interphase.

MITOSIS
- **Interphase** (Protein synthesis, RNA synthesis)
- **Prophase** (Chromatin condensed)
- **Metaphase** (Chromosomes arranged at equatorial plate)
- **Anaphase** (Chromosomes starts moving towards the poles).
- **Telophase** (Chromosomes are at the opposite pole).
- **Cytokinesis** (Division of cell)

Meiosis

It occurs in cells that produce gametes in sexually reproducing organisms. In these organisms, the fusion of an egg and a sperm cell produces a zygote, which develops into a new organism.

DIFFERENCE BETWEEN MITOSIS AND MEIOSIS

MITOSIS	MEIOSIS
1. It occurs in all somatic cells.	1. It occurs only in sex cells.
2. Number of chromosomes remains the same.	2. Number of chromosomes is halved.
3. No exchange of chromosome material takes place.	3. Chromosomal material (chromatin) having genes has crossed over.
4. Daughter cell and parent cell have identical chromosomes.	4. Daughter or son cell has chromosomal material derived in part from the mother cell and in part from the father cell.
5. No genetic variation occurs between generations.	5. Variation in gene combination is seen.

Most of the cells of an organism are diploid (2n). They contain pairs of similar chromosomes, known as homologous pairs. One member of each pair was inherited from the mother by the egg cell and one from the father by the sperm cell. Each species has a characteristic number of chromosomes. Human cells, for example, have a diploid number of 46 or 23 pairs of chromosomes.

The essence of meiosis is that it produces gametes that are haploid (n) that is, they have only half the number of chromosomes found in the other cells of the parent organism.

MORPHOLOGY OF THE PLANT

There are three kinds of organs in plants—roots, stems, and leaves. The reproductive structures-cones and flowers—of higher plants are sometimes referred to as separate organs. Actually they are specialized stems.

For example, the asparagus plant and certain parasitic flowering plants lack leaves. In asparagus, the functions of leaves have been taken over by small, green stem branches. Roots, stems, and leaves are called vegetative organs.

Root Systems

Roots anchor the plant body firmly in the soil. They absorb water and mineral nutrients from the soil, conduct these materials upward into stems, and transport food downward from stems. Many roots store food produced during the growing season, such as carrots and beets. In these, food is accumulated in the roots during the first year, flowers and seeds are produced in the second.

Certain roots arise neither from primary nor secondary roots but from stems or leaves. They are called *adventitious roots*. A new plant can develop from the bulb of the tulip plant because adventitious roots grow from it. This is called *vegetative propagation*. The stems of certain plants, such as the banyan tree, bear aerial roots. These grow downward until they penetrate the ground. They are called *prop roots*. Mangrove trees, which grow along ocean shores in tropical regions, also put forth prop roots. They reach the water and penetrate the sandy bed.

The aerial roots of orchids play an important part in the life of the plant. They serve to anchor to the tree or other supports on which the orchid grows.

They also absorb water from the moisture in the air or from the rain. The *stilt roots* supporting structure in maize and sugarcane.

Stems

The first stem develops from the plumule of embryo. A miniature stem emerges as the seed germinates. Generally; it makes its way upward through the soil and into the air. As long as its growing point remains alive, it becomes longer. In time, branches develop. If the growing point is killed or removed, one or more growing point may be formed below the cut end. Stems that grow above the ground in this way are called aerial stems.

Most essential characteristics of stem is that it bears nodes and internodes and buds is present at the nodes.

In certain plants, such as potatoes, we find fleshy, thickened undergroud stems known as *tubers*. They develop buds - "eyes" of potatoes. Generally the rhizomes and tuber connected to the main stem of the plant and die after the growing season. The tubers remain alive, and in the next growing season they put forth shoots.

A *bulb* is very short underground stem that bears a cluster of thick, overlapping leaves. These leaves store food. Onions, tulips, lilies, and other familiar plants develop bulbs, each of which can give rise to a new plant.

Gladiolus, crocus, and various other plants form underground stems called ***corms***. These resemble bulbs somewhat. However, the stems are much more prominent and the leaves are generally smaller and thinner than those of bulbs.

Like roots, stems serve several purposes. They produce and support leaves, which are the food-making centres of plants. They provide passage ways along which various substances are transported within the plant. Stems also serve as a storage place for foods. And in certain cases, parts of stems propagate plants.

Leaves

The stem and leaves constitute the shoot system of the plant. Leaves are perhaps the most important vegetative organ of the plants. Generally a leaf consists of a *leaf stalk*, or *petiole*, and the *leaf proper*, called *a blade*. In some leaves there are small projections, called *stipules*, at the point where the petiole meets the stem. The petiole contains xylem and phloem and forms part of the conducting system of the plant. Certain leaves have no petioles; the blade grows out from the stem. The framework of all blades is made up of a network of veins. In many trees, each leaf consists of a single blade and petiole. In other trees the leaf blade is divided into several *leaflets* each attached to the same petioles. The latter is called *complex*, and the former, *simple* leaf.

The leaves of most plants have a similar microscopic structure. There is a surface layer of cells, the epidermis, covered on the outside with a waxy coating or cuticle. The hairs found on some leaves are outgrowths of epidermal cells. The epidermis has various openings, or pores, known as stomata (singular, "stoma"). Gases such as carbon dioxide, oxygen, and water vapour pass in or out through these pores. Each stoma is surrounded by a pair of cells called guard cells.

RESPIRATION

All living organism respire. In fact respiration is one of the basic characteristics of living organism so that if an object does not respire, it is considered non-living. Respiration which uses oxygen is called aerobic respiration. Which respiration takes place in absence of oxygen it is called anaerobic respiration. Very little energy is released during anaerobic respiration because glucose is not completely broken down into carbon dioxide and water. It is changed into alcohol or lactic acid.

Respiration in Plants

Plants require much less energy than most animals, and respire more slowly. They do not breathe; diffusion provides sufficient oxygen for their respiratory needs. Atmospheric air moves in and out by simple diffusion, through the stomata of the leaves and the surface tissues in general. Subsequent, the gases enter the inter-cellular spaces. Oxygen is absorbed by the individual cells for use in the energy yielding reactions. As oxygen is utilized, more of it diffuses into the plant. Since carbon dioxide is being continuously formed, its concentration in tissue becomes higher than in the surrounding air. Consequently, it diffuses out of the plant, especially when it is not being used for photosynthesis. Besides leaves, other parts of the plants, such as stems, roots, fruits and seeds, also respire. The respiratory rates of root and shoot apices and germinating seeds are, however, higher since they are actively growing and therefore require much more energy.

Respiration in Animals

Single-celled organisms have no organs for respiration: they simply exchange carbon dioxide and oxygen across their cell membranes. Higher animals, however have special respiratory mechanisms. Insects have a network of tubes (tracheae) that open to the outside and bring oxygen into the body. Fish and several aquatic invertebrates have gills, which permit the exchange of gases with the surrounding water; a pumping mechanism then carries the oxygenated blood through the animal's body. Some fishes and amphibians use their thin, moist, vascular skin for respiratory exchange. Land-dwelling vertebrates have lungs that vary in complexity. The lungs are inflated by various types of pumping mechanisms, which cause oxygen to enter in response to a change in air pressure. Oxygen is transported throughout the body by bonding with haemoglobin pigments in red blood cells. Haemoglobin also acts to carry carbon dioxide from body tissues back to the lungs where it is exhaled.

Human Respiratory System

In human beings lungs are the respiratory organs (pulmonary respiration). Lungs communicate with the atmospheric air through nostrils, pharynx (throat), larynx (voice- box), trachea (windpipe), bronchi and bronchioles. These bronchioles terminate into millions of tiny sacs like structures called alveoli. The thin walls of alveoli are lined with a network of blood capillaries. Alveoli have a far larger surface area than the total skin surface and consequently provide for greater respiratory exchanges.

Lungs are located in the thorax cavity. Diaphragm and the intercostal muscles, help in contraction and expansion of the lungs during breathing.

Respiratory gases are exchanged between the alveolar air and the blood in alveolar capillaries.

Most of the oxygen entering the blood combines with haemoglobin to form oxyhaemoglobin and is thus transported by RBC. The high pO_2 and low pCO_2 in the alveoli haemoglobin takes up large volumes of oxygen in the lungs. On reaching the tissue capillaries, oxyhaemoglobin dissociates to release oxygen; the low pO_2 and high pCO_2 in the tissue enhances this release of oxygen. This oxygen released in the tissue is then utilised in breakdown of food, releasing energy and waste products – CO_2 and H_2O.

TRANSPORTATION SYSTEM

Transportation in Plants

Plants obtain their nourishment from the atmosphere in the form of carbon dioxide, water, and some mineral elements. The water and minerals are generally absorbed from the soil through roots, except in aquatic plants. Carbon dioxide, on the other hand, is obtained from the surrounding air through minute pores in the leaves called stomata. Using the simple substances and the energy from sunlight, the green plants synthesize their own food. Since this activity of synthesizing food, called photosynthesis, is limited to green leaves, the water and mineral elements have to be transported from the roots to the leaves. Also the food synthesized by the leaves has to be transported to the various plant parts, including roots and the growing shoot tips for their active functioning. How the plants manage to transport these substances over long distances, sometimes to heights of more than 100 metres, is a problem that has elicited the interest of a large number of botanists for more than hundred years.

Higher plants obtain inorganic nutrients in the form of liquid or gas. Substances are transported from one part of a plant to another through extremely narrow tubes in the root, stem, and leaves. This tube is called *xylem.* It transport water and dissolved minerals from the roots to the leaves. Another tube is called *phloem* which transport sugar made during photosynthesis from the leaves to growing and storage areas of the plant.

Plant roots take in water and dissolved minerals from the soil through root hairs. Root hairs take in water through a combination of diffusion, osmosis and active absorption. As root hairs take up water their cell sap is diluted and soon becomes a weaker solution than the sap of cells deeper inside the root hairs. Water entering root hairs by osmosis gradually flows further into the root from cell to cell and eventually reaches the root xylem vessels. Water flows into root xylem vessels with sufficient force to push it up into the stem xylem.

Root hairs take in dissolved minerals by active absorption (i.e, transport of molecules against concentration gradient) which requires expenditure of energy (ATP) by the cells.

Transportation in Animals

Circulation is the process by which nutrients, respiratory gases, and metabolic products are transported throughout a living organism.

In unicellular and small multicellular organisms, simple diffusion is often sufficient to transport oxygen and carbon dioxide. The streaming movement of the cell cytoplasm is called *cyclosis,* it is sufficient to conduct larger molecules like sugars, fats, proteins to different parts of the cell. In more complex organisms, however, specialized systems have been developed to provide adequate circulation to all tissues.

In *simple multicellular organisms* like sponges and coelenterates (e.g. jellyfish and hydras) water circulates from the surrounding medium through channels in their bodies. Cells in contact with the water take up food and oxygen directly from it.

In *the flatworm*, which has true circulatory system, a fluid carrying nutrients bathes the animal tissues while moving passively through the spaces between its component cells. Oxygen is taken up directly from the environment at the animal's surface.

The *earthworm*, has a well developed circulatory system. It consists of a network of blood vessel which is in contact with almost all cells of the body.

The insects such as *cockroach* have an *open circulatory system*. The blood pumped by a many chambered heart, passes through a closed vessel, the aorta, only for a part of its circulation. For the rest it flows through the body cavity, the *haemocoel* and tissue spaces.

All vertebrates have *true circulatory system* which has *closed circulation*. In a closed system, blood remains within a network of vessels. It is carried away from the heart through the arteries. Capillaries and veins return the blood back to the heart.

The lung-fishes have a dual circulation consisting of the *systemic circulation,* which carries oxygenated blood to the body tissues and returns deoxygenrated blood to the heart, and *pulmonary circulation,* which pumps deoxygenated blood to the air bladder and returns oxygenated blood to the heart.

Adult amphibians have a dual circulation. The heart is not completely partitioned in amphibians. There is some mixing of pulmonary and systemic circulation occurs in heart. In amphibian exchange of oxygen and carbon dioxide occurs through their moist skin as well as through their lungs, respiratory exchange takes place in both the pulmonary and systemic circulation. As a result, there is less need to avoid mixing of the blood in the heart.

Reptiles have lungs for respiratory exchange and therefore have a more complete separation of the pulmonary and systemic circulation than is found in amphibians. In both birds and mammals there is a complete separation of both ventricle and atrium into a two-sided heart.

In man the heart beats about 72 times per minute. The total volume of blood in the human system is about 5 litres. Approximately 5 litres of blood is pumped out by the heart every minute.

EXCRETION SYSTEM

Excretion is the process by which an organism gets rid of the waste products of its metabolism. Most waste products become toxic, if allowed to accumulate in an organism, and may fatal from organism. Therefore every living thing has some means of getting rid of its waste products. These mechanisms may also be used to get rid of other unwanted substances such as superfluous water, and salts, so as to aid in osmoregulation.

Waste Products

Urine is composed of water (95%), urea (2%) uric acid (0.05%). Amount of urine secreted per day is 1.5 to 2 litres. Protein metabolism results in nitrogenous wastes such as ammonia, urea and uric acid. While the carbon dioxide is eliminated by the respiratory system, the nitrogenous materials are taken care of by the specialized excretory organs.

Excretion in Plants

In simpler forms such as *Spirogyra,* the metabolic by-products simply permeate out into the surroundings. In higher plants, carbon dioxide, water and oxygen diffuse out through the epidermis (as in roots) and stomata of the leaves, and lenticels of the stems and the minerals besides water through the *hydathodes* by *guttation.* The surplus salts are secreted in the form of calcium oxalate crystals in pith and cortex of roots and stems (grapevine, eucalyptus) or fruits (tomato) or as calcium carbonate in the lithocyts of certain leaves (Indian rubber tree). Tannins, resins, mucilage and latex are some other excretory materials stored in plants. Ammonia and other nitrogenous substances are utilized for the synthesis of new compounds. Some roots are also known to excrete mineral salts, sugar, amino acids and hydrolytic enzymes.

Excretion in Animals

The mechanisms that evolved to carry out excretory functions differ greatly in various organisms and environments. An animal living in a desert must be able to conserve water in its body, while a freshwater fish needs the capacity to rid itself of large amounts of water.

In flatworms, *flame cells* constitute the excretory system. The *nephridia* constitutes the excretory organs of invertebrates like annelids (segmented worms).

The excretory organ of molluscs is the *renal gland.* In insects disposal is through a bunch of long tubules called *Malphigian tubules.*

Birds, like reptiles and insects, excrete uric acid into a continuation of the alimentary canal. Some marine birds have, in addition, salt glands (modified tear glands) which remove excess salt from their bodies and discharge the concentrated solution through the nostrils.

Amphibians store large quantities of dilute urine in a large *bladder* which acts as a water reserve when the animal is on land.

Freshwater fish must overcome the problem posed by water entering the body through osmosis and salts leaching out. To compensate, they produce large volumes of dilute urine and take in salts from the water through specialized cells in their gills. Nitrogenous wastes, for the most part, are diffused as ammonia through the skin. Marine fish, on the other hand, lose water through the skin and take in salt by osmosis.

Human Excretory System

The human excretory or urinary system is typical of that of all mammals. It consists of two *kidneys* where urine is produced by filtration, secretion, and reabsorption; the *ureter tubes* that transport the urine; the *bladder* where the urine is stored; and the *Urethra* through which the urine is voided.

In humans, kidneys are paired bean-shaped organs about five inches long. Located in the abdominal cavity, one on either side of the vertebral column. The concave portion lies nearest the backbone and is deeply cleft by the hilus through which arteries, veins, nerves, and lymphatics enter the kidney sinus. A cross-section of the kidneys show them to be made up of a darker *outer cortex* and *inner medulla* composed of rough cones with apex projecting into the sinus.

EXCRETORY ORGANS OF HUMAN BODY

EXCRETORY ORGAN	SUBSTANCES EXCRETED
1. Kidneys	Excretion of nitrogenous wastes, Excess of acids or bases, Osmoregulation and homeostasis, Regulation of mineral salts.
2. Liver	Formation of urea by ornithine cycle, Formation of bile pigments.
3. Sweat glands of skin	Excretion of mineral salts, small amounts of urea, waxes, sterols and a number of hydrocarbons (**sebum**), Osmoregulation.
4. Oil glands of skin	Excretion of carbon dioxide.
5. Lungs	Excretion of water by evaporation.
6. Intestine	Excretion of undigested food with bile pigments, salts like calcium phosphate.

The functional units of kidney are called *nephrons,* which are about a 1,000,000 in each kidney. Each nephron has *Bowman's capsule* at one end (a double-walled cup) and the rest part of the nephron is differentiated into a coiled *proximal convoluted tubule, a* 'U' shaped tin *Henle's loops*, and a *distal convoluted tubule.*

Urine formation begins in Bowman's capsule which encloses a dense cluster of microscopic blood vessels, the *glomerulus.* Under the driving force of blood pressure, plasma filters from the blood. Proteins and about 80 per cent of the water are held back in this process. The filtrate passes through the inner wall of the capsule and moves into the tubule.

THE SKELETAL AND MUSCULAR SYSTEM

A *skeleton* is a part of an animal which provides support for the rest of the body. Nearly every species of multi-cellular animal has a skeleton. Most are made of hard material *e.g.* bone, cartilage, chitin. They are either *exoskeletons* on the outside of the body (*Example:* insect skeletons) or *endoskeletons* inside the body (*Example:* vertebrate skeletons). Some animals have a hydrostatic skeleton which consists of fluid under pressure *e.g.* earthworm.

Bone is a very hard material, found only in vertebrates. It is made up of living cells, calcium phosphate (a mineral salt), and collagen (a protein). ***Cartilage*** is a second skeletal tissue of vertebrates. It is more plastic and resilient than bone, but not so hard. These properties make it a suitable covering for surfaces where bones meet (articular surfaces) at movable joints.

Chitin is the hard substance of which insect exoskeletons are made. It is a type of polysaccharide.

Movement in Animals

In higher animals, the skeletal muscle cause the movement and locomotion of the body by contracting. At least two muscles are needed to move a joint. One called the ***flexor muscle,*** contracts and bends a joint. On the opposite side of the joint there is an ***extensor muscle.*** This straightens the joint. Since flexer and extensor muscles pull a joint in opposite directions they are said to form an *antagonistic system.*

Muscles are attached to bones by tough, inelastic fibres called *tendons.* Tendons have two main functions :

(i) They protect muscle cells from wear, because they, are not the muscle cells pass over the movable ends of the bones and,

(ii) They concentrate the pull of the muscle into a small area.

The pectoral girdle is attached to the vertebral column by tendons, which gives it some mobility. It acts as a shock absorber in vertebrates which spring (*Example,* leopards) or hop (*Example,* frogs).

Joints

Joints occur wherever two or more bones touch. Some *joints are immovable* and are called ***fixed joints,*** Example–those in the skull. Some *joints are slightly movable*, example vertebrae can move slightly against the discs of cartilage in between them and other *joints are freely movable* called ***synovial*** joints, example the limb joints. The bones of freely movable joints are held in place and yet allowed to move freely by bands of fibres called ***ligaments.***

In *hinge joints*, movement occurs in one plane only *e.g.* the knee and the elbow joints. In ***ball-and-socket joints***, movement occurs in three planes *e.g.* the hip, the shoulder. In ***pivot joints*** one bone twists against another. A pivot joint occurs where a peg on the axis vertebra fits into a socket in the atlas vertebra.

In a ***sliding or gliding joint*** the surfaces which rub together are flat *e.g.* the vertebrae joint.

Muscular System

Muscles, the tissues attached to bones, are composed of fibres. They are capable of contracting and relaxing to effect body movement. There are about 630 important muscles in human body, which normally account for 40 per cent of the weight. There are about 100 joints and 10,000 km of blood vessels in the human body. Water constitutes about 70 per cent of human body tissues.

Largest muscle: The bulkiest muscle in the body is *gluteus maximus* or buttock muscles.

Longest muscle: Sartorius (tailor's muscle) is the longest muscle in the body. It has its origin in the upper part of the hip bone, crosses obliquely over the upper portion of the thigh, passes behind the femur and is attached to the tibia in the leg.

Smallest muscle: The smallest muscle in the human body is the *stapedius,* which controls the stapes, an auditory ossicle in the middle ear. It is less than 1/20 of an inch and 0.127 cm long. The ear also contains one of the few tissues, which has no blood supply.

NERVOUS SYSTEM

The nervous system, is an organized group of cells specialized for the conduction of a stimulus impulse from a sensory receptor through a nerve cell network to the site at which the response occurs.

The nervous system enables a multi-cellular animals to respond to changes in their external and internal environment. Nerve tissue is composed primarily of cells called *neurons.*

CENTRAL NERVOUS SYSTEM

(i) Brain

In man it is located in the skull called *cranium.* The brain have following parts as given in table.

The cerebrum of brain is divided into two hemisphere : the *left cerebral hemisphere* and *the right cerebral hemisphere*. Each hemisphere is divided into four lobes

(a) Frontal lobes (b) Temporal lobes
(c) Parietal lobes (d) Occipital lobes

Each lobes is named after the bone of skull under which the part of brain lying.

(ii) Spinal Cord

It is a long narrow tubular structure that extends from the brain to the bottom edge of the first lumbar vertebra. It is covered by the same meninges as the brain and is housed in the neural canal within the vertebral column.

Dorsal and ventral grooves divide the cord into the right and left halves. Running through the centre of the spinal cord is the central canal which is filled with cerebrospinal fluid. A cross-section of the spinal cord reveals an outer region of white matter and inner region of grey matter. The spinal cord has a two fold function: it conducts impulses to and from the brain, and acts as a reflex centre.

Reflex Action

A reflex action is defined as an involuntary action in response to an external or an internal stimulus. It is an inborn automatic response to a stimulus, and is the functional unit of the nervous system.

Reflex actions involving the spinal cord are called *spinal reflexes* and those involving the brain are called *cranial reflexes.*

REPRODUCTION SYSTEM

Reproduction is the production of a new generation of individuals of the same species. It is one of the fundamental characteristics of living organisms. It involves transmission of genetic material from one generation to the next, ensuring that the species survive over long periods of time, even though individual members of the species die. There are two basic types of reproduction, asexual and sexual.

Asexual Reproduction is reproduction by a single organism without production of gametes. It usually results in the production of genetically identical offspring, the only genetic variation arising as a result of random mutation among the individuals.

Sexual Reproduction is the fusion of two gametes to form a zygote, which develops into a new organism. It leads to genetic variation, which is advantageous to the species because it provides the raw material for natural selection and, therefore, evolution. Eventually, new species may form, the process known as speciation. Increased variation can be achieved by the mixing of genes from two different individuals, the process known as genetic recombination.

ASEXUAL REPRODUCTION IN PLANTS

Vegetative Propagation

It is a form of asexual reproduction in which the bud grows and develops into a new plant. At, some stage, the new plant becomes detached from the parent plant and starts to lead an independent existence. Examples: Bulbs, corms, rhizomes, stolons and tubers. A number of methods of artificial propagation of plants are used in agriculture and horticulture. The first three methods discussed below, namely cutting, grafting and layering, are traditional methods, but for commercial purpose they are gradually being replaced by modern methods involving tissue culture.

(a) Cutting

It is a simple procedure in which a part of the plant is removed by cutting and placed in a suitable medium for growth. It produces roots and grows into a new plant.

(b) Grafting or Budding

Grafting is the transfer of a part of one plant, the scion, onto the lower part of another plant, the stock. The scion is chosen for its fruits and the stock for properties such as disease resistance and hardiness. Most rose bushes are propagated by a variation of this method known as budding, in which a bud is used as a scion rather than a shoot.

(c) Layering

Layering is used for plants that produce runners such as strawberries. The runners are pegged out (layered) around the parent plant until they take root and are then cut to them from parent plant.

ASEXUAL REPRODUCTION IN AMOEBA

The single-celled amoeba demonstrates a simple method of asexual reproduction. It divides in half by a process called fission, producing two smaller daughter cells. After a period of feeding and growth, these two daughter cells will themselves divide in half.

(d) Tissue Culture or Micropropagation

It involves the propagation or cloning of plants. The tissue is grown in a special solution; therefore, the process is called tissue culture. It developed from experiments that showed that plant tissues removed from plants could be stimulated to grow in solution by the addition of nutrients and certain hormones, particularly auxins and cytokinins (which are needed for continued cell division). Tissue culture is widely used for the rapid propagation of desired varieties.

Asexual Reproduction in Animals

Asexual reproduction occurs only in relatively unspecialized animals. Members of animal phylum Cnidaria can undergo budding which a new individual is produced as an outgrowth of the parent (as in yeast). Another form of asexual reproduction is fragmentation. This is breaking of an organism into two or more parts, each of which grows to form a new individual. Strong regeneration powers are needed. The bodies of ribbon worms, a group of simple marine worms, break up easily into small pieces, each of which can regenerate a new individual. Starfish can regenerate if accidental fragmentation occurs.

Sexual Reproduction in Plants

The gymnosperms have naked ovules (structures containing a single egg), which develop into exposed seeds after fertilization. The angiosperms have their ovules enclosed in an ovary, which enlarges into a fruit as the seeds develop within it.

Gymnosperms are a numerically small group of plants, consisting chiefly of cone bearing trees such as the pine, fir, cedar, and spruce. They have male cones (which give rise to pollen grains, each containing a male gamete) and female cones (which contain female gametes). In some species, both kinds of cones are found on the same tree; in other, they are borne on separate trees. The pollen grains are carried by wind to female cones, where fertilization occurs.

In angiosperms sexual reproduction occurs in the flower, which is considered as a specially modified shoot. In a flower the ***sepals*** (or ***calyx***) are generally green and protect the other floral organs. The ***petals*** (or ***corolla***) are usually coloured, showy and often fragrant and serve to attract pollinators. The ***stamens*** (or androecium) and ***carpels*** (or gynoecium) are the male and female reproductive structures respectively. In each stamen the another contains four microsporangia which produce a large number of microspore mother cells. Each of this cell by meiotic divisions give rise to four pollen grains. Each pollen grain on releasing produces two male gametes or sperms.

In plant the gynoecium or pistil has three parts: ***ovary*** basal swollen part), ***style*** and ***stigma***. Inside the ovary are present a fixed number of ovules.

The *stamen (male reproductive organ)* bears microsporangia, which contains large number of pollen grains (male gametes). The *ovary (female reproductive organ)* bears megasporangia, which contains embryo sac. The embryo sac have antipodal cells (n), one polar cell (2n), two synergids (n) and an egg (n).

Pollination

It is a process of transfer of pollen grain from anther to stigma. It is two types :

(a) ***Self pollination*** : The transfer of pollen grains from anther to stigma in same flower or in same plant.

(b) ***Cross pollination*** : The transfer of pollen grains from anther of one flower to stigma of another flower in different plant. The pollination is carried out by various agents.

Reproduction in Human Beings

The male reproductive system consists of two testes each of which has two functional components : (i) ***seminiferous tubules***, and (ii) ***interstitial cells*** or ***leydig cells***.) suspended in the pouch of scrotum. The Scrotum have a paired duct system each consisting of *epididymis, vas deferens, ejaculatory duct* and *male* urethra, and *secondary sex organs* including a prostrate, two seminal vesicles, two Cowper's glands and a penis. **Testes produce sperms and secrete testosterone;** prostrate, seminal vesicles and Cowper's gland secrete fluids which mix with sperm to form semen; the duct system conducts the semen to the exterior.

The female reproductive system consists of *two ovaries*, and a duct system of *two fallopian tubes*, and *uterus and a vagina*. ***Ovaries produce oya and secrete oestrogens and progesterone.*** The fallopian tubes conduct the ovum towards the uterus; the uterus lodges the growing foetus and opens to the exterior through the vagina.

Gametogenesis is the formation of gametes for sexual reproduction. Gametogenesis is carried out in the *gonads.* The gametogenesis in male gonad is called *spermatogenesis.* It is the production of sperms in the testes. The gametogenesis in female gonad is called *oogenesis.* It is the formation of ova in the ovary.

Spermogenesis or transformation of spermatogonia (male germ cells present in seminiferous tubules) into spermatozoa occurs in seminiferous tubules in four stages: *(i) Proliferation phase :* In this stage the spermatogonial cells have diploid number of chromosomes (46 in man) which undergo several mitotic divisions to increase their number, *(ii) Growth phase:* The spermatogonia cells increase in the dimensions and are called primary, spermatocytes in this stage, *(iii) Maturation phase;* Primary spermatocytes undergoes first meiotic division to produce two smaller secondary spermatocytes and these two further divide to give four spermatids and; *(iv) Transformation phase;* The spermatid in this final stage acquires a tail and anterior acrosomal cap (head cap) and is transformed into spermatozoan.

Oogenesis is the transformation of oogonia (female germ cells) into ova. It takes place in the Graafian follicle of ovaries and is completed in the three stages: *(i) Proliferation phase:* The oogonia cells which have a diploid number of chromosomes undergo several mitotic divisions in the foetus upto six months; *(ii) Growth phase:* The oogonium increases in size and is transformed into a primary oocyte; and *(iii) Maturation phase:* The primary oocyte undergoes meiosis in two steps. The first reduction division leads to the formation of two unequal daughter cells-the larger constitute the secondary oocyte, whereas the smaller, consisting mainly of the nucleus, forms the first polar body, that subsequently degenerates. An ovum and a second polar body result from the second meiotic division or second maturation division prior to fertilization. Like the first, the second polar body also disintegrates after some time. Thus, a single mature cell is produced from one primary oocyte.

MULTIPLE CHOICE QUESTIONS

1. All organisms require food to obtain:
(*a*) Vitamins (*b*) Proteins
(*c*) Energy (*d*) Fats

2. The protein part of complex enzymes associated with a metallic group is known as:
(*a*) Coenzyme (*b*) Apoenzyme
(*c*) Hormone (*d*) None of these

3. Pepsin acts in:
(*a*) Neutral media (*b*) Acidic media
(*c*) Alkaline media (*d*) None of these

4. Enzymes present in the pancreatic juice are:
(*a*) Pepsin, peptidases and lipase
(*b*) Trypsin, amylase and lipase
(*c*) Lipase, sugar and peptidases
(*d*) None of the above

5. The largest gland in the coelom is:
(*a*) Pancreas (*b*) Liver
(*c*) Thyroid (*d*) Parathyroid

6. Coprophagy is associated with:
(*a*) Frog (*b*) Dog
(*c*) Rabbit (*d*) Scorpion

7. When a man starves, he starts consuming his own:
(*a*) Protein (*b*) Fat
(*c*) Glycogen (*d*) None of these

8. Hormone secretin stimulates the secretion of:
(*a*) Bile (*b*) Salivary juice
(*c*) Pancreatic juice (*d*) All the above

9. Which one of the following enzymes does not function after food passes from stomach to the intestine?
(*a*) Trypsin (*b*) Pepsin
(*c*) Steapsin (*d*) None of these

10. Formation of protein is:
(*a*) Dehydration analysis
(*b*) Dehydration synthesis
(*c*) Both (*a*) and (*b*)
(*d*) None of the above

11. Liver is said to be a digestive gland although it secretes:
(*a*) Many enzymes (*b*) No enzymes
(*c*) Amylase (*d*) Pepsin and trypsin

12. Increased excretion of sodium and ammonium salts by the kidneys is called:
(*a*) Alkaline tide (*b*) Diabetes
(*c*) Haemophilia (*d*) None of these

13. The enzyme invertase converts:
(a) Cellulose into starch
(b) Starch into glucose
(c) Glucose into sucrose
(d) Sucrose into glucose and fructose

14. Digestion of carbohydrates is enhanced by:
(a) Pepsin (b) Trypsin
(c) Amylopsin (d) None of these

15. The most important element for the growth and repair of tissues is:
(a) Vitamins (b) Proteins
(c) Calcium (d) Carbohydrates

16. Actual release of oxygen in the cells is called :
(a) Breathing
(b) External respiration
(c) Internal respiration
(d) None of the above

17. Unlobulater lungs are found in :
(a) Whales (b) Horse
(c) Frog (d) None of these

18. The rate of breathing is lowest when we are :
(a) Eating (b) Sleeping
(c) Playing (d) Running

19. Chloride shift is essential for :
(a) CO_2 transport (b) O_2 transport
(c) N_2 transport (d) All the above

20. A iron-containing protein myoglobin is present in the :
(a) Spleen (b) Lungs
(c) Muscles (d) None of these

21. Amount of air exchanged in breathing can be measured with a :
(a) Thermometer (b) Barometer
(c) Potometer (d) Spirometer

22. Carbon dioxide release is accelerated in lungs by an enzyme knwon as :
(a) Oxidase
(b) Hydrogenase
(c) Carbonic anhydrase
(d) None of the above

23. Which animal has a double trachea?
(a) Snakes (b) Whales
(c) Penguins (d) None of these

24. The organs of sound production in birds is :
(a) Larynx (b) Syrinx
(c) Pharynx (d) Vocal sac

25. Excess of carbon dioxide in the body fluids is known as:
(a) Dysponea (b) Hypercapnia
(c) Apnoea (d) None of these

26. Lack of oxygen in body fluids is known as :
(a) Hyperpnoea (b) Anoxemia
(c) Anoxia (d) Hypoxia

27. In which form CO_2 is carried in the blood?
(a) Potassium carbonate
(b) Sodium carbonate
(c) Magnesium carbonate
(d) None of the above

28. In anaerobic respiration the pyruvic acid in muscles will form :
(a) Acetaldehyde (b) Lactic acid
(c) Acetic acid (d) Alcohol

29. Oxygen dissociation curve of haemoglobin is:
(a) Linear (b) Sigmoid
(c) Hyperblue (d) None of these

30. Which one of the following animal has no blood but respires?
(a) Fish (b) Cockroach
(c) Earthworm (d) Coelentrate

31. Respiratory mechanism is controlled by :
(a) Autonomic nervous system
(b) Sympathalic nervous system
(c) Central nervous system
(d) None of the above

32. The amount of air normally inspired and expired is called :
(a) Residual volume
(b) Tidal volume
(c) Complemental air
(d) None of the above

33. Exchange of gases occurs in :
(a) Alveoli (b) Bronchi
(c) Trachea (d) Bronchioles

34. Ratio of oxyhaemoglobin and haemoglobin in the blood is based on :
(a) CO_2 tension (b) Carbonate tension
(c) O_2 tension (d) None of these

35. The sum of inspiratory and expiratory capacity is known as:
(a) Respiratory capacity
(b) Vital capacity
(c) Lung capacity
(d) All the above

36. Defibrinated blood in:
(a) Blood proteins (b) Blood plasma
(c) Serum (d) All the above

37. Smallest RBC are found in :
(a) Musk deer (b) Frog
(c) Rat (d) None of these

38. The ion that is necessary for coagulation of blood is :
(a) Sodium ion (b) Calcium ion
(c) Iron ion (d) Potasium ion

39. Source of fibrinogen is :
(a) Blood (b) Lymph
(c) Liver (d) Spleen

40. Antibodies are synthesized in :
(a) Blood (b) Liver
(c) Heart (d) Lymph glands

41. Antibodies are produced by :
(*a*) RBC (*b*) Basophils
(*c*) Lymphocytes (*d*) Eosinophils

42. The instrument used to measure the blood pressure is :
(*a*) Thermometer (*b*) Stethoscope
(*c*) Potometer (*d*) Sphygmomanometer

43. The largest lymphatic organ in the body is :
(*a*) Liver (*b*) Pancreas
(*c*) Spleen (*d*) Lymph node

44. William Harvey is known for the discovery of:
(*a*) Blood circulation (*b*) Blood groups
(*c*) Blood clotting (*d*) None of these

45. The blood leaving the lungs is richer in:
(*a*) Carbon dioxide (*b*) Water
(*c*) Oxygen (*d*) Nitrogen

46. The renal portal system is found in:
(*a*) Man (*b*) Whale
(*c*) Rabbit (*d*) Frog

47. ANF (Atrial Natruretic Factor) is:
(*a*) Hormone of the heart
(*b*) An antibody
(*c*) An enzyme
(*d*) None of the above

48. The electrodes of the "pacemaker" are inserted into the:
(*a*) Ventricle
(*b*) Auricle
(*c*) Conducting system
(*d*) None of the above

49. Heart is completely enclosed by a membrane known as :
(*a*) Tympenic (*b*) Venticular septum
(*c*) Pericardium (*d*) None of these

50. The difference between systolic and diastolic pressure is called :
(*a*) Blood pressure (*b*) Pulse pressure
(*c*) Systolic pressure (*d*) None of these

51. Blood pressure is measured usually from the :
(*a*) Branchial vein (*b*) Branchial artery
(*c*) Coronary artery (*d*) None of these

52. The first tap like sound heard at the time of measuring blood pressure represents :
(*a*) Systolic pressure (*b*) Diastolic pressure
(*c*) Both (*a*) and (*b*) (*d*) None of these

53. Double circulation is found in :
(*a*) Amphibians (*b*) Mammals
(*c*) Arthropods (*d*) None of these

54. The life of erythrocytes in mammalian blood is:
(*a*) About 120 days (*b*) About 150 days
(*c*) About 180 days (*d*) About 30 days

55. The process of blood cells formation is called:
(*a*) Haemocytopoiesis (*b*) Hematopoiesis
(*c*) Both (*a*) and (*b*) (*d*) None of these

56. In mammals the function of spleen is :
(*a*) Excretion
(*b*) Blood pressure control
(*c*) Haemopoietic tissue
(*d*) None of the above

57. Lymph differs from the blood in the absence of:
(*a*) Proteins (*b*) WBCs
(*c*) RBCs (*d*) Platelets

58. The largest artery in the body is :
(*a*) Vena cava (*b*) Aorta
(*c*) Ventricle (*d*) Capillary

59. Largest erythrocytes in vertebrates are found in:
(*a*) Whale (*b*) Ostrich
(*c*) Elephant (*d*) None of these

60. Heart attack involves a blockage of the
(*a*) Aorta (*b*) Coronary arteries
(*c*) Alkalemia (*d*) Acidosis

61. The renal organs for excretion and the genital organs for reproduction commonly called as:
(*a*) Excretory organs
(*b*) Reproductive organs
(*c*) Urogenital organs
(*d*) None of the above

62. Kidneys, skin and lungs are:
(*a*) Excretory organs
(*b*) Digestive organs
(*c*) Reproductive organs
(*d*) None of the above

63. Extraction of sodium is done by:
(*a*) Distal tubule (*b*) Proximal tubule
(*c*) Loop of Henle (*d*) None of these

64. Ornithine cycle is concerned with:
(*a*) Formation of urine
(*b*) Formation of urea
(*c*) Formation of blood
(*d*) None of these

65. Which of the following is secreted by kidney?
(*a*) Vitamin K
(*b*) Erythropoietin hormone
(*c*) Erythrocytes
(*d*) Apoenzymes

66. The structural and functional unit of kidney is:
(*a*) Medulla (*b*) Neuron
(*c*) Nephron (*d*) Tubules

67. Urea in human urine is derived from the breakdown of:
(*a*) Uric acid (*b*) Amino acids
(*c*) Glucose (*d*) All the above

68. Waste products of adenine and guanine metabolism are excreted by man as:
(*a*) Urea (*b*) Uric acid
(*c*) Ammonia (*d*) None of these

69. The yellow colour of urine of vertebrates is due to:

(a) Uric acid (b) Urochrome
(c) Melanin (d) None of these

70. Excretory products of foetus comes out through:
(a) Umbilical cord (b) Placenta
(c) Both (a) and (b) (d) Ammiotic fluid

71. The snakes and birds are usually:
(a) Ureotelic (b) Uricotelic
(c) Ammonotelic (d) None of these

72. Diabetes is characterised by increased excretion of:
(a) Proteins (b) Amino acids
(c) Glucose (d) None of these

73. Glucose is completely absorbed in:
(a) Collecting tubule
(b) Loop of Henle
(c) Distal convoluted tubule
(d) Proximal convoluted tubule

74. Haemodialysis is also called artificial
(a) Lung (b) Kidney
(c) Liver (d) Heart

75. Which blood vessel contains the least amount of urea.
(a) Renal vein (b) Hepatic portal vein
(c) Hepatic vein (d) Renal artery

76. Nervous tissue is made up of :
(a) Neurons (b) Nerve fibres
(c) Neuroglia (d) All the above

77. The centre for the control of all activities of an animal is:
(a) Heart (b) Brain
(c) Liver (d) Stomach

78. The system which consists of nerves arising from the brain the spinal cord is called:
(a) Peripheral nervous system
(b) Central nervous system
(c) Autonomous nervous system
(d) None of the above

79. Which one of the following is a motor nerve?
(a) Facial (b) Abducens
(c) Vagus (d) Olfactory

80. The secretion of adrenal glands called:
(a) Aldrin (b) Adrenalin
(c) Sympathin (d) None of these

81. Temperature control centre is located in the:
(a) Hypophysis (b) Hypothalamus
(c) Diencephalon (d) None of these

82. Generally tear glands are functional in child after:
(a) One month (b) Two months
(c) Three months (d) Four months

83. The brain is situated in a long case known as:
(a) Atrium (b) Sinus
(c) Cranium (d) None of these

84. Body temperature, hunger and water balance is regulated by:
(a) Cerebellum (b) Medulla oblongata
(c) Hypothalamus (d) Thalamus

85. In brain the chief centres of intelligence, memory, emotions and ability to learn from experience is present in:
(a) Neopallium
(b) Corpora quadrigemina
(c) Corpora striata
(d) Cerebral hemisphere

ANSWERS

1	2	3	4	5	6	7	8	9	10
(c)	(b)	(b)	(b)	(b)	(c)	(b)	(c)	(b)	(b)
11	**12**	**13**	**14**	**15**	**16**	**17**	**18**	**19**	**20**
(b)	(a)	(d)	(c)	(b)	(c)	(a)	(a)	(a)	(c)
21	**22**	**23**	**24**	**25**	**26**	**27**	**28**	**29**	**30**
(d)	(c)	(c)	(b)	(b)	(b)	(a)	(b)	(b)	(b)
31	**32**	**33**	**34**	**35**	**36**	**37**	**38**	**39**	**40**
(a)	(a)	(a)	(a)	(a)	(c)	(a)	(b)	(c)	(d)
41	**42**	**43**	**44**	**45**	**46**	**47**	**48**	**49**	**50**
(c)	(d)	(c)	(a)	(c)	(d)	(a)	(c)	(c)	(b)
51	**52**	**53**	**54**	**55**	**56**	**57**	**58**	**59**	**60**
(b)	(a)	(b)	(a)	(c)	(c)	(c)	(b)	(b)	(b)
61	**62**	**63**	**64**	**65**	**66**	**67**	**68**	**69**	**70**
(c)	(a)	(c)	(b)	(b)	(c)	(b)	(a)	(b)	(c)
71	**72**	**73**	**74**	**75**	**76**	**77**	**78**	**79**	**80**
(b)	(c)	(d)	(d)	(a)	(d)	(b)	(a)	(b)	(b)
81	**82**	**83**	**84**	**85**					
(b)	(c)	(c)	(c)	(a)					

MOVING THINGS, PEOPLE AND IDEAS

MOTION

If the position of a material system as measured by a particular observer changes with respect to time, that system is said to be in motion with respect to the observer. Absolute motion, has no significance, and only relative motion may be defined.

There are various kinds of motion – one dimensional, two-dimensional and three-dimensional.

Movement of lift from ground floor to sixth floor or an apple, dropped from the branch of a tree before it strikes the ground are examples of motion in one dimension.

A boat sailing on a lake over distances which are small compared to the earth's radius; a carrom coin or a billiards ball in motion; these are examples of motion in two dimensions over a plane. Objects moving on the surface of the earth over distances comparable to the earth's radius are examples of motion in two dimensions, but not over a plane. Finally, the most general motions we can consider are of objects moving in space, involving all the three dimensions.

Movement of birds in the sky, helicopter or flying of kite in windy day are examples of motion in three dimension.

Distance

The actual length of path travelled by a body is called the distance (*S*) travelled or covered by the body. It is a scalar quantity and is measured in metres in SI units.

Displacement

The shortest distance from the initial to the final position of a body is called displacement of the body. Displacement vector is the straight line joining the initial and final position and does not depend on the actual path undertaken by the object between the two positions.

A person starts his journey from point A and moves along ABCDA.

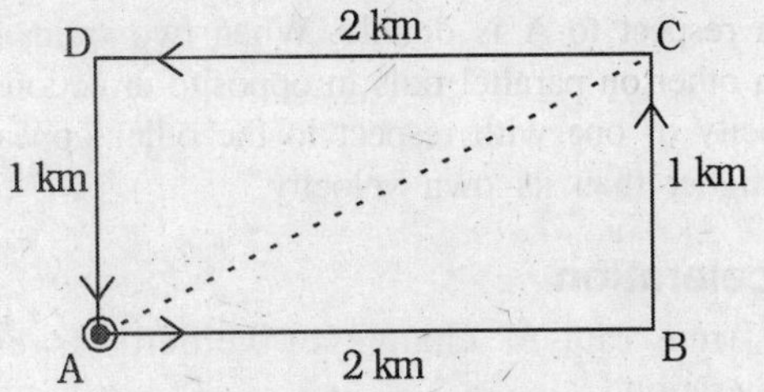

For path AB, distance = 2 km

and displacement = 2 km

For path A-B-C, distance = 3 km

and displacement = $\sqrt{2^2 + 1^2} = \sqrt{5}$ km

For path A-B-C-D distance = 5 km

and displacement = 1 km

For path A-B-C-D-A distance = 6 km

and displacement = zero

When initial and final position coincide the displacement becomes zero.

Speed

Speed is the time rate of change of position. It is measured in metre per second, centimetre per second, kilometre per hour etc. Average speed is the total distance travelled divided by the time taken.

$$\text{Speed} = \frac{\text{distance travelled}}{\text{time taken}} = \frac{s}{t} = \text{m/s}$$

Velocity

The time rate of displacement (change of position vector) of the particle is called velocity. Thus

$$\text{Velocity} = \vec{v} = \frac{d\vec{S}}{dt}, \text{ where } \vec{S} = \text{displacement}$$

The velocity is a vector quantity. Its unit is m/s.

Is is of two types:

(*a*) **Uniform Velocity:** If a body covers equal distances in a particular direction in equal intervals of time, it is said to move with a uniform velocity.

(*b*) **Variable Velocity:** If a body covers unequal distances in a particular direction in equal intervals of time, however small, it is said to move with a variable velocity.

Relative Velocity

Relative velocity is the velocity of one body with respect to another body. Suppose two trains A and B are moving parallel to one another with the same velocity and in the same direction. For a passenger in A, B appears to be stationary and *vice versa.* Thus, the relative velocity of A with respect to B is zero. Also the relative velocity of B with respect to A is zero. If A and B are moving in opposite directions. The relative velocity of A with respect to B is twice the velocity of either. Also the relative velocity of B with respect to A is double. When two trains cross each other on parallel rails in opposite directions, the velocity of one with respect to the other appears to be higher than its own velocity.

Acceleration

The time rate of change of velocity is called acceleration.

Thus acceleration = $\vec{a} = \frac{d\vec{v}}{dt}$

It is a vector quantity. Its unit is m/s^2.

(*a*) **Uniform Acceleration:** If the velocity of a body increases by equal amounts in equal intervals of time, however small, it is said to move with uniform acceleration.

(*b*) **Variable Acceleration:** If the velocity of a body increases by unequal amounts in equal intervals of time, however small, it is said to have variable acceleration. The acceleration will be variable if either the magnitude or direction of velocity changes unequally.

Acceleration Due to Gravity

The acceleration with which a freely falling body moves towards the earth is called *acceleration due to gravity.* If a feather and an iron piece are released from the same height in vacuum, both will reach the ground simultaneously. If they are released in atmosphere, the feather takes a longer time due to air resistance. The force of gravity differs at various locations. It is stronger, for example, at the poles than at the equator.

TYPES OF MOTION

Translatory Motion

A body has translatory motion, if all the particles move with the same velocity and their paths are parallel. There are two types of translatory motion.

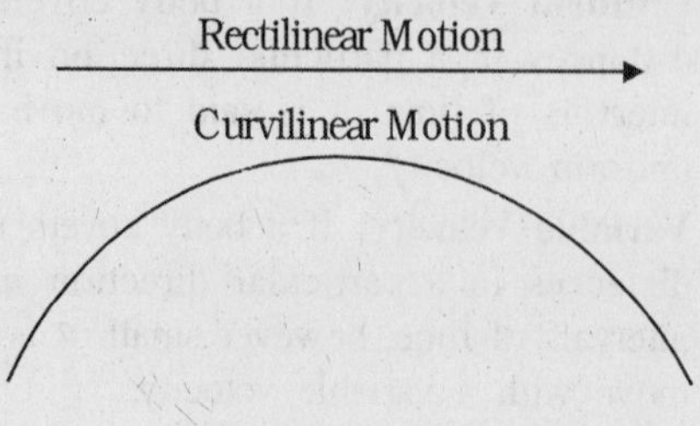

The train moving along a railway track, a body falling freely under the action of gravity, a car moving on the road (except the wheels), are examples of translatory motion. Translatory motion can be along a straight line (rectilinear) or a curved path (curvilinear).

Rotatory Motion

When a body rotates about a fixed axis, the motion is said to be rotatory. All the particles do not move with the same linear velocity. The particles nearer the axis move with less speed and the particles away from the axis move with more speed.

Earth rotating about its own axis, spinning top, rotating fly wheel, the motion of the blades of a fan, are examples of rotatory motion. A ball rolling on the ground, motion ot the cycle wheel, movement of the earth in its orbit around the sun are examples in which these bodies possess translatory and rotatory motions simultaneously.

Circular Motion

Circular motion is a form of periodic (or cyclic) motion. There are many familiar examples of an object moving in a circle at constant speed, such as the moon around the earth, a satellie in circular oribit around the earth, a cyclist on a circular track at constant speed, and so on.

Uniform Circular Motion: An object is undergoing uniform circular motion if it is travelling at a constant speed while moving in a circle. Its main requirement is constant speed and motion in a circle.

For uniform circular motion, we have a velocity which is always tangential, and an acceleration which is along the inward radius. Both velocity and acceleration have constant magnitudes but changing directions. Constant speed does not mean that acceleration vanishes.

Force and Inertia

It is an observable fact that an isolate object at rest do not start moving of their own accord. Effort is required to move the objects. When we push or pull a table, for instance, we are exerting a force on the table. It is the force exerted by a bat that makes the ball move.

Inertia is the inherent property of objects to remain at rest unless acted upon by a force. Also the property of a body to keep moving with constant velocity in the absence of any force acting on it is its *inertia.* Gelileo discovered the *law of inertia.* Bodies moving with uniform velocity would maintain this state of motion forever in the absence of forces acting upon them. Continuing his investigations on the basis of Galileo's findings, Issac ***Newton formulated his three laws of motion*** which form the foundations of mechanics.

The property of a body to continue in its state of rest or that of uniform motion in a straight line in the absence of external force is called inertia. ***Newton's first law of motion is the law of inertia.***

Newton's First Law of Motion

Every body continues in its state of rest or of uniform motion in a straight line unless compelled by some external force to act otherwise.

The state of rest and that of uniform motion are both examples of zero acceleration. They are, as a matter of fact, the only examples of zero acceleration. The first law tells us therefore that in order to change such a state of motion we need a force. If a body is at rest, we will have to apply a force on it to make it move. If a body is moving with constant speed in a straight line and if we want to change its speed, we will have to apply a force on it to make it move. If we just want to change the direction of motion, we still need a force acting normal to this direction.

Whenever a bus is at rest or travelling with constant velocity, the motion is unaccelerated and the force acting is zero. When the bus is speeding up there should be a force acting in the direction of motion; when the bus is slowing down there must be a force acting opposite to the direction of motion.

In case of circular motion with constant speed, even though the speed does not change, the direction of motion continuously changes. The acceleration in this case is directed towards the centre. Since the velocity is changing, there should be a force acting according to the first law. As we shall see this force will have to be in the direction of the acceleration, that is directed towards the centre.

We are quite often made aware of the law of inertia and sometimes with unpleasant consequences. For example if we are travelling in a vehicle like a bus and the brakes are applied suddenly, the bus will come to an abrupt halt. But we tend to keep moving forward according to the law of inertia. We may be thrown forward rather violently as a consequence. Newton's First law of motion gives ideas about (*i*) inertia, and (*ii*) definition of force.

MOMENTUM

The product of mass (*M*) of a body and its velocity ($\vec{v}$) is called momentum ($\vec{p}$). Thus $\vec{p} = M\vec{v}$. Its unit is kg m/s. The momentum of an object can be defined as follows:

$$\text{momentum} = \text{mass} \times \text{velocity}$$

With mass measured in kg and velocity in m/s, momentum is measured in kg m/s. Like force and velocity, momentum is a vector quantity it shows the strength of motion.

Newton's Second Law of Motion

The rate of change of momentum of an object is directly proportional to the force acting, on it and takes place in the direction in which the force acts.

Force acting on a body causes change in its position or state of uniform motion; the acceleration produced is the effect. Newton's second law of motion relates these two quantities–force and acceleration. It states that the force on an object is directly proportional to the product of the mass of the object and its acceleration.

The unit of force is Newton.

The second law comes into play when a driver applies the brakes and the large decelerating force created in this way brings the vehicle rapidly to a stop. In a collision, a car is stopped almost instantaneously. The large deceleration that is developed corresponds to large stopping force. It is this force that damages cars in collisions. The faster a car is moving at the instant of impact, the greater the decelerating force and the more damaging the effect upon the car will be.

Newton's second law of motion gives (*i*) expression of force, and (*ii*) the direction of force.

Impulse

When a force acts for a given time, the quantity force × time is called an *Impulse.* If force is measured in N and time in *s*, impulse is measured in Ns or kg m/s – both amount to the same thing.

$$\text{As, Force} = \frac{\text{Gain or change in momentum}}{\text{Time}}$$

It follows that:

Force × Time = Gain in momentum

in symbols. $Ft = mv - mu$

Application of the Concept of Impulse

1. A cricket player lower his hands while catching a cricket ball. In order to avoid injury he/she increases the time of catch. According to the concept of inpulse, when time of contact increases, the impact of force on hands decreases.
2. Vehicles are provided with shockers.
3. A person receives more injury when falls on a cement floor, than on a sand floor.

Newton's Third Law of Motion

To every action there is always an equal and opposite reaction. It may be noted that action and reaction which occur in pairs act on *different* bodies. If they acted on the same body, the resultant force would be zero and there could never be accelerated motion. Furthermore, the above two forces are found to be equal in magnitude and opposite in direction. For example, if we try to push a heavy door the force we exert on it accelerates it as it opens. Simultaneously we feel the force exerted by the door on us impeding our movement.

Sometimes, we can feel the reacting force. If we fire a rifle, the forward thrust of the projectile is matched by the backward thrust.

Conservation of Momentum

An important consequence of Newton's third law, in combination with the second, is the law of conservation of momentum which states: *When two or more bodies interact with one another, isolated system their total momentum remains constant, provided no external forces are acting.*

Rocket propulsion

One of the spectacular instances in which Newton's third law or the momentum of conservation manifests itself is the flight of a rocket. Here gases produced by the combustion of fuel are ejected and the reaction to this generates the thrust on the rocket. Here is an example in which the mass of the body keeps changing, as the gas escapes from the rocket. The exhaust gases move with an approximately constant velocity with respect to the rocket. If the rate of ejection of gas is constant during firing, then the rate of change of momentum will also be constant. However, as the mass of the rocket keeps decreasing due to the escaping mass of the gases, the acceleration will not remain constant. Both the velocity and the acceleration of the rocket will increase.

FORCE

Force is any influence that tends to change the state of rest or the uniform motion in a straight line of a body. The action of an unbalanced or resultant force results in the acceleration of a body in the direction of action of the force or it may, if the body is unable to move freely, result in its deformation. Force is a vector quantity, possessing both magnitude and direction; its SI unit is the newton.

Balanced and Unbalanced Forces

Despite friction and gravity, objects on Earth can still be at rest or travelling at a constant velocity. In each case, this is because the forces acting are balanced; their effects cancel out and the objects behaves as if no force is acting.

The weight of the aircraft is balanced by the lift from the wings, and air resistance is balanced by the thrust of the engines. As a result, the velocity of the aircraft is constant. If one of the forces were to change, the velocity of the aircraft would change.

An object will accelerate if the forces acting on it are not balanced. Figure below shows a small rocket of mass 200 kg at the point of take off. The rocket engine is producing an upward force of 3000 N; 2000 N balances the weight of the rocket, but the remaining 1000 N is unbalanced. The upward force and the weight therefore have the same effect as a single force of 1000 N upwards. There is said to be a resultant force on the rocket of 1000 N upwards.

The acceleration of the rocket can be calculated as follows:

$$\text{Resultant force} = \text{Mass} \times \text{Acceleration}$$

$$1000\text{N} = 200 \text{ kg} \times a$$

$$\text{This gives: } a = 5 \text{ m/s}^2$$

The rocket therefore has an acceleration of 5m/s^2 upwards.

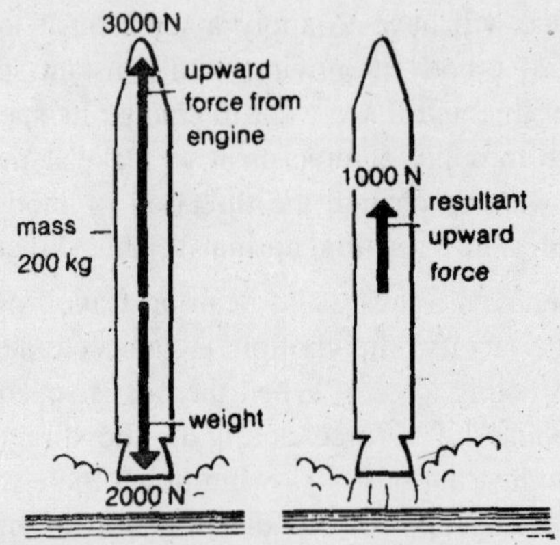

Two forces produce one resultant force.

TYPES OF FORCES

The Gravitational Force

All objects fall because of the gravitational force of attraction exerted on them by the earth. The acceleration due to gravity g is independent of the mass of the object. The force acting is given by F = mg and is the weight of the object. The direction of this acceleration and consequently of F is towards the centre of the earth. This direction therefore varies from point to point on the earth, although we may assume it to be constant over a small region. The value of g which is about 9.8m/s^2 also shows minor geographical variations. The weight of the body varies accordingly, but its mass remains the same.

The Electrostatic Force

Between any two electric charges there always exists a force. Electric charges are classified as positive and negative. When a glass rod is rubbed with a silk cloth, the glass rod becomes positively charged. Similarly, when a rubber rod is rubbed with fur, the rod acquires negative charge. Among elementary particles protons are positively charged while electrons carry negative charge. The electrostatic force is attractive between opposite charges and repulsive between like charges. This is in contrast to gravitation which is always attractive between any two given masses.

The Magnetic Force

The magnetic property of lodestone has been known since ancient times. Similarly the use of a magnetic compass has been in vogue for a very long time. Its needle, which is small magnet, is acted upon by the magnetic field of the earth. This is an instance of the magnetic force in action. The law of force between two magnets or the law of force on a magnet placed in a magnetic field are known, so that these forces can be readily computed.

Mechanical Force

These are the forces that are exerted by active or living objects, e.g. humans, animals, engines, moving objects, springs, etc.

Centripetal Force

When a body moves along a circular path with uniform speed, the magnitude of the velocity remains the same but its direction changes at every point. It means that there is change in velocity. Whenever there is change in velocity, there must be some acceleration. As a body has mass also, a force must act upon the body. This force must act along such a direction that the magnitude of the velocity does not change.

Examples:

(1) When a bucket containing water is rotated in a vertical circle, water does not fall downward even when the bucket is at the highest point (In Fig.). The centripetal force is provided by the motion. Due to this reason water does not fall.

(2) In the case of motion of the moon round the earth centripetal force is provided by the gravitational force of attraction of the earth on the moon. Similarly the force of attraction of the sun on the planets provides the necessary centripetal force and the planets revolve round the sun.

(3) Electrons revolve round the nucleus in various orbits. The electrons do not collapse into the nucleus. The electrostatic force of attraction of the nucleus on the electron provides the necessary centripetal force and the electron revolves round the nucleus.

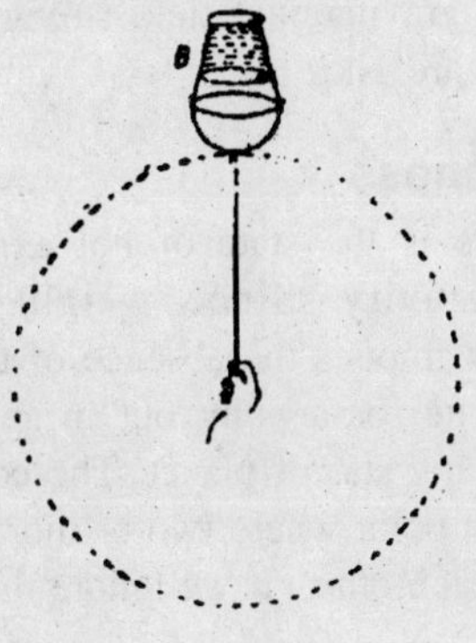

Artificial satellites move round the earth. The force of attraction of the earth on the satellite provides the necessary centripetal force and the satellite revolves round the earth.

Centrifugal Force

Centrifugal Force is a fictitious or pseudo outward force on a particle rotating about an axis which by Newton's third law is equal and opposite to the centripetal force. Like all such action-reaction pairs of forces, they are equal and opposite but do not act on the same body and so do not cancel each other. Consider a mass *M* tied by a string of length R to a pin at the centre of a smooth horizontal table and whirling around the pin with an angular velocity of ω radians per second. The mass rotates in a circular path because of the centripetal force $F_c = M\omega^2 R$ which is exerted on the mass by the string. The reaction force exerted by the rotating mass *M*, the so-called centrifugal force, is $M\omega^2 R$ in a direction away from the centre of rotation.

Centrifugal force, representing an inertia reaction, makes itself felt when a car begins to skid. Suppose we make a left turn too sharply or too quickly, the centrifugal inertia force of the turn becomes greater than the friction of the tyres against the road, and the car will start to skid to the right. The only way to overcome the momentum of the skid is to create a force to overcome it. This we can do by immediately turning the front wheels to the right-that is, in the direction of the skid. The car will then tend to turn in a rightward curve. In this way it sets up a leftward centrifugal force which stops the skid. The car may overbalance and tend to skid leftward again. The driver, therefore, must be prepared to turn the front wheels to the left if this should happen. This manoeuver is done expertly by racing car drivers, who deliberately skid their cars around turns in order to avoid losing speed.

One is likely to skid on an icy road, because on such a road the road friction is reduced to a minimum. The turning of the front wheels will not bring us into an opposite turn as quickly as on a dry road, because the car will have travelled further in the direction of the skid.

A method commonly used to prevent skidding when rounding a curve is to construct the curved roadway so that the outer part of the road is higher than the inner. This construction is called **banking of road**. It brings about the same effect as leaning inward when rounding a flat curve on a bicycle. The cyclist leans inward to balance the effect of centrifugal inertial force. This is called **bending of cyclist**. Of course the automobile cannot "lean inward", but the same effect is produced if the road is banked at the proper inclination.

SCIENCE

A familiar application of inertial force is found in centrifuges, which are devices used to separate one material from another. This device is often used to remove from a liquid the small solid substances it contains. The solids in the liquid, being heavier than the liquid itself, are thrown outward and collect in the bottom of the tube. The machine is then stopped and the clear liquid is poured off. The same principle is used to separate cream from milk in the device known as the separator. In the separator, the milk is passed it to a spinning bowl and is drawn off. The cream, which is lighter, stays near the centre and is drawn off from that point.

GRAVITATIONAL FORCE

Gravitation plays a crucial role in most processes on the earth. Ocean tides are caused by the gravitational attraction of the moon and the sun towards the earth and its oceans. Gravitation drives weather patterns by making cold air sink and displace less dense warm air, forcing the warm air to rise. The gravitational pull of the earth on all objects holds the objects to the surface of the earth. Without it, the spin of the earth would send them floating off into space. The gravitational attraction of every bit of matter in the earth for every other bit of matter amounts to an inward pull that holds the earth together against the pressure forces tending to push it outward. Similarly, the inward pull of gravitation holds stars together. When a star's fuel nears depletion, the processes producing the outward pressure weaken and the inward pull of gravitation eventually compresses the star to a very compact size.

Kepler's law

Early in the seventeenth century, the German astronomer and natural philosopher Johannes Kepler deduced three laws that first described the- motions of the planets about the sun: (1) the planets orbit the sun in elliptical paths, with the sun at one focus of the ellipse (2) The second law states that the areas described in a planetary orbit by the straight line joining the centre of the planet and the centre of the sun are equal for equal time intervals; that is, the closer a planet comes to the sun, the more rapidly it moves. (3) Kepler's third law states that the ratio of the cube of a planet's mean distance, d, from the sun to the square of its orbital period, t, is a constant; that is, d^3/t^2 If is the same for all planets. This means that the square of the period (in years) for one revolution about the sun equals the cube of the mean distance from the sun's centre, measured in astronomical units.

Newton's Law of Gravitation

Newton's law of gravitation was the first theory to accurately describe the motion of objects on Earth as well as the planetary motion that astronomers had long observed, According to Newton's theory, the gravitational attraction between the planets and the sun holds the planets in elliptical orbits around the sun. The earth's moon and moons of other planets are held in orbit by the attraction between the moons and the planets. Newton's law led to many new discoveries, the most important of which was the discovery of the planet Neptune. Scientists had noted unexplainable variations in the motion of the planet Uranus for many years. Using Newton's law of gravitation, the French astronomer Urbain Leverrier and the British astronomer John Couch each independently predicted the existence of a more distant planet that was perturbing orbit of Uranus. Neptune was discovered in 1864, in an orbit close to its predicted position.

Acceleration Due to Gravity

If an object held near the surface of the earth is released, it will fall and accelerate, or pick up speed, as it descends. This acceleration is caused by gravity, the force of attraction between the object and the earth. The force of gravity on an object is also called the object's weight. This force depends on the object's mass, or the amount of matter in the object. The weight of an object is equal to the mass of the object multiplied by the acceleration due to gravity.

$$W = mg$$

The mass of an object does not change as it is moved from place to place, but the acceleration due to gravity, and therefore the object's weight, will change because the strength of the earth's gravitational pull is not the same everywhere. The earth's pull and the acceleration due to gravity decrease as an object moves farther away from the centre of the earth.

Gravitational Field

The gravitational field strength g at a point at a distance r from mass M is defined as the force on the unit mass placed at that point, that is

$$g = \frac{GM}{r^2}$$

Therefore, for an object placed on the surface of the earth, the gravitational field strength = $GM/r^2 = g_0$. The units are Nkg^{-1}.

Weightlessness

Weightlessness is the state of not experiencing the effects of gravity. Since weight is a force, weightlessness implies the absence of this force. But this is only true for a point out in space, infinitely distant from any star of planet. The condition could also apply at a point where two or more gravitational fields cancel each other. If we ignore the attraction of the sun, then there will be a point between the earth and the moon where true weightlessness would occur.

Feeling of Weightlessness

We usually describe a feeling of weightlessness when there is no reaction on a body from the floor. If we stand in a lift that is falling freely we still have a weight but we feel weightlessness because the reaction has been removed. The same feeling is experienced in orbit, since both the spacecraft and the astronaut have the same centripetal acceleration. During training astronauts fly in a plane that describes a parabolic trajectory, and they therefore experience free fall and feel weightless.

FRICTION

Friction is the force that tries to stop materials sliding over each other. There is friction between our hands when we rub them together, and there is friction between our shoes and the ground when we walk along. Friction is caused in two ways. First, rougher surfaces have ridges and bumps which catch in each other. Second, all materials are made up of tiny particles called molecules, and these have a tendency to stick to each other when materials are pressed together.

Friction prevents machinery from moving freely. It also causes any moving parts to heat up. To reduce friction, wheels are often mounted on ball or roller bearings and oil is used to make moving surfaces more slippery. Friction can also be useful. It gives shoes and tyres 'grip' on the ground, and it is used in most braking systems.

Types of Friction

Friction is classified into three types:

- **Static Friction:** The opposing force that comes into play when one body tends to move over the surface of another but the body remains at rest, is knows as static friction. The magnitude of static friction adjusts itself so that it becomes equal to applied force, so it is also called self adjusting force.
- **Limiting Friction:** This is the maximum static friction that comes into play when one body is at the verge of motion over another body.
- **Dynamic/Kinetic Friction:** This is the force of friction that comes into play when one body is moving over another body.

Limiting friction is greatest of all frictions. Kinetic friction is of two types. *i.e.* sliding friction and rolling friction.

The wheel has been considered one of the greatest inventions. It is much easier to cart a heavy load on a trolley with wheels than to push it. Wheels are used extensively in our daily lives for transportation, since they save labour to a great extent. This is because of the reduced friction during rolling as compared to sliding. When a body rolls over a surface the frictional force developed is known as the ***rolling friction***.

Force of Internal Friction is the force which opposes the motion of a solid body in a fluid or the relative motion of two layers of a fluid. This force depends on the area of the surfaces in contact and the speed of the solid body or layers of the fluid.

Advantages of Friction

A frictionless world would not at all be convenient. It would be difficult to sit on a chair without friction. It helps in supporting ladders against a wall, or to start cars and trains. We are reminded of the importance of friction every time we slip on a polished floor. Walking would be impossible if there were no friction between the ground and the soles of our feet or shoes. Quite often, our lives depend on the force of friction in the brakes of an automobile or railway train. When brakes are applied, the car is stopped by the force of friction between the brake-lining and the drum of the wheel.

Disadvantages of Friction

Friction is not wholly beneficial. In machines it wastes energy. As one surface of any body is moved over another, some energy is used up in overcoming the friction (dissipated into heat energy). Wear and tear of machinery is a result of excessive friction; A motor car engine will seize, if it runs short of oil. The pistons and cylinders get so hot on account of excessive friction that they become jammed together.

HEAT AND ENERGY

Energy is the ability to do work. This ability can be in different ways. There are different forms of energy such as mechanical energy (Kinetic energy and Potential energy), heat energy, chemical energy and muscular energy.

The unit of Energy is Joule. It is a scalar quantity. Commercial unit of energy is kWh. 1 kWh = 3.6×10^6 Joules.

Kinetic Energy

The energy of a body due to its motion is called the kinetic energy.

$$K.E. = \frac{1}{2}mv^2$$

where m = mass of the body, and v = velocity of the body.

Potential Energy

The energy of a body due to its position or change in shape is known as potential energy.

$$P.E. = mgh$$

where m = mass of the body, g = Acceleration due to gravity, and h = height through which the body is lifted.

Law of Conservation of Energy

According to this law "energy can neither be created nor can be destroyed". It can only be transformed from its one form to the another form. External combustion engine e.g. steam engine and 'internal combustion engine e.g. diesel engine and petrol engine convert chemical energy into mechanical energy.

Heat

Heat is a form of energy. It is also called thermal energy. It is measured in calories or joules or kilocalories.

1 kcal. = 1000 cal.

1 cal. = 4.18 joules.

1 calorie is the quantity of heat which raises the temperature of 1 gm of water by 1°C.

Temperature

It is the degree of hotness or coldness of an object. It is measured by an instrument called thermometer. Temperature is measured in °C or °F.

There are two fixed temperature scales:

1. Lower Fixed Scale, i.e., melting point of ice (0°C)
2. Upper Fixed Scale, i.e., boiling point of water (100°C)

Normal human body temperature is 37°C or 98.6°F.

Specific Heat

The specific heat of a substance is the amount of heat needed to raise the temperature of 1 kg of it through 1°C.

It is measured in kcal/kg °C or cal/gm °C. The specific heat of water is 1 kcal/kg °C or 4180 J/kg °C. The specific heat of water is higher than all other common substances.

Amount of heat gained or lost by a substance depends on

(*i*) Rise or fall in temperature

(*ii*) The mass of the substance

(*iii*) Specific heat of the substance.

Thus,

Heat gained or lost = mst, i.e., H = mst.

where m = mass of the substance

s = specific heat of the substance

t = temperature difference

Thermal Capacity

The thermal capacity of a body is the amount of heat required to raise the temperature of the whole body by 1°C.

Thermal capacity = mass x specific heat.

Its unit is $\frac{\text{Cal}}{°\text{C}}$ or $\frac{\text{K Cal}}{°\text{C}}$.

Thermal Expansion

Most of the solids, liquids and gases expand on heating. This property of expansion of matter on heating is called thermal expansion.

Expansion of solids on heating plays an important part in our life. We have to take note of the effects of thermal expansion while laying railway tracks, fixing of iron girders while constructing a bridge, fixing telegraph wires, fixing iron rims over wooden wheels and designing clocks and watches that keep correct time in both summer and winter.

We also use the phenomenon of thermal expansion in liquids in the construction of an ordinary thermometer. More sensitive thermometer used for standardization purposes are based on the thermal expansion of hydrogen.

Equilibrium Temperature

When a hot substance is mixed with a cold substance, then the temperature of a hot substance gradually decreases and that of cold substance gradually increases till both the substances attain the same temperature. This temperature is called equilibrium temperature.

Transfer of Heat

There are three different ways in which heat is transferred from a hot body to a cold one.

1. **Conduction:** It is the process by which heat passes from the heated end of a body to its cold end e.g. if we heat one end of metallic spoon then the other end also becomes hot in a few minutes. But if we place one end of a wooden stick in the flame, it starts burning but the other end does not get heated up. This is so because all substances do not conduct heat equally well. Wood, plastics etc are poor conductors of heat, whereas metals are good conductors of heat.
2. **Convection:** Convection is the mode of transfer of heat in liquids and gases which takes place by the actual movement of their molecules. When the movement of heated matter is taking place, we say that convection currents have been set up in them.

These convection currents have many practical applications in our lives.

For example when we exhale air, it gets warm. Being lighter, it rises and moves out through the ventilators and cold fresh air moves in through the windows to take its place. This cyclic movement of air ensures proper ventilation of our rooms.

3. **Radiation:** Radiations are the invisible rays given by a hot body which can even travel through vacuum. The heat of the sun reaches us by radiation.

Change of State

A substance can exist in three physical states: solid, liquid and gas.

The change of substance from solid state to liquid state is called melting or fusion and the temperature at which substance starts melting is called melting point.

The change of substance from liquid state to its gaseous state on heating is called vaporization. The temperature at which liquid starts boiling is called boiling point.

When a liquid converts to solid state, it is called freezing and the temperature is called the freezing point.

When a steam converts to liquid, it is called condensation.

Sometimes, a solid substance may directly convert into the gaseous stage, without passing through the liquid stage. The process is called sublimation.

Latent Heat

Latent heat (hidden heat) of a substance is the amount of heat absorbed or released by a unit mass of the substance to change its state without change of temperature. The unit of latent heat is calories/gram or joules/kg.

Latent heat of fusion of ice is 80 cal/gm, i.e., 80 calories of heat are required to change 1 gm of ice at its melting point (0°C) into water at the same temperature. Latent heat of vaporization of water is 540 cal/gm, i.e., 540 calories of heat are required to convert 1 gm of water at 100°C to steam at the same temperature. Latent heat of steam is equal to the latent heat of vaporization of water.

Superfluidity and Superconductivity

All liquids have viscosity at room temperatures. However, as the temperature goes down, Helium, which is available in Gas form, gets transformed to liquid form and its viscosity becomes zero. This means that no aperture is too narrow for it to flow through. This property is called superfluidity.

Similar phenomenon is observed in case of electrical resistance. The resistance decreases with temperature. This is because in a cold conducting material, the obstacles to flow of current is less. At very low temperatures, the resistance vanishes altogether. This phenomenon is called superconductivity. Newer objects are being discovered which show superconductivity at even relatively higher temperature. Mercury Barium Copper Oxide superconducts at 100° Centigrade or 173° Kelvin. Attempts are being made to develop superconductors which can show zero resistance even at room temperatures.

LIGHT

Light is a form of energy which produces in our eyes the sensation of sight. It has both particle nature as well as wave nature, i.e., light may be considered to give out energy either as a stream of particles called photons (Particle nature) or as a continuous stream of energy along a ray or as wave motion in the medium (Wave nature).

The concept of light particles such as photon is useful in the study of interaction of light with matter e.g. Photoelectric effect.

Light energy is propagated through medium as a wave motion. Light reaches from sun to earth. We know that there is no medium between its path. So light can even travel through vacuum. It always travel in a straight line (rectilinear propagation). The 'Pin-hole Camera' is the application of rectilinear propagation of light.

Reflection of Light

When a light falls on a smooth polished surface, it bounces back. This is called reflection of light. It is of two types:

(1) **Regular Reflection:** When a parallel beam of light falls on a smooth surface, the reflected rays are also parallel to each other.

(2) **Irregular Reflection:** When a parallel beam of light falls on rough surface, it gets reflected in different directions. This type of reflection enables us to see the various objects around us.

The reflection of light always obeys laws of reflection.

An opaque surface like mirrors reflects light according to the laws of reflection which says that angle of incidence of a ray is equal to the angle of reflection.

Refraction

The phenomenon of change in the direction of a beam of light as it passes from one medium to another

SCIENCE

is called refraction of light, e.g. pencil appears to be bent in water.

When light enters rarer medium from a denser medium it goes away from normal.

When light enters denser medium from a rarer medium it bends towards normal.

The optical density of a medium is characterised by the speed of light in that medium. More dense the medium is, less is the speed of light in it. Speed of light in vacuum is maximum with a value of 3 x 10^8 m/s and its optical density is taken as minimum to be equal to one.

When a ray of light enters from one medium to another, the ratio of its speeds of propagation in the two medium (measured in terms of refractive index μ) determines the extent of refraction and change in direction.

More is the ratio of velocity of light in two media, more refractive index and hence change in the direction of propagation.

We see these effects of refraction in our everyday life, e.g.,

(a) Bottom of a pond appears to be raised up, i.e., its apparent depth is less than the real depth.

(b) On refraction through a prism, the white light splits up into seven colours of rainbow, namely, Violet, Indigo, Blue, Green, Yellow, Orange and Red to be remembered by the word "VIBGYOR".

Rainbow: Rainbows are formed by sunlight falling on raindrops. Sometimes two rainbows are seen. The primary rainbow is a coloured band, having red on the outside and violet on the inner side. It is formed due to two refractions and one reflection of light falling on raindrops. The secondary rainbow is formed due to the two refractions and two reflections of the sunlight falling on the raindrops. The rainbows are visible only when the altitude of the sun is less than 42°C.

Refraction Through Lenses: Lenses are transparent and made by grinding glass plates. They have curved spherical surfaces, convex or concave. They have faces of equal or unequal radii.

Convex Lens: The middle portion of these lenses is thicker than the edges. These are also called converging lenses, because they converge a parallel beam of light after refraction through them. It has two real foci. The nature and the position of the image formed by a convex lens depends on the position of the object.

They are used to correct hypermetropia.

Concave Lens: The middle portion of these lenses is thinner than the edges. These are also called diverging lens. Because they diverge the parallel beam of light. It has a virtual focus. A concave lens always forms a virtual, erect and diminished image of an object, no matter where the object is placed in front of the lens.

Concave lens is used to correct myopia.

Power of a Lens

It is defined as the reciprocal of its focal length in metres Its unit is Dioptres (D).

A convex lens has positive focal length, so the power of convex lens is positive.

A concave lens has negative focal length, so the power of concave lens is negative.

Dispersion of Light

When a beam of white light passes through a prism, then it gets split up into its constituent colours. This is called dispersion of light. The image thus formed on a screen is called a spectrum.

The spectrum consists of visible and invisible regions. In the visible region, the order of the colours is from violet to red. The deviation produced for the violet rays of light is maximum and for red rays of light it is minimum. The invisible region of spectrum of wavelength shorter than violet is called ultra-violet and the region of wavelength longer than red is called infra-red.

The refractive index of the material of a prism is given by

$$\mu = \frac{\sin\left(\frac{A+D}{2}\right)}{\sin\frac{A}{2}}$$

where A is the angle of the prism and D is the angle of minimum deviation.

Interference of Light

When two or more wave trains act simultaneously on any particle in a medium, the displacement of the particle.at any instant is due to the superposition of all the wave trains. This phenomenon is called interference of light e.g. We are familiar with the beautiful colours produced by a thin film of oil on the-surface of water and also by the thin film of a soap bubble. This is due to the interference between light reflected from the top and the bottom surface of a thin film.

Holography: In the case of ordinary photographs, the camera lens can be focussed only in a particular plane and the details of field nearer and farther than the focussed plane will not be recorded. This is because ordinary photographs record only the intensity distribution in a particular plane.

But in holography, it is possible to record the amplitude and phase distribution in any plane between the object and the observer. This holographic studies help to obtain the complete field of view as originally observed.

Gabor has introduced for the first time the holographic method of recording and retrieving the image.

Uses of Holography:

(1) It has been used in holographic interferometry.
(2) It is useful in the microscopic examination of certain kinds of specimens.
(3) It is also useful to provide a high capacity system for image storage and re-examination.

Diffraction

Bending of light round the edges of an obstacle within the geometrical shadow is called diffraction. That is why even if we are not able to see the source of the light, we can see the light.

SOUND

We live in a world full of sound. Some of the sounds are pleasant while others are unpleasant. Unpleasant sounds are called "noise". Sound is a conse-quence of the vibrations of any object, vibrating in a material medium. Sound needs a material medium to travel, i.e., it cannot travel through vacuum. It can travel through solids and liquids also. It travels fastest in solids than in liquids and gases. Speed of sound is nearly 330 m/sec through air. Through water, the speed of sound is 1500 m/sec while through steel, the speed of sound is as high as 5000 to 6000 m/sec.

Human ear is quite sensitive to the frequency of the vibrating body producing sound. A normal ear can only hear sounds of frequencies from 20 Hz to 20,000 Hz. This range of frequencies from 20 Hz to 20,000 Hz constitutes the audible range of the normal human ear. We call these sounds as 'sonics'. Sound of frequencies greater than 20,000 Hz are called *ultrasonics*. Sounds of frequencies less than 20 Hz are called *infrasonics* or *subsonics*. Some animals like dogs, leopards, deers, monkeys and bats can hear ultrasonics.

When sound waves strike a surface, they can change their directions and start travelling back. Thus sound can be reflected. Sound also obeys the laws of reflection.

Echo

Echoes are due to reflection of sound. We can observe echoes in many open places like open fields, hills etc. But we cannot here echo in our homes. This is because of the limitation of our ear. The effect of a given sound 'stays on' .in our ear for about 1/15 second. If therefore, a reflected sound reaches our ears before this interval, it mingles with the direct sound and we are not able to distinguish between the two.

To get a clear echo, the reflecting wall etc. should be 11 m away (but it should be open place, too many reflecting surface should not be there). Since sound travels at about 330 m/s, in 1/15 sec, it will travel nearly 22 m. Since it has to travel an equal distance forward and backward, it must travel nearly 11 m either way. This Echo Effect has many applications e.g. to calculate the depth of the well, to measure the depth of ocean, to estimate the distance of an enemy aeroplane etc. Different materials do not reflect sound equally. Different sounds differ from one another in loudness and pitch.

MULTIPLE CHOICE QUESTIONS

1. The passengers in a boat are not allowed to stand because:
(*a*) this will raise the centre of gravity and the boat will be rocked
(*b*) this will lower centre of gravity and the boat will rocked
(*c*) the effective weight of system increases
(*d*) of surface tension effects

2. A person presses the earth least where he is:
(*a*) sitting
(*b*) standing
(*c*) running
(*d*) lying on the ground

3. One litre of cool air weighs heavier than one litre of hot air because of the:
(*a*) increased number of collisions between the molecules
(*b*) increased number of molecules at high temperature
(*c*) greater energy of molecules at high temperature
(*d*) lower energy of molecules at high temperature

4. A bomb is dropped from an aeroplane moving horizontal at constant speed. When air resistance is taken into consideration, then the bomb:
(*a*) flies with the aeroplane
(*b*) falls on earth ahead of the aeroplane
(*c*) falls on earth behind aeroplane
(*d*) falls on earth exactly below the aeroplane.

5. A ball is thrown upwards in a train which is accelerating. The ball will fall
(*a*) Ahead of the thrower
(*b*) Behind the thrower
(*c*) In the hands of thrower
(*d*) Data inadequate

6. The flying of birds is a proof of Newton's:
(*a*) first law
(*b*) second law
(*c*) third law of motion
(*d*) both second and third law

7. A moving bullet hits a solid target resting on a frictionless surface and gets embedded in it. What is conserved in this process?
(*a*) both momentum and kinetic energy
(*b*) kinetic energy alone
(*c*) momentum alone
(*d*) neither momentum nor kinetic energy

8. Fat can be separated from milk in a cream-separator because of:
(*a*) cohesive force (*b*) gravitational force
(*c*) centrifugal force (*d*) centripetal force

9. A cricket player while taking a catch lowers his hands to
(*a*) Increase time of impulse
(*b*) Decrease time of impulse
(*c*) Take catch safely
(*d*) Increase the area of impact

10. Where should be the centre of gravity of a body?
(*a*) It must lie within the body
(*b*) It may be near but not essentially within the body
(*c*) It changes its position from time to time
(*d*) It must be outside the body

11. The process of walking involves
(*a*) Newton's first law of motion
(*b*) Newton's second law of motion
(*c*) Newton's third law of motion
(*d*) Conservation of momentum

12. Which of the following is used to reduce friction
1. Streamlines
2. Use of ball bearings
3. Lubrication
(*a*) 1 & 2 only (*b*) 1 & 3 only
(*c*) 2 & 3 only (*d*) 1, 2 & 3

13. Which law is involved in the act of cleaning a carpet by beating it with a stick?
(*a*) First law of motion.
(*b*) Second law of motion.
(*c*) Law of conservation of energy.
(*d*) Law of conservation of mass.

14. When a body is taken from the earth to the moon:
(*a*) Its weight increases
(*b*) Its weight decreases
(*c*) Its weight remains unchanged
(*d*) It becomes completely weightless

15. Which of the following is the cause of weightlessness experienced while orbiting around earth on a spaceship ?
(*a*) Inertia (*b*) Zero gravity
(*c*) Acceleration (*d*) Centre of gravity.

16. The weight of an object would be minimum when it is placed:
(*a*) at the North Pole
(*b*) at the South Pole
(*c*) at the Equator
(*d*) at the Centre of the Earth

17. As the train starts moving, a man sitting inside leans backwards because of:
(*a*) inertia of rest
(*b*) inertia of motion
(*c*) moment of inertia
(*d*) conservation of mass

18. Electrons revolve round the nucleus because of:
(*a*) cohesive force (*b*) adhesive force
(*c*) centripetal force (*d*) centrifugal force

Directions Qs. 19-27: *In each of the following questions there are two statements Assertion (A) is given followed by a corresponding statement of Reason (R) just below it. Of the statements, mark the correct answer:*
(*a*) If both assertion and reason are true and reason is the correct explanation of assertion.
(*b*) If both assertion and reason are true but reason is not the correct explanation of assertion
(*c*) If assertion is true but reason is false
(*d*) If assertion is false but reason is true.

19. **Assertion (A):** Inertia is the property by virtue of which the body is unable to change by itself the state of rest only.
Reason (R): The bodies do not change their state unless acted upon by an unbalanced external force.

20. **Assertion (A):** If the net external force on the body is zero, then its acceleration is zero.
Reason (R): Acceleration does not depend on force.

21. **Assertion (A):** Newton's second law of motion gives the measurement of force.
Reason (R): According to Newton's second law of motion, force is directly proportional to the rate of change of momentum.

22. **Assertion (A):** Force is required to move a body uniformly along a circle.
Reason (R): When the motion is uniform, acceleration is zero.

23. **Assertion (A):** If two object of different masses have same momentum, the lighter body possess greater velocity.

Reason (R): For all bodies momentum always remains same.

24. Assertion (A): Aeroplanes always fly at low altitudes.

Reason (R): According to newton's third law of motion, for every action there is an equal and opposite reaction.

25. Assertion (A): No force is required by the body to remain in a state of uniform motion or at rest.

Reason (R): In uniform linear motion, acceleration has a finite value.

26. Assertion (A): Mass is a measure of inertia of the body in linear motion.

Reason (R): Greater the mass, greater is the force required to change its state of rest or of uniform motion.

27. Assertion (A): The slope of momentum versus time curve give us the acceleration.

Reason (R): Acceleration is given by the rate of change of momentum.

28. Kinetic energy of a body is directly proportion to its—

(*a*) Weight (*b*) Speed
(*c*) Mass (*d*) Velocity

29. Einstein got his Nobel Prize for

(*a*) His theory of relativity
(*b*) Explanation of Photoelectric effect
(*c*) His theory of atomic heats of solids
(*d*) None of the above

30. If a body moves along a frictionless horizontal surface its weight—

(*a*) does work (*b*) does not work
(*c*) work partially (*d*) none of these

31. A car and a lorry both are moving with equal kinetic energies. If equal breaking force is applied on both, then before coming to rest:

(*a*) a car will cover a greater distance
(*b*) lorry will cover a greater distance
(*c*) both will cover the same distance
(*d*) the distance covered by them will depend only on their respective velocities.

32. The work done by a force:

(*a*) is independent of the frame of reference
(*b*) is same in all reference-frames
(*c*) is same in all inertial frames
(*d*) none of these

33. Identify the correct statement of Work-Energy Theorem.

(*a*) work done by all the forces on a particle to displace it is equal to its change in kinetic energy.
(*b*) work done by all the forces on a particle is equal to its change in mechanical energy.
(*c*) work done by all the forces acting on a particle is equal to change in its potential energy.
(*d*) work done by a force on a particle is equal to change in its kinetic energy.

34. Which of the following statement is true?

(*a*) Kinetic energy and momentum both are conserved in all types of motion.
(*b*) Momentum is conserved in elastic collision but not in inelastic collision.
(*c*) Total kinetic energy is not conserved but momentum is conserved in inelastic collision.
(*d*) Kinetic energy is conserved in elastic collision but not in inelastic collision.

35. Thermal energy is a energy due to—

(*a*) Kinetic energy of molecules
(*b*) Potential energy of molecules
(*c*) Both (*a*) and (*b*)
(*d*) None of these

36. The internal energy of a gas:

(*a*) is the sum total of kinetic and potential energies.
(*b*) is the total transitional kinetic energies.
(*c*) is the total kinetic energy of randomly moving molecules.
(*d*) is the total kinetic energy of gas molecules.

37. Power is measured in—

(*a*) Joules per second
(*b*) Joules per minute
(*c*) Joules per square second
(*d*) None of these

38. It takes much longer to cook on the hills than in the plains, because:

(*a*) due to low atmospheric pressure in the hills, the boiling point of water is raised, and therefore water takes longer to boil
(*b*) in the hills, the atmospheric pressure is lower than that in the plains and therefore water boils at lower temperature
(*c*) in the hills, the atmospheric temperature is low and therefore a lot of heat is lost to the atmosphere
(*d*) in the hills, the humid atmosphere absorbs a lot of heat, leaving very little for the cooking

39. Expansion during heating:

(*a*) occurs only in a solid
(*b*) increases the weight of a material
(*c*) decreases the density of the material
(*d*) occurs at the same rate for all liquids and solids

40. In isothermal expansion of an ideal gas:

(*a*) there is no change in the temperature of the gas
(*b*) there is no change in the internal energy of the gas
(*c*) the work done by the gas is equal to the heat supplied to the gas
(*d*) all of the above

41. The temperature of the sun is measured by:

(*a*) platinum resistance thermometer
(*b*) gas thermometer

(c) pyrometer
(d) vapour pressure thermometer

42. The absolute zero is the temperature at which:
(a) water freezes
(b) all substances exist in solid state
(c) molecular motion ceases
(d) none of these

43. Thermal expansion takes place in a:
(a) solid (b) liquid
(c) gas (d) none

44. Which of the following produces more severe burns?
(a) boiling water (b) steam
(c) hot air (d) sun rays

45. The factor not needed to calculate heat lost or gained when there is no change of state:
(a) weight (b) specific heat
(c) relative density (d) temperature change

46. Melting point of ice:
(a) increases with increasing pressure
(b) decreases with increasing pressure
(c) is independent of pressure
(d) is proportional to pressure

47. Which of the following statement(s) is/are correct?
(1) The boiling point of a liquid is affected by addition of soluble solid.
(2) The boiling point of a liquid is affected by external vapour pressure.
(3) The boiling point is a fixed characteristic of a liquid and does not vary.

Code:
(a) only (3) is correct
(b) only (1) is correct
(c) (1) and (2) are correct
(d) only (2) is correct

48. If the door of a refrigerator is opened while connected to supply, the room gets:
(a) cooled
(b) heated
(c) no effect
(d) Nothing could be said as the temperature is not given

49. Heat is transmitted from higher to lower temperature through actual mass motion of the molecules in:
(a) conduction (b) convection
(c) radiation (d) all the above three

50. The good absorbers of heat are:
(a) poor emitters (b) non-emitter
(c) good emitters (d) highly polished

51. In which process, the rate of transfer of heat is maximum ?
(a) conduction
(b) convection
(c) radiation
(d) in all these, heat is transferred with same speed

52. A piece of metal feels hotter than a piece of wood in summer because:
(a) metal expands more than wood
(b) our body is cooler than metal but warmer than wood
(c) metal is a better conductor of heat than wood
(d) metal gets hotter than wood

53. Which of the following minimises the transference of heat in a thermoflask?
I. Conduction II. Convection III. Radiation
(a) I, II and III (b) II and III
(c) I and II (d) I and III

54. Heat produced in a conductor depends:
(a) directly on time
(b) inversely on time
(c) both (a) and (b) are true
(d) none of the above

55. In summer, water is stored in unglazed earthen pots because:
(a) They are cheap
(b) Evaporation through pores makes the water cooler
(c) Earthen pots do not need as much rinsing and cleaning as metal vessels do
(d) More water can be stored in them

56. In a barometer, mercury is preferred over water because :
(a) Mercury is a good conductor of heat
(b) Mercury is shining and therefore, its level can be read easily
(c) Mercury is available in pure form
(d) Mercury has high density and low vapour pressure

57. Hot water is used in the pipes for heating purposes in the cold countries because:
(a) it has low density
(b) it has poor conductivity
(c) it has high specific heat
(d) it has a considerable value of latent heat of freezing

58. Water-pipes burst in severe winter at hill stations because:
(a) They contract on cooling
(b) Water in the pipe contracts on freezing
(c) Water in the pipe expands on freezing
(d) Pipes expand on cooling

59. Relative humidity is measured by which of the following instruments?
(a) Thermometer (b) Barometer
(c) Hygrometer (d) Lactometer

60. What is the 'critical temperature' of water vapour?
(a) 0°C (b) less than 100°C
(c) 100°C (d) more than 100°C

61. Which of the following statements is wrong?
(a) Sound travels in straight line
(b) Sound travels as waves
(c) Sound is a form of energy
(d) Sound travels faster in vacuum than in air

62. Sound waves do not show in air:
(*a*) polarisation (*b*) diffraction
(*c*) refraction (*d*) reflection

63. With the rise of temperature, the velocity of sound:
(*a*) decreases
(*b*) remains the same
(*c*) increases
(*d*) is independent of temperature

64. Velocity of sound will be:
(*a*) smaller in moist air than in dry air
(*b*) greater in moist air than in dry air
(*c*) same in moist and dry air
(*d*) independent of its density

65. The velocity of sound is largest in:
(*a*) water (*b*) air
(*c*) steel (*d*) vacuum

66. Buzzing of a mosquito is:
(*a*) loud sound (*b*) shrill sound
(*c*) flat sound (*d*) sweet sound

67. Quality of sound depends upon its:
(*a*) wavelength (*b*) frequency
(*c*) amplitude (*d*) overtone

68. Pitch of sound depends upon it:
(*a*) wavelength
(*b*) frequency
(*c*) amplitude
(*d*) periodicity and regularity

69. Doppler's effect of sound is produced when the source and the observer are:
(*a*) moving
(*b*) in relative motion
(*c*) stationary
(*d*) resonance phenomenon

70. The Doppler effect is applicable for:
(*a*) light waves only
(*b*) sound waves only
(*c*) both light and sound waves
(*d*) none of the above

71. To a stationary man the frequency of a sound source moving towards the man appears to be:
(*a*) lower than the original frequency
(*b*) same as the original frequency
(*c*) higher than the original frequency
(*d*) lower as well higher than the original frequency depending upon the speed of the source

72. The same notes being played on the Sitar and Veena differ in:
(*a*) pitch
(*b*) quality
(*c*) both pitch and quality
(*d*) none of the two

73. The walls of the halls built for music concerts should:
(*a*) amplify sound (*b*) transmit sound
(*c*) reflect sound (*d*) absorb sound

74. When we hear a sound, we can identify its source from:
(*a*) amplitude of sound
(*b*) intensity of sound
(*c*) wavelength of sound
(*d*) overtones present in the sound

75. Consider the following statements:
Assertion A: The velocity of sound in the air increases due to presence of moisture in it.
Reason R: The presence of moisture in air lowers the density of air.
Of these statements,
(*a*) both (A) and (R) are true and (R) is the correct explanation of (A)
(*b*) both (A) and (R) are true but (R) is not the correct explanation of (A)
(*c*) (A) is true but (R) is false
(*d*) (A) is false but (R) is true

ANSWERS

1	2	3	4	5	6	7	8	9	10
(*a*)	(*d*)	(*b*)	(*c*)	(*b*)	(*c*)	(*c*)	(*c*)	(*a*)	(*c*)
11	**12**	**13**	**14**	**15**	**16**	**17**	**18**	**19**	**20**
(*c*)	(*d*)	(*a*)	(*b*)	(*b*)	(*d*)	(*a*)	(*c*)	(*d*)	(*c*)
21	**22**	**23**	**24**	**25**	**26**	**27**	**28**	**29**	**30**
(*a*)	(*c*)	(*c*)	(*a*)	(*c*)	(*a*)	(*c*)	(*c*)	(*b*)	(*b*)
31	**32**	**33**	**34**	**35**	**36**	**37**	**38**	**39**	**40**
(*c*)	(*d*)	(*a*)	(*d*)	(*c*)	(*c*)	(*a*)	(*a*)	(*c*)	(*d*)
41	**42**	**43**	**44**	**45**	**46**	**47**	**48**	**49**	**50**
(*c*)	(*c*)	(*a*)	(*b*)	(*c*)	(*b*)	(*c*)	(*b*)	(*b*)	(*c*)
51	**52**	**53**	**54**	**55**	**56**	**57**	**58**	**59**	**60**
(*c*)	(*c*)	(*a*)	(*a*)	(*b*)	(*d*)	(*c*)	(*c*)	(*c*)	(*d*)
61	**62**	**63**	**64**	**65**	**66**	**67**	**68**	**69**	**70**
(*d*)	(*a*)	(*c*)	(*b*)	(*c*)	(*b*)	(*d*)	(*b*)	(*b*)	(*c*)
71	**72**	**73**	**74**	**75**					
(*c*)	(*b*)	(*d*)	(*d*)	(*a*)					

HOW THINGS WORK

ELECTRIC CURRENT AND CIRCUITS

Electric Charge

1. Electric charge is a fundamental property like Length, Mass, and Time. Electric charges are of two types- Positive and Negative.
2. *(i)* A positive ion is an atom from which one or more electrons has been removed, i.e. **positive charge implies the deficiency of electrons.**

   (ii) A negative ion is an atom to which one more electrons has been added, i.e. **negative charge implies excess of electrons.**
3. **Units of Charges:**

   SI system – coulomb

Coulomb's Law

According to this law the electrostatic force F (either attractive or repulsive) between two stationary point charges q_1 and q_2 in free space (i.e. air or vacuum)

(i) is directly proportional to the product of the two charges.

(ii) is inversely proportional to square of the distance between the charges and

(iii) acts along the line joining the two charges. Let r be the distance of charges q_2 from q_1 then

$$F \propto \frac{q_1 q_2}{r^2}$$

or

$$F = C' \frac{q_1 q_2}{r^2}$$

where C' represents constant of proportionality.

Value of constant C depends on two factors.

(a) System of units.

(b) Medium in which charges are placed.

Electric Field

The region in which a charged particle placed at any point experiences a force, is called electric field. Electric field is measured in terms of electric field intensity $(\vec{E})$. The electric field intensity $\vec{E}$ at any point in an electric field is equal to force experienced by unit positive test charge q_0 placed at that point *i.e.*

$$\vec{E} = \frac{\vec{F}}{q_0}$$

Electric Potential

The electric potential at any point in an electric field is defined as the works done on the system against the electric force in moving an unit positive test charge from infinity (i.e. from beyond the electric field) to that point. If W is the work done in bringing the charge q_0 from infinity to given point, then potential at that point:

$$V = \frac{W}{q_0}$$

Electric Current

Electric current is the rate of flow of electric charge through any point of the circuit per unit time. It is denoted by I.

If a charge 'q' flows through the circuit for time 't', then current $I = q/t$.

Current is a *scalar* quantity and its unit is **ampere**.

Electric Resistance

The opposition offered by the substance to the flow of charge is known as electrical resistance. If the potential difference between the ends of the conductor is V and the current in the conductor is I, then the electric resistance of the conductor will be given by $R = V/I$.

Electric Resistance

The opposition offered by the substance to the flow of charge is known as electrical resistance. If the potential difference between the ends of the conductor is V and the current in the conductor is I, then the electric resistance of the conductor will be given by $R = V/I$.

The resistance of the conductor

(i) $R \propto$ length of conductor

(ii) $R \propto \frac{1}{\text{area of cross-section}}$

The Unit of resistance R in the MKS system is 'Ohm'.

Ohm's Law

According to Ohm's law, if physical state of a conductor (such as temperature), are unchanged then the ratio of the potential difference applied at its ends and the current flowing through it is constant.

Effect of Temperature on Resistivity

1. **Resistivity of Metals**
Electric resistance of the metallic wire increases when its temperature is raised. Since the resistance of the wire is given by $R = ml/n\rho^2 A\tau$, where n is the number of free electrons per unit volume of the wire, m is the mass and e is the charge of the electrons.

2. **Resistivity of Alloys**
With rise in temperature the resistivity of alloys also increases. But this increase is much smaller compared to pure metals.

Combinations of Resistances

There are following two combinations of resistances :

(i) **Resistance in Series**

The equivalent resistance of combinations of three resistances in series

$$IR = IR_1 + IR_2 + IR_3$$

or $$R = R_1 + R_2 + R_3$$

(ii) **Resistance in Parallel**

The equivalent resistance of combination of three resistances R_1, R_2, R_3 in parallel

$$\frac{1}{R} = \frac{1}{R_1} + \frac{1}{R_2} + \frac{1}{R_3}$$

Electric Cell

A device which maintains the flow of charges continuously in a circuit is called the electric cell.

E.M.F. of Cell

It is defined in two ways :

(i) **Qualitative Definition.** The potential difference across the terminals of the cell in an open circuit is called the e.m.f.

(ii) **Quantitative Definition.** The energy given by the cell in the flow of unit charge in the whole circuit (including the cell) is called the 'electromotive force (e.m.f.) of the cell. The e.m.f. is a characteristic of the cell which depends upon the nature of the plates and the electrolyte used in the cell. It is not affected by the quantity of the electrolyte or the size of the plates or the distance between the plates.

Suppose during the flow of a charge of q coulomb in an electric circuit, the energy supplied (or the work done) by a cell is W joule then the E.M.F. of the cell is

$$E = (W/q) \text{ joule/coulomb or volt.}$$

Potential Difference

Suppose during the flow of a charge of q coulomb in a part of an electrical circuit, W' joule work is done or W' joule energy is consumed, then the potential difference across that part will be $V = W'/q$ volt. It is measured by a voltmeter.

Combinations of Cells

As a cell is a source of electric current, a single cell cannot give a strong current, hence two or more cells are to be combined to get strong current. The combination of cells is called a 'battery'. Cells can be combined in three ways : (1) In series, (2) In parallel and (3) In mixed grouping.

1. In Series.

Total resistance of the circuit = $(nr + R)$

Let i be the current in the circuit then $i = \dfrac{nE}{nr+R}$

Two cases arise here :

(i) If $nr << R$, then $i = \dfrac{nE}{R}$ (approx), i.e. if the internal resistance of the connected cells is much smaller then the external resistance, then the current given by these cells will be nearly n times, the current given by one cell. Hence, when the internal resistance of the connected cells is much smaller than the external resistance, then the cells should be connected in the series to obtain a strong current.

(ii) If $nr >> R$, then $i = \dfrac{nE}{nr} = \dfrac{E}{r}$ (approx), i.e. if the internal resistance of the connected cells is much greater than the external resistance, then nearly the same current is obtained by n cells as by a single cell. Hence, there is no advantage of connecting cells in series.

2. In Parallel

Total resistance of the circuit = $\left(\dfrac{r}{n} + R\right)$ If the current in the external circuit be i,

then $$i = \frac{E}{(r/n) + R} = \frac{nE}{r + nR}$$

Two cases arise here :

(i) If $\dfrac{r}{n} << R$, *i.e.* if the internal resistance of the cells is much smaller than the external resistance then r can be neglected in comparison to nR. Then from equation (i), $i = \dfrac{E}{R}$ (approx), i.e. the total current will be equal to the current given by a single cell. Hence connecting the cells of small internal resistance in parallel has no advantage.

(ii) If $\dfrac{r}{n} >> R$, i.e. if the internal resistance of the cells is larger than the external resistance,

then the current will be $i = n\frac{E}{r}$ (approx.)

This current is nearly n times the current given by a single cell. Hence, when the internal resistance of the cells is much larger than the external resistance, then the cells should be connected in parallel.

3. Mixed Grouping

Suppose n cells are connected in èach series, and such m rows are connected in parallel. Let E be the e.m.f. of each cell and r be the internal resistance. This battery of cells is sending current in an external resistance R.

$\therefore$ Total resistance of the circuit = $\{(nr/m) + R\}$. Let the current in the external circuit be i, then

$$i = \frac{nE}{(nr/m)+R} = \frac{mnE}{nr+mR}$$

Wheatstone's Bridge

A bridge-arrangement of four resistances devised by Wheatstone by which resistance of a given conductor can be determined is called 'Wheatstone bridge'.

Four resistance P, Q, R and S are connected in the form of four arms of a parallelogram $ABCD$.

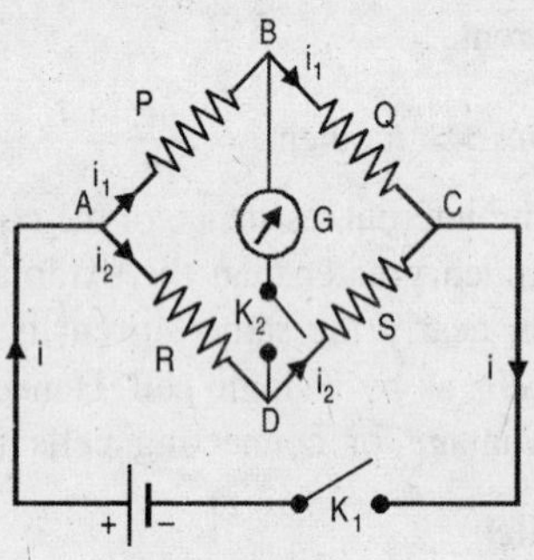

Fig.

$$\frac{\bar{\tau}}{\text{क}} = \frac{\bar{r}}{-}$$

From this formula it is clear that if the ratio of the resistances P and Q, and the resistance R are known, then the unknown resistance S can be calculated.

Chemical Effects of Electric Current

The phenomenon of the conduction of electricity through liquids was first studied by Faraday in about 1833. Pure liquids, with the exception of mercury, are, in general, bad conductors of electricity at ordinary temperatures, but the conductivity of a liquid increases if the solution contains a metallic salt or an acid. *The process of decompositions of a compound by the application of an electric field is called electrolysis.* The liquid containing the compound is called an electrolyte and the vessel containing the electrolyte is called a *voltmeter*.

Faraday's Laws of Electrolysis

The two laws of electrolysis are stated as follows:

(i) The mass of ion liberated from an electrolyte at the respective electrodes is directly proportional to the quantity of electricity which passes through it,

$$W \propto Q$$

But, $\quad Q = It$

where Q is the charge, I is current and t is the time. If I is expressed in amperes and t in seconds, then Q will be in coulombs.

$$\therefore \quad W \propto It \text{ or } W = ZIt$$

where Z is a constant called the electro-chemical equivalent of the substance. The units of Z will be g/coulombs, if W is expressed in grams.

$$\therefore \quad Z = \frac{W}{I \times t} g/C$$

The electro-chemical equivalent of a substance is defined as the mass of the ion in grams liberated at the electrode when when one coulomb of electricity is passed through the electrolyte.

(ii) If the same quantity of electricity passes through different electrolytes, the masses of the ions liberated at the respective electrodes are proportional to their chemical equivalents.

Let W be the mass of ion liberated, then,

$$W \propto \text{chemical equivalent}$$

or $$\frac{W}{\text{Chemical equivalent}} = \text{constant}$$

provided the same quantity of electricity passes through different electrolytes.

Electromagnetic Induction

"Whenever the magnetic lines of force linked with a closed circuit change an induced e.m.f. is always produced in the circuit and lasts only so long as the change lasts." The induced e.m.f. giving rise to such currents is called the induced electromotive force and the phenomenon is called **electromagnetic induction**.

Faraday's Laws of Electromagnetic Induction

(i) The induced emf, e is equal to the negative rate of change of magnetic flux : If $\Delta\phi$ be the change in magnetic flux in a time interval Δt, then the induced emf in the circuit is

$$e = -\frac{\Delta\phi}{\Delta t}$$

In the limit $\Delta t \to 0$, $e = -\frac{d\phi}{dt}$

The negative sign indicated that the induced e.m.f. opposes the change in magnetic flux (Lenz's law).

Transformer

Transformer is a device used to obtain suitable A.C. voltage. It never works on D.C. There are of two types of transformer—

(a) Step-up Transformer. It is used to convert low voltage high current to high voltage low current.

(b) Step-down transformer. It is used to convert high voltage low current to low voltage high current.

Principle. Transformer works on the principle of mutual induction *i.e.* when a magnetic flux linked with one coil changes, an induced e.m.f. is produced in the other coil.

Generator or Dynamo

A device by which we can convert mechanical energy to electrical energy is called Dynamo.

Alternating Current Generator (A.C. Dynamo)

Principle. Alternating current generator is based on the principle of the electromagnetic induction. When a coil is rotated about an axis perpendicular to the direction of uniform magnetic field, an induced e.m.f. is produced across it.

Construction. The A.C. generator consists of the following parts :

(1) Armature. The armature is a rectangular coil *ABCD* consisting of a large number of turns wound over a soft iron core. The soft iron core is used to increase the magnetic flux.

(2) Field magnet. Field magnet is a strong magnet having concave poles. The armature is rotated between the two poles of this magnet so that axis of the armature is perpendicular to magnetic field lines.

(3) Slip ring. The leads from the arms of the armature are connected to the two rings R_1 and R_2 separately. As the armature and hence the leads rotate, the rings R_1 and R_2 also rotate about the central axis.

(4) Brushes. Brushes (B_1, B_2) are used to pass on the current from armature to the external load *R*. As the rings rotate, the brushes remain in constant touch with the rings and always keep on pressing against them.

Working. The working of the a.c. generator is illustrated with the help of five different positions of the armature *ABCD* at time $t = 0, \frac{T}{4}, \frac{T}{2}, \frac{3T}{4}$ and *T* respectively as shown in Fig. below.

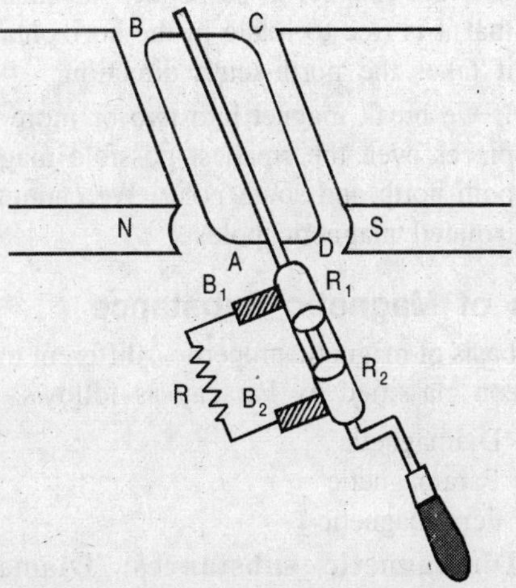

At $t = 0$, the armature *ABCD* is vertical with arm *AB* up and *CD* down. During the interval $t = 0$ to $t = \frac{T}{2}$, arm *AB* moves down and *CD* moves up. The direction of current can be found with the help of Fleming's right hand rule. The current in the armature will flow in the direction *DCBA*.

During the interval $t = \frac{T}{2}$ to $t = T$, just the arm *AB* moves up and *CD* moves down. Hence during this interval, the current in the armature will flow in the direction *ABCD*.

The arms *AB* and *CD* of armature move momentarily parallel to the field. whenever, the armature is vertical, hence the rate of change of magnetic flux is zero. So, the induced e.m.f. $\left(e = -\frac{d\phi}{dt}\right)$ is also zero. Thus at time $t = 0$, $\frac{T}{2}$ and *T*, there is no induced e.m.f. in the coil.

In the horizontal position of armature, the arms cut the magnetic lines of force at once, so the rate of change of magnetic flux is fastest and maximum e.m.f. is induced in this position. Thus at time $t = \frac{T}{4}$ and $\frac{3T}{4}$, the induced e.m.f. produced is maximum.

Hence output e.m.f. across *R* during a complete rotation will vary sinusoidally.

MAGNETS

Magnetism is the natural force that causes magnets to function as they do. A substance that is attracted by a magnet is called magnetic. Iron, nickel and cobalt are strongly magnetic. Copper, wood, glass, etc. are non-magnetic. Some varieties of magnetite, known as lodestone, are natural magnets.

Some of the main properties of magnets are:

(a) A bar magnet attracts iron filings more strongly near its free ends. These ends are called the poles.

(b) If a bar magnet is suspended in such a way that it is free to rotate in the horizontal plane, it takes the north-south direction.

(c) If we break magnet into two or more smaller pieces even the smallest possible magnet has both north and south poles. We cannot obtain isolated magnetic poles.

Types of Magnetic Substance

On the basis of magnetic properties, different materials have been classified by Faraday as follows:

(a) Diamagnetic
(b) Paramagnetic
(c) Ferromagnetic

(a) Diamagnetic substances: Diamagnetic substances are those in which individual atoms do not posses magnetic moment of their own. Cu, Gold and Bismuth are diamagnetic substances.

(b) Paramagnetic Substances: Those substances in which individual atom has a net non-magnetic moment of its own. When such material is placed in external magnetic field, it tries to align individual dipole moments in the direction of field. Al, Pt and Chr are Paramagnetic substances.

(c) Ferromagnetic Substances: Those substances in which each atom has a non-zero magnetic moment, as is a paramagnetic substance. The individuai magnetic moments align themselves is common direction over microscopic volumes.

Ferromagnetic materials, when heated, eventually lose their magnetic properties. This loss becomes complete above the Curie temperature, named after the French physicist Pierre Curie, who discovered it in 1895. The Curie temperature of metallic iron is about 770°C/1300°F. At this temperature ferro-magnet substance gets converted into paramagnetic substance.

Magnetic Poles

A magnet has two poles. When a magnet is brought near a heap of iron fillings the ends of the magnet show the maximum attraction. These ends where the magnetic attraction is maximum are called poles of the magnet.

A magnet suspended freely, always points in $N - S$ direction. The pole which points towards north is called **north pole** (N) and the pole that points towards the south is called **south pole** (S).

The SI unit of strength of a magnetic pole is ampere metre (A m) .

Magnetic Moment

The product of pole strength (m) and effective length ($2l$) of the magnet is called the Magnetic Moment. Thus $M = m \times 2l = 2ml$.

Its units are Ampere-m^2 and it is a vector quantity. Its direction is along the axis of the magnet from north pole of the magnet to the south pole.

Magnetic Field

The region around a pole in which magnetic effect can be experienced is called magnetic field.

Intensity of Magnetic Field

The number of lines of force crossing unit area of the surface, normally is called intensity of magnetic field.

OR

The force acting on unit pole placed in the magnetic field is called intensity of magnetic field.

i.e. $H = (\mu_0/4\pi) \cdot (m/r^2)$

Field Due to a Small Bar Magnet (Magnetic Dipole)

(i) In End-on position

In End-on position the point lies on the axis of the magnet. Let r be the distance of the point P from the centre O of the magnet. Let $2l$ be the length of the magnet and m be its pole strength. Then $NP = (r - l)$, $SP = (r + l)$.

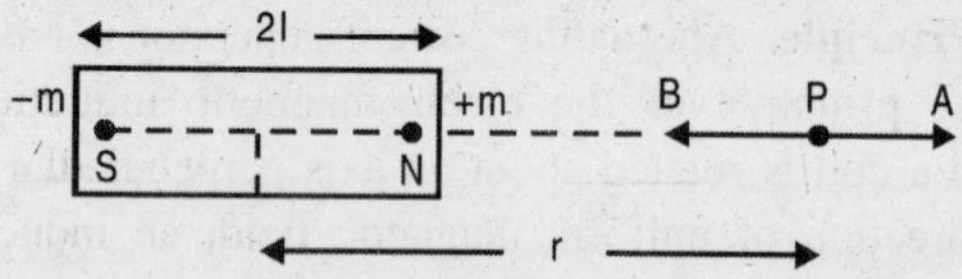

Fig.

The intensity due to the N-pole

$$\vec{PA} = \frac{\mu_0}{4\pi}\frac{m}{NP^2} = \frac{\mu_0}{4\pi} \cdot \frac{m}{(r-l)^2}$$

and, the intensity due to the S-pole,

$$\vec{PB} = \frac{\mu_0}{4\pi}\frac{m}{(SP^2)} = \frac{\mu_0}{4\pi} \cdot \frac{m}{(r+l)^2}$$

Thus, the resultant intensity is

$$B = \frac{\mu_0}{4\pi}\left[\frac{m}{(r-l)^2} - \frac{m}{(r+l)^2}\right] = \frac{\mu_0}{4\pi} \cdot \frac{4mlr}{(r^2-l^2)^2}.$$

$$B = \frac{\mu_0}{4\pi}\frac{2Mr}{(r^2-l^2)^2}$$

for a small magnet $r^2 >> l^2$, hence

$$B = \frac{\mu_0}{4\pi}\frac{2M}{r^3}$$

The direction of $\vec{B}$ is along the line joining the two poles from S pole to N pole.

(ii) Broad side-on position

In broad side-on the point lies on the magnetic equator of the magnet i.e. on the right bisector of the magnet.

Let us consider a magnet NS of pole strength m and length $2l$. P is the point on the right bisector of this magnet such that $OP = r$. Then,

$$SP = NP = (r^2 + l^2)^{1/2}$$

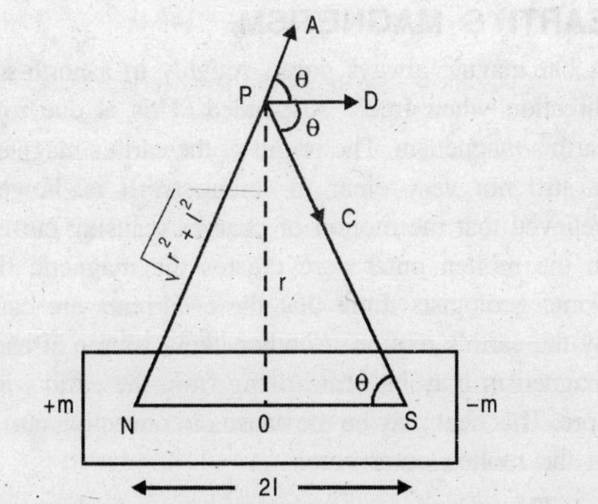

Fig.

Hence intensity of field at P due to N-pole $= \frac{\mu_0}{4\pi} \cdot \frac{m}{(r^2 + l^2)}$ along $\vec{PA}$. The intensity of field at P due to S-pole $= \frac{\mu_0}{4\pi} \cdot \frac{m}{(r^2 + l^2)}$ along $\vec{PC}$.

Each of these intensities can be resolved into two components : (i) along $\vec{PD}$ and (ii) perpendicular to $\vec{PD}$. The components perpendicular to $\vec{PD}$ being equal and opposite neutralise each other while the components parallel to $\vec{PD}$ add up.

Thus the resultant intensity at P is

$$B = \frac{\mu_0}{4\pi} \cdot \frac{m}{(r^2 + l^2)} \cos\theta + \frac{\mu_0}{4\pi} \frac{m}{(r^2 + l^2)} \cos\theta$$

or $$B = \frac{\mu_0}{4\pi}\left[\frac{2m}{(r^2+l^2)} \cdot \frac{l}{(r^2+l^2)^{1/2}}\right] = \frac{\mu_0}{4\pi} \cdot \frac{M}{(r^2+l^2)^{3/2}}$$

For a small magnet $r^2 >> l^2$, hence $B = \frac{\mu_0}{4\pi} \cdot \frac{M}{r^3}$

The direction of $\vec{B}$ is parallel to the axis from N-pole to S-pole.

Classification of Magnetic Substances

Curie and Faraday observed that almost all substances have certain magnetic properties. Placing many substances in magnetic fields he studied their behaviour. On the basis of magnetic behaviour of different materials, he divided them into three categories : (1) diamagnetic substances, (2) paramagnetic substances and (3) ferromagnetic substances.

1. Diamagnetic Substances

(i) When these substances are placed in a magnetic field they acquire feeble magnetism opposite to the direction of the magnetic field.

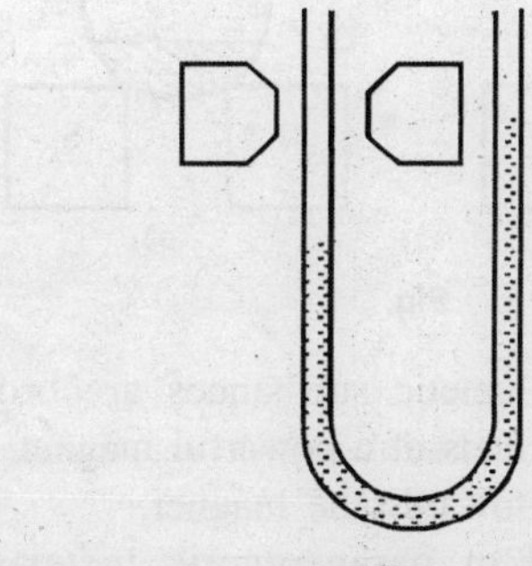
Fig.

(ii) When these substances are brought near the ends of a powerful magnet they are somewhat repelled. They are called 'diamagnetic' substances, and their magnetism is called the 'diamagnetism.'

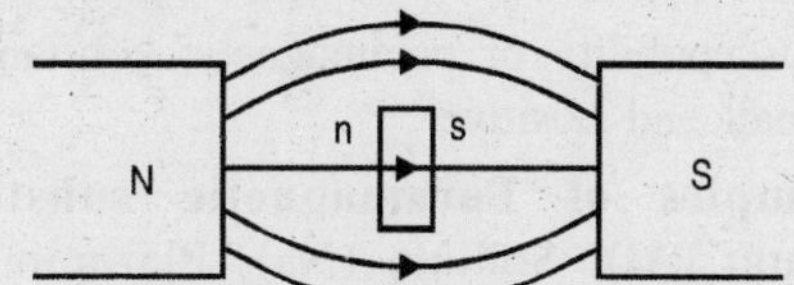

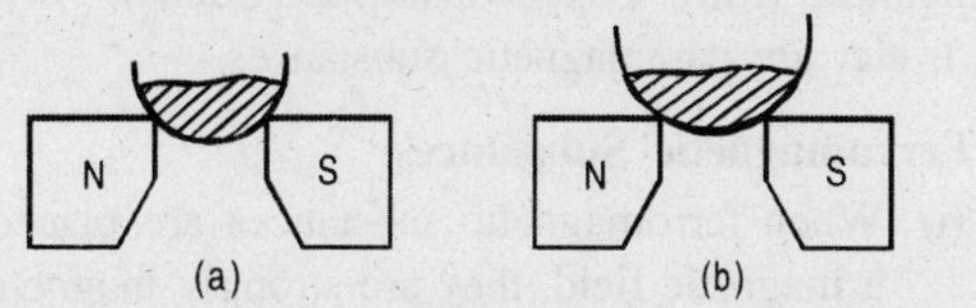

Fig.

(iii) If a diamagnetic solution is poured into a U-tube and one arm of this U-tube is placed between the poles of a strong magnet, the level of the solution in that arm is depressed (Fig. b).

(iv) Permeability of diamagnetic substances is less than 1 (i.e. $\mu < 1$).

(v) Susceptibility of diamagnetic substances is small and negative.

(vi) Susceptibility of diamagnetic substances is independent of temperature.

Examples of Diamagnetic Substance: Bismuth (Bi), Zinc (Zn), Copper (Cu), Silver (Ag), Gold (Au), (Diamond) *(C)*, Salt (NaCl), Water (H_2O), Mercury (Hg), Nitrogen (N_2), Hydrogen (H_2), etc. are diamagnetic substances.

2. Paramagnetic Substances

(i) When paramagnetic substances are placed in a magnetic field, they acquire feeble magnetism in the direction of the magnetic field.

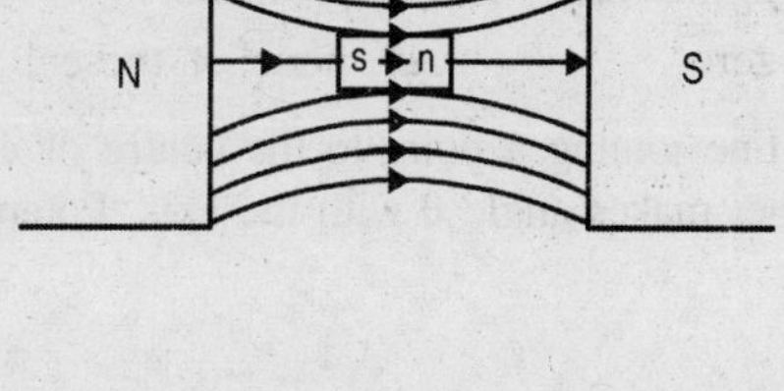

SCIENCE

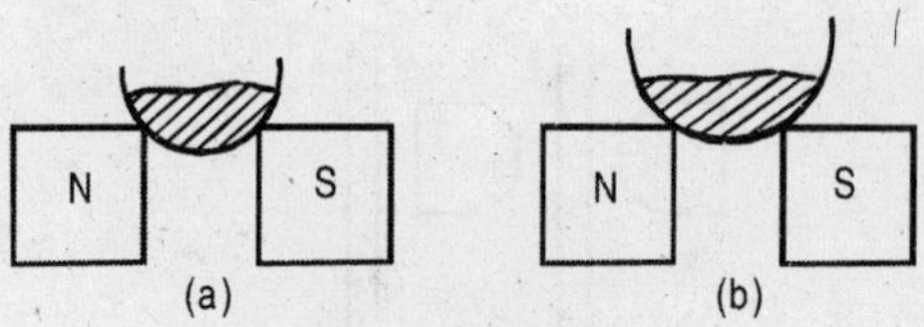
Fig.

(ii) When paramagnetic substances are brought closed to the ends of a powerful magnet, they are attracted towards the magnet.

(iii) When a rod of paramagnetic material is suspended freely between two magnetic poles, then its axis becomes parallel to the magnetic field. The poles produced at the ends of the rod are opposite to the nearer magnetic poles.

(iv) Permeability of paramagnetic substances is slightly greater than 1 i.e. $\mu > 1$.

(v) Susceptibility of paramagnetic substances is small and positive.

Examples of Paramagnetic substances Aluminium (Al), Sodium (Na), Platinum (Pt), Manganese (Mn), Copper Chloride ($CuCl_2$), Oxygen (O_2), etc. are paramagnetic substances.

3. Ferromagnetic Substances

(i) When ferromagnetic substances are placed in a magnetic field, they are strongly magnetised in the direction of the field.

(ii) Ferromagnetic substances are attracted fast towards a magnet when brought closer to either of its ends.

(iii) They possess all the properties of paramagnetic substances with much greater intensity.

(iv) Permeability of ferromagnetic substances is much greater than 1, ($\mu >> 1$).

(v) Ferromagnetic substances follow Curie law i.e. their susceptibility $\chi \propto (1/T)$. At Curie temperature ferromagnetic substances change into paramagnetic substances.

Examples of Ferromagnetic Substances. Iron (Fe), Nickel (Ni), Cobalt (Co), Magnetic (Fe_3O_4), etc. are ferromagnetic substances.

EARTH'S MAGNETISM

A bar magnet always points roughly in a north-south direction when freely suspended. This is due to the earth's magnetism. The origin of the earth's magnetism is still not very clear to scientists. It is, however, believed that the motion of charges (causing currents) in the molten outer core creates the magnetic field. Some geologists think that these currents are caused by the earth's motion. Another likely source of earth's magnetism may be heat arising from the earth's inner core. This heat may be the cause of convection currents in the molten outer core.

The motion of ions and electrons in this molten material would produce a magnetic field. It is probably such convection currents in combination with the rotational effects of the earth that produce the earth's magnetic field.

The earth behaves as if it contained a short bar magnet inclined at a small angle to its axis of rotation, with the south pole of the magnet in the northern hemisphere. At a particular place on the earth, the magnetic north is not usually in the direction of the geographic north. The angle between the two directions is called the declination. Mariners and others who use compasses must allow for declination in determining the true north. The angle, which a freely suspended bar magnet makes with the horizontal, is called the dip of the place. Thus, on the equator, the value of the dip is zero and that on the poles is 90°.

Elements of Earth's Magnetism

There are three elements of earth's magnetism (i) Angle of declination, (ii) Angle of dip, (iii) Horizontal component of earth's field.

Geographic Meridian : A vertical plane passing through the axis of rotation of the earth is called the geographical meridian.

Magnetic Meridian : A vertical plane passing through the axis of a freely suspended magnet is called the magnetic meridian.

MULTIPLE CHOICE QUESTIONS

1. S.I. unit of magnetic permeability is
(a) A-m (b) Am^2
(c) H-m (d) H/m

2. Potential at any point on equatorial line of dipole is
(a) $\mu_0 M/4\pi d^2$ (b) $\mu_0 M/4\pi d^3$
(c) zero (d) none of these

3. The line joining a point to the centre of a short magnet makes angle θ with the axis. Potential at a point distant d from the centre of magnet, on this line is
(a) $\frac{\mu_0 M \sin\theta}{4\pi d^2}$ (b) $\frac{\mu_0 M \cos\theta}{4\pi d^2}$
(c) $\frac{\mu_0 M}{4\pi d^3}$ (d) none of these

4. Magnetic potential at a point distant d from a magnetic pole of strength m is

(a) $\frac{\mu_0}{4\pi}\frac{m}{d}$ (b) $\frac{\mu_0}{4\pi}\frac{m}{d^2}$

(c) $\frac{\mu_0}{4\pi}\frac{2m}{d}$ (d) none of these

5. Which of the following is not a magnetic substances ?
(a) brass (b) iron
(c) cobalt (d) nickel

6. A magnet of magnetic moment M is freely suspended in a constant uniform magnetic field of intensity H. If magnet is delfected by an angle θ from direction of H, the work done is
(a) $MH \cos \theta$ (b) $MH (1 - \cos \theta)$
(c) $MH \sin \theta$ (d) $MH (1 - \sin \theta)$

7. A bar magnet is released into a copper ring directly below it. The acceleration of the magnet will be
(a) equal to the acceleration due to gravity at that place
(b) less than the acceleration due to gravity at that place
(c) greater than the acceleration due to gravity at that place
(d) twice the acceleration due to gravity at that place

8. Force between two magnetic poles depends on
(a) pole strength only
(b) distance only
(c) medium only
(d) all the three above

9. What is the resultant magnetic moment of two magnets, each of magnetic moment M in the following figures :

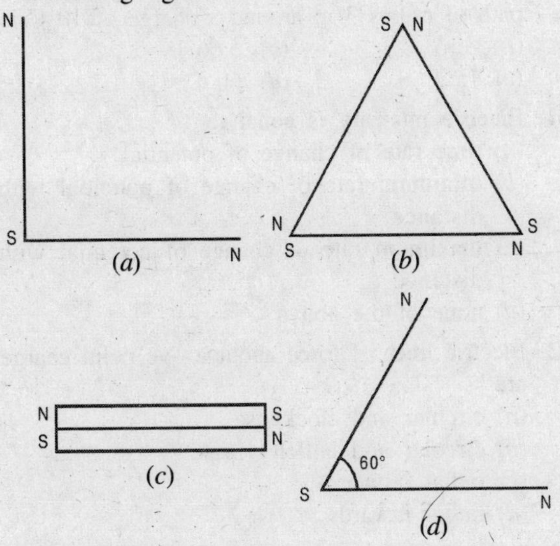

(a) $\sqrt{2}\, M$; zero $\sqrt{3}\, M$; zero

(b) $\sqrt{2}\, M$; zero ; zero; $\sqrt{3}\, M$

(c) $\sqrt{2}\, M$; $\sqrt{3}\, M$; zero ; zero;

(d) none of the above

10. A bar magnet is held at right angles to a uniform magnetic field. The couple acting on the magnet is to be halved by rotating it from this position. The angle of rotation is
(a) 60° (b) 45°
(c) 30° (d) 75°

11. Two magnets of equal magnetic moments M each are placed as shown in Figure. The resultant magnetic moment is

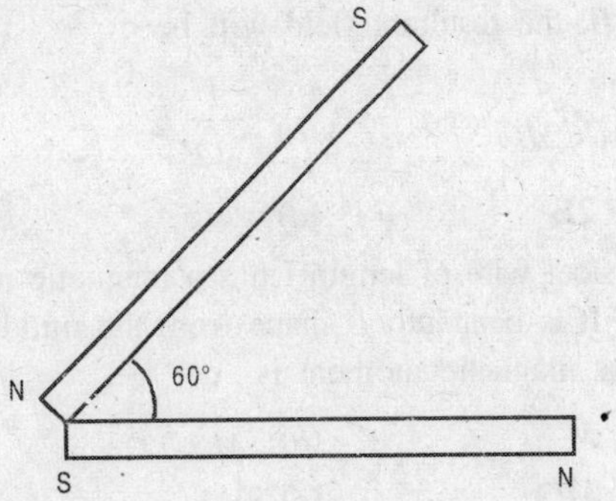

(a) M (b) $\sqrt{3}\, M$

(c) $\sqrt{2}\, M$ (d) $M/2$

12. Two small magnets, each of magnetic moment 10 Am^2 are placed in end of position 0.1 m apart from their centres. The force acting between them is
(a) 0.6 N (b) 0.6×10^7 N
(c) 0.6×10^{-7} N (d) none of the above

13. A non magnetic material is that which is
(a) not attracted by a magnet
(b) repelled by a magnet
(c) not affected even by strong magnetic fields
(d) none of these

14. Can a system have magnetic moment even though its net charge is zero ?
(a) Yes
(b) No
(c) sometimes yes and sometimes no
(d) cannot say

15. The source of magnetic field is
(a) isolated magnetic pole
(b) static electric charge
(c) current loop
(d) none of the above

16. Two magnets have the same length and the same pole strength. But one of the magnets has a small hole at its centre. Then
(a) both have equal magnetic moment
(b) one with hole has smaller magnetic moment
(c) one with hole has larger magnetic moment
(d) one with hole loses magnetism through the hole

17. A thin magnet is cut into two equal parts by cutting it parallel to its length. If the original time period of vibration is 4 sec, the time period of each part in the same field will be
(*a*) 4s (*b*) 2s
(*c*) $4\sqrt{2}s$ (*d*) none of these

18. Two identical coils carrying same current have common centre but have their planes at right angles to each other. If the field due to each coil is *B*, the resultant field will be
(*a*) $\sqrt{2}B$ (*b*) $\frac{1}{\sqrt{2}}B$
(*c*) 2B (*d*) zero

19. A steel wire of length *l* has a magnetic moment *M*. It is bent into *L* shape from the middle. The new magnetic moment is
(*a*) *M* (*b*) $M/\sqrt{2}$
(*c*) *M*/2 (*d*) 2*M*

20. The magnetic moment of a short magnet is 8 Am^2. The magnetic induction 20 cm away from its mid point on the axial line is
(*a*) 1×10^{-4}T (*b*) 2×10^{-4}T
(*c*) 4×10^{-4}T (*d*) 8×10^{-4}T

21. The moment of a magnet is 0.1 Am^2 and the force acting on each pole in a uniform magnetic field of 0.36 oersted is 1.44×10^{-4} N. The distance between the poles of magnet is
(*a*) 2.5 cm (*b*) 5.0 cm
(*c*) 1.25 cm (*d*) 1.17 cm

22. A magnet can be completely demagnetised by
(*a*) breaking the magnet into small pieces
(*b*) heating it slightly
(*c*) droppping into cold water
(*d*) applying a reverse field of appropriate strength

Directions Qs. 23-27: *In each of the following questions there are two statements Assertion (A) is given followed by a corresponding statement of Reason (R) just below it. Of the statements, mark the correct answer:*
(*a*) If both assertion and reason are true and reason is the correct explanation of assertion.
(*b*) If both assertion and reason are true but reason is not the correct explanation of assertion
(*c*) If assertion is true but reason is false
(*d*) If assertion is false but reason is true.

23. **Assertion (A):** Iron behaves as magnet.

Reason (R): In magnet, the molecular magnetrs are aligned in same direction.

24. **Assertion (A):** Basic difference between an electric line and magnetic line of force is that former is discontinous and the latter is continous or endless.

Reason (R): No electric lines of forces exist inside a charged body but magnetic lines do exist inside a magnet.

25. **Assertion (A):** Magnetic moment of an atom is due to both, the orbital motion and spin motion of every electron.

Reason (R): A charged particle produces a magnetic field.

26. **Assertion (A):** Torque experience by the bar magnet is maximum when field is applied perpendicular to magnetic moment.

Reason (R): Torque on a bar magnet depends on the angle between applied magnetic field and magnetic dipole moment.

27. **Assertion (A):** When radius of cirular wire carrying current is doubled, its magnetic moment becomes four times.

Reason (R): Magnetic moment depends on area of the loop.

28. Maximum value of electric intensity due to a charged sphere is at
(*a*) centre (*b*) surface
(*c*) infinity (*d*) none of the above

29. A positively charged rod is brought near an uncharged conductor. If the rod is then suddenly withdrawn the charge left on the conductor will be
(*a*) positive (*b*) zero
(*c*) negative (*d*) none of the above

30. Work done in carrying 2 C charge in a circular path of radius 3 m around a charge of 10 C is
(*a*) zero (*b*) 6.66 J
(*c*) 15 J (*d*) 60 J

31. Electric intensity is equal to
(*a*) time rate of change of potential
(*b*) minimum rate of change of potential with distance
(*c*) maximum rate of change of potential with distance
(*d*) none of the above

32. Electric lines of force about a +ve point charge are
(*a*) circular and clockwise
(*b*) circular and anticlockwise
(*c*) radial outwards
(*d*) radial inwards

33. A charge is moved against electric repulsion in an electric field. Which of the following is correct?
(*a*) work is done by the electric field
(*b*) the potential energy of the charge decreases
(*c*) the strength of electric field decreases
(*d*) none of the above

34. Electric potential is
(*a*) scalar and dimensionless quantity
(*b*) vector and dimensionless quantity
(*c*) scalar and dimensional quantity
(*d*) vector and dimensional quantity

35. Where is the electric potential due to a charged shell constant?
(*a*) outside it
(*b*) inside it
(*c*) both inside and outside it
(*d*) neither inside nor outside it

36. Where does the electric potential due to a charged conducting shell vary inversely as the distance from its centre?
(*a*) both inside and outside it
(*b*) only inside it
(*c*) only outside it
(*d*) neither inside nor outside it

37. For an irregularly shaped charged conductor, the potential is
(*a*) more at the flat parts
(*b*) more at the spherical parts
(*c*) more at the sharp edges
(*d*) same every where

38. A positively charged glass rod is brought near the disc of uncharged gold leaf electroscope. The leaves diverge. Which of the following statement is correct?
(*a*) no charge is present on the leaves
(*b*) positive charge is induced on the leaves
(*c*) negative charge is induced on the leaves
(*d*) positive charge is induced on one leaf and negative charge is induced on the other leaf

39. Two charges are placed a certain distance apart. A metallic sheet is placed between them. What will happen to the force between the charges?
(*a*) increases
(*b*) decreases
(*c*) remains unchanged
(*d*) may increase or decrease depending on the nature of the metal

40. How does the electric field strength vary when we enter a uniformly charged spherical cloud?
(*a*) decreases inversely as the square of the distance from the surface.
(*b*) decreases directly as the square of the distance from the surface
(*c*) increases directly as the square of the distance from the centre
(*d*) increases directly as the distance from the centre

41. From where do the electric lines of force are assumed to originate?
(*a*) positive charge
(*b*) negative charge
(*c*) both from +ve and –ve charges
(*d*) neither from +ve charge nor from –ve charge.

42. Which of the following does not allow the electric field lines to cross each other?
(*a*) they originate from +ve charge and end at –ve charge
(*b*) they do not pass through the conductor
(*c*) they exhibit longitudinal tension and lateral pressure
(*d*) superposition of electric fields

43. Which of the following increases, when the distance between the plates of the charged capacitor is increased?
(*a*) charge (*b*) potential difference
(*c*) capacitance (*d*) none of the above

44. The length of a conductor is doubled and its radius is halved, its specific resistance is
(*a*) unchanged (*b*) halved
(*c*) doubled (*d*) quadrupled

45. Identify the set in which all the three materials are good conductors of electricity
(*a*) Cu, Ag and Au
(*b*) Cu, Si and diamond
(*c*) Cu, Hg and NaCl
(*d*) Cu, Ge and Hg

46. Two unequal resistances are connected in parallel across a cell. Which of the following statement is true?
(*a*) current through smaller resistance is more
(*b*) current through larger resistance is more
(*c*) current is same through both the resistances
(*d*) nothing is definite, as it depends upon the e.m.f. of the cell and the circuit conditions

47. Constantan wire is used for making standard resistance, because it has
(*a*) high melting point
(*b*) low specific resistance
(*c*) high specific resistance
(*d*) negligible temperature coefficient of resistance

48. Which of the following has negative temperature coefficient of resistance?
(*a*) platinum (*b*) tungsten
(*c*) carbon (*d*) nichrome

49. On increasing the temperature of a conductor, its resistance increases because
(*a*) relaxation time decreases
(*b*) mass of the electron increases
(*c*) electron density decreases
(*d*) none of the above

50. In which of the following substances the resistance decreases with an increase of temperature?
(*a*) Copper (*b*) Germanium
(*c*) Silver (*d*) Constantan

51. A metallic resistor is connected across a battery. If the number of collisions of the free electrons with the lattice is some how decreased in the resistor (for example by cooling it,) the current will
(*a*) remain constant (*b*) increase
(*c*) decrease (*d*) become zero

Directions Qs. 52-55: *In each of the following questions there are two statements Assertion (A) is given followed by a corresponding statement of Reason (R) just below it. Of the statements, mark the correct answer:*

(*a*) If both assertion and reason are true and reason is the correct explanation of assertion.
(*b*) If both assertion and reason are true but reason is not the correct explanation of assertion
(*c*) If assertion is true but reason is false
(*d*) If assertion is false but reason is true.

52. **Assertion (A):** If there exists coulomb attraction between two bodies, both of them may not be charged.

Reason (R): In coulomb attraction two bodies are oppositely charged.

53. **Assertion (A):** No two electric lines of force can intersect each other.

Reason (R): Tangent at any point of electric line of force gives the direction of electric field.

54. **Assertion (A):** Electric force acting on a proton and an electron, moving in a uniform electric field is same, where as acceleration of electron is 1836 times that of a proton.

Reason (R): Electron is lighter than proton.

55. **Assertion (A):** As force is a vector quantity, hence electric field intensity is also a vector quantity.

Reason (R): The unit of electric field intensity is newton per coulomb.

56. Voltameter cannot be used to measure
(*a*) current
(*b*) electrochemical equivalent
(*c*) potential difference
(*d*) charge

57. What determines the emf between the two metals placed in an electrolyte?
(*a*) relative position of metals in the electrochemical series
(*b*) distance between them
(*c*) strength of electrolyte
(*d*) nature of electrolyte

58. Same current is being passed through a copper voltameter and a silver voltameter. The rate of increase in weights of the cathodes in the two voltameters will be proportional to
(*a*) relative densities (*b*) atomic masses
(*c*) atomic numbers (*d*) none of the above

59. The potential difference across a conductor is doubled, the rate of generation of heat will
(*a*) become one fourth
(*b*) be halved
(*c*) be doubled
(*d*) become four times.

60. What are the essential requirements for the heater filament?
(*a*) high resistivity, low melting point
(*b*) low resistivity, low melting point
(*c*) high resistivity, high melting point
(*d*) low resistivity, high melting point

ANSWERS

1	2	3	4	5	6	7	8	9	10
(*d*)	(*c*)	(*b*)	(*a*)	(*a*)	(*b*)	(*b*)	(*d*)	(*b*)	(*a*)
11	**12**	**13**	**14**	**15**	**16**	**17**	**18**	**19**	**20**
(*a*)	(*a*)	(*c*)	(*a*)	(*c*)	(*b*)	(*a*)	(*a*)	(*b*)	(*b*)
21	**22**	**23**	**24**	**25**	**26**	**27**	**28**	**29**	**30**
(*a*)	(*d*)	(*d*)	(*a*)	(*c*)	(*a*)	(*b*)	(*b*)	(*b*)	(*a*)
31	**32**	**33**	**34**	**35**	**36**	**37**	**38**	**39**	**40**
(*c*)	(*c*)	(*d*)	(*c*)	(*b*)	(*c*)	(*d*)	(*b*)	(*b*)	(*d*)
41	**42**	**43**	**44**	**45**	**46**	**47**	**48**	**49**	**50**
(*a*)	(*d*)	(*b*)	(*a*)	(*a*)	(*a*)	(*d*)	(*c*)	(*a*)	(*b*)
51	**52**	**53**	**54**	**55**	**56**	**57**	**58**	**59**	**60**
(*b*)	(*b*)	(*a*)	(*a*)	(*b*)	(*c*)	(*a*)	(*d*)	(*d*)	(*c*)

NATURAL PHENOMENA

Introduction

A natural phenomenon is a non-artificial event in the physical sence, and therefore not produced by humans, although it may affect humans (e.g. pathogens, aging, natural disasters, death). Common examples of natural phenomena include volcanic eruptions, weather decay and erosion. Most natural phenomena, such as rain, are relatively harmless so far as humans are concerned.

Various types of natural phenomena occur, these include

- Geological phenomena (volcanic activity and earthquakes)
- Meteorological phenomena (hurricanes, thunderstorms, and tornadoes)
- Oceanographic phenomena (tsunamis, ocean currents and breaking waves)

Natural pheaomena can be classified also on the basis of their origin: as meteorological (hurricanes cyclones, floods, droughts), Topographical (landslides avalanches), tectonic (earthquakes, volcanoes), intestic (locust invasion of crops epidemics) and human (Industrial accidents, nuclear bombs), some disasters are rapid and occur without any warning. Although some phenomena are slow.

The intensity of phenomena is governed by the following factors:

(*i*) Historical and social conditions and a level of economic of a country or region affect their vulnerability. In developing country even potentially modest hazards may prove disastrous. A developed country can tackle disasters easily in comparison to a country with poor economy.

(*ii*) The scope of damage that natural hazards may cause depends upon the type of land use what is exposed or how is exposed determines the amount of damage. Damage by an earthquake in a desert is less than the damaged caused in a densely populated area.

(*iii*) The scope of disasters depends upon the geographical position of a country or an area. Coastal area of Andhra Pradesh and Orissa are more prone to cyclones than centrally located Madhya Pradesh.

(*iv*) Natural hazards are often not so dangerous when taken separately. Drought associated with shortage of food, fodder, water and means of transport are disastrous.

There are some important natural phenomena as follows in detail.

LAND SLIDE

A land slide is the rapid sliding of large masses of bed rocks or rególiths. Whenever mountain slopes are steep there is a possibility of large disastrous landslide, landslides are triggered by earthquakes or sudden rock failures. They can also result when the base of a slope is over steepened by excavation or river erosion. Severe earthquakes in mountainous regions are a major cause of landslides.

In the Himalayas, the Western Ghats and along the river valleys landslides are a common features. Natural removal of soil and rock from slopes is known as mass wasting. Landslide as a hazard has long been recognised by the people living in the mountains. It becomes specially dangerous when there is heavy rainfall or snowfall on the steep hill sides which makes the rocks to slip and break.

The extent of landslides depends on the steepness of the slope, the bedding plane of rocks, the amount of vegetation cover and the extent of folding and faulting of the rocks. It is the rocks that break and carry with it the soil and debris. A major cause which triggers off the landslide is the weight of the overlying material and the presence of a lubricating material like, water, this is known as soilfluction. Freezing and thawing of the rocks on mountain slopes, cause them to break and roll down the slopes. The over bearing weight of snow or ice or water which has seeped into the soft permeable rocks also lead to sleeping and breakage of hill slopes.

Other cause of landslides are the volcanoes and earthquakes. In areas which have sedimentary rock and steep slopes. Tremors dislodge the rock structures and cause falls, often near sea coasts as for example the Kanara coast, cliffs are eroded at the base by sea waves and the rocks jutting out on top break off and fall, Landslides occur frequently during the rains Deforestation as a result of felling of trees for timber and removal of vegetation cover for development activities are also responsible for soil erosion and destabilization of slopes. It is estimated that the construction of just one kilometer long road requires removal of 40,000 to 80,000 cubic metres of debris, which slide down the slopes, killing vegetation and choaking mountain streams.

Humans often make changes in the natural slope for construction of roads and buildings such changes make hill sides more vulnerable to mass wasting and landslides.

Effect of landslides : The landslides cause havoc to man but are the nature's way of getting rid of the excess materials that accumulate on the hill slopes and prevent trees and grasses from finding roots. The formation of new slopes is usually the consequence of landslide and mass wasting. Rivers often get blocked by the debris brought by landslides. The Birahital in Garhwal, for example, way formed in 1983 when 5000 million tonnes of crushed pyrite bearing shale and dolomitic limestone slipped along a 45 degree steep slope filling the valley of the Birahi Ganga and changing the river into a lake. Such lakes are washed out in due course of time.

CYCLONES

A cyclone is an area of low atmospheric pressure. It is storm system of great intensity in which winds spiral inward at great speeds towards the centre of the system. The pressure is lowest at the centre. This closed air circulation is caused by atmospheric disturbances over and above the earth's surface coupled with the earth rotation which in parts a whirling motion to these disturbances. Cyclones of a diameter of 600 km or more is one of the most destructive and dangerous atmospheric storms on the earth with about 6% of the world wide cyclones. The Indian sub continent is the worst cyclone affected areas. There are two types of cyclones (1) Tropical cyclones and other is temperate cyclones.

No universally acknowledged theory of occurrence of tropical cyclone is known today. A tropical cyclone can form when the Horizontal temperature gradients are exceedingly high around a weakly developed area of low pressure. The cyclone is the heat engine whose heater is the oceanic surface.The released heat after condensation converts into kinetic energy for the cyclone. The following are the stages in the formation of cyclones:

1. Temperature of the oceanic surface over 26°C
2. Low pressure dropping below 1000 mb
3. Appearance of a closed isobar.
4. Areas of circular movement, first spreading to a radius of 30-50 km then increasing gradually to 100-200 km and even to 1000 km.
5. Vertically the wind speed first rising to a height of 6 km. then much higher.

Tropical cyclones have large pressure gradients 14-17 mb/100 km, in some cyclones it is as 60 mb/ 100 km. The wind belt can spread to a distance of 10 to 150 km from the centre and at times even further cyclonic circulation at the surface converts into anti cyclonic at the higher level. The tropical cyclones have a warm core. In the centre of the cyclone, there is generally a cloudless spot known as the eye of the storm. The eye is encircled by a cloud of great vertical extent. The average rainfall in a tropical cyclone amounts to over 50 cm., some time rising to over 100 cm.

The cyclone moves forward at an average speed of about 20 km per hour. As soon as the cyclone moves over the land, its energy because of the absence of sea water, starts decreasing. This leads to the death of the cyclones. The cyclone lasts for five to seven days.

The damaging impact of a tropical storm is due to winds of hurricane force, hurricane waves and floods caused by heavy showers.

Majority of the storms inflict heavy losses because of either strong wind or storm waves. In mountainous areas, heavy damage are caused by powerfull surface run offs smashing every thing on their way. Intensity of storm waves depends on wind speed, pressure gradient, topography of sea bottom and profile of coastline. Tropical cyclones entail casualties and losses to life and property in spite of warning system introduced in several areas.

Most of the cyclones have their origin between 10° N and 15° N during the monsoon season. Almost all stroms in the Bay of Bengal have their genesis between 16° N and 21° N and West of 92° E in June. By July the Bay storms form North of 18° N and West of 90°E. It is also note worthy that most July storms move along a westerly track. They are generally confined to the region between 20° N and 25° N and recurvature to the Himalayan foot hills is comparatively rare.

Temperate cyclones: Also known as extra-tropical or wave cyclones temperate cyclones are active over mid latitudinal region between 35° and 65° latitude in both hemisphere.

The temperate cyclones are asymmetrical and shaped liked an inverted '^'. The stretch from 500 km to 600 km. They may go up to 2500 km over North America. They have a height of 8 to 11 Km.

Structure: The North Western sector is the cold sector and the North Eastern sector is the warm sector. As one moves Eastwards in the Northern sector, darknimbus clouds and altro stratus are followed by cirrostratus higher up with cirrus clouds finally at the storm front. In the Eastern sector the extent of cloudiness and rainfall is limited. This sector is generally dominated by cumulonimbus which cause heavy down pour thunder storm lightning and hail storm.

Associated weather : The approach of a temperate cyclone is marked by fall in temperature, fall in the mercury level, wind shifts and a halo around the sun and the moon and a thin veil of cirrus clouds. A light drizzle follows which turns into a heavy down pour. These conditions change with the arrival of the warmfront which halts the fall in mercury level and the rising temperature. Rainfalls stops and clear weather prevails until the cold front of an anticyclonic character arrives which causes a fall in temperature bring cloudiness and rainfall with thunder. After this once again clear weather is established.

The temperate cyclones experience more rainfall when there is slower movement and a marked difference in rainfall and temperature between the front and rear of the cyclone. These cyclones are generally accompanied by anti cyclones.

Reducing impact of damage : Most damage from cyclones is caused by the strong winds torrential rain and high storm tides. Floods generated by cyclonic rainfall are more destructive than the winds. Today due to the significant improvement in the cyclone warning system and adequate and timely steps taken loss of human lives is comparatively less. Other measures like construction of cyclone shelters embankments, dykes, reservoirs and coastal afforestation help immensely. The insurance of crop and cattle also goes a long way in helping people cope with the losses. The warning about the path of cyclone is possible by the satellite images that are available, the computer generated models can predict with fair accuracy the direction and intensity of the winds and direction of the cyclones.

EARTHQUAKES

Earthquakes are considered to be one of the worst natural hazards which often turn into disaster causing wide spread destruction and loss of human lives. The most devastating earth quakes are of tectonic origin. They are associated with large scale strain in the crust of the earth. There may be earthquakes of non tectonic origin. Examples of such earth quakes are those caused by volcanic eruptions, rock bursts, subsidence in mines impounding of reservoirs etc. Damaged caused by such earth quakes are confined to small areas.

Magnitude and intensity are two ways of measuring the strength of an earthquake. The magnitude measured on the richter scale is a measure of the seismic energy radiated by an earthquake the intensity is the measure of damage caused by the earthquake. Based on the study of about 1200 earthquakes of India that occurred in different years, the Indian's meteorological department has divided the country into five zones namely zone I-no risk, zone II-low risk, zone III-moderate risk zone IV-high risk and zone V-very high risk.

About 55% of country is vulnerable to earthquakes. However, the earthquake activity in different parts is not of the same intensity. On the basis of recent experiences, no part of the country is free from earth quakes.

From the earthquake point of view, very high risk areas in India are the Himalayan mountains, North Eastern India, Kachchh, West coast around Ratnagiri and Andaman and Nicobar Islands. The high risk areas are the Ganga plains and Western Rajsthan. While earthquakes can not be stopped or accurately predicted but structures can be designed which can safely resist and negotiate the actions of earthquake ground motion. The study of earthquakes resistant structures has now grown into a multi-disciplinary field of engineering.

Consequences of earthquakes : An earthquake becomes hazard or disaster—only when it strikes the populated area. The impact of an earthquake is always disastrous. The earthquakes make change in the natural environment in a number of ways. Passage of surface waves produce fissures through which sometimes water floods out. This brings enornmous quantity of sand and produces sand dikes. A marked change can also be observed on the drainage system of on area. Rivers somtimes change their courses and cause flood, land slides occur in hilly areas which bring down huge quantities of rock material, leading to mass wasting. Glaciers are breached and their avalanches scatter to for off places new water falls and streams are also created.

Man made structures are not spared from earthquake hazards. Roads, Railways bridges and telephone lines are destroyed, earthquakes have worst effect on towns and cities because of high rise building and huge agglomeration of human population.

Reducing effect of earthquake : In order to reduce the effect of earthquakes the most common method is its constant monitoring and informing people about expected date. This may help evacuation of people from the areas there is need to develop special type of structures and buildings in high risk seismic zones. People may be advised to construct earthquake resistant houses and buildings in such areas.

DROUGHTS

Drought can occur in any area regardless of the amount of rainfall the area may receive or irrespective of its scientific and social advancement. It can occur in small pockets or over a large area. Drought can occur at any time and cause scarcity of water for drinking, irrigation, industry and urban needs. Drought causes deficiency in soil moisture and make the land unproductive. This causes damage to the crops. Droughts are caused due to failure of monsoon or when it is delayed or arrives early or withdraws without giving rain. These circumstances have produced a continuing expansion in India's drought prone areas. Drought is no longer a natural disaster. It is a direct consequence of human activity. The resulting human suffering is enormous and growing.

Drought and aridity are closely related and both indicate a shortage of water. Aridity is a permanent condition where as drought is a temporary situation. Arid and semi arid regions are prone to drought. Droughts based on their cause, nature and character are classified as meteorological hydrological agricultural and ecological. Meterorological, drought, exits when the average annual rainfall is 25 percent less than the usual. On the other hand hydrological drought is one when the water level in the surface and ground falls. The agricultural drought occurs when the soil moisture goes below the level needed to sustain plant growth. Ecological drought occurs when the productivity of a natural ecosystem fails and causes environmental damage like the death of a large number of cattle, wildlife or trees in the forest.

The main cause of drought is the inadequate and uneven distribution of rainfall. West and central India face an uncertainty of rainfall which they receive in the monsoon season. The rainfull is in adequate as well. The scarcity of rainfall triggers off hydrological and agricultural drought. About 19 per cent of the total area of India experiences drought with 12 per cent of the population being affected by it. Drought is a perennial feature in some states of India. About 30 per cent of the country's total area is drought prone, affecting 50 million people and 68 per cent of total sown area annually. The figure on page 203 shows three types of drought prone areas namely extreme, severe and moderate.

Droughts lead to scarcity of food grains (akal), water (jalkal), fodder (tinkal) and often all of these (trikal). The subsequent famine leads to mass migration of humans and live stock. During the famines of 1968-69, in the Thar desert, all the villages between Jodhpur and Pali, spread over 65 square kilometres were abandoned in the famine years between 1812 and 1940, 30 to 80% of the live stock population died. In 1987 a severe drought affected 13 states and two union territories. It affected 2.6 lakh villages, a cropped area of 45.4 million hectares and a population of 285 millions. The failure of monsoon in 2009 led to the creation of droughts in most the Central, Western and Southern states of India.

Reducing impact of Drought : Planning for mitigration of drought may be taken up on war footing. Various devices of remote sensing, satellite mapping and GIS (Geographical Information System) may be used for identifying water qualifiers. Integrated water harvesting programmes with active peoples participation may also be useful. Inter basin transfer of river waters from surplus to deficit areas can also mitigate water crisis to some extent. Some other measures may be building of small dams for collection of water afforestation and use of drought resistant crops. The Panipanchayat in Maharashtra and the Sukhmajari experiment in Haryana are some of the well known efforts made by the people to counter drought.

FLOODS

Floods are a major cause of human misery in India every year. Out of a number of natural disasters that the country has experienced floods are the most important one. India is the most flood effected country in the world next only to Bangladesh. Twenty per cent of the global deaths caused by floods in the world are in India. In spite of the fact that floods are a natural disaster. It often turns out to be a social disaster as the people who are severely affected are generally the poor because they live on the periphery of human habitat. The annual flood affected population has arisen faster than the growth of India's population. The flood affected areas and damages have also increased recently. The reason for this increase is the encroachment of flood plain by the people.

The most flood prone basins in the country are those of the Ganga in Uttar Pradesh, Bihar and West Bengal, the Brahmaputra in Asom, and the Baitarni the Brahmani and Suwarn Reka basins in Orissa. Sometimes floods occur also in Andhra Pradesh, Rajasthan, Haryana and Gujarat.

Flood occurs when a river over flows its banks and spread out over the bordering flood plain. India has a large number of rivers that overflow in certain seasons and remain dry in other seasons. The rivers of north and central India are prone to frequent floods during the monsoon season. They occur when the surface run off is high, drainage water is blocked by landslides or excessive silt is deposited in the river beds. Flash floods in arid areas are associated with cyclonic storms. The coastal belts of India get flooded with the occurrence of cyclones, sea coasts and river estuaries experience flood when the sea level rises or a bore from the enters the river. In urban areas the excessive runoff of storm water drains leads to flooding of low-lying areas.

The Rashtriya Bandh Ayog (RBA) or the national commission of floods set up in 1976, believes that floods have increased in recent years because of human factors like deforestations, drainage congestion (caused by badly planned construction of bridges, roads railway tracks and other developmental activities), reduction in infiltration (because of increased occupation of land by industries and large scale in sanitation), and construction of embankments along rivers. The flood prone area in the country is over 40 million hectares about one-eight of India's land area.

Flood control : Floods are not new in India. The practice of building flood protection embankments along rivers is an ancient one. We had flood protection embankments on the Godavari, the Krisna and the Kaveri deltas and in the Indo-gangetic plain. The nationwide protection programmes, however, began only after independence. At the time of independence in 1947, India had some 5280 km of embankments along different rivers of this 3500 km were in the Sundarbans in West Bengal and 1209 km along the Mahanadi in Orissa. This provided protection to about 3 million hectares of land.

In 1954 a spate of severe floods came. Enormous devastation caused in Uttar Pradesh, Bihar, West Bengal and Asom. Long term programmes for construction of dams and embankments were drawn, central and state flood control boards were set up. Inspite of various measures taken up to minimize the fury of floods. They are still a regular feature in the Ganga and the Brahmaputra basins.

Reducing Impact of flood : The building of embankments was the only was floods could be controlled in the forties. The dams and reservoirs were considered useful to control runoff and reduce flooding. Now there are several other measures to reduce the severity of flood. Felling of trees and deforestation on mountain slopes and in catchment areas need control, weather forecast and flood warning systems be made a regular feature.

TSUNAMI

Earthquakes and volcanic eruptions that cause the sea-floor to move abruptly resulting in sudden displacement of ocean water in the form of high vertical waves are called *tsunamis* (harbour waves) or seismic sea waves. Normally, the seismic waves cause only one instantaneous vertical wave; but, after the initial disturbance, a series of afterwaves are created in the water that oscillate between high crest and low trough in order to restore the water level.

The speed of wave in the ocean depends upon the depth of water. It is more in the shallow water than in the ocean deep. As a result of this, the impact of tsunami is less over the ocean and more near the coast where they cause large-scale devastations. Therefore, a ship at sea is not much affected by *tsunami* and it is difficult to detect a tsunami in the deeper parts of sea. It is so because over deep water the tsunami has very long wave-length and limited wave-height. Thus, a tsunami wave raises the ship only a metre or two and each rise and fall takes several minutes. As opposed to this, when a tsunami enters shallow water, its wave-length gets reduced and the period remains unchanged, which increases the wave-height. Sometimes, this height can be up to 15m or more, which causes large-scale destructions along the shores. Thus, these are also called *Shallow Water Waves*. Tsunamis are frequently observed along the Pacific ring of fire, particularly along the coast of Alaska, Japan, Philippines, and other islands of Southeast Asia, Indonesia, Malaysia, Myanmar, Sri Lanka, and India etc.

After reaching the coast, the tsunami waves release enormous energy stored in them and water flows turbulently onto the land destroying port-cities and towns, structures, buildings and other settlements. Since the coastal areas are densely populated the world over, and these are also centres of intense human activity, the loss of life and property is likely to be much higher by a tsunami as compared to other natural hazards in the coastal areas.

Unlike other natural hazards, the mitigation of hazards created by tsunami is difficult, mainly because of the fact that losses are on a much larger scale.

It is beyond the capacity of individual state or government to mitigate the damage. Hence, combined efforts at the international levels are the possible ways of dealing with these disasters as has been in the case of the tsunami that occurred on 26th December 2004 in which more than 300,000 people lost their lives. India has volunteered to join the *International Tsunami Warning System* after the December 2004 tsunami disaster.

DISASTER MANAGEMENT

Disasters due to cyclones, unlike the ones caused by earthquakes, tsunamis and volcanic eruptions are more predictable in terms of the time and place of their occurrences. Moreover, with the help of development of techniques to monitor the behaviour of cyclones, their intensity, direction and magnitude, it has become possible to manage the cyclonic hazard to some extent. Construction of cycloneshelters, embankments, dykes, reservoirs and afforestation to reduce the speed of the winds are some of the steps that can help in minimising the damages. However, increase in the loss of life and property in countries like India, Bangladesh, Myanmar, etc. in successive storms is largely due to high vulnerability of their population residing in the coastal areas.

SCIENCE

India is vulnerable, in varying degrees, to a large number of natural as well as man-made disasters. 58.6 per cent of the landmass is prone to earthquakes of moderate to very high intensity; over 40 million hectares (12 per cent of land) is prone to floods and river erosion; of the 7,516 km long coastline, close to 5,700 km is prone to cyclones and tsunamis; 68 per cent of the cultivable area is vulnerable to drought and hilly areas are at risk from landslides and avalanches. Vulnerability to disasters/ emergencies of Chemical, Biological, Radiological and Nuclear (CBRN) origin also exists. Heightened vulnerabilities to disaster risks can be related to expanding population, urbanization and industrialization, development within high-risk zones, environmental degradation and climate change.

In the context of human vulnerability to disasters, the economically and socially weaker segments of the population are the ones that are most seriously affected. Within the vulnerable groups, elderly persons, women, children - especially women rendered destitute and children orphaned on account of disasters and the differently abled persons are exposed to higher risks.

To build a safe and disaster resilient India by developing a holistic, proactive, multi-disaster oriented and technology driven strategy through a culture of prevention, mitigation, preparedness and response a national policy on Disaster Management is required.

Disaster Management involves a continuous and integrated process of planning, organising, coordinating and implementing measures which are necessary or expedient for:

- Prevention of danger or threat of any disaster.
- Mitigation or reduction of risk of any disaster or its severity or consequences.
- Capacity building including research and knowledge management.
- Preparedness to deal with any disaster.
- Prompt response to any threatening disaster situation or disaster.
- Assessing the severity or magnitude of effects of any disaster.
- Evacuation, rescue and relief.
- Rehabilitation and reconstruction.

A typical Disaster Management continuum comprises six elements; the pre-disaster phase includes prevention, mitigation and preparedness, while the post-disaster phase includes response, rehabilitation, reconstruction and recovery.

A holistic and integrated approach will be evolved toward disaster management with emphasis on building strategic partnerships at various levels. The themes underpinning the policy are:

- Community based Disaster Management, including last mile integration of the policy, plans and execution.
- Capacity development in all spheres.
- Consolidation of past initiatives and best practices.
- Cooperation with agencies at national and international levels.
- Multi-sectoral synergy.

The objectives of the national policy on disaster management should constitute:

- Promoting a culture of prevention, preparedness and resilience at all levels through knowledge, innovation and education.
- Encouraging mitigation measures based on technology, traditional wisdom and environmental sustainability.
- Mainstreaming disaster management into the developmental planning process.
- Establishing institutional and techno-legal frameworks to create an enabling regulatory environment and a compliance regime.
- Ensuring efficient mechanism for identification, assessment and monitoring of disaster risks.
- Developing contemporary forecasting and early warning systems backed by responsive and failsafe communication with information technology support.
- Promoting a productive partnership with the media to create awareness and contributing towards capacity development.
- Ensuring efficient response and relief with a caring approach towards the needs of the vulnerable sections of the society.
- Undertaking reconstruction as an opportunity to build disaster resilient structures and habitat for ensuring safer living.
- Promoting productive and proactive partnership with media in disaster management.

Disaster Management Act, 2005

The Act lays down institutional, legal, financial and coordination mechanisms at the national, state, district and local levels. These institutions are not parallel structures and will work in close harmony. The new institutional framework is expected to usher in a paradigm shift in Disaster Management from relief-centric approach to a proactive regime that lays greater emphasis on preparedness, prevention and mitigation.

National Disaster Management Authority (NDMA)

The NDMA, as the apex body for disaster management, is headed by the Prime Minister and has the responsibility for laying down policies, plans and guidelines for Disaster Management (and coordinating their enforcement and implementation for ensuring timely and effective response to disasters). The guidelines assist the Central Ministries, Departments and States to formulate their respective Disaster Management plans. It approves the National Disaster Management and Disaster Management plans of the Central Ministries/Departments. It takes such other measures as it may consider necessary, for the prevention of disasters, or mitigation, or preparedness and capacity building, for dealing with a threatening disaster situation or disaster. Central ministries/departments and State Governments extend necessary cooperation and assistance to NDMA for carrying out its mandate. It oversees the provision and application of funds for mitigation and preparedness measures. NDMA has the power to authorize the Departments or authorities concerned, to make emergency procurement of provisions or materials for rescue and relief in a threatening disaster situation or disaster. The general superintendence, direction and control of National Disaster Response Force (NDRF) are vested in and are exercised by the NDMA. The National Institute of Disaster Management (NIDM) works within the framework of broad policies and guidelines laid down by NDMA.

The NDMA is mandated to deal with all types of disasters, natural or man-made. Whereas, such other emergencies including those requiring close involvement of the security forces and/or intelligence agencies such as terrorism (counter-insurgency), law and order situation, serial bomb blasts, hijacking, air accidents, Chemical, Biological, Radiological and Nuclear (CBRN) weapon systems, mine disasters, ports and harbour emergencies, forest fires, oil field fires, and oil spills continue to be handled by the extant mechanism i.e., National Crisis Management Committee.

NDMA formulates guidelines and facilitates training and preparedness activities in respect of Chemical, Biological, Radiological and Nuclear (CBRN) emergencies. Cross cutting themes like medical preparedness, psycho-social care and trauma, community based disaster preparedness, information & communication technology, training, preparedness, awareness generation etc. for natural and manmade disasters also engage the attention of NDMA in partnership with the stakeholders concerned. Resources available with the disaster management authorities at all level, which are capable of discharging emergency support functions, made available to the nodal Ministries/Agencies dealing with the emergencies at times of impending disasters/disasters.

District Disaster Management Authority (DDMA)

The DDMA is headed by the District Collector, Deputy Commissioner or District Magistrate as the case may be, with the elected representative of the local authority as the Co-Chairperson. DDMA acts the planning, coordinating and implementing body for Disaster Management at District level and take all necessary measures for the purposes of Disaster Management in accordance with the guidelines laid down by the NDMA and SDMA. It prepares the District Disaster Management plan for the district and monitor the implementation of the National Policy, the State Policy, the National Plan, the State Plan and the District Plan. DDMA also ensures that the guidelines for prevention, mitigation, preparedness and response measures laid down by the NDMA and the SDMA are followed by all Departments of the State Government at the District level and the local authorities in the district.

Local Authorities

For the purpose of this policy, local authorities includes Panchayati Raj Institutions (PRI), Municipalities, District and Cantonment Boards and Town Planning Authorities which control and manage civic services. These bodies ensure capacity building of their officers and employees for managing disasters, carry out relief, rehabilitation and reconstruction activities in the affected areas and prepares Disaster Management Plans in consonance with guidelines of the NDMA, SDMAs and DDMAs.

National Institute of Disaster Management (NIDM)

The NIDM, in partnership with other research institutions has capacity development as one of its major responsibilities, along with training, research, documentation and development of a national level information base. It will network with other knowledge-based institutions and function within the broad policies and guidelines laid down by the NDMA. It will organize training of trainers, DM officials and other stakeholders. The NIDM will strive to emerge as a 'Centre of Excellence' in the field of Disaster Management.

National Crisis Management Committee (NCMC)

The NCMC, comprising high level officials of the GoI headed by the Cabinet Secretary, deals with major crises which have serious or national ramifications. It is supported by the Crisis Management Groups (CMG) of the Central nodal Ministries and assisted by NEC as may be necessary. The Secretary, NDMA is a member of this Committee.

National Disaster Response and Mitigation Funds

A National Disaster Response Fund is constituted to provide financial help. The National Disaster Response Fund is applied by the National Executive Committee (NEC) towards meeting the expenses for emergency response, relief and rehabilitation, in accordance with the guidelines laid down by the Central Government in consultation with the NDMA.

Similarly, the National Disaster Mitigation Fund (NDMF) is created for projects exclusively for the purpose of mitigation. NDMF is applied by the NDMA as recommended by the Finance Commission from time to time.

Forecasting and Early Warning Systems

It is most essential to establish, upgrade and modernise the forecasting and early-warning systems for all types of disasters. The nodal agencies responsible for monitoring and carrying out surveillance, for specific natural disasters, identify technological gaps and formulate projects for their upgradation, in a time bound manner. All States provide to India Meteorological Department the required infrastructure for upgradation/ establishment of meteorological observation systems. Partnership with the World Meteorological Organisation (WMO), Pacific Tsunami Warning System and other regional and global institutions may also be considered. ICT tools need to be used for data receptions, forecasting and timely dissemination.

Medical Preparedness and Mass Casualty Management

Medical preparedness is a crucial component for any DM Plan. The NDMA, in close coordination with the Ministry of Health and Family Welfare, states and premier medical research institutes formulates policy guidelines to enhance our capacity in emergency medical response and mass casualty management. DM plans for hospitals includes developing and training of medical teams and paramedics, capacity building, trauma and psycho-social care, mass casualty management and triage. The surge and casualty handling capacity of all hospitals, at the time of disasters, is worked out and recorded through a consultative process, by all the states/UTs in the pre-disaster phase. The State and District authorities are encouraged to formulate appropriate procedures for treatment of casualties by the private hospitals during the disasters. These plans addresses post-disaster disease surveillance systems, networking with hospitals, referral institutions and accessing services and facilities such as availability of ambulances and blood banks.

Community Based Disaster Preparedness

During any disaster, communities are always not only the first to be affected but also the first responders. Community participation ensures local ownership, addresses local needs, and promotes volunteerism and mutual help to prevent and minimise damage. Therefore, the efforts of the states/UTs, in this regard need to be encouraged.

The needs of the elderly, women, children and differently abled persons require special attention. Women and youth will be encouraged to participate in decision making committees and action groups for management of disasters. As first responders to any disaster, communities are trained in the various aspects of response such as first-aid, search and rescue, management of community shelters, psycho-social counselling, distribution of relief and accessing support from government/agencies etc. Community plans will be dovetailed into the panchayat, block and district plans.

Media Partnership

The media plays a critical role in information and knowledge dissemination in all phases of Disaster Management. The versatile potential of both electronic and print media needs to be fully utilised. Effective partnership with the media will be worked out in the field of community awareness, early warning and dissemination and education regarding various disasters.

Conclusion

On the basis of the above discussion, it can be concluded that disasters can be natural or the results of human activities, and all hazards need not turn into disasters since it is difficult to eliminate disasters, particularly natural disasters. Then the next best option is mitigation and preparedness. There are three stages involved in disaster mitigation and management:

(*i*) Pre-disaster management involves generating data and information about the disasters, preparing vulnerability zoning maps and spreading awareness among the people about these. Apart from these, disaster planning, preparedness and preventive measures are other steps that need to be taken in the vulnerable areas.

(*ii*) During disasters, rescue and relief operations such as evacuation, construction of shelters and relief camps, supplying of water, food, clothing and medical aids etc. should be done on an emergency basis.

(*iii*) Post-disaster operations should involve rehabilitation and recovery of victims. It should also concentrate on capacity building in order to cope up with future disasters, if any.

These measures have special significance to a country like India, which has about two-third of its geographical area and equal proportion of its population, vulnerable to disasters. Introduction of the Disaster Management Bill, 2005 and establishment of National Institute of Disaster Management are some examples of the positive steps taken by the Government of India.

MULTIPLE CHOICE QUESTIONS

1. Little or no volcanic activity is associated with which of the following plate boundaries?
   (a) Subducting plate boundaries
   (b) Transform plate boundaries
   (c) Divergent plate boundaries
   (d) Converging plate boundaries
2. In India Landslides are common in—
   (a) Himalayan Range
   (b) Western Ghats
   (c) Along the river valleys
   (d) All of these
3. The primary difference between magma and lava is that:
   (a) magma becomes lava anytime it is in a cooling condition.
   (b) they are produced from different parent materials.
   (c) one is below the ground, the other is above the ground.
   (d) one occurs at divergent plate boundaries, the other at convergent plate boundaries.
4. The extent of Landslides depends on—
   (a) steepness of the slope
   (b) the bedding plane of rock
   (c) the amount of vegetation cover
   (d) All of these
5. As the rate of cooling decreases, the sizes of the crystals in an igneous rock:
   (a) decreases (b) increases
   (c) can not predict (d) stays the same
6. Which among the following is the cause of Landslide?
   (a) Earthquakes (b) Volcanoes
   (c) Both (a) and (b) (d) None of these
7. Droughts lead to scarcity of which of the following?
   (a) grains (b) water
   (c) fodder (d) All of these
8. A Disaster Management Continuum at the pre-disaster phase includes which of the following?
   (a) Prevention (b) Mitigation
   (c) Both (a) and (b) (d) None of these
9. The central regions of Earth's core are a solid because
   (a) the composition at the centre of the core is lower in iron.
   (b) the pressure at the centre raises the melting point.
   (c) the magnetic field cannot penetrate into the centre of the core.
   (d) convection does not extend all the way to the centre of the core.
10. L wave is a type of
    (a) P wave (b) S wave
    (c) Body wave (d) Surface waves
11. Consider the following statements regarding general characteristics associated with tropical cyclones :
    1. Tropical cyclones, move with very low velocity over the oceans but become strong while moving over the land areas.
    2. They are confined to a particular period of the year (mainly summer) and normally move from east to west.

    Which of the statements given above is/are correct?
    (a) 1 only (b) 2 only
    (c) Both 1 and 2 (d) Neither 1 nor 2
12. The velocity of P wave near earth surface is
    (a) 15 km/second (b) 6 km/second
    (c) 2 km/second (d) 4 km/second
13. P wave can travel through
    (a) Solid (b) Gas
    (c) Liquid (d) All
14. S wave can travel through
    (a) Solid (b) Gas
    (c) Liquid (d) All
15. S wave can't pass through which part of the earth?
    (a) Crust (b) Mantle
    (c) Outer core (d) Inner core
16. Earthquake prediction can performed on the basis of
    (a) Emission of radon gas
    (b) Shifting of some burrowing animals like ants, termites etc.
    (c) Both (a) and (b)
    (d) None of the above
17. The 'ring of fire' is located in
    (a) Indian Ocean (b) Atlantic Ocean
    (c) Pacific Ocean (d) Antarctica
18. Consider the following statements:
    The Circum Pacific belt is highly prone to the occurrence of earthquakes because it is a zone of
    1. Young fold mountain
    2. Active Volcanoes
    3. Divergent plate boundaries
    4. Convergent plate boundaries

    Which of the statements given above are correct?
    (a) 1, 2 & 3 (b) 1, 2 & 4
    (c) 2, 3 & 4 (d) 1, 3 & 4

SCIENCE

19. The Magma contains which of the following gases
(a) CO_2 (b) Nitrogen
(c) Chlorine (d) All

20. The cyclones of temperate latitudes differ from those of the tropics in a number of ways. Which one of the following is the most prominent of them all?
(a) Their size is far greater
(b) They are caused by frontal systems whereas the tropical cyclones are not
(c) They occur more frequently
(d) The precipitation is more evenly distributed in a temperate cyclone

21. Oceanic waves caused by a earthquake are known as
(a) P wave (b) S wave
(c) L wave (d) Tsunami

22. Which of the following is/are the correct characteristics of primary seismic wave?
(a) It is a longitudinal wave
(b) It is similar to sound waves
(c) It travels with faster speed in solid than in liquid
(d) All of the above

23. Consider the following statements:
1. P-wave are the first seismic waves to reach a place
2. S-waves travel only through liquids
3. Arrival time of P and S-waves is used to locate the epicentre
4. Richter Scale is a logarithmic scale

Which of the statements given above are correct?
(a) 1, 2 & 3 (b) 1, 3 & 4
(c) 1 & 4 (d) 3 & 4

24. The North East of India, comes under which of the following Earthquake zone type:
(a) Zone II (b) Zone III
(c) Zone IV (d) Zone V

25. A tarnado is differ from a tropical cyclone in that it forms over
(a) River (b) Ocean
(c) Land (d) Sky

26. An anticyclone develops in a region of descending air in an area of
(a) High pressure (b) Low pressure
(c) Low temperature (d) High temperature

27. Catastrophic waves are sudden, violent and temporary and are cause by
(a) Earthquakes (b) Volcanoes
(c) Land slides (d) All of the above

28. Taifer is name of tropical cyclone of
(a) Carribbean sea (b) Australia
(c) Philippines (d) Japan

29. The tropical cyclone of Australia is called
(a) Hurricanes (b) Typhoons
(c) Willy-wilies (d) Taifer

30. Baguio is the name given for tropical cyclone of
(a) Philippines (b) Australia
(c) Japan (d) America

ANSWERS

1	2	3	4	5	6	7	8	9	10
(b)	(d)	(c)	(d)	(b)	(c)	(d)	(c)	(b)	(d)
11	**12**	**13**	**14**	**15**	**16**	**17**	**18**	**19**	**20**
(b)	(b)	(d)	(a)	(c)	(c)	(c)	(c)	(d)	(b)
21	**22**	**23**	**24**	**25**	**26**	**27**	**28**	**29**	**30**
(d)	(d)	(b)	(d)	(c)	(a)	(d)	(d)	(c)	(a)

□□□

NATURAL RESOURCES

SOILS

Soil is a natural covering on the Earth's land surface, composed of loose, unconsolidated materials such as tiny mineral particles, decayed organic matter, living organisms, water and air.

Most soils contain four basic components : mineral particles, water, air, and organic matter. Organic matter can be further sub-divided into humus, roots, and living organisms. The values given below are for an average soil.

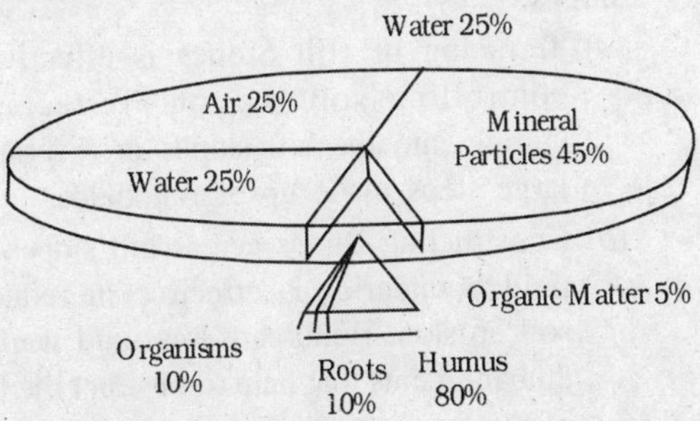

Properties of Soil

The physical and chemical properties of soil determine both the fertility and productivity of soils.

(i) The **physical properties** include texture, structure, and colour.

Soil texture refers to the particle sizes composing the soil. These particles are classified as gravel, sand, silt and clay in decreasing order of size. Four textural types are recognised. These are sand, sandy loam, and clay. All the textural types are combinations of different sizes of particles. Soil texture determines the water condition of the soil affecting the pore space size. In sand as both the particles and the pore spaces are large, it drains rapidly. The particles and pore spaces in clay are small, hence drainage is very slow. Both are poor for plant growth for which loam texture is best.

Soil structure refers to the arrangement in which soil grains are grouped together into larger pieces. Major types of structure are blocky, granular, columnar, prismatic, crumb, and platy. Soil structure influences the absorption of water by the soil, its erodibility, and ploughing.

Soil colour is a minor physical attribute but it is the most readily observed. It indicates the origin and composition of the soil. Increasing quantities of humus produce a range from white, through brown, to black. Black and dark brown colours are typical of soils in the cool and humid areas of temperate latitudes. Soil in the steppe lands and deserts are light brown and grey. Red and yellow colours are quite common in tropical region and both are due to the presence of iron oxides and hydroxides.

(*ii*) **Chemical Properties** of soil include soil water, chemical composition, soil colloids, humus and soil air.

pH and pOH of Soil : The removal of soluble materials from the surface soil to lower by water is called **leaching.** Most plants grown best in soils that are neutral–neither acid nor alkaline (basic)—or nearly so. Acidity usually occurs to some degree in soils of humid regions. Where acidity is high enough to cause trouble, lime is usually added to the soil. Alkaline soils–with an abundance of soluble bases–are most common in the drier parts of the world, where little leaching takes place. Acidity and alkalinity are measured in terms of pH, a numerical value ranging from 0 to 14. Soil pH is the most important chemical properties of a soil and is generally related to the concentration of free hydrogen ions in the soil matrix. Soils with a relatively large concentration of hydrogen ions tends to be acidic. Alkaline soils have relatively low concentration of hydrogen ions. A *pH* of 7 indicates a neutral soil; values slightly below 7 indicate mild acidity and values slightly above 7 mild alkalinity. Maximum soil fertility occurs at the range of 6.0 to 7.2.

Classification of Soils

1. Laterite Soils : These are found in high rainfall areas (e.g. equatorial rain forests) having hot and humid conditions. It is also found in areas of wet and dry conditions. They are characterised by leaching, accumulation of sesquioxides, crust formation, acidic nature and red colour.

2. Red Soils : These soils are also found in tropical areas having high rainfall. They are highly leached having residues of iron and aluminium oxides. This deeply weathered soil is low in fertility.

3. Red and Yellow Soils : Found in regions having high temperature and abundant rainfall. This soil is affected by leaching, podzolization and laterization and has a well developed horizon. It is susceptible to erosion and gives a good response to agriculture when mixed with fertilizers.

4. Black Soils : These soils are formed on the basaltic bed rock formed because of lava flow. Such soils are highly water retentive and are good for production of dry crops.

5. Red Desert Soils : Found in arid tropical areas and is characterised by underdeveloped horizon, coarse texture, and moderate to high fertility. This soil becomes productive when irrigation is applied and salt content is rationalized. The most important characteristic of these soils is the saline nature and encrustation of its surface. Because of excessive dryness lime is brought to the surface.

6. Chernozem : Found in temperate grassland areas of the world which receives low and light precipitation. Thick accumulation of humus gives it a characteristic black colour and therefore it is also known as Black Earth. The moderate rainfall which the region receives resulting in balanced leaching and evaporation, does not allow the humus to percolate. Further it is characterized by clayey texture, basic nature and high fertility.

7. Chestnut : As these are found in the arid margins of the Chernozem belt they have lower humus content, are of lighter colour and fertile than the chernozems.

8. Seriozems : These are found in the mid latitude continental deserts of central Asia and N. America and are characterised by poor horizon development, low humus content, lime concentration and grey colour. Under irrigation they become productive.

9. Podzols : These are found in humid mid latitude forests and the coniferous forest regions having moderate to low rainfall. Melting of snow in these colder regions allow adequate water flow for leaching to take place resulting in high acidity. Thick forest vegetation allows slow organic matter decomposition and subsequent podzolization. Though they have low fertility, but it can be enhanced by the addition of lime and fertilizers.

10. Grey Drown Podzolic Soils : These are found in the mid latitude deciduous forests on the western margin of continents and parts of East Asia. They are characterised by lesser leaching and acidity and more Humus content than podzols. They are reasonably fertile.

11. Tundra Soils : These are found along the polar margins in the Tundra region. These are characterised by acidic reaction, slow chemical and organic changes, homogenous soil profile and low fertility. This is a permafrost region affected by water melting and logging during summers.

SOIL CONSERVATION

Soil can conserved in many ways :

(i) Afforestation is the planting of trees and other vegetation on previously cleared areas like hill slopes and uncultivated land. The roots of trees and plants anchor and hold the soil together and so it is not easily removed by running water and wind. Trees, plants, shrubs and grasses reduce the speed of flowing water and allow the water to be absorbed by the soil. Trees reduce the force of strong winds and prevent the blowing away of soil particles.

(ii) Restricted Grazing of Animals should be paractised. Animals should be moved over different pastures so as avoid the removal of all vegetation from the ground.

(iii) Proper Farming Techniques particularly on hill slopes.

(*a*) Terracing of Hill Slopes is effective in controlling soil erosion. Terracing is cutting into the hill slopes in a series of large steps made up of flat fields.

(*b*) Constructing Bunds across hill slopes and field boundaries is effective in reducing soil erosion. Bunds are low mud walls or embankments that help to obstruct the flow of water.

(*c*) Contour Ploughing should be practised. Contour ploughing is ploughing along the outline of the field in a circular manner. This prevents the soil from being washed away by running water.

(*d*) Strip Cropping is another farming technique that helps reduce soil erosion. Strip cropping is planting of alternate rows of different kinds of crops instead of strips of land uncultivated.

(iv) Flood Control by building dams and multipurpose projects.

NATURAL VEGETATION

Natural vegetation in India is influenced by altitude (in the Himalayan region) and rainfall. On the basis of altitude, the Himalayan region has vegetations of tropical to tundra regions, namely tropical wet-evergreen and semi-evergreen forests, the tropical deciduous, and the thorn forests. India is the 10th in the world and 4th in Asia in plant diversity. It is one of the 12 'mega-diversity' countries of the world. India is also at meeting zone of three major bio-geographic realms, namely the **Indo-Malayan** (the richest in world) the **Euro-asian** and the **Afro-tropical.** India has the two richest bio-diversity spot, one in the Eastern Himalyas and other in the Western Ghats. India's biological diversity which is estimated to be over 46,000 plant species represents about 7% of the world flora and 6.5% of the world fauna respectively.

The distribution of vegetation in the Himalayas is mostly along the vertical plane. The *Shivaliks* or the outer Himalayas are covered with tropical moist deciduous flora of which the ***sal*** is an important species of economic significance. The vegetation followed, at higher elevation are evergreen oak, chestnut and some ash and beech. This is a typical subtropical wet hill vegetation. At higher altitude the vegetation is replaced by *chir* and *chil* trees, representative of subtropical moist hill flora. Pine, cedar, silver fir, and spruce are the most important species found between the altitudes 1,600 metres to 3,300 metres. These conifer trees typical of the dry temperate region found in the inner Himalayan ranges. The conifers are replaced by the shrubs, scrub and grasses of the Alpine variety at 3,500 metres and above.

Classification of Natural Vegetation

The natural vegetation of India is diverse owing to varied biotic conditions as well as unequal rainfall. A noteworthy classification of Indian vegetation is given by Champion and Seth who base it on three factors—temperature, altitude and rainfall. They have evolved eight broad types.

1. Tropical Evergreen or Rain Forests

These are dense forests of luxuriant growth which look evergreen as their trees shed leaves at different times of the year. They are prevalent in areas where the annual rainfall is over 200 cm and the average annual humidity exceeds 77 per cent. The annual temperature is 25°C to 27°C on an average. Mahogany, Bamboo, Ivory Wood, Ebony, Rubber trees are the economically significant trees of these forests. Such forests are found in the north-east, eastern regions of subtropical Himalaya (Tarai), western portions of the Western Ghats and Andaman and Nicobar Islands. The forests are sub-divided as follows.

(*a*) *Tropical Wet Evergreen Forests :* They are found in areas where the annual rainfall is above 250 cm. The many storeyed forests have an undergrowth of bamboos, ferns, canes and climbers. They contain economically valuable species such as Ebony, Rosewood, Iron wood, Champa, Toon, etc. Such forest is found in the north-eastern states, the Andaman and Nicobar Islands and western parts of the Western Ghats.

(*b*) *Tropical Semi-Evergreen Forests :* Found in regions where the annual rainfall is below 200 cm, these forests have evergreen trees mixed with deciduous ones. The mean annual temperature in these forests ranges from 24°C to 27°C and humidity is about 80 per cent. Trees have heavy barks and climbers, and buttressed trunks at many places. Important trees include Champa, Canes, Ferns, Orchids, Rosewood, Benteak, Kadam, Semul, Laurel, etc. These forests occur in regions of upper Assam, lower eastern Himalaya, Orissa, and the Andaman and Nicobars.

(*c*) *Tropical Moist Deciduous Forests :* Also called the Monsoon forests, they occur where annual rainfall is 150 to 200 cm and the mean annual temperature is about 26-27°C. The forests are characterised by few species and the undergrowth is of canes and bamboos. Humidity varies from 60 to 80 per cent. They are found in the interior of the Indian Plateau and the Sivalik east of the Yamuna river. Sal, Teak, Tendu, Sissoo, Mahua, Sandal, Shisham are the important trees. The trees shed their leaves during spring and early summer.

(*d*) *Littoral or Swamp Forests :* Also called tidal forests, these occur in and around the tidal creeks and along the deltas of the rivers Ganga, Mahanadi, Krishna and Godavari. The trees, mainly evergreen, have profuse growth and stilt-like roots. The densest trees are found in the great Sunderban delta which has the sundari trees in abundance. Rhizophora and Nipa fruiticans (a type of palm) also grow in these forests. On the tropical tide-washed coasts where mud and silt have accumulated, dense mangrove forests flourish.

2. Dry Tropical Forests

Such forests are mostly prevalent in regions with an annual rainfall of 90 to 130 cm, a mean annual temperature of 23 to 27°C and humidity ranging between 50 and 60 per cent. They are subdivided into following types.

(*a*) *Tropical Dry Deciduous Forests :* They run from the Himalayan foothills to Kanyakumari and comprise important trees like Bijasal, Teak, Tendu, Amaltas, Khair, Palas, Rosewood and Axlewood. The tracts of these forests have a low canopy of grasses and shrubs in some places which has been cleared for agriculture or casuarina plantations.

(*b*) *Tropical Thorn Forests :* These are mostly prevalent in those areas where rainfall is very low, i.e., 50 cm to 70 cm, the mean annual temperature is 25°C to 27°C and humidity is rather low, i.e., less than 47 per cent. Kutch, Saurashtra, Punjab, Haryana, Rajasthan, the Upper Ganga plains and the Deccan Plateau consist of such forests. Small trees such as Khair, Babul, Thor, Khejra, Kanju, Ak and Neem are found in these forests.

(*c*) *Tropical Dry Evergreen Forests :* From Tamil Nadu to Nellore, such type of forests cover areas where the mean rainfall is about 100 cm, the annual temperature is 28°C and the mean annual humidity is 74 per cent. Trees are 12 m high with canopies. Bamboos are rare and the grass is not conspicuous. The important species of trees are Khirni, Jamun, Kokko, Toddy Palm, Casuarina, Neem, Cane, etc.

3. Riparian Forests

They are common in wet places particularly along river banks and other wetlands where rainfall is less than 50 cm. Short trees and grasses such as Munj and Kans are abundant. Neem, Shisham, Pipal, Babul, Tamarind are common in such regions.

4. Subtropical Broad Leaved Hill Forests

Such forests are common in the highlands of Bastar, Pachmari, Palani Hills, Khasi Hills on the lower slopes of the Himalaya in Assam and West Bengal. The mean annual temperature is about 18°C to 21°C, the mean annual rainfall is about 75 to 125 cm and the humidity is 80 per cent. With an abundance of evergreen trees, these forests are called Shola forests in southern India.

5. Montane Wet Temperate Forests

Generally at a height of 1800-3000 m above sea level especially in the hills of Kerala, Tamil Nadu and the eastern Himalaya, the forests occur in regions with a mean annual temperature of about 11°C to 14°C and a mean annual rainfall of 150 to 300 cm. The important trees are Oaks, Magnolia, Chilauni, Birch, Plum, Michilus, Deodar and Hemlock.

6. Montane Moist Temperate Forests

Such type of forests occur in the temperate eastern and western Himalaya, i.e., in Jammu and Kashmir, Himachal Pradesh, Punjab, Uttarakhand, Sikkim and Darjeeling. They are mainly composed of coniferous species generally 30 to 50 m high Mosses and ferns that grow on trees. The important trees are Pine, Deodar, Silver Fir, Oak, Beach, Rhododendrons, Maple, etc.

7. Alpine Forests

As the name suggests, these forests cover the Alpine areas in the Himalayas, i.e., at a height of 2880 m to 3700 m. They constitute dwarf shrubs of Juniper, Fir, Pine, Birch and Rhododendrons. On the southern Himalayan slopes, the Alpine forests degenerate into a low evergreen scrub. On the northern slopes of the Himalaya, they represent a dry, xerophytic vegetation.

8. Grasslands

Though the Indian grasslands are not comparable to the savanna or steppe, they do occur on wet soil ground and in the sal belt and some hilly areas. They are sub-divided as follows.

(*a*) ***Low-land Grasses :*** Occurring in regions receiving 31 to 200 cm of rainfall where the temperature is high during summers, they are found in the plains of upper India— Punjab, Uttar Pradesh, Haryana, Bihar and north-west Assam. These grasses grow on different soil type and are suitable for cattle-breeding.

(*b*) ***Upland or Hilly Grasses :*** They are found at a height of over 1,000 m in the Himalaya and in the cleared forest areas of the Western Ghats in the Karnataka region. They are found among small tracts of Shola forests in South India.

(*c*) ***Riverine Grasses :*** Found in the northern part of India, they form the Bhabar pastures which are important grazing grounds for buffaloes and cattle.

Forest Policy (1988)

The policy of 1952 was revised in 1988. The main objectives of the revised forest policy of 1988 are: (*i*) preservation of ecological balance and conservation of natural heritage; (*ii*) to control erosion of soil, denudation in catchment areas and extension of sand dunes in the north-west desert region and along the coasts; (*iii*) to provide rural and tribal people their requirement of forest products; (*iv*) utilising products of forestry in the best manner possible; (*v*) increasing the productivity of forests as well as the forest cover by afforestation programmes among others; and (*vi*) involving the people to meet the objectives. In 1988, the Forests (Conservation) Act of 1980 was amended to prevent deforestation and use of forest land for non-forestry purposes. Punishments in case of violations were included. To prevent destruction of forest area by fires, a Modern Forests Fire Control Project was started in 1984 with the assistance of the UNDP.

Mangrove Forest Conservation

Mangroves are salt tolerant plant communities occurring in sheltered coastline areas such as bays, estuaries, lagoons and creeks. They possess some specialised roots called pneumatophores. These pneumatophores contain pores which enable the trees to breathe, when other roots are submerged under water during high tide. Mangrove forests are reservoirs of a large number of plant and animal species associated together over a long evolutionary period and exhibiting remarkable capacity for salt tolerance. India harbours some of the best mangroves in the world. The total area covered by mangroves in India is estimated at about 5,000 sq km. The mangrove forests stabilise the shoreline and act as a bulwark against encroachments by the sea.

Taking into consideration ecological and economic significance of mangroves and threats faced by them due to various anthropogenic activities, the

Government of India launched a scheme on conservation and management of mangroves in 1987. Full central assistance is given under Management Action Plans (MAPs) for undertaking activities like raising mangrove plantations, protection, catchment area treatment, siltation control, pollution abatement, biodiversity conservation, sustainable resource utilisation, survey and demarcation, education and awareness, etc. This is further supplemented by research and developmental activities which can give scientific inputs for smooth execution of MAPs. A National Management Genetic Resources Centre has been established by the Ministry in Orissa.

MINERALS

Minerals are naturally occurring substances having a definite chemical composition. They are grouped into classes, generally as rocks, non-metallic, mineral fuels and metals.

Important Minerals

Minerals are obtained from the rocks of the earth's crust and they have great utility to mankind. They are used to produce a variety of goods and it will not be wrong to say that they form the foundations of the modern civilisation. Occurrence or distribution of minerals in various parts of the world is a function of the geological history and mineral resources of an area are called a product of the geological lottery. Some of the minerals are used as power resources also. Although some minerals are used as power resources also. Although some minerals are found in practically all parts of the world, some areas are richer than the others in these resources. A brief outline of the distribution of some important mineral is provided here.

1. **Aluminium :** A light weight durable metal, aluminium is obtained from bauxite which is its principle *ore* (the raw material of any mineral). Chief producers of bauxite are Australia, Jamaica, Guinea, Brazil, USA and Russia. Production of aluminium from bauxite is a highly energy consuming process. Hence only the countries rich in energy resources are the major producers of this metal. The chief producers of aluminium are China, Russia, Canada, USA, Australia and Brazil.
2. **Asbestos :** It is fibrous mineral produced largely in Canada, Zimbabwe and South Africa.
3. **Copper :** Though found in pure state also, most of the copper is obtained from copper oxides and sulphides which are the chief ores of this metal. It finds applications in a host of areas, electrical equipment and transmission lines being the most important. Chile, USA, Peru, China, Canada and Armenia are the leading producers. China has recently increased production of copper joining the club of the top ten producers. China has recently increased production of copper joining the club of the top ten producers in the world.
4. **Chromium :** It is a metal used for making high quality alloy steel. South Africa and Russia are its leading producers.
5. **Diamonds:** It is a non-metallic precious stone. It is also the hardest substance. The leading producers are South Africa, Republic of Congo and Australia.
6. **Gold :** Gold occurs either in alluvial or placer deposits or as reefs or lobes underground. Due to its non-reactive character it is considered a *noble metal.* South Africa, USA, Australia, China and Canada are the leading producers. Witwaters rand is the most important gold mining region of South Africa.
7. **Iron Ore:** Iron is the most widely used metallic substance and it forms the foundation of modern industrial civilisation. It is also one of the most widely occuring minerals. Commercial ores of iron are magnetite (more than 60% iron), haematite (50% to 65% iron), limonite (less than 50% iron) and siderite. The leading producers of iron ore are China, Brazil, Australia, India and Russia. Iron ore is the basic raw material for the iron and steel industry. It is also one of the most traded minerals in ore form.
8. **Lead :** Lead sulphide or galena is the chief ore of lead. This metal occurs in association with zinc. Chief producers of lead are Australia, China, USA, Peru and Canada.
9. **Manganese :** Manganese is used for making steel. Its main ores are *pyrolusite* and *psilomelane.* Leading producers of manganese are China, South Africa, Australia, Ukraine, Brazil and India.
10. **Mercury:** It is a metal which normally occurs in a liquid state. Chief producers are Spain, China and Italy.
11. **Mica :** It is a non-metallic mineral. It is a bad conductor of heat and electricity and finds application in electrical appliances and a host of other industries. India and USA are the leading producers.
12. **Nickel :** The chief ore of nickel is *pentlaudite.* Nickel finds application in a host of areas including electroplating. The leading producers of nickel are Canada, Australia and USA.
13. **Phosphate:** Rock phosphate is an important raw material for fertiliser industry. Besides rocks phosphate, another source of phosphate

is *guano,* the droppings of the fish eating birds. Chief producers of rock phosphate are USA and Russia. Peru is a major producer of guano.

14. **Platinum :** Like gold, platinum is also a noble metal. It is one of the rarest metals also. Canada, South Africa, Russia and Columbia are the chief producers.
15. **Silver :** It is another precious metal. The most important ore of silver is *argentite.* It occurs mostly in association with lead and zinc. Chief producers of silver are Mexico, Peru, Australia, Chile and Poland.
16. **Sulphur :** It is a non-metallic mineral used in chemical industry. Mexico, USA and Poland are the leading producers.
17. **Salt (Rock Salt):** *Halite* or sodium chloride is the common salt obtained from rocks. USA, China, Russian Federation and Germany are the Chief producers.
18. **Tin :** Tin is found mostly in the form of alluvial or placer deposits. *Cassiterite* or *tinstone* is its cheif ore. China, Indonesia, Peru, Brazil, Malaysia and Bolivia are the chief producers.
19. **Tungsten :** It is a very heavy metal and has a high melting point. It is used for making alloy steel. China, Democratic Republic of Korea, Russia and Bolivia are the leading producers.
20. **Uranium :** Being a radio-active mineral, uranium is the basic raw material for atomic energy. Its chief ores are *uranite* and *pitchblende*. Chief producers are Canada, Australia, Kazakhstan, Russia, Niger and Namibia.
21. **Zinc :** It is another metallic mineral finding application in a variety of areas. One of its chief uses is for galvanizing. *Zinkblende* and *calamine* are the main ores of zinc and it occurs in association with lead. The chief producers of zinc are China, Australia, Peru, Canada, and India.

ENERGY RESOURCES

Coal

A principal mineral fuel, coal is a combustible, solid stratified rock of organic and mineral matter. The organic matter constitutes carbon (60 to 90 per cent), hydrogen (one to 12 per cent), oxygen (two to 20 per cent), nitrogen (one to three per cent) and also small amounts of phosphorus and sulphur. Coal occurs as a sedimentary rock in association with carbonaceous shale, sandstone and even fireclay in a regular succession and in repetitions. Gondwana coal is found as drifted deposits and tertiary coal occurs as *in situ* deposits.

Coal originates from the accumulation of vegetable matter in swampy areas on broad delta, coastal plains and basin lowlands. The vegetable matter is subjected to geological processes that effect physical and chemical changes. The changes can be seen in the darkening of colour, increase in compactness, hardness and carbon content, and decrease in volatility and moisture. The growth *in situ* and drift theories explain the origin of coal. The complex process of coal formation involves physical and bacteriological agencies. Favourable climatic conditions for coal formation are mild temperature to sub-tropical climate with well-distributed moderate to heavy rainfall.

Stages of Coal Formation

Peat is the first stage of coal formation and varies considerably in extent and thickness. It has a high percentage of moisture and volatile matter. Carbon makes up only about one-third of its bulk.

Anthracite, the hardest variety, ranks highest amongst the coals. It has a carbon content of almost 95 per cent with practically no volatile matter. Only about 5 per cent of the world's coal is anthracite.

Economic Uses

Coal, a primary source of heat and power (thermal power), is used in the production of water gas; in metallurgical operations for the purpose of extraction of metals like iron, zinc, etc.; in the production of coal gas, tar, coke, etc.; and to produce different types of varnish and germicides.

Petroleum or Crude Oil

It is one of the important mineral fuels and a complex mixture of hydrocarbon compounds with minor amounts of impurities like nitrogen, sulphur and oxygen. The liquid petroleum is called crude oil, petroleum gas is called natural gas and the semi-solid to solid forms of petroleum are known as asphalt, tar, pitch, bitumen, etc.

For petroleum to accumulate in commercial quantities in an area, the oil must originate in a source bed. A marine shale, once a black mud rich in organic compound, is thought to be a common source rock. The oil then migrates to permeable reservoir rocks after travelling for long distances both vertically and horizontally. The source beds tend to lack the permeability necessary for profitable extraction of the oil. A non-permeable layer must occur above the reservoir bed. A favourable structure must exist.

Economic Uses

The chief use of petroleum is as fuel, particularly in transport operations. The petrochemical derivations of petroleum have a wide range of uses in agricultural, industrial and medicinal industries. It is also used for the purpose of generation of heat and power.

Natural Gas

It generally occurs with oil, but may also occur separately. It is a particularly useful fuel, because it can be controlled for heating purposes. It is used as a fuel; for instance, Compressed Natural Gas (CNG) is used as transport fuel. It is also used in thermal power generation and in manufacture of fertilisers and petrochemicals. USA and the former Soviet region are major producers, others being the Netherlands, Canada, Indonesia, UK.

Nuclear Minerals

Heavy metals; such as uranium, thorium, radium, plutonium and lithium, are the sources of nuclear energy. Uranium is the most important among these metals. The main ores of uranium are pitchblende, uranite, samarskite and thorianite. Canada is the leading producer of uranium. South Africa, Australia, USA, Niger and France are other important producers. Colorado, Utah and New Mexico in the USA are the important areas of uranium deposits. Australia's important uranium areas are Port Darwin, the Rum Jangle and the Radium Hill. The Rand and the Massef Central have significant uranium deposits in South Africa and France respectively. Cornwell in England and Katanga in the Republic of Congo also possess some uranium.

As compared to uranium, the geographical distribution of thorium is much more restricted. Main ores of thorium are monazite, allanite and thorianite. The largest deposits of monazite are in India. Florida coast and Idaho in the USA and coastal areas of South Africa also have thorium deposits.

Beryllium (obtained from beryl, which is found in association with feldspar and mica in pegmatites), zirconium (found in zircon in beach sands) and ilimenite (found in the concentrated form in the beach sands) are other important nuclear minerals.

The first *nuclear power* station was built in Britain in 1956 at Calder Hall. Britain was rapidly overtaken in this field by France and the USA. Nuclear power provides 11 per cent of the USA's electricity supplies. Majority of the nuclear reactors in the US are concentrated in three areas: (*a*) the region between Massachusetts and northern Virginia, accounting for about one-fourth of the country's total capacity; (*b*) the Chicago region; and (*c*) an area extending from Carolina westward across northern Georgia, Alabama and Tennessee state borders.

Hydel Power

Hydro-electricity development is dependent upon the following factors: (*a*) a head of water, waterfalls are useful, a dam may be built to create falling water; (*b*) large amounts of water to make it more economic; (*c*) regular and reliable supply of water; (*d*) presence of lakes which are useful for water storage; (e) space for a reservoir. Heavy capital investment is needed as maintenance costs are also high.

Many hydroelectric power (HEP) generating plants are situated in uplands where the rivers and streams have a steep gradient and waterfalls are common, e.g., in Scandinavia, the Swiss Alps, the Rocky Mountains, the Japanese Alps and the Appalachians. Rivers with a low gradient but a large volume of water can also be used, e.g., the River Shannon in Ireland or the River Volta in Ghana.

Thermal Power

Power produced by burning fuels such as coal, petroleum, or natural gas in thermal generators or specially designed furnaces is thermal electricity. Thermal plants depend on a supply of solid or liquid fuels so they are better situated near coalfields, oil or natural gas fields, or at importing ports where oil is refined. The generation of electricity releases much heat, so a great deal of water is required for cooling purposes. Thus, nearness to a large river, lake, estuary or a coastal site is useful. Also advantageous is a location near the main markets of electricity (such as industrial centres, towns with a large domestic power demand).

The highest number of thermal plants are situated in the densely populated and heavily industrialised areas of western Europe and north-eastern North America. The USA leads as producer and consumer.

Geothermal Energy

This is a kind of energy available as heat emitted from within the earth's crust, usually as hot springs, emissions of dry or wet steam. Geothermal energy can be harnessed for power generation, space heating and other thermal applications.

Geothermal energy is most used in Iceland, where it supplies about 15 per cent of the total domestic demand of electricity, mostly for central heating, which, includes domestic heating for the whole of the capital, Reykjavik. Italy, US, Japan, New Zealand, the Philippines, Turkey and former USSR have also shown keen interest in exploiting geothermal power from steam or hot water sources.

Tidal Energy

The vast potential of energy of the seas and oceans, which cover about three-fourth of our planet, can make a significant contribution to tide over the energy crisis. Ocean contains renewable energy in the form of temperature gradients, waves, tides and ocean currents, which can be used to generate electricity in an environment-friendly manner. Tidal power, wave power and ocean thermal energy conversion are the three most well developed technologies. The realisation of power from ocean at present is limited because of large technological gaps and limited resources. With the present technology only tides can be harnessed on commercial basis.

Tidal power has already been successfully developed on the Rance Estuary in Brittany, France. Other coastal countries have also taken steps to harness this alternative source for producing electricity. However, there are only few sites in the whole world where it could be developed. Further, initial development costs of generating tidal energy are enormous.

WATER

Water is our most abundant resource, covering about 71% of the earth's surface. This precious film of water—about 97% salt water and the remainder fresh—helps maintain the earth's climate and dilutes environmental pollutants. Essential to all life, water makes up 50% to 97% of the weight of all plants and animals and about 70% of your body. Water is also a vital resource for agriculture, manufacturing, transportation, and countless other human activities.

Because of differences in average annual precipitation, some areas of the world have too little fresh water and others too much. With varying degrees of success, we have attempted to correct some of these imbalances. We have captured fresh water in reservoirs behind dams, transferred fresh water in rivers and streams from one area to another, tapped underground supplies, and attempted to reduce water use, waste, and contamination.

Despite these efforts, water is one of the most poorly managed resources on earth. We waste it and pollute it. We also charge too little for making it available, encouraging even greater waste and pollution of this potentially renewable resource.

Supply and Use of Water Resources

World Supply: The world's fixed supply of water in all forms (vapour, liquid, and solid) is enormous. If we could distribute it equally, every person on earth would have 280 billion liters. However, about 97% of the earth's water is found in the oceans and is too salty for drinking, growing crops, and most industrial uses except cooling.

The remaining 3% is fresh water. However, all but 0.003% of this supply is highly polluted, lies too far under the earth's surface to be extracted at an affordable cost, or is locked up in glaciers, polar ice caps, atmosphere, and soil. To put this in measurements that we can understand, if the world's water supply were only 100 liters, our usable supply of fresh water would be only about 0.003 liter.

That tiny fraction of usable fresh water still amounts to an average of 8.4 million litres for each person on earth. This supply is continually collected, purified and distributed in the natural hydrologic (water) cycle. This natural recycling and purification process works as long as we don't use water faster than it is replenished and as long as we don't overload it with slowly degradable and nondegradable wastes.

Surface-water Runoff: The fresh water we use comes from two sources : groundwater and surface-water runoff. Precipitation that does not infiltrate into the ground or return to the atmosphere by evaporation or transpiration is called **surface water** and becomes **runoff**—fresh water that flows on the earth's surface into streams, rivers, lakes, wetlands, and reservoirs. The land area that delivers runoff, sediment, and water-soluble substances to a major river and its tributaries is called a **watershed**, or **drainage basin**.

Surface water can be withdrawn from streams, rivers, lakes, and reservoirs for human activities, but only part of the total annual runoff is available for use. Some of it flows in rivers to the sea too rapidly to be captured, and some must be left in streams for wildlife and to supply downstream areas. In some years the amount of runoff is reduced by below-average precipitation.

Ground water: Some precipitation seeps into the ground, where it accumulates as **soil water** and partially fills pores between soil particles and rocks in the upper layers of the earth's crust. Most of this water is eventually lost to the atmosphere by evaporation from the upper layers of soil and by transpiration from leaves.

Under the influence of gravity, some infiltrating water slowly percolates through porous materials deeper into the earth. There it fills pores and fractures in spongelike, or permeable, layers of sand, gravel and porous rock such as sandstone. This area, where all available pore spaces are filled by water, is called the zone of saturation. These porous, water-bearing layers of underground rock are called **aquifers** and the water in them is **groundwater**.

MULTIPLE CHOICE QUESTIONS

1. Which among the following is known as new alluvium?
(*a*) Khadar (*b*) Bangar
(*c*) Terai (*d*) None of these

2. Which soil is known as regur?
(*a*) Red Soil (*b*) Alluvial Soil
(*c*) Laterite Soil (*d*) Black Soil

3. Which of the following is the characteristics of soil found in the Indo-Gangatic plains?
(*a*) It is rich in Nitrogen
(*b*) It is rich in humus
(*c*) Soil is acidic
(*d*) Soil is highly porous and fertile

4. Which state has very little alluvial soil area?
(*a*) Tamil Nadu (*b*) Haryana
(*c*) West Bengal (*d*) Madhya Pradesh

5. The most important factor in soil formation is?
(*a*) Relief (*b*) Climate
(*c*) Natural Vegetation (*d*) Rock Cover

6. Peaty soil is found in
(*a*) Kerala (*b*) Kashmir
(*c*) Assam (*d*) Gujarat

7. The colour of the red soil is red because it contains
(*a*) Nitrogen (*b*) Iron
(*c*) Potash (*d*) Humus

8. Which type of soil is most suitable for tabacco cultivation?
(*a*) Black soil (*b*) Red Soil
(*c*) Laterite Soil (*d*) All of these

9. The soils which have supported agriculture for centuries without much manuring are
(*a*) red and laterite soils
(*b*) black and alluvial soils
(*c*) laterite and black soils
(*d*) alluvial and laterite soils

10. The ravine erosion is generally not occurs in
(*a*) Andhra Pradesh
(*b*) Uttar Pradesh
(*c*) Rajasthan and Madhya Pradesh
(*d*) Madhya Pradesh

11. Soil erosion in India occures in almost all the littoral states, but it is most serious along the coast of
(*a*) Kerala (*b*) Tamil Nadu
(*c*) Orissa (*d*) Karnataka

12. Which soil needs only little irrigation as it retains soil moisture?
(*a*) black (*b*) red
(*c*) alluvial (*d*) laterite

13. Mountail soil contains a lot of
(*a*) clay
(*b*) humus
(*c*) coarse material
(*d*) iron and aluminium salts

14. Which soil requires the least tilling?
(*a*) black (*b*) laterite
(*c*) red (*d*) None of these

15. Which soil swells when wet and develops cracks when dry?
(*a*) red (*b*) black
(*c*) laterite (*d*) alluvial

16. Tropical moist deciduous vegetation is found in Sahyadris, north-east plateau of the Peninsula, and in the Shivaliks. Which of the following is not a tree species of this group?
(*a*) Teak (*b*) Sal
(*c*) Sandalwood (*d*) Deodar

17. ***Assertion*** **(*A*) :** Most of the 'exotics' plants that have come to India from other country are troublesome weeds which thrive here.
Reason **(*R*) :** They have no 'natural' enemies of their home land to curb them in their new habitat.
(*a*) A and R are true but R is not a correct explanation of A
(*b*) A and R are true and R correctly explains A
(*c*) A is true but R is false
(*d*) A and R both are incorrect

18. Which one of the following statements about forests is not correct?
(*a*) Forests in the equatorial regions of India are less dense than the monsoon forests.
(*b*) Coniferous forests of high latitudes yield soft wood.
(*c*) Large-scale exploitation of forests has caused soil erosion and repeated floods.
(*d*) Between 2000 m. and 3000 m. elevation on the Himalayas deodar, chinar, and walnut are found

19. Where is the Valley of flowers found?
(*a*) Kerala (*b*) Uttarkhand
(*c*) Assam (*d*) Sikkim

20. The evergreen tropical rain forest is found in
(*a*) Assam (*b*) West Bengal
(*c*) Orissa (*d*) All of these

21. First National Park in India was established in
(*a*) 1936 (*b*) 1873
(*c*) 1902 (*d*) 1857

22. A National Institute of Animal Welfare has been established at
(*a*) Delhi (*b*) Faridabad
(*c*) Bengaluru (*d*) Bhopal

23. "Reserved forests" are the forests:
(a) reserved for hunting
(b) reserved for commercial exploitation and prohibited for grazing.
(c) reserved for local use
(d) reserved for growing medicinal herbs

24. The minimum forest cover necessary to maintain ecological balance is
(a) 50% of the total land area
(b) 40% of the total land area
(c) 33% of the total land area
(d) 25% of the total land area

25. The Periyar National Park in Kerala is renowned for
(a) tiger (b) panda
(c) lion (d) spotted deer

26. Which sanctuary has been selected as an alternative home for the Indian lion?
(a) Bandipur Sanctuary (Karnataka)
(b) Ghana Sanctuary (Rajasthan)
(c) Periyar Sanctuary (Kerala)
(d) Chandra Prabha Sanctuary (U.P.)

27. Economically, the most important forests of India are
(a) Tidal forests
(b) Thorn forests
(c) Evergreen forests
(d) Tropical deciduous forests

28. Mudumalai Sanctuary, famous for elephants and deer, is situated in
(a) Assam (b) Gujarat
(c) Tamil Nadu (d) Karnataka

29. Bandipur National Park is situated in
(a) Kerala (b) Assam
(c) Andhra Pradesh (d) Karnataka

30. Which of the following is not under Tiger Project.
(a) Namdapha National Park
(b) Pench National Park
(c) Similipal National Park
(d) Singalila National Park

31. Which one of the following types of coal contains a higher percentage of carbon than the rest.
(a) Anthracite (b) Bituminous
(c) Lignite (d) Peat

32. Pyrolusite and Psilomelane are major ores of
(a) Lead (b) Gold
(c) Rock Salt (d) Manganese

33. Name the major ore of Uranium.
(a) Cinnabar (b) Pitchblende
(c) Argentite (d) Bauxite

34. The Sullivan mines of British Columbia (Canada), are famous for which mineral resource?
(a) Lead (b) Zinc
(c) Aluminium (d) Tin

35. The largest copper deposits are to be found in
(a) Chile and Arizona
(b) Chile and the Congo
(c) Russia and the Congo
(d) Mexico and Zaire

36. Match the following :

	List-I		List-II
A.	China	1.	Salt
B.	South Africa	2.	Diamond
C.	Malaysia	3.	Tin
D.	Ukraine	4.	Petroleum

	A	B	C	D
(a)	1	2	3	4
(b)	2	3	1	4
(c)	2	1	4	3
(d)	1	2	4	3

37. Mark the true statement:
(a) Japan exports iron ore
(b) Iceland imports fish
(c) Egypt exports cotton
(d) All the above statements are true

38. Which one of the followings is also known as noble metal?
(a) Platinum (b) Aluminium
(c) Mangenese (d) Tin

39. Cassiterite is an ore of
(a) Lead (b) Iron
(c) Tin (d) Silver

40. Which among the following is major nickel producer?
(a) Canada (b) USA
(c) Germany (d) India

41. Which among the following is the chief exporter of Manganese?
(a) USA (b) Canada
(c) Russia (d) Mexico

42. Consider the following statements and select the correct answer from the code given below:
1. Brass is a compound of copper and zinc.
2. Magnetite is the most important ore of aluminium
3. Mexico is chief exporter of silver.
4. Zaire is an important producer of uranium.

Codes :
(a) 1 and 2 (b) 2 and 4
(c) 3 and 4 (d) 1 and 4

43. Match List-I with List-II and select the correct answer using the codes given below the lists.

	List-I		List-II
A.	Lignite	1.	Copper
B.	Bauxite	2.	Iron
C.	Magnetite	3.	Aluminium
D.	Pyrite	4.	Coal

Codes :

	A	B	C	D
(*a*)	2	3	1	4
(*b*)	4	1	3	2
(*c*)	4	3	1	2
(*d*)	4	3	2	1

44. Korea is main producer of
(*a*) Lead (*b*) Tungesten
(*c*) Uranium (*d*) Silver

45. Pitchblende is an important ore of
(*a*) Uranium (*b*) Zinc
(*c*) Nickel (*d*) None of these

46. Name the country which uses nuclear energy mostly.
(*a*) France (*b*) Canada
(*c*) USA (*d*) Sweden

47. Major Coal producer in the world is
(*a*) USA (*b*) China
(*c*) India (*d*) Germany

48. Which of the following is the most superior of coals?
(*a*) Anthracite (*b*) Bituminous
(*c*) Lignite (*d*) Peat

49. Bitumen and asphalt are by products of extracting
(*a*) Coal (*b*) Petroleum
(*c*) Uranium (*d*) Tar

50. Which is the major component of natural gas
(*a*) Methane (*b*) Ethane
(*c*) Butane (*d*) Propane

51. Wind power is employed prominently in
(*a*) France (*b*) Holland
(*c*) Saudi Arabia (*d*) Canada

52. Which one of the following is not the oil producing area of the erstwhile USSR?
(*a*) Kuznetsk (*b*) Caucasus
(*c*) Lena basin (*d*) Sakhalin

53. Which one of the following is not suitably matched?
(*a*) Kuzbas – Petroleum
(*b*) Ruhr – Coal
(*c*) Pennsylvannia – Petroleum
(*d*) Shansi – Coal

54. Which one of the following is not the oil producing regions?
(*a*) Volga-Ural (*b*) Honshu
(*c*) Yangtse Valley (*d*) Donbass

55. Geothermal energy is mostly used in
(*a*) Iceland (*b*) New Zealand
(*c*) Japan (*d*) Philippines

56. Gondwana coal field is found in
(*a*) Assam
(*b*) Madhya Pradesh
(*c*) Meghalaya
(*d*) Jammu and Kashmir

57. The nuclear power plant in India, which will provide power mainly for agriculture, is located at.
(*a*) Kalpakkam (*b*) Narora
(*c*) Kota (*d*) Tarapur

58. The major thermal power station fed on natural gas is at
(*a*) Lunej (*b*) Trombay
(*c*) Naharkatiya (*d*) Digboi

59. The oldest coal mine in India is at
(*a*) Dhanbad (*b*) Jharia
(*c*) Raniganj (*d*) Asansol

60. The biggest oil refinery in India is at
(*a*) Vishakhapatnam (*b*) Koyali
(*c*) Barauni (*d*) Mathura

61. The state having the maximum number of oil wells on its land is
(*a*) Gujarat (*b*) Maharashtra
(*c*) Assam (*d*) Goa

62. In the production of tidal energy the maximum potential exists at
(*a*) Bhawnagar (*b*) Digboi
(*c*) Cochin (*d*) Ladakh

63. Which of the following are true with regard to coal in India?
I. Coal is found in sedimentary rocks.
II. The best quality of coal is lignite.
III. The largest and oldest coalfield in India is Raniganj.
IV. The Damodar river valley is popularly known as the Ruhr of India.
(*a*) I and IV (*b*) I, II and III
(*c*) I, III and IV (*d*) II, III and IV

64. Which of the following is true with regard to petroleum?
I. It is found in the anticlines.
II. It is found over underground water.
III. It is found in wide, horizontal rocks.
IV. It is found over impermeable rocks.
(*a*) I and II (*b*) I, II and IV
(*c*) II and IV (*d*) II and III

65. Which of the following was India's first mobile offshore drilling platform?
(*a*) Sagar Kanya (*b*) Sagar Matha
(*c*) Sagar Samrat (*d*) None of the above

66. Which of the following is the oldest atomic power station ?
(*a*) Kalpakkam (*b*) Tarapur
(*c*) Narora (*d*) Kota

67. Match the following

	Atomic Power Stations		**States**
A.	Kakrapara	1.	Rajasthan
B.	Narora	2.	Gujarat
C.	Kalapakkam	3.	Tamil Nadu
D.	Tarapur	4.	Maharashtra
E.	Kota	5.	Uttar Pradesh

Codes :

	A	B	C	D	E
(*a*)	1	2	3	4	5
(*b*)	5	4	3	2	1
(*c*)	2	5	3	4	1
(*d*)	1	4	2	3	5

68. The advantage of micro hydel projects is that they
(*a*) make use of water of the perennial hill streams in irrigation canals
(*b*) prevent floods
(*c*) save water
(*d*) involve less cost

69. Which of the following is not a super thermal power station being setup by the NTPC.
(*a*) Ramagundam (A.P.) and Farakka (W.B.)
(*b*) Rihand and Singrauli (U.P.)
(*c*) Korba and Vindhyachal (M.P.-Chhattisgarh)
(*d*) Badarpur (Delhi) and Ukai (Gujarat)

70. The maximum power in India comes from
(*a*) Thermal power (*b*) Hydro-power
(*c*) Nuclear power (*d*) Solar energy

ANSWERS

1	2	3	4	5	6	7	8	9	10
(*a*)	(*d*)	(*d*)	(*d*)	(*b*)	(*a*)	(*b*)	(*b*)	(*b*)	(*a*)
11	**12**	**13**	**14**	**15**	**16**	**17**	**18**	**19**	**20**
(*a*)	(*a*)	(*c*)	(*a*)	(*b*)	(*d*)	(*b*)	(*a*)	(*b*)	(*d*)
21	**22**	**23**	**24**	**25**	**26**	**27**	**28**	**29**	**30**
(*a*)	(*b*)	(*b*)	(*c*)	(*a*)	(*d*)	(*d*)	(*c*)	(*d*)	(*d*)
31	**32**	**33**	**34**	**35**	**36**	**37**	**38**	**39**	**40**
(*a*)	(*d*)	(*b*)	(*d*)	(*b*)	(*a*)	(*c*)	(*a*)	(*c*)	(*a*)
41	**42**	**43**	**44**	**45**	**46**	**47**	**48**	**49**	**50**
(*c*)	(*c*)	(*d*)	(*b*)	(*a*)	(*a*)	(*b*)	(*a*)	(*b*)	(*a*)
51	**52**	**53**	**54**	**55**	**56**	**57**	**58**	**59**	**60**
(*b*)	(*a*)	(*a*)	(*d*)	(*a*)	(*b*)	(*b*)	(*c*)	(*c*)	(*d*)
61	**62**	**63**	**64**	**65**	**66**	**67**	**68**	**69**	**70**
(*a*)	(*a*)	(*c*)	(*b*)	(*c*)	(*b*)	(*c*)	(*d*)	(*d*)	(*a*)

SECTION b PEDAGOGICAL ISSUES

NATURE AND STRUCTURE OF SCIENCE

Science is a particular way of understanding the natural world. It extends the intrinsic curiosity with which we are born. It allows us to connect the past with the present.

Science is based on the premise that our senses, and extensions of those senses through the use of instruments, can give us accurate information about the Universe. Science follows very specific "rules" and its results are always subject to testing and, if necessary, revision. Even with such constraints science does not exclude, and often benefits from, creativity and imagination (with a good bit of logic thrown in).

Nature of Science

Over the course of human history, people have developed many interconnected and validated ideas about the physical, biological, psychological, and social worlds. Those ideas have enabled successive generations to achieve an increasingly comprehensive and reliable understanding of the human species and its environment. The means used to develop these ideas are particular ways of observing, thinking, experimenting, and validating. These ways represent a fundamental aspect of the nature of science and reflect how science tends to differ from other modes of knowing.

It is the union of science, mathematics, and technology that forms the scientific endeavour and that makes it so successful. Although each of these human enterprises has a character and history of its own, each is dependent on and reinforces the others.

Science presumes that the things and events in the universe occur in consistent patterns that are comprehensible through careful, systematic study. Scientists believe that through the use of the intellect, and with the aid of instruments that extend the senses, people can discover patterns in all of nature.

Science also assumes that the universe is, as its name implies, a vast single system in which the basic rules are everywhere the same. Knowledge gained from studying one part of the universe is applicable to other parts. For instance, the same principles of motion and gravitation that explain the motion of falling objects on the surface of the earth also explain the motion of the moon and the planets. With some modifications over the years, the same principles of motion have applied to other forces-and to the motion of everything, from the smallest nuclear particles to the most massive stars, from sailboats to space vehicles, from bullets to light rays.

Science is a process for producing knowledge. The process depends both on making careful observations of phenomena and on inventing theories for making sense out of those observations. Change in knowledge is inevitable because new observations may challenge prevailing theories. No matter how well one theory explains a set of observations, it is possible that another theory may fit just as well or better, or may fit a still wider range of observations. In science, the testing and improving and occasional discarding of theories, whether new or old, go on all the time. Scientists assume that even if there is no way to secure complete and absolute truth, increasingly accurate approximations can be made to account for the world and how it works.

Although scientists reject the notion of attaining absolute truth and accept some uncertainty as part of nature, most scientific knowledge is durable. The modification of ideas, rather than their outright rejection, is the norm in science, as powerful constructs tend to survive and grow more precise and to become widely accepted. For example, in formulating the theory of relativity, Albert Einstein did not discard the Newtonian laws of motion but rather showed them to be only an approximation of limited application within a more general concept. Moreover, the growing ability of scientists to make accurate predictions about natural phenomena provides convincing evidence that we really are gaining in our understanding of how the world works. Continuity and stability are as characteristic of science as change is, and confidence is as prevalent as tentativeness.

There are many matters that cannot usefully be examined in a scientific way. There are, for instance, beliefs that-by their very nature-cannot be proved or disproved (such as the existence of supernatural powers and beings, or the true purposes of life). In other cases, a scientific approach that may be valid is likely to be rejected as irrelevant by people who hold to certain beliefs (such as in miracles, fortune-telling, astrology, and superstition). Nor do scientists have the means to settle issues concerning good and evil, although they can sometimes contribute to the discussion of such issues by identifying the likely consequences of particular actions, which may be helpful in weighing alternatives.

Sooner or later, the validity of scientific claims is settled by referring to observations of phenomena. Hence, scientists concentrate on getting accurate data. Such evidence is obtained by observations and measurements taken in situations that range from natural settings (such as a forest) to completely contrived ones (such as the laboratory). To make their observations, scientists use their own senses, instruments (such as microscopes) that enhance those senses, and instruments that tap characteristics quite different from what humans can sense (such as magnetic fields). Scientists observe passively (earthquakes, bird migrations), make collections (rocks, shells), and actively probe the world (as by boring into the earth's crust or administering experimental medicines).

NATURAL SCIENCE : AIMS AND OBJECTIVES

Science teaches an understanding of natural phenomena. It aims to stimulate a child's curiosity in finding out why things happen in the way they do. It teaches methods of enquiry and investigation to stimulate creative thought. Children learn to ask scientific questions and begin to appreciate the way science will affect their future on a personal, national, and global level.

The aims of science are to enable children to:

- ❑ ask and answer scientific questions;
- ❑ plan and carry out scientific investigations, using equipment, including computers, correctly;
- ❑ know and understand the life processes of living things;
- ❑ know and understand the physical processes of materials, electricity, light, sound and natural forces;
- ❑ know about the nature of the solar system, including the earth;
- ❑ evaluate evidence and present their conclusions clearly and accurately.

UNDERSTANDING AND APPRECIATING SCIENCE

To understand what science is, just look around you. What do you see? Perhaps, your hand on the mouse, a computer screen, papers, ballpoint pens, the family cat, the sun shining through the window .... Science is, in one sense, our knowledge of all that — all the *stuff* that is in the universe: from the tiniest subatomic particles in a single atom of the metal in your computer's circuits, to the nuclear reactions that formed the immense ball of gas that is our sun, to the complex chemical interactions and electrical fluctuations within your own body that allow you to read and understand these words. But just as importantly, science is also a reliable process by which we *learn* about all that stuff in the universe. However, science is different from many other ways of learning because of the way it is done. Science relies on testing ideas with evidence gathered from the natural world.

Science helps satisfy the natural curiosity with which we are all born: why is the sky blue, how did the leopard get its spots, what is a solar eclipse? With science, we can answer such questions without resorting to magical explanations. And science can lead to technological advances, as well as helping us learn about enormously important and useful topics, such as our health, the environment, and natural hazards. Without science, the modern world would not be modern at all, and we still have much to learn. Millions of scientists all over the world are working to solve different parts of the puzzle of how the universe works, peering into its nooks and crannies, deploying their microscopes, telescopes, and other tools to unravel its secrets.

Science is complex and multi-faceted, but the most important characteristics of science are straightforward:

- ❑ Science focuses exclusively on the natural world, and does not deal with supernatural explanations.
- ❑ Science is a way of learning about what is in the natural world, how the natural world works, and how the natural world got to be the way it is. It is not simply a collection of facts; rather it is a path to understanding.
- ❑ Scientists work in many different ways, but all science relies on testing ideas by figuring out what expectations are generated by an idea and making observations to find out whether those expectations hold true.
- ❑ Accepted scientific ideas are reliable because they have been subjected to rigorous testing, but as new evidence is acquired and new perspectives emerge these ideas can be revised.
- ❑ Science is a community endeavour. It relies on a system of checks and balances, which helps ensure that science moves in the direction of greater accuracy and understanding. This system is facilitated by diversity within the scientific community, which offers a broad range of perspectives on scientific ideas.

APPROACHES AND INTEGRATED APPROACH

Foundational Approach

Foundational Approaches in Science Teaching (FAST) is an interdisciplinary science programme designed to meet the developmental needs of adolescents 12- to 15-years old. While it leans heavily on a curriculum for grades 6-10, the programme has an extensive, required staff development component that prepares teachers to teach science concepts in constructivist ways and helps develop teachers'content knowledge.

The programme emphasizes basic concepts and methods of the physical, biological, and earth sciences and relates these to practical issues of human use of the environment. FAST is designed around three courses of study. FAST 1 focuses on the local environment; FAST 2 addresses matter and energy in the biosphere; and FAST 3 emphasises change over time. The content is organised into three strands: physical science, ecology, and relational study. In the FAST program, students are actively engaged in conducting scientific investigations to discover key concepts and principles. FAST students also explore relationships among the various science disciplines and societal issues.

The structure of the programme develops scientific literacy to provide students (1) the background necessary for understanding and appreciating concerns that arise in a technological world and (2) the essential tools for further study in the sciences. FAST stresses increasing students' ability to communicate what they are learning through the use of oral reports, project work, graphing, flow charts, and diagramming. FAST helps students develop thinking skills, laboratory skills, and increase their knowledge of the foundational concepts.

Foundational Approaches to Science Teaching requires intensive teacher development. Prior to implementation of any course, teachers are immersed in a 10-day inquiry investigation for each FAST course. Each segment models the variety of teaching behaviours inherent within the FAST programme and provides opportunities for discussion of the learning, teaching, and assessing process. In the institutes, certified FAST instructors model constructivist teaching strategies while participants conduct the same investigations their students will conduct. The content focuses on concept development and the issues, challenges, and rewards of inquiry-based instruction. Debriefing of the investigations helps teachers identify instructional strategies used during the investigation. Participants also review issues related to safety, unexpected data or results, alternative procedures, lack of appropriate science equipment, and handling students with special needs.

Integrated Approach

Many science and mathematics teachers in secondary schools are alarmed at the amount of content which needs to be covered in meeting the requirements of the National Curriculum. Much time has already been spent in developing carefully planned programmes to ensure full coverage of the Attainment Targets.

There is considerable overlap between some of the science and mathematics targets: science AT 1 and ATs and 9 in mathematics are the most obvious examples. Clearly there is scope for time to be saved by covering such ATs simultaneously. Three tasks are offered here as examples of how this may be achieved. Although each of the tasks may appear to be "scientific" in style they all contain many of the skills listed in the mathematics ATs 1 and 9 and touch on three main strands of mathematical activity.

Using mathematics

- ❑ planning and working methodically;
- ❑ checking for sufficient information;
- ❑ using trial and improvement methods.

Communicating in mathematics

- ❑ making sense of a task;
- ❑ exploring and recording work systematically;
- ❑ presenting results in an intelligible way to others;

Developing ideas of argument and proof

- ❑ asking the question "What if.....";
- ❑ making and testing predictions;
- ❑ generalising, making and testing hypotheses

In addition, they provide obvious opportunities for the application of measurement skills (AT 8 in mathematics).

The tasks are intended to be carried out by small groups or pairs of pupils. Such "practical interactive settings", according to research carried out by the Assessment of Performance Unit (APU), have been shown to have a number of advantages:

(*i*) They give the pupils an opportunity to talk to other pupils about mathematics.

(*ii*) Pupils often spark ideas off one another—a simple idea can often be elaborated into something more complex in which several pupils have a stake.

(*iii*) Pupils have been known to do better at individual work when they also have experience of group work.

(*iv*) Pupils often find it easier to see what other pupils have difficulty in understanding and can sometimes explain more clearly than can the teacher,

(*v*) Pupils may find it easier to express their difficulties to people of their own age rather than the teacher. They may also be afraid to ask the teacher to explain yet again. They almost invariably say that they like working in a group, not just because of the social aspects, but because more ideas are contributed and evaluated.

(*vi*) Pupils are often more motivated and involved than they normally are during mathematics lessons. Several teachers expressed surprise that pupils had spent 2½ hours working on mathematics without realising it.

(*vii*) Some teachers felt that pupils working on their own often keep to a very narrow channel, whereas in groups pupils can pool ideas.

In addition, APU found that similar tasks offered in both written and practical modes have a much lower non-response rate in the latter case. They also enable teachers to get a better idea of how pupils think.

OBSERVATION/EXPERIMENT/DISCOVERY

Observation in Science

The scientific method requires observations of nature to formulate and test hypotheses. It consists of these steps:

1. Asking a question about a natural phenomenon
2. Making observations of the phenomenon
3. Hypothesising an explanation for the phenomenon
4. Predicting a logical consequence of the hypothesis
5. Testing the hypothesis by an experiment, an observational study, or a field study
6. Creating a conclusion with data gathered in the experiment

Observation plays a role in the second and fifth steps. However the need for reproducibility requires that observations by different observers be comparable. Human sense impressions are subjective and qualitative making them difficult to record or compare. The idea of measurement evolved to allow recording and comparison of observations made at different times and places by different people. Measurement consists of using observation to compare the thing being measured to a standard; an artifact, process or definition which can be duplicated or shared by all observers, and counting how many of the standard units are comparable to the object. Measurement reduces an observation to a number which can be recorded, and two observations which result in the same number are equal within the resolution of the process.

Senses are limited, and are subject to errors in perception such as optical illusions. Scientific instruments were developed to magnify human powers of observation, such as weighing scales, clocks, telescopes, microscopes, thermometers, cameras, and tape recorders, and also translate into perceptible form events that are unobservable by human senses, such as indicator dyes, voltmeters, spectrometers, infrared cameras, oscilloscopes, interferometers, geiger counters, x-ray machines, and radio receivers.

One problem encountered throughout scientific fields is that the observation may affect the process being observed, resulting in a different outcome than if the process was unobserved. This is called the *observer effect*. For example, it is not normally possible to check the air pressure in an automobile tire without letting out some of the air, thereby changing the pressure. However, in most fields of science it is possible to reduce the effects of observation to insignificance by using better instruments.

Considered as a physical process itself, all forms of observation (human or instrumental) involve amplification and are thus thermodynamically irreversible processes, increasing entropy.

Experiment in Science

Experiment method (also called scientific method) refers to a body of techniques for investigating phenomena, acquiring new knowledge, or correcting and integrating previous knowledge. To be termed scientific, a method of inquiry must be based on gathering empirical and measurable evidence subject to specific principles of reasoning. The Oxford English Dictionary says that scientific method is: "a method of procedure that has characterised natural science since the 17th century, consisting in systematic observation, measurement, and experiment, and the formulation, testing, and modification of hypotheses."

Although procedures vary from one field of inquiry to another, identifiable features distinguish scientific inquiry from other methods of obtaining knowledge. Scientific researchers propose hypotheses as explanations of phenomena, and design experimental studies to test these hypotheses via predictions which can be derived from them. These steps must be repeatable, to guard against mistake or confusion in any particular experimenter. Theories that encompass wider domains of inquiry may bind many independently derived hypotheses together in a coherent, supportive structure. Theories, in turn, may help form new hypotheses or place groups of hypotheses into context.

Scientific inquiry is generally intended to be as objective as possible, to reduce biased interpretations of results. Another basic expectation is to document, archive and share all data and methodology so they are available for careful scrutiny by other scientists, giving them the opportunity to verify results by attempting to reproduce them. This practice, called *full disclosure*, also allows statistical measures of the reliability of these data to be established.

Discovery in Science

Discovery science (also known as discovery-based science) is a scientific methodology which emphasises analysis of large volumes of experimental data with the goal of finding new patterns or correlations, leading to hypothesis formation and other scientific methodologies.

Discovery-based methodologies are often viewed in contrast to traditional scientific practice, where hypotheses are formed before close examination of experimental data. However, from a philosophical perspective where all or most of the observable "low hanging fruit" has already been plucked, examining the phenomenological world more closely than the senses alone (even augmented senses, e.g. via microscopes, telescopes, bifocals etc.) opens a new source of knowledge for hypothesis formation.

Data mining is the most common tool used in discovery science, and is applied to data from diverse fields of study such as DNA analysis, climate modelling, nuclear reaction modeling, and others.

The use of data mining in discovery science follows a general trend of increasing use of computers and computational theory in all fields of science. Further following this trend, the cutting edge of data mining employs specialised machine learning algorithms for automated hypothesis forming and automated theorem proving.

INNOVATION IN SCIENCE TEACHING

Teaching affects learning directly and indirectly both. If we disregard the self-efforts of learners, learning and its extent will depend on the level of teaching of the teacher. What a teacher wants to make his students by his teaching depends on what the objectives of his teaching are? It means that as soon as level of teaching changes, its objectives and way of attack also change and evaluation of students also changes accordingly. Educators have determined three levels of teaching and a teacher selects these levels according to the ability and mental levels of students.

(A) Memory level of teaching (MLT)

(B) Understanding level of teaching (ULT)

(C) Reflective level of teaching (RLT)

It must be kept in mind that only one level of teaching is selected at a time. When one level of teaching completes and the teacher receives feedback by the process of evaluation only then he skips to the next level. All these three levels of teaching can be arrived at either in one period or it may take several periods to reach all these levels. Determination of the level of teaching depends on the following factors:

I. Mental and academic level of students.

II. Nature of the content (subject-matter).

III. Skill of the teacher to use different strategies of teaching.

Memory Level of Teaching (MLT)

This is a thoughtless teaching level. This level is concerned with the mere reproduction of learnt material by students through recognition and recall. If subject-matter presented by the teacher is crammed by students, task of this level of teaching is said to be complete. The subject-matter which is easy, interesting and purposeful is learnt by students easily and retained for a longer period of time. On the other hand, difficult, dull and purposeless subject-matter is learnt with difficulty and forgotten hurriedly.

At this level of teaching, without regarding interests, attitudes and freedom of students, the teacher inserts the facts and informations into the minds of learners like an autocrate and learners receive them like a mute audience. This attitude of the teacher makes the teaching teacher centred and low level of interaction is seen between teachers and students. This instructional type of teaching can develop only limited level of cognitive domain and if students are able to reproduce the learnt facts or events in written or oral form, teaching is said to be successful.

In spite of some shortcomings, the advantages of this level of teaching is that this is the foundation stage of understanding or reflective levels of teaching, i.e., we can not adopt any other level of teaching without completing teaching at this level.

Understanding Level of Teaching (ULT)

Successful accomplishment of memory level of teaching is the assumption of ULT. We may call it a necessary supplement to the first level of teaching. By understanding level of teaching the teacher develops the mental capacities of students in such a manner that the students can now understand and apply the laws and principles in a confident manner. Their potentials developed by this level of teaching enable them to solve the problems themselves. The roles of the students do not lag behind the teacher. For example, students can answer the comprehensive questions from the para themselves. They can write the summary of the paragraphs and can draw conclusions on the basis of the facts given in the extract or subject-matter. Doing long mathematical sums by using the numerical tables is also the example of understanding level of teaching.

Reflective Level of Teaching (RLT)

This is the highest level of teaching which starts when understanding level of teaching is over. It is a child centred approach of teaching where students are more active than the teacher and they deliberate consciously over the understood material. By doing so the students present their original views.

M. Bigge has elaborated it in the following words:

"Reflective level of teaching tends to develop classroom atmosphere which is more alive and exciting, more critical and penetrating and more open to fresh and original thinking".

Thus, this level of teaching increases the thinking power of students and when this ability is developed in students fully they can solve the real life related problems by applying reflective thinking and logic. This teaching is basically problem-centred. The teacher extracts the problems from within the text and presents them before his students. After looking at the problem, they become excited and tense. Then they reach to the solution of the problem by applying critical judgement techniques. The knowledge which is obtained by this reflection is original and permanent.

Micro-Teaching

Educational technology believes that teachers are not only born but an ordinary person can be made a successful teacher by giving him training in teacher training institutions. Meaning thereby teaching of any teacher can be improved by drilling different strategies, techniques and skills of teaching. In this way, many teaching skills and techniques have been developed by the science of educational technology in order to transform teaching from art to science. Micro teaching is one of such attempts.

By micro-teaching, teachers are taught teaching skills in such a manner that the application of these skills in teaching not only becomes the habit of the teacher but it also becomes the part of his character. In short, micro teaching is a special technique to bring about a desirable change in the behaviour of the pupil teacher.

Characteristics of micro-teaching

Following characteristics of micro-teaching can be drawn on the basis of the definitions and meaning given above:

1. Micro-teaching is done in a controlled environment of a small sized class of five to seven students.
2. The time period of this teaching is also very short, i.e., five to ten minutes, in which the teacher manifests only one teaching skill repeatedly in order to get it practiced.
3. Video tape facility is also provided in order to give proper feedback to the pupil teacher. With the help of video tapping, the pupil teacher can observe his activities himself and after receiving criticisms from his classmates and the teacher trainer, he can mend his behaviour.
4. In micro-teaching the pupil teacher concentrates on only one teaching skill and this skill is especially shown by him.
5. In micro-teaching the pupil teacher teaches only a small portion of the lesson plan. Thus, teaching behaviour is important here rather than content.

6. In this teaching, class size and teaching time both are reduced thus, all pupil teachers get proper time for the practice of teaching skill.

Components of Micro-Teaching

1. **Controlled Environment :** Here only 5 to 10 students are kept in the class and duration of teaching does not exceed to 15 minutes. In such a short span of time only a small unit of the total lesson is taught to students. In this way, the pupil teacher exerts full control over his students and the subject-matter.
2. **Teaching Skills :** Only one teaching skill is concentrated upon by the pupil teacher in micro-teaching. He may use other skills but they are neglected by the observer.
3. **Pupil teacher :** He is the person in charge of the teaching activity.
4. **Feedback :** Feedback is given to the pupil teacher only after the teaching is over. For this purpose either video recording of the teaching is done or the classmates of the pupil teacher observe his lesson on a set format.
5. **Laboratory :** This teaching is done in a laboratory situation not in the classroom. All the necessary equipments are made available there.

Advantages of Micro-Teaching

1. In this type of teaching the whole lesson is divided into different units and skill is selected according to the nature of unit. It makes the task of the teacher easy.
2. There is no problem of discipline in micro teaching due to controlled atmosphere and small size of the class.
3. Pupil teacher gets feedback immediately after the teaching is over.
4. In micro teaching if one pupil teacher learns skills by practice, other teachers learn the skill by imitation. Thus, all the teachers need not practise the skill by formal teaching in the class.
5. The pupil teacher can evaluate his teaching himself by microteaching when it is tapped on a video.
6. Critical thinking power and observation ability can be developed in all the pupil teachers by micro teaching.
7. Special teaching skills can be developed in all the pupil teachers by it and thus desirable changes in their behaviour can be brought about.
8. This is a successful method for individualized training and thus, individual weakness of teachers can be found out.
9. It can bring professional maturity in students (Pupil teachers).
10. This type of teaching can also be used for research purposes and new teaching strategies and techniques can be developed.

TEXT MATERIALS/AIDS

Text Book

Text book is the area in which the study material is presented prescribed for teaching and learning science.

Characteristics of Good Text Books

A good text books not only teaches but it also tests. A few essential characteristics of good text books are given below:

(*i*) The size of text book should be handy for the students.

(*ii*) The binding should be proper and strong.

(*iii*) The subject matter should be printed on good quality paper.

(*iv*) Heading and subheading should be printed on title page in bold form.

(*v*) Illustration should be attractive. For every young pupil, the picture should be well drawn and realistically coloured and not in black and white.

(*vi*) Clear and unambiguous instruction should be given along side the test and practice and exercise.

(*vii*) The introduction at the beginning and conclusion at the end of the chapter should be given in the text book.

(*viii*) The words and structure are carefully graded.

(*ix*) No difficult words and new words are given in good text book.

(*x*) The words and structure already learnt are repeated in the coming pages so that the students could revise them making them stable in their memory.

(*xi*) The subject matter of text book should provide new information so that students could get new knowledge.

(*xii*) There should be both practice and text exercise at the end of the chapter.

(*xiii*) The practice should be low which the majority of students could solve them easily.

Chalkboard

It is the closest friend of a teacher in the class and about 50% teaching task is completed with the help of the blackboard. Advantages of using a chalkboard in the class are as follows:

(*i*) It is a cheap material aid which does not cost much on its maintenance.

(*ii*) When a teacher writes important points of the lesson on the chalkboard along with his oral teaching and lectures, aural and visual both the senses of students work simultaneously. It increases learning many times.

(*iii*) Writing meaning of difficult words, drawing graphs or diagrams, solving the sums of mathematics, preparing the summary of the lesson, all these works can be done on the chalkboard and they help the students understand the facts, events or terminologies.

(*iv*) Blackboard works as a model for students. This can help the students mend their ways if they imitate the model.

Models

Models are the reflection or copy of the real objects. They are used in the class to clarify the concepts when either real objects are not available or it is not possible to bring real objects to the class. They are also the abbreviated version of real objects. Elephants, lions or other animals or birds can not be brought to the class, hence, it is better to use the models of these objects. Globe is the best example of model to be used in the class.

Through models knowledge of all types of historical, geographical and scientific facts and concepts can be given to students. Models are especially useful for teaching visually handicapped children who perceive the objects by touch. Since, clear dimensions of length, breadth and height are given in the model in a proportionate manner, they are more useful for concept formation than pictures.

How to use models

(*i*) Scale should be used for showing size, shape or structure of the real objects. Apart from this, teacher should also clarify the real shape, size or structure of the real object.

(*ii*) Students should be given opportunity to have a critical view on the model and their views on it.

(*iii*) All students should be given chance to have a close look at the model in the class.

(*iv*) Models should have direct relevance to the lesson and they should develop scientific temperament among learners.

(*v*) Models should be properly explained in the class in order to make the use of models effective.

Pictures

Pictures are used in the class as material aids when neither real objects nor models can be arranged. They are cheap and easily available in the market, therefore, a teacher should not be miserly in using them. Pictures are actually the outlines of the real objects and when they are shown in the class, they give clear concepts about the colour, physique, shape and size of the real objects. Attention of students can easily be drawn to the lesson through them. If pictures related to the lesson are not available in the market, the teacher should sketch them by using pencils and water colours. Pictures are used as material aids for teaching all the school subjects.

Diagrams

They are another option and used when even pictures can not be arranged. They can also clarify the concepts like models or pictures but at a lesser degree. Diagrams are drawn on the chalkboard by using coloured chalks and then students copy it on their notebooks. The biggest advantage of this material aid is that teacher need not spend even a single pie in using this material aid.

They help in clarifying the concepts, laws and principles of science and social sciences.

Graphs

Graphs are especially used in history, geography, science and mathematics. They help the teacher and the students to study, analyse and compare the data, facts or events. Whenever action research is made by a teacher in the class, graphs are used to show the data.

Maps

Maps are the flat representation of the surface of the earth on a paper where many informations are presented through lines, symbols dots, points or letters. They have special significance in teaching history and geography. We can also get information about the size and physical features of a country, state or continent through these maps and distance between different parts of the country or the world can also be read from them. Though printed maps of all states or countries are available in the market yet a teacher draws them also on roler boards. This will enable the students to draw such maps themselves.

Slide Projector

Simple 'slide projector' was known as "magic lantern" in the olden days. The principle here is that when we put the transparent slide on the socket and throw light from behind, the light passes through it and projects the image on the screen.

A slide projector typically consists of a quart, three halogen lamps, light to be reflected by the reflector, a heat filter and lastly, condenser lenses. The heat filter is a thermo crystal which absorbs most of the heat produced by three lamps. A cooling system is also needed which consists of a fan for convecting off the heat, filter and other components. The fan is thermostatically controlled. When projector is switched off, the fan is also switched off.

Classroom uses of the Slide Projector : Slides are prepared for selected topics and the informations contained by them may be in the form of written words, pictures, graphs, sketches, etc. The topic selected should be arranged frame by frame. The ideal ratio of length and breadth of slides is 2 : 3. Each frame should have only one concept for the ease of understanding.

The slides and the film strips are arranged in a sequential order. This arrangement is also coordinated with the teaching learning activity of the class. When slides are shown in the class, curtains are drawn on the windows in order to reduce the entry of natural light in the class.

Before showing these slides, teacher elaborates important points. Once the film is over, the teacher gives his own comments and relates the aid with the lesson to be taught.

Film Strips

They are used before a large group of students either for introducing a lesson or for elaborating some minute object not seen in ordinary situations. Film strips are projected on a big screen through a film projector and then the projector is switched on. Here, very minute objects look very big on the screen and we can study their parts. For example, knowledge about bacteria and viruses can be given to students through these film strips. Sometimes, sound recording is also used along with the film to clarify important points.

Advantages of Film Strips :

(*i*) The order or sequence of film strips is fixed and a teacher can prepare the relevant material to supplement the film according to the sequence.

(*ii*) We can have any part of the film on the screen as long as we desire so. As a result, a teacher can discuss a single topic as long as he needs. Thus, complete control over the equipment and the material is possible.

(*iii*) Handling of film projectors is also not complex. There is no problem of storing them because of their small size. Precautions are, however, needed against fungi or physical damage.

(*iv*) They have become very cheap today and any school can afford the cost of these projectors.

(*v*) They do not require complete darkness in the room as we do in using epidiascope or motion film projectors.

Limitations of Film Strips:

(*i*) They can be used only in small sized classes because of limited focal length. Modern projectors are, however, having large focal length.

(*ii*) Slide projection is not as effective as film projection. Inventions of 3D films have reduced the use of slides even further. In spite of this, fixed order of the film strips creates problem in handling individual frames.

(*iii*) Many schools do not have audio-visual workshops and thus, they depend on the cheap and unstandardized materials available in the market.

Film Projector

16 mm films are generally used for the purpose of training or teaching. These films are planned and executed by a pannel of experts who endeavour to prepare films of good quality.

As far as use of film projector for classroom teaching is concerned, it is very easy. Everything is automatic here. If electricity supply is not restricted, the film will not stop in the middle, after it is put on the projector.

Advantages of motion pictures :

(*i*) Motion pictures can especially be used for training purposes. Take the example of games and sports. If some actions of a player is wrong leading to defeat in the game, it can be corrected by viewing the films. After the game is over, the film of the game is later analysed to be discussed by the experts to bring in new strategies and tactics to counterplay.

(*ii*) In all training courses, perfection is needed everywhere. If action is recorded on films, we can see our own performance and remove our defects.

(*iii*) In the classroom teaching, motion pictures can highlight those aspects also that would have otherwise been missed. For example, by enlarging, close up and action replay techniques, motion pictures can highlight those movements also which are very minute and can be missed in ordinary situations.

(*iv*) Motion pictures are **multi-sensory technique** of instruction. It is because a combination of light, sound and actions are seen here.

(*v*) Motion pictures can develop imaginative and observational capacities of students simultaneously.

(*vi*) Whatever ideals are shown by the models in motion pictures are imitated by pupils and thus, good ideals and etiquettes can be developed in them.

(*vii*) They are helpful in giving clarity of concepts through concreteness and accuracy.

(*viii*) Facts and events related to industry, politics, history and geography and knowledge about scientific inventions, discoveries, laws and principles can be communicated to pupils very effectively through these motion pictures.

Kinescope

It is a sight and sound recording that can be made in the studio from the television screen for repeated use. What transcription is to radio, the kinescope is to TV. They are used for the following purposes :

(*i*) For delayed telecast.

(*ii*) For retelecast of the same programme.

(*iii*) For repeating the telecast when programme could not be seen due to failure of network.

(*iv*) For sending programmes abroad.

Only limitation of kinescope is that live element or spontaneity does not exist here.

It can be used in teaching learning process in the same way as television is used.

Epidiascope

Epidiascope is an equipment that can project all types of materials whether transparent or non-transparent (opaque). It has thus a twin facility and separate mechanism for projecting transparent and opaque materials.

In epidiascope, the word epi means 'upon' dia means 'through' and scope means 'projected material to be seen'.

While projecting a slide, beams pass through the slide and projects its image on the screen. In this way, transparent material is projected.

While projecting the opaque material the light bits upon the object which reflects the image on a very sensitive mirror and reflects the image of the opaque objects on the screen.

Despite the multipurpose functioning of this device, it is not very popular in educational institutions because of its poor quality image, total room darkening, very high need of energy, complexity of its use and poor range. It is to be installed in the middle of the class due to its low range, therefore, causing more interference than aiding something to the lesson. Because of its ability to project opaque objects on the screen, it is also known as opaque projector.

Overhead Projector (OHP)

Built on the basic principle of periscope, OHP is an important audio visual equipment. In the classroom it is placed in front of the teacher above his head to reflect an image on the screen (blackboard). This device consists of a strong energy source, (bulbs), fixed reflectors (mirrors), projection lens and a platen. This projector is called over head because the image goes over the head of the teacher and falls on the screen behind him. The teacher puts one slide over the other in order to give a sense of continuity of the subject matter projected on the screen.

Advantages of OHP : Its advantages lie in its special characteristics given below :

(*i*) No special training is required by the teacher to operate a projector.

(*ii*) OHPs are not very costly as compared to computers or film projectors.

(*iii*) It is handy and portable.

(*iv*) The image formed by the projector is also very bright and every pupil can see it. A 4 × 4 inches slide gives an image of 4 × 4 feet. This enlarged image is very easy to understand.

(*v*) It can create interests in pupils and hence it is a good motivator.

(*vi*) It is the best visual aid available to a teacher to supplement his oral teaching. He uses the screen of OHP as a blackboard without looking back. Transparencies, drawing, diagrams, figures and outlines etc. can be shown on the screen.

Television

TV differs from the radio in the sense that it is audio and visual both. We can see the incident occurring round the globe on it immediately after the occurrence of the incident through telecast. Thus, it is bisensory (multisensory) media. We get news, views and recreation through television in the same way as we do through the transistor but in a more compact and concrete way due to the facility of vision here.

As far as application of TV in education is concerned, it is still in the stage of infancy in India. It was only in 1961 that Indian television (Doordarshan) started a special service for schools in collaboration with the directorate of Education. This programme aimed at supplementing the regular classroom teaching in selected subjects. By 1972 only 400 schools of the capital received this telecast and two lakh students benefited from them. These programmes were telecast in the evening and on Sundays but there was no mechanism developed at that time to measure the effectiveness of such transmitting programmes.

After the introduction of distance education system in India, television is now regularly used as an instructional media. The enactment of Prasar Bharti Act is expected to boost the role of TV in the teaching learning process.

Advantages of television :

(*i*) It heightens the reality more than the physical presence. For example, if someone is watching a cricket match in a stadium, even then he can not see certain situations despite being present there. On the other hand, if he is viewing a match on a TV, he can see and analyse every situation by close up action replay. Thus, television experience may be more real than the actual one. It can show even those details which we can not see with the help of direct experiences. Thus, television can be used for all training programmes and behaviour of the trainees can be modified in the desired manner.

(*ii*) TV experiences are new and versatile. So, they can bring variety to classroom teaching by breaking monotony and strengthening the learning structures by its multisensory approach.

(*iii*) It widens the horizon of pupils' experiences by giving them upto date knowledge of the real situation and by making them conversant with the opinions of others.

(*iv*) It can motivate the pupils for learning by arousing and retaining their interest in the learning situation.

Limitations of Television:

(*i*) Speed of a television can not be changed as we can do in motion pictures.

(*ii*) A TV programme can not be adjusted to teaching and vice versa will have to be done. A teacher can take the help of video recording in such cases.

Tape Recorder and Audio Cassettes

Cassette type audio taps are available now which can play for 90 minutes on both sides. We can listen to our own recorded voice, recorded speeches of politicians and learned people, recorded poems of great composers, songs, music etc by the tape recorder.

Audio cassette recorder is used for the following purposes :

Such types of recording serve the following purposes:

(*i*) **Analysis of verbal messages :** Accuracy, speed and tone of verbal messages are studied here and if perfection is seen, reinforcement to the presenter is given.

(*ii*) **Drill and practice :** Accurate verbal messages are presented before the trainee for drill and practice.

(*iii*) **Teaching of specific skills :** Impressive oral presentation is actually a skill. This skill is taught to students through audio-recording in the individual and group situations.

(*iv*) **Speech improvement :** Style of speaking and phonetics can also be improved by using this technology.

(*v*) **Improvement in vocabulary :** Recorded verbal messages are full of many new words which pupils can learn by listening to the message.

(*vi*) **Recreation :** Many recorded songs and music entertain the listeners and remove their fatigue.

Radio

It is an important and easily accessable audio aid serving three important general purposes "news, views and recreation". It is the cheapest equipment of all and radio broadcast is now reachable to 100% population of the country. Pupils can get information about the incidents in any part of the globe immediately through radio. This increases their general awareness of the world. Students listen the ideas of learned people, politicians and educationists from across the world on the radio. This extends their own views and way of thinking. Apart from these, there are hundreds of programmes of music, songs and plays broadcast on the radio which entertain them round the clock.

Instructional Value of the Radio :

(*i*) It is a powerful means of developing listening comprehension.

(*ii*) It can also help the pupils to acquire correct pronunciation and phonetics like tape recorders.

(*iii*) Conversational style and language can be learned on the radio.

(*iv*) It improves word power of learners.

(*v*) Mass education goals can be achieved through radio broadcast. It was the realization of the people when radio came into being in 1917.

(*vi*) News listened on the radio can improve our general knowledge.

(*vii*) Radio listening does not require literacy. Even illiterates can take the benefit of it.

Radio Broadcast in India : The first radio station was established in India in July 1927 in Mumbai followed by one more station in Kolkata in the same year. This media is now able to penetrate to the remotest villages of the country and is covering more than 99% of the population.

School broadcasting in India was started in 1937. Radio broadcasting is now very much used for mass education as well as the education of school going children in selected areas. Central Institute for educational technology (CIET) under the supervision and control of NCERT produces quality radio broadcast programmes. Adult education Radio Programmes also started in 1956 to educate the adults in the age group of 15-35 in the vicinity of Pune as a project sponsord by UNESCO. Today, broadcast of adult education programmes are many under different titles. When Consumer Protection Act was passed in 1986, consumer education through radio was also given recognition. Today, it is a regular programme of all the radio stations in India. One more regular radio programme is the radio counseling programme of IGNOU which is broadcast from 4-5 pm on every Sunday.

Apart from these, radio broadcast is also making the people aware about various social and economic problems and people are also educated about how they can solve these problems.

Computer

It is the latest electronic device that is audio and visual both. It accepts data, performs operations on that data in sequence (decided by a programme) and outputs the results.

Computer in education : From input devices to output and its storage, computer has a wide range of applicability in education. In computers inputs are converted into output by a programme. Thus, input (data) plus programme form software or instructional programme. Inputs are converted into output in the CPU of the computer.

Computer always works according to the programme given to it. Whatever instruction or programme the students gives to the computers, it will always act accordingly and output will also come out on the same line. Application of computers in education can be understood by the following lines.

Videodiscs

This system is comprised of videodisc, where the information is stored, a video player and a TV set.

It is helpful in teaching learning process in the following ways :

(*i*) Students can get more informations through effective way of presentation.

(*ii*) By forwarding or reversing the CD player, learners can have access to any informations as many times as possible. This repeated action is necessary in understanding complex materials.

(*iii*) Live coverage given by the CD player can provide higher degree of motivation.

(*iv*) Auto stop system provided in the system can help those learners who study till late hours of night.

(*v*) The materials prepared by the effective teachers can be made available in the market for wide use.

Videotext

This system provides an interactive information retrieval service. It allows the home television to work as a computer terminal, which retrieves the textual material and graphic information from a remote data base.

Advantages of Videotext:

(*i*) It is useful for downloading the required information from a remote data base.

(*ii*) It raises the general awareness of learners.

(*iii*) The principal of a school can have access to any information about his or other schools any time if this system is available in the school.

(*iv*) It is especially useful for distance learning. A learner can connect himself with his study centre or regional office any time.

(*v*) It is free from time schedule. We can have any information any time.

(*vi*) Two way interaction between the teacher and the taught is possible here with the help of alphanumeric keyboard. The learner can address to his tutor by typing questions and sending it to the tutor. Once he receives the answer, he gets immediate feedback.

(*vii*) It is faster than telephone or telegram because user need not wait here in queue.

Teleconferencing

Teleconferencing is a two way broadcast system in which learners can interact with the programme through a local telephone. It is a powerful medium of instruction for distance education. In this system three or four subject experts sit at different places and participate in the discussion on the given subject matter. Here learners do not take part in the teaching-learning process directly. They only hear the programme on their radio set or TV. They can however, interact with the experts through telephone which is connected to the radio or TV station where the discussion is being organised.

Thus, teleconferencing involves the use of many media and allows interactive group communication by means of a two way broadcast. All such conferencing need good quality audio device to facilitate immediate interaction among the participants for exchange of views.

Advantages of Teleconferencing :

(*i*) **Effective for distance learning :** When groups of students are scattered over a large area of the country and it is not possible for them to interact with their teachers personally, then learning through teleconferencing is the best option for them.

(*ii*) **Interaction between the teacher and the taught possible :** As far as interaction between teachers and learners are concerned, this approach does not differ in any way from classroom teaching.

(*iii*) **High quality instruction :** Since, very learned people and experts of the subject take part in these discussions, the quality of the programme is never questionable.

(*iv*) **Immediate feedback :** Learners get answer of their questions immediately from the experts and their problem is solved. In this way, they get immediate feedback.

(*v*) **Flexibility :** Experts do not teach here on a pre-determined track. Their instruction and its way of presentation always changes according to the questions asked by learners. Thus, this approach is very flexible.

Internet

It is the abbreviation of international network. The computers connected to this system are automatically connected to world wide website(www). Due to this we can hear and see any programme available on website any time when we want to do so. If we have missed any television or radio programme, we can not have access to that programme again but if that programme is loaded on the website, we can repeatedly hear and see the programme. We will only have to log on the website of the programme producer and it will be available for us. The major advantage of this system is that it has made 24 hour communication possible especially between those countries which have great differences in their local timings such as India and America have a time difference of 10 ½ hours. When there is day time in India, offices are closed in America.

Applications of internet in education :

(*i*) We can get any information any time at home through internet on one hand and we can store the information by creating our own website on the other. Thus, it is not necessary to have immediate print out of the textual matter.

(*ii*) The two talking persons can see each other in face to face situations also through internet. Thus, a teacher can teach millions of students scattered across the world together.

(*iii*) Many educational institutions have created their educational websites. We can download any information about them any time by logging on these websites.

(*iv*) Internet has also its role to play in classroom teaching. Teacher can show any educational programme through internet any time according to his own convenience and he will not have to adjust his time table according to the programme as he does while using radio or television as aids.

(*v*) Latest teaching strategies and latest researches in different fields can be obtained through internet immediately and we need not have to wait for their publication in magazines and journals.

(*vi*) Books, magazines and newspapers are also published on internet and it has made our access to them easy. Any Indian living in Canada even can read "Amar Ujala" or "Times of India" daily.

(*vii*) Research material and encyclopaedias are also published on internet to facilitate learning process.

EVALUATION

Evaluation is the criteria of success or failure of a task done. If it is done at the end of a task, total efforts, including the investment of time and money may be a failure but if it goes side by side of the task, immediate feedback received might alarm the performer to rectify his mistakes and thus there is 100% chance of success of the programme.

Education is also an investment in the sense that time, energy and money are spent to bring about behavioural change in learners. That is why when a teacher performs his teaching works in his class, he also simultaneously finds out whether the changes in behaviour of learners are in concurrence with the learning objectives or not. If it is not so there, then what types of modifications are needed and at what steps of teaching. He also finds out whether the problem lies in his teaching strategies or techniques or it is there in the students itself. Thus, teaching and evaluation run-hand in hand. Evaluation determines the behaviour of students on one hand and testifies to the teaching of the teacher on the other. This very purposeful behaviour of the teacher is called evaluation in education.

Purpose of Evaluation

1. **Giving Details of Students' Progress** : Evaluation tells where a student is standing on the way to his destination of learning, how much he is ahead or behind his classmates, to what extent the behavioural changes occurred in him are acceptable, how far he can apply his present acquired knowledge to his future life or learning situations, at what point he is facing any difficulty and why and so on. Thus, evaluation here works like the diagnostic function of measurement.
2. **Predicting future achievement** : When evaluation covers the aptitude aspect of behaviour, it can predict the future performance of a student or a teacher on the basis of his present performance.
3. **Guidance and Motivation** : When a student comes to know about the actual position of his achievement, he gets motivated to do better. Besides, strengths and weaknesses of students become manifest through evaluation and a teacher can guide them accordingly.
4. **Improvement in the system** : Once proper guidance is given to students by the teacher after evaluation, teaching-learning process gets improved. A teacher can also come to know his own strength and weakness by the process and can change his own behaviour accordingly. Once he gets acquainted with his own shortcomings, he can remove them. Thus, process of evaluation is concerned with inputs and output both.
5. **Discovery of effective teaching strategies** : Evaluation opens the new avenues of action researches in the class. When a teacher does not get the desired result by adopting a particular combination of teaching strategies, he adopts another combination and this process continues until a final effective combination of teaching strategies is discovered.
6. **Classification of Students** : By evaluation process we can classify students into different groups like talented, bright, average, slow learners and poor and adopt different strategies of teaching for different groups. We can also give remedial treatment to weak students in the class only after thorough evaluation of them.
7. **Providing feedback to students and teachers both** : When a teacher comes to know the results of his efforts he gets feedback. If result is good, he is motivated if result is not satisfactory, feedback pushes him to change his behaviour. Similarly, knowledge of progress and the feedback received thereof motivate the students also.

Techniques of Evaluation

Evaluation is broader concept than measurement but no exact evaluation is possible without going through the process of measurement. All the three domains of behaviour are covered by evaluation, e.g.,

1. **Cognitive domain :** Oral, written, essay type, objective type tests, practical examinations and observation techniques etc. are used for evaluating cognitive domain.
2. **Affective domain :** This domain is evaluated by interest inventory, attitude scale, check list, rating scales and observation techniques.
3. **Psychomotor domain :** Performance tests, practical examinations and observation techniques are used to evaluate this domain (See optional paper II for Educational Objectives).

There are basically two techniques of evaluation:

A. Quantitative : These techniques are highly reliable and valid. Important such techniques are as follows:

1. **Oral :** These techniques are basically used at lower grades of teaching. At higher level of education too viva voce is used to test the lower levels of cognitive behaviour. Debates or drama can also be used for this purpose.
2. **Written :** Objective type tests, essay type tests and short answer questions are important written techniques to evaluate cognitive achievement of students. They give more accurate results than oral tests.
3. **Performance tests** : Here some works are assigned to students to accomplish them. Students practically do these works and then output is evaluated.

B. Qualitative : These techniques evaluate the quality of attributes and hence they are highly subjective. Important such techniques are given below:

1. **Cumulative Records :** Such records are prepared by the school to show all-round development of students individually. They reflect the total personality of the child, i.e., marks obtained by students in sessional tests and examinations, their participation in games, sports cultural programmes and other co-curricular activities, their regularity, punctuality, their etiquette.
2. **Anecdotal Records :** These records maintain the description of significant events or works of students. Here informations regarding the behaviour, attitudes or interests of students are systematically cumulated.

3. **Observation :** This is the most common technique of qualitative assessment of students. It is mostly used at lower grades of education. This is the only technique for the evaluation of classroom interaction.
4. **Check list :** This technique is used for evaluating attitude and affective domain of students. Here questions are given to students and they are asked to answer them in yes or no, e.g.,

   Item : 'Do you like doing mathematical sums-Yes/No.'
5. **Rating Scales :** Here some statements are given to students and agreed, indifferent or disagreed are written before the statements. Then students are asked to tick the option according to their own choice.

Types of Evaluation

1. Formative Evaluation : The purpose of formative evaluation is to monitor instructional process to know whether learning is taking place or not. It is designed to enhance and improve teaching-learning process and thus it becomes a continuous process in the school system.

These tests diagnose the weaknesses of students as well as teachers and thus, both of them can get feedback from these tests. Students and teachers both after identifying their difficulties change their behaviour and remove these difficulties. Thus, function of this evaluation is remedial in nature.

The second function of this evaluation is that if evaluation finds teaching-learning process satisfactory, it motivates the teachers and students to work harder for better results.

Tanner (1972) has defined formative evaluation in the following words :

"Formative evaluation refers to the use of tests and other evaluative procedures while the course and instructional programme is in progress."

Both criterion referenced and norm referenced tests are used to take the students to the mastery of the content. These tests are given in the following stages of learning.

I. At the end of each unit of the lesson.
II. At the end of each whole lesson.
III. At the end of each unit of the total course.

Advantages of Formative evaluation :

I. It provides sufficient information to teachers for modifying teaching.
II. It helps in formulating individual and group remedial programmes.
III. It provides feedback to students as well as teachers.
IV. It facilitates retention and transfer of training.
V. It enables the teacher to readjust his teaching according to the needs of the students.
VI. Students can also modify their behaviour after getting feedback from this evaluation.
VII. It gives reinforcement to high achievers.
VIII. It can work as a self-evaluation device for learners.

2. Summative Evaluation : This evaluation takes place at the end of the session to measure over all achievement of pupils. Annual, internal or external examinations are the examples of summative evaluation. The purpose of this evaluation is to certify fail or pass of the product. If formative evaluation is related to the process of teaching, it is related to the product of teaching. Here students are evaluated from the whole syllabus. On the basis of this evaluation, a decision is taken whether a student should be promoted to the next class or he should be kept in the same class again.

On the basis of above discussions we can say that summative evaluation works as a complement to formative evaluation and both of them combined together are necessary for all educational system.

Difference between Measurement and Evaluation:

1. Measurement process may be included in evaluation but evaluation may not necessarily include any measurement.
2. Evaluation is quantitative and qualitative both but measurement is always quantitative.
3. Evaluation is a comprehensive concept while measurement is a narrow concept. It means that measurement has no meaning without involving evaluation at least in psychology and education.
4. Evaluation is a continuous process in education while measurement is only a part of evaluation.
5. Evaluation always aims at improving the situation but measurement does not involve this purpose.
6. Evaluation provides descriptive as well as quantitative data regarding behavioural changes of pupils while measurement converts behavioural changes of pupils into numerals only.
7. Base of remedial teaching is evaluation not measurement.
8. Evaluation is more reliable, valid and objective than measurement.
9. Evaluation covers all the three domains of human behaviour while measurement covers only the cognitive aspects of human behaviour.
10. Evaluation is a value judgement process but measurement has no significance in itself unless data is compared with the criteria or norm.

11. Evaluation is basically concerned with the educational process while measurement is a universal phenomenon.

Characteristics of a Good Test (Evaluation)

If we want to measure an attribute accurately or we want to bring about an improvement in the evaluation process of pupils, we will have to keep this while constructing a test, i.e., test must possess the following characteristics. Good evaluation should also possess these very characteristics.

1. **Objectivity :** Objectivity means two things :
   (a) Whosover takes the test, attempts its items in the same manner. It is called objectivity in the test construction. The items of the test should not create any confusion in the minds of person being measured by the test.
   (b) Items (stimuli) are such that whosover evaluates them arrives at the same conclusion. It is called objectivity of scoring. It means that if marks are not influenced by the subjectivity of examiners, such tests are called objective tests.
2. **Reliability** : If the same test is given to the student again and again at different times, the examiner does not find any variation in the scores obtained by the examinee. It means that a test should assess a situation accurately free from any error.

   The basic difference between objectivity and reliability is that same test is evaluated by different examiners with no variation in scores in the former case but in the later case the same test is evaluated by the same examiner at different times but no variation is seen in the scores obtained.
3. **Validity** : A test should measure only what it is intended to measure, e.g., if a test wants to measure extroversion-introversion of the personality, it should measure nothing other than extroversion-introversion. Thus, purpose is always involved here. The test fulfils the purpose for which it has been designed.
4. **Discriminatory** : A test should be such as to discriminate poor, average and high achievers significantly. This is essential for giving proper guidance to students. It otherwise means that the scores obtained by a group of students in a given test should be such as to lay on normal probability curve.
5. **Comprehensive** : The items included in a test should fully represent all the aspects of a particular attribute so that complete information about a particular trait may be obtained. For example, if we are constructing an achievement test, it should cover all the three domains of human behaviour representing the whole course content or curriculum.
6. **Diagnostic** : A test should enable us to find out all the weaknesses of pupils' behaviour with reference to the course content. If we are able to diagnose the pin pointed difficulties of students, only then we can adopt remedial measures.
7. **Usability** : A test should be very easy to use for the person whosever wants to use it. Following points should be kept in mind for this purpose.
   I. Items included in the test should have the same meaning for different persons taking or evaluating the test. For example, Mr. B should also mean the same thing by the word " Natural instincts" as Mr. A means. It means that questions included in the test should have clear and objective language.
   II. Clear guidance should be given for administration of the test, e.g., maximum time limit should be specified beforehand.
   III. Methods of scoring and interpretation should also be made clear in advance in order to avoide subjectivity.
   IV. Norms or criterion should be given beforehand for the purpose of clear interpretation.
   V. No test in psychology or education can be universal in nature. Hence, its limitations such as the population to which sample belongs should be given.

Grading System

The strongest argument in favour of grading system is that it is a qualitative assessment of achievement of a student not a quantitative one. The strength of personality of a person is determined on the basis of his quality not quantity. Desirable change in the behaviour of a learner is determined on the basis of its quality and grades assigned to behavioural changes is the best parameter of determining quality.

In grading system, grades instead of marks are assigned to the examinee on the basis of quality of his answer. Various grades referring to various qualities are pre-determined. An example will illustrate this point in which various grades ranging from excellent to very poor are given.

Quality	Grades
1. Excellent	O
2. Very Good	A
3. Good	B
4. Satisfactory	C
5. Average	D
6. Poor	E
7. Very Poor	F

On the basis of the quality of the question, the examiner gives various grades to different examinees by keeping the parameters from excellent to very poor into account.

Semester System

When a particular course of study is divided into different equal parts not on the basis of the session but on the basis of months and examination is conducted after the completion of every part it is called semester system. For example, if course of study is of two years, four semesters may be there. A professional course which is of long duration, e.g., 4 ½ years, may have only three semesters of 1 ½ years durations each as we see in medical and engineering courses.

Need and Importance of Semester System :

(i) If it is not possible to divide the course on yearly basis due to technical reasons, the total course of study is divided into different semesters.

(ii) If there is no internal evaluation prevailing in the system, two semesters are arranged in one academic session in order to keep the student alert for their studies.

(iii) When duration of course is very long, ie, 4 ½ years and first part of the course can not be completed in one year, then a semester of one and half years is arranged for the students.

(iv) When so many subject papers are to be taught to students and every subject or paper needs only five or six months to complete, semester system is the best option.

(v) In semester system no arrangement for long vocation is made. Classes are held round the year without giving any break to students except for the period of examination. When course of study requires round the year study, semester system is the best option.

Limitations : Replacing annual system by semester system is nothing but old wine in a new bottle. Its demerits are as given below :

(i) Hectic examination activities are seen very frequently here if duration of a semester is short. It means that purpose of learning is to pass the examination and nothing else.

(ii) It suffers from all those defects which annual system of examination suffers Students starts their study only when the examination is near.

(iii) After the examination is over, students do not start their fresh study before they gets feedback from their examination results. Since declaration of results takes time, at least 20-30 working days are wasted after every semester.

(iv) In semester system papers are not set by internal teachers. They are sent to other universities for setting. This increases clerical work and may cause delay in the examination.

Continuous Internal Assessment

Continuous Internal Assessment (CIA) is a system in which the teacher who teaches the class sets examination papers, evaluates the answer sheets of students, declares the result in the class and gives, feedback to his students. This assessment procedure is not time bound. It goes side by side of teaching as a continuous process for regular improvement of the teaching-learning process. Five or six sessional tests conducted by school in an academic session is an example of CIA. Oral examinations are generally added to written ones in CIA.

Advantages of CIA

I. It gives regular feedback to the teacher who teaches the subject and he can remove his mistakes and weaknesses every time.

II. CIA can give us the trend of progress of a student, whether he is going up or he is coming down or he is stagnant at his progress. This will help the teacher to modify his strategies every time.

III. With the help of CIA the teacher can classify his students into different categories on the basis of their scores in tests and can adopt different strategies for different categories. Thus, backward students will be given more attention by the teacher.

IV. CIA goes along with teaching and only a small part of the syllabus is covered. Thus, it reduces the burden of examination from the shoulder of students. It does not create any stress or strain in the minds of students. They can take the test in an easy manner.

V. CIA motivates the students to study on a regular basis in order to improve achievement at every level. Thus, there is less chance of students', failure in the class. Problem of stagnation at the primary level can be solved by adopting this method.

PROBLEMS IN SCIENCE TEACHING

Science education at secondary level could not attract attention in terms of effort and investment. With increased emphasis on quality of primary education and renewed efforts to check high drop out rate in basic education, secondary level education now needs to be developed for comparatively heavy influx of students. The ESR's included a reform in science education at the secondary level by constructing science laboratories, provision of science equipment, revision of Science Curricula and professional development of Science and Mathematics teachers.

It is an accepted reality that the only road leading to national development passes through the area of education. One cannot name even a single profession where the role of education can be undermined. If education is viewed as the back bone and energising force for the national progress then how can the exalted and pivotal position of the teacher can be ignored who has been assigned the responsibility of education for the future generation. The education standard and professional competence of the teacher would always remain of primary concern and require top priority for having the fruit of educational enterprise in its true spirit.

Teachers are the torch bears in creating social cohesion, national integration and learning society. They not only disseminate knowledge but also create and generate new knowledge. They are responsible for acculturating role of education. No nation can even marginally slacken its efforts in giving necessary professional inputs to its teachers and along with that due status to their stature and profession.

The teacher is of paramount importance in the teaching learning process. He is a pivot in the system of education. The whole education system revolves around him, therefore he must always try to improve his teaching skills and motivate the pupil's while using various methods and techniques of teaching suitable for their learning. Since the teacher has been assigned a Herculean task of being the builders of nation, so he has to come up to fulfil the expectation of the parents, society and students as well. The prime aim of teachers is to impart right education and remove the signs of ignorance from all lifestyles. Yet teachers are expected to end ignorance because this is the only way to way to prosperity and to survive in dignified manner amongst the comity of nations. The educational system of any country hinges on the teacher, who occupies a pivotal position in its evolution as he has been assigned the responsibility of educating the future generation. The growing number of students and reports that are becoming available suggest that better education of teachers may be the most crucial input for the development of human resources in the country.

To develop an individual as a scientist, we will have to develop a suitable science curriculum, Laboratories, for our educational institutions and that will be only possible that we remove the problem faced by science teachers in secondary level.

- No Special classrooms available for science students.
- Classes are over crowded.
- Teachers are not properly trained for teaching the current science text at Secondary level.
- Teachers are not properly trained in practical laboratory work in science subjects at Secondary level.
- Only combined science laboratories are available for the students in school.
- Science teachers have not sufficient number of periods for practical.
- Due to limited time and resources, the study is being delimited to Public secondary schools.
- Design of the study is descriptive in nature. The researcher has to depend upon the literature available and structured questionnaire administered to secondary school science teachers working in the government schools.
- For the collection of data Questionnaire is more efficient in that it requires less time, less expensive and permits collection of data from much large sample. The Questionnaire are developed in the light of the objectives of the study and is responded on the basis of 'yes' 'No' and 'undecided' for obtaining the information from the sample secondary school science teachers.

REMEDIAL TEACHING

Remedial teaching is required to exceptional child. Exceptionals are the separate categories of people who have unique traits and characteristics genetically determined by the environmental factors which make them fundamentally different from the normals. These people are supposed to learn, perceive and adjust in ways which are unique to them.

Characteristics of Exceptional Children

On the basis of the concepts and definitions given

above following characteristics of exceptional children are inferred.

1. Exceptional children are those for whom uniform educational programmes do not suit. Hence, they need special instructional programmes or ancillary services or both.
2. Exceptionality is manifested by performance that is superior or inferior to that of the average children.
3. They deviate from the average (normal) people in both directions, plus and minus of mean physically, psychologically or socially and these deviations are significant to such an extent that their adjustment with the normals in some situations becomes difficult. Thus, exceptionality creates adjustment problem.
4. They come across learning difficulties in normal setting due to the defects and sometimes due to their superior qualities. These difficulties can be removed only by providing special instructional procedures unique to them.
5. If they are retarded or disabled in any area, their performance will be lower than the normal children and if they are superior in any trait significantly, the performance will be higher. Disabled children, however, come to the average performance when they are fully grown up and matured in their experience and drill.
6. The exceptionals are found in every society and culture almost in the same percentage of the total population. Sudden medical factors can, however, increase their numbers all of a sudden, e.g., spread of epidemics can increase their number.

Classification of Exceptional Children

(A) Classification on the basis of area or mode of deviations: This classification is more qualitative than quantitative. Exceptionals can be classified into the following categories on the basis of area of deviation.

1. Intellectual Deviance : Intellectual deviance may be in both directions from the mean. Mentally retarded comes on the minus side and gifted and creative come on the plus side from the mean. These two deviations are given below:

(a) Mental Retardation : They are less than 90 IQ on any intelligence test. They have special learning needs in areas requiring functional use of intelligence and adaptive behaviour. About 0.96% of the school going children is classified in this category.

(b) Giftedness and Creativity : These children possess IQ more than at least 110. Creatives differ from gifted in the sense that creative children perform in superb manner in one or two selected areas in original manner. These two types of children have special learning needs in areas requiring functional use of intelligence and artistic ability. About 3% of school going children come under this category.

2. Sensory Deviance : Here comes the hard of hearing, the deaf and dumb and visually impaired. There may be the people without the sense of taste or touch but we are not concerned with these people because they don't pose any social problem and hence they are not discussed in the category of exceptionals. Two important types of sensory deviance are given below:

(a) Visual Impairment : Under this category only those children legally come whose visual acuity is either zero (blindness) or less than 6/60 after correction (semi blindness). These children have special leaning needs in areas requiring functional use of vision. About 0.4 to 0.6 percent of school going children have been detected as visually impaired.

(b) Hearing Impairment : Audible capacity of these children are very low. Due to this reason, they have special learning needs in areas requiring functional use of hearing. About 0.11% school going children suffer from this problem across the world.

3. Motor Deviance : Crippled, orthopedically handicapped, speech and adjustment defectives, epileptics etc. come under this deviance. Two types of motor lisabilities are given here:

(a) Speech Impairment : Speech impairment is closely associated with hearing impairment because speech learning requires hearing. If speech development is nill or very close to nill, speech therapy or lip reading or reading on fingers is required.

(b) Orthopedic Impairment : These children have special learning needs in areas requiring functional use of hands, arms, feet, legs or other locomotive body parts. About 1% of the school going population is found to be orthopedically handicapped in India.

4. Personality deviance : Here children suffering from behavioural disorders and learning disabilities are included. For example, children suffering from neurosis or psychosis face serious problem of adjustment in social situations. Personality deviance can be classified into two categories:

(a) Leaning Disabilities : These children have special learning needs in areas requiring functional use of listening, speaking, reading, writing, reasoning and arithmetic skills. This is the largest category in special education in terms of percentage. About 4% school going children suffer from this problem. These children are normal in intelligence, even then they are very poor in learning.

(b) **Emotional Disorders :** These children lack proper emotional and social skills. When these children are treated by their peers, mates and teachers in a prejudiced manner, they become more disturbed emotionally and hence they need special attention by the teacher.

5. Educational Deviance : They are significantly different from the normals in academic achievement due to a variety of reasons in both directions. They can be classified into three categories:

(a) **Educationally bright :** Achievement level of these students is very high due to ve.y high level of adaptability to learning, assimilation of thoughts, understanding and memory. They can learn any subject matter in no time and they can retain it for a longer period of time. They are hardworking children in the field of learning.

Though educational achievement is directly related to intelligence yet intellectually gifted and educationally bright children are not the same. The reason is that high achievement in schools may be due to some other reasons also like future aspirations of students, high motivational level, hard labour done by pupils, guidance by parents etc.

(b) **Educationally Backward :** These children are backward by their age mates by 2 to 4 years or grades in the field of education due to repeated failure in different classes. This backwardness may be due to a number of reasons such as defective teaching learning process, low intellectual ability of learners, adjustment or emotional problems in the school. etc. These children need special treatment by the teacher in the classes and if problem is very serious, special classes should be arranged for them.

(c) **Communication Disorders :** These children are very poor in understanding the views of others and equally deficient in communicating their opinions to others either due to low level of intelligence or due to poor level of concentration power to the subject matter.

6. Social Deviance : Juvenile delinquents, (adult criminals) and maladjusted students come under this category. Ethnic minorities and the culturally suppressed people also come under this category. They deviate from the social norms due to a variety of reasons and constitute educational and social problems:

(a) **Maladjusted Children :** These children fail to adjust in their family, in the school and in the society and create the problem of adjustment for others also. If they are not properly dealt with, they will remain maladjusted leading to an isolated life.

(b) **Deprived Children :** Feeling of derivation develops in such a child only after seeing social, economic and cultural inequalities.

(c) **Juvenile Delinquents :** These adult criminals are antisocial elements in the sense that they violate the social norms and legal structure. Committing crime is a fun for them.

7. Traumatic Brain Injury : These injuries are caused by an external physical force or by an internal problem such as strokes. Children who are born with brain injuries are not included in this category.

8. Multiple Deviance : Many exceptional people deviate from the normal in more than one areas like a blind man is deaf also or personality deviance is associated with educational deviance etc. Such a multiple exceptionality is an automatic process also. For example, a sensory handicapped child is very badly treated by some people in the society. The exceptionals react to these behaviours very negatively and in a hateful manner and thus social deviance is slowly developed. These students have special learning needs in more than one areas.

Need and Importance

Provision of special education is a must to fulfil the following requirements in democratic countries.

1. When individual differences in learners are found to such an extent that all of them can not be benefitted in normal classes, they are put into the category of exceptionals for special learning arrangement. This is the responsibility of every democratic country to do its best for the maximum development of all its citizens. The handicapped can not be left unnoticed at the mercy of normal people for begging alms.
2. A severely deviant child is not supposed to take part in the routine activities meant for normal children. He will either be frustrated there or frustrate the others. Thus, the whole teaching learning process will be disturbed. Their proper adjustment of the society needs special leaning arrangements for them.
3. Gifted and talented children are the assets of the society. If they are not given proper opportunity to flourish in their own way, it will be the loss of the society itself.
4. Exceptional can not take the benefit of regular classes due to their unique needs and abilities. They need special curriculum, special teaching

strategy and special teacher to develop them to the fullest extent.

5. Creative and positive deviants are likely to turn into juvenile delinquents in future if they are not treated properly by the family, school and the society resulting in-law and order problem in the society.
6. Handicapped children will become a liability for the society if efforts are not made to educate and rehabilitate them. They can be proved to be productive in those areas where they are not disabled. For example, a blind person can he a good musician or a good teacher (communicator) though he is unable to perform in those areas which require activity of vision.
7. Deviant children generally feel problem of adjustment in normal educational setting. It will create tension in their minds and they may become deviant in other areas also.
8. Special education helps teachers, guardians, researchers and educational administrator to understand the special problems of these children.
9. Blind, deaf and dumb children are not supposed to learn properly in normal educational setting due to their unique respective problems. For example, normal children can learn more if visual aids are used in the class but such aids are useless for a blind child. He will rather need audio aids for increasing his rate of learning and it can not be provided in regular classes.
10. Educational and rehabilitational needs of these children are also different. If they are not properly educated or trained by applying special measures, their rehabilitation will not be possible.

Special Education with Reference to Family and Community

Practical shape of special education is given below:

(A) Special Education in the Context of the Family

A handicapped child first belongs to his family. He is made in future in the manner how he is responded and behaved by the family. The role of special education in the context of the family is being discussed below:

1. Effects of Handicapping Situation: The handicapping situation can influence and thus mould a child in the following ways.

(a) Psychological effects : It may cause the child to be deprived of certain abilities, e.g., the emotional and intellectual development of a two years old normal child will be more than that of a handicapped child. He may several times come to feel that his disability is a punishment and develop feeling of guilt. He may also develop feeling of hatred against his maker and thus he may hate whole human being. In this way he may either be aggressive to the environment or fearful of it.

(b) Physical Effects : Emotional outrage burst in the handicapped may cause physical illness, i.e., psychosomatic or neurotic problems are very commonly seen. Similarly, if child is maladjusted in the family or in the society, his parents may also face the difficulty of adjustment. If he is given more attention in the family than the normals, then the unique relationship developed between the parents and the handicapped child can create new problems for normal children in the family also. Moreover, if the material environment of the child is impoverished as we generally see (handicapped are mostly found in poor families), then the perceptual conceptual bricks with which he should build the whole framework of cognition will be very weak. Apart from these, due to impairment, physical and psychological changes of puberty and growth in height, weight and sexual traits may be delayed.

(c) Parental Reactions to a Defective Child and Development of the Child. Parents react to these children in the following ways:

*(i) **Realistic (coping with the situation)** :* They may adopt a realistic attitude towards the problem and does not try to hide anything. This type of reaction is useful for parents and the child both. They will help and guide the child in the desired manner. They will not put extra burden on the child due to extra expectations.

*(ii) **Denial of the reality of handicap** :* Handicap if occurred in the family is a reality but in most of the time denied by parents due to shame or stigma attached to the disability in the society. It is useful for parents to some extent as it helps them in bringing the mind into balance but excess denial of reality is fatal.

*(iii) **Self pity-more than the desired care for the child** :* This is a type of over protection given to the child on account of pity. He may start questioning or suspecting God, why he has made a blind or paralysed child for him or 'what wrongs did he do that made him liable to be punished in this way' etc. Thus parents may either become atheistic or they may take solace in their religious beliefs.

(iv) Ambivalence-toward the child: Additional responsibilities, anxieties and irritations caused by such children which become a routine part of their life produce ambivalent parental reactions. Parents accept and love their children due to the natural love created by the blood but they also reject and hate them at the same time.

(v) Projection of the difficulty: Anxiety relating to unacceptable feelings of resentment, hatred and hostility can be minimized by blaming someone else for the handicapping situation of their child, e;g., other children, doctors, teachers, or the marriage arranged by their elders in blood relations can be blamed resulting in a handicapped child in the family. This is known as projection. Handicapped are mostly found in muslims due to probably the marriages between close relations.

(vi) Feeling of Guilt and Shame : Shame involve\s the expectation of ridicule or criticism from others while guilt involves self blaming or personal regret. When such feelings develop in parents, they try to avoid social situations resulting in slow social development of the child also.

(vii) Pattern of Mutual Dependency : The future development of the child depends upon the experiences that he receives at home and in the school. If he is fully cared by the parents and given chance to be exposed in social situations, his experiences will hike. Contrary to this if there is big distance between the child and his parents, the child will lose self confidence, though, he will try to develop self confidence in him.

(d) **Sexual Adjustment :**Sexual adjustment to a large extent depends on the social relationship ranging from love and friendship to increasing social horizons. If the child is not getting proper chance of socialization, his sexual adjustment with his/her life partner will always be at stake.

(e) **Economic Adjustment :** Economic self reliance is necessary for self respect and may be essential to lead a married life also. If he is not given extra educational facilities by considering his specific impairment, he will not be fully adjusted in the society vocationally or economically.

2. Guidance and Counselling of Parents of a handicapped child : The family counsellor, the expert in education, paedriatist and the psychologist have their respective role to play in this regard. The service of these experts are needed for proper development of the child. As we know, the influence of the family on the over all development of the child is three times powerful to any other institution. Due to this reason, the idea of a continuous consultative relationship between a well qualified person and the family has been advocated. The major areas of counselling are as follows :

(a) **Intellectual Area :** Here the parents need information concerning the nature and the degree of the exceptionality of the child, i.e., diagnostic information. They are also supposed to know the cause of the handicap to avoid future occurrence of disability in the family, i.e., etiological information. They also need information about how to treat the problem to the maximum level possible and how to educate the child, i.e., remedial informations. Parents need all these three informations together.

(b) **Emotional Area:** The counsellor must remove the parents' fear and anxieties and also their feeling of guilt and shame. He should also endeavour to minimize the emotional vulnerability of the family members though he can not eliminate all these types of tensions altogether. If only the counsellor is able to increase their ability to tolerate them, his job is over.

(c) **Behavioural Area :** The counsellor uses the techniques of psychotherapy to mould the behaviour of parents, to understand the problems and to deal with them more adequately. They are also told by the counsellor how they will behave their handicapped child so that he may properly adjust in the society.

(B) Special Education In the Context of the Community

Democratic base of special education-Equal opportunities of education and employment for handicapped.

Equality of opportunities for handicapped means right to education. It is a human right approved by the UN Charter and it is in this context that handicapped children should be assured the facilities to attain equality and to make them at part with other people. For this purpose, they may be provided with special facilities for assistance, protection and rehabilitation.

This concept is developed on the belief that if they are given the right opportunities and the facilities commensurable with their deviance, they are fully capable of developing their residual capacities, powers and traits to the fullest extent and of becoming economically independent and socially self reliant. They need only special care not alms.

If the above concept is applied to education, they will have the equal right to get education in the same manners as normals have. In Indian context, it has been enshrined in our constitution that each and every child in the age group of 6-14 years has the fundamental right to receive free and compulsory education in the country. Before 2002 it was only a directive principle of the state policy under Article 45(A) of the Indian constitutions.

Since, handicapped lag behind the normals due to a variety of reasons, they are given three percent reservation for the admission in schools and colleges and for employment in government run installations and offices. This reservation is not against the principle of equality because of the following reasons.

(i) They are deficient in some respects leading to poor academic achievement. This deficiency cannot be overcome even by providing facilities to the maximum level possible.

(ii) They need special protection for their economic independence. If such protection is not given to them, they will not be able to survive in today's age of competition and hard struggle for means of livelihood.

(iii) Many backward and deprived communities in India have been endowed with reservation facilities and handicapped are the most backward of all the backwards.

(iv) It is their right to get extra facilities for their education and employment from the state. It is not their fault in any way that they have become handicapped. It may be the fault of their parents or other people of the society. In this sense, if special provisions are not made for them, they will be penalized for no guilt.

(v) If special provisions are not made for them, they may become a burden on the society.

MULTIPLE CHOICE QUESTIONS

1. Which one of the following alternatives is correct in reference to definition of Education technology?
(*a*) It is a self-directed technique which assists in teaching-learning process
(*b*) It is the software of teaching and learning
(*c*) It is only related with the process aspect of education
(*d*) It is the science of arriving at results

2. Education technology has three basic aspects—
(*a*) Inɒut—Process—output
(*b*) Input—organisation—process
(*c*) Input—Process—Communication
(*d*) None of the above

3. Hardware Approach consists of—
(*a*) Understanding of teacher's behaviour and learning principles
(*b*) Exchange among students
(*c*) Reduction in the educational load of the students
(*d*) Only (*b*) and (*c*)

4. Educational technology provides desirable educational situations, therefore it focusses its attention on—
(*a*) Educational objectives
(*b*) Evaluation process
(*c*) Best methods of instruction
(*d*) All the above

5. The contribution of Educational technology in the field of teacher education is—
(*a*) Micro teaching
(*b*) Mini teaching
(*c*) Simulated teaching
(*d*) All the above

6. The teaching process in educational technology has form steps as—
(*a*) Planning—organisation—forwarding and control
(*b*) Planning—preplanning—organisation and control
(*c*) Preplanning—pre-teaching—evaluation and feedback
(*d*) None of the above

7. When educational technology is employed for the obtaining of educational objectives through teaching techniques and tactics it is called—
(*a*) Instructional technique
(*b*) Teaching technology
(*c*) Behaviour technology
(*d*) All the above

8. Programmed Learning can be classified under—
(*a*) Instructional technology
(*b*) Teaching technology
(*c*) Systems Analysis
(*d*) None of the above

9. The Educational technology has reduced the load of the teachers in the area of—
(*a*) Information communication
(*b*) Organisation of Learning experiences
(*c*) Arrangement of Learning experiences
(*d*) Evaluation of Learning experiences

10. The stage comes after the determination of objectives is—
(*a*) Selection and application of teaching
(*b*) Evaluation of the learner activities
(*c*) Feed-back of the learner
(*d*) Reorganisation of learning process

11. Education has established relationship because—
(*a*) Explosion of new knowledge with fast pace
(*b*) The explosive growth in world population
(*c*) Critical change in social perspective due to the development of science and technology
(*d*) All the above

12. The educational technology is the integrated whole of—
(*a*) Medium (*b*) Methods
(*c*) Techniques (*d*) All the above

13. The implication of technology in education is related with—
(*a*) Application of hardwares
(*b*) Application of softwares
(*c*) Application of Systems Analysis
(*d*) None of the above

14. Instructional technology is used for—
(*a*) The students
(*b*) The teachers
(*c*) Both of the above
(*d*) None of the above

15. To bring change in behaviour is the objective of—
(*a*) Instructional technology
(*b*) Teaching technology
(*c*) Behaviour technology
(*d*) None of the above

16. The objective of the development of interaction between the teacher and the students is of—
(*a*) Teaching technology
(*b*) Instructional technology
(*c*) Behaviour technology
(*d*) All the above

17. Development of coginitive aspect of behaviour is the main objective of—
(*a*) Behavioural technology
(*b*) training technology
(*c*) Instructional technology
(*d*) Educational technology

18. Emphasis on Self-learning is given in—
(*a*) Instructional technology
(*b*) Teaching technology
(*c*) Behavioural technology
(*d*) None of the above

19. Effective teachers are prepared through—
(*a*) Educational technology
(*b*) Instructional technology
(*c*) Teaching technology
(*d*) Behavioural technology

20. Immediate feed-back is proved to be very significant in—
(*a*) Micro-teaching
(*b*) Programmed instruction
(*c*) Tele-conferencing
(*d*) Personalised System of Instruction

21. Teaching models are developed on the basis of—
(*a*) Teaching theory
(*b*) Instructional models
(*c*) Learning theories
(*d*) Learning strategies

22. The Teaching models are affected by—
(*a*) Social values
(*b*) Educational philosophy
(*c*) Psychological principles
(*d*) (*a*) and (*c*)

23. Which one of the following is a correct statement?
(*a*) Teaching Models are of 3 types—voluntary, involuntary and acceptable
(*b*) Teaching Models create only voluntary and instructional effect
(*c*) Teaching Models produce only acceptable effects
(*d*) None of the above

24. Which one of the following is a correct statement?
(*a*) A teacher should employ one teaching model at a time
(*b*) A teacher should employ various teaching models during his teaching as per the conditions
(*c*) A teacher should employ new teaching models in order to enhance achievement
(*d*) A teacher should employ and two models in his teaching

25. Behavioral system model focuses upon—
(*a*) Specific voluntary behaviour
(*b*) Specialised behavioural development
(*c*) Specific behavioural changes substitution and previous knowledge
(*d*) None of the above

26. Information model gives importance to
(*a*) Cognitive aspects
(*b*) Affective aspects
(*c*) Psycho-motor domain
(*d*) All the above

27. Micro-teaching is a—
(*a*) Classroom teaching process
(*b*) Teacher-training method
(*c*) Personal-instruction process
(*d*) Group instruction process

28. Micro-teaching is a process which is formulated for—
(*a*) Maximum learning in minimum time
(*b*) Improving teaching skills
(*c*) Improving teaching skills and their development
(*d*) All the above

29. Feed-back is a process which signifies—
(*a*) A child can learn through imitation
(*b*) A child adjust his behaviour in order to his errors
(*c*) A child exhibits specific behaviour patterns
(*d*) A child imitates his elders

30. Which of the following statement is correct for micro-teaching?
(*a*) To use modern techniques for qualitative improvements of the teachers
(*b*) To use modern techniques for the training of specific teaching skills
(*c*) To use modern techniques for individualised instruction
(*d*) To formulate flexible planning and group techniques for specific instruction

31. Micro-teaching is primarily based on the teaching maxim of—
(*a*) From complete to incompleteness
(*b*) From whole to part
(*c*) From concrete to abstract
(*d*) From Abstract to concrete

32. Teaching is an interactional process in which the classroom statements are included. This definition expresses—
(*a*) The nature of teaching in autocratic set up
(*b*) The nature of teaching in democratic set up
(*c*) The nature of teaching is laissez faire set up
(*d*) None of the above

33. Which one of the following is not the quality of teaching?
(*a*) Teaching makes learning process more effective
(*b*) Teaching has psychological foundation
(*c*) Teaching guides the students
(*d*) Teaching can be done by any person

34. The Chief characteristic of good teaching is—
(*a*) to provide Auto-learning conditions
(*b*) to make Effective planning
(*c*) to promote democratic principles
(*d*) All the above

35. Teaching-learning process fundamentally completed in—
(*a*) Class room (*b*) School
(*c*) Society (*d*) Home

36. Learning can be defined as—
(*a*) Acquisition of new knowledge and responses
(*b*) A process of gradual adjustment and accomodation
(*c*) Ability to learn
(*d*) All the above

37. Teaching process's intervening variable is associated with—
(*a*) Content
(*b*) Teaching method
(*c*) Teaching strategy
(*d*) All the above

38. The objective of the remedial activities of the teacher in a classroom is—
(*a*) To diagnose the difficulties of the students
(*b*) To arrange and analyse the content of teaching
(*c*) To relate the content with previous learning of the students
(*d*) All the above

39. The evaluative work of teaching variable is—
(*a*) Construction of a criterion test
(*b*) Evaluation of behavioural change
(*c*) Both of the above
(*d*) None of the above

40. The remedial function of teaching is not associated with—
(*a*) The analysis of teaching problem
(*b*) The determination of previous knowledge of the students
(*c*) The knowledge of individual differences
(*d*) Construction of Criterion-referenced test

41. Interactive stage of teaching includes—
(*a*) Linguistic abilities
(*b*) Students performance
(*c*) Expression of abilities
(*d*) All the above

42. The main teaching activity takes place in pre-active stage of teaching is—
(*a*) Formulation of objectives
(*b*) Selection of content
(*c*) Decision of teaching style
(*d*) All the above

43. The contribution of feed-back and reinforcement is—
(*a*) To enhance the frequency of desired behaviour
(*b*) To create obstacle in desired behaviour
(*c*) They do not express any role in desired changes
(*d*) None of the above

44. The mutual relationship between education and teaching is—
(*a*) Education is a comprehensive concept while teaching is a narrow concept
(*b*) Education is a life-long process but teaching is a class room function
(*c*) Education has national/international perspective but teaching gets its aims from it
(*d*) All the above

SCIENCE

45. Teaching and learning are related—
(a) With deep bond
(b) Fractional share
(c) In vague form
(d) Indirectly to each other

46. The knowledge of teaching-learning helps a teacher—
(a) In attainment of objectives
(b) In developing teaching skills of pupil teachers
(c) In evaluating teaching
(d) All the above

47. The quality of teaching strategy is based on—
(a) Definite teaching model
(b) Teachers skills
(c) Scientific nature to teaching
(d) All the above

48. The micro-teaching is related with—
(a) Teaching strategy
(b) Teaching method
(c) Teaching models
(d) All the above

49. The foundation of democratic teaching strategies is—
(a) Democratic value
(b) Psychological value
(c) Both of the above
(d) None of the above

50. The precaution observed in application of Question-answer strategy is—
(a) The clarity in questions
(b) The inter–relationship in questions
(c) The simplicity in questions
(d) All the above

51. The function of a teacher primarily is that of a—
(a) Service-station attendant, filling students with knowledge
(b) Minister, tending to the personal and spiritual needs of children
(c) Guide, helping the child progress toward maximum growth
(d) Director, organizing and planning worthwhile exprediences for the class

52. Educators feel that the greatest challenge in teaching lies in—
(a) Obtaining adequate financial renumeration
(b) Aiding children to grow and find themselve
(c) Fostering the personal growth of the teacher
(d) Obtaining security in the teaching profession

53. The function of the teacher in the democratic classroom is to—
(a) Allow students completely free choice without any interference or suggestion
(b) Try to prevent situations from arising in which it is necessary for students to choose among alternatives
(c) Tell students, what are intelligent choices among various alternatives
(d) Help students to become more capable of making intelligent choices among increasingly significant alternatives

54. The most important function of the teacher is to—
(a) Maintain a order
(b) Impart subject-matter
(c) Teach problem-solving techniques
(d) Guide pupil's growth

55. The most important task in teaching is—
(a) Making assignments and hearing recitations
(b) Directing pupils in development of experiences
(c) Scoring test papers and giving outgrades
(d) Making monthly reports and keeping records

56. The teacher's responsibility with regard to standards is to—
(a) Set up standards for the members of the class
(b) Help children to set standards for themselves individually and collectively
(c) Enforce for each child the standards set by the school
(d) Set a programme of effective instruction and learning whithout regard to standards

57. The teacher's responsbility with regard to teaching meterials is to—
(a) Choose all teaching materials to be used in his classroom
(b) Accept without question, whatever materials are provided
(c) Use a few materials as possible as to save money
(d) Participate in the selection, ordering and handling of teaching materials

58. Parents expect teachers to show, above all else—
(a) Fairness in evaluating their children
(b) Wide knowledge in subject areas
(c) Sincere interest in their children
(d) Strictness in classroom discipline

59. The best way to establish rapport with your class is to—
(a) Demand the respect due your age and status
(b) Remain aloof, be a figure of authority
(c) Impress your students with your knowledge and skill
(d) Play the role of a guide who desires to help them

60. The best learning procedure in teaching children is to have them—
(*a*) Read about the way an activity can be performed
(*b*) Write about the way an activity can be performed
(*c*) See an activity as it is being performed
(*d*) Perform the activity themselves

61. Indian science teaching is mostly affected by—
(*a*) England (*b*) France
(*c*) Canada (*d*) Germany

62. By which method the students learn to the maximum extent?
(*a*) By seeing (*b*) By reading
(*c*) By listening (*d*) By doing themselves

63. Which quality of the teacher is liked the most by the students?
(*a*) Punctuality
(*b*) Impartiality
(*c*) Love for discipline
(*d*) Dominance

64. What should the teacher do to maintain the interest of students in class teaching?
(*a*) Maximum use of blackboard
(*b*) Extensive use of examples from the practical life
(*c*) Extensive use of teaching materials/aids
(*d*) Giving ample opportunity to students for discussion/delibrations

65. Children with disability must get education because—
(*a*) They are vulnerable
(*b*) They have special needs
(*c*) It is a basic constitutional right
(*d*) They are poor

66. Which of the following is a sensory disorder?
(*a*) Hearing Impairment
(*b*) Mental Retardation
(*c*) Cerebral Palsy
(*d*) Neuro Muscular Disorder

67. Learning depends on—
(*a*) Intelligence (*b*) Parental attitude
(*c*) Peer attitude (*d*) None of these

68. Which of the following can increase the quality of education?
(*a*) To extend one hour time period
(*b*) Service period teacher training
(*c*) Solution and treatment teaching
(*d*) By help-books

69. Which cannot be the stage of learning?
(*a*) Procedure
(*b*) Difference perception
(*c*) Exercise
(*d*) Imagination

70. Which of the following is decisive for teaching work?
(*a*) To make effective the excellence
(*b*) To educate
(*c*) True management of classes
(*d*) Communication with students

71. What will be the indication when a group of students gets more marks in the question paper made by any teacher?
(*a*) It is a group of high achiever
(*b*) Teacher has tought well
(*c*) Question-paper is good
(*d*) None of these

72. Choose the one which best expresses the meaning of the word 'Condone'.
(*a*) Grieve (*b*) Endure
(*c*) Forgive (*d*) Ignore

73. Study of science gives birth of which aspect?
(*a*) Universal (*b*) Social
(*c*) Limited (*d*) National

74. The objectives of science are determined by—
(*a*) experimentation (*b*) Puntuality
(*c*) adequacy (*d*) All of these

75. The main objective of science teaching is—
(*a*) Social (*b*) Cultural
(*c*) Disciplinary (*d*) All of these

76. Schools should be concerned with the development of child, which should include—
(*a*) Acquisition of knowledge by the child
(*b*) Acquisition of life skills by the child
(*c*) Acquisition of skills required by the nation
(*d*) Acquisition of skills required by the healthy person

77. A student gives a partially correct respond to your question. Then you will—
(*a*) Seek further information
(*b*) Provide reinforcement
(*c*) Reframe your question
(*d*) Tell the correct information

78. Which of the following is/are productive skill/skills?
(*a*) Speaking (*b*) Writing
(*c*) Both (*a*) and (*b*) (*d*) None of the above

79. The first step in scientific temperament is—
(*a*) Data Collection
(*b*) Defining Problem
(*c*) Experiancing Problem
(*d*) Analysing Problem

80. An organisation for development of science teaching at state level is—
(*a*) NCERT (*b*) UNESCO & UNICEF
(*c*) SCERT (*d*) All of these

81. Teaching aids are useful because they—
(*a*) help teacher's work
(*b*) activate all senses

SCIENCE

(c) help students to be attentive
(d) make learning more meaningful

82. Teaching would be more effective if the teacher—
(a) Makes his intent purposeful
(b) Is master of the subject
(c) Uses various instructional aids
(d) Declares his objectives in the beginning

83. The word 'Tacit' means—
(a) Formal (b) Fear
(c) Silent (d) Celestial

84. UNESCO organised a survey for science and math teaching first time in India in—
(a) 1948 (b) 1964
(c) 1968 (d) 1945

85. Which of the following can be exhibited in science fair/exhibition?
(a) Films related to science
(b) Picture and models
(c) Informations related to science
(d) All of these

86. The teacher-child relation should:
(a) Allow children to express their feelings
(b) Share their trials and triumphs
(c) Be responsive and reach out to children
(d) All of the above

87. Student's learning difficulties can be best addressed by—
(a) Advising them to work hard
(b) Suggesting private tuitions
(c) Supervised study in the library
(d) Remedial teaching

88. For being successful in life students should be encouraged to—
(a) selective study
(b) casual study
(c) intensive study
(d) learning by rote memorisation

89. Students who bring out alternative solutions and cite the books not prescribed by the teacher should be—
(a) discouraged
(b) encouraged
(c) advised to talk to the teacher outside the class
(d) advised to follow the class notes to score better in the examinations

90. Problem of school dropouts can be effectively tackled by—
(a) reducing curriculum load
(b) teachers empathy
(c) attractive school environment
(d) providing incentives

91. Education helps a child to develop his/her
(a) Emotional intelligence
(b) Social intelligence
(c) Career skills
(d) All of the above

92. Role of a teacher is necessary for the development of:
(a) Educational development of children
(b) Intellectual development of children
(c) Emotional development of children
(d) All of the above

93. Remedial teachers should observe the following when dealing with the behaviour problems of pupils—
(a) should always pay attention to their misbehaviour
(b) always observe the performance of pupils in class and their behaviour in groups
(c) give positive reinforcement to pupils good behaviour
(d) refer the cases to student Guidance Officers/ teachers for follow up action

94. Which of the following is not a type of an experiment?
(a) Trial and Error experiment
(b) Laboratory experiment
(c) Natural experiment
(d) Hypothesis

95. In a teaching-learning process factors related to content are
(a) Nature of contents
(b) Selection of contents
(c) Organization of content
(d) All of the above

96. Usual teaching-learning processes can be supplemented by the following to improve the quality—
(a) Extra coaching
(b) Diagnostic and remedial teaching
(c) Enrichment programmes
(d) Inservice teacher education

97. School based evaluation can solve the problem of—
(a) Mass copying
(b) Student's indiscipline
(c) Unrealistic assessment
(d) Teacher's social reputation

98. What are the factors related to learner that affects the learning
(a) Learners physical and mental health
(b) Level of aspiration and achievement motivation
(c) Readiness and willpower
(d) All of the above

99. In a group situation generallly the performance of a student
(a) Remains same (b) Become better
(c) Deteriorate (d) None of these

100. Pedagogy is considered to be the—
(*a*) Science of Teaching
(*b*) Art of Learning
(*c*) Science of Communication
(*d*) Art of Assimilation

101. Inductive approach of teaching means—
(*a*) initiating the child to new subject
(*b*) teaching through specific instruction
(*c*) group learning as opposed to individualised learning
(*d*) arriving at generalisations with the help of examples

102. In a process of learning, transfer of learning can be
(*a*) Positive (*b*) Negative
(*c*) Zero (*d*) All of these

103. Which of the methods can be adopted by a teacher to develop creativity in his/her students?
(*a*) By giving freedom to respond to pupils
(*b*) By giving opportunity for ego development
(*c*) By encouraging originality and flexibility
(*d*) All of the above

104. Which of the following conditions must be satisfied in order to designate a person mentally retarded?
(*a*) Sub-normal intellectual functioning
(*b*) Very poor adaptive ability
(*c*) Dependability on others
(*d*) All of these

105. The best measure of identifying mildly mentally retarded is—
(*a*) Administration of standardized intelligence test
(*b*) Administration of behaviour test
(*c*) Administration of adjustment test
(*d*) A combination of all

106. Physical trauma during pregnancy may cause
(*a*) Mental retardation
(*b*) Blindness
(*c*) Deafness
(*d*) All of these

107. All of the following may cause mental retardation except
(*a*) Blood incompatibility
(*b*) Action of toxic agent
(*c*) Radio-activity
(*d*) None of these

108. Dullers do not differ from normal children in—
(*a*) Physical characteristics
(*b*) Level of social expectancy
(*c*) Both of these
(*d*) None of these

109. Which of the following things is not required for educating mildly mentally retarded children?
(*a*) Regular counselling
(*b*) Remedial teaching
(*c*) Modification in the curriculum
(*d*) Regular evaluation

110. Teaching of which of the following skills is not suitable to borderline cases?
(*a*) Electric fitting
(*b*) Repairing of electric or electronic equipments
(*c*) Oratory skills
(*d*) Activity based skills

111. Morons are slow in—
(*a*) Physical growth
(*b*) Thinking and planning
(*c*) Taking initiative
(*d*) All of these

112. Unsatisfactory relation of a mentally retarded child with the environment is technically called—
(*a*) Autism (*b*) Maladjustment
(*c*) Pseudo-dullness (*d*) None of these

113. Learning disabled children are—
(*a*) Deficient in using potentials
(*b*) Low in intelligence
(*c*) Slow in activity
(*d*) None of these

114. Learning disability is related to—
(*a*) low listening and comprehension power
(*b*) poor ability of expression
(*c*) poor ability of mathematical operation
(*d*) All of these

115. Learning disabled children perform very poorly in—
(*a*) Academic areas (*b*) Technical areas
(*c*) Both of these (*d*) None of these

116. Problem of learning disability is more complex than that of other disabilities because—
(*a*) Its causes can not be easily ascertained by applying usual tests
(*b*) It is associated to behaviour problems
(*c*) Both of these
(*d*) None of these

117. In your opinion which of the following plans should be adopted for the education of the gifted children?
(*a*) Separate schools
(*b*) Ability grouping
(*c*) Enrichment programmes
(*d*) All of the above

118. In which of the following physical characteristics learning disabled children differ from the normal ones?
(*a*) They are all the time clumsy and awkward
(*b*) Poor coordination of motor abilities
(*c*) Height, weight and health
(*d*) All of these

119. Which of the following methods is most suitable for learning disabled children?
(*a*) Behaviour guidance method
(*b*) Remedial teaching
(*c*) Brain storming
(*d*) None of these

120. In order to improve work habits of learning disabled what should be done?
(*a*) Unattending behaviour should be penalized
(*b*) Close monitoring of the behaviour is needed
(*c*) Cues and prompt should be given
(*d*) All of these

121. Which of the following situations may lead to educational backwardness?
(*a*) Sensory impairment
(*b*) Motor disability
(*c*) Long diseases and health problems
(*d*) All of these

122. Which of the following factors are necessary for the overall development of child
(*a*) Emotional development
(*b*) Physical growth and development
(*c*) Social development
(*d*) All of the above

123. Which of the following measures should be adopted by the teacher to check educational backwardness?
(*a*) Continuous evaluation and regular feedback
(*b*) Remedial teaching
(*c*) Adjustment and behaviour training
(*d*) All of these

124. Teaching by small steps and frequent short assignment techniques are useful for—
(*a*) Slow learners
(*b*) Learning disabled
(*c*) Educationally backward children.
(*d*) Children of all types of disabilities

125. Special schools are required for backward children when—
(*a*) Backwardness is due to any serious physical handicap
(*b*) The size of population of backward children in the society is very large as is the case of Gujarat where the achievement of students in mathematics is always seen very low
(*c*) Both of these
(*d*) None of these

ANSWERS

1	2	3	4	5	6	7	8	9	10
(*d*)	(*a*)	(*d*)	(*d*)	(*d*)	(*a*)	(*d*)	(*b*)	(*a*)	(*a*)
11	**12**	**13**	**14**	**15**	**16**	**17**	**18**	**19**	**20**
(*d*)	(*d*)	(*a*)	(*c*)	(*c*)	(*c*)	(*c*)	(*a*)	(*a*)	(*b*)
21	**22**	**23**	**24**	**25**	**26**	**27**	**28**	**29**	**30**
(*c*)	(*c*)	(*a*)	(*b*)	(*c*)	(*a*)	(*b*)	(*c*)	(*b*)	(*b*)
31	**32**	**33**	**34**	**35**	**36**	**37**	**38**	**39**	**40**
(*a*)	(*b*)	(*d*)	(*d*)	(*a*)	(*d*)	(*d*)	(*d*)	(*c*)	(*d*)
41	**42**	**43**	**44**	**45**	**46**	**47**	**48**	**49**	**50**
(*d*)	(*d*)	(*a*)	(*d*)	(*a*)	(*d*)	(*d*)	(*a*)	(*c*)	(*d*)
51	**52**	**53**	**54**	**55**	**56**	**57**	**58**	**59**	**60**
(*c*)	(*b*)	(*d*)	(*d*)	(*b*)	(*b*)	(*d*)	(*c*)	(*d*)	(*d*)
61	**62**	**63**	**64**	**65**	**66**	**67**	**68**	**69**	**70**
(*a*)	(*d*)	(*b*)	(*c*)	(*c*)	(*d*)	(*a*)	(*b*)	(*a*)	(*a*)
71	**72**	**73**	**74**	**75**	**76**	**77**	**78**	**79**	**80**
(*b*)	(*b*)	(*a*)	(*d*)	(*d*)	(*b*)	(*b*)	(*c*)	(*c*)	(*c*)
81	**82**	**83**	**84**	**85**	**86**	**87**	**88**	**89**	**90**
(*d*)	(*c*)	(*c*)	(*b*)	(*d*)	(*d*)	(*d*)	(*c*)	(*b*)	(*d*)
91	**92**	**93**	**94**	**95**	**96**	**97**	**98**	**99**	**100**
(*d*)	(*d*)	(*a*)	(*d*)	(*d*)	(*d*)	(*c*)	(*d*)	(*b*)	(*a*)
101	**102**	**103**	**104**	**105**	**106**	**107**	**108**	**109**	**110**
(*d*)	(*d*)	(*d*)	(*d*)	(*d*)	(*d*)	(*d*)	(*c*)	(*c*)	(*c*)
111	**112**	**113**	**114**	**115**	**116**	**117**	**118**	**119**	**120**
(*d*)	(*a*)	(*d*)	(*d*)	(*a*)	(*a*)	(*d*)	(*b*)	(*a*)	(*d*)
121	**122**	**123**	**124**	**125**					
(*d*)	(*d*)	(*d*)	(*d*)	(*c*)					

English

SECTION a

COMPREHENSION

INTRODUCTION

Comprehension determines the ability of an examinee to grapple with abstract thoughts hidden in the text. It also judges his ability to draw conclusions from the given set of information that is in the form of running text. This test can be solved by reading the given paragraph and answering the questions that are given below it. Answers may be given either by ticking the right choices in the question paper or filling the relevant boxes (showing options) in the answer sheet with pencil. The passage can vary in length; it could be as small as a paragraph of 50 words or, it could be a type of small essay of nearly 500 words, conveniently divided into some paragraphs. Single paragraphs are also given in many a test. The topic of the paragraph generally deals with abstract subjects whereas figures or tables are generally avoided.

While treating the test from an artistic viewpoint, readers will have to develop the sense of making logical conclusions. These conclusions must be based on the text given in the passage; they cannot imagine phenomenon, conclusions or facts. They have to limit their imagination and the power to comprehend the abstract points (the "fine things" stated in the topic) to the passage only.

In order to solve this test in a scientific manner, readers will have to proceed according to the following steps:

(1) Read the passage and try to grasp the main theme of the story.

(2) Underline the important points.

(3) Read those words carefully that are in bold face letters. Try to connect them to the lines in which, they have been carefully embedded.

(4) Read the questions given below the passage and tick the relevant option in the answer sheet.

(5) Many passages have tests of antonyms and synonyms appended in the end of their questions. Do not imagine the antonym or synonym of the given word or the bold-faced word of the passage. Instead, link that word to the line in which, it is embedded. Try to find out what the author is saying in that line. Now, answer the question (antonym or synonym) keeping in mind the "true spirit" of the word in its sentence.

(6) In many tests, you may be asked to give a suitable title to the passage. Scan through the passage quickly and read the underlined phrases carefully. Give such a title to the passage as would encompass all the vital points of the passage. Do not go beyond the "real essence" of the given passage. Do not use difficult words in the title decided by you.

As an artist, you have to comprehend the fine aspects of the text that you will read. As a logician, you will be required to deduct and conclude.

PASSAGE-1

The villager has customarily been very conservative in his attitude and approach. He is reluctant to change his traditional way of thinking and doing things. His attitude, in many respects, is: "home-made is best". For instance, most cattle-farmers in the villages, prefer to feed their cows and buffaloes with a home-mix comprising local oil-cakes like mustard or cottonseed, pulses, jaggery, salt, etc. It takes numerous visits, hard-convincing, daily trials and experiments to convince the rural cattle-farmer that compound feeds, scientifically formulated, improve the yields of milk, without any incremental costs.

The age-old values and attitudes towards caste, creed, women, time and money take time to change. The villager has traditionally been a believer in the philosophy of 'Karma or fate. He has found it more convenient to blame his economic destitution, poor living conditions, and straitened social status on 'bhagya', 'Karma' or 'fate'. The security that the villagers find in the 'status quo', acts as a disincentive to change and experiment, in the short-run. Many of these antiquated attitudes, value-system and outlooks are changing, due to improved levels of awareness and education. However, the rate of change is sluggish. Attitudes that have fossilised over the centuries, do take time to change.

1. What does the phrase "home-made is best" imply?
(*a*) The best should not be discarded.
(*b*) Whatever is being practised is better than what is new.
(*c*) People should go in for the Swadeshi because it is home-made
(*d*) Change for the sake of change is no good.

2. Which one of the following is not the usual reason offered by an average Indian villager for his poverty?
(*a*) It is God's will
(*b*) It is a result of some of his bad deeds committed in this or the previous birth.
(*c*) It is because of his resistance to new ideas.
(*d*) It is his destiny

3. When will you call a person conservative in his attitude and approach?
(*a*) When he sticks to old ways of thinking and doing.
(*b*) When he would like to try out every new idea before accepting it.
(*c*) When he imputes motives to change agents.
(*d*) When he solves his problems through tried out methods.

4. Why does a villager feel secure in maintaining 'status quo'?
(*a*) Because whatever is known should be the best.
(*b*) Because change is seldom for the better.
(*c*) Because too many people go about advising him.
(*d*) Because of the imagined risk involved in trying a new approach.

5. What is the best method to convince the average Indian villager about the superiority of a new cattle-feed?
(*a*) Discussion
(*b*) Field demonstration
(*c*) Distribution of related literature.
(*d*) Home-visits.

PASSAGE-2

I do not suggest that the cultural side of education should be ignored. On the contrary, I think, it is essential to the production of the sort of adult who best fits the modern world. But I think that what is important in cultural education should be conveyed at any rate in the early stages, by methods far more attrractive than those now usual. History and Geography should be taught at first by means of the cinema. When taught this way, they will give pleasure; attention will be spontaneous and therefore the impression will be less temporary. In spite of reforming movements, there is still among educators a feeling that what is enjoyed without effort cannot have much educational value. I would have children made aware of the manners and customs of tribes and nations utterly remote from their own. Education conducted on these lines would do more than many books to cure provincialism in space and time and to make children realise that actual human beings with actual feelings can be outwardly very different from the people among whom they live, but inwardly composed of the same human material. A Zulu would not appear strange, remote or savage but one like themselves.

1. The writer criticised traditional educators for not
(*a*) using cinema as a method of teaching.
(*b*) making learning an enjoyable activity.
(*c*) imparting information about remote tribes.
(*d*) imparting information about various cultures.

2. The writer thinks that the cultural side of education is needed to make man
(*a*) appreciate one's heritage.
(*b*) appreciate other civilisations.
(*c*) suitable for modern civilisation.
(*d*) admire his environment.

3. The expression "to cure provincialism in space and time" means to get rid of
(*a*) regional feelings (*b*) obscure ideas
(*c*) narrow views (*d*) selfish opinion

4. One of the goals of education should be to make children realise that
(*a*) human culture is diverse.
(*b*) regional cultures should not be ignored.
(*c*) They must respect values of alien culture.
(*d*) there is a unified system of human values underneath cultural diversity.

5. The response of the learners to teaching through cinema is
(*a*) absorbing. (*b*) long-lasting.
(*c*) enthusiastic. (*d*) superficial.

PASSAGE-3

n the technological systems of tomorrow — fast, luid and self-regulating — machines will deal with he flow of physical materials; men with the flow of nformation and insight. Machines will increasingly perform tasks. Machines and men both, instead of being concentrated in gigantic factories and factory cities, will be scattered across the globe, linked ogether by amazingly sensitive, near-instantaneous communications. Human work will move out of the actory and mass office into the community and the home. Machines will be synchronised, as some already are, to the billionth of a second; men will be desynchronised. The factory whistle will vanish. Even he clock, "the key machine of the modern industrial age," as Lewis Mumford called it a generation ago, will lose some of its power over humans, as distinct rom purely technological affairs. Simultaneously, the organisation needed to control technology will shift rom bureaucracy to Ad-hocracy, from permanence to ransience, and from a concern with the present to a ocus on the future.

In such a world, the most valued attributes of the ndustrial age become handicaps. The technology of omorrow requires not millions of lightly lettered men, ready to work in unison at endlessly repetitive obs, it requires not men who take orders in unblinking ashion, aware that the price of bread is mechanical ubmission to authority, but men who can make critical judgments, who can weave their way through novel environment, who are quick to spot new elationships in the rapidly changing reality. It equires men who, in C.P. Snow's compelling terms, "have the future in their bones."

1. The type of society which the author has mentioned makes a plea for
(*a*) a mind assimilative of modern scientific ideas
(*b*) a critical mind having insight into future
(*c*) a mind well-versed in cultural heritage
(*d*) a mind with firm principles of life

2. The future man, according to this passage, must be
(*a*) most adaptative and intelligent
(*b*) most capable of dealing with the changing reality
(*c*) more concerneu with the present than the future
(*d*) trained and obedient

3. Near-instantaneous communications' may be regarded as a symbol of
(*a*) anachronisation
(*b*) mischronisation
(*c*) desynchronisation
(*d*) synchronisation

4. If a person believes that 'the price of bread is mechanical submission to authority', he is
(*a*) a believer in devotion to duty
(*b*) a believer in taking things for granted
(*c*) a believer in doing what he is told, right or wrong
(*d*) a believer in the honesty of machines

5. The technological system of tomorrow will be marked by
(*a*) dehumanisation (*b*) perfection
(*c*) automation (*d*) unpredictability

PASSAGE-4

Education, particularly higher education is the obvious but crucially important instrument for nation building. As Confucious has said;

If you are thinking of one year, plant rice. If you are thinking of a decade, plant trees. If you are thinking of a century, educate the people.

When we set about the task of higher education, we should be absolutely clear in our perception of the goals of education in the specific context of our nation's development. No doubt, one of the important aims of education would be to create the required range and nature of trained manpower assessed to be needed by different sectors of national growth. The entire educational apparatus must be geared progressively to fulfill the requrements of different phases of our growth in every sector—primary, secondary and tertiary. The aim must be to ensure that our country does not experience either paucity, or a surfeit, of trained manpower in any specific segment of our economy. The requirements of our country, as a free, democratic, secular, socialist, nation, aspiring for rapid development, entail a specific recipe for our educational institutions. Today's educational institutions must therefore be developed accordingly and must regulate themselves to give the country the precise nature and quantum of trained manpower as projected by the requirements of our planned economy.

1. The author has quoted thoughts of Confucious to stress
(*a*) importance of planting trees for human beings
(*b*) the worthless efforts in planting rice
(*c*) the benefits of investing in education
(*d*) the need for assessing manpower requirement
(*e*) None of these

2. Which statement cannot be made on the basis of the passage?
(*a*) Higher education should keep in view the requirements of national economy
(*b*) Higher education has not been employed for nation building

(c) All levels of education have a role to play in nation's growth
(d) In our country we need to have a specially planned educational system
(e) The educational system should be modified to suit to our country's needs

3. The writer believes that
(a) there are no problems related to higher education
(b) investment in education is of long-range
(c) higher education should be used to assess manpower needs
(d) aims of higher education in India are absolutely clear
(e) None of these

4. The author's expectations from higher education are essentially
(a) unrealistic (b) confusing
(c) critical (d) vague
(e) reasonable

5. The writer indicates that
(a) higher education did not play any role in national growth
(b) primary education did not play any role in national growth
(c) our nation experiences paucity of trained manpower in many sectors
(d) today's higher education has no precise goals to achieve
(e) None-of these

6. Author has used the word 'apparatus' to indicate the
(a) scientific nature of education
(b) complicated organisation demanded by education
(c) readily visible benefits of education
(d) entire equipment of education to perform particular function
(e) None of these

7. Which of the following has not been conveyed by the passage?
(a) Education at any level can contribute in nation building
(b) Manpower needs in many areas can be fulfilled through higher education
(c) Rapid development of our nation is possible through higher education
(d) Present higher education does not ensure surfeit of trained manpower

8. This passage is likely to be addressed to
(a) politicians only (b) scientists only
(c) students only (d) economists only
(e) cannot be said

9. The title below which expresses the ideas of this passage best is
(a) Manpower Planning in India
(b) Importance of Higher Education
(c) Demands of Higher Education
(d) Role of Higher Education in India
(e) None of these

PASSAGE–5

Using infant mortality as a key indicator of the status of children, we now begin to have the broad features of a hypothesis as to the causes of higher or lower mortality rates. One aspect is the **complex** of factors involving the **access** of mothers to trained personnel and other facilities for child delivery, the nutritional status of pregnant and nursing mothers and the quality of health-care and nourishment which babies receive. The other aspect, indicated by rural-urban differentials, is the possible importance of human settlement patterns in relation to the availability of health-care and related facilities such as potable water, excreta disposal systems, etc. Thus, in a special sense it is much cheaper to make health and other basic services available to a community when it is densely settled rather than widely dispersed.

It is possible to argue, however, that both these sets of factors are closely related to a third one, namely income levels. Poorer mothers and babies have less access to health-care facilities and nourishment than those who are better-off, urban communities are on an average much better-off than rural communities. That economic conditions play a crucial role in determining the status of both mother and child is beyond dispute. But the question really is whether this is the only decisive factor or whether factors such as the availability of medical facilities, health-care programmes and nutritional programmes have an independent role. If so, then the settlement patterns which affect service delivery to the mother and child target groups become a relevant consideration. These are clearly issues of some importance for policy and programme planning.

1. Which of the following can be inferred from the passage?
(a) Infant mortality rate is higher in rural areas as compared to that of urban areas
(b) Income level alone can predict the infant mortality rate
(c) There, now, is more population in urban areas as compared to rural areas
(d) Delivery of services to the mother and child does not depend on the settlement pattern
(e) The rural areas have now become densely-populated

2. Which of the following is the issue of importance for policy?
(a) Relationship of mortality and income levels

(b) Growing rural-urban differentials

(c) Infant-mortality rate and mortality rate interdependence

(d) Dependence of education level of the mother and infant mortality rate

(e) Independence of factors other than income on infant mortality

3. Which, according to the passage, is the other main indicator of the status of children, besides infant mortality?

(a) Educational level

(b) Nourishment level

(c) Weight at birth

(d) Not mentioned

(e) None of these

4. What is the advantage of providing services in the urban areas, as compared to that of rural areas?

(a) The services are cheaply available

(b) Per-capita expenditure for setting up services is much less

(c) There is more awareness about availability of services

(d) The investment can be received in short duration

(e) It is much easier to set up services

5. Which of the following is the **same** in meaning as the word "**access**" as used in the passage?

(a) Passage (b) Outburst

(c) Surplus (d) Demand

(e) Reach

6. Which of the following is not to factor for mortality rate?

(a) Settlement pattern

(b) Type of child delivery

(c) Nutritional status

(d) Potable water

(e) Income level

7. Which of the following is the **same** in meaning as the word "**complex**" as used in the passage?

(a) Building (b) Nature

(c) Composite (d) List

(e) Types

PASSAGE-6

To open up a field of study, draw attention to its vital elements, the lecture is invaluable. To listen to a lecture can be thrilling experience from which the student may gain ideas obtainable in no other way. But possibly to a greater degree than other forms of instruction, lecturing presumes a high order of intellectual competence on the part of learners. The purposes of the lecture are to summarize, to clarify, to stimulate and to humanize the materials of the course. It should synthesize, evaluate, criticise and compare ideas and facts with which students have come in contact through out-of-class assignments.

The effectiveness of lectures could be enhanced by introducing the lecture with a brief review of the work preceding. It should also be indicated how the day's lecture fits into the course pattern. A lecture should seldom be presented in one unbroken discourse. Unless exceptionally interesting, a long lecture **strains** the capacity for concentrated listening, causing intermittent wandering of attention and loss of continuity in thought. The lecture should therefore be organized in a few block or units. As a rule, the exposition should be concluded before the end of the class period so as to allow some time for general discussion.

For students to obtain maximum benefit from a lecture, individual participation in study both precede and follow it. On their own initiative, most students would not engage in preparatory study, hence formal assignments may be necessary. The lecture should be concluded on the assumption that the assignment has been fulfilled. It pays to explore the aids available for teaching a course particularly through lectures, since verbal exposition alone, however **lucid**, has its shortcomings.

1. Which of the following is the best suited title for the passage?

(a) Methods of Teaching

(b) Effective Learning

(c) Contrast Programmes

(d) Lecture-Method

(e) Teaching Without Tears

2. Which of the following is the **same** in meaning as the word "**strains**" as used in the passage?

(a) Spoils

(b) Damages

(c) Drains energy from

(d) Requires greater effort

(e) Puts premium on

3. An uninterrupted discourse type method results into.........

(a) loss of attention

(b) a thrilling experience

(c) stimulation of interest

(d) humanising the course material

(e) None of these

4. Which of the following is **not true** in the context of the passage?

(a) Students on their own take up assignments

(b) Lecture method humanises the course content

(c) There are many methods of teaching

(d) Improvements can be made in the traditional lecture method of instruction

(e) Various aids can be used with lecture method

ENGLISH

5. Compared to other methods, lecturing requires ....
(*a*) more competent trainer
(*b*) bigger number of students
(*c*) higher level of learner
(*d*) a new field of study
(*e*) better presentation of ideas

6. The passage seems to be written chiefly for.........
(*a*) students (*b*) educators
(*c*) parents (*d*) researchers
(*e*) administrators

7. The effectiveness of lectures can be enhanced by which of the following?
1. Breaking it into units
2. Showing its integration in the course
3. In the end giving some time for discussion
(*a*) 1 and 2 only (*b*) 3 only
(*c*) 1 and 3 only (*d*) 2 and 3 only
(*e*) All 1, 2 and 3

8. Which of the following is the same in meaning as the word "**lucid**" as used in the passage?
(*a*) long (*b*) interesting
(*c*) clear (*d*) ideal
(*e*) thrilling

PASSAGE-7

Among the several citrus fruits, acid lime is one of the most, prolific yielder, and this crop can be profitably grown in the tropical plains and hill slopes with scant water resources. It comes up well in sandy loam rich in organic residues and endowed with adequate drainage. Good quality grafts are ideal for raising a healthy and productive lime garden. The grafts yield true-to-parent plants of high yielding potential, and are early bearers. They also bear big fruits all through the year.

However, the longevity of the grafts is less as compared with the trees developed from the seeds, according to experts. Seeds extracted from healthy fruits from proven mother plants will develop into robust plants with longer life. The main field should be thoroughly tilled, and ripe farm-yard manure should be incorporated well with the final ploughing and land levelling. Green manuring will also help in increasing the soil's organic matter content, and in improving the soil structure. A spacing of 6 m by 6 m is recommended for raising acid lime plantation. Pits of 90 cm by 90 cm are to be dug, and filled up with adequate quantities of vermin-compost, coir-pith compost and small amounts of powdered neem cake and bio-fertilizers. About 250 plants can be accommodated in a hectare.

Regular irrigation is essential in the early stages of crop establishment. Drip irrigation, pitcher irrigation and micro-sprinklers have been found to give good results, besides saving considerable quantities of water and energy. In the initial months after planting, sufficient shade should be provided to protect the tender seedlings and grafts from harsh sun. Planting Sesbania (agathi) around the young plants will be effective in ensuring the required shade, besides enriching the soil. Several annual crops such as pulses and vegetables, can be raised as intercrops in the initial years. The plants should be trained to grow vertically by discouraging the lateral shoots and other growths.

Regular pruning to get the desired dome-shape should be done when the plants are still young. The field should be kept free of weed and other unwanted vegetation. Regular manuring should be done twice annually. The nutrients, mostly organic in nature, should be incorporated at the base of the plants, and watered immediately. The plants particularly respond well to liberal application of organic amendments. The micro-nutrient deficiencies will not be noticed in acid lime plantations raised with rich organic nutrients. Plant protection is an important aspect in acid lime cultivation. The plants should be sprayed with cow's urine, vermin-wash and other botanical insecticides to ward off leaf-munching caterpillars and other sucking and chewing pests.

Need-based application after monitoring the field for pest incidence will be rewarding. Spraying should be taken up at an interval of ten days, and it will also improve the fruit setting and fruit development. The plants will establish well and start yielding from the second year of planting. Though the fruits can be had all round the year, some major flushes can be harvested in December-January and July-August seasons. A well nurtured grown-up tree can yield as high as 3000 fruits a year. The profit for the growers depends on the season and the prevailing market rate. With an average price of Rs. 0.35 a fruit, a farmer can realize about Rs. 2.5 lakhs from a hectare of a healthy and well-tended acid lime garden.

1. It can be inferred from the passage that
I. The quality and size of fruits depend upon the longevity of the plants.
II. The yield of grafts is less as compared to the trees developed from the seeds.
III. There is not much of a difference between grafts and the trees developed from the seeds, except in life.
Which of the above statements is/are true?
(*a*) Only III (*b*) Only II
(*c*) I and II (*d*) I, II and III

2. For a good growth of acid-lime crop, all of the following are essential *except,*
(*a*) water-logged tropical plains
(*b*) good irrigation with adequate drainage
(*c*) rich residues of orgainc nutrients
(*d*) hill slopes with poor water resources

3. The author of the passage could be
(a) an agricultural activist
(b) an agricultural expert
(c) a farmer
(d) an analyst

4. Which of the following is necessary for the nascent crop?
(a) Sufficient shade
(b) Regular inrrigation
(c) Regular manuring and application of organic nutrients
(d) Both (A) and (B)

5. The most appropriate insecticide for acid-lime crop is
(a) cow's urine (b) powdered neem
(c) vermi-compost (d) organic residue

PASSAGE-8

We should preserve Nature to preserve life and beauty. A beautiful landscape, full of green vegetation, will not just attract our attention but will fill us with infinite satisfaction. Unfortunately, because of modernization, much of nature is now yielding to towns, roads and industrial areas. In a few places some Natural reserves are now being carved out to avert the danger of destroying Nature completely. Man will perish without Nature, so modern man should continue this struggle to save plants, which give us oxygen, from extinction. Moreover, Nature is essential to man's health.

1. What does "Nature" in the passage mean?
(a) Countryside covered with plants and trees
(b) Physical power that created the world
(c) Inherent things that determine character
(d) Practical study of plants and animals

2. Which one of the following is the correct statement?
According to the passage
(a) Beauty is only skin-deep
(b) Everything is beautiful in its natural state
(c) There is beauty in Nature
(d) Nature is a moral teacher

3. What does the writer suggest?
(a) We should not modernize, so that Nature can be preserved
(b) While modernizing we should be careful not to destroy Nature completely
(c) All Nature has been destroyed by modern living
(d) Carving out Natural reserves will hamper the growth of industries

4. What does "Struggle" in the passage mean?
(a) Man's Struggle to exist in the world
(b) Man's Struggle to save Nature
(c) Man's Struggle to catch up with modern trends
(d) Man's Struggle to conserve oxygen

5. Why a beautiful landscape will fill us with infinite satisfaction'?
(a) We love beauty
(b) It is full of green vegetation
(c) It will ensure our future existence
(d) It will show our command over Nature

PASSAGE-9

Finally, there arises the question as to our leadership potential. Although the entire younger generation by the very definition is a potential storehouse of leadership, I feel that our universities provide the richest reservoir from which the future leaders of this country will be forthcoming. I have had occasion to travel fairly extensively and to visit a number of university centres in the country. It is deeply encouraging to see that despite the economic and other difficulties which these young men and women have to face they are full of energy and idealism. The real question is whether we have the ability and imagination to tap this reservoir, to fan the sparks of youthful idealism into bright flames that would illumine the future of India — the India of our dreams for the building of which countless generations have struggled and sacrified; an India socially emancipated, economically prosperous, politically integrated, militarily strong and spiritually dynamic.

1. Which one of the following is correct?
The writer believes that India is
(a) socially emancipated
(b) economically prosperous
(c) spiritually dynamic
(d) None of the above

2. What is the author's tone in the passage?
(a) Optimistic (b) Autocratic
(c) Pessimistic (d) Partisan

3. Where will the future leaders of the country mainly come from?
(a) The families of present political leaders
(b) The community of social scientists
(c) The universities
(d) The entire younger generation

4. Which one of the following is correct?
For realizing the India of our dreams,
(a) we should have the imagination to exploit our budding leadership potential
(b) we should admire the sacrifices made by several generations
(c) we should bring about more technological advancements
(d) we should provide better facilities for sports

ENGLISH

5. Which one of the following is correct?

   What is deeply encouraging about educated young men and women of India is that

   (*a*) they come from the richest reservoirs of potential leaders

   (*b*) they are full of energy and idealism because of quality education

   (*c*) they are full of youthful idealism and imagination

   (*d*) they are full of energy and idealism in spite of economic and other difficulties they face as students

PASSAGE-10

My own recollection is that I had not had any high regard for my ability. I used to be astonished whenever I won prizes and scholarships. But, I very assiduously guarded my character. The least little blemish drew tears from my eyes. When I merited, or seemed to the teacher to merit, a rebuke, it was unbearable for me. I remember having once received corporal punishment. I did not so much mind the punishment, as the fact that it was considered my desert. I wept piteously. That was when I was in the first or second standard. There was another such incident during the time when I was in the seventh standard. Dorabji Edulji Gimi was the Headmaster then. He was popular among the boys, though he was a disciplinarian. He was a man of method and a good teacher. He had made gymnastics and cricket compulsory for the boys of the upper standards. I disliked both. I never took part in any exercise, cricket or football, before they were made com-pulsory. My shyness was one of the reasons for this aloofness, which I now see as wrong. I then had the false notion that gymnastics had nothing to do with education. Today I know that physical training should have as much place in the curriculum as mental training.

1. Why did the author say that he did ***not*** have any high regard for his ability?

   (*a*) He was a dunce

   (*b*) He always used to miss his classes

   (*c*) He never did well in studies or sports

   (*d*) He was full humility

2. The author's idea that character is a treasure is revealed in which of the statements?

   (*a*) "I won prizes and scholarships"

   (*b*) "When I merited, or seemed to the teacher to merit, a rebuke, it was unbearable for me"

   (*c*) "I very assiduously guarded my character"

   (*d*) "I wept piteously"

3. Why did the author weep piteously?

   (*a*) He felt insulted

   (*b*) Punishment was considered his due

   (*c*) He felt the physical pain

   (*d*) He took the punishment to heart

4. Why did the author dislike gymnastics and cricket?

   (*a*) They cut into his study time

   (*b*) He had to spend money in buying bats, etc.

   (*c*) He felt that physical education could cause injury

   (*d*) He was shy

PASSAGE-11

According to the research findings of a team of American scientists published recently, the sea waves contain as much energy as the world is consuming at present. Scientists have found that, through the application of two major devices called land-based systems and offshore devices, this source of energy can provide huge amount of electricity without cooling towers and pollution.

Land-based systems include tapered channels and fixed oscillating water column (OWC) devices whereas offshore devices include floating OWC devices, buoys, etc. Through these devices the mechanical energy of ocean waves is absorbed and converted into electrical energy. The wave power potential depends on numerous factors such as the device's capability to harness long wavelengths, period of waves and depth of water where they arise.

Compared to conventional power stations which require greater space and are difficult to maintain in critical situations, wave power devices are highly modular, cost effective and easier to upgrade. As the recent findings suggest, sea wave energy has much greater potential to be used for electricity generation than the hitherto known sources of renewable energy. Moreover, most of the renewable energy systems require hundreds of square acres of useful land for their installation. But in case of wave energy devices, space crunch' can never be a serious problem.

1. Which one of the following statements is correct?

   Harnessing energy from sea waves

   (*a*) undermines ecological balance.

   (*b*) requires huge capital.

   (*c*) requires high technical expertise.

   (*d*) results in saving of useful land area.

2. Which one of the following statements is correct?

   Wave power devices

   (*a*) convert wind energy into mechanical power.

   (*b*) convert mechanical energy of ocean waves into electrical energy.

   (*c*) require costly transmission mechanism

   (*d*) entail risk to human life.

3. Which one of the following statements is correct?
   (*a*) Fixed as well as floating oscillating water column devices are required to harness ocean wave energy.
   (*b*) Fixed oscillating water column devices are required for off shore based system.
   (*c*) Floating oscillating water column devices are required for land-based system.
   (*d*) Electricity generated from oceans is independent of the depth of water where waves arise.
4. Which one of the following statements is correct?
   The capacity of system to generate electricity from ocean waves
   (*a*) can be increased only at exorbitant cost.
   (*b*) can be easily upgraded.
   (*c*) can be increased but it requires a great space.
   (*d*) is only a few megawatts.
5. Which one of the following statements is ***not*** correct?
   (*a*) Conventional power stations require cooling towers.
   (*b*) Power generation from ocean waves also adds to pollution like conventional power stations.
   (*c*) Ocean wave energy can meet all the present energy of the world.
   (*d*) Period of waves is one of the relevant factors in power generation from ocean waves.

PASSAGE-12

The most important fact, which a leader who wishes to motivate others should bear in mind, is that an individual has an incessant and gnawing craving for importance. There is no exception to this psychological need. Barring his biological needs, practically all his actions are directed at satisfying his continuing need to feel important. According to William James, the deepest principle in human nature is the craving to be appreciated. The individual who can honestly satisfy this burning hunger for importance on the part of his fellow human beings can literally rule the world. He can motivate and influence any person, big or small, high or low, educated or uneducated, rich or poor, man or woman, provided he is capable of making the other person feel truly important. By discovering the special and particular gifts of an individual, by giving due recognition and sincere appreciation to that singular gift or talent, you can win him or her over to your side easily.

You have to create an eager want on the part of the other individual if you wish to motivate him. In other words, you have to make the horse feel thirsty if your aim is to make it drink. Fortunately for you, there is an inborn, ever-present, gnawing hunger on the part of every human being to gain recognition and appreciation. This want is already there and you don't have to create it. All you have to do is to satisfy this hunger. If you objectively analyse your own motives and needs you will find that this need for recognition is the strong driving factor behind your aspiration to become a leader. It was this urge for importance which made Alexander and Great embark on a world conquest, and made many emperors wage innumerable battles and wars. This urge has driven artists, authors, scientists, inventors and others to attain great heights in their chosen fields and produce the best results.

1. Which one of the following statements is correct?
   (*a*) Many scientists and inventors have excelled because of the availability of research facilities.
   (*b*) Artists and authors have made contribution to society because of their innate genius.
   (*c*) Many athletes have won gold medals in the Olympics because of their coaches.
   (*d*) People in different areas have been successful because of the need of recognition.
2. Which one of the following statements is ***not*** correct?
   (*a*) Hunger for recognition has to be developed over the years in one's personality.
   (*b*) Need to gain recognition is an inborn trait.
   (*c*) Many wars have been waged to satisfy the need to get importance.
   (*d*) Craving for importance is a natural psychological need of every human being.
3. Which one of the following statements is correct?
   (*a*) A successful leader must be able to identify the need of importance of others.
   (*b*) Need for recognition is a trait only of high professionals.
   (*c*) To motivate a person, an increase of his salary is the best strategy.
   (*d*) Monetary success is the driving force for a leader.

PASSAGE-13

Because goldfish can be kept easily in small ponds and aquariums, they make good pets, but like many other pets, they must have proper care and the right kind of place to live.

A two-inch fish requires a minimum of two gallons of water containing sufficient oxygen to support life.

Some oxygen will make its way into the water of an aquarium from the air that touches the surface. Plants in an aquarium also help to furnish oxygen. Snails help to keep an aquarium clean. Thus, with plenty of plants and snails the water is an aquarium does not have to be changed frequently. A large lake may prove to be a quite unsuitable abode for goldfish.

It is important that goldfish not be overfed. They can be fed such things as dried insects in addition to commercially-prepared goldfish food, but they should never be fed more than once a day. Even then, they should not be given more food than can be consumed in about five minutes. This ensures prolonged life.

1. Which one of the following statements is correct?
   (*a*) Snails eat up the goldfish in an aquarium
   (*b*) A large lake may not be a suitable place for goldfish
   (*c*) Plants provide food to the snails in an aquarium
   (*d*) Goldfish come above the surface of water to get oxygen from air
2. Which one of the following statements is *not* correct?
   (*a*) Goldfish can be made goods pets
   (*b*) Plants in an aquarium provide oxygen to goldfish
   (*c*) Goldfish must never be given too much food
   (*d*) Snails make the aquarium clean by eating up goldfish
3. Which of the following helps supply goldfish with oxygen?
   (*a*) Snails
   (*b*) Dried insects
   (*c*) Goldfish food
   (*d*) Plants
4. Which one of the following statement is *not* correct?
   (*a*) Water in an aquarium has to be changed frequently because of plants and snails
   (*b*) Commercially-prepared goldfish is available
   (*c*) The place for the goldfish should be selected with care
   (*d*) Dried insects make good feed for goldfish
5. What is important to remember when feeding goldfish?
   (*a*) Goldfish should be fed more than once a day at regular intervals
   (*b*) Goldfish should be fed with plants and snails
   (*c*) Goldfish should be fed only once a day
   (*d*) Goldfish should be fed only in the evenings

PASSAGE-14

Ah ! whatever could be said was said. All held him guilty. Even his own mother who claimed to understand him the best. All had betrayed him in his hour of need. Yet, there he was, still with a sparkling hope and knew that the truth must prevail. In the cold, dark and damp cell he never for a moment lost faith in God and goodness and was waiting anxiously for an angel to come, plead non guilty for him and free him of his miseries.

1. Three of the following statements indicate that he had a sparkling hope. Which statement does not?
   (*a*) He had never lost faith in God.
   (*b*) He was sure there was goodness.
   (*c*) He could have evidence in his favour.
   (*d*) He knew that the truth must prevail.
2. Whatever others said about him, he
   (*a*) betrayed no one.
   (*b*) thought over the problem.
   (*c*) never lost faith in goodness.
   (*d*) raised his voice against injustice.
3. In the dark dungeon he always waited for
   (*a*) his mother.
   (*b*) the jailer.
   (*c*) the verdict freeing him of his miseries.
   (*d*) the angel to come and plead for him.
4. The truth must prevail means
   (*a*) he was true.
   (*b*) angel will reveal truth.
   (*c*) truth always wins in the end.
   (*d*) we must plead for the truth.

PASSAGE-15

Once while travelling by the local bus, I got a seat beside a very strange man. He seemed interested in every passenger aboard. He would stare at a person, scribble some odd mathematical notations on his long notebook and then move on to the next. Being quite interested in what he was doing I asked him what all those notations meant and then came the startling reply. He saw a man's face not as a single unit but as thousands of squares put together. He was in fact a statistical expert and a budding artist learning the art of graphics.

1. The man was scribbling down
   (*a*) the figures of co-passengers.
   (*b*) the details of thousands of squares put together.
   (*c*) some mathematical formulae and calculations.
   (*d*) some mathematical signs.
2. The man caught author's attention because
   (*a*) he was sitting next to him.
   (*b*) he was staring at every person in the bus.
   (*c*) he would stare at every person and then scribble down some mathematical notation.
   (*d*) he was a budding artist learning the art of graphics.

3. The author found that man's reply quite startling because
   (a) a statistical expert cannot be a budding scientist.
   (b) a budding artist cannot be a statistical expert.
   (c) graphics is still a rare art form and he was learning it while travelling in a bus.
   (d) the fact that "a man's face can be analysed as thousands of squares" was a strange concept.
4. From the passage we gather that
   (a) the author is very inquisitive.
   (b) the author tries to poke his nose in other people's business.
   (c) the author is interested in mathematical notations.
   (d) the author wants to talk to fellow passengers in the bus.

PASSAGE-16

With the inevitable growth of specialisation I see the universities facing two great dangers. First, it is very easy to get so involved in the technical details of education that the object of education is lost. And secondly, in an effort to condition a university to the needs of its students and to the needs of the state it may lose its power to make or mould those students into responsible men, capable of thinking for themselves and capable of expressing the results of their thoughts to others.

1. The author calls growth of specialisation 'inevitable'. Which one of the following statements is likely to be the most correct reason for this inevitability?
   (a) Universities give grants only to do specialised work in different disciplines.
   (b) The professors and researchers in universities are competent only for specialised work.
   (c) Specialisation helps economic growth of the nation.
   (d) In an age of science and technology specialisation becomes necessary.
2. Which one of the following statements most correctly suggests the central theme of the passage?
   (a) The aim of education is specialisation.
   (b) The aim of education is to mould the youth to work for the state.
   (c) The aim of education is to make the youth capable of independent thought and expression.
   (d) The aim of education is to enable the youth to earn a comfortable living.
3. Which one of the following statements most correctly suggests the warning implied in the passage?
   (a) University education should not be concerned with technical details.
   (b) Universities should not subordinate themselves to the interests of tile state.
   (c) Universities should be concerned only with the needs of students.
   (d) Universities should not go in for any specialisation.

PASSAGE-17

We shall go on to the end; we shall fight in France, we shall fight on the seas and oceans, we shall fight with growing confidence and strength in the air, we shall defend our island whatever the cost may be, we shall fight on the beaches, we shall fight on the landing grounds, we shall fight in the fields and in the streets, we shall fight in the hills. We shall never surrender, and even if this island or a large part of it were subjugated and starving, then our empire beyond the seas would carry on the struggle, untill the New World steps forth to the rescue and the liberation of the Old.

1. On the basis of the passage which of the following statements may be said to be correct?
   (a) The speaker is encouraging his men for the conquest of France
   (b) The speaker is aggressive and maniacal war-monger
   (c) The speaker is not satisfied with the conquest of the island
   (d) The speaker is a patriot urging the defence of his motherland
2. The speaker in the passage wants to go on fighting because
   (a) he is a raving lunatic
   (b) he is in a state of utter despair
   (c) he expects help from other quarters
   (d) he is the leader of a suicide squad
3. Which of the following pairs of the phrases helps best to bring out the intention of the speaker?
   (a) "Go on to the end"; "shall never surrender"
   (b) "Growing confidence"; "subjugated and starving"
   (c) "Subjugated and starving"; "fight on the landing ground"
   (d) "Fight in the streets"; "subjugated and starving"
4. The passage consists of repetitive patterns in syntax and vocabulary. The effect of this style is that it
   (a) reveals the speaker's defects in giving a speech

(*b*) produces the impression of bad poetry
(*c*) conveys the speaker's helpless situation
(*d*) reinforces the speaker's basic intention

PASSAGE-18

It is said that once three old men set out on a Journey together. One of them was bald, the second was a philosopher and the third was a barber. At nightfall they decided that each one of them should sit for watch *turn* by turn. The *barber* was to keep watch first of all, the *philosopher* after that and the *bald* man last of all. So, the philosopher and the blad man went to sleep and the barber was on watch. For some time he kept awake but in the end, he felt tired of it and he thought of some *diversion* as otherwise it was difficult for him to *pass* time. Then he took out the razor from his box and shaved the head of the philosopher. At the fixed time he woke up the philosopher and himself went to sleep. when the philosopher got up and felt his head all over, he was startled and said in surprise, "It was my trun but this *wretched* fellow has *awakened* bald man."

1. Why did the philosopher get up?
(*a*) He realised that his head was being shaved off
(*b*) It was his turn to keep watch
(*c*) He was awakened by the barber
(*d*) he had a bad dream

2. Who went to sleep first?
(*a*) The philosopher and the barber
(*b*) The barber and the bald man
(*c*) The bald man and the philosopher
(*d*) The barber

3. Why did the barber shave off the head of the philosopher?
(*a*) The barber was jealous of the philosopher
(*b*) The barber wanted to indulge in some fun
(*c*) The barber wanted the philosopher to keep watch
(*d*) The barber was feeling drowsy

4. Which one of the following is the correct sequence decided upon the three to keep watch turn by turn?
(*a*) Barber – bald man – philosopher
(*b*) Bald man – philosopher – barber
(*c*) Barber – philosopher – bald man
(*d*) Bald man – barber – philosopher

5. Which one of the following statements is ***not*** correct?
(*a*) All the three men decided to keep watch one by one
(*b*) The barber woke up the bald man
(*c*) The head of the philosopher was shaved off
(*d*) The philosopher was startled on feeling his head all over

PASSAGE-19

There can be only two explanations why countries like UK, US, Germany and Japan are willing to spend up to 5.5 million to make the Next Generation Linear Collider (NGLC) : Intellectual snobbery or complete indifference to the problems of the real world. To plan a 20-mile-long tunnel merely to go about smashing atoms, so as to recreate the Big Bang, is a frightful waste of public money. The project has no foreseeable practical application. Already, cyber-savvy cosmologists are engaged in simulating the Big Bang, or the beginning of the universe, in the virtual world, through number crunching and reverse engineering. Thye have successfully created a black hole on the desktop. So why go in for prohibitively expensive experimentation, when the virtual world is just a mouse-click away? Scientific ingenuity, remember, is not confined to reallife experiments; many of today's break-throughs have been inspired by research conductd almost entirely in cyberspace. Moreover, virtual research is 'clean'— without such fallouts as lab accidents and chemical leakages—and costs next to nothing.

1. Countries like UK, US, Germany and Japan wish to spend lot of money.
(*a*) to attend to the problems of humanity.
(*b*) to control AIDS.
(*c*) for defence research.
(*d*) to carry out atomic research.

2. Virtual research is carried out
(*a*) on computers.
(*b*) by experimentation in the field.
(*c*) by spending up billions of dollars.
(*d*) by experimentation in space.

3. Scientific research is not prohibitively costly when conducted
(*a*) by simulation in the virtual world.
(*b*) smashing atoms in a tunnel.
(*c*) making real-life models.
(*d*) using satellites.

4. Reverse engineering
(*a*) is commonly practised in research.
(*b*) is prohibitively expensive experimentation.
(*c*) is not used by cosmologists in the virtual world.
(*d*) is independent of analysis using computers.

PASSAGE-20

Failure and success are the ways of life. Constant efforts despite initial setbacks have brought us from the chrysalis of failures into the bright opportunity of triumphs. The conquest of Everest is a fitting example. Success eluded men for nearly twenty-five years. The leader of an unsuccessful expedition started, "Everest cannot add to its height, but spirit of man heightens even under repulse." Subsequent conquest of Everest has proved the truth of this. Indeed every newborn day is in itself an opportunity teeming with splendid chances for those who are alert, wide awake and aspiring.

1. According to the writer, the conquest of Everest proves that
   (*a*) the spirit of man heightens under demanding circumstances.
   (*b*) man cannot attain the unattainable.
   (*c*) success is always elusive.
   (*d*) the nature is most potent.
2. In this passage, "chrysalis of failure" means that
   (*a*) failure involves a closed situation from which one cannot escape.
   (*b*) failure can be compared to the pupa of the gold-coloured butterflies.
   (*c*) failure is a transitional state.
   (*d*) as an insect emerges in a different shape from chrysalis, so a human being changes after every failure.
3. The very style of the prose suggests that the writer intends the last sentence of the passage to be
   (*a*) poetic
   (*b*) inspiring
   (*c*) vague
   (*d*) contradictory to the first sentence of the passage.
4. The expression "teeming with" in the passage can be replaced by
   (*a*) multiplying (*b*) abounding
   (*c*) fruitful (*d*) promising
5. Every new day brings fresh challenges for a person
   (*a*) who is young
   (*b*) whose head is teeming with bright ideas
   (*c*) who has come out of the chrysalis of failure
   (*d*) who is watchful and daring.

PASSAGE-21

The most important reason for this state of affairs, perhaps, is that India was the only country in the world to truly recognise the achievements of the Soviet Union—rather than merely focus on the debilitating faults that Communism brought to its people. The people of India realised that the achievement of one hundred per cent literacy in a country much, much larger than its own and with similarly complicated ethnic and religious groupings, the rapid industrialisation of a nation that was a primarily agrarian society when the Bolshevik revolution took place in 1917, the attendant revolutionary steps in science and technology, the accessibility of health care (primeval according to Western standards, perhaps, but not according to Indian ones) to the general population, and despite prohibition of the government of the time the vast outpourings in literature, music, art, etc., are momentous and remarkable feats in any country.

In contrast, all that the West focussed on were the massive human rights violations by the Soviet State on its people, the deliberate uprooting and mass migrations of ethnic peoples from one part of the country to another in the name of industrialisation, the end of religion ..... in short, all the tools of information were employed to condemn the ideology of Communism, so much at variance with capitalist thinking.

The difference with the Indian perception, I think here is, that while the Indians reacted as negatively to what the Soviet governments did to its people in the name of good governance (witness the imprisonment of Boris Pasternak and the formation of an international committee to put pressure for his release with Jawaharlal Nehru at its head), they took the pain not to condemn the people of that broad country in black and white terms; they understood that mingled in the shades of grey were grains of uniqueness. (The Russians have never failed that characteristic in themselves; they have twice experimented with completely different ideologies, Communism and Capitalism both in the space of a century).

1. Which of the following statements according to the passage is correct ?
   (*a*) India took heed on the weak faults of Russian policies and system
   (*b*) India seriously commended the achievement of Russia, *i.e.,* cent per cent literacy and rapid industrialization
   (*c*) The process of industrialization had already started when Russian revolution took place in 1917
   (*d*) The literature, art and music received a setback during the communist regime in Russia
2. The West did not focus on:
   (*a*) rapid growth of nuclear weapons in Russia
   (*b*) Massive human rights violation by the Soviet state on its people
   (*c*) deliberate uprooting and mass migration of ethnic people in the name of industria-lization.
   (*d*) Both (*b*) and (*c*)
3. The India perception of the USSR was always
   (*a*) negative
   (*b*) neutral

(c) counter-reactionary
(d) applauding

4. The passage is
(a) descriptive (b) paradoxical
(c) analytical (d) thought provoking

PASSAGE-22

India's role on the international stage was moulded by history rather than by the pomp and circumstances of war. As a separate entity of the British empire, India became a founder member of the League of Nations in the same way as Australia and Canada, and thus acquired a somewhat unique international status long before independence. During the days of the League when India's interests were affected, such as in matters of trade or the position of Indians overseas, the Indian delegation did not hesitate to make known its independent position, for what it was worth. Some Indian delegates were in demand for chairing meetings riddled with contention and controversy, because of their reputation for impartiality and talent for mediation.

These were the small beginnings of India's later entry into the United Nations in 1945, again as a founder member before independence. The drafting of Chapter IX and X of the UN Charter, which deal with international social and economic cooperation, was entrusted to a group that was presided over by an Indian. It is important, however, to bear in mind that fact that the Government of independent India had no part in the drafting of the UN Charter, although in accepted the obligations contained therein. The UN was primarily the creation of three powers—The USA, UK and Russia.

The size, population, resources and potential of India lent it the weight of a medium power in the functioning of the United Nations. The fact that India was among the first nations to liberate itself from the imperialist domination through non-violent means endowed it with a moral obligation to work in and outside the UN for the independence of nations still under colonial rule. India has served on the Security Council for 10 years or 5 terms, on the Trusteeship Council for 12 years or 4 terms and on the Economic and Social Council for 21 years or 7 terms.

1. The title below that best expresses the ideas of the passage is:
(a) India's role at the United Nations
(b) India and Her Neighbours
(c) India's International Prestige
(d) British Colonial Expansion

2. Through a part of the British Empire, India enjoyed great prestige at the League in as much as Indian delegates were in demand for chairing meeting to consider controversial issues. It was because:
(I) Indian delegates were well known for their impartiality.
(II) Indian delegates had talent for mediation.
(III) India was considered a power to reckon with.
(a) I and III are correct
(b) I and II are correct
(c) I and III are correct
(d) only I is correct

3. Which articles of the UN Charter deal with International, Social and Economic Co-operation ?
(a) Articles IX and X
(b) Articles XI and XII
(c) Articles VIII and XIII
(d) Articles VI and VII

4. Which of the following countries does not find any coverage in the passage ?
(a) The USA (b) Britain
(c) The Russia (d) Sri Lanka

PASSAGE-23

Some religious teachers have taught that Man is made up of a body and a soul: but they have been silent about the Intellect. Their followers try to feed the body on earth and to save soul from perdition after death : but they neglected the claims of the mind. Bread for the body and Virtue for the soul: these are regarded as the indispensable requisites of human welfare here and hereafter. Nothing is said about knowledge and education. Thus Jesus Christ spoke much of feeding the hungry, healing the sick, and converting the sinners: but he never taught the duty of teaching the ignorant and increasing scientific knowledge. He himself was not a well educated man, and intellectual pursuits were beyond his horizon. Gautam Buddha also laid stress on morality, meditation and asceticism, but he did not attach great importance to history, science, art or literature. St. Ambrose deprecated scientific studies and wrote, "To discuss the nature and position of the earth does not help us in our hope for life to come". St. Basil said very frankly and foolishly, "It is not a matter of interest for us whether the earth is a sphere or a cylinder or disc." Thomas Carlyle also followed the Christian traditions when he declared that he honoured only two men and no third: the manual labour and the religious teacher. He forgot the scientist, the scholar and the artist. The cynics of Greece despised education at last ?

1. What have the religious teachers taught in the past ?
(a) That man is made up of body only
(b) That man is made up of soul only
(c) That man is made up of bubbles
(d) That man is made up of body and soul together

2. What is food for the soul ?
(*a*) Bread (*b*) Virtue
(*c*) Vice (*d*) Education

3. The following philosophers occur in the passage. But they are not in correct order. Correct the order.
(I) Jesus Christ (II) Gautam Buddha
(III) St. Ambrose (IV) Thomas Carlyle
(V) St. Basil
(*a*) I, II, III, IV, V (*b*) I, III, IV, V, II
(*c*) I, II, III, V, IV (*d*) II, I, III, IV, V

4. Intellectual pursuits have been neglected because:
(I) they are unnecessary and superfluous
(II) they make people dwarf
(III) they lead people to hell
(*a*) Only I is correct
(*b*) Only II is correct
(*c*) Only III is correct
(*d*) Only I and II are correct

5. The style of the passage is
(*a*) narrative (*b*) expository
(*c*) critical (*d*) Analytical

PASSAGE-24

The impact of technical advancement in armaments on man, needs to be analyzed with a rational mind, and heart free from prejudices of any kind towards modernisation. The most noticeable impact of this development certainly has been the loss of immunity from violence for successive generations ever since the invention of gunpowder. In modern times, the presence of technically advanced arms, not only at the fronts but also among the civilian population, has vastly undermined the value of human life, and endangered the very entity of those virtues of self restraint and discretion, on which a peaceful and amiable society rests. However, an unbiased view of the present scenario, would refrain one from attributing the rising trends of violence to the availability of technically superior weapons, for one must not overlook the fact that "Necessity is the mother of invention".

Every stage in the development of armaments has been marked by its distinct impact on society. When man fought with stones and his bare hands, the society was not yet compact. The discovery of metal and the use of spears, knives and arrows indicate the stage of the formation of small kingdoms. Fire continued to be an effective weapon of destruction. When man introduced the cavalry into the army and improved the strategies of making war, some small kingdoms gave away to form empires, but with no revolutionary advances in armaments forthcoming, the political structure of society remained more or less stagnant for the many coming centuries.

The next significant development was the use of gunpowder, which could be used to perform acts which were then thought to be impossible. Gunpowder was used to form the ammunition of several guns and canons. This sudden advances in weaponry not only facilitated the control of a large mass of people by relatively few armed men that helping to form strong empires, but the availability of the new technology to a select few nations enabled the formation of colonies in continents which did not have access to the modernized technologies of warfare. Modern technological advances in armaments aided the formation of nation states in Europe. The extensive use of the fire-power lent a lethal edge to the naval power which proved to be the greatest asset to any nation in the 19th century. Small United Nations States of Europe with strong navies, modern arms and disciplined men gained control of lands in foreign continents far greater in areas than the parent countries.

1. Necessity is the mother of invention means
(*a*) where there is mother there is invention
(*b*) when necessity arises invention is done
(*c*) most of the invention are preplanned
(*d*) nothing happens without creating congenial environment

2. The invention of modern weapons have resulted into
(*a*) loss of immunity from war in the society
(*b*) successive wars for the last two centuries
(*c*) arms race among the nations
(*d*) loss of life and property every now and then

3. Small kingdoms turned into big empires, after
(*a*) the invention of cavalry and canons and its introduction into the army
(*b*) the introduction of nuclear arms into the army
(*c*) the end of the use of knives, arrows and swords
(*d*) the end of the 19th century

4. The style of the passage is
(*a*) informative (*b*) analytical
(*c*) retrospective (*d*) provocative

PASSAGE-25

It was during one of the most dreadful smallpox epidemics in England that Edward Jenner, a country doctor, made a discovery which was to alter the course of history. Jenner noticed that the disease seldom struck those who lived in rural areas and worked around cattle. Most farmers and dairy workers had contracted cowpox and had recovered with nothing more serious than a putsule which left a scar. This observation led Dr. Jenner to think: Why not vaccinate people with cowpox to protect them from smallpox ? On May 14, 1876, Dr. Jenner took a healthy boy, James Phillips, to a dairy maid, Sarah Nelmes, who had a cowpox putsule on her hand resulting from an infection from her master's cow. Dr. Jenner made two shallow cuts on James Phillips' arm and inoculated them with matter taken from the cowpox sore. A putsule developed on the boy's arm formed a scab and healed. In July of the same year. Dr. Jenner inoculated James with matter from a smallpox putsule. During the next two weeks, the doctor watched for signs of smallpox. They did not develop. The vaccination was successful. Dr. Jenner wrote a paper explaining his method of vaccination. At first the doctors were hostile and would not listen to a ridiculous procedure. Many towns people organised anti vaccination campaigns. Gradually, however, the doctors and their patients accepted vaccination.

1. The fact that Edward Jenner was a country doctor, was important in the discovery of smallpox vaccine, because
(*a*) he had enough time to pursue his research in the rural areas
(*b*) he noticed that the disease was prevalent where people worked around cattle
(*c*) he noticed that the disease seldom struck people who worked around the cattle
(*d*) he found that he could convince rural people more easily than city people

2. Dr. Jenner was successful as cowpox virus produces
(*a*) severe infection in humans resulting in deaths
(*b*) a mild infection in humans which is not enough to produce active immunity
(*c*) a mild infection in humans which is enough to produce active immunity
(*d*) no infection in humans

3. Dr. Jenner made his experiment on a healthy boy who
(*a*) died after experimentation
(*b*) could not be relieved of his mark of putsule
(*c*) developed the sings of putsule on his body when he was injected the matter of cowpox
(*d*) was paid for it

4. Passage here is having a/an
(*a*) narrative style
(*b*) analytic style
(*c*) provocative style
(*d*) idiomatic style

PASSAGE-26

The Indian culture of our times is in the making. Many of us are striving to produce a blend of all cultures that seem today to be in clash with one another. No culture can live, if it attempts to be exclusive. There is no such things as pure Aryan culture in existence in India today. Whether the Aryans were indigenous to India or were unwelcome intruders, does not interest me much. What does interest me is the fact that may remote ancestors blended with one another with the utmost freedom and we of the present generation are a result of that blend. I do not want my house to be walled in, on all sides and my windows to be stuffed. I want the cultures of all lands to be blown about my house as freely as possible. But I refuse to be blown off my feet by any. I would have any young men and women with literary tastes to learn as much of English and other world-languages as they like, and then expect them to give the benefits of their learning to India and the world alike like a Bose, a Ray or Tagore. But I would not have a single Indian forget, neglect or be ashamed of his mother tongue, or feel that he or she cannot think or express the best thoughts in his or her own vernacular. Mine is not a religion of the prison house.

1. The author views Indian Culture as
(*a*) pure Aryan culture.
(*b*) a clash of cultures.
(*c*) a continual blend of cultures.
(*d*) the culture of remote ancestors.

2. The author thinks that
(*a*) the Aryans were indigenous to India.
(*b*) the Aryans were unwelcome intruders.
(*c*) the question whether the Aryans were indigenous or not is not of interest.
(*d*) the culture that we have inherited is the Aryan culture.

3. The author wants
(*a*) the cultures of others to be kept out.
(*b*) the cultures of others to replace our old culture.
(*c*) the freedom to blend other cultures with our own.
(*d*) the preservation of the culture of our ancestors.

4. The author wants Indians to
(*a*) learn only English, as much as they like.
(*b*) learn English and other world languages.
(*c*) learn only the mother tongue or the vernacular.
(*d*) English and other world languages in addition to the mother tongue.

PASSAGE-27

As civilization proceeds in the direction of technology, it passes the point of supplying all the basic essentials of life, food, shelter, clothes, and warmth. Then we are faced with a choice between using technology to provide and fulfil needs which have hitherto been regarded as unnecessary or, on the other hand, using technology to reduce the number of hours of work which a man must do in order to earn a given standard of living. In other words, we either raise our standard of living above that necessary for comfort and, happiness or we leave it at this level and work shorter hours. I shall take it as axiomatic that mankind has, by that time, chosen the latter alternative. Men will be working shorter and shorter hours in their paid employment.

1. "Then we are faced with a choice..." what does "then'' refer to?
   (*a*) When automation takes over many aspects of human life
   (*b*) The present state of civilization
   (*c*) The past stage of civilization
   (*d*) After having provided the basic essentials of life
2. What does the passage suggest about the use of technology?
   (*a*) It creates new and essential needs for mankind
   (*b*) It is opposed to the basic essentials of life
   (*c*) It is complementary to a raised standard of living
   (*d*) It is responsible for man's love of comfort and happiness
3. What does increased use of technology imply?
   (*a*) An advanced stage in human civilization
   (*b*) A backward step in human culture
   (*c*) Unnecessary comfort and happiness for mankind
   (*d*) Man's zest for more and more work
4. What does the author suggest?
   (*a*) Man will gradually rise above his present stage in civilization
   (*b*) Man will gradually settle down to the same stage with fewer hours of work
   (*c*) Man will gradually raise his standard of living by working longer hours
   (*d*) Man will gradually earn a given standard of living with the help of technology

PASSAGE-28

It is said that ideas are explosive and dangerous. To allow them unfettered freedom is, in fact, to invite disorder. But, to this position, there are at least two final answers. It is impossible to draw a line round dangerous ideas, and any attempt at their definition involves monstrous folly. If views, moreover, which imply disorder are able to disturb the foundations of the State, there is something supremely wrong with the governance of the State. For disorder is not a habit of mankind. We cling so eagerly to our accustomed ways that, as even Burke insisted; popular violence is always the outcome of a deep popular sense of wrong.

1. What is the central point that the passage emphasizes?
   (*a*) It is unnecessary to define dangerous ideas
   (*b*) Dangerous ideas are born out of the enjoyment of freedom
   (*c*) A well-governed State is unaffected by dangerous ideas
   (*d*) Dangerous ideas originate from man's preoccupation with politics
2. From a close study of the passage, which one of the following statements emerges most clearly?
   (*a*) The author is against the exercise of political freedom
   (*b*) He is indifferent to dangerous and explosive ideas
   (*c*) He welcomes violence as a method to change governments
   (*d*) He warns that violence is the outcome of popular dissatisfaction with the government
3. The author says, 'we cling eagerly to our accustomed ways'. Which one of the following statements may be considered as the assumption of the author?
   (*a*) We are afraid of social changes
   (*b*) Mankind is averse to any disorder
   (*c*) We have developed inertia that makes us incapable of social action
   (*d*) There is an all-round lack of initiative in the society
4. Which of the following statements may most correctly bring out the significance of the opinion of Burke quoted in the passage?
   (*a*) Burke advocated violence against injustice
   (*b*) Burke's opinion coincides with the author's opinion on explosive and dangerous ideas
   (*c*) Burke hated any popular uprising
   (*d*) Burke had no belief in political liberty

PASSAGE-29

The psychological causes of unhappiness, it is clear, are many and various. But all have something in common. The typical unhappy man is one who, having been deprived in youth of some normal satisfaction, has come to value this one kind of satisfaction more than any other, and has therefore given to his life a one-sided direction, together with a quite undue emphasis upon the achievement as opposed to the activities connected with it. There is, however, a further development which is very common in the present day. A man may feel so completely thwarted that he seeks no form of satisfaction, but only distraction and oblivion. He then becomes a devotee of "pleasure". This is to say, he seeks to make life bearable by becoming less alive. Drunkenness, for example, is temporary suicide - the happiness that it brings is merely negative, a momentary cessation of unhappiness.

1. Who is a typical unhappy man?
   (*a*) One who has been deprived of normal satisfaction in youth
   (*b*) One who finds life unbearable and attempts suicide
   (*c*) One who does not mind momentary unhappiness
   (*d*) One who seeks every form of satisfaction
2. "One sided direction" refers to the pursuit of which one of the following?
   (*a*) Drinking and forgetfulness
   (*b*) The satisfaction one had been deprived of
   (*c*) Activities leading to happiness
   (*d*) Every form of psychological satisfaction
3. Which one of the following is the correct statement?
   Drinking helps the unhappy only to
   (*a*) forget their dissatisfaction
   (*b*) get sublime happiness
   (*c*) get the motivational needs fulfilled
   (*d*) concentrate harder
4. What does "becoming less alive" imply?
   (*a*) Neglect of health
   (*b*) Decline in moral values
   (*c*) Living in a make-believe world
   (*d*) Leading a sedentary way of living

PASSAGE-30

What is to be the limit of forgiveness? It would probably have been allowed by many of the ancients that an unforgiving temper was not to be commended. They would have said, we are not to exact a penalty for every nice offence; we are to overlook some things; we are to be blind sometimes. But they would have said at the same time, we must be careful to keep our self-respect, and to be on a level with the world. On the whole, they would have said, it is the part of a man fully to requite to his friends their benefits and to his enemies their injuries.

1. Which one of the following is the correct statement?
   According to the writer we must
   (*a*) ignore an offence if it is nice
   (*b*) forgive people if they bring us nice presents
   (*c*) forgive pretty offenders
   (*d*) not punish each and every offence
2. Which one of the following is the correct statement?
   We must
   (*a*) be blind if we want to forgive others
   (*b*) be blind to the faults of our friends
   (*c*) be indifferent to what others do
   (*d*) overlook certain things
3. Which one of the following is the correct statement?
   In ancient times people were
   (*a*) ordered to lose their tempers
   (*b*) permitted to lose their tempers and not forgive their enemies
   (*c*) told that it was not good to have an unforgiving temper
   (*d*) advised to forgive each and every offence committed by both friends and foes
4. What is the underlying tone of the passage?
   (*a*) We must be forgiving in general
   (*b*) We must forgive our friends
   (*c*) There is no limit whatsoever to our duty to forgive
   (*d*) We must always punish the wrongdoer

PASSAGE-31

The bird egg is a self-contained life-support system for the developing bird embryo. All the nutrients, minerals, energy sources and water utilized by the embryo during its incubation are already present in the freshly laid egg, so that the egg requires only warning by the parents and periodic turning to prevent the adhesion of the embryo to the shell membranes. Still, the egg lacks one crucial requirement : oxygen, which drives the metabolic machinery of the embryonic cells so that they can execute the complex maneuvers of development. How does the egg breathe, taking up oxygen from the surrounding atmosphere and discharging carbon dioxide, the waste product of respiration?

Gas exchange is usually associated with the periodic inhalation of a fluid medium (air or water), which carries oxygen to the capillaries of the lungs or the gills and removes carbon dioxide from the respiratory organ with each exhalation. The lungs or the gills are driven by muscles whose rate of pumping is determined by metabolic demand and controlled by the nervous system. Yet the eggs of birds and other organisms (such as insects, spiders, amphibians and reptiles) show no respiratory movements, and there are no air currents within the egg that could transport oxygen to the capillaries of the growing embryo. Instead the egg "breathes" by diffusion through thousands of microscopic pores in the shell.

Gas moves through the pores by the passive process of diffusion : the tendency for a high concentration of a molecule to run downhill to an area of lower concentration. Diffusion takes place because of the kinetic energy of gas molecules and does not require the direct expenditure of metabolic energy by the embryo : the lower concentration of oxygen inside the egg brings new oxygen in through the pores from the outside, where the concentration is higher. Conversely, the concentration of carbon dioxide inside the egg causes those molecules to diffuse toward the outside, where there are essentially none. These diffusion processes are governed by the available pore area of the shell, the length of the pores and the concentration differences of the gases diffusing across the shell.

The water content of the air within the egg is greater than that of the air outside it, and so the pores will also allow water molecules (which are smaller than oxygen molecules) to diffuse out. Animals have evolved many specialized adaptations for conserving water, but bird eggs seem designed to lose it at a controlled rate. Most of the energy needed for embryonic development is taken from the fat stores of the yolk, and for every gram of fat burned an almost equal mass of metabolic water is generated. Therefore, the relative water content of the egg will increase during incubation unless water is lost. If the relative water content at hatching is to equal that of the freshly laid egg, about 15 per cent of the initial mass of the egg must be lost as water. As breeders of domestic fowl well know, this amount of water loss is essential for successful hatching.

1. The passage is primarily concerned with
(*a*) explaining difficulties involved in cultivating domestic fowl.
(*b*) explaining the origin of passive diffusion as a method of respiration.
(*c*) explaining the processes of gas and water diffusion in eggs.
(*d*) distinguishing between passive diffusion and active respiration.

2. A necessary ingredient in the eggshell's suitability for gas exchange is its
(*a*) opacity (*b*) fragility
(*c*) permeability (*d*) adhesiveness

3. The passage contains information that would answer which of the following questions about fowl-breeding?
I. What function does turning the fertilized egg serve in the hatching process?
II. Why must the egg shed water during the hatching process?
III. What occurs when the amount of water loss during hatching exceeds 15 per cent of the egg's initial mass?
(*a*) II only (*b*) I only
(*c*) I and II only (*d*) II and III only

4. The passage would be most likely to appear in
(*a*) a pamphlet designed to introduce novice breeders of domestic fowl to the advantages of current techniques.
(*b*) an agricultural research report focused on the history of fowl-breeding practices in the United States.
(*c*) a Congressional report urging the appropriation of funds for research into needed improvements in egg-hatching.
(*d*) a scientific journal article highlighting biochemical and physical principles underlying common phenomena.

5. According to the passage, which of the following statements is true of the extent of water loss by the egg during the hatching process?
(*a*) It exceeds the initial mass of the egg by 15 per cent.
(*b*) It is regulated by a specialized adaptation for conserving water.
(*c*) It should compensate for the egg's entire water gain during incubation.
(*d*) It should amount to 15 per cent of the egg's water gain during incubation.

PASSAGE-32

Globalization, liberalization and free market are some of the most significant modern trends in economy. **Most economists** in our country seem **captivated** by the spell of the free market. Consequently, nothing seems good or normal that does not accord with the requirements for the free marekt. A price that is determined by the seller or, for that matter, established by anyone other than the aggregate of consumers seems **pernicious.** Accordingly, it requires a major act of will to think of price-fixing as both normal and having a valuable economic function. In fact, price-fixing is normal in all industrialized societies because the industrial system itself provides, as an effortless consequence of its own development, the price-fixing that it requires. Modern industrial planning requires and rewards great size. Hence a comparatively small number of large firms will be competing for the same group of consumers. That each large firm will act with consideration of its own needs and thus avoid selling its products for more than its competitors charge is commonly recognised by **advocates** of free-market economic theories. But each large firm will also act with full consideration of the needs that it has in common with the other large firms competing for the same customers. Each large firm will thus avoid significant price-cutting, because price-cutting will be prejudicial to the common interest in a **stable** demand for products. Most economists do not see price-fixing when it occurs because they expect it to be brought about by a number of **explicit** agreements among large firms, it is not.

Moreover, those economists who argue that allowing the free-market to operate without interference is the most efficient method of establishing prices have not considered the economics of non-socialist countries. Most of these economics employ intentional price-fixing, usually in an **overt** fashion. Formal price-fixing by cartel and informal price-fixing by agreements covering the members of an industry are common place. Were there something peculiarly efficient about the free market and inefficient about price-fixing, the countries that have avoided the first and used the second would have suffered drastically in their economic development. There is no indication that they have.

Socialist industry also works within a framework of controlled prices. In the early 1970's the Soviet Union began to give firms and industries some flexibility in adjusting prices that a informal evolution has accorded the capitalist system. Economists in the USA have hailed the change as a return to the free-market. But the then Soviet firms were not in favour of the prices established by a free-market over which they exercised little influence; rather. Soviet firms acquired some power to fix prices.

1. The author's primary objective of writing the passage seems to:
(*a*) belie the popular belief that the free-market helps enhance development of industrial societies
(*b*) advocate that price-fixing is unavoidable and it is beneficial to the economy of any industrialized society
(*c*) explain the methodology of fixing price to stabilize free-market
(*d*) prove that price-fixing and free-market are compatible and mutually beneficial to industrialized society
(*e*) create awareness among the general public regarding combating price-fixing by large firms

2. Which of the following statements (1), (2) and/or (3) is/are TRUE in the context of the information given in the passage?
The information in the passage is helpful to:
1. know some of the ways in which prices can be fixed
2. identify the products for which price-fixing can be more beneficial
3. differentiate between the economics of various countries

(*a*) Only (1) (*b*) Only (2)
(*c*) Only (3) (*d*) Only (1) and (2)
(*e*) None of these

3. Considering the literal meaning and connotations of the words used in the passage, the author's attitude towards "Most economists" can best be described as:
(*a*) derogatory and antagonistic
(*b*) impartial and unbiased
(*c*) spiteful and envious
(*d*) critical and condescending
(*e*) indifferent

4. The author feels that price fixed by seller seems pernicious because:
(*a*) people do not have faith in large firms
(*b*) people do not want the Government to fix prices
(*c*) most economists believe that consumers should determine prices
(*d*) most economists believe that no group should determine prices
(*e*) people do not want to decide prices

5. Which of the following statements is **definitely TRUE** in the context of the passage? Price fixing is:
(*a*) a profitable result of economic development
(*b*) an inevitable result of the industrial system
(*c*) the joint result of a number of carefully organized decisions
(*d*) a phenomenon uncommon to industrialized societies
(*e*) a result of joint venture of the Government and industry

6. According to the passage, price-fixing in non-socialistic countries is generally:
(*a*) intentional and widespread
(*b*) illegitimate, but beneficial
(*c*) conservative and inflexible
(*d*) legitimate and innovative
(*e*) conservative and scarce

7. What was the result of the then Soviet Union's change in economic policy in the 1970's?
(*a*) They showed greater profits
(*b*) They had less control over the free-market
(*c*) They were able to adjust to techno-advancement
(*d*) They acquired some authority to fix prices
(*e*) They became more responsive to free-market

8. The author's primary concern seems to:
(*a*) summarise conflicting view points
(*b*) make people aware of recent discoveries
(*c*) criticise a point of view
(*d*) predict the probable results of a practice
(*e*) prepare a research proposal

9. Which of the following statements about the Socialist industry is/are false?
1. It works under certain price restrictions.
2. It has no authority to determine prices

3. It hails the strategy of price fixing, as a major deviation

(*a*) Only (1) is false

(*b*) Only (2) is false

(*c*) Only (3) is false

(*d*) (1) and (2) are false

(*e*) (2) and (3) are false

PASSAGE-33

Educational planning should aim at **meeting** the educational needs of the entire population of all age groups. While the traditional structure of education as a three layer hierarchy from the primary stage to the university represents the core, we should not overlook the periphery which is equally important under modern conditions workers need to rewind, or renew their enthusiasm, or strike out in a new direction, or improve their skills as much as any university professor. The retired and the aged have their needs as well. Educational planning, in their words, should take care of the needs of everyone.

Our structures of education have been built up on the assumption that there is a terminal point to education. This basic defect has become all the more harmful today. A UNESCO report entitled "Learning to Be" prepared by Edgar Faure and others in 1973 asserts that the education of children must prepare the future adult for various forms of self-learning. A viable educational system of the future should consist of modules with different kinds of functions serving a diversity of constitutent. And performance, not the period of study, should be the basis for credentials. The writing is already on the wall.

In view of the fact that the significance of a commitment of lifelong learning and lifetime education is being discussed only in recent years even in educationally advanced countries, the possibility of the idea becoming an **integral** part of educational thinking seems to be *a* **far cry**. For, to move in that direction means such more than some simple rearrangement of the **present** organisation of education. But a good beginning can be made by developing open university programmes for older learners of different categories and introducing extension services in the conventional colleges and schools. Also these institutions should learn to coorporate with the numerous community organisations such as liraries, museums, municipal recreational programmes, health services, etc.

1. According to the passage, the present education structures assume which of the following:

(*a*) Education is a one time process.

(*b*) All people can be educated as per their needs.

(*c*) Discussions on lifelong learning should continue for some more time

(*d*) Present educational planning is very much practical

(*e*) Simple rearrangement of the present educational system is a must

2. According to the author, educational planning should attempt to:

(*a*) decide a terminal point to education

(*b*) train the people at the core

(*c*) fulfil the educational needs of everyone

(*d*) encourage conventional schools and colleges

(*e*) overlook the people on the periphery

3. According to the author, what should be the basis for awarding credentials?

(*a*) Duration of the course

(*b*) Diversity of the topics covered

(*c*) Participation in community activities

(*d*) Real grasp of matter or skill

(*e*) Competence of the course-teachers

4. In the context of the passage, what is the meaning of the sentence "The writing is already on the wall"?

(*a*) The signs of change are already visible

(*b*) Everything is uncertain nowadays

(*c*) It is a mysterious process

(*d*) Changes have already taken place

(*e*) You cannot change the future

5. According to the author, the concept of "lifetime education" is:

(*a*) not practical

(*b*) not desirable

(*c*) in vogue in advanced countries

(*d*) still in formative stages

(*e*) as old as traditional education

6. Which of the following is not true in the context of the passage?

(*a*) 'Learning to Be' defends that there is a terminal point to education

(*b*) Needs of aged and retired should also be considered

(*c*) Lifelong learning is a recent concept

(*d*) Schools and colleges should open extension services

(*e*) 'Workers' knowledge and skills also need to be updated constantly

7. Which of the following best describes the purpose of the author?

(*a*) To criticise the present educational system

(*b*) To strengthen the present educational practices

(*c*) To present a satirical style

(*d*) To present a pragmatic point of view

(*e*) To support non-conventional educational organisations

8. What is the main thrust of the author?
(*a*) One should never cease to learn
(*b*) Traditional systems should be strengthened
(*c*) There is no substitute for the extant system of education
(*d*) Formal education is more important than non-formal
(*e*) It is impossible to meet the needs of everyone

9. Integrating the concepts of lifelong learning with the educational structure:
(*a*) simple rearrangement of present educational organisations
(*b*) longer durations for all formal courses
(*c*) more weightage for actual performance than real understanding
(*d*) closing dawn conventional schools and colleges
(*e*) None of these

10. What should be the major characteristic of the future educational system?
(*a*) Different modules with same function
(*b*) Same module for different groups
(*c*) No modules but compulsory standard programme for all
(*d*) Rearrangement of various course contents
(*e*) None of these

11. According to the author, what measures should open university adopt to meet modern conditions?
(*a*) Open more colleges on traditional lines
(*b*) Primary education should be under the control of the open universities
(*c*) Develop various programmes for adult learners
(*d*) De-recognition of various community organisations
(*e*) Cater to the needs of those who represent 'core'

12. Which of the following is most opposite in meaning of the phrase 'a far cry' as used in the passage?
(*a*) Next to impossible
(*b*) Making loud noise
(*c*) Very funny
(*d*) A reality
(*e*) A theoretical suggestion

13. Which of the following is most nearly the same in meaning as the word 'present' as used in the passage?
(*a*) gift (*b*) existing
(*c*) given (*d*) new
(*e*) outward

14. Which of the following is most opposite in meaning of the word 'integral' as used in the passage?
(*a*) minor (*b*) major
(*c*) essential (*d*) independent
(*e*) unwilling

15. Which of the following is most nearly the same in meaning as the word 'meeting' as used in the passage?
(*a*) satisfying (*b*) contacting
(*c*) representing (*d*) looking
(*e*) approaching

PASSAGE-34

Water plays a versatile role in the functioning of the biosphere. The water cycle has two distinct branches — the atmospheric branch and the terrestrial branch. In the atmosphere, water exists mainly in gaseous form. One the earth, liquid forms and solid forms (ice/snow) predominate.

Water is important to the biosphere in that it is from water that the biosphere **draws** its most abundant element, hydrogen. Hydrogen in the form of carbohydrates constitute a very important source of energy for all living things. Although we have plentiful supply of water in the oceans, it is not of direct use to us. We have to depend upon a small stock of water-less than 1% — contained in our rivers and fresh water lakes and in the subsoil. Even this small proportion can cause havoc to life if it is not properly managed: The reference here is to floods.

We return to the subject of floods again since nature's fury seems still **unabated.** While relief measures are undoubtedly important, attention has to be focussed on the long-term flood control measures. In the past, we had constructed flood moderation reservoirs across catchment areas of rivers, and built 19,260 km. of embankments and 27,850 km. length of drainage channels. Besides, 18,900 villages have been raised above the flood level upto March 1997.

The fact is that long-term flood control measures to be effective should include both traditional methods and afforestation measures. The intensity of floods may be reduced by keeping the drainage channels clear and removing the accumulated silt from reservoirs and river-beds. In fact, the dams built have trapped silt coming from the hills and prevented its large accumulation in river-beds downstream. Hence, the new emphasis on building more dams in the northern rivers should be welcomed. The ambankements also need to be **reinforced.** In many places, they are just made of mud and sand and easily breached by a little gush of water. Other improvements should be in the regulation of water discharge from filled reservoirs and in the flood forecasting system. Even the present warning system, though inadequate, has helped to save many valuable lives and property. Since the States have been **lethargic** in implementing flood control schemes and since most rivers flow through many States, it would be better if flood control is handled by the Centre. The mighty Himalayan rivers are unlikely to be tamed unless we have a basic understanding as to how flood originate. Since 1947, Indian and foreign scientists have been repeatedly emphasizing that the volume of water in the Himalayan rivers in the monsoons are the combined effect of rainfall, snow melt and glacier discharges. Even the first expert committee set up by Mr. Nehru had opined that a serious study of the snow melt and glacier discharges is essential for avoiding flood disasters in the north. But efforts in this direction, during the last 50 years, have been very inadequate. Now that satelite pictures are avilable detailing the snow cover in the Himalayas over large areas and their movements the government would do well to initiate measures to obtain the relevant data from such pictures. Field studies in the Himalayan region would also help flood control measures.

1. Which of the following according to the passage is a new non-traditional method of flood control?
(*a*) Construction of flood moderation reservoirs across catchment areas of rivers
(*b*) Building embankments
(*c*) Laying drainage channels
(*d*) Planting more areas with trees
(*e*) Raising village levels

2. The author speaks approvingly of all of the following EXCEPT .....
(*a*) afforestation measures
(*b*) the last five decades' efforts at studying the Himalayan environment
(*c*) emphasis on building dams
(*d*) inadequate flood warning system
(*e*) traditional methods of flood control

3. The author welcomes building dams in the northern rivers because they ......
(*a*) prevent trapping the silt coming from the hills
(*b*) store water for irrigation
(*c*) store water for power generation
(*d*) store water for navigation
(*e*) do none of these

4. The author's attitude is ......
(*a*) cynical (*b*) critical
(*c*) constructive (*d*) conservative
(*e*) optimistic

5. The author seems to favour ....
1. traditional methods
2. afforestation
3. soil conservation measures
(*a*) (1) only (*b*) (2) only
(*c*) (3) only (*d*) (1) and (2) only
(*e*) (1) and (3) only

6. Which of the following statement(s) is/are definitely TRUE in the context of the passage?
1. A significant proportion of water on the earth is not of direct use to us
2. Water from rainfall, glaciers and snowmelt do not pose any threat to life and property
3. Water exists in atmosphere in the same state as is avilable on the earth
(*a*) (1) only (*b*) (2) only
(*c*) (3) only (*d*) (1) and (2) only
(*e*) (1) and (3) only

7. The difficulty in controlling Himalayan rivers is ....
(*a*) inadequate numbers of dams
(*b*) inadequate number of reservoirs in catchment areas of rivers
(*c*) inadequate length of drainage channels
(*d*) lack of knowledge of snow melt and glacier discharges
(*e*) lack of knowledge of rainfall

8. Which of the following is a new suggestion of the author?
(*a*) Water discharge should be regulated
(*b*) The drainage channels should be cleared up
(*c*) The reservoirs built across the catchment areas of rivers should be desilted
(*d*) The river-beds should be desilted
(*e*) A flood forecasting system should be established

9. A deficiency in the flood control measures contributing to the intensity of floods is the ....
(*a*) clearing up of the drainage channels
(*b*) destiliting of reservoirs built across the catchment areas of rivers
(*c*) weak embankment
(*d*) desilting of rivers-beds
(*e*) lack of a warning system

10. According to the passage, the flood problem arises because ......
(*a*) afforestation and soil conservation measures have not been taken
(*b*) reservoirs across catchments areas of rivers have not been built
(*c*) embankements have not been built
(*d*) drainage channels have not been laid
(*e*) levels of villages have not been raised

11. The author recommends all of the following EXCEPT ....
(*a*) use of data from satellite pictures
(*b*) field studies of rainfall
(*c*) field studies of glacier discharges
(*d*) field studies of snow melt
(*e*) asking states to take flood control measures

PASSAGE-35

Peace and order are necessary, not just in our own country but also at the international level, if we are to secure national progress and development. The different countries in the world are coming closer today due to faster means of transport and communication. Economically, they are become increasingly interdependent. If peace is disturbed in one part of the world, it has adverse effects in other parts of the world as well. Nuclear weapons have already threatened the world with nuclear war. If the conflicts between different nations are not settled in time, they might **culminate** in a nuclear war destroying the whole world. It is therefore in our own interest that the world is free of conflicts. If at all there are any, they must be settled promptly and peace should be restored. That is why we have declared the establishment of international peace and understanding as an objective of our foreign policy.

We need the help and co-operation of other countries for our scientific, industrial and economic development, especially in those fields where we have yet to achieve self-sufficiency. We obtain the latest machinery, technology and financial aid from the developed countries. On our part we, too, offer help to the underdeveloped countries. We are keen on maintaining friendly relations with other countries. Such friendly relations **foster** international understanding.

We have always exerted ourselves to see that the disputes arising between the different nations are settled through peaceful negotiations. We play an active role in the United Nations, the South Asian Association for Regional Co-operation, the Commonwealth of Nations and other such international organisations. We make it a point to participate in the international conferences on issues like energy crisis, environmental imbalance, nuclear arms race, etc. We always offer a helping hand to other nations affected by natural calamities such as famines, earthquakes, floods and so on. We strive to maintain peaceful and friendly relations with our neighbouring countries. Why do we do all this? We sincerely believe that the conflits in today's world should be minimised, making way for better cooperation among the nations. If this is achieved, human resources will no longer be wasted in things like war or aggression. There will be no destruction of wealth. We believe that, in a peaceful world, there will be greater scope for the economic and cultural development of countries.

1. Which of the following statements is NOT TRUE in the context of the passage?
(*a*) International conflicts must be settled promptly
(*b*) We try to maintain friendly relations with our neighbours
(*c*) We participate in many international conferences
(*d*) Friendly relations with other countries foster international understand
(*e*) Each country can be considered isolated and insulated from the effects of other countries

2. Which of the following words is largely SIMILAR in meaning of the word **'culminate'** as used in the passage?
(*a*) Reach the highest point
(*b*) Stretch to the maximum
(*c*) Absolute standards
(*d*) Total destruction
(*e*) Coming of age

3. According to the passage, maintaining friendly relations with other countries facilitate
(*a*) developing international understanding
(*b*) exchange of scientists and technologists
(*c*) strategic planning in defence matters
(*d*) import and export of several vital commodities
(*e*) none of the above

4. If the conflicts between nations do not cease
(*a*) international bodies will have to take up these issues
(*b*) international understanding will not be fostered
(*c*) nuclear war will destroy the whole world
(*d*) the means of transport and communication will be disrupted
(*e*) none of these

5. Which of the following is obtained by us from the developed countries, according to the passage?
(*a*) Fertilisers (*b*) Foodgrains
(*c*) Leather Products (*d*) Technology
(*e*) Crude Oil

6. Which of the following according to the passage, is facilitating the process of different countries coming together?
(*a*) Emerging world order
(*b*) Asian Association for Regional Cooperation
(*c*) Our participation in international conferences
(*d*) Need for self-sufficiency
(*e*) Faster means of transport and communication

7. Minimising the conflicts and making way for better co-operation among the nations will result in
(*a*) useful and purposive utilisation of human resources

(*b*) better utilisation of means of transport and communication
(*c*) culmination of nuclear war destroying the world
(*d*) keenness on maintaining friendly relations with other countries
(*e*) preservation of our national unity and integrity

8. The question "Why do we do all this" is asked in the passage in which of the following contexts?
(*a*) We always offer a helping hand to other nations in improving their technology
(*b*) We endeavour to maintain peaceful and friendly relations with our neighbours
(*c*) We obtain the latest machinery, technology and financial aid from the developed countries
(*d*) We have shaped our foreign policy in a balanced and purposeful manner
(*e*) None of these

9. Does any of the following sentences contain any idea expressed in the passage?
(*a*) We have to make conscious efforts to preserve our national unity
(*b*) Our country is huge in size and population where many languages are spoken
(*c*) We have adopted the objective of democracy in the interest of overall development of our country
(*d*) Citizens must be well-informed about public issues in order to participate meaningfully in public life
(*e*) None of these statements contain any idea expressed in the passage

10. Which of the following words is most OPPOSITE in meaning of the word **'foster'** as used in the passage?
(*a*) advocate (*b*) hinder
(*c*) obviate (*d*) facilitate
(*e*) Jettison

PASSAGE-36

Pisa offers a quiet holiday. Apart from the Leaning Tower Square where the tourists flock, the city is free of the kind of crowds one sees at Florence. An 11-km bus ride brings us to Marina de Pisa, the coastal extension of the city, where the Ligurian Sea and quaint buildings provide a few hours of relaxed walks. However, there is not much of a beach.

Gone is the tension of the previous night, when, flying into Italy in the late hours, my wife and I were a little apprehensive. Compared to Germany where we had spent three weeks, Italy, one thought, was 'unsafe'. The fears were compounded when the night bus from the airport terminated at the railway station, instead of going all the way to our hotel. "Ten Euros," said the cab driver at the station when asked how much the ride to the hotel would cost. Quite sure he was overcharging, we got in nevertheless. At 11.30 p.m. we anyway had little choice. The streets were dimly lit and the driver was uncommunicative. Stopping at a desolate building after we had clearly gone out of the city limits, he announced : "Your hotel." I gave him a 10-Euro bill and turned away. But the cabman stopped me. "Your change, sir," he said, pointing to the meter which read 8-20 Euros.

The small change I got back that day was like receiving the certificate of a nation's honesty. Italy, as it turned out, was just fine.

1. The author and his wife were
(*a*) thrilled at the idea of travelling to Italy.
(*b*) concerned about safety.
(*c*) worried because of high cost.
(*d*) worried because of language problem.

2. The author
(*a*) was cheated by the taxi driver.
(*b*) did not like the etiquette of the taxi driver.
(*c*) was pleasantly surprised by the rectitude of the driver.
(*d*) was irked because the driver was very talkative.

3. Pisa
(*a*) has many traffic jams.
(*b*) is full of business houses.
(*c*) is a quiet town.
(*d*) has major pollution problems.

4. Marina de Pisa
(*a*) is known for its beautiful beaches.
(*b*) is full of churches.
(*c*) has many shopping centres.
(*d*) is a coastal city.

PASSAGE-37

Much of our adult state of fear is linked up with the feeling that I, an individual, have to cope single-handed with a hostile world, the details of which have become far too complicated for me to understand. This feeling of isolation is in part a by-product of the way we have been educated and the stress that is pure on passing examinations. The more 'successful' your education, the more likely you are to feel alone, because the process of segregation has been more complete at every stage you proved how much cleverer you are than all those other fellows, until in the end you stand quite alone and afraid. It ought to be possible to manage things in a different way so that we go forward into the future, collaborating as a team instead of looking around for every possible opportunity to knife each other in the back.

ENGLISH

1. An adult in the modern world is in a state of fear because
   (a) he has developed an individuality.
   (b) he feels lonely in an unfriendly world.
   (c) his life has become complicated.
   (d) he cannot understand the challenge.
2. The modern man feels isolated
   (a) because he has passed through the stress of examinations.
   (b) because he is the by-product of 'successful' social system.
   (c) because he fails to receive education.
   (d) because he nurses his feeling of isolation.
3. The writer thinks that fierce competitiveness in the modern educational system
   (a) makes them neurotic.
   (b) makes man clever.
   (c) does not make man care for his fellows.
   (d) makes man hostile to his environment.
4. Modern education makes man feel segregated
   (a) because of its emphasis on materialism.
   (b) by making him distrustful of others.
   (c) by making him stand on his own.
   (d) by inculcating the fear of society in him.
5. It would be a better educational system
   (a) if it would manage things differently.
   (b) if it inculcates the spirit of togetherness.
   (c) if it teaches collaboration with a team.
   (d) if it does not allows us to knife each other in the back.

PASSAGE-38

Diversity typically provides fresh perspectives on issues, but it makes it more difficult to unify the team and reach agreements. The strongest case for diversity on work teams is when these teams are engaged in problem-solving and decision-making tasks. Heterogeneous teams bring multiple perspective to the discussion, thus increasing the likelihood that the team will identify creative or unique solutions. Additionally, the lack of a common perspective usually means diverse teams spend more time discussing issues, which decrease the chances that a weak alternative will be chosen. However, keep in mind that the positive contribution that diversity makes to decision-making teams undoubtedly declines over time. Diverse groups have more difficulty working together and solving problems, but this dissipates with time expect the value-added component of diverse teams to decrease as members become more familiar with each other and the team becomes more cohesive.

1. Diversity on work team leads to
   (a) human problems.
   (b) creative solutions.
   (c) economy in manufacturing.
   (d) higher turnover.
2. With diversity in work-force there is
   (a) difficulty in reaching a solution quickly.
   (b) difficulty in designing wage formula.
   (c) difficulty in managing international market.
   (d) difficulty experienced in shop-floor management.
3. Advantages of diversity
   (a) are sustained over long periods of time.
   (b) lead to furhter increase with time.
   (c) decline as the members come to know each other.
   (d) decline as the absenteeism increases.
4. Problem-solving tasks can be handled by
   (a) homogeneous groups.
   (b) heterogeneous groups.
   (c) management graduates.
   (d) consultants.

PASSAGE-39

The world of today has achieved much, but for all its declared love for humanity it has based itself far more on hatred and violence than on the virtues that make man human. War is the negation of truth and humanity. War may be unavoidable sometimes but its progeny are terrible to contemplate. Not more killing, for man must die, but the deliberate and persistent propagation fo hatred and flasehood, which gradually become the normal habits of the peole. It is dangerous and harmful to be guided in our life's course by hatreds and aversions, for they are wasteful of energy and limit and twist the mind, and prevent it from perceiving the truth.

1. According to the author, the achievements of the world are not impressive because
   (a) there is nothing much to boast of.
   (b) they are mostly in the field of violence.
   (c) its love of humanity is a pretence.
   (d) the world has not made any achievement.
2. War is the negation of truth means
   (a) wars do not exist.
   (b) wars are evil.
   (c) wars spread and advertise falsehood.
   (d) wars kill human beings.
3. According to the author, the world's declared love of humanity is
   (a) false.
   (b) true.
   (c) non-existent.
   (d) not to be taken seriously.
4. Man should be guided by
   (a) scientific discoveries.
   (b) practical wisdom.

(c) generous human feelings.
(d) materialism.

5. Hatred and aversions are unwholesome as they are
(a) dangerous.
(b) harmful.
(c) narrow.
(d) barries in seeing the truth.

PASSAGE-40

Few people ask from books what books can give us. Most commonly we come to books with blurred and divided minds, asking of fiction that it shall be true, of poetry that it shall be false, of biography that it shall be flattering, of history that it shall enforce our own prejudices. If we could banish all such preconceptions when we read, that would be an admirable beginning.

1. According to this passage, most readers think that poetry is essentially
(a) imagination (b) unrealistic
(c) realistic (d) didactic

2. The author's reference to biography being viewed as something 'flattering' suggests that he thinks that it should be
(a) offensive (b) critical
(c) truthful (d) subjective

3. According to the passage, most books of history are
(a) an objective of the past events
(b) the author's views on the past events
(c) reproduction of the records available from the past
(d) an objective interpretation of the past records

4. According to this passage, most readers
(a) expect too much from books
(b) ignore the objective of the writer
(c) do not know what to expect from a book
(d) are positively inclined towards the author

5. The main intention of the author is to
(a) point out the faults of the readers
(b) define what various kinds of books are
(c) suggest the correct approach to books
(d) enumerate the readers' preconceptions

PASSAGE-41

I couldn't sleep that night. A vague feeling of impending misfortune affected me. My sister and I were twins, and you know how subtle the linsk are between such people. It was a wild night. Suddenly, there bursts forth the wild scream of a terrified woman. I knew that it was my sister's voice. I rushed into the corridor. By the light of the corridor lamp, I saw my sister at the door of her room, her face pale with terror, and her hands groping for help, and her whole figure swaying unsteadily. I ran to her and threw my arms around her, but her knees gave way and she fell to the ground.

1. The author couldn't sleep because
(a) the night was wild
(b) she apprehended some trouble
(c) she knew that some calamity would befall her
(d) she felt uneasy

2. It was well known that
(a) she and her sister were twins
(b) twins have a special bond between them
(c) the relationship between twins is always cordial
(d) twins can sense danger more easily than others

3. She rushed into the corridor because
(a) she heard a terrifying cry
(b) her sister called her to the room
(c) she recognised the voic,e of the person who screamed
(d) she dreamt that her sister needed her help

4. She realised that her sister
(a) was in a state of excitement
(b) needed support
(c) was too weak to walk
(d) was gripped with fear

5. She threw her arms around her sister to
(a) express her affection
(b) prevent her from running away
(c) prevent her from falling down
(d) save her from danger

PASSAGE-42

Because millions of years ago, a little tarsier-like creature began to use its hands and became inquisitive, the long trail of evolution towards man began. Those things are among man's characteristic features. Every year he delves deeper and deeper into the secrets of nature and his responsibilities grow more serious. In an age of mass production and machines, collective reason must control mass hysteria and mass instinct. That is the problem. The atomic bomb has only thrown it into higher relief. In the atomic bomb, man has used the fundamental energy process of the universe for destructive purposes, but that is largely an accident of the time and place. All around we have abundant evidence that without this energy, life itself could not exist.

1. The author believes, that man has evolved from a little tarsier-like creature because
(a) his face resembles that of a tarsier

(*b*) he uses his hands and walks like a tarsier
(*c*) he is curious and walks like a tarsier
(*d*) he is curious and uses his hands like a tarsier

2. The increasing human knowledge of the secrets of Nature has given rise to a problem which
(*a*) involves a huge expenditure
(*b*) makes man more and more irreligious and irreverential
(*c*) is both a boon and a bane
(*d*) necessitates a rational and humane approach to individual and social life

3. The invention of the atomic bomb has made this problem
(*a*) more obscure
(*b*) more prominent
(*c*) more controversial
(*d*) insignificant

4. Man has used atomic energy for destructive purposes because
(*a*) it has no constructive purposes at all
(*b*) he does not know how to sue it constructively
(*c*) its constructive use is too expensive to be practicable
(*d*) the force of circumstances compelled him to do so

5. The author thinks that the use of atomic energy
(*a*) will affect the society adversely
(*b*) is needed for the enrichment of life
(*c*) will ultimately destroy our civilization
(*d*) will lead to the end of the universe

PASSAGE-43

The strength of Indian democracy lies in its tradition, in the fusion of the ideas of democracy and national independence which was the characteristic of the Indian nationalist movement long before Independence. Although the British retained supreme authority in India until 1947, the provincial elections of 1937 provided real exercise in democratic practice before national independence; during the Pacific War India was not overrun or seriously invaded by the Japanese and after the War was over, the transfer to power to a government of the Indian Congress Party was a peaceful one as far as Britain was concerned. By 1947 'Indianisation' had already gone far in the Indian Civil Service and Army, so that the new government could start with effective instruments of central control.

After independence, however, India was faced with two vast problems; the first, that of economic growth from a very low level of production, and the second was that of ethnic diversity and the aspirations of subnationalities. The Congress leadership was more aware of the former problem than of the second; as a new political elite which had rebelled not only against the British Raj but also against India's old social order, they were conscious of the need to initiate economic development and undertake social reforms, but as nationalists who had led a struggle against the alien rule on behalf of all parts of India, they took the cohension of the Indian nation too much for granted and underestimated the centrifugal forces of ethnic division, which were bound to be **accentuated** rather than diminished as the popular masses were more and more drawn into politics. The Congress Party was originally opposed to the idea of recognising any division of India on a linguistic basis and preferred to retain the old provinces of British India which often cut across linguistic States was **conceded** as the basis for a federal 'Indian Union'. The rights granted to the States created new problems for the Central Government. The idea of making Hindi the national language of a united India was **thwarted** by the **recalcitrance** of the speakers of other important Indian languages, and the autonomy of the States rendered central economic planning extremely difficult. Land reforms remained under the control of the States and many large-scale economic projects required a degree of cooperation between the Central Government and one or more of the States which it was found impossible to achieve. Coordination of policies and difficult even when the Congtress Party was in power both in the States and at the Centre; when a Congress Government in Delhi was confronted with non-Congress parties in office in the States, it became much **harder**.

1. Why was central economic planning found to be difficult?
(*a*) Multiplicity of States and Union Territories
(*b*) Lack of coordination in different Government departments
(*c*) Autonomy given to the States in certain matters
(*d*) Lack of will in implementing land reforms
(*e*) Ethnic diversity of the people

2. Which of the following problems India was faced with after Independence?
(*a*) Military attack from a country across the border
(*b*) Lack of coordination between the Central and State Governments
(*c*) Improper coordination of various Government policies
(*d*) Increasing the production from a very low level
(*e*) None of the above

3. Which of the following issues was *not* appropriately realised by the Central Government?
(*a*) Ethnic diversity of the people
(*b*) A national language for the country
(*c*) Implementation of the formulated policies

(*d*) Centre-State relations
(*e*) None of the above

4. Which, according to the passage, can be cited as exercise in democratic practice in India before Independnce?
(*a*) The handing over of power by British to India
(*b*) The Indianisation of the Indian Civil Service
(*c*) A neutral role played by the Army
(*d*) Several democratic institution created by the Indian National Congress
(*e*) None of the above

5. Why was the linguistic reorganisation of the States accepted?
(*a*) The States were not cooperating with the Central Government
(*b*) Non-Congress Governments in the States demanded such a reorganisation of the States
(*c*) No common national language could be emerged
(*d*) Strong pressure from the States were exerted on the Central Government to create such States
(*e*) None of the above

6. Choose the word which is most nearly the **SAME** in meaning as the word **'thwarted'** as used in the passage?
(*a*) opposed (*b*) implemented
(*c*) accepted (*d*) diverted
(*e*) advocated

7. Choose the word which is most **OPPOSITE** in meaning of the word **'conceded'** as used in the passage?
(*a*) criticised (*b*) rejected
(*c*) denounced (*d*) withdrawn
(*e*) accorded

8. Choose the word which is most **OPPOSITE** in meaning of the word **'recalcitrane'** as used in the passage?
(*a*) opposition (*b*) dedication
(*c*) amenability (*d*) vulnerability
(*e*) provocation

9. Which of the following statements is **NOT TRUE** in the context of the passage?
(*a*) The Congress Party was originally opposed to the idea of division of States on linguistic basis
(*b*) Economic development and social reforms were initiated soon after Independence
(*c*) The political elite in India rebelled against the British Raj
(*d*) The Congress leadership was fully aware of the problem of ethnic diversity in India at the time of Independence
(*e*) By 1947, Indian Army was fairly Indianised

10. Choose the word which is most nearly the **SAME** in meaning as the word **'accentuated'** as used in the passage?
(*a*) projected (*b*) exhibited
(*c*) mitigated (*d*) devalued
(*e*) sharpened

11. The provincial elections of 1937 in India showed that the
(*a*) supremacy of British in India was likely to be short-lived
(*b*) India was capable of bringing into practice the ideas of democracy
(*c*) Indian Congress was the single largest party of India
(*d*) British Rule not popular in India
(*e*) Indians were peace-loving people

12. The new government could start with effective instrument of central power after independence because the
(*a*) process of Indianisation of the Indian Civil Service had already started
(*b*) Indian army was organised on the pattern of British Army
(*c*) people of India offered their whole-hearted support to the Government
(*d*) transfer of power to the Indian Congress party was peaceful
(*e*) None of the above

13. Why was India not overrun by the Japanese during the Pacific War?
(*a*) Japan had friendly relations with Britain
(*b*) Japan was interested in India's freedom from the British rule
(*c*) It was not an advantageous proposition for Japan from the military perspective
(*d*) Japan was sceptical about its success in the war
(*e*) None of the above

14. Which of the following statements is **TRUE** in the context of the passage?
(*a*) After Independence, India was faced with the problem of linguistic diversity of the people
(*b*) During the Pacific War, India was invaded by Japan
(*c*) Congress leadership was not as much aware of the problem of ethnic diversity as much as of low production
(*d*) Social reforms were neglected by the Government
(*e*) Land reforms were under the control of the Central Government

15. Choose the word which is most **OPPOSITE** in meaning of the word **'harder'** as used in the passage?
(*a*) slower (*b*) easier
(*c*) shorter (*d*) larger
(*e*) inferior

ENGLISH

PASSAGE-44

The International Monetary Fund has played a significantly enhanced role in promoting global economic growth and stability. In one of the important decisions taken at the Pittsburgh G-20 summit, the IMF has been given the mandate to assist in a new mechanism for a peer review of every country's economic policy framework and performance. Policies of many countries including India are already being reviewed by the IMF and after the G-20 summit the richer countries' policies will be subject to scrutiny. Of course, much will depend on how the IMF goes about fulfilling the mandate. But the decision at the summit is in itself a big step towards ensuring that the policies pursued by the G-20 countries "are collectively consistent with more sustainable and balanced trajectories for the global economy." In a related development, the IMF itself will be restructured and made more democratic so as to reflect the current global economic order rather than what prevailed in 1945 when it was set up. Its executive board will become more broad-based. The IMF's system of quotas— from which the voting power of individual members is derived—will be realigned in such a way that developing countries including India and China, now having a 43 per cent share, get five per cent more. That, however, falls short of the 50 per cent share the developing countries have been asking for. But the G-20 ought to be complimented for finally moving forward on a long-pending agenda of internal reform of the IMF and the World Bank.

The IMF will be able to alter the economic policies of countries that have directly or indirectly contributed to the global economic crisis. At Pittsburgh, there were few concrete suggestions for an orderly unwinding of "global imbalances"—the huge current account deficit of the United States matched by the current account surplus of China. It is not clear whether the IMF will be in a position to influence China's exchange rate policy (leading to a revaluation of the yuan) or the U.S.'s inclination to consume. Obviously, continued global cooperation will be necessary even as the world economy climbs out of the recession. The IMF, which has forecast a gradual recovery, has gained in reputation by its generally deft handling of the crisis. For instance, it mobilized resources swiftly and stepped up lending to the countries in need, thereby containing the crisis. Even more significantly all the loans came without the onerous conditions and advice of the kind that showed a disregard for national sensibilities as it happened during the Asian crisis over a decade ago.

1. "... collectively consistent with ... the global economy" means
   (*a*) framing of policies by G-20 countries in such a way that the global economy shows sustained and balanced performance.
   (*b*) continued growth for G-20 countries must be ensured consistently.
   (*c*) ensuring equal economic growth for all the countries.
   (*d*) None of these
2. The title most aptly suited to this passage is
   (*a*) Handling of global economic crisis - Key role of IMF
   (*b*) G-20 countries - Economic bullies or powerhouses
   (*c*) G-20 countries - Impact of their policies on global economy
   (*d*) Global cooperation key to combating economic crisis
3. Which of the following statements is/are true in the context of this passage?
   (1) In the past needy countries were given loans under stringent conditions.
   (2) As per IMF the recovery from the present economic crisis will be a slow process.
   (3) G-20 countries' policies are exempt from IMF's scrutiny.
   (*a*) 3 only (*b*) 1, 2 & 3
   (*c*) 1 & 2 (*d*) 1 & 3
4. Which of the following has been a key contributing factor to the global economic crisis?
   (*a*) Imbalance in the economic policies of certain rich countries.
   (*b*) IMF's stepped up lending to needy countries that did not have the means to pay back.
   (*c*) The huge current account deficit of US.
   (*d*) China's exchange rate policy leading to a revaluation of the Yuan.

PASSAGE-45

Power utilities in the country face an economic paradox: demand for electricity is running 12 per cent ahead of supply, yet they cannot capitalize on it by extracting higher prices from consumers. An industry association in Karnataka has appealed to the state regulator against a proposed hike in tariff, arguing that there is ample scope for power utilities to cut costs. The argument is not without merit. Utilities can gain immensely by just eliminating pilferage of power and ensuring that they bill and collect money for every unit that they produce and supply. There is a lot of slack, especially at the level of the distribution utilities where unmetered and unbilled supply are chronic problems.

The lack of energy accounting in agriculture is a well-known problem. There is no proper record of the number of irrigation pump sets, as a result of which consumption, distribution and transmission losses cannot be correctly estimated. Efforts to extend metering to the distribution transformer level have made little headway. This is despite the fact that Rs. 7,646 crore has been spent under the Accelerated Power Development Reforms Programme, which was conceived in 2002-03 to address some of these issues. The aggregate technical and commercial losses of state power utilities, basically due to theft or free agricultural supply, are still of the order of 33 per cent, enough to extend significant upward pressure on unit cost. Just halving these losses will obviate the need for utilities to seek periodic tariff increases from the regulators. Regulators should bear these in mind while evaluating the tariff proposals of utilities. They should do their utmost to ensure that the guaranteed 15.5 per cent return on equity to utilities does not necessarily translate into a tariff increase. Their job is not easy given that they have to draw a fine balance between keeping average cost per unit of power down and simultaneously ensuring that the returns are attractive enough to encourage new investment. There is a need to push reforms in the distribution segment; though in theory electricity producers and consumers can now deal directly with each other in the new open access system, in practice they cannot reach out to each other because of steep tariffs and other barriers put up by State utilities that own the transmission and distribution networks. It is time regulators cracked down on such insidious attempts by the state utilities to defeat the open access regime in its infancy.

1. Which of the following is not implied in the passage?

(*a*) There is scope to improve the efficiency in distribution of power.

(*b*) It is certainly possible to increase the price of power without any kind of protest from consumers.

(*c*) Demand for electricity is higher than its supply in the country.

(*d*) None of these

2. Which of the following captions would be the most appropriate for the passage?

(*a*) Controlling price of power through efficient distribution

(*b*) Power Sector: Public-Private Partnership

(*c*) Power Sector: Public or Private?

(*d*) The crux of the matter is power theft

3. There is a lack of energy accounting in agriculture because

(1) there are no qualified Chartered Accountants in rural areas.

(2) there is no proper record of the number of irrigation pump sets.

(3) power is often supplied free to agriculturists.

(*a*) 1, 2 & 3 (*b*) 1 & 3

(*c*) 1 only (*d*) 2 only

4. According to the passage which of the following is true?

(*a*) The utilities can get maximum of 15.5% return on equity.

(*b*) State utilities that own the power transmission and distribution networks are largely to blame for the high price of power.

(*c*) Open Access Regime can never be effective in the power sector.

(*d*) Extracting higher prices from consumers will help cut down their consumption of power.

ANSWERS

PASSAGE-1

1	2	3	4	5
(*b*)	(*b*)	(*a*)	(*a*)	(*b*)

PASSAGE-2

1	2	3	4	5
(*b*)	(*a*)	(*c*)	(*d*)	(*b*)

PASSAGE-3

1	2	3	4	5
(*b*)	(*b*)	(*d*)	(*c*)	(*c*)

PASSAGE-4

1	2	3	4	5
(*c*)	(*b*)	(*c*)	(*e*)	(*e*)
6	**7**	**8**	**9**	
(*d*)	(*d*)	(*e*)	(*b*)	

PASSAGE-5

1	2	3	4	5
(*a*)	(*b*)	(*b*)	(*b*)	(*e*)
6	**7**			
(*b*)	(*b*)			

PASSAGE-6

1	2	3	4	5
(*d*)	(*c*)	(*a*)	(*a*)	(*e*)
6	**7**	**8**		
(*a*)	(*e*)	(*c*)		

PASSAGE-7

1	2	3	4	5
(*a*)	(*a*)	(*d*)	(*a*)	(*a*)

PASSAGE-8

1	2	3	4	5
(a)	(c)	(b)	(d)	(c)

PASSAGE-9

1	2	3	4	5
(d)	(a)	(c)	(a)	(d)

PASSAGE-10

1	2	3	4
(d)	(c)	(a)	(d)

PASSAGE-11

1	2	3	4	5
(d)	(b)	(a)	(b)	(b)

PASSAGE-12

1	2	3
(d)	(a)	(a)

PASSAGE-13

1	2	3	4	5
(b)	(d)	(d)	(a)	(c)

PASSAGE-14

1	2	3	4
(c)	(c)	(d)	(c)

PASSAGE-15

1	2	3	4
(a)	(c)	(d)	(a)

PASSAGE-16

1	2	3
(d)	(c)	(b)

PASSAGE-17

1	2	3	4
(d)	(c)	(a)	(d)

PASSAGE-18

1	2	3	4	5
(c)	(c)	(b)	(c)	(b)

PASSAGE-19

1	2	3	4
(d)	(a)	(a)	(a)

PASSAGE-20

1	2	3	4	5
(a)	(d)	(b)	(b)	(d)

PASSAGE-21

1	2	3	4
(b)	(a)	(d)	(c)

PASSAGE-22

1	2	3	4
(a)	(b)	(a)	(d)

PASSAGE-23

1	2	3	4
(d)	(b)	(c)	(a)

PASSAGE-24

1	2	3	4
(b)	(a)	(a)	(c)

PASSAGE-25

1	2	3	4
(c)	(c)	(c)	(a)

PASSAGE-26

1	2	3	4
(c)	(c)	(c)	(d)

PASSAGE-27

1	2	3	4
(d)	(d)	(a)	(b)

PASSAGE-28

1	2	3	4
(b)	(d)	(c)	(b)

PASSAGE-29

1	2	3	4
(a)	(b)	(b)	(c)

PASSAGE-30

1	2	3	4
(d)	(d)	(c)	(c)

PASSAGE-31

1	2	3	4	5
(c)	(c)	(a)	(d)	(a)

PASSAGE-32

1	2	3	4	5
(b)	(a)	(b)	(c)	(b)
6	7	8	9	
(a)	(e)	(a)	(c)	

PASSAGE-33

1	2	3	4	5
(a)	(c)	(d)	(a)	(a)
6	7	8	9	10
(a)	(d)	(a)	(e)	(e)
11	12	13	14	15
(c)	(d)	(b)	(d)	(a)

PASSAGE-34

1	2	3	4	5
(d)	(b)	(e)	(c)	(d)
6	7	8	9	10
(a)	(d)	(a)	(c)	(a)
11				
(e)				

PASSAGE-35

1	2	3	4	5
(e)	(a)	(a)	(c)	(d)
6	7	8	9	10
(e)	(a)	(b)	(e)	(b)

PASSAGE-36

1	2	3	4
(b)	(c)	(c)	(d)

PASSAGE-37

1	2	3	4	5
(b)	(b)	(b)	(b)	(b)

PASSAGE-38

1	2	3	4
(b)	(a)	(a)	(b)

PASSAGE-39

1	2	3	4	5
(c)	(c)	(a)	(c)	(d)

PASSAGE-40

1	2	3	4	5
(c)	(b)	(d)	(b)	(c)

PASSAGE-41

1	2	3	4	5
(b)	(b)	(c)	(d)	(c)

PASSAGE-42

1	2	3	4	5
(d)	(d)	(b)	(d)	(b)

PASSAGE-43

1	2	3	4	5
(c)	(d)	(a)	(e)	(d)
6	7	8	9	10
(a)	(b)	(c)	(d)	(e)
11	12	13	14	15
(b)	(a)	(b)	(c)	(b)

PASSAGE-44

1	2	3	4
(a)	(a)	(c)	(c)

PASSAGE-45

1	2	3	4
(b)	(b)	(d)	(d)

❑❑❑

SECTION b PEDAGOGY OF LANGUAGE DEVELOPMENT

English is a West Germanic language that arose in the Anglo-Saxon kingdoms of England and spread into what was to become south-east Scotland under the influence of the Anglian medieval kingdom of Northumbria. Following the economic, political, military, scientific, cultural, and colonial influence of Great Britain and the United Kingdom from the 18th century, via the British Empire, and of the United States since the mid-20th century, it has been widely dispersed around the world, become the leading language of international discourse, and has acquired use as *lingua franca* in many regions. It is widely learned as a second language and used as an official language of the European Union and many Commonwealth countries, as well as in many world organizations. It is the third most natively spoken language in the world, after Mandarin Chinese and Spanish.

Historically, English originated from the fusion of languages and dialects, now collectively termed Old English, which were brought to the eastern coast of Great Britain by Germanic (Anglo-Saxon) settlers by the 5th century - with the word *English* being derived from the name of the Angles. A significant number of English words are constructed based on roots from Latin, because Latin in some form was the *lingua franca* of the Christian Church and of European intellectual life. The language was further influenced by the Old Norse language due to Viking invasions in the 8th and 9th centuries.

Significance

Modern English, sometimes described as the first global lingua franca, is the dominant language or in some instances even the required international language of communications, science, information technology, business, seafaring, aviation, entertainment, radio and diplomacy. Its spread beyond the British Isles began with the growth of the British Empire, and by the late 19th century its reach was truly global. Following British colonisation from the 16th to 19th centuries, it became the dominant language in the United States, Canada, Australia and New Zealand. The growing economic and cultural influence of the US and its status as a global superpower since World War II have significantly accelerated the language's spread across the planet.

In many former British colonies, English is still used in the government and as a medium of communication among people who do not have another language in common. In some cases, it is a neutral language that is used to avoid giving any one indigenous language too much prestige. English is often used in India, because it is neutral. It is the language of the government. People who speak English have a certain status in society. English is also very important for international travel. Much of the information, countries disseminate about themselves outside of their borders, is in English.

A working knowledge of English has become a requirement in a number of fields, occupations and professions such as medicine and computing; as a consequence over a billion people speak English to at least a basic level. It is one of six official languages of the United Nations.

One impact of the growth of English is the reduction of native linguistic diversity in many parts of the world. Its influence continues to play an important role in language attrition. Conversely, the natural internal variety of English along with creoles and pidgins have the potential to produce new distinct languages from English over time.

LEARNING

A considerable change in the behaviour of the organism is called learning. When organism comes in contact with his environment certain necessary adjustment in the behaviour is needed. This adjustment in behaviour is the result of acquision of various habits, skills, attitudes and knowledge which is actually learning in simple term.

Thus, learning means change in response or behaviour (modification, elimination or acquisition of responses involving some degree of performance) caused partly or wholly by conscious or unconscious experiences. This learning does not include physiological changes such as fatigue, temporary sensory resistance or non functioning even after continued stimulation.

Definition of Learning

It is very difficult to give a universally acceptable definition of learning because psychologists have defined the concept from different angles on the basis of their experiments. The common feature among these definitions is that learning in psychology has the status of a construct which means an idea or image that can not be directly observed like electrons or genes but they are inferred from the behaviour of the organism.

Melvin H Marx has defined learning in the following words;

"Learning is a relatively enduring change in behaviour which is a function of prior behaviour (usually called practice).

Explanation : According to the definition given above learning has three attributes:

1. Learning is a some what permanent change in behaviour. Changes occurred due to illness, fatigue, maturation or the consumption of intoxicants is not learning.
2. Learning is not directly observable. It is inferred from the behaviour of the organism in the form of construct.
3. Learning is a function of practice and experience. Experiences adds learning and practice gives it an enduring nature.

Some other **definitions** of learning are given below;

"Learning is modification of behaviour through experiences." **— Gates**

"Learning involves the acquisition of habit knowledge and attitudes". **—Crow and Crow**

"Learning is any change in behaviour resulting from behaviour." **—Guilford**

"Learning includes both acquisition and retention." **—Skinner**

Characteristics of Learning

On the basis of the meaning and definitions given above following characteristics of learning can be derived:

1. **Learning is a relatively permanent change in behaviour :** Temporary changes in behaviour brought about due to some accidents or consuming any drugs is not learning at all. Learning is a relatively permanent change in behaviour. It is in this context we can say that reading some selected material to pass an examination is not learning. It is because learnt material is forgotten immediately after the exam.
2. **Learning is a progress or growth of the organism :** Learning is a fundamental need of life. Without it, no progress or growth is possible. This process of growth is unending also. One achievement of the organism motivates him to go f r further achievement and thus excellence in many cases is achieved.
3. **Learning is a life long process :** An organism needs learning (behavioural change) at every moment of life to adjust to new situations at every moment. He can not sit idle at any time. Situations all the time force him for the acquisition of new learning.
4. **Learning is not directly observable :** How much learning has taken place in an organism can not be directly observed. It is inferred from his behaviour which is manifested by some activities, mental or physical.
5. **Learning is the result of experiences :** Experiences are gained at every moment of life. Learning is the other name of these experiences.
6. **Learning is a goal directed process :** Learning is a purposeful activity. It is a goal directed process. Learning which is the result of unconscious efforts of the individual is not learning in actual sense.
7. **Learning is retained through practice :** Practice or exercise is a must to retain learning. If practice is not made, learning will be forgotten and the nature of learning will no longer remain permanent. Thus, learning is acquisition and retention both.
8. **Learning is aroused by individual and social needs :** Learning depends upon our social needs, problems, desires, and ideals. There are certain persons who learn very fast whereas others are slow in learning. It should be noticed that social environment affects learning. It is impossible to learn in the absence of environment.
9. **Learning is active and creative :** Learning is active and creative i.e. learning depends upon the active involvement of the learner. It is said that if the learner is not self active, he cannot learn.

   It is, therefore, said that learning is the result of active involvement and experience from the sender and the receiver both.
10. **Learning is universal :** Humans are not the only organism that learn ie, react to the

environment for adjustment. Animals also go through the process of learning though their speed of learning may be slower than humans.

Basic Processes of Teaching and Learning

Teaching-learning process is the heart of education. On it depends the fulfilment of the aims & objectives of education. It is the most powerful instrument of education to bring about desired changes in the students. Teaching learning are related terms. In teaching-learning process, the teacher, the learner, the curriculum & other variables are organised in a systematic way to attain some pre-determined goal.

Essential Aspects of the Teaching-learning Process

According to Diana Laurillard, there are four aspects of the teaching-learning process:

1. **Discussion**—between the teacher and learner.
2. **Interaction**—between the learner and some aspect of the world defined by the teacher.
3. **Adaptation**—of the world by the teacher and action by the learner.
4. **Reflection**—on the learner's performance by both teacher and learner.

According to **Burton**

1. Teaching can become effective only by relating it to process of learning.
2. Teaching objective cannot be realised without being related to learning situation.
3. We may create and use teaching aids to create some appropriate learning situation.
4. The strategies and devices of teaching may be selected in such a manner that the optimal objectives of learning area achieved.
5. To understand principles, goals, objectives of education in right perspective.
6. Appropriate learning situation condition may be created for congenial and effective teaching.

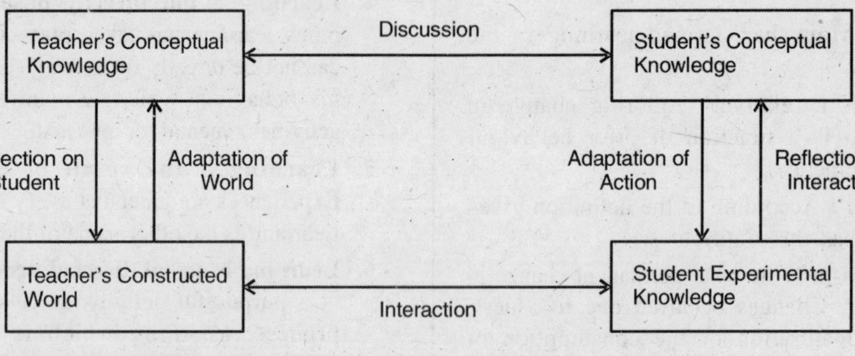

Fig. *Essential aspects of the ideal teaching-learning process*

Approaches to Learning Theories

Aspect	Behaviourist	Cognitivist	Humanist
Learning theorists	Thorndike, Pavlov, Watson, Guthrie, Hull, Tolman, Skinner	Koffka, Kohler, Lewin, Piaget, Ausubel, Bruner, Gagne	Maslow, Rogers
View of the learning process	Change in behaviour	Internal mental process (including insight, information processing, memory, perception)	A personal act to fulfil potential
Locus of learning	Stimuli in external environment	Internal cognitive structuring	Affective and cognitive needs
Purpose in education	Produce behavioural change in desired direction	Develop capacity and skills to learn better	Become self-actualized autonomous
Educator's role	Arranges environment to elicit desired response	Structures content of learning activity	Facilitates development of the whole person
Manifestations in adult learning	Behavioural objectives	Cognitive development	Andragogy
	Competency-based education	Intelligence, learning and memory as function of age	Self-directed learning
	Skill development and training	Learning how to learn	

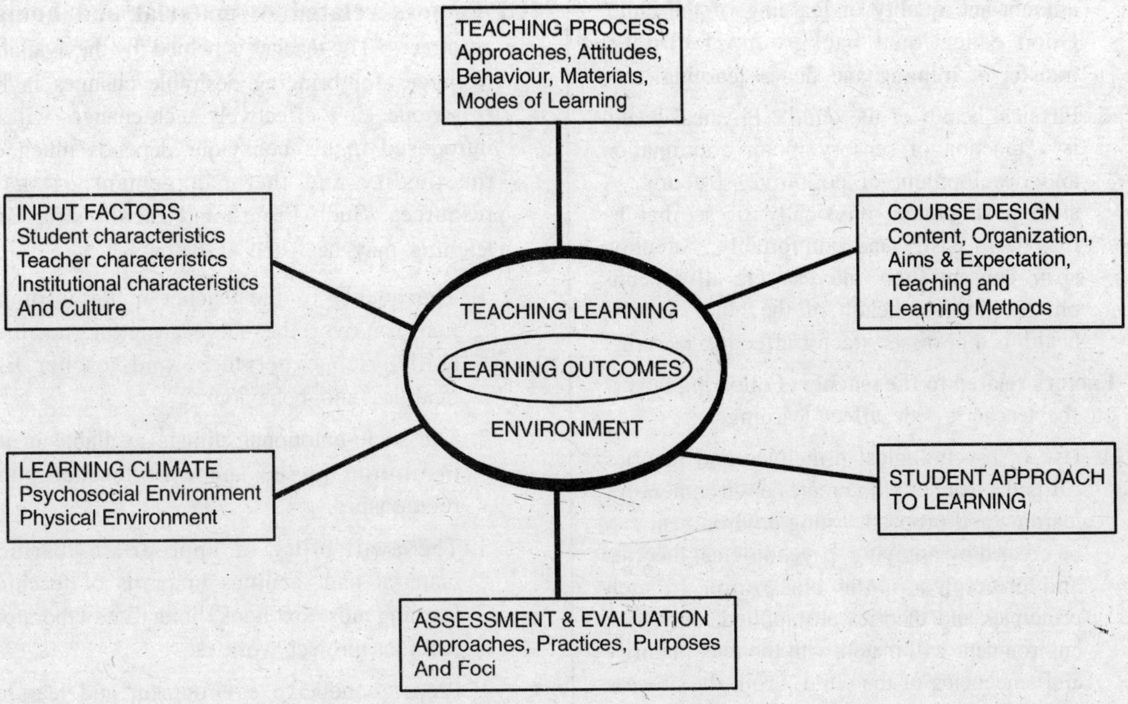

Fig. *Teaching-Learning Environment*

Factors Affecting Learning

Factors affecting learning can be classified into three categories :

(A) Factors belonging to the learner himself
(B) Factors belonging to the teacher
(C) Factors belonging to the material and human resources.

(A) Factors relating to the child : Important such factors are as follows :

1. Motivation level of the child : There is a proverb in Hindi that we can not arrange a market by knitting the shopkeepers with ropes. If learner is not motivated to learn, no learning can take place. If these motives are not there in him, his power of action can not be aroused. If these motives are not there in him, they are given to him from outside. Since, all learners can not be motivated by the same techniques, motives according to the psychology of learners are identified and selected.
2. Intellectual ability of the child : We can not make a mentally retarded child learn by adopting any measure howsoever, it is effective. If level of intelligence of a learner is high, his learning ability will also be high and vice versa provided that he has not become problematic or delinquent because of his superior intelligence.
3. Interest of the child : Children also differ in interests because of the differences in mental tendencies and attitudes to the environment. Interest can also be created by providing incentive to him.
4. Age of the child : Learning efficiency increases with age but to a certain extent till it reaches to the maturity level of a particular age. Maturation of an individual makes a difference in the total learning of an individual. This process is reversed in the old age.
5. Child's willingness to learn : The amount of learning very much depends on the will of the learner to learn. If an inner urge or drive is not there in the child to learn, he will not learn. This will can be developed by raising the aspiration level of students.
6. Availability of guidance facility : Simple trial and error method of learning will not work if guidance is not provided to learners to develop proper insight for learning in them. Guidance can eliminate frustration and tension from their minds and it will work more positively for learning. This guidance should be so much as to facilitate learning. Excessive guidance is an impediment for learning.
7. Background of the child : Socio-economic status of the child's family also affects learning. If educational background of the child is poor and his low family income is a source of continuous tension for the child, a number of factors will work to reduce the

amount and quality of learning of the child. Good educational background facilitates transfer of training and hence learning.

8. Physical health of the child : Physical health is a function of sensory motor coordination and development of cognitive structure. A student should be physically fit so that he may learn easily and comfortably. Attention span, concentration, interests etc all depends on the physical health of the child. Hence, health is a necessary factor affecting learning.

(B) Factors related to the teacher: Following factors on the teacher's side affect learning:

1. Use of psychological principles and theories : It is the teacher who creates environment for learning and proper learning environment can be created by applying psychological theories and principles in the classroom. If such principles and theories are applied, only then environment will match with the age, maturity and tendencies of the child. From the process of child's growth to the procedures of learning and motivation, everything contributes to learning.
2. Professional efficiency of the teacher: The teacher should have full command over the subject that he is to teach along with the knowledge of educational philosophy and psychology. He should be a life long student of his field in order to give more and more to his students.
3. Knowledge of educational technology : Educational technology includes application of mechanical devices into the teaching learning process for the speedy transfer of knowledge to students and use of scientific procedures and practices in the class room. Such a knowledge and his commitment to its use facilitate learning.
4. Knowledge of individual differences : No two individuals are alike with respect to physical, mental or emotional abilities so a teacher has to deal not a class of 40-50 students but 40-50 different individuals. This makes the task of a teacher very difficult and gigantic. The task of a teacher will not be over unless each and every child is satisfied with him.
5. Attitude and personality of the teacher :

   Teaching profession is not a physical job like that of a rickshaw puller. His job is psychological in nature because he deals with human being. Unless his attitude towards humans is not positive and his personality is not structured in the line of learning, learning will not be facilitated.

(C) Factors related to material and human resources: The teacher is helped ;by the available resources for bringing desirable changes in his behaviour. How effectively such changes will be introduced in his behaviour depends much on the quality and the management of these resources. Such things and factors affecting learning may be listed as below:

1. The quality of the teacher in terms of his mastery over the subject matter, teaching skills, rich experiences and teacher like qualities and behaviour.
2. The socio-emotional climate available in the institution in the shape of teacher pupil relationship.
3. The availability of appropriate learning material and facilities in terms of teaching learning aids, text book, library and laboratory facilities project work etc.
4. Proper conducive environment and learning situation like:

   (i) Proper seating arrangement

   (ii) Quite calm and peaceful environment

   (iii) Management and control of factors leading to distraction.

   (iv) Cooperative and competitive group situation

   (v) Learning environment at home

   (vi) Rest and recreation facilities provided to the learner

ACQUISITION

Language acquisition is the process by which the language capability develops in a human. It is the process by which a child acquires its mother tongue. It is the most wonderful feat we perform in our whole life and we do it at an age when we can hardly do anything else. It is an active process by which children, taking cues available to them, construct their own utterances and say things they have never heard of. Language learning is a behaviour acquired by making conscious efforts. It involves certain skills – learning to understand when it is spoken, speaking, reading and writing. It is also forming a certain set of habits. It is acquired by imitation and practice. Since language is a learned activity, we have to learn it and teach it properly.

Distinction between Acquisition and Learning

There are many distinctions between the processes of acquisition and learning.

1. Children within 5 years of age learn their mother tongue through acquisition. A second language, is through conscious effort of learning.
2. Acquisition is an unconscious process where no formal classroom instruction is involved. Learning, however is about conscious knowledge and the application of rules and structures.
3. In language acquisition, the focus is on communication or reception of a message. But in language learning the thrust is on syntax and grammar.
4. The context is usually crucial and meaningful in language acquisition but it need not be important to that extent in language learning.
5. Motivation is a matter of urgent necessity for acquisition. It is not so for second learning.
6. Most importantly, the usual outcome of language acquisition is fluency which is by no means guaranteed in language learning.

It is the process by which humans acquire the capacity to perceive, produce and use words to understand and communicate. This capacity involves the picking up of diverse capacities including syntax, phonetics and an extensive vocabulary. This language might be vocal as with speech or manual as in sign. Language acquisition usually refers to first language acquisition, which studies infants' acquisition of their native language, rather than second language acquisition, which deals with acquisition (in both children and adults) of additional languages.

The capacity to acquire and use language is a key aspect that distinguishes humans from other organisms. While many forms of animal communication exist, they have a limited range of nonsyntactically structured vocabulary tokens that lack cross cultural variation between groups.

A major concern in understanding language acquisition is how these capacities are picked up by infants from what appears to be very input. A range of theories of language acquisition has been created in order to explain this apparent problem including innatism in which a child is born prepared in some manner with these capacities, as opposed to the other theories in which language is simply learned.

Social interactionist theory consists of a number of hypotheses on language acquisition. These hypotheses deal with written, spoken, or visual social tools which consist of complex systems of symbols and rules on language acquisition and development. The compromise between ''nature'' and ''nurture'' is the ''interactionist'' approach. In addition, for years, psychologists and researchers have been asking the same question. What are the language behaviours that nature provides innately and what are those behaviours that are realized by environmental exposure, which as nurture.

The relational frame theory (Hayes, Barnes-Holmes, Roche, 2001), provides a wholly selectionist/learning account of the origin and development of language competence and complexity. Based upon the principles of Skinnerian behaviorism the relational frame theory posits that children acquire language purely through interacting with the environment. The relational frame theorists introduced the concept of functional contextualism in language learning, which emphasizes the importance of predicting and influencing psychological events, such as thoughts, feelings and behaviours, by focusing on manipulable variables in their context. The relational frame theory distinguishes itself from Skinner's work by identifying and defining a particular type of operant conditioning known as derived relational responding, a learning process that to date appears to occur only in humans possessing a capacity for language. Empirical studies supporting the predictions of relational frame theory suggest that children learn language via a system of inherent reinforcements, challenging the view that language acquisition is based upon innate, language-specific cognitive capacities.

Emergentist theories, such as Mac Winney's competition model, posit that language acquisition is a cognitive process that emerges from the interaction of biological pressures and the environment. According to these theories, neither nature nor nurture alone is sufficient to trigger language learning; both of these influences must work together in order to allow children to acquire a language. The proponents of these theories argue that general cognitive processes subserve language acquisition and that the end result of these processes is language-specific phenomena, such as word learning and grammar acquisition. The findings of many empirical studies support the predictions of these theories, suggesting that language acquisition is a more complex process than many believe.

PRINCIPLES OF LANGUAGE TEACHING

Due to the evolution problems of teaching theories, educationists are now mostly concerned with the development of teaching principles rather than theories. These principles are only tested guidelines for a teacher because they are mostly based on learning theories and principles.

1. **Principle of Activity :** This principle states that teaching should mostly go in the direction of students' activities, i.e., teacher should get the students involved physically in his teaching as much as possible. Knowledge which is obtained by the involvement of activity is never forgotten. According to

Mc Dougal, every child has some natural instinct of construction. Because of this instinct he is always in action doing one thing or the other. If a teacher does not get him involved in any activity, he will himself do something without purpose.

Activities are of two types- physical and mental. Both these activities are important in teaching. However, physical activities are preferred to mental ones because acquisition of knowledge is already concerned with mental activities.

The introduction of physical activity into teaching learning process can be understood with an example. We can forget a story read in a book after one or two years but we do not forget the skill of cycling after we have learnt it once. The reason is that activity is involved in the second type of knowledge. So, if a teacher wants to make a knowledge fixed into the minds of learners, he must supplement the theoretical knowledge with the practical one. Even history can be taught by doing activity, by dramatizing the incidents and staging it in the class. Due to the utility of this principle many modern methods of teaching such as Montessori Method, Project method, Kinder Garten method, Problem solving method etc are based on it.

2. **Principle of Interest :** According to this principle, a teacher should teach in the class only when students take interest in it and if this interest does not exist, it should first be created by the teacher. Interests in learning can be created in the class in so many ways. Some of them are given below :

   i. Tell the students the aims of their life.

   ii. Tell them how useful they are for the country.

   iii. Develop curiosity of learning in them.

   iv Clarify the objectives of the lesson before the students.

   v. Teach the subject-matter to students by relating it with their daily life situations.

   vi. Principles of leaning by doing and motivation should be followed.

   vii. Clear cut relation must be established between content, aims and students.

   viii. Lesson should be made interesting by using proper material aids and engineering technology and so on.

3. **Principle of Linking with Life :** It has been seen that every child lives in his own world. Thus, children take interest in those activities and subjects only which have a direct link with their lives. Thus, according to this principle, subject-matter should be taught to students only after it has been linked with the daily life of the child. This enables them to learn at faster rate and with ease. The reason for this is simple enough. When new experiences are integrated with old ones, they also become the part of old experiences. For example, if we want to teach consumer's surplus to students we first of all tell them why or how a commodity is cheap or dear for persons of different incomes. Then we inculcate the concepts of ability to pay and willingness to pay and finally, the concept of consumer's surplus becomes clear to them. If a teacher is fully acquainted with the background of his students only then he can use this principle.

4. **Principle of Definite Aim :** Teaching objectives must be clear before the teacher prior to teaching because only on the basis of these objectives he selects suitable teaching strategies and techniques. For example, if the purpose of a poetry teaching is the appreciation of the poem, then pronunciation and rhythm will be emphasized and if understanding is the aim of poetry teaching, then vocabulary and sense perception will be emphasized. Thus, a teacher must know why he has to do an activity in the class before doing the activity.

5. **Principle of Selection :** Content is selected keeping in view the larger objectives of education. There may be many irrelevant materials in a lesson which are not useful for students. Similarly, many such things may be there in a text-book which do not pace with the level of learner. So, teacher selects only that part of the subject-matter which match the objectives and are meaningful for learners. For example, if a teacher decides that his students should score at least 90% marks in the examination, he selects all those parts which enable the students to score 90% marks in the exam.

6. **Principles of Planning :** A teacher must prepare a lesson plan of the lesson which he is to teach. Planning helps him to identify the expected problems of teaching and select suitable strategies to overcome them. If such a problem arises during teaching about which teacher had not even thought of while preparing the lesson plan, this type of the problem is solved by the teacher on the basis

of his experiences. Planning is actually the name of taking benefit of the experiences of others.

7. **Principle of Division :** If a teacher teaches a lesson after dividing it into different natural parts, his presentation will be effective. But the teacher should keep this fact in mind that every unit of the lesson should be complete in itself and should be able to arouse curiosity for learning of the next unit. This makes the whole lesson eacy and systematic for learners. When a teacher teaches a lesson in this way, he synthesizes these units in a logical sequence also.

8. **Principle of Revision :** Whatever lesson is taught to students, it must be revised by them as well. If it is not done, it will be forgotten soon. Tough subject-matter needs more revisions and easy one needs comparatively less revisions. Home work is given to students only on the basis of this very principles.

9. **Principle of Democratic Dealing :** The behaviour of the teacher should be democratic in the class. It means that he should give full opportunities to students to develop their self thinking and self-expression by respecting their personalities. In democratic dealing teacher is guided by the students and vice-versa. Thus, the teacher develops the lesson with the cooperation of students. He questions them and answers their queries. He also invites them for criticising him at the end of the teaching. All these activities increase the self-confidence of students.

10. **Psychological Principles of Teaching :** These principles are based on psychological researches conducted on lower animals and children. Some of these principles are given below:

    (a) ***Principle of Motivation :*** The task of a teacher becomes very easy if he is successful in motivating his students for learning. Since, motivation is directly related to needs, the teacher must take steps to satisfy their needs. Reward and punishment, praise and blame, arousing and quenching the curiosity of learners, using material aids in teaching, competition and cooperation etc are some important techniques of motivation.

    (b) ***Principle of Recreation :*** Lengthy and dull teaching tasks bore the students and proper enthusiasm on both sides can entertain both of them. In order to reduce the fatigue and boredom of students, teaching task is made interesting. A teacher must make his teaching a means of recreation not a burden on students.

    (c) ***Principle of Individual Differences :*** No two learners are alike in the world in their abilities and interest. So, teaching work is done keeping in view the individual differences of learners. Thus, a teacher has to satisfy at least four groups of students by his teaching simultaneously.
    - Talented and superior students.
    - Weak and dull students.
    - Students of average performance
    - Students with special problems.

    (d) ***Principle of Remedial Teaching :*** It has generally been seen that only those students shun the classes who are educationally backward in any way. This problem of backwardness lies in defective method of teaching and unsystematic classroom management. A good teacher is one who diagnoses his faults of teaching by applying standardized test and adopts remedial measures thereon.

    (e) ***Principle of Sympathy :*** Those teachers who are sympathetic to their students can easily motivate their students for learning. If a teacher is able to develop a feeling in his students that there is none more sympathetic to them than him, the teacher will always be cooperated by his students.

    (f) ***Principle of Reinforcement :*** Reinforcement refers to removing barriers from the way of students and presenting such stimuli before them which increases the rate of responses by learners. The teacher reinforces his students off and on during teaching sometimes verbally and sometimes by giving rewards in order that their enthusiasm for more correct responses increases.

    (g) ***Principle of Training to Senses :*** Five sense organs play a very important role in the acquisition of knowledge. Teacher initiates those activities in the class which are conducive to the development of these senses.

ROLE OF LISTENING

Listening is an active process that has three basic steps.

- **Hearing :** Hearing just means listening enough to catch what the speaker is saying. For example, say you were listening to a report on horses, and the speaker mentioned that no two are alike. If you can repeat the fact, then you have heard what has been said.

- **Understanding :** The next part of listening happens when you take what you have heard and understand it in your own way. Let's go back to that report on horses. When you hear that no two are alike, think about what that might mean. You might think, "Maybe this means that the colour is different for each horse."
- **Judging :** After you are sure you understand what the speaker has said, think about whether it makes sense. Do you believe what you have heard? You might think, "How could the colour to be different for every horse.

How to Become a Good Listener

- Give your full attention on the person who is speaking. Don't look out the window or at what else is going on in the room.
- Make sure your mind is focused, too. It can be easy to let your mind wander if you think you know what the person is going to say next, but you might be wrong! If you feel your mind wandering, change the position of your body and try to concentrate on the speaker's words.
- Let the speaker finish before you begin to talk. Speakers appreciate having the chance to say everything they would like to say without being interrupted. When you interrupt, it looks like you aren't listening, even if you really are.
- Let yourself finish listening before you begin to speak! You can't really listen if you are busy thinking about what you want say next.
- Listen for main ideas. The main ideas are the most important points the speaker wants to get across. They may be mentioned at the start or end of a talk, and repeated a number of times.
- Ask questions. If you are not sure you understand what the speaker has said, just ask. It is a good idea to repeat in your own words what the speaker said so that you can be sure your understanding is correct.
- Give feedback. Sit up straight and look directly at the speaker. Now and then, nod to show that you understand. At appropriate points you may also smile, frown, laugh, or be silent. These are all ways to let the speaker know that you are really listening. Remember, you listen with your face as well as your ears!

ROLE OF SPEAKING

Speaking English is the main goal of many learners. Their personalities play a large role in determining how quickly and how correctly they will accomplish this goal. Those who are risk-takers unafraid of making mistakes will generally be more talkative, but with many errors that could become hard-to-break habits. Conservative, shy students may take a long time to speak confidently, but when they do, their English often contains fewer errors and they will be proud of their English ability. It's a matter of quantity vs. quality, and neither approach is wrong. However, if the aim of speaking is communication and that does not require perfect English, then it makes sense to encourage quantity in your classroom. Break the silence and get students communicating with whatever English they can use, correct or not, and selectively address errors that block communication.

Speaking lessons often tie in pronunciation and grammar which are necessary for effective oral communication. Or a grammar or reading lesson may incorporate a speaking activity. Either way, students will need some preparation before the speaking task. This includes introducing the topic and providing a model of the speech they are to produce. A model may not apply to discussion-type activities, in which case students will need clear and specific instructions about the task to be accomplished. Then the students will practice with the actual speaking activity.

These activities may include imitating (repeating), answering verbal cues, interactive conversation, or an oral presentation. Most speaking activities inherently practice listening skills as well, such as when one student is given a simple drawing and sits behind another student, facing away. The first must give instructions to the second to reproduce the drawing. The second student asks questions to clarify unclear instructions, and neither can look at each other's page during the activity.

Some ideas to keep in mind as you plan your speaking activities.

- **Content :** As much as possible, the content should be practical and usable in real-life situations. Avoid too much new vocabulary or grammar, and focus on speaking with the language the students have.
- **Correcting Error :** You need to provide appropriate feedback and correction, but don't interrupt the flow of communication. Take notes while pairs or groups are talking and address problems to the class after the activity without embarrassing the student who made the error. You can write the error on the board and ask who can correct it.

- **Conversation Strategies :** Encourage strategies like asking for clarification, paraphrasing, gestures, and initiating ('hey,' 'so,' 'by the way').
- **Teacher Intervention :** If a speaking activity loses steam, you may need to jump into a role-play, ask more discussion questions, clarify your instructions, or stop an activity that is too difficult or boring.
- **Quantity vs. Quality :** Address both interactive fluency and accuracy, striving foremost for communication. Get to know each learner's personality and encourage the quieter ones to take more risks.

It is very important that teachers are aware if the aim of a speaking activity is fluency or accuracy, because the role of the teacher is radically different in each activity type.

In accuracy activities, the teacher needs to correct the students if they make mistakes. The whole point of the activity is to form correct sentences, so if a student gets it wrong, it needs to be immediately addressed in the form of correction.

In process oriented fluency activities, however, correcting students can be very counter productive indeed. If we want our students to communicate, we need to give them time and space to do so, in order that they can start to learn to deal with all the demands of oral interaction.

In fluency activities, the teacher becomes more of an organiser, a facilitator, a manager, a guide, a guru. The teacher sets up the activity, explains what needs to be done, organises the necessary groupings, and then lets the learners get on with it.

FUNCTIONS OF LANGUAGE

Six major functions of the English language are:

- A means of conveying information, example, "The Kyneton train is now approaching on platform 4." This example is conveying to those waiting for the Kyneton train that it has now arrived.
- An instrument of action, example, "Don't forget to feed the dog." This example is telling the second person in the conversation to do something.
- To maintain social relationships example, "Good Morning, how are you?" Here we see that this function allows us to make and keep friends. This function is usually more informal than others.
- Acting as a marker of groups example, "He was out for a duck." This example would only be heard by someone talking about the cricket, therefore establishing that the people involved in the conversation are involved with cricket in one way or another, marking them as a group.
- As an instrument of cognitive and conceptual development. This is the power of language to influence thinking. This is why we have many words that mean basically the same thing, because they all have slight differences or are used in different circumstances. For example if you could only say you were happy, but not excited, thrilled, etc, then you would not be able to give as much detail.
- As an art form, language can be purposed towards beauty for beauty's sake.

THE ROLE OF GRAMMAR IN LEARNING A LANGUAGE

It is a question of debate for a long is learning grammar necessary for picking up a new language? Some linguists think grammar rules are usually considered core of any language learning class, without which a student would be completely lost. However, a language acquisition theory from Dr. Stephen Krashen, a renowned linguistics professor, suggests picking up a new language doesn't require any conscious knowledge of grammar; instead, the best and most effective methods of acquiring a new language occur through regular and useful conversation.

Dr. Krashen actually separates the way people learn languages into two separate categories: the ''acquired system'' and the ''learned system''. The acquired points to learning a new language in an almost subconscious manner, mostly through regular communication and interaction using the target language. The learned system, on the other hand, points to the traditional method of learning that many of us are used to, in which we learn conjugations, grammar rules, tenses, etc. The most important conclusion of Krashen's hypothesis, however, is that the ''acquired system'' is more effective and indeed better the ''learned system'' used by most language schools worlwide.

Language, which includes grammar, would emerge as a result of interaction and communication or that it would emerge as a result of comprehensible input. Krashen holds that given a ''natural order'' in acquistion, grammar teaching is unnecessary.

However, the acquisition of a second language is usually achieved in an acquisition—rich environment. In an acquisition—poor environment like China, there isn't much natural exposure to the target language. We cannot expect the students to achieve grammatical competence solely through interaction and communication.

In communicative language teaching, students could assimilates new structures through active practice and use. However, some also felt that ''more able and/or elder pupils wanted, and could benefit from systematic and explicit oresentation of grammatical rules and explanations, and also that grammatical expositions could assist pupils in shifting from rote learning to a more creative use of the target language''. Wilkins (1976) points out that acquiring the grammatical system of the target language is of central importance, because an inadequate knowledge of grammar would severely constrain linguistic creativity and limit the capacity for communication.

CHALLENGES OF TEACHING LANGUAGE IN A DIVERSE CLASSROOM

Language Difficulty

Students in bilingual classrooms manipulate more than one language and are influenced by more than one culture. Their experiences with these languages and cultures influence their learning. The more we understand the personal, socio-cultural, and linguistic backgrounds of bilingual students, the better equipped we will be to provide these students with an effective learning environment. This environment should be one that supports learning in a second language and culture, while fostering a positive attitude and respect for the other language and culture.

The responsibility for English language learning, academic progress, and integration of bilingual learners into the school community should be assumed by *all* personnel at the school, not just by the bilingual staff. School administrators should make certain that bilingual students have opportunities to integrate both socially and academically with monolingual English speakers. The following practices promote the inclusion of all students in a supportive, educational environment:

1. Create participatory, inquiry-based classrooms
2. Maintain high expectations for all students
3. Teach English through content-area instruction
4. Use thematic units
5. Incorporate culturally familiar learning strategies
6. Use a variety of strategies when teaching literacy
7. Provide appropriate and valid assessment
8. Recognize that students use both languages to learn

Errors

English is such a complex language, it is fraught with traps that we all frequently fall into. With this list I hope to clear up at least a few of the confusing words we use every day. This is a list of some of the more common errors people make with English.

Its / It's

As in the case above, the apostrophe denotes an abbreviation: it's = it is. Its means "belongs to it". The confusion arises here because we also use an apostrophe in English to denote possession – *except* in this case; if you want to say "the cat's bag" you say "its bag" not "it's bag". "It's" always means "it is" or "it has". "It's a hot day." "it's been fun seeing you."

Your / You're

Your means "belonging to you". You're means "you are". The simplest way to work out the correct one to use is to read out your sentence.

Practice / Practise

In US English, practice is used as either a verb (doing word), or noun (naming word). Hence, a doctor has a practice, and a person practices the violin. In UK english, practice is a noun, and practise is a verb. A doctor has a practice, but his daughter practises the piano.

Bought / Brought

Bought relates to buying something. Brought relates to bringing something. For example, I bought a bottle of wine which had been brought over from France.

Desert / Dessert

This is a confusing one because in English an 's' on its own is frequently pronounced like a 'z' and two 's's are usually pronounced as a n 's' (for example: prise, prissy). In this case, desert follow the rule – it means a large stretch of sand. However, dessert is pronounced "dez-urt" with the emphasis on the second syllable – ie, something we eat as part of our meal. To make matters worse, when a person leaves the army without permission, it is spelt desert.

Dryer / Drier

If your clothes are wet, put them in a clothes dryer. That will make them drier. A hair dryer also makes hair drier.

Chose / Choose

This is actually quite an easy one to remember – in English we generally pronounce 'oo' as it is written – such as "moo". The same rule applies here: choose is pronounced as it is written (with a 'z' sound for the 's') – and chose is said like "nose". Therefore, if you had to choose to visit Timbuktu, chances are you chose to fly there. Chose is the past tense, choose is the present tense.

Lose / Loose

This one is confusing. In this case, contrary to normal rules of English, the single 's' in loose is pronounced like an 's' – as in wearing trousers that are too loose. Lose on the other hand, relates to loss – for example: "I hope we don't lose this game". A good way to remember this is that in the word "lose" you have lost the second 'o' from loose. If you can't remember a rule that simple, you are a loser!

Literally

This one is not only often used in error, it is incredibly annoying when it is used in the wrong way. Literally means "it really happened" – therefore, unless you live on a parallel universe with different rules of physics, you can not say "he literally flew out the door".

Disorders

Children who have a condition of incomplete or less than normal mental development so that they are unable to adjust to day to day living in a normally efficient, useful, productive and harmonious manner are called mentally retarded. They are, hence, in constant need or care, protection, supervision and help.

Thus, mental retardation is a serious disability. It creates a lot of learning problems before mentally retarded children. These learning problems create obstacle in other areas of life as well. Thus, total life activities are affected by mental retardation.

General Characteristics of Mentally Retarded

On the basis of the definitions given above following common characteristics of mentally retarded children (less than 18 years of age) can be derived:

1. **Limited functioning :** Their level of functioning is very limited. They have difficulty not only in learning but also doing routine life job due to significant loss of conceptual, practical and social intelligence.
2. **Sub average intellectual functioning :** Their intellectual functioning is less than average (below 80 IQ) on an intelligence test. This is the fundamental criterion of diagnosing a mentally retarded child.
3. **Poor performance level :** If someone falls short in his performance of certain tasks from the performance of the majority of children of his own age, he is said to have low mental age or sub-normal intellectual functioning. For example, If eight years old child performs equal to the child of 6 years, his IQ will be (Mental Age/Chronological age × 100) or $(6/8) \times 100 = 75$
4. **Slow acquisition of skills :** Academic (content related) and non academic (action related) both types of skills are acquired by them at a very slow rate.
5. **Low level of adaptive skills. :** They are not only slow in acquiring skills but they are always poor in adaptive skills also.
6. **Early manifestations :** Mental retardation manifests itself before the age of 18. From this perspective, mental retardation is viewed as a disorder of the life period characterized by the slow rate of development.

Characteristics of Exceptional Children

On the basis of the concepts and definitions given above following characteristics of exceptional children are inferred.

1. Exceptional children are those for whom uniform educational programmes do not suit. Hence, they need special instructional programmes or ancillary services or both.
2. Exceptionality is manifested by performance that is superior or inferior to that of the average children.
3. They deviate from the average (normal) people in both directions, plus and minus of mean physically, psychologically or socially and these deviations are significant to such an extent that their adjustment with the normals in some situations becomes difficult. Thus, exceptionality creates adjustment problem.
4. They come across learning difficulties in normal setting due to the defects and sometimes due to their superior qualities. These difficulties can be removed only by providing special instructional procedures unique to them.
5. If they are retarded or disabled in any area, their performance will be lower than the normal children and if they are superior in any trait significantly, the performance will be higher. Disabled children, however, come to the average performance when they are fully grown up and matured in their experience and drill.
6. The exceptionals are found in every society and culture almost in the same percentage of the total population. Sudden medical factors can, however, increase their numbers all of a sudden, e.g., spread of epidemics can increase their number.

Classification of Exceptional Children

(A) Classification on the basis of area or mode of deviations: This classification is more qualitative than quantitative. Exceptionals can be classified into the following categories on the basis of area of deviation.

Intellectual Deviance : Intellectual deviance may be in both directions from the mean. Mentally retarded comes on the minus side and gifted and creative come on the plus side from the mean. These two deviations are given below:

(a) **Mental Retardation :** They are less than 90 IQ on any intelligence test. They have special learning needs in areas requiring functional use of intelligence and adaptive behaviour. About 0.96% of the school going children is classified in this category.

(b) **Giftedness and Creativity :** These children possess IQ more than at least 110. Creatives differ from gifted in the sense that creative children perform in superb manner in one or two selected areas in original manner. These two types of children have special learning needs in areas requiring functional use of intelligence and artistic ability. About 3% of school going children come under this category.

Sensory Deviance : Here comes the hard of hearing, the deaf and dumb and visually impaired. There may be the people without the sense of taste or touch but we are not concerned with these people because they don't pose any social problem and hence they are not discussed in the category of exceptionals. Two important types of sensory deviance are given below:

(a) **Visual Impairment :** Under this category only those children legally come whose visual acuity is either zero (blindness) or less than 6/60 after correction (semi blindness). These children have special leaning needs in areas requiring functional use of vision. About 0.4 to 0.6 percent of school going children have been detected as visually impaired.

(b) **Hearing Impairment :** Audible capacity of these children are very low. Due to this reason, they have special learning needs in areas requiring functional use of hearing. About 0.11% school going children suffer from this problem across the world.

Motor Deviance: Crippled, orthopedically handicapped, speech and adjustment defectives, epileptics etc. come under this deviance. Two types of motor lisabilities are given here:

(a) **Speech Impairment :** Speech impairment is closely associated with hearing impairment because speech learning requires hearing. If speech development is nill or very close to nill, speech therapy or lip reading or reading on fingers is required.

(b) **Orthopedic Impairment :** These children have special learning needs in areas requiring functional use of hands, arms, feet, legs or other locomotive body parts. About 1% of the school going population is found to be orthopedically handicapped in India.

Personality deviance: Here children suffering from behavioural disorders and learning disabilities are included. For example, children suffering from neurosis or psychosis face serious problem of adjustment in social situations. Personality deviance can be classified into two categories:

(a) **Leaning Disabilities:** These children have special learning needs in areas requiring functional use of listening, speaking, reading, writing, reasoning and arithmetic skills. This is the largest category in special education in terms of percentage. About 4% school going children suffer from this problem. These children are normal in intelligence, even then they are very poor in learning.

(b) **Emotional Disorders :** These children lack proper emotional and social skills. When these children are treated by their peers, mates and teachers in a prejudiced manner, they become more disturbed emotionally and hence they need special attention by the teacher.

Educational Deviance : They are significantly different from the normals in academic achievement due to a variety of reasons in both directions. They can be classified into three categories:

(a) **Educationally Bright :** Achievement level of these students is very high due to very high level of adaptability to learning, assimilation of thoughts, understanding and memory. They can learn any subject matter in no time and they can retain it for a longer period of time. They are hardworking children in the field of learning.
Though educational achievement is directly related to intelligence yet intellectually gifted and educationally bright children are not the same. The reason is that high achievement in schools may be due to some other reasons also like future aspirations of students, high motivational level, hard labour done by pupils, guidance by parents etc.

(b) **Educationally Backward :** These children are backward by their age mates by 2 to 4 years or grades in the field of education due to repeated failure in different classes. This backwardness may be due to a number of reasons such as defective teaching learning process, low intellectual ability of learners, adjustment or emotional problems in the school. etc. These children need special treatment by the teacher in the classes and if problem is very serious, special classes should be arranged for them.

(c) **Communication Disorders :** These children are very poor in understanding the views of others and equally deficient in communicating their opinions to others either due to low level of intelligence or due to poor level of concentration power to the subject matter.

Social Deviance: Juvenile delinquents, (adult criminals) and maladjusted students come under this category. Ethnic minorities and the culturally suppressed people also come under this category. They deviate from the social norms due to a variety of reasons and constitute educational and social problems:

(a) **Maladjusted Children :** These children fail to adjust in their family, in the school and in the society and create the problem of adjustment for others also. If they are not properly dealt with, they will remain maladjusted leading to an isolated life.

(b) **Deprived Children :** Feeling of derivation develops in such a child only after seeing social, economic and cultural inequalities.

(c) **Juvenile Delinquents :** These adult criminals are antisocial elements in the sense that they violate the social norms and legal structure. Committing crime is a fun for them.

Traumatic Brain Injury: These injuries are caused by an external physical force or by an internal problem such as strokes. Children who are born with brain injuries are not included in this category.

Multiple Deviance: Many exceptional people deviate from the normal in more than one areas like a blind man is deaf also or personality deviance is associated with educational deviance etc. Such a multiple exceptionality is an automatic process also. For example, a sensory handicapped child is very badly treated by some people in the society. The exceptionals react to these behaviours very negatively and in a hateful manner and thus social deviance is slowly developed. These students have special learning needs in more than one areas.

LANGUAGE SKILLS

There are, in general, four language skills, each based upon the modality of emphasis. These are the Listening, Speaking, Reading, and Writing skills.

Listening Skill

Listening in English is attending to and interpreting oral English. Listening is necessary to develop the speaking skill. The student listens to oral speech in English, then separates into segments the stretch of utterances he hears, groups them into words, phrases, and sentences, and, finally, he understands the message these carry. Listening prepares the students to understand the speech of the native speakers of English as they speak naturally in a normal speed and normal manner.

There are three approaches to listening: interactive (listening to a message and doing something as a consequence) and one-way communication or non-interactive (just listening and retaining the message, in activities such as conversations overheard, public address announcements, recorded messages, etc.) and self-talk. Listening to radio and watching TV and films, public performances, lectures, religious services, etc., generally reflect non-interactive listening. Responding to the commands given reflects interactive listening, which, in fact, is equally widespread in communicative situations. Self-talk is also an important process by which internal thinking and reasoning is carried out.

Role of Listening : In the classroom, students listen in order to repeat and to understand. In listening to repeat, students imitate and memorize linguistic items such as words, idioms, and sentence patterns. This is an important beginning task and focus of listening exercises. However, it is listening to understand that is real listening in its own right.

Students listen to understand as part of using English for communication purposes. In listening to understand, students may be involved in the question-oriented response model of learning or in the task-oriented model of learning. In the question-oriented response model, students may be asked to listen to a sentence, a dialogue, a conversation, a passage, or a lecture and asked to answer questions which may be presented in the form of true/false statements, multiple choice questions, fill in the blank, or short answers. In the task-oriented response model, students may be asked to listen to a passage and accomplish the task described in the passage through interaction with others or by themselves.

Listening Comprehension

The listening skill is the most neglected one, both in first and second language teaching. Teachers tend to focus on the rudimentary elements of listening briefly, and pass over to other aspects of language teaching. Discrimination of sounds and intonations often form the major part of listening practice in the classroom. Listening for content is often assumed. In reality, the listening skill is fundamental to the entire process of mastering and using a language, whether first or second or foreign.

In the past, listening was labeled as a passive skill, along with reading. No doubt, it is a receptive skill like reading. Speaking and writing were considered to be productive skills, but also active skills. While this categorization is somewhat justifiable because the focus of listening is on reception of information, listening itself cannot be fully and correctly characterized only as a passive skill.

There is a need for an active involvement of the self for the efficient performance of listening. The listener is often forced into guessing an approximation to what the speaker is communicating. The listener expects and anticipates what may be the form and content of the immediate message being delivered. He actively avoids the redundancies in the process of listening, focuses himself on the relevant, interesting and/or crucial points, and engages himself in some critical analysis of content. Listening becomes the stepping stone for action. In view of all these and other activities that are involved in listening, we should consider listening as an active skill demanding active participation of the listener.

In essence, listening is not mere recognition of linguistic units and their meanings. It comprises an ability to predict information based on linguistic context, and the situation and topic of the message conveyed by the linguistic code, as well as the expectations about the world. Listening helps also to understand and act according to the emotional state of the speaker.

No one should think that listening comprehension exercises are miniature tests. These generally come in the form of questions to be answered, action to be performed, or objects to be identified, etc. Because this format demands response in the form in which tests are generally prepared and presented, we tend to treat the exercise as a test. Consider listening comprehension only as practice and look for progress in student performance.

Brief listening comprehension exercises with content interesting to the student and which focus upon and incorporate his communicative needs will develop his listening comprehension to a satisfactory level. Students need to be attentive to the tone of the conversation, and should ask questions whenever they find it difficult to understand the conversation.

What is the generally followed form of listening comprehension exercises? Students are given a specific task such as answering questions or solving problems. They listen to the teacher or the recorded material and perform the task asked for. Thus the teacher as well as materials on tape/cassette recorders become the major means to train the students in listening comprehension.

Speaking Skill

Imitation and repetition are important elementary steps in developing speaking skill in English. Imitation and repetition are inter-related, and yet they are distinct.

Imitation helps students to pronounce and produce the English utterance they hear from the teacher as closely as possible to the utterance produced by her. Imitation is not restricted to mere production of the sounds, phrases, and sentences. It includes also the capacity to produce the utterances in the contexts in which the original utterances were produced.

Some of the imitation and repetition exercises may be organized in the following manner: Present some simple sentence, phrase, or word and ask students to repeat after you. If you want them to understand and repeat a conversation, say the questions and the answers and have the students repeat the latter, or perhaps both, signaling the meaning in some way. The meaning can be demonstrated with realia (real objects brought into the classroom), pictures, gestures, or translating.

The teacher may use pictures, gestures, pantomime, translation, guessing, and drawing on the board to make the students understand the meaning. It is important that you use only meaningful words, phrases, and sentences for imitation and repetition. The props you use to explain or demonstrate the meaning should enable the student to learn the meaning with ease, along with the pronunciation.

Substitution of a word, phrase, or sentence by another is an elementary method which helps students to produce new utterances and to develop speaking skill.

Expressions of greeting, gratitude, small talk, introductions and making acquaintance, leave-taking, appreciation, expressions of regret and asking to be excused, etc., are very important communicative acts students need to master. For one thing, such expressions may take on different form and import in English than the ones students are accustomed to in their language and culture.

Simple question-answer dialogues around a given context and object/objects is another elementary method to develop speaking skill in students.

How does a teacher teach a dialogue? There are three types of drills one could use in the class: **choral drill** in which the entire class participates in one voice with the teacher modelling the utterance; **chain drill** in which one student asks the question and another answers, and in this way the entire class participates as a chain; and **individual drill** in which individual students are pointed out and asked to produce the utterance modelled by the teacher.

Eliciting is an important process which teachers must employ to get the class involved in what is going on in the class. For speaking practice eliciting is highly essential. It helps students to focus their attention, to think, and to use what they already know. It helps teachers to assess what the class already knew.

Translation is another helpful device to encourage students to speak in English. The students may be given some sentences in their own native language and asked to translate them and use these to answer or ask questions. There are several other ways of using translation as a tool to develop speaking skill.

Reading Skill

Scholors classify reading into three kinds: extensive reading, intensive reading, and oral reading. Extensive reading is used "to refer to the teaching of reading through reading. In this approach, there is no overt focus on teaching reading. Rather, it is assumed that the best way for students to learn to read is by reading a great deal of comprehensible material." Intensive reading is used to refer to the actual teaching skills in an instructional setting. Students are exposed to a variety of materials and asked to perform activities such as answering comprehension questions on the passage read. They may be trained to look for critical information in the passage they read, and make inferences, etc. Intensive reading is instruction-based and forms the core of teaching reading in the classroom. Oral reading does attract much attention from many teachers, but it is "an integral part of of reading.

At the beginning level, the focus is on the mechanics of reading. The beginner needs to be taught the relationship and the correspondence between the letters of the alphabet and the spoken language.

In a sense, the letters are all abstract symbols. The letter functions as a tag to the sounds it represents. By seeing (reading) the letter, the beginner identifies the appropriate sound value for that letter in that context.

This is not an easy task even for the adult learner. It is possible that the learner may come from a language in which the Roman alphabet similar to the one used in English is being used. And yet the sound values of letters in his language may vary context to context in his language also, which in their turn may be in conflict with the sound values of the letters as used in English.

Or, the learner may come from a language background in which syllabaries are used. That is, he may be accustomed to reading the syllables which more or less retain the same values wherever they are used. However, he will find that in character and chat, cha needs to be read differently.

Or, he may come from a language background where pictograms are used, as in Chinese in which there is no easy and manifest correspondence between the "letter" and the sound.

Keep the following in mind when you begin teaching reading at the beginner's level.

1. The background of the beginner: a child, an illiterate, a moderately educated person.
2. The Reading task involves decoding the system of abstract symbols to discover its relation to the spoken language system.
3. The time taken to master this relationship varies with age, maturation, previous experience, and other social factors.
4. With primary emphasis on mechanics one may master the mechanics of reading in four months.
5. Some recognition problems in English: capital, small, italics, handwriting, left to right, distinction between letters, mirror image problems.
6. Choose the words which express familiar meanings or meanings which can be recognized and retained in memory.
7. Choose only those words which focus on the item to be learned.
8. Do not choose those words which may have the same spelling in English as well as in the learner's language, but are read (pronounced) differently.
9. Do not ignore the stress.

Writing Skill

Writing is an individual effort. Individuals compose their thoughts often in privacy and then reduce their thoughts to writing, using the strict conventions followed in the language. Writing is an individual effort or work, but it must follow the rules laid down. The development of writing even in native English speaking children is conscious and is thus non-spontaneous.

In writing, the discrete nature of linguistic signs should be appreciated consciously. The learner must recognize the sound structure of each word, dissect it and reproduce it in alphabetical symbols, which he must have studied and memorized before. This same deliberate preparedness is needed to put words in a certain sequence to form a sentence.

"Writing is more an individual effort than speaking, while at the same time more rule-bound and therefore more error-prone. . . The speaker does not have to pronounce each word exactly according to one standard of pronunciation or one model of structure, while the writer is expected to produce according to one model of spelling, and usually a reduced range of structures, with 100 percent accuracy".

The writing classes have the potential to help consolidate and improve the students' speaking and reading skills. However, it is important for us to remember that writing is an important skill which can be taught as an end in itself, although none of the language skills is far removed from the other language skills. Focusing on writing as an independent skill helps us to identify the specific problems faced by the learners, and to identify the specific needs of the learners relating to writing. Mechanics of writing are distinct from the mechanics of other skills such as speaking and reading. While reading involves seeing and pronouncing, writing involves association of sounds with mental composition of thoughts and their orderly presentation, and hand movements.

Raimes classifies approaches to teaching writing into five types: controlled to free, free writing, paragraph pattern, grammar-syntax-organization, communicative, and process approaches. In the controlled to free approach, "students are first given sentence exercises, then paragraphs to copy or manipulate grammatically by, for instance, changing questions to statements, present to past, or plural to singular. They might also change words or clauses or combine sentences" (Raimes 1983).

In the free writing approach, students are asked to "write freely on any topic without worrying about grammar and spelling for five or ten minutes. . . . The teachers do not correct these short pieces of free writing; they simply read them and perhaps comment on the ideas the writer expressed" (Raimes 1983). In the paragraph pattern approach, "students copy paragraphs, analyze the form of model paragraphs, and imitate model passages. They put scrambled sentences into paragraph order, they identify general specific statements, they choose or invent an appropriate topic sentence, they insert or delete sentences" (Raimes 1983). In the communicative approach to writing, students are asked to assume the role of a writer who is writing for an audience to read. Whatever is written by a student is modified in some way by other students for better communicative effect. In the process approach to writing, students "move away from a concentration on the written product to an emphasis on the process of writing" (Raimes 1983).

Note that a proper blend of these approaches to writing will give us best results. For example, the controlled to free approach to writing helps us to focus on proper mechanics in the beginning level, whereas communicative approach to writing will be very effective once our students have some control over the mechanics and have acquired a good number of words and sentence structures to help them match these with their thoughts. All successful texts and teachers have always tried to take the best and relevant aspects of every method to suit the learner's level and need.

EVALUATING LANGUAGE COMPREHENSION

Meaning of Evaluation

Evaluation is the criteria of success or failure of a task done. If it is done at the end of a task, total efforts, including the investment of time and money may be a failure but if it goes side by side of the task, immediate feedback received might alarm the performer to rectify his mistakes and thus there is 100% chance of success of the programme.

Education is also an investment in the sense that time, energy and money are spent to bring about behavioural change in learners. That is why when a teacher performs his teaching works in his class, he also simultaneously finds out whether the changes in behaviour of learners are in concurrence with the learning objectives or not. If it is not so there, then what types of modifications are needed and at what steps of teaching. He also finds out whether the problem lies in his teaching strategies or techniques or it is there in the students itself. Thus, teaching and evaluation run-hand in hand. Evaluation determines the behaviour of students on one hand and testifies to the teaching of the teacher on the other. This very purposeful behaviour of the teacher is called evaluation in education.

Purpose of Evaluation

Evaluation has following purposes to serve:

1. **Giving Details of Students' Progress** : Evaluation tells where a student is standing on the way to his destination of learning, how much he is ahead or behind his classmates, to what extent the behavioural changes occurred in him are acceptable, how far he can apply his present acquired knowledge to his future life or learning situations, at what point he is facing any difficulty and why and so on. Thus, evaluation here works like the diagnostic function of measurement.
2. **Predicting Future Achievement** : When evaluation covers the aptitude aspect of behaviour, it can predict the future performance of a student or a teacher on the basis of his present performance.
3. **Guidance and Motivation** : When a student comes to know about the actual position of his achievement, he gets motivated to do better. Besides, strengths and weaknesses of students become manifest through evaluation and a teacher can guide them accordingly.
4. **Improvement in the System** : Once proper guidance is given to students by the teacher after evaluation, teaching-learning process gets

improved. A teacher can also come to know his own strength and weakness by the process and can change his own behaviour accordingly. Once he gets acquainted with his own shortcomings, he can remove them. Thus, process of evaluation is concerned with inputs and output both.

5. **Discovery of Effective Teaching Strategies** : Evaluation opens the new avenues of action researches in the class. When a teacher does not get the desired result by adopting a particular combination of teaching strategies, he adopts another combination and this process continues until a final effective combination of teaching strategies is discovered.
6. **Classification of Students** : By evaluation process we can classify students into different groups like talented, bright, average, slow learners and poor and adopt different strategies of teaching for different groups. We can also give remedial treatment to weak students in the class only after thorough evaluation of them.
7. **Providing Feedback to Students and Teachers Both** : When a teacher comes to know the results of his efforts he gets feedback. If result is good, he is motivated if result is not satisfactory, feedback pushes him to change his behaviour. Similarly, knowledge of progress and the feedback received thereof motivate the students also.

Techniques of Evaluation

Evaluation is broader concept than measurement but no exact evaluation is possible without going through the process of measurement. All the three domains of behaviour are covered by evaluation, e.g.,

1. **Cognitive Domain :** Oral, written, essay type, objective type tests, practical examinations and observation techniques etc. are used for evaluating cognitive domain.
2. **Affective Domain :** This domain is evaluated by interest inventory, attitude scale, check list, rating scales and observation techniques.
3. **Psychomotoı Domain :** Performance tests, practical examinations and observation techniques are used to evaluate this domain (See optional paper II for Educational Objectives).

There are basically two techniques of evaluation:

A. **Quantitative :** These techniques are highly reliable and valid. Important such techniques are as follows:

1. **Oral :** These techniques are basically used at lower grades of teaching. At higher level of education too viva voce is used to test the lower levels of cognitive behaviour. Debates or drama can also be used for this purpose.
2. **Written :** Objective type tests, essay type tests and short answer questions are important written techniques to evaluate cognitive achievement of students. They give more accurate results than oral tests.
3. **Performance Tests** : Here some works are assigned to students to accomplish them. Students practically do these works and then output is evaluated.

B. **Qualitative** : These techniques evaluate the quality of attributes and hence they are highly subjective. Important such techniques are given below:

1. **Cumulative Records :** Such records are prepared by the school to show all-round development of students individually. They reflect the total personality of the child, i.e., marks obtained by students in sessional tests and examinations, their participation in games, sports cultural programmes and other co-curricular activities, their regularity, punctuality, their etiquette.
2. **Anecdotal Records :** These records maintain the description of significant events or works of students. Here informations regarding the behaviour, attitudes or interests of students are systematically cumulated.
3. **Observation :** This is the most common technique of qualitative assessment of students. It is mostly used at lower grades of education. This is the only technique for the evaluation of classroom interaction.
4. **Check List :** This technique is used for evaluating attitude and affective domain of students. Here questions are given to students and they are asked to answer them in yes or no, e.g.,

   Item : 'Do you like doing mathematical sums-Yes/No.'
5. **Rating Scales :** Here some statements are given to students and agreed, indifferent or disagreed are written before the statements. Then students are asked to tick the option according to their own choice.

Types of Evaluation

1. Formative Evaluation : The purpose of formative evaluation is to monitor instructional process to know whether learning is taking place or not. It is designed to enhance and improve teaching-learning process and thus it becomes a continuous process in the school system.

These tests diagnose the weaknesses of students as well as teachers and thus, both of them can get feedback from these tests. Students and teachers both after identifying their difficulties change their behaviour and remove these difficulties. Thus, function of this evaluation is remedial in nature.

The second function of this evaluation is that if evaluation finds teaching-learning process satisfactory, it motivates the teachers and students to work harder for better results.

Tanner (1972) has defined formative evaluation in the following words :

"Formative evaluation refers to the use of tests and other evaluative procedures while the course and instructional programme is in progress."

Both criterion referenced and norm referenced tests are used to take the students to the mastery of the content. These tests are given in the following stages of learning.

(*i*) At the end of each unit of the lesson.

(*ii*) At the end of each whole lesson.

(*iii*) At the end of each unit of the total course.

Advantages of Formative evaluation :

(*i*) It provides sufficient information to teachers for modifying teaching.

(*ii*) It helps in formulating individual and group remedial programmes.

(*iii*) It provides feedback to students as well as teachers.

(*iv*) It facilitates retention and transfer of training.

(*v*) It enables the teacher to readjust his teaching according to the needs of the students.

(*vi*) Students can also modify their behaviour after getting feedback from this evaluation.

(*vii*) It gives reinforcement to high achievers.

(*viii*) It can work as a self-evaluation device for learners.

2. Summative Evaluation : This evaluation takes place at the end of the session to measure over all achievement of pupils. Annual, internal or external examinations are the examples of summative evaluation. The purpose of this evaluation is to certify fail or pass of the product. If formative evaluation is related to the process of teaching, it is related to the product of teaching. Here students are evaluated from the whole syllabus. On the basis of this evaluation, a decision is taken whether a student should be promoted to the next class or he should be kept in the same class again.

On the basis of above discussions we can say that summative evaluation works as a complement to formative evaluation and both of them combined together are necessary for all educational system.

CONTINUOUS AND COMPREHENSIVE EVALUATION

Continuous and Comprehensive Evaluation refers to a system of school based assessment that covers all aspects of student's development. It emphasizes two fold objectives.Continuity in evaluation and assessment of broad based learning.

CCE helps in reducing stress of students by :

- Identifying learning progress of students at regular time intervals on small portions of content.
- Employing a variety of remedial measures of teaching based on learning needs and potential of different students.
- Desisting from using negative comments on the learner's performance.
- Encouraging learning through employment of a variety of teaching aids and techniques.
- Involving learners actively in the learning process.
- Recognizing and encouraging specific abilities of students, who do not excel in academics but perform well in other co-curricular areas.

Teachers should Keep in Mind

- Use a variety of tools (oral, projects, presentations).
- Understand different learning styles and abilities.
- Share the assessment criteria with the students.
- Allow peer and self assessment.
- Give an opportunity to the student to improve.

Important Points

- CCE will cover the scholastic and co scholastic areas of school education.
- The two types of assessment referred to in the circular are formative and summative. The periodicity of the two types of assessment are four and twice a year respectively.
- Formative Assessment totals to 40% weightage.
- Summative Assessment totals to 60% weightage.

- There are nine grades in Part A of Scholastic assessment and Part B of the same assessment has five grades.
- Summative assessment covers non academic areas like attitudes and skills and there are three grades.
- If a student secures Grade 6 in the academic areas his/her marks would range from 51% to 60%.
- CCE advocates absolute grading. This means that Grade 9 would imply an A2 grade.
- The academic term will be divided into two terms.

TEACHING LEARNING MATERIALS

Text Book

Text book is the area in which the language material is presented prescribed for teaching and learning English.

Characteristics of Good Text Books

A good text books not only teaches but it also tests. A few essential characteristics of good text books are given below:

(*i*) The size of text book should be handy for the students.

(*ii*) The binding should be proper and strong.

(*iii*) The subject matter should be printed on good quality paper.

(*iv*) Heading and subheading should be printed on title page in bold form.

(*v*) Illustration should be attractive. For every young pupil, the picture should be well drawn and realistically coloured and not in black and white.

(*vi*) Clear and unambiguous instruction should be given along side the test and practice and exercise.

(*vii*) The introduction at the beginning and conclusion at the end of the chapter should be given in the text book.

(*viii*) The words and structure are carefully graded.

(*ix*) No difficult words and new words are given in good text book.

(*x*) The words and structure already learnt are repeated in the coming pages so that the students could revise them making them stable in their memory.

(*xi*) The subject matter of text book should provide new information so that students could get new knowledge.

(*xii*) There should be both practice and text exercise at the end of the chapter.

(*xiii*) The practice should be low which the majority of students could solve them easily.

Chalkboard

It is the closest friend of a teacher in the class and about 50% teaching task is completed with the help of the blackboard. Advantages of using a chalkboard in the class are as follows :

(*i*) It is a cheap material aid which does not cost much on its maintenance.

(*ii*) When a teacher writes important points of the lesson on the chalkboard along with his oral teaching and lectures, aural and visual both the senses of students work simultaneously. It increases learning many times.

(*iii*) Writing meaning of difficult words, drawing graphs or diagrams, solving the sums of mathematics, preparing the summary of the lesson, all these works can be done on the chalkboard and they help the students understand the facts, events or terminologies.

(*iv*) Blackboard works as a model for students. This can help the students mend their ways if they imitate the model.

Models

Models are the reflection or copy of the real objects. They are used in the class to clarify the concepts when either real objects are not available or it is not possible to bring real objects to the class. They are also the abbreviated version of real objects. Elephants, lions or other animals or birds can not be brought to the class, hence, it is better to use the models of these objects. Globe is the best example of model to be used in the class.

Through models knowledge of all types of historical, geographical and scientific facts and concepts can be given to students. Models are especially useful for teaching visually handicapped children who perceive the objects by touch. Since, clear dimensions of length, breadth and height are given in the model in a proportionate manner, they are more useful for concept formation than pictures.

How to use models

(*i*) Scale should be used for showing size, shape or structure of the real objects. Apart from this, teacher should also clarify the real shape, size or structure of the real object.

(*ii*) Students should be given opportunity to have a critical view on the model and their views on it.

ENGLISH

(*iii*) All students should be given chance to have a close look at the model in the class.

(*iv*) Models should have direct relevance to the lesson and they should develop scientific temperament among learners.

(*v*) Models should be properly explained in the class in order to make the use of models effective.

Pictures

Pictures are used in the class as material aids when neither real objects nor models can be arranged. They are cheap and easily available in the market, therefore, a teacher should not be miserly in using them. Pictures are actually the outlines of the real objects and when they are shown in the class, they give clear concepts about the colour, physique, shape and size of the real objects. Attention of students can easily be drawn to the lesson through them. If pictures related to the lesson are not available in the market, the teacher should sketch them by using pencils and water colours. Pictures are used as material aids for teaching all the school subjects.

Diagrams

They are another option and used when even pictures can not be arranged. They can also clarify the concepts like models or pictures but at a lesser degree. Diagrams are drawn on the chalkboard by using coloured chalks and then students copy it on their notebooks. The biggest advantage of this material aid is that teacher need not spend even a single pie in using this material aid.

They help in clarifying the concepts, laws and principles of science and social sciences. Their role in teaching languages is very limited.

Graphs

Graphs are especially used in history, geography, science and mathematics. They help the teacher and the students to study, analyse and compare the data, facts or events. Whenever action research is made by a teacher in the class, graphs are used to show the data.

Maps

Maps are the flat representation of the surface of the earth on a paper where many informations are presented through lines, symbols dots, points or letters. They have special significance in teaching history and geography. We can also get information about the size and physical features of a country, state or continent through these maps and distance between different parts of the country or the world can also be read from them. Though printed maps of all states or countries are available in the market yet a teacher draws them also on roler boards. This will enable the students to draw such maps themselves.

Slide Projector

Simple 'slide projector' was known as "magic lantern" in the olden days. The principle here is that when we put the transparent slide on the socket and throw light from behind, the light passes through it and projects the image on the screen.

A slide projector typically consists of a quart, three halogen lamps, light to be reflected by the reflector, a heat filter and lastly, condenser lenses. The heat filter is a thermo crystal which absorbs most of the heat produced by three lamps. A cooling system is also needed which consists of a fan for convecting off the heat, filter and other components. The fan is thermostatically controlled. When projector is switched off, the fan is also switched off.

Classroom uses of the Slide Projector : Slides are prepared for selected topics and the informations contained by them may be in the form of written words, pictures, graphs, sketches, etc. The topic selected should be arranged frame by frame. The ideal ratio of length and breadth of slides is 2 : 3. Each frame should have only one concept for the ease of understanding.

The slides and the film strips are arranged in a sequential order. This arrangement is also coordinated with the teaching learning activity of the class. When slides are shown in the class, curtains are drawn on the windows in order to reduce the entry of natural light in the class.

Before showing these slides, teacher elaborates important points. Once the film is over, the teacher gives his own comments and relates the aid with the lesson to be taught.

Film Strips

They are used before a large group of students either for introducing a lesson or for elaborating some minute object not seen in ordinary situations. Film strips are projected on a big screen through a film projector and then the projector is switched on. Here, very minute objects look very big on the screen and we can study their parts. For example, knowledge about bacteria and viruses can be given to students through these film strips. Sometimes, sound recording is also used along with the film to clarify important points.

Advantages of Film Strips :

(*i*) The order or sequence of film strips is fixed and a teacher can prepare the relevant material to supplement the film according to the sequence.

(ii) We can have any part of the film on the screen as long as we desire so. As a result, a teacher can discuss a single topic as long as he needs. Thus, complete control over the equipment and the material is possible.

(iii) Handling of film projectors is also not complex. There is no problem of storing them because of their small size. Precautions are, however, needed against fungi or physical damage.

(iv) They have become very cheap today and any school can afford the cost of these projectors.

(v) They do not require complete darkness in the room as we do in using epidiascope or motion film projectors.

Limitations of Film Strips:

(i) They can be used only in small sized classes because of limited focal length. Modern projectors are, however, having large focal length.

(ii) Slide projection is not as effective as film projection. Inventions of 3D films have reduced the use of slides even further. In spite of this, fixed order of the film strips creates problem in handling individual frames.

(iii) Many schools do not have audio-visual workshops and thus, they depend on the cheap and unstandardized materials available in the market.

Film Projector

16 mm films are generally used for the purpose of training or teaching. These films are planned and executed by a pannel of experts who endeavour to prepare films of good quality.

As far as use of film projector for classroom teaching is concerned, it is very easy. Everything is automatic here. If electricity supply is not restricted, the film will not stop in the middle, after it is put on the projector.

Advantages of motion pictures :

(i) Motion pictures can especially be used for training purposes. Take the example of games and sports. If some actions of a player is wrong leading to defeat in the game, it can be corrected by viewing the films. After the game is over, the film of the game is later analysed to be discussed by the experts to bring in new strategies and tactics to counterplay.

(ii) In all training courses, perfection is needed everywhere. If action is recorded on films, we can see our own performance and remove our defects.

(iii) In the classroom teaching, motion pictures can highlight those aspects also that would have otherwise been missed. For example, by enlarging, close up and action replay techniques, motion pictures can highlight those movements also which are very minute and can be missed in ordinary situations.

(iv) Motion pictures are **multi-sensory technique** of instruction. It is because a combination of light, sound and actions are seen here.

(v) Motion pictures can develop imaginative and observational capacities of students simultaneously.

(vi) Whatever ideals are shown by the models in motion pictures are imitated by pupils and thus, good ideals and etiquettes can be developed in them.

(vii) They are helpful in giving clarity of concepts through concreteness and accuracy.

(viii) Facts and events related to industry, politics, history and geography and knowledge about scientific inventions, discoveries, laws and principles can be communicated to pupils very effectively through these motion pictures.

Kinescope

It is a sight and sound recording that can be made in the studio from the television screen for repeated use. What transcription is to radio, the kinescope is to TV. They are used for the following purposes :

(i) For delayed telecast.

(ii) For retelecast of the same programme.

(iii) For repeating the telecast when programme could not be seen due to failure of network.

(iv) For sending programmes abroad.

Only limitation of kinescope is that live element or spontaneity does not exist here.

It can be used in teaching learning process in the same way as television is used.

Epidiascope

Epidiascope is an equipment that can project all types of materials whether transparent or non-transparent (opaque). It has thus a twin facility and separate mechanism for projecting transparent and opaque materials.

In epidiascope, the word epi means 'upon' dia means 'through' and scope means 'projected material to be seen'.

While projecting a slide, beams pass through the slide and projects its image on the screen. In this way, transparent material is projected.

While projecting the opaque material the light bits upon the object which reflects the image on a very sensitive mirror and reflects the image of the opaque objects on the screen.

Despite the multipurpose functioning of this device, it is not very popular in educational institutions because of its poor quality image, total room darkening, very high need of energy, complexity of its use and poor range. It is to be installed in the middle of the class due to its low range, therefore, causing more interference than aiding something to the lesson. Because of its ability to project opaque objects on the screen, it is also known as opaque projector.

Overhead Projector (OHP)

Built on the basic principle of periscope, OHP is an important audio visual equipment. In the classroom it is placed in front of the teacher above his head to reflect an image on the screen (blackboard). This device consists of a strong energy source, (bulbs), fixed reflectors (mirrors), projection lens and a platen. This projector is called over head because the image goes over the head of the teacher and falls on the screen behind him. The teacher puts one slide over the other in order to give a sense of continuity of the subject matter projected on the screen.

Advantages of OHP : Its advantages lie in its special characteristics given below :

(*i*) No special training is required by the teacher to operate a projector.

(*ii*) OHPs are not very costly as compared to computers or film projectors.

(*iii*) It is handy and portable.

(*iv*) The image formed by the projector is also very bright and every pupil can see it. A 4 × 4 inches slide gives an image of 4 × 4 feet. This enlarged image is very easy to understand.

(*v*) It can create interests in pupils and hence it is a good motivator.

(*vi*) It is the best visual aid available to a teacher to supplement his oral teaching. He uses the screen of OHP as a blackboard without looking back. Transparencies, drawing, diagrams, figures and outlines etc. can be shown on the screen.

Television

TV differs from the radio in the sense that it is audio and visual both. We can see the incident occurring round the globe on it immediately after the occurrence of the incident through telecast. Thus, it is bisensory (multisensory) media. We get news, views and recreation through television in the same way as we do through the transistor but in a more compact and concrete way due to the facility of vision here.

As far as application of TV in education is concerned, it is still in the stage of infancy in India. It was only in 1961 that Indian television (Doordarshan) started a special service for schools in collaboration with the directorate of Education. This programme aimed at supplementing the regular classroom teaching in selected subjects. By 1972 only 400 schools of the capital received this telecast and two lakh students benefited from them. These programmes were telecast in the evening and on Sundays but there was no mechanism developed at that time to measure the effectiveness of such transmitting programmes.

After the introduction of distance education system in India, television is now regularly used as an instructional media. The enactment of Prasar Bharti Act is expected to boost the role of TV in the teaching learning process.

Advantages of Television :

(*i*) It heightens the reality more than the physical presence. For example, if someone is watching a cricket match in a stadium, even then he can not see certain situations despite being present there. On the other hand, if he is viewing a match on a TV, he can see and analyse every situation by close up action replay. Thus, television experience may be more real than the actual one. It can show even those details which we can not see with the help of direct experiences. Thus, television can be used for all training programmes and behaviour of the trainees can be modified in the desired manner.

(*ii*) TV experiences are new and versatile. So, they can bring variety to classroom teaching by breaking monotony and strengthening the learning structures by its multisensory approach.

(*iii*) It widens the horizon of pupils' experiences by giving them upto date knowledge of the real situation and by making them conversant with the opinions of others.

(*iv*) It can motivate the pupils for learning by arousing and retaining their interest in the learning situation.

Limitations of Television:

(*i*) Speed of a television can not be changed as we can do in motion pictures.

(*ii*) A TV programme can not be adjusted to teaching and vice versa will have to be done. A teacher can take the help of video recording in such cases.

Tape Recorder and Audio Cassettes

Cassette type audio taps are available now which can play for 90 minutes on both sides. We can listen to our own recorded voice, recorded speeches of politicians and learned people, recorded poems of great composers, songs, music etc by the tape recorder.

Audio cassette recorder is used for the following purposes :

Such types of recording serve the following purposes:

(*i*) **Analysis of verbal messages :** Accuracy, speed and tone of verbal messages are studied here and if perfection is seen, reinforcement to the presenter is given.

(*ii*) **Drill and practice :** Accurate verbal messages are presented before the trainee for drill and practice.

(*iii*) **Teaching of specific skills :** Impressive oral presentation is actually a skill. This skill is taught to students through audio-recording in the individual and group situations.

(*iv*) **Speech improvement :** Style of speaking and phonetics can also be improved by using this technology.

(*v*) **Improvement in vocabulary :** Recorded verbal messages are full of many new words which pupils can learn by listening to the message.

(*vi*) **Recreation :** Many recorded songs and music entertain the listeners and remove their fatigue.

Radio

It is an important and easily accessable audio aid serving three important general purposes "news, views and recreation". It is the cheapest equipment of all and radio broadcast is now reachable to 100% population of the country. Pupils can get information about the incidents in any part of the globe immediately through radio. This increases their general awareness of the world. Students listen the ideas of learned people, politicians and educationists from across the world on the radio. This extends their own views and way of thinking. Apart from these, there are hundreds of programmes of music, songs and plays broadcast on the radio which entertain them round the clock.

Instructional Value of the Radio :

(*i*) It is a powerful means of developing listening comprehension.

(*ii*) It can also help the pupils to acquire correct pronunciation and phonetics like tape recorders.

(*iii*) Conversational style and language can be learned on the radio.

(*iv*) It improves word power of learners.

(*v*) Mass education goals can be achieved through radio broadcast. It was the realization of the people when radio came into being in 1917.

(*vi*) News listened on the radio can improve our general knowledge.

(*vii*) Radio listening does not require literacy. Even illiterates can take the benefit of it.

Radio Broadcast in India : The first radio station was established in India in July 1927 in Mumbai followed by one more station in Kolkata in the same year. This media is now able to penetrate to the remotest villages of the country and is covering more than 99% of the population.

School broadcasting in India was started in 1937. Radio broadcasting is now very much used for mass education as well as the education of school going children in selected areas. Central Institute for educational technology (CIET) under the supervision and control of NCERT produces quality radio broadcast programmes. Adult education Radio Programmes also started in 1956 to educate the adults in the age group of 15-35 in the vicinity of Pune as a project sponsord by UNESCO. Today, broadcast of adult education programmes are many under different titles. When Consumer Protection Act was passed in 1986, consumer education through radio was also given recognition. Today, it is a regular programme of all the radio stations in India. One more regular radio programme is the radio counseling programme of IGNOU which is broadcast from 4-5 pm on every Sunday.

Apart from these, radio broadcast is also making the people aware about various social and economic problems and people are also educated about how they can solve these problems.

Computer

It is the latest electronic device that is audio and visual both. It accepts data, performs operations on that data in sequence (decided by a programme) and outputs the results.

Computer in education : From input devices to output and its storage, computer has a wide range of applicability in education. In computers inputs are converted into output by a programme. Thus, input (data) plus programme form software or instructional programme. Inputs are converted into output in the CPU of the computer.

Computer always works according to the programme given to it. Whatever instruction or programme the students gives to the computers, it

ENGLISH

will always act accordingly and output will also come out on the same line. Application of computers in education can be understood by the following lines.

Videodiscs

This system is comprised of videodisc, where the information is stored, a video player and a TV set.

It is helpful in teaching learning process in the following ways :

(*i*) Students can get more informations through effective way of presentation.

(*ii*) By forwarding or reversing the CD player, learners can have access to any informations as many times as possible. This repeated action is necessary in understanding complex materials.

(*iii*) Live coverage given by the CD player can provide higher degree of motivation.

(*iv*) Auto stop system provided in the system can help those learners who study till late hours of night.

(*v*) The materials prepared by the effective teachers can be made available in the market for wide use.

Videotext

This system provides an interactive information retrieval service. It allows the home television to work as a computer terminal, which retrieves the textual material and graphic information from a remote data base.

Advantages of Videotext:

(*i*) It is useful for downloading the required information from a remote data base.

(*ii*) It raises the general awareness of learners.

(*iii*) The principal of a school can have access to any information about his or other schools any time if this system is available in the school.

(*iv*) It is especially useful for distance learning. A learner can connect himself with his study centre or regional office any time.

(*v*) It is free from time schedule. We can have any information any time.

(*vi*) Two way interaction between the teacher and the taught is possible here with the help of alphanumeric keyboard. The learner can address to his tutor by typing questions and sending it to the tutor. Once he receives the answer, he gets immediate feedback.

(*vii*) It is faster than telephone or telegram because user need not wait here in queue.

Teleconferencing

Teleconferencing is a two way broadcast system in which learners can interact with the programme through a local telephone. It is a powerful medium of instruction for distance education. In this system three or four subject experts sit at different places and participate in the discussion on the given subject matter. Here learners do not take part in the teaching-learning process directly. They only hear the programme on their radio set or TV. They can however, interact with the experts through telephone which is connected to the radio or TV station where the discussion is being organised.

Thus, teleconferencing involves the use of many media and allows interactive group communication by means of a two way broadcast. All such conferencing need good quality audio device to facilitate immediate interaction among the participants for exchange of views.

Advantages of Teleconferencing :

(*i*) **Effective for distance learning :** When groups of students are scattered over a large area of the country and it is not possible for them to interact with their teachers personally, then learning through teleconferencing is the best option for them.

(*ii*) **Interaction between the teacher and the taught possible :** As far as interaction between teachers and learners are concerned, this approach does not differ in any way from classroom teaching.

(*iii*) **High quality instruction :** Since, very learned people and experts of the subject take part in these discussions, the quality of the programme is never questionable.

(*iv*) **Immediate feedback :** Learners get answer of their questions immediately from the experts and their problem is solved. In this way, they get immediate feedback.

(*v*) **Flexibility :** Experts do not teach here on a pre-determined track. Their instruction and its way of presentation always changes according to the questions asked by learners. Thus, this approach is very flexible.

Internet

It is the abbreviation of international network. The computers connected to this system are automatically connected to world wide website(www). Due to this we can hear and see any programme available on website any time when we want to do so. If we have missed any television or radio programme, we can not have access to that programme again but if that programme is loaded on the website, we can repeatedly hear and see the programme. We will only have to log on the website of the programme producer and it will be available for us. The major advantage of this system is that it has made 24 hour communication possible especially between those countries which have great differences in their local timings such as India and America have a time difference of 10 ½ hours. When there is day time in India, offices are closed in America.

Applications of internet in education :

(*i*) We can get any information any time at home through internet on one hand and we can store the information by creating our own website on the other. Thus, it is not necessary to have immediate print out of the textual matter.

(*ii*) The two talking persons can see each other in face to face situations also through internet. Thus, a teacher can teach millions of students scattered across the world together.

(*iii*) Many educational institutions have created their educational websites. We can download any information about them any time by logging on these websites.

(*iv*) Internet has also its role to play in classroom teaching. Teacher can show any educational programme through internet any time according to his own convenience and he will not have to adjust his time table according to the programme as he does while using radio or television as aids.

(*v*) Latest teaching strategies and latest researches in different fields can be obtained through internet immediately and we need not have to wait for their publication in magazines and journals.

(*vi*) Books, magazines and newspapers are also published on internet and it has made our access to them easy. Any Indian living in Canada even can read "Amar Ujala" or "Times of India" daily.

(*vii*) Research material and encyclopaedias are also published on internet to facilitate learning process.

REMEDIAL TEACHING

Remedial Teaching (RT) means that help is offered to pupils who need (pedagogical/didactic) assistance. These are often children who function at a lower than average level because of a certain learning- or behavioural problem/disorder, but RT can also be offered to pupils who achieve at a higher than average level, they too can do with the extra attention and care. The best known learning disorder is dyslexia.

The help includes the pupil who is being put forward for RT to the remedial teacher is examined by means of an intake conversation, checks, tests and/or observations. The remedial teacher tries to form a picture of the pupil also by way of talks with the group teacher and the parents in order to discover where the problem lies. When this is clear (diagnosis) a therapy plan is drawn up. In a therapy plan it states amongst others which aims should be achieved. The treatment that ensues is called remedial teaching. It is help that is completely specialized in the problem of the pupil, it is custom-made.

The therapy plan is drawn up for a fixed period of time. Remedial teaching is usually given during 6 weeks to 3 months, once or twice a week at school or in the remedial teacher's own practice. The aim being that the pupil can join his own group again after this period of time (or possibly after a continuation).

Remedial teaching is offered at many schools. However, a school is allowed to establish its own priorities and is not obliged to offer remedial teaching. There has to be a course of care though, the organization of which is determined by the whole team, although the directives and rules are laid down by the Ministery of Education an Science (OC&W).

Quizzing students more often is another commonly used method in a well balanced remedial teaching program. Taking the extra time to check each individual's progress gives the teacher an opportunity to regroup if necessary. It can also take the overall test pressure off students who tend to "freeze" when tested on larger amounts of material. From elementary to college, the best remedial teaching programs will include constant feedback from its students. This kind of communication provides a comfort level between student and teacher which leads to a more proficient, positive and rewarding outcome for both.

Too often, a lack of understanding among parents, school administrators and teaching staff gets in the way. Proper training of teachers and administrators go beyond their degree of specialties. Listening to each other, and to parents and children who live with specific special needs, is a huge first step in creating an exemplary remedial teaching program as opposed to another "one size fits all" classroom. Requesting conferences, discussing individual strengths and weaknesses, and respecting each others expertise and opinions are all important pieces, and are defining points of the best remedial teaching programs.

Need and Importance of Special Education

Provision of special education is a must to fulfil the following requirements in democratic countries.

1. When individual differences in learners are found to such an extent that all of them can not be benefitted in normal classes, they are put into the category of exceptionals for special learning arrangement. This is the responsibility of every democratic country to do its best for the maximum development of all its citizens. The handicapped can not be left unnoticed at the mercy of normal people for begging alms.
2. A severely deviant child is not supposed to take part in the routine activities meant for normal children. He will either be frustrated there or frustrate the others. Thus, the whole teaching learning process will be disturbed. Their proper adjustment of the society needs special leaning arrangements for them.
3. Gifted and talented children are the assets of the society. If they are not given proper opportunity to flourish in their own way, it will be the loss of the society itself.
4. Exceptional can not take the benefit of regular classes due to their unique needs and abilities. They need special curriculum, special teaching strategy and special teacher to develop them to the fullest extent.
5. Creative and positive deviants are likely to turn into juvenile delinquents in future if they are not treated properly by the family, school and the society resulting in-law and order problem in the society.
6. Handicapped children will become a liability for the society if efforts are not made to educate and rehabilitate them. They can be proved to be productive in those areas where they are not disabled. For example, a blind person can he a good musician or a good teacher (communicator) though he is unable to perform in those areas which require activity of vision.
7. Deviant children generally feel problem of adjustment in normal educational setting. It will create tension in their minds and they may become deviant in other areas also.
8. Special education helps teachers, guardians, researchers and educational administrator to understand the special problems of these children.
9. Blind, deaf and dumb children are not supposed to learn properly in normal educational setting due to their unique respective problems. For example, normal children can learn more if visual aids are used in the class but such aids are useless for a blind child. He will rather need audio aids for increasing his rate of learning and it can not be provided in regular classes.
10. Educational and rehabilitational needs of these children are also different. If they are not properly educated or trained by applying special measures, their rehabilitation will not be possible.

Special Education with Reference to Family and Community

Practical shape of special education is given below:

(A) Special Education in the Context of the Family

A handicapped child first belongs to his family. He is made in future in the manner how he is responded and behaved by the family. The role of special education in the context of the family is being discussed below:

1. Effects of Handicapping Situation: The handicapping situation can influence and thus mould a child in the following ways.

(a) **Psychological Effects :** It may cause the child to be deprived of certain abilities, e.g., the emotional and intellectual development of a two years old normal child will be more than that of a handicapped child. He may several times come to feel that his disability is a punishment and develop feeling of guilt. He may also develop feeling of hatred against his maker and thus he may hate whole human being. In this way he may either be aggressive to the environment or fearful of it.

(b) **Physical Effects :** Emotional outrage burst in the handicapped may cause physical illness, i.e., psychosomatic or neurotic problems are very commonly seen. Similarly, if child is maladjusted in the family or in the society, his parents may also face the difficulty of adjustment. If he is given more attention in the family than the normals, then the unique relationship developed between the parents and the handicapped child can create new problems for normal children in the family also. Moreover, if the material environment of the child is impoverished as we generally see (handicapped are mostly found in poor families), then the perceptual conceptual bricks with which he should build the whole framework of cognition will be very weak. Apart from these, due to impairment, physical and psychological changes of puberty and growth in height, weight and sexual traits may be delayed.

(c) **Parental Reactions to a Defective Child and Development of the Child.** Parents react to these children in the following ways:

(i) ***Realistic (coping with the situation) :*** They may adopt a realistic attitude towards the problem and does not try to hide anything. This type of reaction is useful for parents and the child both. They will help and guide the child in the desired manner. They will not put extra burden on the child due to extra expectations.

(ii) ***Denial of the reality of handicap :*** Handicap if occurred in the family is a reality but in most of the time denied by parents due to shame or stigma attached to the disability in the society. It is useful for parents to some extent as it helps them in bringing the mind into balance but excess denial of reality is fatal.

(iii) ***Self pity-more than the desired care for the child :*** This is a type of over protection given to the child on account of pity. He may start questioning or suspecting God, why he has made a blind or paralysed child for him or 'what wrongs did he do that made him liable to be punished in this way' etc. Thus parents may either become atheistic or they may take solace in their religious beliefs.

(iv) ***Ambivalence-toward the child:*** Additional responsibilities, anxieties and irritations caused by such children which become a routine part of their life produce ambivalent parental reactions. Parents accept and love their children due to the natural love created by the blood but they also reject and hate them at the same time.

(v) ***Projection of the difficulty:*** Anxiety relating to unacceptable feelings of resentment, hatred and hostility can be minimized by blaming someone else for the handicapping situation of their child, e;g., other children, doctors, teachers, or the marriage arranged by their elders in blood relations can be blamed resulting in a handicapped child in the family. This is known as projection. Handicapped are mostly found in muslims due to probably the marriages between close relations.

(vi) ***Feeling of Guilt and Shame :*** Shame involve\s the expectation of ridicule or criticism from others while guilt involves self blaming or personal regret. When such feelings develop in parents, they try to avoid social situations resulting in slow social development of the child also.

(vii) ***Pattern of Mutual Dependency :*** The future development of the child depends upon the experiences that he receives at home and in the school. If he is fully cared by the parents and given chance to be exposed in social situations, his experiences will hike. Contrary to this if there is big distance between the child and his parents, the child will lose self confidence, though, he will try to develop self confidence in him.

(d) **Sexual Adjustment :**Sexual adjustment to a large extent depends on the social relationship ranging from love and friendship to increasing social horizons. If the child is not getting proper chance of socialization, his sexual adjustment with his/her life partner will always be at stake.

(e) **Economic Adjustment :** Economic self reliance is necessary for self respect and may be essential to lead a married life also. If he is not given extra educational facilities by considering his specific impairment, he will not be fully adjusted in the society vocationally or economically.

2. Guidance and Counselling of Parents of a handicapped child : The family counsellor, the expert in education, paedriatist and the psychologist have their respective role to play in this regard. The service of these experts are needed for proper development of the child. As we know, the influence of the family on the over all development of the child is three times powerful to any other institution. Due to this reason, the idea of a continuous consultative relationship between a well qualified person and the family has been advocated. The major areas of counselling are as follows :

(a) **Intellectual Area :** Here the parents need information concerning the nature and the degree of the exceptionality of the child, i.e., diagnostic information. They are also supposed to know the cause of the handicap to avoid future occurrence of disability in the family, i.e., etiological information. They also need information about how to treat the problem to the maximum level possible and how to educate the child, i.e., remedial informations. Parents need all these three informations together.

(b) **Emotional Area:** The counsellor must remove the parents' fear and anxieties and also their feeling of guilt and shame. He should also endeavour to minimize the emotional vulnerability of the family members though he can not eliminate all these types of tensions altogether. If only the counsellor is able to increase their ability to tolerate them, his job is over.

(c) Behavioural Area : The counsellor uses the techniques of psychotherapy to mould the behaviour of parents, to understand the problems and to deal with them more adequately. They are also told by the counsellor how they will behave their handicapped child so that he may properly adjust in the society.

(B) Special Education in the Context of the Community

Democratic base of special education-Equal opportunities of education and employment for handicapped.

Equality of opportunities for handicapped means right to education. It is a human right approved by the UN Charter and it is in this context that handicapped children should be assured the facilities to attain equality and to make them at part with other people. For this purpose, they may be provided with special facilities for assistance, protection and rehabilitation.

This concept is developed on the belief that if they are given the right opportunities and the facilities commensurable with their deviance, they are fully capable of developing their residual capacities, powers and traits to the fullest extent and of becoming economically independent and socially self reliant. They need only special care not alms.

If the above concept is applied to education, they will have the equal right to get education in the same manners as normals have. In Indian context, it has been enshrined in our constitution that each and every child in the age group of 6-14 years has the fundamental right to receive free and compulsory education in the country. Before 2002 it was only a directive principle of the state policy under Article 45(A) of the Indian constitutions.

Since, handicapped lag behind the normals due to a variety of reasons, they are given three percent reservation for the admission in schools and colleges and for employment in government run installations and offices. This reservation is not against the principle of equality because of the following reasons.

(i) They are deficient in some respects leading to poor academic achievement. This deficiency cannot be overcome even by providing facilities to the maximum level possible.

(ii) They need special protection for their economic independence. If such protection is not given to them, they will not be able to survive in today's age of competition and hard struggle for means of livelihood.

(iii) Many backward and deprived communities in India have been endowed with reservation facilities and handicapped are the most backward of all the backwards.

(iv) It is their right to get extra facilities for their education and employment from the state. It is not their fault in any way that they have become handicapped. It may be the fault of their parents or other people of the society. In this sense, if special provisions are not made for them, they will be penalized for no guilt.

(v) If special provisions are not made for them, they may become a burden on the society.

MULTIPLE CHOICE QUESTIONS

1. The linguistic aims of teaching English relate to:

(*a*) Cognitive domain
(*b*) Affective domain
(*c*) Rational domain
(*d*) Logical domain

2. The process by which we remove obscurity of meaning from a phrase or statement in English, is called:

(*a*) Explanation (*b*) Exposition
(*c*) Illustration (*d*) Assignment

3. What is the purpose of silent reading?

(*a*) To enable students to read silently
(*b*) To pave the way for extensive reading
(*c*) To bring students back to the passage after the exposition and explanation
(*d*) All the above

4. Teaching devices are the:

(*a*) Tools for teachers
(*b*) Tools for students
(*c*) tool for school evaluation
(*d*) Tools for parents

5. Which one of the following is not merit of Bilingual method:

(*a*) It gives emphasis on speech practice
(*b*) It develops the habit of independent reading
(*c*) Audio-visual aids are not much needed

(*d*) It is suited to all the type of school located in rural or urban areas

6. Which method follows maxims simple to complex:
(*a*) translation-cum-grammar method
(*b*) Structural approach
(*c*) Bilingual method
(*d*) Direct or natural method

7. Illustrations can be classified as:
(*a*) Verbal and visual
(*b*) Oral and material
(*c*) Both of the above
(*d*) None of the above

8. Sentence method is opposite to the method
(*a*) Alphabetic method
(*b*) Syllabic method
(*c*) Story method
(*d*) No one

9. Introductory questions are put by the students in order to:
(*a*) Correlate part and present experiences
(*b*) Seek active help from the teacher
(*c*) Present some problem
(*d*) Examine the performance

10. We, as English teacher, evaluate pupil performance for
(*a*) Upgrading the students
(*b*) Motivating the students
(*c*) assessing teacher's performance
(*d*) All the above

11. Communicative Language Teaching focuses on
(*a*) successful communication through translation
(*b*) appropriate use of grammatical structures
(*c*) structure and form more than on meaning
(*d*) communication only through the oral language

12. In the Direct Method of language teaching
(*a*) Teaching is done only in the laguage to be taught
(*b*) Reading and writing are taught first and then listening and speaking are taught
(*c*) New points are taught in the written language
(*d*) The teacher translates direct from the first language to the foreign/second language

13. Which one of the following is the main limitation of the substitution method:
(*a*) There is no sequence and therefore children learn any isolated sentences
(*b*) This method cannot be used for teaching grammar systematically
(*c*) It lays a greater stress in oral work than on written work, which is equally important
(*d*) All of these

14. Teaching steps for Group-work Method of English teaching are:
(*a*) Determining the work project
(*b*) Group formation
(*c*) Conduction of group work
(*d*) All of these

15. Debate is a:
(*a*) Formal Presentation
(*b*) Arguments between two groups
(*c*) Norm-based
(*d*) All of these

16. What is not true about Communicative Language Teaching?
(*a*) There is no authoritative universally accepted model of Communicative Language Teaching
(*b*) It is an integration of grammatical and functional teaching
(*c*) The goal of Communicative Language Teaching is to develop linguistic competence
(*d*) Communicative competence includes both grammatical and social linguistic competence

17. Poetry must primarily be taught for the sake of
(*a*) Meaning (*b*) Music
(*c*) Grammar (*d*) Sound system

18. The Principle of Gradation means:
(*a*) Go from easy to difficult
(*b*) Choose only difficult items to teach
(*c*) Choose only easy items to teach
(*d*) Choose only relevant and significant items to teach

19. Grammar should be taught
(*a*) as means to achieve good command of listening, speaking, reading and writing skills
(*b*) as an end in itself
(*c*) as a means to achieve good command of only speaking and reading skills
(*d*) as a means to achieve good command of writing skills only

20. In Communicative Language Teaching
(*a*) Meaning is insignificant
(*b*) Meaning is paramount
(*c*) Function and Form are paramount
(*d*) Form is paramount

21. The Principle of Selection is based on the assumption that
(*a*) only a few selected and trained teachers can teach a language
(*b*) it is not possible to teach the whole language within the prescribed time period and the other constraints

(c) it is possible to select those who want to learn the target language
(d) only a few selected learners can learn the target language

22. The teaching of Composition is related to
(a) Listening Skills
(b) Speaking Skills
(c) Reading Skills
(d) Writing Skills

23. In the Bi-Lingual method, the use of the mother tongue has been
(a) avoided (b) restricted
(c) encouraged (d) eliminated

24. The psycho-linguists uphold this view that in the process of second language learning the use of mother tongue is
(a) a catylist (b) a hindrance
(c) a medium (d) a convenience

25. The following points are applicable to
1. Selection and gradation of words and structures
2. creation of learning situations
3. Exploitation of learning situations
4. Maximum participation of the learners in language-learning
5. Emphasis on spoken aspect and drills
(a) The Direct method
(b) The Structural Approach
(c) The Translation-cum-method grammar
(d) The bi-lingual method

26. The rule of grammar are taught by the teacher of classical Method in a
(a) deductive manner
(b) inductive manner
(c) functional manner
(d) situational context

27. The teaching of English in India, is facing the main problem of
(a) Use of excessive teaching aids
(b) Use of traditional and old method
(c) Lack of good books
(d) Bodh (b) and (c)

28. Which one is the teaching technique
(a) Interview (b) Note making
(c) Review (d) All of these

29. Aims and objectives of Teaching English are different from each other in relation to:
(a) Time perspective (b) Purpose
(c) Nature (d) All of these

30. The teaching of grammar must be according to the changes and:
(a) development that take place in a language
(b) undevelopment that take place in school curriculum
(c) (a) and (b)
(d) None of the above

31. The aim of teaching English to Indian school children is:
(a) to understand it when spoken
(b) to speak it and to write it
(c) to understand the English language when written
(d) All the above

32. The rapid reading has the aims:
(a) Recreational aim
(b) Literary and linguistic aim
(c) Intellectual aim
(d) All the three mentioned above

33. The interest among the students towards English can be sustained with the help of:
(a) Audio-visual aids
(b) Mass-media
(c) Language Laboratory
(d) All of these

34. Value and importance of teaching English is:
(a) English is the Lingua franca language of the world
(b) It is the language through which we can exchange our views with the people of other countries
(c) If very long association with Indian life has made it a language of many Indians
(d) All of these

35. Principle of activity in English teaching promotes the quality of:
(a) Learning by doing
(b) Learning through cramming
(c) Learning by the teachers
(d) Learning by the assignments

36. Communication skill is:
(a) Individual (b) Specific
(c) General (d) All of these

37. Poetry increases a child's.....to beauty.
(a) Interest (b) Behaviour
(c) Awareness (d) Sensitiveness

38. In inductive method we proceed from:
(a) Simple to complex
(b) Reading to writing
(c) Poetry to prose
(d) All of these

39. Which of the following should be kept in mind while formulating homework policies formulation
(a) Ineffective and mechanical drills should be used often
(b) Contents of homework should not be of a great variety

(c) Exercise books available in the market should be done first
(d) Teachers should make good use of the homework as a tool for evaluation and feedback

40. Remedial teachers should observe the following when dealing with the behaviour problems of pupils
(a) should always pay attention to their misbehaviour
(b) always observe the performance of the pupils in class and their behaviour in groups
(c) give positive reinforcement to pupils' good behaviour
(d) refer the cases to Student Guidance Officers/ Teachers for follow up action

41. Teaching and testing are:
(a) Possible (b) Similar
(c) Inseparable (d) Unique

42. Communicative approach emphasises on learning by
(a) Play (b) Use
(c) Imitation (d) Training

43. Language has relevance only in.....context:
(a) Spoken (b) Written
(c) Social (d) Emotional

44. "Language acquisition can be automatically attained" favoured by
(a) congnitivists
(b) behaviourists
(c) both of the above
(d) None of the above

45. Positive interference is a kind of.............. interference
(a) target language
(b) foreign language
(c) pictorial language
(d) native language

46. The study of language has four aspects. Which one is not a such aspect?
(a) Grammar aspect
(b) Graphic aspect
(c) Semantic aspect
(d) Phonetic aspect

47. The kinds of drill work in English teaching are:
(a) Repetition and chain drill
(b) Substitution and completion drill
(c) Question-answer and transformation drill
(d) All of these

48. Intensive reading lays stress on mastery of:
(a) Words (b) Grammar
(c) Language (d) Usage

49. Speech training is paid more emphasis by the
(a) Translation method
(b) Direct method
(c) Bilingual method
(d) Grammar method

50. Writing is a representation of speech:
(a) Morphological (b) Graphical
(c) Linguistical (d) Phonetical

51. Which of the following is not a language skill?
(a) Reading (b) Writing
(c) Thinking (d) Speaking

52. By which method the students learn to the maximum extent?
(a) By seeing
(b) By reading
(c) By listening
(d) By doing themselves

53. Which quality of the teacher is liked the most by the students?
(a) Punctuality
(b) Impartiality
(c) Love for discipline
(d) Dominance

54. What should the teacher do to maintain the interest of students in class teaching?
(a) Maximum use of blackboard
(b) Extensive use of examples from the practical life
(c) Extensive use of teaching materials/aids
(d) Giving ample opportunity to students for discussion/delibrations

55. Children with disability must get education because—
(a) They are vulnerable
(b) They have special needs
(c) It is a basic constitutional right
(d) They are poor

56. Which of the following is a sensory disorder?
(a) Hearing Impairment
(b) Mental Retardation
(c) Cerebral Palsy
(d) Neuro Muscular Disorder

57. Learning depends on—
(a) Intelligence
(b) Parental attitude
(c) Peer attitude
(d) None of these

58. Which of the following can increase the quality of education?
(a) To extend one hour time period
(b) Service period teacher training
(c) Solution and treatment teaching
(d) By help-books

59. Which cannot be the stage of learning?
(*a*) Procedure
(*b*) Difference perception
(*c*) Exercise
(*d*) Imagination

60. Which of the following is decisive for teaching work?
(*a*) To make effective the excellence
(*b*) To educate
(*c*) True management of classes
(*d*) Communication with students

61. What will be the indication when a group of students gets more marks in the question paper made by any teacher?
(*a*) It is a group of high achiever
(*b*) Teacher has tought well
(*c*) Question-paper is good
(*d*) None of these

62. Choose the one which best expresses the meaning of the word 'Condone'.
(*a*) Grieve
(*b*) Endure
(*c*) Forgive
(*d*) Ignore

63. Change the following active voice into passive one :
Does the noise disturb you?
(*a*) You are disturb by the noise.
(*b*) Are you disturbed by the noise?
(*c*) You are disturbing by the noise.
(*d*) Are you disturbing by the noise?

64. A statement that can have a double meaning—
(*a*) Verbose (*b*) Ambivalent
(*c*) Epigraph (*d*) Ambiguous

65. We should always observe from the stand point of others. This is a —
(*a*) Simple sentence
(*b*) Complex sentence
(*c*) Compound sentence
(*d*) Phrase

66. Schools should be concerned with the development of child, which should include—
(*a*) Acquisition of knowledge by the child
(*b*) Acquisition of life skills by the child
(*c*) Acquisition of skills required by the nation
(*d*) Acquisition of skills required by the healthy person

67. A student gives a partially correct respond to your question. Then you will—
(*a*) Seek further information
(*b*) Provide reinforcement
(*c*) Reframe your question
(*d*) Tell the correct information

68. Which of the following is/are productive skill/skills?
(*a*) Speaking
(*b*) Writing
(*c*) Both (*a*) and (*b*)
(*d*) None of the above

69. Language acquisition can be automatically attained favoured by—
(*a*) Cognitivists
(*b*) Behaviourists
(*c*) Both of the above
(*d*) None of the above

70. Which of the following grammar teaching method disturbs the teaching of a text book or composition writing at times?
(*a*) Deductive Method
(*b*) Inductive Method
(*c*) Inductive Deductive Method
(*d*) Incidental Method

71. Teaching aids are useful because they—
(*a*) help teacher's work
(*b*) activate all senses
(*c*) help students to be attentive
(*d*) make learning more meaningful

72. Teaching would be more effective if the teacher—
(*a*) Makes his intent purposeful
(*b*) Is master of the subject
(*c*) Uses various instructional aids
(*d*) Declares his objectives in the beginning

73. The word 'Tacit' means—
(*a*) Formal (*b*) Fear
(*c*) Silent (*d*) Celestial

74. One who is well-versed in the science of languages is called a—
(*a*) Philosopher
(*b*) Theologist
(*c*) Philologist
(*d*) Zoologist

75. Choose the correctly spelt word—
(*a*) Coloqial
(*b*) Coloquial
(*c*) Colloqial
(*d*) Colloquial

76. Choose what expresses the meaning of 'Pull the wool over one's eye'—
(*a*) Delay (*b*) Encourage
(*c*) Suppress (*d*) Deceive

77. Student's learning difficulties can be best addressed by—
(*a*) Advising them to work hard
(*b*) Suggesting private tuitions
(*c*) Supervised study in the library
(*d*) Remedial teaching

78. For being successful in life students should be encouraged to—
(*a*) selective study
(*b*) casual study
(*c*) intensive study
(*d*) learning by rote memorisation

79. Students who bring out alternative solutions and cite the books not prescribed by the teacher should be—
(*a*) discouraged
(*b*) encouraged
(*c*) advised to talk to the teacher outside the class
(*d*) advised to follow the class notes to score better in the examinations

80. Problem of school dropouts can be effectively tackled by—
(*a*) reducing curriculum load
(*b*) teachers empathy
(*c*) attractive school environment
(*d*) providing incentives

81. Choose the synonym of voracious—
(*a*) Hungry
(*b*) Wild
(*c*) Quick
(*d*) Angry

82. Choose the misspelt word—
(*a*) Command
(*b*) Appraise
(*c*) Behaviour
(*d*) Mentenance

83. Remedial teachers should observe the following when dealing with the behaviour problems of pupils—
(*a*) should always pay attention to their misbehaviour
(*b*) always observe the performance of pupils in class and their behaviour in groups
(*c*) give positive reinforcement to pupils good behaviour
(*d*) refer the cases to student Guidance Officers/teachers for follow up action

84. Use stress and rhythmic patterns and intonation patterns of the language and 'use vocabulary appropriately' are the micro-skills involved in which of the following?
(*a*) Speaking
(*b*) Listening
(*c*) Reading
(*d*) Writing

85. Problems in language learning arise due to lack of—
(*a*) methodology of teaching
(*b*) availability of materials
(*c*) teaching of mother tongue
(*d*) teacher's competence

86. Usual teaching-learning processes can be supplemented by the following to improve the quality—
(*a*) Extra coaching
(*b*) Diagnostic and remedial teaching
(*c*) Enrichment programmes
(*d*) Inservice teacher education

87. School based evaluation can solve the problem of—
(*a*) Mass copying
(*b*) Student's indiscipline
(*c*) Unrealistic assessment
(*d*) Teacher's social reputation

88. Choose the correct meaning of the idioms: Hobson's choice—
(*a*) feeling of insecurity
(*b*) accept or leave the offer
(*c*) excellent choice
(*d*) no choice at all

89. Choose the meaning of the **bold** phrase in the sentence—

He has been working **on and off** for several years on this project.
(*a*) at intervals (*b*) rarely
(*c*) painstakingly (*d*) continuously

90. Pedagogy is considered to be the—
(*a*) Science of Teaching
(*b*) Art of Learning
(*c*) Science of Communication
(*d*) Art of Assimilation

91. Inductive approach of teaching means—
(*a*) initiating the child to new subject
(*b*) teaching through specific instruction
(*c*) group learning as opposed to individualised learning
(*d*) arriving at generalisations with the help of examples

92. Which of the following is an appropriate order for learning of a language?
(*a*) Listening → Speaking → Writing → Reading
(*b*) Speaking → Listening → Writing → Reading
(*c*) Listening → Speaking → Reading → Writing
(*d*) Listening → Reading → Speaking → Writing

93. The primary functions of language are—
(*a*) Expression of feeling, meaning, communication and thinking
(*b*) To control over other people, as language is a social act

(*c*) Both (*a*) and (*b*)
(*d*) None of these

94. Which of the following conditions must be satisfied in order to designate a person mentally retarded?
(*a*) Sub-normal intellectual functioning
(*b*) Very poor adaptive ability
(*c*) Dependability on others
(*d*) All of these

95. The best measure of identifying mildly mentally retarded is—
(*a*) Administration of standardized intelligence test
(*b*) Administration of behaviour test
(*c*) Administration of adjustment test
(*d*) A combination of all

96. Physical trauma during pregnancy may cause
(*a*) Mental retardation (*b*) Blindness
(*c*) Deafness (*d*) All of these

97. All of the following may cause mental retardation except
(*a*) Blood incompatibility
(*b*) Action of toxic agent
(*c*) Radio-activity
(*d*) None of these

98. Dullers do not differ from normal children in—
(*a*) Physical characteristics
(*b*) Level of social expectancy
(*c*) Both of these
(*d*) None of these

99. Which of the following things is not required for educating mildly mentally retarded children?
(*a*) Regular counselling
(*b*) Remedial teaching
(*c*) Modification in the curriculum
(*d*) Regular evaluation

100. Teaching of which of the following skills is not suitable to borderline cases?
(*a*) Electric fitting
(*b*) Repairing of electric or electronic equipments
(*c*) Oratory skills
(*d*) Activity based skills

101. Morons are slow in—
(*a*) Physical growth
(*b*) Thinking and planning
(*c*) Taking initiative
(*d*) All of these

102. Unsatisfactory relation of a mentally retarded child with the environment is technically called—
(*a*) Autism
(*b*) Maladjustment
(*c*) Pseudo-dullness
(*d*) None of these

103. Learning disabled children are—
(*a*) Deficient in using potentials
(*b*) Low in intelligence
(*c*) Slow in activity
(*d*) None of these

104. Learning disability is related to—
(*a*) low listening and comprehension power
(*b*) poor ability of expression
(*c*) poor ability of mathematical operation
(*d*) All of these

105. Learning disabled children perform very poorly in—
(*a*) Academic areas (*b*) Technical areas
(*c*) Both of these (*d*) None of these

106. Problem of learning disability is more complex than that of other disabilities because—
(*a*) Its causes can not be easily ascertained by applying usual tests
(*b*) It is associated to behaviour problems
(*c*) Both of these
(*d*) None of these

107. Educationally, learning disabled look similar to—
(*a*) Dullers (*b*) Backward children
(*c*) Both of these (*d*) None of these

108. In which of the following physical characteristics learning disabled children differ from the normal ones?
(*a*) They are all the time clumsy and awkward
(*b*) Poor coordination of motor abilities
(*c*) Height, weight and health
(*d*) All of these

109. Which of the following methods is most suitable for learning disabled children?
(*a*) Behaviour guidance method
(*b*) Remedial teaching
(*c*) Brain storming
(*d*) None of these

110. In order to improve work habits of learning disabled what should be done?
(*a*) Unattending behaviour should be penalized
(*b*) Close monitoring of the behaviour is needed
(*c*) Cues and prompt should be given
(*d*) All of these

111. Which of the following situations may lead to educational backwardness?
(*a*) Sensory impairment
(*b*) Motor disability
(*c*) Long diseases and health problems
(*d*) All of these

112. Which of the following is an important cause of educational backwardness at primary level of education in India?
(a) Poor school organisation
(b) Lack of accountability
(c) Attitude of the masses towards education
(d) All of these

113. Which of the following measures should be adopted by the teacher to check educational backwardness?
(a) Continuous evaluation and regular feedback
(b) Remedial teaching
(c) Adjustment and behaviour training
(d) All of these

114. Teaching by small steps and frequent short assignment techniques are useful for—
(a) Slow learners
(b) Learning disabled
(c) Educationally backward children.
(d) Children of all types of disabilities

115. Special schools are required for backward children when—
(a) Backwardness is due to any serious physical handicap
(b) The size of population of backward children in the society is very large as is the case of Gujarat where the achievement of students in mathematics is always seen very low
(c) Both of these
(d) None of these

116. Audio-visual materials reduce:
(a) Time (b) Interest
(c) Effort (d) Verbalism

117. Intensive reading is
(a) Loud reading
(b) Silent reading
(c) Both (a) and (b)
(d) None of these

118. A Blue print contains details information of:
(a) Normative (b) Effective
(c) Formative (d) Integrated

119. What is the aim of extensive reading?
(a) Enriching the student's knowledge
(b) Cultivating a taste for reading
(c) Both (a) and (b)
(d) None of these

120. The general aims of teaching are:
(a) Fluid (b) Fixed
(c) Pragmatic (d) Dogmatic

121. The aim is that the child should learn to do the task both accurately and quickly' the statement fits to which of the following stage?
(a) Acquisition
(b) Maintenance
(c) Generalization
(d) Fluency

122. To make language natural it must be:
(a) Spoken (b) Read
(c) Write (d) None of these

123. Why Choral Recitation is necessary in teaching poetry?
(a) It helps them in overcoming shyness
(b) It heightens aural effect
(c) Both (a) and (b)
(d) None of these

124. Which one is the theory based on the habit formation that says that human or any creature gives response due to stimulus or human learn due to stimulus?
(a) Classical conditioning
(b) Operant conditioning
(c) Stimulus conditioning
(d) None of these

125. The way through which the art of using skill and practice is given to learn it than it is called
(a) learning (b) acquisition
(c) erudition (d) recitation

ANSWERS

1	2	3	4	5	6	7	8	9	10
(a)	(a)	(d)	(a)	(b)	(d)	(c)	(a)	(a)	(d)
11	12	13	14	15	16	17	18	19	20
(d)	(a)	(d)	(d)	(d)	(a)	(b)	(a)	(a)	(b)
21	22	23	24	25	26	27	28	29	30
(b)	(d)	(b)	(b)	(b)	(a)	(d)	(d)	(d)	(a)
31	32	33	34	35	36	37	38	39	40
(d)	(d)	(d)	(d)	(d)	(b)	(d)	(a)	(d)	(a)
41	42	43	44	45	46	47	48	49	50
(c)	(b)	(c)	(a)	(b)	(a)	(d)	(a)	(b)	(b)

51	52	53	54	55	56	57	58	59	60
(*c*)	(*d*)	(*b*)	(*c*)	(*c*)	(*d*)	(*a*)	(*b*)	(*a*)	(*a*)
61	**62**	**63**	**64**	**65**	**66**	**67**	**68**	**69**	**70**
(*b*)	(*b*)	(*b*)	(*d*)	(*a*)	(*b*)	(*b*)	(*c*)	(*a*)	(*d*)
71	**72**	**73**	**74**	**75**	**76**	**77**	**78**	**79**	**80**
(*d*)	(*c*)	(*c*)	(*c*)	(*d*)	(*d*)	(*d*)	(*c*)	(*b*)	(*d*)
81	**82**	**83**	**84**	**85**	**86**	**87**	**88**	**89**	**90**
(*a*)	(*d*)	(*a*)	(*a*)	(*d*)	(*d*)	(*c*)	(*d*)	(*a*)	(*a*)
91	**92**	**93**	**94**	**95**	**96**	**97**	**98**	**99**	**100**
(*d*)	(*c*)	(*c*)	(*d*)	(*d*)	(*d*)	(*d*)	(*c*)	(*c*)	(*c*)
101	**102**	**103**	**104**	**105**	**106**	**107**	**108**	**109**	**110**
(*d*)	(*a*)	(*d*)	(*d*)	(*a*)	(*a*)	(*b*)	(*b*)	(*a*)	(*d*)
111	**112**	**113**	**114**	**115**	**116**	**117**	**118**	**119**	**120**
(*d*)	(*d*)	(*d*)	(*d*)	(*c*)	(*d*)	(*a*)	(*c*)	(*c*)	(*b*)
121	**122**	**123**	**124**	**125**					
(*d*)	(*a*)	(*c*)	(*a*)	(*a*)					

❑❑❑

हिन्दी

हिन्दी

SECTION a

भाषा बोध

भूमिका

भाषा बोध के द्वारा व्यक्ति की समग्र अवबोधन क्षमता का मूल्यांकन किया जाता है। इससे अभ्यर्थी की समझ क्षमता एवं दिए गए अवतरण में छुपे गूढ़ विचारों को ग्रहण करने की क्षमता आंकी जाती है। इसके द्वारा अभ्यर्थी के निर्णय लेने की क्षमता की भी जांच की जाती है। ऐसा दिए गए प्रतिपाद्य के हृदयंगम द्वारा ही संभव है। इस प्रकार भाषा बोध व्यक्तित्व के बहुआयामी पहलुओं के परीक्षण की पद्धति है। इसके द्वारा भाषा-ज्ञान, निहितार्थ की समझ एवं अवबोधन क्षमता, निर्णय क्षमता एवं सही निष्कर्ष तक पहुंचने की क्षमता की जांच एक साथ की जाती है। जाहिर है, इतने सारे परीक्षणों के द्वारा व्यक्तित्व का समग्र उभार एवं निखार प्रकट हो जाता है। ऐसे में भाषा बोध के प्रश्नों को हल करने में अतिरिक्त सावधानी एवं सचेतता आवश्यक है। इस प्रकार के प्रश्नों के सही उत्तर देने के लिए निरंतर अभ्यास की आवश्यकता होती है।

उद्धरण को पढ़कर उसके मूलभाव या निहितार्थ को समझने की कोशिश करनी चाहिए। एक बार पढ़कर मूलभाव को समझने में कठिनाई हो तो उसे एक से अधिक बार पढ़ें। जबतक निहितार्थ समझ में न आए उसे दुबारा एवं तिबारा पढ़ें। निहितार्थ समझ लेने पर प्रश्नों का उत्तर देना आसान हो जाता है।

उद्धरण को पढ़ते समय महत्वपूर्ण बिंदुओं को रेखांकित करते चलें। ऐसे में मूल बिंदुओं को शीघ्रता से दुहरा सकते हैं। हो सकता है समयाभाव के कारण मूल अवतरण को बार-बार पढ़ना संभव न हो।

प्रश्नों के उत्तर दिए गए अवतरण पर ही आधारित हों। अपनी पूर्व की जानकारी के आधार पर निष्कर्ष न निकालें। यह संभव है कि अवतरण में दी गई जानकारी आपकी पूर्व की जानकारी या राय से भिन्न हो। ऐसे में अपनी जानकारी को अवतरण में दी गई सूचना के साथ घालमेल न करें। ऐसा करना आत्मघाती कदम हो सकता है।

कभी-कभी अवतरण में किसी शब्द के समानार्थक या विपरीतार्थक शब्द पूछे जाते हैं। ऐसे प्रश्नों के उत्तर देने में जल्दबाजी न करें। जाहिर है किसी एक शब्द के कई समानार्थक एवं विपरीतार्थक शब्द हो सकते हैं। ऐसे में उपयुक्त शब्द का चुनाव आवश्यक है। इसके लिए लेखक के मूल कथ्य और विचार को समझना आवश्यक है।

दिए गए अवतरण के लिए उपयुक्त शीर्षक लिखना एक चुनौतीपूर्ण कार्य होता है। यह प्रश्न काफी आसान भी है और कठिन भी। आसान इसलिए कि इनका उत्तर दिए अवतरण के आधार पर ही देना होता है और कठिन इसलिए कि अवतरण के मूल भाव को समझे बिना विषयांतर हो जाने की संभावना अक्सर बनी रहती है।

और, सबसे जरूरी चीज है—अभ्यास! अभ्यास के बिना आसान प्रश्न भी कठिन लगने लगते हैं। भाषा-बोध के प्रश्नों को हल करने के लिए भाषा में अभिरुचि एवं समझ विकसित करनी चाहिए।

उद्धरण-1

समकालीन भारत की अर्थव्यवस्था एक बड़ा विरोधाभास है। वह उत्कृष्ट उपलब्धियों और गंभीर विफलताओं का विचित्र संयोग है। स्वतंत्रता के बाद से भारत ने अपने आर्थिक पिछड़ेपन से ऊपर उठने में उल्लेखनीय प्रगति की है। वह जो 1950 के दशक में एक अत्यंत निर्धन देश था और 1960 के दशक के मध्य में सहायतार्थी देश था, वही आज विश्व की चौथी सबसे बड़ी अर्थव्यवस्था (क्रय-शक्ति क्षमता के आधार पर) के रूप में उभरा है। हमारी अर्थव्यवस्था विश्व की सबसे तेजी से संवर्द्धित होने वाली अर्थव्यवस्थाओं में आ गई है। अब यह देश विश्व ज्ञान अर्थव्यवस्था में एक अग्रणी खिलाड़ी बन गया है, जिसके पास अपार बौद्धिक पूंजी और तेजी से बढ़ने वाली सॉफ्टवेयर और सूचना प्रौद्योगिकी सेवाएं हैं। यद्यपि

हमारा देश विश्व के पांच सबसे अधिक तेजी से संवर्धित होने वाली अर्थव्यवस्थाओं के समूह में शामिल हो गया है फिर भी हम मानव विकास सूचकांक (ह्युमन डेवलपमेंट इंडेक्स) की दृष्टि से सबसे निचले 20 देशों में हैं। यद्यपि देश अपनी संवृद्धि दर और प्रौद्योगिकीय करामातों का जश्न मना रहा है, फिर भी वह सामाजिक विरोधाभासों तथा विकास के विरोधाभास और विडंबनाओं से गुजर रहा है। इस प्रकार समकालीन भारत में 'दो भारत' हैं।

1. भारतीय अर्थव्यवस्था को 'एक बड़ा विरोधाभास' क्यों माना जाता है?
   A. वह साक्षरता का निम्न स्तर होने के बावजूद सूचना प्रौद्योगिकी सेवाओं में एक अग्रणी खिलाड़ी है।
   B. कृषि जन्य उत्पादन की विपुलता के बीच गरीबी है।
   C. यह निम्न मानव विकास वाली एक सबसे बड़ी अर्थव्यवस्था है।
   D. सामाजिक विरोधाभासों के साथ ही उसकी वैज्ञानिक उपलब्धियाँ हैं।

2. भारत को विश्व ज्ञान अर्थव्यवस्था में एक अग्रणी खिलाड़ी क्यों कहा जा रहा है?
   A. विज्ञान और प्रौद्योगिकी में भारत के ज्ञान का आधार विश्व के सर्वोत्तम में से है।
   B. भारत के पास मानव बौद्धिक पूंजियों और सूचना प्रौद्योगिकी सेवाओं के विशाल भंडार हैं।
   C. भारत विश्व की पांच सबसे तेजी से संवर्द्धित होने वाली अर्थव्यवस्थाओं तथा प्रौद्योगिक भंडारों में से एक है।
   D. भारत के पास मानव पूँजी और वैज्ञानिक ज्ञान निर्यात संभाव्यता का विशाल भंडार है।

3. लेखक का 'दो भारत' से क्या तात्पर्य है?
   A. एक भारत है जिसके पास अपार बौद्धिक पूंजी है जबकि एक दूसरा है जो मुख्यतया निरक्षर है।
   B. एक भारत है जहाँ संवृद्धि में उछाल है तो वहीं व्यापक अभाव और विपन्नता वाला भारत भी है।
   C. एक प्रगतिशील मानसिकता वाला भारत है तो वहीं वह भारत भी है जो सामाजिक तौर पर दकियानूसी है।
   D. एक ऐसा भारत है जिसमें विशिष्ट उपलब्धियों के साथ ही विशाल विफलताएं हैं।

उद्धरण-2

भारतीय गणतंत्र में कानून एवं व्यवस्था राज्यों का विषय है इसीलिए मुख्यमंत्रियों को केंद्रीय दृष्टिकोण से लैस करने के क्लास को जरूरी समझा जाता है। विकास की दिशा में असमानता को दूर करने की कोई कारगर योजना भले ही नहीं दिखती हो लेकिन नक्सलियों से निपटने के लिए विशेष पुलिस फोर्स का गठन जरूरी बताया गया है। अब तक नक्सल प्रभावित क्षेत्रों के बारे में सरकारी कार्रवाईयों का अनुभव भी यही रहा है कि यहां पुलिस एक्शन तो बड़े पैमाने पर शुरू हो जाते हैं लेकिन नक्सली गतिविधियों की जड़ों में जो आर्थिक, राजनैतिक, सामाजिक असमानता के कारण को सत्ता जिम्मेदार मानती है, उसे दूर नहीं कर पाती है। भारत में यह खास तौर से देखा जाना चाहिए कि नक्सलियों की गतिविधियां उन्हीं राज्यों में हैं जहां दूसरी हथियारबंद शक्तियां नहीं हैं और जहां क्षेत्र विशेष की चरित्र वाली संसदीय शक्तियां अपनी पहचान खो चुकी हैं। इस तरह देश में किसी न किसी रूप में हथियारबंद समूहों की मौजूदगी की स्थितियां लगातार न केवल बनी हुई हैं बल्कि अंग्रेजों के जाने के बाद से विकसित हुई हैं। इस समय आंतरिक सुरक्षा और आदिवासी को खासतौर से जोड़कर देखा जा रहा है।

1. भारत में नक्सलवाद
   A. कानून एवं व्यवस्था की समस्या है।
   B. राज्यों की समस्या है।
   C. आर्थिक पिछड़ेपन एवं सामाजिक असमानता से उपजी समस्या है।
   D. हथियारबंद समूहों की समस्या है।

2. उपर्युक्त उद्धरण के आधार पर सही कथन का चयन कीजिए।
   A. नक्सलवाद से निपटने के लिए राज्य सरकारों के पास कोई स्वतंत्र कार्य योजना नहीं है।
   B. आर्थिक विकास की तुलना में विशेष पुलिस फोर्स पर अधिक निर्भरता की सरकारी नीति।
   C. नक्सलवाद की समस्या अंग्रेजों की फूट डालो और राज करो की नीति का ही परिणाम है।
   D. A एवं B दोनों।

3. निम्न में से कौन नक्सलवाद के उदय का कारण है?
   A. आर्थिक पिछड़ापन
   B. सामाजिक असमानता
   C. क्षेत्र विशेष की चरित्र वाली संसदीय शक्तियों का पहचान खोना
   D. उपरोक्त सभी।

उद्धरण-3

भारत के पूर्वी एशिया से गहरे ऐतिहासिक और सांस्कृतिक संबंध रहे हैं। प्राचीन काल में कई भारतीय सम्राटों ने दक्षिण पूर्व एशियाई देशों में भारत की संस्कृति का प्रचार किया। बौद्ध धर्म भी सम्पर्क का एक माध्यम बना। ये संबंध अठारहवीं शताब्दी तक रहे, लेकिन ब्रिटेन के आधिपत्य में आने के बाद अंतर्राष्ट्रीय जगत् में भारत एक स्वतंत्र खिलाड़ी नहीं रहा।

आजादी के बाद भारत ने फिर से पूरब की ओर देखने का प्रयास किया और नई दिल्ली में अप्रैल 1947 में 'एशियाई

बंधुत्व' कायम करने की इन आरम्भिक कोशिशों की परिणति 'हिन्दी चीनी भाई-भाई' जैसे नारों और बांडुंग सम्मेलन व गुटनिरपेक्ष आंदोलन के रूप में सामने आई, लेकिन चीन के साथ 1962 के युद्ध और शीतयुद्ध कालीन घटनाओं ने भारत को एक बार फिर पूरब से दूर कर दिया। पिछली शताब्दी में कई भारतीय इतिहासकारों ने नये साक्ष्यों के आधार पर दक्षिण-पूर्वी एशियाई देशों को भारत के 'सांस्कृतिक उपनिवेश' के रूप में पेश करके उन देशों में गलत संदेश दिया, क्योंकि कुछ ही समय पहले औपनिवेशिक गुलामी से आजाद हुए इन देशों में राष्ट्रवादी भावनाएं उफान पर थीं। भारत की पूर्वोन्मुखी नीति का वर्तमान स्वरूप 1992 में सामने आया जब शीतयुद्ध की समाप्ति हो चुकी थी और भारत आर्थिक उदारीकरण का मार्ग अपना चुका था। इस बार व्यापार और वाणिज्य संबंध का मुख्य आधार बने।

1. प्राचीन काल में भारत के पूर्व एशियाई देशों के साथ संबंध का मुख्य आधार क्या था?
A. व्यापार
B. राजनीतिक संबंध
C. धर्म
D. A एवं C दोनों

2. उपरोक्त उद्धरण के आधार पर निम्न में से कौन-सा कथन सही है?
A. प्राचीन काल में भारत के पूर्वी एशियाई देशों के साथ घनिष्ठ व्यापारिक संबंध थे।
B. मुसलमानों के आगमन के बाद भारत अंतर्राष्ट्रीय जगत में अलग-थलग पड़ गया।
C. गुट निरपेक्ष आंदोलन द्वारा एशियाई बंधुत्व को बढ़ावा दिया गया।
D. भारत की पूर्वोन्मुखी नीति का वर्तमान स्वरूप 1980 के दशक में सामने आया।

3. सांस्कृतिक उपनिवेश से लेखक का क्या अभिप्राय है?
A. सांस्कृतिक तौर पर समान होना
B. दूसरे की संस्कृति से प्रभावित होना
C. सांस्कृतिक विसंक्रमण
D. सांस्कृतिक आच्छादन

4. एशियाई देशों के साथ भारत के संबंध में सबसे बड़ी बाधा रही है–
A. राजनीतिक प्रतिस्पर्धा
B. सीमित व्यापार
C. इतिहास की गलत व्याख्या
D. उपरोक्त सभी

उद्धरण-4

अंतर्राष्ट्रीय मुद्राकोष के एक अध्ययन के मुताबिक भारत में रेमिटेंस इसलिए बढ़ा है, क्योंकि भारत से ऑस्ट्रेलिया, कनाडा और अमेरिका जाने वाले भारतीय प्रवासियों की संख्या तेजी से बढ़ी है। इन प्रवासियों में कुशल पेशेवरों की संख्या काफी है, जिन्हें वहां ऊंचा वेतन हासिल होता है। इससे भारतीय प्रवासियों की औसत आय बढ़ी है, लिहाजा भारत में रेमिटेंस ज्यादा आने लगा है। इन दिनों दुनिया के विकसित देशों के आर्थिक विकास की जो रिपोर्टें प्रकाशित हो रही है, उनमें बताया जा रहा है कि प्रवासी भारतीय विकसित देशों के सबसे महत्त्वपूर्ण विकास सहभागी बन गये हैं। कारण यह है कि दुनिया के विकसित देश प्रवासी भारतीयों को अधिक सम्मान देते हुए उन्हें अपने देश में रोकने के लिए हरसंभव प्रयास कर रहे हैं। आर्थिक सहयोग और विकास संगठन (ओईसीडी) के द्वारा जारी की गयी प्रवासी रिपोर्ट में भारतीयों को दुनिया का सबसे योग्य प्रवासी बताया गया है। रिपोर्ट में कहा गया है कि विकसित देशों में जाने वाले विभिन्न देशों के प्रवासियों में सेवा भावना, परिश्रम और ईमानदारी के परिप्रेक्ष्य में सबसे ज्यादा योग्य समुदाय भारतीय समुदाय ही है। उच्च कौशल सम्पन्न लोगों में सबसे ज्यादा (40 प्रतिशत से भी ज्यादा) संख्या भारतीयों की है।

1. विकसित देशों में भारतीय प्रवासियों को सम्मान की दृष्टि से देखा जाता है, क्यों?
A. प्रवासी भारतीय इन देशों की विकास प्रक्रिया में सहभागी हैं।
B. प्रवासी भारतीय इन देशों में भारतीय संस्कृति एवं मूल्यों का प्रसार कर रहे हैं।
C. A एवं B दोनों
D. दोनों में से कोई भी नहीं।

2. उपरोक्त उद्धरण के आधार पर निम्न में से कौन-सा कथन सही है?
A. विकसित देश प्रवासी भारतीयों को अपने यहां रोकने का हर संभव प्रयास करते हैं।
B. अन्य देशों की तुलना में भारतीय प्रवासी उच्च कौशल से संपन्न हैं।
C. विदेशों में भारतीयों के साथ भेदभाव किया जाता है।
D. A एवं B सही हैं।

3. लेखक के अनुसार भारत में रेमिटेंस बढ़ने का मुख्य कारण है–
A. भारत में सेवा क्षेत्र का विकास
B. प्रवासी भारतीयों द्वारा देश में भेजा जाने वाला धन
C. भारत में विदेशी निवेश में वृद्धि
D. उपरोक्त सभी

4. भारतीयों को दुनिया का सबसे योग्य प्रवासी माना जाता है, क्यों?
A. ये उच्च कौशल संपन्न हैं।
B. ये परिश्रमी एवं ईमानदार हैं।
C. इनमें सेवा भावना अधिक दिखती है।
D. उपरोक्त सभी

उद्धरण-5

आतंकवाद और तोड़फोड़ की तमाम घटनाएं, जिन्हें देश की संप्रभुता और स्थायित्व के दुश्मनों द्वारा अंजाम दिया जाता है, आंतरिक सुरक्षा की समस्या पैदा करती हैं। व्यापक पैमाने

पर हिंसा, जैसे मजहबी या जातीय दंगे, लोक व्यवस्था की परिधि में एक व्यक्ति या व्यक्तियों के एक समूह द्वारा किये जा रहे अपराध आते हैं। इन दोनों वर्गों के अपराधों की जांच-पड़ताल अलग-अलग तरीके से की जाती है। सबसे पहले कानून एवं व्यवस्था के मुद्दे को लेते हैं। यह निराशाजनक है कि आपराधिक मामलों की संख्या और उनके घटित होने की आशंका बढ़ती जा रही है, लेकिन न तो जांच-पड़ताल और कानूनी कार्रवाई के तौर-तरीके में बदलाव आ पा रहा है और न ही पुलिस बल का आचार-व्यवहार बेहतर हुआ है।

देश में बहुत बड़ी संख्या में मामले दर्ज नहीं कराए जाते या फिर पुलिस दर्ज नहीं करती। भारत में हर मिनट भारतीय दंड संहिता से संबद्ध औसतन तीन अपराध और विशेष व स्थानीय कानूनों से संबंधित छह अपराध होते हैं। महिलाओं के साथ होने वाले अपराधों की स्थिति तो विचलित कर देने वाली है। हर 15 मिनट में एक महिला के साथ छेड़छाड़, हर 29 मिनट में एक दुष्कर्म की घटना और हर 77 मिनट में दहेज हत्या होती है। इनमें भी केवल 30 फीसदी दर्ज मामलों पर ही अदालती कार्रवाई होती है।

1. निम्न में से कौन-सी समस्या आंतरिक सुरक्षा के लिए खतरा है?
A. आतंकवादी घटनाएं B. मजहबी हिंसा
C. जातीय दंगे D. उपरोक्त सभी

2. उपरोक्त उद्धरण के आधार पर निम्न में से कौन-सा कथन सही नहीं है?
A. देश में आपराधिक मामलों की संख्या में वृद्धि हुई है।
B. पिछले कुछ वर्षों में कानूनी कार्रवाई के तौर तरीकों में बदलाव हुआ है।
C. पुलिस का नजरिया भी इन वर्षों में बदला है।
D. B एवं C दोनों

3. महिलाओं के साथ होने वाले अपराध मुख्य रूप से किस श्रेणी में आते हैं?
A. राजनीतिक अपराध B. कानूनी अपराध
C. सामाजिक अपराध D. B एवं C दोनों

4. देश में बढ़ते अपराध का मुख्य कारण है–
A. कानून एवं व्यवस्था की खामियां
B. अपराधियों का राजनीतिक संरक्षण
C. सामाजिक जागरूकता का अभाव
D. उपरोक्त सभी

उद्धरण-6

एडम स्मिथ को मुक्त बाजार की अवधारणा का प्रतिपादक माना जाता है। उनकी मान्यता थी कि यदि आर्थिक प्रक्रिया में राज्य कोई हस्तक्षेप न करे तो उत्पादन में विकास होता जायेगा और एक 'अदृश्य हाथ' उसके लाभों को निम्नतम स्तर तक पहुंचा देगा। आजकल जिस उदारीकरण की नीति का बोलबाला है, उसका अर्थशास्त्रीय तात्त्विक आधार एडम स्मिथ ने अपने प्रसिद्ध ग्रंथ 'वेल्थ ऑफ नेशंस' में 1776 में प्रस्तुत किया था। भूमंडलीकरण इस उदारीकरण का ही स्वाभाविक अनुज, बल्कि उदारीकरण का अंतर्राष्ट्रीय अवतार है। इसका सीधा तात्पर्य यह है कि आर्थिक प्रक्रिया एक स्वायत्त प्रक्रिया है और उसमें हस्तक्षेप विकास को बाधित करता है।

अर्थशास्त्रीय दृष्टि से भी मुक्त बाजार की प्रतिस्पर्धा कीमतों को कम रखने और आर्थिक सेवाओं को अधिक कुशल बनाने में सहायक होगी, जिसका स्वाभाविक परिणाम होगा उपभोक्ता अर्थात् समाज को कम कीमत में अधिक कुशल उत्पाद या सेवा मिलना। बाजार में प्रतिस्पर्धा की कमी एकाधिकारवादी आर्थिक प्रक्रिया का रास्ता सुगम करती है और इसके चलते वह उपभोक्ता के बजाय उत्पादक के लिए अधिक लाभकारी हो जाती है। आदर्श बाजार वह है जिसमें ग्राहक और उत्पादक दोनों पक्षों को मोलतोल करने की पूरी स्वतंत्रता और शक्ति हो और ऐसा केवल मुक्त बाजार की अर्थव्यवस्था में ही संभव है।

1. मुक्त बाजार की अवधारणा का क्या अभिप्राय है?
A. बाजार की गतिविधियों में सरकार का हस्तक्षेप न होना
B. बाजार की अंतःक्रिया में मांग एवं पूर्ति का हस्तक्षेप न होना
C. बाजार का बाह्य आर्थिक प्रभावों से मुक्त होना
D. A एवं C दोनों

2. उपरोक्त उद्धरण के आधार पर सही कथन का चयन कीजिए।
A. मुक्त बाजार की अवधारणा का प्रतिपादक एडम स्मिथ था।
B. वेल्थ ऑफ नेशंस का प्रकाशन 1876 में हुआ।
C. भूमंडलीकरण बाजार की गतिविधियों से स्वतंत्र आर्थिक क्रिया का समर्थक है।
D. A एवं C दोनों

3. आधुनिक आर्थिक तंत्र के बारे में निम्न में से कौन-सा कथन सही है?
A. बाजार प्रतिस्पर्धा के कारण कीमतों में कमी आती है।
B. भूमंडलीकरण के कारण बाजार की प्रतिस्पर्धा में कमी आई है, क्योंकि बड़ी कंपनियों ने बाजार पर अपना आधिपत्य कायम कर लिया है।
C. भूमंडलीकरण के कारण आर्थिक सेवाओं में अधिक कुशलता आई है।
D. A एवं C दोनों

4. एकाधिकारवादी आर्थिक क्रिया के लिए उत्तरदायी कारण है–
A. बाजार में प्रतिस्पर्धा की कमी
B. राज्य का आर्थिक क्रियाओं में हस्तक्षेप
C. बाह्य बाजार का हस्तक्षेप
D. A एवं C दोनों

उद्धरण-7

तिब्बत पर पूरी तरह शिंकजा कसने के लिए चीन सभी हथकंडे अपना चुका है। चीन ने बड़ी संख्या में हान वंशी चीनियों को तिब्बत में बसाया है। इससे वहां की जनांकिकी चीन के पक्ष में जाने का खतरा है। चीन जानबूझकर तिब्बत में हान वंशियों की वास्तविक संख्या नहीं बताता। यही सिलसिला चलता रहा तो वह दिन दूर नहीं जब तिब्बती बौद्ध अपने ही देश में अल्पसंख्यक बन कर रह जाएंगे। चीन ने 2006 में तिब्बत को चीन से जोड़ने वाले रेलमार्ग की शुरूआत की जिसका स्थानीय बौद्ध लोग काफी विरोध कर रहे हैं। उनका आरोप है कि नए रेलमार्ग से चीन को तिब्बत पर शिकंजा कसने में न केवल आसानी होगी, बल्कि तिब्बतवासी सांस्कृतिक और आर्थिक रूप से और अधिक हाशिये पर आ जाएंगे।

तिब्बतियों पर जिस तरह के कहर ढाये जा रहे हैं उससे बहुत ज्यादा आश्चर्य नहीं करना चाहिए, क्योंकि साम्यवादी चीन को दमन के अलावा कोई दूसरा तरीका नहीं आता। चीन किसी भी लोकतांत्रिक आंदोलन को सख्ती से निपटाने में विश्वास करता है। दूसरी ओर भारत, बहुभाषी, बहुधर्मी और बहुसांस्कृतिक देश होने के कारण यह जानता है कि लोकतांत्रिक ढांचे के बिना स्थायी शांति संभव नहीं है। किसी आंदोलन को सैन्य शक्ति के सहारे दबाया तो जा सकता है, लेकिन उसे पूरी तरह खत्म नहीं किया जा सकता। चीन द्वारा तिब्बत पर अर्द्धशताब्दी से ज्यादा तक जबरन कब्जा करने के बावजूद तिब्बतियों के दिल में आजादी की ज्वाला अभी तक जल रही है और दलाई लामा के जीवित रहते हुए तो चीन अपनी साम्राज्यवादी मंशाओं को पूरा नहीं कर सकता।

1. तिब्बत पर अपना प्रभाव बढ़ाने के लिए चीन ने कौन-सा कदम उठाया है?

A. तिब्बत में बड़ी संख्या में हानवंशी चीनियों को बसाया जा रहा है।

B. तिब्बत के चीन में विलय का प्रस्ताव पारित कर दिया है।

C. तिब्बत को चीन का स्वायत प्रदेश घोषित कर दिया है।

D. उपरोक्त सभी

2. तिब्बत में चीन द्वारा निर्मित रेलमार्ग का विरोध किया जा रहा है, क्यों?

A. इससे तिब्बत पर चीन के प्रभाव में वृद्धि होगी।

B. तिब्बतवासी सांस्कृतिक एवं आर्थिक रूप से अधिक हाशिये पर चले जाएंगे।

C. भारत के साथ तिब्बतियों का संबंध टूट जाएगा।

D. A एवं B दोनों

3. तिब्बत में स्थायी शांति कैसे कायम हो सकती है?

A. चीन के प्रभाव में कमी लाकर

B. उसे चीनी प्रभाव से मुक्त स्वायत प्रदेश का दर्जा देकर

C. लोकतांत्रिक ढांचे की स्थापना द्वारा

D. B एवं C दोनों द्वारा

4. उपरोक्त उद्धरण के आधार पर सही कथन का चयन कीजिए।

A. चीन तिब्बत में अपने सांस्कृतिक प्रभाव का विस्तार करना चाहता है।

B. चीन ने तिब्बत में बड़ी संख्या में चीनियों को बसाना शुरू किया है।

C. चीन अपने प्रभाव क्षेत्र में किसी भी प्रकार के लोकतांत्रिक आंदोलन का विरोधी है।

D. उपरोक्त सभी

उद्धरण-8

आज की सियासत की सबसे बड़ी सच्चाई यह है कि हम गठबंधन यानी अलायंस के जमाने में चल रहे हैं। कोई नहीं जानता कि यह दौर कब खत्म होगा। ऐसे समय में गठबंधन धर्म को सबसे बड़े मंत्र की तरह दोहराया जाता है। गठबंधन बनाने और चलाने के चैलेंज का अहसास सबको है, लेकिन क्या वजह है कि इसके बावजूद हमारे देश में पॉलिटिकल अलायंस का कल्चर उस तरह से मजबूत नहीं हो पा रहा जैसा यूरोप के कई देशों में है। हमारे यहां अलायंस हमेशा कमजोर रहते हैं। उनका वजूद अक्सर खतरे में पड़ता दिखता है, जैसा हाल में दिखा। साझेदारी को लेकर तनाव पैदा होते रहते हैं और समर्थन के नाम पर सियासी ब्लैकमेलिंग का बोलबाला है। हमारे अलायंस रजामंदी का खेल नहीं मजबूरी का सौदा लगते हैं।

हमें यह नहीं भूलना चाहिए कि केंद्र में गठबंधन सरकारें कई कारकों का मिलाजुला नतीजा होती हैं। अगर कांग्रेस का कमजोर होना एक कारक है, तो बीजेपी को भी कुछ क्षेत्रों के अलावा पूरे देश में स्वीकार नहीं किया जाना गठबंधन सरकार को एक प्रभावी तंत्र के रूप में स्थापित करने वाला कारक है। इन दोनों विषयकों के अलावा अपने-अपने राज्यों में मजबूत जनाधार वाले क्षेत्रीय दलों का उभरना भी इन्हीं कारकों में शामिल है। यूपी में समाजवादी पार्टी, बहुजन समाज पार्टी, बिहार में जनता दल (एकीकृत), उड़ीसा में बीजू जनता दल, पंजाब में अकाली दल, आंध्र प्रदेश में तेलुगू देशम पार्टी, तमिलनाडु में एआईएडीएमके और डीएमके कुछ ऐसे क्षेत्रीय दलों के उदाहरण हैं जो क्षेत्रीय के साथ-साथ राष्ट्रीय राजनीति में भी अपनी महत्त्वपूर्ण भूमिका निभाते हैं। 2009 के लोकसभा चुनावों में क्षेत्रीय दलों का महत्व कुछ कम हुआ है और कांग्रेस पार्टी का विस्तार हुआ है। यह देश के लिए बहुत शुभ लक्षण है।

1. भारत में राजनीतिक गठबंधन की सबसे बड़ी कमी क्या है?

A. इनमें बड़े और छोटे दल एक साथ शामिल होते हैं।

B. हमारे यहाँ राजनीतिक गठबंधन वैचारिक समानता के आधार पर नहीं बनते बल्कि मजबूरी का सौदा होते हैं।

C. A एवं B दोनों।

D. दोनों में से कोई भी नहीं।

2. हाल ही में भारत में कई गठबंधन सरकारें बनी हैं। इसके लिए कौन-सा कारण उत्तरदायी है?

A. कांग्रेस का सिमटता जनाधार

B. कांग्रेस के प्रभावी विकल्प के रूप में किसी अन्य पार्टी का न उभर पाना

C. क्षेत्रीय पार्टियों का उभरना

D. उपरोक्त सभी

3. यूरोपीय देशों की तुलना में भारत में गठबंधन की संस्कृति कमजोर रही है, क्यों?

A. भारत में राजनीतिक दलों की बहुलता।

B. राजनीतिक दलों के बीच वैचारिक मतभेद।

C. संकीर्ण राजनीतिक हित एवं मानसिकता।

D. उपरोक्त सभी।

4. उपरोक्त उद्धरण के आधार पर सही कथन का चयन कीजिए।

A. 2009 के लोकसभा चुनाव में क्षेत्रीय दलों का महत्व कुछ कम हुआ है।

B. इस चुनाव में बिहार एवं बंगाल में कांग्रेस जनाधार का विस्तार हुआ है।

C. क्षेत्रीय पार्टियों को करारी हार का सामना करना पड़ा।

D. उपरोक्त सभी।

उद्धरण-9

कर्त्तव्य एक नैतिक बंधन है। यह एक तरह से ऋणी होने के समान है, जिस सामाजिक प्राणी के साथ हम रह रहे होते हैं। हमें अपने साथ रहने वालों के लिए इसकी अनुमति मिलनी चाहिए। हमारे जीवनवृत्ति का अधिकार संकेत देता है कि यह हमारा कर्त्तव्य है कि हम उन साथ रहने वाले प्राणियों को भी अपने समान ही जीवन की परिस्थितियां उपलब्ध कराएं। वास्तव में अधिकार और कर्त्तव्य परस्पर संबद्ध हैं। किसी एक के संबंध में अधिकार दूसरे का कर्त्तव्य हो सकता है। अधिकार और कर्त्तव्य एक सिक्के के दो पहलू हैं। हमें दूसरे के ओहदों का हमेशा ख्याल रखना चाहिए। नैतिक कर्त्तव्य, वैद्यानिक अधिकार की अपेक्षा ज्यादा प्रभावी होते हैं। नैतिक कर्त्तव्य वह कर्त्तव्य है जो लोगों को नैतिक स्तर पर बांध कर रखती है। यह हमारा नैतिक कर्त्तव्य है कि हम गरीबों की मदद करें क्योंकि वह एक प्राणी और समाज का अंग है।

हमें उन परिस्थितियों के निर्माण के लिए हमेशा प्रयास करना चाहिए जिनसे मानवता का कल्याण हो सके। यह हमारा अनुकरणीय कर्त्तव्य है कि हम अपने माता-पिता की आज्ञा मानें और उन्हें सम्मान दें। यह कर्त्तव्य जिम्मेवारी की चेतना से पैदा होता है जो कि प्रत्यक्षतः हमारे अंतःकरण से संबंधित है। इस प्रकार से यह एक नैतिक कर्त्तव्य है जिसमें कोई व्यक्ति बिना वैधानिक बंधन के ही ऋणी है।

कर्त्तव्य की चेतना, सही तरीके से सभ्यता के विकास की सर्वश्रेष्ठता है। पाखंड कर्त्तव्य की चेतना के एकदम विपरीत है। पाखंड में जहां दुरात्मा का समावेश है, वहीं कर्त्तव्य में यथार्थता और विश्वस्तता का समावेश है।

1. गद्यांश के अनुसार वैधानिक कर्त्तव्य है:

A. नैतिक कर्त्तव्य की अपेक्षा अधिक महत्त्वपूर्ण

B. नैतिक कर्त्तव्य की अपेक्षा कम महत्त्वपूर्ण

C. नैतिक कर्त्तव्य की अपेक्षा अधिक प्रभावी

D. नैतिक कर्त्तव्य की अपेक्षा कम प्रभावी

2. निम्न में से कौन-सा वाक्य गद्यांश के अनुसार सही नहीं है?

A. पाखंड में दुष्टता का समावेश

B. पाखंड का कर्त्तव्य के विपरीत होना

C. कर्त्तव्य में यथार्थता का समावेश

D. कर्त्तव्य की चेतना का सभ्यता के विकास के लिए महत्त्वपूर्ण न होना

3. निम्न में से किन नैतिक कर्त्तव्यों का उल्लेख गद्यांश में नहीं किया गया है?

A. नैतिक कर्त्तव्य हमारी मातृभूमि से बढ़कर है

B. नैतिक कर्त्तव्य हमारे माता-पिता से बढ़कर है

C. नैतिक कर्त्तव्य गरीब से बढ़कर है

D. नैतिक कर्त्तव्य मानव-कल्याण में योगदान है

4. निम्न में से कौन नैतिक कर्त्तव्य से संबंधित नहीं है?

A. जिम्मेवारी की चेतना

B. सद्विचार

C. पाखंड

D. यथार्थता

5. हमें माता-पिता के प्रति आज्ञाकारी और सम्मानपूर्ण होना चाहिए, क्योंकि:

A. यह जिम्मेवारी की चेतना है

B. यह वैधानिक बाध्यता है

C. यह सभ्यता है

D. यह पाखंड है

उद्धरण-10

ऐसे महान् चिन्तकों को जिनकी शिक्षाएँ वैश्विक हैं, अपने समय के संदर्भ से ही समझा जा सकता है। बुद्ध को व्यापक रुप में गलत समझा गया है। व्यवहारवादियों, अज्ञेयवादियों, निरीश्वरवादियों तथा नैतिक मानवतावादियों ने उन्हें अपने दर्शन का प्रचार करने वाला माना है। बुद्ध की शिक्षाओं को भारत की ईसा-पूर्व छठी शताब्दी को समझकर ही ठीक प्रकार से समझा जा सकता है क्योंकि उनका आविर्भाव उसी शताब्दी में हुआ था किन्तु ऐसा करना अपेक्षाकृत कठिन कार्य है।

ईसा-पूर्व छठी शताब्दी के भारत में बहुत प्रकार की विचारधाराएँ और सम्प्रदाय थे तथापि सभी सम्प्रदाय आत्मा के पुनर्जन्म, कर्म के दर्शन एवं मानव के चरम लक्ष्य निर्वाण के

विषय में सहमत थे। बुद्ध ने इन सिद्धान्तों को स्वीकार किया है, यद्यपि उन्होंने धार्मिक सिद्धान्तवाद को अस्वीकार किया है, किन्तु उनका योगदान नैतिकता तथा सदाचार की उत्कृष्टता को महत्वपूर्ण मानने में था। उन्होंने हृदय को शान्ति प्रदान करने की आवश्यकता तथा नैतिकता के नियमों के अनुसरण पर विशेष बल दिया। दुःखों का अन्त शरीर की भूख को शान्त करने तथा हमारे संवेगों पर दृढ़ता से नियंत्रण करने से हो सकता है।

बुद्ध की रुचि ईश्वर में नहीं थी बल्कि मनुष्य और मानव-प्रयासों में थी। अपनी साधना और अपने प्रयत्नों से मानव अपने आपको देवत्व की ऊँचाई तक उठा सकता है, यद्यपि भक्ति-सम्बन्धी तत्त्वों के बिना भी बुद्ध की शिक्षाएँ मुख्य रूप से धार्मिक हैं। बुद्ध के अन्दर आध्यात्मिक गहराई, नैतिक दृढ़ता तथा बौद्धिक स्पष्टता का भण्डार समाहित है। समय के व्यतीत होने के साथ-साथ उनके द्वारा की गई मानवता की सेवा का विश्वव्यापी समादर हो रहा है। उनका संदेश सभी काल के लिए सार्थक है।

1. बुद्ध ने अधिक महत्व प्रदान किया
   A. ईश्वर को न कि मनुष्य को
   B. मनुष्य तथा ईश्वर दोनों को
   C. न ईश्वर को और न मनुष्य को
   D. मनुष्य-मात्र को न कि ईश्वर को

2. महान विचारकों को ठीक से किसके द्वारा समझा जा सकता है?
   A. ई॰ पू॰ छठी शताब्दी के भारत को समझने से
   B. जिस काल में वे रहे हैं उस काल की सापेक्षता में उन्हें समझने से
   C. बुद्ध की शिक्षाओं का ठीक-ठीक समादर करने से
   D. उनके विचारों और दर्शन का अध्ययन करने तथा समझने से

3. बुद्ध ने किस पर जोर दिया?
   A. ईश्वर की भक्ति पर
   B. कर्मकाण्ड पर
   C. प्रार्थना पर
   D. आचारशास्त्र तथा नैतिक नियमों पर

4. परिच्छेद के अनुसार बुद्ध की शिक्षाएँ मुख्य रूप से धर्मसम्बन्धी हैं,
   A. आध्यात्मिक गहराई के कारण
   B. नैतिक दृढ़ता के कारण
   C. क्योंकि विशुद्ध रूप से बौद्धिक नहीं हैं
   D. उपर्युक्त सभी के कारण

उद्धरण-11

मनुष्य का सुखी जीवन संतुलित प्राकृतिक पर्यावरण पर निर्भर करता है। मानव की बढ़ती जनसंख्या और तज्जन्य आवश्यकताएँ प्रकृति के संतुलन को बिगाड़ रही हैं। पर्यावरण में दूषित तत्त्वों की मात्रा आवश्यकता से अधिक बढ़ जाती है तो पर्यावरण का यह असन्तुलन प्रदूषण का रूप ले लेता है। मानव की आवासीय, औद्योगिक नगरीकरण, कृषि उत्पादन में वृद्धि करने की समस्याओं ने प्रकृति के संतुलन को बिगाड़कर प्रदूषण को बढ़ाया है। यातायात-साधनों की वृद्धि, वृक्षों की अंधाधुंध कटाई से वातावरण में ऑक्सीजन की कमी और कार्बन डाइ-आक्साइड की वृद्धि हो गई है। पॉप संगीत और रॉक संगीत तथा हॉर्न बजाने से ध्वनि प्रदूषण बढ़ रहा है। वातावरण को प्रदूषित कर हम अपनी मृत्यु को स्वयं ही निमंत्रण दे रहे हैं। प्रदूषण की वृद्धि के लिए मानव ही उत्तरदायी है। अतः इसके निवारण के लिए सर्वप्रथम अपने मानसिक प्रदूषण को दूर करना होगा। वृक्षारोपण, पेयजल-शुद्धीकरण, रासायनिक विस्फोटों पर नियंत्रण, कर्णभेदी ध्वनि विस्तारक यंत्रों, वाहनों और संगीत को रोकने के उपायों से मानव जीवन को प्रदूषण मुक्त बनाना होगा, तभी मानव जीवन सुखमय हो सकता है।

1. 'अपनी मृत्यु को स्वयं निमंत्रण देने' का अभिप्राय क्या है?
   A. आत्महत्या करना
   B. जीने की इच्छा छोड़ देना
   C. हताश हो जाना
   D. वातावरण को प्रदूषित करना

2. मानव जीवन को सुखी कैसे बनाया जा सकता है?
   A. औद्योगीकरण से
   B. जनसंख्या नियंत्रण से
   C. संतुलित पर्यावरण से
   D. यातायात साधनों की वृद्धि से

3. कर्णभेदी संगीत से किस प्रकार का प्रदूषण होता है?
   A. वायु प्रदूषण   B. ध्वनि प्रदूषण
   C. पर्यावरण प्रदूषण   D. मानसिक प्रदूषण

4. 'वृक्षारोपण' से प्रमुख लाभ क्या है?
   A. मृदा संरक्षण
   B. जड़ी-बूटियों, औषधियों की पूर्ति
   C. वातावरण में वायुशुद्धि
   D. रेगिस्तान वृद्धि की रोकथाम

5. पर्यावरण असन्तुलन के लिए कौन उत्तरदायी है?
   A. मानसिक प्रदूषण
   B. ध्वनि प्रदूषण
   C. वृक्षों की अंधाधुंध कटाई
   D. प्राकृतिक प्रकोप

उद्धरण-12

विकसित देशों के लोगों की अपेक्षा अविकसित देशों के लोगों की सोच ग्राम्यता के उत्प्रेरकों के सम्बन्ध में एकदम भिन्न है। वहाँ यह एक प्रकार से मानव के जीवित रहने की क्रिया के लिए केवल भौतिक आवश्कता है। तीसरी दुनिया के देशों में, जो मुख्य रूप से ग्रामीण हैं, उनका एकमात्र आधार ग्रामीण

हिन्दी

विकास ही है, जिसके द्वारा मानव जीवन को इसके वर्तमान अवमानव स्तर से ऊपर उठाया जा सकता है। उन देशों में शताब्दियों से ग्रामीण जीवन जहाँ का तहाँ खड़ा अवरोधित है। उस ग्रामीण जनसंख्या की दशाओं को सुधारने के लिए कुछ नहीं किया गया जो अन्य चार पैर वाले प्रतिरूपों की तुलना में मामूली ढंग से भिन्न है। अविकसित एवं अर्द्धविकसित देशों में अज्ञान, कुस्वास्थ्य तथा गरीबी ग्रामीण जीवन के पर्याय बन गये हैं। लेकिन सबसे दुःखद स्थिति यह है कि इस प्रकार की मानव जनसंख्या ने ऐसा स्वीकार कर लिया है कि यह दुरवस्था अपरिवर्तनीय है। यह एक ऐसी स्थिति है जिसकी कोई दवा नहीं है। उनके जीवन से आशा की सभी किरणें दूर हो गयी हैं। इस प्रकार के देशों में, ग्रामीण विकास किसी प्रकार की भौतिक अथवा अभौतिक विकास के लिए अपरिहार्य शर्त है। इसलिए इन सभी देशों का प्रबुद्ध वर्ग ग्रामीण विकास के प्रश्न पर निरन्तर बढ़-चढ़कर रुचि ले रहा है।

उनके स्वतंत्रता संघर्ष की विरासत का यह एक अंग भी था। भारत जैसे देश में, इस बात को सभी जानते हैं कि स्वतंत्रता आन्दोलन में ग्रामीण विकास की कोशिश एक अविभाज्य अंग था। गाँधीजी जैसे नेताओं को भली-भाँति यह एहसास था कि वास्तविक भारत अवरोधग्रस्त ग्रामों में निवास करता है। शहर जो ज्यादातर पश्चिमी उपनिवेशवाद की उपज हैं, केवल दिखावटी दर्शनीय वस्तुएँ हैं। तब भी दो प्रकार की दुनिया थी – वह जहाँ तड़क-भड़क के जीवन वाले जो शाही रुचियों के सुविधासम्पन्न कुछ गिने-चुने सम्भ्रान्त क्षेत्रवासी रहते थे। वे क्षेत्र छोटे-छोटे टापू जैसे थे जिनको धूल-मिट्टी और गंदगी के विशाल समुद्र ने घेर रखा है और बहुसंख्यक लोग उन स्थानों का प्रतिनिधित्व करते थे।

भारत नगरों से किसी भी तरह अपरिचित नहीं रहा। प्राचीन भारत में, नगर देश के अंगभूत भाग थे जो मूलरूप से शेष सारे देश और समग्र समाज से सम्बन्धित थे। वे संस्कृति के सुमन की भाँति तथा राष्ट्र की कलात्मक उत्कृष्टता के परिचायक थे। आधुनिक नगर केवल दूसरों के शिकार करने वाले परजीवीमात्र हैं जो देश को कमजोर बना रहे हैं।

इसीलिए गाँधीजी ने 'गाँवों की ओर लौट चलो' यह ग्राम आन्दोलन प्रारम्भ किया था। उनके मतानुसार यह आन्दोलन ही भारत को स्वतंत्रता दिलवा सकता था और स्वतंत्रता को सुरक्षित रख सकता था। राष्ट्र की स्वतंत्रता के लिए अपनायी गयी उनकी रणनीति में ग्रामीण विकास गर्व का स्थान रखता था। इस प्रकार ग्रामीण विकास का उद्गम स्वतंत्रता संग्राम के मूल में सन्निहित है।

1. इस परिच्छेद के सन्दर्भ में निम्नलिखित में से कौन-सा कथन सत्य नहीं है?
   - A. तीसरी दुनिया के देशों की ग्रामीण जनता की यह सोच है कि उनकी अवमानवीय स्थिति सुधर नहीं सकती।
   - B. तीसरी दुनिया के देशों के लोगों का जीवन-स्तर केवल ग्रामीण विकास द्वारा उठाया जा सकता है।
   - C. आधुनिक नगरों में रहने वाले अधिकांश धनाढ्य लोग वास्तव में ग्रामीण विकास के सम्बन्ध में चिन्तित हैं।
   - D. किसी भी प्रकार की अन्य उन्नति और विकास के लिए ग्रामीण विकास सर्वप्रथम आवश्यक है।

2. लोग ग्रामीण विकास में अत्यधिक रुचि ले रहे हैं क्योंकि–
   - A. उन्हें इसकी अपरिहार्यता का अनुभव हो चुका है
   - B. वे घोर स्वास्थ्य-समस्याओं से दुःखी हैं
   - C. निकट भविष्य में कुछ भी सार्थक करना सम्भव नहीं है
   - D. अब वे इसके सम्बन्ध में आशावादी हो गए हैं

3. ग्रामीण विकास को भारत के स्वातंत्र्य आन्दोलन का एक अंग समझा गया था, क्योंकि–
   - A. केवल ग्रामों में ही शाही रुचि निवास करती थी
   - B. देश मुख्य रूप से ग्रामों से बना था
   - C. गाँधीजी पश्चिमी उपनिवेशवाद के विरुद्ध थे
   - D. उस समय वास्तविक भारत ब्रिटिश हुकूमत के मातहत था

4. परिच्छेद के सन्दर्भ में निम्नलिखित में से कौन-सा कथन सत्य है?
   - A. तीसरी दुनिया के अधिकांश देशों का त्वरित गति से नगरीकरण हो रहा है।
   - B. भारत का स्वतंत्रता आन्दोलन ग्रामीण विकास का अंगभूत समझा जाता है।
   - C. ग्रामीण जनता अपनी दशा सुधारने के बारे में बहुत आशावादी है।
   - D. वर्तमान सन्दर्भ में अज्ञान, निर्धनता तथा रुग्ण-स्वास्थ्य ग्रामीण जीवन के अविभाज्य अंग हैं।

5. निम्नलिखित में कौन-सा कथन आधुनिक नगरों वाली दो विपरीत दुनिया का सबसे उपयुक्त वर्णन करता है?
   - A. कुछ धनी लोग और अधिक गरीब लोग
   - B. चमक-दमक का क्षेत्र और धनाढ्य लोग
   - C. वाणिज्यिक तथा औद्योगिक शोषण
   - D. पश्चिमी उत्पादों के संरक्षक तथा शाही रुचियों के पोषक

उद्धरण-13

शिष्टजनों द्वारा अनुष्ठित आचरण मात्र कल्पना-उद्भूत सामाजिक शिष्टाचार नहीं है अपितु गंभीर वैज्ञानिक रहस्यों से ओत-प्रोत ऐसा संस्कार है जो मानव जीवन में गुणाधान प्रक्रिया को प्रशस्त करता है। भारतीय संस्कृति में शिष्टाचार का श्रीगणेश सामाजिक व्यवहार के सिंहद्वार – अभिवादन से होता है। ईश्वराभिवादन, पूज्यजनों को प्रणाम, नमस्कार, प्राञ्जलि, अञ्जलिपुट, प्रणिपात, नामोच्चारणपूर्वक नमन, प्रदक्षिणापूर्वक सम्मान तथा साष्टांग प्रणाम पर्यायभेद से अभिवादन के ही विविध रूप हैं। प्रतिदिन

या विशिष्ट अवसरों पर कर्म में सफलता और दीर्घायुष्य-प्राप्ति हेतु माता-पिता तथा गुरुजनों को अभिवादन करना केवल भारतीय संस्कृति में ही विद्यमान है। अध्यात्म-विज्ञान की मान्यता है कि किसी वरेण्य व्यक्ति के आगमन पर प्राणस्पन्दन की गति ऊर्ध्वमुखी होकर ऊर्जस्वित हो जाती है। उनका आशीर्वाद प्राप्त कर प्राण ऊर्जावान् बन जाते हैं। आज अन्य क्षेत्रों की भाँति शिष्टाचार के विधि-विधान में प्रदूषण और अवमूल्यन निर्बाध गति से हो रहा है। 'हाय', 'ही', 'हेलो' करने वालों को भला हाथ जोड़कर मस्तक झुकाना कैसे रास आ सकता है? त्याग-वैराग्यसम्पन्न अल्पवयस्क या वयोवृद्धों को अभिवादन करना हमारी पुरातन आचार-पद्धति है।

1. शिष्टाचार का प्रथम सोपान क्या है?
   A. कुशलक्षेम पूछना B. मुस्कराते हुए बात करना
   C. अभिवादन करना D. भेंट देना

2. गुरुजनों को अभिवादन करने का कौनसा कृत्य विधिसम्मत नहीं है?
   A. चरण स्पर्श करना
   B. हाथ जोड़कर सिर झुकाना
   C. साष्टांग प्रणाम करना
   D. हाथ मिलाना

3. आशीर्वाद ग्रहण करने का वैज्ञानिक रहस्य क्या है?
   A. मन प्रसन्न हो जाता है
   B. प्राण ऊर्जस्वित हो जाते हैं
   C. असम्भव कार्य सम्भव हो जाता है।
   D. हमारा आत्मविश्वास बढ़ता है

4. सामाजिक कुशलता प्राप्त करने का सिंहद्वार क्या है?
   A. श्रीगणेश का पूजन
   B. सहभोज का आयोजन
   C. प्रत्येक व्यक्ति को अपना गुरु मानना
   D. विधिपूर्वक यथायोग्य अभिवादन

5. 'सबहिं मानप्रद आप अमानी' का अभिप्राय है–
   A. स्वयं सम्मान की चाह न कर सबको सम्मान देना
   B. सबके मान की परवाह करने से पहले अपनी चिन्ता करना
   C. मान पाकर आपा न खोना
   D. अपने सम्मान के समान दूसरों का भी सम्मान करना

उद्धरण-14

शैक्षिक योजना का उद्देश्य सभी उम्र के वर्ग समूहों की कुल जनसंख्या की शैक्षिक आवश्यकताओं की पूर्ति करना होना चाहिए। निस्संदेह प्राथमिक स्तर से विश्वविद्यालयी स्तर तक शिक्षा का तीन स्तरीय पदानुक्रम परम्परागत शिक्षा की संरचना का सार भाग है तथापित हमें परिधीय शिक्षा जो उतनी ही महत्त्वपूर्ण है, की अवहेलना नहीं करनी चाहिए। आधुनिक अवस्थाओं के अंतर्गत, कार्यकर्त्ताओं को अपने उत्साह को तरोताजा करने की आवश्यकता है अथवा उन्हें एक नई दिशा में बढ़ने या अपने कौशलों को विश्वविद्यालयी प्रोफेसर के स्तर तक बढ़ाने की आवश्यकता है। सेवानिवृत और वृद्धों की भी अपनी आवश्यकताएँ होती हैं। शैक्षिक योजना ऐसी होनी चाहिए जिसमें प्रत्येक की आवश्यकताओं को ध्यान में रखा जाए। शिक्षा की हमारी संरचना इस मान्यता पर आधारित है कि शिक्षा का एक सीमावर्ती बिन्दु होता है। आजकल यह मूलभूत त्रुटि और अधिक हानिकारक बन गई है। एडगर फौरे तथा अन्य सदस्यों द्वारा रचित युनेस्को का 'लर्निंग टू बी' नामक प्रतिवेदन, जो 1973 में प्रकाशित हुआ, यह दावा करता है कि बच्चों की शिक्षा द्वारा स्व-अधिगम के विभिन्न रूपों के लिए भावी प्रौढ़ तैयार होने चाहिएँ। एक व्यवहार्य भावी शिक्षा पद्धति में ऐसे मोड्यूल होने चाहिए जिसमें विभिन्न प्रकार के प्रकार्य सम्मिलित हों और वह विविध सामाजिक अवयवों के लिए उपयोगी हों। और प्रमाण-पत्रों का आधार अध्ययन अवधि न होकर निष्पादन होना चाहिए। इसकी इबारत पहले से ही दीवार पर लिखी हुई है।

इस बात या तथ्य को ध्यान में रखते हुए कि जीवन-पर्यन्त अधिगम या आजन्म शिक्षा के प्रति प्रतिबद्धता के महत्त्व को आजकल शैक्षिक रूप से विकसित देशों में भी विवेचित किया जा रहा है, परंतु इस बात की सम्भाव्यता कि यह विचार शैक्षिक चिंतन का अभिन्न अंग बन जाए बहुत दूर की बात है। क्योंकि इस दिशा में आगे बढ़ने का अर्थ है वर्तमान शैक्षिक संगठनों की पुनर्व्यवस्था से कुछ अधिक करना। कम-से-कम विभिन्न वर्गों के वयस्क अध्येताओं के लिए मुक्त विश्वविद्यालयी प्रोग्राम विकसित करके और परम्परागत महाविद्यालयों और विद्यालयों में प्रसार-सेवाएँ आरंभ करके इसका शुभारंभ किया जा सकता है। साथ ही इन संस्थाओं को चाहिए कि असंख्य सामुदायिक संगठनों, जैसे पुस्तकालय, संग्रहालय, म्युनिसिपल मनोरंजन कार्यक्रम, स्वास्थ्य सेवाएँ आदि, के साथ सहयोग करते रहें।

1. परिच्छेद के अनुसार, वर्तमान शैक्षिक संरचनाएँ निम्नलिखित में से किसको मान्यता देती हैं?
   A. सभी व्यक्तियों को उनकी आवश्यकताओं के अनुसार शिक्षित किया जा सकता है
   B. वर्तमान में शैक्षिक योजना बहुत अधिक व्यवहार्य है
   C. शिक्षा एक निश्चित समय में पूर्ण होने वाली प्रक्रिया है
   D. जीवन-पर्यन्त शिक्षा (अधिगम) पर चर्चाएँ चलती रहनी चाहिए

2. दिए गए परिच्छेद के संदर्भ में निम्नलिखित में से कौन-सा सही नहीं है?
   A. जीवन-पर्यन्त शिक्षा एक आधुनिक अवधारणा है
   B. कर्मियों का ज्ञान तथा उनके कौशलों का निरंतर रूप से अद्यतन होते रहना चाहिए
   C. 'लर्निंग टू बी' नामक ग्रंथ इस बात का समर्थन करता है कि शिक्षा का एक सीमांत बिन्दु होता है
   D. विद्यालयों तथा महाविद्यालयों में भी विस्तार सेवाएँ आरंभ की जानी चाहिए

3. जीवन-पर्यन्त शिक्षा को शैक्षिक संरचना के साथ समेकित करने का अभिप्रेत होगा–
   A. परम्परागत विद्यालयों और महाविद्यालयों को बंद कर देना
   B. सभी औपचारिक पाठ्यक्रमों के लिए अधिक समयावधि
   C. वर्तमान शैक्षिक संगठनों का सामान्य पुनर्व्यवस्थापन
   D. इनमें से कोई नहीं
4. लेखक का मुख्य बल किस बात पर है?
   A. परम्परागत पद्धतियों को सुदृढ़ किया जाना चाहिए।
   B. औपचारिक शिक्षा, गैर-औपचारिक शिक्षा से अधिक महत्त्वपूर्ण है
   C. व्यक्ति को सीखना कभी बंद नहीं करना चाहिए
   D. मुक्त शिक्षा प्रणाली का कोई विकल्प नहीं है
5. लेखक के अनुसार, 'जीवन-पर्यन्त शिक्षा' की अवधारणा है
   A. इतनी पुरानी जितनी परम्परागत शिक्षा होती है
   B. जो अभी भी निर्माण अवस्था में हो
   C. जो विकसित देशों में प्रचलित है
   D. जो व्यवहार्य अथवा वांछनीय न हो

उद्धरण-15

मानव-जीवन के सौ वर्षों को चार भागों में बाँटा गया है। वास्तव में सम्पूर्ण जीवन सतत प्रयत्न करते हुए व्यक्तित्व का विकास करने के लिए है। व्यक्तित्व के विकास की दिशा अवस्था के अनुसार बदलती है। विशेष प्रकार की योग्यताओं को विकसित करने के लिए अनुकूल वातावरण की आवश्यकता पड़ती है। आश्रम-व्यवस्था के अनुसार जीवन-भार श्रम करते हुए मानव अधिकाधिक सफलता प्राप्त कर सकता है। जीवन का प्रथम आश्रम ब्रह्मचर्य अधिक से अधिक ज्ञान करने के लिए था। ब्रह्मचर्याश्रम में जो ज्ञान प्राप्त किया जाता है उसी की मात्रा के अनुरूप जीवन की सफलता होती है। इसी के बल पर गृहस्थाश्रम में वह अधिक से अधिक धन कमा कर लोक-कल्याण कर सकता है। मनुष्य की आध्यात्मिक प्रवृत्तियाँ स्वान्तः सुखाय होती हैं। इनके द्वारा वह वानप्रस्थ और संन्यास में शान्ति प्राप्त करता है।

1. वास्तव में सम्पूर्ण जीवन किसलिए है?
   A. सतत प्रयत्न करते हुए व्यक्तित्व के विकास के लिए
   B. श्रम करते हुए सफलता प्राप्त करने के लिए
   C. अधिक से अधिक धन कमाने के लिए
   D. अधिक से अधिक ज्ञान प्राप्त करने के लिए
2. व्यक्तित्व के विकास की दिशा कैसे बदलती है?
   A. योग्यताओं के विकास के अनुसार
   B. अनुकूल वातावरण के अनुसार
   C. अवस्था के अनुसार
   D. सतत प्रयत्नों के अनुसार
3. प्राप्त ज्ञान की मात्रा के अनुरूप क्या होता है?
   A. जीवन की सफलता B. सुख की प्राप्ति
   C. धन की प्राप्ति D. शान्ति की प्राप्ति
4. लोक-कल्याण कब अधिक किया जा सकता है?
   A. ब्रह्मचर्याश्रम में B. वानप्रस्थ में
   C. गृहस्थाश्रम में D. संन्यास में
5. मनुष्य शान्ति किसके द्वारा प्राप्त करता है?
   A. ज्ञान के द्वारा
   B. धन के द्वारा
   C. लोक-कल्याण के द्वारा
   D. आध्यात्मिक प्रवृत्तियों के द्वारा

उद्धरण-16

इन्द्र यह सुनकर स्वयं महर्षि दधीचि के आश्रम में गए और उन्हें मजबूरी कह सुनायी। ऋषि जग-कल्याण के लिए सहर्ष अपना शरीर त्यागने के लिए तैयार हो गए। उनकी हड्डियों से त्वष्ठा ने वज्र बनाया। इस वज्र को हाथ में लेकर इन्द्र दुगुने उत्साह से वृत्रासुर के सम्मुख गए। उनके मेघरूपी रथ के गर्जन से एक बार वृत्रासुर का कलेजा काँप गया। उनके साथ चलते हुए मरुत जोर-जोर से उनकी जयजयकार कर रहे थे। इन्द्र ने सबसे पहले अपने वज्र से वृत्रासुर की माया को काट दिया। फिर भी वह दैत्य बड़ा शक्तिशाली था। अपनी माया से विछिन्न होकर भी वह बहुत देर तक इन्द्र से जूझता रहा। लेकिन अन्त में इन्द्र ने वज्र के प्रहार से वृत्रासुर का सिर काट दिया। वृत्रासुर के मरते ही रुका हुआ जल बह निकला, नदी-नाले फिर से भर उठे और देखते-ही-देखते खेत लहलहा उठे।

1. महर्षि दधीचि एक ऐसे ऋषि थे जिन्होंने :
   A. देवताओं की रक्षा के लिए अपने शरीर का त्याग किया था
   B. योग बल से अपने शरीर को त्याग कर वृत्रासुर के वध हेतु वज्र बनाने के लिए इन्द्र को अपनी अस्थियाँ सुलभ करा दी थीं
   C. वृत्रासुर के वध में इन्द्र की सहायता की थी
   D. वृत्रासुर का वध किया था
2. हमें इस अवतरण से यह प्रेरणा मिलती है कि परोपकार के लिए आवश्यकता पड़ने पर :
   A. अपने शरीर भी दे देना चाहिए
   B. अपना सर्वस्व दे देना चाहिए
   C. अपनी अस्थियाँ दे देनी चाहिए
   D. अपनी सम्पत्ति दे देनी चाहिए
3. इस गद्यांश का उपयुक्त शीर्षक हो सकता है :
   A. दधीचि का आत्मदान
   B. दधीचि का सर्वस्व दान
   C. वृत्रासुर वध
   D. इन्द्र का कोप
4. निम्नलिखित में से सही कथन पर निशान लगाइए :
   A. वृत्रासुर इन्द्र का प्रतिद्वन्द्वी था
   B. वृत्रासुर एक आततायी राक्षस था

C. वृत्रासुर एक महाप्रतापी राक्षस था, जिसने जलावरोध कर रखा था
D. वृत्रासुर उपर्युक्त में से कोई नहीं था

इस उद्धरण में प्रयुक्त निम्नलिखित शब्दों के सही अर्थों पर निशान लगाइए :

5. महर्षि
A. मुनि
B. ऋषि जो ब्राह्मण न हो
C. ऋषि जो ब्राह्मण हो
D. ऋषियों का एक पद विशेष

6. जगकल्याण :
A. संसार का हित
B. संसार की भलाई
C. संसार को सुख देना
D. संसार के लिए आनन्द की व्यवस्था करना

7. वज्र :
A. एक प्रकार का बाजा
B. एक प्रकार का शस्त्र
C. एक प्रकार का आघात
D. पत्थर गिरना या बिजली गिरना

उद्धरण-17

आचार्य शुक्ल जी के गंभीर निबंध 'चिंतामणि' में संग्रहीत हैं। उनमें दो प्रकार के निबंध हैं, एक तो भावों के विश्लेषण से सम्बन्ध रखने वाले निबंध जो भाव-विषयक होते हुए भी आवश्यक नहीं हैं वरन् उच्चकोटि के विचारात्मक हैं, दूसरे साहित्यिक जिनमें कुछ सैद्धांतिक आलोचना से संबंध रखते हैं, जैसे—'साधारणीकरण और व्यक्ति वैचित्र्यवाद' और कुछ व्यावहारिक आलोचनाओं के हैं, जैसे 'भारतेन्दु हरिश्चन्द्र'। आचार्य शुक्ल जी के मनोवैज्ञानिक निबंधों की भी अन्विति उनकी आलोचनाओं से की जा सकती है, वे भारतीय रस सिद्धान्त पर अवलम्बित हैं और उनका सम्बन्ध जीवन सागर के निजी अवगाहन से है। इन निबंधों के भावों का विश्लेषण पर्याप्त मात्रा में हुआ है किन्तु जीवन से चुने हुए उपयुक्त उदाहरणों के कारण यह विश्लेषण दुरूह नहीं होने पाया है। 'लज्जा और ग्लानि' का आधार भारत की आत्मग्लानि है, 'लोभ और प्रीति' का अन्तर समझ लेने पर जायसी के 'रत्नसेन' के प्रेम की आलोचना भली प्रकार समझी जा सकती है।

—काव्य के रूप, डॉ. गुलाब राय

1. उक्त गद्यांश का सम्यक् अनुशीलन करने से पता चलता है कि लेखक ने :
A. शुक्ल जी को समझने में काफी प्रयास किया था
B. शुक्ल जी के साहित्य का सम्यक् अध्ययन किया था
C. शुक्ल जी से दिशाबोध ग्रहण किया था
D. शुक्ल जी को समीप से देखा था

2. डॉ. गुलाब राय की शैली थी :
A. कथा शैली
B. भावना प्रवण शैली
C. विवेचना प्रधान शैली
D. विश्लेषणात्मक शैली

3. डॉ. गुलाब राय ने आचार्य शुक्ल की शैलियों का जो वर्गीकरण किया है वह :
A. अत्यन्त वैज्ञानिक है   B. शोधपूर्ण है
C. सर्वांगीण है   D. यथातथ्य है

4. उक्त गद्यांश के लिए उचित शीर्षक होगा :
A. आचार्य शुक्ल की निबंध-शैली
B. शुक्ल जी की निबंध-कला
C. निबंध कला और शुक्ल जी
D. हिन्दी के श्रेष्ठ निबंधकार शुक्ल जी

5. अन्विति का अर्थ है :
A. अनुरक्ति   B. तालमेल
C. आलोचना   D. अर्चना

उद्धरण-18

चीन में न तो वर्ण व्यवस्था थी न जाति-पाँति का भेदभाव। परम्परा के अनुसार सम्मान के मुख्य पात्र क्रमशः विद्वान्, राज्य पदाधिकारी, योद्धा और अध्यापक थे। साधारण लोगों में नौ श्रेणियाँ थीं। अन्न उत्पन्न करने वाले, माली, लकड़हारे, पशु-पक्षी पालने वाले, बुनकर, नौकर-चाकर, कारीगर, व्यापारी और फुटकर काम करने वाले। कुलीनों तथा साधारण लोगों में अथवा श्रेणियों और व्यवसायों में ऊँच-नीच का भेद कायम था। पर यह विभेद नगण्य-सा था। अपनी योग्यता के अनुसार मनुष्य का स्थान घटता-बढ़ता था। लोग आपस में विवाह आदि बिना किसी बाधा के करते थे। चीनियों में विद्वान् और सेनापति विशेष आदर के पात्र समझे जाते थे। हिजड़े, भाँड, गुलाम, हरकारे, वेश्याएँ नीचे के स्तर के लोग थे। चीन में गुलामों की दशा उतनी खराब नहीं थी जितनी रोम तथा यूरोप के देशों के मध्य युग में थी। गुलामों से घरेलू काम कराये जाते थे। उनकी विशेष जाति नहीं थी। उन्हें यद्यपि खरीदा-बेचा जा सकता था तथापि उनसे न तो नीच काम कराए जाते थे और न उन्हें सताया जाता था।

—विश्व इतिहास, डॉ. रामप्रसाद त्रिपाठी

1. उक्त उद्धरण के अध्ययन से पता चलता है कि मध्यकालीन चीन में :
A. जाति प्रथा प्रचलित थी
B. सामाजिक जीवन काफी समुन्नत था
C. सामाजिक जीवन वैभवपूर्ण था
D. वर्ण-व्यवस्था से रहित था

2. उक्त उद्धरण का उपयुक्त शीर्षक हो सकता है :
A. मध्यकालीन चीन का सामाजिक जीवन
B. मध्यकालीन चीन में सामाजिक व्यवस्था
C. चीनी समाज में विविधता
D. चीनी समाज में गिरावट

3. उक्त गद्य खण्ड का सारांश एक पंक्ति में इस प्रकार व्यक्त किया जा सकता है :
A. अन्य तत्कालीन समाजों की तुलना में मध्यकाल में चीन का सामाजिक जीवन समुन्नत था

B. चीन का मध्यकालीन समाज विकास के शिखर पर था
C. चीन मध्यकालीन राज्यों में अग्रणी था
D. मध्यकालीन चीन का सामाजिक जीवन विकासोन्मुख था

4. चीन के सामाजिक इतिहास का अनुशीलन करने से पता चलता है कि चीन में :
A. सामाजिक भेदभाव अवश्य था भले ही वहाँ वर्ण-व्यवस्था नहीं थी
B. समाज के सभी सदस्य एक-सा जीवन नहीं जीते थे
C. चीनी समाज गुलामों को उत्पीड़ित करता था
D. मध्यकालीन चीन में नागरिक सुविधाओं का अभाव था

5. चीन में विशेष आदर के पात्र समझे जाते थे :
A. हिजड़े और भाँड B. विद्वान् और वेश्याएँ
C. विद्वान् और सेनापति D. कारीगर और व्यापारी

उद्धरण-19

आज से सप्तदशक पूर्व सम्पादकाचार्य पराड़करजी ने कहा था—हम सब सम्पादक पत्रों की उन्नति चाहते हैं। पर हमें स्मरण रखना चाहिए कि इस उन्नति के साथ-साथ हमारी स्वातंत्र्य-हानि अवश्यम्भावी है। उन्नति व्यापारी ढंग से ही हो सकती है; इसके लिए पूँजीपति और संचालक व्यवसाय की आवश्यकता है। इनके कथनानुसार और भी पत्र का सम्पादन करना असम्भव हो जाता है। इंग्लैण्ड और अमेरिका के पत्रों में स्पष्ट देखा जाता है कि इनके समाचार स्तम्भ, मनोरंजन स्तम्भ जितने ही अच्छे हो रहे हैं, उनके सम्पादकीय स्तम्भ उतने ही निकम्मे बनते जा रहे हैं। लन्दन के 'टाइम्स' जैसे दो-तीन पत्र इसके अपवाद हैं। पर साधारण नियम वही है जो बताया जा चुका है। एडिटर की अपेक्षा मैनेजिंग एडिटर का प्रभाव और गौरव अधिक बढ़ गया है। भावी हिन्दी समाचार-पत्रों में ऐसा ही होगा। पत्र निकालकर सफलतापूर्वक चलाना बड़े-बड़े धनियों अथवा सुसंघटित कम्पनियों के लिए संभव होगा। पत्र सर्वांगसुन्दर होंगे। आकार बड़े होंगे, छपाई अच्छी होगी, मनोहर, मनोरंजक और ज्ञानवर्द्धक चित्रों से सुसज्जित होंगे, लेखों में विविधता होगी, कल्पकता होगी, गम्भीर गवेषणा की झलक होगी और मनोहारिणी शक्ति भी होगी, ग्राहकों की संख्या लाखों में गिनी जाएगी। यह सब कुछ होगा पर पत्र प्राणहीन होंगे। पत्रों की नीति देशभक्त, धर्मभक्त अथवा मानवता के उपासक महाप्राण सम्पादकों की नीति न होगी—इन गुणों से सम्पन्न लेखक विकृत मस्तिष्क समझे जाएँगे, सम्पादक की कुर्सी तक उनकी पहुँच भी न होगी। वेतनभोगी सम्पादक मालिक का काम करेंगे और बड़ी खूबी के साथ करेंगे। वे हम लोगों से अच्छे होंगे। पर आज भी हमें जो स्वतन्त्रता प्राप्त है वह उन्हें न होगी। वस्तुत: पत्रों के जीवन में यही समय बहुमूल्य है। इंग्लैण्ड और अमेरिका के पत्रों ने उन्हीं दिनों सच्चा काम किया था जब उनके आकार छोटे थे, समाचार कम होते थे, ग्राहक थोड़े होते थे पर सम्पादक की लेखनी में ओज था और प्राण था। उन देशों की इस उन्नति के बहुत कुछ कारण वे ही सम्पादक थे जिनसे धनी घृणा करते थे, शासक क्रुद्ध रहा करते थे और जो हमारे ही जैसे, एक पैर जेल में रखकर धर्मबुद्धि से पत्र सम्पादन किया करते थे। उनके परिश्रम से और कष्ट से पत्रों की उन्नति हुई पर उनके वंश का लोप हो गया। अब संचालक और व्यवस्थापक सर्वेसर्वा हैं, सम्पादक कुछ नहीं है।

(ध्रुवतारा, अप्रैल-जून, 1996 के सौजन्य से)

1. नीचे लिखे विकल्पों में से कौन-सा उपर्युक्त गद्यांश की विषयवस्तु का सही प्रतिपादन करता है?
A. समाचार-पत्र B. समाचार-पत्र के स्वामी
C. सम्पादक का महत्त्व D. लेखक

2. इंग्लैण्ड और अमेरिका के समाचार-पत्रों की क्या विशेषता है?
A. मनोरंजन स्तम्भ अच्छे हैं
B. सम्पादक स्तम्भ अच्छे हैं
C. रंग-बिरंगे हैं
D. सस्ते हैं

3. 'सर्वांगसुन्दर' का क्या तात्पर्य है?
A. सभी गुणों का होना
B. समाचार-पत्र हर प्रकार से अच्छा हो
C. सबसे श्रेष्ठ
D. सबको लुभाने वाला

4. समाचार-पत्रों की उन्नति कैसे हो सकती है?
A. अच्छी मशीन लगाने से
B. व्यापारी ढंग से
C. सम्पादक के कारण
D. पूँजी लगाने से

5. स्वातन्त्र्य-हानि का क्या अर्थ है?
A. स्वतन्त्रता का नाश
B. पराधीनता
C. मनमानी करने पर रोक
D. कृपा

उद्धरण-20

हम विज्ञान युग में जी रहे हैं। हमसे ये आशा नहीं की जाती कि हम अविश्वसनीय मतों अथवा एकांतिक दैवी-संदेशों को सोचे-समझे बगैर आसानी से स्वीकार कर लेंगे। आज के युग में विज्ञान और प्रौद्योगिकी के नित-नूतन आविष्कार हो रहे हैं। प्रकृति के रहस्यों पर से आवरण क्रमश: हटता जा रहा है। यह युग मानववाद का भी है, जिसमें वे धर्म जो मानवीय बुराइयों तथा सामाजिक अपराधों के प्रति संवेदनशील नहीं हैं, आधुनिक व्यक्ति के गले नहीं उतरते। वे धर्म जो विभेद, वैमनस्य और अनैतिकता को बढ़ावा देते हैं तथा एकता, सद्भावना और सामंजस्य को प्रोत्साहित नहीं करते, वे मनुष्य को मनुष्य से लड़ाकर धर्मद्रोहियों के हाथ में अस्त्र बन जाते हैं। विज्ञान की प्रकृति कभी धर्म-विरोधी नहीं

रही है। धार्मिक मतों के पक्ष में मुख्य तर्क प्राय: ब्रह्मांड संबंधी वस्तुपरक विचारों पर आधारित होते हैं। प्राकृतिक धर्म कभी भी किन्हीं आप्त स्रोतों, इल्हामों या परंपराओं पर निर्भर नहीं करता, वह तो अनुभूत अनुभव सिद्ध प्रत्यक्ष तथ्यों के अध्ययन और व्यावहारिकता पर अवलंबित होता है। वैज्ञानिक विधि का अनुसरण करते हुए, प्राकृतिक तथ्यों का सर्वेक्षण करके, युक्तियुक्त तर्क देकर परमसत्ता-विषयक सिद्धान्त का प्रतिपादन किया जाता है। वैज्ञानिक धर्म में ब्रह्मांड को समझने की जिज्ञासा पर बल दिया जाता है। प्राकृतिक ऊर्जा व पदार्थों के जन्म तथा विनाश को समझ सकने की इच्छा होती है। विकास का क्रम ऊर्ध्वमुखी रहा है : यह अप्राण से सप्राण तक; सप्राण से संवेदनशील तक; संवेदनशील से सज्ञान जीवन तक विकसित होता है। सज्ञान प्राणी को आध्यात्मिक प्राणी के रूप में आत्मविकास करना पड़ता है। आध्यात्मिक प्राणी—विशुद्ध ज्ञानी या विचारवान् प्राणी से उतना ऊँचा होता है जितना ज्ञानवान प्राणी संवेदनशील प्राणी से उन्नत होता है। विज्ञान की चेतना में कहीं यह संकेत नहीं मिलता कि पदार्थ से ही सृष्टि का आरंभ हुआ था। परमाणु को विखंडित करने वाले मनुष्य का मन निश्चय ही परमाणु से कहीं अधिक श्रेष्ठ है। प्रकृत की व्यवस्था और प्रगति के अवलोकन से स्पष्ट हो जाता है कि अगणित क्रमबद्ध प्रणालियों का संचालन, किसी सर्वद्रष्टा परम-आत्मा द्वारा किया जा रहा है।

—(ध्रुवतारा—जनवरी, मार्च, 1996 के सौजन्य से)

1. वर्तमान युग का मनुष्य कैसे धर्म को सही समझ सकता है?
A. जो भय पैदा करे
B. वैज्ञानिक व सद्भावना पैदा करने वाला हो
C. जो वैमनस्य और अनैतिक को बढ़ावा दे
D. जो परंपरा पर आधारित हो

2. 'संवेदनशील' का सही अर्थ चुन कर बताएँ।
A. दूसरे को दु:ख देने वाला
B. दूसरे का कष्ट महसूस करने वाला
C. दूसरे का संदेश देने वाला
D. दूसरों की भलाई सोचने वाला

3. 'आशा', 'अविश्वसनीय', 'प्रोत्साहित' तथा 'यह' शब्दों को क्रिया, विशेषण, सर्वनाम तथा संज्ञा के क्रम में व्यवस्थित करिए।
A. आशा, अविश्वसनीय, प्रोत्साहित, यह
B. यह, आशा, अविश्वसनीय, प्रोत्साहित
C. अविश्वसनीय, प्रोत्साहित, यह, आशा
D. प्रोत्साहित, अविश्वसनीय, यह, आशा

4. 'सामंजस्य' शब्द का सही अर्थ चयन करें :
A. सामना करना
B. आलस्य दूर करना
C. भेद-भाव हटाकर एक करना
D. अपना पक्ष प्रबल करना

5. उपर्युक्त गद्यांश में से 'प्राचीन' शब्द का विलोम चुनिए।
A. आधुनिक B. नित-नूतन
C. पारंपरिक D. ऊर्ध्वमुखी

उद्धरण-21

शान्ति और विश्वकल्याण की इसी उदात भावना के कारण युगों-युगों से विश्व हमारी संस्कृति हमारे साहित्य और हमारे विश्वबंधुत्व की ओर आकर्षित रहा है। इसी से प्रेरित होकर लोग भारत से सम्पर्क बढ़ाने के लिए हमारी राष्ट्रभाषा को सीखते-पढ़ते रहे हैं। उसी का सुफल है कि सोवियत संघ से लेकर अमेरिका तक, दक्षिण अफ्रीका से लेकर एशिया तक, यूरोप से लेकर कनाडा तक लाखों-लाखों विदेशी भारत प्रेमी लोग आज हिन्दी पढ़-लिख रहे हैं। इसलिए नहीं कि हिन्दी विश्व की तीसरी सबसे बड़ी भाषा है, इसलिए भी नहीं कि भारत विश्व का सबसे बड़ा लोकतंत्रीय देश है, इसलिए भी अधिक नहीं वह निर्गुट राष्ट्रों का एक मुखिया देश है, बल्कि सबसे अधिक इसलिए कि भारत के प्रति समीपता से उन्हें आत्मिक शान्ति प्राप्त होती है। वे भौतिकता से आध्यात्मिकता की ओर उन्मुख होते हैं। वे मनोविकारों से ऊपर उठकर स्वस्थ चिंतन में प्रवृत्त होते हैं और सबसे अधिक इसलिए कि भौतिकवाद की जिस कुन्ठा ने उन्हें ग्रसित कर रखा है उससे त्राण पाने का मार्ग उन्हें भारतीय संस्कृति और भारत की वाणी से सहज में ही सुलभ हो जाता है। क्योंकि हिन्दी आक्रान्ताओं की नहीं, आक्रमणों से मुक्ति पाने का सन्देश है। वह विश्व के साम्राज्यवादियों की भाषा नहीं, उनके द्वारा शोषित, सताए, लूटे और दलित बनाए जाने वाले लोगों की आत्मा की अदमनीय अनुगूंज है। वह समता का सन्देश देती है। वह सहअस्तित्व का पाठ पढ़ाती है। विश्व को युद्धों की विभीषिका से बचाकर उन्हें शांति का कर्त्तव्य बोध कराती है।

विश्व के लोगों के लिए हिन्दी वह भाषा है जो उन्हें वही देती है जिसकी वे तलाश में हैं। इसीलिए हम हिन्दी को भाषा नहीं विचार कहते हैं, संस्कृति कहते हैं और हम उसे मानवता का शांतिपाठ मानते हैं क्योंकि हिन्दी तलवार के बल पर नहीं, संतों के वचनामृत से फैली है। उसने द्वेष और छल से राष्ट्रों और व्यक्तियों का शोषण नहीं किया है। उसके साहित्य की पंक्ति-पंक्ति में प्रेम का सन्देश बिखरा हुआ है। वह प्रेम जो मनुष्य को मनुष्य से जोड़ता है और आत्मा को परमात्मा से जोड़ता है। इसलिए हिन्दी को हम जोड़ने वाली कड़ी कहते हैं, तोड़ने वाली हथौड़ी या छैनी नहीं। पढ़िए सूर को, तुलसी को, गाइए मीरा को और गुनगुनाइए कबीरा को, सुनिए मैथिलीशरण गुप्त को, प्रसाद को, महादेवी या निराला को। इन सभी महात्मा कवियों में आपको मानवीय संवेदना और प्रेम का एक ऐसा मधुर संगीत सुनाई देगा जो आपकी आत्मा को रसविभोर कर देगा। हिन्दी के उदात्त साहित्य में रस है, कामुकता नहीं, बौद्धिकता है, परन्तु जड़ शुष्कता नहीं, आनन्द की अनुभूति है, विरह के आँसू हैं, लेकिन जीवन की दुखान्त परिणति और कलुषित आक्रोश नहीं।

हिन्दी अपने इन्हीं गुणों के कारण विश्वमंच पर आज आदर से प्रतिष्ठित है। स्वार्थ और स्वामित्व की कुटिल विश्वनीति कितनी ही उसके मार्ग में बाधाएं उपस्थित करे, उनका कुहासा हिन्दी के दिव्य प्रकाश को फैलने से नहीं रोक सकता। क्योंकि हिन्दी के पीछे अन्य साम्राज्यवादी भाषाओं की तरह परपीड़न और शोषण का इतिहास नहीं है। उसने उपनिवेशों का शोषण करके अपने देश

और अपनी भाषा को ज्ञान-विज्ञान के मारक अस्त्र प्रदान नहीं किए। साम्राज्यवादी भाषाओं ने औपनिवेशिक देशों को जनता को ही नहीं वहां की संस्कृति, कला और साहित्य को भी दबाया है तथा उनके उत्कर्ष और विकास की खिल्ली उड़ाई है। उनके बुद्धिजीवियों और रचनाधर्मियों को सदैव अपने से हीन समझा है। जहां-जहां ये साम्राज्यवादी गए वहां-वहां अपनी संस्कृति और भाषा को थोपते रहे। जब वहां से हटे तो ऐसा कुचक्र रच गए कि वहां के शासक, श्रीमंत और बुद्धिजीवी इस तरह मानसिक दासता के चक्र में फंस गए कि उन्हें अपनी भाषा, कला, साहित्य-संस्कृति सब दीन-हीन लगने लगे। लेकिन भारत और अन्य देशों के साम्राज्यशाही चुंगल से छूटने के बाद शनैः-शनैः यह व्यामोह छूटने लगा है। राष्ट्रों में स्वाभिमान और स्वावलम्बन की प्रवृत्तियां उभर रही हैं। यह प्रक्रिया भाषा के क्षेत्र में भी प्रारंभ हुई है। राष्ट्रों में अपनी-अपनी भाषाएं अपना स्थान बना रही हैं और सम्पर्क सूत्र के रूप में अब अंग्रेजी ही नहीं अनेक देशों में विशेषकर तीसरी दुनिया के देशों में हिन्दी की भी छवि निखर कर ऊपर आने लगी है।

1. विदेशी आज हिन्दी सीख-पढ़ रहे हैं, क्योंकि :
A. हिन्दी विश्व की तीसरी सबसे बड़ी भाषा है
B. विदेशी हमसे सम्पर्क बढ़ाना चाहते हैं
C. भारत विश्व का सबसे बड़ा लोकतंत्रीय देश है
D. भारत निर्गुट राष्ट्रों का एक मुखिया देश है

2. विश्व हमारी संस्कृति की ओर आकर्षित हुआ :
A. शान्ति और विश्वकल्याण की उदात्त भावना के कारण
B. हमारी परमाणु शक्ति के विकास के कारण
C. अन्तर्राष्ट्रीय व्यापार मेलों के आयोजन के कारण
D. अनेक धार्मिक स्थलों के संरक्षण के कारण

3. हिन्दी मनुष्य को वही देती है :
A. जिसे वह नहीं चाहता है
B. जिसकी उसे चाह नहीं है
C. जिसकी उसे तलाश है
D. जिसे वह चाहती है

4. हिन्दी भाषा नहीं विचार है क्योंकि :
A. वह विश्व को सह-अस्तित्व का पाठ पढ़ाती है
B. वह विश्व को संत बनने का उपदेश देती है
C. वह विश्व को असंत बनाती है
D. वह विश्व को शान्ति का कर्तव्य-बोध कराती है

5. हिन्दी का मुख्य सन्देश है :
A. आक्रान्ताओं से मुक्ति पाने का सन्देश
B. कुन्ठा से ग्रसित होने का सन्देश
C. आक्रमणों से मुक्ति पाने का सन्देश
D. अकर्मण्यता का सन्देश

उद्धरण-22

अभिप्रेरण की संकल्पना अत्यंत जटिल है। इसका संबंध अनेक अभिलाषाओं, इच्छाओं, आवश्यकताओं एवं अनुभूतियों से है। वस्तुतः अभिप्रेरण की पूरी संकल्पना इन्हीं बलों पर आधारित है। यदि अभिप्रेरणा के विविध पक्षों का गंभीर अध्ययन करें तो यह सहज ही स्पष्ट हो जाता है कि यह वस्तुतः एक प्रकार की वैयक्तिक एवं आंतरिक भावना है या व्यक्ति विशेष के अंतःकरण में उत्पन्न होने वाला एक तरह का मनोवैज्ञानिक क्रम है। यह एक व्यावहारिक संकल्पना है जिससे मनुष्य का व्यवहार किसी निश्चित लक्ष्य की ओर निर्देशित और अग्रसर होगा। यह एक निरंतर चलती रहने वाली प्रक्रिया है। पर यदि एक ओर यह सकारात्मक हो सकती है तो दूसरी ओर नकारात्मक भी हो सकती है। प्रेरणा से व्यक्ति का व्यवहार प्रभावित होता है। प्रेरणा अभिप्रेरण के मूल में है। दूसरे शब्दों में यह अभिप्रेरण का मूलतत्व है। प्रेरणा के कारण व्यक्ति को कार्य करने की दिशा मिलती है। अतः किसी लक्ष्य या पुरस्कार की प्राप्ति के लिए ऊर्जा बढ़ाने की चाहत ही अभिप्रेरण है। यह एक ऐसी शक्ति है जिससे सुप्त ऊर्जा सक्रिय हो जाती है और व्यक्ति कार्य के प्रति उत्साहित एवं उन्मुख हो उठता है। मस्तिष्क किस प्रकार कार्य करता है इसे पूरी तरह समझ पाना अब संभव नहीं हो पाया है।

किंतु यह अवश्य ही सत्य है कि किसी भी व्यवस्था/तंत्र में मानवीय अंतःक्रिया की गुणवत्ता से ही संतोषजनक परिणाम मिल पाना संभव होता है। यह किसी ऐसे प्रतिफल की मांग द्वारा निर्धारित नहीं होती जिसे समाज में अनिवार्यतः हमेशा महत्व दिया जाता है बल्कि इसके मूल में एक ऐसे प्रतिफल की मांग होती है जो किसी खास संदर्भ में आवश्यक होता है। अतः यह समझना अपरिहार्य है कि अभिप्रेरण की वास्तविक दिशा क्या है? इसके लिए विभिन्न प्रकार की पद्धतियां अपनाई जाती हैं जिन्हें सामूहिक रूप से अभिप्रेरण-निर्देश की संज्ञा दी जाती है। इनमें से सबसे महत्वपूर्ण निर्देश वह है जिसके द्वारा यह ज्ञात करने की चेष्टा की जाती है कि अभिप्रेरित व्यक्ति या व्यक्ति समूह दायित्व से दूर भाग रहा है अथवा दायित्व के प्रति अभिमुखन दर्शा रहा है।

इस प्रकार के निर्देशों की दूसरी कोटि वह है जिनके जरिए यह निर्धारित करने का प्रयास किया जाता है कि अभिप्रेरण का मूलभाव स्वःअंतर्मुखी है अथवा अन्य-बहिर्मुखी है। तात्पर्य यह है कि अभिप्रेरित व्यक्ति स्वकेन्द्रित, आत्मसंतुष्टि पर आधारित प्रयोजनों के लिए अभिप्रेरित होता है या दूसरे व्यक्ति अथवा व्यक्तियों के लिए अभिप्रेरित होता है। तीसरे अभिप्रेरण निर्देश का आधार समानता और अंतर तथा चौथे निर्देश का आधार समग्र विवरण है।

1. अभिप्रेरण एक व्यावहारिक संकल्पना है जिससे मनुष्य का व्यवहार किसी निश्चित लक्ष्य की ओर निर्देशित और :
A. आधारित होता है B. अग्रसर होता है
C. निर्धारित होता है D. रूपायित होता है

2. अभिप्रेरण का संबंध अनेक अभिलाषाओं, इच्छाओं, आवश्यकताओं एवं :
A. अनुभूतियों से है B. भावनाओं से है
C. प्रकृति से है D. उत्थान से है

3. प्रेरणा के कारण व्यक्ति को कार्य करने :
A. का आधार मिलता है B. की शक्ति मिलती है
C. की दिशा मिलती है D. की दृष्टि मिलती है

4. दूसरे अभिप्रेरण-निर्देश के मूल में है :
A. व्यक्ति का अभिमुखन
B. व्यक्ति का दृष्टिकोण
C. व्यक्ति का लक्ष्य
D. व्यक्ति की लक्ष्य चेतना

5. अभिप्रेरण निर्धारित होता है :
A. प्रतिकार की मांग से
B. प्रतिकृति की मांग से
C. आवश्यक प्रतिफल की मांग से
D. प्रतिवाद से

उद्धरण-23

शस्त्र की परंपरा आगे बढ़ती जाती है। मानव की मूल प्रकृति में असुरक्षा का भय समाया रहता है। इसी भय से शस्त्र और सेना का जन्म होता है। प्रत्येक मानव किसी देश का निवासी है। देश रक्षा उसका प्रमुख कर्त्तव्य है। वह जन-जीवन, आत्म सम्मान और अपने धर्म की रक्षा करना, सर्वोपरि मानता है। युद्ध एक आवेश और मजबूरी है। युद्ध दीर्घकालीन जीवन शैली नहीं होता। युद्ध द्वारा आवेश की उत्तेजना का विरेचन हो जाता है। युद्ध केवल राष्ट्र के लिए खतरे में ही प्रासंगिक होता है, युद्ध की हिंसा में विनाश है शांति की अहिंसा में ही विकास है। युद्ध के बिना सारे विश्व जीवन का कार्य संभव है पर शांति के बिना असंभव। जब तक शस्त्रों का अस्तित्व है तो उसकी परंपरा अनिवार्यत: बढ़ती जाएगी। पूर्व प्रस्तर एवं प्रस्तर युगों में पत्थर के चाकू, कुल्हाड़ी और गदा जैसे शस्त्र थे। कालांतर में तीरकमान, भाले, तलवार, बंदूक, तोप, बारूद व विस्फोटक बम एवं परमाणु बम की परंपरा चलती गई। सभी देश एक-दूसरे से भयभीत होकर, शस्त्र निर्माण पर, देश की संपत्ति लुटाते जा रहे हैं। हिंसा से भय और भय से हिंसा का अन्तहीन, गतिमान अधोगामी चक्र चलता रहता है। मौलिक शस्त्र तो हमारा मन है, जो वाणी और कर्म द्वारा शस्त्रों की परंपरा को चलाता है, क्रिया-प्रतिक्रिया की मानसिक चेतना ही शस्त्र और अशस्त्र होती है। डार्विन के विकासवाद की आधारशिला संघर्ष और आक्रामकता है। डार्विन 'अस्तित्व के लिए संघर्ष और श्रेष्ठ का कायम रहना' विकास की प्रक्रिया मानते हैं। इस विचारधारा को खंडित सत्य ही मानना होगा। संसार के अनेक धर्म, आत्मा, को जड़-द्रव्य की कारा से विमुक्ति के लिए, सतत संघर्षरत मानते हैं। जड़-द्रव्य के आवरणों का निरंतर विरल होते जाना ही चेतना का अंत: प्रकाशन है। यही मानव का सच्चा विकास है। सामाजिक चेतना की मूल प्रेरणा का स्रोत प्रेम और सहयोग में निहित है। शस्त्र द्वारा तो हम भयजनित तनावयुक्त संतुलन को अस्थायी आधार पर कायम रखने का प्रयास करते हैं। तनाव अपनी सीमा पार करके स्वयं अशांति व मरणेच्छा में बदल जाता है। यह मन का बांध टूटते ही विनाश जन्म ले लेता है। मन से भय भगाकर ही हम सचमुच नि:शस्त्र हो सकते हैं। मन के अभय होने पर सच्ची शांति प्राप्त होती है।

1. नीचे दिए विकल्पों में से कौन-सा उपयुक्त गद्यांश की विषय वस्तु का प्रतिपादन करता है?
A. शस्त्र परम्परा B. वास्तविक विकास
C. नि:शस्त्रीकरण D. शस्त्र और शांति

2. 'प्रासंगिक शब्द का सही अर्थ चुनकर बताएं।
A. तराजू की डंडी से संबंधित
B. दरबान
C. मामले से जुडा हुआ
D. साथ निभाने वाला

3. शस्त्र व सेना के जन्म का मूल कारण है :
A. असुरक्षा
B. शक्ति प्रदर्शन
C. वैभव एवं समपन्नता
D. साम्राज्यवादी महत्वाकांक्षाएं

4. शस्त्रों की परंपरा चलाने वाला वास्तविक शस्त्र क्या है?
A. ज्ञान B. बल
C. उत्साह D. मन

5. उपर्युक्त गद्यांश में से 'चेतन' का विलोम चुनिए।
A. विरेचन B. गतिमान
C. जड़ D. जन्म

उद्धरण-24

भारत की सांस्कृतिक शक्ति लोगों को आकर्षित करती है। सिकन्दर पूरब की ओर आया, तो उसने राज कायम कर लौटने का रास्ता पकड़ा। बाबर आया, तो वह भी लौटने की तैयारी में था। फिर भी उसे भारत ने आकर्षित किया। भारत में पश्चिम के लोग अपने लिए बेहद शांतिप्रिय बसेरा पाते हैं। निकोलोई-श्वेतास्लाव रोरिख, नारा रिचर्ड, एल्फ्रेड बुर्फल ऐसे अनेक नामी गिरामी लोगों ने, जो बीसवीं शताब्दी में ऊँचाइयों पर पहुँचे, बिना किसी संकोच के भारत को अपना घर बनाया। सरला बहन और मीरा बहन गांधी जी की दो शिष्याएं थीं। मीरा बहन ने पक्षी कुंज में अपना निवास बनाया था, जहां से वह हर समय हिमालय की बर्फ से लदी चोटियां देखती थी। मुंबई शहर को एक जर्मन विद्वान लाइफर ने आवास चुना।

भारतीय संस्कृति अपनी शक्ति उस वैविध्य से पाती है, जिसे मोटे तौर पर हम बहुलतावाद के रूप में देखते हैं। तथापि वैविध्य में गुणसूत्रों में जो लोकव्यापी होने का सामर्थ्य रहता है, वही तत्व संस्कृति का जीवनदायी तत्व निर्धारित हो जाता है। यानी भारतीय संस्कृति को सजीव और सक्रिय रखने की प्रक्रिया के भीतर गुणों को आत्मसात कर अपना बनाने की जो प्रवृत्ति है, यही वह मूल बिंदु है, जिसका बोध कर हम आसानी से कह सकते हैं कि भारतीय संस्कृति वैश्वीकरण, विश्व बाजार या नयी प्रौद्योगिकी से जन्मे कल-पुर्जो के अति उपयोगकर्ता सभ्यता के हमले भी झेल लेगी।

1. पश्चिमी दुनिया के लोगों के भारत की ओर आकर्षित होने का मुख्य कारण क्या है?
A. भारत की संपदा
B. भारत की आकर्षक जलवायु
C. भारत की बहुलतावादी संस्कृति
D. उपरोक्त सभी

2. निम्न में से किसने मुम्बई को अपना आवास स्थल बनाया?
   A. लाइफर B. सरला बहन
   C. एल्फ्रेड बुर्फल D. उपरोक्त सभी
3. भारतीय संस्कृति को जीवनदायी तत्त्व मिलते हैं–
   A. लोक जीवन से
   B. सांस्कृतिक आदान-प्रदान से
   C. सांस्कृतिक विक्षेप से
   D. B एवं C दोनों से
4. उपरोक्त उद्धरण के आधार पर निम्न में से कौन-सा कथन सही है?
   A. भारत की संस्कृति ने सर्वदा ही विदेशियों को अपनी ओर आकर्षित किया है।
   B. भारत की संस्कृति अन्य संस्कृतियों से श्रेष्ठ है।
   C. भारत की संस्कृति एक बंद संस्कृति रही है।
   D. A एवं B दोनों

उद्धरण-25

अफ्रीका में चीन के बढ़ते हुए प्रभाव से अमेरिका को एक और चिंता ने घेर लिया है। इराक, ईरान और उत्तरी कोरिया के बारे में तो अमेरिकी शासक खुलकर बात करते आये हैं, किंतु चीन से मुचैटा लेने के मामले में वे भारी सावधानी बरतते हैं। आखिर वे चीन के भारी कर्जदार तो हैं ही और शायद ये भुलाना भी आसान नहीं है कि किस प्रकार दशकों तक चीन से शत्रुता रखने के बाद उन्हें शीतयुद्ध जीतने के लिए पाकिस्तान की मध्यस्थता के माध्यम से, चीन की ओर मित्रता का हाथ बढ़ाना पड़ा था। चीन जैसी बड़ी ताकत से अपने रिश्तों में विश्व की सोल-सुपरपावर भी वो रुख नहीं अपना सकती, जो वह इराक जैसे बरसों से पिटे-पिटाए देश के साथ अपना सका था, यह बात समझना कठिन नहीं है।

लेकिन फिर भी अगर खतरा बढ़ने लगे, प्रतिस्पर्धा से कतराना संभव न रहे और वामपंथियों का दबाव बढ़ता चला जाये तो आखिर कब तक उनका राष्ट्रपति हाथों पर हाथ रखकर बैठा रह सकता है? इसीलिए तमाम उलझनों के बावजूद पूर्व राष्ट्रपति बुश को चीन की चुनौती की ओर ध्यान देने के लिए विवश होना पड़ा।

1. अमेरिका के लिए सबसे बड़ी चुनौती क्या है?
   A. चीन का बढ़ता आर्थिक प्रभाव
   B. शीत युद्ध के बाद सुपर पावर बने रहने की चिंता
   C. दक्षिण पंथ का विस्तार
   D. उपरोक्त सभी
2. चीन से मुचैटा लेने में अमेरिका अक्सर सावधानी बरतता है, क्यों?
   A. चीन की बड़ी पूँजी अमेरिका के बाजार में लगी हुई है।
   B. अमेरिका चीन के साथ बेहतर संबंध बनाना चाहता है।
   C. चीन शीत युद्ध के दौरान तटस्थ रहा था।
   D. A एवं C दोनों
3. निम्न में कौन-सा कथन सही है?
   A. चीन एशिया एवं अफ्रीका में अपने प्रभाव क्षेत्र का विस्तार कर रहा है।
   B. अमेरिका चीन के साथ संबंध खराब न हो जाए, इसलिए उत्तरी कोरिया के खिलाफ खुलकर कुछ नहीं कहता।
   C. शीत युद्ध के दौरान अमेरिका ने चीन की ओर मित्रता का हाथ बढ़ाया था।
   D. अमेरिका को वास्तविक खतरा विश्व आतंकवाद से है।
4. अमेरिकी राष्ट्रपति बुश को चीन की चुनौती की ओर क्यों ध्यान देना पड़ा?
   A. चीन के बढ़ते आर्थिक प्रभाव के कारण
   B. चीन द्वारा पाकिस्तान को मिलने वाले समर्थन के कारण
   C. उत्तरी कोरिया का चीन द्वारा समर्थन के कारण
   D. वामपंथ के बढ़ते दबाव के कारण

उद्धरण-26

समकालीन विश्व राजनीति में पश्चिम एशिया एक ऐसे क्षेत्र के तौर पर कुख्यात हो चुका है जहां केवल आतंक, अशांति और अराजकता का बोलबाला है। दूसरे विश्व युद्ध के बाद से ही मिडिल ईस्ट या पश्चिम एशिया कई छोटे-बड़े युद्ध और अनगिनत हिंसक झगड़े झेल चुका है। हाल ही में फतह और हमास द्वारा फिलिस्तीन के अलग-अलग इलाकों पर कब्जा करने के बाद तो पश्चिम एशिया का सामरिक वातावरण और उलझ गया है। अगर आतंक के खिलाफ विश्वव्यापी जंग की बात करें तो वर्तमान हालात यही इशारा कर रहे हैं कि अगर अमेरिका यह जंग हार नहीं रहा तो जीत भी उससे कोसों दूर है। पूरा पश्चिम एशिया समस्याग्रस्त है और अमेरिकी विदेश नीति के पास इन समस्याओं से जूझने के लिए कोई ठोस रणनीति नहीं है।

फिलहाल सबसे विकट समस्या इराक को लेकर है। इराक पर हुए अमेरिकी हमलों के कई साल गुजर चुके हैं। लेकिन वहाँ अभी तक शांति कायम नहीं की जा सकी है। रोजमर्रा के शिया-सुन्नी झगड़ों और अमेरिकी आधिपत्य के खिलाफ जिहादी हिंसा ने इराक को जर्जर बना दिया है। दोनों प्रमुख सम्प्रदायों को समान रूप से स्वीकार्य एक राजनीतिक व्यवस्था अभी नहीं पनप पाई है। दरअसल इराक को शिया, सुन्नी और कुर्द इलाकों में बाँटने की केवल औपचारिक घोषणा होना ही शेष है। अमेरिका के लिए गले की फांस बन चुका इराक दुनिया भर में जिहादियों के लिए प्रशिक्षण केंद्र में तब्दील हो चुका है। सितम्बर 2010 में अमेरिकी राष्ट्रपति बराक ओबामा ने ऑपरेशन 'इराकी फ्रीडम' खत्म होने की घोषणा की है। अब वहाँ स्थिति और बिगड़ सकती है। आत्मघाती हमलों में बेगुनाह

इराकियों का मरना जारी है। अलकायदा दिन-प्रतिदिन अपनी ताकत में इजाफा कर रहा है। कट्टरपंथियों की फौज खड़ी हो रही है।

1. इराक में अमेरिका के लिए सबसे बड़ी चुनौती क्या है?
   A. इराक में एक प्रतिनिधि सरकार स्थापित करना
   B. इराक में शांति कायम करना
   C. इराक में गठबंधन सेना के बीच समन्वय स्थापित करना
   D. उपरोक्त सभी
2. उपरोक्त उद्धरण के आधार पर सही कथन का चयन कीजिए।
   A. फतह एवं हमास गुट की सक्रियता के कारण पश्चिम एशिया की समस्या और भी उलझ गई है।
   B. इराक में अमेरिका विरोधी जिहादी गुट लगातार सक्रिय हैं।
   C. इराक पर अमेरिकी हमले के बाद वैश्विक आतंकवाद में कमी आई है।
   D. A एवं B दोनों
3. इराक में शांति स्थापना में सबसे बड़ी बाधा क्या है?
   A. अल कायदा की इस क्षेत्र में बढ़ती गतिविधियाँ
   B. शिया-सुन्नी झगड़े
   C. जिहादी हिंसा
   D. A एवं C दोनों
4. पश्चिमी एशिया की पहचान निम्न में से किसके कारण है?
   A. अरब-इजराइल युद्ध के कारण
   B. इराक युद्ध के कारण
   C. सीरिया में होने वाली शांति प्रक्रिया के कारण
   D. उपरोक्त सभी के कारण

उद्धरण-27

किसी भी लोकतांत्रिक समाज का भविष्य, उसकी प्रगतिशीलता, वैज्ञानिकता और संवेदनशीलता पर निर्भर करता है। लोकतंत्र में मताधिकार योग्य व्यक्ति के चयन की कारगर व्यवस्था नहीं है। मतदाता की बौद्धिकता, वैज्ञानिकता और संवेदनशीलता ही सही निर्णय लेने में सहायक हो सकती है वरना चुनाव में तमाम हत्यारे अपराधी और गुंडे चुने जा सकते हैं। हमारे देश के ज्यादातर मतदाताओं में इन गुणों का अभाव है। वह मोबाइल युग में परम अवैज्ञानिक है। हम मतदाताओं की बौद्धिकता का अंदाज ऐसे लोगों को देखकर आसानी से लगा सकते हैं जो ओझा-तांत्रिक और नीम-हकीमों के चक्कर में फंसकर तिल-तिल मरने को मजबूर हैं। वह यह समझ पाने की स्थिति में नहीं है कि ओझा-तांत्रिक, नीम- हकीम वगैरह उनकी अज्ञानता का लाभ उठाकर, शोषण कर रहे हैं।

हम वर्तमान शिक्षा व्यवस्था में पनपे उस गरीब समाज को देखकर बौद्धिकता की असलियत जान सकते हैं, जो अपनी औलादों की बलि देकर कल्याण ढूंढ़ता है। जो पढ़ने-पढ़ाने का हक मांगने के बजाय, उन्हें 'मिड-डे-मिल' खाना खिलाकर धन्य हो रहा है। बौद्धिकता की असलियत समाज के उन वयस्क मतदाताओं से जानी जा सकती है, जो असामाजिक तत्वों, अपराधियों के गले में माला डालकर उनकी जय-जयकार करते हैं। ये मतदाता वैज्ञानिकों या समाजशास्त्रियों को चुनने के बजाय फूलनदेवी, मलखान सिंह, मुख्तार अंसारी या शहाबुद्दीन जैसे लोगों को चुनते हैं।

1. उपरोक्त उद्धरण के आधार पर सही कथन का चयन कीजिए।
   A. भारतीय मतदाता पिछड़ी सोच वाला और अवैज्ञानिक है।
   B. भारतीय लोकतंत्र में मताधिकार, योग्य व्यक्ति के चयन की कारगर व्यवस्था नहीं है।
   C. भारतीय मतदाता अशिक्षित है।
   D. उपरोक्त सभी।
2. लोकतंत्र का भविष्य किस पर निर्भर करता है?
   A. समाज की प्रगतिशीलता पर
   B. सामाजिक संवेदनशीलता पर
   C. A एवं B दोनों पर
   D. सामाजिक सुव्यवस्था पर
3. भारतीय लोकतांत्रिक व्यवस्था का सबसे बड़ा अंतर्विरोध क्या है?
   A. भारत में गरीबी एवं असमानता व्याप्त है।
   B. समाज में भूखमरी एवं अज्ञानता है।
   C. बौद्धिकता के युग में ज्यादातर मतदाता घोर अवैज्ञानिक हैं।
   D. उपरोक्त सभी।
4. चुनाव में अपराधी किस्म के लोगों का चुना जाना किस बात का संकेत है?
   A. जनता की तटस्थता का
   B. जनता की अबौद्धिक निर्णय क्षमता का
   C. जनता की सक्रिय भागीदारी का
   D. प्रशासनिक विफलता का

उद्धरण-28

देह-प्रदर्शन स्वेच्छा से किया जाए या सामाजिक दबाव के कारण, लेकिन उसके दुष्प्रभावों को नजरअंदाज नहीं किया जा सकता है। नारियों से छेड़छाड़, अश्लील हरकतें, बलात्कार, यौन अपराध, देह व्यापार आदि बुराइयों की जड़ देह प्रदर्शन है। यदि पुरुषों से यह पूछा जाए कि क्या नारी के देह-प्रदर्शन से तुम को लज्जा महसूस नहीं होती है तो उनका तर्क होता है कि जब नारी को देह-प्रदर्शन करने में लज्जा नहीं आती है तो हमको देखने में लज्जा क्यों आएगी? देह-प्रदर्शन करने वाली नारी को समाज में हेय दृष्टि से देखा जाता है। ऐसी नारी को सिर्फ देह मानकर उसे इस्तेमाल किया जा रहा है।

आजकल माता-पिता के लिए लड़की की परवरिश करना चुनौतीपूर्ण होता जा रहा है क्योंकि यौन अपराधों की संख्या में वृद्धि होती जा रही है। माता-पिता सोचते हैं कि यदि हम

बेटी की इज्जत की रक्षा न कर पाए तो बेटी को जन्म देने का क्या फायदा होगा? माता-पिता की यह सोच कन्या भ्रूण-हत्या का महत्त्वपूर्ण कारण है। जो नारी आर्थिक लाभ के लिए अंग प्रदर्शन करती है उसका यौवन व आकर्षण समाप्त हो जाने पर वह कुंठित हो जाती है। विषादग्रस्त होकर वह आत्महत्या भी कर सकती है। नारी देह के प्रति पुरुषों का आकर्षण यौवनावस्था में होता है, इसमें स्थायित्व नहीं होता है। ऐसी नारियाँ आकर्षणहीन हो जाने पर स्वयं को एकाकी महसूस करती हैं तथा कई प्रकार के मानसिक रोगों से ग्रस्त हो जाती हैं।

1. नारी देह-प्रदर्शन का स्वाभाविक परिणाम है–
A. उनके साथ छेड़छाड़
B. अश्लील हरकतें
C. यौन अपराध
D. उपरोक्त सभी

2. नारी देह-प्रदर्शन की बढ़ती प्रवृत्ति का मुख्य कारण है–
A. नारी की स्व इच्छा
B. सामाजिक दबाव एवं लोलुपता
C. शिक्षा का माहौल
D. A एवं B दोनों

3. लेखक के अनुसार कन्या भ्रूण-हत्या का महत्वपूर्ण कारण क्या है?
A. महिलाओं के साथ होनेवाला यौन शोषण
B. बच्चियों का उचित परवरिश न हो पाना
C. सामाजिक असुरक्षा की भावना
D. उपरोक्त सभी

4. उपरोक्त उद्धरण के आधार पर सही कथन का चयन कीजिए।
A. आर्थिक लाभ के कारण नारी में शरीर-प्रदर्शन की प्रवृत्ति बढ़ती जा रही है।
B. नारी के देह-प्रदर्शन के पीछे सामाजिक दबाव एक मुख्य कारण है।
C. अंग-प्रदर्शन करनेवाली नारियों को यौवन का आकर्षण समाप्त हो जाने पर कुंठा का सामना करना पड़ता है।
D. उपरोक्त सभी।

उद्धरण-29

'वर्तमान इतिहास में दो प्रवृत्तियां दिखाई देती हैं। एक प्रवृत्ति की दिशा वर्चस्व (हेजीमनी) की ओर है जो मानव-अस्तित्व (सरवाइवल) के लिए खतरा बन कर पागलपन के सैद्धांतिक चौखटे में तर्कपूर्ण ढंग से काम कर रही है। दूसरी प्रवृत्ति इस विश्वास को समर्पित है कि 'एक नयी दुनिया संभव है', जिन शब्दों से विश्व सामाजिक मंच प्रेरित है, जो शासक विचारात्मक प्रणालियों को चुनौती दे रहा है और जो विचार, कर्म और संस्थाओं का नया सृजनात्मक विकल्प बनाना चाहता है। इनमें कौन-सी प्रवृत्ति जीतेगी, कोई इसकी भविष्यवाणी नहीं कर सकता है। यह प्रक्रिया समूचे इतिहास में दिखाई देती है।'

चोमस्की का कहना है कि अस्सी के दशक में मुख्यधारा के अमेरिका, खासकर मध्य अमेरिका से संबंधित जो मानव एकता आंदोलन चले उन्होंने साम्राज्यवाद के इतिहास में नयी जमीन जोड़ी। इससे पहले कभी भी शासक समाज के लोग बड़ी संख्या में दुष्टतापूर्ण हमले के शिकार लोगों के साथ रहने और उन्हें कुछ मात्रा में सुरक्षा प्रदान करने नहीं गये थे। वैसे आम जनता में मानव अधिकारों की यह जागरूकता 1960 के दशक में तेज हुई थी और कई क्षेत्रों में जन-सक्रियता ने अपना सभ्यताकारी प्रभाव डाला। इससे अल्पसंख्यक समूहों, स्त्रियों, भावी पीढ़ियों के अधिकारों के आंदोलन और फिर पर्यावरण सुरक्षा के आंदोलन विकसित हुए थे।

1. वर्तमान इतिहास की दो महत्वपूर्ण प्रवृत्तियाँ कौन-सी हैं?
A. आशा एवं निराशा की।
B. हिंसा एवं सभ्यता की।
C. विश्व वर्चस्व की एवं एक नई दुनिया बसाने की।
D. साम्राज्यवाद एवं उदारवाद की।

2. आज मानव अस्तित्व के लिए सबसे बड़ा खतरा क्या है?
A. वर्चस्व की प्रवृत्ति
B. हिंसा की प्रवृत्ति
C. अधीनस्थता की प्रवृत्ति
D. उपरोक्त सभी

3. मानव एकता आंदोलन ने किस रूप में सकारात्मक भूमिका निभाई?
A. इसने शासक वर्ग की मानसिकता में बदलाव लाया।
B. इसने साम्राज्यवाद के इतिहास में एक नई जमीन जोड़ी।
C. इसने मानव अधिकारों को और भी सशक्त बनाया।
D. उपरोक्त सभी।

4. उपरोक्त उद्धरण के आधार पर सही कथन का चयन कीजिए।
A. हेजीमनी मानव अस्तित्व को बनाए रखने में सहायक है।
B. 'एक नई दुनिया संभव है' का विचार शासक विचारात्मक प्रणाली के लिए खतरा है।
C. मानव एकता आंदोलन का आरंभ दक्षिण अमेरिका से हुआ।
D. उपरोक्त सभी।

उद्धरण-30

इंडिया के लिए कॉमनवेल्थ गेम्स की सफलता ने एक साथ कई काम किए हैं। गेम्स शुरू होने से पहले दुनिया भर में बनी देश की नेगेटिव छवि धुलकर पॉजिटिव हो गई। इंडिया में निवेश करने वाले इन्वेस्टर्स अब शायद बेधड़क यहां पैसा लगाएंगे। ऑस्ट्रेलियाई और अंग्रेज अब शायद एक हिंदुस्तानी को नीचे नजर से न देख पाएं। इस सफलता ने भविष्य में ओलंपिक गेम्स जैसे बड़े आयोजन को लेकर भारत की दावेदारी को भी पुख्ता किया है। भारतीय खिलाड़ियों ने 71 देशों में

दूसरा स्थान हासिल कर देश के युवाओं को दिखाया है कि कैसे खेल भी उसके लिए नाम और रुतबे का जरिया बन सकते हैं। खेलों के आयोजन में हजारों करोड़ रुपये खर्च जरूर हुए मगर इससे देश की दो पीढ़ियों के करोड़ों लोगों में खेलों के प्रति नया जज्बा भी पैदा हुआ है। इन खेलों ने हमारे कई खिलाड़ियों को गुमनामी से निकाल कर रोशनी के घेरे में खड़ा कर दिया। दीपिका कुमारी, कृष्णा पूनिया, सुरंजय, ओंकार सिंह, जिन्हें मुट्ठी भर लोग ही जानते थे, अब नेशनल हीरो बन गए हैं। इनमें कई खिलाड़ी ऐसे हैं जिन्होंने अपने माता-पिता की सुरक्षित और बेहतर करियर अपनाने की नसीहतों के खिलाफ जाकर खेलों को अपनाया। गेम्स ने देश को उनकी कामयाबी दिखाई, उन्हें अपने देशवासियों के सामने अपनी मेहनत और अपनी जिद का उत्सव मनाने का मौका दिया।

देश की गरीब जनता की जरूरतों को भुलाकर एक सर्कस शो पर करोड़ों रुपये फूंकने की दलील देने वाले गेम्स के आलोचक आगे की बजाय पीछे देखते हुए ऐसा कह रहे हैं। वे यह नहीं समझ रहे कि भारत का एक बड़ी ताकत बनने का दावा सिर्फ आंकड़ों में कैद नहीं रहना चाहिए, तमाम क्षेत्रों में दिखना चाहिए। गेम्स की कामयाबी ने यही किया है। उसने इंडिया के फ्यूचर की तस्वीर पेश की है–आत्मविश्वास से भरा, बुनियादी सुविधाओं से लैस, सफलता का जश्न मनाता हुआ इंडिया।

1. कॉमन वेल्थ गेम्स की सफलता का सबसे बड़ा लाभ क्या हुआ है?
   A. भारतीय खिलाड़ियों ने अंतर्राष्ट्रीय स्तर की खेल प्रतिभा का प्रदर्शन किया।
   B. खेल के आयोजन में करोड़ों रुपये का घोटाला हुआ।
   C. गेम्स के दौरान खिलाड़ियों को स्तरहीन सुविधाएँ उपलब्ध कराई गईं।
   D. भविष्य में ओलंपिक खेल जैसे बड़े आयोजन को लेकर भारत की दावेदारी पुख्ता हुई है।

2. आलोचकों की नजर में कॉमनवेल्थ गेम्स एक सर्कस शो क्यों था?
   A. क्योंकि इसमें सर्कस की तरह तमाशे हुए।
   B. आयोजन की तैयारी पूरी न हो पाने के कारण गेम्स एक तमाशा बनकर रह गया।
   C. इसमें देश की गरीब जनता की जरूरतों को भुलाकर अनावश्यक खर्च किए गए।
   D. उपरोक्त सभी

3. 'गुमनामी से निकालकर रोशनी के घेरे में खड़ा कर दिया' पदबंध का अर्थ बताइए–
   A. अचानक प्रसिद्धि मिलना
   B. अचानक बड़ी धनराशि मिलना
   C. रोशनी से चकाचौंध होना
   D. ऊँचा पद प्राप्त होना

4. उपरोक्त उद्धरण के आधार पर सही कथन का चयन कीजिए।
   A. कॉमनवेल्थ गेम्स से दुनिया भर में देश की अच्छी छवि बनी है।
   B. इससे दुनिया भर के निवेशक भारत में निवेश के लिए प्रोत्साहित होंगे।
   C. इससे युवाओं में एक नई स्फूर्ति पैदा हुई है।
   D. उपरोक्त सभी।

उद्धरण-31

देश में खाद्यान्न भंडारण की समस्या ने विकराल रूप धारण कर लिया है। इसकी भयावहता का अंदाजा इसी बात से लगाया जा सकता है कि एफसीआई के गोदामों में 67,542 टन अनाज नष्ट हो गया। इसकी कीमत 60 हजार करोड़ रुपए बताई गई है। सुप्रीम कोर्ट ने इसमें दखल देते हुए कहा है कि गोदामों में अनाज सड़ाने की जगह इसे गरीबों में बाँट देना चाहिए। सुप्रीम कोर्ट ने 12 अगस्त, 2010 को केन्द्र सरकार को आदेश देते हुए कहा कि वह फूड कॉरपोशन ऑफ इंडिया के गोदामों में अनाज सड़ाने की जगह गरीबों को मुफ्त बाँट दें।

जस्टिस दलवीर भंडारी और जस्टिस दीपक वर्मा की बेंच ने कहा कि और अनाज न सड़ने पाए, इसके लिए सरकार तुरंत कदम उठाए। वह उतने ही अनाज की खरीदारी करे, जितने को संभाल सकती है। साथ ही कोर्ट ने केन्द्र से प्रत्येक राज्य में एक बड़ा गोदाम और अलग-अलग जिलों व संभागों में विभिन्न गोदाम बनाने की व्यवस्था करने को कहा। इसके अलावा सरकार से यह सुनिश्चित करने को भी कहा कि उचित मूल्य की दुकानें पूरे महीने खुली रहें। कोर्ट ने सरकार को निर्देश दिया है कि वह 2010 के आंकड़ों के आधार पर बीपीएल (गरीबी रेखा से नीचे), एबीपीएल (गरीबी रेखा से ऊपर), एएवाई (अंत्योदय अन्न योजना) परिवारों का नए सिरे से सर्वे कराए। अधिकारी फायदे बांटने के लिए एक दशक पुराने आंकड़े पर भरोसा नहीं कर सकते।

बेंच ने अपना पहले का आदेश दोहराया कि एबीपीएल परिवार सब्सिडी वाला अनाज न हासिल करने पाएं। अगर सरकार उन्हें लाभ देना ही चाहती है तो उन परिवारों को दे, जिनकी सालाना आय 3 लाख रुपये से कम हो।

सुप्रसिद्ध अर्थशास्त्री डॉ. अमर्त्य सेन द्वारा 1981 में लिखी गई 'पावर्टी एंड फैमीन एंड एस्से ऑन इनटाइटिलमेंट एंड डिप्राइवेशन' (गरीबी और अकाल और पात्रता और वंचना पर निबंध) कृति में तर्क दिया गया कि अधिकांश मामलों में भूख और अकाल अनाज की उपलब्धता की कमी के कारण नहीं पड़ते, बल्कि उनका कारण असमानता और वितरण व्यवस्था की कमी होती है। उन्होंने जो बात 1981 में कही थी, संभवतः वह 2010 में भी सही है। हालांकि स्वतंत्रता प्राप्ति के बाद विगत तिरसठ वर्षों में भूख और वंचना से लड़ने के क्रम में हमने काफी अनुभव प्राप्त किया है।

1. अनाजों के भंडारण को लेकर सर्वोच्च न्यायालय ने कौन-से आदेश दिए हैं?
   A. सरकार भंडारण के बराबर क्षमता के अनाज का ही क्रय करे।

B. सरकार अलग-अलग जिलों एवं संभागों में गोदाम बनाने की व्यवस्था करे।
C. उचित मूल्य की दुकानें महीने भर खुली रहें।
D. उपरोक्त सभी

2. देश में खाद्यान्न भंडारण की समस्या का मुख्य कारण क्या है?
A. खाद्यान्न भंडारण की सीमित क्षमता
B. अत्यधिक खाद्यान्नों की खरीद
C. समय पर खाद्यान्नों का वितरण न हो पाना
D. उपरोक्त सभी

3. प्रसिद्ध अर्थशास्त्री अमर्त्य सेन के अनुसार भूख एवं अकाल का कारण है–
A. राष्ट्रीय कृषि उपज में कमी
B. कृषि निर्यात की असमानता
C. अनाजों के उपयुक्त वितरण की समस्याएं
D. A एवं C

4. कोर्ट ने किस आधार पर बीपीएल, एबीपीएल एवं एएवाई परिवारों का सर्वे कराने को कहा है?
A. 2011 की जनगणना के आधार पर
B. 2005 के आंकड़ों के आधार पर
C. 2007 के योजना आयोग के आंकड़ों के आधार पर
D. 2010 के आंकड़ों के आधार पर

उद्धरण-32

वैश्वीकरण की दौड़ में क्षेत्रीय संगठनों का महत्व बढ़ा है। आज विश्व की स्थिति यह है कि राष्ट्र अपने आपसी मतभेदों को भुलाकर व्यापार एवं आर्थिक क्षेत्रों में एक-दूसरे को सहयोग कर रहे हैं। राष्ट्रों की पारस्परिक निर्भरता पहले की अपेक्षा काफी बढ़ी है। सार्क विश्व की 22 प्रतिशत आबादी को अपने दामन में रखने वाला विश्व का सबसे बड़ा क्षेत्रीय संगठन है। भारत विश्व की उभरती हुई आर्थिक शक्ति है। सार्क के सदस्य देश आपस में एक-दूसरे का आर्थिक सहयोग करें तो इस क्षेत्र से गरीबी, भुखमरी, अशिक्षा को सदा के लिए समाप्त किया जा सकता है। आज यूरोपियन संघ एवं आसियान जैसे क्षेत्रीय संगठनों ने जो आर्थिक सफलता पायी है। उससे सार्क के नेताओं को प्रेरणा लेनी चाहिए। इन क्षेत्रीय संगठनों ने आर्थिक एकजुटता के बल पर काफी उपलब्धियाँ हासिल की हैं। अब यह स्थिति स्पष्ट हो चुकी है कि आर्थिक विकास में क्षेत्रीय वैश्वीकरण की भूमिका अतिमहत्वपूर्ण है।

जनवरी 2009 में इस्लामाबाद में हुए सम्मेलन में इस तरह की स्पष्ट अभिव्यक्ति सामने आई। इस सम्मेलन में सार्क देशों ने 2012 तक दक्षिण एशियाई स्वतंत्र व्यापार क्षेत्र (साफ्टा) बनाने की इच्छा व्यक्त की है, लेकिन इस दिशा में अभी तक कोई ठोस कार्य नहीं हुआ है। साफ्टा के बारे में छोटे-छोटे देशों को यह भ्रम पैदा हो गया कि इससे भारत को ही अधिक लाभ होगा, जबकि सच्चाई यह नहीं है। उदाहरणस्वरूप अभी हम भारत, श्रीलंका के मुक्त व्यापार को देखें। दोनों देशों के बीच मुक्त व्यापार पिछले तीन वर्ष से चल रहा है। श्रीलंका का भारत को निर्यात 135 प्रतिशत सालाना की दर से बढ़ा है। इस तुलना में भारत का श्रीलंका को निर्यात 32 प्रतिशत की दर से बढ़ा है। अपितु मुक्त व्यापार के होने से श्रीलंका भारत की अपेक्षा अधिक लाभ की स्थिति में है। यही बात नेपाल एवं भूटान के साथ हैं। पाकिस्तान एवं बांग्लादेश के साथ भारत का व्यापार उतना नहीं बढ़ा है जितना बढ़ना चाहिए। इन देशों के असहयोग के कारण भी साफ्टा को लागू करने में कठिनाई है।

1. वैश्वीकरण के कारण क्षेत्रीय संगठनों का महत्व बढ़ा है–
A. क्योंकि वैश्वीकरण के दौरान विभिन्न देशों के बीच व्यापार बढ़ा है।
B. राष्ट्र अपने आपसी मतभेद को भूलाकर आर्थिक क्षेत्र में एक-दूसरे को सहयोग कर रहे हैं।
C. सभी राष्ट्रों ने व्यापार को सीमाकर मुक्त कर दिया है।
D. अंतर्राष्ट्रीय बाजार में डॉलर का मूल्य घटा है।

2. उपरोक्त उद्धरण के आधार पर सही कथन का चयन कीजिए।
A. हाल के वर्षो में राष्ट्रों के बीच पारस्परिक निर्भरता बढ़ी है।
B. सार्क दुनिया का सबसे बड़ा क्षेत्रीय संगठन है।
C. सार्क देशों में दुनिया की लगभग 1/4 आबादी रहती है।
D. उपरोक्त सभी।

3. सार्क देशों के बीच आपसी व्यापार में पर्याप्त वृद्धि नहीं हुई है, इसका क्या कारण है?
A. सार्क देशों के बीच व्यापार प्रतिबंध
B. आपसी सहयोग का अभाव
C. पश्चिमी देशों पर अत्यधिक निर्भरता
D. व्यापारिक निवेश का अभाव

4. साफ्टा को लेकर सार्क देशों में कौन-सा भ्रम फैला हुआ है?
A. इससे भारत को अधिक लाभ होगा।
B. भारत एक आर्थिक महाशक्ति बन जाएगा।
C. भारत का प्रभाव दुनिया के अन्य देशों में बढ़ जाएगा।
D. भारतीय रुपया और भी मजबूत होगा।

उद्धरण-33

महामशीन के महाप्रयोग का उद्देश्य परमाणु कणों की आपसी टक्कर को देखना है, जिनसे नए कण बन सकते हैं। उनका वेग और ऊर्जा मापकर मालूम हो सकता है कि आखिर शुरू में ब्रह्माण्ड कैसे बना और बाद में कैसे उसकी उत्पत्ति हुई। एलएचसी के इस प्रयोग में परमाणु कणों की बहुत अधिक वेग से अब तक की सबसे अधिक ऊर्जा से टक्कर हुई। आशा की जा रही है कि अब वैज्ञानिक भौतिकी की अनेक गुत्थियों को सुलझा लेंगे।

50,000 करोड़ रुपए की लागत से बना लार्ज हैड्रॉन कोलाइडर (LHC) 2008 में असफल हो गया था। उस समय इस सबसे बड़े एटम स्मैशर में दो शक्तिशाली चुम्बकों के बीच विद्युत कनेक्शन फ्यूज हो गया था। इन चुम्बक प्रोटॉनों को स्टीआर कहते हैं। इस खराबी से सुरंग में बड़े जोर का विस्फोट हुआ था, लेकिन इस बार का प्रयोग सफल रहा। एलएचसी प्रसिद्ध ईश्वरीय कण 'हिग्स बोसोन' के चिह्न की भी पहचान करेगा। बताया जाता है कि इसी कण के कारण ब्रह्माण्ड की सभी चीजों को पिण्ड भार मिलता है। इसके अलावा रहस्यमयी 'ब्लैक होल' की भी पहचान की जाएगी, जिससे काफी हद तक ब्रह्माण्ड बना है, लेकिन इसमें अंधेरा होने के कारण अब तक इसके दर्शन नहीं हुए हैं। वैज्ञानिकों का कहना है कि एलएचसी में जब कणों की टक्कर हुई, तब अनेक ऐसे मिनी बिग बैंग बने, जैसे आज से 13 अरब, 70 करोड़ वर्ष पहले बने थे।

इन असाधारण खोजों के अतिरिक्त मशीन बिग बैंग के पहले और बाद के कणों की नकल करेगी। गुरुत्वाकर्षण के रहस्य भी जानने के प्रयत्न किए जाएंगे। इस अनुसंधान में लगे वैज्ञानिकों का कहना है कि जब कणों की बीमों की टक्कर हुई तब सभी डिटेक्टरों ने अपने परमाणु कणों के बहुरंगी मार्गों की पहचान की। ये कण प्रत्येक दिशा में कार्यशील थे। भौतिकविद् का कहना है कि जब उप परमाणु कण बड़े वेग से आपस में टकराते हैं तो वे टूटकर नए तत्व बनाते हैं। आशा की जा रही है कि इसमें से एक तत्व हिग्स बोसोन होगा जिससे हमारे ब्रह्माण्ड बनने की गुत्थी सुलझेगी। वैज्ञानिकों का कहना है कि प्रयोग में उत्सर्जित ऊर्जा फील्ड को यदि ऊष्मा में बदल दिया जाए तो यह सूर्य की सतह से भी ज्यादा गर्म होगा।

1. महामशीन ब्रह्माण्ड की उत्पत्ति की जाँच किस आधार पर करेगा?
   A. परमाणु कणों की आपसी टक्कर से उत्पन्न वेग के आधार पर
   B. परमाणु कणों के बीच आपसी आकर्षण के आधार पर
   C. परमाणु कणों की आपसी टक्कर से उत्पन्न वेग एवं ऊर्जा के आधार पर
   D. परमाणु कणों के गुरुत्वाकर्षण के आधार पर

2. लार्ज हैड्रॉन कोलाइडर की पिछली असफलता का क्या कारण था?
   A. चुम्बकीय विद्युत कनेक्शन का फ्यूज होना
   B. हिग्स बोसोन कण का रिसाव
   C. परमाणु कणों के बीच तीव्र विकर्षण
   D. परमाणु कणों का विस्फोट

3. ब्रह्मांड के पिंडों का पिंड भार किस पर निर्भर करता है?
   A. पिंड के द्रव्यमान पर
   B. पिंड के घनत्व पर
   C. हिग्स बोसोन कण पर
   D. A एवं B दोनों पर

4. हिग्स बोसोन कण का निर्माण होता है–
   A. जब उप परमाणु कण तीव्र वेग से आपस में टकराते हैं।
   B. परमाणु कणों के बीच तीव्र आकर्षण बल के कारण।
   C. परमाणु कणों के बीमों के साथ टक्कर से।
   D. A एवं B दोनों

उद्धरण-34

विज्ञान शब्द की परिभाषा तथा इसके विस्तार, और प्रौद्योगिकी से इसके भेद को भी स्पष्ट रूप से समझ लेना जरूरी है। मानव जाति के भविष्य की कुंजी जिन कुछ शक्तिशाली ताकतों के हाथ में है, उनमें से विज्ञान संभवतः एकमात्र ऐसी ताकत है, जिसे एक अनूठा स्थान प्राप्त है क्योंकि वस्तुतः निरपवाद रूप से इसे सभी स्वीकार करते हैं। उन गिने-चुने व्यक्तियों के मामले में भी, जो विज्ञान के प्रति नफरत रखने वाले दिखाई देते हैं, उनके साथ भी एक बार बातचीत करने पर यह तथ्य उभरकर सामने आएगा कि वे वास्तव में विज्ञान के विरुद्ध नहीं हैं, बल्कि प्रौद्योगिकी के विरुद्ध हैं, जिसका सम्बन्ध मानव की विविध जरूरतों को पूरा करने के लिए विज्ञान के निष्कर्षों के अनुप्रयोगों से है।

वर्तमान समय में विज्ञान से हमारा अभिप्राय है हमारे विश्व तथा इसके परिवेश का मौलिक ज्ञान, उस ज्ञान का इसके सभी पहलुओं में, नियंत्रित तथा निरन्तर अनुसरण करना, इसके लिये जरूरी नहीं कि उसका प्रयोग सार्वजनिक प्रयोजनों के लिए किया जाए। प्रौद्योगिकी से हमारा आशय विज्ञान को मानव सेवा में लगाने के विभिन्न तरीकों से है, उन तरीकों का संकेन्द्रित अध्ययन जिनमें चीजों को मानव-प्रयोजन के लिए रचा या बदला जा सकता है। दोनों में स्पष्ट अन्तर करने के लिए इस समय आण्विक विज्ञान तथा टेक्नोलॉजी के सर्वाधिक लोकप्रिय क्षेत्रों से उदाहरण दिए जा सकते हैं। जब भारी धात्विक तत्व यूरेनियम के केन्द्रक का विखंडन या विस्फोटन होता है तब उससे निःसृत होने वाले कणों की संख्या तथा प्रकृति का मापन विज्ञान द्वारा ही किया जाता है। लेकिन, जब इस वैज्ञानिक ज्ञान का प्रयोग विद्युत उत्पादन के लिये परमाणु बिजली घर डिजाइन करने तथा बनाने अथवा एक परमाणु बम डिजाइन करने और बनाने के लिए किया जाता है तो यह प्रौद्योगिकी होती है। इस प्रकार, यह प्रौद्योगिकी ही होती है जो नैतिक रंग ले लेती है और इसे नैतिक या अनैतिक कहा जा सकता है। विज्ञान तटस्थ या नैतिकता से परे होता है और वह नैतिक-आचार या मानव कल्याण के विरुद्ध नहीं होता, हालांकि एक वैज्ञानिक एक मनुष्य तथा टेक्नोलाजिस्ट होने के नाते इसके विरुद्ध हो सकता है।

1. लेखक
   A. विज्ञान के प्रति बेहतर रवैया अपनाये जाने के लिए वकालत करने की कोशिश कर रहा है
   B. यह सुझाव देने की कोशिश कर रहा है कि हम विज्ञान का सार्वजनिक हित के लिए प्रयोग करें
   C. भौतिक विज्ञान के बजाय नैतिक विज्ञान का अध्ययन करने की कोशिश कर रहा है

D. विज्ञान तथा प्रौद्योगिकी (टेक्नोलाजी) के बीच भेद करने की कोशिश कर रहा है

2. लेखक के अनुसार, विज्ञान

A. एकमात्र ऐसी ताकत है, जो मानवजाति के भविष्य का निर्धारण करती है

B. मानव की नियति को निर्धारित करने वाली चन्द एक ताकतों में से एक है

C. भविष्य में मानवजाति की एकमात्र चिन्ता होगी

D. उन अनेक बाधाओं में से एक है जो मनुष्य की प्रगति में रुकावट डालती है

3. यह अवतरण

A. आलंकारिक है B. वर्णनात्मक है

C. वृत्तात्मक है D. व्याख्यात्मक है

4. यूरेनियम केन्द्रक के विस्फोट के अध्ययन को

A. आधुनिक प्रौद्योगिकी (टेक्नोलाजी) का एक उदाहरण कहा जा सकता है

B. विद्युत-सिद्धांतों का एक अनुप्रयोग कहा जा सकता है

C. ऐसा अध्ययन कहा जा सकता है जिसके कोई भौतिक निहितार्थ नहीं हैं

D. समूची मानवजाति के कल्याण के लिए महत्त्वपूर्ण कहा जा सकता है

उद्धरण-35

बच्चे किसी देश के सामाजिक तथा राजनीतिक दर्शन का अंग होते हैं। उनके प्रति जो रवैये अपनाये जाते हैं वे इस बात का निर्धारण करने में महत्त्वपूर्ण कारक होते हैं कि क्या उनकी जरूरतें पूरी होंगी तथा उनके अधिकार उन्हें मिलेंगे। भविष्योन्मुख कोई भी समाज इस बात का ध्यान रखेगा कि विपदा के समय बच्चों का ख्याल रखा जाये। इस समय विश्व के अनेक भागों में बच्चों को शांति तथा भाई-चारे की भावना के साथ पाले-पोसे जाने का कोई अवसर प्राप्त नहीं है। युद्ध तथा आतंकवाद के जो अत्यधिक भयावह रिकार्ड मिलते हैं वे हमेशा अपने घरों के खण्डहरों तथा अपने परिवारों के शवों के पास रोने के लिए बचे हुए शिशुओं या छोटे बच्चों की (या इतने सहमे हुए बच्चों की जो रो भी नहीं पाते) तस्वीरें होती हैं। ऐसे देशों में जहां लड़ाई-झगड़ा चल रहा हो या ऐसे समाजों में जहां ऐसी कार्यवाहियों को मनमोहक ढंग से पेश किया जाता हो, वहां बच्चों का निर्बाध रूप से खेलना जीवन की घटनाओं तथा/या ऐसी घटनाओं की सामाजिक स्वीकृति को परिलक्षित करेगा, जो हम सभी को यह सोचने पर मजबूर कर देगा कि क्या इस प्रकार के राष्ट्रीय दर्शनों से प्रभावित करोड़ों बच्चों को शांति की भावना के साथ बड़े होने के उनके अधिकार मिलने की कोई संभावना है। और निश्चय ही, "जाति, रंग, लिंग, राष्ट्रीय या सामाजिक मूल के धर्म" पर अकेले या कुछेक के मेल पर आधारित भेदभाव करोड़ों बच्चों को, जरूरतों की सार्वत्रिकता के बावजूद, जिन पर अधिकार आधारित होते हैं, इन अधिकारों से वंचित रखता है।

1. निम्नलिखित में से कौन-सा कथन बच्चों में शांति तथा भाई-चारे की भावना के विकास के लिए सहायक नहीं है?

A. जब वयोवृद्ध बच्चों को युद्ध के संत्रासों का अनुभव करने के लिए छोड़ देते हैं

B. जब प्रौढ़ लोग जातीय भेद-भाव का व्यवहार करते हैं

C. जब किसी देश का राजनीतिक दर्शन विश्वव्यापी भाई-चारे की वकालत करता है

D. जब समाज युद्ध के कार्यकलापों को मनमोहक ढंग से पेश करता है

2. प्रौढ़ों का बच्चों के प्रति एक कर्त्तव्य है। किसी समाज विशेष में बच्चों की देखभाल कितनी अच्छी तरह से होती है इसका पता इस बात से चल सकता है कि

A. विपदा के समय उनके लिए क्या किया जाता है

B. वे प्रौढ़ों का कितना ख्याल रखते हैं

C. प्रौढ़ उनके अधिकारों के प्रति कितने संवेदनशील हैं

D. समाज कितना समृद्ध है

3. लेखक की धारणा है कि

A. युद्धों के बावजूद बच्चे शान्तिपूर्वक रहने के अपने अधिकारों को प्राप्त कर लेते हैं

B. बच्चों के अधिकार सामाजिक दशाओं पर निर्भर होने चाहिए

C. बच्चों को शांति की भावना के साथ बड़ा होने का अधिकार है

D. राष्ट्रीय दर्शन बच्चों के अधिकारों का समर्थन करते हैं

4. युद्ध सम्बन्धी कार्यकलापों

A. का समाजों द्वारा परिहार किया जाता है

B. को समाजों द्वारा परिलक्षित किया जाता है

C. की समाजों द्वारा निन्दा की जाती है

D. को समाजों द्वारा स्वीकार किया जाता है

उद्धरण-36

हम सभी चिकित्सा विज्ञान के क्षेत्र में हुई कतिपय उल्लेखनीय खोजों से परिचित हैं। मिसाल के तौर पर, हम वेक्सीनों की खोज के बारे में जानते हैं। हम चेचक तथा पोलियो जैसे रोगों की रोकथाम को समझ सकते हैं। हम अनेक साधारण एंटीबायोटिक्स के बारे में भी जानते हैं। यह जानकारी कि हम उपदंश रोग पर पेनिसिलीन और तपेदिक पर आइसोनाइजिड से काबू पा सकते हैं, कुछ हद तक आश्वासनदायक है। हम इस विश्वास के आधार पर निश्चय ही अपने आपको झूठी तसल्ली दे सकते हैं कि संक्रामक रोग अब कोई खतरा नहीं रहे हैं। लेकिन यह सत्य नहीं है और समाचारों तथा मेडिकल जर्नलों में हाल में छपे समाचार हमें संक्रामक रोगों के विभिन्न तथा कभी-कभी 'नए' खतरों की याद दिलाते हैं।

ऐसे समाचारों में अपेक्षाकृत अधिक यथार्थवादी दृष्टिकोण को स्वीकार किया गया है। इस दृष्टिकोण का निहितार्थ यह

है कि संक्रामक रोग बने रहेंगे और यह कि उनके अन्दर कुछ ऐसी क्षमताएं हैं कि वे उन्हें खत्म कर देने की हमारी कोशिशों के खिलाफ लड़ सकते हैं। कतिपय मानव-व्याधियों, जैसे सुजाक रोग, तत्त्व-गुण (Strains) विकसित हो गए हैं जिन पर कतिपय एंटीबायोटिक्स का कोई असर नहीं होता।

1. चेचक तथा पोलियो जैसे रोगों की रोकथाम किसकी खोज के कारण संभव हो सकी है?

A. पेनिसिलीन B. आइसोनाइजिड

C. वेक्सीन D. एंटीबायोटिक्स

2. चिकित्सा विज्ञान के क्षेत्र में खोजों के द्वारा अब तक क्या संभव नहीं हो पाया है?

A. चेचक तथा पोलियो की रोकथाम

B. पेनिसिलीन की सहायता से उपदंश रोग के फैलाव पर नियंत्रण करने की संभावना

C. संक्रामक रोगों का उन्मूलन

D. आइसोनाइजिड की सहायता से तपेदिक के फैलाव पर नियंत्रण करने की संभावना

3. कुछ संक्रामक रोग उन्हें खत्म कर देने के हमारे प्रयासों के खिलाफ कैसे लड़ते हैं?

A. अन्य क्षेत्रों में अंतरित होकर

B. वेक्सीनों को प्रभावहीन बनाने की शक्ति विकसित करके

C. पहले की तरह भ्रांतिजनक बने रहकर

D. मानव-तंत्रिका में गहरे पैठ कर

4. यह अवतरण

A. सूचना देने वाला है B. वृत्तात्मक है

C. नाटकीय है D. प्रोत्साहक है

उद्धरण-37

प्रत्येक व्यवसाय अथवा व्यापार, कला और विज्ञान की अपनी तकनीकी शब्दावली होती है, जिसका कार्य अंशतः उन प्रक्रियाओं और वस्तुओं को दर्शाना होता है जिनके नाम सामान्य अंग्रेजी में नहीं मिलते और अंशतः पारिभाषिक शब्दावली में पूर्ण यथार्थता प्राप्त करना होता है। किसी भी प्रकार की तकनीकी बातचीत में ऐसी विशिष्ट भाषिका अथवा शब्दजाल की आवश्यकता होती है। विज्ञान अथवा कला विशेष के अध्येताओं के लिए सर्वविदित होने के साथ-साथ गणितीय सूत्र जैसी सूक्ष्मता रखते हैं। साथ ही, वे समय बचाते हैं, किसी प्रक्रिया का वर्णन करने की अपेक्षा उसका नाम लेना अधिक किफायती है। ऐसे हजारों पारिभाषिक शब्द बहुत अच्छी तरह इन शब्दकोशों में संकलित किए गए हैं, फिर भी, कुल मिलाकर, वे अंग्रेजी भाषा की मूल शब्दावली के बजाय उसके आस-पास ही ठहरते हैं। फिर भी विभिन्न व्यवसाय अपनी विशिष्ट शब्दावली की दृष्टि से पर्याप्त भिन्नता लिए हुए हैं। व्यापार, हस्तकला, कृषि और मछलीपालन जैसे अन्य व्यवसायों में जहाँ लम्बे समय से भारी संख्या में लोग लगे हैं, तकनीकी शब्दावली बहुत पुरानी है। इसमें अधिकतर स्थानीय शब्द मिलते हैं अथवा ऐसे आयातित शब्द हैं जो हमारी भाषा में घुल-मिल गए हैं। अतः अनेक रूपों में पूर्णतः तकनीकी होते हुए भी ये शब्दावलियां बोलने में अधिक परिचित-सी हैं और अन्य अधिकांश तकनीकीय तुलना में अधिक सहजता से समझी जाती हैं।

कानून, औषधि, धर्मविज्ञान और दर्शन की विशिष्ट भाषिका भी अपने प्राचीन रूप में परिष्कृत व्यक्तियों में पर्याप्त परिचित हो गई है, और प्रचलित शब्दावली में काफी योगदान कर चुकी है फिर भी प्रत्येक व्यवसाय आज भी ऐसी बहुत-सी तकनीकी शब्दावली लिए हुए है जो मूलतः विदेशी हैं। यह अनुपात पिछले पचास वर्षों में अधिक बढ़ा है विशेषतः यांत्रिक कलाओं, प्राकृतिक विज्ञान और राजनीति विज्ञान के विभिन्न क्षेत्रों में। यहाँ पूरी आजादी से नए शब्दों को शामिल कर लिया गया है और व्यर्थ हो जाने पर छोड़ दिया गया है। अधिकतर नए पद विशिष्ट बातचीत तक सीमित रहे हैं, कभी-कभी ही सामान्य बातचीत अथवा साहित्य जुड़ पाए हैं। पर आज कोई भी व्यवसाय, जैसा कि पहले सभी थे बंद निकाय नहीं हैं। वकील, चिकित्सक, वैज्ञानिक और पादरी अपने साथी सृजनकर्त्ताओं से जुड़ता है और ऐसा नहीं है कि मात्र व्यावसायिक रूप से ही मिलता है। बल्कि आज का प्रचलित विज्ञान प्रत्येक व्यक्ति को आधुनिक विचारों और खोजों से जोड़ता है। कोई भी महत्त्वपूर्ण प्रयोग चाहे वह दूर अथवा क्षेत्रीय प्रयोगशाला में किया गया हो, समाचार-पत्रों में तुरंत प्रकाशित हो जाता है और हर एक व्यक्ति उसके बारे में ऐसे ही बात करना शुरू कर देता है जैसे विकिरण किरणों और बेतारी तार-संचार के बारे में बात करता है। अतः हमारी सामान्य बोली सदैव नए तकनीकी शब्दों को अपना रही है और उन्हें प्रचलित कर रही है।

1. तकनीकी शब्दावली बढ़ाई जा सकती है :

A. नए शब्द बनाकर, विदेशी भाषाओं से शब्द ग्रहण करके और पुराने हुए शब्दों को निकालकर

B. नई अवधारणाओं के लिए नए शब्द गढ़कर

C. नए शब्द ढालकर और विदेशी भाषाओं से शब्द आयात करके

D. विदेशी शब्दों का अपनी भाषा में अनुवाद करके

2. प्रचलित विज्ञान, प्रत्येक व्यक्ति को परिचित कराता है

A. आधुनिक विचारों और नवीन खोजों से

B. नवीन खोजों और आविष्कारों से

C. आधुनिक विचारों, नवीन खोजों और तकनीक से

D. विज्ञान और तकनीक में नए विकास से

3. तकनीकी शब्दावली सभी की भाषा का अंग बन गई है :

A. व्यावसायिकों के प्रयासों द्वारा

B. विदेशी भाषा पढ़कर

C. प्रचलित वैज्ञानिक लेखों और समाचारपत्रों द्वारा

D. भाषा के परिवर्तनों द्वारा

4. तकनीकी शब्द हैं :

A. संक्षिप्त, किफायती और नामात्मक

B. नवीन, कठिन पर आवश्यक

C. भाषा की मूल शब्दावली से चुने हुए

D. सभी द्वारा सामान्य रूप से समझे जाने वाले

उद्धरण-38

मैं इस अंधविश्वास को जानता हूँ कि आत्म-ज्ञान जीवन की चौथी अवस्था में ही सम्भव है और वह है संन्यास। पर इस बात को सभी जानते हैं कि जो इस अमूल्य अनुभव को जीवन के अन्तिम क्षणों के लिए टालते हैं वे आत्म-ज्ञान प्राप्त नहीं करते बल्कि द्वितीय और दयनीय बचपन के समान बुढ़ापे को प्राप्त करते हैं और पृथ्वी पर एक भार की तरह जीते हैं। मुझे पूरी तरह याद है कि जब मैं 1911-12 में पढ़ाता था तब भी इसी विचार को मानता था भले ही इसी तरह की भाषा में उसे अभिव्यक्त न किया हो।

तब किस प्रकार यह आध्यात्मिक प्रशिक्षण दिया जाना था? मैंने बच्चों को भजन याद कराये और उनका अभ्यास कराया और उन्हें नैतिक शिक्षा की पुस्तकों से पढ़कर सुनाया। पर यह सब मेरे लिए संतोषजनक नहीं था। जब मैं उनके और अधिक निकट आया तो पाया कि अध्यात्म का प्रशिक्षण केवल पुस्तकों के माध्यम से नहीं कराया जा सकता। उसी प्रकार जैसे शारीरिक प्रशिक्षण व्यायाम के माध्यम से दिया जाता है और बौद्धिक अभ्यास के द्वारा, अतः अध्यात्म का प्रशिक्षण भी अध्यात्म के अभ्यास से संभव था। और अध्यात्म का प्रशिक्षण पूर्णतः अध्यापक के जीवन और चरित्र पर निर्भर करता है। अध्यापक चाहे विद्यार्थियों के बीच में है अथवा नहीं उसे सदैव अपने व्यवहार और चरित्र का ध्यान रखना है।

1. ऊपर उधृत पाठ सामग्री के लिए सर्वाधिक उपयुक्त शीर्षक है :

A. बौद्धिक अभ्यास B. अंधविश्वास

C. आध्यात्मिक विकास D. प्रशिक्षण

2. व्यापक स्तर पर आत्म-ज्ञान के बारे में लोगों के बीच अंधविश्वास है कि यह

A. अनवरत प्रक्रिया है

B. केवल संन्यास द्वारा संभव है

C. केवल आरम्भिक जीवन में संभव है

D. एक मिथक है

3. लेखक के अनुसार बच्चों का आध्यात्मिक प्रशिक्षण मुख्यतः किसके चरित्र पर निर्भर है?

A. अभिभावकों के B. अभिजात वर्ग के

C. सामाजिक नेताओं के D. अध्यापकों के

4. लेखक का बुढ़ापे के बारे में पहले विचार था कि यह

A. एक गुण है B. एक अभिशाप है

C. विचारों की स्मृति है D. संतोष है

उद्धरण-39

क्या विद्यार्थियों द्वारा प्राप्त किये गये परिणामों से अध्यापन-कार्य का मूल्यांकन किया जा सकता है? कुछ हद तक अध्यापकों को इसी प्रकार आँका जाता है, प्रायः सामूहिक रूप से, किसी संस्थान की ख्याति के रूप में। परन्तु इसमें कुछ कठिनाइयाँ हैं। विशेष रूप से उल्लेखनीय कठिनाई, जिसे स्क्राइवन (1988) ने 'हार्वर्ड फैलेसी (भ्रामकता)' के नाम से वर्णित किया है, इस प्रकार है :

...यह मान लेने की भ्रामकता कि हार्वर्ड में पढ़ाई अच्छी होती होगी क्योंकि यहां के स्नातक अपने बाद के जीवन में अच्छी तरक्की करते हैं ...इन आँकड़ों से यही परिणाम निकाला जा सकता है कि हार्वर्ड में मस्तिष्क को स्थायी हानि नहीं पहुँचाई जाती–सामान्यतया। बाकी की युक्ति केवल इतनी-सी है कि प्रतिभाशाली विद्यार्थियों का चयन कर कक्षाओं में भेजा जाए और उनके मार्ग में कोई रुकावट खड़ी न की जाए। उन्हें पुस्तकालय, प्रयोगशाला, पीयर ट्यूटरिंग और परिवार के प्रभाव या नाम के प्रति आदर का उपयोग करने दिया जाए। अध्यापकों का योगदान यदि कोई है तो वह अवशेष जो दूसरे कारणों से अलग करने के बाद बचता है जैसे कि ...'पुराने विद्यार्थियों के जाल' और नाम की मान्यता का नौकरी के लिए चयन और पदोन्नति पर प्रभाव। यद्यपि हार्वर्ड प्रमाण्यतः एक महान विश्वविद्यालय है तथापि निश्चित रूप से यह प्रमाण्यतः एक महान अध्यापन विश्वविद्यालय नहीं है बल्कि केवल एक भव्य रूप से सुसज्जित विश्वविद्यालय।

दूसरे देशों के विश्वविद्यालयों को स्पष्टतः हार्वर्ड के स्थान पर रखा जा सकता है। लेकिन फिर भी यदि एक जैसे संस्थानों के एक जैसे पाठ्यक्रमों के परिणामों की तुलना करना सम्भव हो तो भी सफलता का श्रेय दूसरे कारणों को देने की बजाय अध्यापन को देने के बारे में स्क्राइवन का तर्क विचारणीय रहेगा। किसी प्रकार के 'मूल्य-जुड़े' पैमाने से भी यह सम्भव नहीं होगा और ऐसे पैमाने या तो इतने अपक्व होंगे कि उनका कोई अर्थ ही नहीं होगा या फिर इतने जटिल होंगे कि जाँचने और आँकने के लिए पढ़ाने और सीखने की केन्द्रित गतिविधियों के मुकाबले में बहुत अधिक समय की आवश्यकता होगी। एक ही संस्थान में एक वर्ष के परिणामों की अगले वर्ष के परिणामों से तुलना करने में भी कठिनाइयाँ सामने आती हैं क्योंकि विभागों में और विद्यार्थियों में परिस्थितियाँ बदलती रहती हैं।

1. इस परिच्छेद का शीर्षक क्या हो सकता है?

A. हार्वर्ड विश्वविद्यालय में अध्यापन

B. विद्यार्थियों के परिणामों से अध्यापन-कार्य का मूल्यांकन

C. संस्थानों की प्रतिष्ठा

D. अध्यापकों के मूल्यांकन के लिए अवशिष्ट पद्धति

2. हार्वर्ड फैलेसी (भ्रामकता) का अर्थ है :

A. यह मान लेना कि प्रतिष्ठित संस्थानों में पढ़ाई अच्छी होती है

B. जो कुछ हार्वर्ड में भ्रामक रूप से किया जा रहा है

C. कि हार्वर्ड में प्रतिभाशाली विद्यार्थियों को दाखिला दिया जाता है और अच्छे परिणाम प्राप्त किये जाते हैं

D. कि हार्वर्ड में जो अध्यापन कार्य होता है उसमें बहुत-सी भ्रामकतायें हैं

3. विद्यार्थियों की उपलब्धियों में अध्यापकों के योगदान को स्क्राइवन के अनुसार किस बात से आँका जाना चाहिए?

A. स्नातकों द्वारा बाद के जीवन में अर्जित उपलब्धियों से

B. विद्यार्थियों के दाखिले के लिए संस्थानों द्वारा निर्धारित मानदण्डों से

C. बाकी सभी कारणों को निकालने के बाद बचे अवशिष्ट प्रभाव से
D. संस्थानों में उपलब्ध सुविधाओं से

4. स्क्राइवन के अनुसार हार्वर्ड की प्रतिष्ठा किस कारण से है?
A. इसका प्रचुर मात्रा में सुविधाओं से सम्पन्न होना
B. प्रतिभाशाली विद्यार्थियों को दाखिला और उनके मार्ग में रुकावट न डालना
C. इसका एक महान अध्यापन विश्वविद्यालय होना
D. इसके अपक्व और अर्थहीन तरीके जिनसे अध्यापन-कार्य की प्रभाविकता को माना जाता है

उद्धरण-40

संतान को बुढ़ापे की लाठी माना जाता है, परन्तु जब यह लाठी ही सहारा देने के बजाय मां-बाप को प्रताड़ना देने के लिए इस्तेमाल होने लगे तो संबंधों का क्या होगा? समाज और सरकार परम्पराओं को तोड़कर पैदा की जा रही विकृतियों की कब तक उपेक्षा कर सकते हैं? जाहिर है कि इन हालात में समाज व कानून के हस्तक्षेप की तैयारी पुख्ता हो जाती है। संसद द्वारा पारित द मेंटिनेन्स एंड वेलफेयर ऑफ पेरेंट्स एंड सीनियर सिटीजन बिल, 2007 एक प्रकार से ऐसा ही एक हस्तक्षेप है। बस देखना यही होगा कि इस हस्तक्षेप के लिए निर्धारित प्रावधानों का किस हद तक व कितना प्रभावी तरीके से इस्तेमाल होता है।

कानून तो बन गया है परन्तु इस पर अमल की चुनौतियां कम नहीं होंगी। कितने प्रताड़ित अभिभावक कानून के इस संरक्षण के प्रति जागरूक बन सकेंगे और कितने इस कानून के प्रावधानों के इस्तेमाल का संकल्प कर सकेंगे, उनका सचमुच इस्तेमाल कर न्याय हासिल कर सकेंगे? यहां पर समाज व सामाजिक एवं स्वयंसेवी संगठनों की भूमिका महत्त्वपूर्ण हो जाती है। उन्हें न केवल जागृति उत्पन्न करनी होगी बल्कि कानून के सदुपयोग के लिए सक्रिय भूमिका का निर्वाह भी करना होगा। यदि एक दफा इस कानून के अच्छे नतीजे सामने आने लगे तो ये मां-बाप की उपेक्षा की राह पर चलने वाली संतानों के लिए निषेधात्मक उपाय के रूप में भी प्रतिष्ठित हो सकेंगे।

1. सरकार को नया बिल संसद में क्यों लाना पड़ा?
A. इसके लिए सरकार पर दबाव डाला जा रहा था।
B. संसदीय समिति ने इस बारे में सुझाव सरकार के सामने रखे थे।
C. संतान द्वारा माता-पिता की उपेक्षा एक आम प्रचलन बनता जा रहा था।
D. A एवं C दोनों

2. नए कानून पर अमल के लिए सरकार को क्या करनी चाहिए?
A. न्यायिक प्रक्रिया में सुधार लानी चाहिए।
B. पुलिस कार्रवाई में तेजी लानी चाहिए।
C. जन-जागृति पैदा करनी चाहिए।
D. उपरोक्त सभी।

3. इस कानून को लागू करने में कौन-सी चुनौतियाँ हैं?
A. अभिभावकों को कानून के प्रति जागरूक बनाना।
B. कानून का सदुपयोग सुनिश्चित करना।
C. इससे जुड़े अपराध को रोकना।
D. A एवं B दोनों।

4. उपरोक्त उद्धरण के आधार पर सही कथन का चयन कीजिए।
A. संसद द्वारा पेरेंट्स एंड सीनियर सिटीजन बिल, 2008 में पारित किया गया।
B. यह कानून 65 वर्ष से अधिक उम्र के माता-पिता पर लागू होता है।
C. माता एवं पिता में से कोई भी इस कानून के तहत् अपना हक मांग सकता है।
D. इस कानून को सफल बनाने में स्वयंसेवी संगठनों को सक्रिय भूमिका निभानी होगी।

उद्धरण-41

भारत में नारी की स्तुति प्राचीनकाल से की जाती रही है "यत्र नार्यस्तु पूज्यन्ते रमन्ते तत्र देवता," इत्यादि के रूप में। यहाँ तक कि असुरों पर विजय प्राप्त करने हेतु भी देवताओं को नारी की शरण में जाना पड़ा था और देवी दुर्गा ने ही असुरों का संहार किया था। विद्या की देवी महासरस्वती, धन की देवी महालक्ष्मी और दुष्टों का नाश करने वाली महाकाली की आराधना की जाती है।

आधुनिक काल में भारत की आजादी की लड़ाई में महिलाओं ने पर्दा-प्रथा का त्याग कर देश को स्वतंत्रता दिलाने हेतु बढ़-चढ़कर हिस्सा लिया। आजाद भारत में महिलाओं को वोट देने का समान अधिकार दिया गया। हम सब जानते हैं कि आज की महिला जीवन के किसी भी क्षेत्र में पुरुषों से पीछे नहीं है। सर्वत्र अपनी विजय पताका फहरा रही है। माता-पिता ने भी समयानुसार आकाश छूने की आजादी दे दी है।

यह तो है महिला की तस्वीरों का एक पहलू। अब जरा दूसरे पहलू पर भी दृष्टि डालें। आज भी महिला शोषण का शिकार हो रही है। आश्चर्य की बात तो यह है कि यह शोषण अनपढ़, गाँव की महिलाओं के साथ ही नहीं, पढ़ी लिखी, ऊँचे पदों पर प्रतिष्ठित महिलाओं के साथ भी जारी है। फिर चाहे वह यौन शोषण हो, समाज द्वारा किया गया शोषण हो, अंधविश्वास के कारण हो या पुरुषों द्वारा अपना वर्चस्व बनाए रखने के कारण हो, महिलाएँ इसे सहने को अभिशप्त हैं। वैज्ञानिक शोधों को नकारते हुए संतानहीनता का दोष उसे ही भोगना पड़ता है। विधवा नारी को दी जाने वाली प्रताड़ना भले ही पहले जैसी कठोर न हो, पर वह एक सामान्य नारी न रहकर अशुभ का सूचक बन जाती है, इसलिए शुभ कार्यों में उसकी उपस्थिति वर्जित है। हालाँकि अब इस सोच में परिवर्तन आने लगा है, पर यदि वह निःसंतान है, तो परिवार के कार्यों में हाथ बंटाने के सिवाय उसका महत्व नही आंका जाता।

1. आज समाज में किन महिलाओं को प्रताड़ना झेलनी पड़ती है?
   A. विधवा B. निःसंतान
   C. अशिक्षित D. A एवं B दोनों
2. निम्न में से कौन महिलाओं के शोषण का सर्वाधिक प्रमुख रूप है?
   A. यौन शोषण
   B. संपत्ति में हिस्सेदारी न मिलना
   C. उन्हें घर के कामों तक ही सीमित रखना
   D. A एवं C दोनों
3. आजादी के बाद महिलाओं की स्थिति में क्या बदलाव आया है?
   A. महिलाओं को वोट का अधिकार मिला।
   B. सती प्रथा का निषेध किया गया।
   C. शिक्षा एवं जीवन के अन्य क्षेत्रों में भी उन्हें समानता मिली।
   D. A एवं C दोनों
4. उपरोक्त उद्धरण के आधार पर सही कथन का चयन कीजिए।
   A. प्राचीन काल में नारी को सम्मान की दृष्टि से देखा जाता था।
   B. आजादी की लड़ाई में महिलाओं ने बढ़चढ़कर भाग लिया।
   C. आज भी महिलाएँ यौन शोषण से सर्वाधिक पीड़ित हैं।
   D. उपरोक्त सभी

उद्धरण-42

साठ के दशक में ही कनाडा के दार्शनिक मार्शल मक्लूहन ने कहा था कि संचार व्यवस्था में अभूतपूर्व प्रगति के कारण दुनिया एक 'वैश्विक गांव' में बदल जायेगी। वर्तमान भूमंडलीकरण मक्लूहन की इस भविष्यवाणी का कार्यान्वियन लगता है। उल्लेखनीय है कि भूमंडलीकरण का वर्तमान प्रयोग मूलरूप से इंटरनेट से प्रेरित है और यही इसे अतीत में भूमंडलीकरण की दिशा में किये गये अन्य प्रयोगों से भिन्न कर देता है। वर्तमान भूमंडलीकरण एक ऐसी घटना साबित हुई है, जिसे समझने के लिए दुनिया की विभिन्न भाषाओं में अब तक कुल सात हजार पुस्तकें प्रकाशित हो चुकी हैं। हालांकि अभी भी इस परिघटना के बारे में अंतिम रूप से कुछ कहना मुश्किल माना जाता है। केवल एक ही बात पर आम सहमति है कि यह एक पेचीदा और बहुआयामी विकास प्रक्रिया है।

अर्थशास्त्र के आधुनिक विद्यार्थी इसे आर्थिक संसाधनों का सबसे सुंदर और प्रभावी विनियोजन मानते हैं और दुनिया में संपन्नता की वर्तमान लहर के लिए भी जिम्मेदार मानते हैं। इतना ही नहीं, कुछ लोगों की राय में तो भूमंडलीकरण के कारण दुनिया से युद्ध के खतरे भी मिट जायेंगे, क्योंकि देशों के बीच पारस्परिक व्यापार की जड़ें गहरी होने से उनमें युद्ध के प्रति आकर्षण खत्म हो जायेगा। दुनिया में प्रतिष्ठा हासिल करने के प्रतिमान बदल रहे हैं और देशों की पहचान सैनिक उपलब्धियों के बजाए आर्थिक सफलताओं से होने लगी है। युद्ध का स्थान आर्थिक प्रतियोगिता ने ले लिया है।

लेकिन भूमंडलीकरण के विरोधी इसे यूरोपीय अमेरिकी विकास मॉडल का महज एक आरोपण मानते हैं। उनका मानना है कि भूमंडलीकरण दुनिया को पश्चिमी देशों के हितों के अनुरूप ढालने की कोशिश है। पश्चिमी देशों द्वारा प्रतिपादित यह एक नयी किस्म की बाजार विचारधारा है जो निष्ठुर, सर्वग्रासी और निरंकुश है और जिसकी इतिहास में कोई मिसाल नहीं है। यह यूरोप और अमेरिका के दुनिया के संसाधनों पर स्थायी नियंत्रण स्थापित करने की पहल है।

1. भूमंडलीकरण है–
   A. एक पेचीदा और बहुआयामी विकास प्रक्रिया।
   B. इंटरनेट आधारित व्यापार संजाल।
   C. गरीब देशों के शोषण का एक नवीन आर्थिक तंत्र।
   D. उपरोक्त में से कोई नहीं।
2. भूमंडलीकरण के कारण दुनिया में युद्ध का खतरा कम हुआ है, कैसे?
   A. सभी देश आर्थिक उन्नति में लग गए हैं।
   B. पारस्परिक व्यापार की जड़ें गहरी होने से उनमें युद्ध के प्रति आकर्षण कम हो रहा है।
   C. युद्ध के खिलाफ अंतर्राष्ट्रीय जनमत गोलबंद हो रहा है।
   D. उपरोक्त सभी
3. भूमंडलीकरण को निष्ठुर एवं सर्वग्राही व्यवस्था क्यों कहा जा रहा है?
   A. इसके अंतर्गत दुनिया को पश्चिमी देशों के हितों के अंतर्गत ढालने की कोशिश की जा रही है।
   B. इसका लाभ सिर्फ अमेरिका और पश्चिमी देशों को मिल रहा है।
   C. भूमंडलीकरण के कारण अंतर्राष्ट्रीय वित्तीय संस्थाओं की भूमिका घटी है।
   D. उपरोक्त सभी
4. निम्न में से कौन भूमंडलीकरण का प्रभाव नहीं है?
   A. आर्थिक संसाधनों का बेहतर विनियोजन
   B. आर्थिक समृद्धि
   C. प्रतियोगी अर्थव्यवस्था
   D. नियोजित अर्थव्यवस्था

उद्धरण-43

तकनीकी रूप से भारतीय करेंसी परिवर्तनीय नहीं है। वह रेवेन्यू में परिवर्तनीय है, कैपिटल में नहीं। अगर आप विदेशों में जाकर बैंकों से कहें कि आप के पास भारतीय करंसी है, उसके बदले आपको डॉलर चाहिए तो ऐसा नहीं होगा। आपको डॉलर खरीदना पड़ेगा। इसका मतलब यह हुआ कि पूंजी में भारतीय करेंसी परिवर्तनीय नहीं है। इसी तरह हमें विदेशों में बैंक खाता खोलने के लिए डॉलर या पाउंड की जरूरत होगी।

हमें पहले रुपये को डॉलर या पाउंड में उसे बदलना होगा, तब जाकर हम उसे जमा करा सकते हैं। इसी तरह से विदेशों में शॉपिंग से लेकर किसी वस्तु की खरीदारी, आप किसी भी देश में डॉलर या पाउंड में कर सकते हैं। लोग उसे स्वीकार कर लेंगे, मगर वे रुपये को स्वीकार नहीं करेंगे। मगर रुपए का सिंबल बनने के बाद रुपए की कैपिटल में पूर्ण परिवर्तनीयता जल्द हो जाएगी। जिस तरह से भारत में आज डॉलर को लेने में कोई परहेज नहीं करता, वैसे अमेरिका में रुपये को लेने में कोई परहेज नहीं करेगा।

सवाल यह उठता है कि आखिर इसकी जरूरत क्या है। एक समय ब्रिटेन का कारोबार विश्व में काफी फैला था। कारोबार ब्रिटिश मुद्रा में होता था। ब्रिटेन ने इस विशिष्टता को कायम करने के लिए उसका प्रतीक चिह्न बनाया। अमेरिका ने भी यही रणनीति अपनाई। अपनी मुद्रा डॉलर की पहचान और वर्चस्व अंतर्राष्ट्रीय बाजार में स्थापित करने के लिए उसने अपनी मुद्रा का प्रतीक चिह्न बनाया। कई अन्य देशों में डॉलर मुद्रा का प्रचलन है, जापान के बाद 1999 में यूरोपीय देशों ने अपनी नई मुद्रा यूरो का प्रचलन शुरू किया, अपने खास प्रतीक चिह्न के साथ।

यह कारोबार के वर्चस्व की लड़ाई है। जिन-जिन देशों की मुद्रा के प्रतीक चिह्न हैं, उनके साथ कारोबार की पहली शर्त यह है कि कारोबार उनकी मुद्रा में होगा। एक्सपोर्ट से लेकर इंपोर्ट सब कुछ उनकी मुद्रा में होगा। अमेरिकी डॉलर ने विदेशी मुद्रा विनिमय बाजार में अपनी धुरी इस कदर बना ली है कि अन्य देशों की मुद्राओं की कीमत डॉलर के मुकाबले ही तय होती है। हालांकि यूरोपीय देश यूरो के द्वारा इस मिथ को तोड़ने की कोशिश में हैं, मगर अन्य देशों के साथ अमेरिका का कारोबार यूरोपीय देशों की तुलना में इतना अधिक है कि डॉलर का वर्चस्व बना हुआ है।

1. भारतीय करेंसी परिवर्तनीय है–
A. अमेरिकी डॉलर के साथ
B. राजस्व खाते पर
C. पूँजी खाते पर
D. सभी पर

2. देश की अपनी करेंसी का क्या लाभ है?
A. इससे देश का कारोबार देश की मुद्रा में ही होगा।
B. इससे देश का निर्यात बढ़ेगा।
C. इससे देश का आयात प्रतिस्थापित होगा।
D. इससे राष्ट्रीय उत्पाद में वृद्धि होगी।

3. दुनिया में अमेरिकी डॉलर के वर्चस्व का क्या कारण है?
A. अमेरिकी डॉलर अन्य देशों की मुद्रा की तुलना में अधिक महँगा है।
B. अमेरिकी डॉलर अन्य देशों द्वारा स्वीकृत मुद्रा है।
C. अन्य देशों के साथ अमेरिका का कारोबार अधिक है।
D. विदेशी विनिमय बाजार में डॉलर का कोई प्रतिस्थापन नहीं है।

4. पूँजी खाते पर रुपये के परिवर्तनीय होने का क्या लाभ है?
A. इससे भारतीय रुपये को डॉलर एवं अन्य विदेशी मुद्राओं में बदलना आसान हो जाएगा।
B. इससे देश में निवेश को बढ़ावा मिलेगा।
C. भारतीय निर्यात में वृद्धि से व्यापार संतुलन देश के पक्ष में होगा।
D. उपरोक्त सभी

उद्धरण-44

'आधार' से जुड़े विचार नए नहीं हैं। अमेरिका में काफी समय पहले सामाजिक सुरक्षा कार्यक्रमों से संबंधित लोगों को 'सामाजिक सुरक्षा नंबर' देने की सोच ने आकार लिया था और वहां पचास वर्षों से भी अधिक समय से ऐसे पहचान पत्र का इस्तेमाल हो रहा है। हाल ही में वहां पर सीनेट के कुछ सदस्यों ने यह प्रस्ताव रखा कि देश में बायोमेट्रिक सामाजिक सुरक्षा कार्ड शुरू किया जाए। इस प्रस्ताव को अमेरिका के नागरिक समूहों एवं निजता संबंधी वकीलों के जबर्दस्त विरोध का सामना करना पड़ा। आज से कुछ समय पहले ब्रिटेन सरकार ने भी बायोमेट्रिक राष्ट्रीय पहचान योजना शुरू की थी, लेकिन ब्रिटेन की नई सरकार इस योजना को खत्म करने, बल्कि एकत्रित बायोमेट्रिक आंकड़ों को ध्वस्त करने की सोच रही है। वहां कहा जा रहा है कि यह पूरी कवायद निरर्थक, नौकरशाही संबंधी और निजता में हस्तक्षेप करने वाली थी।

भारत में 'आधार' को सरकारी सेवाओं के समस्त रोगों की रामबाण दवा के रूप में पेश किया जा रहा है। अपेक्षा की जा रही है कि यह पहचान पत्र शिक्षा के अधिकार के तहत दाखिले की निगरानी करेगा। यह सार्वजनिक वितरण प्रणाली की दरारों को बंद कर देगा और वित्तीय समायोजन, ग्रामीण रोजगार गारंटी योजना, प्रस्तावित खाद्य सुरक्षा कानून तथा गरीबी-उन्मूलन से जुड़ी अन्य योजनाओं को लागू कराने में भी अचूक साबित होगा। फर्जी लाभार्थियों को छांट सकने वाली अनूठी पहचान संख्या की अवधारणा यकीनन आकर्षक है, लेकिन चिंता की बात यह है कि यह नंबर गलत पहचान या योजनाओं के क्रियान्वयन के रिसाव की समस्या को हल करने में कितना कारगर होगा। एक ऐसी व्यवस्था, जिसमें सरकारी अनुदान संबंधी ज्यादातर लाभ परिवार केंद्रित हैं, बल्कि बड़ा परिवार एक नेमत-सा हो, उसमें निजी सूचनाओं पर आधारित 'आधार' कैसे लाभप्रद हो सकता है?

1. सामाजिक सुरक्षा से जुड़ी राष्ट्रीय पहचान योजना निम्न में से किस देश में लागू की जा चुकी है?
A. भारत B. ब्रिटेन
C. संयुक्त राज्य अमेरिका D. उपरोक्त सभी

2. अमेरिका में बायोमेट्रिक सामाजिक सुरक्षा कार्ड योजना का विरोध किया जा रहा है, क्यों?
A. इससे अमेरिका की राष्ट्रीय सुरक्षा खतरे में पड़ सकती है।
B. इंटरनेट आधारित योजनाओं में इसके दुरूपयोग की संभावना बढ़ सकती है।
C. इससे व्यक्ति की निजता प्रभावित होगी।

D. इससे अमेरिका की गोपनीय खुफिया रिपोर्ट सार्वजनिक हो सकती है।

3. उपरोक्त उद्धरण के आधार पर सही कथन का चयन कीजिए?

A. अमेरिका के कुछ सीनेटरों ने देश में बायोमेट्रिक सामाजिक सुरक्षा कार्ड का विरोध किया है।

B. अमेरिका के नागरिक समूह सुरक्षा कार्ड योजना का समर्थन कर रहे हैं।

C. ब्रिटेन की नई सरकार कुछ समय पहले शुरू की गई बायोमेट्रिक राष्ट्रीय पहचान योजना खत्म करने पर विचार कर रही है।

D. भारत सरकार ने भी इस योजना के खतरे को देखते हुए इसे स्थगित करने का निर्णय हाल ही में लिया है।

4. भारत में शुरू की गई आधार योजना का मुख्य लाभ क्या है?

A. इससे सार्वजनिक वितरण प्रणाली की खामियों को दूर करने में मदद मिलेगी।

B. इससे सरकारी खर्च पर नियंत्रण रखा जा सकेगा।

C. इससे रोजगार गारंटी योजना के लाभार्थियों को उचित लाभ मिल सकेगा।

D. A एवं C

उद्धरण-45

3जी मोबाइल सेवा टेलीकॉम जगत में क्रान्ति लेकर आई है। यह सेवा इन्टरनेट टेलीविजन, वीडियो ऑन-डिमांड, आडियो-वीडियो फोन कॉल और क्रांफ्रेंसिंग के साथ ही तीव्र गति डाटा आदान-प्रदान जैसे तेज सम्पर्क और एप्लीकेशन की सुविधा प्रदान करेगी। वीडियो फोन कॉल में एक-दूसरे को देखते हुए बातचीत की जा सकती है। कम्पनियों की योजना के अनुसार, शुरुआत में वे 100 चैनलों का लाइव टीवी शुरू करेंगी, जिसमें बाद में 100 और चैनल जोड़ दिए जाएंगे। तेज गति की ऑनलाइन गेमिंग, पिक्चर इन पिक्चर और फोटो अपलोडिंग भी सम्भव हो जाएगी। मोबाइल पर ईमेल एकाउंट या किसी वेबसाइट खुलने में देरी तब बीते जमाने की बात हो जाएगी। 2जी सेवाओं में फिलहाल प्रयुक्त किए जा रहे फोन सेटों में ईमेल एकाउंट का खुलना ज्यादा आसान हो जाएगा। चूंकि 3जी युक्त मोबाइल सेटों में सेवा प्रदाता कम्पनी से प्राप्त संकेत अधिक शक्तिशाली होंगे इसलिये सभी तरह की सेवाओं की गति अधिक होगी। जबकि 2जी सेवाओं में आडियो कॉल्स के साथ एमपीथ्री, एफएम, रिंगटोन और औसत गति का जीपीआरएस और टेक्स्ट मैसेजिंग (एसएमएस) का लाभ ही मिलता था। दूरसंचार विभाग के अनुसार, फिलहाल मोबाइल सेवा में उच्च श्रेणी के ब्रॉडबैंड इंटरनेट की गति 256 केबीपीएस होती है जबकि 3जी पर ब्रॉडबैंड की शुरुआत ही होगी 384 केबीपीएस से जो वर्तमान उपलब्ध संरचना में 3.2 एमबीपीएस तक जा सकती है। भारत में फिलहाल व्यापक रूप से जिस 3जी मोबाइल प्रौद्योगिकी की प्रतीक्षा की जा रही है, वह तीसरी पीढ़ी की है। इस समय बीएसएनएल और एमटीएनएल को छोड़कर सभी निजी मोबाइल ऑपरेटर कम्पनियाँ दूसरी पीढ़ी (2जी) प्रौद्योगिकी की सेवाएं उपलब्ध करा रही हैं।

1. 3जी मोबाइल सेवा को टेलीकॉम जगत में एक क्रान्ति के रूप में क्यों देखा जा रहा है?

A. इससे तीव्र गति से डाटा का आदान-प्रदान संभव हो पाएगा।

B. इससे ऑन लाइन टिचिंग संभव हो पाएगा।

C. मानसून की सटीक भविष्यवाणी की जा सकेगी।

D. उपरोक्त सभी

2. 3जी सेवा का प्रमुख लाभ क्या है?

A. डाटा का शीघ्र आदान-प्रदान।

B. टी.वी. चैनल सेवाओं का विस्तार।

C. पिक्चर इन पिक्चर एवं फोटो अपलोडिंग।

D. उपरोक्त सभी।

3. निम्न में से कौन-सी सुविधा 2जी सेवाओं पर आधारित नहीं है?

A. टेक्स्ट मैसेजिंग B. जीपीआरएस

C. एमपी थ्री D. वीडियो ऑन डिमांड

उद्धरण-46

बीपीओ के क्षेत्र में भारत जैसे देश की सफलता ने विकसित देशों को चौंका दिया। अमेरिका के राष्ट्रपति चुनाव में आउटसोर्सिंग एक बड़ा मसला बना। भारत के ज्ञान के आगे अमेरिका जैसा सशक्त देश सहम गया। अमेरिकी राष्ट्रपति बराक ओबामा कई बार अपने भाषण में भारत और चीन जैसे देश की उच्च स्तरीय बौद्धिक संपदा से खौफ जता चुके हैं। बराक ओबामा ने तो अमेरिकी कंपनियों को सख्त आदेश दिए कि बाहर नौकरी देने वाली कंपनियों को किसी तरह की सरकारी रियायत नहीं दी जाएगी, लेकिन विकसित देशों का यह खौफ आउटसोर्सिंग को रोक नहीं पाया, हां इसके लिए चुनौतियां जरूर बढ़ गई हैं। खासकर वैश्विक आर्थिक मंदी के बाद भारत की ओर जा रही नौकरियों को लेकर पश्चिमी देश अपनी भौंहें टेढ़ी करने लगे, लेकिन एक बार वैश्विक कारोबार में अपने पांव जमाने के बाद भारतीय श्रम शक्ति को नजरअंदाज करना आसान नहीं है। फिर भी यह सच है कि आज चुनौतियां ज्यादा बढ़ गई हैं। जरूरत है इन चुनौतियों का मुकाबला कर, वैश्विक कारोबार में अपने पांव जमाए रखने की। आज के भारतीय युवा को इस क्षेत्र से काफी उम्मीदें हैं। भारत केपीओ का भी अगुआ बन रहा है। कल के सॉफ्टवेयर कुली आज के परामर्शदाता हैं। विकसित दुनिया की एक बड़ी जरूरत बन गए हैं। इस कामयाबी को बरकरार रखने और बढ़ाने की जरूरत है। आशा की जानी चाहिए कि भारत आने वाले दिनों में दुनिया का सबसे बड़ा केपीओ बाजार बन जाएगा।

1. भारत की कौन-सी सफलता विकसित देशों को चौंकानेवाली है?

A. एशिया में एक महत्वपूर्ण आर्थिक शक्ति के रूप में भारत का उभरना।

B. भारत द्वारा रुपये के नए चिह्न को अपनाना।
C. भारत में बीपीओ क्षेत्र की सफलता।
D. भारत का बढ़ता विदेशी मुद्रा भंडार।

2. अमेरिकी सरकार ने आउटसोर्सिंग को रोकने के लिए कौन-से कदम उठाए हैं?
A. आउटसोर्सिंग करनेवाली कंपनियों पर अतिरिक्त टैक्स
B. आउटसोर्सिंग करनेवाली कंपनियों को मिलने वाली सरकारी रियायत में कटौती
C. आउटसोर्सिंग पर पूर्ण प्रतिबंध
D. आउटसोर्सिंग रोकने के लिए यूरोपीय संघ के साथ समझौता

3. आनेवाले दिनों में भारत को दुनिया का सबसे बड़ा केपीओ बाजार बन जाने की संभावना व्यक्त की जा रही है, क्यों?
A. भारत को बीपीओ क्षेत्र की सफलता का लाभ मिलेगा।
B. भारत के पास उन्नत कोटि का मानव संसाधन उपलब्ध है।
C. केपीओ बाजार में भारत का कोई प्रतिद्वन्द्वी नहीं है।
D. उपरोक्त सभी

4. अमेरिका के राष्ट्रपति चुनाव का मुख्य मुद्दा क्या था?
A. इराक में शांति स्थापना
B. संयुक्त राष्ट्रसंघ की सुरक्षा परिषद् में सुधार
C. आउटसोर्सिंग
D. अमेरिकी राष्ट्रीय सुरक्षा

उद्धरण-47

विकास की दौड़ में देश का भीतरी संतुलन भी बहुत ही महत्वपूर्ण है। आज भारत के सन्दर्भ में परोक्ष रूप से संवैधानिक व्यवस्था के सामने समय की चुनौती है, परीक्षा है प्रजातन्त्र और गणतन्त्र की दुहाई देने वाले राजनीतिक दलों की, उनके निर्वाचित सदस्यों की और व्यवस्था का संचालन करने वाली शासकीय नौकरशाही की वे अपने कर्तव्यबोध में कितनी कर्मठता, पारदर्शिता, ईमानदारी और राष्ट्रीय भावना को तरजीह देते हैं।

हम कभी कर्ज से मुक्त और सम्पदा से युक्त एक राष्ट्र थे, हम समूचे विश्व को एक नई राह दिखाने की क्षमता वाले सक्षम राष्ट्र थे, परन्तु जो हुआ है और आज जो हो रहा है वह देश के हित में कम नेताओं के और उनके वंशजों के व पूँजीपतियों के हित में अधिक हो रहा है। देश का, जो विकास होना था वो हुआ या नहीं, न तो किसी को इसका ठीक-ठाक पता है और न ही किसी को यह सब देखने में रुचि है इतना तो अवश्य है कि नेताओं की स्वहितकारी पंचवर्षीय योजनाएं अच्छी तरह से बनती चली गई हैं और उनका भारी विकास होता चला गया है। एक अनुमान के अनुसार हमारे देश के नेताओं का एक लाख करोड़ रुपए से अधिक काला धन स्विस बैंकों में और छद्म सम्पत्तियों में रखा और निवेशित किया गया है। इतने धन से भारत की तस्वीर बदली जा सकती है, कुछ हद तक गरीबी दूर की जा सकती है, परन्तु यह धन आम जनता की गरीबी दूर करने के लिए नहीं है, बल्कि यही धन आम जनता से छीनकर उन्हें गरीब किया गया है इस देश को कर्जदार बनाया गया है और भारी विषमता की इस खाई को रचा गया है।

1. लेखक ने आम जनता की गरीबी का कारण किसे बताया है?
A. संसाधनों का सही उपयोग न हो पाने को।
B. धन के दुरूपयोग को।
C. जनता के धन के विदेशों में पलायन को।
D. उपरोक्त सभी।

2. लेखक ऐसा क्यों मानता है कि आज जो विकास हो रहा है वह देश का कम, नेताओं का ज्यादा है?
A. विकास का लाभ आम जनता को नहीं नेताओं को मिला है।
B. नेताओं ने विकास की प्रक्रिया को अपनी ओर मोड़ लिया है।
C. नेता ही विकास के सबसे बड़े नियंता हैं।
D. नेता देश का विकास नहीं चाहते।

3. भारत में विकास की सबसे बड़ी विसंगति क्या है?
A. देश में प्रजातंत्र की जड़ लगातार कमजोर हुई है।
B. संपदा से युक्त राष्ट्र आज सबसे बड़ा कर्जदार बन गया है।
C. देश का धन बड़ी मात्रा में विदेशों में भेजा जा रहा है।
D. A एवं C दोनों।

4. संवैधानिक व्यवस्था के सामने सबसे बड़ी चुनौती क्या है?
A. शासन में कर्तव्य बोध एवं पारदर्शिता का अभाव।
B. राष्ट्रीय भावना का कमजोर पड़ना।
C. नागरिकों में कर्मठता का अभाव।
D. उपरोक्त सभी।

उद्धरण-48

एक आर्थिक विचार के रूप में ब्रिक की धारणा का प्रतिपादन वर्ष 2001 में अमेरिका की वित्तीय कम्पनी गोल्डमैन सैच (Goldman Sachs) के अर्थशास्त्री जिम ओ नील (Jim O' Niel) ने किया था। नील ने इन चार देशों की उभरती अर्थव्यवस्थाओं को आगे आने वाले भविष्य के लिए महत्त्वपूर्ण माना था। इस धारणा का विधिवत् प्रतिपादन उनके द्वारा 2003 में लिखित रिपोर्ट 'Dreaming with BRICS : The path to 2050' में यह माना गया था कि इन चार देशों ने वैश्विक पूँजीवाद के आलोक में अपनी राजनीतिक व आर्थिक व्यवस्थाओं में परिवर्तन कर लिया है। इस रिपोर्ट के अनुसार वर्ष 2050 तक भारत व चीन विश्व में निर्मित वस्तुओं व सेवाओं के अग्रिम आपूर्तिकर्ता देश होंगे। इसी प्रकार रूस तथा ब्राजील

2050 तक विश्व में कच्चे माल के अग्रिम आपूर्तिकर्ता देश होंगे। इस प्रकार इन देशों की अर्थव्यवस्थाएं एक-दूसरे की पूरक होंगी। इसी प्रकार वर्ष 2005 में प्रकाशित गोल्डमैन सैच की एक अन्य रिपोर्ट में यह भविष्यवाणी की गई थी कि इन चारों देशों की अर्थव्यवस्थाएं इतनी तेजी से विकसित हो रही हैं कि वर्ष 2050 तक ये चारों अर्थव्यवस्थाएं वर्तमान विश्व के धनी देशों की अर्थव्यवस्थाओं से आगे निकल जाएंगी। लेकिन इस रिपोर्ट का तर्क यह नहीं था कि ये चारों अर्थव्यवस्थाएं एक आर्थिक सहयोग संगठन का निर्माण करेंगी।

वर्तमान में इन चारों देशों में विश्व की 40 प्रतिशत जनसंख्या निवास करती है तथा इन चारों का क्षेत्रफल विश्व के भौगोलिक क्षेत्रफल का 25 प्रतिशत है। साथ ही इन चारों का सकल राष्ट्रीय उत्पाद (GDP) 15.43 ट्रिलियन डॉलर है। इन चारों देशों में आपसी सहयोग की सम्भावना इसलिए अधिक है कि जहाँ रूस में तेल व प्राकृतिक गैस व ब्राजील में खनिज पदार्थों विशेषकर लौह अयस्क की अच्छी मात्रा है, वहीं भारत व चीन तकनीकी व निर्माण के क्षेत्र में आगे हैं।

1. लेखक ने किन अर्थव्यवस्थाओं को भविष्य के लिए महत्त्वपूर्ण माना है?

A. ब्राजील, रूस भारत, चीन
B. चीन, भारत, द. अफ्रीका, रूस
C. ब्राजील, भारत, रूस, द. अफ्रीका
D. रूस, भारत, चीन, जापान

2. 2050 तक किन देशों के निर्मित वस्तुओं एवं सेवाओं के अग्रिम आपूर्तिकर्ता होने की संभावना व्यक्त की गई है?

A. भारत एवं ब्राजील B. भारत एवं चीन
C. ब्राजील एवं रूस D. चीन एवं ब्राजील

3. निम्न में से कौन-सा कथन सही है?

A. इस शताब्दी के अर्द्धांश तक ब्रिक राष्ट्रों की अर्थव्यवस्था विकसित देशों की अर्थव्यवस्था से आगे निकल जाएगी।
B. ब्रिक राष्ट्रों के बीच आपसी व्यापारिक प्रतिस्पर्धा बढ़ेगी।
C. ब्रिक राष्ट्र दुनिया के सर्वाधिक निर्यातक राष्ट्र के रूप में उभरेंगे।
D. A एवं C दोनों

4. ब्रिक राष्ट्रों के बीच सहयोग की अधिक संभावना किस कारण से है?

A. सभी राष्ट्र सहयोग के लिए प्रतिबद्ध हैं।
B. इनकी अर्थव्यवस्था एक-दूसरे की पूरक है।
C. इनकी अर्थव्यवस्था एक-दूसरे की प्रतिस्पर्धी है।
D. सभी ने सीमा शुल्क रहित व्यापार का समर्थन किया है।

उद्धरण-49

भारत की सामाजिक संस्थाओं में जाति प्रणाली के घृणितम स्वरूप के दंश समाज के एक वर्ग ने शताब्दियों तक झेले हैं। जाति व्यवस्था से ही समाज में ऊँच-नीच की भावना पैदा हुई है। कर्म के आधार पर विकसित हुई वर्णव्यवस्था में बौद्धिक दृष्टि से श्रेष्ठतर तथा शिक्षा-दीक्षा का कार्य करने वाले लोग ब्राह्मण, समुदाय (राज्य) की रक्षा करने वाले लोग क्षत्रिय, कारोबारी लोग वैश्य तथा उत्पादन करने वाले लोग शूद्र कहलाए। यह वर्गीकरण जन्मगत न होकर कर्मगत था। कालान्तर में समाज में कर्म के ही आधार पर जातियाँ और उप-जातियाँ बनीं। बुद्धिबल, बाहुबल तथा धनबल के आधार पर कतिपय जातियों ने स्वयं को श्रेष्ठतम (ऊँचा) तथा अन्यों को निम्नतम (नीचा) मान लिया। तथाकथित नीची जातियों पर तरह-तरह की निर्योग्यताएं थोपी गईं यथा नीची जातियों के लोगों पर जूते पहनने, पगड़ी बाँधने पर प्रतिबन्ध लगा दिया गया। वे तथाकथित ऊँची जातियों के कुओं से पानी नहीं ले सकते थे; मन्दिरों में प्रवेश नहीं कर सकते थे; तथाकथित नीची जाति की महिलाएँ कमीज (ब्लाउज) नहीं पहन सकती थीं उन्हें साड़ी लपेट कर ही अपना शरीर ढंकना पड़ता था। तथाकथित नीची जातियों के लोग बराबरी के साथ चारपाई पर नहीं बैठ सकते थे। उनकी छाया तक पड़ जाने पर ब्राह्मण स्वयं को अशुद्ध मानकर स्नान करते थे। महाराष्ट्र में दलितों को सार्वजनिक स्थान, सड़क आदि पर थूकने के भी अधिकार नहीं थे। प्रताड़ना के विकृततम रूप में दलितों को अपने गले में कटोरा बाँधकर चलना पड़ता था ताकि यदि वे थूकें तो उसी कटोरे में थूकें और अपनी बस्ती में जाकर कटोरा साफ करें। कतिपय नीची जातियों के लोगों को अपनी कमर से एक झाड़ू बाँधकर चलना पड़ता था ताकि जिस रास्ते से वे चलें वह स्वतः ही साफ होता रहे। इस प्रकार की अमानवीय कुप्रथाओं तथा दलितों के सामाजिक उत्पीड़न के विरुद्ध उन्नीसवीं और बीसवीं शताब्दी में अनेक समाज सुधार आन्दोलन चले। महात्मा गांधी के अछूतोद्धार आन्दोलन तथा डॉ. बी.आर. अम्बेडकर के प्रयासों से स्वाधीनता आन्दोलन के दौरान ही जाति व्यवस्था पर कड़े प्रहार किए गए। भारतीय राष्ट्रीय कांग्रेस तथा अन्य समाज सुधारकों के प्रयास से जनगणना में जाति का उल्लेख किया जाना बन्द कर दिया गया। भारतीय जाति व्यवस्था की कुरीतियों को दास प्रथा, रंगभेद, सती प्रथा, बालिका भ्रूण हत्या के समकक्ष ही अमानवीय करार दिया गया। इन समस्त प्रयासों के चलते ही संविधान के मौलिक अधिकारों में समानता के अधिकार के तहत जाति, धर्म, लिंग, भाषा अथवा क्षेत्र के आधार पर किसी भी व्यक्ति के प्रति भेदभाव किए जाने को निषेध कर दिया गया। अस्पृश्यता को मौलिक अधिकारों के हनन की संज्ञा देते हुए एवं असंवैधानिक मानते हुए एक संज्ञेय अपराध भी माना गया।

1. समाज में ऊँच-नीच की भावना का मुख्य आधार क्या है?

A. जाति व्यवस्था B. वर्ण व्यवस्था
C. सांप्रदायिक विभाजन D. उपरोक्त सभी

2. निम्न में से कौन सामाजिक श्रेष्ठता का आधार है?

A. बुद्धि B. बाहुबल
C. धन D. उपरोक्त सभी

3. भारतीय समाज में निचली जाति पर कौन-सी निर्योग्यता आरोपित नहीं की गई थी?
   A. ऊँची जाति के कुओं से पानी न भरना
   B. पगड़ी बाँधना
   C. जूते पहनना
   D. मंदिरों में प्रवेश
4. जाति-व्यवस्था को असंवैधानिक माना गया है–
   A. संविधान की प्रस्तावना में।
   B. मौलिक अधिकार खंड में।
   C. राज्य के नीति निदेशक भाग में।
   D. उपरोक्त सभी में।

उद्धरण-50

भारत में प्राचीन काल से ही उत्तम कोटि के सूती वस्त्रों का उत्पादन होता आया है। यहाँ का मलमल अपनी विशेषता के लिए विश्वविख्यात रहा है। 17वीं शताब्दी तक भारत में उत्तम कोटि के सूती वस्त्रों का बड़े पैमाने पर उत्पादन होता था। अंग्रेजी साम्राज्य ने अपने देश के प्रभुत्व को स्थापित करने के उद्देश्य से ब्रिटेन में उत्पादित वस्त्र को भारतीय बाजार में उतार कर भारतीय वस्त्र उद्योग को नष्ट कर दिया था। इसके फलस्वरूप भारत यूरोपीय देशों के कच्चे माल की पूर्ति का केन्द्रमात्र बनकर रह गया। धीरे-धीरे भारतीय ग्रामों में फैला परम्परागत वस्त्र उद्योग नष्ट होने लगा।

राष्ट्रपिता महात्मा गांधी की दृष्टि लुप्तप्राय होते जा रहे ग्रामीण उद्योगों की ओर गई। उन्होंने स्वदेशी वस्त्र उत्पादन के कार्य को पुनर्जीवित करने के उद्देश्य को ध्यान में रखते हुए वर्ष 1925 में अखिल भारत चरखा संघ की स्थापना से खादी कार्य का सूत्रपात किया। गांधीजी का लक्ष्य खादी उद्योग के माध्यम से शोषण मुक्त समाज की रचना करना था। एक बार गांधीजी ने कहा भी था, "यदि मुझे कोई हाथ-कताई से बेहतर सुविचारित व्यापक कार्यक्रम बतलाए तो मैं आज चरखा का त्याग कर दूँगा। परन्तु अभी तक न तो मैंने देखा है और न ही मुझे दिखाया गया है। यदि ऐसा कोई सुविचारित कार्यक्रम है, तो उसे जानने के लिए मैं उत्सुक हूँ।"

वर्ष 1947 तक यह उद्योग गांधीजी के मार्ग निर्देशन में रहा। स्वतंत्रता प्राप्त करने के पश्चात् सरकार ने इस उद्योग को आवश्यक संरक्षण प्रदान किया। खादी ग्रामोद्योग आयोग अधिनियम, 1946 द्वारा उद्योगों के विकास के लिए एक विशेष आयोग स्थापित किया गया। आयोग का काम खादी ग्रामोद्योग सम्बन्धी कार्यक्रमों की योजना बनाना तथा उनके कार्यान्वयन में सहायता देना है। खादी ग्रामोद्योग के क्षेत्र में काम करने वाले लोगों को प्रशिक्षण देने के अलावा आयोग ऐसी एजेंसियों के लिए वित्त की व्यवस्था करता है, जो इसकी पात्र होती हैं। उन्हें कच्चा माल जुटाता है तथा खादी ग्रामोद्योग के उत्पादों की बिक्री का प्रबन्ध करता है।

1. भारतीय वस्त्र उद्योग के नष्ट होने का मुख्य कारण क्या था?
   A. भारतीय वस्त्र उद्योग की गुणवत्ता लगातार घटती जा रही थी।
   B. भारतीय वस्त्रों की कीमत बाजार में लगातार बढ़ती जा रही थी।
   C. भारतीय वस्त्र उद्योग को ब्रिटेन में उत्पादित सस्ते कपड़ों से मुकाबला करना पड़ रहा था।
   D. B एवं C दोनों।
2. खादी उद्योग को बढ़ावा देने का गांधी का मुख्य उद्देश्य क्या था?
   A. देशी उद्योग को बढ़ावा देना।
   B. खादी को लोकप्रिय बनाना।
   C. भारतीय उद्योग को आत्मनिर्भर बनाना।
   D. शोषण मुक्त समाज की स्थापना करना।
3. 17वीं शताब्दी में भारत प्रसिद्ध था–
   A. उन्नत कोटि के सूती वस्त्रों के लिए।
   B. मलमल वस्त्र के लिए।
   C. A एवं B दोनों के लिए।
   D. रंगरेजी के लिए।
4. खादी ग्रामोद्योग आयोग का गठन किस उद्देश्य से किया गया?
   A. खादी ग्रामोद्योग के विकास के लिए योजना बनाना।
   B. इस उद्योग में काम करनेवाले लोगों को प्रशिक्षण देना।
   C. इन उद्योगों में निर्मित वस्तुओं की विक्री के लिए।
   D. उपरोक्त सभी।

उत्तरमाला

उद्धरण-1

1	2	3
D	B	A

उद्धरण-2

1	2	3
C	D	D

उद्धरण-3

1	2	3	4
C	C	D	D

उद्धरण-4

1	2	3	4
A	D	B	D

उद्धरण-5

1	2	3	4
D	D	B	A

उद्धरण-6

1	2	3	4
A	A	D	A

उद्धरण-7

1	2	3	4
A	D	D	D

उद्धरण-8

1	2	3	4
B	D	D	A

उद्धरण-9

1	2	3	4	5
D	D	A	C	A

उद्धरण-10

1	2	3	4
D	B	D	B

उद्धरण-11

1	2	3	4	5
D	C	B	C	A

उद्धरण-12

1	2	3	4	5
C	A	B	D	A

उद्धरण-13

1	2	3	4	5
C	D	B	D	A

उद्धरण-14

1	2	3	4	5
A	C	D	C	B

उद्धरण-15

1	2	3	4	5
A	C	A	C	D

उद्धरण-16

1	2	3	4	5
B	B	C	C	C
6	**7**			
A	B			

उद्धरण-17

1	2	3	4	5
B	C	D	A	B

उद्धरण-18

1	2	3	4	5
D	B	A	A	C

उद्धरण-19

1	2	3	4	5
C	A	B	B	A

उद्धरण-20

1	2	3	4	5
B	B	D	C	A

उद्धरण-21

1	2	3	4	5
B	A	C	D	C

उद्धरण-22

1	2	3	4	5
B	A	C	A	C

उद्धरण-23

1	2	3	4	5
D	C	A	D	C

उद्धरण-24

1	2	3	4
C	A	A	A

उद्धरण-25

1	2	3	4
A	D	C	D

उद्धरण-26

1	2	3	4
B	D	B	A

उद्धरण-27

1	2	3	4
D	C	C	B

उद्धरण-28

1	2	3	4
D	D	A	D

उद्धरण-29

1	2	3	4
C	A	D	B

उद्धरण-30

1	2	3	4
D	C	A	D

उद्धरण-31

1	2	3	4
D	A	C	D

उद्धरण-32

1	2	3	4
B	D	B	A

उद्धरण-33

1	2	3	4
C	A	C	A

उद्धरण-34

1	2	3	4
A	B	D	C

उद्धरण-35

1	2	3	4
B	C	C	B

उद्धरण-36

1	2	3	4
C	C	B	A

उद्धरण-37

1	2	3	4
C	A	C	A

उद्धरण-38

1	2	3	4
C	B	D	B

उद्धरण-39

1	2	3	4
B	A	C	B

उद्धरण-40

1	2	3	4
C	C	D	D

उद्धरण-41

1	2	3	4
D	D	D	D

उद्धरण-42

1	2	3	4
A	B	A	D

उद्धरण-43

1	2	3	4
B	A	C	A

उद्धरण-44

1	2	3	4
D	C	C	D

उद्धरण-45

1	2	3
A	D	D

उद्धरण-46

1	2	3	4
C	B	B	C

उद्धरण-47

1	2	3	4
C	A	B	D

उद्धरण-48

1	2	3	4
A	B	A	B

उद्धरण-49

1	2	3	4
A	D	A	B

उद्धरण-50

1	2	3	4
C	D	C	D

SECTION b भाषा विकास का शिक्षा शास्त्र

भाषा चाहे कोई भी हो वह, भाव, विचार तथा अनुभवों को अभिव्यक्त करने का सर्वोत्तम साधन है। भावों का प्रकाशन व्यक्ति कई प्रकार से करता है, जैसे—अंग संचालन द्वारा, वस्तु अथवा चित्र दिखाकर, विभिन्न क्रियाकलापों के माध्यम से और भाषा व्यवहार द्वारा। परन्तु केवल अंग संचालन और विभिन्न क्रियाओं द्वारा भावों की अभिव्यक्ति में वैसी पूर्णता नहीं होती जैसी ध्वनि संकेतों द्वारा होती है।

व्यक्ति अपने भावों तथा विचारों की अभिव्यक्ति दो रूपों में करता है—बोलकर और लिखकर। मौखिक तथा लिखित रूप में विचारों को प्रकट करने के लिए भाषा का सहारा लिया जाता है। भाषा ध्वनि प्रतीकों से निर्मित होती है। अतः भाषा को सार्थक ध्वनि प्रतीकों की व्यवस्था कहा जाता है जिसके द्वारा किसी समाज के लोग आपस में अपने भावों तथा विचारों का आदान-प्रदान बोलकर या लिखकर करते हैं।

भाषा की निम्नलिखित विशेषताएँ होती हैं:

1. भाषा एक अर्जित सामाजिक निधि है, अर्थात् प्रत्येक व्यक्ति को इसे सीखना होता है और यह समाज में रहकर ही संभव होता है। कोई व्यक्ति इसे जन्म से ही प्राप्त नहीं कर लेता है। वह जिस समाज में रहता है, उस समाज की भाषा वह सीख लेता है। भाषा का यह अर्जन उसी प्रकार होता है जैसे बालक अन्य सामाजिक आचरण या क्रियाकलापों को सीखता है।
2. भाषा विविध रूपी होती है। जहाँ एक ओर भाषा के अनेक रूप उसके बोलने वाले समाज के वर्ग तथा स्तर-भेद के अनुसार होते हैं, वहीं, उस समाज के इतिहास और भूगोल (भौगोलिक वितरण) के अनुसार भी भाषा के अनेक रूप होते हैं। इस प्रकार सामाजिक वर्ग-भेद के अनुसार विभिन्न जातियों या सामाजिक वर्गों की विभिन्न बोलियाँ होती हैं और वर्ग में स्तर-भेद के अनुसार उच्च, मध्य और निम्न वर्ग की बोलियाँ होती हैं। इन सभी भौगोलिक, सामाजिक आदि बोलियों में मानक बोली भी एक होती है, जिसे उच्च स्तर पर शिक्षा, साहित्य, राजकाज, जनसंचार, पत्रकारिता आदि के क्षेत्र में प्रयुक्त किया जाता है।
3. भाषा संप्रेषण अर्थात् अभिव्यक्ति और बोधन का सर्वश्रेष्ठ साधन है, जो मूलतः सामाजिक और पारंपरिक होती है।

अधिगम एवं अधिगम के सिद्धान्त

हिलर्गाड के अनुसार "सीखना (अधिगम) वह प्रक्रिया है जिससे कोई क्रिया आरम्भ होती है अथवा सामना की गयी परिस्थिति से प्रतिक्रिया के द्वारा परिवर्तित की जाती है। बशर्ते क्रिया के परिवर्तन के लक्षण स्वाभाविक प्रतिक्रिया की प्रवृत्तियाँ, परिपक्वता अथवा जीव को अस्थायी दशाओं के आधार पर न समझाई जा सकें।"

अधिगम (सीखने) के प्रमुख सिद्धान्त

सीखने की प्रक्रिया को और अधिक स्पष्ट करने के लिये विभिन्न मनोवैज्ञानिकों ने विभिन्न सिद्धान्त प्रस्तुत किये हैं, जिनमें प्रमुख हैं—

1. अन्तर्दृष्टि द्वारा अधिगम का सिद्धान्त अथवा पूर्णाकार सिद्धान्त।
2. संयोजनवाद या सम्बन्धवाद अथवा परीक्षण द्वारा भूल-सुधार सिद्धान्त।
3. स्किनर का क्रिया प्रकरण अनुकूलन का सिद्धान्त।
4. पावलोव का क्लासिकी सिद्धान्त।

अन्तर्दृष्टि द्वारा सीखने का सिद्धान्त

अन्तर्दृष्टि द्वारा सीखने के सिद्धान्त का प्रतिपादन जर्मनी के मनोवैज्ञानिक कोहलर ने किया। पहले इस सिद्धान्त के वैज्ञानिक पक्ष को समझाने के लिए पशुओं पर प्रयोग किये गये थे। बाद में इनका प्रयोग मनुष्यों को समझाने के लिये किया गया। कोहलर ने चिम्पैंजी (Chimpanzees) पर प्रयोग किये। उन्होंने इन चिम्पैंजियों को प्राकृतिक स्थिति में रखकर उनकी बुद्धि पर प्रयोग किये और यह निष्कर्ष निकाला कि पशु भी बुद्धि का प्रयोग करते हैं। ऐसी स्थिति में यदि मनुष्य को रख दिया जाए तो वह भी उस प्रकार के व्यवहार करेगा।

अन्तर्दृष्टि से तात्पर्य है समस्या के सभी पक्षों को गम्भीरता से देखना। अन्तर्दृष्टि से सीखने में इकाई (Whole Unit) का उसके अंगों की अपेक्षा उसके भागों का अधिक महत्व होता है। इस विधि में भूल और प्रयास विधि का प्रयोग भी होता है। इस विधि के आवश्यक तत्व हैं– सम्पूर्ण इकाई का ज्ञान या बोध, स्पष्ट उद्देश्य, सामान्यीकरण की शक्ति आकस्मिक समाधान की सूचना, वस्तुओं का नया रूप, सीखने का स्थानान्तरण तथा व्यवहार में परिवर्तन आदि।

अन्तर्दृष्टि का शैक्षिक महत्व

(*i*) **कठिन विषयों में उपयोगी :** कठिन से कठिन कार्यों को करने और सीखने के लिये सूझबूझ का सिद्धान्त अधिक लाभकारी रहता है। उदाहरणार्थ–विज्ञान व गणित विषय।

(*ii*) **अभिप्रेरणा का महत्व :** यदि सीखने से होने वाले लाभों का पहले से ज्ञान हो जाये तो बालक अपनी सूझबूझ और बुद्धि का भरपूर प्रयोग करेगा। अतएव अभिप्रेरणा का इस विधि में भी बहुत महत्व है। इससे बच्चों में कार्य सीखने की रुचि भी बनी रहेगी।

(*iii*) **बौद्धिक शक्तियों के विकास में सहायता :** बालकों के बौद्धिक विकास के लिए उनकी अन्तर्दृष्टि या सूझबूझ बहुत सहायक होती है। अतः इस विधि से अधिक से अधिक कार्यों को करने के लिये बालकों को प्रोत्साहित करना चाहिए।

(*iv*) **पाठ्यक्रम निर्माण में उपयोगिता :** पाठ्यक्रम के निर्माण में अन्तर्दृष्टि अथवा सूझ-बूझ प्रक्रिया को ध्यान में रखकर पाठ्यक्रम के विभिन्न अंगों को एकीकृत किया जाता है। दूसरे शब्दों में एकीकृत पाठ्यक्रम, इस सिद्धान्त के परिणामस्वरूप बनाया जाता है कि सारा विषय एक इकाई के समान हो।

(*v*) **वैज्ञानिक खोजों के लिए उपयोगी :** वैज्ञानिक खोजों के लिये अन्तर्दृष्टि का सिद्धान्त ही सहायता करता है। इसके बिना खोज कार्य नहीं हो सकते।

संयोजनवाद या सम्बन्धवाद

इस सिद्धान्त को उद्दीपन-अनुक्रिया एवं प्रसन्नता-दुख का सिद्धान्त भी कहा जाता है। इस सिद्धान्त का प्रतिपादन सन् 1968 में अमेरिका के मनोवैज्ञानिक **थार्नडाइक** (Thorndike) ने किया था। इस सिद्धान्त के अनुसार मनुष्य एवं पशु प्रयास एवं भूल के द्वारा बहुत कुछ सीखते रहते हैं। व्यक्ति प्रयास करता जाता है और परिणामस्वरूप धीरे-धीरे उसकी सीखने की प्रक्रिया होती रहती है। प्रयास एवं भूल द्वारा सीखने के लिये मनुष्य को प्रेरणा, बाधा, निरर्थक प्रतिक्रियायें, सफलता का आकस्मिक अवसर, उचित अनुक्रियाओं को स्थायी रखना तथा लक्ष्यों की प्राप्ति आदि तत्त्वों की आवश्यकता होती है तभी वह इस सिद्धान्त के अनुसार सीख सकेगा। इस सिद्धान्त के कुछ दोष भी हैं जैसे इस विधि द्वारा सीखने में बुद्धि का अधिक प्रयोग नहीं होता। सीखने में समय अधिक लगता है। सूझ-बूझ का प्रयोग भी कम होता है। यह विधि पिछड़े बच्चों के लिए ही उपयुक्त है, प्रतिभावान बालक इस विधि को अधिक पसन्द नहीं करते।

संयोजनवाद का शैक्षिक महत्व

(*i*) **अभ्यास द्वारा सीखना :** अभ्यास मनुष्य को परिपक्वता की ओर ले जाता है। अभ्यास प्रयास और भूल विधि की मुख्य विशेषता है।

(*ii*) **कौशल अर्जित करना :** छोटा बालक कई कौशल प्रयास और भूल विधि से ही सीख पाता है, जैसे–बैठना, खड़े होना, चलना, भागना। शिक्षण में भी बालक लेखन में गलतियाँ करके ही सुधार लाता है।

(*iii*) **प्रेरणा पर बल :** इस सिद्धान्त में प्रेरणा पर अधिक बल दिया जाता है। बालकों को सीखने से पहले अभिप्रेरित करना अति आवश्यक है।

(*iv*) **सूझबूझ द्वारा सीखना :** प्रयास और भूल विधि में सूझ का प्रयोग भी होता है। कई समस्याओं में इनका सम्मिश्रण करना पड़ता है।

(*v*) **दोहराना :** किसी कार्य को सीखने के लिये उसे दोहराना आवश्यक है। प्रयास और भूल विधि में कार्यों का दोहराव होता रहता है।

(*vi*) **सरल से कठिन की ओर :** इस सिद्धान्त द्वारा कार्य सरल पक्ष से प्रारम्भ किया जाता है और कठिनाई की ओर धीरे-धीरे बढ़ा जाता है। इससे कमजोर व पिछड़े बालकों को लाभ होता है।

सक्रिय अनुबन्धन का सिद्धान्त

पावलोव के अनुकूलित अनुक्रिया की तरह ही स्किनर (Skinner) ने सक्रिय अनुबन्धन के सिद्धान्त का प्रतिपादन किया। सक्रिय अनुबन्धन इस सिद्धान्त पर आधारित है कि व्यवहार के किसी एक पक्ष को पुरस्कृत किया जा सकता है।

सक्रिय अनुबन्धन का आधार पुनर्बलन है। पुनर्बलन का अर्थ निम्न प्रकार है–

सक्रिय अनुबन्धन का अर्थ है–जब किसी पुरस्कार से कोई अनुक्रिया हो तो उसी अनुक्रिया के दोहराये जाने की प्रवृत्ति रहती है।

''सक्रिय अनुबन्धन में किसी भी घटना का उद्दीपन जो किसी प्रकार की अनुक्रिया उत्पन्न करता है, पुनर्बलन कहलाता है।''

इस प्रकार बार-बार दिया जाने वाला पुनर्बलन भावी व्यवहार का निर्णायक हो जाता है।

उदाहरणार्थ, खाने की मेज पर यदि कोई भूखा व्यक्ति 'कृपया शब्द कहता है तो उसे खाना दे दिया जाता है। हर बार यह बात दोहराई जाती है और इस बात की सम्भावना बढ़ जाती है कि जब वह व्यक्ति भूख लगने पर 'कृपया' शब्द कहेगा तो उसे 'खाना' मिल जायेगा। इस प्रकार 'भोजन' उसके 'कृपया' अनुक्रिया के लिए सकारात्मक पुनर्बलक कहलायेगा।

अतः स्किनर ने यह अवधारणा विकसित की कि सक्रिय अनुबन्धन एक अधिगम प्रक्रिया है जिसमें जब अनुक्रिया संभावित होती है, उस समय सक्रियता की शक्ति बढ़ जाती है।

स्किनर के अनुसार समस्त व्यवहार सक्रिय पुनर्बलन के द्वारा होता है। जीवन के हर क्षेत्र में पुनर्बलन द्वारा ही परिवर्तन आते हैं। अतः जब भी किसी व्यवहार को पुनर्बलित किया जाता है तो उस व्यवहार की पुनरावृत्ति के अवसर अधिक होते हैं।

सक्रिय अनुबन्धन का शैक्षिक महत्व

स्किनर का मानना है कि सक्रिय-अनुबन्धन द्वारा शिक्षण-प्रक्रिया को प्रभावी बनाया जा सकता है। इसी सिद्धांत के अनुसार पशुओं को भी प्रशिक्षित किया जा सकता है। शिक्षा के क्षेत्र में सक्रिय अनुबन्धन का महत्व निम्नलिखित है–

(i) **व्यवहार को स्वरूप प्रदान करना :** सक्रिय-अनुबन्धन के सिद्धांत द्वारा शिक्षक विद्यार्थियों के व्यवहारों को वांछित स्वरूप एवं दिशा प्रदान कर सकता है। इस कार्य के लिये शिक्षक को उद्दीपन नियन्त्रित करना पड़ेगा।

(ii) **निदानात्मक शिक्षण :** स्किनर के अनुसार कई जटिल तथा मानसिक रोगियों को सक्रिय अनुबन्धन द्वारा प्रशिक्षित किया जा सकता है तथा उनका अधिगम प्रभावशाली बनाया जा सकता है।

(iii) **परिणाम की जानकारी :** यदि छात्रों को उनके प्रयासों के परिणाम का ज्ञान करा दिया जाए तो छात्र अपने कार्य में अधिक उन्नति कर सकते हैं। गृह कार्य की जाँच करके उसमें संशोधन करने से छात्र उन्नति कर सकता है।

(iv) **अधिक्रमित अधिगम :** स्किनर ने इस सिद्धान्त का प्रयोग अभिक्रमित अधिगम के लिए किया है। इसी सिद्धान्त द्वारा शब्द भण्डार में भी वृद्धि की जा सकती है।

(v) **पुनर्बलन का महत्व :** सक्रिय अनुबन्धन में पुनर्बलन का बहुत महत्व है। पुनर्बलन के विभिन्न रूप हो सकते हैं, जैसे– पुरस्कार, दण्ड, परिणाम का ज्ञान आदि।

अनुकूलित अनुक्रिया सिद्धान्त

इस सिद्धान्त द्वारा अनुबन्धन से सीखा जाता है। इस सिद्धान्त का प्रतिपादन **पावलोव** और **वाटसन** ने किया था। इस विधि के अनुसार सम्बद्ध स्थिति से भी अधिगम अधिक हो जाता है। दूसरे शब्दों में अनुकूलित या अनुबन्धित अनुक्रिया से तात्पर्य है–कृत्रिम उत्तेजना या उद्दीपन के प्रति स्वाभाविक क्रिया का पैदा होना। रूसी वैज्ञानिक वाटसन ने खरगोश पर प्रयोग करके और पावलोव ने कुत्ते पर प्रयोग करके यह सिद्ध कर दिया कि अनुकूलित या अनुबन्धित अनुक्रिया द्वारा पशु काफी कुछ सीखते हैं। यदि मानव को उन्हीं परिस्थितियों में रखा जाए तो वे भी पर्याप्त मात्रा में सीखते हैं। इस विधि में प्रमुख आवश्यक तत्व हैं: अनुक्रिया का प्रभुत्व, दो उद्दीपनों में समय का सम्बन्ध, उद्दीपनों की पुनरावृत्ति और उद्दीपनों की क्षमता आदि। इस सिद्धान्त के प्रमुख दोष हैं– यान्त्रिकता पर अधिक बल, अस्थायित्व तथा मनुष्य की अपेक्षा पशुओं पर किये गये अधिक प्रयोग।

अनुकूलित या अनुबन्धित अनुक्रिया पर अनेक कारक प्रभाव डालते हैं, उनमें प्रमुख हैं अभ्यास, प्रेरक, समय, बाहरी रुकावटें, बुद्धि, आयु व मानसिक स्वास्थ्य आदि। इन कारकों के प्रभाव से अनुकूलित अनुक्रिया की गति अधिक अथवा कम हो सकती है।

अनुकूलित अनुक्रिया सिद्धान्त का शैक्षिक महत्व

(i) **समायोजन में सहायक :** अनुबन्धन क्रिया छात्रों को नये-नये वातावरण में समायोजन में सहायक सिद्ध होती है।

(ii) **भ्रम दूर करना :** अनावश्यक भ्रमों और वहमों को दूर करने के लिये इस विधि का प्रयोग किया जाना आवश्यक है।

(iii) **भाषा के प्रशिक्षण में सहायक :** अनुकूलन या अनुबन्ध भाषा के प्रशिक्षण में बहुत उपयोगी होती है। उचित भाषा के प्रयोग से बालक उसके प्रयोग के लिए अनुकूलित हो जाता है।

(iv) **भय, प्रेम तथा घृणा को जागृत करना :** इस विधि के द्वारा छात्र तथा अध्यापक के मध्य भय, प्रेम तथा घृणा के भाव जागृत किए जाते हैं। एक अध्यापक यदि छात्र को मारता-पीटता है तो छात्र उसके नाम से ही घृणा अथवा भय के भाव प्रदर्शित करेगा, यह उसका अनुबन्धन होता है।

(v) **दंड पुरस्कार का सिद्धान्त :** दंड और पुरस्कार अनुकूल या अनुबन्ध पर बहुत निर्भर करता है। बुरे कार्यों के लिए दंड व अच्छे कार्यों के लिए पुरस्कार का मिलना बालक के अनुकूल या अनुबन्ध के लिये परम आवश्यक है। उचित समय पर दिया गया दंड या पुरस्कार बालक के व्यवहार को परिवर्तित करता है या उसमें संशोधन लाता है।

अधिगम को प्रभावित करने वाले कारक

अधिगम को प्रभावित करने में अनेक कारकों की अन्तक्रियाएँ होती हैं। कुछ कारक ऐसे होते हैं जिनसे सीखने की प्रक्रिया तीव्र होती है और कुछ कारक इस प्रक्रिया को मन्द कर देते हैं और कुछ इसमें बाधा उत्पन्न करते हैं। अतः उन्हीं कारकों को प्रोत्साहित करने की आवश्यकता होती है जिनसे सीखने की प्रक्रिया तीव्र होती है। अधिगम को प्रभावित करने वाले प्रमुख कारक निम्नलिखित हैं–

(1) अभिप्रेरणा : बालक हर उस क्रिया को रुचि पूर्वक शीघ्रता में सीखता है, जिसके लिए उसे प्रेरित किया जाता है। प्रेरणा बालक को क्रियाशील बनाती है। प्रयास, रुचि, प्रतिक्रिया सब प्रेरणा के परिणाम हैं।

सीखने की प्रत्येक क्रिया में प्रेरकों और लक्ष्यों का घनिष्ठ सम्बन्ध होता है। प्रेरक किसी व्यक्ति की वे शारीरिक और मानसिक दशाएँ हैं जो उसे किसी कार्य को करने के लिए अग्रसरित करती है।

(2) **पुरस्कार एवं दण्ड :** पुरस्कार एवं दण्ड प्रेरणा के साधनों में से एक साधन है। पुरस्कार बालकों को अच्छे कार्य करने और सीखने की प्रेरणा देते हैं। इनके द्वारा बालकों की सीखने की गति को तीव्र किया जा सकता है। दण्ड अनुचित कार्यों को करने से रोकने के लिये तथा उनको वांछित व्यवहार करने के लिए दिया जाता है।

(3) **स्पर्धा और सम्मान :** स्पर्धा बालकों की सीखने के लिए एक अच्छी प्रेरक शक्ति है। प्रतियोगिताओं में भाग लेकर सम्मान प्राप्त करने की भावना बालकों को कुछ न कुछ नया करके दिखाने को सदा प्रेरित करती है। इस प्रकार वे कुछ न कुछ सीखते हैं और अपने व्यवहार में सुधार करते हैं।

(4) **उचित वातावरण :** वातावरण का सीखने की प्रक्रिया में महत्त्वपूर्ण योग होता है। वातावरण आन्तरिक भी होता है और बाह्य भी। आन्तरिक वातावरण का निर्माण विषय-कक्षों की स्थापना करके किया जा सकता है। विज्ञान प्रयोगशालाएँ इतिहास-कक्ष, भूगोल-कक्ष, भाषा-कक्ष आदि सभी में प्रकाश और वायु का उत्तम प्रबन्ध, बैठने और कार्य करने की सुविधाएँ प्रदान करके उचित वातावरण बनाया जा सकता है। इसी प्रकार बाह्य वातावरण शान्त और स्वच्छ होना चाहिए। विभिन्न प्रकार के मौसम भी सीखने की प्रक्रिया को प्रभावित करते हैं।

(5) **अध्यापक का व्यवहार :** अध्यापक का स्वयं का व्यवहार सीखने की प्रक्रिया को प्रभावशाली बनाता है। अध्यापक का सहानुभूति पूर्ण स्नेहपूर्ण और मित्रतापूर्ण व्यवहार छात्रों में आत्म-विश्वास की भावना उत्पन्न करता है और वे उत्साहपूर्वक सीखने में प्रदत्त होते हैं। इसके विपरीत अध्यापक का कटोर और पक्षपातपूर्ण व्यवहार छात्रों को सीखने में निरुत्साहित कर देता है। अध्यापक को व्यक्तिगत विभिन्नताओं को ध्यान में रखकर छात्रों को नए से नए ज्ञान देने का प्रयास करना चाहिए।

(6) **इच्छा शक्ति :** सीखने के लिए बालक में दृढ़ इच्छा-शक्ति का होना अनिवार्य है। इसी प्रकार अध्यापक में भी सिखाने की दृढ़ इच्छा शक्ति होनी आवश्यक है। यदि बालक सीखने के लिए तत्पर नहीं है तो उसे बलपूर्वक सिखाने का प्रयास नहीं करना चाहिए।

(7) **ध्यान और रुचि :** बालकों का ध्यान और रुचि सीखने की प्रक्रिया को प्रभावपूर्ण बनाने में सहायक होती है। ध्यान और रुचि का अभाव सीखने की प्रक्रिया को मन्द कर देता है।

भाषा अध्यापन के सिद्धान्त

शिक्षण एक जटिल सामाजिक प्रक्रिया है और शिक्षक इसमें महत्त्वपूर्ण भूमिका का निर्वहन करते हैं। शिक्षण कुछ सिद्धान्तों पर आधारित होता है–

1. विषय का प्रभावी प्रस्तुतीकरण। व्याख्या स्पष्ट होनी चाहिये। छात्रों में कौतुहल एवं जिज्ञासा जागृत करनी चाहिये ताकि वे विषय में रुचि लें।
2. छात्रों की समस्याओं का समाधान करना चाहिये और उन्होंने पाठ को ठीक से समझा है कि नहीं इसके लिये उपयुक्त प्रश्न पूछने चाहिए।
3. विषय वस्तु को तर्क संगत ढंग से Organise एवं Arrange करना चाहिये।
4. शिक्षण लोकतंत्र के सिद्धान्तों पर होना चाहिये अर्थात् इसमें शिक्षक एवं छात्रों के बीच close interaction होना चाहिये ताकि वे अपने संदेह, विचार एवं धारणा को व्यक्त कर सकें।
5. एक Resourceful शिक्षक जिसमें शिक्षण अभिरुचि एवं शिक्षण के प्रति विशुद्ध लगाव हो, अपने छात्रों के प्रति लाभदायक होता है।
6. शिक्षण छात्रों में रुचि एवं कौतुहल जगाने वाला होना चाहिये यह छात्रों को प्रेरित करने वाला होना चाहिये इसके लिये Innovative Teaching Methods एवं दूसरे तकनीकों को प्रयोग किया जा सकता है।
7. सीखने के लिये मनोवैज्ञानिक एवं भौतिक वातावरण होना चाहिये।
8. संप्रेषण क्षमताएं शिक्षण के लिये निर्णायक होती हैं। इसमें वाचन क्षमता के अतिरिक्त वाचिक मुद्रायें जैसे gesture, expression इत्यादि भी महत्त्वपूर्ण होते हैं।
9. छात्र एवं शिक्षक के बीच सम्बन्ध मधुर होने चाहिये एवं एक विश्वास होना चाहिये।
10. आधुनिक तकनीकों, तरीकों एवं उपकरणों का प्रयोग भी होना चाहिये क्योंकि ये छात्र में सीखने की उत्सुकता पैदा करते हैं।
11. कक्षा में सीखने योग्य वातावरण बनाने के लिए छात्रों की आवश्यकताओं को ध्यान में रखना आवश्यक है।
12. अच्छे व्यवहार एवं प्रदर्शन के लिये ईनाम देने चाहिये एवं दुर्व्यवहार के लिए दंड। सामान्यतः दण्ड देने से बचना चाहिये।

अध्यापन विधि

प्रस्तावना विधि

इस विधि को विन्यास-प्रेरणा विधि भी कहते हैं। इसका सम्बन्ध पाठ को शुरू करने से होता है। यदि पाठ का प्रारम्भ प्रभावशाली है तो पाउ की सफलता प्रायः निश्चित हो जाती है। पाठ की प्रस्तावना में शिक्षक की कल्पना, सृजनात्मक आदि शक्तियाँ अधिक सक्रिय रहती हैं।

पाठ-प्रस्तावना विधि के तत्व–इससे सम्बन्धित सूक्ष्म-पाठ (Micro-Lesson) तैयार करने के लिये निम्नलिखित तत्वों की ओर ध्यान देना अति आवश्यक है–

(1) **पूर्व-ज्ञान :** नयी विषय-वस्तु को पढ़ाने से पहले विद्यार्थियों के पूर्व ज्ञान को जान लेना अति आवश्यक होता है। पूर्व-ज्ञान में उसी उप-विषय (Topic) के बारे में जानना चाहिए जिस उप-विषय के लिये शिक्षण-कार्य शुरू किया जाना हो। इससे विद्यार्थी नयी विषय-वस्तु को पढ़ाने में रुचि लेंगे।

(2) **उचित शृंखला बद्धता :** पाठ को शुरू करते समय प्रयोग में लाये जाने वाले विचारों (Ideas), प्रश्नों (Questions) तथा कथनों (Statements) आदि में तारतम्यता (Coordination) का होना आवश्यक है।

(3) **विद्यार्थियों में रुचि एवं अभिप्रेरणा पैदा करने की क्षमता :** शिक्षक में इतनी क्षमता होनी चाहिए कि वह विद्यार्थियों में रुचि और अभिप्रेरणा जागृत कर सके।

(4) **कथनों का विषय-वस्तु और उद्देश्यों से सम्बन्ध :** पाठ को प्रारम्भ करते समय जिन-जिन कथनों का प्रयोग किया जाना चाहिए, उन कथनों का सम्बन्ध नई पढ़ाई जाने वाली विषय-वस्तु से अवश्य होना चाहिए तथा उस विषय-वस्तु का सम्बन्ध पूर्व-निर्धारित उद्देश्यों से होना चाहिए।

(5) **उद्देश्य और सहायक सामग्री :** पाठ के उद्देश्यों को ध्यान में रखकर ही विभिन्न प्रकार की सहायक सामग्री का प्रयोग किया जाता है। कक्षा में एक जैसे शिक्षण कार्य से विद्यार्थी ऊब (Bore) जाते हैं। दृश्य-श्रव्य सामग्री के उचित चयन और आकर्षक प्रयोग से विद्यार्थी की वह ऊबाऊ प्रवृत्ति काबू में की जा सकती है।

व्याख्यान विधि

कक्षा में शिक्षक अपने विचार तथा ज्ञान विद्यार्थियों तक पहुँचाने के लिये व्याख्यान विधि का प्रयोग करते हैं। कक्षा में अधिक समय तक शिक्षक व्याख्यान विधि का ही प्रयोग होता है। इस व्याख्यान विधि में अधिक दोष होने के बावजूद भी इसी का प्रयोग अधिक होता है। संक्षेप में अपने विचारों, प्रत्ययों और सिद्धान्तों को शाब्दिक रूप (Verbal Form) में पहुँचाना ही व्याख्यान कहलाता है।

व्याख्यान विधि के घटक

(1) व्याख्यान शुरू करने की योग्यता
(2) व्याख्यान में प्रयुक्त भाषा का सरल होना
(3) पाठ की गति
(4) दृश्य-श्रव्य सामग्री का प्रयोग
(5) शिक्षण-बिन्दुओं को दोहराना
(6) अन्तः क्रिया में परिवर्तन होना
(7) रुचिकर युक्तियों (Interesting Tactics) का प्रयोग
(8) आवाज का स्पष्ट होना
(9) कथनों का स्पष्ट एवं सम्बद्ध होना
(10) व्याख्यान समाप्त करने की योग्यता का होना

वाद-विवाद विधि

शिक्षण प्रक्रिया में कई बार विषय-वस्तु को स्पष्ट करने के लिये वाद-विवाद पद्धति की सहायता लेनी पड़ती है। शिक्षक किसी बिन्दु (Point) को विद्यार्थियों के सामने प्रस्तुत करके उनसे उनके विचार व्यक्त करने को कहता है। विद्यार्थी अनुक्रिया स्वरूप एक-एक करके अपने विचार प्रस्तुत करने लगते हैं। इस प्रकार कक्षा शिक्षण में वाद-विवाद का वातावरण उत्पन्न करना अध्यापक की योग्यता का एक हिस्सा है। वाद-विवाद कौशल में निपुण शिक्षक ही एक सफल तथा प्रभावशाली शिक्षक माना जाता है।

वाद-विवाद कौशल में अन्य कई कौशल भी सक्रिय होते हैं। जैसे–प्रश्न पूछने का कौशल, उद्दीपन परिवर्तन कौशल मौन एवं अशाब्दिक संकेत पुनर्बलन आदि। वाद-विवाद कौशल के अभ्यास से ही इन विभिन्न कौशलों का अभ्यास हो जाता है।

वाद-विवाद विधि के घटक

(1) उचित वातावरण का निर्माण
(2) प्रश्न पूछना
(3) उद्दीपन परिवर्तन
(4) विद्यार्थी संभागिता में वृद्धि
(5) मौन एवं अशाब्दिक संकेत
(6) अन्तः क्रिया शैली परिवर्तन
(7) आलोचनात्मक सजगता में वृद्धि
(8) व्याख्यान कौशल का विकास
(9) पुनर्बलन

प्रदर्शन विधि

शिक्षण की सम्पूर्ण प्रक्रिया केवल मौखिक रूप में ही नहीं चल सकती। विषय वस्तु स्पष्ट करने के लिये शिक्षक को कुछ न कुछ क्रिया कक्षा में करके दिखानी ही पड़ेगी। कई बार शिक्षक को प्रदर्शन विधि का सहारा लेना पड़ता है। विशेषकर विज्ञान के विषयों में तो प्रदर्शन (Demonstration) शिक्षण का आवश्यक अंग है। उदाहरणार्थ, यदि कक्षा में किसी गैस (Gas) को तैयार करने की विधि बतानी है तो शिक्षक गैस बनाने की विधि का प्रदर्शन कक्षा में करेगा, फिर दूसरे छात्रों को स्वयं करने के लिये कहेगा। यही प्रदर्शन (Demonstration) कहलाता है।

प्रदर्शन विधि के घटक

(1) विषय वस्तु से सम्बद्धता
(2) छात्र संभागिता
(3) प्रयोग सम्बन्धी वस्तुओं और सामग्री का उपयोग
(4) प्रदर्शन की उपयुक्तता
(5) प्रदर्शन दृष्टिगोचरता
(6) कार्य-कारण सम्बन्ध स्थापित करना
(7) परिणाम निकालने की क्षमता

दृष्टांत विधि

कक्षा में जटिल प्रत्ययों (Complex Concepts), विचारों आदि को सुगम बनाकर विद्यार्थियों को समझाना पड़ता है। इस कार्य के लिये शिक्षक दृष्टांत कौशल का प्रयोग करता है। शिक्षक जब किसी विषय-वस्तु को सरल तथा स्पष्ट बनाने के लिये चित्रों, स्पष्टीकरणों, उदाहरणों आदि का सहारा लेता है तो इसे दृष्टांत कौशल या दृष्टांत व्याख्या कौशल कहते हैं।

दृष्टांत प्रयोग के उद्देश्य—

(1) पाठ को रुचिकर बनाना
(2) अज्ञात ज्ञान को ज्ञात के साथ सम्बद्ध करना
(3) जटिल तथा अपरिचित ज्ञान को सरल तथा परिचित बनाना
(4) विद्यार्थियों की कई इन्द्रियों का प्रयोग करना

दृष्टांत विधि के घटक

(1) सरल उदाहरणों का चयन
(2) उदाहरणों का रुचिकर होना
(3) उदाहरण आदि के लिये उपयुक्त माध्यम का चयन
(4) उदाहरण के लिये उपयुक्त विधियों का चयन
(5) दृष्टांतों की उपयुक्त संख्या
(6) उदाहरणों की संप्रत्ययों एवं विचारों से सम्बद्धता
(7) विद्यार्थियों द्वारा दृष्टांत या उदाहरण दिये गये
(8) विद्यार्थियों का संप्रत्यय बोध

व्याख्या विधि

कक्षा में सभी बालक एक जैसे नहीं हुआ करते। अर्थात् कुछ बालक बुद्धिमान होते हैं, कुछ सामान्य बुद्धि के, कुछ परिपक्व तथा कुछ अपरिपक्व होते हैं। सभी को ज्ञान प्रदान करना ही शिक्षक का कर्त्तव्य होता है। विषय-वस्तु को सरल बना कर विद्यार्थियों के समक्ष प्रस्तुत करना और उसे ग्रहण करने योग्य बनाने के कौशल को ही व्याख्या कौशल (Skill of Explanation) का नाम दिया गया है। इसका प्रयोग सभी विषयों में अनिवार्य माना गया है। इसके प्रयोग के बिना विषय-वस्तु का प्रस्तुतीकरण सम्भव नहीं होता। इसमें विषय-वस्तु से सम्बन्धित कथनों में इस तरह के शब्दों का प्रयोग किया जाता है जिनसे वे कथन अपना अर्थ स्पष्ट रूप से दर्शाने लगते हैं। कई बार एक कथन में से यदि एक भी शब्द हटा लिया जाये तो वह कथन अस्पष्ट रह जाता है।

व्याख्या विधि के घटक

(1) कथनों में तारतम्यता : व्याख्या के दौरान प्रयोग हुए कथनों में आपसी तालमेल होना अति आवश्यक होता है, अन्यथा व्याख्या 'खिचड़ी' सी बन जायेगी।

(2) असम्बद्ध कथनों का अभाव : विषय-वस्तु के प्रस्तुतीकरण के दौरान विषय-वस्तु से सम्बन्धित कथनों का ही अधिकतर प्रयोग किया जाये।

(3) भाषा में धारा-प्रवाह : शिक्षक व्याख्या के लिये प्रवाहपूर्ण भाषा बोले तथा प्रवाह इतना होना चाहिये कि सभी विद्यार्थी सुगमता से उसके विचारों को सुन तथा समझ सकें।

(4) परस्पर जोड़ने वाले शब्द : विभिन्न विचारों या कथनों को परस्पर जोड़ने वाले शब्दों, मुहावरों या कड़ियों का समुचित प्रयोग करना अति आवश्यक है। जैसे 'इसलिये' परिणामस्वरूप आदि।

(5) उपयुक्त शब्दों का प्रयोग : व्याख्या में किसी वस्तु या घटना आदि के लिये शिक्षक उपयुक्त शब्द का प्रयोग करे अन्यथा असमंजस की स्थिति में पड़ सकता है।

श्रवण की भूमिका

बालक की अधिकांश भावी शिक्षा उसकी श्रवण शक्ति पर ही अवलम्बित होती है। जनधारणा तो यहाँ तक है कि वीर अभिमन्यु ने चक्रव्यूह भंग करने की शिक्षा अपनी माता के गर्भ में उस समय सीख ली थी जब अर्जुन सुभद्रा को व्यूह-भंग करने की विधि सुना रहे थे।

वैदिककालीन और उत्तर वैदिककालीन जितना भी साहित्य था वह सुनकर ही याद किया जाता था। यही कारण है कि वेद को श्रुति भी कहा जाता है। ऋषि-मुनि विभिन्न वैदिक शाखाएँ अपने ज्ञान को वंश परम्परा में सुनकर ही स्मरण रखते थे। यही शाखाएँ तत्कालीन पुस्तकें और उन शाखाओं के बहुसंख्यक शिष्य ही उन पुस्तकों के बोलते पृष्ठ थे।

श्रेष्ठ श्रोता श्रेष्ठ बुद्धि वाला भी होता है। बालक में अच्छे श्रोता के लक्षणों का विकास प्रयत्न पूर्वक करके उसके ज्ञान में असाधारण वृद्धि की जा सकती है।

अच्छा वक्ता होने के लिए अच्छा श्रोता होना आवश्यक है। श्रवण चिंतन-मनन करने एवं अपना मंतव्य स्थिर करने का श्रेष्ठ साधन है। चिंतन-मनन से वाणी में प्रखरता आती है और अभिव्यक्ति में तीक्षणता।

श्रवण की शिक्षा के महत्त्व को देखते हुए प्राथमिक, माध्यमिक, उच्चतर-माध्यमिक तथा विश्वविद्यालय के स्तर पर भी इसकी परीक्षा का प्रावधान किया जाता है। प्राथमिक स्तर पर यह भाषाकला शिक्षण के रूप में, बड़ी कक्षाओं तथा विश्वविद्यालयों में इसे भाषणमाला (Speech Courses) के रूप में तथा उद्योग के क्षेत्र में इसे संपर्क और प्रबंध पाठ्यक्रम के रूप में स्थान दिया जाता है।

मौखिक अभिव्यक्ति (बोलने) की भूमिका

शिक्षा के क्षेत्र में बोलचाल की शिक्षा या मौखिक अभिव्यक्ति का ऐतिहासिक महत्त्व है। वैदिक युग का समग्र ज्ञान मौखिक रूप से ही गुरु-शिष्यों में चलता रहा।

बौद्ध तथा जैन काल में भी शिक्षा का मुख्य माध्यम बोलचाल ही रहा। मिस्र, यूनान तथा इंग्लैंड आदि के शिक्षा शास्त्र के इतिहास के अवलोकन से ज्ञात होता है कि इन देशों में भी मौखिक अभिव्यक्ति का शिक्षा में प्रमुख स्थान था।

ब्रिटिश शासन काल में शिक्षा के क्षेत्र में बोलचाल की शिक्षा का ह्रास हुआ क्योंकि उनको क्लर्कों की आवश्यकता थी, स्वतंत्र रूप से विचार अभिव्यक्त करने वालों की नहीं।

भारत के स्वतंत्र होने के बाद प्रजातांत्रिक प्रणाली में बोलचाल की शिक्षा के महत्त्व को पुनः स्थापित किया गया। कुशल वक्ताओं द्वारा ही प्रजा के हितों की रक्षा संभव है।

भाषा शिक्षण के प्रायः सभी स्तरों पर बोलचाल की शिक्षा का महत्त्व है। आरंभिक कक्षाओं में तो बोलचाल की शिक्षा की और भी अधिक आवश्यकता होती है। आरंभिक कक्षा में बालक सामाजिक, आर्थिक, धार्मिक तथा बौद्धिक दृष्टि से भिन्न-भिन्न परिवारों से आते हैं। वे भिन्न-भिन्न प्रकार की बोलियाँ बोलते हैं। पर उन्हें अध्ययन में एक मानक भाषा की आवश्यकता होती है। स्वभावतः पठन से पहले मौखिक अभिव्यक्ति पर बल देना आवश्यक है।

बोलचाल में पटुता, मधुरता एवं प्रभावोत्पादकता कई रोजगारों के लिए आवश्यक होती है। ऐसे क्षेत्र में उन्नति के लिए स्पष्टता एवं व्यावहारिकता आवश्यक होती है।

भाषा का कार्य एवं महत्त्वः बच्चों के लिए एक साधन के रूप में भाषा

भाषा व्यक्ति, समाज, राष्ट्र तथा अन्तर्राष्ट्रीय विकास के लिए संजीवनी है। इस प्रकाश-स्रोत के अभाव में सर्वत्र अज्ञान और अंधकार है। सद्-असद्, करणीय-अकरणीय, गमनीय-अगमनीय का बोध भाषा ही कराती है।

1. भाषा व्यक्ति और उसके व्यक्तित्व के विकास का महत्त्वपूर्ण आधार है। व्यक्ति अपने अन्तस् को भाषा के माध्यम से अभिव्यक्त करता है। इसी अभिव्यक्ति के साथ उसके अन्दर छिपी अनंत शक्ति अभिव्यक्त होती है। जिसकी अभिव्यक्ति जितनी स्पष्ट होगी उसके व्यक्तित्व का विकास भी उतने ही प्रभावशाली ढंग से होगा।

   भाषा के माध्यम से ही व्यक्ति बाह्य जगत का ज्ञान प्राप्त करता है। मूक और बधिर व्यक्ति के व्यक्तित्व का पूर्ण विकास इसलिए संभव नहीं हो पाता कि वह भाषा-सी अलौकिक देन से वंचित रह जाता है।
2. भाषा के माध्यम से समाज के दैनिक व्यापार सम्पन्न होते हैं, संस्कृति भी अनुजीवित रहती है। जीव-जगत, आत्मा-परमात्मा, लोक-परलोक, प्रकृति-पुरुष आदि के विषय में निर्धारित धारणाएँ आज भी भाषा के माध्यम से हमारे पास संचित हैं।

   विभिन्न जातियों, धर्मों, क्षेत्रों के लोगों के बीच में एकता का आधार भी भाषा ही है।
3. राष्ट्र के विस्तृत भू-भाग के शासन का संचालन भाषा के माध्यम से होता है। राष्ट्रों के बीच विचार-विनिमय, व्यापार, सांस्कृतिक आदान-प्रदान का साधन भी कोई न कोई भाषा ही होती है। यदि भाषाएँ न होतीं तो विभिन्न राष्ट्रों के महापुरुषों की विचारधारा राष्ट्र विशेष तक सीमित होकर रह जाती।
4. प्रत्येक भाषा में साहित्यिक और कलागत विविधताएँ होती हैं। गद्य तथा पद्य साहित्य के महत्त्वपूर्ण अंग हैं। इसी प्रकार कहानी, निबन्ध, जीवनी, आत्मकथा, संस्मरण, पत्र लेखन, नाटक, उपन्यास आदि साहित्य की कुछ महत्त्वपूर्ण विधाएँ हैं। भाषा शिक्षण के माध्यम से इन विधाओं का परिचय विद्यार्थियों को दिया जाता है। इसी प्रकार छन्द और अलंकार भाषा के कलापक्ष को निखारते हैं। ये भाषा में एक नए रक्त का संचार करते हैं। भाषा शिक्षण इन महत्त्वपूर्ण अवयवों की ओर विद्यार्थी का ध्यान आकर्षित करता है। सुनने और पढ़ने के विविध अवसरों से इस पक्ष की सराहना करने तथा बोलने और लिखने के माध्यम से इनका प्रयोग करने के अवसर मिलते हैं।
5. जीविका उपार्जन मानव की आधारभूत आवश्यकताओं में से है। साधारण श्रमिक से लेकर उच्च पदों तक की सफलता के लिए भाषा कौशल की आवश्यकता होती है। तकनीकी युग में साधारण श्रमिक को देश-विदेश के कितने शब्द दैनिक व्यवहार में लाने पड़ते हैं। भाषा की कुशलता उसे अपने व्यवसाय की आधारभूत शब्दावली को समझने में सहायक होती है। कार्यालयों में काम-काज करने वाले बाबुओं को टाइप, आशुलिपि, टिप्पण आदि में भाषा का कुशल प्रयोग ही सहायक होता है। अध्यापन व्यवसाय में भाषा की निपुणता ही विद्यार्थियों के व्यक्तित्व को प्रभावित करती है। जीवन का कोई भी ऐसा कार्यक्षेत्र नहीं जहाँ भाषा जीविका-उपार्जन में सहायक न होती हो।

विचारों के संप्रेषण के लिए भाषा के अध्ययन में व्याकरण की भूमिका

1. उच्चारण की शुद्धता के लिए व्याकरण का अध्ययन आवश्यक है। अतः अन्य शास्त्र न पढ़ने पर उतनी हानि नहीं होती जितनी व्याकरण न पढ़ने से। उच्चारण भेद के कारण अर्थ का अनर्थ हो जाता है।
2. व्याकरण से भाषा की रचना, शब्दों की व्युत्पत्ति, शब्दों का शुद्ध प्रयोग आदि के विषय में जानकारी प्राप्त होती है।
3. किसी भाषा के पूर्ण ज्ञान के लिए व्याकरण का ज्ञान होना परम आवश्यक है।
4. व्याकरण भाषा के नियमों का पता लगाकर इसके सिद्धांतों को स्थिर करता है।
5. तुलनात्मक विधि से अन्य भाषा सीखने में व्याकरण के अध्ययन से मदद मिलती है।

कक्षा में भाषा अध्यापन की चुनौतियाँ

विविधता वाले क्लास में शिक्षण की चुनौतियाँ

कक्षा में विभिन्न पृष्ठभूमि वाले छात्र होते हैं। इनकी मातृभाषा एवं ज्ञान का स्तर भिन्न-भिन्न होता है। इनके उच्चारण एवं बोलचाल में इनकी मातृभाषा का प्रभाव अधिक होता है। अध्यापन आरंभ करने से पहले अध्यापक को छात्रों के पूर्व ज्ञान का पता होना चाहिए। ऐसा न होने

पर छात्र एवं अध्यापक के बीच दूरी बनी रहती है। बच्चों के पूर्व ज्ञान का पता लगने पर पाठ का आरंभ उसी से संबंधित करके होना चाहिए। इससे बच्चों को यह अनुभूति होती है कि जो ज्ञान वे प्राप्त करेंगे उसका संबंध पिछले ज्ञान से है। जहाँ तक संभव हो अध्यापक को मानक भाषा का प्रयोग करना चाहिए।

बच्चों में वैयक्तिक भिन्नता प्रकृति प्रदत्त होती है। कोई बच्चा भावुक होता है तो कोई कम संवेदनशील। किसी का हृदय पक्ष प्रबल होता है तो किसी का बुद्धि पक्ष। ज्ञान की ग्रहणशील शक्ति भी सबमें समान नहीं होती। अध्यापक को सभी की प्रकृति को उदारता से स्वीकार करना चाहिए और सभी को सम्मान देना चाहिए।

क्लास में तीव्र बुद्धि छात्र अक्सर बाजी मार ले जाते हैं। वे शिक्षक का अधिकांश समय अपने लिए अर्जित कर लेते हैं। ऐसे में क्लास में उनका एकाधिकार स्थापित हो जाता है। शिक्षक को चाहिए कि वह क्लास में ऐसा माहौल बनाए जिसमें सभी छात्र निर्भीक होकर प्रश्न पूछ सकें एवं अपनी शंका का निवारण कर सकें।

ऐसे क्लास में अध्यापक को शिक्षण की विभिन्न युक्तियों का प्रयोग करना चाहिए। जैसे– स्लाइड, मानचित्र, ग्राफ, तस्वीर, वीडियो आदि। ये अलग-अलग पृष्ठभूमि के छात्रों को संतोषप्रद निदान प्रस्तुत करते हैं।

भाषागत कठिनाइयाँ एवं दोष

1. पंचम–अक्षर का प्रयोग

ङ, ञ, ण, न्, म क्रमशः कवर्ग, चवर्ग, टवर्ग, तवर्ग तथा पवर्ग के पंचम अक्षर हैं। जिस समय ये व्यंजन स्वर विहीन होते हैं तो इनको विकल्प से अनुस्वार या वर्ण पर बिन्दी के रूप में लिखा जाता है। लेखन और प्रकाशन सुविधा के लिए विकल्प से अनुस्वार को प्रोत्साहन देना अच्छा है लेकिन भाषा के सीखने वाले को पंचम अक्षर नियम का ज्ञान अवश्य होना चाहिए।

नियम अनुसार प्रत्येक वर्ग के किसी वर्ण से पहले यदि स्वर विहीन पंचम वर्ण आए तो सवर्गी अर्थात् उसी वर्ग का पंचम वर्ण लगेगा अन्य का नहीं। नीचे इस बात को शुद्ध और अशुद्ध शब्दों के उदाहरण देकर स्पष्ट किया गया है–

	शुद्ध	अशुद्ध
अड्ग/	अङ्ग/अंग	अण्ग
शड्ख/	शङ्ख/शंख	शञ्ख
पञ्जा/	पंजा	पन्जा
पञ्छी/	पंछी	पन्छी
झण्डा/	झंडा	झन्डा
ठण्डा/	ठंडा	ठन्डा
आनन्द/	आनंद	आन्नद
कम्पन/	कंपन	कम्पन

2. इ की मात्रा का प्रयोग

अर्धव्यंजन के कुछ उदाहरण ऐसे हैं जिनके साथ ह्रस्व "इ" की मात्रा का योग विशेष प्रकार से होता है। "इ" की मात्रा एक नहीं बल्कि दो व्यंजन पीछे चली जाती है। जैसे–

1. पण्डित
2. मस्जिद
3. अग्नि
4. चिट्ठियाँ
5. पश्चिम

3. संयुक्त वर्ण का लेखन

संयुक्त वर्ण देवनागरी लिपि की विशेषता है। इनकी आवश्यकता शुद्ध उच्चारण के लिए अनुभव की गई। नीचे संयुक्त वर्णों की एक सूची दी जा रही है–

क् + क = क्क – पक्का
क् + म = क्म – रुक्मणी
क् + र = क्र – क्रम
क् + ष = क्ष – क्षमा
क् + त = क्त – भक्त
क् + ल = क्ल – क्लेश
क् + श = क्श – नक्शा

4. र के योग संबंधी अशुद्धियाँ

ट ड न ह आदि ध्वनियों में र का योग वर्ण के नीचे होता है। जैसे–ट्रंक। ड्रामा। द्रष्टा। ह्रास आदि। क, ग, फ, स आदि वर्णों में इसका योग खड़ी पाई के साथ होता है। जैसे–

ग्राम पात्र
क्रम फ्राक

5. र और ऋ में भ्रम

ऋ की मात्रा प्रायः अक्षर के नीचे लगाई जाती है, जबकि र की मात्रा अक्षर से संयुक्त होती है।

- "ऋ" मात्रा वाले शब्द–
  गृह। पृथक। वृथा। शृंगार। सृष्टि। वृद्धि।
- "र्" युक्त शब्द–
  ह्रास। ग्रह। स्रष्टा। ब्रज।

6. रेफ (र्) का प्रयोग

'र्' से बनने वाले शब्दों के पठन और लेखन दोनों में भूल हो जाती है। र् जिस वर्ण के साथ जोड़ा जाता है उससे पहले बोला जाता है। जैसे–मर्मज्ञ। ऐसे कुछ शब्द नीचे दिए जा रहे हैं।

मूर्ख मार्ग दीर्घ
अर्जुन निर्झर कर्ण
दर्द निर्धन दर्पण, आदि।

यदि किसी शब्द में र् के बाद दो या दो से अधिक अर्ध वर्ण हों तो र् का योग पूर्ण वर्ण पर ही होता है, जैसे–वर्त्स्य। यहाँ र् त् से पूर्व उच्चरित होता है।

7. कहीं-कहीं अनुस्वार और अनुनासिक में भी भ्रम होता है। यथा:–

शुद्ध	अशुद्ध
चाँद	चांद
दाँत	दांत
हँसना	हंसना

8. वचन परिवर्तन

एकवचन को बहुवचन बनाते समय अंत की दीर्घ ई तथा ऊ ह्रस्व हो जाते हैं। यथा :–

एकवचन	बहुवचन
नदी	नदियाँ
बिन्दी	बिन्दियाँ
भालू	भालुओं
हिन्दू	हिन्दुओं

9. लिंग परिवर्तन सम्बन्धी

(क) लिंग परिवर्तन के समय "इन" प्रत्यय जुड़ने पर जो स्त्रीलिंग रूप बनाया जाता है उससे अंत की दीर्घ "ई" बहुधा ह्रस्व हो जाती है। जैसे–

धोबी — धोबिन
स्वामी — स्वामिन

(ख) हिन्दी में स्त्रीलिंग के रूप कुछ स्थितियों में स्वतंत्र होते हैं, "ई" प्रत्यय लगा कर नहीं। यथाः–

सम्राट — साम्राज्ञी
कवि — कवयित्री

10. संधि

दो शब्दों में संधि करते समय भी उनमें आने वाले परिवर्तन के प्रति सावधान रहने की आवश्यकता होती है। नीचे इसी प्रकार के कुछ उदाहरण दिए गए हैं :–

सत् + गति = सदगति
निर् + अपराध = निरपराध
जन्म + अष्टमी = जन्माष्टमी
महत् + त्व = महत्त्व
निः + रोग = नीरोग
निः + काम = निष्काम

11. समास

दो शब्दों का सामासिक रूप बनने पर उनमें परिवर्तन हो जाता है। प्रथम शब्द के अंत की दीर्घ "ई" ह्रस्व "इ" में परिवर्तन हो जाती है। यथा–

मंत्री + मंडल = मंत्रिमंडल
खेती + हर = खेतिहर

12. विभक्ति चिह्न

हिंदी में विभक्ति चिह्नों के प्रयोग में एकरूपता नहीं है। कभी ये शब्द के साथ लिखे जाते हैं तो कभी उससे अलग। हिंदी के विभक्ति-चिह्न सभी प्रकार के संज्ञा शब्दों में प्रातिपदिक से पृथक् लिखने चाहिए, जैसे– राम ने, रावण को, सीता से आदि। सर्वनाम शब्दों में ये चिह्न प्रातिपदिक के साथ मिलाकर लिखे जाने चाहिए, जैसे–मैंने, उसको, इसकी, उसपर।

सर्वनामों के साथ यदि दो विभक्ति चिह्न हों तो उनमें से पहला सर्वनाम के साथ एवं दूसरा पृथक लिखा जाना चाहिए, जैसे–

उसके लिए
उसपर से
इसमें से

13. प्रत्यय प्रयोग

कुछ प्रत्ययों के योग से मूल शब्द में परिवर्तन आ जाता है। उदाहरण के लिए "इक" प्रत्यय के योग में पूर्व स्वर की वृद्धि होती है :–

मंगल	मांगलिक
समाज	सामाजिक
इतिहास	ऐतिहासिक
भूगोल	भौगोलिक
एक	ऐकिक
उद्योग	औद्योगिक

14. क्रियापद

संयुक्त क्रियाओं में सभी अंगभूत क्रियाएँ पृथक्-पृथक् लिखी जानी चाहिए, एक साथ नहीं, जैसे–

खाया करता है।
कर सकता है।
जा सकता है।
चलता रहेगा।
मिला करता था।
हंसा करता था।
बढ़ रहा होगा, आदि।

15. अव्यय

सम्मान सूचक अव्यय जी और श्री के प्रयोग में द्विरूपता मिलती है, कभी तो ये शब्द के साथ मिलाकर लिखे जाते हैं तो कभी शब्द से अलग, जैसे–

गांधीजी – गांधी जी
श्रीराम – श्री राम

ये शब्द अव्यय के साथ मिलाकर ही लिखे जाने चाहिए।

समस्त पदों में प्रति, मात्र, यथा आदि जैसे अव्यय शब्द के साथ ही लिखने चाहिए, जैसे–

प्रतिदिन
मानवमात्र
यथाशक्ति, आदि

न कि इस रूप में –

प्रति-दिन
मानव मात्र
यथा शक्ति।

16. श्रुति मूलक 'य' एवं 'व' का प्रयोग

हिंदी में स्वर ध्वनियों के विकल्प में श्रुति मूलक 'य' एवं 'व' का प्रयोग किया जाता है। ऐसे में स्वर ध्वनियों के प्रयोग को ही जारी रखना चाहिए। जैसे–

शुद्ध	–	**अशुद्ध**
गए	–	गये (य-श्रुति)
नई	–	नयी (य-श्रुति)
हुआ	–	हुवा (व-श्रुति)

पर जिन शब्दों के मूल में 'य' ध्वनि है, उसके स्थान पर स्वर का प्रयोग उचित नहीं है, जैसे–

शुद्ध	–	अशुद्ध
अव्ययी भाव	–	अव्यई भाव (स्वर)
दायित्व	–	दाइत्व (स्वर)

17. विदेशी ध्वनियाँ

अंग्रेजी एवं अरबी-फारसी के वे शब्द जो हिंदी के अंग बन चुके हैं और जिन विदेशी ध्वनियों का हिंदी ध्वनियों में रूपांतरण हो चुका है, वे हिंदी रूप में ही स्वीकार किए जा सकते हैं, जैसे–

हिंदी	अरबी-फारसी
कलम	क़लम
जिद	ज़िद
किला	क़िला

परंतु जहाँ उसका शुद्ध विदेशी रूप में प्रयोग अभीष्ट हो अथवा उच्चारणगत भेद बताना आवश्यक हो, वहां हिंदी में प्रयुक्त शब्द के नीचे नुक्ते लगाए जा सकते हैं। जैसे–

हिंदी	अरबी-फारसी
गजल	ग़ज़ल
फनकार	फ़नकार
जिस्म	ज़िस्म

शारीरिक-मानसिक विकार (Disorder)

विद्यालयों में ऐसे बच्चे भी प्रवेश पाते हैं जो शारीरिक एवं मानसिक रूप से बाधित होते हैं। शारीरिक रूप से बाधित बच्चों में प्रायः तीन प्रकार की असमर्थताएं पाई जाती हैं–दृष्टि संबंधी, श्रवण संबंधी एवं वाक् संबंधी। ऐसे बच्चों को सुनना, बोलना, पढ़ना तथा लिखना सीखने संबंधी विशेष आवश्यकताएँ होती हैं।

सामान्यतः मानसिक विकलांगता वो विकलांगता जो औसत से निम्न मानसिक कार्यक्षमता का उल्लेख करती है। इसका आरंभ बालक के विकास की अवधि में होता है और यह निम्न में से एक या अधिक से अनुकूल व्यवहार की कमी द्वारा संबंधित रहती है–

(*i*) परिपक्वता, (*ii*) अधिगम, (*iii*) सामाजिक समायोजन।

स्किनर ने मानसिक रूप से विकलांगों को अनेक नाम दिए हैं, यथा–अल्पबुद्धि (Mentally Deficient), विकल बुद्धि (Mentally Handicapped), धीमी गति से सीखने वाले (Slow Learners), पिछड़े हुए (Backward) और मूढ़ (Dull)।

दृष्टि बाधित

दृष्टि बाधित बालक सामान्य से कम, निम्न या शून्य दृष्टि वाले होते हैं। इन बालकों की समस्या यह होती है कि वे कक्षा में श्याम-पट्ट (Black Board) पर अंकित लेख या दृश्य सहायक सामग्री को तथा अपनी पुस्तक पठन में कठिनाई का अनुभव करते हैं।

दृष्टिहीन छात्र

वे बालक जिनकी दृष्टि एक्यूटी 20/200 होती है तो उन्हें शैक्षिक कार्य के लिए नेत्रहीन समझा जाता है। इससे कम होने पर अथवा इसी प्रकार की कोई अन्य अक्षमता होने पर बालक अंधे समझे जाते हैं। अंधे बालक को अपनी अन्य इन्द्रियों पर निर्भर रहना पड़ता है। जिन बालकों में बहुत कम दृष्टि होती है वे रंगों का भेद कर सकते हैं। एक बालक को तभी अंधा मानना चाहिए जबकि डाक्टर ने उसकी ऐसी स्थिति बतायी हो। डाक्टर द्वारा बताए गए चश्में को पहनने से इनकी दृष्टि में सुधार हो सकता है समय-समय पर आंखों की परीक्षा लेना भी जरूरी है। अध्यापक को देखना चाहिए कि बालक ने चश्मा पहना है अथवा नहीं, चश्मा ठीक दशा में है अथवा नहीं। चूंकि अंधा बालक हमेशा अपनी अन्य इंद्रियों पर निर्भर रहता है, उसकी अन्य इंद्रियों के स्वास्थ्य की परवाह करनी चाहिए।

अंधे बालकों की समस्या अधिक विकट होती है। वे सामान्य विद्यालय व सामान्य कक्षाओं में शिक्षित होने में अधिक असुविधा का सामना करते हैं। उन्हें विद्यालय में आने-जाने, लिखने-पढ़ने जैसी क्रियाओं में दूसरों की सहायता लेनी पड़ती है। वे दूसरे व्यक्तियों के उपहास के पात्र बनते हैं जिससे उनमें हीन भावना का उदय होता है।

बधिर

कानों के द्वारा सुनने में बाधा से उत्पन्न अयोग्यता व्यक्ति विशेष को श्रवण विकलांग बनाती है। यह विकलांगता ऐसे बालकों की श्रवण शक्ति दोषयुक्त होने से उन्हें शब्दिक या बोलकर अभिव्यक्त करने में असमर्थ बनाती है। यही कारण है कि बहरे लोग गूंगे (Deaf) भी होते हैं। अतः सामान्य स्कूलों में शैक्षिक शिक्षण की अपेक्षा श्रवण विकलांगों की शिक्षा हेतु पृथक गूंगे-बहरों के विशिष्ट विद्यालयों की व्यवस्था की जाती है। जहां प्रशिक्षित अध्यापक विशिष्ट उपकरणों की सहायता से उनका विशिष्ट शिक्षण करते हैं।

प्रकार– बहरेपन अथवा श्रवण बाधिता को प्रायः दो प्रकारों में बांटा जाता है–

(*i*) बधिर या बहरे (Deaf) (*ii*) ऊंचा सुनने वाले (Hard of Hearing)। इन दोनों प्रकारों में भाषा को सीखने की योग्यता भिन्न-भिन्न होती है। ऊंचा सुनने वालों को श्रवण सहायक यंत्रों (Hearing Aids) की सहायता से शिक्षित किया जा सकता है किन्तु बधिरों की जिन्होंने कभी वाणी या भाषा सुनी ही नहीं, शिक्षा व्यवस्था विशिष्ट प्रकार की होती है।

शारीरिक रूप से विकलांग

जब तक शरीर स्वस्थ्य नहीं होगा तब तक मनुष्य सामान्य रूप से कार्य नहीं कर सकता। शारीरिक स्वास्थ्य उसके कार्य व विकास को प्रभावित करता है। शारीरिक अक्षम अथवा अपंग बालक शारीरिक रूप से विकलांग कहलाते हैं। अपंग बालक चिरकालिक बीमार बालकों से संख्या में कहीं अधिक होते हैं। ऐसे बालक निरंतर असफल होते हैं और अंत में विद्यालय आना छोड़ देते हैं। अपंग और बीमार दोनों ही प्रकार के बालक विशिष्ट बालकों की श्रेणी में आते हैं। अतः वे विशेष शिक्षा के अधिकारी हैं।

विकलांगता के प्रकार

(*i*) मेरूदण्ड का वक्र
(*ii*) मेरूदण्डीय द्विशाखी
(*iii*) मांसपेशीय डायसट्रोफी
(*iv*) लूले-लंगड़े, हथकटे
(*v*) एक या इससे अधिक अंगों का लकवा।
(*vi*) पांवफिरा
(*vii*) प्रमस्तिष्कीय पक्षाघात
(*viii*) विकृत नितंब

अधिगम अयोग्य बालक

अधिगम अयोग्य बालक वे बालक होते हैं, जो शारीरिक और बौद्धिक रूप से दुर्बल ओर पिछड़े तो नहीं होते किंतु सुविधाओं के अभाव में वे अधिगम (Learning) नहीं कर पाते। उन्हें वह वातावरण नहीं प्राप्त होता जो एक सामान्य बालक को प्राप्त होती है। अतः वे पिछड़ जाते हैं एवं उनका अधिगम स्तर गिर जाता है। अधिगम न कर पाना अथवा कम कर पाना सुविधाओं के अभाव के कारण होता है।

भाषा कौशल

श्रवण (Listening)

भाषायी कौशलों में श्रवण एक महत्त्वपूर्ण कौशल है। शिशु के जन्म से ही इस कौशल के सीखने का क्रम आरंभ हो जाता है।

सुनना एक प्रकृति प्रदत्त शक्ति है। इसका लाभ वही उठा सकते हैं जिनकी श्रवणेन्द्रिय ठीक हो। इसमें विकार होने से श्रवण दोष उत्पन्न हो जाते हैं।

सामान्यतः श्रवण का अर्थ किसी ध्वनि, बातचीत, वाद्य-संगीत आदि के सुनने से लिया जाता है। किन्तु यह सुनने का बहुत सीमित अर्थ है। भाषा शिक्षण के संदर्भ में ''श्रवण'' का अर्थ सुनकर भाव-अधिगम या भावग्रहण करना है।

श्रवण में किसी कथन को ध्यानपूर्वक सुनने, सुनी हुई बात पर चिन्तन-मनन करने, अपना मंतव्य स्थिर करने और तदनुसार आचरण या व्यवहार करने जैसी जटिल प्रक्रियाएँ सम्मिलित हैं।

श्रवण कौशल के विकास के अवसर

विद्यार्थियों को मोटे तौर पर निम्नलिखित स्थितियों में सार्थक श्रवण के अवसर प्राप्त होते हैं:

(1) कक्षा शिक्षण के दौरान
(2) सहशैक्षिक क्रियाओं के दौरान
(3) कक्षेतर कार्यकलापों के दौरान

(1) कक्षा शिक्षण के दौरान

कक्षा शिक्षण के दौरान विद्यार्थियों को बालगीत, कविता, कहानी आदि के माध्यम से श्रवण कौशल के विकास के अवसर उपलब्ध कराए जाते हैं।

(2) सहशैक्षिक क्रियाओं के दौरान

सहशैक्षिक क्रियाओं द्वारा भी श्रवण शक्ति का विकास कराया जा सकता है। उदाहरण के लिए जिस एकांकी को विद्यार्थियों ने कक्षा में पढ़ा है उसका कक्षाभिनय कराया जा सकता है। इससे विद्यार्थियों को श्रवण लाभ होगा और साथ ही साथ मनोरंजन भी। ऐसे श्रवण बाधित विद्यार्थी जिन्हें कुछ कम या ऊँचा सुनता है, उन्हें इन कार्यक्रमों में विशेषरूप से सम्मिलित कर लाभान्वित किया जा सकता है।

सहशैक्षिक कार्यक्रमों के आयोजन से विद्यार्थी उत्तरोत्तर लाभान्वित हो सकते हैं:

1. समाचार वाचन
2. कविता वाचन प्रतियोगिता
3. कहानी प्रतियोगिता
4. वाद विवाद प्रतियोगिता
5. आशुभाषण प्रतियोगिता

(3) कक्षेतर कार्यकलापों के दौरान

कक्षेतर कार्यकलापों द्वारा भी श्रवण कौशल का विकास कराया जा सकता है, जैसे–

1. **आकाशवाणी कार्यक्रम द्वाराः** अनेक राज्यों में आकाशवाणी से विद्यार्थियों के लिए कार्यक्रमों का प्रसारण होता है। कक्षा के अनुसार इन कार्यक्रमों का लाभ विद्यार्थी उठा सकते हैं। शिक्षण अभ्यास के दौरान अध्यापन को आकाशवाणी के कार्यक्रम के अनुसार आयोजित किया जा सकता है।
2. **दूरदर्शन द्वाराः** दूरदर्शन के कुछ उपयोगी कार्यक्रमों को देखकर सुनने के लिए विद्यार्थियों को प्रोत्साहित किया जाना चाहिए।
3. **वृत्त चल-चित्रों द्वाराः** वृत्त चल-चित्रों को दिखाकर सुनने के अवसर देना भी विद्यार्थियों के लिए लाभदायक हो सकता है।
4. **टेप-रिकार्ड द्वाराः** उपयोगी कार्यक्रमों को टेप-रिकार्डर पर रिकार्ड करके विद्यार्थियों को सुनाना।
5. **साप्ताहिक छात्र सभाओं द्वाराः** विद्यार्थियों को इन सभाओं में सम्मिलित होने को प्रेरित करना चाहिए।

मौखिक अभिव्यक्ति (Speaking)

अपने भावों और विचारों को प्रभावी ढंग से सार्थक शब्दों में बोलकर व्यक्त करने को 'मौखिक अभिव्यक्ति' कहते हैं। इसमें वक्ता तथा श्रोता दोनों का होना आवश्यक होता है। प्राथमिक तथा उच्च प्राथमिक कक्षा में पहुँचते-पहुँचते बालकों में मौखिक अभिव्यक्ति संबंधी योग्यता का उचित विकास होने से उनके व्यवहार में कुछ परिवर्तन आ जाते हैं। मौखिक अभिव्यक्ति को प्रभावी बनाने के लिए निम्नांकित पक्षों पर ध्यान देना आवश्यक होता है–

1. शुद्ध उच्चारण 2. उचित गति, बलाघात तथा अनुतान 3. उचित हाव-भाव 4. निस्संकोच भावाभिव्यक्ति 5. विचारों में क्रमबद्धता।

1. शुद्ध उच्चारण : शुद्ध उच्चारण शिक्षित व्यक्ति का लक्षण है। वक्ता के शुद्ध उच्चारण का श्रोता पर गहरा

प्रभाव पड़ता है। श-स, न-ण, छ-क्ष, व-ब, त्र, द्य, प्र, आदि ऐसी ध्वनियाँ या व्यंजन गुच्छ हैं जिनका अशुद्ध उच्चारण उपहास का कारण बनता है। उच्चारण के समय एक-एक वर्ण या शब्द स्पष्ट रूप से व्यक्त होना चाहिए।

2. **उचित गति, बलाघात तथा अनुतान :** बोलने की गति तेज, मन्द या सामान्य होती है। यदि वक्ता तेज गति से भावाभिव्यक्ति करता है तो श्रोता को भाव ग्रहण करने में कठिनाई होती है। बहुत धीमे बोलने से भी विचारों का तारतम्य टूट जाता है। अतः भावाभिव्यक्ति की गति सामान्य होनी चाहिए।
   अपने किसी कथ्य को प्रमुखता देने के लिए वक्ता एक वाक्य में किसी अक्षर/शब्द पर बल देता है ताकि श्रोता को भाव विशेष की गंभीरता या विशेषता का पता लग जाए।
3. **उचित हाव-भाव :** श्रोता पर वक्ता के उचित हाव-भाव या अंग संचालन का भी प्रभाव पड़ता है। हाव-भाव या अंग संचालन से अभिप्राय है गर्दन घुमा कर दाएँ और बाएँ बैठे श्रोताओं को निहारना ताकि वे वक्ता से निकटता का संबंध अनुभव कर सकें, मुखाकृति पर भावानुकूल हर्ष, उत्साह, करुणा, क्रोध आदि भाव लाना, हाथ की मुद्राओं द्वारा अपनी बात को प्रभावोत्पादक बनाना। अंग संचालन के समय यह ध्यान रहे कि उसमें किसी प्रकार का बनावटीपन न आए। इसी प्रकार हाव-भाव उचित सीमा तक रहने चाहिए।
4. **निस्संकोच भावाभिव्यक्ति :** आरम्भ से ही बच्चों को बिना झिझके बोलने के लिए प्रोत्साहित करना चाहिए। यदि किसी कारणवश वे अपनी बात प्रकट करने में झिझकते हैं तो उस कारण का पता लगाकर उसे दूर करने का प्रयास करना चाहिए। कक्षा में विद्यार्थियों को समय-समय पर बोलने के लिए प्रेरित करते रहना चाहिए।
5. **विचारों में क्रमबद्धता :** शुद्ध उच्चारण के साथ अपने भावों व विचारों को सुव्यवस्थित तथा क्रमबद्ध रूप में प्रकट करना मौखिक अभिव्यक्ति को प्रभावी बनाता है।

मौखिक अभिव्यक्ति के रूप

मौखिक अभिव्यक्ति के मोटे-तौर पर दो रूप हैं—अनौपचारिक तथा औपचारिक। घर-परिवार, हाट-बाजार, यात्राकाल तथा खेल-कूद आदि स्थानों पर व्यक्तियों के बीच जो बातचीत होती है वह अनौपचारिक वार्ता कहलाती है। अनौपचारिक अभिव्यक्ति की शब्दावली, वाक्य विन्यास तथा विषय बहुत अधिक व्यवस्थित नहीं होते। औपचारिक अभिव्यक्ति का विषय सीमाबद्ध होता है। विचारों में शृंखलाबद्ध व्यवस्था होती है तथा शब्दावली और वाक्य विन्यास में शुद्धता पर ध्यान रखा जाता है।

औपचारिक मौखिक अभिव्यक्ति को दो उप भागों में बांटा जा सकता है—साहित्यिक तथा व्यावहारिक।

साहित्यिक मौखिक अभिव्यक्ति से अभिप्राय है—साहित्यिक विधाओं के रूप में अपने विचारों को श्रोताओं के सामने प्रस्तुत करना, जैसे—कहानी, नाटक, कविता-पाठ, भाषण, वाद-विवाद आदि।

हम समाज में अनेक व्यक्तियों से मिलते हैं, उनका स्वागत करते हैं, उनके प्रति धन्यवाद ज्ञापन करते हैं तथा परिचय अथवा विदाई के समय शिष्टाचार के कुछ शब्दों का प्रयोग करते हैं। यह औपचारिक मौखिक अभिव्यक्ति का व्यावहारिक पक्ष है।

मौखिक अभिव्यक्ति का विकास

अनौपचारिक रूप में बातचीत करने से भी बालक विचारों को प्रकट करना सीखता है। विभिन्न स्थितियों—खेलकूद के मैदान में, रेलवे स्टेशन पर, मेले में, प्रदर्शनी में वह बातचीत में भाग लेता है और अभिव्यक्ति की नई-नई शब्दावली सीखता है।

प्रौद्योगिकी के इस युग में मौखिक अभिव्यक्ति को विकसित करने के लिए ध्वनि यंत्रों की सहायता भी ली जाती है।

बाल सभा के समय माइक्रोफोन पर बुलवाने का अभ्यास करवाना चाहिए। आजकल कहानियों तथा कविताओं को कैसेट रूप में प्रस्तुत करने का प्रचलन हो गया है। सुनी हुई कहानी या कविता को टेपरिकार्डर पर टेप करवाया जा सकता है। विद्यार्थी आदर्श वाचन भी सुन सकते हैं और अपना वाचन भी। इस प्रकार अपने पठन का आदर्श वाचन से मिलान कर अपनी कमियों का पता लगा सकते हैं और अपने वाचन में स्वयं सुधार कर सकते हैं।

पठन (Reading)

पठन भाषा के चार कौशलों (सुनना, बोलना, पढ़ना, लिखना) में से एक कौशल है किन्तु पठन-योग्यता पर ही बहुत कुछ अन्य कौशलों (सुनकर समझना, बोलना, लिखना) का उत्तरोत्तर विकास संभव है। हम जितना ही अधिक पढ़ते हैं उतना ही अधिक समझने की शक्ति बढ़ती है। परिणामतः उतना ही अच्छा बोल और लिख सकते हैं।

पठन भाषा-ज्ञान का ही नहीं, अपितु समस्त विषयों के ज्ञानार्जन का मुख्य साधन है। इस कारण उसका अर्थ व्यापक हो गया है और वह शिक्षा का पर्याप्य बन गया है।

पठन के प्रकार

पठन के दो प्रकार हैं—सस्वर और मौन। सस्वर पठन में शब्दों का उच्चारण, वाक्यों का सार्थक शब्द समूहों में विभाजन, अनुतान, विराम चिह्न, प्रवाह आदि महत्त्वपूर्ण हैं क्योंकि वह मौखिक अभिव्यक्ति के बहुत निकट है। मौन पठन में स्वरहीनता, पठन गति, तथा अर्थग्रहण पर विशेष ध्यान दिया जाता है।

सस्वर

सस्वर पठन एक कौशल है। सस्वर पठन दूसरों के लिए किया जाता है, अतएव यह औपचारिक है। इसके अंतर्गत निम्न बातों पर ध्यान दिया जाता है—

- शब्दों का शुद्ध उच्चारण
- शुद्ध बलाघात
- अनुतान, वाक्यों का सार्थक पदबंधों में विभाजन
- विराम चिह्नों का प्रयोग
- सामग्री की प्रकृति के अनुकूल भावपूर्ण वाचन, आदि।

मौन पठन

मौन पठन में अर्थग्रहण पर बल होता है। इसीलिए यह ज्ञानार्जन का मुख्य आधार है।

मौन पठन विभिन्न संदर्भों में अपने लिए ही किया जाता है। अतएव यह अनौपचारिक है। इसके अन्तर्गत सभी प्रकार की शैक्षिक, कार्यालयी, व्यावसायिक, अनौपचारिक सामग्री का पठन सम्मिलित है। मौन पठन में पठन की गति तीव्र होती है।

लेखन (Writing)

लेखन एक कला है जो दो चरणों में विकसित होती है। पहला चरण भाषा की ध्वनियों को लिपिबद्ध करके उनको शुद्ध, सुपाठ्य एवं सुंदर रूप में प्रस्तुत करने की कुशलता से संबंधित है तो दूसरे चरण में लिपि-प्रतीकों के माध्यम से अपने भावों/विचारों की सुस्पष्ट, अर्थपूर्ण एवं प्रभावी अभिव्यक्ति की योग्यता सन्निहित है।

लेखन के प्रकार

सामान्यतया यह अभ्यास तीन प्रकार का होता है : सुलेख, अनुलेख और श्रुतलेख।

1. **सुलेख :** सुन्दर लेख को सुलेख कहते हैं। यह लेखन का प्रथम और आवश्यक गुण है। सुलेख लिखते समय वर्ण के विभिन्न अवयवों की बनावट, उनकी स्पष्टता तथा सुडौलता, वर्णों में स्वर-मात्राओं का उचित योग, वर्ण से वर्ण और शब्द से शब्द के बीच की उचित दूरी, सीधी शिरारेखा आदि बिन्दुओं पर भी विशेष ध्यान दिया जाता है।
2. **अनुलेख :** अनुलेख से अभिप्राय है पुस्तक की सामग्री को ज्यों का त्यों देखकर लेख लिखना। अनुलेख का मुख्य उद्देश्य है–शुद्ध वर्तनी सहित लेख का अभ्यास कराना।
3. **श्रुतलेख :** सुनकर लिखे गए लेख को श्रुतलेख कहते हैं। इसका उद्देश्य वक्ता द्वारा उच्चरित ध्वनियों को कान लगाकर सुनना तथा तदनुरूप उचित गति स्पष्टता एवं शुद्धता से लिखने का अभ्यास करना है।

   श्रुतलेख सूक्ष्म ध्वनि भेद वाले वर्णों तथा ड-ढ, ढ-ढ़, ड-ड़ आदि का लेखन अथवा ह्रस्व-दीर्घ मात्रा के श्रवण अभ्यास के लिए देना आधिक उपयुक्त रहता है।

भाषा बोध एवं प्रवीणता का मूल्यांकन

मूल्यांकन विद्यार्थी के ज्ञानात्मक, भावात्मक तथा मनोप्रेरित (साइकोजेनिक) क्षेत्र को परखने के लिए निरन्तर चलती रहने वाली वह प्रक्रिया है जिसमें मानक तथा अमानक परीक्षा-साधनों का प्रयोग करते हुए निदानात्मक तथा उपचारात्मक पद्धति अपनाकर विद्यार्थी के गुण-दोषों का वर्णन किया जाता है। इस पद्धति के अनुसार विद्यार्थी के भावी चलन के बारे में भविष्यवाणी की जा सकती है।

मूल्यांकन का क्षेत्र परीक्षा से विस्तृत है। परीक्षा या मापन केवल यह बता सकता है कि किसी विशेष समय में परीक्षार्थी की बौद्धिक क्षमता की स्थिति क्या है। मूल्यांकन में परीक्षार्थी की स्थिति विशेष के अतिरिक्त उस स्थिति का कारण और उसके सुधारने के उपायों पर भी विचार किया जाता है।

मूल्यांकन उद्देश्य आधारित होता है। मूल्यांकन के लिए ऐसी विधियों का प्रयोग किया जाता है जिसका हर बिन्दु किसी न किसी उद्देश्य की जाँच करता है। भाषा के मूल्यांकन के लिए भी इस प्रकार की विधियों का प्रयोग किया जा सकता है।

मूल्यांकन उद्देश्य प्रेरित होता है। भाषा के विभिन्न कौशलों–सुनना-बोलना, लिखना-पढ़ना–के मूल्यांकन के समय भी इन बातों का ध्यान रखना चाहिए।

मूल्यांकन के उद्देश्य

(*i*) शिक्षण विधियों की उपयुक्तता की जांच।
(*ii*) पाठ्यक्रम में उचित संशोधन करना।
(*iii*) छात्रों की दुर्बलताओं एवं योग्यताओं की जानकारी प्राप्त करना।
(*iv*) छात्रों का वर्गीकरण करना।
(*v*) छात्रों में अधिगम (Learning) की मात्रा ज्ञात करना।
(*vi*) शिक्षकों की कुशलता एवं सफलता का मापन।
(*vii*) इस बात की जानकारी प्रदान करना कि छात्रों की विभिन्न व्यक्तिगत एवं सामाजिक आवश्यकताओं की पूर्ति किस प्रकार की जा सकती है।
(*viii*) छात्रों को उचित शैक्षिक एवं व्यावसायिक मार्ग निर्देशन प्रदान करना।
(*ix*) छात्रों को अपनी समस्याएं समझने एवं उनकी प्रगति के संबंध में जानकारी प्रदान करना।
(*x*) अनुदेशन (Instruction) की प्रभावशीलता ज्ञात करना एवं उसके अनुरूप अपनी क्रियाओं (Activities) का नियोजन (Planning) करना।

शैक्षिक मूल्यांकन की आवश्यकता

(*i*) मूल्यांकन एक अनवरत प्रक्रिया है। एक आदर्श परिस्थिति में एक ओर शिक्षण अधिगम प्रक्रिया तथा दूसरी ओर मूल्यांकन प्रक्रिया साथ-साथ चलती है।
(*ii*) मूल्यांकन केवल विषयगत उपलब्धि से ही संबंधित नहीं है बल्कि इसके अंतर्गत बालक के विचारों, रुचियों, क्षमताओं, आवश्यकताओं, सोचने एवं तर्क-वितर्क करने के तरीकों, व्यक्तिगत एवं सामाजिक जागरूकता आदि को भी उचित महत्त्व प्रदान किया जाता है।
(*iii*) मूल्यांकन के अंतर्गत् शिक्षण की अपेक्षा अधिगम पर अधिक बल दिया जाता है।

(iv) मूल्यांकन के अनुसार प्रक्रिया का केंद्र बिंदु बालक होना चाहिए न कि विषय-वस्तु।

(v) मूल्यांकन में हमेशा यह मानकर चला जाता है कि उद्देश्य पूर्व-निर्धारित एवं परिभाषित होते हैं।

(vi) यह मूल्यांकन बालक की मनोवैज्ञानिक आवश्यकताओं, रुचियों, सोचने के तरीकों, तर्क-वितर्क करने के तरीकों, व्यक्तिगत एवं सामाजिक दायित्वों के निर्वाह करने की क्षमताओं आदि के अनुरूप होता है।

(vii) मूल्यांकन एक प्रक्रिया है। छात्रों के आकस्मिक अनियंत्रित निरीक्षण की ओर कोई ध्यान नहीं दिया जाता।

(viii) मूल्यांकन शिक्षा की अपेक्षा अधिगम पर अधिक बल देता है।

सतत् आंतरिक मूल्यांकन

सन् 1948-49 में विश्वविद्यालय कमीशन ने सुझाव दिया कि विद्यार्थी के वर्ष भर सतत् आंतरिक मूल्यांकन को भी उसकी योग्यता के आकलन में महत्त्व दिया जाए। इसके लिए पाक्षिक, मासिक, त्रैमासिक छमाही, परीक्षाएं ली जाएं और उनके अंक वार्षिक परीक्षा में जोड़े जाएं।

सतत् मूल्यांकन की आवश्यकता के कारण

(i) शिक्षक को छात्रों के लिए निर्धारित उद्देश्यों– ज्ञान, अवबोध, कौशल आदि के समुचित विकास का ज्ञान होता है।

(ii) इससे शिक्षक को उसके विद्यार्थियों के अधिगम के निरंतर विकास का संचित ज्ञानार्जन का आभास होता है, जिसे वह एक समयावधि में उन्हें प्रदान करता रहा है।

(iii) निश्चित समयावधि के अंत में निर्दिष्ट व निर्धारित पाठ्यक्रम में छात्र अधिगम व निष्पत्ति का ज्ञान होता है।

सुनने की योग्यता का मूल्यांकन

सुनने की योग्यता के मूल्यांकन के लिए निम्नलिखित श्रुतसामग्री का प्रयोग किया जा सकता है:–

1. सस्वर वाचन
2. वार्तालाप
3. वाद-विवाद
4. कविता
5. कहानी
6. आकाशवाणी तथा दूरदर्शन से प्रसारित कार्यक्रम
7. टेप पर रिकार्ड की गई सामग्री

सुनने की योग्यता के मूल्यांकन के समय बालक में हुए निम्नलिखित परिवर्तनों की ओर ध्यान देना चाहिए:–

1. वह सुनने के शिष्टाचार का कितना पालन करता है?
2. वह कितनी तन्मयता से सुनता है?
3. वह कितने मनोयोगपूर्वक सुनता है?
4. क्या वह बलाघात व अनुतान के उतार-चढ़ाव के अनुसार अर्थ ग्रहण कर पाता है?
5. वह श्रुत सामग्री के विषय, महत्त्वपूर्ण विचारों, भावों तथा तथ्यों को कितना समझता है?
6. वह श्रुत सामग्री के केन्द्रीय भावों को कितना ग्रहण कर पाता है?
7. वह भाषा एवं शैली की दृष्टि से साहित्यिक अंशों की व्यापक तुलना कर पाता है या नहीं।
8. वह श्रुत सामग्री के सुन्दर स्थलों को पहचान कर पाता है या नहीं।

सुनकर अर्थ ग्रहण करने की योग्यता का मूल्यांकन हमारे विद्यालयों में नहीं के समान है। यही कारण है कि बालसभा, विद्यालय के उत्सव, पास-पड़ोस के उत्सव, राजनीतिक भाषणों आदि का श्रोताओं पर वांछित प्रभाव नहीं पड़ पा रहा है। विद्यालयों का दायित्व है कि वे भाषा के इन महत्त्वपूर्ण गुणों की ओर विद्यार्थियों का ध्यान आकृष्ट कराएँ।

मौखिक अभिव्यक्ति की योग्यता का मूल्यांकन

मौखिक अभिव्यक्ति का मूल्यांकन करते समय विद्यार्थी के निम्नलिखित गुणों का मूल्यांकन होना चाहिए:–

1. सुश्रव्य वाणी में बोलना।
2. शुद्ध उच्चारण, उचित बलाघात और अनुतान के उतार चढ़ाव के अनुसार बोलना।
3. उचित विराम या उचित प्रवाह के साथ बोलना।
4. व्याकरण सम्मत भाषा का प्रयोग करना।
5. क्रमबद्धता, सुसम्बद्धता बनाए रखना।
6. प्रसंगानुकूल उचित शब्दों, मुहावरों और सूक्तियों का प्रयोग करना।
7. भावानुकूलन ढंग से विचारों को प्रकट करना।
8. विचारों को अपनी भाषा में व्यक्त करना।
9. विषय की एकता बनाए रखना।
10. प्रसंगानुसार उचित गति के साथ बोलना।

मौखिक अभिव्यक्ति का मूल्यांकन प्राथमिक कक्षा से उच्च कक्षाओं तक निरन्तर चलता रहना चाहिए। इससे विद्यार्थियों को साक्षात्कार के समय सफलता प्राप्त करने में सहायता मिलेगी।

पढ़कर अर्थग्रहण करने की योग्यता का मूल्यांकन

आज विद्यालयों में पढ़कर अर्थ ग्रहण करने की शक्ति के मूल्यांकन पर ही अधिक बल दिया जाता है। हमारी परीक्षा प्रणाली इसके लिए अनेक अवसर प्रदान करती है। इस योग्यता के मूल्यांकन के लिए विद्यार्थी के निम्नलिखित पक्षों की ओर विशेष ध्यान रखना चाहिए:–

1. मनोयोगपूर्वक पढ़ पाने की क्षमता।
2. ग्रहणशीलता की स्थिति बनाए रखना।
3. भावानुरूप सस्वर वाचन करना।
4. शुद्ध उच्चारण, बलाघात व अनुतान के उतार-चढ़ाव।
5. शब्दों, मुहावरों तथा उक्तियों का प्रसंगानुकूल भाव ग्रहण।
6. छन्द, अलंकार, प्रस्तुत-अप्रस्तुत तथा मूर्त-अमूर्त विधानों को पहचान पाना।
7. भावपक्ष की दृष्टि से सुन्दर स्थलों की पहचान कर पाना।
8. महत्त्वपूर्ण विचारों, भावों, तथ्यों का चयन करना।

9. पठित सामग्री का सारांश तथा केन्द्रीय भाव ग्रहण कर पाने की क्षमता।
10. लेखक के मनोभावों को समझ पाना।

पठित सामग्री की अर्थग्रहण कुशलता के मूल्यांकन के लिए मौखिक तथा लिखित दोनों प्रकार की परीक्षाओं का प्रयोग किया जा सकता है।

लिखित अभिव्यक्ति की योग्यता का मूल्यांकन

लिखित अभिव्यक्ति का हमारी परीक्षा पद्धति में महत्त्वपूर्ण स्थान है। फिर भी अधिकांश विद्यार्थियों की लेखन अभिव्यक्ति संतोष जनक नहीं है। इस असंतोषजनक स्थिति का प्रमुख कारण यह है कि हमारे मूल्यांकन के मापदण्ड बहुधा दोषपूर्ण होते हैं। जिन पक्षों का मूल्यांकन होना चाहिए वे उपेक्षित रह जाते हैं। मूल्यांकनकर्ता लिखित अभिव्यक्ति के मुख्य उद्देश्यों को सम्मुख रख कर प्रश्न पत्र का निर्माण नहीं करते तथा परीक्षक भी इनके प्रति उदासीन भाव से कार्य लेते हैं।

विद्यार्थी की लिखित अभिव्यक्ति का मूल्यांकन करते समय निम्नलिखित उद्देश्यों को ध्यान में रखना चाहिए:–

1. शुद्ध वर्तनी का प्रयोग।
2. विराम चिह्नों का सही प्रयोग।
3. व्याकरण सम्मत भाषा का प्रयोग।
4. प्रसंगानुकूल उचित शब्दों, मुहावरों, लोकोक्तियों का प्रयोग।
5. विषय तथा अभिव्यक्ति के अनुकूल शैली का प्रयोग।
6. यथोचित अनुच्छेदों का निर्माण।
7. क्रमबद्धता बनाए रखना।
8. उचित गति से लिखने की क्षमता।
9. लेखन में मौलिक शैली का प्रयोग।

लिखित अभिव्यक्ति के मूल्यांकन के लिए अनुच्छेद लेखन, निबंध लेखन, कहानी लेखन, पत्र लेखन, सारांश लेखन आदि विधियाँ अपनाई जा सकती हैं।

शिक्षण-अधिगम सामग्री

शिक्षण प्रक्रिया को सुचारू रूप से संपन्न करने के लिए अनेक प्रकार की सामग्री की आवश्यकता होती है। मोटे तौर पर शिक्षण में प्रयुक्त सामग्री को दो वर्गों में रखा जा सकता है। पहले वर्ग में वह सामग्री आती है, जिसका शिक्षक तथा शिक्षार्थी दोनों ही नियमित रूप से प्रयोग करते हैं, जैसे–पाठ्यपुस्तक, पूरक पुस्तक तथा अभ्यास-पुस्तिका (विशेषतः प्राथमिक स्तर पर)। वस्तुतः इस प्रकार की सामग्री शिक्षण प्रक्रिया का अभिन्न अंग है, क्योंकि शिक्षक तथा शिक्षार्थी दोनों को ही इसके प्रयोग की आवश्यकता होती है।

दूसरे वर्ग में वह सामग्री आती है जो कक्षा में प्रस्तुत विषयवस्तु को विद्यार्थियों के लिए सुस्पष्ट, सुबोध, सुग्राह्य एवं सजीव बनाने में शिक्षक की सहायता करती है। इसके अंतर्गत श्यामपट्ट, चार्ट, चित्र, मॉडल जैसे–पारंपरिक उपकरण तथा स्लाइड, पारदर्शी चित्र, टेप (कैसेट) जैसे आधुनिक उपकरण और रेडियो, दूरदर्शन, चलचित्र जैसे जनसंचार माध्यम आते हैं।

पाठ्यपुस्तक

शिक्षण प्रक्रिया में पाठ्यपुस्तक का अपना एक विशिष्ट स्थान है। वास्तव में यह संपूर्ण शिक्षण प्रक्रिया की आधारशिला है। यह एक ओर अध्यापक का शिक्षण-विषय के पाठ्यक्रम की सीमा के संदर्भ में मार्गदर्शन करती है तो दूसरी ओर विद्यार्थी के सम्मुख लक्ष्य का स्वरूप स्पष्ट करती है।

जब हम मातृभाषा का अध्ययन करते हैं तो पाठ्यपुस्तक का महत्त्व और भी बढ़ जाता है, क्योंकि मातृभाषा का विषय क्षेत्र अत्यंत व्यापक और बहुमुखी होने के कारण उसकी पाठ्यपुस्तक की सामग्री व्यापक एवं विविधतापूर्ण होती है। इतना ही नहीं, मातृभाषा की पाठ्यपुस्तक में समाहित सामग्री में वैचारिक तथा भाषिक दोनों पक्षों का ध्यान भी रखना होता है और साथ में विविध साहित्यिक रूपों एवं विधाओं का समावेश भी करना होता है।

किसी भी पाठ्यपुस्तक के दो पक्ष होते हैं :

1. भाव पक्ष, तथा
2. कला पक्ष

1. **भाव पक्ष :** पाठ्यपुस्तक इस उद्देश्य से तैयार की जाती है कि उसके अध्ययन से विद्यार्थियों में अपेक्षित योग्यताओं का विकास हो सके। ये योग्यताएँ शिक्षण उद्देश्य कहलाती हैं। इन शिक्षण उद्देश्यों के अन्तर्गत विभिन्न प्रकार की विषयवस्तु का ज्ञान, भाषाई कौशल और सद्प्रवृत्तियाँ आती हैं। पाठ्य-सामग्री के भाव पक्ष के संदर्भ में उस विषय के शिक्षण उद्देश्यों का अत्यंत महत्त्व है। इस संबंध में निम्नलिखित तीन बातों को ध्यान में रखा जाता है :
   (*i*) भावों का चयन।
   (*ii*) भावों का क्रमिक स्तरीकरण।
   (*iii*) भावों का प्रस्तुतीकरण।

2. **कला पक्ष :** पाठ्य-सामग्री के कला पक्ष के अंतर्गत उसके बाहरी और आंतरिक दोनों रूप आते हैं। बाहरी रूप के अंतर्गत पुस्तक को आकार तथा उसकी मोटाई ऐसी होनी चाहिए जिससे उस आयु वर्ग के बच्चों को उसे एक स्थान से दूसरे स्थान तक ले जाने में सुविधा हो और पुस्तक को हाथ में उठाकर पढ़ने में भी असुविधा न हो।

   पुस्तक की छपाई, शुद्ध वर्तनी एवं चित्र रूप पक्ष के अंतर्गत ही आते हैं। छोटे बालकों के लिए टाइप का आकार बड़ा होना चाहिए। बढ़ती हुई कक्षाओं में यह आकार छोटा होता जाता है।

   पुस्तक की वर्तनी के संबंध में सबसे प्रमुख बात यह है कि शब्दों की वर्तनी शुद्ध हो। दूसरी बात भिन्न रूपों वाले– अ, फ, क्ष, झ आदि जैसे अक्षरों का मानक रूप ही पूरी पुस्तक में प्रयुक्त हो। चाहिए, जाए, लाए जैसे शब्दों को पुस्तक में एक ही रूप में प्रस्तुत किया जाना चाहिए।

पाठ्य सामग्री में चित्र बहुत महत्त्वपूर्ण होते हैं। पाठ्य-सामग्री में केवल वे चित्र दिए जाने चाहिएँ जो उनका अंग बन सकें और उसके पूरक हों। इनमें से कुछ चित्र काल्पनिक होते हैं और कुछ तथ्यात्मक। छोटी कक्षाओं की शिक्षण सामग्री में फोटो तथा तस्वीर वाले चित्र अधिक उपयोगी होते हैं और बड़ी कक्षाओं की सामग्री में कार्टूनों तथा रेखा वाले और तथ्यात्मक फोटो आवश्यक और उपयोगी हैं। चित्रों का स्थान भी इसी आधार पर निर्धारित किया जाता है जिससे उनका लिखित सामग्री के साथ तादात्म्य स्थापित हो सके। यदि किसी चित्र को बार-बार देखने की आवश्यकता हो तो वह सामग्री के बीच में देना चाहिए। यदि कोई चित्र सामग्री की पृष्ठभूमि के रूप में कार्य करता हो तो उसे पूरे पृष्ठ पर फैलाना चाहिए। यदि लिखित सामग्री को पढ़ने की प्रेरणा देना चित्र का उद्देश्य हो तो वह सामग्री के प्रारंभ में दिया जा सकता है। चित्रों के रंग भी बहुत महत्त्वपूर्ण होते हैं।

बहुआयामी स्त्रोत

चित्र

भाषा के कठिन एवं गहन स्थलों को स्पष्ट करने में चित्रों तथा चित्र-शृंखलाओं की उपयोगिता सर्वमान्य है। चित्रों से अभिव्यक्ति में विस्तार एवं गहनता आती है। चित्र शब्दों और कहानियों का प्रतिनिधित्व करते हैं। क्रियाशील चित्र-शृंखला रचना और कहानी शिक्षण का श्रेष्ठ साधन है। शब्दों और चित्रों का समन्वय भाषा शिक्षण की प्रक्रिया को जीवंत बना देता है।

रेखाचित्र

इसके अंतर्गत चार्टों, पोस्टरों, कार्टूनों, हास्य-व्यंग्य चित्रों, मानचित्रों आदि का समावेश होता है। फ्लैनलग्राफ पर क्रमबद्ध रूप में व्याकरण के लिंग, वचन, कारक, क्रिया, विशेषण आदि के भेदों को चार्ट के रूप में प्रदर्शित किया जा सकता है। मानचित्रों के प्रयोग से प्रदेशों का भाषावार वर्गीकरण दिखाया जा सकता है। पोस्टर, कार्टून और हास्य-व्यंग्य चित्र किसी व्यक्ति, विचार एवं स्थिति के चित्र होते हैं जिनका जनसमूह पर गहरा प्रभाव पड़ता है। इनसे उपहासात्मक किंतु विचारपरक हास्य-व्यंग्य एवं अतिश्योक्तिपूर्ण स्थलों के गूढ़ भावों का स्पष्टीकरण होता है। ये विचारों को क्रमबद्ध तथा गतिमय रूप में प्रस्तुत करते हैं।

फ्लैश कार्ड

ये शिक्षण के प्रभावशाली दृश्य उपकरण हैं। ये चित्रात्मक और लिखित दोनों प्रकार के हो सकते हैं।

वर्णमाला-शिक्षण में फ्लैश कार्डो का विशेष महत्त्व है। एक वर्ण को सिखाने के लिए फ्लैश कार्ड पर अनेक शब्द दिए जाते हैं जो उस वर्ण से आरंभ होते हैं।

इनमें शब्दों के साथ उनके चित्र भी दिए जाते हैं। आरंभिक कक्षाओं में शब्दों और वाक्यों के चित्र सहित फ्लैश कार्ड अधिक उपयोगी सिद्ध होते हैं। इनसे किसी एक वस्तु, घटना या तथ्य की झलक एक दृष्टि में प्रस्तुत की जा सकती है।

मल्टीमीडिया सामग्री

ग्रामोफोन और लिंग्वाफोन

इनके रिकार्डो द्वारा उच्चारण के विभिन्न अभ्यासों के अंतर्गत बलाघात, सुर, विवृत्ति और अनुतान का सहज रूप में अभ्यास कराया जा सकता है। इनमें महापुरुषों के भाषणों, उत्कृष्ट कवियों की कविताओं और नाटकीय संवाद को सुना जा सकता है। उच्चारण, सस्वर पाठ और भाषण कला की प्रवीणता प्राप्त करने में इनका प्रयोग विशेष उपयोगी है।

टेप

उत्कृष्ट वक्ता के भाषणों, गीतों, नाटकीय कथनोपकथन, कविताओं और भाषा कौशलों विशेषतः उच्चारण और वाचन पाठों का अंकन करके "प्लेबैक उपकरण" (रिकार्ड प्लेयर) द्वारा जब चाहे, तब सुना और सुनाया जा सकता है।

रेडियो

शिक्षण का एक अत्यंत उपयोगी एवं सुलभ साधन है। समाचार, नाटक, भजन, गीत, संगीत, कहानियों, कविताओं, संवादों आदि की आकर्षक एवं प्रभावशाली प्रस्तुति से विद्यार्थी मनोरंजनात्मक ढंग से शुद्ध उच्चारण एवं आत्मप्रकाशन की क्षमता विकसित कर सकते हैं।

दूरदर्शन और चलचित्र

दूरदर्शन और चलचित्रों के कार्यक्रम देश-विदेश की घटनाओं, कार्यकलापों और दृश्यों को सजीव एवं यथार्थ रूप में प्रस्तुत करते हैं। दूरदर्शन आधुनिक युग की सबसे बड़ी देन है। इसके कार्यक्रम हमारी सामाजिक संस्कृति की झलक प्रदर्शित करते हैं। इनसे राष्ट्र के नागरिकों और विद्यार्थियों में एकता और सद्भावना उत्पन्न होती है और वे राष्ट्र की मुख्य धारा में समाहित होने की प्रेरणा ग्रहण करते हैं।

इनके माध्यम से जन शिक्षा का आसानी से प्रचार-प्रसार और विस्तार किया जा सकता है। ये जीवन के सभी पक्षों से संबंधित कार्यक्रमों का प्रसारण करते हैं। इनके द्वारा समाज की मान्यताओं, जीवन मूल्यों, सांस्कृतिक परंपराओं आदि की जानकारी विद्यार्थियों को प्राप्त होती है। इसके अतिरिक्त भाषाई पाठों का प्रसारण भी दूरदर्शन पर होता है जिससे विद्यार्थी सरल एवं रोचक वातावरण में पाठ की विषयवस्तु को अनायास ही सीख लेते हैं। इन कार्यक्रमों से शिक्षकों और छात्राध्यापकों को कक्षा शिक्षण में प्रयुक्त होने वाली विधियों, तकनीकों और उपागमों का भी व्यावहारिक ज्ञान प्राप्त होता है।

उपचारात्मक शिक्षण

विशेष आवश्यकता वाले बच्चों की कठिनाइयों की पहचान कर उन कठिनाइयों को दूर करते हुए शिक्षण कार्य करना उपचारात्मक शिक्षण कहलाता है। अध्यापक छात्रों के दोषों में यथासंभव सुधार लाने तथा उसकी भाषा संबंधी कठिनाइयों को दूर करने के लिए निम्नलिखित उपचारात्मक सहायता कर सकते हैं:

1. ऊँचा सुनने/कम सुनने तथा मानसिक रूप से बाधित बच्चों को कक्षा में अगली पंक्ति में बैठाने की व्यवस्था करनी चाहिए ताकि वे अध्यापक के चेहरे के हाव-भाव को ध्यान से देख सकें तथा उसके द्वारा कही गई बात को अच्छी तरह समझ सकें।
2. पढ़ाते समय शब्दों को ऊँची और स्पष्ट आवाज में तथा उचित गति से बोलना चाहिए।
3. श्रवण शक्ति तथा स्मरण शक्ति की कमी को पूरा करने के लिए अधिकाधिक दृश्य संकेतों तथा दृश्य सामग्री जैसे–चार्ट, चित्र, मॉडल आदि का प्रयोग करना उचित होता है। मनोरंजक कार्यकलापों का आयोजन करके ऐसे विद्यार्थियों को कक्षा में अतिरिक्त श्रवण के अवसर प्रदान किए जा सकते हैं। जैसे–चित्र कार्डों को दिखाकर छोटी-छोटी कहानियाँ तथा बालगीत अभिनयपूर्ण ढंग से सुनाना और घटनाओं का वर्णन करना आदि।
4. कठिन शब्दों या वाक्यांशों के अर्थ को स्पष्ट करने के लिए उसे बालक के अनुभव या ठोस वस्तु या परिस्थिति से जोड़कर।
5. श्रवण कौशल के विकास के लिए लघु प्रश्न पूछने की पद्धति अपनानी चाहिए।
6. संवेगात्मक तथा सूक्ष्म संकल्पनाओं को समझाने के लिए कक्षा में क्रियात्मक परिस्थितियाँ निर्मित करना, जैसे–प्रसन्नता, नाराजगी, घृणा, आशा, निराशा आदि भावों की अभिव्यक्ति को नाटकीय स्थिति में ढालकर व्यक्त करना।

मौखिक अभिव्यक्ति संबंधी दोषों तथा उनके कारणों का पता लगा लेने के पश्चात् अध्यापक उन्हें सुधारने के लिए निम्नलिखित उपचारात्मक उपाय कर सकते हैं :

1. तुतलाने वाले बच्चों को ध्वनियों का निरंतर उच्चारण अभ्यास कराना चाहिए।
2. हकलाने तथा मानसिक रूप से बाधित बच्चों को यथासंभव बोलने तथा सस्वर पठन का अतिरिक्त अवसर देना चाहिए। उनका मनोबल ऊँचा करने के लिए उन पर व्यक्तिगत रूप से ध्यान देना चाहिए। उनके साथ प्रेम एवं सहानुभूति का व्यवहार करना चाहिए।
3. अन्य बच्चों को उनके साथ घुलने-मिलने के लिए प्रोत्साहित करना चाहिए।
4. कक्षा में उनके प्रति उदारतापूर्ण दृष्टिकोण अपनाना चाहिए।
5. कठिन ध्वनियों का शुद्ध उच्चारण सिखाने के लिए टेप-रिकार्डर, ग्रामोफोन, रेडियो, टेलीविजन आदि दृश्य-श्रव्य साधनों का प्रयोग करना चाहिए।

पठन कौशल संबंधी दोषों को दूर करने के लिए निम्न प्रयास किए जाने चाहिए।

- इन बच्चों को अभ्यास और आवृत्ति की आवश्यकता सामान्य बच्चों से अधिक होती है। अतः इन्हें वर्णों एवं मात्रा चिह्नों का बार-बार अभ्यास कराना चाहिए।
- जिन वर्णों या शब्दों की पढ़ने की अशुद्धियाँ वे अक्सर करते हैं उनकी सूची बनाकर उन वर्णों की मूर्त या ठोस वस्तुओं के माध्यम से पढ़ना सिखाएँ, जैसे–वर्ण विशेष की आकृति, चित्र, फ्लैश कार्ड दिखाकर उसे पढ़ने का अभ्यास कराना।
- सही सस्वर वाचन करने पर इन बच्चों की तुरन्त प्रशंसा करें।

लेखन संबंधी दोष को दूर करने के लिए निम्न उपाय किए जाने चाहिए–

1. 5 वर्ष से अधिक आयु का बच्चा शारीरिक और मानसिक रूप से लिखना सीखने के योग्य हो जाता है। इस अवस्था से पूर्व लिखना सीखने का अभ्यास नहीं कराना चाहिए।

2. व्यक्तिगत स्तर पर अशुद्धि संशोधन के बिना लेखन दोषों का निराकरण कठिन होता है। प्राथमिक स्तर पर तो इस ओर विशेष ध्यान देने की आवश्यकता है।

3. विद्यार्थी जिन शब्दों को अशुद्ध लिखता है बहुत संभव है उसका कारण अशुद्ध उच्चारण हो। यथा–श-ष-स, प्र-पर, छ-क्ष, त्र-तर आदि का उच्चारण अशुद्ध होने से लेखन में भी दोष आ सकता है। अतः इन ध्वनियों से युक्त शब्दों के शुद्ध उच्चारण और लेखन का अभ्यास कराया जाना चाहिए।

4. शब्दों के शुद्ध उच्चारण को सुनने, उचित गति से लिखने तथा अशुद्धियों की जाँच के लिए श्रुतलेख श्रेष्ठ साधन है। इसका अभ्यास छात्रों को नियमित रूप से कराया जाना चाहिए।

5. हर बच्चे की अपनी शारीरिक और मानसिक सीमा होती है। प्रत्येक बालक के प्रति स्नेह और सम्मान का बर्ताव किया जाए और उसे उचित विधि से लेखन के प्रति प्रोत्साहित किया जाए। विशेष आवश्यकता वाले विद्यार्थियों को लेखन सिखाने के लिए और भी सावधानी बरतनी चाहिए।

बहुविकल्पीय प्रश्न

1. निम्नलिखित में से रचनात्मक शिक्षण की विधि नहीं है–
   A. कक्षा नियम विधि B. आदर्श अभिनय विधि
   C. व्याख्या विधि D. भाषा संसर्ग विधि
2. निम्नलिखित में मातृभाषा शिक्षण का सिद्धान्त नहीं है–
   A. आवृत्ति का सिद्धान्त
   B. पुनर्बलन का सिद्धान्त
   C. चिन्तन मनन का सिद्धान्त
   D. नियोजन का सिद्धान्त
3. मातृभाषा हिन्दी शिक्षण में विस्तृत ज्ञान से अभिप्राय है–
   A. भाषा के तत्वों का ज्ञान
   B. हिन्दी साहित्य का ज्ञान
   C. विषय में रुचि एवं लगन
   D. ये सभी
4. निर्देशित स्वाध्याय प्रणाली का सोपान है–
   A. नियोजन B. क्रियान्वयन
   C. मूल्यांकन D. ये सभी
5. माध्यमिक स्तर पर कविता शिक्षण की प्रणाली है–
   A. अर्थ बोध B. गीत
   C. व्याख्या D. उद्दीपन
6. गद्य शिक्षण करते समय छात्रों के शब्द भण्डार में वृद्धि पाठ योजना के किस सोपान के अन्तर्गत की जाती है?
   A. उत्प्रेरणात्मक उपक्रम B. आदर्श वाचन
   C. विचार-विश्लेषण D. आत्मीकरण
7. किस विधि के द्वारा पढ़ाने पर पद्य के गुण-दोषों की आलोचना करनी पड़ती है?
   A. व्यास विधि B. तुलना विधि
   C. खण्डान्वय विधि D. समीक्षा विधि
8. निम्नलिखित में से किस विधि में व्याकरण का सैद्धान्तिक ज्ञान न देकर व्यावहारिक पक्ष पर अधिक बल दिया जाता है?
   A. आगमन विधि
   B. निगमन विधि
   C. आगमन-निगमन विधि
   D. भाषा-संसर्ग विधि
9. कोई छात्र स्वर संधि के बनाने में गलती करता है। आप इस दिशा में सुधार हेतु क्या उपाय करेंगे?
   A. निदानात्मक परीक्षण B. उपचारात्मक शिक्षण
   C. सामान्य शिक्षण D. अभिभावकों को शिकायत
10. विद्यार्थियों को गृह कार्य देने से विद्यार्थियों को लाभ है–
    A. घर पर नियमित रूप से स्वाध्याय करने का अभ्यास
    B. स्वयं चिन्तन-मनन की शक्ति का विकास
    C. अतिरिक्त समय का उपयोग एवं विद्यालय एवं घर के वातावरण का सान्निध्य
    D. उपर्युक्त सभी
11. 'गाल बजाना' मुहावरे का अर्थ है–
    A. हल्ला करना B. थप्पड़ मारना
    C. ड़ीग हांकना D. बहाने बनाना
12. 'अमावस्या' का विपरीतार्थ शब्द है–
    A. प्रतिपदा B. प्रदोष
    C. चतुर्दशी D. पूर्णिमा
13. विद्यालयी पाठ्यक्रम में त्रिभाषा सूत्र का क्रियान्वयन इस प्रकार है–
    A. निम्न प्राथमिक स्तर
    B. उच्च प्राथमिक स्तर
    C. निम्न माध्यमिक स्तर
    D. ये सभी
14. 'दिग्गज' का सन्धि विच्छेद है–
    A. दिक् + गज B. दिग् + गज
    C. दिग + गज D. दिग्ग + ज
15. जिस विधि में पहले उदाहरण प्रस्तुत किए जाते हैं, उसे कहते हैं–
    A. आगमन विधि B. निगमन विधि
    C. समवाय विधि D. प्रश्नोत्तर विधि
16. कविता-शिक्षण के अन्त में सस्वर पाठ के सोपान का उद्देश्य है–
    A. काव्यमय वातावरण में पाठ का समापन
    B. ककाव्यपाठ का अभ्यास करवाना
    C. कविता के भावों से अवगत करवाना
    D. काव्य के प्रति रुचि उत्पन्न करना
17. शिक्षक पाठ्य-पुस्तकों का उपयोग करता है–
    A. अध्ययन में B. पाठ्-योजना में
    C. कक्षा अनुदेशन में D. उपरोक्त सभी में
18. मूल्यांकन प्रक्रिया अपनायी जा सकने वाली विधियाँ (तकनीक) हैं–
    A. निरीक्षण व साक्षात्कार
    B. पड़ताल सूची व प्रश्नावली

C. संचित अभिलेख व सामयिक जांच
D. उपर्युक्त सभी

19. पद्यपाठ का सर्वाधिक महत्त्वपूर्ण सोपान है–
A. भाव विश्लेषण B. प्रस्तावना
C. आदर्श वाचन D. समभावी कविता

20. 'कमर कसना' मुहावरें का अर्थ है–
A. कमर बाँधना B. बीमार होना
C. हार मान लेना D. तैयार होना

21. मातृभाषा शिक्षण का सिद्धान्त निम्नलिखित में है–
A. अभिप्रेरणा का सिद्धान्त
B. रुचि का सिद्धान्त
C. क्रियाशीलता का सिद्धान्त
D. उपरोक्त सभी

22. सामान्यतः जिन विषयों का शिक्षण विद्यालय में होता है, वह कहलाता है–
A. शिक्षण B. पाठ्यक्रम
C. अधिगम D. समायोजन

23. उपचारात्मक शिक्षण का उद्देश्य है–
A. छात्रों की त्रुटि का पता लगाना
B. छात्रों का पिछड़ापन दूर करना
C. विषय के प्रति रुचि उत्पन्न करना
D. छात्रों की प्रगति का ज्ञान प्राप्त करना

24. उपचारात्मक शिक्षण की आवश्यकता होती है–
A. दृष्टि दोष वाले बालकों के लिए
B. कक्षा स्तर के अनुकूल प्रगति न करने वाले बालकों के लिए
C. आदिवासी बालकों के लिए
D. सृजनशील बालकों के लिए

25. भाषा शिक्षण में अधिगम-सामग्री का प्रमुख दायित्व है–
A. कम समय में अधिक ज्ञान दिया जाना
B. छात्रों का ध्यान पाठ में केन्द्रित होना
C. शिक्षकों द्वारा शिक्षण कार्य में कम मेहनत किया जाना
D. विषय-वस्तु के कठिन स्थलों का उचित स्पष्टीकरण करना

26. नैदानिक परख पत्र बनाने की आवश्यकता है–
A. प्रतिभाशाली बालकों की पहचान के लिए
B. छात्रों की कमजोरी पता लगाने के लिए
C. छात्रों का वर्गीकरण करने के लिए
D. छात्रों की प्रगति की जानकारी प्राप्त करने के लिए

27. राष्ट्र भाषा किसकी प्रतीक है?
A. राष्ट्रीय एकता की B. बन्धुत्व की
C. प्रेम की D. वसुधैव कुटुम्बकम् की

28. हिन्दी में एक ध्वनि के लिए–
A. एक ही संकेत है B. दो संकेत हैं
C. तीन संकेत हैं D. उपर्युक्त कोई नहीं

29. हिन्दी भाषा के मौखिक व्यवहार में शब्दों के शुद्ध उच्चारण निर्भर करते हैं–
A. बोलने के बल पर
B. बोलने के सुर पर
C. बोलने के अनुतान पर
D. उपर्युक्त सभी पर

30. एक भाषा बोलने वाले लोगों में क्या भावना पाई जाती है?
A. द्वेष की भावना
B. विचार अभिव्यक्ति की भावना
C. सहानुभूति की भावना
D. राष्ट्रीयता की भावना

31. उच्च प्राथमिक स्तर पर पढ़ाई जाने वाली भाषा होगी–
A. मातृ भाषा या क्षेत्रीय भाषा
B. संघीय या सह-संघीय भाषा
C. विदेशी भाषा
D. उपर्युक्त A तथा B

32. मानक भाषा के लिये अनिवार्य शर्त है–
A. व्याकरण सम्मत होना
B. वृहद समाज द्वारा प्रयोग करना
C. शिक्षित वर्ग की प्रिय भाषा होना
D. उपर्युक्त सभी

33. सामान्य बालक के उच्चारण पर सर्वाधिक प्रभाव पड़ता है–
A. समाज का B. परिवार का
C. मित्र मण्डली का D. वर्तनी का

34. एक शिक्षक कक्षा में कविता के वाचन पाठ का आयोजन कर रहा है। वह किस प्रकार के भाषायी कौशल के विकास का उपाय कर रहा है–
A. अभिव्यक्ति
B. अर्थग्रहण
C. अभिव्यक्ति एवं अर्थग्रहण
D. उपर्युक्त में से कोई नहीं

35. शिक्षक की क्रिया से सम्बन्धित है–
A. आदर्श वाचन B. अनुकरण वाचन
C. समवेत वाचन D. मौन वाचन

36. भाषा का गहन एवं व्यापक अध्ययन करने हेतु उपयोगी है–
A. गद्य B. पद्य
C. व्याकरण D. रचना

37. ध्वनियों के द्वारा व्यक्ति अभिव्यक्ति करता है–
A. निबन्ध लेखन B. कविता
C. संवेग D. उक्त सभी

38. सस्वर वाचन शिक्षण की विधि नहीं है–
A. साम्य विधि B. साहचर्य विधि
C. संशोधन विधि D. अनुकरण विधि

39. छात्रों को श्रुत-लेख देने का क्या लाभ है?
A. वर्तनी सम्बन्धी त्रुटियाँ न करना
B. गति के साथ सुन्दर लिखना

C. सुनकर अर्थ ग्रहण करना
D. उक्त सभी

40. काव्य में रुचि विकसित करने हेतु उत्तम है–
A. पुस्तकें खरीदना B. अन्त्याक्षरी प्रतियोगिताएँ
C. व्याकरण का ज्ञान D. उक्त सभी

41. व्याकरण शिक्षण की विधि नही है–
A. सूत्र विधि B. सहयोग विधि
C. कथन विधि D. भाषा संसर्ग विधि

42. वाचन सिखाने की सबसे प्राचीन पद्धति है–
A. वाक्य ज्ञान B. अक्षर ज्ञान
C. व्यंजन ज्ञान D. शब्द ज्ञान

43. अशुद्धोचरण का कारण हो सकता है–
A. क्रोध में बोलना
B. भयभीत होकर बोलना
C. शब्दों को चबा-चबाकर बोलना
D. उक्त सभी

44. सस्वर वाचन बड़ा लाभप्रद है क्योंकि इससे–
A. समय व्यंतीत करने में सुविधा रहती है
B. उच्चारण में शुद्धता आती है
C. छात्र प्रतियोगिता करना सीखता है
D. उक्त सभी

45. कक्षा-6 के हिन्दी शिक्षण में प्रयुक्त किये जा सकने वाले सामुदायिक साधन हैं–
A. सामाजिक व राष्ट्रीय पर्व
B. मेले, तमाशे
C. सार्वजनिक स्थल
D. उक्त सभी

46. गद्य की रूढ़िगत पठन विधि का दोष है–
A. छात्र की वाचन सम्बन्धी अशुद्धियों को ठीक नहीं कराया जाता
B. छात्र गद्यांश का अर्थ नहीं समझ पाते
C. वाक्य प्रयोग, मुहावरे, पर्यायवाची शब्दों का अर्थ स्पष्ट नहीं कराया जाता
D. उपर्युक्त सभी

47. विद्यालय में मातृभाषा हिन्दी शिक्षक की प्रमुख भूमिका होनी चाहिए–
A. विद्यालय समुन्नयन योजना प्रभारी
B. गृह कार्य के जाँच प्रभारी
C. शैक्षिक एवं सह-शैक्षिक कार्यो के आयोजन प्रभारी
D. उपर्युक्त सभी

48. वार्तालाप संवाद में होना चाहिए–
A. स्पष्टता व शुद्धता B. प्रभावोत्पादकता
C. स्वाभाविकता D. उक्त सभी

49. उच्चारण दोष को दूर करने का उपाय है–
A. शारीरिक उपचार B. विश्लेषण
C. वाचन D. प्रयोगशाला

50. एक भाषा बोलने वाले लोगों में क्या भावना पाई जाती है?
A. द्वेष की भावना
B. विचार अभिव्यक्ति की भावना
C. सहानुभूति की भावना
D. राष्ट्रीयता की भावना

51. भाषा शिक्षण का सामान्य उद्देश्य है–
A. छात्रों में सृजनात्मक शक्ति का विकास करना
B. भावानुकूल भाषा प्रयोग, स्वर निर्माण, अंग संचालन का अभ्यास करना
C. छात्रों में शुद्ध, सरल, स्पष्ट ढंग से आत्मविश्वास की योग्यता उत्पन्न करना
D. उपर्युक्त सभी

52. हिन्दी भाषा के रूढ़िगत शिक्षण विधि में–
A. शिक्षक की भूमिका प्रमुख और छात्रों की भूमिका गौण बन जाती है।
B. छात्रों को विचाराभिव्यक्ति की स्वतन्त्रता नहीं मिल पाती।
C. छात्र, पाठ में संभागिता के अभाव के कारण निष्क्रिय अधिक हो जाते हैं।
D. उपर्युक्त सभी

53. खेल द्वारा शिक्षण विधि के अन्तर्गत उच्च कक्षाओं के लिए–किस विधि का उपयोग उत्तम है?
A. उच्चस्तरीय विभिन्न प्रतियोगिताओं के खेल
B. परिभाषाओं की होड़ का खेल
C. समस्या-पूर्ति का खेल
D. उपर्युक्त सभी

54. भाषा शिक्षण की प्रायः नवीन पद्धतियों द्वारा किन बातों पर विशेष बल दिया गया है–
A. बालक की स्वतन्त्रता
B. बालक की रुचि
C. क्रियाशीलता
D. इनमें से सभी

55. निम्नलिखित में से कौन-सा विशिष्ट गुण शिक्षक को प्रेरणा का स्रोत बनने में सहायक है?
A. व्यवहार कुशलता
B. उत्तम शिक्षण विधियों का ज्ञान
C. प्रभावशाली व्यक्तित्व
D. शैक्षिक/सह-शैक्षिक क्रियाओं में रुचि

56. कविता शिक्षण का मुख्य उद्देश्य है–
A. भावों का अनुभूति रहित होना
B. भावों की अनुभूति कराना
C. आनन्द का संचार करना
D. उपरोक्त से कोई नहीं

57. भाषा शिक्षण में किस विधि का प्रयोग अधिक लाभकर होता है–
A. प्रश्नोत्तर विधि B. खेल विधि
C. डाल्टन विधि D. इनमें से कोई नहीं

58. 'दयालु' का विपरीतार्थक है–

A. नीच B. क्रूर

C. निकृष्ट D. दुष्ट

59. निम्न में से किस विधि द्वारा भाषा शिक्षण के उद्देश्य, अर्थग्रहण, अभिव्यक्ति तथा सृजन शक्ति तीनों साथ-साथ पूरे होते हैं–

A. किंडरगार्टन पद्धति B. डॉल्टन पद्धति

C. प्रोजेक्ट पद्धति D. मॉण्टेसरी पद्धति

60. माध्यमिक स्तर पर भाषा शिक्षण का निम्न में से उद्देश्य है–

A. छात्रों को द्रुत गति से सस्वर तथा मौन पठन करने की प्रेरणा देना

B. उसमें अभिनय संवाद की योग्यता उत्पन्न करना

C. उन्हें व्याकरण का उच्च ज्ञान प्रदान करना

D. उपर्युक्त सभी

61. उद्देश्यनिष्ठ मूल्यांकन की विशेषताएँ हैं–

A. वस्तुनिष्ठता और विभेदकारी

B. व्यापकता और व्यवहारिकता

C. विश्वसनीयता और वैधता

D. उपरोक्त सभी

62. नाटक शिक्षण के सोपान हैं–

A. उद्देश्य-निर्धारण B. पूर्व ज्ञान

C. प्रस्तावना D. उपरोक्त सभी

63. शब्द व्याख्या की प्रमुख विधि है–

A. उद्‌बोधन विधि B. प्रवचन विधि

C. स्पष्टीकरण विधि D. उपर्युक्त सभी

64. निम्नलिखित में से कौन-सी विधि रचना शिक्षण की विधि नहीं है?

A. चित्र रचना विधि B. शब्द प्रधान विधि

C. सूत्र विधि D. खेल विधि

65. शब्द भण्डार में वृद्धि के लिए उत्तम है–

A. पद्य शिक्षण B. गद्य शिक्षण

C. नाटक शिक्षण D. उपन्यास शिक्षण

66. शैक्षिक भ्रमण का दूसरा नाम है–

A. शिक्षण-घूमना B. क्षेत्र-पर्यटन

C. शिक्षण भ्रमण D. शैक्षिक तकनीकी

67. व्याकरण शिक्षण पाठ के प्रकार होते हैं–

A. औपचारिक व्याकरण पाठ

B. व्यावहारिक व्याकरण पाठ

C. प्रासंगिक व्याकरण पाठ

D. उपरोक्त पाठ

68. निम्न में से निबन्ध शिक्षण की विधि है–

A. चित्र वर्णन विधि

B. रूपरेखा विधि

C. प्रवचन प्रश्नोत्तर विधि

D. उपर्युक्त सभी

69. जो दूसरों के अधीन है–

A. स्वाधीन B. पराधीन

C. परदेशी D. परामर्शदाता

70. लिखित अभिव्यक्ति की विधा है–

A. पत्र लेखन B. संस्मरण लेखन

C. कहानी D. उपर्युक्त सभी

71. निम्नलिखित में शिक्षण योजना बनाने का लाभ है–

A. शिक्षण योजना से अध्यापक का कार्य क्रमबद्ध हो जाता है।

B. अध्यापक पाठ के भिन्न-भिन्न अंगों में समायोजन कर सकता है।

C. इस विधि से छात्रों का मूल्यांकन भली-भांति किया जा सकता है।

D. उपर्युक्त सभी।

72. निम्नलिखित में दृश्य-श्रव्य उपकरण है–

A. रेडियो B. टेलीग्राफ

C. दूरदर्शन D. ग्रामोफोन

73. मूल्यांकन से अभिप्राय है–

A. निरन्तर/सतत् चलने वाली प्रक्रिया

B. वांछित व्यवहारगत परिवर्तन की जानकारी

C. उद्देश्यों की पूर्ति का सीमांकन

D. उपर्युक्त सभी

74. 'ध्वनि साम्य विधि' द्वारा–

A. उच्चारण व हाव-भाव सिखाया जाता है

B. ध्वनि में समानता रखने वाले शब्दों को एक साथ सिखाया जाता है

C. अनुकरण करना सिखाया जाता है

D. उपरोक्त में से कोई नहीं

75. निम्न में से कौन-सी शब्दार्थ विधि का विकसित रूप है?

A. तुलना विधि B. गीत विधि

C. व्याख्या विधि D. व्यास विधि

76. आदर्श हिन्दी शिक्षक के लिए आवश्यक है–

A. व्याकरण का ज्ञान होना

B. हिन्दी साहित्य का ज्ञान होना

C. शुद्ध उच्चारण करना

D. उपरोक्त सभी

77. 'कान में तेल डालना' का अर्थ है–

A. कान की बीमारी B. कुछ न सुनना

C. चुप बैठ जाना D. बहरा होना

78. प्रायोजना विधि का आधारभूत सिद्धान्त है–

A. रोचकता B. उद्देश्य

C. क्रियाशीलता D. ये सभी

79. सहायक पुस्तकों के उद्देश्य होते हैं–

A. भाषा का ज्ञान कराना

B. बौद्धिक क्षमताओं का विकास

C. साहित्यिक तथा स्वास्थ्य मनोरंजन का विकास

D. उक्त सभी

80. शिक्षण को सहायक सामग्री बनाती है–

A. रोचक B. प्रभावी

C. बोधगम्य D. उक्त सभी

81. अध्यापक को कक्षा में अपनी आवाज को रखना चाहिये–

A. पर्याप्त ऊंची B. धीमी

C. मध्यम D. कभी धीमी कभी तेज

82. यदि कुछ विद्यार्थी परीक्षा में फेल हो जाते हैं तो यह गलती है–

A. अध्यापकों की B. प्रधानाध्यापक की

C. स्वयं छात्रों की D. पाठ्यपुस्तकों की

83. वह अध्यापक जो अपने छात्रों का ध्यान आकर्षित करने में सफल न हो रहा हो तो उसे चाहिये कि–

A. वह अपनी शिक्षण विधि का मूल्यांकन करके उसमें सुधार लाये

B. वह अपने पद से त्यागपत्र दे दे

C. वह अपने शिष्यों में गलती ढूंढे

D. वह डिक्टेशन देना आरम्भ कर दे

84. यदि पीछे बैठने वाले सदैव बातचीत में ही व्यस्त हों तो अध्यापक को चाहिये कि वह–

A. उन्हें जो कुछ वे कर रहे हैं करने दे

B. उन्हें दन्ड दे

C. उन्हें आगे बिठाये और उन पर नजर रखे

D. उपरोक्त कोई नहीं

85. अध्यापक को

A. अध्यापन आरम्भ करने से पूर्व पाठ का परिचय कराना चाहिये

B. अपनी भाषा में दक्ष होना चाहिये

C. अपने विषय में निपुण होना चाहिये

D. उपरोक्त सभी

86. यदि अध्यापक छात्र के प्रश्न का उत्तर देने में असमर्थ हो तो उसे चाहिये कि वह

A. कहे कि वह जानकारी प्राप्त करने के बाद उत्तर देगा

B. शिष्यों को डांटे-फटकारे

C. कहे कि प्रश्न ही गलत है

D. उपरोक्त कोई नहीं

87. निम्न शिक्षण-प्रक्रियाओं को क्रम में लिखो :

(*i*) वर्तमान ज्ञान को पिछले ज्ञान से सम्बद्ध करना

(*ii*) मूल्यांकन

(*iii*) पुनर्शिक्षण

(*iv*) उद्देश्यों की संरचना

(*v*) सामग्री को प्रस्तुत करना

A. (*i*), (*ii*), (*iii*), (*iv*), (*v*)

B. (*ii*), (*i*), (*iii*), (*iv*), (*v*)

C. (*v*), (*iv*), (*iii*), (*i*), (*ii*)

D. (*iv*), (*i*), (*v*), (*ii*), (*iii*)

88. दूरदर्शन सामग्री का प्रयोग :

A. ध्यान केन्द्रण तथा ज्ञान को बढ़ाता है

B. अध्यापक के बोझ को कम करता है

C. स्मरणशक्ति में वृद्धि करता है

D. उपरोक्त सभी

89. यदि छात्र आपकी बात नहीं समझ पा रहे हैं तो

A. आपको उन्हें संकेत (prompt) देना चाहिये

B. सामग्री को सरल बनाना चाहिये

C. उदाहरण देकर समझाना चाहिये

D. उपरोक्त सभी

90. सूक्ष्म शिक्षण लाभदायक है :

A. प्राथमिक कक्षा के छात्रों के लिए

B. जूनियर कक्षा के छात्रों के लिए

C. 10 + 2 कक्षा के छात्रों के लिए

D. उच्च तथा प्राथमिक दोनों कक्षाओं के छात्रों के लिए

91. यदि छात्र आप पर फब्तियां कसते हैं तो आप

A. उन्हें दन्ड देंगे

B. उन्हें कॉलेज से निकाल देंगे

C. उनकी परीक्षा-पुस्तिकाओं का मूल्यांकन करते समय आप उनसे बदला लेंगे

D. उनकी परीक्षा-पुस्तिकाओं का मूल्यांकन के समय भी आप गैर-जानिबदार रहेंगे

92. शिक्षण में छात्रों की सर्वाधिक भागीदारी सम्भव है :

A. व्याख्यान विधि द्वारा

B. चर्चा विधि द्वारा

C. पुस्तक विधि द्वारा

D. ऑडियो-विजुअल एड द्वारा

93. नये आये अध्यापक की सफलता के लिए निम्न में से कौन-सा घटक सर्वाधिक महत्त्वपूर्ण है?

A. विद्वता

B. संप्रेषण योग्यता

C. अध्यापक का व्यक्तित्व तथा उसकी छात्रों तथा कक्षा से मेल खाने की अभिक्षमता

D. संगठनात्मक योग्यता

94. निम्न सभी एक प्रभावशाली शिक्षक की विशेषताएं हैं केवल एक को छोड़कर :

A. स्टैन्डर्ड को बनाये रखने पर जोर देना

B. लक्ष्यों के स्पष्टीकरण हेतु सामूहिक चर्चा पर बल देना

C. समस्या उत्पन्न करने वाली परिस्थितियों के तुरन्त नियन्त्रण पर जोर देना

D. कक्षा के छात्रों के साथ विभेदात्मक व्यवहार करना

95. एक प्रभावशाली शिक्षण का तात्पर्य नहीं है :

A. अध्यापक उत्साहपूर्वक पढ़ाता है

B. अध्यापक अपने छात्रों में गलती ढूंढता है

C. अध्यापक शिक्षण पर अधिक तथा कक्षा-नियन्त्रण पर कम जोर देता है

हिन्दी

D. अध्यापक की रुचि विषय-सामग्री को छात्रों को समझाने में है न कि पाठ्यक्रम पूरा करने में

96. उच्च प्राथमिक कक्षाओं में कविता शिक्षण की किस विधि का प्रयोग किया जाता है?
A. तुलना विधि B. व्यास विधि
C. व्याख्या विधि D. प्रश्नोत्तर विधि

97. प्रजातान्त्रिक समाज वह है, जो
A. स्वतन्त्रता, समानता, बन्धुत्व तथा न्याय के सिद्धान्तों का पालन करता है
B. सूझ-बूझ रखने वाले व्यक्तियों का तिरस्कार नहीं करता है
C. समान शिक्षा के अवसर में विश्वास रखता है
D. उपरोक्त सभी

98. एक प्रभावशाली अध्यापक पालन करता है :
A. प्रजातान्त्रिक समाज के नियमों का
B. स्वतन्त्र समाज के नियमों का
C. तानाशाही समाज के नियमों का
D. परिस्थितियों के अनुसार सभी का

99. सहायक शिक्षण सामग्री के रूप में टी. वी., रेडियो से उत्तम है क्योंकि
A. यह मंहगा है
B. इसमें दो इन्द्रियां–सुनना तथा देखना दोनों साथ-साथ प्रयोग होती हैं। जिसके फलस्वरूप लड़कों को अधिक आसानी से समझ में आता है
C. यह छात्रों द्वारा आमतौर पर पसन्द किया जाता है
D. उपरोक्त सभी

100. सबसे बड़ा उत्तरदायित्व जो स्कूल में काम करने वालों पर आता है वह यह है कि
A. वे बच्चों तथा समाज दोनों की आवश्यकताओं में सामन्जस्य स्थापित करते हैं जिससे दोनों को लाभ होता है
B. वे बच्चों को नौकरी पाने के योग्य बनाते हैं
C. वे स्कूल के कार्यक्रमों को बच्चे की आवश्यकता तथा रुचि के अनुसार तैयार करते हैं
D. A तथा C दोनों

101. सबसे उत्तम शिक्षा कार्यक्रम वह है जो कि
A. बच्चों की आवश्यकतानुसार हो
B. बच्चों की योग्यतानुसार हो
C. बच्चों की रुचि के अनुसार हो
D. उपरोक्त सभी

102. लेक्चर देते समय यदि कक्षा में कुछ व्यवधान (शोर) हो रहा हो तो अध्यापक को चाहिये कि वह
A. थोड़ी देर चुप रहे फिर पढ़ाना आरम्भ करे
B. कक्षा में जो कुछ हो रहा है उसकी कोई चिन्ता न करे
C. शोर शराबा करने वाले लड़कों को दन्ड दे
D. उपरोक्त सभी

103. Learning (सीखना) का सबसे समुचित अर्थ है :
A. ज्ञान देना
B. व्यवहार में परिवर्तन
C. व्यक्तिगत रूप से माहौल में ढलना
D. हुनर की प्राप्ति

104. अन्तिम विश्लेषण में शिक्षण को विशेष रूप से समझना चाहिये :
A. प्रश्न पूछने तथा ज्ञान के मूल्यांकन की प्रक्रिया
B. विद्यार्थियों की गतिविधियों को निर्दिष्ट करना
C. विद्यार्थियों के वाचन का श्रवण
D. उपरोक्त सभी

105. अध्यापक के कार्य हैं :
A. बच्चे का मार्गदर्शन करना, प्रगति में उनकी सहायता करना तथा मूल्यांकन
B. घर का काम चेक करना, उनका मार्गदर्शन करना तथा आगे का काम देना
C. उपरोक्त दोनों
D. कोई नहीं

106. कक्षा में अध्यापक है :
A. समूह का अध्यक्ष
B. समूह का निर्देशक
C. समूह का नेता तथा मार्गदर्शक
D. उपरोक्त सभी

107. अध्यापक का प्राथमिक उत्तरदायित्व निहित है :
A. शैक्षिक अनुभवों को सुनियोजित करने में
B. नीतियों को लागू करने में
C. छात्रों का रिकार्ड रखने में
D. उपरोक्त सभी

108. अपने विद्यार्थियों से गहरा तालमेल बनाने के लिए आपको
A. उनका मार्गदर्शन करना चाहिये
B. उनके साथ खुलेपन का व्यवहार करना चाहिये
C. संप्रेषण में सक्षम होना चाहिये
D. उपरोक्त सभी

109. मौखिक मार्गदर्शन सबसे कम प्रभावशाली है :
A. अभिवृत्ति के शिक्षण में
B. अवधारणा तथा तथ्य के शिक्षण में
C. परस्पर सम्बन्ध के शिक्षण में
D. हुनर (skills) के शिक्षण में

110. अध्यापन आरम्भ करने से पूर्व शिक्षक को चाहिये कि
A. वह अपने विद्यार्थियों के वर्तमान तथा भूत के विषय में जाने
B. वह विद्यार्थियों के मस्तिष्क पर काम कर रहे वातावरण के विचलनों से भिज्ञ हो
C. वह अपने विद्यार्थियों की जिज्ञासा को उजागर करने में सक्षम हो
D. उपरोक्त सभी

111. किसी स्कूल/कॉलेज में शिक्षा की गुणवत्ता को मापा जा सकता है :
A. उपलब्ध बुनियादी सुविधाओं द्वारा
B. उपलब्ध जनशक्ति, अध्यापक तथा प्रधानाचार्य के माध्यम से
C. छात्रों की शैक्षिक प्रगति के माध्यम से
D. उपरोक्त सभी द्वारा

112. UNESCO प्रकाशन की व्याख्या के अनुसार अध्यापक के अन्दर कौन-सा व्यावसायिक गुण होना चाहिये?
A. अपने विषय में दक्षता तथा शिक्षण में निपुणता
B. शिक्षण-पद्धति में प्रतिक्षण नयापन
C. व्यवसाय के प्रति न्याय व ईमानदारी
D. उपरोक्त सभी

113. शिक्षण का पहला चरण है :
A. पहले से योजना बनाना
B. पाठ्यसामग्री को सुसंगठित करना
C. विद्यार्थियों की बैकग्राउन्ड को जानना
D. कोई नहीं

114. यदि कोई छात्र कक्षा में बेहोश हो जाता है तो आप सबसे पहले क्या करेंगे?
A. प्रधानाचार्य के कार्यालय की ओर दौड़ेगे तथा सहायता के लिए कहेंगे
B. बच्चे के माता-पिता को टेलीफोन करेंगे तथा उनकी प्रतीक्षा करेंगे
C. उसे प्रथम सहायता चिकित्सा देंगे तथा किसी निकट के डॉक्टर से सम्पर्क करेंगे
D. उस लड़के को घर भेजने का प्रबन्ध करेंगे

115. यदि सामान्य लड़कों के साथ आपको किसी नेत्रहीन को पढ़ाने का अवसर मिले तो आपका व्यवहार कैसा होगा?
A. आप सहानुभूति से उसकी देख-रेख करेंगे
B. आप उस पर कोई अतिरिक्त ध्यान नहीं देंगे क्योंकि इससे शेष छात्रों की क्षति होगी
C. आप उसको आगे की सीट पर बिठायेंगे और अपने अध्यापन को उसकी क्षमतानुसार इस प्रकार सुनियोजित करेंगे कि उससे अन्य छात्रों को क्षति न हो
D. उपरोक्त कोई नहीं

116. एक नया अध्यापक, जिसके साथ कक्षा में कुछ बच्चे गलत ढंग से व्यवहार करते हैं, वह उनसे निपटेगा
A. दण्डात्मक तरीकों को अपना कर
B. अपने अन्दर सुधार लाकर और उसे छात्रों के सामने अच्छे अन्दाज से पेश करके
C. प्रधानाचार्य से सलाह के बाद अपनी कक्षा को बदल कर
D. उन्हें स्कूल से निकाल देने की धमकी देकर

117. यदि कोई लड़का पीछे बैठता है और श्यामपट को ठीक से नहीं देख पाता है, परिणामस्वरूप वह बार-बार खड़ा होकर देखता है और बैठ जाता है। इस केस के सम्बन्ध में आप क्या निष्कर्ष निकालेंगे?
A. अपने सहपाठियों की तुलना में वह छात्र नाटा है
B. श्यामपट पर रोशनी की चमक पड़ रही है
C. बच्चा दूरदृष्टि दोष रखता है
D. A और C दोनों

118. बच्चे की श्रवण-क्षमता में विकार हो सकता है यदि
A. वह असामान्य रूप से बहुत जोर से बोलता है
B. बातचीत के दौरान वह वक्ता के निकट आ जाता है
C. वह अध्यापक से आमतौर पर फिर से कहिये, फिर से कहिये, कहता रहता है
D. उपरोक्त सभी

119. यदि कोई छात्रा आपसे अपनी डाक आपके पते पर मंगाने के लिए कहती है तो
A. आप उसे इसकी अनुमति नहीं देंगे क्योंकि यह आपके सिद्धान्तों के विरुद्ध है
B. आप उसे अपना पता नहीं देंगे कि कहीं यह आप के विरुद्ध कोई चाल न हो
C. आप उसे इसकी अनुमति दे देंगे क्योंकि एक अध्यापक के नाते आपको ऐसा करना चाहिये
D. आप उसे व्यक्तिगत लगाव के कारण इसकी अनुमति दे देंगे

120. यदि कोई उच्च जाति का अध्यापक किसी नीची जाति के छात्र के साथ भेदभाव करता है तो उसका व्यवहार
A. उसके अपने धर्मानुसार सही है
B. राष्ट्रीय सोच तथा समय की जरूरत के विरुद्ध है
C. संवैधानिक प्रावधानों के विरुद्ध नहीं है
D. UNESCO के अध्यापकों के व्यवसायवाद के नियमों के विरुद्ध नहीं है

121. पद्य पाठ का सर्वाधिक महत्त्वपूर्ण सोपान है–
A. प्रस्तावना B. भाव विश्लेषण
C. समभावी कविता D. आदर्श प्रस्तावना

122. 'कलेजा मुंह को आना' मुहावरे का सही अर्थ है–
A. बहुत दुखी होना B. क्रोध करना
C. धोखा खाना D. मूर्ख बनना

123. आकाश का विलोम है–
A. धरती B. पाताल
C. गगन D. नभ

124. निम्न में से कौन एक भिन्न है?
A. अहं B. दर्प
C. अहंकार D. निराला

125. सहिष्णुता शब्द है–
A. विशेषण B. अव्यय
C. भाववाचक संज्ञा D. सर्वनाम

126. उल्लास का समानार्थक शब्द है–
A. उत्साह B. दुःख
C. प्रसन्नता D. ताजगी

127. सज्जन शब्द का संधि विच्छेद है–

A. सज् + जन B. सः + जन
C. सत् + जन D. सा + जन

128. पर्यावरण का शब्दार्थ है–

A. जलमंडल B. स्थलमंडल
C. वायुमंडल D. वातावरण

129. निम्नलिखित में से रचनात्मक शिक्षण की विधि नहीं है–

A. कक्षा नियम विधि B. आदर्श अभिनय विधि
C. व्याख्या विधि D. भाषा-संसर्ग विधि

130. समवाय विधि प्रयुक्त होती है–

A. निबंध शिक्षण में B. कहानी शिक्षण में
C. कविता शिक्षण में D. उपरोक्त सभी में

131. निम्न में कौन दृश्य-श्रव्य उपकरण है–

A. दूरदर्शन B. टेलीफोन
C. ग्रामोफोन D. रेडियो

132. बालकों के शब्दकोष होने चाहिए–

A. भाषात्मक B. काव्यात्मक
C. चित्रात्मक D. मनोविश्लेषणात्मक

133. सक्षम शब्द का समानार्थक है–

A. समर्थ B. शक्तिशाली
C. कायर D. निर्माता

134. विहंगम दृष्टि का अभिप्राय है–

A. एक झलक B. गहन दृष्टि
C. गहन चिंतन D. इनमें से कोई नहीं

135. विधाता की अनुपम रचना है–

A. मानव B. समुद्र
C. वन D. पृथ्वी

136. नीरस का संधि विच्छेद है–

A. नी + रस B. नि + रस
C. निः + रस D. नीः + रस

137. अक्षर बोध प्रणाली से छात्रों का

A. उच्चारण शुद्ध होता है
B. वाक्यों का क्रमबद्ध ज्ञान होता है
C. विवरण दोष नहीं आ पाता है
D. उपरोक्त सभी

138. नैदानिक परीक्षण का उद्देश्य है–

A. छात्र की कमजोरियों का पता लगाना
B. छात्र में सद्वृत्तियों का विकास करना
C. छात्र की अभिव्यक्ति में सुधार लाना
D. छात्र की भाषा संबंधी क्षमता का मूल्यांकन करना

139. निर्देशित स्वाध्याय प्रणाली का सोपान है–

A. नियोजन B. क्रियान्वयन
C. उपरोक्त दोनों D. कोई भी नहीं

140. पेडागॉजी कहलाता है–

A. शिक्षण विज्ञान
B. सीखने की कला
C. शिक्षण-अधिगम विज्ञान व कला दोनों
D. संप्रेषण विज्ञान

141. निम्नलिखित में से कौन सा वैकल्पिक पाठशाला का अर्थ नहीं है?

A. चरवाहा विद्यालय
B. विद्यालय से बाहर रहे बच्चों की शिक्षा
C. आसपास/पड़ोस के बच्चों की शिक्षा उनके पड़ोस में
D. निर्माण कार्य के पास बच्चों की शिक्षा

142. निम्नलिखित में से कौन सी बात कौशल सीखने की एक प्रावस्था नहीं हो सकती है?

A. संविधि B. भेद बोध
C. अभ्यास D. कल्पना

143. शिक्षण कार्य के लिए निम्नलिखित में से कौन सबसे अधिक निर्णायक है?

A. अधिगम को प्रभावी बनाना
B. ज्ञान देना
C. कक्षा का संप्रबंधन
D. छात्रों के साथ संप्रेषण

144. गरीबों की मदद करना एक कर्त्तव्य है, क्योंकि

A. हम गरीब हैं
B. हम अमीर हैं
C. हम उस समाज से संबंध रखते हैं
D. हम उनकी अच्छाई चाहते हैं

145. 'हमें दूसरे के ओहदों का हमेशा ध्यान रखना चाहिए।' यह एक है–

A. साधारण वाक्य B. जटिल वाक्य
C. मिश्रित वाक्य D. मुहावरा

146. वर्ण को कहते हैं–

A. मौलिक ध्वनि B. लघुत्तम अक्षर
C. मूल ध्वनियां D. वृहत्तम अक्षर

147. नीलकंठ शब्द किस वर्ग का है?

A. रूढ़ि B. योगरूढ़
C. यौगिक D. इनमें से कोई नहीं

148. बुढ़ापा क्या है–

A. भाववाचक संज्ञा B. व्यक्तिवाचक संज्ञा
C. क्रिया विशेषण D. जाति वाचक संज्ञा

149. प्रत्यय कहाँ जोड़े जाते हैं?

A. शब्द के आरंभ में
B. शब्द के अंत में
C. शब्द के बीच में
D. शब्द के उस भाग में जहां उपयुक्त लगे

150. नमस्ते में कौन सी संधि है?

A. व्यंजन संधि B. स्वर संधि
C. विसर्ग संधि D. इनमें से कोई नहीं

151. संचय का संधि विग्रह है–
A. सत् + चय B. सम् + चय
C. सं + चय D. सः + चय

152. जन्मांध में कौन सा समास है?
A. तत्पुरुष B. द्वन्द्व
C. बहुव्रीहि D. अव्ययीभाव

153. अकथ का विपरीतार्थक शब्द होगा–
A. कथनीय B. मान्य
C. कथ्य D. चिंतनीय

154. अक्ल का दुश्मन का क्या तात्पर्य है?
A. बेवकूफ B. महामूर्ख
C. पागल D. बुद्धिहीन

155. हमारी परीक्षा प्रणाली में सुधार का सर्वोत्तम तरीका होगा–
A. आंतरिक मूल्यांकन B. बाह्य मूल्यांकन
C. उपरोक्त दोनों D. इनमें से कोई भी नहीं

156. निम्नलिखित में से दृश्य-श्रव्य सामग्री है–
A. टेलीविजन B. ग्रामोफोन
C. रेडियो D. टेपरिकार्डर

157. भाषा शिक्षण की किस विधि का प्रयोग लाभकर होता है?
A. प्रश्नोतर विधि B. खेल विधि
C. डाल्टन विधि D. इनमें से कोई नहीं

158. कविता किसका विषय है?
A. अनुभूति का B. विधा का
C. रस का D. आनन्द का

159. सम्प्रेषण की कुशलता बढ़ती है–
A. अंतःक्रिया से B. अनुभव से
C. धन से D. प्रशिक्षण से

160. रूपरेखा शिक्षण विधि का संबंध है–
A. गद्य शिक्षण से B. कहानी शिक्षण से
C. व्याकरण शिक्षण से D. रचना शिक्षण से

161. जीवन में सफल होने के लिए छात्रों को क्या करने के लिए प्रोत्साहित करना चाहिए?
A. चयनित अध्ययन B. आकस्मिक अध्ययन
C. गहन अध्ययन D. कण्ठस्थीकरण करके सीखना

162. बुनियादी शिक्षा का विचार निम्न में से किसने दिया?
A. डॉ. जाकिर हुसैन B. डॉ. राजेन्द्र प्रसाद
C. महात्मा गांधी D. रवीन्द्रनाथ टैगोर

163. बालिकाओं की शिक्षा को प्राथमिकता देनी चाहिए, क्योंकि–
A. लड़कियाँ लड़कों की अपेक्षा अधिक होशियार होती हैं
B. लड़कियाँ संख्या में लड़कों से कम हैं
C. भूतकाल में लड़कों की तुलना में लड़कियों के साथ भेदभाव किया गया है
D. केवल लड़कियां ही सामाजिक परिवर्तन का नेतृत्व करने में सक्षम हैं

164. सम्मिलित (Inclusive) शिक्षा की सफलता निर्भर करती है–
A. समुदाय के सहारे पर
B. शिक्षण-अधिगम सामग्रियों की उच्च कोटि की गुणवत्ता पर
C. पाठ्य-पुस्तकों की उत्कृष्टता पर
D. अध्यापकों में अभिवृत्यात्मक परिवर्तन पर

165. पाठ्य-सहगामी क्रियाओं का आयोजन करना किसका दायित्व होना चाहिए?
A. प्रधानाध्यापक का
B. इस कार्य के लिए नियुक्त अध्यापक का
C. उन अध्यापकों का जो इसमें रुचि रखते हैं
D. सभी अध्यापकों का

166. छात्रों के अनुतीर्ण रहने पर समझना चाहिए कि
A. व्यवस्था ही असफल हो गई है
B. अध्यापक की असफलता है
C. पाठ्य-पुस्तकों की असफलता है
D. व्यक्तिगत छात्र की असफलता है

167. छात्रों का सामयिक परीक्षण होना चाहिए ताकि
A. छात्रों की प्रगति उनके अभिभावकों को सूचित की जा सके
B. नियमानुसार निर्धारित अभ्यास करवाया जा सके
C. छात्रों को अंतिम परीक्षाओं के लिए प्रशिक्षित किया जा सके
D. परिणामों से प्राप्त प्रतिपुष्टि के आधार पर सुधारात्मक उपाय अपनाए जा सकें

168. गृहकार्य जांचने का सबसे अच्छा उपाय है–
A. प्रबुद्ध छात्रों द्वारा इसे संपन्न करा देना
B. कक्षा में सामूहिक रूप से उत्तरों की जांच करा देना
C. नमूने के आधार पर इन्हें जांच डालना
D. नियमित रूप से स्वयं अध्यापक/अध्यापिका द्वारा उनकी जांच करना

169. कण्ठ का विशेषण है–
A. कण्ठी B. काठी
C. कण्ठक D. कण्ठ्य

170. निम्न में कौन सी वर्तनी शुद्ध है?
A. श्रीहरी B. पूजनीय
C. मनः कामना D. कवित्री

171. इनमें कौन सा वाक्य अशुद्ध है?
A. मैंने थोड़ी देर बाद जाना है
B. आप सपरिवार आमंत्रित हैं
C. कृपया हमारे घर आइए
D. आप जब भी आएं, मुझसे मिलें

172. अभिमुख होने के अर्थ में किस मुहावरे का प्रयोग है?
A. छत्तीस का आंकड़ा होना
B. एक और एक ग्यारह होना
C. निन्यानवे का चक्कर
D. तिरेसठ की तरह होना

173. 'बतरस लालच लाल की
मुरली धरी लुकाई
सौंह करैं, भौंहनि हंसै
देन कहैं नट जाँइ।'
यहां नट शब्द का क्या अर्थ है?
A. नाटक करना B. छिप जाना
C. मना करना D. झगड़ा करना

174. 'कमर टूट जाना' का अर्थ है–
A. कमर की हड्डी टूटना
B. घबरा जाना
C. असफल होना
D. शक्ति या साहस न रहना

175. हमारे जीवन का उद्देश्य है कि दूसरों की सहायता करें। यह किस प्रकार का वाक्य है?
A. संयुक्त B. सरल
C. साधारण D. मिश्र

176. 'लाली मेरे लाल की ....' यहां लाल से क्या अभिप्राय है?
A. बेटा B. कीमती पत्थर
C. ईश्वर D. मनुष्य

177. नीरव में कौन सी संधि है?
A. स्वर संधि B. व्यंजन संधि
C. विसर्ग संधि D. दीर्घ संधि

178. मधुकर का समानार्थक शब्द क्या है?
A. शहद B. भ्रमर
C. रीछ D. रोटी

179. हथेली पर सरसों जमाना का क्या अर्थ है?
A. जादू दिखाना B. काम झटपट कर लेना
C. अच्छी खेती करना D. असंभव कार्य कर लेना

180. विकलांग बच्चों के साथ किस प्रकार का व्यवहार किया जाना चाहिए?
A. उन्हें सामान्य विद्यालयों एवं सामान्य बच्चों से दूर रखा जाए
B. सामान्य बच्चों की तरह उन्हें भी अवसर दिए जाएं
C. उन्हें एक जिम्मेदारी समझ कर दया की भावना से उनकी सहायता की जाए
D. विशेष सुविधाएं प्रदान कर उन्हें सामान्य विद्यालयों में समाकलित की जाए

181. 'सीता हँसती है' वाक्य में कौन सी क्रिया है?
A. अकर्मक B. द्विकर्मक
C. विकर्मक D. सकर्मक

182. 'राम से बैठा नहीं गया' यहां कौन सा वाच्य है?
A. भाव वाच्य B. कर्मवाच्य
C. कर्तृवाच्य D. मिश्रवाच्य

183. तत्पुरुष समास में कौन-सा पद प्रधान होता है?
A. पूर्व पद B. अन्य पद
C. उभय पद D. उत्तर पद

184. ब्रजभाषा का विकास किस भाषा से हुआ?
A. अर्धमागधी B. शौरसेनी
C. पालि D. पैशाची

185. विकलांग बच्चों के संदर्भ में प्रारंभिक शिक्षा के सार्वभौमिकरण के लिए कौन सी अधिकतम आयु निर्धारित की गई है?
A. 11 वर्ष B. 14 वर्ष
C. 16 वर्ष D. 18 वर्ष

186. विकलांग बच्चों की समेकित शिक्षा का निहितार्थ है–
A. कुछ शिक्षा सामान्य विद्यालयों में हो और कुछ विशेष विद्यालयों में हो
B. ऐसे बच्चों को केवल विशेष अध्यापक ही पढ़ाएँ
C. सामान्य बच्चों के साथ ही उनकी पढ़ाई का प्रावधान हो
D. विकलांगता के अनुरूप विशेष विद्यालयों में दाखिला

187. देवनागरी लिपि किस भाषा की लिपि है?
A. तमिल B. पंजाबी
C. हिन्दी D. उर्दू

188. हिंदी का सबसे बड़ा गुण यह है कि–
A. इसमें वैज्ञानिक आविष्कारों को स्वीकार करने की क्षमता है
B. इसने अपने को दूसरी भाषाओं के संपर्क से अलग रखा है
C. इसने संस्कृत के साथ अन्य भाषाओं के शब्दों को भी अपनाया है
D. यह भारत की सबसे समृद्ध भाषा है

189. हिंदी राष्ट्रभाषा इसलिए रही क्योंकि–
A. गांधीजी इसके पक्षपाती थे
B. यह अंतरप्रांतीय भाषा थी
C. यह सार्वजनिक व्यापार की भाषा थी
D. यह देश में उत्तर से दक्षिण और पूरब से पश्चिम तक परस्पर बातचीत और विचार-विनिमय के लिए प्रयोग में लाई जाती थी

190. राष्ट्र भाषा में–
A. हिंदू संस्कृति के गुण होने चाहिए
B. राजभाषा के गुण होने चाहिए
C. सामासिक संस्कृति के गुण होने चाहिए
D. शुद्ध भाषा के गुण होने चाहिए

191. हिंदी के उदात्त साहित्य का मूल है–
A. रस B. कामुकता
C. कलुषित आक्रोश D. दुखान्त परिणति

192. प्रासंगिक शब्द का सही अर्थ चुनकर बताएं–
A. तराजू की डंडी से संबंधित
B. दरबान
C. मामले से जुड़ा हुआ
D. साथ निभाने वाला

193. उद्देश्य निष्ठ मूल्यांकन की विशेषताएँ हैं–
A. वस्तुनिष्ठता और विभेदकारी
B. व्यापकता और व्यावहारिकता
C. विश्वसनीयता और वैधता
D. उपरोक्त सभी

194. देवनागरी लिपि अन्य लिपियों की तुलना में कहीं अधिक–
A. ध्वन्यात्मक है B. कलात्मक है
C. वैज्ञानिक है D. उपरोक्त सभी

195. वाद-विवाद प्रतियोगिता में आपको निर्णायक बनाए जाने पर आप–
A. साथी निर्णायक के निर्णय के अनुरूप निर्णय करेंगे
B. प्रभावी वक्ता को प्रमुखता देंगे
C. अपने विद्यालय के छात्र को प्रमुखता देंगे
D. छात्र नेता को प्रमुखता देंगे

196. आप कक्षा में धीरे-धीरे सीखने वाले छात्र के लिए क्या करेंगे?
A. अन्य छात्रों की अपेक्षा अधिक गृह कार्य देंगे
B. उसको पारितोषिक प्राप्त करने को प्रोत्साहित करेंगे
C. उसका व्यक्तित्व शिक्षण करेंगे
D. उसका कारण जानकर उपचारात्मक विधि अपनाएंगे

197. एक अच्छे अध्यापक के लिए संतोष की वस्तु है–
A. उच्च पद B. धन
C. आदर-सम्मान D. जन समर्थन

198. कक्षा में शिक्षक को अधिकाधिक प्रश्न पूछने चाहिए, क्योंकि इससे–
A. प्रधानाचार्य प्रसन्न होते हैं
B. कक्षा का अनुशासन बनता है
C. छात्रों को अभिव्यक्ति का अवसर मिलता है
D. शिक्षक को अभिव्यक्ति का अवसर मिलता है

199. अपेक्षा का विपरीत शब्द है–
A. अनादर B. आदर
C. सत्कार D. उपेक्षा

200. अंधाधुंध शब्द का अर्थ है–
A. तीव्र गति से B. धीमी गति से
C. विवेक रहित D. विवेक सहित

उत्तरमाला

1	2	3	4	5	6	7	8	9	10
D	C	D	D	C	D	D	D	B	D
11	12	13	14	15	16	17	18	19	20
C	D	D	A	A	C	D	D	A	D
21	22	23	24	25	26	27	28	29	30
D	B	B	B	D	B	A	A	D	C
31	32	33	34	35	36	37	38	39	40
D	D	B	A	A	A	D	C	D	B
41	42	43	44	45	46	47	48	49	50
C	B	D	B	D	D	C	D	D	A
51	52	53	54	55	56	57	58	59	60
D	D	D	D	C	B	B	B	A	D
61	62	63	64	65	66	67	68	69	70
D	D	D	C	B	B	D	D	B	D
71	72	73	74	75	76	77	78	79	80
D	C	D	B	C	D	B	D	C	D
81	82	83	84	85	86	87	88	89	90
A	C	A	C	D	A	D	A	C	D
91	92	93	94	95	96	97	98	99	100
D	B	C	C	B	C	D	A	B	D
101	102	103	104	105	106	107	108	109	110
D	A	B	B	A	C	A	D	D	D
111	112	113	114	115	116	117	118	119	120
D	D	A	C	C	B	D	D	A	B
121	122	123	124	125	126	127	128	129	130
B	A	B	D	C	A	C	D	D	A

131	132	133	134	135	136	137	138	139	140
A	C	A	A	A	C	A	A	C	C
141	142	143	144	145	146	147	148	149	150
A	A	A	C	A	C	B	A	B	C
151	152	153	154	155	156	157	158	159	160
B	A	A	D	C	A	B	A	D	D
161	162	163	164	165	166	167	168	169	170
C	C	C	A	D	A	D	D	D	B
171	172	173	174	175	176	177	178	179	180
A	D	C	D	A	A	C	B	D	B
181	182	183	184	185	186	187	188	189	190
A	C	D	B	D	D	C	C	D	C
191	192	193	194	195	196	197	198	189	200
A	C	D	D	B	D	C	C	D	C